Mastering
Windows® SharePoint®
Services 3.0

C.A. Callahan

WILEY

Wiley Publishing, Inc.

Acquisitions Editor: Thomas Cirtin
Development Editor: Lisa Thibault
Technical Editors: James Kelly, Kevin Lundy, Daniel Galant, Vanessa Williams
Production Editor: Christine O'Connor
Copy Editor: Kathy Carlyle
Production Manager: Tim Tate
Vice President and Executive Group Publisher: Richard Swadley
Vice President and Executive Publisher: Joseph B. Wikert
Vice President and Publisher: Neil Edde
Book Designer: Maureen Forys and Judy Fung
Compositor: Aptara
Proofreaders: Nancy Hanger, Nancy Riddiough, Ian Golder, and Amy McCarthy
Indexer: Ted Laux
Cover Designer: Ryan Sneed
Cover Image: Pete Gardner / Digital Vision/ gettyimage

For general information on our other products and services or to obtain technical support, please contact our Customer Care Department within the U.S. at (800) 762-2974, outside the U.S. at (317) 572-3993 or fax (317) 572-4002.

Wiley also publishes its books in a variety of electronic formats. Some content that appears in print may not be available in electronic books.

Library of Congress Cataloging-in-Publication Data

Callahan, C. A., 1967–
    Windows SharePoint services 3.0 / C.A. Callahan.
        p.   cm.
    Includes index.
ISBN 978-0-470-12728-5 (paper/website)
1. Intranets (Computer networks)   2. Web servers.   I. Title.
TK5105.875.I6C345   2008
004.6'82–dc22   2007032142

10 9 8 7 6 5 4 3 2 1

Mastering
Windows® SharePoint®
Services 3.0

Dear Reader

Thank you for choosing *Mastering Windows SharePoint Services 3.0*. This book is part of a family of premium quality Sybex books, all written by outstanding authors who combine practical experience with a gift for teaching.

Sybex was founded in 1976. More than thirty years later, we're still committed to producing consistently exceptional books. With each of our titles we're working hard to set a new standard for the industry. From the paper we print on, to the authors we work with, our goal is to bring you the best books available.

I hope you see all that reflected in these pages. I'd be very interested to hear your comments and get your feedback on how we're doing. Feel free to let me know what you think about this or any other Sybex book by sending me an email at nedde@wiley.com, or if you think you've found a technical error in this book, please visit http://sybex.custhelp.com. Customer feedback is critical to our efforts at Sybex.

Best regards,

Neil Edde
Vice President and Publisher
Sybex, an Imprint of Wiley

To Charles for his patience, strength, and determination. This will teach you to brag about a book before it is written. Thanks for having my back.

Acknowledgments

I'd like to thank the people who helped me out during the, at times, overwhelming quest to write this book. Most books are not written alone, but this particular book has a fair number of people who stepped up to assist when deadlines were tight and the work was hard. I'd like to show my gratitude for:

The reviewers, who reviewed my edits for me after I had pneumonia and found myself in the terrible predicament of having no time to do them personally: Karla Carter (Chapters 5 and 6), Brian Bridson (Chapters 4 and 9), Gareth Rowlands (and his wife Sheila Graven, Chapters 3 and 14), James Finley, (who reviewed his own work, Chapter 13), and, of course, Charles Firth, who reviewed Chapters 7, 8, 10, 11, and 12 (good job, man).

The people who tackled the task of writing a Chapter or two: Ron Freeman, who wrote Chapter 14 at lightning speed; Bill Chapman, who laid the foundation of Chapter 11, and Charles Firth, who filled it in; James Finley who wrote Chapter 13; and Charles Firth again for also writing Chapters 7 and 8 (now you can see why the book is dedicated to him).

The editors, Lisa Thibault (development) and Jim Kelly (technical), for their tireless efforts to provide comments and feedback. The production editor, Christine O'Connor, who didn't expect the whirlwind of reviewers and technical editors; yet handled the situation with kindness and grace. The additional, and extraordinary, technical editors; Vanessa Williams (thanks for the advice and support); Daniel Galant, who truly is gallant (thanks for answering my call for help); and Kevin Lundy, who inherited a lot of work at the very end of the project and did an amazing job. And, especially, Kathy Carlyle, to whom I've never even spoken; for doing a fast, outstanding job as copy editor. Thank you for that.

I appreciate the efforts you all have made. For better or worse, we have created a book. Each person on this page left their mark on the work they did, and I thank them for it.

About the Author

CA Callahan, MCSE, MCSA, MCT, is the founder and principal trainer for CallahanTech, providing customized training and courseware for businesses and IT professionals. A Microsoft Certified Trainer since the Windows NT Server days, Callahan teaches fellow IT professionals about the latest Microsoft technologies. She's a frequent presenter at conferences and expos, including Windows/Office Connections and LinuxWorld/NetworkWorld Expo; with a brief stint instructing hands-on labs at Microsoft TechEd. Previously, she traveled across the US on behalf of Microsoft to do TechNet Security Briefings, and has become passionate about network access security, disaster recovery, and virtualization. An avid beta tester, she has participated in such notable betas as Server 2003 (as well as SP1 and R2), Server 2008, Vista, Virtual Server, and Data Protection Manager. Callahan is a contributing author of *Windows Vista: The Missing Manual* with David Pogue as well as *Mastering Windows Server 2003* and its *Upgrade Edition for SP1 and R2* with Mark Minasi.

Contents at a Glance

Introduction . . . . *xxi*

Part I • Preparing for Windows SharePoint Services 3.0 . . . . **1**

    Chapter 1 • Windows SharePoint Services 3.0 Under the Hood 3

    Chapter 2 • Installation 31

Part II • Using Windows SharePoint Services 3.0 . . . . **133**

    Chapter 3 • Introduction to the SharePoint Interface 135

    Chapter 4 • Introduction to Web Parts 159

    Chapter 5 • Introduction to Lists 201

    Chapter 6 • Introduction to Libraries 323

    Chapter 7 • Sites, Subsites, and Workspaces 417

    Chapter 8 • Site Collections and Web Applications 497

Part III • Administering Windows SharePoint Services 3.0 . . . . **563**

    Chapter 9 • Central Administration: Operations 565

    Chapter 10 • Central Administration: Application Management 613

    Chapter 11 • Users and Permissions 653

    Chapter 12 • Maintenance and Monitoring 711

Part IV • Special Topics in Windows SharePoint Services 3.0 . . . . **805**

Chapter 13 • STSADM: A Look at the SharePoint Command Line Tool .807

Chapter 14 • Migrating from WSS 2.0 to WSS 3.0 865

Chapter 15 • Advanced Installation and Configuration 901

Appendix • The Bottom Line 1013

Index *1035*

Contents

Introduction .... *xxi*

Part I • Preparing for Windows SharePoint Services 3.0 .... **1**

Chapter 1 • Windows SharePoint Services 3.0 Under the Hood **3**
Software Requirements 4
Installing SharePoint: Single Server and Server Farm 6
SharePoint Sites and Databases 9
    Content Databases 10
SharePoint Service Accounts and Services 11
    Service Accounts 11
    SharePoint Services 13
User Account Modes 14
Authentication Types 15
Authentication Methods 16
SharePoint Search 16
SharePoint and Email 20
Alternate Access Mapping 21
Managed Paths 21
User Accounts and Permissions 22
Hardware Requirements 22
    Performance Planning 23
    Storage Planning 25
    Software Limitations 27
The Bottom Line 29

Chapter 2 • Installation **31**
Preparing for the SharePoint Installation 31
    IIS 6.0 with SMTP 32
    ASP .NET 2.0 and .NET Framework 3.0 35
    Setup Account 37
    Service Accounts 42
Basic Installation 45
    Confirming the Installation of the Windows Internal Databases 50
    Checking IIS for Web Site Creation 51
    Checking SharePoint's Services 55
    Checking the Central Administration Site 56

Advanced Server Farm Installation.. 57

    Launching Central Administration 71

    Checking the SharePoint Databases... 73

    Confirming Database Creation.. 73

    Confirming the Changes to IIS... 77

    Confirming SharePoint Services and Local
    Security Groups.. 80

    Checking the Index Files 86

    Finalizing the Server Farm Installation.. 89

    Post-Installation Configuration Tasks 113

The Bottom Line.. 130

Part II • Using Windows SharePoint Services 3.0 .... **133**

Chapter 3 • Introduction to the SharePoint Interface **135**

Team Site Home Page.. 135

    Home Page Anatomy.. 136

Content Pages... 150

    A Quick Look at a List... 151

    A Quick Look at a Document Library 152

    The Action Bar 153

The Bottom Line.. 156

Chapter 4 • Introduction to Web Parts.. **159**

Exploring Web Parts... 159

Using Edit Mode.. 161

    Move a Web Part 163

    Remove a Web Part from a Zone 164

    Add a List View Web Part... 166

    Reset Page Content 167

Working with Web Parts 168

    Default Web Parts 169

    Add User-Aware Web Parts... 171

    Change Web Part Settings... 172

    Add a Built-In Web Part... 176

    Configure a Built-In Web Part.. 176

    Export a Web Part 181

    Import a Web Part to a Single Page 184

    Import a Web Part to a Site Collection Gallery... 189

    Add a Web Part from a Site Collection Gallery 192

    Close a Web Part.. 193

    Return a Closed Web Part to a Page.. 194

    Delete a Web Part... 195

The Bottom Line.. 198

Chapter 5 • Introduction to Lists **201**

What Is a List? 201

    Views 201

    Common Data 202

    Explore a List 204

Create a New List Item 205

View a List Item 208

Edit a List Item 212

Modify a List View 213

    Add an Existing List Field to a View 215

    Remove a Field from a View 216

    Change the Order of Fields in a View 216

Modify a List 218

    Add a Field to a List 221

    Change the Order of Fields in a List 224

Enter Data via Datasheet View 229

Create a New List View to Group by Category 236

Create a New View to Filter by Category 243

Customize a List 244

    Enable Incoming Email 248

    Enable Content Approval 253

    Check the RSS Feed Settings 256

    Set Alerts 258

Explore Prebuilt Lists 264

    Calendar 264

    Links 267

    Tasks 269

    Team Discussion 273

Create New Lists with Existing Templates 278

    Issue Tracking 279

    Surveys 291

    Contacts 297

Create a Custom List 310

    Edit an Existing Field 312

    Add a Person or Group Field 313

    Add Single-Line Text and Currency Fields 314

    Add a Lookup Field 315

    Add a Custom Site Column 315

The Bottom Line 321

Chapter 6 • Introduction to Libraries **323**

What Are Libraries? 323

Upload a Document 326

Create a New Document 328

Add a Required Field to a Library 332

Edit a Document with a Required Field 334

Opening or Viewing the Library with Windows Explorer 338

Require Check Out... 343
   Check Out a Document.. 344
   Check In a Document... 350
   Discard Check Out... 351
   Manage Checked Out Files.. 352
Versioning.. 355
   Create a New Minor Version of a Document..................................... 358
   Create a New Major Version of a Document..................................... 359
   Unpublish a Major Version... 361
   Restore a Previous Version of a Document.. 362
   Content Approval.. 365
Create a Document Library... 376
   Replacing a Library's Template with an Existing Template.................... 379
Send To.. 383
Content Types.. 393
   Enable Content Types... 395
   Create a New Content Type.. 396
Picture Library... 405
Wiki Page Library... 407
Form Library.. 410
The Bottom Line... 414

Chapter 7 • Sites, Subsites, and Workspaces.. 417
Definitions and Concepts.. 417
Creating a New Subsite... 419
Site Settings.. 422
   Users and Permissions.. 423
   Look and Feel.. 424
   Galleries... 439
   Site Administration.. 443
   Site Collection Administration.. 458
Additional Default Site Templates... 464
   Team Site.. 464
   Document Workspace... 465
   Wiki.. 466
   Blog.. 470
   Meeting Workspace... 472
Even More Sites.. 484
   Application Templates.. 484
   Self-Service Site Creation.. 491
The Bottom Line... 496

Chapter 8 • Site Collections and Web Applications................................. 497
Site Collections.. 497
   Creating a Site Collection.. 498
   Site Collection Site Settings... 501
   Configuring Site Collections.. 504

Web Applications.. 516
  Creating a New Web Application 517
  Web Application Settings 525
  Content Databases... 535
  Anonymous Access 540
  Host Headers... 547
  Alternate Access Mapping... 550
The Bottom Line.. 560

Part III • Administering Windows SharePoint Services 3.0 .... **563**

Chapter 9 • Central Administration: Operations **565**
Central Administration Organization.. 565
Operations.. 569
  Topology and Services... 571
  Security Configuration Settings... 575
  Logging and Reporting... 581
  Global Configuration 587
  Backup and Restore 602
  Data Configuration 609
The Bottom Line... 610

**Chapter 10 • Central Administration: Application
            Management** **613**
Overview... 613
Sharepoint Web Application Management.. 615
  Create Or Extend Web Application 615
  Remove SharePoint from an IIS Web Site.. 617
  Delete Web Application 618
  Define Managed Paths.. 619
  Web Application Outgoing E-Mail Settings...................................... 621
  Web Application General Settings.. 622
  Content Databases... 625
  Manage Web Application Features... 628
  Web Application List.. 628
Application Security... 628
  Security for Web Part Pages 628
  Self-Service Site Management.. 628
  User Permissions for Web Application.. 629
  Policy for Web Application 629
  Authentication Providers 637
Workflow Management.. 639
  Workflow Settings... 639
SharePoint Site Management... 639
  Create Site Collection 640
  Delete Site Collection 640

Site Use Confirmation and Deletion 642

Quota Templates 644

Site Collection Quotas and Locks 645

Site Collection Administrators 646

Site Collection List 647

External Service Connections 647

Records Center 647

HTML Viewer 648

Document Conversions 649

The Bottom Line 650

Chapter 11 • Users and Permissions **653**

What Are Users, Groups, and Permissions? 653

Individual Permissions 656

Permission Levels 663

Manage Permission Levels 666

Users and Groups 675

Editing Site Administrators 676

Viewing People and Groups 678

Creating a New SharePoint Group 683

Adding a Domain User or Domain Group to a SharePoint Group 686

Removing a Domain User or Domain Group from a

SharePoint Group 688

Viewing All People 689

Applying Permissions 691

Inheritance 691

Change Subsite Permissions 694

Change List or Library Permissions 701

Change List Item or Library Item Permissions 703

Planning User Access 705

User Access at the Web Application Level 706

User Access at the Site Collection Level 706

The Bottom Line 709

Chapter 12 • Maintenance and Monitoring **711**

Performance Monitor 711

Adding a Counter to System Monitor 712

Creating a Counter Log 715

Setting a Performance Counter Alert 723

IIS Logs 726

Event Viewer 729

Common Application Event Errors 730

Backing Up and Restoring SharePoint 732

Back Up SharePoint 734

Restore SharePoint 738

Back Up a Site Collection 746

Restore a Site Collection 750

Export and Import Site Collections and Subsites.. 751

Back Up an Individual Subsite to a Template.. 758

Restore an Individual Subsite from a Template.. 763

Back Up a List or Library Template... 766

Restore a List or Library Template... 768

Backup and Restore Using Other Tools... 771

Back Up the IIS Metabase... 771

Restore the IIS Metabase... 773

Back Up a Web Application by Saving its Configuration File........................... 774

Restore a Web Application Using a Configuration File................................. 775

Back Up Virtual Directories and SharePoint's folders.................................. 777

Restore a Virtual Directory from Backup.. 783

Backup Standalone Server Databases.. 785

Backup Your SQL Databases in a Server Farm Install.................................. 789

Restore a SQL Database.. 792

Suggested Recovery Scenarios... 795

For a Full Recovery of a Single Server Installation..................................... 795

For a Web Front End Server... 797

For a Full Recovery of a Server farm... 798

The Bottom Line.. 802

Part IV • Special Topics in Windows SharePoint Services 3.0 .... **805**

Chapter 13 • STSADM: A Look at the SharePoint Command Line Tool.......... **807**

STSADM Setup Information 808

STSADM.EXE Inline Help.. 810

STSADM-Only Tasks 813

Site Template Management with *STSADM.EXE* 814

Adding a Template to the Server Farm 814

Listing the Site Templates for the Farm 815

Deleting Site Templates.. 816

Managing Web Parts with STSADM... 817

Adding a Web Part Package.. 818

Listing Web Part Packs 820

Removing Web Part Packages.. 820

Managing Features and Solutions with STSADM.. 821

Adding Solutions... 823

Deleting Solutions... 824

Deployment of Solutions... 824

Upgrading Solutions... 826

Adding Features... 826

Activating/Deactivating Features... 826

Web Application Management 828

Creating a Web Application... 830

Removing Web Applications.. 833

Listing Your Web Applications 833

Ongoing Management and Maintenance 834
!New Content Icon 837
Database Management 837
Connecting and Disconnecting Databases 840
Search Management 843
Searching Content in More Than One Language 844
Managing the Search Service 845
Moving the Index 845
Action! 846
Site and Subweb Management 848
Listing Site Collections and Sites 849
Creating Site Collections and Sites 852
Renaming a Site 854
Deleting Site Collections and Sites 854
Security Management 854
User Management 856
SharePoint Group Management 857
Permission Policy Management 858
Site Locks 858
Farm Management 859
The Bottom Line 863

Chapter 14 • Migrating from WSS 2.0 to WSS 3.0 .... **865**
Migration Basics 866
The Joy of Justification: Why Migrate? 866
Which Way to the New World? Types of Upgrades 867
Preparing for the Migration: What do I Need in Place? 871
Check the Software 872
Define Your Key Sharepoint Users 873
Define Your Regression Testing 873
Document Everything 873
Communication Is Key 873
Evaluate Custom Web Parts 874
Keep Rollbacks in Place 874
Consider Improving the System 875
Performing the Migration: Can I Get My Hands Dirty Now? 876
Migration In Place 879
Gradual Migration 884
SQL Server Database Move Migration 894
Database Move Migration: WMSDE to WID 898
Post-Update Steps: Testing for success 899
The Bottom Line 900

Chapter 15 • Advanced Installation and Configuration **901**
Advanced Installation 901
Active Directory Account Creation Mode SharePoint Installation 902
Using SharePoint in Active Directory 911
Installing an Additional SharePoint Server on a Server Farm 923

Advanced Configuration... 942
    Network Load Balancing the Server Farm... 942
    Using SSL with SharePoint 961
    Using Kerberos for Authentication.. 977
    Directory Management Service 984
The Bottom Line..1012

Appendix • The Bottom Line **1013**
Chapter 1: Windows SharePoint Services 3.0 Under the Hood 1013
Chapter 2: Installation 1014
Chapter 3: Introduction to the SharePoint Interface 1015
Chapter 4: Introduction to Web Parts..1016
Chapter 5: Introduction to Lists 1017
Chapter 6: Introduction to Libraries 1018
Chapter 7: Sites, Subsites, and Workspaces..1020
Chapter 8: Site Collections and Web Applications 1021
Chapter 9: Central Administrations: Operations 1023
Chapter 10: Central Administration: Application Management 1024
Chapter 11: Users and Permissions 1026
Chapter 12: Maintenance and Monitoring...1028
Chapter 13: STSADM: A Look at the SharePoint Command Line Tool 1029
Chapter 14: Migrating from WSS 2.0 to WSS 3.0 1031
Chapter 15: Advanced Installation and Configuration......................................1032

Index...*1035*

Introduction

This book started off as a single 200-page chapter in someone else's book. Almost a year later, and a different version of SharePoint, this book was born.

Mastering Windows SharePoint Services 3.0 was intended for IT administrators to get a handle on Windows SharePoint Services 3.0. Most of us don't have time to waste struggling with the ins and outs of a new product. We just need it to work. SharePoint is a really complicated beast; poorly documented, with oddly named settings, in even odder places. It's not for the faint of heart.

SharePoint is several things at once. It is a developer's platform, leveraging ASP .NET 2.0 and the Windows Workflow Foundation. It is a robust front end over the power of SQL 2000 or 2005 on the backend. And finally, it's a web collaboration tool, a useful front end to help increase the productivity of the IT worker. It's a network product, installs on a server, and inevitably ends up being the responsibility of the server administrator.

When I started using Windows SharePoint Services (WSS), I just couldn't find any detailed, accurate, WSS-only documentation. There was almost nothing reliable out there that was for administrators using WSS (not the paid for SharePoint Server product). Most of the documentation, especially the books, that I could find about WSS were written for developers. There was almost nothing for the busy administrators who have an entire network to run, for whom WSS is just another server role.

So when I was asked to write about WSS for IT professionals, I couldn't say no (well, I considered it, but I finally agreed because the cause was good). That's why this book is here. I wrote it because it was the book I needed when I started out. It is the book I would have bought if it had been available when I was looking. I tried to fill it full of suggestions, tips, tricks, and concepts that would help you navigate through the maze of hype about SharePoint to reach the truth—what it really is, what it really does, and how to use it. The intent was not particularly to hold your hand, but to show you, administrator to administrator, what Windows SharePoint Services 3.0 is all about.

Contents of the Book

So, intrepid IT Professional, Administrator, Student of all things server related, this book was written for you. It takes you through what an administrator should know, part by part, chapter by chapter:

Part I: Preparing for Windows SharePoint Services 3.0

Chapter 1, "Windows SharePoint Services 3.0 Under the Hood": The concepts you need to be prepared for before installing SharePoint; from what installations to expect, to performance and capacity planning, to features that may take extra effort or resources to use.

Chapter 2, "Installation": The different ways to install SharePoint, how to do it, and why.

Part II: Using Windows SharePoint Services 3.0

Chapter 3, "Introduction to the SharePoint Interface": The landmarks and terminology of the interface itself.

Chapter 4, "Introduction to Web Parts": What web parts are, what they are for, where you can put them, what the built in ones do, and how to configure them. All without leaving the browser. No development here.

Chapter 5, "Introduction to Lists": What lists are, really. How they work, what they do, how to customize them, build your own, and reuse preexisting lists and templates. Takes a glance at workflows.

Chapter 6, "Introduction to Libraries": What libraries are. How they work, how to customize them, how to make your own. There are several types of libraries, not all of them work they way you expect them to.

Chapter 7, "Sites, Subsites, and Workspaces": What subsites and workspaces are, how to create them, and how to use them. What site templates are, and how to use the application templates for SharePoint version 3.0 from Microsoft.

Chapter 8, "Site Collections and Web Applications": What site collections and web applications are. Moving up to the big stuff; learn how and why to create new site collections or even new web applications, extend existing web applications, and how alternate access mapping works.

Part III: Administering Windows SharePoint Services 3.0

Chapter 9, "Central Administration: Operations": The first of two reference chapters covering the Central Administration pages and how to administer SharePoint. Explains what Central Administration is, and how to use it. What settings are on the Operations page and what each one does, from Servers on the server farm, to Data retrieval service.

Chapter 10, "Central Administration: Application Management": Primarily about how to manage web applications, this reference chapter covers what settings are on the Application Management page in Central Administration. How to use them, when to use them, and what they're for.

Chapter 11, "Users and Permissions": An in-depth look at individual permissions and their levels, user and group management, and configuration of authorization options. Includes using Policy for Web Applications to secure web applications, restricting site collections using permissions and groups, as well as securing lists and list items.

Chapter 12, "Maintenance and Monitoring": How to monitor, back up and restore Share-Point. How to recover from disaster; from using the recycle bin to recover a lost list item, to rebuilding the server farm.

Part IV: Special Topics in Windows SharePoint Services 3.0

Chapter 13, "STSADM: A Look at a SharePoint Command Line Tool": How to manage SharePoint using the command line administrative tool, STSADM. See how to do more than the Central Administration web site will allow—there's always more power at the command line.

Chapter 14, "Migrating from WSS 2.0 to WSS 3.0": How to migrate to Windows SharePoint Services 3.0 from Windows SharePoint Services 2.0. Get tips and tricks about the different types of migration options.

Chapter 15, "Advanced Installation and Configuration": How to do some of the more advanced configuration, from network load balancing to using Active Directory Account Creation mode to enabling Directory Management Service. Do the fancy administrative tasks that others hesitate to do.

In order to write about SharePoint, I found myself writing about *doing* SharePoint. So there are lots of screenshots and step by step instructions. The way to learn about SharePoint is by using it. It really doesn't make sense until you do. So this isn't a high level book all about the theory of SharePoint—that would be too easy. No, this is largely a real life scenario, tutorial kind of book, chronicling what I know about SharePoint, as quickly as possible.

This book is intended to give you solid insight into how things work, how to do them, and how to understand them well enough that you can take ownership of SharePoint as an IT administrator. It was a slow, painstaking process to explore all those dark places, set all of those settings, and take all of those screenshots. But the hope is; that if I do it here, however briefly, you will see how it works and then you can apply it in your environment. Of course, despite my best efforts, there were simply some topics I could not cover in the time I had to write the book. But I wanted to give you enough information, enough confidence, that if there was something I didn't do in the book, you would be able to do it without me.

Because of the time constraints, not all chapters were written by me; I had to ask for help. Four remarkable men came forward to give me a hand, and I would like to thank them. Charles Firth, when it looked like I simply would never, ever finish, stepped up and wrote two chapters: Chapter 7, "Sites, Subsites, and Workspaces," and Chapter 8, "Site Collections and Web Applications." Chapter 8 turned out to be a beast, overlapping my content in Chapter 10 considerably. Bill Chapman gave me a hand with Chapter 11, "Users and Permissions." He laid the groundwork for quite a bit of information, and Charles built on it from there. James Finley wrote Chapter 13, the STSADM chapter. I have to give him full credit for that chapter. He did a thorough job introducing the command line tool and covering all those odds and ends that you just can't do in Central Administration. And finally, Ron Freeman, who wrote the Migrating from WSS 2.0 to WSS 3.0 chapter, Chapter 14. That chapter had some serious hardware requirements, crossing multiple machines, as well as multiple versions of SharePoint. Thanks again to those fine gentlemen for the work they did.

Behind the scenes: The making of Mastering Windows SharePoint Services 3.0

As for the writing of the book: It was done entirely on a MacBook Pro, running Bootcamp, written entirely using a virtual machine running Word 2003 (the publisher's template required it).

For those who like the nitty gritty details, here is a run down of the background of the book as far as network and resources go. The SharePoint network I used throughout the book was run on the MacBook Pro in either Virtual PC 2005 or on a Virtual Server R2. My coauthors accessed virtual machines configured like my own using my Virtual Server in order to have screenshots and step by steps that matched the domain, server, and user naming structure that I was using for the book.

Well, mostly.

James Finley's in New Zealand (which is on the other side of the planet from where I am writing), and internet access to my machines was a bit intermittent. So if his screenshots aren't identical to my set up, that's why.

The network configuration for the book:

Internal Active Directory Domain: dem0tek.lcl

Email domain: dem0tek.com (and a brief foray during a sidebar with dem0share.com)

Servers:

RR1.dem0tek.lcl: It was the SQL 2005 server for SharePoint. For convenience sake, it was also the Routing and Remote Access Server for the virtual network. I installed Word 2003 and Snag It (by Techsmith) on that machine and wrote all of my content there.

DC1.dem0tek.lcl: It was the domain controller and the POP3 email server. For the Directory Management Services section of Chapter 15, I rebuilt the network, and installed Exchange 2003 on DC1 to manage email as well.

SP1.dem0tek.lcl: First SharePoint server on the network. It was the Basic installation server used in chapter 2.

SP2.dem0tek.lcl: Second SharePoint server on the network. This server is the one installed using the Advanced, Server Farm Configuration and used RR1 for its SharePoint databases. Used for most of the book, it should be familiar to readers.

SP3.dem0tek.lcl: SharePoint server installed specifically to play second fiddle to SP2. SP3 was the server added to the SharePoint server farm in chapter 15 to demonstrate load balancing and SharePoint services management.

SP4.dem0tek.lcl: Used in Chapter 15 as well, this SharePoint server was installed to use Active Directory Account Creation mode. And a fine job it did at that.

There are a number of user accounts that show up throughout the book but in fact there are numerous users for the dem0tek network that didn't really get any recognition. Doing my best to create fictitious names that were truly fictitious, I created names in a few broad categories, most notably herbs and semi-precious stones (believe it or not). The herbs were, by and large, the Information workers (although several of them, particularly Saffron, are power users). The semiprecious stones were staff and IT technicians. Because most of my work was done at the administrative level, I tended to login as an administrator or site collection owner, but there were other accounts available to log in with if necessary. You might recognize Saffron, Jasper, and Citrine when you see them.

So now you know what was going on in the background during the writing of this book. For more information, questions, or suggestions, please feel free to email me at callahan@callahantech.com. I've also got a blog if you'd like to stop by at http://servergrrl.blogspot.com. I created it specifically to support this book. It is there that I will write all the stuff that I didn't get a chance to here (including late breaking information, like changes caused by Service Pack 1 or Server 2008); add more concepts, fix any errata that may turn up (hey, we're all human here), and more. And if this book ends up with a second edition, you can hear about it there, and even offer me suggestions as to what should be in it, that second time around.

There's SharePoint and There's SharePoint

I tend to refer to Windows SharePoint Services 3.0 (WSS 3.0) as SharePoint in this book for readability, convenience, and because I am not fond of using the same acronym in practically every sentence for more than a few hundred pages. However, there are two kinds of SharePoint: Windows SharePoint Services and Microsoft Office SharePoint Server 2007 (MOSS). And because of that, you will see WSS being used only when I need to make it clear which kind I am referring to. It should stand to reason that I will default to SharePoint meaning WSS, since that is the topic of the book.

There is a lot of confusion about the difference between WSS and MOSS. Many people seem to confuse the two. Remember, MOSS is an add-on to WSS. Users who have access to MOSS tend to consider WSS only as a means to use the more extensive MOSS. They never realize that the features they use daily are not the parts they paid for.

Just to be clear, using WSS and MOSS is not entirely an either/or situation. They are basically two different products, but there is a relationship there.

WSS is free and is a complete product by itself. After WSS is installed, it will work perfectly fine on its own.

However, if you buy and install MOSS, WSS 3.0 is installed first and then MOSS is installed *on top of* WSS (this is an automated part of the MOSS installation). Microsoft Office SharePoint Services 2007 requires Windows SharePoint Services 3.0 to be installed before it will even run.

WSS does not need MOSS, but MOSS does need WSS. Windows SharePoint Services 3.0's functions are the foundation of all things MOSS. Without WSS, MOSS would not work. They are considered to be two different products, but MOSS is an add-on to WSS. When you pay for MOSS, you pay for the extras it offers in addition to the usefulness of WSS.

WSS 3.0 Features

So what can WSS 3.0 really do? Here's a brief overview of WSS capabilities. There may be features like smart tags that you might not be familiar with right now, but don't worry, they are covered in depth later in the book. This is to give you an idea of what to look forward to, clearly define what WSS can do without MOSS, and possibly introduce you to something that you might need that you didn't realize it was capable of.

Real-Time Presence and Collaboration   If Microsoft Office (2007 is recommended) is installed and Microsoft's instant messenger is running, Online Presence will allow users to see if their buddy's from SharePoint are online. In addition, Smart Tags will be available wherever a user name is displayed, offering users a menu to send email or instant messages, and to call that user. Office Communicator and Live Communication Server also help facilitate Online Presence.

Consistent User interface   With WSS 3.0, the SharePoint interface has been improved, enhancing the consistent look and feel of SharePoint sites, lists, and libraries with automatic *breadcrumbs*, improved Quick Launch bar, Tree view, Top link bar for navigating sites, and more descriptive menus. The enhancements allow users to more easily navigate backward and forward through sites and pages.

Collaboration Site Templates   WSS 3.0 includes easy-to-use, easy-to-create team sites, document workspaces, meeting workspaces, blogs, wikis, and even blank sites.

Wikis New to WSS 3.0, this site template is a creative forum for brainstorming, using knowledge bases, or simply gathering ideas. Wikis make it easy to create, edit, annotate, link pages, and track contributions and changes in a dynamic, collaborative environment.

Blogs Also new to WSS 3.0, this site template is a publishing-oriented site intended for posting articles, making comments, and archiving, with RSS feed generation.

People and Groups List Another new feature for WSS 3.0, this list is a unified place to find people, add users, manage permissions, and create groups. It integrates with lists and libraries, and offers people-picker functionality. It allows more customizable fields for user information and is security filtered.

Calendars Enhanced for WSS 3.0, calendars allow shared views of events; supporting recurring events, all day events, and richer calendar views.

Email Integration In addition to being able to send out invitations, notifications, and alerts, WSS 3.0 can enable lists such as discussions, libraries, and announcements to receive incoming email and process them as list items. WSS 3.0 has extensible support for custom email handlers to add incoming email to custom lists as well. SharePoint's incoming email can integrate with Active Directory and Exchange 2003 to create contacts for list and libraries, as well as SharePoint group distribution lists.

Task Coordination Enhanced with a Gantt Chart view for project tasks, the Tasks list supports lightweight task management with task assignment, scheduling, prioritizing, task relationships, and status.

Surveys Can be used to collect statistical data that is generated by user responses to custom lists of questions. WSS 3.0 Surveys come with useful graphical views and supports branching logic.

Document Collaboration Libraries allow users to save, upload, and store documents (as well as pictures, forms, and other files) online. Document libraries support required check out, versioning (major and minor), multiple content types, Explorer view, and workflows.

Issue Tracking Like task coordination, this type of list supports issue assignment, status, priority, issue relationship, and scheduling. It also comes with a default, three-part workflow, and category assignment.

Mobile Device Support Using a simplified text layout, WSS 3.0 can support page rendering on international and North American web-enabled phones. Most content pages have an alternate page rendered specifically for Mobile Device user access.

Office Integration WSS 3.0 was built in conjunction with Office 2007 to offer the most integrated features ever available with SharePoint. Users can easily access and edit files stored in SharePoint, create links between lists and Access 2007, or upload and download lists and data from Excel 2007. Office also enhances smart tag and presence capabilities. Outlook 2007 further integrates with SharePoint, synchronizing with document libraries, calendars, and lists. It offers read/write access to calendars, tasks, discussions, and documents, and it can create meeting workspaces from Outlook Calendar events, and rollup views of calendars and lists across sites. It offers a unified view of tasks between Outlook and those in SharePoint. Office 2003 integration is still supported, but Office 2007 was designed to offer more robust features.

Search Search is managed by SharePoint in this new version, which offers a simple, clear, yet powerful user interface for search queries. Searches can include a site collection, or be narrowed down to just one list. Lists, libraries, and sites can be secured so that they are unsearchable, and search results will display only content that the user has the right to see. Users can query for keywords in the text of documents and lists, as well as in the metadata of SharePoint items.

Content Management   When users edit a document, enhanced content management (integrated between Office 2007 and WSS 3.0) offers a content panel that makes it easier for users to edit the document properties while working on the document in Word.

Alerts   Users can set alerts for changes in any list or library, and they can be notified by email when those changes occur, eliminating the need to check the list or library manually.

Task Notification   This feature allows users to receive email notification if a task is assigned to them. Further, there is a new web part that can be used to display all tasks assigned to a user when they log in.

RSS Feeds   New to WSS 3.0, every list and library is RSS enabled. This feature allows users with RSS-enabled readers to view changes to lists or libraries without visiting the SharePoint site.

Recycle Bin   Also new to WSS 3.0, this feature enables users to restore items that were accidentally deleted. Administration of the lifecycle of deleted items is also available. In addition, there is a secondary recycle bin, for administrative recovery of items accidentally deleted from the Recycle Bin itself, for added security.

Backup and Restore (with VSS)   Backing up and restoring SharePoint is another new feature available in the administrative interface for WSS 3.0, with improved functionality utilizing Windows Server 2003's Volume Shadow Copy technology.

List Indexing   Another new addition to WSS 3.0, this feature improves performance and capacity of large lists through the indexing of specific list columns.

Content Types   Also new to WSS 3.0, Content types are generally list item templates, and can be associated with their own workflows and metadata and used in any list or library. Content types can also specify file types and their templates for document libraries, allowing users to be able to create several different types of files from the New button in one library.

Workflows   Brand new to WSS 3.0 (thanks to the Windows Workflow Foundation), customizable structured workflows are supported for document libraries and lists. Workflows are a process management feature that triggers actions based on the status of library or list items.

Folder Organization   Allow items to be organized in folders in documents libraries and lists in WSS 3.0. Folder organization can be used to make huge libraries or lists easier to view and manage or comfort users who are more familiar with file shares.

Item Level Security   New to WSS 3.0, each item can have its own Access Control List, which offers more granular security.

Centralized Configuration Management   Using ASP.NET 2.0, SharePoint supports a central administrative site. This site has been almost complete overhauled for WSS 3.0, per user feedback, is more logically organized, and has additional support for delegation and isolation of duties.

Site Management   Sites can be easily deployed using site templates and definitions. They are easily customized, and they can be saved as templates to be used elsewhere. Also, new to WSS 3.0, site hierarchies can be reorganized, which means that subsites can be moved from under one site and placed under another. WSS 3.0 also offers additional support and security for sites using

Alternate Access Mapping and Zones   This allows SharePoint to respond to alternate addresses and apply the correct authentication requirements depending on the address's zone.

Monitoring   This feature provides usage analysis and diagnostic logging to enable administrators to better manage SharePoint resources.

ANXIETY, TREPIDATION, AND LICENSING

Windows SharePoint Services 3.0 is considered to be a server component, like Internet Information Services (IIS), and it uses the server's license model. No additional licensing is required.

However there is one possible caveat. There is something called an External Connector license required when external users are going to be authenticating to the domain and using SharePoint. In that case, the external user is using an account that is not a licensed account for that server, or using a machine that is not licensed for server access, depending on the server's licensing model. Since those users are not covered under the Server's license, they must be covered elsewhere, thus the External Connector license comes into play.

The External Connector license is a per server license for Windows Server 2003. It is purchased per server, not per client. This means, a server with this license can legally allow an unlimited number of external clients to authenticate and access its resources.

Keep in mind that a license is required for external users who are authenticating and using the resources on the SharePoint server. Due to the fact that the SharePoint server is an IIS web server, there is no license required for users if they are accessing the server anonymously, such as someone who is only looking and doesn't need to contribute to the site.

The scenario in which the External Connector license (or any other license) is required varies, so definitely contact Microsoft Licensing to see whether or not the External Connector license is a requirement for you.

MOSS 2007 Features

In addition to WSS 3.0, Microsoft Office SharePoint Server 2007 offers features especially geared toward large business and enterprise customers. MOSS, as its former name SharePoint Portal Server implies, is fundamentally designed to pull together unrelated resources so they can be accessed from one portal location. Focused on business intelligence, processes, and document management; MOSS 2007 offers the following additions to Windows SharePoint Services' extensive functionality:

Portal Site Templates   Additional site templates are especially geared toward centralizing user access to other locations and applications: Enterprise, Corporate Internet presence site, Application Portal Site, and a Roll Up portal site. Enhanced CSS support is also available for extensive corporate branding of portal sites.

Socialization and Personalization   Offers personalized public My Sites for each user. As well as web parts, such as the SharePoint sites and documents roll up web part (which can list colleagues, friends, and members of a common distribution group), and a social networking web part (which uses information from colleagues' my site information to aggregate common interests). Convenient content authoring and publishing for users is also available through the browser.

Enhanced Search   MOSS offers more robust search capabilities across enterprise content sources (sources beyond a single site collection, such as file shares, websites, other SharePoint servers, public folders, and Lotus Notes databases) and supports 200 different file types, relevance ranking, people search, and extensive search indexing administration and control.

Business Document Management   With additional workflow features built-in (approvals, feedback, and signature collection), MOSS has enhanced document management sites with document libraries that enforce information rights policies with integrated rights management, auditing and retention policies, and legal document processing, as well as record repositories for archiving inactive documents.

Business Processes and Forms   The enterprise version of MOSS offers enhanced support for business form use and management. Users can fill out InfoPath forms from the browser. Integrated heavily with InfoPath 2007, MOSS supports design-once development. It has a Form Import Wizard and centralized forms management and control.

Business Intelligence   MOSS features an integrated business dashboard that assembles and displays information from different sources. The Enterprise version also offers integrated spreadsheet publishing and management, Excel services, data connection library, business data catalogs, business data web part and actions, a Report Center, and Key Performance Indicators.

Single Sign-On   This feature integrates with Microsoft systems and line of business applications. It requires a separate credentials database. It allows users to log on to a portal site and have their credentials passed to other backend applications.

As you can see, MOSS is pretty powerful, but it becomes pretty obvious how much of MOSS's functionality actually lies in the hands of WSS, and why it's useful to understand WSS first.

MICROSOFT OFFICE SHAREPOINT SERVER 2007, MORE VERSIONS THAN A BARREL OF VISTAS (ALMOST)

Microsoft went hog wild to get their money's worth from MOSS. You can get a good deal on MOSS if you are a nonprofit organization or an academic institution. However, acquiring MOSS can still be expensive if you are not careful. To ease the burden of buying a product that may be overpowered for your needs, Microsoft added to the confusion by offering several different kinds of MOSS.

(Keep in mind that this information is offered to you to let you know what you would be getting into if you chose to use MOSS in your environment. However, WSS is still free and uses the Server's licensing model, no extra CALs required.)

MOSS has one core product-Microsoft Office SharePoint Server 2007. It can run as a Standard MOSS server or an Enterprise MOSS server, depending on what Client Access Licenses (CAL) you have (sneaky huh?). Interestingly, the CALs drive what features are available to the clients.

The Standard CALs don't give you everything that the Enterprise ones do. And yes, that basically makes sense. That way, a Standard company doesn't need to pay for Enterprise features it may never use. But here's the catch: in order to use those Enterprise features, you must first buy standard CALs and *then* purchase Enterprise CALs as well. If you are an Enterprise customer, you can't just choose to buy the Enterprise CALs to support the Enterprise features. You must have a Standard *and* an Enterprise CAL for each user to use the Enterprise features.

In addition, you can buy separate types of MOSS altogether. MOSS for Search is basically WSS with the enhanced, enterprise-wide search capabilities of MOSS. Adding enhanced search capabilities to WSS will cost you the price of MOSS for Search *and* the Client licensing fees. MOSS for Internet Sites is meant to be used if your SharePoint server is Internet facing, and it is an add-on to WSS. It is licensed per-server license and, logically, doesn't use CALs. It is basically the Server 2003 External Connector license for SharePoint.

If you are confused, just keep in mind:

◆ To use MOSS you must buy it, of course. But when you buy it, you are really buying the core MOSS server license.

◆ Once you buy MOSS, you must buy a CAL for each client in your business to access it. Just to use MOSS, you need the Standard CAL for each user. To use the Enterprise features, you must *also* have Enterprise CALs for each user.

◆ If MOSS is going to be accessed through the internet by people who are not employees, you must have MOSS for internet sites for each server serving the public.

◆ The other MOSS family products, such as MOSS for search or Microsoft Office Forms Server, are MOSS installations that are slightly modified or limited in order to use or enhance a particular feature of MOSS. They are for the business that doesn't need (and may not be willing to pay for) all of the MOSS features. These products still use CALs though, even though they are not the full fledged product.

For quick reference, Microsoft offers the following MOSS core products:

◆ Microsoft Office SharePoint Server 2007, Server License. This is the core SharePoint server 2007 license. You can't have MOSS without it.

◆ Microsoft Office SharePoint Server 2007 Client Access License, Standard Edition. There must be at least a Standard CAL for each client in order for them to even use MOSS.

◆ Microsoft Office SharePoint Server 2007 Client Access License, Enterprise Edition. This license is an add-on to the Standard Edition. You must have a standard CAL for each enterprise CAL. This license allows a client to use business intelligence enterprise services such as performance management dashboards and electronic forms.

◆ Microsoft Office SharePoint Server 2007 for Internet Sites. This software may be used only for Internet-facing websites. The license is per server, so it doesn't need separate CALs. Is basically the External Connector server license for MOSS. However, it was not meant to be taken advantage of by internal users.

◆ Microsoft Office SharePoint Server 2007 for Search. This MOSS is an odd addition to the Microsoft Office SharePoint Server family. It isn't really a full-blown MOSS server. When you buy it, you are literally adding MOSS search features to a standard WSS install.

◆ Microsoft Office Forms Server 2007. This addition to the Microsoft Office SharePoint Server family is an add-on to WSS that creates better support for building InfoPath forms and displaying them for client use *without* the client needing to install InfoPath. It does have some enhanced InfoPath integration to create, edit, or upload forms. You pay for the web browser support for displaying InfoPath forms rather than buying InfoPath for the clients on your network that need it. It may seem like a single-trick pony, but it could save you money if you know it's there. This functionality can be enabled as part of the Enterprise features of MOSS itself. Forms server simply isolates that capability for customers who don't want to pay for full-blown MOSS.

A Brief History of SharePoint

It's great to see a solid list or two about what products do, even if you don't recognize some of the features or can't see how they relate to you in the beginning. A features list can provide food for thought and a good reference for later. However, when reading a list of what something can do, you might not realize how incredible some of those features are or how this version really kicks the butt of the version before it. To really understand SharePoint, it helps to know its humble beginnings and how it got to its current greatness.

Windows SharePoint Services started out as SharePoint Team Services (STS) version 1 and was a feature that could be found only on the FrontPage 2002 CD (or as part of Office XP). It worked on both Windows XP and Windows Server 2000 and was basically a demonstration of how powerful sites and applications using IIS and FrontPage Server Extensions could be. STS set up IIS Web Sites with really useful and nifty lists, with the familiar document library, discussions, events, tasks, contacts, and links. It was pretty basic, but even at that level of usability, it was a hit. Despite it being so new, it was also surprisingly customizable using FrontPage.

Of course, people complained about STS. It stored documents in a file share and metadata in the content database, and it used a mix of ISAPI and FrontPage extensions to create pages, aspects on the pages, and web parts. It was a mishmash of bits, but it was a great start.

Meanwhile, in a different development track, Microsoft was trying to capitalize on the growing portal market by releasing SharePoint Portal Server 2001 (SPS). According to legend, this product was created independently and ironically only resembled STS's functionality with added features. The two products were very different under the hood. SPS did not have many of the behind-the-scenes limitations of STS, and it was sort of a precursor to some of the backend functionality later found in the newer version of STS (WSS). SPS was *definitely* not free. Generally, it required a server license and a CAL for each user. Later, with the introduction of WSS, SPS version 2 was built to depend on WSS, while still costing extra money. This charging structure is still in place today, with a free, foundation SharePoint product, and then the much more expensive add-on Server product.

When Windows SharePoint Services came out, it was practically a rebuild of STS, but it did have STS at its foundation. The name change from SharePoint Team Services indicated that the product was not limited to team activities and may have helped encourage people to consider WSS a server product, and as such, affected by the Server's licensing model. However, to this day, some of the program files still bear the initials STS.

WSS put the documents and other data in the same database as the metadata, and mostly used ASP.NET for the pages and components of its various parts. The later versions of WSS don't work well with those FrontPage extensions on the IIS server. WSS uses its own very customized version of those extensions and will not install (or at least not properly) if the FrontPage extensions are enabled in IIS. WSS stepped out as a non-FrontPage–dependent product, being downloadable from the Internet or built-in as a server role in Server 2003 R2. The primary tool used to customize it was still FrontPage, but ironically people actually complained about having to buy FrontPage to edit it properly. Ah, how soon they forget that they used to have to buy the FrontPage CD to even get SharePoint.

Service Packs were released for WSS, which meant it was going places. Service Pack 1 was released to provide numerous error fixes and performance and security enhancements. Then due to customer interest and the fact that version 3 was so far on the horizon, Service Pack 2 was released to appease the masses and whet their appetite for the version to come. This Service Pack made some significant changes to SharePoint's performance; rolling together numerous hotfixes, correcting a number of undocumented (in the knowledgebase) issues, and improving the overall functionality of SharePoint itself.

There were still some functionality that could use improvement, such as a lack of security filtering (users could actually access settings pages, but not save the settings), no convenient way to tell what account was logged in, navigating between sites and subsites could be inconvenient, and the Administrative site layout made it difficult to find settings.

After Service Pack 2, came the long awaited Windows SharePoint Services 3.0, an upgrade of epic proportions. WSS 3.0 takes advantage of the strength and flexibility of ASP .NET 2.0, and requires the new Windows Workflow Foundation to offer workflow functionality to things such as document collaboration or issue tracking. Adding new and improved features that users have been clamoring for (such as required document check out, improved navigation, security filtering, improved Central Administration layout, wikis, blogs, RSS feeds, and content types), WSS 3.0 is significantly different from its predecessors.

In an ironic twist, Microsoft has "repurposed" good old FrontPage as the primary customizing tool of choice when working on SharePoint. It is no longer being sold solely as a web development tool and has been split into two different products, with one half of it being renamed "SharePoint Designer," and intended for use specifically for customizing SharePoint. It was once the only way you could get STS, and is now specifically marketed to only edit SharePoint. Fitting don't you think?

WHAT VERSION IS IT?

Due to SharePoint's varied past, there is some confusion concerning what WSS was actually called before version 3.0.

Microsoft considers the first WSS to be the second version of SharePoint Team Services, which is why the WSS installer is traditionally named stsv2.exe. But officially Microsoft always refers to whatever version of WSS someone is using as Windows SharePoint Services, even if they admit that the installer is called stsv2.exe and when you *install* the product, it calls itself Windows SharePoint Services 2.0.

So how do you tell the versions apart? Well, Windows SharePoint Services before any service packs, has the version number in Site Settings of 6.0.2.5530. If you were looking for that version online, you would find the installer file (called STSV2.exe) if you did a search for Windows SharePoint Services.

When you install Service Pack 1, the version number changes to 6.0.2.6361. Some people may have even called that version Windows SharePoint Services 1.0, which is considered a mistake. According to Microsoft there never was a 1.0 version. As far as they are concerned it's either referred to as

Windows SharePoint Services 2.0 or Windows SharePoint Services without a version, period. At least until WSS 3.0. To install this Service Pack 1 version of WSS, you would reasonably enough, search for Windows SharePoint Services with Service Pack 1. And when you found it, the installer would be called stsv2.exe (do you see a pattern here?).

When Service Pack 2 is applied to Windows SharePoint Services, the version number becomes 6.0.2.6568. This is also exactly the same version number as the Windows SharePoint Services server role on the Windows Server 2003 R2. This is the version known colloquially as Windows SharePoint Services 2.0.

And if you do want to download Windows SharePoint Services 2.0, you have to use the Windows SharePoint Services with Service Pack 2 installer (also called stsv2.exe) instead.

To make matters worse, each installation of WSS actually has two different representations of its version numbers. In Site Settings (internal to WSS), each version of Windows SharePoint Services prior to version 3 used a number syntax of 6.0.2.XXXX, with the last four digits actually pertaining to the version.

But if you ever went to Add\Remove Programs (which is obviously external to WSS), you would first notice that, no matter if installation is the base Windows SharePoint Services or Windows SharePoint Services with a Service Pack, WSS will always show up as Windows SharePoint Services 2.0. The next thing you'll notice, if you click on Support Information for the Windows SharePoint Services entry, is that the version number will be displayed as 11.0.XXXX.0, with next to the last set of digits indicating the version number.

So that brings us to Windows SharePoint Services 3.0. This version has a completely new installation interface that indicates from the start that it's Windows SharePoint Services 3.0. The installer is no longer refers to STS at all and is called SharePoint.exe. Further, the product, after installation, is depicted as Windows SharePoint Services 3.0 in Add\Remove Programs. And finally, the version number that is displayed in Site Settings is almost exactly the same as the version number displayed in the Support Information for Windows SharePoint Services 3.0, ending the discrepancy between the two. The version number, in case you are wondering, is 12.0.0.4518 in Site Settings, and 12.0.0.4518.1016 in Support Information.

So for the record, SharePoint Team Services was version 1.0. Windows SharePoint Services, regardless of Service Pack, was version 2.0. And now, Windows SharePoint Services 3.0 is explicitly referred to by that version number. Now you know.

So that's where SharePoint comes from and what it's capable of doing today. This book will cover the ins and outs of Windows SharePoint Services 3.0 to give you the best bang for your buck, the most information about what you can get out of the free version before you go out and buy the expensive add-on.

Now that you understand what SharePoint can do, let's get into what SharePoint is made of, what makes it tick, what you need to know before installing it, and what to look out for when trying to make it work.

Part I

Preparing for Windows SharePoint Services 3.0

Chapter 1

Windows SharePoint Services 3.0 Under the Hood

You've heard of Windows SharePoint Services 3.0. You've probably seen webcasts and presentations about it, but what is it and why should it matter to you?

Windows SharePoint Services (WSS) 3.0 is a nifty web-based collaboration, data management, communication, idea-creating, problem-solving tool that costs you nothing. Windows SharePoint Services, which is usually referred to in the singular, needs to run on Windows Server 2003 (Service Pack 1 or higher, or Release 2 if you have it) and should be a server role in Server 2008 (which is in beta at the writing of this book).

WSS has its needs, its shortcomings, and its weaknesses, but overall, it is a surprisingly useful, flexible, powerful web-based tool for any administrator. The best part is that using it doesn't require any web-development skills at all. As a matter of fact, this book is being written for IT admins specifically because they seem to be the people who are ultimately responsible for managing SharePoint, without really being trained for it. This book should help fill in some of those holes in training.

So what is SharePoint? SharePoint comes in two flavors: WSS 3.0 and Microsoft Office SharePoint Server 2007 (MOSS). WSS 3.0 is free and is considered a Windows Server 2003 server role which falls under the server's license model. However, MOSS, which installs on top of the free version, costs thousands of dollars (depending on volume license) and requires a Client Access License (CAL) for each user. The free version doesn't require separate client licenses for each user and is the foundation for SharePoint. The paid for version just adds more functionality to the foundation. So yes, Windows SharePoint Services is free and the foundation for the more expensive MOSS components.

What does SharePoint do? It presents a web interface for people to collaborate, communicate, and share data in an environment that is consistent, easy for administrators to control, designed to store data and documents, and is very scalable. SharePoint can be installed on a single server or it can be installed on numerous web front end servers sharing the client load on what is called a SharePoint *server farm*.

Fundamentally, SharePoint is a bunch of web pages with web parts and lists on top of a database. However, SharePoint takes advantage of that simple framework and uses it to offer lists, libraries, workspaces, wikis, blogs, and web parts. With these tools, you can offer shared calendars, discussions, file libraries, surveys, and more. For process management, you can require document checkout, content approval, and versioning. You can even establish workflows to trigger alerts and other changes based on where documents or list items are in a process. Lists and libraries can be set up with their own email accounts, so people can email entries without going to the SharePoint site.

SHAREPOINT DOESN'T DO SHARE POINTS?

WSS uses *content* databases to contain its data. It's a great way to store and organize large numbers of records, documents, photos and more. However, it is not intended to be a web front end for aggregating file shares, despite the fact that file shares are also sometimes called share points. So SharePoint does not have anything to do with share points. There are web parts and other page attributes that can point to file shares, but that is not the primary purpose of SharePoint.

This book will cover the ins and outs of Windows SharePoint Services 3.0 to give you the best bang for your buck and the most information about what you can get from the free version before you buy the expensive versions.

In this chapter, you'll learn how to:

◆ Determine the software and hardware requirements you need for installing SharePoint Services 3.0

◆ Identify the three ways of installing SharePoint Services 3.0

◆ Set up the necessary accounts that SharePoint needs to run

◆ Recognize the new features and requirements of SharePoint

Software Requirements

To make all that SharePoint goodness possible, the following roles and technologies must be installed and running on the SharePoint server. These are the underlying technologies that make SharePoint function. Without them, SharePoint won't even install.

Internet Information Services (IIS) 6.0 (or Higher)   SharePoint is web-based because IIS allows a Windows Server (2003 or higher) to host websites and service HTTP requests from clients. Many SharePoint capabilities are dependent upon and colored by the functions and needs of IIS. For example, IIS contains Web Sites, that hold web pages. In SharePoint, IIS's Web Sites are considered to be *Web Applications*, formerly called *virtual servers* in WSS 2, and contain web pages organized into sites and subsites, called *site collections*. SharePoint Web Applications are considered containers and security boundaries for those site collections, largely because of the built-in properties of IIS's Web Sites and their management (for example, specifying application pools and whether or not anonymous access is allowed). Those settings may be configured in SharePoint, but are applied at the IIS Web Site (ala web application). This explains why anonymous access is enabled at the web application level and then trickles down to each site collection contained within. The IIS server role must be installed before SharePoint can be installed.

An additional SharePoint feature that depends on IIS is incoming email, which requires that the SMTP service is enabled in IIS.

ASP.NET 2.0   ASP.NET is required to create and run web parts and other components of Share-Point web pages (as well as compile the pages themselves). It must be installed and enabled in IIS before SharePoint will install properly. ASP.NET 1.1 will also need to be installed for backward compatibility. ASP .NET 2.0 can be installed separately, or as part of the .NET Framework 3.0 installation.

.NET Framework 3.0   Required in order to install SharePoint, this service contains the Windows Workflow Foundation, a useful part of list management and document processing.

Windows Workflow Foundation   Although not something that can be installed by itself, this part of the .NET Framework 3.0 is required for SharePoint to work properly.

IT'S NOT FOR WORKSTATIONS

SharePoint can't install just anywhere on just any operating system. It requires Windows Server 2003 SP1 (Standard, Enterprise, Data Center, or Web Edition) or higher. It also requires. NTFS It is not recommended to install, it won't install on FAT32. It supports x86 and x64, although the installer for either version is still sharepoint.exe, so be careful what you download. SharePoint on a domain controller. Also, Windows Server 2003 Web Edition cannot host a database, but it can hold SharePoint. Therefore you can install SharePoint as a web front end server on the Web Edition of Windows Server 2003, but you cannot install the standalone version.

In addition, somewhere on the network, depending on how you install it, there has to be a version of SQL server for SharePoint to access. There are basically two types of SQL you can use:

SQL Server   SharePoint supports either SQL 2000 with at least SP3 or SQL 2005. This pricey package is a database powerhouse. Network aware, it can be made to support clustering and more. It is ideal for handling the huge amounts of data a large server farm might generate. SQL Server is possibly overkill for small offices who are considering SharePoint. However, if you already have SQL Server 2000 SP3 or 2005 on your network, then by all means use it.

SQL Server 2005 Embedded Edition   This edition is also called the Windows Internal Database. If you don't have SQL handy (and don't want to shell out the cash to install and use it), you can do the poor man's single SharePoint server install, as discussed in Chapter 2, "Installation." This will install SQL Server 2005 Embedded Edition (SSEE) during SharePoint's initial setup. SSEE is a local only (cannot be remotely accessed), free database, which is a modified version of SQL Server 2005 Express and essentially the newer version of WMSDE. With SSEE, SharePoint can create and manage its databases just fine. The catch is that the embedded version of SQL cannot support any other SharePoint servers accessing it. It is not as robust as its big brother SQL 2005, and it has no graphical tools built in with which to manage and update it.

CLIENT-SIDE SHENANIGANS

Of course, from the client side, users will need a browser to access the SharePoint sites. Microsoft says that SharePoint has two levels of browser support: Level 1 and Level 2. Level 1 browsers support Active X controls, namely Internet Explorer 6.0, 7.0, or higher. Level 2 refers to all other browsers.

SharePoint is optimized for Level 1 browsers (no surprise there) and supports everything you might ever want to do in SharePoint. Level 2 browsers support only non–Active X activities and are generally limited to reading and adding text to fields. Your performance may vary, depending on what customization and development has been done on your sites. The bottom line is, Microsoft wants you to use IE to use SharePoint—that and Office 2007, of course.

Office 2007 is incredibly integrated with SharePoint; half the things you can do with SharePoint you can do *better* with Office 2007. Office 2003 can do integration too, but not as completely as Office 2007.

It's important to realize how pivotal SQL is to SharePoint. In addition to hosting nifty-looking websites, SharePoint's real primary purpose is to store and access data from its databases. SharePoint is really an extensive database front end. It's all about lists (and a special kind of list called a Library). Lists contain data in records and fields (or, visually, rows and columns). Therefore, SharePoint logically requires databases on the back end to hold all that data.

As you know, SharePoint does not necessarily need to be installed on the same server as the databases themselves, although it can be if you need it. That is the beauty of SQL server: it can be accessed remotely. This means that a SharePoint server just needs to be pointed at a nearby SQL server to create and use a database there. This is convenient for several reasons, such as separating resources and storage, helping eliminate the SharePoint server as a single point of failure, and scalability. If a SQL database can be accessed by one SharePoint server, then it stands to reason (with maybe a little tweaking) that other SharePoint servers can access the same database. This is what makes server farms possible. Using this approach, multiple installations of SharePoint can be pointed to the same configuration and content databases, so they can do load balancing and share the same consistent configuration and administration settings.

This is obviously why SharePoint requires SQL. This is also where you see a functional split between installing SharePoint to be hosted by a single server and installing SharePoint to be managed across a server farm. Single server installations only need local access to a database, and they can easily use SSEE to accomplish that. A server farm requires a remote SQL server that all SharePoint front end servers can share.

So there you have it, that's SharePoint's foundation; IIS 6.0 or higher, ASP .NET 2.0, .NET Framework 3.0, and SQL Server 2000 SP3 or higher (or you can let SharePoint install SSEE). These roles and technologies, working in tandem, power SharePoint. The strengths and weaknesses of this underlying infrastructure lend their particular traits to SharePoint. Knowing about them teaches you both how SharePoint works and how to manage it, especially when it comes to troubleshooting.

Now that you know SharePoint's critical components, there are other considerations you need to cover before you install it.

Installing SharePoint: Single Server and Server Farm

SharePoint may come in two sizes, but it can actually be installed three different ways: Basic, Stand-alone Server, and Server Farm. The last two options are under the heading "Advanced."

Basic The Basic install assumes that you are going to use only one server *ever* to run SharePoint and that you don't have a copy of SQL handy to use for its databases. What it does in that case is install SharePoint assuming all necessary services are going to run locally and that you need it to install the free "Windows Internal Database," which is Microsoft's nickname for its SQL Server 2005 Embedded Edition database (SSEE).

DESKTOP DATABASE PRIMER

MSDE was Microsoft's free desktop database engine, originally for developers to run on their workstations to develop SQL applications without having to have a copy of the expensive version of SQL. It had a 2GB limit, could have a maximum of only five concurrent users, could not be accessed remotely, had no search indexing capabilities, and had a few more limitations.

WMSDE, or MSDE (Windows), was created by Microsoft to be the built-in database back end for some of their free but necessary products, such as Microsoft's Windows Server Update Service (WSUS) and Windows SharePoint Services 2.0. The WMSDE version of MSDE unlocked the 2GB limitation, but it still did not have full-search indexing or remote access capabilities.

WMSDE was sort of "embedded" in those free Microsoft products, meaning it was transparent, installed invisibly; and was a critical part of those products, so much so that they installed it automatically (well, WSS 2.0 did if you told it to).

This explains why the newest version of WMSDE that installs with the SharePoint version 3.0 Basic install is called SQL Server 2005 Embedded Edition (SSEE) or Windows Internal Database (WID). It is a slightly modified version of the WMSDE update, called SQL Server 2005 Express Edition, which has been surprisingly improved and supports search, remote access, and Windows authentication.

If you perform the SharePoint Basic installation, the SSEE database cannot be used by any other SharePoint server on the network. You will not have remote access. There is absolutely no way that you can do a more complicated, multiple server installation of SharePoint using the SSEE database. Unfortunately, an SSEE database is not quite as robust as SQL server databases. For most people, this only means that as the databases fill up more quickly and become more awkward and slower, so it is important to closely monitor the content database of a Basic installed SharePoint server (use database site quotas and quota templates for site collections judiciously). That being said, a lot of small to medium businesses use the Basic install of SharePoint without any problems, and they have the bonus of saving so much money by not buying SQL. Basically, if you plan to never have more than 10 separate web applications in your company, and plan to have only one SharePoint server, then using SSEE would be fine for you. Web applications (and their databases) will be discussed in greater detail in Chapter 8.

Advanced *Stand-alone.* This installation is essentially the same as the Basic install. Use this installation method if you intend to install SharePoint on one server only, and you want SharePoint to install and use the SSEE database. The only difference between this install type and Basic is that it gives you the option to specify the location of your index files, as well as define your feedback (because you may want to let Microsoft know about your day to day SharePoint experience).

Web Front End (Server Farm). This installation method actually includes a few kinds of SharePoint topologies. At its simplest, this is the method of installation you use if you don't want SharePoint to install SSEE because you have, and are going to use a SQL Server. That's because Basic and Stand-Alone install SSEE without your involvement. If you have a SQL server on your Windows network (2000 SP3 or 2005) and you want to use it to house your SharePoint databases, then the Server Farm install is the only type that lets you specify where your databases will go.

The other reason you would use the Server Farm installation method would be if you want a server farm topology. A SharePoint server farm uses more than one server to support Share-Point. This can be simply one SharePoint server and one SQL server; or it can be scale up to a more complex topology, such as several SharePoint severs (generally called web front end servers) and an SQL database cluster. The simplest server farm consists of a database server and a server with SharePoint installed on it, so the two functions are separated between two servers. Together they are a server farm. Of course, there is more to it than that. Usually, people create bigger server farms which means more SharePoint servers all using the same SQL databases. This is appropriate if they have a lot of SharePoint sites and they want to spread HTTP requests between servers to improve performance; meaning multiple SharePoint servers, and even multiple, clustered database servers.

If you choose to do a Server Farm installation, you can specify whether the SharePoint server you are installing is the first on the farm or if you want that server to be part of an existing server farm (see Figure 1.1). The first SharePoint server on a server farm is kind of like the first domain controller in a domain. Because it's the first, it tends to hold all the services and is the one used to set up the databases. Choosing to add the server to an existing server farm means that the installation will install only the files needed to make that new server a web front end server to help support the first server with client requests.

FIGURE 1.1
Starting a new server farm, or connecting to an existing farm

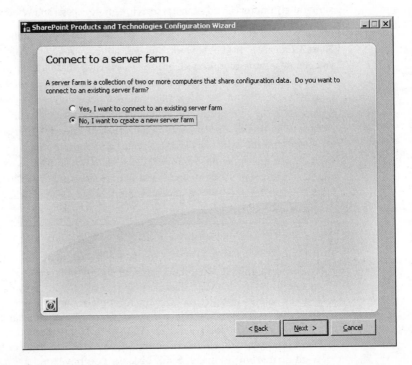

Server farms work in this configuration because the databases that hold all the information of the SharePoint sites already exist on the SQL server. All you have to do at that point is specify which configuration databases the new server will share with the first server, and presto change-o, you've got a new SharePoint server with the same configuration and content.

> **THE GORILLA IN THE ROOM**
>
> Something that isn't mentioned much is that server farms, in addition to having front-end servers that all access the same databases, are usually configured using Windows Network Load Balancing software, DNS round robin, or a hardware load-balancing device. Real, server farm, load-balancing functionality requires additional setup using something other than SharePoint. Installing additional SharePoint front-end servers is only one part of it.
>
> To make matters worse, there is little current documentation about how to do load balancing. So check out Chapter 15 for a brief demonstration of how to simply do network load balancing with SharePoint.

The differences between the kinds of SharePoint installations are not the stuff of rocket science. However, if you intend to do more than run everything on one server, or if you don't want to end up with the SSEE database, you really need to understand those differences before you install SharePoint.

SharePoint Sites and Databases

SharePoint needs at least two different IIS Web Sites (otherwise known as SharePoint web applications) to function. These web applications contain the web pages that you will access to either administer SharePoint or actually use SharePoint's lists, sites, and libraries.

The Central Administration Web Application   This web application controls the configuration and administration of all servers on the server farm, as well as all web applications. This site is set up on a completely different and unique port than the standard one for HTTP. If you do a server farm installation, you can specify the port or use the one suggested. If you do a Basic or Stand-Alone installation, then the port will be chosen at random for you during installation and configuration. The range is somewhere between 1023 and 32767. The unique port helps obscure this site from anyone surfing the standard ports on the server.

The SharePoint Site   The default name for the first SharePoint web application (that isn't dedicated to Central Administration) is usually SharePoint-80. It will contain the first top-level site for SharePoint, just to get you started (or in a server farm installation, you will have to create if yourself). Web applications were meant to contain site collections, which are literally collections of sites, starting with a top-level site, but can also include additional subsites. Web applications can contain as few as one site collection with one top-level site, or many site collections, each with multiple subsites. Because a web application is essentially a container for your SharePoint sites, when you configure settings at the web application level, they can affect *all* sites contained therein.

> **I THOUGHT THERE WOULD BE ONLY TWO**
>
> Keep in mind that these are the web applications that are created during SharePoint installation. You can create more if you'd like. If you inherit a SharePoint server and find that more than two web applications are being used by SharePoint, that's fine. Someone probably added more for a good reason (see Chapter 8 for more information as to how and why to create additional web applications), and now you are responsible for them. Congratulations.

Each SharePoint web application needs at least one content database to contain its data. The Central Administration web application also accesses the server farm's configuration database (which stands to reason, because that is where all the configuration settings are for SharePoint). Because SharePoint is capable of performing full-text, site-collection wide searches, Search also has its own database.

The Sharepoint Databases   This means that four databases must be created when SharePoint is installed. I am using the default names, but you can change them depending on how you install SharePoint.

SharePoint_Config_(GUID):   This is the configuration database for SharePoint. It holds all of the configuration data and settings for the entire server farm. The thing that makes separate Share-Point servers all members of the same server farm is that each of them use the same configuration database. This makes it possible for all of those servers to have the same configuration settings. When you do a single server installation, the database will be called SharePoint_Config_(GUID). If you do a server farm installation, the suggested default (which you can easily change) is simply SharePoint_Config.

WSS_Search_Servername   This is the database that contains all of the search data acquired when the index (or content access) service crawled through the SharePoint site collection. Search is an interesting beast in SharePoint, both overly simple and potentially complex.

WSS_Content   This is the content database for the first web application made in SharePoint for SharePoint sites. It will contain information about the site collections that the web application contains, and it will contain all of the list, library, and web part metadata, documents, and attachments. Keep in mind that you can have more than one content database for a web application, and chances are good that you will grow out of the first one pretty quickly.

SharePoint_AdminContent_(GUID):   This is the content database for the Central Administration web application. Because the Central Administration website is just like any other SharePoint website, it is prone to the same strengths and weaknesses. Site settings can be changed, including those for the master page. Novices should not do this. As a matter of fact, no one should. They could potentially delete the document library folder containing the Help files and more.

Content Databases

Although each web application gets its own content database, web applications can contain more than one site collection, and each site collection can contain multiple sites that can contain lists and libraries that *can* get really big (I'm not guaranteeing anything, I'm just saying, over and over, that they *can*). Frankly, using a single database to contain large sites full of data can be an invitation for that database to become really slow and unwieldy. There is always a reasonable limit to how much any one database can hold, and its surprising how quickly that limit can be reached. Don't think of it as a bad thing; it just means that people are using the sites. To help you cope, SharePoint allows you to add extra content databases to web applications to keep up with the ever-increasing data load. This is why it is possible to have several content databases for one web application. In addition, you can configure database capacity settings (by limiting the number of site collections per database and the size in MB of the site collections themselves), so that you can be warned when a database is getting too big and be prepared to add a new database.

Overall, this means that SharePoint uses IIS Web Sites as web applications to hold site collections. Web applications can contain multiple site collections, each site collection can hold many sites, and each site can have many lists and libraries. As a result, a SharePoint server farm can have many web applications, each with several content databases. However, there can only be *one* configuration database for each server farm. The configuration database specifies the configuration for the whole farm and, therefore, must be only one.

SharePoint Service Accounts and Services

After it installs, SharePoint creates and enables certain services and application pools. To be able to do their jobs, these services need to run with some sort of account context. Depending on how you install SharePoint, you may have to create domain accounts to apply to those services. If you want SharePoint to work, it will help to know what the services are, what they do, and what access those accounts need while remaining secure.

Service Accounts

Here are the accounts you need for SharePoint to install and work:

Setup Account (Basic or Stand-alone install)   In order to install SharePoint, you must be logged in on the server with an administrative account. If your server is not in a domain, this account needs to be the local Administrator. In order to install SharePoint, you must be logged in on the server with an administrative account. On a domain, the account can be a domain admin. The account must be able to install software locally, and should also be allowed to add and start services on the server.

All other service accounts used by SharePoint are set up automatically (local system or network service) with a Stand-alone or Basic installation. It really is the easiest installation, in addition to being the cheapest. Although it is not super scalable, it is convenient.

THE CHEESE STANDS ALONE

You don't have to install SharePoint to support multiple servers in a domain environment. You also can install SharePoint on a stand-alone server in a workgroup with no domain controller. The easiest way to do this is to install SQL server (or let SharePoint install the SQL 2005 Embedded Edition for you) on the server that will house SharePoint. Then it can do all the database management it requires without needing to access anything on a different server. To use incoming email features, the server will also need to have SMTP enabled. Local users and groups will be used to give users access to SharePoint in that scenario, rather than going through a domain controller. It just goes to show that SharePoint is scalable down as well as up.

Another bonus of a single-server install with SQL 2005 Embedded Edition is that you don't really need to worry about specifying domain permissions or specific SQL permissions of the SharePoint service accounts. If you choose a Basic install, database and services set up will be done for you by SharePoint using the administrative account you used to log in. It will specify that all services will run using local system or network service server accounts.

Setup Account (Server Farm)   In a domain Server Farm install, the setup account should be a domain admin (you can use local Administrator accounts to install SharePoint on each individual server, but it is easier simply to use one setup account that is a domain admin). This account should be allowed to install SharePoint on any server in the domain, and it must be able to access the SQL server that SharePoint will be using to build databases.

On the SQL server, the setup account must have these SQL server security roles on the target SQL server: Logins, Securityadmin, and Dbcreator.

Database Access Account   Also known as the *server farm account* or *configuration database account*, this account is powerful and critical to SharePoint. It does not need to have administrative privileges; but it should be a domain account. All other rights for this account will be configured automatically by the setup account during installation. The setup account adds the database access account to the SQL server's Logins, Dbcreator, Securityadmin roles. This is why the database access account ends up being the owner (DBO) of most of the SharePoint databases.

THE DBO EXCEPTION

Oddly enough the database access account does not become the DBO of the configuration database for the server farm because the setup account creates that database during installation and then assigns ownership of it to the database access account. This means that, by default, the setup account is the DBO, but the database access account holds an owner role.

This account is the Central Administration application pool identity. This means that it is *the* account that accesses and changes the configuration database for the server farm. It is also the account used to power the SharePoint Timer Service, which is in charge of any jobs that need to be started and stopped at different times (such as getting incoming mail, managing quotas, and alerts). This account should be guarded and not used for anything else.

Content Database Account   Also known as the *web application account*, or web application *application pool account*, this is the account that uses the content database of a web application. There should be one of these per web application—although under some circumstances (as is the case in businesses with security policies that limit service accounts), web applications can share an account. This account should be a domain user and otherwise is given (and requires) database ownership of all content databases associated with a web application.

Search Account   This account should be a domain user. It directly accesses the Search database. Because it takes the questions entered into the Search field in SharePoint and queries the Search database records with them, it is considered the query account.

Content Access Account   Also known as the *index, gatherer,* or *crawler account*, this account analyzes all of the content in SharePoint site collections. It must be a domain user, and it will automatically be given full read rights to all web applications. It also has access to the Search database to write in the information it has gathered.

Optional SharePoint Admin Account   I also suggest you consider a general purpose SharePoint administrator account. This account should be a domain admin (or at least local admin for each SharePoint server), so it can install tools locally on all SharePoint servers on the farm, run the SharePoint command line tools, and can be used as a default administrator for central administration and new site collections you may create. It comes in handy for me when I need to troubleshoot a site or a setting in Central administration. I always know that account's name and password, and it is usually the first owner of most site collections I create (of course, this may not be allowed to remain after handing the collection over to its rightful owner, but it's convenient during setup).

IF THE SQL DBA DOESN'T PLAY NICE

If the person in charge of the SQL databases is not comfortable giving the SharePoint server admin the power to create databases on their SQL server, don't worry. If you prebuild the databases that the SharePoint server will require, SharePoint will happily connect at the correct points of setup to the preexisting database without unduly empowering non-database administrators to create databases of their own. Check out the "Deploy using DBA-created databases" TechNet article for more information about how to configure the databases and handle service accounts in that situation. There are versions of the document for both WSS and for MOSS, but they are basically identical. Go to the Windows SharePoint Services 3.0 Technical Library, Deployment for Windows SharePoint Services 3.0 technology, End to end deployment scenarios, "Deploy using DBA-created databases."

SharePoint Services

The following services are created and required by SharePoint. It might be handy to know what they are before you conduct your first installation.

SPAdmin (Windows SharePoint Services Administration)   This is the administrative service for SharePoint. It runs on every SharePoint server locally and is in charge of checking the configuration database for changes. It keeps track of what server on a server farm is running what service, and is used by sharepoint to access local resources per server. This services runs as the WSSADMIN process in Task Manager.

SPTimerV3 (Windows SharePoint Services Timer)   This is the service in charge of actually triggering and running jobs for SharePoint. Because it uses the database access account identity, it usually doesn't have administrative permissions on the local server; however, it does have ownership permissions to do what it needs to do on both the configuration and content databases. If it needs to do something administrative on the local machine, it calls on the SPAdmin account to do it. This service runs as the OWSTIMER process in Task Manager.

SPSearch (Windows SharePoint Services Search)   This is the Search service for SharePoint. It runs on the SharePoint servers that are running the Search service. This service runs the mssearch process in Task Manager.

SPTrace (Windows SharePoint Services Tracing)   This service also installs on each SharePoint server locally. It is used for error tracking and analysis, and controls the trace logs. This service runs as the wsstracing process in Task Manager.

SPWriter (Windows SharePoint Services VSS Writer)   This service integrates with SQL's VSS writer service, inherited from SPS 2003, and works with SharePoint's backup and recovery capabilities. It makes it possible to use Windows Volume Shadow Copy when doing backups. This services runs as the SPWRITER process in Task Manager, and only starts when necessary. So it's not always running.

SQL SERVICES

SharePoint is dependent upon SQL, so it should go without saying that if it is installed to use the SSEE database locally, that version of SQL should be running locally as well.

User Account Modes

Most people don't even realize they have a choice when it comes to selecting a user account mode. By default, SharePoint will install using the Active Directory Domain Account mode. However, hidden deep behind an Advanced Settings button at the end of SharePoint's installation is the option to choose a different option when it comes to how SharePoint handles user accounts. When they say "advanced," they mean it. Setting up account modes is a one-shot deal. You get one chance to choose your user account mode when you install the first SharePoint server in the server farm (or a Stand-alone server). Then that information gets locked in the configuration database of the whole farm, affecting the whole farm with no way to change it. *You cannot undo the account mode decision once you make it.* So choose with caution. There are two choices and they both are based on Windows Active Directory user accounts.

There are two User Account Mode options. The default user account mode is the one with which we are all familiar—Active Directory Domain Account Mode. The other account mode (Active Directory Account Creation Mode) is more complicated to set up and is actually considered a different SharePoint deployment. That other user account mode is the one that must be selected during installation in order to be enabled—otherwise the default, Domain Account mode will be enforced.

Domain Account Mode   This mode is selected by default during SharePoint setup, SharePoint lets the administrators add users to SharePoint based on their Active Directory or Local Users accounts. In other words, first you have user accounts in Active Directory (which is what you probably have already), and then you can add them to SharePoint.

Active Directory Account Creation (ADAC) Mode   When this mode is selected during SharePoint setup, SharePoint allows administrators to create user accounts in Active Directory when they add them to SharePoint. That's right. When you add users to SharePoint, it adds the users to a special Organizational Unit (OU) in Active Directory. This was meant for ISPs or companies that had a lot of external partners or offsite users who needed authenticated access to the server content. Therefore, instead of creating user accounts in Active Directory and then adding them to SharePoint, Active Directory Account Creation mode does it the other way around by adding the user to SharePoint, which adds them automatically to Active Directory. See Chapter 15 for more information as to how to use ADAC and what happens when you do.

Sounds interesting, doesn't it? But keep in mind that it is a potentially complicated procedure from which there is no going back. See Chapter 15 for a step by step look at Active Directory Account Creation mode.

Authentication Types

In conjunction with IIS, SharePoint supports several different ways to allow users to authenticate. They are not exclusive; you can choose to apply multiple types of authentication to a web application. IIS will apply the most restrictive method first. If that fails, it will try the second most-restrictive method, and so on until it finally refuses the client or lets them log in.

A Rose by Any Other Name . . .

You may have noticed that SharePoint uses the same terminology in several different ways in several different places. Here is a quick rundown on some of them:

Authentication Provider: (sometimes referred to as Membership Providers): Usually refer to the services that provide authentication like SQL Forms based authentication or Windows authentication.

Authentication Method: The method that authentication is sent to the Windows Authentication Provider, such as NTLM or Kerberos. In IIS, authentication methods also refer to using other authentication types like basic, digest, and integrated Windows to authenticate users to a particular Web Site.

Authentication Source: Where the authentication accounts are stored and accessed by the Provider. Examples of this are Active Directory or the database used by Forms based authentication.

Because SharePoint has gone through several different versions by this time, and over time it has changed its terminology. However, the SharePoint command line tool, STSADM, does occasionally reflect some of the older terms. So don't be surprised if you see, when working at the command line, the following examples:

◆ Sites collections are called "Sites."

◆ Sites are often called "Webs."

◆ Subsites are referred to as "Subwebs."

◆ Server Farms are often referred to as Web Farms.

◆ Web Applications are called "Virtual Servers."

Windows Integrated Authentication   This authentication method requires the user to have a domain account or a local account on the SharePoint server. This, of course, is the method that Microsoft prefers and the one used throughout this book.

Digest   This also works with Active Directory, but it sends the username and password as hashed values. It can be used if Windows Integrated Authentication is blocked by a firewall or not being passed by a proxy server. It is also available on WebDAV servers.

Basic   This method will send authentication information across a network as cleartext, which is obviously not a great idea.

Anonymous Access   This method allows users to establish an anonymous connection with IIS by using an anonymous or guest account.

Authentication Methods

In addition to those authentication types, SharePoint offers two Windows authentication methods during installation. These protocols don't just govern how authentication data is passed on the network for users trying to access SharePoint; they govern how SharePoint service accounts themselves access resources:

NTLM This secure protocol encrypts usernames and passwords over the network. It simply sends data to the authenticating authority and back. This protocol does not require additional configuration, and it is suggested for most SharePoint scenarios.

Kerberos This secure protocol encrypts data but handles authentication differently than NTLM. Kerberos is based on *ticketing*. A username and password are passed to an authentication server, which sends back a ticket to allow the authenticated user to access network resources. The user *and* the authentication server (or Key Distribution Center) must trust each other. This means that service principal names must be set for the SharePoint servers and the database access account so resources on the network can be accessed by SharePoint on behalf of the user. The account and the servers must be trusted for delegation in some circumstances.

Microsoft suggests using NTLM, because using Kerberos requires the database access account to have a service principal name, which could be a greater danger to the network if that account is compromised. And even though outside the network, authentication is tighter with the mutual authentication process of Kerberos, using to authenticate can be a problem due to time synchronization. There is one catch though: in some situations, search's index service cannot authenticate using Kerberos and therefore cannot index sites that require it. For more information about Kerberos and how to configure it, see Chapter 15, "Advanced Installation and Configuration," for more details.

IFILTERS

Don't despair if you are thinking about collaborating on files other than those made in Microsoft Office using SharePoint. Some vendors use Index Filters (IFilters) so that Search can index their document types. Check with your vendor first to see if they have an IFilter you can use to recognize their file types for searching.

SharePoint Search

The Search feature is new to Windows SharePoint Services. In the old days, you could enable Search in SharePoint (WSS 2 and lower) only if you were using a full-blown SQL server. This was because SharePoint was simply using SQL's built-in full-text search and indexing features to do searches, which could add a significant performance load to the SQL server. This meant that if you did the Typical install of SharePoint, which is now called Basic, and used WMSDE for the database, the Search field simply would not be available in SharePoint (see Figure 1.2). WMSDE does not have the search capabilities of SQL server.

FIGURE 1.2
In WSS 2.0, a Typical install could not search

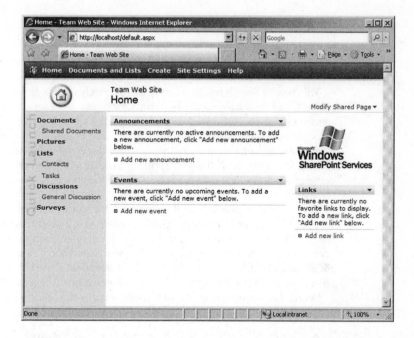

WSS 3.0 uses the same SharePoint search service that the older version of MOSS used. This means that you can perform full-text searches of site collections, including Office files, *even* if you did a Basic install of SharePoint and are using the SSEE database (see Figure 1.3). SharePoint is doing the searching now, not SQL. This helps lower the performance stress of the SQL server as well.

FIGURE 1.3
In WSS 3.0, a Basic Installation has a search field

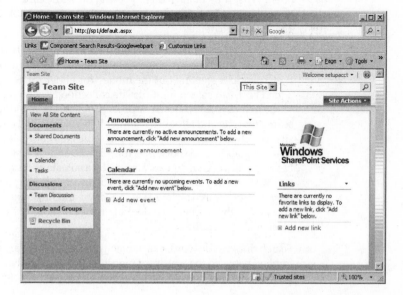

Search basically does two things:

- It responds to search queries.

- It crawls through site collections and indexes data.

This is why Search has two services, the search service and the index service (or content access service), and their corresponding service accounts. Both services use a Search database; the index service merges its collected data with it, and the search service queries it. Only one index service can exist on a server farm, but there can be more than one server running the search service on a farm. (Each server would share the index service.) The index service requires read access to all content databases of all the web applications that will be searched. When a web application is being created, you can assign a search server to service its content database. This is useful if you have more than one server running search.

The index service will scan the content databases of the web applications per the schedule you set up when you enable Search. The changes that it finds, are temporarily stored in index files on the SharePoint server that is running the index service, then merges them with the Search database after a set period of time. Meanwhile, the search service, when responding to a user query, will check the index files and the database to be sure that all results are accurate. This is why there can be only one server running the index service on a farm, because those files have to be in one place.

Search has some strengths and weakness that you should know about before you install SharePoint:

- Search only returns search queries per site collection. That means if you are looking for a document and you have several site collections, you need to know what site collection it's in or search each site collection until you find it. Site collections are a hard-search boundary.

- Search doesn't have much of an administrative surface. The GUI settings are limited to what service accounts use, the Search database name, and how often the site collections will be indexed. Indexing is primarily incremental, but even that can strain resources if you do it too often. What little management you can do with search is through the SharePoint command line tool STSADM. See Chapter 13, "STSADM: A Look at the SharePoint Command Line Tool" for more details.

- Search can search *only* site collections (or more precisely content databases). It cannot search file shares, email servers, or other locations. If you want to search content outside site collections, consider shelling out the money for either MOSS or MOSS for Search (which for the added cost, can search multiple site collection or even multiple SharePoint servers).

    Search uses a top-down approach. When you conduct a search query on a site, it will search that site and all subsites under it. If you conduct a search query on a site at the top of a site collection (the first site created in a site collection), it will search the data contained in its Search database and index files for that site and then systematically check all other subsites below it. However, if you are already on a subsite and start to search, it will search from there and work its way down the subsites below it, ignoring the sites above it in the collection. In other words, Search always searches *down* and never *up*. Unless you absolutely know which subsite has the data you are looking for, you should always perform searches from the top level of a site collection.

- Search does whole word, exact match queries. If there are multiple words in a query, AND is implied between the words (orange juice is considered orange AND juice, and would return only results that contain both values). Punctuation is ignored, as is the word "and itself."

However, strangely, the word OR is neither ignored nor recognized as a part of the query logic and is treated like part of the query text itself.

◆ Unfortunately, Search doesn't accept wildcards or Boolean logic, but it does allow for keyword exclusions or additions by using the plus (+) or minus (–) signs. Search will also support property filtering. Property filtering means that search can recognize some field names and properties, such as filetype, contenttype (used for libraries particularly), author, title, or subject. To filter in the search field by property, the syntax is property:query, such as filetype:txt will result in all text files in the site collection.

◆ Searches can be scoped. This is a simple concept that just means that when you are in a list, library, or folder, the little dropdown list next to the Search field offers you the option to search that one location or the entire site.

◆ The search results are displayed on a page organized by modified date or relevance (the default is relevance). This can further allow you to narrow down the search query. Results are displayed with the link to it, and some summarizing information. The page even displays the length of time the query took to complete (Figure 1.4).

FIGURE 1.4
Search results page

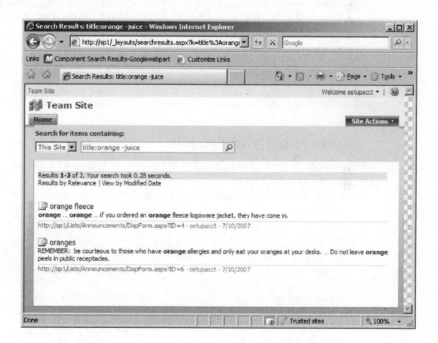

◆ In a server farm, there should be only one search service account and one index (content access) service account. However, if you have a large and busy server farm, it might be good to have a server dedicated to searching, or you could run more than one server with the search service enabled. Search prefers Windows Authentication and may cause errors in an anonymous environment. In addition, the index service prefers NTLM authentication, so it can have problems accessing a web application that requires Kerberos.

◆ Sites and lists can be excluded from indexing, if you'd like them to be unsearchable such as lists with item level security, which may cause some items to be displayed for those who can't open them.

◆ Search can perform *security trimming*, which means it includes security information when it is indexing site collections and excludes items from a query based on the permissions of the person asking.

INDEXING AND GATHERING

The search service's index service appear to be hand-me-downs from SPS 2003 and MOSS. This is why WSS 3.0's Search is independent from SQL. The index service is a powerful feature that you don't need to monitor. It takes care of itself and does its own thing with WSS. (MOSS has added configuration features for indexing.) Its only content sources are the content databases that SharePoint uses. It uses IFilters and protocol handlers to parse documents, filter out formatting, and find words in documents. It can distinguish between relevant words and irrelevant words or "noise." It can handle only 64MB of indexed words. If it maxes out, it doesn't really notify you; it just doesn't index any more of the document, which is another reason to keep uploads and document files from becoming bloated. It allows whole word searches and keyword inclusion/exclusion, but it doesn't support stemming, wildcards, or Boolean logic.

The IFilters that come with SharePoint can handle Office 2007 file types, text files, HTML, and TIFF files (which is the file type usually used for scanning faxes and documents).

SharePoint and Email

Sharepoint integrates with email more than ever. This is why you should consider how you'll configure email when you're planning to install SharePoint.

In addition to being capable of sending alerts and notifications (which requires properly configured outgoing email), SharePoint needs to be set up to receive incoming email. This is because several lists and libraries can be enabled to receive email. The primary benefit is that you can send a new item to the list without going to the SharePoint site if you know that list's email address. And you can do of this from the comfort of your email program. No need to open a browser.

To manage incoming email, the SharePoint server needs to have the SMTP service set up locally. You should have that enabled before you install SharePoint. When SharePoint receives email, it pulls it from the default drop directory that SMTP uses or from the directory you specify. It gives it to the correct list or library, which parses the email for the subject line, message body, and other pertinent header information. It then applies the information to the appropriate fields in the list record.

Incoming email has another interesting new feature called SharePoint Directory Management Service. This service integrates SharePoint with Active Directory. To use it, you need to create a unique OU, give the server farm account extensive access to it, and assign the content database accounts local administrative rights to the SharePoints server. SharePoint can allow users to create distribution lists that show up in the OU and add the list and library incoming email aliases to the Exchange global address list (GAL). Of course, this obviously requires Exchange, and more specifically Exchange 2003 because it integrates so deeply with Active Directory.

DON'T LET THEM SCARE YOU

Despite occasional documents stating otherwise, SharePoint Directory Management Service does not have to be running for SharePoint to be able to do incoming email. In its simple straightforward way, incoming email works fine without it. If you don't want to increase the complexity of your SharePoint install, don't use SharePoint Directory Management Service. It is an option, not a requirement. Its biggest strength is that it allows Exchange users to have the SharePoint lists' addresses show up in the global address book. It simply adds contact records and distribution lists to the specified OU in Active Directory. For more about Directory Management Service, see Chapter 15.

Alternate Access Mapping

When you initially install and start using SharePoint, accessing it by using the NetBIOS name of the server works fine, but what if you want to be able to access it from the internet? You can't resolve that server name among all the other machine names on the internet, so you need it to resolve to a DNS name. Alternate Access Mapping is about mapping a SharePoint web application to an alternate name other than the default. That means that you can have an internal, default name of http://sp2 and a different, internet URL of http://sharepoint.dem0tek.com, and both actually point to the same server.

Alternate Access Mapping (AAM), specifies alternate access of a web application by internal URLs, public URLs, and zones. An Internal URL is what the web application responds to. A Public URL is what the web application returns to the user in the address bar, and in the links for all search results. Web applications can have five public URLs associated with it (at which point they are called *zones*). So you can have a Default zone (that's the default URL for the web application which is usually the root path for all the site collections it might contain), an Intranet zone, Internet zone, Extranet zone, and a Custom zone.

There is also another use for AAM, extending web applications. Sometimes you might want to have two web applications using the same content database (and therefore accessing the same websites, lists, etc.). This can give users two ways to access the same data and is useful if you want to have two different types of authentication for the content, depending on what URL the user uses. Because the extended web application is just sharing the same content database as an existing web application, it is considered just another URL used to access the first web application's content. This is why an extended web application is not given its own name but is considered a *zone* of the existing web application. In that case one of the Public URL zones is taken up with the URL of the extended web application.

So when planning your URL structure and how users are going to access SharePoint, keep AAM in mind.

Managed Paths

When planning for SharePoint it's a good idea to keep in mind how you would like to structure your site collections. Site collections are composed of a top-level site and all the sites that stem from it (called subsites). The top-level site is usually accessed by using the web application's URL and then the path to the top-level site's home page. When creating a site collection, you must decide what its URL path will be. When you create your first site collection in a web application, you can give it the *root* address for that web application, or you can specify a path. What this means is if you create the first web application on server SP2, then its URL can be http://SP2, using port 80, which is the root address for the URL. But if you create a second site collection in that web application, it needs to have a different path, because it can't use the same URL. This is where Managed Paths comes in. By default SharePoint has a "sites" managed path for additional site collections. The URL for that path would be, on the same server, `http://sp2/sites/`. What this means is if you create that additional site collection, it can be something on that path, such as `http://sp2/sites/something`.

You can, of course, create your own, depending on your required topology. This is useful if you are planning to have one web application, say, per region, and then site collections for each office. Then you might consider creating a managed path for the London office, Beijing office, Helsinki, etc.

Site collections are useful for being a user account or permissions boundary because you can add users once to the top-level site, apply their permissions, and they are available as users in all subsites as well; but for that site collection only. The other site collections are unaffected by the comings and goings of users in any other site collection.

Another thing to consider with managed paths is that if you have additional non-SharePoint Web Sites or web software you want to run in the same IIS Web Site virtual directory, SharePoint automatically ignores it if it is on a path not specified in Managed Paths.

User Accounts and Permissions

In order for anyone to use SharePoint, there must be users. SharePoint leans toward organizing users and permissions based on the users' roles. So if you have a site owner, he would need to have full control of the site, but a member would only need to be able to be a contributor.

SharePoint controls the user permissions that can be applied at the web application level. So if necessary, you could actually block certain permissions entirely from ever being applied to users in the site collections the web application contained. At the site and site collection level, permissions can be combined to create permission levels, which are then applied to users or groups.

Individual Active Directory Users can be added to SharePoint, but you can also simply add domain security groups as well. Doing so let's you add a number of users to SharePoint that might require the same permission levels, at one time. It is also easier for SharePoint to handle because has limitations on how many separate security principals it can manage at one time. It's actually considered SharePoint best practice to use AD security groups to add users rather than individual domain users for that reason.

SharePoint uses SharePoint Groups to organize users. There are three SharePoint groups built in: Members, Visitors, and Owners; but you can also make your own. When you create a SharePoint group, you assign permission levels to the group. Then, when you add a user, you choose the SharePoint group they should belong to, and that group's permission levels automatically apply to that user. So when planning your user management strategy keep permissions, permission levels, and SharePoint groups in mind.

Hardware Requirements

Trying to pin down the exact hardware requirements for a product like SharePoint is tough. There are many different ways to use it; therefore, there are many ways to configure the resources.

Microsoft has some suggestions for SharePoint server's recommended and minimum requirements. These recommendations are for average server loads. In my experience, the recommendations work pretty well as long as your network is healthy and well configured.

Processor   2.5GHz minimum, dual processors, 3GHz recommended.

RAM   1GB minimum, 2GB or more recommended.

Disk   3GB, NTFS. More disk space is recommended, depending on your storage needs. The 3GB reflects only what SharePoint needs and does not include the needs of the operating system, any SQL databases (if you are going to do a single server install), or anything else running on the server.

ALL IN ONE

Disk space is a particular issue if you are running SQL and SharePoint on the same server, as they would be in a Stand-alone installation. You will need to plan for the storage space of the SharePoint pages in IIS, SMTP mail storage (if you enable incoming email), the indexing files used for search, all the storage space that your site's lists and libraries will use, and all the other databases SharePoint uses. As you can see, the space that SharePoint might need for its files is not the only space you'll need. In this case, everything is stored in one place. Size it well and guard it carefully.

DVD Drive   Not really required for SharePoint, but useful.

Display   1024 × 768 on the client (800 × 600 is too small. It forces some pages to require way too much scrolling.)

Network   56 kilobits per second (Microsoft's minimum), 1 gigabit per second is suggested.

These recommendations are just starting points; however, they are more than adequate for most simple SharePoint Server Farm installations. Most single server or simple Server Farm installations can probably handle 1,000 people creating an average load on the SharePoint server, without seeing a lag in operations per second. Commonly, each gigahertz of processing power in a SharePoint server can handle about nine operations per second.

Performance Planning

You might be wondering how you determine operations per second? There are formulas to help you figure that out.

Essentially, you need to know:

1. How many people are supposed to use SharePoint? (Users)

2. What percentage are *really* going to use it? (Percent active users)

3. How many operations per day they do on average (how many documents edited, list entries added, searches done, etc)? (Operations)

4. How many hours do the users work in SharePoint on average? (Work Hours)

5. Whether an average work day has particular peaks in performance? (Peak Factor)

To calculate the operations per second, multiply items 1, 2, 3, and 5 together, then divide that number by the number of hours those people are going to be working a day by 360,000 (which is 100 percent conversion × 60 minutes per hour × 60 seconds per minute). Altogether that will show you how many operations per second your server needs to efficiently handle.

To show you what I mean and illustrate that the above hardware requirements are probably adequate for your needs, assume your office has 1,000 people who are going to use SharePoint and 60 percent of them will be actively using SharePoint daily. You estimate that each user probably performs about 50 operations a day. (Most of them will spend more time editing a document than retrieving it from the document library or uploading it.) Let's say your office has, at maximum, 9 hours of work time a day and a peak factor of 4. *Peak factor* is a scale between 1 and 5 that refers to how often or how likely there are to be peaks in normal daily usage. One indicates that there is practically no particular time of peak usage during a business day, and 5 indicates that practically the entire day is a peak use time. I never go less than 4, just in case.

MEMBERSHIP IN CLUB SHAREPOINT IS NOT ALL-INCLUSIVE

Many businesses do not need to allow every employee access to SharePoint. Therefore, when you determine who will use the SharePoint sites, don't just include everyone in the company. To help ensure that your calculations are as accurate as possible, consider exactly who will do what.

Let's summarize the data we have:

Users: 1,000

Percent active usage: 60

Operations: 50 (per person, per day)

Work hours: 9

Peak factor: 4

And the formula that uses that information is:

Users × Usage × Operations × Peak ÷ (360,000 × WorkHours), or in our case,
   $1,000 × 60 × 50 × 4 ÷ (360,000 × 9)$

That will bring you to the operations per second that your server needs to deliver for your users. In this case, that number is 3.7 operations per second (OPS).

Given the standard formula above, 2.5GHz and 1GB of RAM should be able to handle at least 10 operations per second (Microsoft has mentioned that it feels confident that that hardware can handle 18 operations per second). All *you* need is 3.7 operations per second for 1,000 people doing 50 operations a day. You can see why I think the starting hardware requirements are sufficient for most small to medium businesses.

Of course, I don't really trust Microsoft's ideal that a 1GHz server can handle 9 operations per second. However, under normal circumstances, I could comfortably see at least 10 operations per second being safely handled by the 2.5GHz starting specifications given—especially with 1GB or more of RAM. Remember, just like the processor, RAM is important, if only so the server can render pages efficiently. Keep in mind that each web application a server hosts does increase the amount of RAM the server uses. More web applications, means more RAM.

Be cautious though. SharePoint often rapidly increases in use, and an increase in the percentage of people using it. As SharePoint catches on, you might find yourself at peak usage more often than not. That's why you need to monitor how your SharePoint server handles the stress of use, just in case.

PERFORMANCE MONITORING

You might assume that SharePoint has performance monitoring tools—but it doesn't. It doesn't need them. Windows Server 2003 already has a Performance Monitor for that sort of thing. SharePoint does have a Usage Analysis utility, but it only reports usage activity on sites and web pages. Performance Monitor is easy to use, well-documented, and should be a regular part of your server maintenance arsenal.

As an added bonus, there are performance counters specific to SharePoint that can be used in conjunction with the usage analysis data to manage your SharePoint server. They give you all the more reason to use Performance Monitor to monitor your SharePoint servers. See Chapter 12, "Maintenance and Monitoring," for more details.

ADDITIONAL PERFORMANCE CONSIDERATIONS

You'll want to keep an eye on these items that will increase your processor's load.

Alerts   Users can set alerts on changes in a list or library. Alerts are scheduled and, therefore, keep the SharePoint Timer Services busy. Limit the number of alerts your users can have running at any given time. It will save your processor. Alerts can be configured with a user limit, or disabled altogether.

Indexing   The server that will be indexing site collection content will have to support the increased load on the processor. If you can, try not to index every 5 minutes or less. Instead, consider indexing every hour or at certain times of the day, which would be better. This can be difficult if you expect SharePoint to almost instantaneously index and search new items; just keep it in mind if you are trying to squeeze as many operations per second as you can from your server.

Usage Analysis   Sharepoint can analyze site usage, and deliver detailed reports. However, analyzing the usage logs takes a considerable amount of processor power for the SharePoint. Try to schedule the analysis to occur during a long downtime, usually sometime around 3:00 A.M.

Web Parts   Your developers may go crazy with the power of web parts. Be careful; some web parts (depending on what they do and how they were coded) can be resource hogs. Stay well below 50 web parts per page—and that includes the hidden ones. Home pages, where web parts are usually found, can be overwhelmingly busy.

Storage Planning

When you're considering performance issues, don't forget to plan for adequate storage. If you plan to have SharePoint and the SSEE database on the same server, you'll need extra RAM because SQL uses quite a bit. But more specifically, it will require much more storage space than SharePoint alone. Even if your SharePoint databases—particularly the content database, which holds all of SharePoint's precious content—are stored on a different SQL server, planning for storage is still important.

Consider this, the maximum default size allowed for document uploads is 50MB. In my experience, a 100-page Word document is about 5MB. So, a maximum of 50MB is usually more than sufficient for a Word document. Of course, you can adjust the size; this is just a good default. But of course, if you upload more than Word files, you may need to change that limit.

It goes without saying that storage needs will depend on how your users will use the lists and libraries on your SharePoint sites. Assume they are creating marketing materials to send out every quarter, and they are storing them and collaborating on them in a document library. If they create five major documents each quarter, that would be 20 large documents per year, possibly up to 10MB per document. That could be 200MB of space for those documents alone. If other people manage the images in a picture library, and the material had 10 large, full color pictures per document, that could be 2,000MB (2GB) per year for that picture library in addition to its related document library. You could need gigs and gigs of hard drive space—and that doesn't include versioning.

If you have Versioning enabled in your document libraries, there will be multiple copies (as many copies as you allow when you set up versioning) of each document. Therefore, if versioning (say four major versions, and three minor versions per document) were enabled in the previous scenario, then at least 1.4GB per year would be needed for versioning in the marketing document library alone. Keep in mind that versioning can be allowed for most lists as well.

Most list entries, when stored in the content database, are tiny—just a few KB, if that. However, if you enable attachments for the libraries, those files (by default less than 50MB) will be saved with those list items, increasing the size of your content database in ways you may not have intended. And don't forget about incoming email. If you configure an incoming email enabled list or library to save original emails, those emails (including attachments) need to be stored in the content database too.

You also need to consider that, depending on what you allow, users can easily create their own document workspace subsites from a document if they need additional team work to collaborate. When a document workspace is spun off of a document, it takes a copy of the original document with it. An additional site will need to be stored in the content database, and a copy of that document with its own versions will be stored on that site. That document will eventually be *merged up* to the original document workspace. However, until then (and until you delete the document workspace when it's done) that document (and its workspace) is yet another thing requiring storage. You can also allow users to create their own site collections (with Self-Site Creation), this adds yet more storage overhead to the SharePoint content databases.

Finally, remember that the more stuff you have in SharePoint, the more stuff you will have in the Search database. It holds the indexed search data for documents, list entries, and page content (it *does not* index attached files); that data is stored on the SharePoint server itself and merged regularly into the Search database. To make sure that it returns only the entries that the user making the query is allowed to see, Search also records the Access Control List information for every indexed entry.

Generally Search is only allowed to store indexed word entries that equal about 40 percent of the original document's size, with a maximum of 64MB of stored words for a single document. That is well over the 50MB limit, but that's a maximum hard limit regardless. That means if you have 20 documents in a library, the search database can have (maximum) 1.3GB of entries in the Search database for that library alone. Of course, if the documents themselves are never over 50MB, and Search sticks to its 40-percent limit for each document, then that would be no more than 20MB of indexed entries per document, and therefore (going with our scenario) about 400MB stored in the Search database for that one document library.

When you're deciding how much storage space your SharePoint server should use in SQL, consider this:

◆ You need to have an idea of what your users are going to do. Estimate how many documents they are going to be collaborating on and storing. Think about what lists they will be using, and how they will be used.

◆ Plan how you are going to manage attachments and versioning.

◆ Plan how you are going to manage user websites—especially ones generated for document and meeting workspaces.

◆ Plan on using site collection quota templates to keep site collection storage in check (in addition to limiting site collections per content database). Remember the Recycle Bins as well. The End user Recycle Bin contents at the site level are part of the site collection's quota, so keep an eye on it. But the second stage, site collection level Recycle Bin can have a quota that is a certain percentage of its site collection's quota, but keep in mind that is in *addition* to the site collection's quota. That can cause an unexpected increase in storage requirements if you aren't prepared. Remember to empty your recycle bins to save space.

Once you can estimate what you need, double that space. At least, always have 25 percent more space than you expect to need. Always leave room to bloat. You will never go wrong.

It's great if SharePoint works, but if you have no more room to store SharePoint's data, the users will be upset.

Keep in mind that your environment may be different; after you install your SharePoint server, make sure you monitor the activity. Create a test group that represents a small but measurable sample of your expected users. See how many of them use the server, when they use it, how they use it, and how much they store on the server. Then multiply the increase in resources based on their activities by an estimate of how many more users will be doing the same sorts of things when the server goes live. If you don't think the suggested hardware will be up to the task, improve it. Plan for at least 10 percent more growth than you expect—just in case. It's better to find out that your system is not adequate now than to find out when everyone is using it.

For goodness sakes, storage is cheap. Use RAID to make your storage fault tolerant; mirror the web servers. If there is drive failure, you'll be grateful you did.

SPEAKING OF STORAGE

Although I am primarily referring to SharePoint's hardware needs, do not neglect SQL's needs. If you are going to use SQL, understand that it is as important as the SharePoint server itself in the performance of your SharePoint sites. Do not skimp on the hardware, particularly RAM and storage. Using RAID drives and even clustering are great ideas to help keep all that important data available.

Software Limitations

In addition to its hardware limitations, SharePoint has its software limitations. Microsoft beat the heck out of some servers to see how they performed; they found that when certain objects reached a maximum number, performance degraded significantly. This list of limitations is referred to as the *guidelines of acceptable performance*. These guidelines are something to keep in mind if your simple SharePoint Server Farm install becomes a large, busy server farm. These limitations are probably caused by a combination of the OS, IIS, and SQL performance limitations impacting SharePoint. These limits are something to remember when you are planning your SharePoint objects, such as site collections, lists, and users.

Table 1.1 provides a list of object limitations you need to know. At this point you may not really realize the importance of some of these objects, but you will. It's always good to know up front what limitations there might be for something in case you might end up being responsible for it.

TABLE 1.1: Guidelines for Acceptable Performance

Object	Number for Acceptable Performance
Website	250,000 per site collection, but performance can degrade as more sites are added.
Subsite	2,000 per website. This limit is due to the fact that enumerating the subsites of a site degrades after 2,000.
Document	5 million per library maximum, depending on the size of the documents. Keep in mind that viewing items in a large list or library can slow performance. Use list indexing, and consider making list or library views that filter content to 1,000 items or less per view.
Document Size	Generally, the maximum is 50MB. This can be set to a larger number, but it is not suggested.
List	2,000 per website. They become difficult to enumerate past that point.
Field Type	256 per list (not a hard limit, the performance just degrades at that point).
Web Part	50 per page. If they are complex web parts, the maximum decreases.
Columns	2,000 for libraries, and 4,096 for lists. Not a hard limit, but performance does degrade.
Users in Groups	2 million per website. Do not add users individually if you can help it, because many more can be added using MS security groups.
Security Principals	2,000 per website. The ACL size limits the number of users and groups in a website, but it does not affect the number of users in a group.
Indexed Documents	50 million per search index. One index server is supported per search server or server farm.
Search Servers	One search server can support up to 100 content databases. The number of search servers on a farm is based on the number of web applications being supported.
Content Databases	100 per web application. Performance degrades after adding 100. Consider creating a different web application before that point.
Site Collections	50,000 per web application (or about 50,000 per database). This is a soft limit but it causes performance degradation.
Web Applications per SharePoint Server	64. This is an IIS limitation, not SharePoint directly. It also could vary depending on load.
Web Server to Database Server Ratio	8 web servers to 1 database server. The performance degrades, but it can vary depending on environment.
Web Server to Domain Controller	3 web servers per DC, depending on how much authentication is being done.
Web Applications per SharePoint Server (Basic Install)	10 (the approximate number based on performance limitations of the embedded database).

Enumerating content in libraries and lists can be resource intensive. To ease that burden, if you have more than 2,000 items per list or library, you can limit the number of items viewed by default to 1,000, index a field in the list (only index if the list is very large, because indexing speeds up viewing a list but does add a resource load), or consider breaking up the flat list or library by using folders to organize the items to improve performance (it's okay if this makes little sense now; it will come up again).

These hardware and software factors should help you avoid the slow decay of your SharePoint server's performance. Remember to monitor, monitor, monitor. It does no good to have logs if you don't read them. Be prepared for the need to scale out or upgrade before someone else has to tell you to. If you ever overestimate the performance requirements, it's good to know that too.

So that's it. You've seen behind the curtain of SharePoint and learned about its requirements, limitations, and services. Now you are ready to get started.

The Bottom Line

Determine the software and hardware requirements you need for installing SharePoint Services 3.0   SharePoint has some stringent software and hardware requirements. Be sure you know what you need before you become the proud owner of your own SharePoint server or servers. SharePoint depends on Windows 2003 SP1 server components and services in order to function.

> **Master It**   What software must be on the server before you install SharePoint?

Identify the three ways of installing SharePoint Services 3.0   Choose the best of the three ways of installing SharePoint Services 3.0 for you. With SharePoint, how you choose to install it defines how it works. Making the wrong choice can come back to haunt you. Know what you're in for and choose the correct installation type for your business.

> **Master It**   If you were going to install SharePoint on one server (no existing SQL server) for a small business of about 50 people, what installation type would you choose?

Set up the necessary accounts that SharePoint needs to run   When SharePoint is installed on a domain, it needs user accounts to assign to its services. Knowing what permissions and roles those accounts require will help you avoid problems when installing and running SharePoint.

> **Master It**   What is a Database Access Account? Is it known by any other names?

Recognize the new features and requirements of SharePoint   SharePoint has features that require additional planning and setup to function properly. Make sure you know what they are and what they require.

> **Master It**   What new feature of WSS 3.0 requires SMTP to be running locally on the SharePoint server?

Plan for hardware requirements   Don't let SharePoint outgrow its hardware before it really gets started. Prepare for growth. Establish your company's baseline operations per second and storage needs before installing SharePoint.

> **Master It**   What is the formula to calculate the operations per second that a SharePoint server would be doing in a given environment?

Chapter 2

Installation

Generally, installing a new software product is not the most important part of the process, and you might be wondering why a chapter might be devoted to it.

This is why: SharePoint can function differently depending on how it's installed. Also, to install SharePoint at all, the server must be prepared properly to handle its collaborative goodness. Without preparation, there will be no SharePoint. SharePoint has to be prepared for, then installed properly, and finally, minimally, some settings must be configured in order to simply use the product. Therefore devoting some pages to preparation, installation, and post-installation configuration makes much more sense.

In this chapter, you will learn how to:

◆ Prepare for the installation of SharePoint

◆ Install SharePoint using the Basic and Advanced, Stand-Alone, and Advanced Server Farm installation options

◆ Determine what gets created when SharePoint installs

◆ Perform the initial configuration tasks after a SharePoint install (and understand why you perform them)

Preparing for the SharePoint Installation

In order to install SharePoint, you'll need to make a few preparations. This section will discuss the little things that SharePoint requires before it can install and do its thing.

To recap (for those of you who read the last chapter) a SharePoint installation requires the following technologies:

◆ Windows Server 2003 (Service Pack 1 or higher)

◆ Internet Information Services (IIS) 6.0 (or higher), ASP.NET enabled

◆ ASP.NET 2.0 (which gets installed as part of .NET Framework 3.0)

◆ .NET Framework 3.0

◆ SMTP services (for incoming email support)

.NET Framework 3.0 should be downloaded from the Internet from the Microsoft website.

Microsoft changes its URLs from time to time, so simply go to Microsoft's website and search for ".NET Framework 3.0". Select the download page for .NET Framework 3.0; it should list `dotnetfx3setup.exe` as the installation file. That will work fine for the installation, but the server will require Internet access for the first half of the process.

WHY IS INTERNET ACCESS REQUIRED?

The redistributable installer package requires Internet access because the installer listed on that page for download is the *bootstrap installer*. It is not the full redistributable package it says it is. A bootstrap installer is designed to download quickly; therefore, it does not contain all the files needed to do a full .NET Framework 3.0 install. Instead, it accesses the Internet during installation and fetches the files it is missing, most notably the files specific to the server's architecture, either x86 or x64.

To get the full redistributable package for .NET Framework 3.0 (with all the installation files included), scroll to the Instructions section on the download page that contains the links to the x86 and x64 Redist packages. The full installation packages are called `dotnetfx3.exe` for x86 and `dotnetfx3_x64.exe` for x64. Be very careful to choose the correct installation package for the architecture of your server.

IIS 6.0 with SMTP

Internet Information Services (IIS) 6.0 is required in order for SharePoint to even have a web interface. Windows Server's web server capability is due to IIS, and therefore, so is SharePoint's. Another feature of IIS is the capability to send and receive email using SMTP (Simple Mail Transport Protocol). There has been a long precedent of web servers ofering email capabilities, so it is understandable that IIS would also support SMTP. And, it's just as understandable that SharePoint would take advantage of that IIS capability as well. If you were to have more than one SharePoint server in the server farm, you only need to enable SMTP if the server will be supporting incoming email.

Installing IIS 6.0 with SMTP services requires two stages. The first stage is to install IIS and enable ASP.NET and the second stage is to install the SMTP service. There are a few different ways to do it; however, for convenience, I am going to use the Configuration Wizard to enable IIS 6.0 with ASP.NET and then use Add/Remove Programs ➤ Windows Components to enable SMTP. (Alternatively, you could open the Manage Your Server window and use it to trigger the Configuration Wizard to add the IIS role.) Obviously, you should be logged in with an account that has the right to install software locally.

KEEP THE SERVICE PACK OR INSTALLATION FILES HANDY

Your server may need to access either the Service Pack (1 or 2, depending on what you have installed) files or the server installation files when enabling IIS. Be sure you have them handy during this process because you may be prompted for the Service Pack files.

To install IIS 6.0, just follow these steps:

1. Open the Configuration Wizard (Start ➤ Administrative Tools ➤ Configure Your Server Wizard).

2. Click Next twice, once for the Welcome screen and once for the Preliminary steps screen.

3. Select Application Server from the list of Roles (IIS is considered an application server), and click Next.

4. On the Application Server Options screen, select Enable ASP.NET and click Next (see Figure 2.1).

FIGURE 2.1
The Application Server options

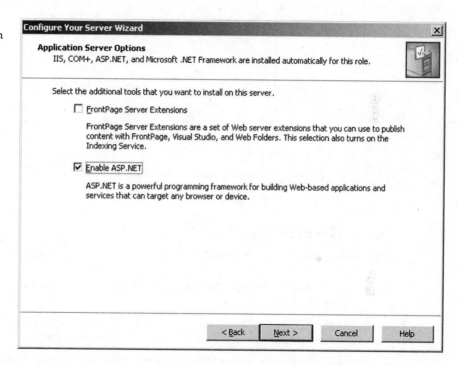

Make sure that the summary of selections includes: Install Internet Information Services, Enable COM+ for Remote Transactions, Enable Microsoft Distributed Transaction Co-ordinator (DTC) for Remote Access, and Enable ASP.NET are listed (see Figure 2.2 for confirmation).

5. To install and configure IIS, click Next.

6. When the wizard indicates that the installation is complete, click Finish.

The Manage Your Server page will indicate that you indeed have a new application server role on the server. Close out of this page.

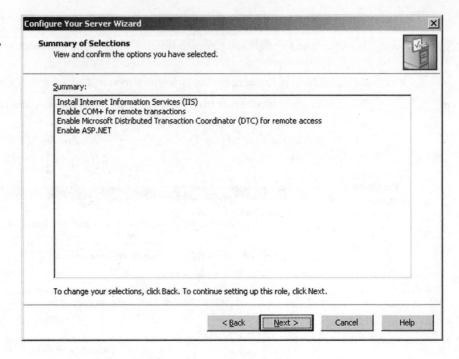

FIGURE 2.2
The Application
Server summary

ENABLE IIS SMTP SERVICE

The next stage in this process installs the IIS SMTP service. To install it, follow these steps:

1. Go to Add or Remove Programs by clicking Start ➢ Control Panel ➢ Add or Remove Programs.

2. In the Add or Remove Programs window, click the Add/Remove Windows Components icon (it will take a moment for the components list to populate).

3. Once the Windows Components Wizard opens, click Application Server. (Do *not* remove the Application Server check mark. If you do, cancel out and try again. Unchecking the Application Server will cause the wizard to remove IIS). Once you have selected Application Server, click the Details button—because it has additional component parts that can be installed.

4. In the Application Server dialog box (see Figure 2.3), select Internet Information Services (IIS) and click Details.

5. In the Internet Information Services (IIS) dialog box, place a check in SMTP Service checkbox. (The box does not turn gray, which means this component, unlike the two previous components, does not have additional components.)

6. Click OK to accept your selection and back out of the Internet Information Services (IIS) dialog box.

FIGURE 2.3
The Application Server
dialog box

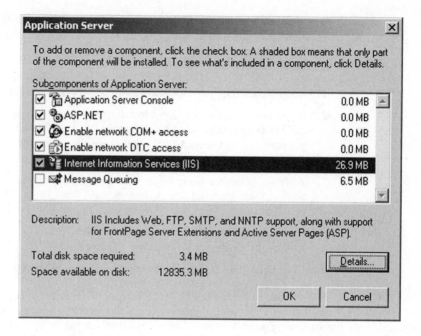

7. Click OK on the Application Server dialog box.

8. Click Next in the Windows Components Wizard. The wizard will begin installing the SMTP services.

When the wizard is done, you should check to see that the IIS and the SMTP service were installed properly.

Open the IIS management console by choosing Start≻ Administrative Tools ≻ Internet Information Services (IIS) Manager. As soon as it opens, you may have to click the plus sign next to the listing for the local computer in the tree pane on the left side of the console; then you should see a node for the Default SMTP Virtual Server below it. This means that the SMTP service has been enabled.

To confirm that ASP .NET has been enabled, select Web Service Extensions. You will see in the content pane on the right that ASP.NET v1.1.4322 is installed and enabled. This is good because, when ASP .NET 2.0 is installed, it will be enabled as well.

ASP .NET 2.0 and .NET Framework 3.0

The next step in preparing to install SharePoint is to install ASP.NET 2.0 and .NET Framework 3.0. ASP .NET 2.0 is a critical component of SharePoint, enabling it to create .aspx web pages, as well as web parts and other page attributes. And .NET Framework 3.0 is required to enable the SharePoint workflow capabilities.

When you install the .NET Framework 3.0, it installs the Windows Workflow Foundation and ASP .NET 2.0 as well. When ASP .NET 2.0 is installed, it will also, as a convenience, be enabled in IIS 6.0 if ASP .NET 1.1 is already enabled there.

Bear in mind that installing .NET Framework 3.0 will take a little time; how much will depend on your hardware. If you are using the `dotnetfx3setup.exe` installer, the server must have Internet access to install this component.

To install .Net Framework 3.0, follow these steps:

1. Double-click the installer package you downloaded earlier.

2. If you are using the Bootstrap Installer, accept the license agreement for .NET Framework 3.0. The page will indicate how large the file is and how long it should take to download. If you aren't using the Bootstrap Installer, simply accept the license agreement and installation will begin.

   After accepting the license agreement, the installation setup window will minimize to the System Tray. To avoid any problems, don't work on anything else until the installation is complete.

3. Wait for the installation process to complete. After it's finished, you can check Windows Update for further updates for .NET Framework 3.0 if you'd like.

4. Click Exit to finish the .NET Framework 3.0 installation process.

If you'd like to verify that .NET Framework 3.0 installed (other than the event logs or Add/Remove Programs, of course), check the Services console, and scroll down to Windows Presentation Foundation Font Cache 3.0.0.0, which wasn't on your server before the installation. To prove that the server is now Windows Workflow Foundation–capable, navigate to Program Files ➢ MSBuild ➢ Microsoft folder and you will see a brand new Windows Workflow Foundation folder.

Further, to confirm that ASP .NET 2.0 was installed and enabled in IIS, open the IIS manager console and click on the Web Service Extensions node. You'll see that ASP .NET v2.0.50727 has been enabled (Figure 2.4).

FIGURE 2.4
ASP.NET 2.0 in the IIS console

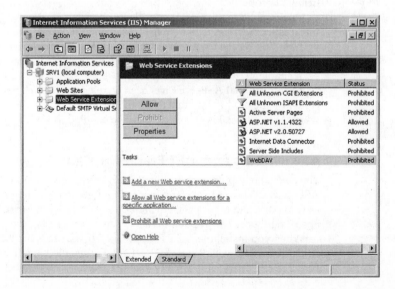

Setup Account

As I've mentioned before, the account you are using to install SharePoint matters (either as the account you are logged in with, or as the account you use to run the installer). To install SharePoint the account must have the rights and permissions to install software and start services locally on the server. If you are installing SharePoint on one server, the setup account only needs to have the rights and permissions to install software on that server. SharePoint can use local system or network service accounts to run all of its other services, and access its databases locally.

If you intend to install SharePoint in a server farm configuration (with SharePoint and SQL on separate servers), the setup account should have the right to install software on all servers in the domain that will be running SharePoint. It must also have Logins access to the SQL server (or server instance to be used by SharePoint, if you are running more than one) as well as hold the DBCreator and SecurityAdmin roles. The setup account creates the configuration database and gives the other service accounts rights to their required databases in SQL.

THE SPECIAL ROLES OF THE SETUP ACCOUNT IN A SERVER FARM CONFIGURATION

If you're planning to use SharePoint in a Server Farm configuration, the account used to install SharePoint on the servers needs to have the rights and permissions to install software on each server locally. You can use an account that has been added as a local Administrator to each server, or you can make the setup account a member of the Domain Admins group for the Active Directory domain.

In a Server Farm configuration, the setup account must also be assigned special roles on the SQL server. If you are not responsible for these tasks, you can simply ask the appropriate Active Directory administrator to create an account that is in the Domain Admins group, and then ask the SQL DBA to add that account to the Logins, DBCreator, and SecurityAdmin roles.

However, if you need to do it, here's how.

To add a user to Active Directory and add them to the Domain Admins group, follow these steps:

1. Open the Active Directory Users And Computers console by choosing Start ➢ Administrative Tools ➢ Active Directory Users and Computers.

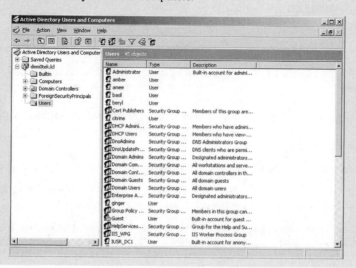

2. Click the Users node, and then click the Add Users button (it looks like a head with a sparkle on the back of it).

3. In the New Object-User dialog box, enter the First Name and User Logon Name. I'm using `setupacct` for both. Despite the fact that this account doesn't have a first and last name, you must enter something for one or the other. If you only add a logon name, the Next button will remain grayed out.

4. Click Next, and enter a password. I suggest you uncheck "User must change password at next logon." Depending on your environment's password policy, you might want to check the Password Never Expires and User Cannot Change Password checkboxes. That way, if the account is compromised, the attacker cannot change the password to one that you don't know.

5. Click Next when you have finished setting up the password. Confirm that the name, logon name, and password settings are correct, and click Finish. The account you created will be highlighted in the console.

6. To add the new setup account to the Domain Admins group, right-click the username and select Add to a group from the popup menu.

7. In the Select Group dialog box, verify that you are selecting from the correct location (it should be your domain).

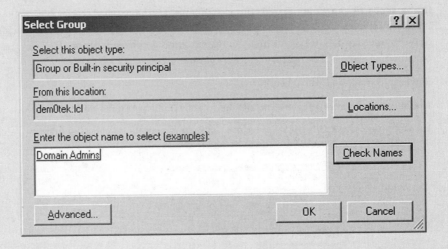

8. In the Enter The Object Name To Select field, enter **domain admins** and click the Check Names button. Domain Admins should become title capitalized and underlined, which means that Check Names found it. Click OK.

9. A dialog box should come notify you that the Add To Group operation was successful. Click OK.

To add the setup account to the correct roles in Microsoft SQL Server 2005, follow these steps (the same roles apply in SQL 2000 sp3 but the interface is a bit different):

1. On the Server running SQL, open the SQL Server Management Studio console by choosing Start ➤ All Programs ➤ Microsoft SQL Server 2005 ➤ SQL Server Management Studio.

2. Make sure you are connecting to the correct server (and server instance if necessary) and server type (in this case, database engine), with the correct authentication, username, and password. Click Connect (my example server is RR1, and I am using the default account for Windows Authentication). See the following figure for more information.

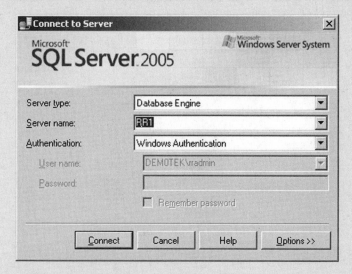

Keep in mind that you need to add the setup account to the SQL Server Logins role, so it can be added to the SecurityAdmins and DBCreator roles.

3. To do this, open the Security node.

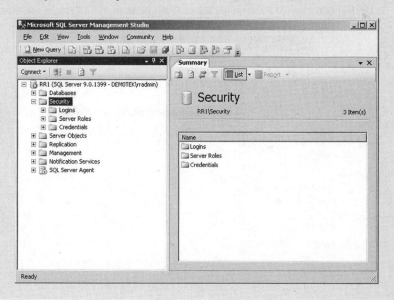

4. Right-click the Logins node or right-click Logins on the Summary page in the detail pane. In the popup menu, select New Login.

5. In the New Login window that appears, enter the name of your setup account in the *domain\\ username* format in Login Name field (my domain is dem0tek, and my setup account is setupacct).

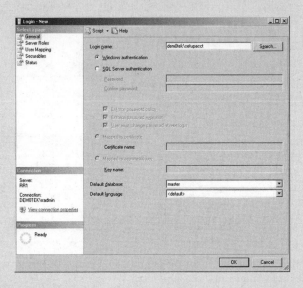

6. While you're creating the setup account as a Login role, you can add it to the necessary server roles. To do this, select Server Roles on the Select a Page pane on the left side of the New Logins window.

7. Check DBCreator and SecurityAdmin in the Server Roles list, and click OK. That should take you back to the SQL Server Management Studio console. Your setup account should be a Logins account and the setup account should be added to the SQL Logins, DBCreator, and SecurityAdmin roles.

Verify that your SQL server is prepared for remote access from the SharePoint server. If SQL is not ready for remote access, SharePoint will not be able to access the server to create the databases it needs. If you try to do a server farm install and keep failing, no matter how perfect your settings, follow these steps to create the configuration database:

1. Check to see if Remote Connections is set up. In SQL 2005, you'll need to use the SQL Server Surface Area Configuration Tool. You can select it by choosing Start ➢ All Programs ➢ Microsoft SQL Server 2005 ➢ Configuration Tool ➢ SQL Server Surface Area Configuration.

2. In the SQL Server 2005 Surface Area Configuration window, in the Configure Surface Area For Localhost section, select Surface Area Configuration For Services And Connections.

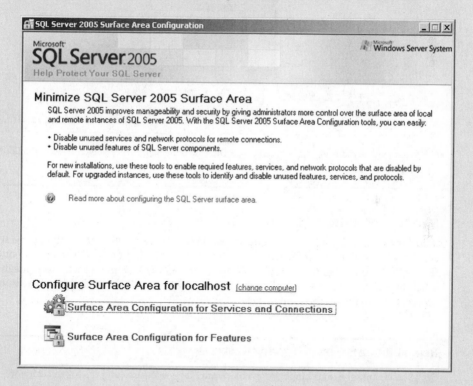

3. In the window that opens, in the services and connections list on the left, make certain that you are using the correct server instance (mine is the default MSSQLSERVER instance), then select Remote Connections. In the configuration area on the right of this selection, you'll specify whether or not SQL 2005 will allow remote connections, which SharePoint needs. Choose Local and Remote connections, and then select Using TCP/IP and Named Pipes (because locally that is what SQL uses). This will make SQL available to SharePoint.

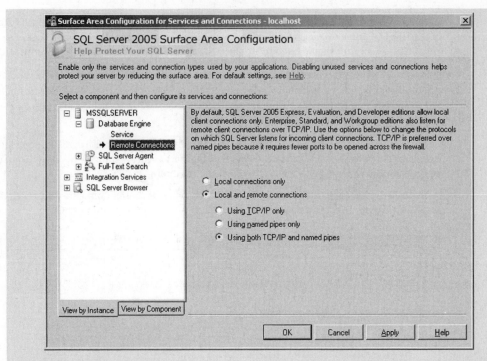

4. When you've made your selections, click OK. Close the SQL Server 2005 Surface Area Configuration window.

Service Accounts

Additional accounts should be specified during the configuration of SharePoint in a server farm scenario. In a single server environment, the local service and network service accounts will work fine as the account identities for all of SharePoint's services. Domain accounts come into play only when the SharePoint services may need to access resources (like databases on a remote SQL server) that are not on the local server.

BEING UNIQUE IS USEFUL BUT NOT NECESSARY

Each SharePoint service and application pool requires a user context (or service account identity) to access resources with. I tend to have a domain user account for each one, but those services and application pools don't *require* unique accounts, as long as the account they all use has the correct permissions for whatever the services do.

As a matter of fact, in some networking environments where controlling the number of domain accounts is an issue, it is reasonable to create one domain account that you apply to all services except the database access account—that account is so powerful it should never be applied to any other service.

However, like myself, you may prefer to separate tasks by using separate service accounts. If one service crashes, it won't take the others with it (by tying up the service account identity). Furthermore, it helps keep services more secure. If a unique account is compromised, it can do less damage than the one über account on which all services depend.

For a server farm installation, in addition to the setup account, the Database Access (server farm), Search, Index (content access), and Content Database Access services also require an account context in which to run.

My example of the domain user accounts I will be using to install SharePoint is listed below and shown in Figure 2.5.:

FIGURE 2.5
The Domain accounts for SharePoint

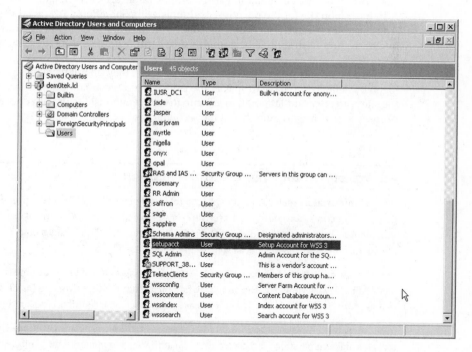

Database Access Account *Wssconfig*. This account is the server farm or database access account and will be the owner of the configuration database. It will create all the other databases used by SharePoint, add the necessary accounts to SQL, and give them the correct database access. It also is the SharePoint Timer service account, and the application pool identity for Central Administration.

Search Account *Wsssearch*. This account is one of the owners of the search database, and it answers search queries.

Content Access Account   *Wssindex.* This account is one of the owners of the search database. It crawls and indexes SharePoint content. It must have read access to all search enabled content databases.

Content Database Account   *Wsscontent.* This account owns and accesses the content database of a web application, such as the first SharePoint site.

Remember that defining these accounts is necessary only if SQL and SharePoint are going to run on different servers. Otherwise, you can still use separate accounts if you'd like, but if SQL and SharePoint are running on the same server, the local service and network service accounts will work fine.

When SharePoint initially installs, someone needs to configure it. Therefore, when Central Administration (the first SharePoint site made so you can further configure and manage SharePoint) is created, the setup account and (just in case) built-in Administrators are added as Farm Administrators by default. Farm Administrators are users that are added to the Central Administration site for the purpose of administering SharePoint. It's called Farm Administrators even if SharePoint is installed on only one server. You can add additional users to Central Administration to be authorized as Farm Administrators (or remove them) as needed.

When you create other sites (and site collections), they do not have these accounts available for log in by default. You have to specify the primary and secondary administrators for the site before the site is created. At that point, to get into the site, you must log in with one of those accounts (the primary is obviously required, and the secondary isn't).

A SharePoint Administration Utility Account

Many administrators may use their own accounts to manage SharePoint, but I prefer to keep my SharePoint administrative account separate from my personal domain account. Because of this, I have a Domain Admins account called *shareadmin* that I use specifically to manage and administer the server the SharePoint Services runs on, as well as SharePoint itself.

The account doesn't need to be a Domain Admin, as long as it is a local Administrator for each of the SharePoint servers. However, the point is to have an account with the right to install software, run tools, manage server roles (such as IIS) and services locally on all SharePoint servers on the domain.

In addition, to administer SharePoint, I add the account to Central Administration as a Farm Administrator. This makes it possible for the account to be authorized to manage SharePoint, create and configure new web applications, site collections, do backups, and more. This account, with those rights and permissions, can use the SharePoint command line tool, STSADM, to manage SharePoint from the command line. It also can install and administer SharePoint features and solutions, web parts, and other SharePoint specific utilities.

Finally, there are times, when I am creating new site collections, testing new templates, or taking over a site collection, I might use that account as a primary or secondary site collection administrator. This makes it possible to log into the site collection, configure and test it before replacing the account with the rightful owner's account when all work is complete.

Overall, my SharePoint admin account is used for all of my SharePoint needs. It allows me to go from the desktop of the server running SharePoint, to the command line to use STSADM to configure and manage SharePoint, to the SharePoint administrative interface, all without having to change logins.

This account may not fit all network security models, but I have found it useful enough that I thought it was worth mentioning to someone who, in the beginning of their experiences with SharePoint, might find it useful too.

At this point you should be all set to install SharePoint. You should have installed IIS 6.0 with ASP.NET enabled and the SMTP service, .NET Framework 3.0 and ASP.NET 2.0. You should have also set up the necessary service accounts, depending on the installation you plan to do. We're going to do a Basic installation first. It will demonstrate how to install SharePoint in a single server environment. In this case, the installation will be entirely automated, all services will be configured to use local service and network service accounts, and a SSEE database engine will be installed to handle all of SharePoint's database needs.

After that installation is confirmed, we'll do a more advanced server farm installation. This type of installation is not as automated, and will require you to specify the location of the SharePoint databases, as well the user accounts that the services will be using. After configuration, the post installation tasks will be covered. These tasks will be the same regardless of installation type.

INSTALLING ON SERVER 2008

The preparation and installation steps for this chapter are being done in Windows Server 2003 Service Pack 1(Service Pack 2 would be fine as well). Preparing for SharePoint is different, and easier, on Windows Server 2008. If you are installing SharePoint as a server role in Server 2008, the steps to prepare are built into the server role set up process. See the TechNet article "Install Windows SharePoint Services in the Windows Server 2008 operating system." Otherwise please consult the Help files for the Windows SharePoint Services server role on your server for more information. Keep in mind that the IIS version on Server 2008 is 7.0 and therefore will require that IIS 6.0 Management Compatibility be enabled for backward compatibility.

Basic Installation

When you choose to do a Basic installation of SharePoint, you are choosing to have a single server SharePoint configuration, installing SQL Server Embedded Edition locally. This will cause all databases and services used by SharePoint to be set up automatically, using local accounts. The installation will occur in two parts, which is standard operational procedure for SharePoint version 3.0: the installation itself, and then the configuration. However, with the Basic and standalone installations, configuration will be handled without you.

Remember that this server will need the resources to handle both SharePoint and its databases on one machine. Plan accordingly.

Before you install SharePoint, make certain that you are logged in with the setup account. In my example, that would be the *setupacct* account created earlier in the chapter. This account will, by default, be the SharePoint Farm Administrator in Central Administration, and be the Primary Administrator of the first SharePoint web application and site collection.

To install this version of SharePoint on a Server 2003 SP1, SP2, or R2 server, you must download the Windows SharePoint Services 3.0 installer from Microsoft. You can search the Microsoft site for "Windows SharePoint Services 3.0 download" and select the download details for Windows SharePoint Services 3.0. The installer file should be called `SharePoint.exe`.

ARCHITECTURE SPECIFICS

There are separate SharePoint installers for x86 and x64, despite the fact that the actual installation files have the same name. The x64 `SharePoint.exe` file is 85.6 MB, and the x86 `SharePoint.exe` file is 77.7MB. So, despite the fact that they have the same name, they contain differing amounts of code. I wouldn't risk using the wrong architecture version of the file.

---

1. While logged in as your setup account, double-click the `SharePoint.exe`. Accept the terms of the license agreement and click Continue (you can't continue without agreeing).

2. The Choose the Installation You Want screen will display two options: Basic and Advanced. (See Figure 2.6.) The Basic button is used to install a single server using the default settings.

FIGURE 2.6
The SharePoint Basic and Advanced installation options

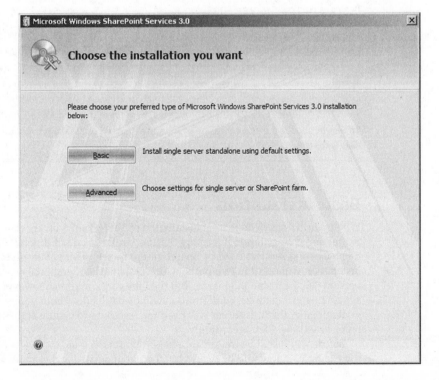

The Advanced button offers two additional installation options, Server Farm and Stand-alone (which is surprisingly similar to the Basic installation).

3. To perform the Basic installation, click the Basic button.

MAY I HELP YOU?

The little question mark in a circle icon in the bottom-left corner of the installer window for SharePoint is the Help icon. Clicking it is the only way to get help during the installation process. I wonder why they made it so tiny? Maybe they were hoping it wouldn't be needed.

From this point on, the installation process will continue without your intervention. However you will be prompted (see Figure 2.7) to start the SharePoint Products and Technologies Configuration Wizard, after the installation files have been copied and update files applied.

4. There is no reason to delay configuration. Therefore, make sure that the box is checked to run the SharePoint Products and Technologies Configuration Wizard, and click Close.

5. The Welcome screen for the Wizard will appear. Click Next to continue.

FIGURE 2.7
The SharePoint
Configuration Wizard
prompt

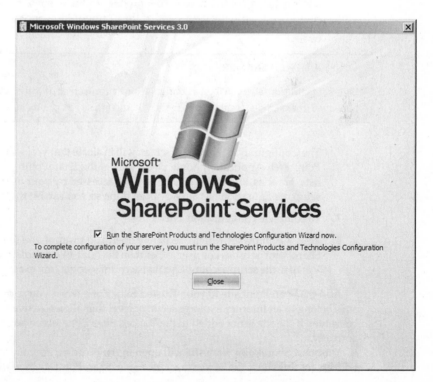

A dialog box will warn you that some services are going to be reset during configuration (Figure 2.8)—the most important one being the Internet Information Services (IIS). If you are hosting any other websites on this machine, service will be interrupted during this process.

FIGURE 2.8
The Service Reset
warning

6. To continue the configuration process, click Yes in the dialog box.

The Configuration Wizard will begin to perform 10 configuration tasks including: creating the configuration database, securing resources, registering SharePoint Services and features, provisioning the web applications, creating sample data, installing application content files, and finalizing configuration. This process will take some time, depending on the server's resources. Eventually it will stop at the Configuration Successful screen.

CONFIGURATION FAILURE

If the configuration fails, you'll get a Configuration Failure screen. It will contain information about what happened (for example, losing access to the SQL server), so you can fix it.

The Configuration Successful screen will indicate that you will be taken to the default SharePoint Web Application home page. This is the SharePoint site that contains all the pages, lists, libraries, and web parts that will be accessed by your users, all ready to go. A lot of the setup configuration has already been done so you can hit the ground running.

7. To complete configuration, click Finish.

8. Your web browser will immediately open and prompt you to log in (Figure 2.9). Right now SharePoint only has one user (other than the built-in Administrators): the account you used to install it, the setup account. Use that account to login (my example is dem0tek\setupacct).

Add the SharePoint site to your Trusted Sites Zone when you're prompted to do so. Trusted sites belong to an Internet Explorer security level that allows ActiveX controls to run on your computer. If the site is not added to the Trusted Sites Zone, some page properties may not function correctly.

Your new SharePoint team site will open in the browser. As you can see in Figure 2.10, the address for this site is the server machine name. SharePoint starts identifying itself by the machine

FIGURE 2.9
The login screen

FIGURE 2.10
The SharePoint Team
site

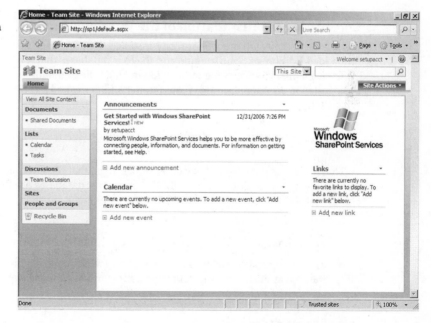

name of the server on which it is loaded. In this case, that is *SP1*. Because the SharePoint site (as you will see later) is set to port 80, it is listening for any HTTP traffic for the server and will respond with the SharePoint content if anyone asks. You can have SharePoint respond to other kinds of addresses, such as a fully qualified domain name (FQDN), but for right now the machine name is the default.

SharePoint can seem a little anticlimactic when you first see it. With a Home tab at the top, the navigation bar on the left that displays the lists, sites, people, Recycle Bin, and document library that are set up during installation. In the center of the page is the web part area, with a few web parts there for you to get a feel for them. At the top right are the Welcome menu (indicating your login name, which is useful if you've forgotten who you are logged in as), the Search field, and the Help icon. SharePoint is not supposed to be busy and intimidating; but easy on the eyes, uncluttered, and easy to use. If you are not intimidated, then SharePoint has achieved its objective.

That's it. That's all it takes to install SharePoint using the Basic option. You can immediately begin to use and manage it without any additional effort. All databases and services were created and configured automatically for you.

However, I don't know about you, but helplessly watching a wizard do mysterious things to my server, regardless of the immediate outcome, makes me nervous. One of the first things I do, after the product is installed and running, is check to see what actually changed on the server in order for the product to function properly. It's also helpful to get to know what a good installation looks like, under the hood, so you'll recognize what's missing should an install go bad. So, now that SharePoint is up and running, let's see what actually happened during the SharePoint Basic installation.

Confirming the Installation of the Windows Internal Databases

During the Basic installation, SharePoint installed the Windows Internal Database (SQL Server Embedded Edition, or SSEE) engine and the four databases that it requires.

To check this, you are going to have to search a little in the file system. One of the flaws of the Basic install is the databases are created under a folder called SYSMSI, in the Windows folder. The full path is

```
%winddir%\SYSMSI\SSEE\MSSQL.2005\MSSQL\Data
```

That folder contains the databases (and their logs) that SSEE requires: `master`, `model`, `mssqlststemresource`, and `temdb`. The other four databases are the ones created and used by SharePoint. As you can see in Figure 2.11, those files are:

- The AdminContent database for the Central Administration website

- The Configuration database for the server (which controls the configuration of SharePoint, the web applications, site collections, sites, and even some web parts)

- The Content database for the SharePoint site itself

- The Search database

FIGURE 2.11
SharePoint's SSEE
databases

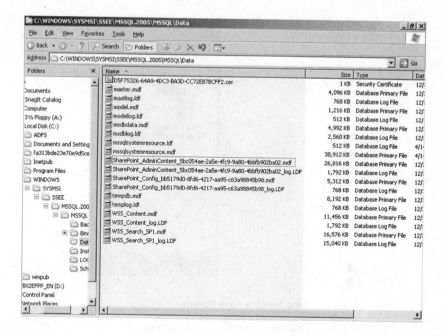

You may have noticed that the AdminContent and Config databases have nice long GUIDs tacked onto their name. That's just what happens when SharePoint creates them, and it is nothing to be concerned about. It simply insures that the database names are unique.

Checking IIS for Web Site Creation

The next thing to check is IIS to see if SharePoint has created the Web Sites the way it was supposed to create them. The default Web Site should be stopped (so it doesn't interfere with SharePoint using port 80 for the SharePoint sites), and a SharePoint-80 Web Site, as well as a Central Administration Web Site, should have been created.

You should recognize these web application names from Chapter 1; SharePoint-80 is the name of the default web application SharePoint creates during the Basic installation. This web application contains the default top-level site you accessed when the installation completed. Central Administration is, as the name implies, the web application containing the top-level site used to configure all SharePoint server, or server farm, settings.

To check the changes SharePoint made in IIS, perform the following steps:

1. Open the IIS management console by choosing Start ➤ Administrative Tools ➤ Internet Information Services (IIS) Manager.

2. In the console tree pane, click the plus next to your server name, and then click the plus sign next to the Web Sites node. Notice in Figure 2.12 that the default Web Site has been stopped (SharePoint stopped it to avoid harming whatever might be stored there) and that two new Web Sites have been created: SharePoint Central Administration v3 and SharePoint-80.

FIGURE 2.12
New Web Sites in IIS

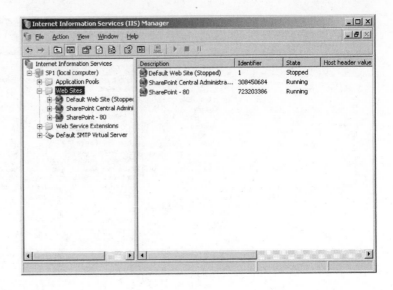

FIGURE 2.12
New Web Sites in IIS

CHECKING THE APPLICATION POOLS

You may remember from the previous chapter that when SharePoint creates web applications (IIS Web Sites), those web applications have to have application pools that require an account identity to function properly. Those accounts are the ones that can be given the permissions the application pools require. Because SharePoint is using only one server, these accounts should be built-in local accounts because they do not need to access anything other than the local server's resources.

To confirm the application pool of the Central Administration Web Site, click the plus sign next to the Application Pools node, right-click the SharePoint Central Administration v3 application pool, and select Properties (see Figure 2.13). In the SharePoint Central Administration Application Pool Properties dialog box, select the Identity tab.

FIGURE 2.13
The IIS Web application pool popup menu

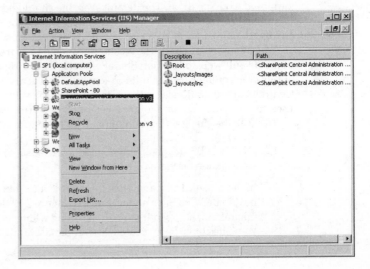

FIGURE 2.14
The Application
Pool Identity

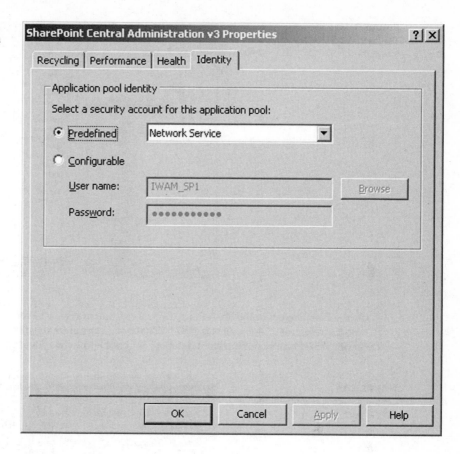

The selected Application Pool Identity is a predefined Network Service account (see Figure 2.14). This is perfectly acceptable for a Basic installation. Close the dialog box.

You can confirm that the SharePoint-80 website is using the correct application pool and identity by following the same steps.

CONFIRMING CENTRAL ADMINISTRATION'S APPLICATION POOL AND PORT

You might recall that Central Administration uses a different port number than the SharePoint site does. With the Basic install, that port is assigned automatically. To confirm what that number is, go to the properties of the Central Administration v3 Web Site. While you're there, make sure that that web application is using the correct application pool. Even though the correct pool exists, someone can change the pool the Web Site is using. It's always good to know where to go to confirm that the correct one is selected.

In the IIS management console, you should be able to see the Web Sites available on your server. Right-click the SharePoint Central Administration v3 Web Site (see Figure 2.15) and click Properties.

FIGURE 2.15
The Central Administration's Web
Site in IIS

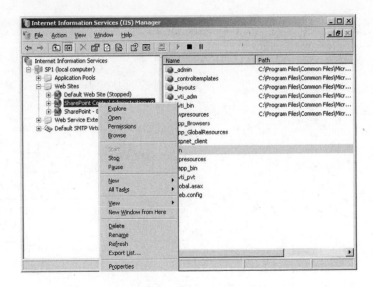

On the Web Site tab in the SharePoint Central Administration v3 Properties dialog box, note the TCP port. (In Figure 2.16, the port is 36971.) That port was automatically assigned. Don't change it; if you do, SharePoint's configuration database will not know that you did.

FIGURE 2.16
Central Administration's unique
TCP/IP port

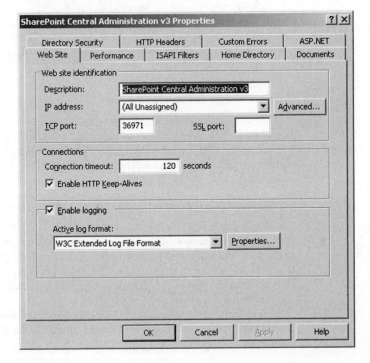

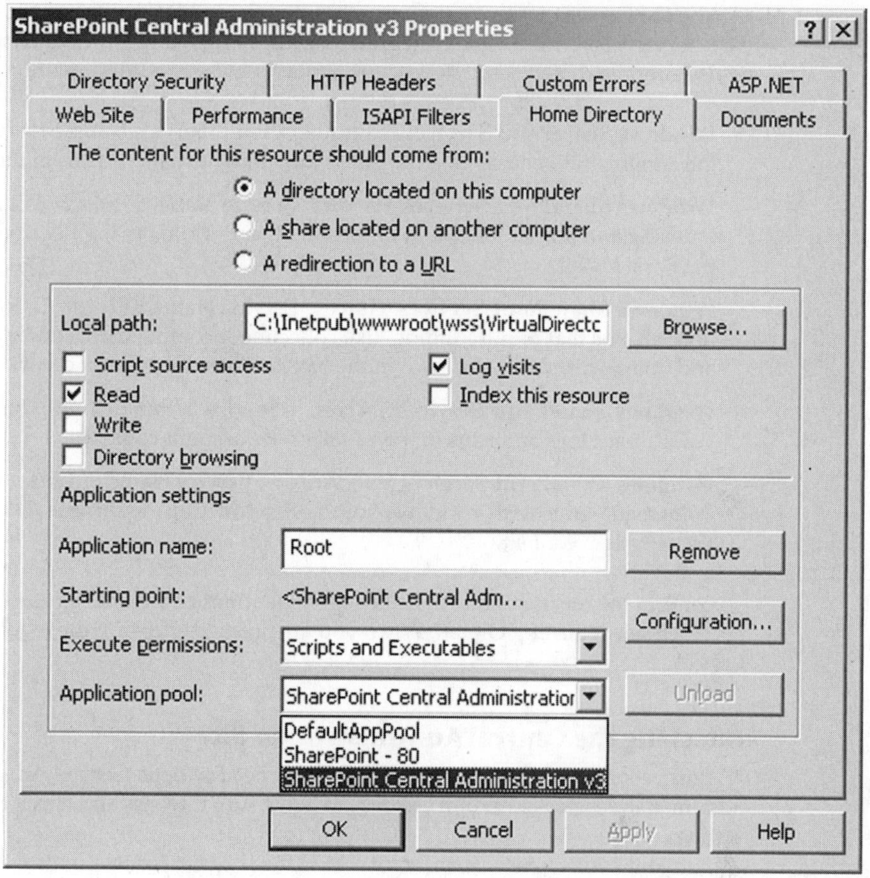

FIGURE 2.17
Central Administration's application pool

SharePoint Central Administration v3 Properties ? ✕

| Directory Security | HTTP Headers | Custom Errors | ASP.NET |
| Web Site | Performance | ISAPI Filters | Home Directory | Documents |

The content for this resource should come from:

      ◉ A directory located on this computer

      ○ A share located on another computer

      ○ A redirection to a URL

Local path: `C:\Inetpub\wwwroot\wss\VirtualDirectc`   Browse...

☐ Script source access   ☑ Log visits
☑ Read   ☐ Index this resource
☐ Write
☐ Directory browsing

Application settings

Application name: `Root`   Remove

Starting point: \<SharePoint Central Adm...

Execute permissions: `Scripts and Executables` ▼   Configuration...

Application pool: `SharePoint Central Administratior` ▼   Unload

                       DefaultAppPool
                       SharePoint - 80
                       SharePoint Central Administration v3

OK   Cancel   Apply   Help

You don't really need to remember the port number to access the site from the local server, because it is listed in the Administrative Tools menu. However, it's useful to know in order to access the site from a machine on the network other than the SharePoint server.

This dialog box also has the tab that let's you see what application pool this Web Site is using. Click the Home Directory tab, and check the Application Pool field at the bottom of the page (Figure 2.17). It should be SharePoint Central Administration v3, which you should recognize from the application pools earlier in this section.

You can use the same steps to confirm that the SharePoint-80 Web Site is using the SharePoint-80 application pool.

Checking SharePoint's Services

Finally, to make certain that SharePoint has created, registered, and is running all of the correct services, open the Services console by going to the Start menu ➢ Administrative Tools ➢ Services.

You should see that the SQL Server 2005 Embedded Edition service is running. Its associated SQL Server VSS Writer, which integrates backup and restore with Windows Volume Shadow Copy is also running. If you scroll down, you should see the five Windows SharePoint Services.

Windows SharePoint Services Administration   Service Name *SPAdmin*, this service performs the administrative tasks that the Timer job cannot do, and it runs in the Local System context.

Windows SharePoint Services Search   Service Name *SPSearch*, this service provides full-text indexing and search for SharePoint content, and it runs in the LocalService account context for the Basic Install.

Windows SharePoint Services Timer   Service Name *SPTimerV3*, this service is the one that does all jobs that require timing, like collecting incoming mail, sending alerts and notifications, and doing workflows and runs in the NetworkService account context.

Windows SharePoint Services Tracing   Service Name *SPTrace*, this service supports SharePoint's trace logs and runs in the LocalService account context.

Windows SharePoint Services VSS Writer   Service Name *SPWriter*, this service allows SharePoint to integrate with Windows Volume Shadow Copy and the SQL VSS Writer and runs in the Local System context.

To confirm the service names and the logon identities of these services, double-click each service and then select the Log On tab. When you are finished checking the logon information, click Cancel.

Checking the Central Administration Site

To finish confirming this installation, you only need to open Central Administration (the other administrative site SharePoint created) to make sure it works and check the server's configuration settings.

For your convenience, SharePoint added the shortcut for the Central Administration site to the Administrative Tools menu on the server where you installed SharePoint. The shortcut allows you to access the Central Administration website without knowing the port number.

To open the Central Administration site, select Start ➢ Administrative Tools ➢ SharePoint 3.0 Central Administration.

Log in using the setup account you used to install SharePoint (that account is just about the only member of SharePoint at this point, because you haven't added anyone else). In my example, that account would be dem0tek\setupacct.

After you log in, the Central Administration site's home page should appear. Notice that its design is similar to the SharePoint site's home page. The configuration settings are divided between server farm operations and web application management, both of which are located on their own pages, accessible by the navigation bar on the left of the page, or the tabs above it. At the center/right of the navigation bar is the web parts area of the page, containing web parts such as Administrator Tasks, Farm Topology, and Resources. Currently, at least eight administrator tasks are generated by default after each installation of SharePoint (to keep you from forgetting to do some of the initial setup tasks that SharePoint may require to work properly). We will go over some of these tasks at the end of this chapter in the Post-Installation Tasks section. Feel free to go to that section and finish configuration there. In the Farm Topology web part is a list of servers that are in the server farm (in a Basic installation there can be only one), and what services are running on each.

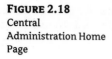

FIGURE 2.18
Central
Administration Home
Page

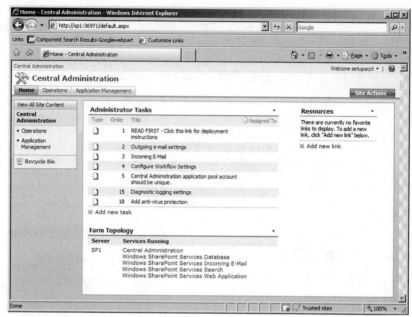

At the top right of the Central Administration home page, SharePoint indicates the account with which you are logged in (this nice feature was not available in the previous version). Also on the top right is the Help icon, so subtle you could miss it (Figure 2.18).

Advanced Server Farm Installation

Verify that your pre-installation preparations are complete. In particular, prepare the domain accounts that you plan to use for your SharePoint Services. Confirm that your server is a member of the domain. Make sure that you know the name (and possibly the instance name where applicable) of the SQL server that will contain the SharePoint databases.

Once you are prepared, make sure that you are logged in to the server where you will be doing the installation as your SharePoint setup account. (My example's is setupacct, or more accurately dem0tek\setupacct, because dem0tek is the fictitious domain for this book and setupacct is a domain user.) Or prepare to run the SharePoint installer using the setup account's context.

Remember that to install SharePoint on a Server 2003 Service Pack 1 or R2 server, you must download the Windows SharePoint Services 3.0 installer, SharePoint.exe from Microsoft (you can search the Microsoft site for "Windows SharePoint Services 3.0 download" and select the download details for Windows SharePoint Services 3.0). Make certain that you are using the version of the installer file that is correct for your server's architecture.

Once you've downloaded the SharePoint installer, and logged in as your setup account, follow these steps:

1. Double-click SharePoint.exe.

2. On the Software License Terms page, check the box at the bottom of the screen next to accept the terms of the agreement. If you don't agree, you can't install SharePoint. Click Continue.

3. On the next SharePoint installer screen, you'll see two buttons to select the type of installation you will be doing. You are going to install a server farm, so you need to choose settings for a SharePoint farm and, therefore, must click Advanced.

4. The next screen has three tabs: Server Type, Data Location, and Feedback (see Figure 2.19). The Basic installation does not offer this screen.

On the Server Type tab, you are offered the opportunity to specify how you want SharePoint to be installed on this server. You can choose to do a Stand-Alone installation (which is exactly like a Basic installation except you can indicate where the search index files are stored on the server, and you can enable the Customer Experience Improvement Program's feedback mechanism). You also can choose the Web Front End option. This option is known as a *Server Farm installation* (or SharePoint Farm, because it will be a farm of SharePoint servers). When you install SharePoint in a server farm configuration, the SharePoint server will be a web server, serving up SharePoint web pages while a different server hosts SQL.

FIGURE 2.19
Advanced installation options

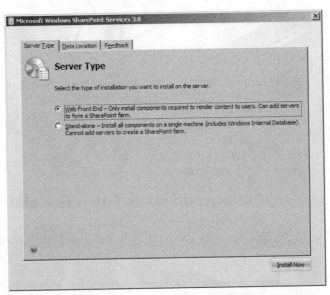

SERVER FARM IN A SINGLE BOX

When you install SharePoint in a server farm configuration, it is expected that the SharePoint server will be dedicated as a web front end server and a different server will support the SQL databases necessary for SharePoint to function.

However, you can have SQL (2000 sp3 or higher) server running on the server where you intend to install SharePoint. This can be useful if you are trying to combine roles to save on hardware resources. It allows you to have a single server dedicated to SharePoint and its databases, giving you the chance to expand to a server farm (by installing SharePoint as addition web front end servers in the farm) with all servers pointing to the first server's databases in SQL if necessary.

On the Data Location tab, you can specify where the index files will be stored for this installation. If you are planning to enable the Search service on this server and use it to do indexing, then it is a good idea to locate those index files on a different drive or partition other than the system files. The index files can become very large because they can contain lists of all the up-to-date, unique words in your SharePoint content. This includes both field data for the lists and libraries (considered *metadata* in SharePoint) and full text data from library documents.

You can sign up for the Customer Experience Improvement Program on the Feedback tab. This program sends anonymous data back to Microsoft about how SharePoint is being used, whether or not it is working, and other data. This program requires regular access to the Internet. If you want to help Microsoft by sending them information about your use of SharePoint and report to them when errors are encountered, choose the recommended option.

STAND-ALONE'S DIRTY LITTLE SECRET

You might wonder why there is a Stand-Alone Installation option when that is what the Basic installation actually is. The Stand-Alone Installation option can be a little misleading. You might think that the difference between a Stand-Alone installation and a Basic one is that the Basic installation installs the Windows Internal Database (WID) as well as SharePoint and, therefore, the Stand-Alone installation would probably indicate that SharePoint is installing on a server that also hosts an existing instance of SQL, with no WID needed. However, that is not the case. That theory is practical and logical, but it is not the way things work.

Although it may seem illogical, both the Stand-Alone and Basic Installation options install SharePoint and the Windows Internal Database (SSEE). There is actually no difference between the Basic and Stand-Alone installations except for the three-tab installation screen. This screen is supposed to give the person doing the Stand-Alone installation a chance to choose its data location.

If you read through the "Basic Installation" section, you know that type of installation installs the SSEE databases in a folder under %SYSVOL%—usually in c:\WINDOWS. You have no choice in that. The Stand-Alone option was supposed to give you the chance to specify a different installation location for the databases, such as a different partition or drive (it has to be local) and a different location for the index files.

However, there is a flaw in the SharePoint installation process. On the Data Location tab, you can specify only where the index files will go, but you should also be able to specify where the database files should go. This is indicated by the Help file that is associated with the Data Location tab of the installation screen.

However, as of the writing of this book, this option does *not* install the databases in the location you specify. It only puts the index files there.

Really, this is the only difference between the Stand-Alone installation and Basic. Hopefully, soon, Microsoft will release a service pack that will fix this oversight, bringing the interface into alignment with the Help file's content.

Earlier you learned that the Advanced Installation option Server Type allows you to choose between a Stand-alone installation of SharePoint and a Web Front End or Server Farm installation, and that these advanced types of installation allow you to configure your feedback to Microsoft, and where the index files go. Specifying the location of the index files does make it easier to find and monitor them.

To do that, follow these steps:

1. On the Server Type tab, select Web Front End.

2. Go to the Data Location tab. By default, the data location for the index files is under Program Files and buried deep beneath the Common Files folder. You can keep that default location, although you may want to make note of it, or you can specify a different location. You can enter the path to the new location, or you can browse to it.

3. In my example I've decided to specify a different location for the index files as a folder that I created on the server called *indexfiles*. To do this, I just click the Browse button, click the plus sign next to the Local Disk, select the indexfiles folder (see Figure 2.20), and click OK. The path `c:\indexfiles` will appear as the data location. You can use whatever folder is appropriate for you to do this; if you have a different local drive or partition, all the better. Simply enter the path to the location you've chosen, or browse to it.

FIGURE 2.20
The index files data
location

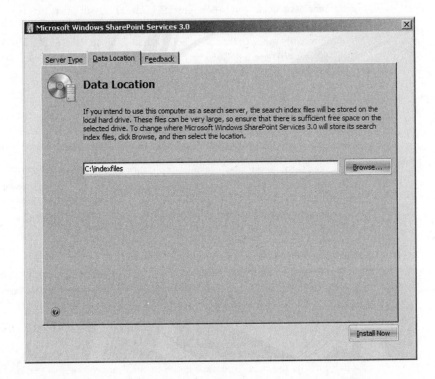

4. Go to the Feedback tab, where you can select the option to sign up to give Microsoft anonymous reports of how SharePoint is working, select the first option on the Feedback tab. By default, it is set to I'll Choose Later, so you do have the option to worry about it after

SharePoint is up and running. This example isn't going to be sending data back to Microsoft at this time, so I am going to keep the default.

5. If the settings of all tabs are as you'd like them (make certain that Web Front End is selected on the Server Type tab), click the Install Now button to continue.

   The installation will continue without any other input from you. When the installation completes, it will trigger the SharePoint Products and Technologies Configuration Wizard, which is the second part of this process.

6. If you want to wait and configure SharePoint later, you can deselect the Run the SharePoint Products and Technologies Configuration Wizard now checkbox. When you click Close SharePoint, it will not continue configuring. For my example, keep the checkbox checked and click the Close button to trigger the configuration process.

WHY WAIT?

If you are installing SharePoint on several servers at one time (building the whole server farm at once), it is suggested that you install SharePoint on each of them first, then wait and configure each server one at a time. This allows the configuration database to acknowledge each server and their services systematically. This is why you can do the install and then delay the actual configuration of the server until some other time.

The Configuration Wizard will start with a Welcome screen. As you can see in Figure 2.21, it requires the name of the database server (or server instance), database where the server farm configuration data will be stored, and a username and password for the database access account that will administer the server farm. Click Next.

FIGURE 2.21
The SharePoint Configuration Wizard
Welcome screen

7. A dialog box will appear and warn you that the Internet Information Services, SharePoint Administration Service, and SharePoint Timer Service services may need to be started or reset during the configuration process (see Figure 2.22). If this server is also currently serving web pages in IIS other than SharePoint, there may be momentary pause as the IIS service is restarted. To continue configuring SharePoint, click Yes in the dialog box.

FIGURE 2.22
The Reset Services
Warning dialog box

8. The next screen asks if you'd like to connect to an existing server farm, or if you would like to create a new server farm (Figure 2.23). This server will be the first in the server farm, so select No, I Want to Create a New Server Farm. Click Next.

FIGURE 2.23
Connect to existing farm
or create new one

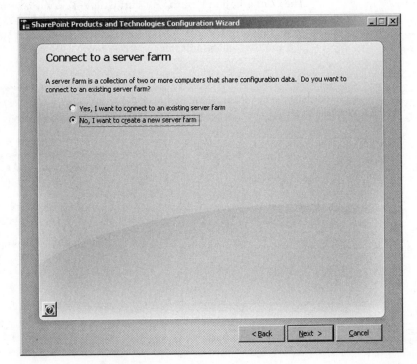

You should be on the Specify Configuration Database Settings at this point. As you can see, there is a field for the database server and a field for the database name. SharePoint has conveniently put the default name, *SharePoint_Config*, in the database name field for you. You can change it if you'd like but I am staying with the default in my example for clarity's sake.

9. In my example, the SQL 2005 server is called *RR1*, so I will enter *RR1* in the database server field, and keep *SharePoint_Config* as the database name. Enter the correct server name or instance in the database server field for your environment.

10. In the Specify Database Access Account section, you will choose the Windows account that SharePoint will use to connect to the configuration database. As a best practice, always use a domain name (if you are using Active Directory) and username. Also, and this is SharePoint thing, always use the *domainname\username* format. If you are going to be using SQL and SharePoint on the same server, and want to use a local account, you have to use the *localmachinename\username* format.

   As you can see in Figure 2.24, my example uses the domain user account created specifically for this purpose: dem0tek\wssconfig. Don't forget to enter a password, of course.

FIGURE 2.24
Specify the database access account

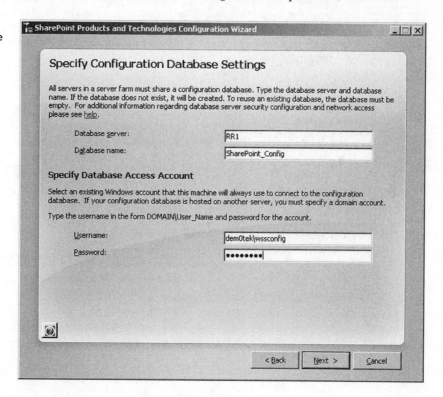

11. After you've filled in the database server, database name, and database access account fields, click Next to continue.

MAKE CERTAIN THE SETUP ACCOUNT IS CORRECTLY CONFIGURED IN SQL

If your setup account was not set up properly in SQL, this screen is where you'll find out. Unless SQL was prepared with preinstalled databases with the correct settings, your setup account must be able to create databases, add the database access account to the SQL Logins, DBCreators, and SecurityAdmins roles, and give it ownership of the Central Administration databases. After we finish the installation, I am going to go through the steps to check the settings on the SQL server. You may want to skip to that part to see if your settings match mine (the Confirming Database Access account settings section). If you forget to set the surface area of your SQL server to allow remote connections, that could also cause a problem. Make sure that has been done on the SQL server. If not, no matter how your account is set up, you will not be able to access the server to create databases.

12. The next screen allows you to configure the configuration database's Central Administration site port number. The Basic installation assigned the port randomly for you. However, although this installation suggests a random port, it also allows you to choose a port number between 1024 and 65535. To be specific, you can choose any port between 1 and 65535, but many of the ports up to 1023 are taken by common protocols. Use a higher port if you can. As you can see in Figure 2.25, my example suggests 9220. The Configuration Wizard suggests truly random port numbers, so they are unlikely to be something your server is using for anything else.

FIGURE 2.25
The default port for
Central Administration

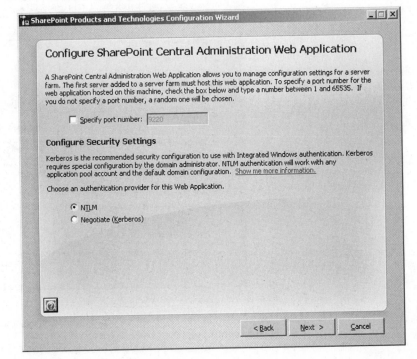

VERIFYING PORT NUMBER USAGE

Let's say that you have an appropriate port number that might be easier to remember than the random one SharePoint chooses for you. Before you assign an alternate port number for your new Central Administration site, you may want to be absolutely certain that your server is not using that port for anything.

The quick and easy way to confirm that is to use an often forgotten tool that comes with Windows Server 2003—*PortQuery*. The executable is .portqry.exe and you can find it on the Windows Server CD in the Support folder, in the support.cab file). If you have Internet access, use the newer version, portqryv2.exe, which is available as a download from Microsoft. This command-line tool is used to query the ports of a server to see if a port is being filtered (by a firewall usually), has a service listening to it (and therefore not available for assignment to anything else), or has nothing listening to it (and therefore is available for you to use).

PortQuery is a tool primarily meant to troubleshoot services such as Active Directory and Exchange. However, in this case it will be used to see if the port I want to use for Central Administration is being used by some other service. To do this, I open a command prompt and navigate to the folder where I installed portqry (or portqryv2), which is usually on the local drive in the portqry or portqryv2 folder. Then I run the portqry command with the following switches:

```
portqry -n IPaddressofserver -p both -e yourport
```

This means that I am running the portqry executable, with the -n, or name switch (this is not optional and can use the machine name, FQDN, or IP address; otherwise, it defaults to 127.0.0.1), -p or protocol switch (I like to check for both TCP and UDP just in case), and the -e or endpoint switch, which is used to specify the port I'm checking.

In this case, the IP address of my SharePoint server is 172.24.63.4, and the port I am going to check is 9876. As you can see, there are no services listening on port 9876 using TCP or UDP.

```
Command Prompt                                                    _ | □ | ×

C:\PortQryV2>portqry -n 172.24.63.4 -p both -e 9876
Querying target system called:

 172.24.63.4
Attempting to resolve IP address to a name...

IP address resolved to SP2.dem0tek.lcl
querying...
TCP port 9876 (unknown service): NOT LISTENING
UDP port 9876 (unknown service): NOT LISTENING
C:\PortQryV2>
```

Port Query is an invaluable troubleshooting tool and definitely should be a standard in your server toolkit.

If you use PortQuery frequently, or you have to teach junior administrators how to use it a little too often, you might want to consider the graphical user interface add-on called the PortQueryUI tool. It is simple to install. Download the PortQryUI.exe installer and double-click it. It will install the necessary files to a folder called PortQryUI on the local drive. Then simply navigate to the PortQryUI folder using Windows Explorer or the command prompt, and run the PortQueryUI.exe executable. The interface is easy to use, and it has convenient predefined queries for common services and a means to manually specify your ports. For easy access, you can create a shortcut to it on the Desktop, which is what I do.

To use PortQueryUI to check if any services are listening to port 9876, just specify the port you want to check, make certain you are checking both TCP and UDP, and click Query. It will generate the same report that the command-line PortQuery tool did, but in an easy-to-use interface. Check out the predefined queries for hours of fun.

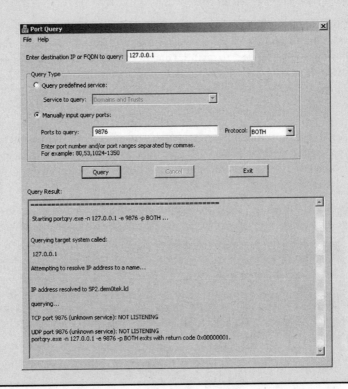

13. To make things easier, if you've checked the port availability on your server, you can ignore the default SharePoint suggests and specify the port you can remember more easily (I am going to use **9876**) for the Central Administration site. To specify the port, check the Specify port number checkbox, which enables the port number field, where you can add the specific port number.

By the way, if you want to change your Central Administration site port number, after this process is complete you will have to rerun the SharePoint configuration wizard, disable the Central Administration site, then re-enable the site to specify a new port. Just changing it in IIS will not let the configuration database for the farm know it has been changed.

14. The Configure Security Settings section of the Configure SharePoint Central Administration Web Application screen is where you can choose the authentication provider used with Windows Integrated Authentication. Kerberos is the most secure method, the one Microsoft suggests, and therefore the most difficult to set up. The default is NTLM, which is perfectly useable in an Intranet environment and the one that requires no additional setup (see Figure 2.26). For my example I'm going to use NTLM because it is the most likely choice for 95 percent of the networks out there.

FIGURE 2.26
Configure the
SharePoint security
settings

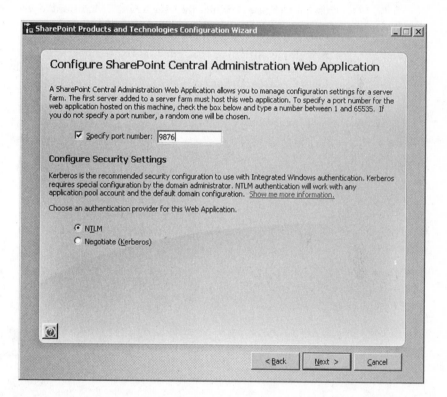

> To learn more about using Kerberos as your authentication method with SharePoint, go to Knowledge-Base article 832769. With SharePoint version 3.0 (or MOSS 2007 for that matter), you no longer have to run the script the document refers to initially, but you do have to complete the "Configure a service principal name for the domain user account" and "Configure trust for delegation for Web parts to access remote resources" sections. Enabling Kerberos is also covered in Chapter 15, "Advanced Installation and Configuration."

15. If you are certain that all the settings are correct, note your port number and click Next. This will take you to a summary screen in the Configuration Wizard. It summarizes your settings (which is useful) and has an Advanced Settings button. The Advanced Settings button is used in this case to change the User Account Mode for the server farm. This screen also gives you the option to go back and fix any mistakes or typos.

The Central Administration URL in Figure 2.27 is my *servername* and the port is 9876 (i.e., `http://sp2:9876/`). The Central Administration URL is what you will enter in your browser's (preferably Internet Explorer 6 or higher) address bar to access Central Administration.

FIGURE 2.27
Configuration Settings summary

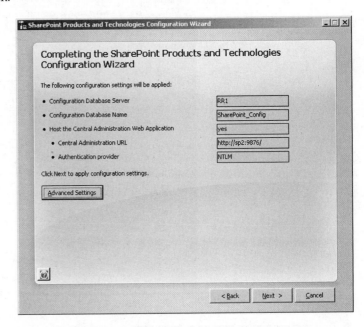

16. If all the settings listed in the configuration settings summary are correct (no typos), and you have completed all configuration steps to your satisfaction, continue installing SharePoint by clicking Next.

SharePoint will be configured by stepping through 9 different tasks, including initializing, creating the configuration database (which may take a while), creating help collections, securing resources, registering SharePoint Services, registering features, provisioning the SharePoint central admin web app, installing application content files, and finalizing SharePoint configuration.

SERIOUSLY CONSIDERING ACTIVE DIRECTORY ACCOUNT CREATION MODE?

SharePoint does not do authentication on its own. It requires Windows, or some other authentication provider (such as forms based or single sign on for MOSS), to perform the authentication for the user account. SharePoint queries the provider about that user; then, if the provider approves it, the user is allowed to use SharePoint. Once the user logs in, then SharePoint can apply its permissions to secure that user's access to its resources. Central Administration in particular must use Windows integrated authentication (although you can use other kinds for your web applications if you wish). But if SharePoint is running on a domain and using Windows Authentication, it can use Active Directory (AD) to store the user accounts that can be added to SharePoint. That's called Domain Account mode, and is the standard user account mode for SharePoint.

If that doesn't work for you (maybe because the people who will contribute and manage SharePoint will be from outside the company), there is Active Directory Account Creation (ADAC) mode. This mode (as you may recall from Chapter 1) uses AD for authentication but in this case you specify an Organizational Unit (OU) for SharePoint to create AD user objects when a user is added to SharePoint. In other words, with Domain User Account mode, you have to have the user in AD, then you can add them as a user in SharePoint. With ADAC you add the user to SharePoint, then they are added as users in the OU you made for SharePoint in Active Directory. If you are using ADAC, only users created in the OU are available as users in SharePoint; you cannot add a user from elsewhere in AD that isn't in that OU.

The tricky thing about choosing a user account mode is that the Domain Account mode is the default mode. The explicit option to choose it is not available. It is simply assumed by SharePoint during installation without administrator intervention. Many may not even know that ADAC exists. As a matter of fact, if you do a Basic or Stand-Alone installation there is no way for you to choose your user account mode anyway.

To enable Active Directory Account Creation mode for SharePoint, you *must* click the Advanced Settings button on the Configuration Settings Summary screen to get to the settings. It is so very easy to miss the settings for Active Directory Account Creation mode that I suspect Microsoft would like to encourage us not to use it.

If you are going to enable ADAC for your user accounts, keep in mind a few things (and read Chapter 15, "Advanced Installation and Configuration" for more):

◆ You cannot upgrade a SharePoint server to MOSS if it is running in ADAC mode. MOSS doesn't support it.

◆ You cannot change your mind. If you decide the setup is too hard and you would rather go back to the default Domain Account mode, you are out of luck. During a SharePoint installation, you choose one user account mode or the other, and that is it for the whole farm forever. The setting is unchangeably burned into the configuration database. You cannot change it without reinstalling. This is why the Basic install just goes for the default Domain Account mode automatically.

◆ You have to set the minimum password age to zero (which means never). If you set it to something else, users cannot change their own passwords. When a user is added to SharePoint with this user account mode, the user is sent their username and password. Because passwords are assigned to them, it is best practice to allow users to change them to something more personally private and relevant. They can't do that if Active Directory is using a minimum password age of anything other than zero.

◆ If you use ADAC mode, you must learn how to manage a lot of SharePoint administration using the command-line tool STSADM. (STSADM is a really powerful command; Chapter 13, "STSADM: A Look at the SharePoint Command-Line Tool," is dedicated to it.) The HTML interface has features that depend on Domain Account mode. It won't let you create site collections in the GUI, or allow users to create their own site collections (called *Self-Service Site Creation*). The potential inconvenience of this is enough to make administrators think twice about using ADAC mode.

◆ As you know, running any IIS Web Sites on a Domain Controller, let alone SharePoint, is not recommended. But specifically, ADAC mode is not supported on a Domain Controller.

◆ There are also some additional steps to setting up the ADAC user account mode, in addition to having an OU in Active Directory specifically for the SharePoint users, the database access account must be delegated the right to create/delete/manage user accounts and read all user account information in that OU.

17. When the configuration tasks are complete, the Configuration Successful screen will appear. This final screen of the Configuration Wizard lists the configuration settings that have been applied (notice there is no Back button in Figure 2.28). Write down these settings or print the screen to document them. You may know them by heart now, but how well will you remember them in a year?

   If your configuration was not successful, this screen will give you an idea of what went wrong so you can fix it and try again.

FIGURE 2.28
The configuration is successful

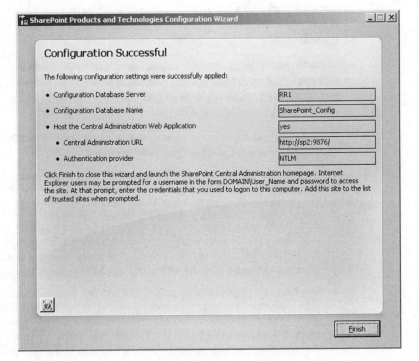

Launching Central Administration

When the configuration is complete, SharePoint is not quite installed; you still need to create an actual site. Before we move on, we first need to confirm everything is in order and working as expected. When you close the Configuration Wizard, Internet Explorer will automatically open and take you to Central Administration. This site naturally requires authentication, so you'll need to log in. Perform the following:

1. As you know, Central Administration automatically has a few accounts that can log in and begin to administer SharePoint. They are the setup account (because it installed SharePoint), the local server's built-in Administrators group, and the database access account. In my example, to be consistent, I am going to use my setup account to login, which is a domain account called setupacct. As you may have noticed, SharePoint prefers the domain\username format for accounts, so use that format to log in with your setup account (see Figure 2.29).

FIGURE 2.29
Log in to Central Administration

WHO ADMINISTERS SHAREPOINT MATTERS

When you log in to SharePoint using the setup account at this point, you are using an account that has both Farm Administrator rights to the farm by default (because it installed SharePoint), and it is allowed to do local administrative work on the local server. This allows it to make changes in IIS, such as adding Web Sites and changing security settings. It is a good idea to add at least one other account that is also a local administrator or domain admin of the SharePoint server/servers so they can configure all settings necessary in SharePoint.

If you log into Central Administration with an account that is allowed to administer SharePoint as a Farm Administrator, but is not a local administrator, or a member of the Domain Admins group, then some of the settings for SharePoint will not be available. You will be unable to work with the services running on the server or create new web applications, for example.

FIGURE 2.30
Prompt to add Central Administration to trusted sites

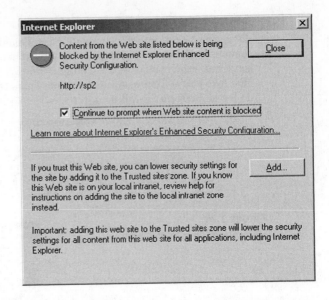

2. You may then be prompted to add the website to Trusted sites (Figure 2.30). Click Add, and use the Add dialog box to add the site to the Trusted Sites list. The Central Administration site will then come up in the browser.

So far you've got the Central Administration site up and running (Figure 2.31). This means that you have the means to configure SharePoint settings and save them in the configuration database, which is good, but you're not really done with the installation process yet. So before we really get into exploring the site, there are some changes to confirm. So let's see what the installation actually did on the back end.

FIGURE 2.31
Central Administration

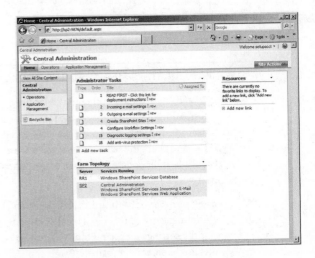

Checking the SharePoint Databases

As you know, SharePoint needs four databases. However, right now SharePoint is in limbo because it is not done being configured. It has created the configuration database and the Central Administration web application. This means that SharePoint currently has two databases. Those databases should have the setup account as the DBO (the original database owner) and the database access account as the database owner (assigned by the setup account during installation—it was basically handed off as soon as the setup account could add the database access account to SQL).

On the SQL server, you need to check the following:

◆ For the existence of the new databases.

◆ If the database access account was added to SQL.

◆ If the database account has the correct security assigned for both databases.

INTERFACE DIFFERENCES

Note that this book uses SQL 2005. Yours might be SQL 2000 SP3 or higher. If so, your interface might be slightly different than what is discussed in this chapter.

ACCESS DENIED?

Even if you are not allowed to access the SQL server (because that is the role of your company's DBA), the information provided in this section can help you understand what happened on the SQL server.

Confirming Database Creation

To get started, follow these steps:

1. Go to the SQL server and access the SQL management console (in my example, that's the SQL Server Management Studio) and connect to the server.

2. See if the two databases for the Central Administration site are there.

   To do that (make sure your Object Explorer is open), click the plus sign next to Databases. It should list the databases that are available on this server (see Figure 2.32). In my example, there are two new databases: `SharePoint_AdminContent`, with a long GUID alphanumeric string at the end of it, and `SharePoint_Config`, or whatever you named your configuration database during the SharePoint installation and configuration.

FIGURE 2.32

The SharePoint databases in SQL Server 2005

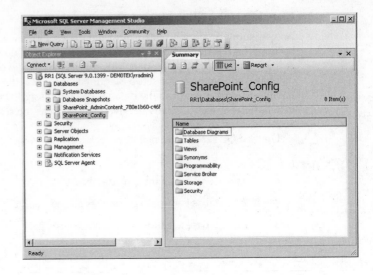

CONFIRMING DATABASE ACCESS ACCOUNT SETTINGS

The next thing to do is check to see if the database access account has been added to SQL properly and if the databases have the correct security settings. Remember that the setup account was added to SQL prior to installation, but that it was supposed to add the database access account as a login to SQL.

1. To confirm this, see what accounts are listed under Logins for the server by clicking the plus sign next to Security in the Object Explorer, and then select the Logins node. Under the contents of that node, your database access account should be listed (`wssconfig` is shown in Figure 2.33).

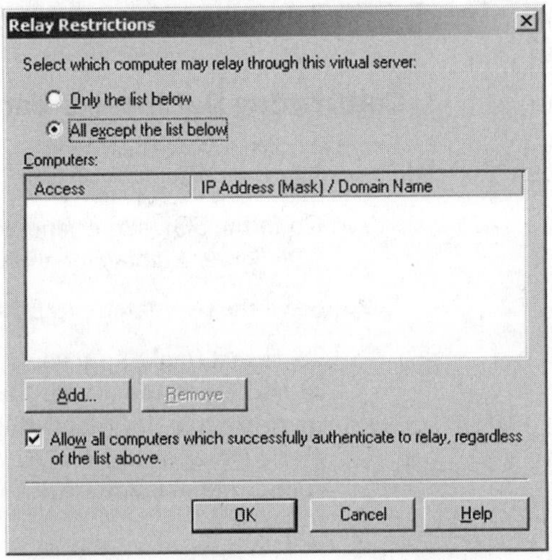

FIGURE 2.33

The SQL logins

2. To see if your database access account has the correct server roles, double-click its name in the Logins list. A Login properties window will open for that account.

3. Select Server Roles from the list on the left (see Figure 2.34). You should see in the details list of server roles that that account has DBCreator and SecurityAdmin privileges.

FIGURE 2.34

Login Properties Server Roles

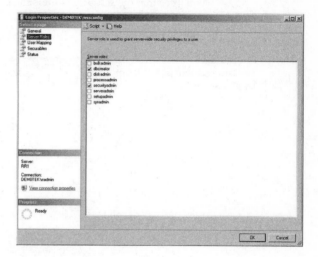

4. Click OK or Cancel to close the Login properties window.

CONFIRMING CENTRAL ADMINISTRATION DATABASE SETTINGS

Next we need to see if the Central Administration databases have the correct user settings, then select them and check their security.

1. To do this, start with the SharePoint_AdminContent database, select it in the Object Explorer, select Security, and then open the Users node (see Figure 2.35).

FIGURE 2.35

The AdminContent database's Users node

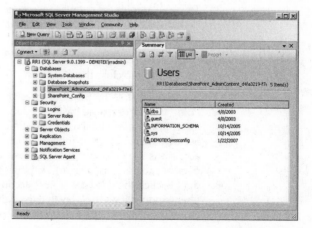

The setup account is not listed under Users; only the database access account is listed. That's because, for the two Central Administration databases, the setup account is the DBO, or ultimate owner of the databases.

2. To prove this, double-click the DBO displayed in the Users list. In the properties window, you'll see that the setup account is the login name for the DBO (Figure 2.36). Click Cancel to close the DBO User information.

FIGURE 2.36

The Setup account is the DBO of AdminContent

3. To see what roles the database access account holds for the AdminContent database, double-click the account name in the Users list. In the User Information window that opens, scroll down through the database role membership list. You'll see that the account is a db_owner, so the database access account has ownership rights to the database (see Figure 2.37).

4. Click Cancel to close the window.

5. To check the role that the setup account and database access account hold for the Share-Point_Config database basically do what you did for the AdminContent database. Select the configuration database, SharePoint_Config in this case, in Object Explorer. Open the Security node, and then open the Users folder. Double-click dbo to verify that the setup account is the DBO for that database, and then close the window. Then to verify that the database access (server farm) account is a database owner of the SharePoint_Config database, double-click the database access account listing and scroll down the Role Members in the User window. It will display that the database access account is the db_owner of this database as well.

FIGURE 2.37

The Database Access account is `db_owner`

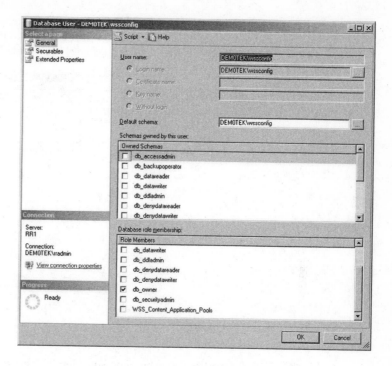

Now you know the following:

◆ The configuration databases were created in SQL.

◆ The setup account created them.

◆ The database access account is allowed to log in, be a DBCreator and SecurityAdmin, and own the two databases created by the setup account.

After this, the setup account will have nothing to do with SharePoint really. All other databases will be created by the database access account, which will also govern the other service accounts' access to those databases.

There you go. That's what SharePoint did in SQL. Now it's time to see what SharePoint did in IIS.

Confirming the Changes to IIS

On the SharePoint server, open IIS by choosing Start ➤ Administrative Tools ➤ Internet Information Services (IIS) Manager. We need to confirm that the application pool for the Central Administration web application (Web Site) is correct, that there is a Web Site for Central Administration and its application pool is correct, as well as confirm the port number for the site. To complete these tasks follow these steps:

1. To confirm the Central Administration application pool, select Application Pools in the tree pane on the left of the console.

2. In the action pane, there should be two application pools (see Figure 2.38): one is the default that loads when IIS is installed, and the other should be SharePoint Central Administration v3 (if this server is hosting other websites in your environment, there may be more).

FIGURE 2.38
Application pools after the SharePoint Server Farm installation

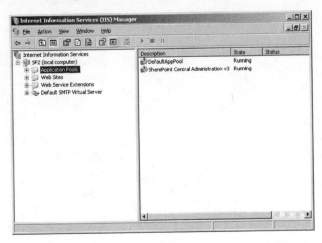

3. Right-click the SharePoint Central Administration v3 application pool, and select Properties from the popup menu.

4. In the Properties dialog box, go to the Identity tab. On that tab, the Application Pool Identity should be the one you assigned during the SharePoint Configuration Wizard (my example is dem0tek\wssconfig, as you can see in Figure 2.39).

FIGURE 2.39
SharePoint Central Administration's Application Pool Identity

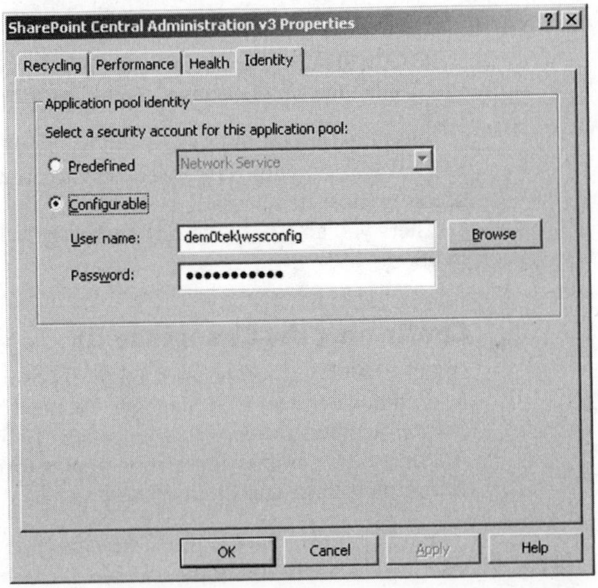

5. Click Cancel to close the Properties dialog box.

6. To confirm that the Central Administration site has the correct port and application pool, select Web Sites in the tree pane of the console. In the action pane, you'll see that the SharePoint Central Administration v3 site is listed, as well as the Default Web Site. (See Figure 2.40 for an example.)

FIGURE 2.40

Central Administration Web Site

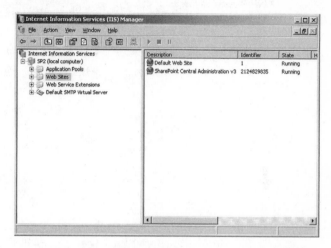

7. Right-click SharePoint Central Administration v3, and select Properties. In the Properties dialog box for the Web Site (Figure 2.41), the TCP port is the one assigned during SharePoint configuration. My example is **9876**.

FIGURE 2.41

Central Administration Web Site properties

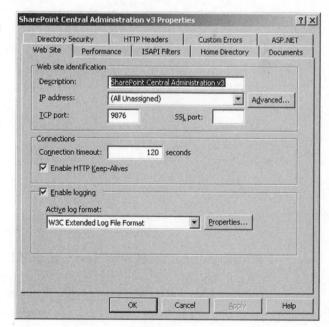

8. Click the Home Directory tab and go to the bottom of that dialog box to see that the application pool listed for this Web Site is the SharePoint Central Administration v3 pool (Figure 2.42).

FIGURE 2.42
Central
Administration's
application
pool

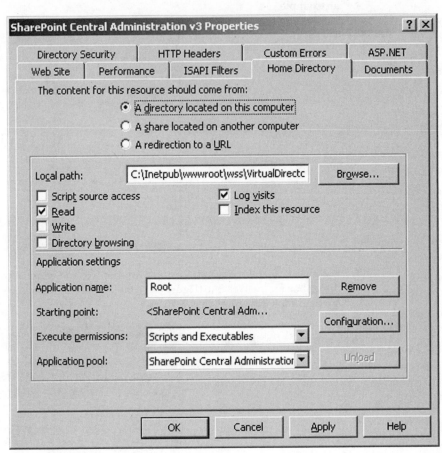

9. Click Cancel to close the Properties dialog box. Since we are done checking IIS for the moment, you can close the console as well.

Confirming SharePoint Services and Local Security Groups

SharePoint adds services to the server in order to function. It's good to know what services are running and what they do so you can better troubleshoot SharePoint should something go awry.

Which is why it is time to check the SharePoint Services. Keep in mind that they are not all on yet because the Search service has not been enabled.

To check the services, open the Services console by choosing Start ➢ Administrative Tools ➢ Services. In the console, scroll down through the services to the Ws. The SharePoint Services will be listed:

Windows SharePoint Services Administration   Performs local administrative tasks for SharePoint and runs in the local system context.

Windows SharePoint Services Search   Provides search services, is currently disabled (because we haven't configured it yet), and although it says it is a local service now, it will be using the account you assign it when it is configured because it has to be able to access the SQL server on the domain.

Windows SharePoint Services Timer   The über service that manages all tasks that require timing, including workflows, alerts, usage analysis, and more. This service runs in the context of the database access account (dem0tek\wssconfig in Figure 2.43).

FIGURE 2.43
The Time
Service
account
context

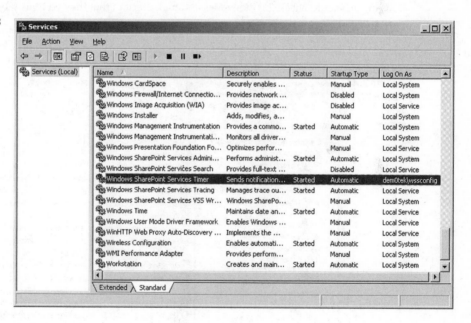

Windows SharePoint Services Tracing   Manages SharePoint trace logs locally and runs as a local service.

Windows SharePoint Services VSS Writer   Assists in backup and restore and integrates with volume shadow copy. It runs in a local system context.

In addition to installing services, SharePoint also creates three local security groups:

WSS_WPG   Members get read access to local SharePoint resources. Usually contains the service accounts that require access to content databases and the search service account.

WSS_Admin_WPG   Members have write access to the local SharePoint resources. This group must have access to the log file location so SharePoint can write to them. If you move the log files, be certain this group has read and write access. By default, built-in administrators, the setup account and the server farm account are members. Any account you add to Central Administration as a Farm administrator will be a member.

WSS_Restricted_WPG   The only member of this group by default is the server farm account. This group is required for the WSS Administration Service to function.

To view these groups, go to Start ➢ Administrative Tools ➢ Computer Management. In the console, select Users and Groups under System Tools, then select Groups (Figure 2.44). To check their membership, simply double click them.

It is not recommended that you add users to these groups manually. It is best to leave these to SharePoint.

Before we move on to the initial configuration tasks to finish installing SharePoint in a server farm, we should check the index files and make certain that they were installed in the location we specified during installation.

FIGURE 2.44
SharePoint local groups

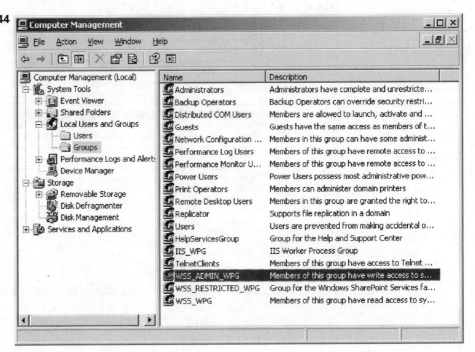

DCOM ERROR SILLINESS

After I install SharePoint, I occasionally get a DCOM error in the system event log. This is very likely because SharePoint forgot to give the database access account Local Activation rights to the IIS WAMREG admin Service DCOM application.

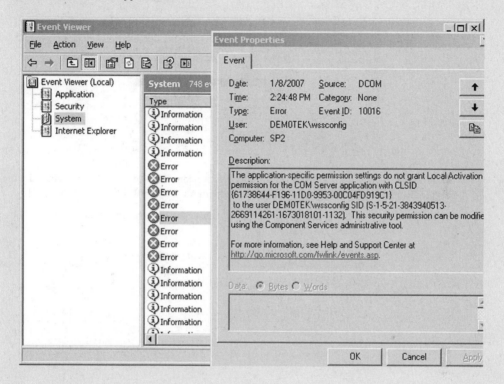

To fix it, follow these steps:

1. Note the CLSID of the offending DCOM application and open the Component Services console by choosing Start ≻ Administrative Tools ≻ Component Services.

2. In the console, make sure Component Services is selected in the tree pane, and then open the Computers folder in the action pane.

3. Open My Computer in the action pane, and then open the DCOM Config folder.

4. To confirm that the error is referring to the IIS WAMREG admin service (although that has always been the culprit for me), change the view of the action pane to Detailed, and scroll through the DCOM applications until you find the CLSID that matches the one you noted earlier. (You must scroll because there is unfortunately no "Find" tool in Component Services.) In my case, it was the IIS WAMREG Admin Service.

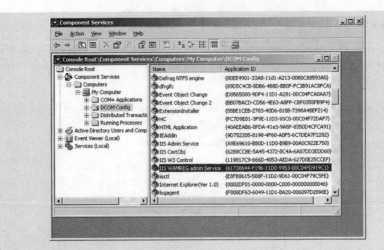

5. To give the database access account Local Activation rights to this DCOM, right-click the DCOM application and select Properties in the popup menu.

6. In the Properties dialog box, go to the Security tab. In the Launch and Activation Permissions section, select Customize and click Edit.

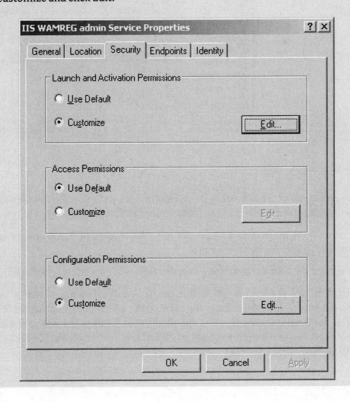

7. In the Launch Permission dialog box, you need to add the database access account and then give it local launch and activation permissions. Click Add, enter the name of your database access account in the dialog box, and click OK. The account should be added to the Group or Usernames in the Launch Permission dialog box.

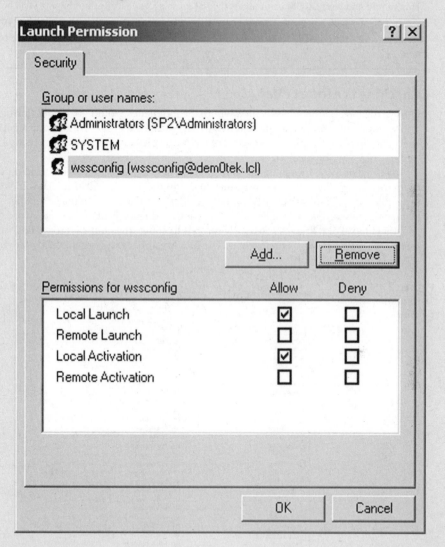

8. With that account selected, allow the Local Launch (if it isn't allowed already) and Local Activation permissions, then click OK.

9. Click OK in the Properties dialog box for the DCOM application.

10. To make absolutely certain that the application updates correctly, refresh all components by right-clicking the My Computer icon in the tree pane, and selecting Refresh all components in the popup menu. Then close the Component Services console.

This should end your DCOM error about the database access account not having local launch and activation permissions. You may also need to add the content database account for each of your SharePoint web applications to the DCOM to the list of those allowed to launch the DCOM application and activate it locally.

Checking the Index Files

During the installation, we specified where the index files would go. Under normal circumstances, you would want them on a different drive than your system files for optimum performance and space, but in my example I chose to store the index files in a folder called, creatively enough, `indexfiles` on the local drive.

To see what those files look like, navigate in Windows Explorer to the location you specified for them (my index files are in the indexfiles folder in the C: drive). Inside that folder created for the index files SharePoint has created a Config folder and filled it with many text files, most of which start with the word *noise* (see Figure 2.45). They hold records of all the *noise* words, like "the" or "a", that SharePoint knows. It uses the records to compare against words it finds and the XML files of the indexed words themselves. The files are apparently organized by language, except jpn seems to be English words.

FIGURE 2.45
The Indexfiles folder contents

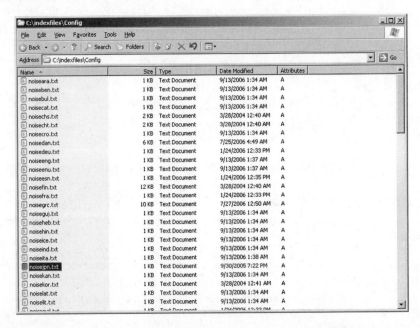

This folder and its files can be tracked to see how large they get and even what changes are made. Keep in mind that those configuration index files were added during installation, regardless of whether or not this server is going to actually be running a search. When search is configured, an Application folder will be added to hold the files needed to index SharePoint content.

Now there are no mysteries about what SharePoint has created, what it needs, and how it installs. All that is left is to finish configuring it and then you'll be ready to roll.

PSCONFIG, THE WIZARD BEHIND THE CURTAIN

Now that you've seen how the installation and configuration wizard works, I'll let you in on a secret: all it is doing is using a command called PSCONFIG at the command line. Behind that nice, appealing interface, PSCONFIG is hard at work doing the installation.

What does that mean to you? It means that you can use that command too. And because it is a command, you can script it to automate installations.

You may have noticed that the installation had two parts: the installation of the necessary files, or *binaries* as they are called, for SharePoint (using your standard `setup.exe`), and then the configuration of SharePoint (which is done with `psconfig.exe`).

If you wanted to install SharePoint with the PSCONFIG command line tool, then don't complete the configuration of SharePoint after the file installation. Clear the "Run the SharePoint Products and Technologies Configuration Wizard" box when that screen comes up, and click Close. This means the files you need to configure SharePoint and truly install it are in place, and now all you have to do is complete the process.

SharePoint puts its command line tools in the **%Program Files%\Common Files\Microsoft Shared\web server extensions\12\bin** folder on the local server. To use the PSCONFIG command, open a command prompt (Start ➢ Run, type **cmd**, click OK), and navigate to that bin folder.

To see what PSCONFIG can do, type *psconfig/?* at the command prompt. It will offer you three command options:

   `-cmd [`*`parameter`*`]`

This command indicates that PSCONFIG should run as a command based on the specified parameter. Parameters can be further modified by additional options.

   `-help`[*`parameter`*]

This lets you get help information about a particular parameter and how to use it.

   `-?`

This is the equivalent of using/? after the command and simply displays the syntax and parameters used with the command.

The parameters that can be used for PSCONFIG are:

◆ `Setup`: This parameter literally just runs the SharePoint setup. You can use the LCID option (to specify language) with this parameter.

   Keep in mind that `Setup.exe` is an executable in its own right, and can run on its own with its own options. For example, to repair an installation, you would run `Setup/repair` at the command line first, then PSCONFIG's setup. `Setup.exe` is what is used to install the SharePoint binaries.

◆ `Standaloneconfig`: Installs SharePoint as a Stand-alone server, with the Windows Internal Database. This also uses the LCID option.

◆ **Configdb**: Is used to specify the configuration database for the installation, with additional parameters to specify whether it should create a database, connect to an existing database, or disconnect. With this parameter you can specify the domain for the farm, its organizational unit (if it will be using Directory Management Service), and even specify the database for the Central Administration site. This parameter is used if you are doing a command line installation of a SharePoint server that will be part of an existing server farm.

◆ **Helpcollections**: Installs the SharePoint help file collections.

◆ **Secureresources**: Is supposed to enforce security on the SharePoint resources, like files, folders, and registry keys.

◆ **Services**: This parameter is used to register SharePoint services and has two additional modifiers: `install`, which registers the SharePoint services on the local server, and `provision`, which installs, and registers the SharePoint services for a Stand-alone server, setting them as online.

◆ **Installfeatures**: Although the command line tool STSADM can also do work with SharePoint features, this parameter is used to register the SharePoint features for the server farms that are on the local server.

◆ **Adminvs**: This parameter is used to create a new Central Administration web application, and has additional options to specify the port and type of authentication. This parameter also has the option to `unprovision`, or remove a Central Administration web application.

◆ **Evalprovision**: Does a Basic SharePoint installation. Intended to install SharePoint conveniently for evaluation, it has three options: `provision`, which simply installs SharePoint; `port`, which allows you to specify the port used by the default SharePoint web application (if not specified, 80 will be used); and `overwrite`, which will overwrite an existing IIS Web Site with the new web application. Normally, if you specify a port that is already in use by SharePoint, it will be shut down and SharePoint will create its own Web Site without disturbing the first one. With `overwrite` enabled, it will replace the existing web application.

◆ **Applicationcontent**: This parameter copies the web application binaries, files, and other shared application data for SharePoint to the web applications. This is good if you feel those files have been removed or corrupted.

◆ **Quiet**: A standard installation parameter, it will run the configuration wizard steps without output. The data is written to a psconfig.exe[date].log file.

◆ **Upgrade**: This parameter is what SharePoint uses to upgrade (or migrate) existing WSS 2.0 installations. This parameter has the option to do side by side or in-place upgrades. It has an option, `reghostonupgrade`, which reverts customized pages to the WSS defaults. Other parameters, such as `force`, `wait`, and `finalize`, are used to control the upgrade process. For more on upgrading SharePoint, see Chapter 14, "Migrating from WSS 2.0 to WSS 3.0."

The syntax for using PSCONFIG is:

```
psconfig.exe -cmd [parameter] -parameteroption
```

An example of this is: `psconfig.exe -cmd setup -lcid <1033>`.

If you are going to use PSCONFIG to automate the installation of servers in your server farm, make certain that the installation of binaries (the initial installation step before configuration) has been run on each server to install the necessary files PSCONFIG requires locally. You can string parameters together to have one long command, but keep in mind that they execute in a certain order. The order I have them above is the order they run, with upgrade going last. So keep that in mind.

So for those of you who don't like the graphic user interface, or were wondering how to automate your SharePoint installation, explore PSCONFIG; it might be what you've been looking for.

Finalizing the Server Farm Installation

When you install SharePoint using the Advanced Web Front-End option (or Server Farm in common parlance), the files required for installation are copied to the server and initialized. Then the Configuration Wizard kicks off to set up the configuration database, sets the database access account, chooses the port number and authentication method, and applies the user account mode (by default or not).

Then the Configuration Database is created; all of those settings are recorded within it, and then the Central Administration site and its content database are created. Finally, when the Configuration Wizard finishes successfully, the Central Administration site is accessed through the web browser.

SharePoint moves from the Configuration Wizard to the Central Administration sites because, with the Advanced Server Farm installation, you explicitly have to create the web application (i.e., the Web Site in IIS) and first site collection for SharePoint. It won't do that for you because you might want a specific name or header for your first web application or site collection, you might want to specify an SQL server for the content database, or you might want to do network load balancing and need to specify your network load balance IP address.

Unlike the Basic Installation, which creates the SharePoint web application and site collection by default just after it sets up the configuration database, and Central Administration, Advanced Web Front End only sets up SharePoint to the first SharePoint web application and site collection (Central Administration) and then stops, waiting for you to go the rest of the way. That's why we are not done configuring SharePoint for this Advanced install.

As you can well imagine, any SharePoint server, regardless of what installation option you choose, is going to require configuration to "make it your own." Because many of the initial configuration tasks are the same, single server or server farm, they will be discussed at the end of the chapter, independent of installation concerns. And this is why we are going to do only two configuration tasks in this section:

- Enable the Search service (and apply the correct service accounts)

- Create the SharePoint web application (and check to see what that does) and the first Share-Point site collection

This will make search possible on all subsequent web applications on the Farm, and it will make it possible for you to use SharePoint to do more than administration. To perform the necessary configuration steps to get this installation up to the point that the Basic Installation ends, you'll need to use Central Administration.

You should have Central Administration up, but if you don't, open Internet Explorer to navigate to http://*yourservername*:port (where the port number is the one you assigned to Central Administration during installation). You can also use the shortcut to the site on the Administrative Tools menu: select Start ➤ Administrative Tools ➤ SharePoint 3.0 Central Administration. Either option will take you to the Central Administration site if you closed it during the previous sections. Log in using the setup account.

FIGURE 2.46

The Central Administration interface

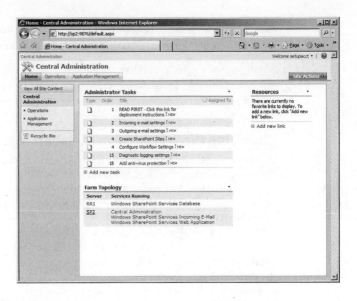

Now, with Central Administration open, let's take a quick look at the interface (Figure 2.46).

Near the top left of the page is the wrench and hammer icon for Central Administration (a carry-over from earlier versions of SharePoint) and the title of the site, Central Administration. Below that are three tabs that are a navigation mechanism to get to the three pages of Central Administration: Home (which is where we are), Operations, and Application Management.

Below the tabs, on the left, is the new and improved Quick Launch bar, another navigation feature. This bar is organized to let you quickly get to the Operations and Applications Management pages—and the Recycle Bin in case you delete something by mistake. You can also view all site content from the top link in the Quick Launch bar—which is useful if you've built a list or library and forgotten to add it to the Quick Launch bar.

In the middle of the page, the convenient web parts summarize Administrator Tasks, display Farm Topology (which shows what servers are running what SharePoint-specific service), and offers a way to display links to resources that you might like to add to the home page of the Central Administration site (such as KnowledgeBase articles). We will be using the Administrator Tasks list in just a moment.

The top right of the page offers the Welcome menu, which indicates who you are logged in as (a very useful feature for anyone who does a lot of testing and uses multiple accounts). You can use it to log off, log in as a different person, or modify your user information. Next to that, on the right is the ubiquitous Help button. Just below that is the Site Actions tab. When it is selected, a menu drops down to allow you to edit the web parts that are on the page, create a new page for the site if necessary, and more particularly, manage the site's settings.

EVER WONDER ABOUT HELP?

Where are the document files for help? How many there are? How to delete them (just kidding)?

Usually, Help files are essentially independent of the product to which they apply; they are a separate set of files usually combined into a .chm file. But this is not so in the case of SharePoint version 3.0.

For this version of SharePoint they are now contained in a document library called HelpFold on the Central Administration site. You should be very careful about the permissions and rights applied to this folder so no one accidentally deletes it. The HelpFold library is an interesting example of a library that contains hundreds of files of different types.

As a matter of fact, it is so large that it triggers a notice on the Settings page about learning how to manage large libraries.

The HelpFold library is, obviously, not listed on the Quick Launch bar on the Central Administration site. To get to it, use the View All Site Content link at the top of the Quick Launch bar.

In the All Site Content page, you'll see the HelpFold document library.

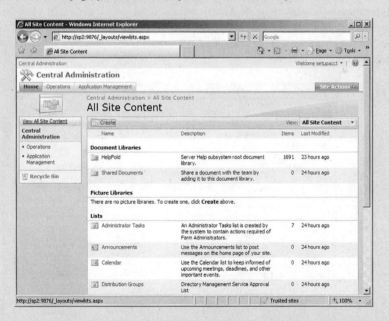

If you open it by simply clicking the HelpFold link, you'll see that Microsoft has decided to organize the Help files by folder. Don't be surprised if the folders are several layers deep. To look inside a folder, click on the folder name (for example, Content). If you selected Content, you'll see that it is further organized based on the language the Help files are in; mine is 1033.

If you click the folder name (1033), two more folders will open; they are MS_WSS (standard Help files for SharePoint) and MS_WSS_ADMIN (the Help files specific to Central Administration and administration in general). If you click on one of those folder names, you will end up on a page listing many files. The page has a navigation component just above the list items that indicates that it is showing 1 to 100 items. Click the right arrow.

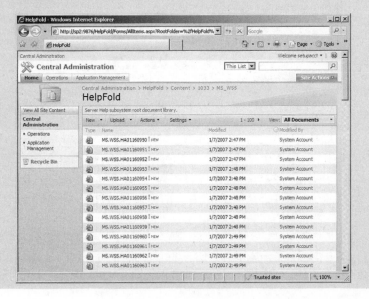

Now you can see items 101 to 200. If you keep going, it stops at around 266 for MS_WSS. That's right, there are 266 Help documents for WSS—not to mention those metadata files, the images files, and more.

Keep this list safe. Chances are that you, or some other SharePoint administrator, will need these files later.

Now that you are a little more familiar with the interface, let's focus on some post-installation, initial-configuration tasks. We are going to finish configuring SharePoint and then stop and confirm the changes the configuration wrought—such as enabling Search, creating a web application, and creating a site collection.

Before we begin, let's check out the Administrator's Task list on the Central Administration home page. Although my example strays from it a little, it is useful to remind you of critical administration that you may have overlooked. The list is organized, generally, by what Microsoft feels is a priority. These listed items are active, and they can change depending on what you enable, disable, or add to SharePoint. You will be using it on and off during these initial tasks because they help you find important configuration settings before you are completely familiar with the Central Administration layout.

THE READ FIRST TASK

The most important task in the Administrator's task list is the Read First task, which gives you access to the Quick Start Guide.

The Quick Start Guide mentions some things that really must be configured before you start using SharePoint that are not on the Administrator Tasks list for some reason. I am going to be doing most of the necessary tasks listed, except Alternate Access Mapping, which I will cover later. Regardless, you should know your resources, and the Quick Start Guide is a good resource.

To open the Read First task to get the deployment instructions, just move your mouse over that task's title until it highlights and click.

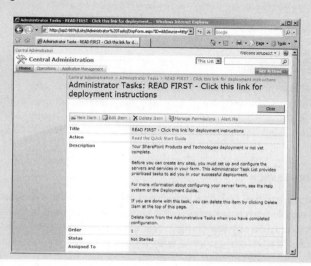

On the Read First task page, you'll notice the Title, Action, and Description sections. As you can see in the description, there are additional tasks that need to be performed. If you click the Read The Quick Start Guide link in the Action area, you will be taken to the Quick Start Guide and shown what those tasks are.

The Quick Start Guide is organized, not surprisingly, by how you install SharePoint. Because we are doing a server farm installation, choose the "Learn how to deploy Windows SharePoint Services 3.0 in a server farm environment" link to learn about the settings necessary for your SharePoint server.

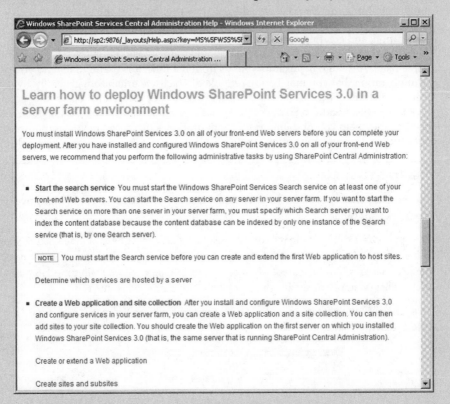

There you will see that you should always start your search service before you create the SharePoint web application that it will be searching. This is why, despite it not being on the Task list, I am going to have you do that next.

CONFIGURING SEARCH

The first administrative task that you must perform, regardless of what the Administrator's Task list says, is enable Search, because Search should be configured before you create a SharePoint site. If you are going to do any searching in SharePoint, there must be at least one server in the farm that is running the Search service. If your farm gets larger, you can enable Search on a different server later.

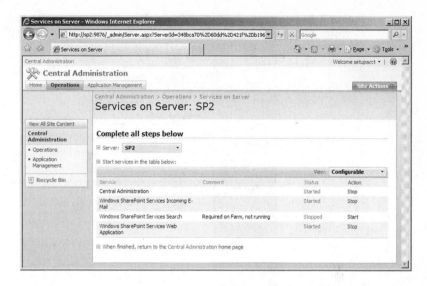

To enable Search, go to the Farm Topology list on the home page of the Central Administration site, and click on the server name for your SharePoint server (my example is *SP2*).

This will bring you to the Services on Server page. To be specific, you are configuring the SharePoint server, which falls under the heading of Operations among the SharePoint administration tasks. This is why the breadcrumb above the title of the page (see Figure 2.47) leads back from this page to Operations and then back to the Central Administration home page.

On this page, you can see the Services running on this server and, most particularly, that the Search service is stopped because it has not been configured. Note that it is required for the server farm.

To configure and start the service, click Start in the same row as the Windows SharePoint Services Search in the Service table.

NO WORRIES

You might notice the red warning text at the top of the Search service configuration page. Unless you are using SSL on this website, all data you are sending to the server is unencrypted except the NTLM or Kerberos managed login information. The fact that this data includes account names and passwords being passed to the configuration database is what causes concern here. If this is an issue within your company, consider using SSL to secure the Central Administration web application. You shouldn't be configuring your SharePoint servers from the Internet (which is where SSL really is important), but using SSL will protect the data that goes between the client and the web server. Currently, I am configuring SharePoint *on* the SharePoint server, and even though the information is not encrypted, I should still be okay.

In the Configure Windows SharePoint Services Search Service Settings page, you'll see Service Account, Content Access Account, Search Database, and Indexing Schedule sections (see Figure 2.48).

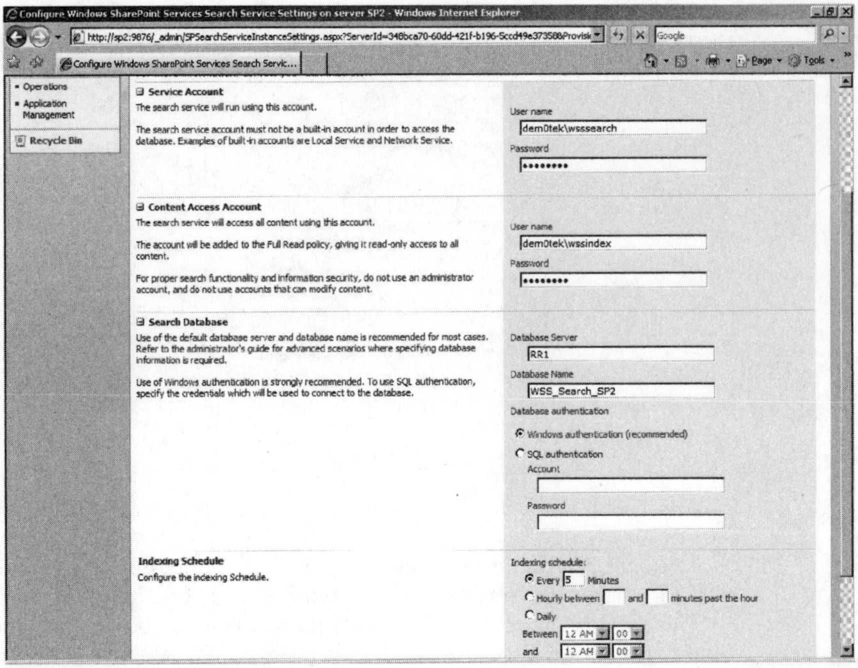

FIGURE 2.48
Configure the
Search Service
settings

Proceed with these steps:

1. In the Service Account section, use the service account you created to do search queries and access the search database. My example uses the dem0tek\wsssearch account for this very reason. This account is just a domain user; SharePoint (or more particularly the database access account) will give it the correct permissions to do its job.

2. For the Content Access Account, the account that will be reading all content for the site collections that will be searched, I am going to use dem0tek\wssindex.

3. The Search Database section should have filled in my SQL server name and created a default name for the search database, WSS_Search_SP2. It also defaults to Windows Authentication, which is the default authentication scheme on my SQL server. I am going to keep all of the defaults. If your SQL server uses SQL authentication, select that option and enter the required user name and password.

4. In the Index Schedule section, you can set the schedule that indexing must follow. The default is every five minutes, which is really convenient. However, indexing does take up valuable server resources, not to mention fills the Application log in Event Viewer with entries every five minutes, so you might want to schedule it either during a *certain* amount of time every hour, or even only during certain hours (supposedly during the off hours) of the day.

   I, however, am not going to be stressing the server unduly if I choose to have SharePoint index my sites every five minutes. And it is nice to be able to search for something very soon after it was posted to SharePoint. So we can keep the setting at the five minute interval in this case.

When you have finished configuring Search, and are certain that all your data is correct, click OK. You might get an Operation in Progress page if it takes a moment to enable the service, create the search database and add the Search service's accounts to it.

That should bring the Services On Server page back up, and now the Windows SharePoint Services Search service should be started (see Figure 2.49).

FIGURE 2.49
The Search service is started

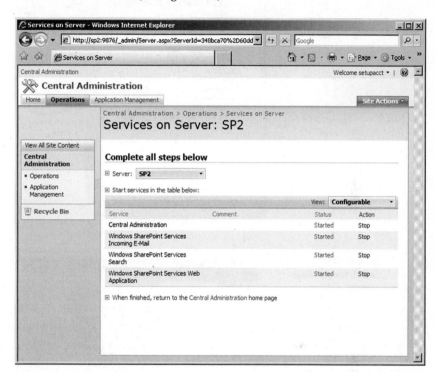

STILL NOT STARTING?

If the service still shows up as stopped, you may have clicked on the Search service name as opposed to the Start link. Doing that would configure Search, but not really *start* it. To start it, click Start in the Action column for the Search service, enter the password for both service accounts, and click OK again. That should properly start the service.

Now that you have enabled Search, when you create the SharePoint web application, its sites will be searchable.

If you were to go to the SQL server and check the server's databases, you would find a new search database (see WSS_Search_SP2 in Figure 2.50).

If you check that database's users, the DBO will be the database access account, and whatever you specified as the content access and Search Service accounts will also have ownership rights to the database, as you can see in the database DB_Owner Role Properties window in Figure 2.51.

FIGURE 2.50
The new Search
database

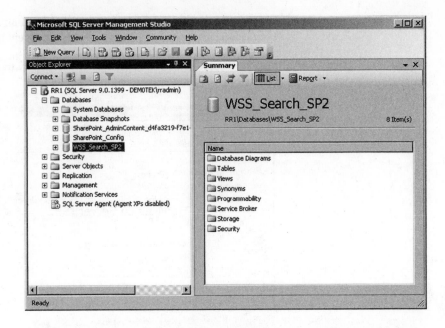

FIGURE 2.51
Search the database
owners

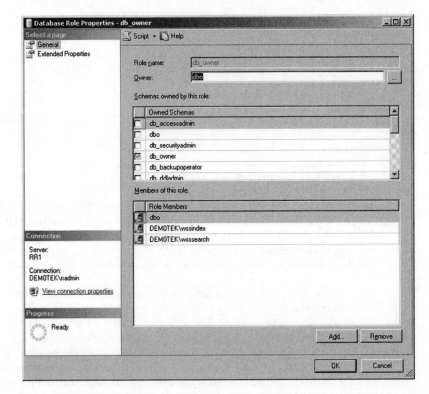

If you were to check the Services console, and scroll to the Windows SharePoint Services Search service, you would see that it is enabled and now uses the Search Service account. Now that Search has been enabled, you can move on to creating the web application and site collection that will contain the content to be indexed and searched.

CREATING SHAREPOINT'S FIRST WEB APPLICATION

To create a SharePoint site, you must first create a web application (IIS Web Site) to put it in. Remember, web applications contain collections of sites. They are the boundary for security, the port number, the header address, and other IIS-specified settings. Web applications control a lot of the settings that are critical to the site collections and sites users will be working in. In order to create a web application on a SharePoint server, the account doing so must be Farm Administrator *and* must have the right to add Web Sites to IIS, meaning it should be a local administrator of the server (or a domain admin).

To create a SharePoint web application, follow these steps:

1. Click on the Home tab at the top-left of the page to go back to the Central Administration home page and use the Administrator Tasks list.

2. On the home page, select the Create SharePoint Sites task in the Administrator Tasks web part.

CREATING A SITE OR A WEB PAGE

It may seem misleading that you selected Create SharePoint Sites as a task to create a web application, but here's the deal. Remember that web applications contain sites. You can't actually create a site unless there is a web application in which to put it. The task is referred to as "creating a site" because goal-oriented people, or people trying to access their SharePoint site after installation, are going to be looking around for a way to create that site, regardless of the steps preceding the goal. Therefore, the task refers to *creating a site*, when at first it is going to take you to the Create New Web Application page.

---

3. On the Task page, take a look at the description of the task (Figure 2.52). To conveniently create a new web application, click Create new Web Application in the Action section of the task. Creating a new web application is the first step toward creating a site, because the site first has to have a web application to contain it. You can't use Central Administration's web application because it must be dedicated to configuration.

   This will take you to the Create New Web Application page. As you can see in the breadcrumb above the page title, this is normally accessed by selecting Application Management ➢ Create or Extend Web applications ➢ Create New Web Application.

4. In the Create New Web Application page (Figure 2.53) you'll find the following sections: IIS Web Site, Security Configuration, Load Balanced URL, Application Pool, Reset Internet Information Services, Database Name and Authentication, and Search Server. As you can imagine, there will be a lot of settings.

FIGURE 2.52
Create a new site task

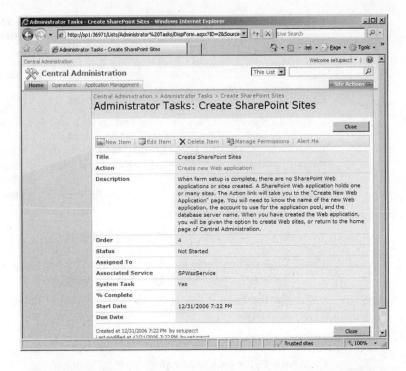

FIGURE 2.53
Create a new web application

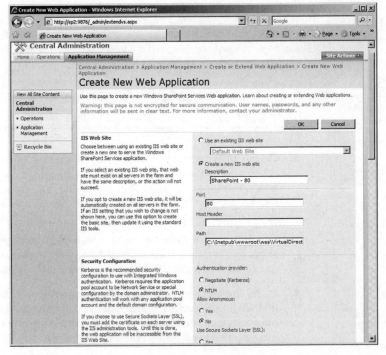

We're going to go through each setting, one at a time, until the new SharePoint web application is ready to be created. At the end of the list I will recap what settings were used for your convenience.

IIS Web Site   To start, you need to set up the IIS Web Site. The settings interact with IIS to create an IIS Web Site with the settings available in this interface. If necessary, you can go to IIS directly once the web application is set up to check.

Use An Existing Site   You could create a website in IIS and then use it for a SharePoint web application in SharePoint. That's basically doing a run around on SharePoint, not letting it create one for you, but using one you built yourself. If you do select an existing IIS Web Site to use as a SharePoint web application, SharePoint won't be aware of it, so you must create it manually on every SharePoint server in the farm so its contents will be replicated properly for load balancing. I really don't suggest you do that.

Create A New IIS Web Site   The second option is the safest and what we are going to use for this example. It lets SharePoint create a new IIS Web Site. Its default description (which will be the IIS Web Site description as well) is `SharePoint - 80`. You can change the default if you'd like. The thing about creating a new web application using Central Administration is it will be noted in the configuration database and replicated to all other SharePoint servers on the farm.

Port   It goes without saying that it is easier to allow users to access SharePoint by just typing in the server name, and not specify a port number (such as `http://servername:1234`). But if you require it, you can use that familiar server name and specify a particular port number for people to access the site.

Host Header   If you'd like this web application to use port 80, but go by a name other than the default `servername`, feel free to create a host header. (For more information about host headers, check IIS's Help files or read Chapter 8, "Site Collections and Web Applications".) A *host header* will let IIS redirect user requests to the correct web application while still using port 80. For my example, this is the only web application on the server on port 80, so there is no need to supply a host header at this time. However, if you need to add another web application to this server, you can use a host header to differentiate traffic between the two web applications if they are using the same port. This option is obviously easier for the users because they do not have to memorize a port number.

Path   The virtual directory path can be set if you don't want the default. This directory is used by IIS to store the files necessary to display web pages. By default, virtual directories are stored on the local drive under `inetpub\wwwroot`. However, if you want to specify some other path, feel free to do so. My example doesn't.

Leave the default settings for the IIS Web Site section as they are for this example.

Security Configuration   You'll see the following options:

Authentication Provider   Here you can choose what kind of authentication method to use. Your options are Kerberos or NTLM. The default is NTLM. Each web application can have its own security configuration, regardless of the authentication method chosen for the server farm during the configuration phase of installation. The method chosen then really only strictly applies to Central Administration, and explains why anonymous wasn't an option. When you create a new web application, you can apply different authentication provider requirements. If you want to use Kerberos authentication instead of NTLM, the application pool for this web application will have to be configured for Kerberos, meaning set up with a service provider name and potentially configure trust for delegation for both the SharePoint server and the content database's service account (see Microsoft's KnowledgeBase article 832769 for details or visit Chapter 15, "Advanced Installation and Configuration").

Allow Anonymous   This setting will enable IIS to allow guest access to the web application if necessary (or disable it, depending on whether you choose Yes or No). Once this is enabled on a web application, it can be selectively applied to the site collections, sites, lists, and libraries. My example does not enable anonymous for this web application.

Use Secure Sockets Layer (SSL)   SSL encrypts data transferred between a server and client, and it requires that the server have an SSL certificate. Enabling this option is a two-step process. First, you enable it in SharePoint by selecting Yes, and then you go into IIS and add the certificate there. Be aware that this web application will be inaccessible until the certificate is added to the IIS server. There are many articles and resources online concerning SSL. To learn how to add SSL certificates to IIS, consult IIS help or see Chapter 15, "Advanced Installation and Configuration." The default for this setting is No, which is fine for this example.

EVERY WEB APPLICATION FOR ITSELF

Each web application can have its own authentication provider and method, allow (or not allow) anonymous, and enable SSL. Part of the reason for this is that authentication provision and SSL are actually the bailiwick of IIS, and SharePoint just uses what's available for IIS Web Sites to manage itself.

The fact that a web application is a security boundary is a good thing to keep in mind when designing for SharePoint. There may be valid reasons to allow anonymous access to certain site collections, while absolutely forbidding the option for others. This is good reason to create two different web applications to separate secure content for authenticated users from content that could be set to be accessed by anonymous users and/or authenticated users. In addition, you might have content that must be secured on the wire between the client and the SharePoint server, so you want those sites to be protected by an SSL certificate.

Load Balanced URL   If you anticipate a heavy user load on your SharePoint servers, you may be planning to utilize network load balancing between your web front end servers. SharePoint supports NLB to some degree by replicating all web applications between servers in a server farm, using alternate access mapping and a load-balanced URL.

When you use load balancing, one URL is used to point to a web application. The load-balancing software or device will manage access to this web application, spreading the load between the balancing front-end servers. In a server farm, the SharePoint servers are the spitting image of each other (well, in relation to IIS and SharePoint related files, not physically identical) and are specifically set up for load balancing. If one server is too busy responding to client requests, the load balancer will redirect that address to the next server in line to take the request.

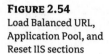

FIGURE 2.54
Load Balanced URL,
Application Pool, and
Reset IIS sections

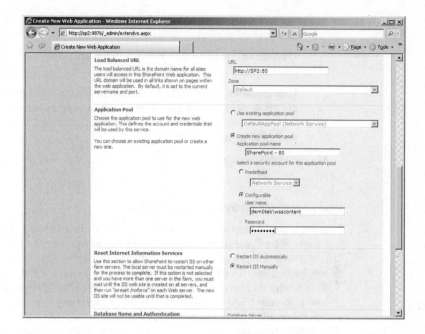

By default, this setting is the default URL or host header specified in the IIS Web Site section (as you can see in Figure 2.54). For this example we are working with just one server in the server farm, so load balancing will not really be an issue at this point. For more about load balancing, see Chapter 15, "Advanced Installation and Configuration."

Application Pool   This section defines the service account that will be used to access this web application's content database.

Use Existing Application Pool   You can use an existing IIS application pool. However, best practice is to specify a domain account especially for the web application. Although using an existing application pool is an option, it is not selected by default.

Create New Application Pool   This setting is selected by default, and it has a default application pool name: `SharePoint-80`. You can keep the default name or change it if you wish. For this example, the default is fine.

SECURITY ACCOUNT REMINDER

The application pool for this web application is going to read and write data to the content database for the sites contained there. It will be using the account that will access and store all your list content and document libraries files. This application pool security account is important for that reason. It should not be an account used for any other task if at all possible.

Select A Security Account For This Application Pool   This setting has two options: Predefined and Configurable.

> **Predefined**   means that you can use a built-in account, such as local service or network service, which is not recommended.
>
> **Configurable**   means you need to configure a unique account specifically for this application pool. Make sure that Configurable is selected. Enter a username using the domain\username format in the User Name field, and enter the account's password in the Password field.

My example uses the Content Database account that was created earlier: dem0tek\ wsscontent.

RESET INTERNET INFORMATION SERVICES

Creating a new website in IIS requires an IIS reset. In a server farm scenario, that means that each and every SharePoint server's IIS must be reset to replicate the new web application to each one. This is where you can give permission to restart all the other SharePoint servers' IIS automatically or not. Regardless, IIS will have to be reset manually on the local server.

This is why there are two options: Restart IIS Automatically and Restart IIS Manually. If you choose to Restart IIS Manually, which is the default (just to be cautious, you may not want to restart IIS on all of your SharePoint servers simultaneously), you will need to go to each SharePoint server and run iisreset/noforce at the command prompt. This will reset IIS and pull the web application changes from the originating server.

Because this example has only one server, we are going to have to reset manually regardless, so leave the default Restart IIS Manually selected.

Database Name and Authentication   This section allows you to specify the database server and database name for the web application (Figure 2.55).

> **Database Server**   Enter the name of the SQL server that will hold the content database for this web application here. It should already contain the name of the SQL server (or server instance) you used for the configuration database. In my example, it is *RR1*, which is correct.
>
> **Database Name**   This is the field for the database name for this web application. The default is WSS_Content. That is fine for this example. If there is already a WSS_Content database on the SQL server, this option will have a long GUID appended to it to insure it is unique.
>
> **Database Authentication**   The options here are to use either Windows Authentication or SQL Authentication. The default is Windows Authentication. Because this SQL server is set up for Windows Authentication, that setting is perfect for my example. However, if your SQL server is set for SQL Authentication, you will need to use the SQL account and password.

Search Server   The final section contains a field in which you specify the server that is running the Windows SharePoint Services Search service. In a large SharePoint server farm, more than one server can do search queries to spread the load.

In this example, there is only one. Therefore, in the dropdown list, the local server's name (my example is *SP2*) is the only server on the list. If it isn't selected, select it so Search will be able to index the web application's content database.

FIGURE 2.55
Database Name And Authentication, and Search Server sections

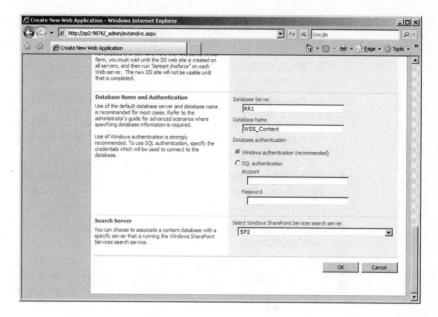

Here's a recap for this example of how to create a new web application:

1. In the IIS Web Site section, perform the following:

   a. Select Create a new IIS Web Site.

   b. Either leave the default description or create one.

   c. Leave the port at 80.

   d. Leave the Host Header blank.

   e. Keep the default path.

2. In the Security Configuration section, perform the following:

   a. Leave the Authentication Provider at NTLM.

   b. Do not Allow Anonymous.

   c. Do not use Secure Sockets Layer (SSL).

3. In the Load Balanced URL section, leave the default URL as listed.

4. In the Application Pool section, perform the following:

   a. Select Create new application pool.

   b. Select Configurable.

   c. Enter the username and password of the Content Database Service account you created. My example uses dem0tek\wsscontent.

5. In the Reset Internet Information Services section, leave Restart IIS Manually selected.

6. In the Database Name And Authentication section, perform the following:

   a. Make sure the Database Server field contains the name of your SQL server—and the instance if required.

   b. Leave the default database name or change it if you wish.

   c. Leave Windows Authentication selected as your database authentication. If your SQL server only does SQL authentication, then enter the account name and password for it in the appropriate fields.

7. In the Search Server section, choose the server running the Search service on your server farm. Because this *is* the only server on the server farm, select the local server's name in the dropdown list.

8. If all of your settings are correct, click OK at the bottom of the page to create the SharePoint web application.

   The Operation In Progress page will appear while it accesses IIS, creates the IIS Web Site, creates the content database, assigns the content database account to the database, configures the settings, creates the virtual directory for the IIS Web Site, and populates it with the SharePoint site's necessary files.

9. The Application Created page will appear in the browser (see Figure 2.56). To finish creating the new web application, you will need to reset IIS. To do this, open a command prompt by choosing Start ➢ Command Prompt (or Start ➢ Run, and enter **cmd**).

FIGURE 2.56
The Application
Created page

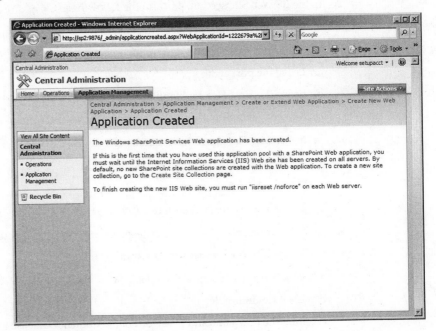

10. At the command prompt, enter **iisreset/noforce** and press Enter. The IIS service will attempt to stop, and then attempt to restart, and then restart successfully.

CONFIRMING WEB APPLICATION CREATION

To confirm that the new web application was created in IIS, open the IIS Manager console, click the plus sign next to the local computer, and click the plus sign next to Web Sites in the tree pane. Notice in Figure 2.57 that the default website has been stopped because it was using port 80 and our new web application needed that port. It kindly stopped the default website in case there was something there that you might need before it created the SharePoint web application, rather than just writing over it.

Select SharePoint-80 (or whatever you used as the description when you created your new web application). The files necessary for the SharePoint web application are listed in the action pane.

When you are finished confirming the new SharePoint web application, close IIS.

If you were to check SQL at this point, you would see that a new content database has been created (my example is WSS_Content).

If you check the database roles for the content database on the SQL server, the content database account will be listed (Figure 2.58). Of course, the DBO for the database will be the database access account.

FIGURE 2.57
Confirm the new web application

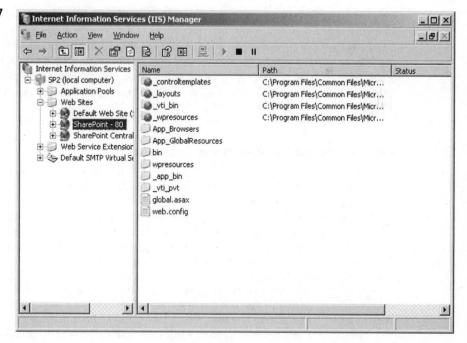

FIGURE 2.58
The Content Database account

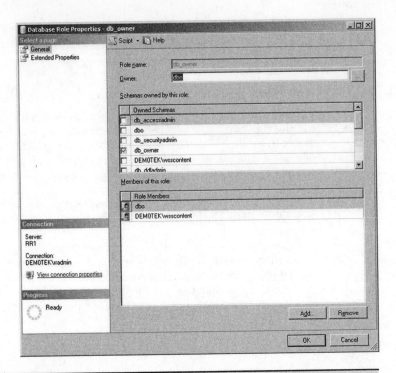

A SQL 2005 MANAGEMENT STUDIO GOTCHA

If you had the Studio console open when you created the web application and you check to see if the content database was created, the new database may not show up in the console. Even if you do a refresh, it still may not show up. However, if you close the Studio console and then reopen it, it will be there. Therefore, before you panic, be sure to close and reopen the Studio window to confirm that the content database has been created.

CREATING THE FIRST SHAREPOINT SITE COLLECTION

When you create a site collection, you are really creating the first, top-most site in the site collection. A *site collection* is just a combination of sites that has to start somewhere—just as a domain starts with a domain controller.

Don't be surprised if it seems as if you are creating only one site, because you are. Site collections start with one top site and build outward—or maybe more precisely, downward. These sites are usually created from the SharePoint templates—or even SharePoint applications you downloaded from the Internet. You can also customize the templates if you'd like, but for now, we will use the standard templates.

Not all sites are created equal. The first site in a collection is the one that all other sites in a site collection hang off of. Because it is the first site, it is considered a *parent*, and all subsites that are created under it are *children*. Because of this, the children sites can inherit settings from the parent site. The top-level site has management settings that affect the whole site collection. That's why the first site in a site collection is so important.

FIGURE 2.59
The Create Site Collection page

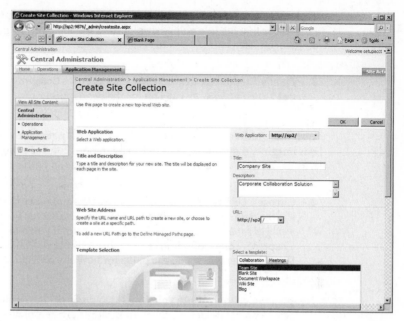

The Application Created page in SharePoint mentioned that you needed to create a new site collection, and it offered a convenient Create Site Collection link. To create a new site collection, follow these steps:

1. Click on the Create Site Collection link on the Application Created page to go directly to the page to create a new site collection.

FINDING THE APPLICATION CREATED PAGE

If you navigated away from the Application Created page, you'll need to go to the Application Management page, and click on the Create Site Collection link under SharePoint Site Management to get to the Create Site Collection page.

The Create Site Collection page (see Figure 2.59) contains the Web Application, Title and Description, Web Site Address, Template Selection, Primary and Secondary Site Administrator, and Quota Template sections.

Web Application This dropdown menu already lists the new web application (`http://sp2`) because that is the only web application available to contain a site collection. It is displayed, reasonably enough, by default.

2. Because the new web application is the web application where we want to put the new site collection, keep the default.

Title and Description   Use something neutral but descriptive for the title and description. Remember that the title will be displayed at the top of every page of this site. These settings can be changed later.

3.   Enter a Title and Description. My example uses **Company Site** for the title and **Corporate Collaboration Solution** for the description.

Web Site Address   There are two default URL paths for site collections at this point (as you can imagine, that can be modified). The options for this example, at this point, are to have the URL be `http://sp2/` or `http://sp2/sites/SiteName`.

4.   Choose a URL for the site collection. My example uses the first option, making this top-level site the default site accessible by just using the server's web address. Those URLs are called *managed paths,* and you can add your own later if you'd like. (We'll cover this topic in depth in Chapter 8, "Site Collections and Web Applications.") Managed paths allow you to be more flexible when you set up the paths for new site collections.

Template Selection   Here you'll find two types of sites, Collaboration and Meeting. These are the two different site definitions with multiple site templates based on each. Feel free to take a look at the different options. When you select a tab, it will list the templates under that definition, and when you select a template, a brief description will appear to the left of it with a nice graphic that looks absolutely nothing like the finished site.

5.   Select a site template from the list. My example will use the Team Site template for the first SharePoint site. This is the site template that the Basic installation uses for its top-level site. It's the default, standard, and trustworthy, and it will be the site template used for most of this book.

Primary Site Collection Administrator   This section allows you to select a domain user account (remember, you are using the default Domain Account User mode for this SharePoint server farm) for the primary site collection administrator. It doesn't have to be the setup account. As a matter of fact, it shouldn't be. That account should be dedicated to installation only. This setting let's you assign administration of a site collection to someone other than yourself.

ONLY TWO MAY ENTER

Keep in mind that the accounts specified in the Primary and Secondary Site Collection Administrators will be the only members of the new site (other than the server farm and content database account, which should never be used to log in). It is supposed to be a security improvement over the previous version of SharePoint because the setup account and the built-in Administrators are not available by default as members of new sites. Don't assume you can log in as the setup account to the SharePoint site because it installed SharePoint. That only works for Central Administration.

If, for some reason, you need to access a site collection and the primary or secondary administrators are not available, you can use the Site collection administrators link in Central Administration. There you can see who the primary and secondary administrator accounts are, and you can replace one of them (or both) with an account you can use to access whatever site collection you need. You can also, of course, add more site collection administrators after the top-level site is created, but initially these two site collection administrators are the only two who can log in.

The User Name field (otherwise known as a *People Picker* field, I am not kidding), has a check name, and a Browse button, which looks like an address book. If you enter a username in the field, you can confirm that it is spelled correctly by clicking the check name icon to the right of the field.

6. Enter an account name for the primary site collection administrator. This account does not need to have special administrative rights to the local server, it can be any domain user you feel needs to be the administrator of the site collection. My example uses my `shareadmin` account for the SharePoint site collection administrator account.

No Need to Specify a Domain

Notice that, because of the People Picker, you don't need to specify the domain, such as `dem0tek\`
`shareadmin`. The picker is Active Directory–integrated, so it's fine just to use the username. The People Picker will resolve it for you.

Secondary Site Collection Administrator   In this section, you can add another user account. This is user account is also notified about the site collection if the primary administrator is on vacation or dropping the ball.

Mind you, these accounts are literally going to be the only members of the whole SharePoint site collection. No other user will be able to log in until you add more people to the site. In this example, we don't need a second administrator for the site.

Quota Template   This setting is used to limit the amount of storage space in Megabytes the site collection (meaning this site and all subsites combined) require on the hard drive. We haven't configured any quotas yet, so this setting is not relevant right now. However, you can set up quotas later and then apply it to this site collection at that time (quotas will be covered in more detail in Chapter 7, "Sites, Subsites, and Workspaces").

7. If you have completed all your settings for this site collection, click OK.

   You may need to wait for the operation to complete, but eventually you will get to the Top-Level Site Successfully Created page (Figure 2.60).

8. On the Top-Level Site Successfully Created page, click the link to your new top-level site. My example is `http://sp2`.

9. A new browser window should open. You should be prompted for a username and password (depending on how you have your browser configured). Use the account you specified as a site collection administrator when you created the site to log in.

FIGURE 2.60

The Top-Level
Site Successfully Created
page

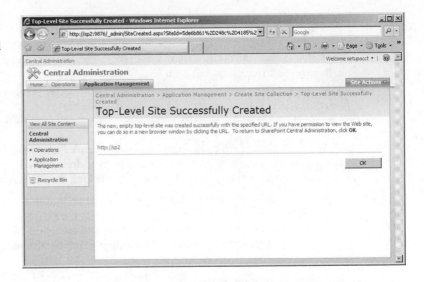

As soon as you log in, you'll see your fresh new site collection's top-level site. Notice that it is sporting a nice conservative Team Site template. Figure 2.61 illustrates our Company Site, and the description of the page is listed above the Web Parts area of the page.

FIGURE 2.61

The new top-level site

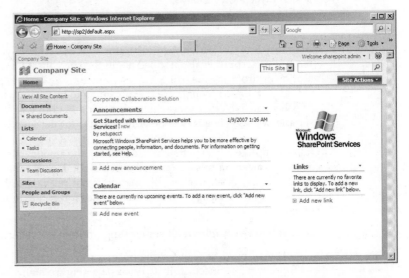

The Announcements web part has a "Get Started with Windows SharePoint Services!" entry, which was apparently written by the setup account. This is because the setup account actually created the site (the account still logged in on this server), so its name is on the sample data for the site despite the fact that that account is not a member of the site.

Congratulations! You have created a SharePoint web application and site collection and because of that you now know how to create other web applications and site collections (although we go into far greater depth in Chapter 8). You also can now appreciate the convenience of doing a Basic Install, because it does all of that for you.

You are almost done configuring SharePoint, and it is almost time to start working with it. However, before we do that, we'll need to finish the initial configuration tasks that require attention.

Post-Installation Configuration Tasks

Regardless of how you chose to install SharePoint, at least three more configuration tasks should be done before you start using it.

In order for notifications and alerts to work, outgoing mail must be configured. To allow lists and libraries to receive incoming mail, that must be configured also. And, in order for anyone else to use SharePoint, you need to add users. For any of these to work, we need to set them up on the server first.

CONFIGURING OUTGOING EMAIL

To configure outgoing mail in SharePoint, take a look at the Administrator Tasks on the home page of Central Administration (Figure 2.62). You should still have it open; if not, select Start ➢ Administrative Tools ➢ SharePoint 3.0 Central Administration, and then log in. You may notice that the Create a SharePoint Site task is gone; because when that task was accomplished, it was removed from the list.

FIGURE 2.62
The Administrator
Tasks list changes

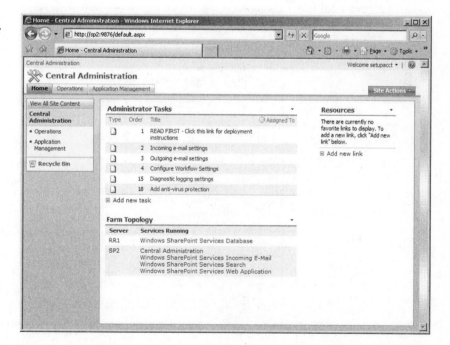

THE CONVENIENCE OF ADMINISTRATOR TASKS

The Administrator Tasks list gives a new administrator a list of common tasks that need to be configured when SharePoint is installed. More importantly, it provides *a way* to get to those settings when you don't yet know your way around Central Administration.

Keep in mind that Central Administration is organized into two pages:

Operations. These settings are used to manage the SharePoint server or server farm.

Application Management. These settings are used to manage web applications and their site collections.

However, until you get the hang of it, you might not be sure what settings fall under which heading. This is why the Administrator Tasks were created.

For more information about what each settings link does on those Central Administration pages, check out the Central Administration reference Chapters 9, "Central Administration: Operations" and 10, "Central Administration: Application Management."

To continue configuring outgoing email, follow these steps:

1. Select Outgoing E-Mail Settings in the Administrator Tasks list, because it's convenient. It should open a page that contains the Outgoing E-Mail Settings task (see Figure 2.63).

FIGURE 2.63
The Outgoing
E-Mail Settings
task

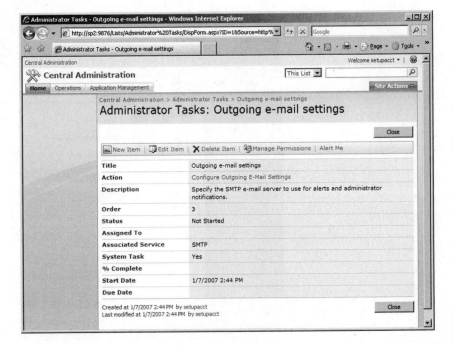

2. To configure those settings, click Configure Outgoing E-mail Settings in the Action section. This will take you to the configuration settings for outgoing email, which are listed under Topology And Services on the Operations page.

The Outgoing E-Mail Settings page has only one section: Mail Settings. It has the fields for Outbound SMTP Server, From Address, Reply To Address, and the Character Set. The default is Unicode UTF-8.

3. For outbound email, you need a valid SMTP server.]My example is running on the DC1.dem0tek.lcl domain controller on my internal network. You also need to specify a From address. Because this account doesn't need to receive email, the From address doesn't need to be a real email address. However, you also need to specify a Reply To address, which *does* need to be a real email account so it can receive replies. See my example settings in Figure 2.64.

FIGURE 2.64
The Outgoing E-Mail settings

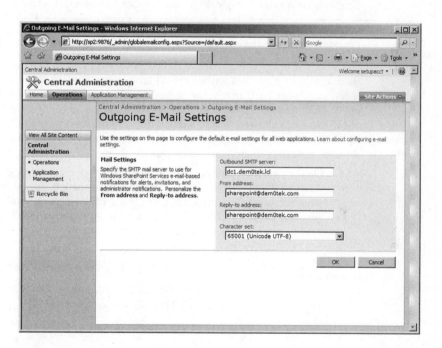

For this example, the outgoing configuration is going to be:

Outbound SMTP server: DC1.dem0tek.lcl

From address: sharepoint@dem0tek.com

Reply To address: sharepoint@dem0tek.com

4. Make sure that your settings are correct for your environment, and click OK to configure outgoing email. That should take you back to the Central Administration home page. Notice that the Outgoing E-Mail Settings task is gone from the Administrator Tasks list.

Déjà Vu All Over Again

Why can you set outgoing email on the Operations page and on the Application Management page? You just configured outgoing mail for the server farm. Those settings are now the default outgoing email settings for the whole server, every web application, and every site for SharePoint. However, you can set outgoing email individually on each web application as well, if you'd like.

The fact that some configuration tasks can be done both at the server farm level and at a web application level can be confusing. For your convenience, you can configure things like outgoing email at the server farm level. Think of it as setting server farm defaults. Configure it once, and those configurations apply to all web applications, websites, etc. all over the farm. However, to be flexible, you can also configure settings for things like outgoing email on a web application by web application basis as well.

Don't think of it as confusingly redundant; think of it as remarkably flexible.

CONFIGURING INCOMING EMAIL

SharePoint uses incoming email to receive email for incoming email-enabled lists, and it redirects those emails to those lists so they can add those emails as list items. This requires the SharePoint server and, more particularly, the SharePoint Timer service to know where to get the incoming email addressed to its lists, what the email alias for the server is going to be, and whether or not the SMTP service is allowed to accept email from anyone or only SharePoint members, to avoid spam.

This time, you are not going to use the Administrator Tasks list to get to the incoming email settings. Instead, you are going to go directly there.

1. On the Central Administration home page, click Operations (either the tab at the top of the page, or the link in the Quick Launch bar on the left side of the page). On the Operations page (Figure 2.65), the settings are listed under general headings such as Topology And Services, Security Configuration, Logging And Reporting, Global Configuration, Backup And Restore, and Data Configuration.

FIGURE 2.65
The Operations page

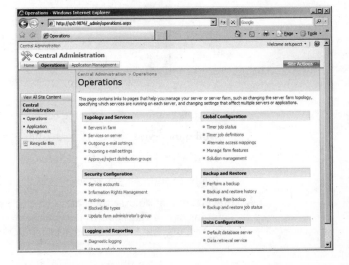

2. In the Topology and Services section, click Incoming E-Mail Settings. This will take you to the Configure Incoming E-Mail Settings page.

This page has four sections. The descriptions of these sections are so verbose that the page is pretty long, even if the settings themselves are pretty sparse (see Figure 2.66). Don't ignore the descriptions though, they are informative.

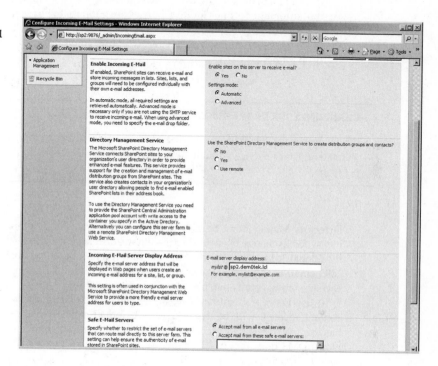

Enable Incoming E-Mail   This section has two settings: "Enable sites on this server to receive e-mail" and Settings Mode.

The first setting is pretty self-explanatory. It is currently set to No, which is why all other settings on the page are grayed out. To enable incoming email, change the setting to Yes. Once you set "Enable sites on this server to receive e-mail," all the other settings will become available.

Settings Mode has two options: Automatic and Advanced. If you are using the IIS SMTP service to handle incoming mail for SharePoint, you can use the Automatic Settings mode because it automatically knows what folder the IIS SMTP service uses for incoming email by default (it's called a *drop folder*).

TIMER SERVICE TIMING

The SharePoint Timer service checks for incoming email approximately every 30 seconds.

If you are not using the SMTP service to handle incoming email, or you have specified in SMTP that incoming email should not go to the default folder, you must use the Advanced Setting mode. This means that you need to specify the folder that SharePoint should check for new email.

3. Select Yes to enable Incoming email. My example uses the IIS SMTP service locally for incoming email, and the drop folder location has not changed. This means that it will use the Automatic Settings mode. Chances are good that your server, if you have been following along, will be using the default drop folder location as well, so select Automatic Settings mode as well. If not, select Advanced Settings mode, and specify the custom location of the drop folder.

CHANGING YOUR DROP FOLDER

If you do change the drop folder that SharePoint should check for emails, make sure that the SharePoint Timer Service account, which is the database access account, has the right to access the folder.

Directory Management Service (DMS)   This service is an interesting one. It is meant to make it easy for Exchange users to find the email address of lists that have incoming email enabled in the Global Address List and create distribution lists based on SharePoint groups. On Exchange 2003 email-enabled Active Directory networks, it literally adds a contact object to the OU for each incoming email enabled list, group, site, or library.

To use DMS, you must create an OU in Active Directory where distribution groups and contact records will be created for the email-enabled lists. The database access account has control delegated to it to create, delete, and manage user accounts in that OU. To work, DMS does require Exchange (2003) and the schema extensions that Exchange adds in Active Directory.

My example will not enable this service at this point because we should do a straightforward configuration to make sure incoming email works. However, you can come back and enable DMS any time, so it's okay to set up incoming email first without it, makes sure it works, and then come back and do DMS later (if you're running Exchange 2003).

4. Do not enable Directory Management Services at this time. For information about how to configure DMS, check out Chapter 15, "Advanced Installation and Configuration."

Keep in mind that there are documents out there that imply that you must enable DMS to get incoming email to work. That is not correct. It works perfectly fine without it.

Incoming E-Mail Server Display Address   In this section, the E-Mail Server Display Address field indicates what will be displayed as the server address for the incoming mail. The default is this SharePoint server's FQDN. This means that when you enable a list or library to receive incoming email, and you specify the list's email alias, it will allow you to add a unique name@ to your server's FQDN, such as *list@server.domain.com*.

USING FQDN FOR THE INCOMING EMAIL ADDRESS

There is a slick reason that the FQDN of the server is used for the incoming email address. When your users send email in the internal network to that address, your internal mail server will go to DNS to figure out where to put the email. The SharePoint server is listed in DNS by FQDN, so it will be sent there without the hassle of additional DNS entries. Make sure your internal email server is set up to relay email to the SharePoint server, and that the SMTP service in IIS on the SharePoint server is accepting those relays (it accepts all by default).

There are issues with that if you want to have people outside the office send email to the SharePoint lists and libraries (you'll need to do additional configuring and change the display address to use an external email address). However, for internal email, using the server name is a convenient workaround.

5. Enter the appropriate server FQDN for the SharePoint server. In my example the server's FQDN is SP2.dem0tek.lcl. It is an internal network address only, so it uses a non-Internet standard top-level domain name. In this case it is correct to accept that as the domain portion of the incoming email address for lists and libraries.

SAFE EMAIL SERVERS

The settings here allow you to specify if SharePoint will accept email from any email server or from only certain specified servers.

6. Leave it at Accept Mail from All E-Mail Servers if you don't have any rogue email servers in your office. However, if that is a problem you can list only the specific email servers from which SharePoint will accept email. Just keep in mind that you can come back and change the list at any time

7. When you have finished configuring your incoming email settings, click OK.

SPECIFYING A DIFFERENT DOMAIN ALIAS FOR INCOMING EMAIL

If you want your incoming email address default to be something that external clients might be able to use, then using the FQDN of the SharePoint server for the email alias is probably a bad idea.

There are four parts to specifying a different domain alias for incoming email: the SMTP service on the SharePoint server, DNS on your network, your office email server, and setting the incoming email address on the SharePoint server to the new domain alias.

To start, you need to decide what you want the address to be; for my example, I am going to use dem0share.com.

Then follow these steps:

1. Go to the IIS management console by choosing Start ➢ Administrator Tools ➢ Internet Information Services (IIS) Manager.

2. Verify that you can see the nodes under your local computer in the tree pane of the console.

3. Click on the plus sign next to Default SMTP Virtual Server node. Select Domains. The local server will be listed as a default domain.

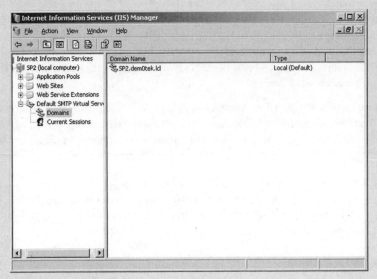

4. If you want to list a different domain that the SMTP service will recognize and accept email from besides the default local server name, right-click Domains in the tree pane or action pane. In the popup menu, select New. From that menu, select Domain. That will trigger the New SMTP Domain Wizard.

5. Because you are creating a new alias for the SMTP server to accept, select Alias and click Next.

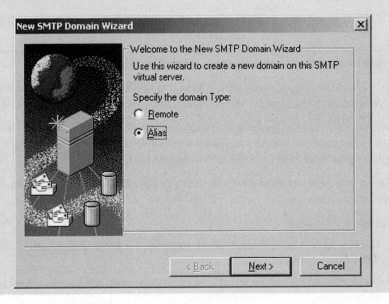

6. On the next screen, enter the domain alias you want the SMTP service to accept. My example uses **dem0share.com**.

7. When you are done entering your domain alias, click Finish. You should now see your new domain alias in the IIS console.

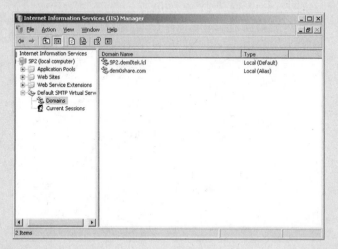

Next, you need to let DNS know what the new domain alias is by creating a new Forward Lookup zone. Then you need to create records there to point at the SharePoint server. Follow these steps:

1. Open the DNS Management console by choosing Start ➢ Administrative Tools ➢ DNS.

2. Right-click the Forward Lookup Zones node, and select New Zone.

3. In the New Zone Wizard Welcome screen, click Next. Choose Primary zone for the zone type, and click Next.

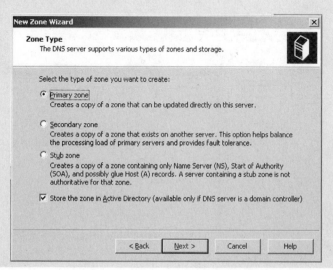

4. On the next screen in the wizard, you can choose how the new zone information will replicate to other servers in the domain. My example uses the default. Click Next.

5. In the Zone Name field, enter your domain alias. My example uses **dem0share.com**. Click Next.

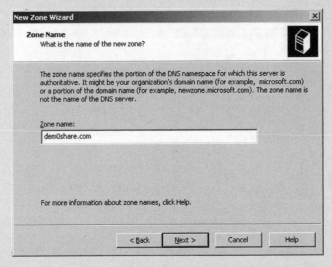

6. In the Dynamic Update screen, choose the update process that best suits your network. My example uses the default. Click Next.

7. The Completing The New Zone Wizard screen will display the new zone name, the lookup type (forward), and the fact that it's an Active Directory–Integrated Primary zone. Click Finish to complete the process.

You should now have a new zone listed under Forward Lookup Zones in the DNS console. My example is dem0share.com.

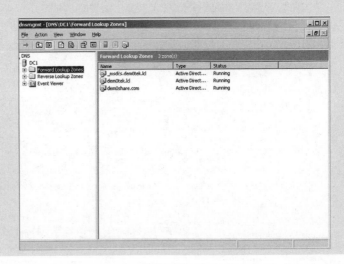

In the zone, you need to create a host record to let DNS know that there is a machine with the name of your SharePoint server using the domain alias. Then with that record, you can create an MX record to let DNS know that that host is a mail server. To do that, follow these steps:

1. To add a host record for the SharePoint server to the new zone, double-click the new zone to open it.

2. Right-click in the action pane of the console, and select New Host (A) from the popup menu.

3. In the dialog box, enter the machine name of the SharePoint server in the Name field. In the IP Address field, type the IP address of your SharePoint server.

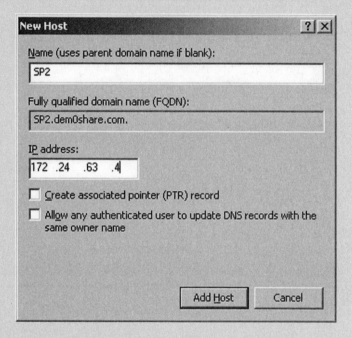

Don't worry about the two boxes at the bottom of the dialog box. In this example I don't want just any authenticated user to update the record, and I don't have a reverse lookup zone, so I don't need a pointer record. To add the host record to your new zone, click Add Host.

(Mind you, if your environment requires it, you can add a cname or alias record to map the new domain name to the SharePoint server instead of a host record. That means the MX record will have to refer to the server in its native, internal domain.)

4. A popup will tell you the host was added successfully. Close that popup, and close the New Host dialog box.

5. You need to create an MX record for the SharePoint server. Right-click in the action pane, and select New Mail Exchanger (MX) from the popup menu.

6. In the FQDN field, enter the name of the host record you just created. My example is sp2.dem0share.com. You can set the mail priority if you'd like. My example uses the default

of 10. When you're done, click OK. Your DNS server now knows what to do with requests for email addressed to your new domain alias.

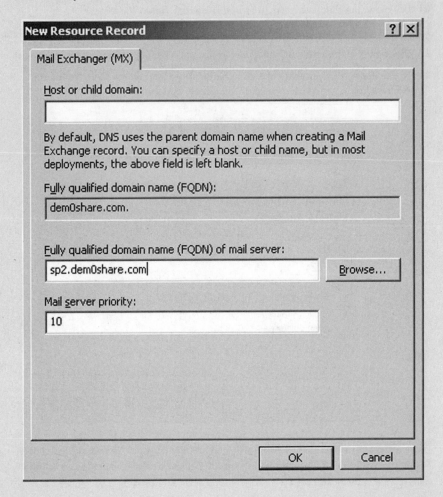

Now you need to make sure that your email server can forward email to your SharePoint server. For Exchange, you need to create an SMTP connector that points to the new MX record in your new DNS zone. For Server 2003's built-in POP3 with SMTP (which is what I am using for this example), you need to enable relay on the SMTP service for that server. That means you would go to the IIS management console, right-click the default SMTP virtual server, and go to properties in the popup menu and:

1. In the Properties dialog box, select the Access tab. Click Relay to specify how to handle relaying email. You can either specify the address of the SharePoint server and select Only The List Below, or you can leave the list blank and select All Except The List Below (meaning that it would exclude whatever was in the list below and that if it's blank, all relays will be allowed).

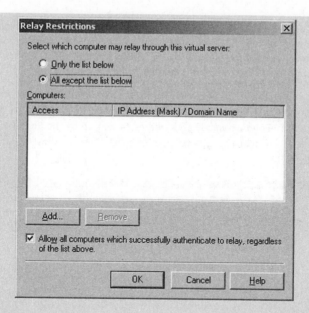

2. When you're done specifying the relay, click OK to get out of the Relay Restrictions dialog box. Then click OK to close the Default SMTP Virtual Server Properties dialog box. You can close IIS too if you'd like.

Finally, you need to go back to the SharePoint server and make the incoming email address for the server match your new domain alias. Follow these steps:

1. In SharePoint Central Administration, go to the Operations page and click the Configure Incoming E-Mail Settings link.

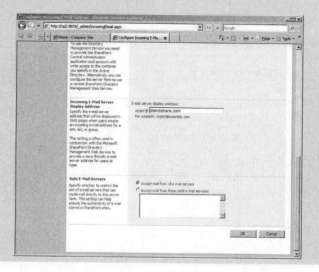

2. On the Configure Incoming E-Mail Settings page, scroll down to the Incoming E-Mail Server Display Address section, and change the address in the field to your new domain alias. My example uses dem0share.com. After you change the incoming email alias and click OK, it will take you to the Operations page of Central Administration.

Later, when you enable incoming email on libraries or lists (something we do in Chapter 5, "Introduction to Lists"), and a user in the office sends email to that list, the email will go to the drop folder on the SharePoint server. Then it will be picked up by the SharePoint Timer service, parsed, and placed in the correct list. My example emailed "Test of Alias" to an incoming email enabled Announcements list.

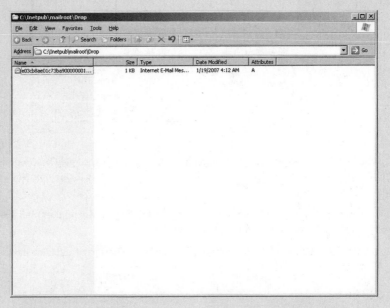

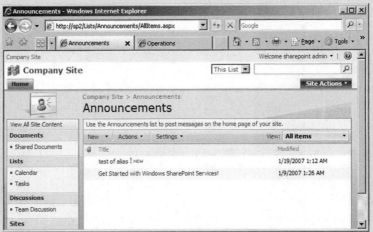

Now you can configure your libraries and certain lists to receive incoming email for an address other than the server's internal network FQDN. Not all lists can do email; they don't have fields that map to a simple email header. However, a developer could create some custom email event handlers if you wanted.

If you did not set up incoming email in Central Administration, the option to configure incoming email in the settings for the lists or libraries in SharePoint will not appear. So if you have to troubleshoot incoming email for a SharePoint site, you should recognize this problem when you see it.

ADDING USERS

Obviously, SharePoint won't be very useful if no on can use it. So to get up and running, let's add a user.

1. To add users to a SharePoint site collection, simply go to the home page of the top-level site (in my example that would be `http://sp2`).

2. Click on the People and Groups link near the bottom of the navigation bar (called a Quick Launch bar) on the left side of the home page.

    It will open the People And Groups page (see Figure 2.67). On the left side of the page is a navigation bar listing the SharePoint groups available for the site collection. They are groups in which to add user accounts (or domain security groups containing user accounts) that you want to give certain permissions to.

    An administrator creates a group and assigns permission levels to it. Then you add users to the groups, giving those users those permissions. By default there are three SharePoint groups: Members (who are allowed to contribute to the site), Visitors (who are only allowed to read what is on the site), and Owners (who are users with full, administrative control of the site collection).

    When you go to the People And Groups page it automatically displays the contents of the site Members group, since that's usually where you will be adding the most users. In this example I would like to add a user so they can start contributing to the site, so this page is perfect.

3. To add one or more users, click the New button.

    On the Add Users page, there are three sections: Add Users, Give Permission, and Send E-Mail. In the Add Users section is the Users/Groups field (this is a larger People Picker field than the one for specifying administrators for site collections earlier in the chapter). This field allows you to add multiple entries separated by semicolons. You can also use the address book button at the bottom right of the Users/Groups field and browse the Active Directory for user accounts and security groups. Or you can type in the name of the user, users, or even domain security group you'd like to add to SharePoint.

4. Click in the Users/Groups field. In my example I am going to add the user `saffron` to the site Members group (see Figure 2.68 for my example).

FIGURE 2.67
People and Groups
page

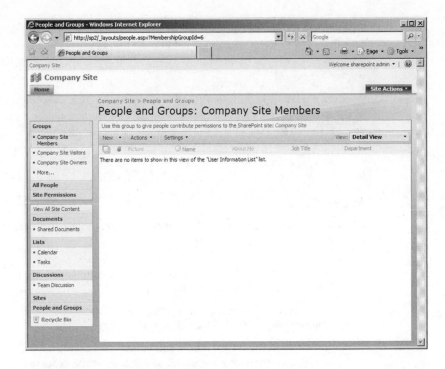

FIGURE 2.68
Add Users page

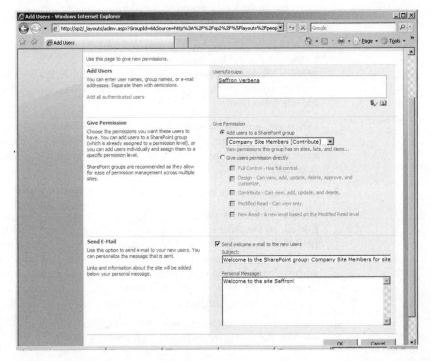

MANAGEMENT TRICK

Although I am keeping it simple here, it is a good idea to consider adding users to SharePoint as part of a domain security group rather than as individuals. Because there are only so many security objects that SharePoint can handle, if a user is added to SharePoint as part of a domain security group, they are considered part of that security object instead of an individual object to be managed.

In the Give Permission section, you can either specify the SharePoint group the user(s) should be a member of, or you can select the permission level(s) they should have explicitly. In this example, keeping the default of Company Site Members selected is appropriate. The point of clicking the New button on the Members page was for this default.

5. In the Give Permission section, in the Add Users To A SharePoint Group field, keep the selection for the Members group for the site.

6. In the Send E-Mail section you can choose to send an email invitation to the user. My example is going to allow the email message to be sent.

7. If all the settings are in order, click OK to add the user to SharePoint.

As you can see in Figure 2.69, Saffron was added to my site's Members group and can now log in to the site as a contributor. This should give you an idea as to how easy it is to add users to SharePoint. For more information about SharePoint groups, creating custom SharePoint groups, as well as using and creating permission levels, see Chapter 11, "Users and Permissions."

FIGURE 2.69

New User in site Members group

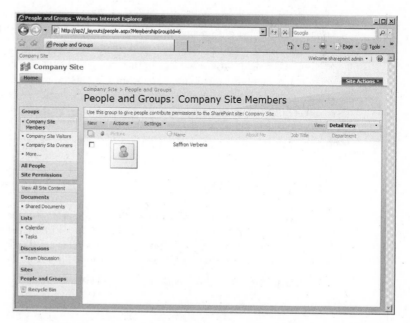

You are ready to move on to using Windows SharePoint Services 3.0, administering it, or customizing it. SharePoint is up and going. You know what it takes to prepare for SharePoint, to install SharePoint, what happens after you do install it, and how to do the post-installation, initial configuration tasks.

You may have noticed that there are links on the Administrator Tasks list that you have not touched. That is because they are not really a priority. SharePoint will work fine if they are left alone for right now. The workflow and diagnostic logging settings are enabled by default. You can adjust those settings later. The Add Antivirus Protection setting requires that you purchase SharePoint-aware antivirus protection. All of these settings and more are going to be explained in Chapter 9, "Central Administration: Operations."

ADDING A NEW FARM ADMINISTRATOR

It stands to reason that you might want to add users to Central Administration so more people can administer SharePoint. It is a little different than adding users to normal SharePoint sites. To start there is really only one SharePoint group for Central Administration. By default, any users added to the site are considered Farm Administrators.

In addition, there is no link for People And Groups in the Quick Launch bar like there is for most SharePoint sites. Instead the People And Groups page is accessed through the site settings.

To get There: click on the Site Actions button on the right side of the page above the web part area. That will open a Site Settings page for the site. Go to the Users And Permissions category and click on People And groups. This will bring you to the People And Groups: Farm Administrator's page. From here you can add users just as you would for a normal site.

Keep in mind that if an account you add as a Farm Administrator is not a local administrator of the server (or a member of Domain Admins), then they will not see all the settings that a local/domain admin can. For Operations, they will be unable to manage services on the server because that requires administrative rights. In Site Settings for the site itself, they cannot be site collection administrators by default, and therefore cannot do site collection administration. And in Application Management, they cannot create or extend web applications. So if ever a farm administrator complains that they cannot see all of the settings some other farm administrator can, chances are good that they are not allowed to administer the local server either.

The Bottom Line

Prepare for the installation of SharePoint   SharePoint does have certain software and hardware requirements before it can be installed. In addition, some of those requirements vary depending on the type of installation you choose. It is good to know what to install, how to install them, and in what order to be prepared for installing SharePoint.

Master It   Does SharePoint require SMTP?

Install SharePoint using the Basic and Advanced, Stand-Alone, and Advanced Server Farm Installation options There are several types of SharePoint installations available; Basic, which is a single server installation in which installs without intervention with all default settings and uses a Windows Internal Database; Advanced, Stand-alone, which is essentially the Basic Installation but you have a few basic configuration options before configuration begins; and Advanced, Web Front End (Server Farm) installation, which allows you to manage all configuration options and specify the SQL server that will manage the databases. Each installation type has its strengths and weaknesses, and it's good to know about them before you begin.

Master It Can you install and use SharePoint if you don't have a SQL server on your network?

Determine what gets created when SharePoint installs From Basic to Server Farm, it is good to know every step of the way the repercussions of each installation, configuration and service that SharePoint adds and/or enables.

Master It What is one way to confirm that the SharePoint services are running properly on the server?

Perform the initial configuration tasks after a SharePoint install (and understand why you perform them) After installation, SharePoint can require additional configuration before you can call it your own. It is good to know what the necessary settings are to quickly get SharePoint up and running to the point where an administrator can start working on it.

Master It Does incoming email require Directory Management Service to function?

Part II

Using Windows SharePoint Services 3.0

Chapter 3

Introduction to the SharePoint Interface

When you look at a SharePoint site for the first time, you might think it looks like a normal website—and it is. The beauty of SharePoint is its simple usefulness as well as its versatility. At first glance, you can see many of SharePoint's standard features. Most of the attributes of a SharePoint web page are focused on ease of navigation and consistency of design. It may not be a blinking, glittering, extravaganza of art and animation, but it gets the job done.

Remember that the point of SharePoint is to be easy for the users to use, navigate, and understand, while being really flexible in terms of it's usefulness. Consider it a framework, filled with potential, but not truly complete until you make it your own.

In this chapter you'll learn how to:

◆ Identify SharePoint's navigation tools and figure out how to use them

◆ Find a list or library

◆ Use the Quick Launch bar

◆ Use a breadcrumb

◆ Understand a content page

Microsoft has particular terminology for most of SharePoint's web page features and attributes. In order for us to have a common language, I will point out this terminology as we go.

From the start, let's take a look at the SharePoint top-level site we created when installing SharePoint (either Basic or Advanced, Server Farm). I chose to use the Team Site template for my top-level site because it is a good, standard starting point. It has the most commonly used lists, libraries, and web parts, as well as standard navigation tools that are a good introduction point for all things SharePoint. Later on in Chapter 7, "Sites, Subsites and Workspaces," you will look at the other templates available for sites straight out of SharePoint's box, but for now, the Team Site template is my favorite for a top-most entry to the rest of your site collection.

Team Site Home Page

The home page of any site is like the foyer of a building. It is intended to be the entrance everyone uses to get into the site. It has navigational elements, like a building directory, that allow you to see at a glance where else you can go in the site and how to get there. In addition, like a bulletin board in a foyer, the home page has an area to display announcements and other information that administration might feel visitors would find important. To see what I mean, let's open the Team Site home page:

1. Open Internet Explorer (if you're not already there), and enter the address of your SharePoint site, if you followed the defaults for your first site collection or used the Basic option for installation, use the machine name of your SharePoint server in the Address bar. Press Enter.

   Keep in mind that if you used the defaults, that the SharePoint-80 web application (or IIS Web Site, depending on how you look at it) is listening for all port 80 traffic directed to the server. That's why you only need to use the server's name to pull up the SharePoint site. This traffic will direct the users to the site at that root address. In my example, that is the Team site.

2. You may be prompted to log in to get to the SharePoint site. Use the *domain\username* format, and use the account you specified as the primary site administrator (the owner of the top-level site). For example, my account is dem0tek\shareadmin.

Once you are logged in, ASP.NET will take a while to compile the page, and then the home page of your first SharePoint site collection in your first SharePoint web application will appear (see Figure 3.1).

FIGURE 3.1
A typical SharePoint home page

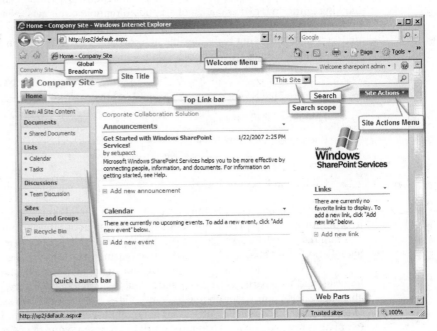

Home Page Anatomy

Now that we're on the home page, you can see that it does have some navigational elements, letting you know what other pages or sites are available from here. There is an area in the center/right of the page for announcements and other information. In order for us to have a common language as to what these features are called, let's dissect its parts. Remember, this is the interface for a home page created with the Team Site template. You may have chosen a different template for your top-level site, so your home page may look different on your server. Don't worry about it. Every site template in SharePoint has the same underlying capabilities, but they are laid out differently based on what they are meant to do, such as blogging, meeting management, or document management. Don't be alarmed if your site doesn't look exactly like mine. Many of the navigation features are the same.

On the Team site, there are certain common features for most pages. Across the top of the Home page is a light blue bar that contains the name of the site on the left (that is a global breadcrumb, and lets you come back to this page from anywhere in the site collection), and the Welcome Menu and Help button on the right. There is also an icon (that you can change) and the Title of the site on the left of the page below the light blue bar, with a search field to the right of that. Below the Search field is a Site Actions tab (actually, it's a drop down menu button, disguised as a tab).

Each of these components has a purpose. Leter, they will be covered individually in more depth, but here's a quick reminder as to where everything is and what they were meant to do:

GRAPHICALLY CHALLENGED OR SECRETLY USEFUL?

You might wonder why the title of the page is listed in a smaller font right above the larger, bolder title of the page. That's because the top blue bar never changes, regardless of what list, library, page, or subsite you are using. (This is a good reason to think seriously about your site names.) This bar is considered the "global breadcrumb" and can be used by a user to get back to the top-level site from a subsite, even if it doesn't inherit its Top Link bar from its parent site. In the previous version of SharePoint, it was easy to get "trapped" in a subsite (or a subsite of a subsite) below a top-level site with no navigation tool to get back to the top. As a result, Microsoft is now dedicated to using breadcrumb navigation wherever possible. Just remember, breadcrumbs only tell you where you've been. That's why SharePoint uses other navigation tools to get you where you're going, without having to actually *type* in the Address bar.

Search Field   The Search field is on the right side of the page, across from the site title and icon. It has a scope dropdown list, which allows you to search the site for something or to narrow that search when you are in a list or library to *just* that list or library (for faster, more direct results).

Top Link Bar   On the left, below the title and icon for the site is the Top Link bar.
This bar is intended to make navigation easier. It offers tabs for each site in the collection, starting with the home site (the first of all tabs made in that Top Link bar). This Top Link bar can, obviously, be edited. It can be inherited by subsites for consistent navigation (or not, your choice). Right now, the only tab listed there is Home, which is the site's home page and the one we're on. Whenever you go to a list or another page from the home page, you can easily go back to the home page by clicking the Home tab.

Site Actions Menu   The Site Actions menu is on the opposite side of the page from the Top Link bar's Home tab. This tab shows up if you have the right to edit the home page or administer the site. It is an administrative feature, so it is governed by SharePoint's security filter, which means that your login controls what you see. The average user with only the permission to read content on the site will not see the Site Actions menu because they cannot do anything with it. This is a vast improvement over the previous version of SharePoint, where users could see all the powerful, tempting links to administrative tools and settings but weren't told they couldn't use them until the users clicked on them and waited for the Access Denied page to load in the browser. The Site Actions menu contains links used to configure site settings, edit the page, or create lists, libraries, or subsites.

Quick Launch Bar   The Quick Launch bar is on the left side of the content area of the page itself. It is a focal point for navigating around the lists, libraries, and subsites of a SharePoint site collection. It displays available lists, libraries, and subsites for the site collection, in addition to links to the user Recycle Bin and the People and Groups page. Although this is a useful element to offer users a convenient way to access site content, you can elect to have items not appear in the Quick Launch bar, if you would like to make it a bit less convenient to access them. Keep in mind all site lists, libraries, and subsites are displayed on the All Site Content page as a fall back should something be accidentally missing from the Quick Launch bar.

Web Parts   On the center/right side of the home page, you'll find the page's real content: the *web parts*. Home pages for SharePoint sites are often called *web part pages* because they are the only pages in the out-of-the-box site templates that are meant to primarily contain web parts. Other pages can have web parts, but Home pages were the only ones meant to showcase them by default.

Web parts are little ASP.NET (2.0 or 1.1 for backward compatibility) controls designed to display the content of a page, list, folder, library, etc. Unassumingly powerful, these web parts can actually pull data to display almost anything displayable on the Internet and more. Out of the box, there are web parts that display a summary view for each list and library created in SharePoint. They give you an "at a glance" view of new entries for the list they contain and an opportunity to check out the entry or list at a single click.

By default, the Team Site template home page has several lists already made to give you an idea of what it can do. It gives you an effective starting point to simply get up and running. Because those lists exist, the home page can also be populated by those list's web parts. Web parts automatically generated by the Team Site template include: Announcements, Calendar (as you can see in Figure 3.1), additional little web parts to hold an image, and a web part for links you might like to add to the home page. You can add, remove, or rearrange web parts in this area to make it more relevant to your users. This will be the first place they will look when they browse to this site before going to the library or list where they need to work.

TYPES OF PAGES

Now that we've gotten an idea of each part of the Home page, let's examine the way SharePoint differentiates between the types of pages it offers its users. All pages in SharePoint, out of the box, are built from templates and definitions that already exist in SharePoint. The web part page is one kind of SharePoint page. It has a section for containing and displaying web parts, as you saw with the Home page.

Another kind of page is a *content page*. This kind of page is used to display the contents of lists and libraries (it can also hold Web parts as well, but that is not its primary purpose). Remember SharePoint's function is to be the front end that displays data that is actually stored in a database on the backend. That means that content pages enable you to view a list or library's associated table's data, manipulate that view (or report, which is essentially what a view is), add data to the underlying table, and even remove data. All data, such as announcements, tasks, events in a calendar, even document files in a library, are stored in tables in the content database. Both web part and content pages comply with the site design for the pages, displaying page attributes such as the Quick Launch bar and the features in the header area of the page, such as the Welcome Menu, Search, and site title.

In addition to web part and content pages are *administration*, *setting*, or *application* pages. These pages are the ones stored in the _layout directory for the site, and are the site management pages used to list settings, actually configure those settings, or create site objects. Site Settings, the Recycle Bin page, and the Create page are good examples of those administration pages. You will be able to identify this type of page because it generally doesn't have the normal layout that web part or content pages do, meaning there is no search field and no Quick Launch bar.

Finally there is one page that doesn't really fit any of the previous categories, and that's the All Site Content page. It looks like a page that just lists all site contents, organized by type of content, such as lists, libraries, or discussions. This page does have a view field like a content page, and the navigational elements of a normal web part or content page, but it has no search field. So it is not quite a content page (despite literally displaying the site's contents) and not quite an administrative page, but something in between. We will be checking it out in detail later in the chapter, so you can see what I mean.

Now that we have some common terminology, let's take a closer look at some of the active features of the SharePoint home page.

WELCOME MENU

At the top right of the Home page is the Welcome menu. This feature is a nice addition for anyone who used the previous version of SharePoint because it indicates with which account you are logged in. If you move your cursor over it and click, a dropdown menu will appear, as shown in Figure 3.2

FIGURE 3.2
The Welcome menu

FIGURE 3.3
The My Settings User
Information page

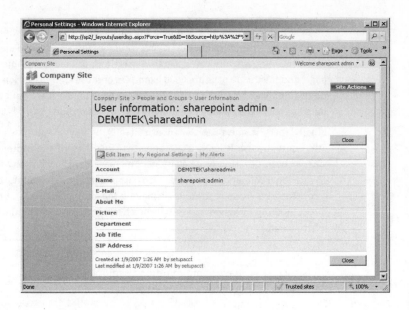

My Settings   The My Settings Welcome menu option opens a User Information page that contains the user information for the account with which you're logged in (see Figure 3.3). This is a convenient place to confirm your email account and change it if needed. You can also use it to add and edit personal information such as department, photo, job title, etc.

Sign In As Different User   The Sign In As Different User menu item allows you to log out of SharePoint without closing the browser, and log in as a different user. This is useful to test the rights of particular users.

DUAL IDENTITY

There is a flaw when you log in as a different user in SharePoint. If, you are still logged in on your computer with your account, and log into SharePoint with a different account, you may get errors trying to access web parts and pages that use Windows Explorer to view folder content. This is because, although you are logged in as person A (in SharePoint), you may be really using Internet Explorer as person B (on the local computer). When the option to use Windows Explorer to see files through IE becomes an issue, IE checks its local user's rights, not the person you are logged into SharePoint as. Therefore, this can be a problem when troubleshooting a user's access issues. Your local user could have more rights than that person and, therefore, have no problem accessing folders, or you could have fewer rights. Just remember this if you have any problems with Explorer view.

Sign Out   Sign Out actually just tries to close the web browser (see Figure 3.4). If you click OK in the dialog box, it will close the browser. If you click Cancel, it will remain at the Sign Out page, at which time you can use the Go back to site link (the small text just above the title of the page) to trigger a prompt to log back in.

FIGURE 3.4
The Sign Out page

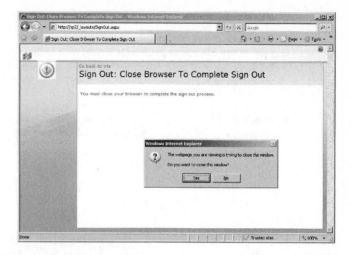

Personalize This Page   This link is interesting. SharePoint allows users to create a personal view (or version) of the home page by letting them rearrange, remove, or add existing web parts to the web part content area. This gives them a little flexibility and allows them to see what is most important to them as soon as they log into the site. If a user does not have the right to personalize their view of the home page, this menu option will not be available. This link will place the page in Edit mode, showing the different Web Part zones (the columns where you can place web parts above one another). In each zone there is a button to add more web parts (see Figure 3.5). We will be looking much more closely at web parts and what you can do with them in the next chapter. If a page has been personalized, then *Personal View* can be an additional menu option beneath Personalize this Page, indicating the user is viewing the shared version of the page. They can use the option to switch to viewing their personalized version.

FIGURE 3.5
Personalizing the home page

HELP

The Help icon is to the right of the Welcome menu, and takes you to the Help page (Figure 3.6). Like many Microsoft products, SharePoint Help is pretty hit or miss. As of the writing of this book, occasional help documents actually suggest checking online for better, more up-to-date information.

FIGURE 3.6
The Help page

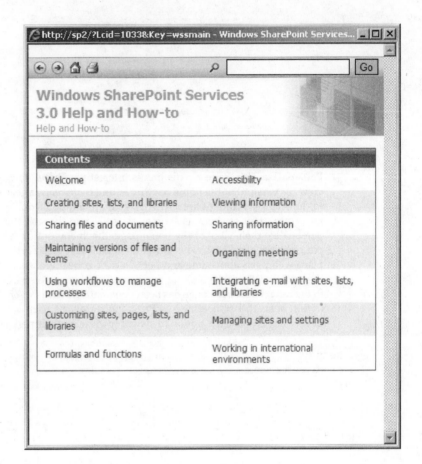

SEARCH

The Search field is below the Welcome menu and Help icon on the top right of the page. This field directly relates to the Search service that we enabled in Chapter 2, "Installation." To use it, just enter the word (or words) for which you are looking. Search doesn't perform partial word matching or Boolean logic, but it can do additions or exceptions. You can include or exclude words using the plus (+) or minus (−) signs (for example, "orange −juice +zest"). The Search scope dropdown field to the left of the Search field tells SharePoint to broaden or narrow the search scope. If you are in a list or library, you can narrow your search scope to that list using the Scope dropdown list. If you are in a list but want to broaden your search to include the whole site (just in case), you can specify This Site.

WHAT EXACTLY DOES SEARCH SEARCH?

Search will index list item contents (the contents of all fields of all lists and libraries) as well as the contents of files stored in libraries, as long as those file types can be indexed. Indexing uses ifilters (get it? index **filters**) specific for the file type they will be indexing. SharePoint can index Office files, as well as HTML and TIFF automatically. To index other kinds of files, you'll need to get ifilters for them.

Keep in mind that searches are performed top down in a site collection; therefore, subsites can show up in a search of a site, but only from that point in the hierarchy down. Searches scoped for a site can't search for text in the sites above itself. To search an entire site collection, always start at the top-level site.

Another thing to remember is that searches are limited by site collection. You can't find something in one site collection by looking for it in another. So pay attention to how you design your site collections. If users clearly understand what goes in which site collection, figuring out where to search should be easy.

MOSS 2007 FOR SEARCH

Microsoft was clever about searching. They took the expanded search capabilities of MOSS (which they knew was a tempting feature, but not enough to make the whole package worth the money), isolated them, packaged them, and resold them as MOSS for Search. This new package can be added to WSS 3.0, and gives administrators who just want the MOSS-style search capabilities without the MOSS enterprise features the ability to stay with Windows SharePoint Services but get all of the MOSS search capabilities. Those Search capabilities include searching across site collections' searching non-SharePoint locations, such as file shares and the ability to have more indexing control. Users can also modify the way Search performs and organizes results by best bets, partial words, and more. All they have to do is buy the license for MOSS for Search, and then all the Client Access Licenses, of course.

After you enter your search query in the Search field and click the "go Search" button (it looks like a magnifying glass), the Search service will query the index files for the most recent changes. It will then query the Search database looking for web pages that contain the words queried. It will generate a results page with links to the pages that contain a match. The user can then decide which results they want to click on to find the content they are seeking. There can be some redundancy in the results returned. Anything—the document contents, that document's record in the library, the content page of the document library itself—that contains the queried words will show up as a result.

SITE ACTIONS

The Site Actions menu is the tab beneath the Search field on the right of the page. This menu offers the user a list of options to manage the site, depending on the rights of the account with which they are logged in. If the user only holds the right to view the site and read list entries and documents, the Site Actions menu won't appear to them. If you're following along from the previous chapter, you're logged in as the site administrator if you did a Server Farm install. Alternatively, if you performed the Basic install, you are logged in with the setup account permissions. In either case, you have the right to access the Site Actions menu. Actually, you have something of an obligation to access it, because it is where you access the site settings that let you configure and manage this site and aspects of the whole site collections (by virtue of being the only site in the collection at this point). If you open the Site Actions menu, you'll see the following menu options shown in Figure 3.7.

FIGURE 3.7
The Site Actions menu

Create   The Create link opens the Create page for the site, with the ubiquitous Site Title, Welcome menu, Help, Home tab, and Site Actions menu in the header (or top) area of the page. There is no Search option for the Create page, what you see is what you get. On this page is listed, in categories, all the lists, other pages, as well as sites and workspaces, that can be created (see Figure 3.8).

FIGURE 3.8
The Create page

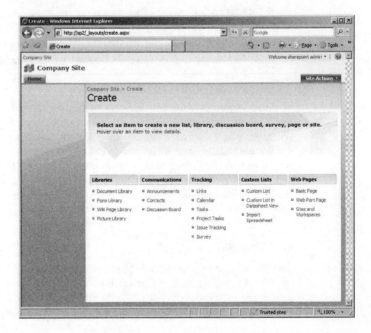

If you clicked the Site Action menu on this page, you might also notice that the Edit This Page option is missing. This is because this is not a web part page, which is what that menu option edits. Ironically, the Create option is still on the Site Action menu, even though it would take you to this very page if you chose it. This is because attributes such as the Site Action menu are standard for most pages, regardless—even if you are already on the page to which the menu item refers.

Edit Page   This link lets you edit the web parts on this page for everyone to view. (It gives you the impression that you can edit the *whole* home page, but that's not the case). When you edit the page from the Site Actions menu, it edits the Shared view of the web parts on the page, meaning that this will be the default view of this page for anyone logging into the site without a personal version set up. It works just like the Personalize This Page option, except the changes you make to the web parts will be the default for all users who didn't personalize. (See Figure 3.5 for an idea of what it looks like when you are editing a web part page.)

Site Settings   This menu option is critical because it is the only way, from the home page, to get to the underlying configuration settings for this site. It is not available to those who don't have the right to manage the site. If you selected this option, it would take you to Site Settings page, which contains the links available for configuring this site's settings (Figure 3.9).

FIGURE 3.9
The Site
Settings page

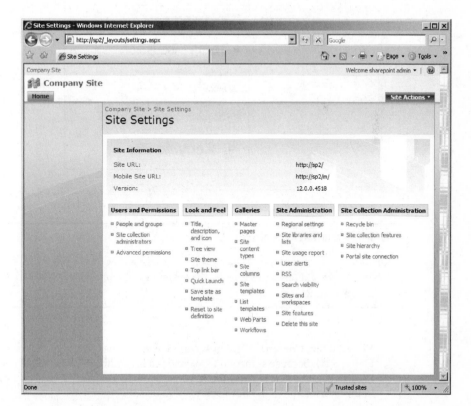

QUICK LAUNCH BAR

The Quick Launch bar was meant for you to customize—at least to the extent of deciding what lists, libraries, and subsites you want to display there for the users to access easily. A few links always remain the same and cannot be removed from the bar (Figure 3.10). You can also change the order or add links to the Quick Launch Bar if you'd like.

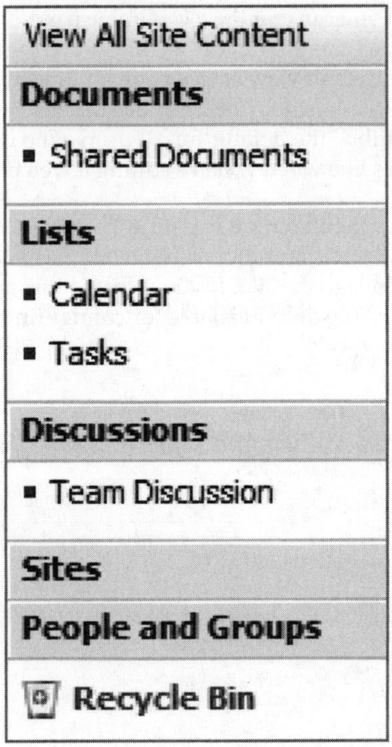

FIGURE 3.10
An example of the
Quick Launch bar

View All Site Content

Documents

- Shared Documents

Lists

- Calendar

- Tasks

Discussions

- Team Discussion

Sites

People and Groups

Recycle Bin

IT'S ALWAYS THERE FOR YOU

The Quick Launch bar follows you almost anywhere you go on the team site, sticking like glue to the left side of every library and list page. The only time it disappears is when you are configuring settings of the site, libraries, or lists.

View All Site Content   This link is used to give you (and the users) access to all site content (see Figure 3.11). Because someone who creates a list or library can choose not to add it to the Quick Launch bar, this helps avoid the issue of "How to get to a list that isn't displayed conveniently in the Quick Launch bar but I still need to use it?"

FIGURE 3.11
The All Site
Content page

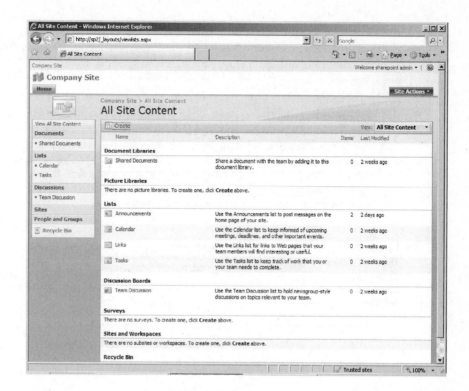

Otherwise known as "I know I left that list around here somewhere," the View All Site Content link takes you to a page that contains everything associated with a particular site. The list of contents is grouped by type: List, Library (two kinds actually, in case you might have document libraries or picture libraries), Discussion (which is actually a kind of list), Survey, and Subsites (known as sites and workspaces, because a workspace is a subsite with a template meant to be focused on a specific work task). Even the Recycle Bin can be accessed for the All Site Content page because, it's part of the site's contents.

Notice that this page has the Quick Launch bar on the left. A breadcrumb (`Company Site>All Site Content` in our example) above the page's title indicates that you are now in the All Site content page, from the Company site (the home page of my Team site). All the links to go back the way you came are active in the breadcrumb, but the one indicating the page you're on isn't. This is why, for example, Company Site is blue, but All Site Content is gray in my breadcrumb.

On the right of this page, below the title, is the View menu. This menu gives you the option to filter the view of the contents to a particular category.

NO SEARCHING AVAILABLE

Strangely, the View All Site Content page does not have the Search field available. If your site becomes full of all kinds of lists, libraries, and subsites, you will not be able to do a quick search through the list here. You'll have to use IE's browser "Find on this Page" capability for that. To be fair, you can't search any of the configuration settings pages, for some reason. However, the View All Site Content page isn't really a configuration page. It's just another peculiarity of SharePoint.

Documents, Lists, Discussions, Sites, and Surveys Headings   Most people consider the Documents, Lists, Discussions, and Sites links to be just organizational headings on the Quick Launch bar, indicating that everything in its section of the bar is of a certain type, but that is not the case. Those heading links also provide a quick way to get to the View All Site Content page, with the view on that page filtered to display only that header's type of list, library, or site (Figure 3.12). Several headings, such as Surveys, Pictures, and Sites, do not show up on the Quick Launch bar until their type of content gets created on the site.

FIGURE 3.12
The View All Site Content page filtered to show only lists

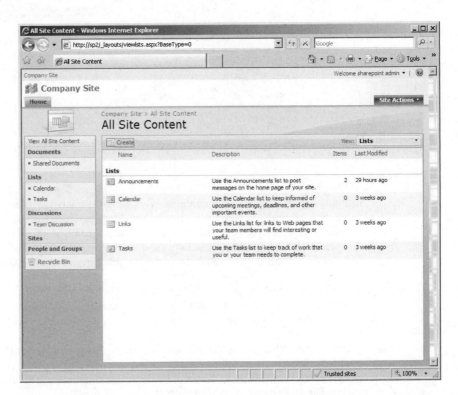

create a survey (which we will do in Chapter 5, "Introduction to Lists"), the Surveys heading shows up on the Quick Launch bar. Therefore, if a site has no surveys (and never did) that heading is not there, and if it does (or did), it is.

The same goes for picture libraries. The Picture Library heading doesn't show up on the Quick Launch bar until you've created one. Even if you delete the actual picture library, its heading will remain once it's been created.

People and Groups   The People and Groups link in the Quick Launch bar takes you to the People and Groups page in Site Settings where you can view (and edit if you have the appropriate permissions) a list of users for the site. (Figure 3.13). The theory is that by letting users see who else is a member of the site, they will have a convenient way to find those users' email addresses and other user information. This may explain why this version of SharePoint no longer has a default Contacts list pre-created for the Team Site template as it did for previous versions.

FIGURE 3.13
The People and Groups page

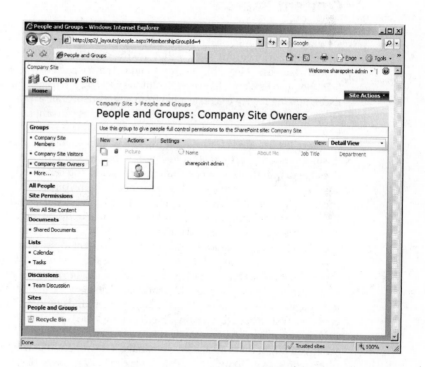

New for SharePoint 3.0, the Recycle Bin is where all deleted items go for a specified amount of time (the default is thirty days). If a user deletes an item from the recycle bin, it will go to a "second stage," site collection Recycle Bin controlled by the site collection administrator (all of this is configurable, but this is the default). After the items go to the site collection Recycle Bin, only a site collection administrator can recover the item. From there, the items are permanently deleted. Accidentally deleting important documents was a big problem with the previous version of SharePoint, so this is why the Recycle Bin makes its debut with two stages already built in.

To insure that users can't go trolling through the Recycle Bin looking at what others have thrown away, Security filtering applies to the Recycle Bin as well. This means that, usually, you can see only what you've deleted.

However, if you are a site collection owner, you can see all deleted items at the site collection level, so you can recover them for someone else's sake. Because the site level Recycle Bin only shows users the items *they* deleted, it is usually called the End users' Recycle Bin.

Content Pages

List and library content is displayed on content pages. These pages are designed specifically for viewing and managing lists. Lists and libraries are often differentiated from each other in common SharePoint parlance, but frankly they are the same thing. A *list* is a table of data stored in the content database. This table has rows and columns. Each row is a record, and each column is a field. Because lists are made up of columns and rows, it's easy for Microsoft to integrate them with Excel, making it easy to create a list from a spreadsheet or export an existing list to a spreadsheet. Of course, you have to have Microsoft Excel for this (no other spreadsheet program is compatible to my knowledge), but the point is still made.

Every list has fields for keeping track of who created a record, if that record is modified, when it was modified, and by whom. Because of this, you can track changes in a record, making it possible to trigger alerts when changes are made. You can trigger an alert based on whether anything changes in a list or whether or not an item you created or modified is changed. Further, because SharePoint knows when a new record is created or modified in a list, it's pretty easy to do RSS feeds from there. As a result, lists are capable of doing alert and RSS feed actions.

Lists are made unique by their intent. When you make a discussion list, for example, it's for specific discussion-related things, such as discussion topics and replies. As a result, certain records (generically referred to as *list items*) can be marked as replies for other records that are considered topics. That means that records in a discussion can be differentiated between topics and replies.

Document libraries, on the other hand, are lists that are intended to focus on the management of documents (other libraries simply manage other kinds of files). This means that their records contain a field meant to contain a file. That file's file type and name are considered the focus of the record, and those fields are the first two generally displayed. Activities in a library are specific to what you might do to add, edit, or manage a document that might be stored in a record there. In other words, even libraries are lists. Lists can vary because they are intended to be used for different reasons. Generally they share the same content page layout, most of the tools, and other features of the interface. But they do have their differences, depending on what they were meant to be used for. This becomes somewhat important as the actions available per list vary depending on that list's intent.

For example, Discussions and Document Libraries should be used for different reasons and in different ways. Therefore, the interface for these two kinds of lists should differ to some degree, despite the standard content page interface. To see what I mean, let's open a Discussion type list and then open the Document library and see what differences there are. This will familiarize you with both the content page interface and how they may vary.

A Quick Look at a List

Click the Team Discussion link in the Quick Launch bar. It will open the Team Discussion page (Figure 3.14). The layout of this page has the standard site header content (Welcome menu, Help, Search, etc.) and the Quick Launch bar down the left side of the page. In the content area, are the following parts:

FIGURE 3.14
The Team Discussion content page

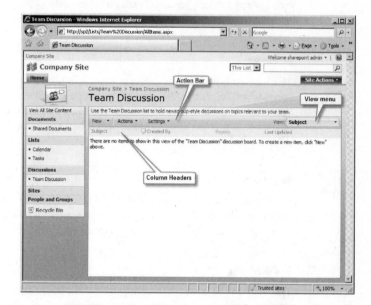

WHERE ARE THE LIST ITEMS?

Right now the content page as seen in Figure 3.14 is empty. You just need to see the attributes of these pages at this point. You'll see how to fill them during the next several chapters.

Action Bar The Action bar refers to the buttons across the top of the content area that indicate what can be done to (or with) the contents of this list. Each item in the bar is actually a menu button, with additional options underneath it. Discussion lists have New, Actions, and Settings buttons on their Action bar. These are standard buttons for the Action bar, with pretty standard options underneath.

New The New button simply gives you the option of creating a new record for this list (otherwise known as an *item* generically, and *discussion topic* when referred to in the context of a discussion list). When you click it, you will end up on a page that lets you fill in the fields for a discussion. The New button is a direct indication of whatever new items the list is capable of creating.

BUTTON VERSUS MENU

The New button can actually have more items beneath it depending on the list, so don't be surprised if you come across a multitasking New button. Generally, like most things Microsoft, there is a default action a New button will take if you just click it rather than clicking its dropdown arrow. That's one of the reasons I call these things "buttons" rather than "menus." So when you see a button with a dropdown arrow next to it, realize that although it has a default action, there may be more under there than you think. This is where being curious comes in handy. Don't be afraid to check the down arrow of any buttons, just in case they offer something unexpected.

ACTIONS

The Actions button drops down a menu containing options that offer to export the list to a spreadsheet, view the RSS feed of the list page and subscribe to it if you'd like, and set up Alerts. Some lists also allow you to view the list data itself in datasheet view. That means change the view of the list so it looks like a spreadsheet. The Discussion list is simply one of those lists that do not support that action.

SETTINGS

The Settings button acts just like the Site Actions menu, only it pertains to settings for this list, not for the whole site. This button drops down a menu containing options to create a new column or view for the list, or simply go to the more extensive Settings page to configure further list settings.

VIEW MENU

The View menu is a way to manipulate the view of this list's data. Right now the default is Subject, and as a matter of fact that is the only view for this particular list. Also on the View menu is, reasonably enough, a link to modify the Subject view or create a new one.

COLUMN HEADERS

The column headers below the Action bar indicate the fields that are available in the list for this view. (Remember, views are like reports. You don't need to display all the fields available in a list for a report.) This list view has fields for Subject, Created by, Replies, and Last Updated. What's not shown on the list is the Body field of the item. To see the contents of the body of the discussion item, you would, logically, click on that item and open it to read it (very much like an email message in an inbox). The column headers, very much like an Excel spreadsheet, can be clicked to sort the list items, and even filter through the items to narrow down your search.

A Quick Look at a Document Library

To see the differences and similarities between a list and a library content page, let's check out the Shared Documents library (Figure 3.15). To do this, click the Shared Documents link in the Quick Launch bar. It will open into the Shared Documents content page. The layout of this page has the same standard site header content that the Team Discussion did and the Quick Launch bar down the left side of the page. In the content area are the following items:

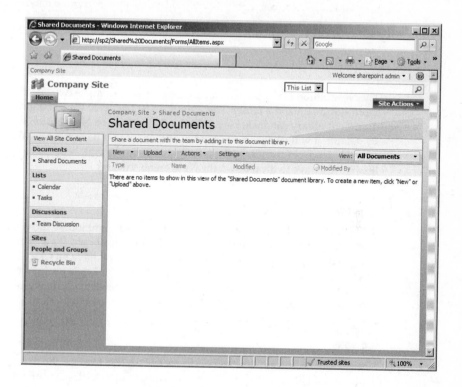

The Action Bar

Document library Action bars contain New, Upload, Actions, and Settings. There are some significant differences between the Action bar of a library and the Action bar of a list.

Microsoft assumes that libraries can potentially be used to store many files and not necessarily in a straightforward, everything-in-one-long-list kind of way. In other words, administrators may want to break up a library into organizational subsets. For example, say you have a Marketing library, with marketing documents. And those documents the library will contain, were originally stored on a common fileshare, organized by campaigns.

In order to make it more convenient and familiar to the users, you can *also* organize the Marketing document library by campaign by using folders, as if the library (whose contents are really stored in a database) were a fileshare. This gives the users a document storage structure with which they are familiar.

In addition, users may want to add many files to a library at once. So the capability exists to create documents one by one, upload one or many documents at once, or even drag and drop documents from a fileshare or local folder to a document library. These options, which are pretty critical to a library, are not necessary for a discussion list, and therefore are not available for that list's interface.

SOMETHING ABOUT FOLDERS

Keep in mind that you can enable folder organization in other lists, but only in document libraries where it is enabled by default.

NEW

The New button in the Shared Documents library can make two "new" things in the library: a Word document and a folder. This ability is just the tip of the iceberg concerning the things a document library can make, but it does indicate that the New button can do more than one thing. By default, it will create a new Word document, if you have a compatible word processor. That's why the down arrow next to the New button is important, because to make a new folder in the library, you have to drop down the New menu to select it.

UPLOAD

A library always has an Upload button. This is to accommodate those documents that you've already made elsewhere and now want to add to the library. It's as simple as that. You can choose to upload a file, or upload multiple files at once (if you have an Office 2003 or 2007 product installed on the computer you are uploading from), which is useful when you are building a library from existing documents on a file share somewhere. If the file already exists in the library, you will be prompted to overwrite it.

ACTIONS

The Actions button still lets you set alerts and an RSS feed for the library, but it specifically indicates that libraries have different activities than a discussion. Again, because Microsoft knew that you might need to add many items to the library in one go, the Actions button's menu has two options that are particularly focused on bulk work: the Edit In Datasheet option and Open With Windows Explorer. Editing in datasheet can be done in some lists that might contain many items, like Contacts or Announcements. However, being able to open a list with Windows Explorer is specific to libraries.

   Edit in Datasheet: Because a library is a list, it can be opened and viewed (the library records itself, not the documents it holds) like a spreadsheet—indicating again that a list is just a table, with rows for records and columns for fields. In the same vein, the library can also be exported to a spreadsheet, just like the discussion list. The Edit in Datasheet option lets you create a bunch of library records as if you were creating them in Excel, which is much faster than clicking the New button, typing in the fields, clicking the Save button on that page, going back to the library, clicking the New button, and so on, to create the same number of records.

   Open with Windows Explorer. As mentioned, libraries are capable of having Windows Explorer-style web folders. This view affords users more comfortable with using fileshares a chance to look at the library as if it were a folder in the filesystem (rather than a table in a database). Also, some people felt it was not easy to upload files using the Upload Multiple Files page. They wanted to be able to select a bunch of files in a file share window and drop them into the library or even a particular folder in a library. You can do this with Open with Windows Explorer.

What it does is open the library as an Explorer window. Then you can open the file share window, select the files you want, and then drag and drop them into the library's Explorer window. A lot of copying will commence, and then voilà! The files will be in the library (see Figure 3.16 for my example of first and second documents in the library).

FIGURE 3.16
The Open With Windows Explorer window

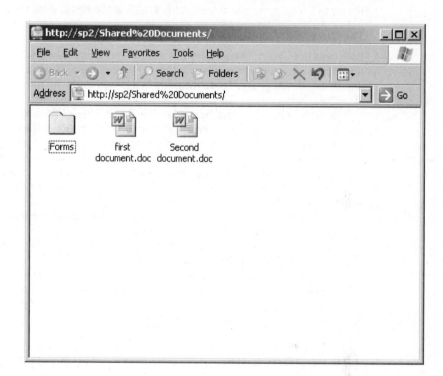

THE FORMS FOLDER

An interesting thing about viewing a document library using Windows Explorer is it contains, without your assistance, a folder called Forms. This folder contains the forms that are used for the library, such as those for different ways to view the content of the page or the form used to upload files. Within the folder, the `Webfldr` file is actually the "Explorer view" listed in the View menu. The Repair Form, a troubleshooting tool, can be found in here as well, and it's worth keeping in mind. This page will allow you to reconnect a document if it somehow becomes disconnected with its content type's template.

SETTINGS

The Setting button (and its dropdown menu) is exactly like a normal list's settings, containing the Create A Column, Create View, or Go to the Document Library's Settings page.

THE VIEW MENU

This menu contains the views of this particular library. You can customize the views that come with this list and even create your own. Remember, a view is just a way of reporting the data in the underlying table. By default, the view is All Documents, but there is also an option to view the library in Explorer view, (since Explorer is already being used for file copying).

THE COLUMN HEADERS

Each item in a library, like any list, is a record. This record has fields that contain data. In a library, records contain more than fields with text in them, they include one field that is required to contain a file. That's the point of a library and why libraries are unique among SharePoint lists.

The fields being displayed in the All Documents view of the library records are Type (which pertains to the type of file the record contains), Name (which is the filename of the file the record has), Modified (when the file or record was last modified), and Modified By (what user account made the modification). There are other fields in the library record that have to do with who created the record and when it was created, but they are not intended to be displayed in this view. Views can be modified or created to display as many or as few of the fields as you'd like.

Normally, these fields are considered *metadata* about the document. However, due to the fact that most files (like Word files) refer to their metadata as *properties*, that's what they are called in a document library. Properties, metadata, or record fields, this data can be sorted or filtered in the page by clicking on the column headers.

From either content page (Shared Documents or Team Discussion), it's easy to get back to the home page. You can use the breadcrumb above the page title, or you can click the Home tab in the Top Link Bar bringing you back to the home page where you started. At this point, you are ready to be introduced to the individual aspects of SharePoint.

The Bottom Line

Identify the SharePoint navigation tools and figure out how to use them   SharePoint makes a point of ensuring that a user always has a way to get where they need to go without using the Back button in the browser. Recognizing these features makes navigation easier and increases productivity.

Master It   List three different ways to get back to the Home page should you be in a list or library.

Find a list or library   SharePoint uses the Quick Launch bar as a quick, convenient, and consistent way for users to find the SharePoint lists and libraries they need to access.

Master It   How do you find a list or library if it is not on the Quick Launch bar?

Use the Quick Launch bar   The Quick Launch bar is more than a list of lists. It also contains an easy way to navigate through all contents of a site, access people and groups, check the Recycle Bin, and create new site contents.

Master It   By default, when SharePoint is initially installed, the Quick Launch bar does not have Surveys as a heading. Why?

Use a breadcrumb   Windows SharePoint Services 3.0 has instituted a navigational device that keeps track of where a user has been. This dynamic horizontal list lets a user jump back to where they started very conveniently without using the web browser's Back button.

Master It   Is there such a thing as a global breadcrumb? What is it?

Understand a content page   Every list and library has a content page. This kind of page has a consistent layout to make working with it easy for users.

Master It   What is an Action bar? What's on it, and why would it be different in a library than it would be in a list?

Chapter 4

Introduction to Web Parts

Web parts are interesting additions to SharePoint. They were meant to be a convenient way to display things on the home page of SharePoint sites. They came in so handy that now they can be added to most of the pages of a SharePoint site. They needed to be resizable, movable, and self-contained. Somewhat like Konfabulator widgets, or sidebar gadgets, web parts are independent little applications that pull and display information from anywhere data might be available, such as the content database, file shares, or web pages. Numerous companies have been built on customizing SharePoint web parts into all kinds of useful things, probably well beyond the expectations of the original SharePoint developers.

In this chapter, you'll learn how to:

- Identify web parts
- Use Edit mode
- Distinguish between Personal and Shared views
- Work with web parts
- Export and import web parts

Exploring Web Parts

Let's first explore the out-of-the-box, no-need-for-coding web parts that any administrator can use. They are useful and often underused.

To start, you need to be on the home page of your SharePoint site, so open IE and browse to your SharePoint server. (Mine is SP2.) Before the page loads, you'll probably need to log in. (The example uses the SharePoint site collection administrator: dem0tek\shareadmin.) Once the site is up, you should be on the home page. Remember, that home pages are web part pages by default in SharePoint, but you can add web parts to most content pages. You can even create web part pages if you need to. However, the most convenient page to customize is the Home page.

In the Web Part area of the Home page, you should see four web parts:

- The Announcements List View web part
- The Calendar List View web part
- The Image web part (where the SharePoint Services graphic is located)
- A Links List View web part

Notice that each List View web part has a title that corresponds with the title of the list, an area below the title where (as you can see with the Announcements web part in Figure 4.1) the items in the list would be displayed, and an Add a new Item link, which will take you to the new item page for that list.

FIGURE 4.1
Home Page web parts

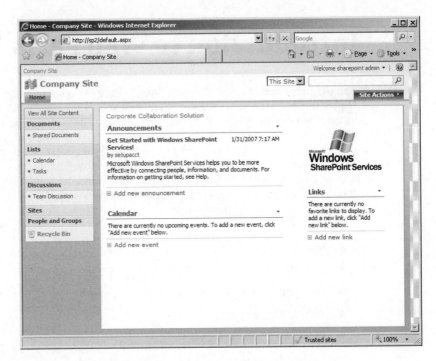

CORPORATE COLLABORATION SOLUTION

You may have noticed the words "Corporate Collaboration Solution" at the top of the web parts area of the Home page in Figure 4.1. When a site is created, and you fill in the description for the site, this is where the description goes. You may want to consider that when a creating your sites. For the purposes of the book, I may not always fill in the description field, but the option is always there for you to use as you see fit.

The Image web part is a simple web part that was meant to display an image file. It's as easy as that. As a matter of fact, that brings me to an important concept. Web part developers rapidly realized that they were creating the same type of web parts over and over, with only the content of the web parts making them unique. There were web parts that contained list information, web parts that were meant to put a picture in the web part area of a page, and web parts that displayed content from a file or folder. Developers, therefore, created *web part frames*, or templates, to be filled with content later. Now you have built-in web parts that were meant to be customized. Two of my favorites are the Content Editor and Page Viewer web parts, which are meant to contain the content you create (via HTML or a Rich Text Editor) or the content of any file folder, document, or web page you specify.

Using Edit Mode

To change, move, delete, or add a web part, you need to put the web part area of the page into Edit mode. There are two ways to do that, depending on whether you want to change the way you personally view the web parts on the home page (Personal version) or if you want to change the way everyone views the web parts on the home page (Shared version). Edit mode looks almost identical regardless of which version you are changing, so pay attention to which one you are editing by checking the information bar that occurs whenever you are in Edit mode. It will indicate what version of the page you are editing.

WHACKY TERMINOLOGY

SharePoint has some terminology that it uses redundantly and in blatant conflict. I am talking about views and versions.

When you are talking about Personal and Shared views of pages that contain web parts, SharePoint refers to them as both views and as *versions*.

However, when you are talking about List Views, you are referring to the way that the underlying data for the list is displayed as in a report or chart. List views are also used to display data in a List View web part.

Then there is the word "Version." When you are talking about versions in terms of Lists, well, that's when the list is configured to keep a version of a list item or file each time that item or file is edited. So there are versions of list items or documents, and versions of web part page views.

I hope that clears things up, and helps explain why it might seem that I am using the terms interchangeably. I am only doing what Microsoft teaches me. In this chapter I am trying to use version in terms of Shared or Personal views because I also mention List View web parts in this chapter as well. In later chapters of the book, views mainly refer to Lists and Libraries, and versions are used in terms of list items and files.

Changing, moving, adding, and removing web parts from a page are all done the same way, regardless of whether you are in the Personal or Shared version of the page. I am going to start in my Personal version because it has one option that the Shared version does not have, the ability to roll back the changes to match the public, shared version. To edit the web part area of a page for your personal viewing only, you enter Edit mode from the Personalize this Page menu item on the Welcome menu.

To do this, select the Welcome menu (top right of the page, next to the Help button). In the dropdown menu, select Personalize this Page. That will cause the web part area to go into Edit mode (see Figure 4.2).

FIGURE 4.2
The home page in Edit mode

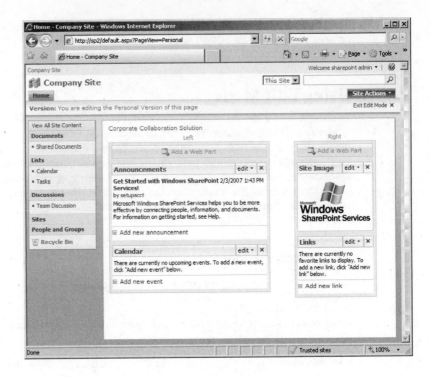

An information bar at the top of the web part area states "You are editing the Personal Version of this page." That's good to know. You don't want to personalize the Shared version of the web page and ruin the consistent and familiar arrangement that users know and love. Pay attention to that information bar when you're editing web parts.

WHO ADDED WEB PARTS TO MY PERSONAL VERSION OF THE PAGE?

Don't be surprised if a web part shows up one day in your Personal version, when you know you did not put it there. A Personal version is based on the Shared version and is intended to essentially augment the Shared version. If a web part is added to the Shared version after you develop your Personal version, the new web part will appear in your Personal version as well. You will still be able to move it around, close it, or minimize it, depending on how the web part is configured.

What exactly happens in Edit mode? First, the web part area breaks into separate Web Part *zones*. These zones can stretch to contain as many web parts as you'd like. Although I find them pretty restrictive, they were intended to help organize the look of your web parts. I suggest you use those web parts sparingly. Fit as many as you can without having to scroll; users don't really like to scroll. On the Team Site home page, the two Web Part zones (as you can see in the Figure 4.2) are labeled Left and Right.

At the top of each zone is an Add a Web Part button, which opens its own window listing possible web parts to add to the zone. In addition, each web part's title bar has changed a bit. They are now slightly orange (in the default theme for the site), with an Edit button and a Close button. If you click the Edit button, it can bring up a work pane on the right of the page (right over the right Web Part zone). This work pane will contain tools and properties specific to that particular web part.

Move a Web Part

Moving a web part from one zone to another is easy and uncomplicated. Simply move your cursor over the title bar of the web part you'd like to move, and then drag it to the location in the other Web Part zone where you'd like to put it and drop it. The catch is, you can't just drop the web part anywhere. It has to be put above, below, or between existing web parts in a zone. A horizontal I-beam marker lets you know where SharePoint thinks you're putting the web part. (The I-beam is very much like the indicator that appears when you are dragging and dropping a file in a list of files or moving text in a document.)

So with that in mind, and with the web part area in Edit mode, move the Image web part (called Site Image in my example) from the right Web Part zone to the left Web Part zone. It's easy; just follow these steps:

1. Move your cursor over the title of the web part until it turns into a four-headed pointer (see Figure 4.3).

FIGURE 4.3
The right Web Part zone with a cursor over the title

2. Click and drag that title over to the other Web Part zone, and drop it between the other existing web parts. (Mine is going to go between the Announcements web part and the Calendar web part.) When you drop the web part, it will resize to match the width of the new zone (see Figure 4.4).

FIGURE 4.4
The new location for the
Image web part

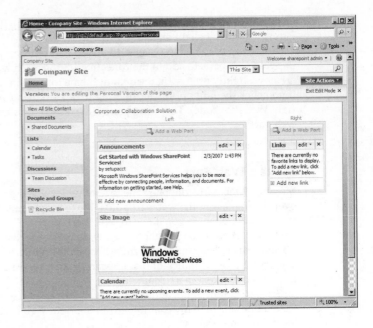

Remove a Web Part from a Zone

If you have a web part you don't want to see on the home page, you can close it. This will remove it from the page, so it won't take up space and you won't see it. To close a web part, simply click the Close button (X) in the title bar.

For example, to remove the Links web part from the page (it's empty at the moment), simply click the X in its title bar. This closes the web part and removes it from the page, but it doesn't delete it from the available web parts should you want to put it back. With it gone the right Web Part zone is empty (Figure 4.5).

To see what Personal version of the home page looks like now that you have moved the Image web part and closed the Links web part you'll need to close out of Edit mode. To do that, simply click the Exit Edit Mode link on the right side of the information bar. You will then get to see the effects of your handiwork (Figure 4.6).

Notice that there is no real indication that you are looking at your Personal version of the page. This can be a challenge when trying to troubleshoot why a user can or cannot see a web part. The best way to be sure which version you are looking at is to use the Welcome menu. It is dynamic, and it will indicate which version you are in by offering a chance to change to the other version state. In other words, if you are in your Personal version of a page that you have edited, the Welcome menu should have two new menu items: Show Shared View (indicating that you are looking at the Personal version of the page) and Reset Page Content. SharePoint keeps track of the changes you made to your Personal version. If you messed up and want to return that web parts page to its original state, you can use that menu item to do so.

To see what the page looks like in the Shared version of the page select that menu item from the Welcome menu. It will take you to the original Shared version, where none of your changes (the moved Image web part or the deleted Link web part from the page) are in effect.

To return to the Personal view version, simply go to the Welcome menu and select it. Your personalized version of the page should return.

FIGURE 4.5
An empty right Web
Part zone

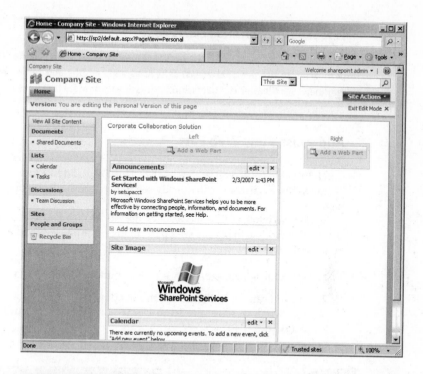

FIGURE 4.6
The new Personal
version of the home
page

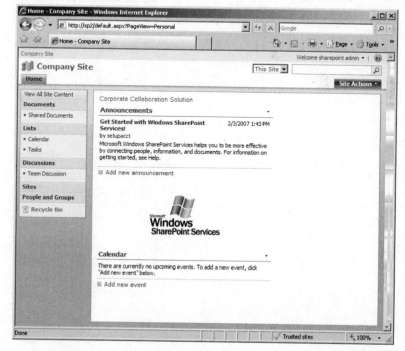

PERSONAL VERSION AND PERMISSIONS

If the possibility for abuse of the personal version of pages is getting you down, you can disable the permission to use personal views, as well as deny adding and removing personal web parts for site members. See Chapter 11, "Users and Permissions" for more information.

Add a List View Web Part

If you'd like to add a web part to one of the Web Part zones in your Personal version, simply go into Edit mode (Welcome ➤ Personalize This Page). I'd like to add the List View web part for the Team Discussion list, so I can quickly see if there are any new topics right on the home page.

To do that, while in Edit mode, click the Add a Web Part button at the top of the Web Part zone in which you'd like to place a web part. In my example, let's add a web part to the left zone, beneath the List View web part of the Calendar list:

1. Click the left zone's Add a Web Part button. It will open an Add Web Parts to Left window.

2. As you can see in Figure 4.7, the window in the top section is called Lists and Libraries. In that window, select the Team Discussion web part by putting a check in its checkbox, and click Add.

FIGURE 4.7
The Add Web Parts To Left window

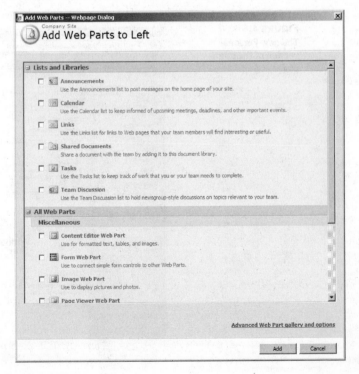

This will, unfortunately, add the Team Discussion List View web part to the top of the left zone, but you can easily drag and drop it to fit snugly below the Calendar web part.

3. Once you have moved the Team Discussion web part to the bottom of the left Web Part zone, click Exit Edit Mode in the information bar below Site Actions. You should now see, in your Personal version of the page, a Team Discussion List View web part (see Figure 4.8) listed beneath Calendar.

FIGURE 4.8

A new Team Discussion web part

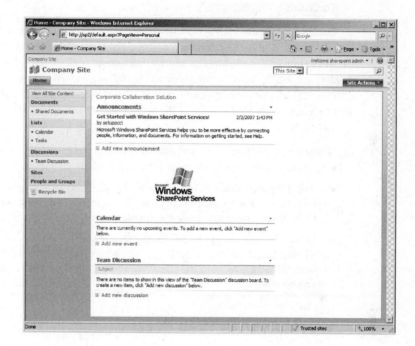

That's how easy it is to add prebuilt List View web parts to a web parts page. Keep in mind that every time you create a new list or library, that a corresponding List View web part is created. This makes it possible for you (or your users) to add a List View web part for any list or library, to any page that can hold web parts on the site.

Reset Page Content

It's possible that you might regret the changes you have made to your personal version. If that happens, it's easy to undo all of the changes you made to personalize the page. Simply go to the Welcome menu and select Reset Page Content.

Selecting Reset Page Content will undo all the changes you have made and make your Personal version of the page match the Shared version; and as such, this option to reset is available only with the Personal version. Over time you may make extensive changes to your Personal version of the page. If you reset your page content, it will undo *all* the changes you have made, even the ones you wanted to keep. You will get a Warning dialog box reminding you that all changes will be undone (Figure 4.9).

FIGURE 4.9
A Reset Page
Content Warning
dialog box

TO CHANGE THE SHARED VIEW

Changing the Shared view version of a page is done in the same way as changing the Personal version of one. Simply click the Site Actions menu (instead of the Welcome menu), and select Edit Page. The page will go into Edit mode, and the information bar will indicate that you are editing the shared version of the page. Again, the Web Part zones will be outlined and have an orange button at the top to add a web part. All web parts displayed will show their title bars, and an Edit and Close button will be available. All changes made in Edit mode of the Shared version will change the web parts for all users who share that view.

You can move, add, modify, and remove web parts in this view just as you could with the Personal version, except for two things:

◆ This is the view that will be used by and be available to everyone by default. If you make changes here, you are doing so without a safety net (in front of everyone who logs into the site). If you make a mistake and want to reset to the original content, you will have to undo your changes manually.

◆ There is no Reset Page Content for the Shared version of the page. That feature only exists for the personalized version because that version is *based on* the Shared version. You can restore closed web parts to the page by using the closed Web Parts Gallery, but there is no one-click undo for the Shared version of a page.

Working with Web Parts

Now that you know the difference between Personal and Shared versions of a page and you know how to move, remove, and add existing web parts to a page, it's time to start really working with them. To do that, though, you need to understand how web parts are organized. They are generally organized by *galleries*. There are site collection galleries, server galleries, and the "recycle bin" of galleries, the *closed web parts*. That gallery contains all the web parts you may have closed from viewing on a web page, but otherwise aren't done with it yet (closed web part galleries are per page). Getting to web part galleries isn't that easy, unfortunately. To use web part galleries, you first need to access the Add Web Parts page by going into Edit mode, then clicking a Add a Web Part bar. Then click the link "Advanced web part gallery and options" located at the bottom of the page. This will open a tool pane with the galleries listed. We will be doing this together later in the chapter.

NO GALLERY FOR ONLINE WEB PARTS

The previous version of SharePoint had another gallery for online web parts. That gallery is not available in this version of SharePoint. Although the possibility of using online, dynamically updating web parts is still open, Microsoft is just not going to be responsible for offering them or maintaining a gallery for them, at this point. So if you were wondering where that gallery went, well, now you know.

To make web parts available in SharePoint (that aren't already there by default), you can import them to the site collection or server galleries. The *Site Collection Gallery*, as its name implies, holds the web parts for an entire site collection. This means a top-level site and all its subsites can add web parts from that gallery. If you have a different site collection, it will not have those imported web parts by default (which stands to reason). The Site Collection Gallery usually is named after the top level site (in my case, that would be Company Site).

If you import a web part to the Server Gallery, however, the web part will be available to all site collections in the web application or even all web applications on the server farm, depending on how it is added to SharePoint.

Default Web Parts

A number of web parts come with SharePoint by default. They are organized into two groups, Lists and Libraries, and All web parts (which strangely does not include lists and libraries):

Lists and Libraries   The List and Library List View web parts were designed to conveniently display the contents of their list or library and give users an easy way to add items to those lists. By default, these lists are available for a Team site:

◆   **Announcements:** Can be used to post messages on the home page of the site.

◆   **Calendar:** Allows you to keep up-to-date on shared events, meetings, and deadlines.

◆   **Links:** Used to display links that may be useful for other site members.

◆   **Shared Documents:** Displays documents in the Shared Documents library.

◆   **Tasks:** Allows users to keep track of tasks that need to be completed.

◆   **Team Discussion:** Allows users to keep track of the topics being discussed in this newsgroup-like list.

NEW LISTS AND LIBRARIES GET LIST VIEW WEB PARTS TOO

Templates exist for other lists and libraries, as well as the option to create custom lists from scratch. These List View web parts are for the lists and libraries that were prebuilt when the top-level site was created. They are not the limit of the lists and libraries you might end up with, and for each, a List View web part is automatically created.

All Web Parts   Most of these web parts are empty templates of a type of web part that requires some configuration to function properly. The exceptions to that rule are the following three web parts:

◆   **Site Users:** This web part is a kind of List View web part for the People and Groups list. By default it gives you a quick way to click on a site group to bring up a list of users contained therein. The catch is that it defaults to display, innocently, the different SharePoint groups, even though the user logged in is not permitted to view the contents of those groups. This leads them to click on a group and be denied access. To offset this, you can configure the web part to display the SharePoint group for the current user. In addition, like all List View web parts, there is a link to add a user, even for a user who might not have the right to add users.

The user will be refused when they attempts to add a user to the site (to avoid this you can set the web part to display no toolbar—this will disable the add a user link).

◆ **User Tasks:** This web part displays any tasks that are assigned to the current user. This means, depending on who is logged in and viewing the home page, the User Tasks web part will display the tasks only for that user. The interesting thing about this web part is it will pick up tasks from any task list, as long as the Tasks List template was used to create it. It won't recognize a custom list, even if you call it "Tasks."

◆ **Relevant Documents:** This web part displays any document or picture a user modified in any library, except a wiki library, on the site. It is site specific. This web part can be configured to display library files that the user has modified, created, or checked out, although by default it shows only those modified by the user.

AGGREGATING CONTENT

Both the User Tasks and Relevant Documents act as item aggregators for their content. They combine all the tasks or files relevant to a user, regardless of the task list or library the item is actually in.

The rest of the miscellaneous web parts are considered the built-in web part templates:

◆ **Content Editor Web Part:** This web part can be configured to hold a rich-text document containing tables, images, text, or hyperlinks, or HTML. It is used to add rich, static content to a web part page.

◆ **Form Web Part:** This web part is a simple, one-field form that can be used to look up information from a different List View web part. The web part makes it convenient to do a quick search of information in a web part (such as for an event in the Calendar) right on the home page.

◆ **Image Web Part:** This web part is meant to contain an image file. That's it.

◆ **Page Viewer Web Part:** This web part is actually pretty nifty. It can display the contents of a file, folder, or web page. This means that you can link this web part to a file share on the network, and make those files available to the users (provided they have the right to access that folder).

◆ **XML Web Part:** This web part was meant to display XML (or transformed XML) pages.

As an administrator, when you are moving, adding, or removing web parts from a page, you first need to decide whether you want the change to occur in your Personal version or the Shared version of the page. Not all users are allowed to change the Shared version of a page, but everyone can be affected by it. By default, only the site owners group members are allowed to change the Shared version. This means that, as an administrator, you have a responsibility to the users to lay out the Shared version of the web parts on your pages well.

I am going to prepare my Company site for users by adding the User Tasks and Relevant Documents web parts. When users log in, they will quickly see the tasks and files relevant to them. Then I'll configure the settings for the Relevant Documents web part so it will be more informative for the user.

Finally I'll look into the advanced options concerning adding web parts, work with a built-in web part, and visit the galleries (as well as take a quick look at importing web parts). This all will be done in the Shared version of the home page, of course, for maximum impact.

To edit the Shared version of the home page, click the Site Actions menu, and select Edit Page. You will now be in Edit mode of the Shared version (as the information bar will tell you).

Add User-Aware Web Parts

To start adding user-aware web parts, let's add the User Tasks and Relevant Documents web parts to the right Web Part zone.

1. Click on the Add a Web Part button at the top of the right zone. This will open an Add Web Parts to Right window. Because there are checkboxes next to each preexisting web part (or web part template), you can select more than one. This is a convenient feature when you are quickly populating a page with web parts.

2. In this example, the web parts that need to be added to the Shared version of the home page of the company site are not part of the Lists and Libraries group. Locate the User Tasks and Relevant Documents under All Web Parts, Miscellaneous.

3. Select the User Tasks web part and the Relevant Documents web part by placing checks in their checkboxes (see Figure 4.10). Click Add.

FIGURE 4.10
Add multiple web parts to the right zone

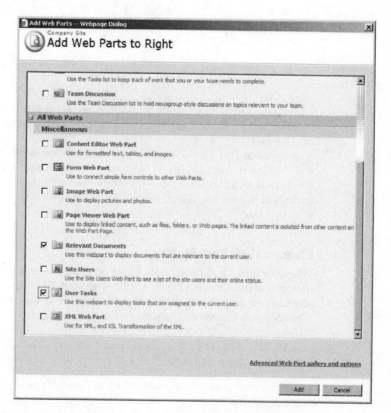

4. They are now located at the top of the right Web Part zone of the home page. If you want them below the site Image web part, drag and drop them just beneath that Image web part.

5. To see what the users will see, exit Edit mode by clicking Exit Edit Mode in the information bar. Notice that the new web parts widen the right zone a little (Figure 4.11).

FIGURE 4.11
New web parts in the right Web Part zone

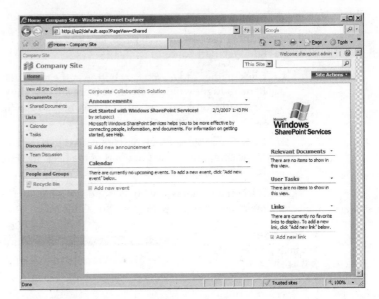

The two web parts are ready for users. Now when a user gets assigned a task, it will show up in the User Tasks web part, and when they modify a document, it will show up in Relevant Documents.

It would also be nice to display any document that someone might have checked out. This way, it will be listed in their Relevant Documents if they forget about it. To ensure that the Relevant Documents web part is configured to show checked out documents, we will have to check its settings. If it is not configured to also display the documents that the user has checked out, we can set it to do so.

Change Web Part Settings

When you add a web part to a Web Part zone, it may require some additional customization. To do that, you will need to modify or edit the web part. Choosing to modify or edit a web part opens a tool pane on the right side of the page (smack dab on top of the right Web Part zone, actually) containing the properties and settings for that web part.

REMEMBER YOUR VERSION!

Remember what page version you were in when you added a web part when it comes time to configure it. Some settings for web parts are not available if you are not editing it in the original page version.

To edit a web part's settings, simply click the down arrow on the right side of the web part title. In this example, we'll edit the Relevant Documents web part.

The Modify Web Part menu will drop down (see Figure 4.12), displaying these options:

FIGURE 4.12
Modify the Web Part
dropdown

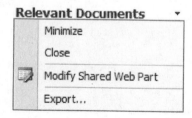

Minimize Rolls up the web part as if it were a window shade. It hides the contents and shows the title bar of the web part. This option is useful for conserving vertical space on a crowded web page. The Minimize menu item becomes Restore when the web part is minimized.

Close Closes the web part in this view, but keeps it available for reuse on this page in the closed Web Parts Gallery. Web parts are often extensively configured, so this feature allows for an accidental closure without forcing someone to re-create and reconfigure that web part again. Keep in mind that the closed Web Part Gallery is unique per page.

Modify Shared Web Part Allows you to see the properties, and configure the settings of, a web part. It opens the tool pane for that web part on the right side of the page. Unfortunately, it obscures the right Web Part zone.

Export Saves the web part (and its settings) to a web part definition (`.dwp`) file so you can export a great web part elsewhere. Not all web parts can be exported.

MISSING MODIFY

Only those users allowed to modify web part settings will see the down arrow in the title of a web part. If it is missing, you don't have the right to change web parts in the page version you are using. Otherwise you can edit a web part's settings while in Edit mode by clicking on the Edit button in the web part's title bar.

To modify the web part, choose Modify Shared Web Part. (The word "shared" is a nice reminder that this is going to impact more than just your Personal version of the page.)

This will trigger a Web Part tool pane to pop out of the right side of the page. The contents of a web part's tool pane vary, depending on that web part. As you can see in Figure 4.13, the Relevant Documents tool pane contains sections for:

Appearance This section contains settings that allow you to change the title of the web part, the web part's width and height, and the chrome state and type. Which controls the title bar and border around a web part or its "chrome."

Layout These settings control whether or not the web part is hidden or displayed, if the web part content is aligned with the right margin or left, what zone the web part is in, and in what order the web part is placed in a zone. Web parts that do a task programmatically, such as trigger reminders, but otherwise have nothing to display should be hidden.

FIGURE 4.13
Relevant Documents
Web Part Tool Pane

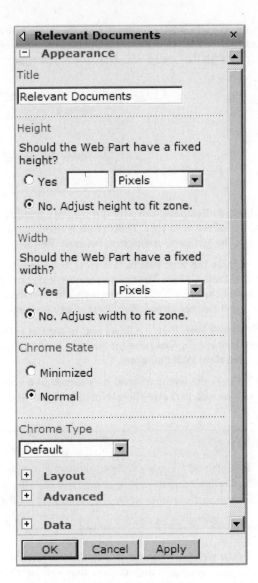

Advanced   This section varies greatly depending on the web part. Primarily, it is focused on what users are allowed to do with the web part (minimize, close, hide, move), even if they can edit it in their Personal version. You can also specify the title of the web part as a URL, so a user is taken to a specific page when its title is clicked. You can specify the location of the icons used by the web part, specify how to export the web part, even specify the error message that comes up if someone tries to import the web part and it fails.

Data   This section is not available for most web parts. It is used to manage what data is displayed in the web part, such as limiting how many items will be displayed in the web part at one time, or what kind of data will be included in the web part's display.

To configure the web part to display checked out documents we are going to change a data setting for the Relevant Documents. In the tool pane, go to the Data section (click the Data heading to open the section), as shown in Figure 4.14.

FIGURE 4.14
The Data section

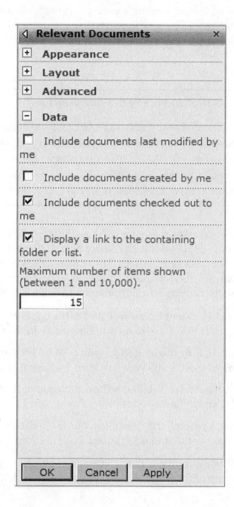

In the Data section, you can set the Relevant Documents web part list to include documents last modified by me, created by me, or even checked out to me (the "me" indicates that it is relative to the user logged in at the time). In addition, it offers to make each listed item a link to itself in its appropriate library, and limits the documents displayed to 15.

To include the documents that have been checked out on the Relevant Documents list, add a check to the box next to the option that includes documents checked out to me. Also, it might be a good idea to conserve space in the web part by only listing the documents the user is actively working on and has checked out. Therefore you might not want to display every document the user has modified. To do that, clear the checkbox for including documents last modified by me. Once you have configured your settings, click OK. That should bring you back to the web page.

Add a Built-in Web Part

The built-in web part templates are a convenient way to add additional web parts to the home page. For example, we could add a reminder that vacation requests are due for most employees. To add content to a page using a web part is easy. The only limitation is the design of the Web Part zones themselves. To be sure to reach as many users as possible, the reminder should be placed on several pages (Shared version of course) of the site. In this case, let's put it on the home page and the Calendar page.

ALL NON-ADMINISTRATIVE PAGES ARE WEB PART PAGES

Remember, all non-administrative pages in Windows SharePoint Services 3.0 are web part pages. This means that web parts can be added to any list, library, or home page you might have. It really gives you more flexibility and control over what information is displayed where. However, it can also be tempting to make list pages too busy or confusing. I suggest that you refrain from putting much, if anything, on pages that contain lists or libraries so users can concentrate on the tasks at hand.

To create a vacation reminder let's use the Content Editor web part. This web part uses content from a rich-text or HTML file to display data. It doesn't have a complex editorial environment, but it is useful. For this example, let's add a Content Editor web part to the web page, give it a unique title, and then set it so the users cannot close it in their personal versions. Then to configure it we need to go into the Rich Text Editor and add some content.

1. To add a Content Editor web part to the page, you need to be in Edit mode. Click Site Actions and select Edit Page to go into Edit mode in the Shared version of the page.

2. While in Edit mode, decide which Web Part zone you want to add the web part to. I am going to use the left Web Part zone because that's where people's eyes tend to go first.

3. Click the Add a Web Part button at the top of the left Web Part zone. That will open the Add Web Parts to Left window.

4. In the All Web Parts, Miscellaneous list is the Content Editor web part. Put a check mark in the box next to it to select it, and click the Add button at the bottom of the window.

This will bring you back to the home page in Edit mode, with the new Content Editor web part listed at the top of the left Web Part zone (see Figure 4.15).

Configure a Built-In Web Part

As you can see in Figure 4.15 the new web part requires configuration. It's empty of content, just a shell based on the Content Editor Web Part template. To add content to this web part, you will need to open the tool pane.

You can open the tool pane for this web part by clicking the down arrow in the web part's title bar and selecting modify shared web part, or, if you are in edit mode, just click the Open The Tool Pane link listed in the web part itself.

Of course, the tool pane opens on the right of the page, covering the web parts beneath it. The first section of the tool pane is the Content Editor section (Figure 4.16). The headings for the Appearance, Layout, and Advanced sections are below that, of course.

FIGURE 4.15
The new Content Editor
web part

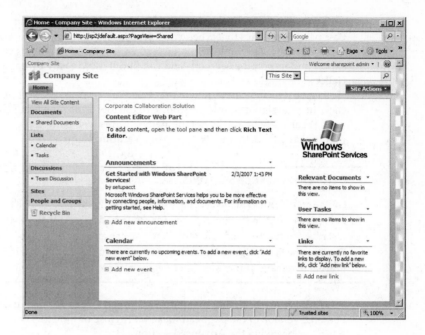

FIGURE 4.16
The Tool Pane Content
Editor section

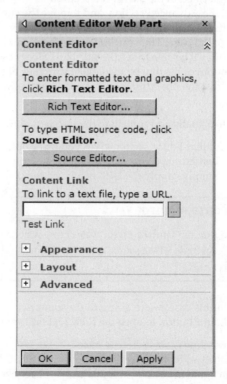

Before editing the content of the web part, you must do something about the web part name. Best practice dictates that when you add and configure a web part on a web page, you must give it a unique name. This makes it possible to easily identify it among other web parts in a gallery, export and import it elsewhere, and can find it more easily by name in the Closed Web Parts Gallery.

To give the web part a unique title, open the Appearance section of the tool pane. To do that, click the plus sign next to Appearance in the tool pane. The first field in that section is the Title field. It currently holds the default name for this web parts type. Enter a unique name for this web part in that Title field. My example uses **Vacation Request**.

OTHER APPEARANCE SETTINGS

For the other settings in this section, you could specify the exact fixed height and width for this web part, but I prefer to let the web part fit the zone automatically. This allows the web part to best fit the zone regardless of the user's screen resolution. You can also decide whether or not the web part will have a title bar (the Site Image web part is set to not have a title bar, for example) or borders. I would like the title bar to remain. This is why I am leaving those settings at this point.

While we are here, this web part needs to be locked so those users who have a right to use a Personal version of the page cannot actually close or hide this while in their Personal version. That setting is located in the Advanced section.

Open the Advanced section, and remove the check marks from the Allow Close and Allow Hide settings. This disables the user's right to close or hide this web part, even in their Personal version of the page. They can still minimize it, but they cannot say they didn't realize it is there because they'll be able to see the title bar. Once those settings are complete, click the Apply button at the bottom of the tool pane to make sure they are applied before we continue.

Now that the pre-editing configuration of the web part is done, we can move on to content editing:

1. To actually add content to the web part, scroll back up to the top of the tool pane if necessary.

The Content Editor section gives you three options to add content to the web part. You can use the Rich Text Editor, create HTML source material (or cut and paste from some HTML source code), or simply supply the URL of an existing file.

IF THE CONTENT EDITOR FAILS

Be aware that the Content Editor web part was not really meant to display web pages that contain `<form>` tags in its HTML source code. For that use, the Page Viewer web part, which is better able to render web pages.

---

2. In this case, we're going to do some rich-text editing, so click the aptly named Rich Text Editor button to open the Rich Text Editor window (see Figure 4.17).

The window is an obviously scaled-down word processor. If you move your cursor over the tools in the two toolbars, you'll see that you can add tables, links, or images, as well as format text. You aren't going to be able to build a style sheet here, but you can create a simple document.

FIGURE 4.17
The Rich Text Editor

3. We are going to essentially put up a flyer to remind users to turn in their vacation requests in this example. To this end, enter some text to that effect in the editor (see my example in Figure 4.19 for more ideas). Feel free to format the text as you'd like.

4. To insert an appropriate vacation image into the document, click the Insert Image button. The Insert Image dialog box (see Figure 4.18) will appear.

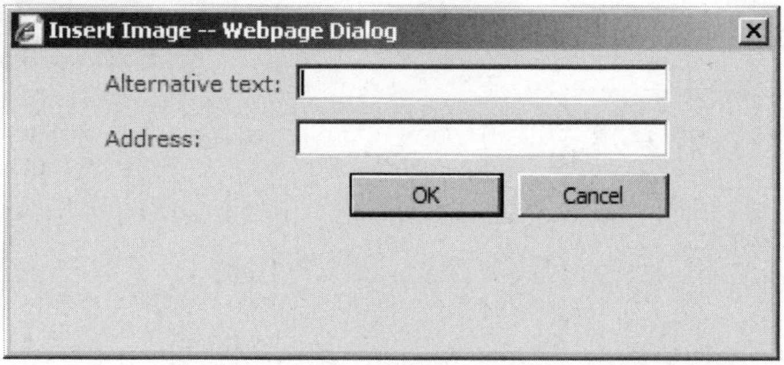

FIGURE 4.18
The Insert Image dialog box

In this dialog box, you can add alternative text (in case the user can't see the image) and you can enter the path to the image you want to use. The previous version had a Browse button, but this one doesn't because the address needs to be accessible from other machines on the network.

This editor is web-based, so the path to the file cannot be a simple windows file system path, it has to comply with `http://`, `ftp://`, `file://`, or the UNC `\\` protocols.

5. With this in mind, I copied the `Azul.jpg` desktop wallpaper, which is normally located in the `%windir&\Web\Wallpaper` folder, to a shared folder on my server named imageshare. To use it in my Vacation Request web part, I am going to give the image an alternative text of **vacation view**, enter the address of `file://sp2/imageshare/azul.jpg`, and click OK.

SO EVERYONE CAN SEE IT

Make sure that the all users have read permission on the location for any image or other content you might add to a web part or else the content will fail to render.

---

6. This should add a huge image of a tiny island with palm trees on it surrounded by beautiful blue ocean waters, with a sail boat in the distance. Of course, it will need to be resized by clicking on the image, then grabbing one of the corner handles, and dragging it until it is the size that suits you. Of course, if you are using a different image file, your experience may vary. But it's still a good idea to keep in mind the area of the web part page you have available for the image and resize the image accordingly.

7. Once your text is formatted and your image resized (see Figure 4.19). Click the Save button on the bottom left of the editor.

FIGURE 4.19
A Vacation Request

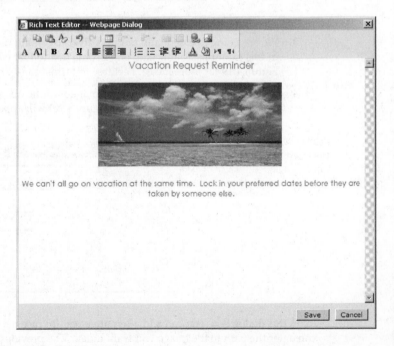

8. To see what it looks like on the page, click Exit Edit Mode in the information bar.

FIGURE 4.20
A new Vacation Request
on the home page

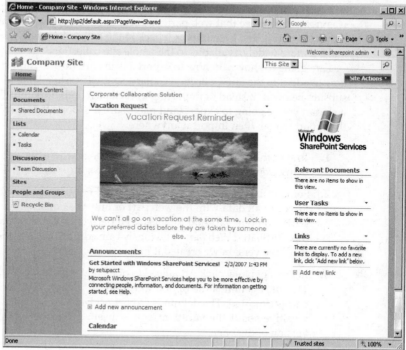

That's it! See Figure 4.20 for the finished product. Users who are allowed Personal versions can move the web part on the page; they can minimize it, but they shouldn't be able to close or hide it.

By now you know how to add a built-in web part to a web page and how to configure it. All built-in web parts have basically the same requirement: they require content. This means that they usually need to be pointed to a source so they can display its contents, such as an XML page, folder, or text file. The Content Editor web part needs to be configured the most because it gives you the resources to actually build the content right there if you'd like, rather than having to point to a preexisting object. The real trick to the built-in web parts is the tool pane; explore all the settings and see where they take you.

Export a Web Part

Now that you've gotten the feel for what it takes to customize a web part, you can understand why you might want to export a copy. It backs up the web part, and it makes it possible to use it elsewhere. For example, let's take that web part we created and put it on the Calendar page. The process could take several steps, depending on whether or not you want to re-create the web part on other pages of the site. If you don't want to create it again from scratch, you can export it (thus the Export field under Advanced in the tool pane carries a little more weight) and then import it to the page where you want to display it.

When you use a built-in template to create a web part, it is unique to the page upon which it was created. To reuse that web part, you would have to package it as a web part definition file (.dwp), export it, and then import it back to the page where you want to put it or, if you want to make it more widely available, to the whole site collection.

I am going to show you how to export a web part, how to import it to a different page, and then how to add it to the Site Collection Gallery, so it will be available to any page on the site, or any subsites below it (instead of importing to each page individually). The first step is to access the web part you're going to export (and make sure it exports the correct data), then export it. After the export we can then import it anywhere.

1. To start the process you need to be on the page where the web part is that you want to export. In my example that would be the Home page.

2. Some web parts point to personal data. If they do, there will be an option in the tool pane to export all data with the web part or only the nonsensitive data. To check the export data setting on our Vacation Request web part, click the down arrow in its title bar and select Modify Shared Web Part. (Obviously I am editing this in the Shared version of the page since that's the version we created it in.)

3. In the tool pane, click Advanced to open that section. Scroll down to the Export Mode field. This field contains the option to export all data or nonsensitive data only when this web part is exported. The default is Export All Data, which is good in our case. There is nothing sensitive about the vacation request itself. Close the tool pane and return to the Shared version of the page.

4. Exporting a web part is as easy as clicking the down arrow in the title bar of the web part. You can be in either version of the page, or in Edit mode (click Edit in the title bar in that case). Either way, the dropdown has an Export option. This option will export a web part to a DWP file.

WE DON'T NEED NO STINKING EXPORT...

List View Web Parts do not have Export available from the drop down menu in their title bar. This is because they are created specifically for the site that holds the List they refer to and won't work anywhere else because that exact list won't be there. Thus they shouldn't be exported.

---

5. When you click Export, a dialog box will ask if you want to save or find a program to run the web part (see Figure 4.21). Click Save to save the export file. It will use the title of the web part as the default name (in this case, Vacation_Request.dwp).

6. Select a location to save the web part, my example saves the web part in my imageshare folder (see Figure 4.22). When it is imported, it will be added to SharePoint from the location where you put it. As long as SharePoint can access it at the time of import, it's okay.

7. So as long as you can access the location to import the web part to the SharePoint server next, and you are okay with the default name (otherwise, change it), click Save, to finish the web part export.

FIGURE 4.21
The Export dialog box

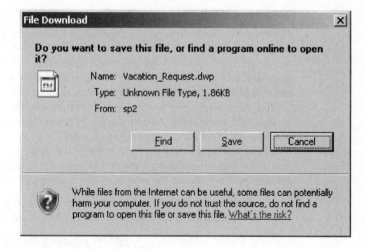

FIGURE 4.22
The Save Web Part
dialog box

BACKING UP A WEB PART

Coincidentally, exporting a web part is a useful way to back up a particularly cool web part. If the web part you have in SharePoint gets corrupted, you can always blow out the bad one and replace it by importing the backup copy you exported.

Import a Web Part to a Single Page

Now that you have successfully exported the web part, you can import it. Remember that although there is one way to export a web part to a DWP file, there are two ways to import a DWP; to a single page, or to the site collection. Importing the newly exported web part to the Calendar page will take several steps, some of which may seem a bit off the beaten path. This is one of the areas of SharePoint that isn't really convenient to use.

To import a web part to a page, such as the Calendar page, you first need to navigate to it, then go into Edit mode there. At that point you'll need to open the Add a Web Part page by clicking on a Add a Web Part bar over the selected zone. Of course, the web part we want to add isn't easily available among the existing web parts for the page, so you'll have to go to the advanced options link at the bottom of the Add Web Parts page. From there, you will need to use the tool pane to import the DWP file for the web part (don't worry, I'll walk you through it).

1. This example uses the Calendar page for the imported web part, so go to the Calendar page by clicking the Calendar link in the Quick Launch bar.

    As you can see in the Calendar page (see Figure 4.23), the page is focused on the calendar, its Action bar, and its View menu. In most instances, adding more web parts to this environment is not a good idea. However, this is where users schedule events and we should remind them to keep their vacation times in mind. Let's add the web part to the top of the page at least temporarily.

FIGURE 4.23

A Calendar page

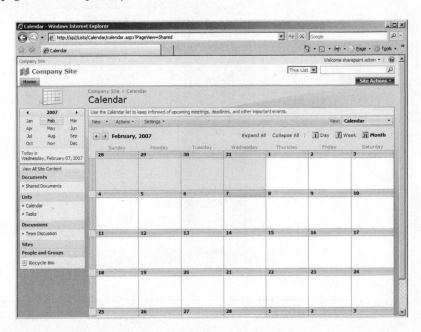

Believe it or not, the entire content area used by the Calendar (and the one used by any other list or library) is just a big web part. This means that all content pages are web part pages, albeit meant to hold only one web part. You might note that the Calendar's chrome is set to not have a title bar and down arrow, as other web parts do. This means, to modify it, you must go into Edit mode on that page.

BEWARE OF PERSONAL VERSION AND CONTENT PAGES

Unfortunately, because the content of a content page for a list or library is a web part it also means that if a user has the right to have Personal page versions, they can close the list or library on a page while in their Personal version of it. Be prepared for the support calls if you have users who try to edit the Personal version of a list or library. You may want to go into the advanced properties of all lists' and libraries' web parts tool panes and disallow the right edit in Personal View, close, or hide, just in case.

2. To import a web part to a page, click on Site Actions, and go to Edit Page.

3. With the page in Edit mode (Figure 4.24), the Calendar List web part title shows up. Make sure you are in the Shared version of the page. Notice there is only one big Web Part zone here, so click the only Add A Web Part button on the page.

FIGURE 4.24
A Calendar page in Edit mode

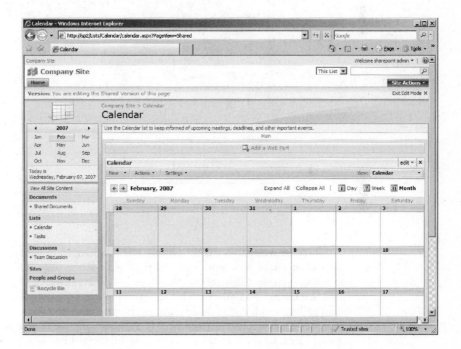

In the Add Web Parts To Main window, take a look through the list of web parts. You can see the built-in Content Editor Template web part, but not the Content Editor web part we configured on the home page. This is because it belongs only on the home page at this point.

4. To add the web part we exported to this page, click the Advanced Web Parts Gallery and options link at the bottom of the window (see Figure 4.25).

FIGURE 4.25
The Add Web Parts To
Main window

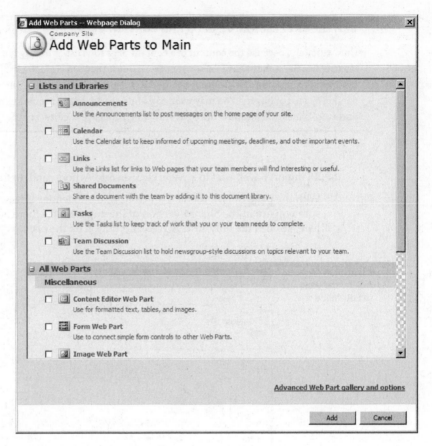

Of course, you might expect another window to open to this fancy new, advanced gallery. However, a tool pane opens on the right side of the page. This is the interface from the previous version of SharePoint; it shows the different web part galleries in the top section. The Site Collection Gallery (called Company Site in my example) is selected by default, with that gallery's web parts listed below, as shown in Figure 4.26.

As you can tell, this environment is cramped. The list of web parts for the site collection should look familiar. It has the Lists And Libraries List View web parts mingled with the built-in and miscellaneous web parts. The list, because it is cramped, will have a Next link to let you page to whatever links could not fit on the opening page of the tool pane.

My server has 14 web parts in the Site Collection Gallery, and I haven't closed any of them yet (so nothing is listed in the Closed Web Parts Gallery). I do not have any imported to the server farm or web application; if I had imported any web part packages, they would show up in the Server Gallery. The interesting thing about this interface is you can drag and drop a web part from this tool pane to the Web Part zone. You can also choose a zone and add a web part using the Add button.

FIGURE 4.26
The tool pane for
advanced options

All of that is nice, but you may have noticed that there is no Import button or link. That is because you are in the Add Web Parts mode of this tool pane. Yes, this tool pane does more than display web parts. Currently, it is in Browse mode. If you go to the top of the tool pane, you'll see the title "Add Web Parts" with an X to close. Below that is a Browse bar with a down arrow on the right. This indicates that if you click on the Browse bar, it'll drop down.

5. Click on the Browse bar. Doing so will display a dropdown list of Browse, Search, and Import.

You've seen Browse. Search just gives you a field into which you type a web part name so that it can search the galleries for you.

Import lets you import a web part to the page. It will not go into one of the galleries to be used elsewhere. This is a one shot, local page import feature.

6. To import the web part, just select Import from the dropdown list.

The tool pane will change to Import mode and display a field for you to enter the location and name of the web part file you want to import.

7. Browse to the location and select the web part you want to import. (My example is the Vacation Request web part on the local drive in the imageshare folder). Once you've supplied the path and filename, click the Upload button. This will upload the web part to be used on this page.

   When the upload is complete, the web part will appear in the tool pane under the newly created Uploaded Web Parts heading (see Figure 4.27).

FIGURE 4.27

Uploaded web parts

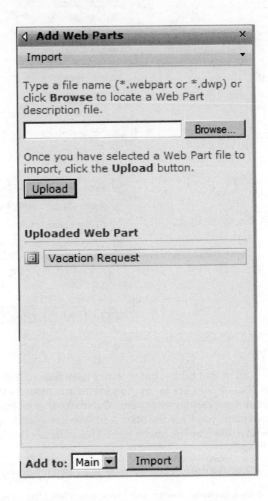

8. To finish the import, make sure the web part you are adding is selected. In my example it's the only web part there. Click Import at the bottom of the pane, notice that it will be added to the Main web part zone.

9. The web part (in my case it's Vacation Request) should show up in the Web Part zone of the page, above the Calendar. Click Exit Edit Mode to see what your handiwork has wrought (see Figure 4.28).

FIGURE 4.28
An imported Vacation
Request

Import a Web Part to a Site Collection Gallery

Now you know how to import a web part to a page. But what if you wanted to import a web part to a site collection, so all pages on all the sites in the collection could have the web part available to them? That would be no problem. Just import the web part to the Web Parts Gallery for the top-level site. Then, instead of importing the web part for a single page, the web part would be available to be added to any page on any site in the site collection.

1. To add the web part you originally exported (or any .dwp web part file for that matter) to the entire site collection's gallery, you need to go to the top-level site's settings. (The first SharePoint site is the top-level site for our current site collection by default, because it is the *only* site in the collection.) Go to the Site Actions menu, and click Site Settings (you can be on any page of the site to do this).

2. Click the Web Parts link under Galleries on the Site Settings page (see Figure 4.29).

The miscellaneous web parts are listed on the Web Parts Gallery page (Figure 4.30). None of the List View web parts are listed, though. They are made unique for each list upon its creation, are site specific, and are not available for export from or import to any other site. The site gallery is basically a list, and the web parts are considered to be "documents."

3. To import a web part to this gallery, click the Upload button. It will open a standard upload page (see Figure 4.31) that has a field for you to specify the file, or as it's called here, document, and a checkbox to indicate whether or not you want to overwrite an existing web part if it has the same name.

4. Click the Browse button and browse to the web part file you'd like to import (my example is Vacation Request).

5. When you've selected the web part and it appears in the Name field, click OK.

FIGURE 4.29
The Site Settings page

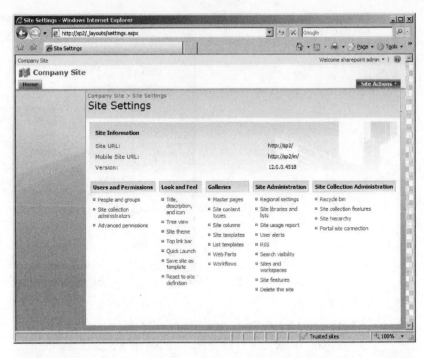

FIGURE 4.30
The Site Web Parts Gallery

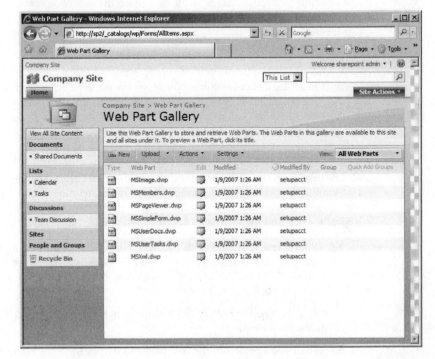

FIGURE 4.31
The Upload page

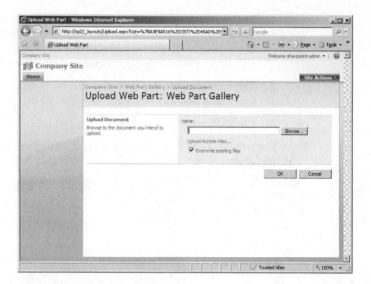

6. A Web Part Gallery page for the web part will open (my example is Web Parts Gallery: Vacation Request). It will contain fields for the metadata of the web part, such as name, title, and description. It will also contain settings to specify how the web part will be displayed in the Add Web Parts windows. You can group the web part under the default web parts, or you can create your own group name for it (Figure 4.32).

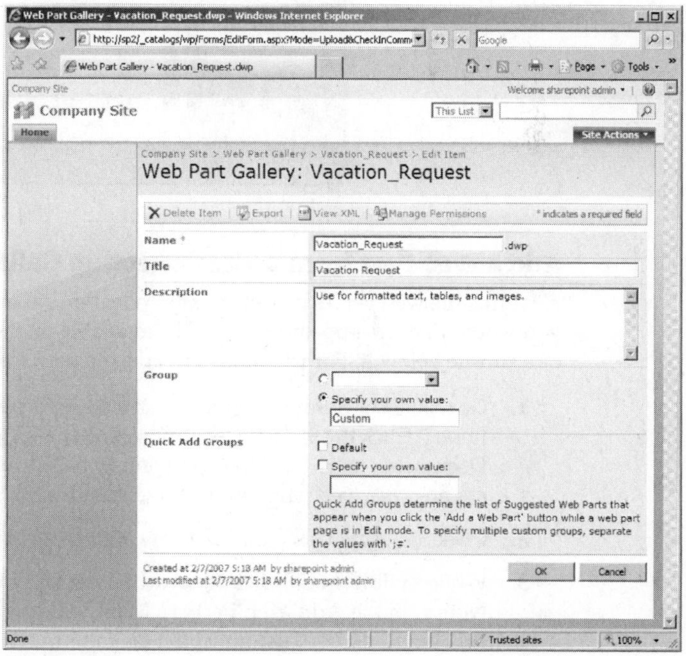

FIGURE 4.32
The uploaded Vacation
Request Web Part
properties page

7. My example keeps the name and title, but notice the description. It is obviously the same description as the Content Editor Web Part template. It's a good idea to change the description to be a little more accurate. Instead of "Use for formatted text, tables, and images," let's enter "**Vacation request reminder web part.**"

8. These settings for this web part can be changed, but for now let's list the web part under Custom in the Add Web Parts window. To do this, specify the value **Custom** for the Group.

9. Click OK when you're done.

The new Vacation Request web part is now part of the site collection's list of web parts. Notice in the Group column, that Custom is listed (Figure 4.33).

FIGURE 4.33
A new web part in the Web Parts Gallery list

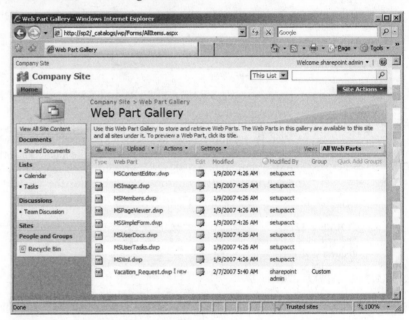

Add a Web Part from a Site Collection Gallery

Now that the web part is part of the site collection gallery, you don't have to import it to every page you would like it to appear on. It will be available on the Add Web Parts page anywhere on the site or a subsite below it. For example, let's add the new web part to a different web page on the site.

1. Go to a list or library to which to add the web part, my example uses the Shared Documents library. Click the Shared Documents link in the Quick Launch bar. While you're in the Shared Documents page (or whatever content page you have chosen), you might notice that there are no other web parts on the page, besides the Shared Documents list itself.

2. Click Site Actions. To add the new web part to this page, select Edit Page.

3. While in Edit mode, click the Add a Web Part button at the top of the main Web Part zone. Notice, in the Add Web Parts to Main window, that there is a new web part group under All Web Parts. It's Custom, and it contains our web part (see Figure 4.34) complete with new description.

FIGURE 4.34
A new web part in the
New Web Part group

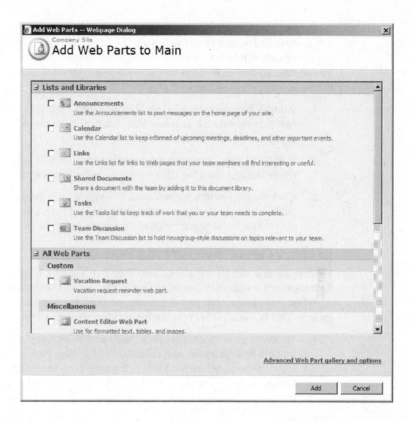

4. Put a check mark beside the web part you'd like to add (in my example that would be Vacation Request) and click Add to add it to the Web Part zone. The web part should appear above the Shared Documents list.

To see your handiwork, click Exit Edit Mode.
The new, imported web part should be proudly located above the Shared Documents content.

There are some things to keep in mind when adding web parts to a content page:

♦ Views of content pages have their own page. This means that if you add a web part to a particular view of a list or library's content, the web part will only display in that view. If a user switches to a different view of the content, and the web part has not been added to that view, then the web part won't be there.

♦ If a user has the right to use Personal versions, they can create a personal view of a content page as well. If you do not want the web part to be closed, hidden, or edited in a Personal version of the page, configure its advanced settings to not allow close, hide, or edit in Personal View.

Close a Web Part

Now that we've added the web part to the Shared Document's "All Documents" view of the content page, you probably realize that you don't necessarily want the web part to stay there permanently. This brings us to another useful skill, how to remove web parts from a page.

To remove a web part from the page, we could do one of two things: we can delete it or we can just close it. Deleting it removes it from the page but not the gallery. Closing it just closes it on the page, but moves it to the closed Web Parts Gallery, in case of accidental closure, especially if you've customized its settings and you want to recover it rather than re-create it again. For this example, let's just close the web part.

1. Allow Close was disabled on this web part earlier in the chapter, so it cannot be closed. It can only be deleted. To allow this web part to be closed, click Edit in the web part's title bar, and select Modify Shared Web Part.

2. In the tool pane, open the Advanced section, enable Allow Close, and click the OK button at the bottom of the pane (this is also a convenient way to confirm a web part can be closed).

3. Click the Edit button in the Vacation Request's title bar (if you weren't in Edit Mode you could click the title bar's down arrow instead), and then select the now available Close option. At that point, the web part should disappear from the page with no warnings or prompts.

Return a Closed Web Part to a Page

We now have a web part in the Closed Web Part Gallery. This gives us a chance to demonstrate how to return a web part that might have been accidentally closed.

When you close a web part it is removed from the page but added to the Closed Web Parts gallery. This is a kind of recycle bin for accidentally closed web parts.

1. To return an accidentally closed web part to its rightful place on the page, it, just make sure you are in Edit mode, and click the Add A Web Part button. In the Add Web Parts To Main window (remember that Main is the only zone for this page), click the Advanced Web Parts Gallery and Options link. In the Add Web Parts tool pane, you'll see that there is one item in the Closed Web Parts Gallery (Figure 4.35).

FIGURE 4.35
A new web part in the Closed Web Parts Gallery

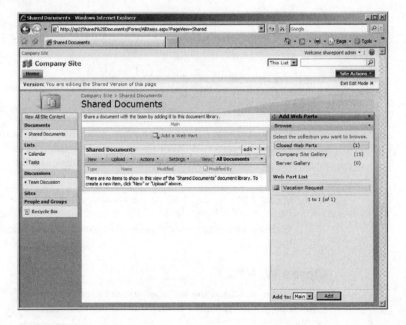

2. If you select the Closed Web Parts Gallery, the web part you closed (mine is Vacation Request) will appear in the Web Part list for that gallery.

3. You can replace the web part by dragging and dropping it back to the top of the Web Part zone.

4. Once the web part is back where it belongs, close the tool pane by clicking the X in the pane's Add Web Parts title bar.

You should be back in Edit mode in the Shared Documents folder, with the newly returned web part back at the top of the Web Part zone. If you were to check the Closed Web Parts Gallery now, it would be empty because you returned the closed web part.

Delete a Web Part

Of course, simply closing web parts to remove them from pages just moves the web part from the page to the Closed Web Parts gallery. To permanently delete the web part (except for its copy in the site collection gallery, should there be one), you will need to delete the web part instead of closing it.

1. To see what happens when you delete a web part, click Edit in the Vacation Request web part's title bar, and select Delete (if you weren't in Edit mode, you could click the down arrow in the web part's title bar and select delete from the menu as well). A dialog box will warn you that the web part will be deleted permanently (see Figure 4.36).

FIGURE 4.36
The Delete Warning dialog box

2. Go ahead and click OK.

When a web part is added to a page, it can be modified to be appropriate there. When you delete it, you are deleting the unique copy on that page, not the original in the Web Parts Gallery.

To see if the imported web part is still in the site collection gallery, there are a couple of ways to check, but the easiest is to see if it's in the Add Web Parts window (you could also go to the Web Parts Gallery and check, but this is easier while in Edit Mode).

1. Click the Add A Web Part button at the top of the main Web Part zone.

2. The Add Web Parts To Main window will open. The Vacation Request web part is safely located in the Custom section of the All Web Parts list (Figure 4.37).

You've exported a web part to a .dwp file. You imported the web part to a page and then imported the web part to a Site Collection Web Gallery. You saw the galleries listed, added the imported web part to a page from the Site Gallery via the Add Web Parts page, closed it, and deleted it.

FIGURE 4.37
A deleted web part is
still in the gallery

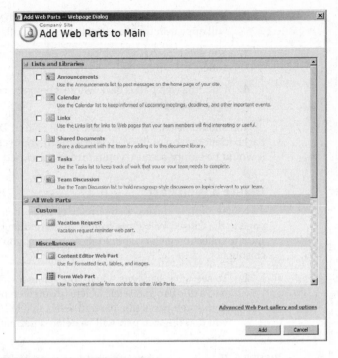

You should realize that there are many, many more things you can do with web parts. This was just an opportunity to get your feet wet. Web parts are easier to use, easier to control, and more useful than most administrators might think at first glance. Because web parts are so prevalent in SharePoint, they are critical components to understanding SharePoint overall.

ADDING WEB PARTS TO THE WHOLE FARM IN ONE GO

There is a third way to import web parts. If the web part is *packaged*, meaning it is in a `.cab` file with some other files such as a `manifest.xml` and some assembly and resource DLLs, you can use the command line to deploy it to an entire web application or to an entire SharePoint server farm (or single web application if you prefer). Usually the web part package extension, despite being a .cab file, is *.wpp* or *.wsp*. They all work the same way.

If you download a web part from a third-party vendor, the only way to make it available to your SharePoint users and administrators is by using the STSADM command to add the web part package to either a specific web application (by specifying the web application's URL), or to all web applications on the server/server farm by omitting the URL.

Let's say you need to import a demo web part package that a member of your team downloaded. The web part will need additional configuring when it is imported, but that team member has the instructions. You just need to be able to get it into SharePoint the easy way.

1. Find the `STSADM.exe` command on your SharePoint server. (It is usually located in the %Program Files%/Common Files/Microsoft Shared/web server extensions/12/Bin folder.)

2. Open a command prompt, and navigate to the `stsadm.exe` file.

3. Use STSADM to run the `addwppack` operation with the filename switch pointing to the web package you need to import. The exact syntax is

   ```
   STSADM -O ADDWPPACK -FILENAME -GLOBALINSTALL -FORCE
   ```

   ◆ `Stsadm -o addwppack -filename`.
   STSADM is the command, *-o* indicating an operation action, with *addwppack* being the add web part package operation. Replace *-filename* with the filename and path of the cab file containing the web part and associated bits.

   ◆ `-globalinstall`.
   Puts the web part in the global assembly cache, which is easier from a security standpoint.

   ◆ `-force`.
   Overwrites a previous import with the new settings.

4. Optionally, you can add a URL switch if you want to import this web part package to only one web application. (Let's omit it at this time.) If you don't specify a URL then the web part package will be added to SharePoint at the server farm level and therefore will be available to all web applications.

Once the operation completes successfully, the web part will appear in the Server Gallery on all of the sites collections in all of the web applications in the server farm.

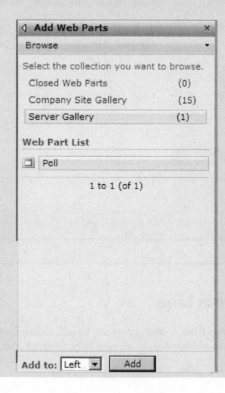

It will also show up in Central Administration for the server farm under Solution Management, although the web parts are not a solution per se. A solution is a .cab file with a WSP file extension that can be used to deploy web parts, template files, assemblies, code access security policies, site definitions, or features. And since a web parts package is a cab file containing a web part, I guess it is considered a teeny, tiny little solution. Vendors often package their web parts in .cab files, so it's a good thing to know how to deploy web parts in this way. And now you know all three ways to add web parts to your SharePoint sites.

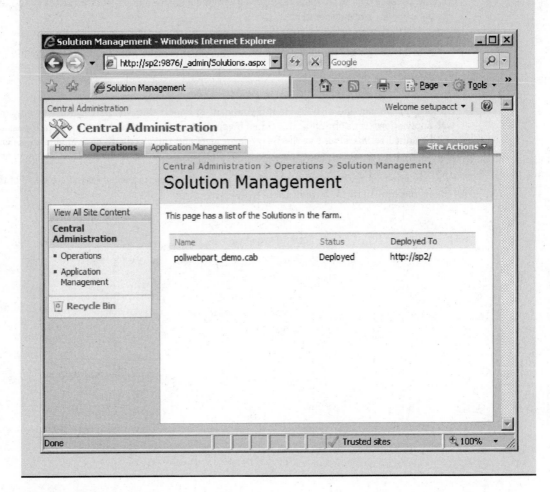

The Bottom Line

Identify Web Parts Web parts are small, independent applications intended to quickly and conveniently display the contents of lists, libraries, folders, or pages.

Master It What are List View web parts?

Use Edit Mode   In order to work on web parts in SharePoint, the page containing the web parts should be in Edit mode. Edit mode is a page state in which web parts can be moved, removed, added, imported, and edited. No data entry occurs in Edit mode.

Master It   How do you enter Edit mode to edit a Shared version of a page? How do you know for certain that you are editing the Shared version?

Distinguish Between Personal and Shared Versions   SharePoint offers the luxury of allowing users to have their own Personal version of any page that can contain web parts, in which they can rearrange, remove, or add web parts to their pages for their convenience.

Master It   How can a user tell if they are viewing the Personal or Shared version of a page?

Work with Web Parts   Adding, moving, removing, and customizing web parts while in the browser are all possible with SharePoint. There are built-in List View web parts to quickly populate the home page with web parts relevant to users. There are also built-in web part templates to easily customize web parts right in the browser, with no coding necessary.

Master It   How do you change the title of a web part?

Export and Import Web Parts   Web parts aren't just static little applications. You can customize them, export them to a web part definition file, and import them to a different page or site collection.

Master It   How do you export a web part?

Chapter 5

Introduction to Lists

Lists are part of the foundation of SharePoint. SharePoint is a Web front end laid over a SQL database back end for the purpose of collaboration on shared data and documents. So, SharePoint is a nice, consistent Web interface to give users an easy way to enter, organize, find, and display data stored in SQL.

This chapter is meant to give you, the administrator, an overview of what lists can do and how to use them (and how the users will be using them), so you have an idea of what to expect when asked about lists and how to use, create, manage, and customize them in the course of your work day.

In this chapter, you'll learn how to:

- ◆ Use and modify a list
- ◆ Modify a view and create a view
- ◆ Create a list from a template
- ◆ Create a custom list

What Is a List?

To start, lists are located in SharePoint sites. Lists offer a consistent interface for data entry. The data in the lists is stored in their site's content database and is available for users to pull up and even manipulate via list views. Each list has at least an All Items view, which is a page that displays the contents of the list; as such it's considered a content page. You can usually navigate to a list using the Quick Launch bar on most pages of a site. Sites are stored in Web applications, and every Web application has at least one content database.

The *content database* contains the relational databases (or what I call, for convenience's sake, "tables") that contain the lists' data. Every time you create a list, you create a table in the content database for it. That table is displayed in the SharePoint Web interface as a list because it has rows and columns, which translate to records (otherwise known as *list items)* and fields.

Views

Each list is displayed on a content page. A *content page* is simply a way to display the contents of a given list. Usually, when you generate a display of a database's contents, the display is called a report. In SharePoint, it's called a *view*. You can create surprisingly useful views using SharePoint's built-in view customization tools, which give you all kinds of control over how to display and manipulate the data that you put into a list. The trick is that a content page is defined by a view, and a list can have several ways to view it, which means (unbeknownst to the users) that a list can have several different content pages, each specific to a different way to view the data.

IT DOESN'T LOOK LIKE A DIFFERENT PAGE

Another reason each view can seem to be on the same page is that the page header and Quick Launch bar never change, making you think you are on the same page and that you only changed the view. Look in the Address bar as you switch views on a list. You'll see that you are going to a different page for each view. It's just that SharePoint has the header and Quick Launch bar as a common design theme for all pages. This common element can be misleading. The thing that is different between the pages is the view of the contents. That's why they're called *content pages*.

Let's say you need to keep information about your inventory, your clients, and what you sell to them. Many companies have this loop, where they buy inventory, store inventory, and have clients to whom they sell that inventory. Therefore, the tables containing information about inventory, clients, and sales would be pretty standard.

You might want to organize the information in an Inventory list in several different ways, so you can quickly view items grouped by vendor or by category. To better manage your data, you can create different views of that Inventory list and then use those views when you wish.

When you create a view, SharePoint puts it on its own page; therefore, when you change to a different view of a list, you are opening a different page. This becomes important only if you are adding Web Parts to a particular view of a list. When you change the view, the Web Parts disappear because the Web Parts were on the other view's content page. You can choose to have a particular view be the default view for a list so the users see that view first when they navigate to the list. Any list can have multiple views, but they all have to have a default view. If a user has the right to, they can create their own personal views of a list, visible only to them. This allows them to create their own custom reports of the list data.

So you know that lists are tables in the content database. You also know that you can manipulate the data in a list by creating different views, and that each view of a list is in fact its own page. But, there is something else that is important about lists simply being tables in the content database: how they can be connected by common data.

Common Data

Lists can sometimes reasonably contain the same data. A Vendor list would have the company name, contact information, address, etc., of the companies from whom you purchase inventory. The Inventory list would probably have a field to track where you purchased an item from, which as luck would have it, would be the vendors. Therefore, these two tables would have a field with common data. Because of this, SharePoint allows you to have a field that is formatted—not as a number, currency, or text—but as a lookup field that displays the data that was entered into a common field in a different list. This means that you can create a vendor field in the Inventory list and have that field be linked to the vendor company name field in the Vendor list, using the Lookup Field format.

A *lookup field* is commonly used to keep someone from having to type the same data over and over if it is already available in a different table. This allows you to create a field that already has the vendor company name in it, so a user can simply click on the field and select the correct company from the dropdown for the inventory item. This is generally done to avoid typing errors and misspelling on the part of the data entry person.

For an administrator, or someone who is designing these lists, the concept of common field data is something to keep in mind. It is possible to have an Inventory list, Customer list, and a Vendor list and then create a Sales list that has lookup fields for the Customer name, Vendor name, Salesperson name (from the People and Groups list of the SharePoint users), and Inventory name. Then all the data entry person actually has to type in is the price of the items sold. The Sales list becomes a kind of middle list, linking three other lists in a way that the other lists wouldn't otherwise have in common.

In addition to the ability to use lookup fields to access field information from one list to another, lists also have the ability to be "connected" using their corresponding List View Web Parts (the Web Parts you learned about in Chapter 4, "Introduction to Web Parts"). Using List View Web Parts, you can put the Web Parts of the Customer list and the Sales list on the home page (or any other page that can contain web parts). Then, create a connection between the Sales list and Customer List Web Parts so if you click on a sales record, the corresponding Customer record will come up in the Customer List Web Part (so maybe you can call those customers to make sure they are happy with their orders).

In other words, as long as the connected list's Web Part is on the page, and the field you are using to connect the two Web Parts is displayed, you can connect the Web Parts of two lists to filter the view of one with the selected record of the other, synchronizing their data to make them both more useful. All this is possible because lists are fundamentally tables of data. They can be treated just like any other table of data. They are meant to contain information that users might want to edit, add to, and display as they see fit. Straight out of the box, they can be connected in a simple, rudimentary way using common data.

Lists can even be displayed as a datasheet if the user has Microsoft Office installed. Datasheet view is essentially a little spreadsheet. This view makes it easier to add a lot of data at one time, and it allows the user to more easily conceptualize the fact that the list is a table, which can lead to them more effectively manipulating the data by using Excel or Access. In addition, users can set alerts on items in a list so that they are notified by email if there is a change. They can even subscribe to an RSS feed (Real Simple Syndication feed) of a list to keep informed of any changes.

As for the list items, they can be set to do versioning, which is very useful in most lists. Versioning means that each time a field's contents in a list item changes; SharePoint saves a copy of the list item so you can roll back in case the change was a mistake. Although versioning is useful in common lists, it really comes into its own with document libraries. Document libraries are, after all, just document focused lists. With versioning enabled in a document library, each time changes to a document are saved, they are saved as a new version of the document (and its list item). You can also set lists to require content approval, which can limit what users can see, or you can limit what users can edit in a list (everything or just their own items). When a list or library has content approval enabled, the new content must be approved first (by someone with the permissions to do so) before the item is available to everyone using the list or library.

Lists can be secured, so they can have the same permissions as the site they're on, or they can have their own unique users and permissions. This means that if a group of users are allowed to contribute to the site, they are automatically allowed to contribute to the list, or the list can be set to only allow contributions from specific users. Even individual list items can be uniquely secured within a list if necessary (such as locking the "Rules and Regulations for this List" item in a list from editing). Security has come a long way.

All in all, even the simplest list can have an array of settings, features, and capabilities in SharePoint. SharePoint has a number of different lists that are ready to use by default, and you can create innumerable lists from scratch if you wish. This means you can use the existing default lists, or list templates straight out of the box, so to speak, to create lists. As a matter of fact, you can make a list based on a template, and customize the heck out of it, or you can simply make a completely new list if you wish.

Explore a List

To start, let's take a look at a list. One of the simplest lists created in the Team Site template is the Announcements list. Interestingly, the site template does not display that list on the Quick Launch bar. Therefore, the easiest way to see its content page is to use the Announcements List View Web Part.

To access a list from its Web Part, go to the home page or wherever the web part is located, and click on its title. In this case, click on Announcements in the Announcements Web Part's title bar. This will take you to the Announcement's list content page (Figure 5.1).

FIGURE 5.1

The Announcements list

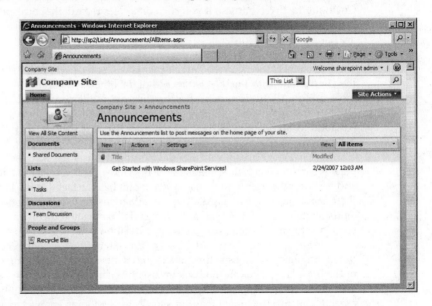

On the content page of the Announcements list, you can see the sample "Get Started with Windows SharePoint Services!" list item.

Notice that, in the content area of the page, the field headings are Title and Modified (and a column to indicate if there is a file attached to a list item). Above the content area is the Action bar, which contains the New, Actions, and Settings menu buttons, as well as the View menu. (The default view for this list is All Items. This means all records item available for the list, not necessarily all of the fields available for each item.) Above the Action bar is the title of the list and above that is the navigation breadcrumb, which indicates that the page you are on is the Announcements page and you got there from—for this example—the Company Site home page. On the left, of course, is the ever-present Quick Launch bar.

The Action bar (as you may recall from Chapter 3, "Introduction to the SharePoint Interface,") has three buttons. They can have dropdown menus associated with them so you can do additional actions on the list. In this list, these buttons contain the following:

New   Simply creates a new item for this list. If you click on the button, or if you click the dropdown arrow and select the New option from the menu, it will do the same thing.

Actions   Contains the actions you can take on the list. Doing anything in a datasheet in a list requires the local machine to have at least one Office product installed (preferably Excel or Access 2007). This makes it possible for SharePoint to understand what a datasheet-which is really a tiny spreadsheet—is. This displays the list items in a spreadsheet format, so you can enter data in a bulk way more easily. You can also filter columns of data in a more complicated way than you can in a normal List view. Also under Actions is the option to export the list's data to a datasheet (which exports the list as it is to Excel so you can work on it there). This menu also has options for keeping tabs on changes made to items in the list by using View RSS Feed and Alert Me (which can create an alert that triggers an email to your account based on what kind of changes to the list you want to track).

Settings   Contains the option to create a new column (otherwise known as a *field*), create a new view, or go into the more in-depth List Settings.

If there are any list items, they'll be displayed beneath the headings. To sort any list items you might have, you can click on a column heading. To open a list item and view its contents, simply click on its title, or whatever field in the item that appears to be a link. You might also notice that when you move your mouse over that list item's linked field that a box appears around it. This is the list item's selection box. That box helps compensate for the fact that right clicking isn't available for list items in Internet Explorer. If you click on the selection box of an item, a menu pops down, offering you approximately the same actions that the action bar offers plus actions specific to that individual item.

Create a New List Item

To create a new list item, click the New button in the Action bar. On the New Item page (see Figure 5.2), you'll notice that, although the list showed an attachment column, a title column, and a modified column, when you create a new item, there are other fields in that record: Body and Expires (and the Attach File link) to be exact. Because the Modified date field is a default field that you cannot change, it's not available for data entry. Keep in mind that the view of the list generally doesn't have all the fields available for the record. It shows what Microsoft thought would be relevant for the Announcements list.

To prove this point, let's fill out these new item fields and return to the Announcements list.

The title of my new Announcement item will be "Welcome to my site!" The body of the text is going to contain a welcome to new members. Although I am going to be assuming that you are following along, you can enter whatever data you'd like.

Below the Body field is a field called Expires. This field is what causes announcements in the Web Part to only display current items. If you leave the Expires field blank, the announcement will always be displayed in the Announcements Web Part on the home page. Because this is a welcome announcement I don't want it to expire, so leave the Expires field blank and click OK to go back to the Announcements list.

In the Announcements list, a new item is displayed (see Figure 5.3 for my new "Welcome to my site!"). Notice that the Body of the list item is not displayed in this view. There is also no Expires field listed.

FIGURE 5.2
The Announcements:
New Item Page

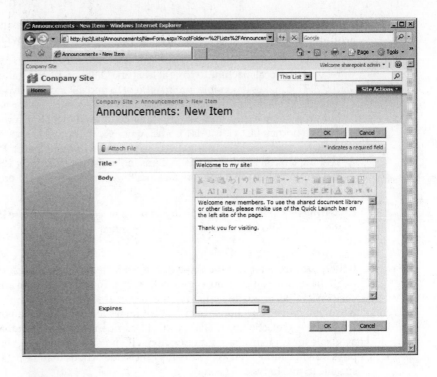

FIGURE 5.3
A new announcement

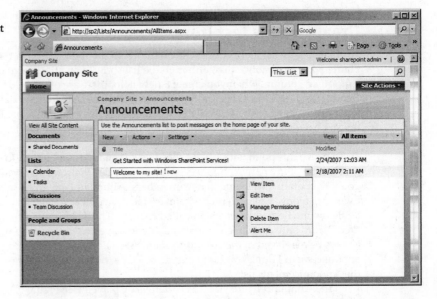

THE NEW ICON

A green exclamation mark (!) is assigned to all new list items in SharePoint, and a little green "NEW" appears next to them for the first 24 hours of their existence. It should disappear after a day. If the !NEW icon bothers you, check out KB article 825510. Even though the article is for previous versions of SharePoint, the operation and parameters are still there.

As you read in Chapter 3, the Action Bar buttons are active and have menu items under them. There is also always one field in every list item that is "linked" to the list item. This means that if you click on that linked item, the item's view page opens. (That page has an Action bar that makes things like, edit item, available to the user.)

SECRETS OF A LINKED FIELD

The linked field for an item is usually the "name" or "title" field. Keep this in mind when you are messing with the way a list is viewed, because if the name or title fields are not displayed, the user may not be able to access that list item to edit or view item contents. There is a way around it, by using an Edit icon for each list item. However, it is still good to know that there are limitations to what fields are automatically (and inflexibly) assigned as the link for an item.

The Action bar is largely focused on things you can do in the list, such as editing or deleting; however, for each item, there needs to be a group of links to work on it specifically. Which is why each list item has a dropdown menu, as I mentioned earlier in the chapter.

The options on the dropdown list will, of course, depend on your permissions for the list, permissions for that particular item, and even in some cases, what kind of list it is. Keep in mind that, if you cannot access the drop down menu of an item (because it is an Active X control, so your browser may not support it), you can also access the item specific commands by going into that item's view page.

LIMITED PERMISSIONS?

I am logged in as *shareadmin* on my server. That account is the primary site owner, so I have all possible rights to all items at this point. This is why I have all the options possible to work on any list, list item, site, Web Part, etc. If you are working on a list in SharePoint and don't have all the options I do, the chances are good that you are logged in and working with an account with limited permissions.

To trigger the Item dropdown menu in the Announcements list, move your mouse pointer over the Title of the new Announcement item (in other lists, be sure to move your mouse over the field that is linked). It will trigger a box around the Title field (which I call a selection box for want of a better term). If you move your mouse pointer off of the Title text itself (which is an active link to view the item's contents) but keep the pointer in the box and click, the dropdown menu will appear (as shown in Figure 5.3).

This menu should have the following items:

View Item   This menu option is what occurs when you click the title for an item. It takes you to the page displaying the contents of that item record.

Edit Item   This menu option opens the Edit page for that item so you can change or add data to the editable fields (fields such as Created Date or Last Modified are automated and cannot be accessed or changed by a user). This page, in particular, illustrates that there can be many more fields of data for an item than may be displayed in a List view. Sometimes there just simply isn't enough room on a screen for all of the data stored in a list item.

Manage Permissions   New to this version of SharePoint, this menu option allows you to specify permissions and security at an item by item level. Not only can you decide who can log on and use a site, or decide who sees and uses lists, but you can even specify, within the same list, which items can be seen and used by whom. Security's that granular.

Delete Item   Does exactly as you'd expect. Click it, and you get a warning that this item will be deleted. Then the item goes to the user's Recycle Bin for the site.

Alert Me   Gives you an easy way to create an *alert* (an email is sent to you alerting you to changes based on the alert settings) on a list. It seems like it means per item because it is on that item's dropdown menu, but actually you configure Alerts to check on changes on the list, or on items that were created, modified by you, or (in the case of this particular list) if an expiration date changes. Alerts trigger emails to your account (if your account has an email address associated with it, and if outgoing email is set up properly in SharePoint). As a matter of fact, alerts are associated with a user's SharePoint account, accumulate per site, and can be managed from that user's User Information page.

LIMIT YOUR ALERTS

Alerts are managed by the SharePoint Timer Service, and do take some processor effort to generate and track. For this reason, it is common practice to limit the number of alerts that a user can have going at any one time. This setting is configured at the Web Application level (Central Administration/ Application Management/Web application general settings/Alerts section). The default maximum is 500. But commonly that number is changed to something far lower, particularly if you are using multiple Web applications for your sites.

Regardless, keep that limit in mind before teaching the users to go alert crazy. It may be better for them to subscribe to an RSS feed on a list to track changes instead.

View a List Item

To view the item's contents, just click View Item on the dropdown menu, or click the item's Title while on the content page for the list (if the list item has a List View web part you can view an item by clicking on its title).

In the window for that item's contents, you'll see the data you entered for this new item earlier in the fields Title, Body, and Expires (which in my case is blank). Notice at the bottom of the page, in Figure 5.4, that there is also other item information not contained in an editable field, namely the name of the person who created or modified the item, and the item's create and modify dates.

On this view item page, there is an Action bar. However, this one is simpler than the Action bar for the list itself. Each link on the bar is just a link to a page to do something with the list item itself. Some of these options simply echo what was in the dropdown list for the item, such as Edit, Delete, Manage Permissions, and Alert Me for the item. The New Item link is the new addition to the bar in this environment, and simply is a convenience for the user to add a new item from here.

To close the item and go back to the list, click Close. This will take you back out to the Announcements list. Keep in mind that the Close button works like a Back button. Because you were on the Announcements list when you viewed the item's contents, the Close button will take you back to the list's content page. But if you had viewed the item from, say, the home page, the Close button takes you back to the home page from the View Item page.

To prove that point, now that you are on the List view of Announcements, navigate to the home page by either clicking the site name (Company Site in my example) in the content breadcrumb, or click on the Home tab in the top-link bar.

Back on the home page of the site; notice that the Announcements Web Part has a new entry (see Figure 5.5) because we put it there by creating the new item.

FIGURE 5.5
A new item in Announcement's
Web Part

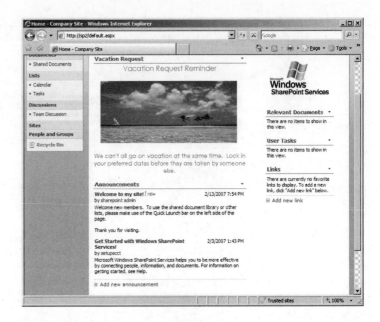

To get back to the item's view itself, simply click on the item's title in the Announcements List View Web Part. It will take you back to the View Item page, so you can see that item's full contents.

THREE ACTIVE LINKS FOR A LIST VIEW WEB PART

A List view web part has at least three active links: the title of the Web Part itself, which will take you to that list's default content page; the title of a list item, which will let you view the contents of that item; and the name of the user who created the item is also an active link, which will bring you to that user's User Information page. If the toolbar of the web part has not been disabled, there may be an Add new Item link at the bottom of the web part as well.

To get back to the home page after viewing the contents of the item, simply click Close. You will end up back on the home page, both proving that Close takes you back to the point before you viewed the item, and showing a quick trick on how to use SharePoint's navigation quirks to your advantage.

Obviously, the easiest way to get to the Announcements list from the home page is to click on the title of the Web Part. However, what if you have a list that wasn't set to show up in the Quick Launch bar and it didn't have a List View Web Part on the home page? How would you get to it? Use the View All Site Content link on the Quick Launch bar.

The All Site content page (Figure 5.6) lists everything that contains content like lists, libraries, subsites and workspaces (which are just subsites with a single task focus, such as a document or meeting), surveys and discussions (which are lists as well), and the Recycle Bin. The All Site content page view can be filtered to display only certain types of content containers. For example, you can filter the view of the page to display only lists by clicking the View menu and selecting Lists. The page contents will become limited to only those items meant to be under the Lists heading (Figure 5.7).

FIGURE 5.6

The All Site Content page with the Views menu

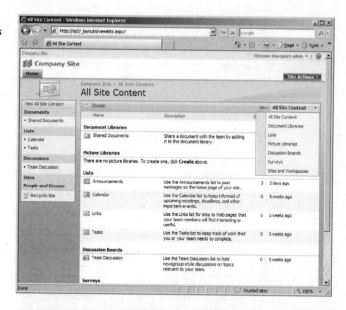

FIGURE 5.7

The All Site content page filtered by the Lists view

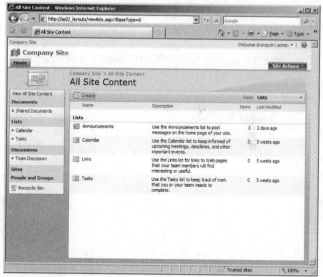

To get to the Announcements list without using the Web Part, click on the link for Announcements on the All Site content page (this is made easier if the page is filtered to display only lists).

Once back on the Announcements list, let's edit the list item we created earlier. You saw in the Announcements List View Web Part that our new list item was displayed. That is because it had not expired. SharePoint has a few variables that it recognizes automatically. Two of them are [Today] which is equal to today's date, and [Me] which is equal to the user account of the person logged in. The Expires field basically works under the covers to filter the Announcements List

View web part by knowing what today's date is and calculating whether or not the date you put in the Expires field is prior to today's date (< [Today]) . If it was yesterday or earlier, the item will not display in the Web Part. It will not be deleted from the list, it will simply not be displayed on the home page.

To demonstrate this, we are going to edit the new item we created earlier. We are going to add a date that was yesterday (or earlier, maybe your birth date or something).

Edit a List Item

As an example of how to edit a list item, let's edit the new Announcement list item that we created in the previous section of the chapter. To do so, follow these steps:

1. Move your mouse over the list item's title, and click in the selection box.

2. From the dropdown menu, select Edit Item.

3. In the Edit Item page, enter yesterday's date in the Expires field. (You can feel free to enter your birth date instead of yesterday's date—but I'm not volunteering mine . . .)

4. Click OK.

Back on the content page, nothing changed. The content page of the Announcements list stayed the same because it isn't filtering its data, even though you added a date that had already passed in the Expires field. But go back to the home page (using the breadcrumb or Home tab in the top-link bar), and you'll see that the Announcements List View Web Part no longer has the new list item displayed (Figure 5.8). This is because the Web Part view is filtered to show items only when the Expires field either contains a date equal to today, is in the future, or is blank. This let's you see the point of the list's List View Web Part, and demonstrate how that web part's view is filtered by its expires field.

FIGURE 5.8
A new item expired in
Announcement Web Part

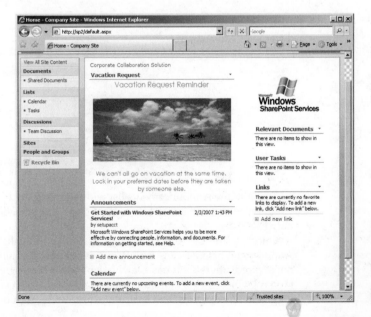

Go back to the Announcements list (click the title of the list in the web part), and you'll see the item is still there. The default view is effective, letting you know what the title of the announcement items are and when they were most recently modified. But what's missing is when they are scheduled to expire. That would be a useful thing to be able to see at a glance. In order to do that, we are going to have to add the Expires field to the current view (the most convenient view since it is the default).

To add a field to the current view, we are going to have to modify that view.

Modify a List View

To modify an existing view, simply click on the View Menu, and select Modify This View (Figure 5.9).

FIGURE 5.9
The View dropdown menu to modify the view

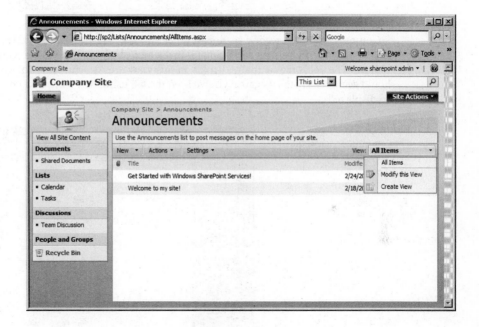

This may be the first time you've seen the Settings page for a view. So let's stop here a second and examine some of the sections. Knowing what the sections are will let you recognize this information when you make changes to lists and views.

The Name section contains the name of the view and the name of the page for that view. The name of the view will be part of the URL for that page. So remember to keep you list names short because addresses have a 255-character limit.

Strangely, as you may notice in Figure 5.10, there is a RSS Feed link next to the Web Address field. It will take you to the RSS Feed page for the list. It really has nothing to do with the way you've got this view set up, and is there in case you get the sudden urge to test your RSS Feed.

FIGURE 5.10
The first section
of the Modify
View page

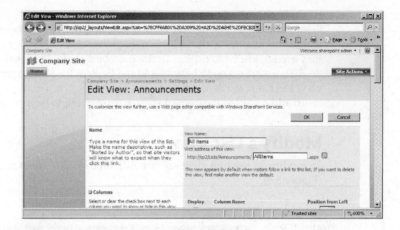

Columns are in the second section of this Edit View page (Figure 5.11). These are the fields for the list item (this helps prove that a list is just a table, because behind the scenes a field is called a column). The fields that actually display in this view are Attachments, Title, and Modified. That should seem reasonable because you've seen the list using this view, and you know those fields are displayed.

FIGURE 5.11
The Columns section of the
Edit View page

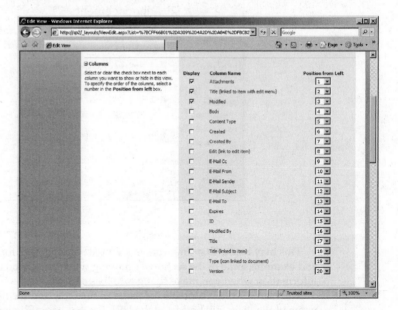

What may not be so familiar is that the list items have many more possible fields than even the ones you used when you did the data entry for the new item. Title, Body, and Expires are the only fields for this list into which you can enter data. All the other fields for this list are automated and will be filled because something happened in the software itself (such as, when the record was created, who created it, what was modified, when it was modified, and who modified it). Other automated fields can be those used by email. If a list is incoming-email enabled, then incoming list items will be received via email, and that needs to be recorded in the list item. This means that there can be fields for Email From, Sender, Subject, To, and Cc. If those fields aren't in the list of columns for your announcements list, that means that you haven't enabled incoming mail for that list yet. I enabled Email for an example in Chapter 2; therefore, it is set up in my example here (once created, even if you disable incoming email for a list, the fields remain). We will be enabling email on a list a little later in the chapter, by the way, so if you don't have the email inspired fields in your list yet, if you follow along, you'll see how to get them later. In addition, there is the ID field, which automatically gives the list items unique, consecutive numbers, the Type field (just in case this list has multiple types of new items that can be created), and the Version field (in case versioning is enabled).

The next several sections have to do with fancying up the view itself. Remember, a view is a sort of report of the data. That means, like most reports, you can organize what data is displayed and how it is displayed by using Sort, Filter, Total, and Style. You can organize data in folders in a view, and you can also specify whether or not this view will be available as a view on a mobile phone or PDA. (SharePoint can be mobile compatible. The catch is the mobile device needs to be able to access the local network.)

We are not going to be getting that fancy with the view just yet. You simply need to know what was available on this page.

So now that we are caught up with the Edit View settings, let's keep it simple and just add the Expires field to the existing view.

Add an Existing List Field to a View

To add the Expires field, while on the list settings page, simply put a check mark next to the field (Expires in our example) listing in the Columns section, and click OK.

That will take you back to the Announcements list. Notice now that the list is displaying a new column, Expires, at the far end of the list (Figure 5.12). Now you can see at a glance when an announcement is due to expire.

FIGURE 5.12
The Expires field has been added to All Items view

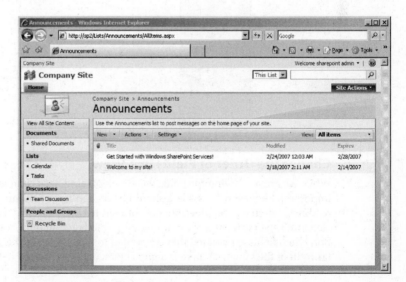

Remove a Field from a View

To further modify this view let's remove the Modified date field and replace it with the Created by field. I find it easier to search for a announcement based on who I remember it being created by rather than when it might've been modified. To make these changes to the view by removing a column and adding another column, go back to the View menu. While in the All Items view, simply click on the View menu and select Modify This View.

In the Columns section on the Edit View page for this list, remove the check mark next to the Modified field name (that removes it), and put a check mark next to the Created By field to add it (Figure 5.13). If you clicked OK, the Modified Data would be removed from the current view and Created by would be added. However, because Created by is being added at this point, it will be positioned at the far right or last place in the field order. I would rather it were located where the Modified Data was. So before we click OK, let's change the order of our fields to specify the location of the Created By field.

FIGURE 5.13
Adding and removing fields from default view

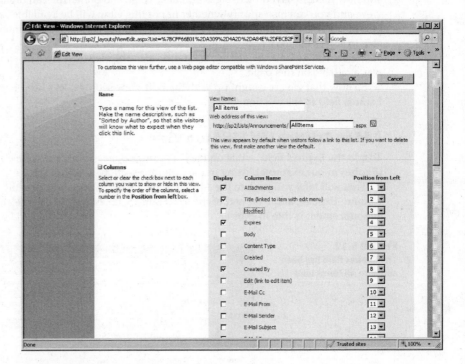

Change the Order of Fields in a View

While we are modifying the fields we are displaying, let's change their order. Field order is important. Highest priority data should be the left most column in a record (unless the user is reading a language that does not go from left to right, if that is the case, adapt accordingly). Generally, the more important or unique a field is for an item, the closest to the left it should be. But, when fields are created they are added to the bottom of the list of fields (putting them on the far right of the view), so there is a good chance they will need to be rearranged to be optimally located.

In this example, let's place the Created By field third from the left, and have the Expired field be last, or the one furthest to the right.

To do this, notice the Position From column in the Columns section of the Edit View page, with its dropdown boxes that contain numbers. The Attachments field is first from the left, then Title, then Modified (which you know is true because you've seen this view in action on the list).

To change that order, just make sure the Position From field numbers are in the order you'd like. In this case, the Created By field should be third and the Expires field fourth. To do this, make certain that the number of the position for the Created By field is 3 and the position of the Expires field is 4.

Once your positions are complete, click OK to finish editing the view, and go back to see the fruits of your labor.

Back on the Announcements list, in the All Items view, notice that the Created By field is displayed, the Modified field is not (it still exists, it's just not being used in this view), and the Expires field is now in the fourth position (see Figure 5.14).

FIGURE 5.14
The fields are rearranged in the All Items view

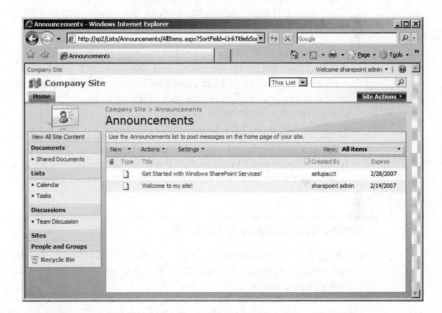

WHAT'S THAT CIRCLE THING?

Did you notice the little circle next to the heading of the Created By column? That's the Online Presence icon. If Online Presence is enabled on the Web application this site is in, and you are looking at the list from a computer with Office installed and Windows Messenger (or now Windows Live Messenger) running, the names of the people in the column will have a little circle next to them if they are in your buddy list. The circle will be green if the person is online. Of course, that person has to have Office too and be using Messenger.

Modify a List

List views are good for manipulating the view of the data in a list, but it is only as useful as that data it displays. In order to make the Announcements list more useful, let's categorize announcements so we can see at a glance what would be informational, emergency, or celebratory. We could even filter announcements by their category, letting us know quickly how many are important to read.

To do this we need to modify the list itself (instead of modifying a view of the list's data) by adding a column. There is a convenient menu option to do this.

On the Announcements list, click the Settings button and select Create Column from the dropdown menu. This will bring you to the Create Column page. Let's take a second to get familiar with the layout of this page before continuing.

This page has two sections of settings: Name and Type and Additional Column settings. The Name and Type section is important because the column type you choose here defines what settings will be available in the Additional Column Settings section below. Additional column settings vary depending on the type of field you choose.

The Name and Type section has the Column Name field and radio buttons to choose the type or format the field will be. Those options are:

Single line of text   This type of field accepts text only (meaning, the characters in this field are handled like text, even formulas) and will display it on a single line. It can be configured for a maximum number of characters and have a default value. Ironically, the maximum number of characters is 255, despite the fact that it is unlikely that you will be able to see all of those characters on a single line.

Multiple lines of text   This type of text field doesn't have a character limit, but instead can enforce a line limit. It is also able to support rich text, or even enhanced rich text (including tables, images, and hyperlinks). If the field has modifications, it also has the option of whether to replace the original text with the changes or append it.

BEFORE YOU CONSIDER APPENDING

Choosing to allow text to be appended in a multiple lines of text field requires versioning be enabled on a list. Versioning is used in this case to keep track of who modified the text in the multiple line text box and whose text is whose.

This means, to allow appending text in this field, you must enable versioning first. This is one of the many instances in SharePoint where you may have to halt your current configuration plan to go configure something else first.

Choice (Menu to Choose From)   This type of field is for offering the user a choice among a set list of options that you supply. It can be set to offer those choices by radio button, dropdown list, or checkbox (which means the user can choose several of the options rather than just one). There is also a setting to allow the user to fill in the field with a value rather than pick one of the choices.

Number (1, 1.0, 100)   This field type will only accept numbers. You can specify the decimal places, minimum/maximum, default value, and if the value is represented as a percentage.

Currency ($, ¥, €)   This is a numbers-only field that also formats the content to display as currency. It allows you to choose from a list of currency formats. Like Number, Currency also can be configured for decimal places and minimum/maximum value.

Date and Time   This field formats the content to a date and time value. You can specify whether or not it just displays a date or a date and time. You can have the field default to today's date and time or specify a default.

Lookup (Information Already on This Site)   The lookup field allows SharePoint to do something that has been done in Access for years: pull data from a column in one table and use it in another. If you have a Vendor list on your site that contains data in a column, such as Vendor Name, you can create a lookup field in a different list that refers to the Vendor Name field from the Vendor list. The field will display the data in a dropdown list, so you can just pick from what is in the column that is being looked up (or referred to from the chosen, originating list). This field is configured when you first choose the list from which to get information. Once you choose the correct list, you choose the column in that list from which to get the information. You also can configure this field to allow multiple selections for the field. This will lay out the field as two list boxes, rather than a dropdown, where you can choose data from the box on the left (which pulls from the list you are looking up) and click the Add button to put your choice(s) in the box on the right, which adds the data to the field.

Yes/No (Checkbox)   This field is literally a checkbox. If it is checked, the value is Yes; if it is not checked, the value is No. It's that simple. You can also specify a default value of either Yes or No.

Person or Group   This field pulls directly from the People And Groups list for the site, like a lookup list for site user accounts. You can configure whether or not you want to allow multiple selections for this field; allow the selection of People only or People and Groups (it defaults to People only); limit the field to All users or a particular group of users (also really useful); and how to show the selection in the field, which is exactly like a lookup field in so far as you can choose from the data that would be listed in the User Information for the selection (such as Account, Email, Job Title, even Name with presence, picture or picture with details).

Hyperlink or Picture   Interestingly, this field is formatted to accept only a URL. That is because this field is going to be accessed from across a network, so the address must be formatted for network access from a browser (such as HTTP, FTP, or FILE) and the location must be accessible from across the network (such as the virtual directory of a website or a file share) must be accessible by the users.

If you choose to use this field as a hyperlink, it will simply display a link. If you choose to use this field to contain a picture, you enter the path to access the picture file from across the network and then that picture will be displayed in the field. This means the picture needs to be stored somewhere accessible across the network, because it is not actually stored in the item record, unfortunately. SharePoint assumes that you will most likely have the picture stored in a Picture Library for the site. That's one of the unique features of a Picture Library, each picture stored in it is given a path. However, you aren't forced to use a library if the picture is somewhere else on the network.

VERSATILITY, THY NAME IS HYPERLINK (OR PICTURE)

This is another example of how SharePoint limits the potential of a feature by naming it. The Hyperlink or Picture field is meant to interpret a path to a file and open it, or it is supposed to simply display a path as a link. This means that this field can be used to open a file share or file (and/or save that file locally as well).

The Hyperlink or Picture field can be used to access a file share somewhere on the network that might contain someone's collection of work or maybe open their resume, open a file store of previous works, or open an archived report from an old assessment.

Of course, most lists can allow for attached files for an item, but this field can be useful if you don't want that item stored in the content database. It still ends up associated and accessible within the item record.

Calculated (Calculation Based on Other Columns)   This really powerful field enables you to use complex formulas to perform calculations. As a matter of fact, it is formatted to do calculations, so you can't actually type in a calculation field when doing data entry. SharePoint just does math in the background and uses the field to display the results.

You can use field names (from this list only, unfortunately), known variables like [Today] or [Me], common math, and even complex formulas and functions ranging from text and logical functions to trigonometry.

The Calculated field has a Formula box with a convenient Insert Column box next to it listing all the list fields created so far. This means if you want to calculate using another field in the list, you need to create that other field before you create the calculated field. Enter the formula you want to be calculated in the Formula box, and double-click the field name you want to add to the formula (which puts itself in the formula for you). You can also specify the data type that the formula is going to return, such as currency, number, or single line of text. Yes/No is also an option.

CLEVERNESS RECYCLED

Field templates, sometimes known as field *definitions*, can be shared between lists on a site. Meaning you can set up a field that you want to include in other lists as a *site column*, and make it available to be reused elsewhere on the site. I find it particularly useful for calculated fields.

However, if you are going to use a calculated field as a site column, and it refers to other fields in its calculations, make certain that those fields exist in the new list. Otherwise, logically, the calculation will fail.

It makes sense, and this way you at least *can* share the calculation field's template with other lists, as opposed to making it from scratch every time you needed it. Using and rolling your own site columns are covered later in this chapter.

All fields in a list can be configured to be required to contain data. When a user is adding a new item record to the list, they won't be able to finish it until there is a value in a required field.

Most data fields can also have a default value and/or a calculated default value. The calculated value in that case must be a simple calculation (no field references, just variables, functions, formulas, or simple math). Using a calculation value for a field is nice because the field can have a simple calculation in it (like a default expires date for example), or you can type something in it instead. Calculated fields don't have that option. They are fields meant to do calculations based on the content of other fields or the value of a variable at the time the item record was created. They weren't meant to be available for the users to change.

In addition, all fields have a setting for being added to the default view. If you don't want that field to be added to the current, default view of the list, remove the check from the Add to Default View box when you are creating the field. This is simply a convenience. You can add or remove fields from a view at any time.

Add a Field to a List

Now that you are familiar with all the settings in the Create Column page (via the Settings button on the Action bar), let's add a Category field to the Announcements list. This field should require the person entering the data for a new announcement to choose a category for it.

1. In the Name and Type section (Figure 5.15), enter the name of the field. My example uses **Category**.

FIGURE 5.15

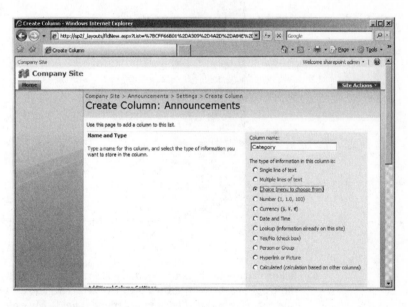

2. From the data types listed, select the type of field Category is going to use. Because this field is supposed to allow users to apply a category to an announcement, my example uses Choice.

   That will change the settings in the Additional Column settings section. In this case, the settings are related to formatting the field for Choice data.

3. The Additional Column Settings section has the ubiquitous Description field. When we add a description to a field, it ends up on the data entry form for the item right below the field. It

can be considered help text, used to assist users in understanding what they are supposed to enter in the field. However, in some cases, if the field's contents are self explanatory, the description can be distracting and take up space. For this example I am not going to enter a description. I can always edit the field's properties and change it later if I need to.

4. There is an option to require information in this field. My example requires the users to choose a category when they create an announcement. As such, this option is going to be Yes.

5. Next is the text box in which we actually type the choices. It seems a bit low tech, but we can replace the placeholder text with our choices. For my example I am going to use **Informational**, **Emergency**, **Celebratory** (see Figure 5.16). Each choice should be entered per line, and you can easily have more than three choices if you wish.

FIGURE 5.16
Adding choices to the Category field

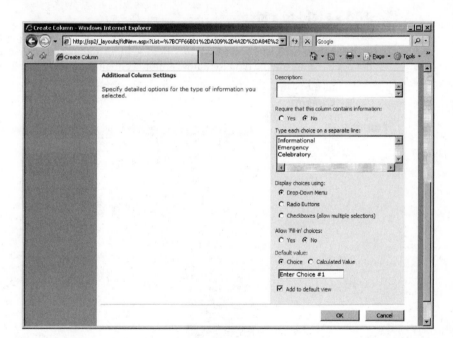

6. Below that are the options that determine how the choices will be displayed: in a group with radio buttons, in a dropdown menu, or with checkboxes so users can choose more than one (the data is stored in the comma-delimited field). My example uses the dropdown menu.

7. You can also decide whether or not you will let users fill in the field with their own value. In this example, the users shouldn't do that because the announcement items will be filtered by a category. So set the Allow Fill-In Choices to No.

8. You can choose to have a default value among the choices or a calculated value. You may notice that the default value is listed as Enter Choice #1. If you leave it that way, just as you press the OK button, the default value will change to the first choice in the list. If you want the default value to be different, simply type it in the default value field yourself. My

example uses the first choice because **Informational** is likely to be a good default. Also at the bottom of the page is the option to add the field to the default view. Leave it checked so that this field is listed in the All Items view for the list. It will be added, by default, as the last field, or the one furthest to the right, in the view.

9. When all settings are finished, click OK to complete the column-creation process.

There should now be a Category field in the List view of the Announcements list. For the previously created items, there will be no data in the category field. All new records will have at least the default value of Informational (or whatever you chose for the default).

Let's add a category value to the new item we created earlier in the chapter:

1. To edit an item simply move the mouse pointer over the item's title, click in the selection box, and select Edit Item from the dropdown menu.

   In the Edit Item page that appears, notice that there is a new field below Expires, called Category. Notice, as well, that the field is blank. Default values for a record item are propagated at the *creation* of a record. Therefore, if the field and its default value were made after the record was made, it will be blank and will not have a default value, as all new items would. As matter of fact, if you open the item (as we have) to edit, and you try to click OK to close the item, you will be prompted to add a value to the field because it can't be saved and closed without a choice selected in the Category field.

2. To choose a value for this announcement, click the down arrow in the Category field (see Figure 5.17). Choose Celebratory (or whatever you'd like) from the dropdown menu.

FIGURE 5.17
The new Category field

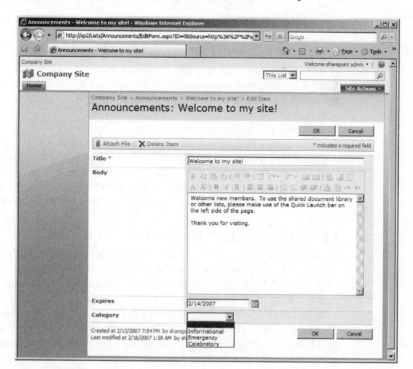

3. Then click OK to finish editing the item. Back on the Announcements list, you can see that Celebratory is listed under Category for the new item (Figure 5.18).

FIGURE 5.18
A new category for Announcements

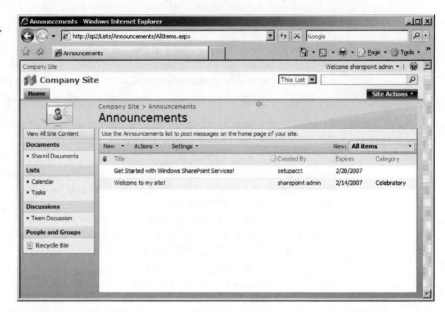

You may notice, when we were editing that new item that the category field was added to the bottom of the item's list of fields. However, it would be better if that field wasn't last on the list. Since it is required, I would like to put it near the top of the data entry page for the item record, so users will be more likely to see it and use it without being forced to because it's required. Because of this, we need to rearrange the fields in the list.

You may remember that we rearranged fields earlier in the All Items list view, but we didn't actually change the order of the underlying fields of the list. We didn't need to. But now that we are considering data entry, what order the fields are in in the underlying list becomes important.

To change the order of a list's fields, we must modify the list itself by using List settings. The List settings page is a significant configuration page. Right now we are just going to mess with the order of list fields. The other settings we'll get to in a later in the chapter.

Change the Order of Fields in a List

To start, we need to go to the List Settings page, so click on the Settings button in the list's Action bar and select List Settings from the menu.

The List Settings page has several sections. The topmost section is the List information, and it also has links to all the important settings pages for this list. The second section is devoted to all column- related activities, such as adding, removing, editing, ordering, and indexing columns. The third section relates to the list's views, focusing on the views that exist (in case you want to edit them), creating new views, or making new views with an existing view as a base, which is convenient.

EXTRA DATA

If you are on a list with content types (covered in Chapter 6, "Introduction to Libraries") enabled, there may be a content types section displayed on the list settings page as well. The Columns section will then be below that. With content types enabled on a list, the list can contain more than one kind of list item. Useful for those lists that might contain both sales quotes and sales orders for example. The two different kinds of list items might contain different fields, fields in a different order, or have different settings enabled.

We are going to focus on the Column section. All of the current fields in this list are in this section. They are displayed in the order they fall when you are creating or editing an item. You can see their data type and whether or not they are required. Also in this section are:

Create column   This field links to the same Create Column page as the Create Column menu item from the Action bar's Settings button. You use it to create a new field for the list.

Add from existing columns   This option lets you choose from the site's existing shared columns. Shared columns are pre-made fields, essentially field templates, that can be added to lists anywhere in the site collection. Fields that you create for lists cannot just be added to this list of site columns, you need to create them from the Site Columns gallery page. If you want a share a clever field you created to be used across the site collection, you have to create it specifically to be shared; not in a list, and then decide to share it. Many columns are already set up to be shared across the site by default. These columns are pulled from the prebuilt lists and List templates of a Team site (or whatever site template you are using).

Column ordering   All of the fields for this list (there are more than you'd think) and their order are displayed on the page for this option.

Indexed columns   *List indexing* is new to this version of SharePoint, and it is a pretty big concept. If you have a list that will become very, very large, you might consider indexing. When you have a huge list, SharePoint can take forever to show all the items in an All Items list view. Microsoft suggests either limiting the views by a hard limit (like only showing 100 records at a time) or filtering the view by a particular field, so the user only sees a subset of all items. However, if a list is so large that even filtering is difficult because sorting through all of those records takes a long time, then you index a field. One suggestion is to find a field in the list that you would like to filter items in the list by (in this case, you could filter the view of the Announcements to only show items with the Category of Emergency) and index that field. This works because indexing causes SharePoint to keep an analysis of that field on its mind (so to speak) for that list at all times, making it faster to index the whole, gigantic list by it.

If you are certain that the Announcements list is going to quickly become huge (thousands of item records), you could index the Category field. Then you could create a view of the list that filters by category. This would allow SharePoint to pull up and organize the item records more efficiently because it has already analyzed that column's data. The catch is that it would take up RAM and processor resources to always keep that column analyzed (and it would stress the database engine itself a little). The more indexed columns, the more resources it takes to index that list. Therefore, you should index only one or two fields per huge list, because too many indexed columns on a huge list diminishes the value of even bothering to index. This is because the resources required to index more than one or two field in a list would actually slow the list down.

Along those lines, only index lists that you really need to index. Indexing takes up server resources. If you aren't having any speed issues working with a list, chances are it isn't too big, so don't index it. Microsoft suggests that a view have no more than 1,000 to 2,000 items in it per list. Keep that in mind, and filter views to at least that number to avoid having a list drag to a halt when someone tries to go to its content page.

So now that you know a little about managing list columns, let's change our column order.

TIPS FOR MANAGING HUGE LISTS

If you are going to have humungous lists of data, you might want some advice. Some of this information may be beyond what we have done so far, but just keep it in mind as you progress through the book. It could be useful.

◆ Limiting the number of items that can be displayed in a view (like limiting it to 100 at a time) does not really help the performance of a list, as far as parsing all the items, as much as indexing does, neither does limiting the number of fields in a view. It's the number of item records that matters, not the fields in the records themselves. It does help in terms of waiting for all items to render in the browser though, so it is limiting items in a view is better than nothing.

◆ Views do have some sorting, filtering, and grouping options that can be a little complex. Filtering a list with an OR parameter negates the usefulness of an indexed column because SharePoint has to deeply analyze and do comparisons with some other field in the list as well as the indexed one.

◆ Like a library, a list can be organized by folders, with list items stored in those folders. This organization can help break up the view of items, and it can help manage large lists. Then you can create views for each folder, further filtering the data (remember to index the field on which the filter is based). Folders with a thousand or more item records basically will negate any performance improvements though, so be careful. Basically, a thousand is the magic number, give or take. Try to avoid it if you can.

◆ When filtering a view, make sure the primary, first column being filtered is the indexed one. You can filter, sort, and group by a lot of columns in a view, but make sure that the main focus of the filter is the indexed column and that the filter significantly reduces the items viewed.

◆ A list can have more than one indexed field, but it is not recommended. Take for instance, if you had two different, popular ways to view a list, each focusing on filtering by a certain field, then you could index those focus fields for the sake of the two different views, as long as they both reduce the number of items to around a thousand or less (preferably far less).

To change the order of the List's fields:

1. Click the Column Ordering link in the Columns section. The Change Field Order page that appears has only one section. It simply displays the fields for the list. The Category field we created is at the end of the list, logically, because it was the last one made.

2. In my example, the Category should go between the Title of the announcement and the Body of the announcement. To do this, click the down arrow in the Position from the Top dropdown box for the Category field and change the number to 2. This will instantly change the order of the fields, placing Category in the second position (see Figure 5.19).

FIGURE 5.19
Changed field order of Category

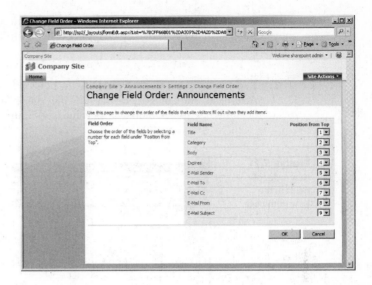

3. To finish, click OK.

This will take you back to the List settings page. In Figure 5.20, you can see that the Category field is the second field in the list. However, the point is to see how it changes the order of data entry for the item, so in the breadcrumb at the top of the page, click Announcements to get back to the Announcements List content page.

FIGURE 5.20
The List Settings page with newly positioned fields

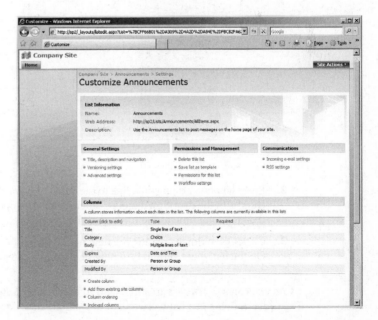

The fields are not in a different order on the Announcements list page. This is because we didn't move Category in the view, we moved it in the list itself. To prove this, create a new item and add some data:

1. To create an item (and therefore see the new order of the fields), click the New button in the Action bar. The Category field is now the second field on the page, and that the category has defaulted to Informational as its value (see Figure 5.21).

FIGURE 5.21
New order of fields in the New Item page

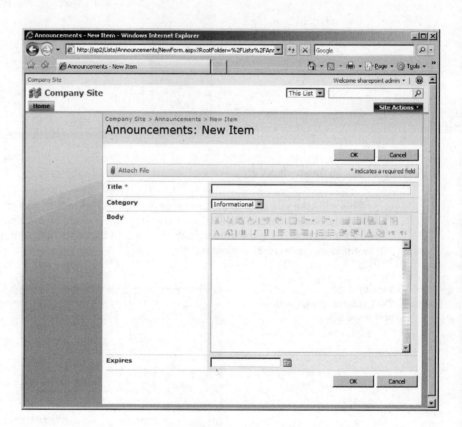

2. Enter whatever data you'd like to the Title field. For the Category, select Emergency from the choices in the dropdown menu. Enter data in the Body field and feel free to enter an Expires date for sometime in the future (see Figure 5.22).

3. Click OK to finish creating the new item. This will take you back to the Announcements list. On the list, there should be a new item and its category.

As you can see, it's easy to add a field to a list and change the order of the fields for data entry. The order of fields in a list were meant to facilitate data entry.

FIGURE 5.22
The new emergency
announcement

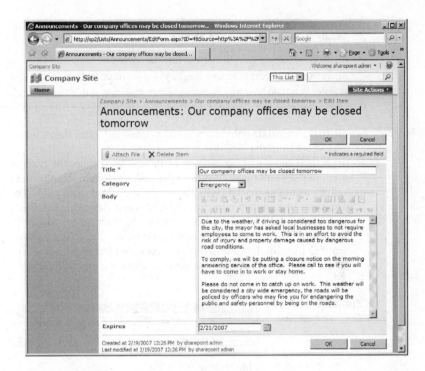

However, what if you have to do bulk data entry, such as entering several announcements at one time? With the New button method, you'd have to enter each item individually. If you want to populate a list quickly, you need to use datasheet view.

Enter Data via Datasheet View

The datasheet view of a list uses an Office feature to make a small spreadsheet out of the List view so you can enter data more quickly. This means you'll need to have at least one Office product (Word, PowerPoint, Excel, etc., preferably Office 2007) installed on the computer you are using to access SharePoint to be able to work with a list in Datasheet view. If you try to edit a list in Datasheet view, you will get a dialog box warning you that the list cannot be displayed (Figure 5.23).

FIGURE 5.23
Datasheet warning
dialog

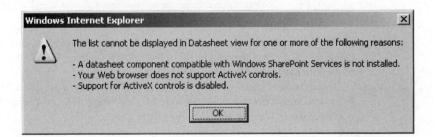

WEB "ACCESS"-IBLE DATA SHEET

If you have Access 2007 installed, the List view will turn into an Access Web datasheet. (This makes sense in a way, because Access is a database product; it should work with SharePoint to manage data.) If you don't, but do have an Office product installed, you'll get a simple, Excel-like datasheet.

To do bulk data entry for a list in a datasheet, click the Actions button and select Edit In Datasheet from the dropdown menu.

As you can see in Figure 5.24, Datasheet view takes the current view you are using on the content page and makes it into a spreadsheet of data. That the fields in the current view are what will be available for data entry is a very important distinction. The datasheet depends on the view you were using when you chose to edit. Most views don't bother to display every single field a list item can contain, which makes it difficult to enter data in all of the fields of a list in Datasheet view. Because of this, people sometimes create views that actually show all relevant fields that you might want to fill with data simply to be used when Datasheet view is employed. In my example, the All Items view doesn't display the Body field, so we can't fill in the Body field in the Datasheet view.

FIGURE 5.24
The Datasheet view

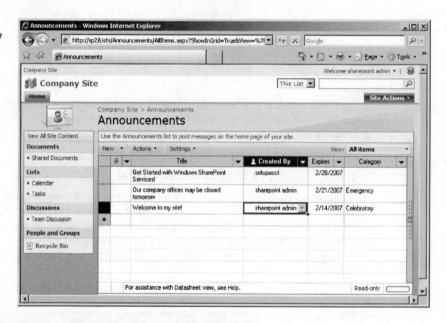

For demonstration purposes, let's populate several fields of Announcement titles and categories with the intention to fill in the Body field later. This will give us enough data in the list to explore more complex views later in the chapter.

The datasheet itself has standard rows and columns, a border across the top containing the field headings, a border along the side for selecting rows, indicating a new row, and the top-right corner of the border for selecting the entire sheet.

CUSTOM FILTERING

All of the field headings have a down arrow next to them. This is a standard spreadsheet feature that allows you to filter and sort a field from that dropdown. You can also use it to perform custom filtering. Just click the down arrow of the column you'd like to filter, and select Custom Filter. That will bring up the Custom Filter dialog box in which you can do three levels of complex filtering of that field's data in the list.

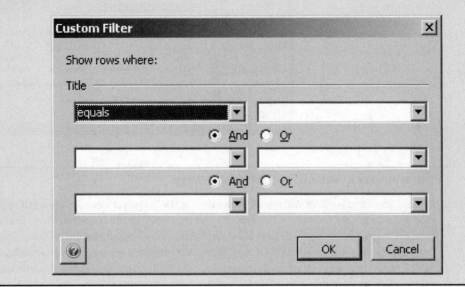

When a list is in Datasheet view, it acts like any spreadsheet. You can add and delete rows and columns, fill columns, cut and paste, etc. In addition, fields that contain multiple-choice data simply drop down for you to choose from the list just as you did in the New Item window. As a matter of fact, because the Choice field has a default value, informational, it will autofill with that value if you skip over it to go to the next row.

To add a new item record, simply go to the last row of the datasheet and start typing in the fields. You'll find that you can type in the Title field but not in the Created By field. Why not? Well, Created By is basically a field that gets filled based on your login information. It wasn't meant to be editable. Fields that are calculations or otherwise are system fields populated by data SharePoint generates (Created By, Modified By, Creation Date, to name a few) will show up as Read Only in the datasheet when you try to enter data into them (see Figure 5.24).

After you've filled the Title, Expires and Category fields (see Figure 5.25 for an example), simply move to the next row to fill in a new list item record. It's that simple. Adding items in bulk is pretty easy. Remember, you can cut and paste data from Excel or Access to the datasheet as well. Of course, because the datasheet is based on the All Items view, we cannot access the Body field from here, but you get the point. Data entry using the Datasheet view is definitely more convenient than clicking the New button when you need to enter a lot of data.

FIGURE 5.25
Bulk data entry in a datasheet

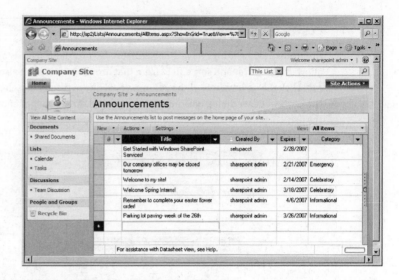

THE MULTIPLE LINE FIELD AND DATASHEET VIEW

Assume, for example, you want to do all your data entry in Datasheet view. Sooner or later you are going to add the Body field (or some other multiple-line text field) to the Datasheet view. That might be a problem. When you add the Body field to a view so you can see it in Datasheet view, it may be set to Read Only, especially if you are using Office 2007. Office 2007 products are sensitive about multiple-line text fields and how they are handled. So if you are using one of Office 2007 products and are having a problem entering data into a multiple-line field in Datasheet view, this sidebar is for you.

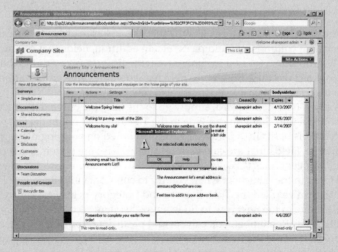

The interesting thing about multiple-line text fields and Datasheet view is that a datasheet creates completely blank records when you start on a row. When a multiple-line text field is not set to allow

Append (which lets the field be edited and added to once it has been saved), the field in Datasheet view is locked as Read Only.

To make it possible to append a Body field in Datasheet view, you must allow Append changes to existing text in the multiple-line text field's settings. To make matters more complicated, you must enable versioning on the list.

Versioning is list wide and causes the list to keep a copy of every change of every list item, which increases the complexity and size of the list. Consider the ramifications of this just to be able to do bulk data entry for a multiple line text field—do the costs outweigh the benefits? However, if this is your preferred method of data entry, or the list is going to have versioning set on it anyway, go ahead.

To change the settings of a multiple line list:

1. Go to Settings on the Action bar and select List Settings.

2. To enable versioning on the list to be able to append data to the multiple-line text field, select Versioning Settings in the General Settings category on the Customize page.

3. In the List Versioning Settings page, select Yes in the Item Version History section of the page, and click OK. (The additional settings aren't that relevant because you are enabling versioning only so that you can type in a field.) That will bring you back to the Edit List Settings page. Now you can set multiple lines of text fields to be editable in Datasheet view.

4. Select the multiple-line column you'd like to edit in the Columns section.

5. On the column's Settings page, select Append Changes To Text (it is the last setting on the page) and click OK.

That should make it possible to perform data entry, even in the Body field, in Datasheet view. If the multiple-line text field is still Read Only after enabling versioning and append, check your text type for that field. If it is enhanced, drop it to rich text, that may enable editing in the datasheet at last.

While using Datasheet view, you can do a few new things. The Actions menu changes to offer you new options:

Show in Standard View   Returns the Datasheet view of the list back to Standard view.

New Row   Inserts a new row at the bottom of the datasheet.

Task Pane   Opens a task pane on the right side of the datasheet for integration tasks with Excel or Access (even if you don't have them installed).

Totals   Adds a Totals row to the bottom of the datasheet, making it possible to go to the bottom of a column and choose to calculate the data there. The Totals possible for each column depends on that column's contents and data type.

Refresh Data   If anyone working on the list has cut and pasted a lot of data, has calculated fields that are not quickly updating, or has this data linked with data in Excel or Access, refreshing the data will reload the list data and pick up those changes.

If you click on the bar on the right side of the Datasheet view (interestingly, it has a textured area as if you need to grip it better with your mouse), the Task pane of the Office integration tasks for this datasheet will open. See Figure 5.26 for an example.

FIGURE 5.26
The Datasheet Task pane

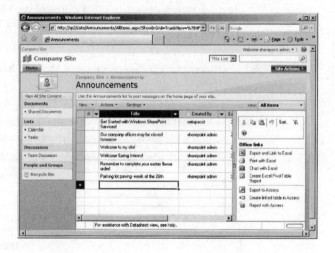

To close the Task pane, you can either select Task Pane in the Actions menu or click the grippy bar on the right side of the datasheet again.

The Total row in Datasheet view is really convenient should you need to sum, average, or count items in a list by column. First, add the Total row by selecting Totals in the Actions Menu dropdown. Then click in the field in that row that corresponds with the column you'd like to total. A dropdown arrow will appear in the selected field, allowing you to choose from the calculations available there. For example, if you want to see the latest expiration date for the Announcements list, enable the Totals row, then click in the field for the Expires column, and select Maximum. This may generate a set of number symbols (####,) but that only means the column is not large enough to display the total. If you increase the width of the column (move your mouse over the right edge of the column header until the pointer turns into a double-headed arrow and then drag the column until it is a few characters wider than it was), the correct maximum date will appear (Figure 5.27).

FIGURE 5.27
The Maximum Date in the
Total row

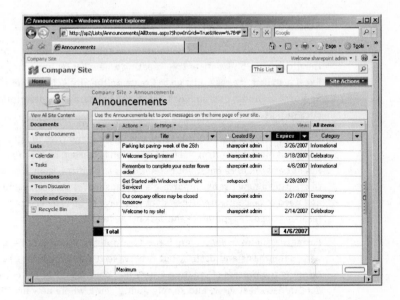

If you were to go back to Standard view (Actions ➤ Show In Standard View) with that total field enabled, the total would be displayed at the top of the list.

If you find a list with a total that is hugging the top, as in Figure 5.28, and don't want it there, simply change the view to Datasheet (Actions ➤ Edit In Datasheet), then go to the Actions menu, select Totals to remove the Totals row which will remove the field calculation as well. When you go back to Standard view, the total won't be at the top of your list. (If you like there, don't remove it.) Getting a quick summary of a column of data in a list using datasheet view is one of those conveniences that not everyone knows how to do.

FIGURE 5.28
The Total displayed in
Standard view

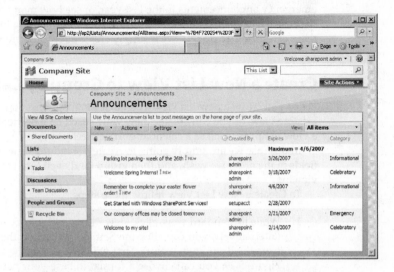

That should give you an idea of the possibilities of bulk data entry using Datasheet view. Let's return to Standard view and customize some views to filter the new data we've entered.

SUPER BULK DATA ENTRY

If you already have a lot of data in an Excel spreadsheet and no existing list to put it in, then consider the ultimate in bulk data entry—creating a new list by importing a spreadsheet. As long as you have Excel installed, it's easy. Just go to Create on the Site Actions menu. On the Create page, select Import Spreadsheet under Custom Lists. Fill in the list name and description, browse to the spreadsheet, and click Import.

What that does is start a wizard that opens Excel and tries to figure out what fields in the spreadsheet will be in the list. Confirm the field selection is correct, or specify the field range and click Import. You might be asked to re-enter your credentials to confirm, then SharePoint will create the list. The catch to creating a new list by importing a spreadsheet is that sometimes the field formats are not perfect and need to be configured (then data will have to be copy and pasted back in for that column because resetting the data type wipes the data in the field).

Formatting fields in SharePoint is pretty simplistic. Phone numbers, for example, can't be set to display with parenthesis and dashes, but otherwise it can save a lot of time importing all of that data by skipping the process of creating a new list, creating all of the correct fields, cutting and pasting the data in datasheet view, and simply giving you a whole new list filled with the data you need to get started.

For more about creating new list, check out the Create a Custom List section of this chapter.

To return to Standard view, simply go to the Actions menu, and select Show in Standard View.

Back in standard view we now have considerably more data with which to work. When a list begins to fill up with data, it is natural to want to filter the data to be able to more easily focus on the items you want to work with. For example, you may want to see if there is a pattern of emergency announcements in the last year, or see how many celebrations there have been. Because the list items can be categorized, it's a natural thing to want to filter or organize the list by these categories. To do this, we'll simply create a few new views.

Create a New List View to Group by Category

When you create a new list view you have some options. You can create a view based on an existing view, or you can create a new view based on a particular view format, which is essentially a view template, such as a calendar or datasheet.

In this case we are simply going to create a standard view (such as the All Items view), add the fields in the order we wish, and then group (and even total) the information by category for easy viewing.

To Create a New List View follow these steps:

1. While in Standard view, click View menu, and select Create View from the dropdown menu (alternatively, you can click the Settings button on the Action bar, and select Create View from the dropdown menu). That will take you to the Create View page. As you can see in Figure 5.29, you can choose a format to base your new view on, or you can start from an existing view.

FIGURE 5.29

The Create View page

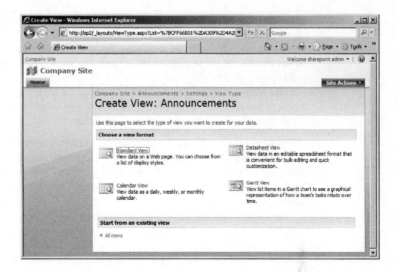

The view formats are as follows:

Standard View   This is your standard report format, with the option to organize the data by groups, total, filter, etc.

Datasheet View   If you find yourself in Datasheet view more often than not, you might want to consider creating a Datasheet view in which to work. This view is also good if you are going to be doing regular bulk data entry, because you can create the view with all of the fields you plan to use.

Calendar View   This view uses any date field a list item might have to display that item on a particular date, such as a deadline. (This works great for birthdays and anniversaries as well.) The Calendar view can be displayed in week, month, or day format.

Gantt View   New to this version of SharePoint, *Gantt view* is exactly like a Calendar view, but on its side. Like a calendar, this view focuses on dates. This view requires that there be two date fields to create a range of time, such as a start and end date, or the period of time a project or event is schedule to last. As long as you have two date fields of some sort, and one always precedes the other (like a creation date and a modified date), a Gantt view might be for you.

2. We are going to use a Standard view to group our data, so select Standard View from the group of view formats. The Create View page that appears is very similar to the Edit View page for a standard view. There is a Name section, Audience section, Columns, etc. Here's a rundown of what to expect, by section.

Name   This section allows you to name the view. Keep in mind that a view name will be used in the Web address for that page, so try to keep the name to a single word, and keep that as short as possible. Remember that when you create a view or site and use two words or more in its name, the spaces are represented by %20 in the Web address. This means that "The Technical Resource Filter View" will end up with a page address of `The%20Technical%20Resource%20Filter%20View`. Given that SharePoint only allows 255 characters in a Web address you will need to keep your names descriptive but short, minimizing spaces. This is another reason why, once you've gotten the hang of SharePoint, planning the names of List views can be important for some large SharePoint deployments. Keep in mind that you can edit the page address by editing the view. There is a field there to change the page as it will appear in the URL.

The Name section also contains a setting for making the view the default view. The default view is the one that will be the one that opens when a user opens the list, such as from a List View web part, or from the Quick Launch bar.

Audience   Like web part pages, lists can have views that are specifically meant to be shared and views meant to be personal. This section lets you decide whether or not this view is going to be public or personal. As with viewing a Web Parts page, you can create a view of a list (and so can users who have the correct permissions) that only you can see (Personal) or that everyone can see (Public).

Personal views are good for creating complex or obscure views that relate only to what you are doing with a list or library, and they help you avoid having a huge list of views from which a user must choose. When you create a view, you can set it to Public so that every user who accesses the list can use that view; or you can set it to Personal so that only you can use it. One of the Public views must be a default so that when a visitor drops by, they see the default until they choose another view.

Columns   In this section, you choose the existing list fields that will appear in the view, and you determine the order in which they are placed. Remember, a list can have many fields, and you can choose not to display all of them in your view. A computer screen can display only so many fields across; as such, determining which fields to display and which to not display is an art in itself. Usually, the more important a field is, the farther to the left side it is displayed.

IF YOU CAN'T SEE IT, YOU CAN'T FILTER BY IT

Keep in mind that if you are creating or modifying a View and you'd like to filter, group, sort, or total by a particular field, it has to be displayed in the view. You cannot modify the data a view uses by a field that isn't actually going to appear in the final display.

Sort   This section lets you specify the sort order of the items in the view. Unfortunately, in SharePoint you can only sort by two fields. So if you wanted to sort by more, you're out of luck. (This has been a disappointment for me a time or two.)

Filter   Filtering lets you display only the list items with data that matches a particular criteria. If you have very large lists, it's important that you limit the number of visible records, as it takes considerable server power to display large lists to clients (which means it can take a long time for a list page to generate as the system chugs through trying to parse the view). To this end, most people create Filtered views that significantly limit the number of records displayed at one time. Seriously consider this option when designing lists you expect to hold 1,000 records or more. Another nice thing about filtering is you can filter by more than two columns of criteria. You can simply keep adding more columns to filter by until you're done. The criteria for filtering is standard but useful, including greater than, less than, equal to, not equal to, contains, and begins with. And can be combined with additional fields with the logic of And or Or to link them.

CREATE DEFAULT PUBLIC VIEWS

Keep in mind that if you have a list that contains thousands, or even tens of thousands of items, it's best to create default Public views that limit the number of items displayed automatically. Doing so will help the list come up more quickly for users navigating to that list. Alternatively, you can create a Private view for each user and teach them how to filter with it to better manage and manipulate the data in the lists for themselves.

Group By Organizes the items displayed in the view by groups. Like Sort, Group By has a two-column limit. The criteria by which to group are standard. Choose the first column to group by and determine the sort order, and then choose the second column and its sort order. A nice thing about grouping is you can choose whether the groups are collapsed or expanded by default. (If a group is collapsed, a plus sign will appear next to the heading for the group. When you click it, the items in that group will be exposed.) For those huge lists, the number of groups to be displayed per page can be limited. The default is 100.

Totals This is very much like the Total row in Datasheet view. You select what fields you'd like to calculate totals from those selected to display in the view. The data type for those columns will define what calculations can be done for the field. Totals for those columns will be displayed, oddly enough, at the top of the list, not the bottom. Be prepared for that.

Style Pertains to the limited offerings of formatting for the view. You can use Basic, Boxed, Newsletter, Shaded, Preview Pane, or Default.

PREVIEW PANE AS A STYLE?

Preview Pane is an odd style and cannot be used with Grouped By, because it basically lists the title for the items on the left and leaves the majority of the content area in the middle of the page available to display the contents of a list item. Then, if you hover your mouse over a list item title, the contents of that item will be displayed. It will display only the fields that are meant to be visible in the view, but it is pretty dramatic. It's an interesting way to display items in a discussion list, but otherwise I haven't been able to find a good reason to use it.

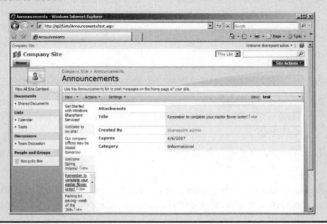

Folders   If folders are used to organize items in a list, you can choose to have this view be folder aware and only display the items in the open folder (and if you want to see items in a different folder, you will have to go to it to apply this view to them). Otherwise, you can set the view to be *flat* or folder unaware, and therefore, if the view is applied, it will display all items in the list that comply with its criteria, regardless of what folder they might be in. If list items are organized by folder in order to manage a large list, consider ensuring that the view is set to be folder aware, or show items inside folders, in order to continue to limit the number of items displayed in the view at one time.

Item Limit   This section allows you to specify how many items can be displayed per page for this view, or even a cut-off limit for all items to be displayed in this view, period. The default is 100 items per page, with no cut-off limit.

Mobile   If you'd like the view to be available for mobile devices, you can enable it in this section. Make note of the long and possibly complicated Web address for that view.

SPEAKING OF MOBILE

If your mobile device uses DNS and can access the network the SharePoint server is on, it can easily access a pared down version of the SharePoint web pages. See Chapter 15, "Advanced Installation and Configuration" to see it in action.

Now let's group our view by category and list the latest expiration date (using the Totals field in Datasheet view).

3. Name the List view. My example uses **GbCategory**. Remember to keep the name short but memorable; my example uses a view naming scheme. All grouped by views are prefaced with a Gb, and filtered lists start with an F, and so on, with the field that is the focus being the largest part of the name. The most important part of the naming process is to keep it short, so use the scheme that works for you.

4. Also in the Name section is the option to make the view the default view for the list (instead of All Items). This isn't necessary in this example, but might be a great idea if you are trying to cut down on the number of items automatically populating the content page of a list every time a user goes to that list. However, we are not going to make this list the default at this time.

5. For the audience, we are going to keep this a public view.

6. For the columns, we are going to keep the ones already selected based on the All Items view. They work for us at the moment. Remember you can always modify a view later if you want to change it.

7. We are not going to sort or filter our view data, but we are going to use Group By. Click the plus sign in the Group By section to expand it.

8. In the Group By section, in the First Group By The Column dropdown list, select Category in this example. By default, groups are sorted in ascending order. That's fine, so leave the default.

9. Click the plus sign in the Totals section to expand it, and click the down arrow in the Total field next to Expires. Select Maximum from the calculations there (Figure 5.30).

FIGURE 5.30
The Group By and Totals sections

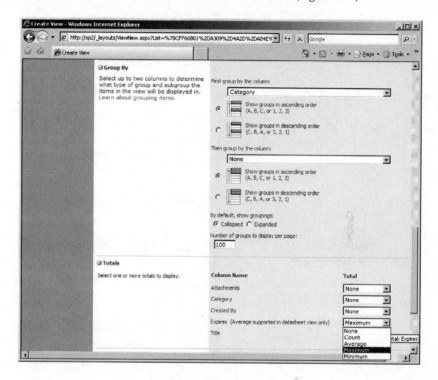

10. Expand the Style section and choose Shaded. This will shade the background of every other group to help them stand out a little.

There is no need to enforce an item limit on the list, because it's simply not that big. The list itself isn't organized by folder, and my example does not use any mobile devices to access the list. That means that, after choosing the style for this view, we're done.

11. Click OK to create the new List view.

In Figure 5.31, you can see that the GbCategory view displays the categories collapsed, with the calculation (which is the maximum expires date) at the top right of the list, in the Expires column. Also notice, in the Address bar, that the filename for the view is GbCategory.aspx.

As for the categories, you might have noticed that there is a blank category (of which there is only one item). To see what list item might be grouped by that category, click the plus sign next to the category heading to expand it.

In my example, the Get Started with Windows SharePoint Services! announcement that was generated as soon as the site was built, was created before the Category field was added. Because of this, that list item has no category assigned (see Figure 5.32). This example is a good one if you ever need to search through a list of items to see if there is any data missing in a field. Group by that field (sorting ascending), and the blanks will come out on top. Then you can edit them, adding the necessary data, until there are no more blanks.

FIGURE 5.31

The new GbCategory view

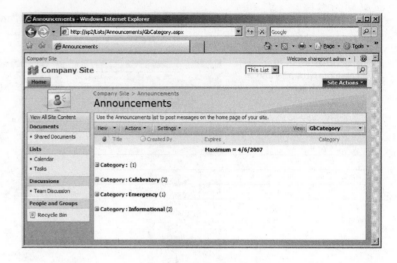

FIGURE 5.32

The expanded group

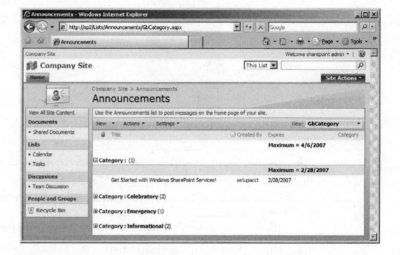

Another useful thing about this view, as you can see in Figure 5.32, is that a calculation is listed for each grouping as well. In my example, only the latest expiration dates for each category appear, but this can be useful for doing total profit or averages; in this case we can scroll to the Emergency announcements, expand that group, and see the most recent expires data and the announcements that are still active.

Now that you've seen how easy it is to create a new standard view and exploit some of the reporting power of that format, let's create another standard view. Only this time, it is going to filter out all list items that don't match our criteria.

When you're in a list you can search for a particular item. You can click on the header of a column and try to sort items. However, the fastest way to isolate several items that have data in common is to use filtering. Remember, you can filter by as many columns as you'd like until you get your desired results. What's even better is that you can create a View to be used to filter a list's content display, and simply modify it over and over as you need. Making it less of a static view and more of an ad hoc one. Not only that, but filtering is one of the best practice methods to open and use very large lists.

Create a New View to Filter by Category

Let's create a new Standard view to use as our filtering tool for the list.

1. Click on the View menu, and select Create View.

2. Then select Standard View on the Create View page.

3. On the Create View: Announcements page, name your view something short but memorable. My example uses **MainFilter**, and it is not the default view.

4. We could make this view private, but select the Public view option so other users can take advantage of it if they know how.

5. In the Columns section, leave the default columns selected. We can change this at any time by just modifying this view later.

6. Scroll down to the Filter section, where we are going to do our work. You can see that the setting selected for this view is currently Show All Items In This View. To apply the filter settings we are going to configure, we must select Show Items Only When The Following Is True setting.

7. Beneath that in the Filter section, are the Show the items when column, Criteria, and Data fields. In this example, we are going to filter by the Category column, so select that in the first field.

8. The second field in the section is the Criteria field. If we click on it, a list of possible criteria to filter the field by drops down (see Figure 5.33 for an example). In this case, we want to choose Contains because we want to filter the Category field by its contents. For the Data or Argument field that the criteria are going to work against, type **info**. Informational is one of the Announcement categories and using part of the word demonstrates that SharePoint doesn't require an exact match for this criteria.

FIGURE 5.33

The Filter criteria for a new view

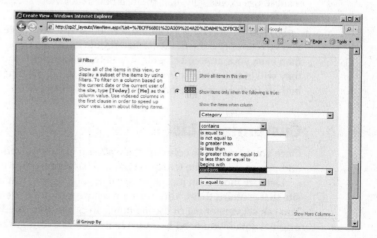

9. We could continue with other criteria and arguments by clicking the And or Or radio buttons, which would indicate that you want to combine the filtering criteria of more than one set, and you could always add more. However, filtering by one argument in the Category field works in this case.

10. Click OK to create and apply the new view.

The view in my example isolated the two informational items that were created earlier in the chapter, and displays them exclusively in Figure 5.34. To turn off the view and see all items in the list, simply click on the View menu and select the All Items view.

FIGURE 5.34
New MainFilter view

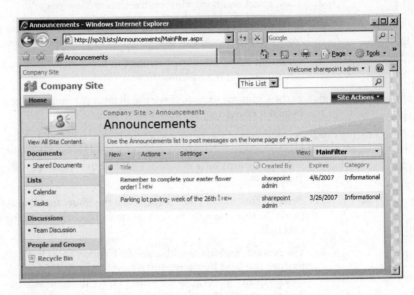

Keep your filter view in mind, and when you need to filter the list, just go to the view, and modify it to match whatever criteria you have in mind. If you keep using a Filter view that you want to use exclusively, just create a new Filter view specifically for it. Even consider setting its audience to private, so no one else can see it or change it.

So, you've worked with announcements. You now have the List views the way you like them, you've rearranged the fields for better data entry, and you've added a category field. Now, more than ever, your announcements are useful. People will read them with renewed interest (or at least they will in this scenario, your mileage may vary). It's time to customize the list further, increasing both its usefulness, and the control you can have over it.

Customize a List

Once you have a list's columns the way you like them, and you've created your views (both public and personal), it's time to expose the real backbone of the lists, their settings.

Lists are more than just columns, data, and views. You can secure them independently of the site that contains them; you can even secure individual items differently than those around them. You can set versioning of the list items, in case someone edits data incorrectly (you won't lose the original data if you need to return to it). You can configure item management rights, set content approval, and allow incoming mail. Lists, particularly for this version of SharePoint, can be more complicated than you think.

One setting that greatly enhances the convenience of a list is Incoming Email. When this setting is enabled, users can simply email in any announcement they need to make. New to this version of SharePoint, certain lists and libraries are email enabled in order to make it easier for users to add items to a list without having to open a browser or leave their email client.

To enable incoming email for a list, as well as other configuration settings, you have to go to the list's List Settings.

Before we set a few things, like incoming email or content approval, let's take a look at the Settings portion of the Lists Settings page. Sure, we've been to the List Settings before, but only to mess with columns and views—now it's time to look into the links at the top of the settings page.

To reach the List Settings, click Settings in the Action bar of the list (the one we're working on is Announcements), and select List Settings from the dropdown menu.

IT HELPS TO BE ALLOWED TO MANAGE THE LIST

It should go without saying that you need to be logged in as site administrator (like I am with *shareadmin*) or someone with the right to manage the list to configure list settings. But just in case you've forgotten, I thought I'd mention it.

In the List Information section at the top of the List Settings page for the Announcements list (called Customize Announcements), you'll see that the Name, Web Address, and Description for the list is displayed. In Figure 5.35, note the address. The list is part of the path, but the page itself is actually the AllItems.aspx page. This is because that is the default view for this list.

FIGURE 5.35
Customize Announcements page

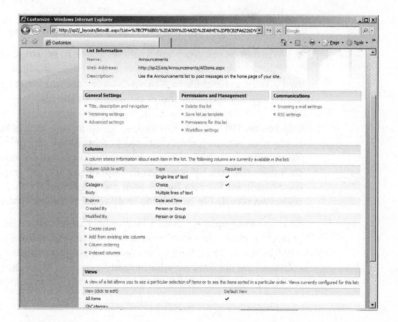

Beneath the list information are the categories of list settings starting with General Settings on the left, then Permissions and Management, and finally Communications on the right. Often the configuration page beneath these settings is not that complicated; they simply give you a chance to either enable or disable a particular feature, such as RSS feeds or incoming email.

Under the General Settings are the following items:

Title, description, and navigation   This configuration page contains three fields: one for the name of the list so you can change (it will not, however, change the name in the path of the Web address), the description (to be edited as well), and the option to change whether or not this list is displayed in the Quick Launch bar.

Versioning settings   This page has three sections: Content Approval, Item Version History, and Draft Item Security. With Content Approval you can require approval for new and changed items before they are published as content. With Item Version History you can keep a copy of a list item every time it is modified. With Draft Item Security, if you allow major and minor (draft) versions, you can limit who can see the draft versions until they are published as a major version. Versioning, especially as it works with content approval will be covered in more detail in Chapter 6, "Introduction to Libraries."

Advanced settings   This is the most complex and least-intuitive configuration catch-all page. These settings include sections for:

◆ Enabling content types (more on those in Chapter 6, "Introduction to Libraries") for this list.

◆ Item-level permissions (if items can be read or edited by everyone, read or edited only by the author, or, if no one can edit an item once it has been created).

◆ Allowing attachments for each list item (useful if you want to add a resumé or other file to a list entry).

◆ Whether or not you want to enable folder organization for the list.

◆ Whether or not you want to allow Search to return results for this list.

In the Permissions and Management category are links that either do something to the list or configure explicit accounts and permissions for the list:

Delete this list   Click this link to go to a page that gives you the option to delete this list. Remember, lists are SharePoint objects; therefore, if you delete them, they will go to the SharePoint Recycle Bin for a while before actually being removed. If you want a list permanently deleted, so it does not take up space on the site or the server's hard drive, you have to remove it from the SharePoint Recycle Bin as well (and don't forget to remove it from the second stage, site collection recycle bin in order to truly reclaim the list's storage space).

Save list as template   Basically, any list can be made into a template for later use. Making the perfect list can be time-consuming, and when you're done, you might want to back it up to use on a different site. By making a template of a list, you can ensure the design (or even the design and contents) are not only saved, but easily available to be used anywhere else in the site collection. List templates are saved to the List Template Gallery on the top-level site. Templates are saved as .stp files and can be used to back up lists against catastrophe (see Chapter 12, "Maintenance and Monitoring").

Permissions for this list   Most lists inherit their permissions from their parent site, so this link goes to a page listing the users and groups that have access to the site. It's here that you can actually break inheritance and set up unique permissions for a list. Permissions are complex and warrant their own chapter (refer to Chapter 11, "Users and Permissions"), but suffice it to say you can specify what groups, even what permission levels are specifically allowed for this list from those available for the site collection. It's also here that, if you choose to work with unique permissions, you can decide whether a user can make an access request if they were refused access to something on the list.

Workflow settings   This is an interesting configuration page. Out of the box, Windows Share-Point Services 3.0 has only one sample workflow (but you can make many more using SharePoint Designer). The sample workflow that comes with Windows SharePoint Services 3.0 was actually designed to work only with a type of list called "Issue Tracking." It was meant to generate a Tasks list item when a new Issue is created and a second task to review the first one.

Workflows are first added to a site like task-oriented templates that lay out a process in which a change of state in a list or a library item can trigger an email, alert, or new list item. A workflow is a flow of actions that continue the human process of working with documents, tasks, or data. A workflow template can be made available to lists on a site, and then you can apply them as an instance with a unique name and settings to a particular list (or library).

BAD FIT, BUT STILL POSSIBLE

Ironically, the sample Three-State workflow does work for our Announcements list to a degree, because the workflow only requires a trigger field, which in this case needs to be a Choice field with three choices in it. Therefore, this list qualifies for the sample workflow.

However, the Three-State workflow was meant to create a Tasks list item (in a specified Tasks list on the site) when triggered by the selection of an item in a Choice field (such as New, Started, Completed). Then it should email the person to whom the task is assigned to let them know they have a new task, then create another task if the Choice field state changes again. We have no reason to add a list item to a Tasks list for an announcement, but the option was there if we needed it. Later in this chapter, we will create a list that's better suited to demonstrating the sample workflow.

Workflows for lists are managed by the SharePoint Timer Service and, therefore, do consume server resources to run. Keep that in mind when you are deciding to apply a workflow to a list.

Finally, in the Communications category are the following items:

Incoming e-mail settings   This link takes you to the page where you can enable incoming email for this list (if incoming email is enabled in Central Administration first). Not all List templates can support this feature. Incoming Email means that you can send email to this list and have this list parse the email's fields and apply them to existing fields in the list itself. The Announcements list has fields that easily map to email fields: Body, Subject, Created By, and Announcements. Not surprisingly, an entry can be emailed to the Announcements list rather than the users having to open their browser, go to the site, authenticate, go to the list, and click New to create a new item. With Incoming Email enabled, users just need to know the email address of the list. Then they can email an announcement to the list, and it will be correctly managed and made into a list item.

Incoming Email settings include enabling the incoming email, specifying the email address (actually, the incoming email domain portion of the address is configured in Central Administration for the entire farm, so the specific alias for the list is set here), whether to allow attachments, save the original email, or save email invitations to the list (should the list be invited to something, usually only done intentionally for discussion lists or announcements). You can also set whether or not the list applies its permissions to the received email items, meaning the list can accept all email as a new item from anyone or accept it only from those allowed to contribute to the list. This helps avoid spam.

RSS settings   RSS feeds for lists are new with this version of SharePoint. All lists have an option to subscribe to an RSS feed by selecting View RSS Feed in the Actions dropdown menu. RSS feeds can be enabled or disabled at the Central Administration level for each web application. Then RSS can be further controlled at the site-collection level, site level, and even by list. RSS tends to be enabled by default and, at the list level, displays all of the contents of an entry unless you set it to truncate the multi-line text field (in this case that would be the Body field) to 256 characters. No more, no less. You can modify the title and description for the RSS feed for the list, or you can leave the default list name and description there. You can even change the image that shows by default if you'd like. Although if you do change the image, make it easy on yourself and put the image in the folder on the SharePoint server where all the images for the site reside: `%program files%\common files\microsoft shared\web server extensions\12\templates\images\`. Other settings specify what fields will display for the feed and the item limits of maximum items to show in the feed (default is 25) and maximum days to include an entry (default is 7).

Now that you've had a quick overview of each link for the List Settings pages, let's configure the list.

Enable Incoming Email

To make it possible for users to add items to a list by email, you must configure the incoming email settings. Incoming email must be enabled and configured at the Central Administration, Operations level of SharePoint before it can be enabled at the list level.

1. On the list you would like to email enable, make certain that you are in Customize page for that list.

2. In the Communications category, select Incoming Email Settings.

3. The Incoming E-mail Settings page that appears (see Figure 5.36) has five sections. In the first section, Incoming E-Mail, select Yes to enable this feature. This will enable you to type in the E-Mail Address field (if the No is selected, you can't type in the field even though it's not grayed out).

FIGURE 5.36

The Incoming E-mail settings

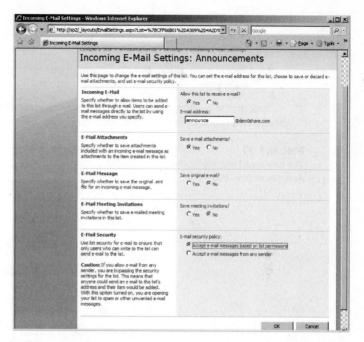

4. Enter an email alias for the list. In my example I'm going to keep it short and call it **announce**.

5. In the second section, you can choose to save attachments with the list item when it is created from the incoming email. In case someone has a photo, directions, or document they need to keep with the announcement item, let's keep this option at Yes.

6. If you don't want to keep a copy of the email sent to this list, make sure that the Save Original E-mail setting is No in the E-Mail Message section. If email successfully gets made into a list item then you have a copy of its contents in the list already, and you could clog up the SMTP Drop folder on your server with all the mail the list has ever received. Therefore, I don't save emails. However, the option to do so is there if you need it.

INCOMING MAIL USES SMTP

You may remember from the first two chapters of the book, that incoming mail uses IIS's SMTP service to gather email sent to its Drop folder on the local drive of the SharePoint server (unless you configure it otherwise). One server services all incoming email. This is why it refers to the SMTP Drop folder in the settings.

---

7. In case someone wants to invite a list to a meeting, there is an option to save email meeting invitations for the list in the E-Mail Meeting Invitations section. It is set to No by default. Let's leave it that way.

8. The final setting is for the list's email security policy. The list can accept all email from anyone who gets the address right (bypassing the list's own security), or it can use the list's

permission settings to block emails from people who don't have the right to contribute to the list. Unless there is a good reason not to, select Accept E-mail Messages Based On List Permissions. This helps the list avoid being spammed.

9. Once you've completed configuring your settings for incoming email, click OK at the bottom of the page.

Back on the Customize page for the Announcements list, the email address for the list is now displayed in the List Information section (Figure 5.37).

FIGURE 5.37
The new email address for the Announcements list

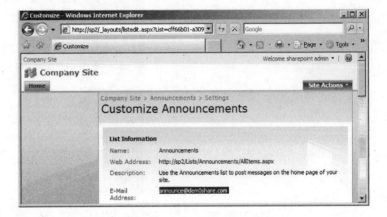

If you have an email client handy (and you are logged in as someone with permission to contribute to the list), you can send an email to the list using the new email alias you specified (see Figure 5.38). This will add a new item to the list via email.

FIGURE 5.38
Email sent to Announcements email alias

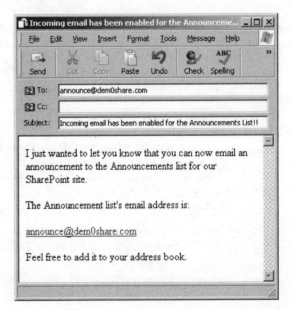

The SharePoint Timer job is in charge of checking the SMTP Drop folder every few minutes to gather email for SharePoint and then distributing it to the correct lists. Therefore, in a few minutes the email will be added to the Announcements lists without any special treatment (Figure 5.39).

FIGURE 5.39
A new list item is created via Incoming Email

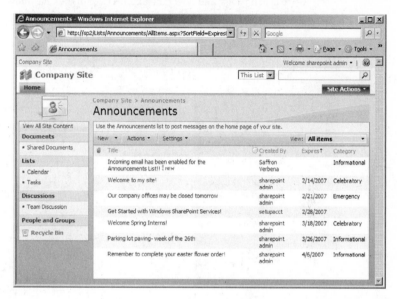

HOW TO AVOID BLANK DATE VALUES

You might have noticed in Figure 5.38 that there is no Expires date, but the category is set to Informational. The Expires date is blank because there is no means to specify the expiration date in the email. The email simply has To, From, Time Sent, Subject, and Body Of message fields. It has no Expires field to fill out. SharePoint does not read the body of the message, so it won't see an expiration date if you added one to the message. However, you could type one in the message, and edit the message later to add it to the correct field in the list.

Because the Expires field was blank, you might think that the Category field should be blank also. No, it was set to have a default value for every new list item. Because of this, as soon as the email was made into a list item, the category was filled with the default value.

To avoid a blank Expires date, consider putting a default value in the field so that when a new item is created, it defaults to a specified expiration. This is actually a effective example of why you might want to use a default calculated value in a field.

In my example, I would like to have the default expiration date be the date the item is created, plus five days. This will give the new announcements five days by default to be displayed on the Announcements List View Web Part on the home page of the site before timing out. Otherwise, all announcements that were emailed will never expire, fill up the home page with announcements, and possibly obscure important items.

To add a default calculated value to the Expires field and avoid cluttering the Announcements List View web part, follow these steps:

1. Go to List Settings, and select the Expires field in the Columns section of the page.

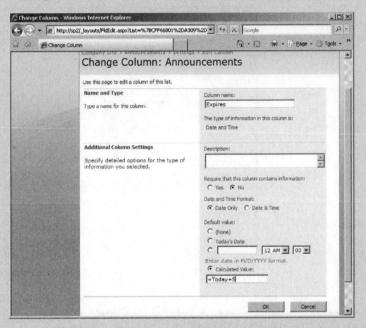

2. On the Expires field Change Column page, scroll to the bottom of the Additional Column Settings section.

3. For a default value, select Calculated Value and enter = [Today] +5 in the field.

Now when a new item is created in the Announcements list, even if no one explicitly adds a value to the Expires field, a default of five days from the day of creation will be the expiration date unless you specify otherwise.

Incoming email almost certainly makes a list more convenient to use. And when a list becomes easy to use, it can become a little too popular. This is why you might need to consider adding content approval to the list so that no one can add an announcement without your approval (or the approval of someone to whom you have given list management rights). When content approval is enabled, as you will see in a moment, all new items or new changes to a list item are considered pending and can be set to be invisible to anyone viewing the list until the they are approved (by someone allowed to do that sort of thing). The announcements list is a good candidate for content approval.

Why? Well, the list is part of the site, and, therefore, inherits the site's permissions (until configured to do otherwise). The site allows site members to contribute to the lists and libraries on the site. This also opens the list for the possible prankster to create a fake emergency announcement just to cause a stir. To avoid this there needs to be a delay between the time a user creates an item and the time the item is published. Hence, the need for content approval, which essentially hides a list item (if you set it to) until it can be approved by the appropriate person or people.

Enable Content Approval

The Announcements list is particularly vulnerable to abuse because it can be very popular as a web part for the home page, and a perfect candidate content approval. To enable Content Approval for the Announcements list, follow these steps:

1. Go to the Customize page for that list.

2. From there, select the Versioning Settings link (it is not very intuitive) in the General Settings category.

The first section of the page (see Figure 5.40) has two options for Content Approval settings: Yes and No. Everything else is invisibly enabled under the hood. Once you opt for Yes in the Content Approval section, all changes to items in the list will be set to Pending (this includes the creation of new items) until someone who is allowed to approve list items (such as site administrators or someone granted the Approve Items permission) changes the status of the item from pending to either approved or rejected. All items in the Pending (or Rejected) state are considered drafts and are visible by default only to those who created them or are allowed to approve them, although that can be changed.

FIGURE 5.40
List Versioning Settings page

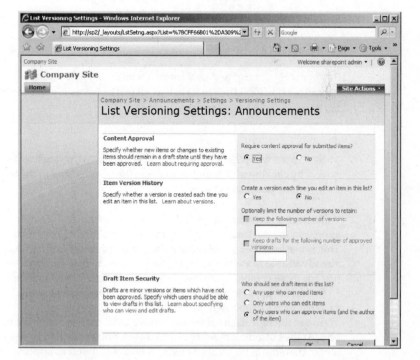

ENABLE VERSIONING

While you're on the List Versioning Settings page, you can also enable versioning. Although versioning is a setting you can enable, and it is meant to work with content approval, the two settings are different and work independently.

Fundamentally, using Content Approval is about whether or not an item can be seen, meaning that changes to items, or the creation of new items, are held in a pending (and potentially unviewable to the public) state until they are approved. Content Approval does delay the viewing of items until approval but it doesn't increase the amount of storage the list requires. Versioning means that all changes to all items in the list are saved as separate copies of the item in chronological order on the off chance that you might need them. Saving a copy of those items each time a change is made can really increase the amount of storage space a list can take up on the server. Keep that in mind before you set versioning on all of your lists. If you don't need it, don't do it. Versioning will be covered pretty extensively (in conjunction with content approval as well) in the next chapter, "Introduction to Libraries."

3. For my example, we are only going to enable Content Approval for the Announcements list here, so click Yes in the Content Approval section. When you do, notice that Draft Item Security at the bottom of the page becomes available to change. The default, which allows only the author and the approvers to see pending items, is fine.

4. Click OK to commit to setting Content Approval.

DON'T ENABLE CONTENT APPROVAL

Do not enable Content Approval if you intend to edit a list in Datasheet view. Content Approval locks the entire list to Read Only in Datasheet view. The fact that items can be in a pending or rejected state can be too confusing for that view.

5. To see what changes have occurred on the list, go back to the content page of Announcements by clicking on Announcements in the breadcrumb at the top above the title of the Customize Announcements page.

Back on the content page of the Announcements list, a new Approval Status column will appear in the All Items view (Figure 5.41). You might notice that almost all items are approved. This is because they were already there when you set Content Approval. Because they were already visible to everyone, SharePoint assumes they are approved. From now on, new items (except those created by users allowed to approve items) will be Pending until approved.

Content Approval adds two new views to the list, a new field to each item, and a new option to each list item's dropdown menu.

To see the new list item options, move your mouse over a list item title and click in the selection box. At the bottom of the dropdown menu, you'll see that the option to Approve/Reject is listed there. This shows up for those users who are allowed to approve or reject items.

FIGURE 5.41
The new Approval Status column

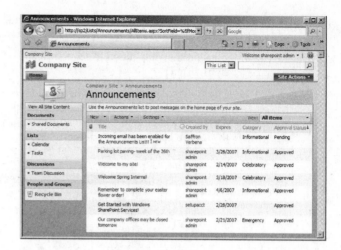

The Approval state of a list item can be changed at any time by someone with the right to do so.

1. To demonstrate this, select Approve/Reject in an Item's dropdown menu. (You can also choose to approve or reject an item by first clicking on it to view it, and choosing Approve/Reject Item then in the Action bar.)

   A page offering you two sections will open. One section lets you choose the approval status of the item; the other lets you make a comment. Approved items are marked approved in the Approval Status field and are visible to anyone able to view the list. Rejected and pending items are not visible to anyone reading the list except the users allowed to approve items and the creator of the item.

2. In this case, reject the item and enter a comment that the content needs to be updated (see Figure 5.42). Click OK to go back to the content page of the list. On the list, that item's Approval Status is Rejected.

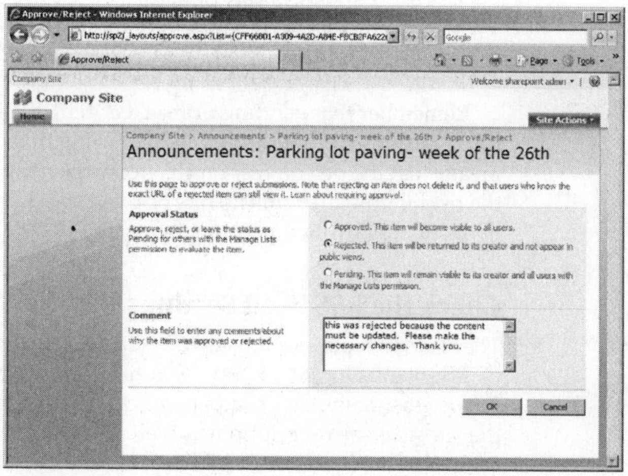

FIGURE 5.42
Rejecting a list item

Content Approval created two new List views by which to filter the list. The List views will be filtered by the submissions of the person logged in and the Group By Approval Status.

3. Click on the View menu to see the two new views, Approve/Reject Items and the submissions, listed.

4. Choose the Approve/Reject Items view to see the list items grouped by approval status, with a column for the Approver Comments (Figure 5.43). My example has one pending item and one rejected item. You can always approve the item later, with a comment by following the same steps you did to reject it.

FIGURE 5.43
The Approve/Reject
Items view

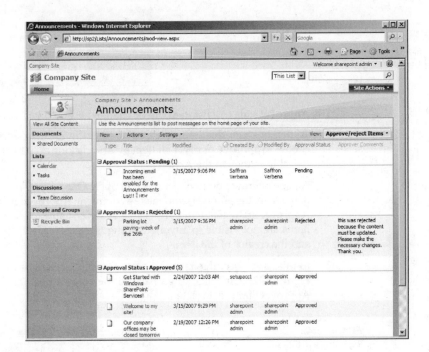

Remember that pending or rejected items will currently not be visible to all users until the items are approved (but they are all visible to those with approval rights and the owner). This means that the person responsible for approving items must keep up with the task of doing so, lest the list fill up with items no one else can see. The Submissions view is for the users to see the list items filtered by their pending items.

Check the RSS Feed Settings

There are two options to keep up with the changes made in a list: RSS Feed and Alerts.

RSS stands for Real Simple Syndication (or Rich Site Summary to some people). In SharePoint, RSS is essentially XML made up of channel tags which contain elements such as title, URL link of the site, website description, as well as elements for each item and their optional sub-elements such as author, category, and comments.

RSS readers are used to keep contact with RSS feeds to which you have subscribed (Internet Explorer has an RSS reader feature). They regularly check for changes by doing regular updates, although some browsers don't perform updates effectively and force you to update manually. Subscribing to an RSS feed for a list allows you to be alerted when there is a change to the list without having to directly visit the list to see those changes.

To check the settings for the RSS Feed of the Announcements list:

1. Go to the List Settings from the Settings button on the Action bar.

2. On the Customize Announcements page, select the RSS settings link in the Communications category.

   On the Modify List RSS Settings page, as you'll see in Figure 5.44, RSS is already allowed for the list by default because it is on by default in the Site Collection.

FIGURE 5.44
The RSS settings

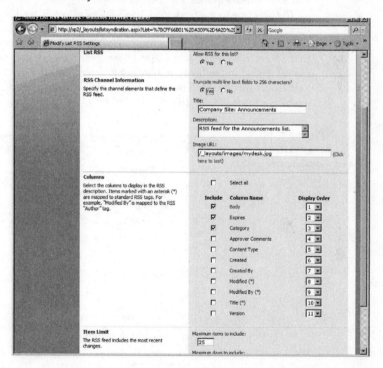

In the RSS Channel Information section of the page, you can see the title, description, and even an image you can specify for the feed. You can truncate longer multi-line fields to 256 characters, and the person reading the feed can click the link for the item to read its full contents.

3. My example leaves the defaults for the RSS channel as they are, except truncation is enabled for the longer multi-line fields (such as the Body field of an announcement). That makes it easier to skim down a RSS feed, while looking for relevant items.

4. All the columns available to be displayed from the Announcements list are in the Columns section. My example leaves the defaults fields as they are.

5. In the Item Limits section, let's leave the defaults. The maximum number of entries displayed on the feed page is 25, and it displays those items that have changed in the last seven days.

6. At the bottom of the page, you could click the Default button to reset the default values for the RSS settings. However, because we made a change (truncating multi-line fields) that we want to keep, click OK to commit the settings and go back to the Customize page.

To actually subscribe to an RSS feed for a list, you first need to go back to the List content page (click Announcements in the breadcrumb above the Customize Announcements page title). Then, while on the list, click the Actions button in the Action bar and select View RSS Feed.

That will take you to the RSS Feed page for the list. The RSS Feed page lists the items in the list. An area at the top of the page describes the page and gives you a link to subscribe to the feed. On the right is the area that gives you a Search field to search within the feed page, as well as a way to sort the items by author, date, or title.

To subscribe to the feed, click the Subscribe to this feed link in the yellow area at the top of the RSS Feed page (see Figure 5.45). When you subscribe to a feed in Internet Explorer 7.0, the browser picks up on the subscription and gives you an opportunity to check your feeds by going to the Favorites Center (click the yellow star on the top left of the browser window, or use the menu). Each kind of browser handles RSS feeds differently, so your performance may vary. Remember that the feed needs to be checked occasionally; therefore, if your computer is offline for a while, your feeds will likely be out of sync—remember to refresh in that case.

FIGURE 5.45
The RSS feed for the Announcements list

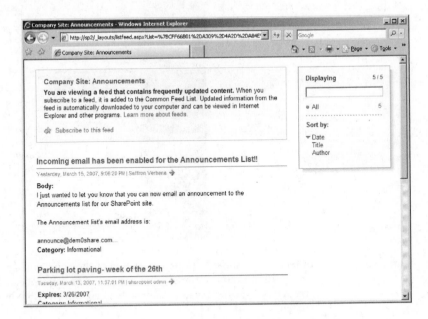

Set Alerts

Another way to keep up with changes made to a list is to set email alerts. User alerts are set and managed at the web application level and are limited web application wide, not by site or site collection. It can also be completely disabled at that level as well. Unlike an RSS feed, *alerts* actively notify you by email when there is a change made to a list item. You can decide what kind of change can trigger the alert, to a certain degree. You can also control when the alerts are sent, from immediately to once a week. SharePoint actively sends you an email when the notification is triggered, causing SharePoint to use more resources that the more passive RSS feeds do. However, using alerts does mean that you will be more likely to notice any changes than if you use RSS, which requires you to open the browser or feed reader to see the update. Another plus to alerts is that you can set an alert for someone else, so they can be informed when a new item or changes to an item might involve them.

So, how do you set up an alert? Well, alerts can be created from any list or library:

1. Go to the Action bar on the content page, click the Actions button, and select Alert Me from the dropdown menu (You can also set alerts from the drop down menu of any list item).

2. On the New Alert page that appears (see Figure 5.46,—this is one of those long configuration pages so the title is cut off in order to show all the settings), the first section gives you a chance to give a more descriptive name for the alert. The default title for the alert is the list name (or list item) from which it stems. For now, let's keep that title.

FIGURE 5.46
The New Alert page

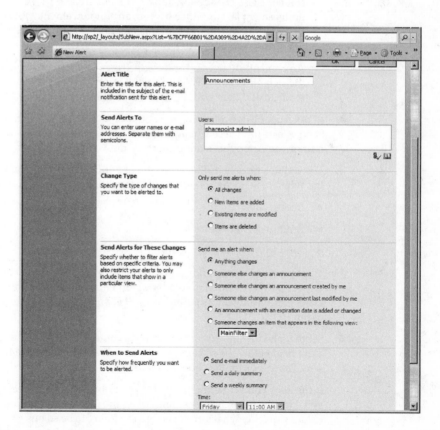

3. In the Send Alerts To section, the default email address is fine. You can see that you are allowed to enter not only someone else's email address but also as many other people's email addresses as you like. Use semicolons to separate them. Be careful. Alerts can keep the SharePoint Timer Service very busy. Teach users to limit alerts to only those lists that are the most important to them. The desire to alert *other people* might overcome their caution, however, particularly if they know that everyone is limited in the number of alerts they are allowed. Encourage them to keep the number of alerts they set for *anyone* to a minimum.

There are basically two different change triggers (or a combination of both) that can cause an alert to be sent:

♦ **Change Type:** This section is available if you set the alert for the list, list items don't have this section. If an item in the list changes in a certain way, you can send a notification. These notifications can be triggered by any changes in the list, when a new item is added, when existing items are modified, or if an item or items are deleted. (That last one is good for administrators.)

♦ **Send Alerts for These Changes:** This trigger uses a more specific criteria to launch a notification: if anything changes on the list, someone else changes an announcement, someone else changes an announcement created by you, someone else changes an announcement last modified by you, an announcement with an expiration date is added or changed (unique to the Announcements list because it refers to expiration), or changes are made to an item when in a particular view.

Any and all changes is the default Trigger setting for an alert. In other words, if we keep the default Change Type and Send Alerts for These Changes, then any change that is made to any item will cause an email to be sent.

4. In my example we are going to set the Change Type to Existing items are modified. Set the Send Alerts for These Changes to filter those modifications down to When Someone else changes an Announcement created by me.

5. The settings for scheduling when email notifications based on the criteria will be sent are in the When to Send Alerts section of alert settings. The options are:

♦ Immediately

♦ Send In A Daily Summary

♦ Send In A Weekly Summary

You can set up an exact day and time of the week for the weekly option, and an exact time of day for the daily option. Immediate alert emails send a separate email for every single alert. Daily and weekly alerts summarize all changes (based on the alert criteria) for that length of time.

6. Set the schedule for this alert to daily summary. When we select Send a daily summary, the Time field below the setting will become available to choose the time the summary will be sent. For this example, choose 2:00 P.M.

If the alert you are setting up is simply informational, a weekly summary might work for you. I tend to go for a daily summary for most of my alerts, under the assumption that I need to know quickly what's going on but am going to be so busy, day to day, that I'll only have a short time to get to alerts once a day. Use your best judgment when it comes to scheduling alerts. Try to balance the need to know about changes immediately with the need not to unnecessarily tie up the SharePoint Timer Service with sending out too many alerts.

7. When you've finished with your settings, click OK to finish configuring the new alert.

NO EMAIL ASSOCIATED

If the account you are using does not have an email address associated with it in SharePoint, a warning will pop up, giving you the opportunity to set your email address.

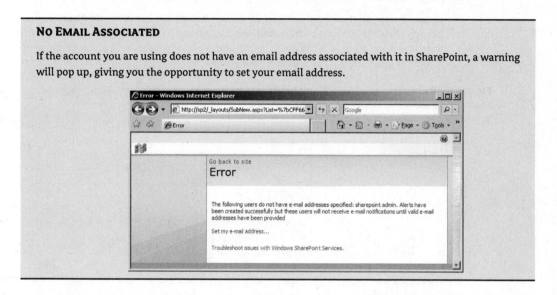

Once you are back to the list, you can feel safe knowing that you will be alerted should any of your items be changed on this list. As a matter of fact, you can log in as a different user and change the Announcement list items specifically to generate an email alert. See Figure 5.47 for an example of a daily summary (well, only one thing happened in that time period, but you get the point).

FIGURE 5.47
Daily Summary email alert

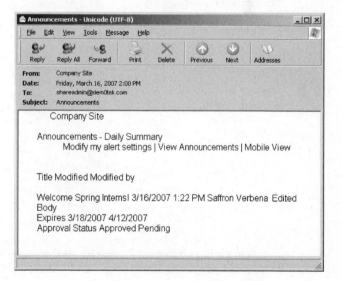

However, as the weeks pass, you may forget exactly how you set up your alert for this list. What if you want to make a change? What if you want to delete the alert because you don't need it anymore? How do you bring up the alerts you've created?

It's easy. There are several ways to access a user's alerts. The two most convenient ways are:

◆ Create a new alert on any list (just go to the Action bar on the content page of any list or library, click the Actions button, and select Alert Me in the dropdown menu). At the top of the New Alert page is a link to see what alerts already exist for the account you are logged in with (Figure 5.48). This link will take you to the My Alerts on this site page for that user.

FIGURE 5.48
View existing alerts on this site link for a new alert

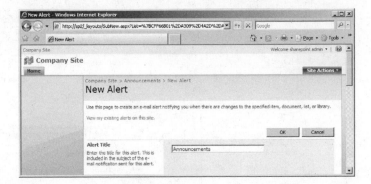

◆ Alerts are associated with a user's user information. Go to your account's user information directly by clicking on the Welcome menu at the top of any page of the site in the site collection. In the dropdown, select My Settings. This will take you to the User Information page (Figure 5.49).

FIGURE 5.49
The User Information page, My Alerts

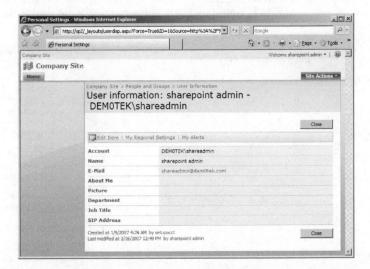

On the User Information page for your account, there is a link to My Alerts in the Action bar. If you click My Alerts, it will open the My Alerts On This Site page (Figure 5.50).

FIGURE 5.50
The My Alerts On This Site page

The alerts will be organized by frequency. You can delete a selected alert here or select an alert to edit it. This is the central location for all of this account's alerts for this site, regardless of the list.

As a matter of fact, this is also where you can create an alert for a list. Simply click Add Alert in the Action bar. It will take you to a page where all existing lists for the site are displayed (Figure 5.51). Just select the radio button next to the list or library you'd like to create an alert for, and click Next at the bottom of the page. You will be taken to a New Alert page for that list or library, where you can make your notification settings.

FIGURE 5.51
The Add Alert page for the whole site

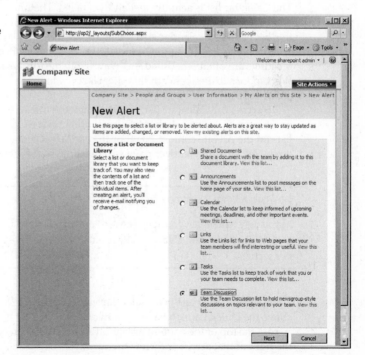

So you now know how to use a list in SharePoint. You've seen how to add a list item individually and in bulk using datasheet view. You've learned about adding fields to a list, created new views, enabled incoming email for a list, configured RSS, set up content approval, and created an alert. Now that you have the fundamentals of lists down, it's time to explore the other lists that are available on the Team site.

Explore Prebuilt Lists

SharePoint creates several more lists by default for the Team Site template. These lists are there for a reason, because they are each well suited to demonstrate the usefulness and flexibility of lists.

Each list that is prebuilt for the Team Site template was created from a template. You can use that template to create your own lists and modify them to suit yourself. You can also take the prebuilt lists and modify them as you did Announcements earlier in the chapter.

One of the preexisting lists for the Team Site template is Announcements. You're familiar with the simple items for this list. The Announcements list, practically more than any other (except maybe the Links list), was meant to be displayed in its List View Web Part. The special field, or trait, for this list is the Expires field. Even though it is nothing more than a date field, the Web Part for this list uses a view that filters the items to display so only items that have not expired will be shown on the home page.

We'll go into each of the other prebuilt lists now: Calendar, Links, Task, and Team Discussion.

Calendar

The Calendar list is actually just an Events list. The unique thing about it is that the default Public view is a Calendar view that organizes events not by title, but by date in a calendar layout. Also, this list has a few calendar-specific fields, such as All Day event and Recurrence. This list also specifically integrates with Outlook (2007 preferably). Because this list has to do with dates, and meetings are often scheduled this way, list items for this list can be used to create new Meeting Workspace subsites beneath this site. Users cannot use this feature unless they have the right to create subsites.

To access the Calendar list, you can click the title of the Calendar List View Web Part on the home page of the site, click the Calendar link on the Quick Launch bar, or select Calendar from the lists on the All Site content page for the site. The Calendar link in the Quick Launch bar is usually on the left side of whatever page you're using, so it is convenient.

ADDING A WEB PART TO CALENDAR VIEW

As you may remember, you added a Web Part to the Calendar View page for this list in Chapter 4. Under normal circumstances, a Vacation Request notice would not be located on the page, so I removed it for this section.

By default, the page is in Calendar view (Figure 5.52). Notice on the top left of the window, above the Quick Launch bar, is a mini calendar in Year view, per month for your convenience. Across the top of the content area is an Action bar, with New, Actions, and Settings buttons. On the right of that area is the View menu.

FIGURE 5.52
The Calendar list

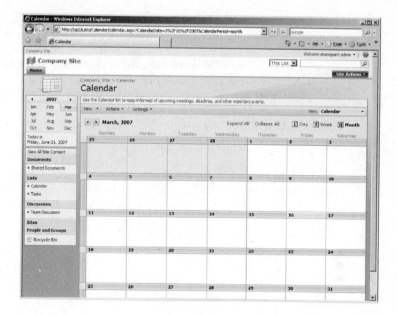

If you click View menu, you'll see that there are views for All Events and Current Events. Because this is really an Events list, these views are not a surprise. If you select the Event view, you'll find that it is the Standard view for the list (Figure 5.53). Notice that the column headers are Title, Location, Start Time, End Time, and All Day Events (for those items that are flagged as all day). There are also columns for recurrence, whether or not the item has an attachment (such as directions or itinerary), or if it is associated with a meeting workspace.

FIGURE 5.53
All Events View for the Calendar list

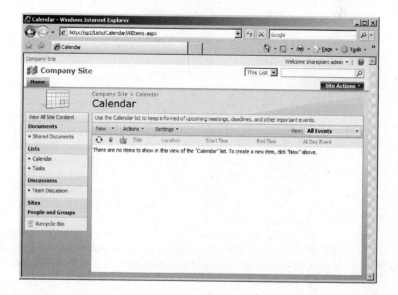

To add an item to this list, as you would with any other, simply click New on the Action bar. In the New Item page that appears, there are three fields; Title, Start Time, and End time, that are required. Their field names are marked with a red asterisk. These fields must contain data or else you can't use the OK button to save the item. You can also attach a file to this event item by using the Attach file link in the action bar.

See Figure 5.54 for my example of the data entered for a Calendar Event item, St. Patrick's Day (usually March 17th). It is set to be an all-day event. This means that the duration (although not listed) will be 12:00 A.M. to 12:00 P.M. from the start date of the event to the end date of the event.

FIGURE 5.54

Create a new Calendar Event item

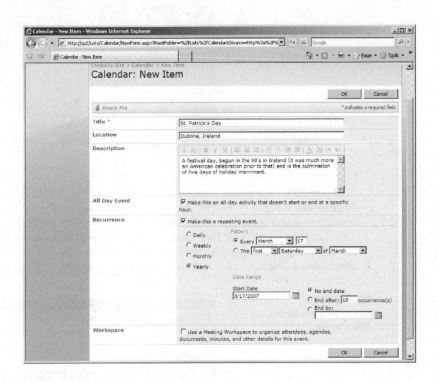

A Calendar Event item also has an interesting setting for making the item a repeating event. The setting is dynamic, which means when you check the Make this a repeating event checkbox, new settings will appear to help configure the way the event repeats. Because the event we are creating is an annual holiday, set it as a yearly, repeating event. Because it is a holiday, do not create a meeting workspace to focus on the event.

After the item is created, it will be displayed as an Event item in the Calendar List content page. Notice that, in the All Events view, the facts that the item is recurring and it is an all-day event are indicated (Figure 5.55).

To view the event in the Calendar view, click the View menu, and select Calendar from the dropdown. The event will be listed in the calendar. In Calendar view, notice in Figure 5.56 that you can view the dates of the calendar by day, week, or month. The default is Month view, but that can be modified.

FIGURE 5.55

A new event item in Calendar list, All Events view

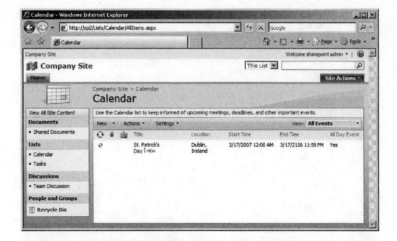

FIGURE 5.56

New Event item in Calendar view

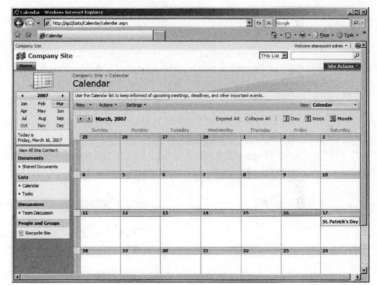

Links

Like Announcements, this simple list was specifically created to be displayed in a web part. Links demonstrates the use of a hyperlink field.

1. To get to the Links list, you can either click the title of the Links List View web part on the home page of the site or go to the All Site content page from the Quick Launch bar.

2. Once you are on the content page for Links, click New to create a new item.

3. You can see in Figure 5.57 that there are only a few fields: a hyperlink field (with a link to click to test the URL to make sure it works), a description for the URL, and a multiple line field for notes about the link. If you click OK, the item will appear in the list's content page.

FIGURE 5.57
A New Links list item

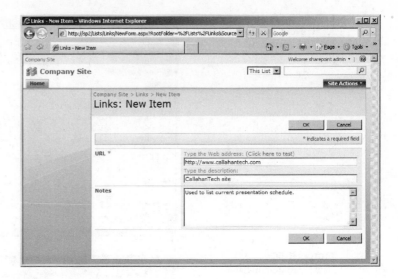

This list doesn't have fancy views or a lot of fields. It was meant to be a utility to add more interaction on the home page. The items in this list were meant to be displayed in a Web Part so the users don't have to go to the list directly.

4. Go back to the home page of the site (click the Home tab in the top-link bar). The link will appear in the right Web Part zone for the page.

5. To create another list item from there, just click Add New Link at the bottom of the Web Part (Figure 5.58). It will take you to the New Item page for that list.

FIGURE 5.58
New link item on the home page

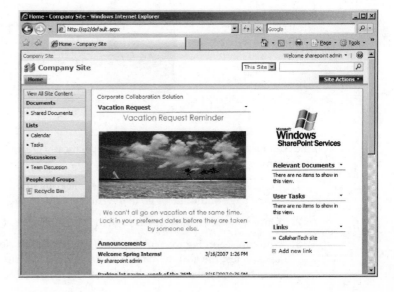

LINKS AREN'T JUST FOR WEB PAGES

A hyperlink field is actually just a *path field*, a field that will hold a path or address that, when selected in the Web Part, will open whatever is at the end of that path.

This means that the hyperlink field for a Links item does not have to be a Web address. It can be a path to a document or image in a public share, or even a folder if all users have access to it. Hyperlink fields are not something to be ignored. Get creative. Imagine what you could offer your users with a link on the home page.

Tasks

A Tasks list actually has several nifty traits. Tasks items demonstrates Choice fields and the People and Groups field. It also has two date fields as well. To get to the prebuilt Tasks list on a Team site, click on the Tasks link under the Lists heading in the Quick Launch bar.

To create a new task, just click New in the Action bar. The New Item page (Figure 5.58) displays all kinds of interesting fields:

Title   The only required field. A Title field is standard for most lists. The first field created by default is the Title field, because it's required it cannot be deleted.

Priority   A Choice field. This particular field has three options: High, Normal, and Low.

Status   Another Choice field. It has five options ranging from Not Started to Waiting on Someone Else.

% Complete   This field is a number field formatted to be displayed in percentage value.

Assigned To   This field uses the People and Groups field and is essentially a lookup field to the People and Groups list for the site (as well as anyone in Active Directory in most cases). It uses the People Picker field (yes, that's its name) that you use to type in the name of the person or group the task is assigned to. You can enter a username and check it with the Check Names button, or use the Browse button and actually browse the Active Directory users for the domain. This means that you can assign a task to someone who isn't a member of the site. In addition (really working the user management aspect of SharePoint), you can assign tasks to SharePoint groups or even security groups in Active Directory rather than a single person. You cannot assign a task to two or more users in this field however. Only one user or group is allowed to be used with this type of People Picker field.

ASSIGNING TASKS TO NON-SHAREPOINT USERS

If you don't want to be able to assign tasks to someone who doesn't have an account in SharePoint, check out Chapter 13, "STSADM: A Look at the SharePoint Command Line Tool," concerning using the `setproperty` operation and the property name of `peoplepicker-onlysearchwithinsi tecollections`.

Description This field is a rich-text multiple-line field.

Start Date A standard date field.

Due Date Another standard date field. However, if you fill in both the start and due date of a task, you can create a Gantt view to track the task's progress.

Figure 5.59 illustrates a sample Tasks item. Feel free to fill the fields with a Start Date and Due Date within the next several weeks.

FIGURE 5.59
New task item

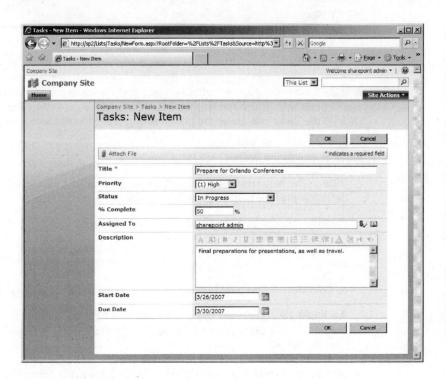

Back on the Tasks list, the All Items view is not necessarily impressive by default. However, because of the useful fields that are contained in a task (Assigned To, Start Dates, End Dates, and Priority), there are several really useful views for this list.

Click on the View menu at the top of the content area for this list. You'll see several more views for this list that you haven't already seen:

Active Tasks This Standard view is filtered by the Status field, if its value is not equal to Completed.

By Assigned To This Standard view is sorted by Assigned To and then Status.

By My Groups This view is odd because it is also sorted by Assigned To and Status, and it seems to be exactly the same as By Assigned To. However, beneath the covers, this view filters by Group assignments. If the tasks were never assigned to groups, and/or never to a group your login is a member of, this view won't display anything for you.

Due Today   This view will display all tasks due today by virtue of filtering by Due Date being equal to the variable [Today]. Interestingly, it is sorted by item ID, which is a default field created for most lists that simply gives each item a consecutive number to ensure that at least one field of the item record is unique. This *does* mean it sorts by when the tasks were put into the list, not by Title of task or Due Date.

My Tasks   This view literally filters the Tasks list if the value of the Assigned to field equals the variable [Me]. It is also sorted by Status and Priority for your convenience.

The Tasks list is also a good example of why you should conscientiously enter data in all of the necessary fields of a list item. Those fields can only be sorted, filtered, grouped, etc., if they have data in them. Views can be powerful, but they are not really relevant if the data is not there.

CREATE A GANTT VIEW FOR THE TASKS LIST

One of the reasons someone would create a Gantt Chart view for a list would be to track a series of tasks—say, making preparations to attend a conference. As long as those tasks have start and end dates, they can have a Gantt view.

To create a Gantt view of the Tasks list:

1. Click the View menu (or the Settings button) and select Create View.

2. In the Create View page that appears, select the Gantt View format.

3. In the Create View page for a Gantt view, the only settings that are different from the Standard view is the Gantt Columns section. Otherwise, you name the view (keep it short), decide on whether or not it will be public (my example is public), and decide which fields will be displayed. (Pay attention to which columns you want to use in this view.)

The Gantt Column section of the settings has four fields available to configure:

◆ **Title:** This field is what is going to be displayed next to the graphic representing the start and end dates. Usually, it is the title of the list item.

◆ **Start Date:** This is the Start Date field for the graphic representation of the duration of the task in the Gantt View. This field's data must always precede the date that you will use for the end date.

◆ **Due Date:** The end date for the task, represented graphically in the Gantt View. This field must have a date that, for every list item, occurs after the Start Date.

◆ **Percent Complete:** This field lets the Gantt View indicate by color how far along a task is toward completion. This field is not necessary for the Gantt View to function properly. This field needs is to be a Choice data-type field.

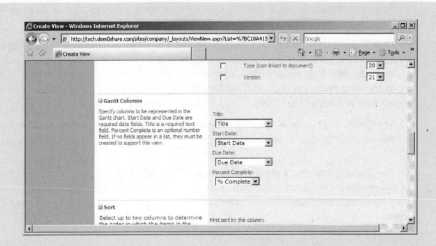

4. For my example Gantt Column values, use the traditional Title field for the Title, Start Date for the Start Date, and Due Date for the Due Date. For the Percent Complete field, choose the Percent Complete field. As you can see, the Gantt View was meant to work with a Tasks list.

5. Once the settings for the view are complete to your satisfaction, click OK to create your view.

The Gantt view is interesting because the top of the view is a horizontal calendar, with a bar of varying colors indicating its nearness to completion. This view assumes that, as you work on a task, you will come back and update the task with your most current percentage of completeness. However, this sideways calendar doesn't show anything concerning data about the task except its title. This might make you wonder why you needed to have those columns listed near the top of the settings for the new view.

That's because those fields are listed at the bottom of the view. You might need to scroll down, but there is a *second* section that displays the additional fields so you can see the details of the item listed near the Date bar.

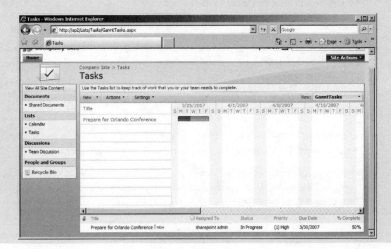

The Tasks list was meant to be used in conjunction with the Issue Tracking list. With this combination, you can create Issue items, which can be resolved by assigning Tasks to a user or group. That is why there is a sample workflow meant to be used with an Issues list that creates an item in the Tasks list and sends an email to the person or group to whom the task is assigned.

By the way, the Project Tasks List template creates a Tasks list with a Gantt view. The only difference between Tasks and Project Tasks is the Gantt view. After creating a quick Gantt view for the existing Tasks list, you've made it into a Project Tasks list. This helps demonstrate that the List templates are a little contrived; they were just examples that Microsoft created to give you ideas of what you can do with lists.

Team Discussion

Due to the content types and folders, the Team Discussion list changed between the last version of SharePoint and the most current one. The Team Discussion list seems innocuous enough. All collaborative sites should have at least one discussion forum. However, this list works differently.

Of course, every prebuilt list on the Team site is supposed to be useful and also demonstrate something useful about list design. A Discussion list has two different types of items in it:

◆ The post that starts a thread, usually referred to as a *post*, *thread*, *topic*, *subject*, or *discussion*.

◆ The reply, generally only called a reply (funny that . . .).

In a SharePoint Discussion list, these two types of items are literally two different content types.

SHAREPOINT, THE NEW GREEN

SharePoint is all about recycling. It has templates of sites, lists, and libraries so you can reuse them. If you create or customize a list to perfection, SharePoint gives you the option to make a template of it for the site collection, so you can reuse it too. No effort needs to be doubled there.

As a matter of fact, if you create a field for a list that is ideal, and you know that you will want to format a field just like it for a different list, you can make it a "site column," which is sort of a template for a field so you can apply its formatting to other lists.

Given SharePoint's proven interest in recycling, it stands to reason that SharePoint also goes one step further and has content types. Content types are a sort of list item template and can be created from list items that you really like: create a list, which will have a list item (which you know is a record in that list's underlying table) with all the fields, or metadata, that you want. If it really works for you, and you can see the need for it in other lists, you can then go to the content type gallery and create that list item as a content type, and use that content type in other lists. You can create a new list, enable content types, choose the list item you want to use for that list, and never have to re-create any of those fields.

Content types are usually based on an existing base content type (like the Item content type for all lists, which contains a Title field, period). So to create your favorite content type just pick the existing content type that suits what you are trying to create, then add some of those premade site columns to flesh it out, and eureka, you've got your own custom list item.

Because of this, you can have a list that contains the list items from several other lists in it, like sales quote, sales order, and bill of sale all in one list. You can create custom Content Type list items, Document Library items, or folders for your new lists if you desire.

Conceptually, content types are a perfect fit for Libraries. Libraries, in earlier versions of SharePoint, could have only one file template associated with its items at a time, and only one kind of record or library item per library. That meant that if you clicked the New button in a library, it would open a new file based on the library's one template (like a Word document, for example) associated with a new library item.

However, if you wanted to be able to create a new Word document or Excel spreadsheet, you had to have two different library items: one associated with one kind of template and another associated with the other template. These library items could also have their own unique fields because of the template associated with them (the way many worksheets an Excel workbook would have, or what Style template a Word document would use).

This is a good reason why, in this version of SharePoint, content types were introduced. Enabling content types for a library lets you have several different kinds of document library items in one document library, so you can have one item that supports creating a particular new document from a contract template, another item that supports creating a new slide presentation based on a PowerPoint template, and so on.

I don't think they are quite finished polishing the concept yet, as you can see with Team Discussions, but it is a step in the right direction.

So SharePoint recycles lists, libraries, and sites with templates. It has a recycle bin (or two) to protect the accidental deletion of items. It even allows the recycling of well made list items with content types, and useful fields with site columns. That's SharePoint, very effort conscious.

Content types for lists and libraries could honestly fill a book of their own. I will be going into it a little in the Chapter 6, "Introduction to Libraries." I suggest you experiment with content types to see how they might improve your lists for your organization.

Content types will be covered more extensively in Chapter 6, but suffice it to say that most lists and libraries have one kind of content. In a list's case, this means that an Announcements list has one kind of item, an announcement. Link lists have one kind of item, a link. Tasks lists have a task, and so on. In previous versions of SharePoint, views change, but the underlying content stayed the same; when you clicked the New button, a single kind of new item was created that was specific to that list.

Now, with the current version of SharePoint, when you create a list or library, you can use more than one content type, meaning a list can contain the list item for a Tasks list and a list item for a Calendar list. That makes it difficult to do Standard views, but it does give you considerable flexibility when making complex lists. Each content type has its own fields and can even have its own workflows associated with it. There is even a unique content type for folders, so their contents can automatically inherit certain fields and traits.

Usually multiple content types are used by Libraries because the users might want to be able to click the New button on the Action bar and choose from a list of templates from which to create a new library document: Excel Spreadsheet, Word Document, PowerPoint Slides, etc.

However, in the case of the Discussion list, it does seem to be the way that Microsoft decided to demonstrate how to use content types in a list.

To use the Team site's Discussion list, just click the Team Discussion list in the Quick Launch bar. Once at the list, you'll see it's a Standard view, the default of which is called Subject, indicating that the view is focused on listing discussion subjects. If you click the View menu (which you may feel compelled to do because that's what we've done with other lists), you will see that there is no other view available. That won't always be the case, but first you must add a discussion to the list to see the list's true magic.

To add a new discussion item, click New on the Action bar. The New Item page for a new discussion item is pretty simple, all things considered. There is only a Subject field (required), a Body field, and the means to add an attachment (which means there's an Attachment field for the item too).

The first discussion item in this example is going to be a welcome message (see Figure 5.60). After adding text to the Subject and Body fields, just click OK to create your new discussion item.

FIGURE 5.60

A new discussion item

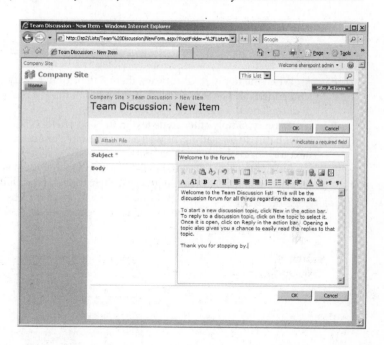

Back at the Team Discussion list, you may notice that the discussion item looks pretty standard for a list item: Subject, Created By, Last Updated fields, and a Reply field that indicates the number of replies the discussion has had.

To reply to a discussion, you first need to view it. Then on the Action bar of the View Item page, you will see a button to Reply. Strangely, Reply is not an option if you click on the selection box of the discussion item and look through the options of its dropdown menu. You can Reply to a discussion only by viewing the contents of the discussion item.

To view a discussion item, click the item's Title field (which is the linked field for this item) or move your mouse over the item and select View Item in the dropdown menu. Once you are viewing that item's contents, click the Reply button in the Action bar (Figure 5.61).

FIGURE 5.61
View a discussion item to make a reply

When the Reply page appears, there will be only a Body field (with the original discussion text embedded) and no Subject field. Because it is simply a reply to the subject of the discussion topic, it doesn't need a subject.

To reply, simply enter some text in the Body field. Notice that it is a multiple line, rich text field, so you can do formatting, as well as insert a table or image if you wish. When you are done adding text to your reply, click OK to finish.

Back at the Team Discussion list, you can see that there is now one reply (see Figure 5.62). This is where using this list could get a little frustrating. Normally, it is easy to see a discussion topic and its replies listed right at the surface, so to speak, of a list. There may be a plus sign next to a topic that might need to be clicked to dropdown the replies, but usually the topics and their replies are right there.

FIGURE 5.62
Team Discussion list item with one reply

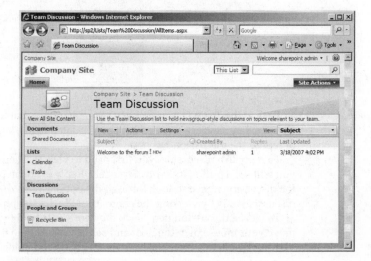

However, in this example of a discussion group, you have to first open the discussion to see a reply. The reply is buried beneath the discussion (or more precisely, it is stored in the discussion). To see the one reply to the welcome discussion topic, click the topic's title.

When you click on a discussion item that has replies, the View Item page for a discussion item turns into a different page altogether. Remember, the discussion item is really a folder content type. That means it can contain things. The odd thing about folder content types in a SharePoint list is, it not only is a container for other list items, but it also can have its own metadata, it's own data fields. This presents a problem, so when you move your mouse over the subject of a discussion and click View Item from the dropdown menu, it shows you the discussion's metadata or *properties*. But if you actually click on the discussion's subject (which is usually link to view an item), it actually opens the discussion folder and shows you the items it contains. In this case, the discussion folder will show the some of the fields of its properties (this was added to the default view of the folder to give context to the replies) and the discussion's replies. As you can see in Figure 5.63, both the discussion topic and the reply are displayed, but you can still view the properties of either item by clicking their View Properties link.

FIGURE 5.63
Discussion with reply

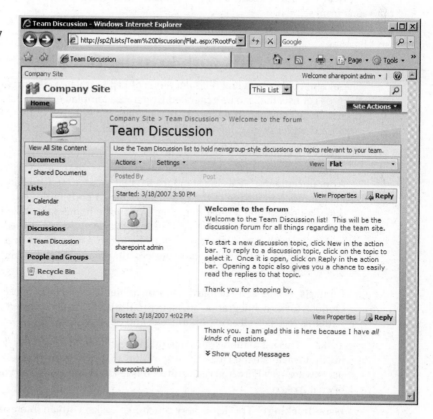

Now that you are viewing the discussion and can see the reply, notice that the view is Flat in the View menu. There is also a Threaded view, which indents the replies so you can see if someone is replying to a reply or to the original discussion. This is the view that most people expect to see on the List itself, rather than in the page for each individual discussion.

SHARED DOCUMENTS IS A LIST

Shared Documents, as you may have noticed in the Quick Launch bar, is an existing list. But I am not going into it in this chapter. This is because Shared Documents is a sample of a kind of list called a Document Library. That list's purpose is purely for the storing, creating, and editing files, and its extensive attributes reflect that. Because of this, it will be getting its own chapter. For information about Shared Documents, see Chapter 6, "Introduction to Libraries."

So hopefully you've gotten a feel for lists; adding items, the action bar, views, and datasheets. Now it's time to create some lists; several from template (and customize them of course), and one from scratch.

Create New Lists with Existing Templates

SharePoint contains several different kinds of List templates. The preexisting lists were some of the types of lists that can be generated from these templates. Most lists were meant to do a particular task, demonstrate the use of new data types, or integrate with Office 2007. Lists are organized under three categories, Communications, Tracking, or Custom Lists.

The current List templates for the Team site are:

Announcements This is a standard list that focuses on displaying simple contents for its Web Part on the home page of the Team site. It has a Body, Title, and Expires field. The expiration date will determine if a list item displays on the home page. Like most lists, because it is fundamentally a table, it can be opened in Datasheet view, exported to Excel, and even opened in Access. In this case, you can export the list to Access to work on it independently of Share-Point, or even export the data to Access, do data entry there, and synchronize the data with SharePoint.

Contacts This is a standard list, but its fields correspond closely to the contact records in Outlook for easy integration and synchronization. You can connect to Outlook (preferably 2007) with this list, as well as export to Excel and open with Access.

Tasks This list demonstrates several interesting field data types. It works with the Issue Tracking list to facilitate the Three-State workflow that comes with SharePoint, and it has an interesting user-aware Web Part. You can connect this list to Outlook 2007 so you can see it there, or you can open it in Access.

Issue Tracking This list is very much like Tasks, with an interesting use of some of the more complex field data types. It is the one list for which the sample Three-State workflow was built, which was designed to take an issue and trigger a task item to be created in the Tasks list based on assignment. This list integrates with Outlook, Access, and Excel. This list also has versioning enabled to allow its comment field to append new data to the field.

Links   This simple list is meant to be used in a List View web part. It demonstrates the power of the Hyperlink field by allowing you to type a path to a file, or location, to be opened when a user clicks on it. Even this list can be exported to Excel or opened with Access.

Shared Documents (and Other Libraries)   The Sample Document library is from the Document Library template. There are also more Library lists, such as the Picture library, Wiki library, and Form library. All of them are focused more on files associated with list items than on the data stored in list items. Document library items can also spawn their own Document Workspace subsite. This kind of list is meant to integrate with Office because the templates associated with Library List items are Office templates such as Word, Excel, PowerPoint, or even InfoPath. In addition, like any list, a Document library can also be opened in Access, exported to Excel (well the metadata anyway), and connected to Outlook.

Team Discussion   This list demonstrates, in an interesting way, the use of content types in a list. You may prefer the previous version's Discussion list; the way threads are displayed is a little awkward in this version. This list, like any other, integrates with Office by connecting to Outlook, opening with Access, and being able to have its list items exported to Excel.

Surveys   This is an unique list because it has no default fields, so when you create the survey, all questions (using standard field data types) must be custom created. It uses an interesting set of graphical views. This version of surveys also support rudimentary branching logic. This list doesn't integrate with Office, but its data can be exported to Excel to be managed there.

Calendar   This is an Events list that demonstrates the use of the Calendar view. It has several custom fields, such as Recurrence. Calendar items can be used to spin off Meeting Workspaces. The Calendar list integrates with Outlook in particularly.

Project Task   This list is exactly the same as a standard Tasks list, except it has a Gantt view. This list, like most others, integrates with Outlook, Access, and Excel.

Let's take a look at the List templates we haven't covered yet: Issue Tracking, Surveys, and Contacts. I am going to do an overview of Issue Tracking and Surveys, saving Contacts for last, because Contacts lends itself most easily to the bread and butter of using a template, customizing it to suit your needs.

Issue Tracking

The Issue Tracking list is meant to capture data about troubleshooting *issues*, which are not uncommon in any collaborative solution. It is very much like a Tasks list except that it has an interesting use for the lookup field: it looks up itself.

To create an Issue Tracking list from an existing template:

1. Go to the Create page by clicking the Site Action menu, and selecting Create from the dropdown menu. (As you know, there are several ways to get to the Create page, but this is the easiest.)

2. Once at the Create page (Figure 5.64), you can move the mouse over the link for Issue Tracking (in the Tracking category) and see that its description is displayed in the area above the template categories.

FIGURE 5.64
The Create page

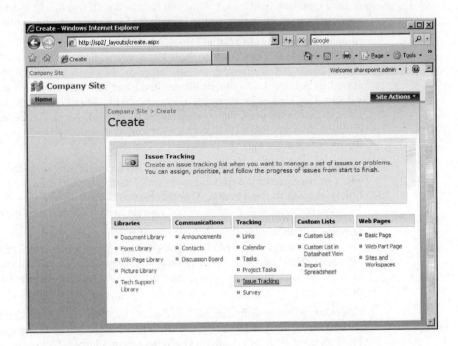

ISSUE TRACKING LISTS ARE MEANT TO BE REVISITED

The items in an Issue Tracking list are supposed to be used to track an issue to completion, which means this is not a *static* list. Most lists, tables, databases, and even spreadsheets, contain data that can be stored permanently and never changes.

Lists such as Issue Tracking are meant to be revisited, and the items can be edited to reflect changes in the status of an issue. This is an important point. If you've ever tried to keep an Issue list and it failed, with nothing ever seeming to be started or finished, it might be because a user, while actually working on the issue, had to also remember to go in and update the list item but failed to do so. The only way an issues list will work is if everyone actually participates in keeping it *dynamic*.

---

3. To create an Issue Tracking list from a template, just click its link on the Create page. That will take you to the New page (see Figure 5.65).

4. For the Name and Description, fill in the Name and Description fields with something appropriate. Remember that the name of the list will be part of the URL for the list itself, so keep it short and try to avoid spaces.

FIGURE 5.65
The New page

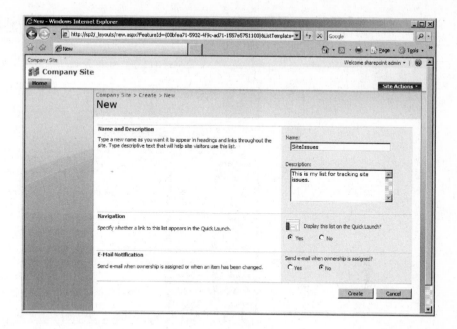

5. For the Navigation setting, we can choose to have the list show up on the Quick Launch bar or not. My example has it on the Quick Launch bar, so keep the default, Yes.

6. For email notification, we could have the list send an email message should ownership of the list item be assigned to someone other than the person who is creating it now. It is not necessary to notify those assigned to an issue by email in my example so keep the default for No; however, this setting is useful in most circumstances. In this case, this list is going to work in conjunction with a Tasks list in the next section, which will be sending emails to assignees. Keep in mind that SharePoint has to use processor and RAM resources to email and send notifications because those functions are performed by the Timer job.

7. Once our settings are complete, click OK to create our Issue Tracking list.

The new Issue Tracking list should come up with the list's name and description (see Figure 5.66). This list comes with three views: All Issues, Active Issues (filters out the closed Issues), My Issues (filters by the [Me] variable).

To really see what the Issue Tracking list is all about, create a new item by clicking the New button in the Action bar. This will take you to the New Item page (Figure 5.67).

Enter a Title (which is required). The Assigned To field is a People and Groups data field. Assign the issue to the user account under which you are logged in by clicking in the field and entering your username. The Issue Status, which is simply a Choice field, can be Active, Resolved, or Closed. Leave it Active for now. The Priority field (also a Choice data field), can be left at Normal.

Feel free to enter a description in the Description field. Under normal circumstances, this field would be very important for resolving the issue and for use as historical data later.

FIGURE 5.66
The new Issue Tracking list

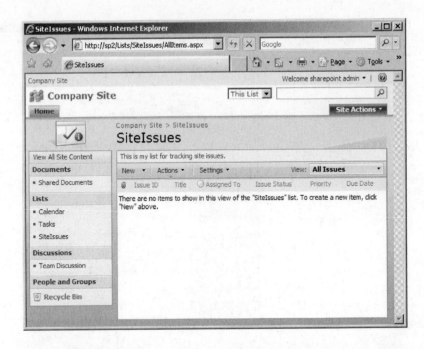

FIGURE 5.67
Creating a new Issue item

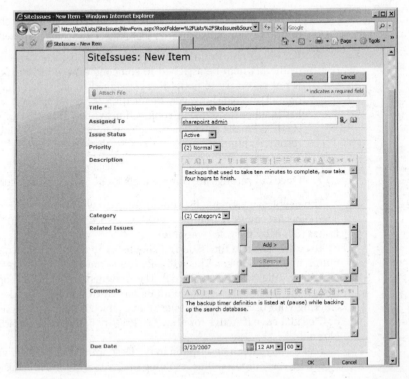

The Category field is actually strangely unfinished in comparison to the other fields, as if to encourage you to customize it. It does contain three, generally nondescript, categories. Leave it at the default of Category2.

The Related Issues field is a lookup field with the option to allow you to choose more than one item from the lookup. An interesting thing about this particular lookup field is that it points, not to the value of a field in a different list, but to the value of the Title field of this list. This allows you to track multiple Issue items that might relate to one another in some way. This is pretty clever, and it illustrates an essential way to demonstrate lookup fields. Right now there is no value to select because this is the first item in this list.

The Comments field is simply another multiple-line rich-text field. Again, this field would be a good place to add documentation about the issue.

Finally, at the bottom of the page is Due Date. Feel free to give the item a due date of the end of the week (or some time in the future), then click OK to finish creating your new Issue item.

If you were to create another Issue item, the first item's title would appear in the Related Issues field (in Figure 5.68) which is a multiple choice lookup field that refers to the title field of it's own items. To select that item's title, you need to get it to appear in the box on the right. To do that, either double-click your selection, or select it from the Related Issues list on the left, and then click the Add button to move it to the right. If there had been more items in the list, you could pick and choose among the items to have them relate to your new issue. Remember, the point of this lookup field is not just to look up the value of a field, but to allow you to choose more than one.

FIGURE 5.68
Created another Issue item to use the Related Issues field

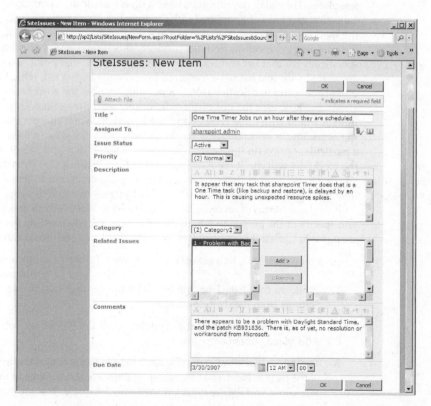

You have created, used, and viewed the Issue Tracking list, but you aren't done with it yet. The interesting thing about the Issue Tracking list is that Microsoft chose it to demonstrate workflows.

USE THE THREE-STATE WORKFLOW

You had to install .NET Framework 3.0 because of the Windows Workflow Foundation. However, here is the catch: To really use more than the one, sample WSS workflow available out-of-the-box, you must use SharePoint Designer (or Visual Studio). Yes, you must buy another product to be able to use all of the features of a free product. However, for workflows it's worth the price.

Workflows are a pretty simple and nifty concept. You know that you have lists. You know that you have libraries. What if you wanted to automatically create a task in a Tasks list when a document is marked *Ready For Review* (this would be a custom field you'd create in the library) and you want the user to see that they have a new task when they log in and view their User Tasks Web Part on the home page?

You could do it with a *workflow.* A workflow is simply a programmatic process that is triggered by an event or change in its associated list. The trigger can send an alert, create a new list or list item, or change the state of a field. Workflows were meant to make SharePoint's document management and collaboration more useful.

Issue Tracking was meant to demonstrate that. Workflows are added to SharePoint as templates. They may have been created with a specific list in mind, but they are added to a site collection as a kind of template (with the intent that you then go to the list that you want to apply the workflow to and set it up there). On a list that you would like to apply the template, you select the template in Workflow Settings (under List Settings), and then name it and configure it specifically for that list and what you want it to do. At that point, a workflow instance is associated with that list to be triggered by a change in that list, which can then effect changes in other lists—send notifications, etc., depending on how the workflow is designed.

My example uses the out-of-the-box sample workflow called Three-State. This workflow utilizes a field with three choices and the Tasks list. When an item is created in a list with which this workflow is associated, the workflow will check the state of a choice field you specify to see if a particular option (in this case, Active) is selected. If that option is in fact the value of that field, the workflow will check the Assigned To field and create a new item in a specified Tasks list for the site that is assigned to that person for the issue. When that task item is set as completed, the Issue item that spawned it gets its Issue Status field value changed to the second option (Resolved).

If the Issue Status of an Issue item is changed to Resolved, an email is sent to either someone you specify or the person to whom the issue was assigned, telling them to review this issue and change it to Closed if necessary (which is the third stage of the workflow).

To demonstrate this, let's set up a Three-State workflow for our new Issue Tracking list.

1. While on the Issue Tracking list, click the Settings button in the Action bar, and select List Settings from the dropdown menu.

2. On the Customize page that appears, click the Workflow Settings link in the Permissions And Management category.

3. The Add a Workflow page (Figure 5.69) has five settings. (Note that the button at the bottom of the page is Next, not OK, meaning there are more pages to this process.) The first section, Workflow, will list the different workflow templates that are available for that site collection. Right now there is only one, so select Three-State.

FIGURE 5.69
The Add A Workflow page

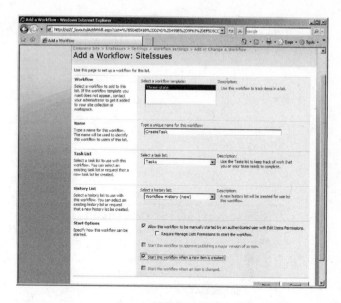

4. In the Name section, you are supposed to type a meaningful name for the workflow that will be applied to this list. In this example it will be named CreateTask.

5. Because this workflow creates tasks, the next section, Tasks List, asks you to specify the Tasks list it should use to create a task item. You can actually use this process to create a new Tasks list specifically to hold the task items created by this workflow if you'd like by clicking on the field in the Tasks List section and selecting New Task List from the dropdown. However, my example doesn't use the existing Tasks list for anything special, so let's keep the existing Tasks list as the Tasks list in which this workflow will generate items.

6. Like most things in SharePoint, a workflow can have a history, essentially a log, to record what it has been doing. If a workflow history is already available, you can choose it from the dropdown. This is the first time we've used workflows, so there is no existing workflow history. We'll have to create a new one, so keep the default.

   Workflows can be called to action by several triggers, such as manually being started (and you can decide who can do that), triggered by the creation of an item, change of an item, or when a document is approved.

7. Because this Issue Tracking list already has some items, we will need to manually start a workflow for them. We can allow anyone who can edit an item to start a workflow for an item, or we can limit that option to only those who have permission to manage a list. My example allows anyone with edit rights to start a workflow on an item if they wish. However, I'd also like to start the workflow when a new task item is created from this point on as well, to avoid any human error.

8. Click Next to continue creating your workflow instance.

9. On the next page, you customize the workflow. This workflow requires a Choice field with at least three options available. The Issue Status field it has three states (Active, Resolved, and Closed) so it is perfect for this workflow. Keep that field choice and its three options (see Figure 5.70).

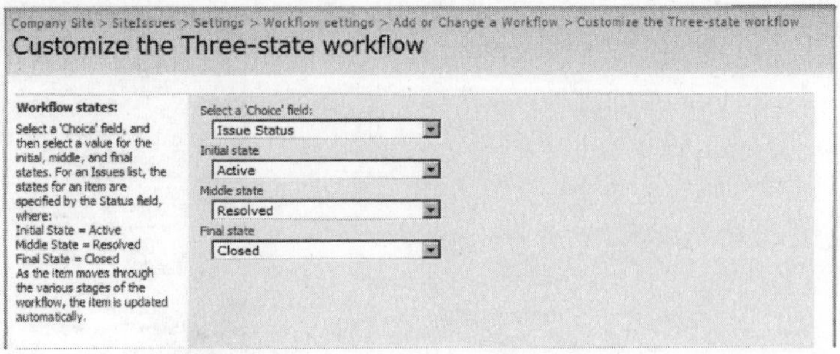

FIGURE 5.70
The Choice field section of Customizing the workflow

ONE WORKFLOW CAN GO A LONG WAY

The Three-State workflow can work with any list that has at least one Choice field with three options available, and either an Assigned To field or one person to whom all tasks are sent. If you are creative, this versatility will allow you to use the Three-Point workflow with a host of other uses—as long as you want the a task item to be created in a Tasks list.

When an item is created in this Issue Tracking list, the default value in the Issue Status field is Active. This is considered the initial state for this workflow.

The settings to specify what happens when the workflow is initiated are in the second section of this page (Figure 5.71). This section lets you specify what data is used for the new task item's fields as well as the email details that will be sent to the Task assignee.

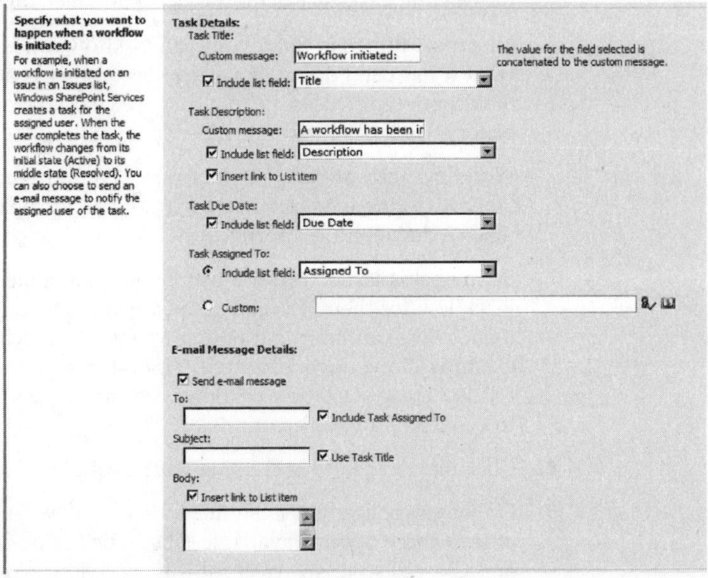

FIGURE 5.71
The "Specify what you want to happen when a workflow is initiated" section

10. The default value for the Title field of the Task Item title generated from an issue is that issue's ID number. Change that value to **Title**, because the Issue Title is much more descriptive than its ID field and would make a better title for the new task item.

11. The Task Description can be derived from the Description field of the issue and the Due Date will come from the issue's Due Date. The new task assignment can be set from the value in the issue's Assign To field, or you can specify someone explicitly. My example uses the Assign To field value.

12. Finally in this section, the workflow gives you the option to send an email to the assignee to let them know they have a new task. You can specify to whom the email is sent or allow it to default to the assignee using the Task title (which, if it is the ID number, is not very descriptive). You can even customize the body of the message if you'd like, but make certain a link to the task is included for the recipient's convenience. For this example, the defaults of sending the email to the assignee, using the task's title as the subject of the email, and putting the task's link in the email body are good enough for me.

In the third section of the Customize Workflow page, you decide what to do when the issue is Resolved (which is considered the middle state of the workflow). This step creates a new task for the assignee to review the task they were originally assigned to be sure it can be closed. When that task is completed, the original Issue Status field value is changed to Closed.

13. This means that this section is used to specify the new Task Title, Task Description, Task Due Date, and the assignee. It is also used to specify whether or not an email is sent, to whom it is sent, and what is contained in the Subject and Body fields (see Figure 5.72). The default settings for the task title, description, due date, assignee, and email are all correct for this example, so keep the defaults.

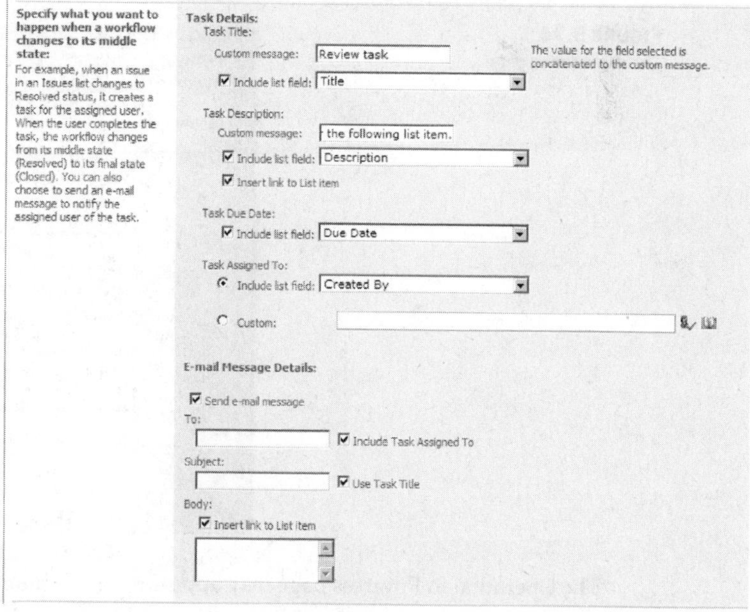

FIGURE 5.72
Specify what happens at the middle stage of the workflow

14. When all of your settings are the way you'd like them (you can edit them later if they don't work for you), click OK to finish creating your workflow instance for this list. That should put you back on the Issue Tracking list, ready to use the Three-State workflow.

This workflow was set to be started either manually or when a new item is created. To start the workflow on an existing item, move your mouse over the item, click in the selection box, and select Workflows, which now appears in the dropdown menu (see Figure 5.73).

FIGURE 5.73
The Workflows option on the dropdown for list item

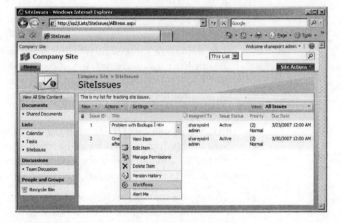

On the Workflows page (Figure 5.74), you can select from the workflow instances that might be available for the list to be started for this list item. You can also see what workflows are currently running on this item and which ones have completed. To start the workflow for the item, just click the button for the workflow.

FIGURE 5.74
The Workflows page

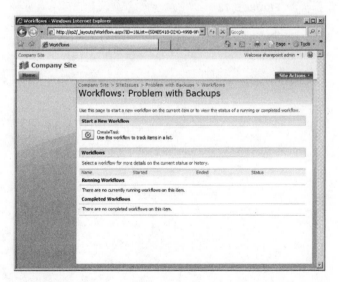

The Operation In Progress page may appear for a few moments while the workflow starts for that item.

Back on the Issue Tracking list, there is a new field indicating that the CreateTask workflow is in progress. To see if a Task Item was created in the Tasks list, click on that list's link in the Quick Launch bar (if it isn't in the Quick Launch, go to the All Site Contents page and select it there). As you can see in Figure 5.75, a new Workflow-initiated task has been created.

FIGURE 5.75

A new workflow-initiated task

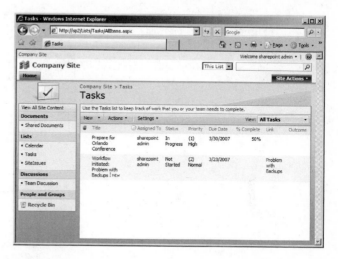

If you open the task item (see Figure 5.76), you'll see the description of the task and a link in that description to the originating issue. This item also has a notice saying that it will email the assignee the contents of the item, in case this is a security issue.

FIGURE 5.76

Contents of the task item

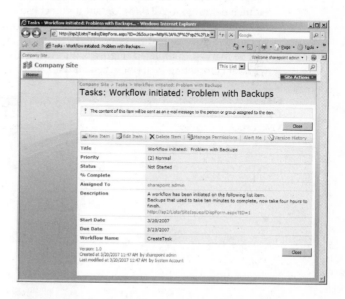

To cause the second stage of the workflow to trigger, we need to set this Task item to be completed, so click Edit Item in the Action bar of the item's View page (which you should have open). In the Edit page, change the Status field value to Completed, and click OK. When the task item is completed, the originating Issue Item status will change to the second state, which is Resolved.

Back on the Issue Tracking list, the originating Issue item's status will change to Resolved instead of Active (see Figure 5.77).

FIGURE 5.77
The Issue item is now resolved

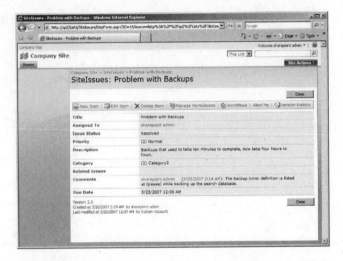

As you may remember, when the first task is complete, and the Issue item changes to Resolved, a second task is created to review the first task's description, resolution, etc. before closing the issue. To check this and finish the workflow, go back to the Tasks list (click on its link on the Quick Launch bar or go to All Site Content if you chose to make a custom list). You will see the second task initiated by the workflow (Figure 5.78). If you edit the item and change its status to Completed, the originating Issue item's status will be set to Closed and its CreateTask workflow will be marked Completed (Figure 5.79). Alternatively, if someone sets the Issue's status to closed, without completing the review task, it will still complete the workflow.

FIGURE 5.78
The second workflow-created task in the Tasks list

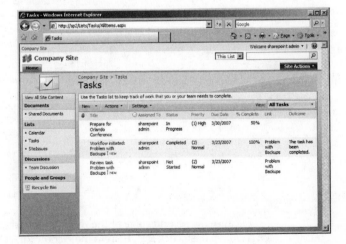

FIGURE 5.79

The originating Issue item is closed and the workflow is completed

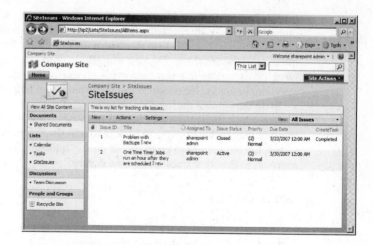

STATUS CHECK

If for some reason you were worried that your workflow for a list item was not working, or you wanted to know why a workflow wasn't completed, you can check the workflow's status by moving your mouse over the list item, clicking in the selection box, selecting Workflows from the dropdown, then on the Workflows page, selecting the running workflow. That workflow's status page will open, allowing you to see a report of that workflow's activities. If the workflow seems to be malfunctioning, it is here that you can deactivate it, which removes it from the item and causes it to delete the tasks it has made.

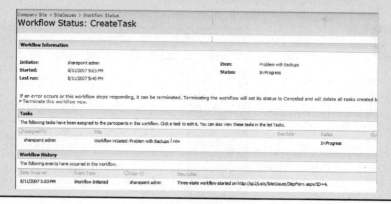

Surveys

The next List template that SharePoint offers is Surveys. *Surveys* are unique lists in that each field is considered a question. Surveys have a unique graphic view, and certain fields (or questions) can use a very rudimentary kind of branching logic. Namely, the Choice or Yes/No fields.

Surveys usually display a list of questions that you create so the user can answer the questions, and you can graph of the results. Surveys can be set so that users cannot see the names of the other participants while they are viewing the data, and users can be blocked from doing the survey more than once. With this latest version of SharePoint, you can create your questions, and when you are done, go back and set the *flow* of the questions. For example, say you have a Yes/No question. If the answer is Yes, you want the user to just move on; however, if the answer is No, you want the user to fill in a text field explaining why they chose No before moving to the next question. Basically, No needs to use the explanation field, but Yes can skip it.

To do that, create the Yes/No Question and the text field that basically says "If no, please explain why," then move on, creating the other questions of the survey. Then, when you are done creating the question fields, go back in to edit the columns, and set the Yes/No answer to branch, setting the No answer to go to the "If no . . ." question, and setting Yes to skip that request and move on to the other questions in the survey.

CREATE A SURVEY

To create a survey, follow these steps:

1. Click Create on the Site Action menu.

2. On the Create page that appears, click the link for Survey in the Tracking category.

   The New page that opens will have the same settings as any other new list—Name, Description, and Navigation. In addition, it will have Survey Options settings: Show User Names in Survey Results and Allow Multiple Responses. This is where you decide whether the survey will be anonymous to other users and whether you will allow users to retake the survey.

3. For this example, name the survey **SimpleSurvey**, (or whatever you'd like) and put a link for it on the Quick Launch bar. Don't show user names, and don't allow multiple responses, then click Next. You will immediately start to create the first field for the survey, which is considered a question (see Figure 5.80).

FIGURE 5.80
The new Question page for a survey

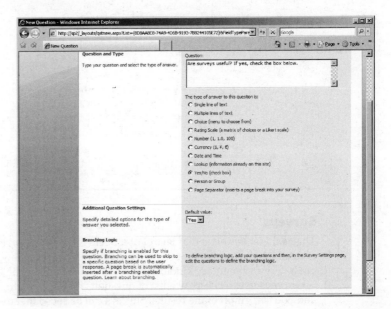

4. My example uses a simple Yes/No question. Type some text (such as **Are surveys useful? If yes, check the box below**), and select Yes/No for the type of answer.

YOU HAVE TO TELL THEM EVERYTHING

Surveys are very, well, primitive. For example, the Yes/No option for a question merely displays the question and a blind checkbox. That's it, no explanation is offered in the interface as to what the checkbox is about; therefore, you'll need to define what the box value actually is in the question. Such as "Check the box below if you are over 18 years of age."

---

5. In the Additional Question Settings section, you have to choose a default value. Yes is the default. Keep it for this example.

   The last section on the New Question page actually has no settings; it's the Branching Logic section that simply reminds you that you can use it after all the questions have been created.

6. At the bottom of the page, you can click the Finish button to create this question and finish creating the survey right now, Next Question to start on the next one, or Cancel. Click Next Question to finish this question and start on the next one.

7. For the Next Question, we are going to create the multiple-line text field where we ask the user to explain why they answered No. In the Question field, type your request for an explanation. Select Multiple Lines of Text for the answer type to give them room to tell you.

8. In the Additional Question Settings section for this type of answer, you can determine if this answer is required (the answer is required in my example), specify how many lines of text this answer is allowed (6 is fine), and determine the type of text for this field (plaintext, rich text, or enhanced rich text). This survey doesn't need enhanced rich text for images and tables, so plaintext (the default) will work.

   That's it for this question's settings, so click Next Question to create the next one. If you answer Yes, you'll go directly to this question. If you answer No, you'll go to this question after you explain the answer.

9. As the meeting point after the branching logic for this example, let's simply ask **Is it easier to do a survey if you know your answers are anonymous**? and make it a choice question.

10. In the Additional Question settings section, require the answer. For my example the choices will be: **Yes, No, and "It makes no difference."** You can display the choices in a dropdown list, with radio buttons, or with checkboxes (to choose more than one). Let's go with the Radio button default. Don't allow a fill-in value (because there are always jokers out there, and it will skew the average). Keep the default value as Choice, because that means that Yes will be the default because it is the first choice.

11. That's enough questions to demonstrate the point, so finish creating the survey by clicking Finish at the bottom of the page. That will take you, not to that list's content page, but to its Customize page (see Figure 5.81), because you may want to rearrange the questions or do branching logic.

FIGURE 5.81
The new survey's Customize
page

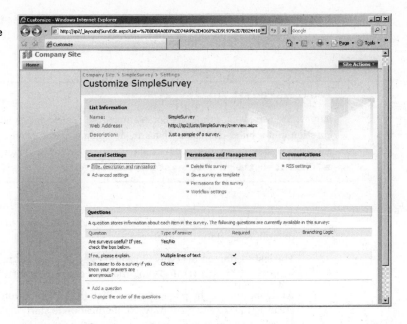

BRANCHING LOGIC

Survey questions are laid out in a linear pattern. Question two follows question one and so on. But with branching logic you can cause questions to stop going in order temporarily, skipping to a different question in the list based on the answer given.

1. For this example, to enable branching logic if the answer is No to the first question, select that question in the Questions section of the page. My example uses "Are surveys useful? If yes, check the box below."

2. Once the question has been selected scroll to the bottom of the Edit Question page, to the Branching Logic section (see Figure 5.82). There are two possible choices to apply the branching logic to, Yes and No. For the choices in this case there are three options, do not branch, or either jump to the second question, which is an explanation question, or jump to the last question which is a choice question. If the answer to the first question is No, then the user should simply move on to the next question (the explanation). However, if the answer to the first question is Yes, the user should skip over the second question and go directly to the last one.

FIGURE 5.82
The Branching Logic
section

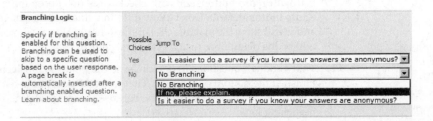

3. To do this, you can branch the Yes answer by selecting the last question in the Jump To field, so you can skip over the "If no, please explain" question. For the No answer, either you can not branch, which would cause it to simply go to the next question, or you can specify that it go to the explanation question directly.

4. Once you've set your branching logic, click OK to finish editing the question. Back on the Customize page for the survey, there should be a check mark next to the first question, indicating that it uses branching logic.

USE A SURVEY

To see how surveys work, as well as branching logic, let's create a Survey list item. Go to the Survey list (SimpleSurvey in my example) by either clicking its link in the breadcrumb above the page title, or clicking on the survey's link in the Quick Launch bar. Notice that there is a new Surveys heading in the Quick Launch bar now that a survey has been built.

The survey list's default view is a little nonstandard (Figure 5.83). The New button in the Action bar is now called a Respond To This Survey button. It is literally the same thing; SharePoint is just staying with a theme. Remember, this is just a list that is presented a little differently. To create a new Survey list item, click Respond To This Survey.

FIGURE 5.83

A new Survey list

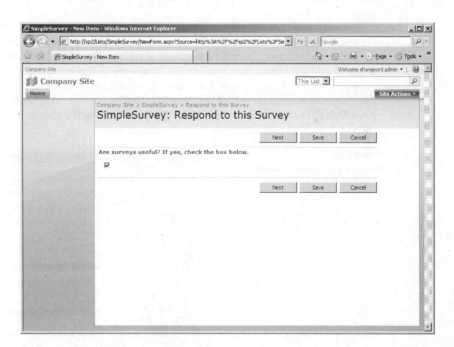

Unlike most new Item pages, Surveys are meant to display their fields in a group until a branch in logic. This means that the first question is displayed by itself, waiting for you to choose Yes or No so it can decide what to display next (see Figure 5.84 to see the first question).

FIGURE 5.84
The first question in a new survey

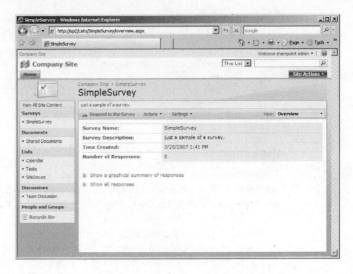

Notice that there is a question and a checkbox (checked by default, of course). That's it. No explanation as to what the box is for unless you provide it in the text of your question. Keep that in mind.

If you answer Yes to this question, it will jump to the last question of the survey; if you answer No (clear the checkbox) and click Next, it will go to the next question, and the one that follows in a normal linear manner. There is no jumping. To demonstrate that, clear the checkbox, so the answer is No. Then click Next.

And as you can see in Figure 5.85, the rest of the questions in the list are displayed on the same page because there is no branching logic to interrupt the flow. Also notice, at the bottom of the page, that the name of the person creating and modifying the survey item is obscured because we chose not to show names.

FIGURE 5.85
The rest of the survey questions

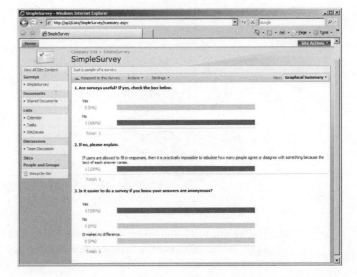

To complete the survey click Finish.

Back on the Survey List content page, there is one response in the Overview View of the list (the overview is essentially a summary of what the survey is about). If you had more than one response to the survey, it would mean more, but you can view all responses or a graphical representation of the responses in the Graphical Summary, so you can track trends and opinions (Figure 5.86). To get back to the overview, use the View menu and select Overview. To get to the normal List view of the survey items, select All Responses.

FIGURE 5.86
A graphical
summary of the
survey

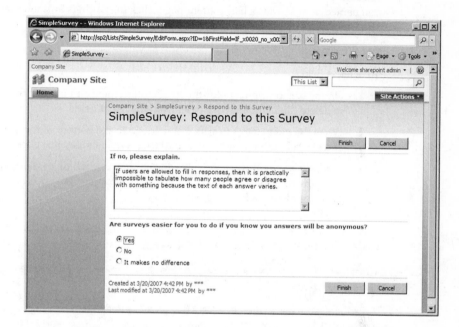

Contacts

The Contacts list doesn't have a workflow associated with it, doesn't do branching logic, nor does it have a fancy graphical summary. It is just a normal Contacts list, useful to practically everyone— with some customization, of course. And because the ever familiar Contacts list is so easy to modify, that is what this section is going to focus on; not just the list, but some of the things you can do with it.

To create a Contacts list:

1. Click Site Action near the top right of any content page or the home page, and then select Create from the dropdown menu.

2. In the Create page that opens, select Contacts from the Communications category. This list is going to be used for customer contacts for this example, so on the New list page, let's name it **Customers**. Feel free to give it a description, and add it to the Quick Launch bar.

3. When you've completed these settings, click OK. This will take you to a standard list content page.

To see what fields a Contacts list has, feel free to click New in the Action bar (and cancel when you're done). There are a lot of fields to fill out for a contact item. Take special notice of the Full Name field. Even if you fill in the First Name and Last Name fields, you'll need to type the Full Name of the contact manually. You can edit that field so the full name is pulled from the values of the First Name and Last Name fields. This will save time when entering data into the list, and when it is pulled into Access or Excel to generate mailing lists, the Full Name field can be used for addressing.

To accomplish this we need to delete the original Full Name field and add a new Full Name calculated field. Go back to the list (if you aren't already there). On the Customers (or whatever you named your Contacts list) content page, click the Settings button in the Action bar and select List Setting.

DELETE A FIELD

To delete a field:

1. On the Customize page for the list, scroll to the Columns section. Select the field you want to delete (Full Name in our case) from the list of fields.

2. When the page opens to edit that field, go to the bottom of the page. In addition to the OK and Cancel button is the Delete button. It's that simple, just click Delete.

3. A dialog box will warn you that the column and all of its data will be deleted. You don't have any data to lose yet, so click OK. This, however, is a good example as to why you want to customize a list *before* you enter data.

OOPSY, IF YOU DELETE SOMETHING BY MISTAKE

When SharePoint says that something you are about to delete is going to be permanently deleted, like list columns, it means it.

But what about those things you delete that go to the SharePoint (not the one on the desktop) Recycle Bin? For lists, list items, documents, templates, and even subsites, there is hope. They're all objects that can be safely recovered from the SharePoint Recycle Bin. If you delete something you want to restore back to its original location, you have (by default, this can be changed) 30 days to pull it from the site's Recycle Bin. After that, it's gone.

The Recycle Bin has two stages: the Recycle Bin that everyone can access from the Quick Launch bar and the higher level safety net Recycle Bin at the site collection level. All Recycle Bins from every site in a collection empty into the big one at the site collection level. So if you delete something from a site level Recycle Bin, that deleted item gets a stay of execution by first going to the site collection level Recycle Bin for 30 days (by default).

To restore something, like a list item or document, that you have accidentally deleted from the site, click Recycle Bin at the bottom of the Quick Launch bar (if you are on an Administrative page, you'll have to go back to a content or home page).

In my example, several list items and some site templates have been deleted. To recover one of these items, I just put a check mark in the box next to it, and click Restore Selection in the Action bar. This will put the item back where it started.

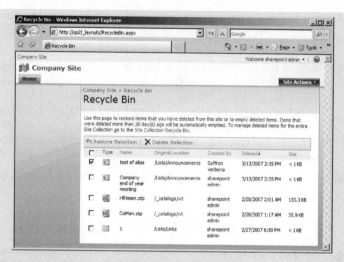

Something to keep in mind is that if you are tidying up and deleting a lot of objects (list items, sites, etc.), they will still take up space, first at the site level, and then (if you delete them from the first Recycle Bin) at the site collection level Recycle Bins. To empty the Recycle Bin, simply select the items you would like to remove and select Delete Selection from the Action bar. From that point, you then delete them from the site collection level Recycle Bin to make the deletion truly permanent.

If you are the site collection administrator, remember that the site collection level Recycle Bin also takes up storage space and holds items that have been deleted from the site level for a pre-set length of time. The site collection level Recycle bin has a storage limit that is set as a percentage of the storage quota for the content database. That means that second stage Recycle Bin can be quite large in addition to the space the content databases uses. Keep track of it carefully.

Always keep the Recycle Bin in mind when accidents happen. It is a mini backup and restore plan.

Once the Full Name field is deleted, it's time to create the new and improved full name field. We'll use this field to demonstrate calculation. Because calculated fields aren't available to be typed in, it won't show up on the New Item page when users are doing data entry.

CREATE A CALCULATED FIELD

1. To create a column, go to the Column section of the Customize page for the list and click Create Column.

2. The Create Column page has two sections: Name and Type and Additional Column Settings. The second section is dynamic and changes depending on what you choose as your data type in the first section. Because the original Full Name field has been deleted, that name is available for use in this list, so you can name the new field **Full Name**.

3. For the data type, choose Calculated, which is at the bottom of the list. Once Calculated is selected, the Additional Column Settings section will change to reflect the needs of a calculated data type.

4. For the description, you can use **Combined First Name and Last Name fields**. Try to always describe any calculated fields so that you will be reminded later what the field was intended to do.

5. Because calculated formulas in lists often refer to values in other fields of a list, there is a convenient Insert Column field populated by the field names of the list right next to the roomy Formula box. We are going to use a formula to *concatenate* (string together two or more text values) the data in the First Name and Last Name fields to create the value of the Full Name field. This is a common text calculation. You can explore the help files for more formulas, because this calculated field can do all kinds of functions, even trigonometry if necessary.

6. To do the concatenation (see Figure 5.87), click in the Formula box. The formula for concatenating fields is:

```
[First Name]&" "&[Last Name].
```

Normally, like Excel, SharePoint formulas start with an equal sign. However, because we are going to use a box specifically for formulas to create the field, the equal sign is understood. Field names are always in brackets, the ampersands (&) indicate the concatenation, and we are inserting a space (which has to be in quotes) between the two words. If you don't insert the space, the first and last name will run together into one word.

FIGURE 5.87
Calculated Field
Settings

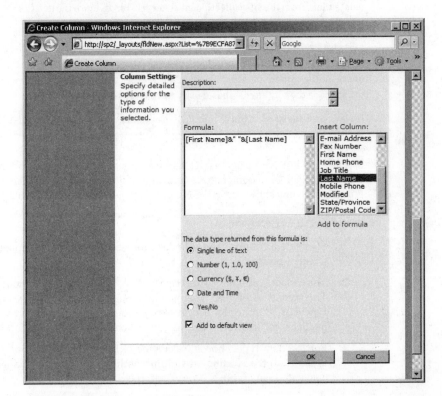

7. You can choose the data type that will be returned by the formula. A single line of text is good for our purposes, but, depending on the formula, you could also choose something like data and time, or even Yes/No if it works for you (but it won't at the moment, because the value we are using needs to be text).

8. Be sure to check the Add To Default View box and click OK.

9. Back on the Customize page, in the Columns section, your new column will be listed. You can change the order of the column so it is closer to the First Name and Last Name fields if you'd like; however, because users will not be entering data in that field, it really only needs to be in the right place in whatever views you create.

To see the new field in action, go back to the List's content page (you'll see a new column for Full Name at the end of the list in the content area, just waiting for data) and click New on the Action bar. Enter whatever data you'd like for the new contact item (see Figure 5.88 for my example). Notice that there is no Full Name field to enter data into, not even at the very bottom of the page.

FIGURE 5.88

New contact item data

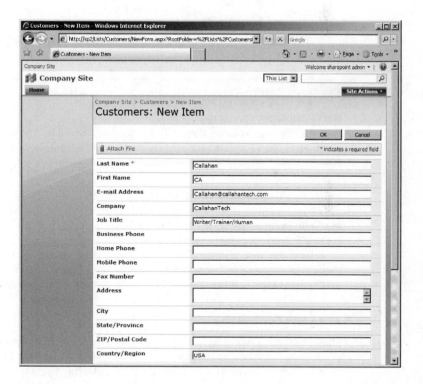

10. Click OK to finish.

On the list's content page, you can see that the First Name and Last Name fields are combined in the Full Name field (Figure 5.89) on the far right of the view.

FIGURE 5.89
The Full Name
field in the List
view

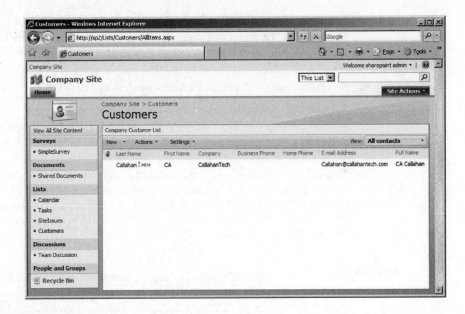

USE ONE FIELD TO VIEW TWO NAMES

If you want to get fancy, consider modifying this view by removing the First Name and Last Name fields from the view and replacing them with just the Full Name field. The data can still be entered normally when you create a new item, but your *view* will be of the full name in one field to save horizontal space.

This contact list is full of useful fields, but there is another field I would like to add. In appreciation of our customers, we try to find out their birthdays for a more personal touch. Our marketing staff sends out automated cards to clients to celebrate their birthdays, so we have collected dates for many of our customers.

A Birth day field is one that can be useful in several different kinds of lists. This brings us to the concept of *site columns*. Site columns are templates of common fields. If you create a field you like and expect to use in other lists, make it a site column. Then you can use it elsewhere.

ADD A SITE COLUMN TO A LIST

SharePoint has a pretty large number of site columns already available based on its numerous preexisting lists and List templates. It's convenient to know that those fields are already there for you use before you end up making something like them yourself. Many standard fields; like Company, Due date, Address, are already available as site columns. Unfortunately, you can't just select a column you've created in a list and make it a shared field; you have to set it up specifically from the Site Column Gallery page to make it available to more than one list. To use its convenience, you have to plan for it. In other words, if there are fields you plan to use over and over, create those fields as site columns specifically, and then create your lists.

In our case, the Birthday site column already exists; we just need to add it to our list.

To create a new field for a list from a site column:

1. Go to Settings on the Action bar, and select List Settings.

2. On the Customize page, scroll to the bottom of the Columns section and click the Add from existing site columns link. Site columns are organized in groups, although I tend to just stay on the All Groups so I can search through all available site columns. Some of the preexisting groups (you can make your own site columns groups to organize your site columns in a way that will be intuitive to you) are Base Columns, Core Contact and Calendar Columns, Core Task and Issue Columns, and the like.

   The columns available under All Groups are pretty numerous—and at this point, probably pretty familiar. Most fields in most SharePoint lists have been made site columns as well, which is really convenient. Just remember, you can't have two fields in a list with the same name, so don't try to add a field with a name you already have in a list. Also, if a field is calculated and refers to another field in the list to do its calculations, the field's calculation won't work unless the field, or fields, it refers to are also in the list.

3. In the list of available site columns, you'll see the Birthday field listed (Figure 5.90). Just double-click it, or click the Add button to move it from Available Columns to the Columns to add box. (When you do that, the field will disappear from the Available Columns box. This helps enforce the fact that a field cannot be added twice to a list.)

FIGURE 5.90
Add a site column

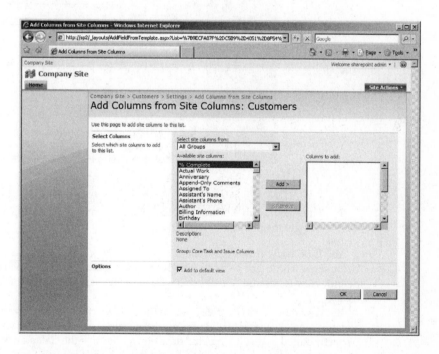

4. This column does not need to be added to the default view of the list, so remove the check from the Add to Default View option and click OK.

5. Back on the Customize page, you should see the Birthday field (formatted for Date and Time) in the Column section. Go back to the list's content page and edit the item you created earlier (move your mouse over the item, click on the selection box that comes up, and select Edit Item in the popup menu).

6. On the Edit Item page, you'll have to scroll down (because when a field is added to a list, it is appended to the bottom of the existing set of fields), but the Birthday field is right there (Figure 5.91).

FIGURE 5.91
New Birthday field from Site Column

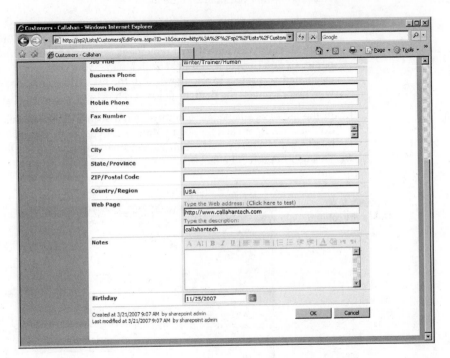

7. Enter your birth date in the field (well, my example doesn't have the correct year for me, but you get the point) and click OK.

You'll be back at the Customers content page. There is, of course, no Birthday field listed because we chose not to add it to the default view. And the reason we didn't add it to the default view is because not all users who view the list need to see the birthdays of their clients so easily.

But now that we have a date field on this list, we can create a view by birthday so you can see at a glance what customer birthdays are approaching. As a matter of fact, there is a view format perfectly suited to displaying birthdays conveniently—the Calendar View. And, to add to that, why not make the view Personal, so only you can see the birth dates easily? This helps avoid the customer receiving duplicate cards because someone else saw the Birthday Calendar view and thought they'd help out.

ROLL YOUR OWN SITE COLUMN

Site columns are pretty useful, and they become even more useful when you create your own. In my case I'd like to create a date field that the users can enter an expiration date into, but otherwise I want the field to have a default value of the date the list item is created plus ten days.

Site column are the property of an entire site, so once created on the site they can be added to any list on the site. To create a site column:

1. Go to the Site Action menu and select Site Settings.

2. In the Galleries category, select Site Columns. The Site Columns Gallery page will display all of the site columns, organized by their groups.

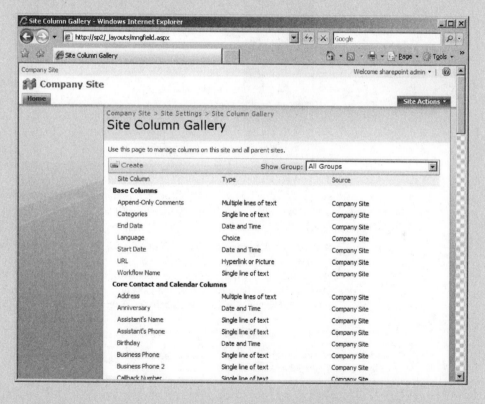

3. To create your own, just click Create. This will take you to a page filled with the standard sections for creating a new field, except this page has a section to specify to which site column group you want to add this field. You can create your own group to put your columns in, but I tend to keep my columns in the default Custom Columns group so they can be located easily.

4. In this example, I am going to create an Expiration field. This field is essentially a date field, except it has a default calculation value of today's date plus 10 days ([Today]+10). You learned how to create fields earlier in this chapter.

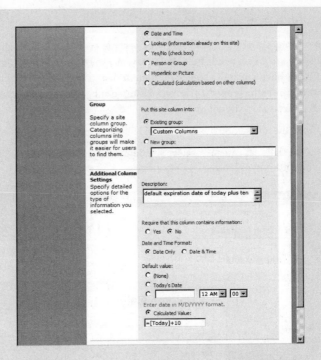

5. Once you've set up the field the way you like it, click OK. The new site column will show up in the Custom Columns group and be ready for use anywhere that a list needs that field in this site collection.

Keep in mind that if you want to tweak a site column once it's in a list, you can't (well, maybe you can rename it or change its description). Using a Site Column on a list is simply the application of a column definition or template, they were not meant to be customized after the fact, unfortunately. To customize a Site Column you have to do it at the gallery level. And when you do that, those customizations will then affect the Site Column's settings site wide.

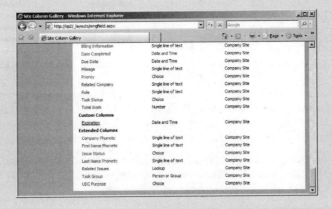

CREATE CALENDAR VIEW

A Calendar view of a list is just another way to display the list items. If you click the link for the item listed on a date, it will simply go to that list item's View page to see its content. However, unlike a Standard view, a selection box will not appear around the item when you hover over it. This explains why the same links that show up in the Selection Box popup are also listed in the Action bar of the View page of an item, so you can access the same actions should you be without the Selection Box menu.

To create a Calendar view:

1. Click the View menu and select Create View (you could also go to Settings and click Create View if you'd like).

2. In the Create View page that opens, choose the Calendar View format.

3. For the View name, my example uses **Birthdays**.

4. For the Audience, choose Create a Personal View.

5. Because we are tracking a single date, use the Birthday field for both the Begin and End fields for the Time Interval section.

6. In the Calendar Columns section, you can choose what kind of information is listed (within the limited amount of space you have in the calendar format) for each kind of display: Month, Week, and Day. For the Week and Day view (because those displays give you room for a second line), you can have two lines of information about the list item displayed for the date on which it will appear. My example doesn't need subheadings, so we'll use Full Name as the field for the Month View Title, Week View Title, and Day View Title (Figure 5.92).

FIGURE 5.92
Settings for new Calendar View

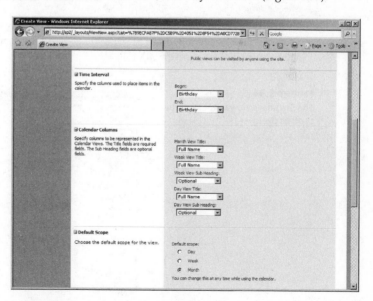

7. The Default Scope for the calendar is going to be Month View (which is the default selection for that section).

8. This view can also be filtered (if only for managing large lists); however, we don't need to do that here, so we can leave it alone.

9. Once you've completed all your settings, click OK to finish.

The Birthdays view is done and available on the Customers List content page. If you scroll to your birth month, you'll get to see what day your birthday will be (Figure 5.93).

FIGURE 5.93
The Birthdays Calendar view

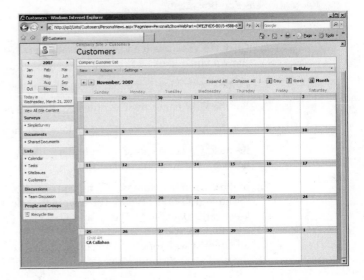

Because this is a Personal view, this view will not be available to someone else. I created the Birthday view when logged in as *shareadmin*. So if I log in as someone else, the Birthday view won't be available (Figure 5.94).

FIGURE 5.94
The Birthdays view is not available
to other users

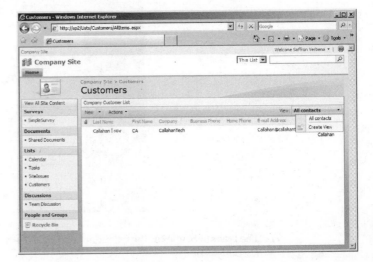

ADVANCED SETTINGS

Now that the list is available for data entry by the users, you might want to consider some permission management. To keep users from intentionally or accidentally messing up the other users' client data, you might want to limit what list items can be edited by whom. Furthermore, there may be a list item or two that you don't want anyone other than yourself to change.

IDENTITY SWAPPING

To log in as a different user, go to the Welcome menu and select Sign In as a Different User. This will trigger a Log In prompt so you can enter that other user's credentials. Remember though, if there are Web Parts or explorer views displaying folder content, the permissions of the user you are actually logged in as will take precedence over the SharePoint login. This means you might be able to view content that the other user cannot. Keep this in mind if you are testing their access.

There are two ways to manage the edit permissions of list items:

◆ Go to Advanced Settings in the List Settings and select to do Item-level Permission, such as allow only Edit access to users for the list items they created.

◆ Choose to manage the permissions of an item (which has some caveats).

This chapter explains the Advanced Settings, Item-Level Permissions for a list. However, if you want to explore managing the permissions for lists and individual items in more detail, visit Chapter 11, "Users and Permissions" which is dedicated to users and permissions.

To manage the edit or view permission of list items as a whole:

1. Go to Settings on the Action bar, and select List Settings on the dropdown menu.

2. On the Customize page that opens, click the Advanced Settings link in the General Settings category. The Advanced settings are pretty much standard for all lists, so what you learn here can be applied to other lists as well. This page has five sections:

Content Types   Enabling Content Types lets a list have more than one kind of item in it.

Item-Level Permissions   This is the section we need to work with now. As you can see in Figure 5.95, this section lets you set the Read permission for each item to let users read all items or only items they created, as well as set the Edit permissions to allow users to edit all items on the list, only their own, or none. (Being able to edit none of the items is a good setting for surveys if you want a candid response that cannot be changed later.)

Attachments   This section lets you enable or disable file attachments for list items. Attachments can be useful for customer contact items (such as directions, contracts, or even pictures) so that if you are promoted, your replacement can get an idea of what the customer looks like or how to get to their office.

Folders   For my example, we don't need to organize the Customers list in folders. Most lists are flat for easy viewing. However, in some cases, using a second level to organize list items is a good idea, so this option is available.

FIGURE 5.95
Item-level Permissions
for the Customers list

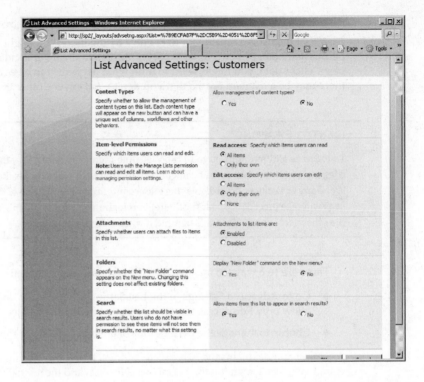

Search   This option is set to Yes by default. If you don't want this list's contents to show up in search results, set it to No.

3. For our purposes, everyone should be able to see all the Customer contacts, but only be able to edit the ones they entered themselves, so change the Edit Access setting in the Item-Level Permissions to Only Their Own.

4. For all other settings, leave the defaults as they are, especially Search. Leave Search set to Yes because we don't want the sales staff to have an excuse not to call a customer, and if they can't search for a number they may not call it.

5. If your settings for this page are complete, click OK to finish.

Now if users add items to this list, they will be able to edit those items. However, they cannot edit anyone else's. Remember, you can always go back and change these settings. If circumstances change and you need to lift that restriction, you know where to go to do so.

So, we've explored the existing lists and list templates of a SharePoint site, as well as customized them, but we've never created a custom list. And now, it's time.

Create a Custom List

To create your own list from scratch, you can either import a spreadsheet from Excel or you can create a standard list and set up the fields yourself before adding data. My example will show you the more difficult one of the two: how to create a custom standard list. Creating a list has at least two steps. First you create the list, then you create the fields for the list. You will need to create the fields from scratch, unless you use site columns. It's at this point you begin to see the true value of site columns.

1. Go to Create on the Site Action Menu.

2. On the Create page that appears, select Custom List in the Custom Lists category.

   The New list page has only two sections (Figure 5.96) which should look familiar to you if you've created a list from a template before: Name and Description and Navigation. In the Name and Description fields, enter the data pertinent to this list. Remember to keep the Name for the list short because it will be part of the Web address for the list and its views. For Navigation, leve the default of displaying the list on the Quick Launch bar.

FIGURE 5.96
Creating a new custom list

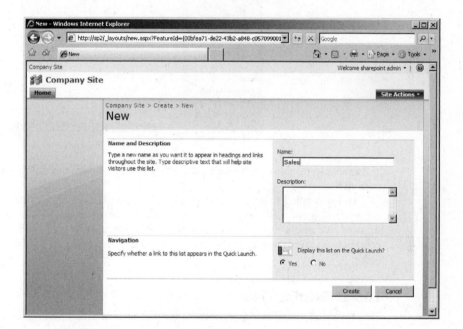

3. In this case, let's call this list **Sales** and leave the description blank (you can always change it later by going into the list's settings and selecting Title, description, and navigation).

4. For Navigation, leave the default and ensure that this list will have a link to it in the Quick Launch bar.

5. To complete the custom list creation, click Create.

That's it; you are at your new list's content page. As you can see in Figure 5.97, there are already two fields in this list: Attachment and Title. The attachment field is indicated by the little paper clip icon. An ID, created by, and modified by field also are created, but they are not displayed in the default view. That title field gets created whether you want it or not. It is the default first field and required.

FIGURE 5.97
A new custom list

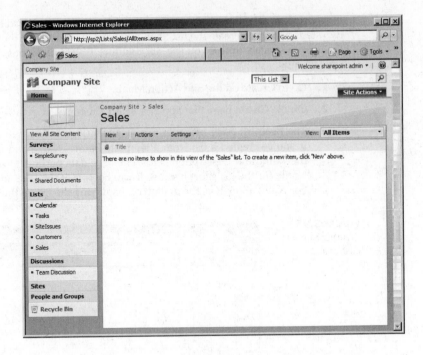

Let's wrap up this chapter by adding several useful fields and doing some fun things with your custom list.

This list is going to be pretty simple. Let's edit an existing field (might as well not waste it) and create a Salesperson field so we can assign sales orders to people. We should also have text fields for item sold and a currency-formatted cost field. And, while we're at it, let's use the site column created in a sidebar earlier in the chapter called Expiration for an expiration date on the sales order.

Edit an Existing Field

There were a few fields already created for this custom list by default. One of them is required automatically and can't be deleted; the Title field. Although Title is as good a name as any for a default single line text single line text field, it would better suit this list if it were renamed.

1. Click the Settings button on the Action bar and select List Settings.

HEY, WHERE'S INCOMING E-MAIL?

There is no link for Incoming E-Mail in the Communications category on the Customize page for this custom list. Custom lists don't have the built-in email handlers that many of the prebuilt lists do. This is why custom lists cannot do incoming email. Do not despair though. You know what the prebuilt lists are about, so find one that does do email and customize it.

Since the Title field is already there, we are going to change it a little so it fits the list better. Because it is a built-in field, and it generally is the field used to open a list item, it's best to try to keep the field and just rename it. We are going to use the field as a Sales Order field.

2. To edit the Title field, click on its link in the Column section. That will open the Change Column page. Go to the first section and change the name to **Sales Order**.

3. Because all of the defaults are fine (require the field and maximum number of characters), just click OK. Notice that you can't change the data type for the field, it has to be a single line of text. However there are some settings you can change. If the field created by you, you'd have been able to do more editing.

That should change the name of the Title field to Sales Order, making it a little more relevant. And now we are ready to create the other fields for this list.

Add a Person or Group Field

On to creating the Salesperson field. We *could* make this field a simple text field and have the users just type in the name of the sales person for the sales orders. But why have the users type anything in, and possibly introduce typing errors, when they could use the Person or Group field to simply look up the name?

1. To start, click Create Column in the Columns section of the Customize page (see Figure 5.98).

FIGURE 5.98
The new Salesperson field

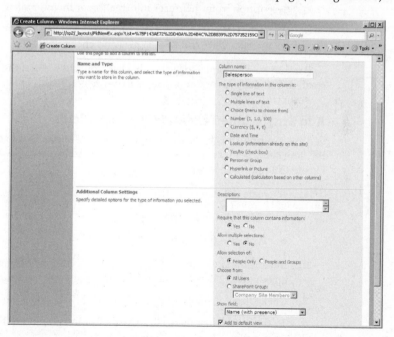

2. In the Create Column page, create the Salesperson field (see Figure 5.98). For the Column name, use **Salesperson** (obviously).

3. For the data type, choose Person or Group.

4. For the Additional Column settings, require that this field contain information. Do not allow multiple selections (only one salesperson gets commission per sale), and allow this field to have only a person's name (People only).

PEOPLE PICKER PICKED A PECK OF PERSONS

The People Picker field that the Person or Group field type uses accesses the site's (and even the domain, if it is set to) permission information, which includes groups as well as individual users. However, you can limit this field to just show SharePoint users, which is what I am going to do.

You can allow the field to choose from a particular site group, or allow it to access all groups (SharePoint or Active Directory) to resolve the username that is entered.

5. My example doesn't have SharePoint groups set up in such a way that specify a group for users will work, so the setting is fine as it is on All Users.

Because the Person or Group field is essentially a lookup field for the People and Groups list, you can actually decide what data from the user information of the person you are selecting will appear in the field. If you type a username in the field, the value returned could be their name with the Presence button next to it (if you have that enabled), or maybe the picture or description from their user information or their email address.

6. Leave the default set to Name (with presence, in case someone is accessing SharePoint while using Office 2007 and Messenger) and click OK.

Back on the Customize page for this list, you can see that the new Salesperson field has been created. There are several more fields to create before this list is done.

Add Single-Line Text and Currency Fields

For this example, this list is also going to need a simple field to display the name or description of the item being sold, as well as one that lists the item's cost. (See Figure 5.98 for an idea of what the Create Column page looks like.)

1. To create the Item Sold field, click Create Column and enter the following values:
   - Column Name: **Item Sold**
   - Type: **Single line of text**

2. In Additional Columns, require that this column contain information and otherwise keep all defaults (255 character maximum, no default value, and add to default view).

3. Click OK.

4. To create the Cost field, click Create Column and enter the following values:
   - Column Name: **Cost**
   - Type: **Currency**

Require that this column contain information.

5. Specify a minimum value for this column at **5.00**. This means that the item will not be able to be saved unless the value of this field is greater than or equal to 5.00.

6. Leave the decimal and default values as they are.

7. Leave the Currency format at the US default.

8. Click OK.

The next two fields for this Custom list are a little fancier. The first one is a Customer lookup field. This field is meant to connect to the Customers contact list so the data entry person won't need to type in a customer name if it already exists in the Customers list.

Add a Lookup Field

1. To create the Customers field, click Create Column.

2. For the Column name, use **Customer**. Choose Lookup for the data type.

3. In the Addition Column Settings section, require that this column contain information.

4. Also in that section, select Customers in the Get Information From field. This selects the list that the lookup field will be accessing.

5. Choose Company as the column to which the lookup field will connect. (It will default to a value of the first company in the Customer list unless you specify otherwise.)

6. Do not allow multiple selections beneath the In this Column field because there should be only one customer per sales order. Allowing multiple selections makes it possible to choose more than one item from the Company field of the Customers list (this option is used in the Issue Tracking list). Keep it in mind for other lists you might make, but it's not appropriate here.

7. Keep all other defaults and click OK.

The final field to create for this list is the Expiration field. This is a site column that we created earlier in the chapter and doesn't need to be created manually. This is also a good example of why you would create a site column (convenience) and how it can be used in whatever lists you'd like on the site.

Add a Custom Site Column

One of beautiful things about Site Columns is their ease of use. Yes, it's a little inconvenient to have to go directly to the Site Column Gallery to create your own Site Columns (rather than just clicking a setting on a field you've already created and tested in a list to add it to the gallery). Regardless, Site Columns can't be beat for their convenience when creating or modifying lists.

1. To add the Expiration field (which was the custom column we added to the Site Columns gallery earlier in the chapter) to the Sales list, simply click Add from existing Site Columns in the Columns section of the Customize page.

We'll be taken to the Add Columns from Site Columns page (see Figure 5.99), where we can select Custom Columns from the Site Columns Groups dropdown menu. This is the group that contains the site column we added earlier in the chapter.

FIGURE 5.99
Add Custom Site Column

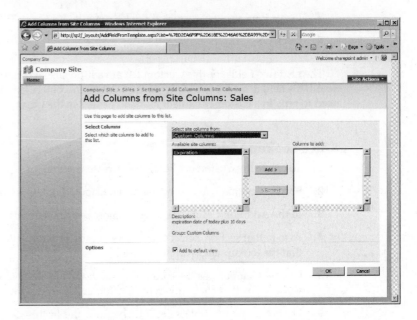

2. Select Expiration from the Available Site Columns list, and click the Add button. Allow the column to be added to the default view.

3. Click OK to finish.

INDEX COLUMNS

I didn't set any column indexing in the exercise because that is primarily done only in the case of extremely large (around 10,000 items) lists. However, if you are planning to have huge lists, consider indexing columns. Indexing a column in a large list helps the server organize and filter those list items more quickly. Indexing is resource intensive, and you should index as few columns per list as possible, because the amount of RAM it takes to index a column begins to take its toll.

To maximize how quickly a list can propagate a view when a user accesses it, it is a best practice to create views that limit the number of items seen at one time. To make those views work better, they should filter by a field that is indexed. Try to use the same indexed field as the main focus in as many views as possible. Index additional fields only if they are going to be the focus of views that cannot contain the original indexed column.

To set a column to be indexed, go to the list's List Settings, go to the Columns section, and select Indexed Columns. There you can select a column (or columns) to be indexed or remove indexing from a column.

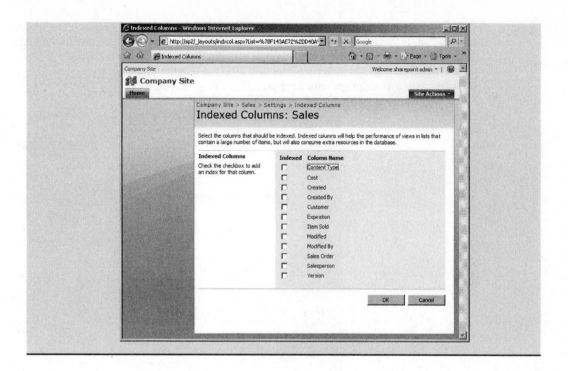

That's it. The Custom List is complete. To give it a test run, go to the List's content page (click the list name in the breadcrumb above the customized page title), and then click New on the Action bar (see Figure 5.100).

FIGURE 5.100
The finished new custom list

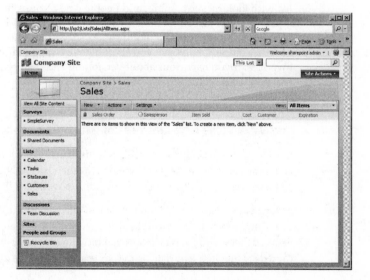

In Figure 5.101, you can see the required fields, indicated with a red asterisk. The Salesperson field is a People Picker. The Customer field is a dropdown list, indicating that it is a lookup field and that it is defaulting to the first (and only) list item in the Customers list. Finally, you can see that the Expiration field is there, is a date field, and has a default date of today plus 10 days (complete with a description, which can be removed later if you'd like).

FIGURE 5.101

A new item for the new custom list

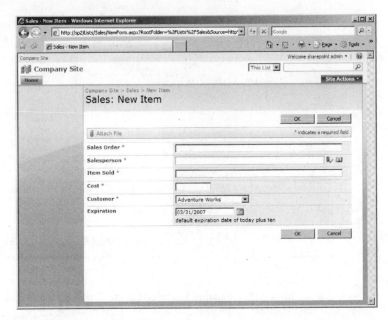

So there you have it. If you add data to the item and click OK, you'll see the fields that were meant to be added to the default view, complete with their data. That's it. Your very own custom list with lookup, site column, and People And Groups fields.

That should just about do it for your introduction to lists. You've covered built-in lists, List templates, custom lists, list modification, views, and more. Lists have many options and can become complex; however, you should have enough information to experiment and make your own lists. If you're curious about versioning and using content types, continue to Chapter 6 for more on those features.

LIST VIEW WEB PARTS AND THE COMMON FIELD CONNECTION

In addition to the ability to use lookup fields to access field information from one list to another, lists also have the ability to be "connected" using their corresponding List View Web Parts (the Web Parts you learned about in Chapter 4, "Introduction to Web Parts").

As long as they have a field in common, you can connect the Web Parts of two lists to filter the view of one with the selected record of the other; synchronizing their data makes them both more useful. This helps List View web parts be more dynamic, allowing users to capitalize on the commonalities among the data of the site's lists right on the home page.

This means you can put the Web Parts of the Customers list and the Sales list on the home page. Then, create a connection between them so if you click on an item in the Sales web part, the corresponding Customer web part will change to show only records that match the common field data from the selected Sales list item.

To make this happen, you have to make certain the List View web parts you want to connect are on the same page, and are each displaying the common field they will use for the connection. To insure the field will be in the web part, either add it to the default view for the list, or create a view with the field displayed. Then in the tool pane for the web part, assign it as the selected view.

On the page that contains the web parts you want to connect, click on the Site Actions menu, and select Edit Page (I am assuming you are going to want this to do this in Shared View). This will put the page and web parts in Edit Mode (the connections option only shows up in the dropdown menu of a web part in Edit Mode).

In the title of the web part you want to do the filtering (in this case it's Sales) click the edit button, and in the dropdown menu click Connections. This will popout a menu. This menu has two options:

◆ Provide Row. If this option is selected this web part will be the one that filters the other by what item is chosen from its contents.

◆ Get Sort/Filter From. If this option is selected, the contents of the web part will be filtered to match the common field data from the item selected in the other web part.

Since we are going to filter the Customers web part by what we select in Sales, that means that the Sales web part is the row provider. Select Provide Row To. Then, because the Customers web part will be the one on the page being filtered, select Customers.

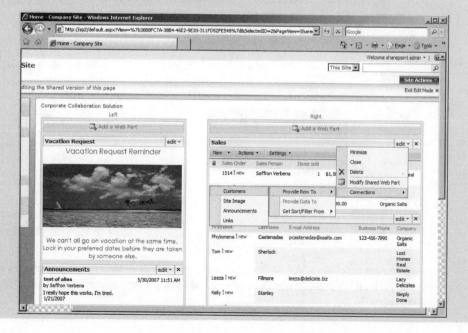

It will trigger a popup window (you may have to set your browser to allow it). Chose the field that the Sales web part will use to filter the Customers web part. In this example it's the Customer field.

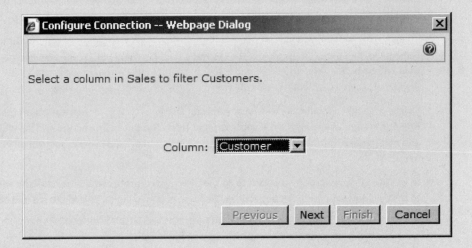

Click Next. You will then need to choose the field with the common data that the other web part (Sales) will be filtered by (in this case that would be the Company field). When you've chosen that you can click Finish.

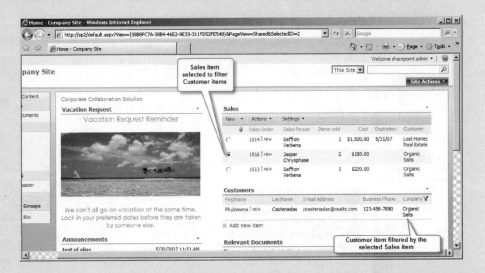

If you want to get fancy, you can have one web part be the row provider and filter several other List View web parts on the page. So when one record in the row provider is chosen, it filters all of the connected web parts.

To remove a connection, go to either connected web part, go back through the steps as if you were connecting them (Edit Mode ➢ edit menu ➢ Connections), choose the correct connection type, then select the web part from the list you are disconnecting from. When the popup comes up, click the Remove Connection link at the top of the window. There will be a warning dialog box prompting you to confirm it's okay. Click OK and the connection will be broken.

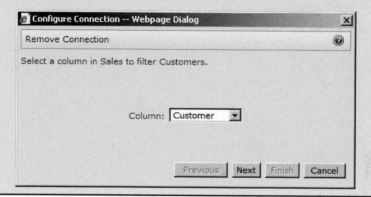

The Bottom Line

Use and Modify a List   Lists are the collaboration core of SharePoint. With the content stored in a database, lists can be used to track data, hold discussions, manage issues, and more.

Master It   How do you get to a list if it isn't displayed on the home page? And, once you find it, how do you get to the list's settings to modify it?

Modify a view and create a view   SharePoint uses views to display the content of lists. Much like reports, views can be modified to display any field in a list, in any order. Custom views can be created, with four different View formats to choose from.

Master It   What are the View formats, and which would you choose to display data grouped by a particular field?

Create a list from a template   SharePoint has, in addition to a few convenient, pre-built lists, has ready to go templates of common lists. This makes it very easy to simply create a new list based on an existing template, then customize it; rather than having to create one like it from scratch.

Master It   What list template creates a list that is meant to work with the Three-State Workflow? How would you go about creating that list?

Create a custom list   In addition to the pre-built lists and the templates, SharePoint has the option to create custom lists from scratch. Lists can be custom made in two ways: by importing from an Excel Spreadsheet, or by manually building one. All lists require at least one field (by default the *Title* field) and include system generated columns for *ID*, *Created By* and *Modified By*.

Master It   You're creating a custom list for the Human Resources department to help manage employees. You've created the list, added a field for them to lookup employees from Active Directory, and another column for their department. As part of the process, you've decided to photograph all employees. These pictures are stored in a Picture Library and can be viewed by HR personnel. You'd like to provide HR a way to display these pictures on the list. You also want to indicate if the employee is full time or part time. How would you go about adding this information to the list?

Chapter 6

Introduction to Libraries

SharePoint libraries are lists intended to be used for managing documents. Their list items are focused on the files attached to them, with features specific to handling the creation and editing of those files, such as requiring check in/check out, versioning, and content approval. Libraries make it easier for users to work together on documents in a consistent and secure manner.

Libraries are often the most compelling reason people even consider using SharePoint. They are generally the foundation of the collaborative work users might need to accomplish; be it sharing documents, spreadsheets, slideshows, or forms.

In this chapter, you'll learn how to:

◆ Create a document library

◆ Use the different kinds of libraries

◆ Set check out, content approval, and versioning

◆ Manage content types

What Are Libraries?

Libraries are lists that are essentially known by the kinds of files they will contain: documents, pictures, forms, and wiki documents.

There are four different types of libraries:

Document Library   Using the name "Document Library" for this type of library rather obscures what it really is. A Document library is a list that creates a new file of some type whenever you create a new list item. The file type depends on what template you associate with the list itself (and doesn't have to be a document template). If you enable content types, the file type depends on what type of library list items (and their associated template) you want to have available for the list. This list also has features such as content approval, versioning, RSS, and incoming email. In addition, libraries can also mark their list items as checked in or checked out, locking the list item and its attached file as read only on check out and unlocking the item upon check in to the library. This feature is unique to libraries. Document libraries also have an Explorer view that lets you see the contents of the library as file system icons instead of list items. SharePoint document libraries are supposed to replace file shares; the Explorer view helps make users comfortable with the transition. This view makes it easy to drag and drop files that need to be stored in a library from a file share. In addition, document libraries can make good use of content types and folders that may not be clearly useful for other types of lists.

Forms Library   This type of library requires Microsoft Office InfoPath, preferably InfoPath 2007. InfoPath is a program that creates forms for users to fill out. More specifically, it lets you design your own form templates; when a user opens the template, it creates a *form instance,* which allows the user to fill the form with data. InfoPath files are XML files, and they require InfoPath to be installed locally on the machine from which you will be using the library. This type of library is useful for companies that process vacation requests, purchase orders, and other kinds of InfoPath forms that need to be filled out by the users. Because InfoPath forms are based on templates, if you move files from one form library to another, you'll need to relink it to its template.

Picture Library   This type of library was meant to contain image files. As a matter of fact, this kind of library was meant to store images you can access elsewhere on the site, because each image file itself is given a direct URL that can be referred to in an image Web Part or hyperlink field of a list item (such as an item in a Contacts list). You may have noticed that images aren't inserted into fields of Web Parts (such as the Content Editor), or RSS pages; instead these features all refer to an image's location and display the image from there. No embedding is necessary. Picture libraries were meant to be one of those locations used to store those images to be referred to later. Remember, image files in a picture library are stored in the content database, so they are convenient to the entire site and are backed up when the content databases are backed up. A picture library uses the picture manager that is installed with Office (preferably 2007, but 2003 has one too) to edit images and add multiple images to the library, if the user does not have an Office product on their machine, they will only be able to upload one picture at a time to the library. Other interesting things about the picture library are that it has several unique views and the ability to display its contents in a slideshow.

Wiki Library   This library is meant to be the primary focus of a wiki site, and it is basically a document library of HTML files that support the wiki syntax when linking to other files in the same library. This library is unique in so far as it displays the contents of the wiki file called Home instead of displaying its contents in a list on its content page. To actually access the content page for the library, you can click on the library's link in the content breadcrumb. This sort of library has versioning enabled by default, and it does not allow content types. Unlike the other library types, it does not allow Explorer view, meaning you cannot drag and drop multiple files into the library. Wiki libraries have no means to simply upload existing pages.

Creating a library is easy; but before you create one, you need to do some planning first. You should ask yourself these questions:

◆ Is there a maximum file size that you want to be allowed on SharePoint sites? The default is 50MB; is that acceptable? If not, it will need to be changed, and that change needs to be considered when planning for SharePoint storage requirements.

◆ Does the library require special permissions, or do certain files require special permissions?

◆ Does the library require check out/check in, versioning, or content approval?

◆ Should the library have a single kind of file template associated with it, or should it have content types enabled so you can have several kinds of templates available to be created from the same library?

◆ Is the list going to contain 10,000 documents or more? If so, should this library be organized as a list, or should you use folders? (When creating a view for a list containing folders, remember to decide whether or not the view should display content from those folders in the library's default view.)

◆ Like any list, a library item has fields such as Name, Title, Created By, etc. What kinds of fields do you want for your library items? They will become the metadata or properties associated with the file attached to the library item, so you should decide what kind of data will be used in the file's properties.

LIBRARY PLANNING FOR WORKFLOWS

Like any list, a library can have new fields for categorizing, organizing, and creating workflows. For example, if you create a choice field called Status with three choices in it and an Assigned To field, you can apply the three-state workflow to the library and create tasks in a Tasks list (with email notifications) for each document. That could be used to enforce a review process. If your company is going to have custom document management workflows, consider their needs when creating your libraries.

To get a feel for libraries in general, let's use the document library that is created by default for the Team site called Shared Documents. To get to the Shared Documents Library, simply click its link in the Quick Launch bar (Figure 6.1).

FIGURE 6.1
Shared documents in the Quick Launch bar

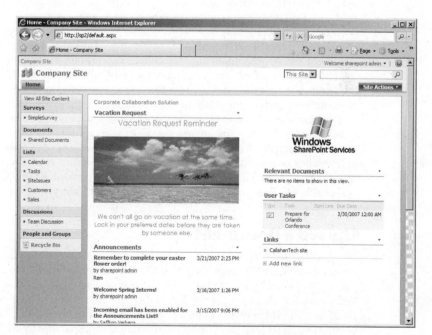

FIGURE 6.2
The Shared Documents
content page

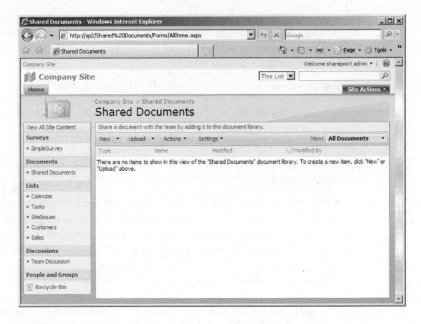

FIGURE 6.2
The Shared Documents
content page

The Shared Documents content page (see Figure 6.2) looks very much like any list. It has a content area to display the library items, the fields for the All Documents view (the all items, default view for the library at this point) are Type, Name, Modified, and Modified By. The Type field will display an icon relating the type of file or template used for the library item. This is useful if you are uploading or creating different files of different types in this library. People can accidentally name two different kinds of files the same name, such as the ProjectPlans Word document and an accompanying ProjectPlans PowerPoint presentation. You can tell them apart by their file type icon. This is why that column in the All Documents view is needed. The buttons on the Action bar are a little different because of the introduction of the Upload button. Otherwise the New, Actions, and Settings buttons are where you would expect them in any standard list.

Libraries can be used to create new documents—depending on how the templates those new documents will be based on are managed—or you can upload existing files to the library. Keep in mind that templates were meant to manage only what is newly created in a library. The template or templates associated with the library are not a limitation on the types of files (text files, image files, audio files, etc.) that can be *uploaded* there. You can upload any kind of existing file (unless it is explicitly blocked administratively) to a document library.

Upload a Document

To upload a file (or files if you'd like to upload more than one at a time) to the library, just click the Upload button, which opens the Upload Document page (see Figure 6.3). It has a check box for overwriting existing files. This option allows you to save over an existing file and add the changes you've made to that file's version list. Notice also that, if you wanted to, you could upload multiple files, which would open a page where you can browse to a location and select more than one file to upload (you can also choose to upload multiple files by clicking the down arrow next to the Upload button and choosing it from the dropdown).

FIGURE 6.3
The Upload
Document page

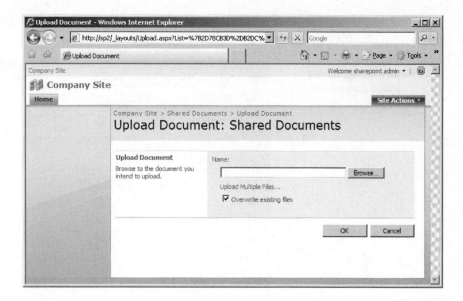

My example keeps things simple and uploads only one file (named *uploaded* in this case). Simply browse to the file you'd like to upload, select it, and click Open in the Choose File dialog box. Once the path for the file is listed on the Upload Document page, click OK to add the file to the document library.

When you add a file to a document library, it actually creates a library list item and adds the file to it. In Figure 6.4, you can see by the icon in the Type column that the file type for my example's new library item is a Word document. SharePoint will try to figure out what the file type is and indicate it; otherwise, it will display a default file icon. The name of the file is the linked field for the library item.

In a standard list, if you click the linked field of an item, it would open the item's View page and display that list's field contents. But because a library is so focused on the files associated with the library item, the linked field is linked to the *file* not the library item itself. Meaning, in this case, if you click on that library item's linked field, it will trigger the appropriate application to open the file and allow you to work on it. Otherwise, to see the fields of the library item you have to specifically select View properties from the item's dropdown menu.

In addition to the Name field, there are the Modified Date and Modified By fields, which are automatically filled in upon creation of the library item and any edits made to the item or its attached file. There are other fields that can be used for an item in this library as well, such as item ID, file size, or version, but they are not available in the default All Items view for the

Documents Library (I mention them in case you'd like to use them in a custom view of your own).

FIGURE 6.4
An uploaded file in a
shared document library

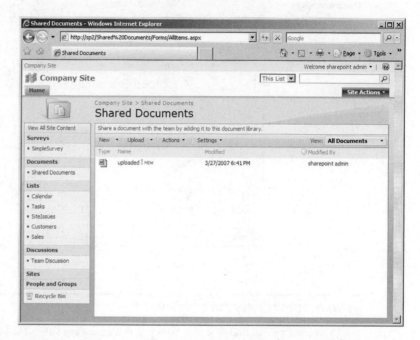

By default the Shared Documents document library uses a Word 2003 document template. This is why, while working in the Shared Documents library, I will literally be working with documents. But keep in mind that you can have a document library focused on PowerPoint presentations just as easily as you can Word documents. Then you would be creating and working on presentations instead of documents. Don't be limited by the name of the type of library or my simple example, document libraries can use other kinds of templates and therefore focus on other kinds of files.

Create a New Document

When you create a new document in a library, rather than uploading an existing one, it creates a new file based on the template associated with the library; opening the file in the correct application (you must have that application installed locally) so you can work on it. When you save the file to the library for the first time it also creates the library item for the file, and populates the item's fields with data that is considered part of the properties of the file associated with it.

To create a brand-new document based on the library's template, you can follow these steps:

1. Click the New button on the Action bar.

2. You very likely will get a dialog box ironically warning you that some files can harm your computer, and that you are opening a `template.doc` file from the SharePoint server. Click OK if that Warning dialog box appears.

3. A Word document will open. Simply type some text into the document and save it.

FIGURE 6.5
Saving a new document to the Shared Documents Library

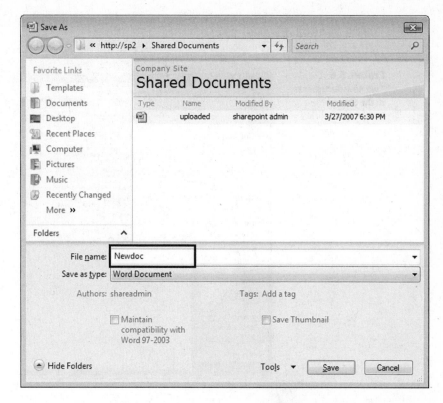

4. You'll be prompted to name the file; my example uses **Newdoc** (Figure 6.5). In the Save As dialog box, the file is being saved to the Shared Documents folder on the SharePoint server, which is `http://sp2` in my example. Notice that the uploaded file is already displayed in the library and that the name of the file you are saving should be in the File name field (I've outlined the file name in Figure 6.5 for your convenience).

5. Name the file and click Save.

6. Close the Word document.

[COMPATIBILITY MODE]

Interestingly, despite the fact that Windows SharePoint Services version 3.0 is intended to be compatible primarily with Office 2007, the default template for the document library is from Office 2003; probably for backward compatibility. If you create a new document in the Shared Documents Library or any library using the default Word template and get a dialog box warning you that the file format will be changed, that's why. This is also why Word 2007 might have [Compatibility Mode] displayed in the title bar. Feel free to keep backward compatibility or not. In my case, I am going with the 2007 file type.

As you can see in Figure 6.6, two documents are now in the Shared Documents Library. Both of them are Word document files.

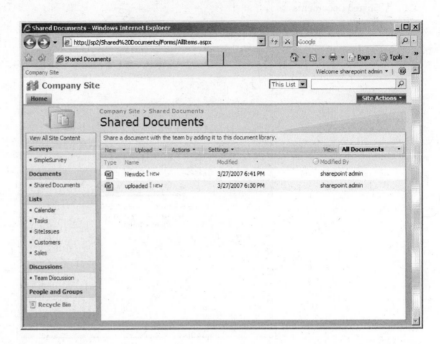

Each document name field is capable of triggering a selection box and dropdown menu to edit, view properties, and do other individual item tasks. To see what tasks are available for a document library item, move your mouse pointer over the Name field of the new document you created (Newdoc in my example) and click in the selection box. This will trigger a dropdown menu with some familiar list item options and some new ones. On the dropdown will be the following options:

View Properties   This menu option is used to see the metadata, or field data, for the library item. It corresponds to the View Item option in a standard list; however, in this environment, you should think of the item fields as document properties.

Edit Properties   This option lets you edit the metadata of the library item.

Manage Permission   This option lets you apply unique permissions to this particular library item.

Edit in Microsoft Office Word   As the option says, it allows you to open the library item's attached file for editing in Microsoft Word. For this to work, of course, you must have Word installed locally on the machine with which you are browsing the site. This menu item is also triggered when you simply click the name of the library item. If the file had not been a Word document, the menu item would reflect that (if SharePoint can identify the file type).

Delete   This is the option that removes the document and its library item from the library and puts it in the Recycle Bin (I mean the SharePoint site's user Recycle Bin, not the one on the workstation desktop). Remember that when things are deleted from lists or libraries, they are not completely gone until they are either removed from the Recycle Bin as well or the Recycle Bin times out and all items of a certain age are deleted (30 days by default).

Send To   This menu option actually has a few functions. Items in a library can be sent to other libraries and locations. As SharePoint and its document libraries have evolved, libraries have become more connected to other libraries and site resources; a document workspace can be generated from a document in a library, or finished documents from a library can be sent to a final archive library.

By default, Send To offers the options to email a link (create an email with a link to the document), create a document workspace, download a copy, or send a copy of the document to another location (like a different library). There is also an option in the overall library settings to define a custom library or location to use as a default place to send a copy of the document. Documents sent to a different library can be updated with changes from the original library. The secondary location is generally meant to be an archive. What that means is the secondary location cannot update changes made to the document copy there *back* to the original library. The updates are only one way.

Check Out   This option locks a document from being checked out as read only for everyone but the person checking it out. This helps limit the amount of overlapping work that might be done on a document simultaneously. When a user is done with a document, they can check it back in, making it available to be edited by someone else. Check out is not required by default, but it can be set to be so. If Check out is required, then no document can be edited unless it is Checked out. That means that to edit a document, a user must check it out, otherwise it will be read only. Check out can be overridden by someone with the permission to do so, usually an administrator or list manager.

Alert Me   This setting is the same one for standard lists, and means that you can configure email notification if there are changes made to library items, based on a limited criteria, such as changes made only to documents you created, or all document.

Most people focus on the documents in a library, but they are just attachments for the library list items. You can create fields for any library item just as you could any list. You can require that those fields be filled out before the item and its document are saved. This makes it possible to require users to enter data that can be used to track documents, search for them, or trigger workflows.

WORD 2007, OR NOT?

You can tell which Word documents are formatted for 2007 and which aren't. In the Type column, documents that are formatted as .docx have an extra blue outline behind the stylized W at the top-left of the icons. Word 2003 and lower documents, documents that use the .doc extension, have no extra blue mark near their W on the top left of their icons.

FIGURE 6.8
Edit Properties of
Library Item

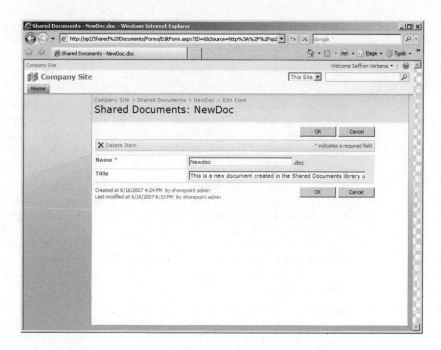

Right now there are very few editable fields for this library. To see what those fields are, in the item selection box dropdown menu, select Edit Properties. In Figure 6.8, you can see that the Name and Title fields are available for data entry. Name is the only required field. In fact, the Name field gets propagated with the filename of the document you upload or create from template in the library. The Title is not required; therefore you generally don't get prompted to fill the Title field in when you create a document. As a matter of fact, for your convenience, when you save a document to a library SharePoint will use at least a portion of the first sentence to fill the Title field for you if you don't fill it in yourself.

Add a Required Field to a Library

One of the nice things about having a library item associated with a document is its fields. Those fields are considered the document's properties. So if you want additional fields that better identify a document, then add them to the library item. Better yet, you can force a field to be filled in when a user creates a new document in the library, making certain that the field is effectively used. To force a field to be filled in when creating, uploading, or editing a file in a library (if the item doesn't have the field filled yet), you need to set that field as required. My example creates a Project field that requires the user to enter a value so anyone can see at a glance which projects are associated with which documents.

Adding fields to a library is exactly like adding fields to a list, although how the library handles fields is different, as you'll see in a moment.

1. Simply click Settings in the Action bar, and select Document Library Settings from the drop-down menu.

2. On the Customize page that appears, in the Columns section, click Create Column. (There seem to be only four columns by default for this library, but that is not the case; the columns displayed are the only ones that are editable.)

3. As you can see in Figure 6.9, in this example the column should be named **Project**. Keep the data type Single Line of Text, give it a description, and require that the field contain information, which is the whole point of this required field. Otherwise, keep the default maximum characters, make sure to leave the default value blank, and add the field to the default view. Remember that adding a field to default view ensures that the field shows up in the default view of the library.

FIGURE 6.9

Create Column Properties

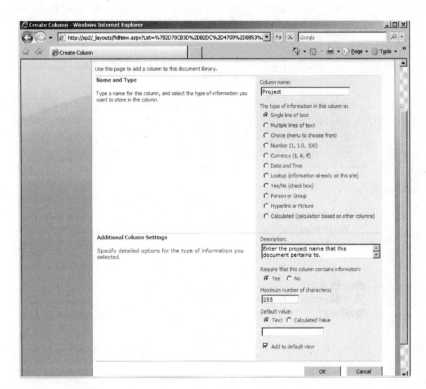

4. Once the settings are complete, click OK to finish creating the new Project field.

5. On the customize page for the library (where you should be able to see that the new field is in the Columns list and is required), click the Shared Documents link in the breadcrumb to get back to the library's content page. Project should be a new column heading on the right of the content area.

Of course, the field will be blank for the two documents already in the library because they were created before the field was. However, because the field is required, if these documents are edited, the field will have to contain data before their changes can be saved—and of course, this field will need to be filled in for new documents as well.

Edit a Document with a Required Field

To prove that we can't save a document that doesn't have required fields filled in, let's edit the document we created.

1. To edit a document in a document library, simply click on it or use the selection box dropdown menu and select Edit in Microsoft Office Word.

2. A Warning dialog box will come up reminding you that you will be opening a file; make sure it displays the filename you want, choose to edit the document, and click OK.

Word might prompt you for your SharePoint login. Your login does two things. It confirms that you can access the location of the file. And if you want to use the task pane to work with the document, your login tells Word who you are so it can propagate the pane with the correct data.

WHAT, NO LOGIN PROMPT?

If you are feeling left out because you didn't get prompted to login, fear not. If you are logged into the client computer with the same account used to access the library, and the site's address is a local intranet zone in that computer's Internet Explorer, then you may not get the prompt to login because it will pass the local user's credentials transparently.

If you open the document in Word 2007, you will see a set of fields at the top of the page area, or you might get a warning like the one in Figure 6.10. If you get the warning, click the Edit Properties button. It will open the Document information panel and display the editable fields for the document library.

FIGURE 6.10
The Properties warning in
Word 2007

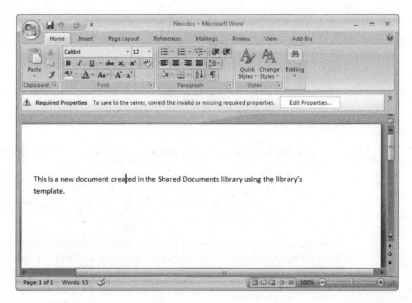

PANELS AND POPUPS

I am using Word 2007; however, if you are using a previous version of Word, a popup box will appear when you save changes instead of an information panel. You can enter your data changes in the popup box.

SERVER PROPERTY FIELDS

The fields for the library are considered Server Property fields, because most Word documents come with properties of their own, such as summary, author, tags, etc. If you use the document properties, rather than the server document properties, they will not show up in SharePoint. Make sure that you are looking at the Server properties to actually access the document library fields for the document.

In Figure 6.11, the Project field is marked with a red asterisk (it looks gray in the book, but trust me, it's red). This means it must contain data if you want to save the changes you will be making to this document.

FIGURE 6.11
Document Properties–Server fields for a library document

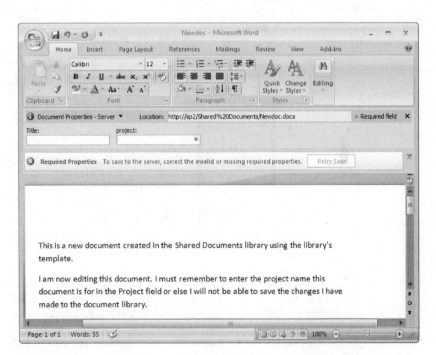

For example, edit the document but don't fill in the required field, and then click Save to save your changes. You will immediately get an Error dialog box warning you that this file cannot be saved because some properties are missing or invalid. This means, in this case in particular, that you did not fill in the Project field. To fix the issue, click the surprisingly large Go to Document

Information Panel button in the dialog box. It will take you back to the Document Information Panel so you can enter what data is required.

In the Document Information Panel, enter data into the Project field. In my example I used, conveniently, the word **Example** as the data in the Project field. Then click the convenient Retry Save button which will be located just below the Document information panel. Now that the field has data in it, the Save function will work fine. Close Word and go back to the Shared Documents Library in SharePoint.

Back in SharePoint, as you can see in Figure 6.12, the Newdoc (or whatever you named your document) now has data in its Project field. If your users are using Word 2007, encourage them to use the Document Information Panel. This allows them to conveniently see the library item fields for the document and easily manage data there. The Document information panel generally doesn't open automatically unless there is an empty field that requires data. To open it, select Office Button ➢ Prepare ➢ Properties. Remember that there are two kinds of properties: Word and Server (SharePoint). Be sure the users are on the Document Properties–Server information.

FIGURE 6.12
The new document with Project field data in the library

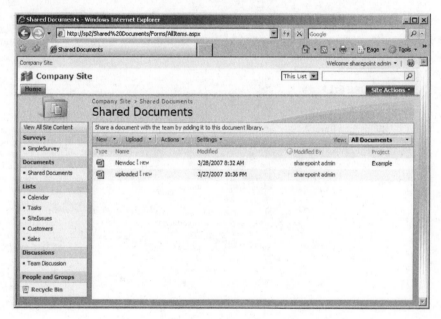

Also realize that, now that there is a required field, if you upload a file to the Shared Documents Library you will be prompted to fill in the required field before the upload can finish. To demonstrate this, click Upload on the Action bar and upload a file (my example is called Sample2003 which was created in Word 2003). After you choose a file to upload and click OK, the Properties page for the document item will come up, prompting you to enter data in the required field (as you can see in Figure 6.13).

When you upload a file that requires its fields to contain data, the file will be in a checked-out state (unavailable for everyone else but you) until you fill in the required fields. Basically, the document can be uploaded, but it's not considered "done" until all the necessary fields are filled out.

FIGURE 6.13
The Library Item Properties
page during file upload

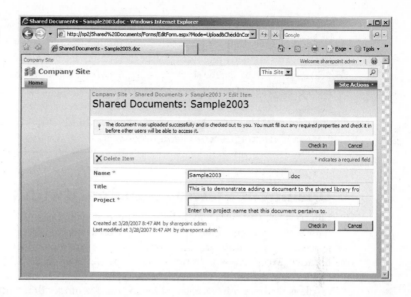

REQUIRED FIELDS AND WORD 2003

Required fields actually work better in Word 2003 than they do in Word 2007 for two reasons. The first is that when a field is required, it doesn't show up as an error in the interface and is, therefore, less likely to cause any user anxiety. If a field is required, it simply pops up a box when the document is being saved, or the application is closed, prompting the users to enter data in the required fields.

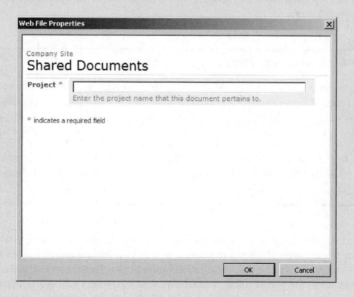

The second reason required fields work better in Word 2003 is that when a field is required for a document in a library, every time the file is edited, the prompt to enter data in the fields pops up during the Save process. This regularly reminds the user those fields are there. It also allows the user to easily change fields, such as changing the status of a document from editing to completed, despite the fact that those fields contain data. The user isn't obligated to change the data; they can just save it as is. Word 2007 does not remind the users of the required fields (at least not consistently) if the field is not empty. That means that once a field has data, the user must remember to edit the field manually if there is a required field that contains information that needs to be updated.

Opening or Viewing the Library with Windows Explorer

Libraries have an extra way of being viewed as well. Because SharePoint was originally used mainly for document management, Microsoft knew that companies would need a quick, familiar, and easy way to dump documents from a file share into a document library. Because of this, libraries (except the wiki library) can be opened or viewed with Windows Explorer.

Opening the library with Windows Explorer literally opens a Windows Explorer window and displays the library like a Web folder so you can simply drag and drop files into the library from a location on the local machine or a network share. You may think that's no big deal; but remember, a library is actually a table in the content database. This feature allows you to see the library as if it were a shared folder for those users unfamiliar with the concept of a list holding their files.

If you don't want to open a separate window, you can use the Explorer View from the View menu to display the library's contents as files and folders in the content area of the page. In Explorer View, the content area takes on the look and feel of a Windows Explorer window. Both Open with Windows Explorer and Explorer view do the same thing– show the library's contents as file system icons—they just conveniently give you the option of displaying those items in two different ways.

THE UNFORTUNATE PRICE OF PROTECTION

If you are trying to use Explorer View on a Vista workstation, you might need to disable Protected mode in Internet Explorer (IE). Protected mode does not allow Explorer View to work, forcing IE to open an Explorer window to display the library's contents instead of opening in the content area of the page.

You can disable protected mode to get Explorer View to work properly, but Internet Explorer 7 will really disapprove of not using protected mode, and as a rule, it's not considered best practice to go without it. Therefore, you might want to consider learning to love viewing a library's contents in a Windows Explorer window and doing without Explorer view in the browser.

Unfortunately, there is one little, maybe inconsequential, thing to worry about with viewing any library with Explorer: the library stores its template and standard view pages (like `allitems.aspx` or `upload.aspx`) in the library in a folder called Forms. Most users will not be able to see the Forms folder, but administrator/owners will (particularly if they have their folder options set to show hidden files). So teach them to be careful not to accidentally drag and drop files into that folder. Keep in mind that the Forms folder is a system folder, adding another folder to the library with the same name can cause intermittent issues with the original folder. You can use the Forms folder to access and easily edit the template for the library, as well as access the standard ASPX pages for the library like `AllItems.aspx` (which is the All Documents default view for the library).

There are two ways to use Explorer in a library:

◆ Open the Explorer view of the library in the content area of the list's page.

◆ Open a separate Explorer window with the contents of the library displayed there.

To open Explorer to display the library's contents in a separate window (Figure 6.14), click Actions in the Action bar, and then select Open with Windows Explorer. You may be prompted for your SharePoint login credentials again to make certain you have the right to have access to the library as a Web folder.

FIGURE 6.14
The Open with Windows Explorer window

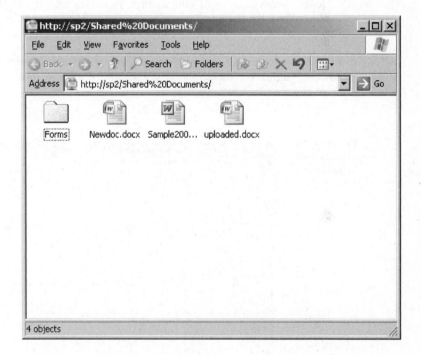

PERMISSIONS AND EXPLORER VIEW

Your login permissions on the local computer will impact which user account SharePoint will use when accessing a resource. Because Explorer is part of the operating system, it will use the locally logged in account as the context allowed to access that library, regardless of the credentials you use to login to SharePoint in the browser.

This is generally not a problem for most users. If their workstations are part of the domain, then they are logged into that machine with the same login that they would use in SharePoint. However, if you are testing what Explorer view might look like for a user with lesser permissions than you have, it might look like, from your machine, they have access to more than they actually do. You need to log on locally as that user, and then access SharePoint to see the full effect of their permissions. This also affects the way Page View Web Parts work if they are accessing shares where permissions might be an issue.

To experience Explorer View in the library's content page, simply click the View menu and select Explorer View. Then the contents of the library (plus a folder called Forms if you are logged in as the site administrator) should be displayed as files and folders in the content area (see Figure 6.15).

To easily move files from a file share to the library, simply drag and drop them into the Explorer View. For example, a document named "Security and Permissions Management" was dragged and dropped from a folder on my hard drive to the library in Figure 6.16 (I am assuming you already know how to drag and drop). Transferring files this way is essentially treated as uploading them and, therefore, they will be considered checked out by you (or whoever "uploaded" them), and unavailable to other users until data is entered into the required fields and the files are checked in.

FIGURE 6.15
Explorer View in the content area

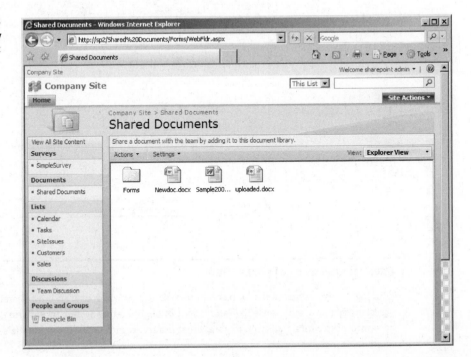

FIGURE 6.16
A document added to the library using Explorer View

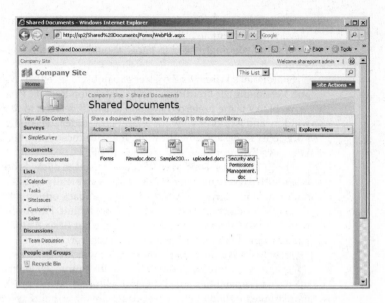

BULK LOADING

It's easy to add multiple documents to a library, either using Explorer View or doing an upload of multiple files using the Upload button on the Action bar. If you upload multiple files at once, remember that if they have required fields, they are checked out until you fill in those fields and then you can check them in. Keep in mind that an uploaded file is not visible to any other user until it is checked in.

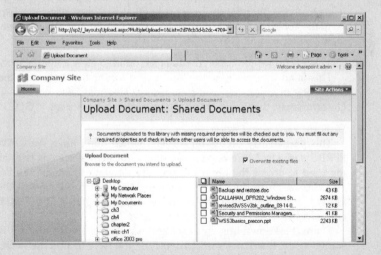

You can easily use Datasheet view to fill in fields in bulk. Doing so makes it easier to enter data into the Project column than it would be to enter each item individually. Datasheet view, and manipulating Views in general, are covered in detail in Chapter 5.

Of course, as an administrator, you are not only going to need to know how to use Explorer View, you are going to need to be able to troubleshoot it as well. Because of this, there are some details that you might need to know about how Explorer View works with SharePoint in order to support it.

SharePoint's Windows Explorer capability uses either WebDAV (Web Distributed Authoring and Versioning) or FrontPage Server Extension Remote Procedure Call protocol (FPRPC).

WebDAV is the preferred method and will be used to serve up both the Windows Explorer window and Explorer view for SharePoint under the conditions that the site is not using custom ports, SSL, or Basic Authentication. If any of those conditions are met, then the generation of Windows Explorer view will fail over to FPRPC.

FrontPage Extensions over RPC was meant to allow FrontPage and other Office products to work with documents over HTTP, and wasn't really meant to be used as a means to expose web folders to the enterprise. Although it is a fallback option for Explorer view access to libraries, WebDAV is obviously better suited as the default. However, FPRPC does work in those cases where the site must use a port other than 80 or Basic Authentication (which isn't a suggested authentication option for SharePoint in general).

WebDAV's Windows Explorer view or window is more integrated with the OS and therefore it has a more feature rich appearance, with a more 3D look, and the context menus that have all the normal capabilities. FPRPC is more limited, with a pre-XP look, and the context menus have more limited options. So if a user complains that their Explorer view looks weird, their system may have defaulted to using FPRPC to produce the view for some reason, rather than WebDAV.

Occasionally there are some common problems using Explorer with SharePoint. Here is a short list and some solutions:

◆ The Common Tasks Bar shows up on the left side of the Explorer View.

Explorer view is controlled by the user's Folder Option settings on the computer they are using to access SharePoint. To get rid of that bar, open Windows Explorer on that computer, go to the Tools menu and select Folder Options. Set the folder to use Windows classic folder view.

◆ The user is prompted for credentials too often to view a library with Explorer.

This is an Internet Explorer thing. The fix for this is to add the library to the Trusted Sites zone in IE on the user's computer. This may also happen if FPRPC is being used. Unfortunately, that is not entirely unexpected behavior for FPRPC.

◆ Explorer View won't work.

This particularly occurs on servers, which don't have WebDAV enabled by default or FPRPC natively. Make certain that the WebClient service is running on the computer being used to access the library. If you do not want to enable the WebClient service, install an Office 2003 product (or FrontPage 2003), which will install the capability to support FPRPC, and means that the machine will default to using FPRPC to do Explorer View exclusively.

There is a known bug concerning the WebClient service— if it is started, stopped, then started again, it will not work properly. If you have to stop the WebClient service, be sure to reboot before restarting. Server 2008 should not have this issue.

For more details, such as how to force the use of one protocol or the other, there is an excellent whitepaper concerning Explorer View called "Understanding and Troubleshooting

SharePoint Explorer View" online, and is available as a Microsoft download. Go to www.microsoft.com/downloads, and search by the whitepaper's title. Although it was created before this version of SharePoint was released, it still effectively explains the underpinnings of Explorer View as it currently works.

Require Check Out

As I've mentioned before, a document that is marked Checked Out (in a standard view a checked out document is indicated by a green arrow on the bottom-right corner of the Document Type icon) is set to be read only for everyone but the person who checked the item out. When you check out a document, you are allowed to edit it, but no one else is until it's checked back in.

Requiring Check Out is a good thing. In the previous version, Check Out was voluntary, users could choose to check out a document, but they could also forget to check it out as well. With this version, Check Out can be configured to be required. If it is set, then users cannot open a document without explicitly choosing to check it out for editing (which locks it for everyone else), or to open it only for reading. If you don't check out a document when Check Out is required, then all you can do is read it and changes made to it can not be saved back up to the library.

You Can Use Force

Don't panic. As an administrator, you can force a document to be checked in if someone leaves the company with a document checked out, or simply forgets to check a document back in for too long.

Keep in mind that there is an issue with allowing Check Out to be voluntary. A user can choose to check out a document they are editing by clicking on Check Out on the document's selection box dropdown menu before opening it, or by choosing to check the document out when prompted by Word when it is being opened. However, this can be a hit or miss thing if a user doesn't bother to check out a document while editing it, because they can still edit the document even if it is not checked out, and, meanwhile, so can everyone else. This means if Require Check Out is not enabled, and the user forgets to check out the document; while they are editing it, someone else can also open the document and edit a copy of it as well. This can cause essentially two versions of the document to exist, one with the edits of one person, one with the edits of the other. The last person to save the document will have their edits displayed as the most recent document, making the other person's edits seem as if they have been "lost" because they were saved as an "older" version of the document.

To require that a document automatically prompts to be checked out when someone edits it and cannot
be checked in by anyone but that person, you must enable the requirement under the library settings.

A setting at the bottom of the Versioning Settings page allows you to require Check Out. The Versioning Settings page actually has all kinds of useful settings that we will revisit later in the Versioning section.

FIGURE 6.17
The Require Check
Out setting

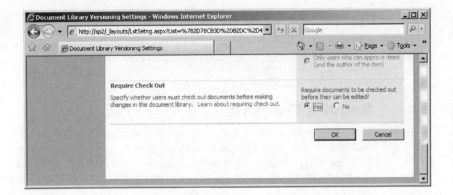

To access the Require Check Out setting:

1. Click on Settings in the library's Action bar, and select Document Library Settings in the dropdown menu.

2. On the Customize page that appears, select Versioning Settings under the General Settings category.

3. On the Versioning Settings page, scroll to the bottom, to the Require Check Out section (see Figure 6.17), and select Yes to require documents be checked out before they can be edited.

4. Then click OK to finish. That should take you back to the Customize page for the library.

5. To return to the content page, click on the name of the Shared Documents Library in the breadcrumb.

Check Out a Document

Back on the Library content page, let's see what happens if we try to edit one of the documents that now require check out. There are two ways to check out a document:

◆ Manually do so by selecting Check Out in the dropdown menu of a document's selection box.

◆ When check out is required, simply open the document.

For example, click on the new document you created earlier (my example is Newdoc) to edit it in Word.

DON'T GET TOO COMFORTABLE

If you are checking out a document to edit in Word 2003 you should manually check it out from the dropdown menu because it may not prompt you for check out while opening the file like Word 2007 does.

FIGURE 6.18
The dialog box for
choosing Read Only
or Check Out and
Edit a library
document

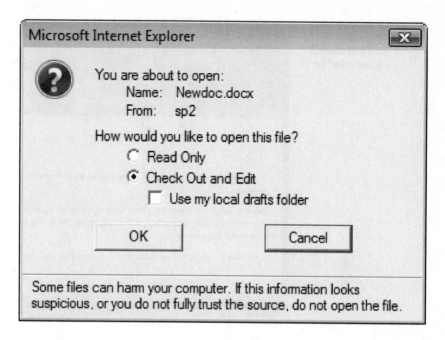

As you can see in Figure 6.18, with Require Check Out enabled, when you prepare to open a library document, the prompt won't just ask you if you want to read or edit the document; it will ask if you want to read or check out *and* edit the document (Figure 6.18).

SAVING A DOCUMENT LOCALLY

SharePoint also can let you save a copy of the document locally in case you need to work offline. I would rather not have two copies of the document at any one time, so I do not save a draft copy to a local folder. However, if that is allowed in your environment, it lets the users to work on a document they have checked out while disconnected from the network. After working on the document locally, once they are connected to the network and able to access the SharePoint server, they can save their changes to the library. When they do, they will be prompted to check the document back in if they are done working on it.

To edit the document, you must check it out. Follow these steps:

1. Select Check Out and Edit from the two options, and click OK. This will open the file in Word to be edited. You may be prompted for your login credentials.

2. Make some changes and then Save and Close the document (in my example, see the last paragraph in Figure 6.19).

FIGURE 6.19
Change a
document while
it is checked out

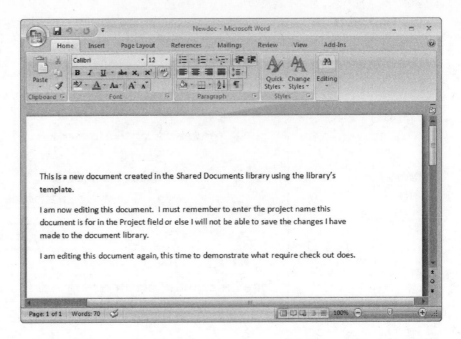

3. When you try to close the program, you will be prompted (see Figure 6.20) to check in the document so others can see the changes. If you save but don't check in the document, it will still be set to Read Only for everyone else, allowing you to continue to edit the document without anyone else accessing it until you are check it in. Also, your changes will not be visible to anyone else until the document is checked in, despite saving them. To see what that means, leave the file checked out by clicking the No button.

FIGURE 6.20
The Check In
prompt after
editing a
document

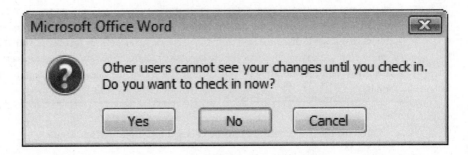

Back on the Shared Documents Library content page, Newdoc (or whatever you named your new document) is marked as checked out. If a different user tries to open or edit a document that someone else has checked out, they are warned that the document is read only. They will not see the changes made to the document by the person editing it until it is checked in.

Log in to your computer as a different user with access to the Shared Documents Library (my example uses the user account Saffron). Open Internet Explorer, browse to the SharePoint server (in my example, that's `http://sp2`), sign in as that different user, and go to the Shared Documents Library. Then try to edit the document you were just working on as the previous user.

READING LAYOUT

SharePoint might open the document in Full Screen reading layout mode. It does this on purpose, for some reason, when you are opening a document from a SharePoint library. Generally it occurs when the document is in Read Only mode, but not always.

In Word 2007, you are warned almost as soon as the document opens that you are not the one who has this document checked out. It offers you, ironically, a button to check out the document (see Figure 6.21). Notice that the last paragraph that you edited as the previous user is not in the version of the document that this user is seeing. SharePoint was right; the changes that are made while the document is checked out are not available to other users.

FIGURE 6.21
Checked Out Document

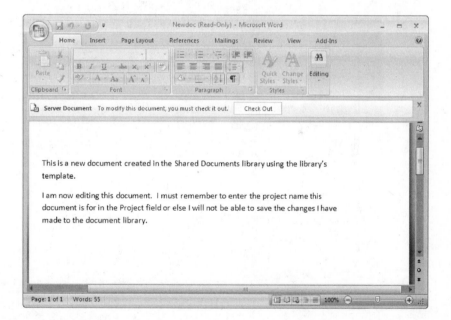

SEEING IS BELIEVING

Speaking of seeing changes, if you are logged in as a user other than the one who dragged and dropped files to the library using Explorer view, you may not be able to see those documents at all, until their properties are fixed and they are checked back in.

For example, I dragged the Security and Permissions Management document into the Shared Documents Library earlier in the chapter. I was warned that whatever I added to the library that way was going to be checked out because there was a required field (Project) that needed data.

I have not filled the required field yet, so the document is still checked out. When I am logged in to SharePoint as `shareadmin` (the account I was using to do that demonstration), I can see the document in the library.

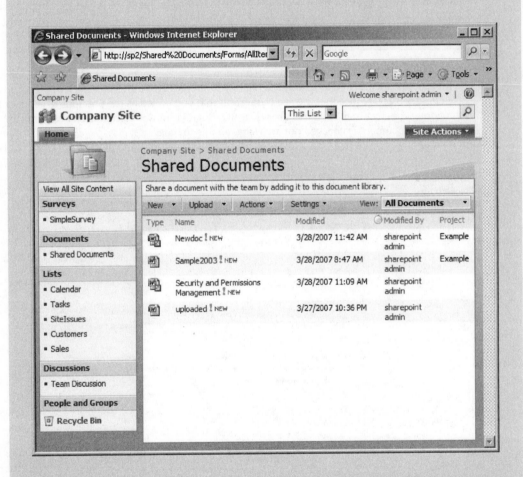

However, when I am logged in as a different user (Saffron, for example), I cannot see that document because it has never been checked in to the library. Because the document has no versions that can safely be given to users while the document is checked out, it simply does not show up for them in the page. The only fix for this problem is to fill in the required field and check the file in. Once checked in the file becomes visible.

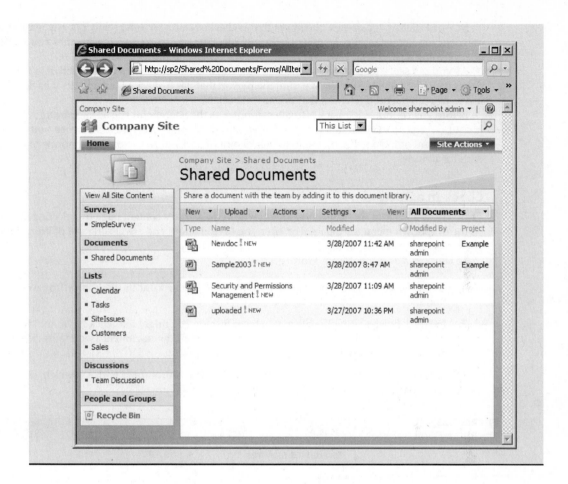

If you click the Check Out button, a dialog box informs you that the document is checked out by someone else (Figure 6.22) and that you can open the file as Read Only or be notified when the document is checked in. Meanwhile you could save a copy of the file locally and work on it there; however, that is not a good idea because it doesn't show all the current changes of both your copy and the version currently being edited by the person who has it checked out.

FIGURE 6.22
Read Only or Notify Dialog
Options

In Word 2003, if you open a document that is checked out, you don't really get any warnings. It only lets you know that the document is Read Only after you try to save the changes you made after opening it.

As you can see, if a document is checked out, and a different user wants to edit it, it is definitely not going to be available for change until the person that has it checked out, checks it back in. That leaves us with the need to check that document back in.

Before you continue, log back into the computer as the SharePoint site administrator (dem0tek\shareadmin in my example) or whatever account you were using when you checked the document out. Open IE and log in to SharePoint (if necessary), so you can continue to work with the libraries.

Check In a Document

There are two ways to check in a document: within the Library content page by selecting Check In on the dropdown menu for the item or after you save changes and are closing out of Word (which is the more often used option).

To check in a document from Word:

1. Open the document you created and still have checked out in the library (my example is Newdoc).

2. In Word, finish editing the file in whatever fashion you might like, click Save, and then close Word. Once again you will be prompted to check in the document (see Figure 6.20 if you aren't familiar with the prompt).

3. This time, instead of clicking No, click Yes. You will be prompted with a Check In dialog box for a comment about this version of the document (Figure 6.23).

FIGURE 6.23
Check In Comment Dialog box

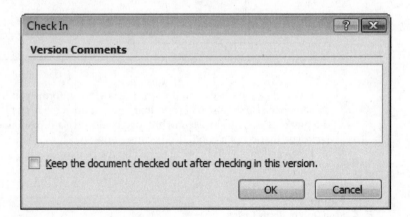

4. Type a comment in the box. If you are using Word 2007, do not check Keep the document checked out after checking in this version, because versioning isn't enabled yet (we will be doing that later in the chapter).

5. Click OK to finish.

CHECKING IN WHILE STAYING OUT

You might think this is a contradiction of terms, keeping the document checked out after checking it in, but you can save a copy of your changes as a version of the document in the library, then keep it checked out to work on it some more. This let's you make a backup version of the document in the library, just in case.

In the Shared Documents Library, the Newdoc (or whatever you named it) now has no green arrow indicating it is checked out. It is free to be checked out by other contributors.

If another user accesses the document now, it will show all changes, including those withheld from everyone else while the document was checked out. This really indicates why no one should be using the document until the user who checked it out is finished editing it.

Discard Check Out

What happens if someone checks out a document for too long? What would happen if documents are left checked out because of a user emergency or because the user left the company? To recover a document that is checked out by someone else, you can log in as that user and check in the document for them, or you can go into the Document Library settings and discard their check out.

As you know, you can have items that may be checked out with no saved changes and no versions in the library (as can be the case if a file is dropped into a library in Explorer View). However, if a document has been changed at least once in a library, then it can be "rolled back" to the state it was before it was checked out most recently. This is useful in those situations when the document must be returned to the library to be checked out by others. In that case, the administrator or someone with the permission to Override Check Out can click on the offending document's selection box, and select Discard Check Out in the dropdown menu (Figure 6.24).

FIGURE 6.24
Discard Check Out in the item dropdown menu

This will check in the document and discard the changes made while the document was checked out (basically reverting it to its most recent version before check out). Remember, this includes changes made to the property fields for the library item while checked out as well.

Manage Checked Out Files

If the document has never been checked in, if it was uploaded by someone, left checked out, and otherwise has no versions to roll back to, then it needs to be managed in a different way. To change that file from checked out to checked in requires that someone take ownership of it:

1. Go to Settings on the Action bar for the library, and click Document Library Settings.

A BIT OF SLEIGHT OF HAND

To do this exercise, I logged in as a user (dem0tek\saffron) other than our usual SharePoint admin (dem0tek\shareadmin) and dragged a document into the library without entering data in the Project field. That left the document checked out without any changes. Then I logged back in as my shareadmin to continue this process. This will create a document that the administrator could take ownership of. Under normal circumstances you would probably have numerous documents in a library for you to wrest ownership from its originator.

---

2. In the Customize page, click Manage checked out files under the Permissions and Management category.

   On the Checked Out Files page (Figure 6.25), you'll note that although there may be many checked out files in the library, only those with no checked-in version are listed. Earlier in the chapter, a document was dragged into the library using Explorer view. It should still be waiting for you to enter data into its required field so you can check it in. However, you already own that library item, so you don't need to take ownership of it (it's in the Files checked out to me section). Note that the file is a link and has no checkbox next to it to select it. That's because to check that document in, all you need do is simply check it in yourself. If you have documents that are still checked out, but don't belong to you, they will be listed under Files checked out to others. In my example the document checked out by someone else is *NeedsCheckin*. To check in that document, you need to take ownership of it, then check it in yourself. To take ownership of a document put a check in the checkbox next to it, and then click Take Ownership of Selection in the Action bar.

3. You'll be prompted with an Are You Sure dialog box; click OK if you're sure.

4. Then go back to the Shared Documents content page (click Shared Documents in the breadcrumb). The document item will show up in the content area of the library (for your view only, since now you own it).

5. To check in the document in this case, you still need to fill the required field. So add data to the Project field by moving your cursor over the document's name, clicking in the selection box, and from the dropdown menu selecting Edit Properties.

6. In the Edit Properties page, enter some data into the Project field and click OK.

FIGURE 6.25
The Checked Out Files page

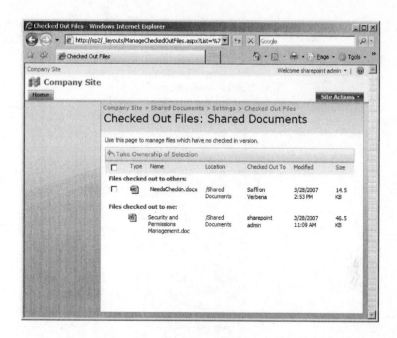

7. To check the document in, simply hover your cursor over its Name field, click on the selection box, and select Check In (you cannot discard check out because there is no previous version to go back to) from the dropdown menu (Figure 6.26).

FIGURE 6.26
A document being checked in after a change in ownership

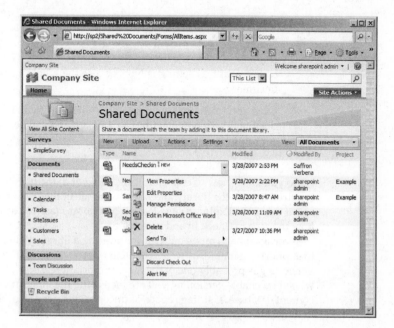

FIGURE 6.27
Check In page

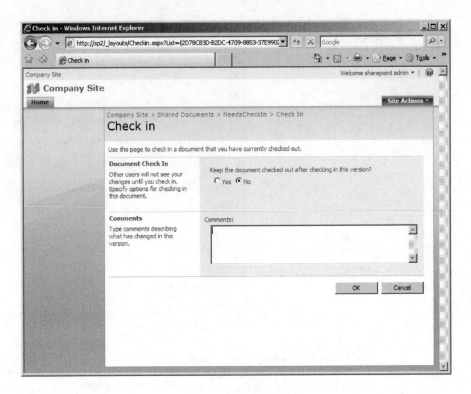

8. Selecting Check In will trigger a Check In page (Figure 6.27) where you can enter a comment and decide to keep the document checked out after checking in this version. Make certain that that setting is No, because the whole point of this exercise was to check in the document.

9. Once you've entered your comment, click OK to finish checking in this document item. The document will no longer be checked out and can be worked on by other people allowed to contribute to the library.

So you know how to create, upload, and edit a document. You've learned how to add a required field to the library and know what affect that has on saving documents. You've learned about using the Explorer View feature of a library (as well as Open with Windows Explorer), and how to manage Check In and Check Out.

Now it's time to move on with configuring a library. A library can be configured, as you know, to support versioning, as well as content approval, content types, even incoming email and RSS. Versioning is probably one of the more important features of a document library. Remember that when you enable versioning you are increasing the amount of space the library takes up in the content database. If storage space or uncontrolled growth of the database is an issue, then you may want to consider at least limiting document versions.

Versioning

All lists can do versioning (which means that the versioning you learn here can be applied to other lists as well). SharePoint keeps a copy of a list item whenever a change is made so the user can "roll back" to the previous version of the item if necessary.

In a library, that means that every time a document that is attached to a library item is edited and the changes saved to the library, it is considered a new version of the document and its library item. Versions are saved (you can enforce how many) to the Version History of that library item, and versions can be restored or deleted there. Restoring a version of a document means that that version is going to be considered the most recent version and will be moved to the top of the list in the history—and be the version that gets opened when you click the link for that document in the library. The version that is being replaced as the most recent gets pushed down one place in the list—it is not deleted. SharePoint currently also supports major and minor (or draft) versions of an item. Major version numbers are whole numbers, like 1.0 or 2.0. Minor versions are indicated with decimal numbers like 1.1, 1.2, etc.

When documents are edited, saved, and checked into a library, they are considered a minor version until you choose to publish the version as a major version. That elevates the version number from a minor version, such as version number 1.2, to whole number, such as version 2.0. If you enable content approval on a library that also has versions enabled, documents will remain as minor versions until they are approved (more on that in a few pages).

To enable versioning, follow these steps:

1. Go to Settings on the Action bar of the library's content page, and select Document Library Settings in the dropdown menu.

2. On the Customize page, click the Versioning Settings link in the General Settings category.

The Versioning Settings page has a content approval section. In the case of a library, you can choose to have a document remain in a draft state until approved. This can be useful with document management. However, we are not going to do content approval just yet.

Other sections for this page are Document Version History, Draft Item Security, and one you've already seen, Required Check Out.

Document Version History is where you actually set how versioning will be handled by this library. It's here that you actually enable versioning, and configure it to use major versions, major and minor versions, and whether or not to limit the number of those versions.

Enabling major and minor (draft) versions unlocks the Draft Item Security section. That is where you can also limit the ability to see a minor version of a document to anyone who can read items in the lists, only people who can edit items, or only those allowed to approve items if you enable content approval.

At this point, we are only going to enable versioning without content approval. After you see how versioning works, you'll see what approval does to versioning.

3. In this library, let's allow the creation of both major and minor versions. Limit the number of versions allowed per document in this library to six major versions and only five of those can have drafts. See Figure 6.28 for the settings. And for draft item security, let's allow anyone who can read items in the library to be able to see minor versions of documents. This will change when you enable content approval.

FIGURE 6.28
Versioning settings

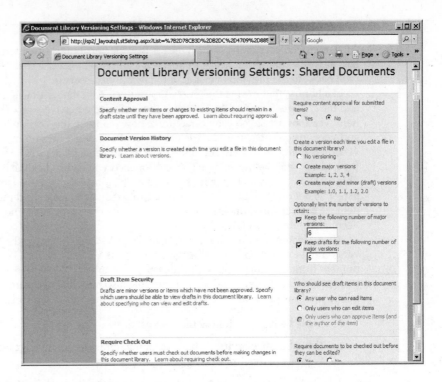

4. Once the settings are complete, click OK at the bottom of the page to finish enabling versioning.

5. Now that versioning is enabled in the library, let's go to the library's content page and start creating document versions. To do this, click the Shared Documents link in the breadcrumb above the title of the page.

NO MINORS ALLOWED

If versioning is enabled but Major and Minor versioning is not selected, then all versions are major versions and use a whole number versioning scheme.

When you're on the Shared Documents content page, bring up the selection box for one of the library items and click to access the dropdown menu. In addition to the standard menu items, there is now a Version History option (Figure 6.29).

On library items that are not checked out, there also is a publishing option. Publishing takes a draft or minor version and makes it a major version. If the document only has a major version available or the most recent version of the document is a major version, the menu will display "Unpublish this version." If the most recent version of a document is a minor version, "Publish a Major Version" will display so you can elevate it to major.

FIGURE 6.29
The Version options for library items

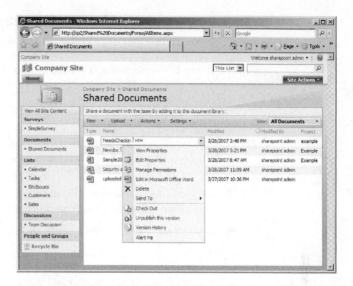

My example is going to use the uploaded file from earlier in the chapter. It currently only has one version; this is why its publishing option in the item selection menu is Unpublish this version. To check, go to Version History for this document and see.

1. Click on the selection box for the uploaded document—or whatever document you'd like to use in your library (my example is literally *uploaded*). In the dropdown menu, select Version History.

2. In the Versions Saved page, you can see that there is only one version of this document in my example (Figure 6.30). Because it is the only version, it is a major version by default. Major versions are indicated by the highlighted color of the background surrounding the entry (it varies depending on the theme you use).

FIGURE 6.30
The Versions Saved page for
`uploaded.docx`

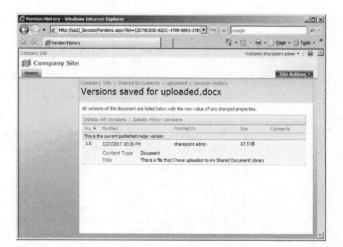

Create a New Minor Version of a Document

Now that you've verified that there is only one version of this document in this library, it's time to make more. Versions occur when you edit a file in a library (or its library item). The most practical way to create another version of a library item is to open the item's file and edit, just as any user would.

1. Click on the Shared Document link in the breadcrumb to go back to the content page (if you aren't already there).

2. From there, click on the filename for *uploaded* or the file with which you want to work. This will trigger a Warning dialog box for you to confirm the filename, and offer you the option to read or check the file out and edit it. Select the Check Out and Edit option, and click OK.

3. In Word, edit the document and add whatever text you'd like. The file Uploaded in my example also requires that the Project field contain data, so make certain it's filled in too.

4. When you are done, save the changes and close Word.

5. When you are prompted, choose to check in the document (Figure 6.31). Remember that you will be prompted to choose minor or major when using Word 2007. With 2003, it will save the document as a minor version by default.

FIGURE 6.31
Check In with Versions enabled

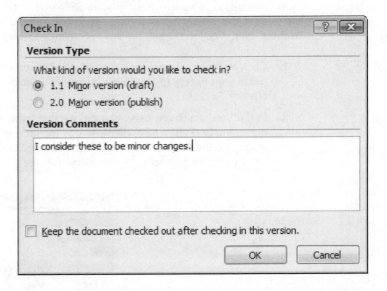

When you check in the edited document in a library that has major and minor versions enabled, SharePoint asks you which version you'd like this document version to be.

6. For my example, I would like to make this a minor version. So make sure that 1.1 Minor version is selected and add a comment. Do not keep the document checked out, and click OK.

7. On the Shared Documents Library content page, the file is there and is not checked out. If you move your cursor over the filename, click on the selection box, and take a look at the

dropdown menu, you'll see that where it said Unpublish this version, it now says Publish a Major Version. This is because the most recent version of the document is a minor version. To prove this, click Version History in the dropdown menu.

8. On the Versions Saved page, you can see that there are now two versions of the document, 1.0 and 1.1 (Figure 6.32). The most recent, and minor version is at the top of the list (and will be the version associated with the Name field if you click on it).

FIGURE 6.32
The Version History for recently edited item

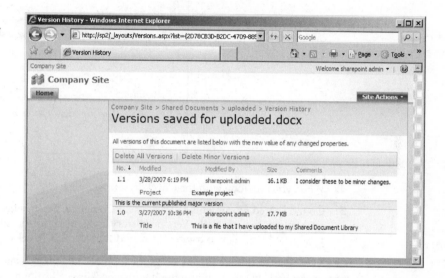

Create a New Major Version of a Document

If you edit the document again, you will see that the most recent version, despite its minor status, will be the one that opens. This means you can edit it untill you feel it is ready to be considered a major version of the document. You can promote a minor version of a file to a major version by publishing it. This is often done if you change your mind about the appropriateness of the version type you chose when you checked a document in. Usually though, a minor version of a document simply needs to be edited, and then the changes are checked in as a new, major, version. To create a new major version of a document:

1. Go back to document library (Shared Documents in this example), and click the filename for the library item you are working on (mine is *uploaded*). When prompted, check out and edit the item.

2. Once the item is open, you'll see that the changes made in the recent version are there. Add additional text (format it if you like, whatever suits you), save the file, and then close out of Word.

3. You will be prompted to select the version type for the changes you just made to the document. Notice in Figure 6.33, that there are three version options for the document: new Minor version (Draft), new Major version (Publish), and Overwrite the current minor version. Select Major version, and add some comments. If you choose to publish the version, the Keep the document checked out option is grayed out.

FIGURE 6.33
The Check In prompt

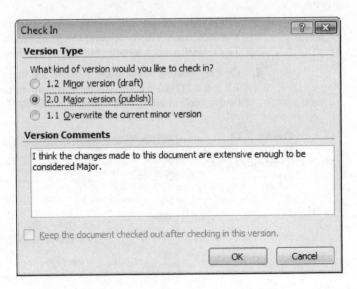

4. When you are done with the Check In settings, click OK.

5. On the Shared Documents Library, the document is not checked out, but otherwise it looks unchanged. To see how the Version History looks, bring up the selection box for the document you just edited, click to trigger the dropdown menu, and select Version History.

On the Versions Saved page (Figure 6.34), the topmost 2.0 version is now the major version. The current major version will be highlighted with a background color appropriate for the site theme to indicate at a glance that it is not a minor version.

FIGURE 6.34
The Versions Saved page with a new major version

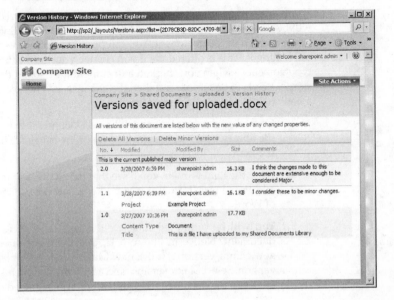

In Versions Saved page you can do several things with the saved versions of the document. You can restore any one of the previous versions to the top of the list (and therefore that version gets edited when you click the linked field for a document in the library).

You can delete a previous version, but not the current version. A current version of a document will need to be replaced at the top of the list before it can be deleted. This is usually done by creating a different new version or by restoring a previous version of the document to the top of the list. On the Versions Saved page you can also view the properties of the document for each version if you'd like. This is where having users fill in Status or Progress fields would come in handy to track the progress of a document via its fields.

To delete, restore, or view the properties of a version on the Versions Saved page, just move your cursor over the version's date and time (which is the linked field for this list) and click the down arrow in the selection box that appears around it. In the dropdown menu are Restore, View, and Delete for the previous versions. If you select the most recent, major version of the document (Figure 6.35), it will not have a Delete option and will have an Unpublish this version option—just as it would on the library's content page for the document.

FIGURE 6.35
The selection menu for the current version of the document

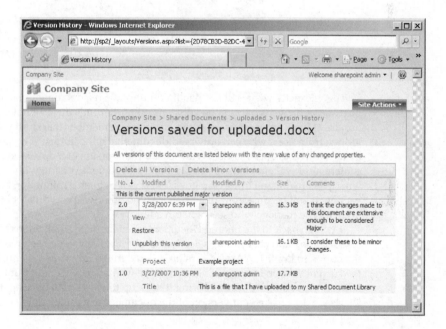

Unpublish a Major Version

If you unpublish a major version of a document, it is demoted to a minor version. To see how this works, in the selection menu of the current, published version of the document, select Unpublish This Version. The document version will not be removed from the top of the list; it will still be the most current version and the one that will be edited back on the content page; however, its version number will go from a whole number to a decimal number, 2.0 to 1.2 in my example (Figure 6.36).

FIGURE 6.36
Unpublishing a
published version of a
document

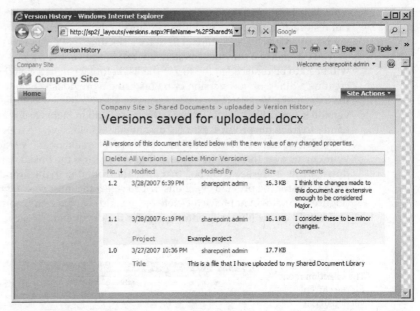

This is exactly what will happen if you unpublish a document you've selected on the content page. Essentially, it changes the version's number from a major whole number to a minor decimal number. Minor numbers are considered drafts. Remember that draft numbered documents can be hidden from users who can only read documents in the library. If content approval is enabled, those allowed to approve items can see a minor version of a document. Therefore, if you have content approval enabled, don't unpublish a document version without being sure that you know what you are doing. For the same reason, if you publish a minor version of a document to a major version, it will become viewable by those who otherwise couldn't see it in draft form. Keep that in mind as you manage who sees what in a library.

If you go back to the Shared Documents content page (click Shared Documents on the breadcrumb), and click on the selection box for the file you've been working with, you will see that the option to Publish A Major Version is listed in the dropdown menu, because we unpublished the current version to a minor version. If we wanted to, we could publish the current version of the document, which would bring it back up to version 2.0 once again. However, at this time, let's leave the most recent version of the document in a minor state.

Restore a Previous Version of a Document

Let's say that the edits for the most recent version of this document are going in the wrong direction and you need the document to be restored to previous edits. To restore a previous version of the document to the top of the version list, you first need to check it out.

Why do we need to check out a document before we restore a previous version of it? Because we set Require Check Out on all document items in the library. That means that if we are going to roll back all changes to a document and its properties, we need to check out the document.

In this two-step process, click on the selection box for the library item we've been working with (my example is *uploaded*), and select Check Out from the dropdown list. That will simply add a green arrow to the bottom-right side of the content type icon for the document. The next step is to go to Version History by moving your cursor over the same document name, clicking the selection box, and selecting Version History from the dropdown menu.

In the Versions Saved page for the document, notice that simply checking out a document causes it to generate a minor version without even opening the file yet.

To restore a previous version (my example uses 1.1), simply move your cursor over the time and date for the version until you get a selection box, and then click the down arrow. In the dropdown menu, select Restore. You will be warned that you are going to replace the current version with the selected version. That's fine, so click OK.

You'll see that the most current version of the document is a copy of the old version 1.1 (it will be the same size), but it will have been renumbered to assume the most current version number available. To verify that it is the correct version (the less current one, the one that does not have our major version, final changes), click the Time and Date link for it.

That will open the document, and because you checked it out, it will open without prompting you because it is not Read Only. Take a look; the last edits you made in the document should be missing. So if those edits weren't what you wanted, you could continue the document from this point.

We are just looking, and won't be making any changes at this time, so close the document, leave the document checked out, and go back to the Versions Saved page.

VERSION WARNING

If you open a version of a document that isn't the most recent, Word 2007 will warn you that there are newer versions and try to encourage you to make a copy. Although I appreciate the warning about the version being less than new, I can't understand Microsoft's intentions with the option to make a local copy of the older version of a document.

Why are they encouraging people to make local copies of a document, and an obsolete one at that? SharePoint is supposed to encourage users to only work on a document in one place, using only the correct version, at all times. So why offer to make a local copy of previous edits?

Again I can appreciate the warning, but as for making a copy, I'd only do so if I fully intended to use that version of the document to create new versions from those changes forward.

Now that we've had our fun, we can return version 1.2 back to its rightful place at the top of the Versions list and delete the version we just created. To do that, just move your cursor over the date and time for version 1.2, click on the selection box, and select Restore from the dropdown menu. You might be prompted with a warning; click OK if you get one.

That will leave the truly most recent version as the correct one. When you make a previous version of a document the official, most recent version by restoring it, that version doesn't have a real version number while it is still checked out. Therefore, to truly put the restored the version we want on the top of the version history list, we need to check it in.

After restoring a version, it sits in limbo, uncertain as to its version number until you assign it. Depending on how you check it in, the version can overwrite the version it replaced, have its own minor version number (leaving its predecessor alone), or it can be made a major version (again, not overwriting anyone).

CONFIRM YOUR VERSION

If you need to confirm the version is correct, simply click on the date and time for the version and open the document in Word. Once you've confirmed that it is the right version, simply close Word without making any changes.

So to finish off committing to the restored version, check in the document you've been working on by going back to the Library content page (Shared Documents on the breadcrumb), clicking the selection box around the document you need, and then selecting Check In from the dropdown menu.

This will trigger a Check In page (Figure 6.37). Notice that there are three options concerning how to handle the current version number for this version. In this example, let's publish it as a major version (committing 2.0 as the version number) and make a comment, and then click OK to check in the document.

FIGURE 6.37
The Check In page with version options

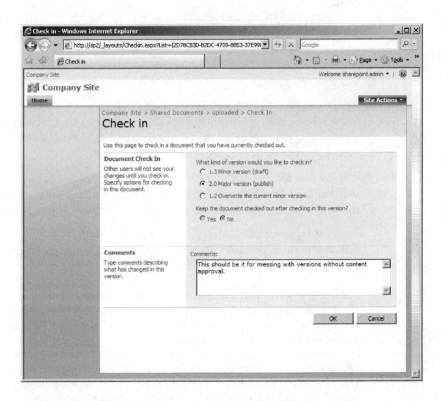

If you were to go to back to the Version History of the document you've been working with, you should be familiar with each version, including the most current major version you just checked in and the original version of the document with which you started. Versions are useful;

just remember that you can restore an older version to the current version position, but that doesn't delete the version that was replaced. That version won't be deleted unless you require it.

To delete a version, simply go to the Version History of the document, move your mouse over the version's Modify date and time, click on the selection box, and select Delete. You'll then be prompted with a warning that the version will be sent to the SharePoint End users' Recycle Bin. Click OK and the version will be deleted. Heck you can even delete all minor versions or all versions altogether in the Version History page (except the most current, which can't be deleted from this page).

VERSION LIMITS

Just a word about those limits you set for the maximum number of major and minor versions kept for items in a library. They are not as exact as you might hope. Version History focuses on the major versions, and will generally keep only the limit you imposed, plus one (the most recent major version). If you reach beyond that one over limit, the oldest minor and major versions will be deleted.

As for minor versions, a lot of people think that the second setting for limiting versions directly limits draft versions. It doesn't. Major versions can have up to 511 draft versions a piece. What the draft limitation literally does is limit the number of major versions that will be allowed to have drafts. Go over that number, and the oldest major version will lose its drafts.

Hopefully you've gotten an idea as to how versions work, what major (publish) and minor (draft) versions are, and how to manage them. However, minor versions are just a concept without content approval. So let's take a look at how content approval works and why minor versions are referred to as drafts.

Content Approval

Content approval means that new items or new versions of items in a list or library require approval before they can be seen by everyone able to view a list. With a normal list, new items start out with the status of pending. Then a person with the right to approve list or library items can decide to either approve or reject an item and add comments to explain their decision. If an item is approved, it becomes viewable by everyone who can read list or library items. If an item is rejected, it remains pending and can be seen only by the administrator, someone who can approve items, and the creator of the item. This means that new items go through the simple process of pending approval then being either approved, and therefore visible to all or rejected, and therefore continuing not to be visible to all.

If you use content approval in conjunction with versions in a library, then drafts can come into play (if you enable them). No longer does content approval have just the approval levels of Pending, Rejected, and Approved; in a library with versioning, it has Draft, Pending, Rejected, and Approved.

ENABLE CONTENT APPROVAL

When you enable content approval, major and minor versions work differently than they do without it. When a document is checked in as a minor version, its approval status is Draft. (Word

2003 checks in new documents as a minor version by default.) If that document is published as a major version (which is sort of a nod toward approving the contents), its status becomes Pending. Only Pending versions can be approved, you cannot approve a minor version. That's why you either have to choose to save your changes as a major version on check in or publish a minor version to a major version in order to move toward approval. When that Pending document is approved, that's it. It's approved and everyone can finally see it.

When a document is a major version and it is pending, you can either approve or reject it. If a major version is rejected, it is indicated as such and treated as if it is still pending, meaning that others can't see that version of the document and it is still not editable by anyone but the owner or people allowed to view draft documents.

SEEKING APPROVAL

The approval process may sound a little complicated, but it works like this: When you are jotting down ideas for a document and creating a really rough draft of what you have in mind, you might want to save a copy to the library for safekeeping. If you don't want everyone to read it, you can save it as a minor version. That makes it a draft in the library that is not ready for approval yet and not visible to average contributors of the list—if you set draft item security correctly.

You keep working on it, fleshing it out. You then save your changes to the library again, but this time you save the changes as a major version. Now they are pending approval, so the people on your staff who can approve items in the library are aware that they need to look at the document now.

Then one of them reads the pending document and either approves it for everyone to work on or rejects it from general consumption with a comment so you can see what you need to fix in order for the document to be ready to be contributed to.

Every time a user opens the document and edits it, a new version is saved, in which they can decide whether their changes are minor or major, and the approval process starts again.

That's basically the point of Content Approval and versioning on a practical level.

To enable content approval on a library, follow these steps:

1. Go to that library's content page, click Settings in the Action bar, and select Document Library Settings from the dropdown menu.

2. On the Customize page, click the Versioning Settings link in the General Settings category.

The Versioning Settings page will appear (Figure 6.38). It has two sections for content approval. The first section of the page, aptly named Content Approval, is where you choose Yes or No to require content approval for submitted items. The Draft Item Security section is where you can configure who can see a draft or unapproved document item (this is where Draft Item Security comes into its own).

FIGURE 6.38
Setting Content
Approval and Draft
Item Security

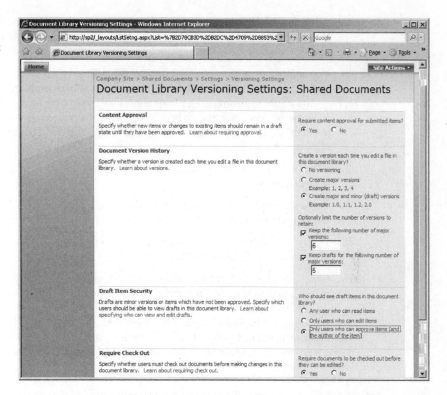

3. To configure your Content Approval settings on this page, click Yes in the Content Approval section.

4. In the Draft Item Security section, select Only Users Who Can Approve Items and the author of the item for this example.

5. All other settings on this page have already been configured, so click OK.

The Shared Documents Library should now be set to require content approval. There is a new column in the All Documents view indicating the Approval Status of the items, and two new views (Approve/reject items and My submissions) to help you keep track of approved items. All items that are a major version in the library prior to enabling content approval are automatically approved—because everyone has been looking at it anyway. Minor items are considered drafts.

Let's create a new document item and see how content approval works. In this demonstration, you are going to create the document as a SharePoint site collection administrator (assuming that is who you are logged in as now). Later you can log in to a workstation as a normal user with edit permissions on the library to see what that user would see, but you will be working in the library with administrative privileges.

1. Click the New button on the Action bar to create a new document. A dialog box should ask if you want to check out and edit because required check out was enabled on the library earlier. Check out and edit the document.

2. You might get a Warning dialog box reminding you which document template you are opening. You can safely ignore the warning about the template and click OK.

   You might be prompted for your SharePoint username and password because Word needs to know who you are in case you want to use the Shared Workspace task pane. This occurs particularly if you are logged into SharePoint with an account that doesn't match the one with which you logged into the computer.

3. When the document opens, enter a relevant value in the Project field in the Document information panel.

4. In the document itself, enter some sample text, such as "It was a dark and stormy night." Format it if you'd like.

5. When you finish the document, click Save, name the document (my example uses `approvaltest`), and then close Word.

6. Check in the document as a minor version, enter a comment (my comment is "keeping it minor", do not keep the document checked out), and click OK.

As you can see in Figure 6.39, the new document is in the Shared Documents Library with its approval status listed as Draft. All other documents are approved because their most current versions were major versions (and they were already visible) when content approval was enabled.

FIGURE 6.39
The new draft document in the Shared Documents Library with content approval enabled

You can see that the new document is a draft version because you own the document and you have approval rights. However, if you happen to log on to a different workstation using a standard user account with edit permissions and look at the Shared Documents Library, you will be unable to see the new document. It literally will not show up in the library because it is a draft (minor) version and not approved (Figure 6.40).

FIGURE 6.40
The new document is missing from the user view of Shared Documents

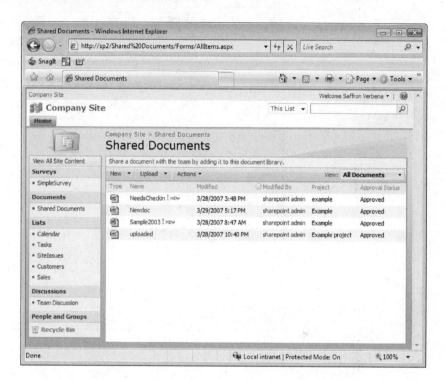

Let's see what can be done with the new document as far as content approval and versioning (you, of course, need to be logged in as someone allowed to do content approval):

1. Move your cursor over the new document's filename and click on the selection box.

2. In the dropdown menu, you have the standard options, nothing that indicates content approval is enabled. As you can see in Figure 6.41 that Approve/Reject is not listed. That's

because you can't approve or reject a draft; only major versions are allowed to be approved or rejected.

FIGURE 6.41
The options available for a draft version of a document

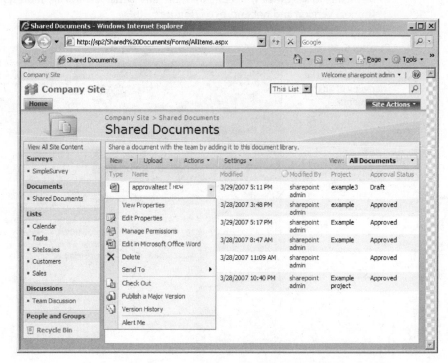

ELEVATE A MINOR VERSION TO A MAJOR VERSION

There are no options that really indicate that you can do content approval on a draft version of a document. However, if you were to elevate this draft version of a document to a major version, the approval status will change from Draft to Pending, which will allow you to approve or reject a document.

3. In the dropdown menu of the selection box of the new document, select Publish a Major Version. A Publish Major Version page will appear. As you can see in Figure 6.42, the Comment box has the comments you made when you created the version, so you can add to them if you'd like before making this minor version a major version. You don't get a new blank Comment box because you are not creating a new version of the document; there were no changes made to it or its properties. You are just changing the version number. There is also a Warning bar saying that despite elevating this minor version to a major version, it will still be invisible to the public (library users without approve rights) until it is approved.

FIGURE 6.42
Publish Major Version

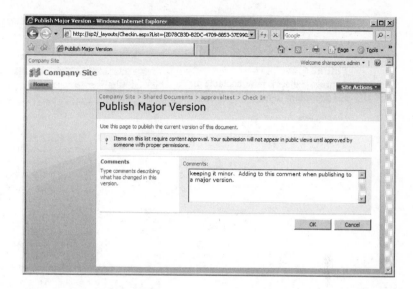

4. Add to the comment about the change in version if you'd like, and click OK. On the library's content page, you can see that the new document has Pending approval status (Figure 6.43).

FIGURE 6.43
The approval status change for the new document

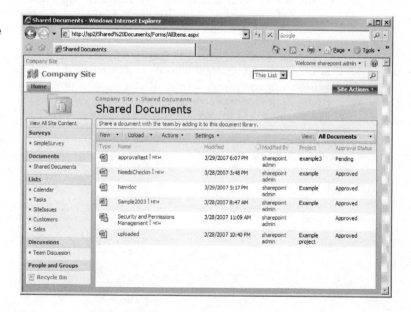

5. Check out the item's selection menu. It will have two new options. Move your cursor over the name of the file, click on the selection box, and look at the dropdown menu. Now that the current version of the document item is a major one, you can Approve/Reject the item or Cancel Approval (Figure 6.44).

FIGURE 6.44
Approve/Reject is now available for the document item

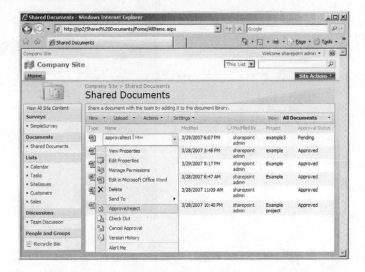

6. Before you change the approval status of this version of the document, verify that there is only one version of the document. Move your cursor over the document name, click on the selection box, and select Version History from the dropdown menu.

As you can see in Figure 6.45, there is only one version for this document, and the version number is 0.1. Although you might think that publishing a document to a major version may change the version, with content approval enabled it doesn't. Publishing a document, only moves the document from a Draft state to a Pending approval state. If you go from draft to major, or even save a document as a major version, the version will not actually change to a whole number until it is approved.

FIGURE 6.45
Version of Pending document

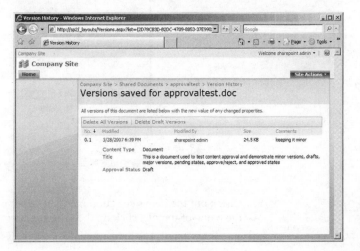

To make matters worse, this is exactly what drives draft item security. People who are not allowed to see draft versions cannot see a version of a document if it is not approved. Period. Pending, Rejected, or Draft are not viewable by anyone who can't approve items and isn't the creator of the items with our current draft item security setting. If the version is not a whole number, and draft item security is set to allow only authors and approvers to see a draft version, then users will not be able to access or even know about a draft version of a document until it is made a major version and then approved. This process is supposed to help prevent a document from exposing data that might still be speculation or poorly worded and revealing it to less-informed, less-qualified, and possibly less-secure library users.

WHAT DO YOU MEAN ACCESS DENIED?!

There is an interesting glitch in the way the library displays versions when content approval is enabled and Draft Item Security is set to allow only those who can approve items to view drafts. If a document was approved in the past, even if its current version is in a draft stage, that past version will be displayed to all users as Approved. Users may be tempted to click the document so they can edit it.

When they do, the document will fail to open. With luck, those users will realize that the most recent version of the document is in a draft state waiting for approval. Otherwise, the document looks approved and is not checked out, but mysteriously cannot be edited.

This means that any status and version of a document will be invisible to the user except the approved one. But, if a document was ever approved in the past, then that is the state a non-approving user can see—even if it is obsolete. Even if the more current, better version is waiting for approval.

In other words, with Draft Security set to allow only the author or approvers to see draft items, a new document that is in a draft state and has never been approved will be completely invisible to users without the right to approve items (or if they are the item creator) until the item is approved and suddenly appears in the library. However, if a previous version of the document was *ever* approved, the document will not be able to be invisible. As a matter of fact, it will not correctly display its status (Pending, Rejected, or Draft) to non-approving users because they are not supposed to see the status. All they will see, mistakenly, is the approved version of the document listed.

This is unfortunate. It can make trying to figure out what can be edited and what can't be edited very frustrating. One way around this problem is to let users who can edit items see draft versions of documents, so they at least know when a document's current version is a draft. However, if they do that, that means they can access it too.

Now you know that a minor version of a document is considered a draft and cannot be approved. Only versions waiting to be major can be approved—or rejected for that matter. Most people edit a document several times, save the changes as minor versions, and then when they are comfortable, either check in their final changes as a major version or take their most current minor version and publish it to a major version. What can confuse people is the fact that if they indicate a version should be major, all that does in a content approval–enabled library, is change its status to Pending, meaning the document is going to major as soon as it is approved.

THE COOKIE JAR ON THE HIGH SHELF

Versioning and content approval aren't exactly security filtered, which means that the Unpublish a Version and Approve/reject options show up on an item's selection menu even if the person logged in doesn't have the right to use it. When they try to use it—and they will—an Access Denied page will encourage them to log in as a different user, which implies that their user login doesn't have the credentials to complete the task. Be prepared to recognize this error if you get help desk calls because a user wants to reject a coworker's document and was denied. Users will assume that that they should be able to do it because the option was on the menu.

To approve a document item that is pending, follow these steps:

1. Move your cursor over the document item, click on the selection box, and select Approve/reject in the dropdown menu.

ANOTHER WAY TO APPROVE/REJECT

You can also Approve/reject a version by viewing a document item's properties and clicking the Approve/reject button in the Action bar. You can do basically anything in the item selection menu that you can do in the Action bar for the item view.

2. The Approve/Reject page (Figure 6.46) has three options: Approved, Rejected, and Pending, which is the current state. To approve this version, select Approved, and enter some text in the comment box. Click OK.

FIGURE 6.46
The Approve/Reject page

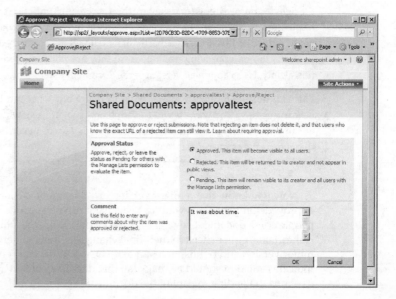

On the content page for the Shared Documents Library, the document (`approvaltest` in my example) is now Approved in the Approval Status field. If you were to log in to a workstation as a normal site member and go to the Shared Documents Library, it would finally be visible to that user. Notice the username in the Welcome menu in Figure 6.47.

FIGURE 6.47
The `Approvaltest` approval status

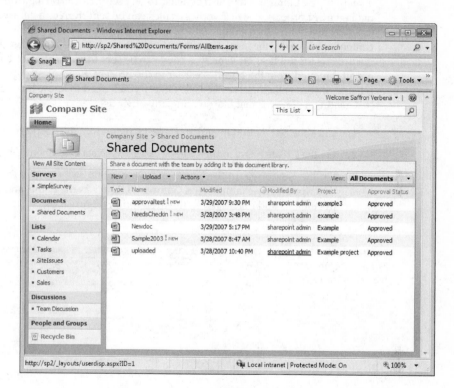

You know what versions are, you know what content approval is, and more importantly, you know how they work together. You should have some idea as to how to use these features in your business, or if they should be used at all. Eventually though, you are going to outgrow the existing Shared Documents Library. To prepare for that eventuality, let's create our own document library so we can customize the library's template and explore content types.

Create a Document Library

Because document libraries are so useful, and so versatile, chances are good that you are going to need to create more than one. Keep in mind that although you can upload any allowed file type to a library, libraries can be created to focus on a particular type of file, custom template, or group of content types. Libraries have also evolved to be used to focus on a particular part of the document management process. Because copies of files can be sent from one library to another, a document can start in a library focused on writing and editing, then a copy can be sent to a library focused on content approval by the legal department, and then on to the library used for preparing documents for publication. Finally, a copy can be sent to an archive for backup, while the originals are all removed from the libraries earlier in the process. Regardless of how libraries fit into the scheme of your collaborative needs, it's likely you'll need to know how to create more than one.

Creating a library is just like creating any other list:

1. Click the Site Action menu, and select Create from the dropdown.

2. On the Create page, in the Library category, select Document Library.

3. On the New page, in the Name and Description section, give the new library a name and description. My example uses CompanyLibrary as the name, and it uses "Official company documents and materials" as the description (Figure 6.48).

FIGURE 6.48
The new Document
Library settings

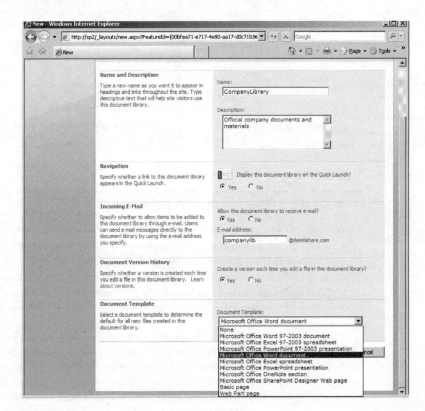

SHORT NAMES ARE BEST

Keep in mind that you should keep a list or library name short if you can, because the library name (like any list) will be part of its URL. URLs for SharePoint can have a maximum of 255 characters. You'll be amazed how quickly that maximum can be reached. Bear this in mind also if you are creating Folders, keep their names as short as possible.

4. In the Navigation section, you will be offered the choice of whether or not to display a link for this library on the Quick Launch bar. Keep the default in order to display this library on the Quick Launch bar. However, if you wanted this library to be unavailable from the Quick Launch bar, this is where you would set it No.

In the Incoming E-Mail section, you have the option to enable incoming email for this library. Most libraries can receive files attached to email and translate them into document library items.

5. This library should be email-enabled, so select Yes to allow this document library to receive email . This setting is useful for those busy employees who may have their email up, but may not want to browse, log in, and navigate to the library to upload a file. They can simply email the library with the document attached, and that will be added to the library automatically.

6. My example uses the email alias `companylib` for the library. You can, of course, enter any alias you'd like; just be sure it is short enough to be convenient to type and reasonably descriptive. It helps if it is easy to remember too.

ENABLING INCOMING MAIL

Incoming email cannot be enabled for any list or library on a site if it is not configured at Central Administration first.

You can also conveniently enable Document Versioning while creating a document library, so it is ready to start versioning before the first document is added.

7. In the Document Version History section, select Yes to create a version each time a document is edited in the library.

8. The Document Template section contains powerful and sometimes overlooked settings for a document library. For one thing, it is unfortunately named. It isn't just for documents. In Figure 6.41, you can see that there are more templates to base a document library on than one that just makes documents. Yes, you can choose a Word document, but you can also choose a PowerPoint Presentation, an Excel Spreadsheet, OneNote sections, and even SharePoint Designer 2007 Web pages. You can also use libraries for Basic Web pages and Web Part pages. (The library's ability to have a template for Web pages is what makes wiki libraries possible.)

For this library, we are going to use a Word 2007 document template. However, in my example we are going to replace it with some existing company letterhead that was made elsewhere. Templates for letterhead and document forms are common in businesses, and it's easy to replace a library's template with one of your own. Then, when users create new documents in the library, they will already have the formal company letterhead.

WATCH OUT FOR DIFFERENT VERSIONS

Do not use an Office 2007 template for documents if not everyone who is going to use those documents has 2007 or the file format converter for 2007 installed.

9. Choose Microsoft Word Document in the Document Templates dropdown list.

10. Click Create to finish. You should end up on the content page of your new document library. In the Quick Launch bar in Figure 6.49, you can see that CompanyLibrary is listed. The Address bar indicates that you are on the `CompanyLibrary/Forms/AllItems.aspx` page. This view is the default view for the library, which you should recognize if you've used Explorer view to access any library's Forms folder.

FIGURE 6.49
The new CompanyLibrary content page

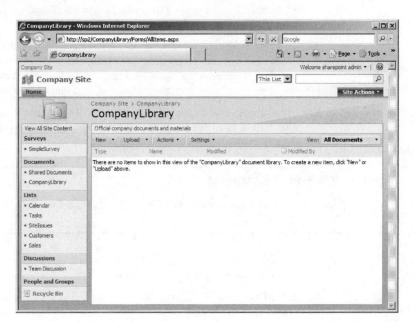

CUSTOMIZE THE DEFAULT TEMPLATE

What do you do if you don't have an existing template, but would like to customize the blank template for the library? Click the Edit Template link under the Document Template field in the Advanced Settings page of a library. This will open the template in its corresponding Office product, where you can customize it to your heart's content. When you are done, save it. The changes will be saved to the template file for the library in the library's Forms folder. This means that when you next use the New button in the library, it will create a document from your new and improved template.

Replacing a Library's Template with an Existing Template

Before you create any documents in this library, let's replace that blank Word template with one of your own. There are two easy phases involved in using your own template for a library. Phase one adds the template to the Forms folder in the library. Phase two configures the template setting for the library to point to the new template.

1. Make sure you have the template file you want to use handy. Then either click Actions on the Action bar in the content page of the library, and select Open with Windows Explorer, or you can click the View menu and select Explorer View. Either way, use Explorer to display your library's contents.

2. Because you are an administrator, you can see the Forms folder in the library. Open the Forms folder because this is the default location for the library's template.

3. Drag and drop (or copy and paste if you prefer) your existing template into the Forms folder. If you can't see the Forms folder, try setting your Windows Explorer folder options to show hidden folders, or try viewing the site from a Windows XP machine. The new template should appear in the Forms folder (see Figure 6.50). My example uses a template called dem0tekred.

FIGURE 6.50
A new template in the Forms folder

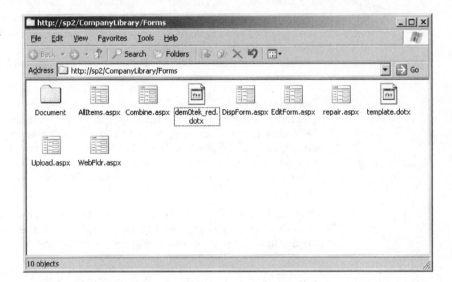

4. Now that the template is in the library's Forms folder, you can configure the library to use it. Click Settings on the Action bar and select Document Library Settings.

5. On the Customize page, select Advanced settings in the General Settings category.

Although we are only going to change the document template at this time, take a quick look at what the advanced settings for a document library are:

Content Types By default, the content types are not enabled on document libraries. This means that the library itself is associated with one kind of library item and one particular template file. That means the library was meant to use one kind of library item (like a list item, you could have different library items with different fields or workflows for example) and create and store a certain kind of file, such as PowerPoint presentations, Excel workbooks, or Word documents. When you click the New button in a library associated with one template, it tries to open a file based on its associated template.

If you want a library to be able to create, edit, and store different kinds of library items and/or files, enable content types. When you do this, you can choose to have several kinds of library items, each associated with its own template and using its own fields too. This means that the library stops being associated with one template (and the Document Template settings grays out) and leaves the template association to the content types instead.

OFFICE FILES ARE A MUST

Unless you've configured SharePoint to support HTML viewing, if you don't have the necessary Office program installed on your computer, SharePoint will fail to open that file. You cannot edit a file from a library without the appropriate program running locally. You can save the file, open it in a program that will work (but is not recognized by SharePoint as a Microsoft Office product) to edit it, save the file, and then upload it to the library again. However, SharePoint, being a Microsoft product, is specifically designed to work with other Microsoft products.

Document Template   This is the section with which you are going to be working. Here you can specify the path to the template you would like to use for this library. Make sure the path is accessible to all users (and in our case it is because we put the template in the Forms folder of the library). The Edit Template link is under the field for the document template. Use this link to open the template's Office product to customize the template. When you are done, save the file and close it. The template for the library will then use your custom changes for all new items.

Browser-Enabled Documents   Because some files can be displayed in either the browser or its client application, this setting lets you specify whether you want the item to always display in the browser or open its appropriate application when applicable. If no client application is available, it will default to the browser.

Custom Send To Destination   Because you can send a copy of a file from one library to another, you can specify a default library to send to that users can easily click on in the item selection menu. This makes it easy—if the library they are working in has an archive library or a legal department library that the document needs to be passed to when it's done it will be displayed on the document's Send To menu. Send To keeps tabs on copied documents and gives you the option to update the copy in a new library when the document is checked in with changes in the original library. The Destination name is what appears in the dropdown, and the URL is actually the Web address of the other library.

Folders   Some users feel more comfortable if they can find their files in folders. Some companies need to have more structure than a mere flat list or library to store their data. When you have huge libraries and lists (around 10,000 items), it helps to break up the view of the data by storing some of it in folders within the list or library. Libraries have folders enabled by default. They can be created (if you have the permissions to) by clicking the down arrow of the New button and selecting New Folder from the dropdown menu. You can disable this feature if you'd like, and enable it later if necessary.

Search   This option is set to Yes by default. It lets you specify if this library should be searchable or if it should be exempt from being indexed by Search and available for searching. Keep in mind that if someone does not have the right to view the library, they cannot search that library's contents. Search is aware of access control, and it will not display results to a user that they are not allowed to see.

6. To finish setting up your template, go to the Document Template section. In the Document Template field, change the filename for the template from `Template.dotx` to the filename of the template you put in the Forms folder. My example is `dem0tekred.dotx` (Figure 6.51) so the field should have the path `CompanyLibrary/Forms/dem0tekred.dotx`. Keep all other default settings as they are and click OK. That will take you back to the Customize page.

FIGURE 6.51
Assigning a Custom Document Template

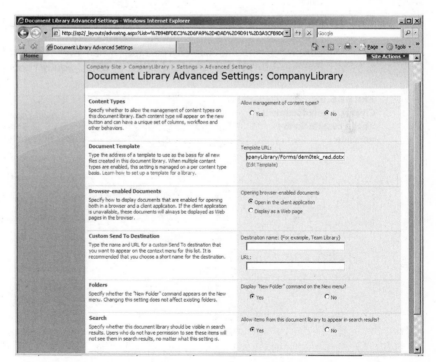

LIST EMAIL

The email address you specified for incoming email while creating the library is listed on the Customize page in the List information area for your library. In my example, that is `companylib@dem0share.com`.

List Information

Name:	CompanyLibrary
Web Address:	http://sp2/CompanyLibrary/Forms/AllItems.aspx
Description:	Official company documents and materials
E-Mail Address:	companylib@dem0share.com

7. To test your new template for the library, click the library's name in the breadcrumb above the title for this page to get back to the content page.

8. On the library's content page, click the New button to create a new document based on your template. If it prompts you about opening a file, it is referring to your template file. Click OK.

9. My example uses Dem0tek letterhead as the template (Figure 6.52). Enter some text into your new document. Save the document. Name it (my example is *Congratulations*). Close Word. Remember that you enabled versioning when you created the library. Also keep in mind that you didn't specify major or minor versions, require check out, or content approval.

FIGURE 6.52
Creating a new document using a custom library template

On the Library content page, you'll see your new document based on the custom template you assigned to the library.

Now you have a library dedicated to creating Word documents using a custom template. After you've worked on the documents in this library, you might want to send a copy to another library to be archived or viewed by a larger group of people. So let's take a look at what Send To can offer to make managing files between libraries easier.

Send To

This version of SharePoint, 3.0, has a Send To feature that makes it convenient to copy a file from one library to another. When you're working with a great many documents, using one library to store everything might not be a good idea. The number of finished documents can far exceed the number of documents in progress. Because of this, people often have *archive libraries*, where finished projects can be moved to simplify the organization of the primary library. From that idea also springs things such as a legal library, where documents can be copied to after editing to be checked by the legal department. Sending documents from one library to another in some environments is a natural part of the process. Send To was designed to address this process.

SEND TO CAPABILITIES

Send To can send documents to other libraries on a site, to a different library somewhere in a site collection, or to a library in a different Web application if you are using Office 2007 (other Office products aren't Web application–aware).

Send To has a few options:

Other Location   This option allows you to send a copy of a document from one library to another. You can specify a default location for this option to encourage users to send finished copies to a particular library. Specifying a default Send To location for a library is especially useful if there is one library that most documents will be copied as part of a document management process.

Email a Link   You can email a link to the document to someone if you'd like them to read or edit the document.

Create Document Workspace   Like its predecessor, SharePoint 3.0 offers the option to create a workspace subsite to work on a particular document. This site is a mini Team site that is specifically focused on working on a single document only. Because the document or file is copied to the library in the workspace from the original, that copy is able to be easily copied back to the original library when you are done. Creating a document workspace will be covered in Chapter 7, "Sites, Subsites, and Workspaces." Workspaces are really easy to make if a user is allowed to create subsites.

Download a Copy   This option simply lets you quickly download a copy of a document to your machine in case you may be going offline.

The most useful and most frequently used option when you're using Send To is sending a copy of a document to another library (Other Location). That option seems half finished, and it can be a little misleading.

You can send a copy of a document from one library to another using two different methods: unlinked or linked. A *linked* copy can be updated with whatever changes were checked in from the originating document. That way the archived copy does not become obsolete, or out of sync with the original. An *unlinked* copy is completely independent from the original and should not be changed when the original changes.

SharePoint lets you specify whether a copy should be linked or unlinked by choosing, oddly enough, whether or not you can prompt for updates. This option is unfortunately worded. At no time does SharePoint actually prompt you to update copies of a document after you check it in. This inconsistency makes the feature seem unfinished somehow. Perhaps after a service pack or two, this option will be complete. For now, if you want a document to send its changes to a copy that might be stored in a different library, you need to remember to force it yourself.

Microsoft intends this option to be used to send a finished copy of a document to a different library to be archived. That means that the destination library should not be actively editing the document. To this end, the destination or target library for the document copy must *not* require check out or updating from original document will not work.

As an example, let's send a copy of a document from the Shared Documents Library to the CompanyLibrary as a reference for future documents and keep it linked. That way, when you change the document in the originating library (Shared Documents) you can update the copy in the destination library (CompanyLibrary).

To send a copy of a document in the Shared Documents Library to the CompanyLibrary (or whatever you named your library), follow these steps:

1. Go to the Shared Documents Library. Find the document you'd like to send to the other library. My example uses the Newdoc we created earlier in the chapter.

2. Simply move the cursor over the document name, and click on the selection box. In the dropdown menu, select Send To. The Send To options will pop out.

3. Select Other Location (Figure 6.53).

   The Copy page, will open. It has two sections: Destination and Update (See Figure 6.54).

   The Destination section, is where you specify the location of the library where you'd like to put the document copy. My example has only two libraries on the site. We are sending a copy from the Shared Documents Library, so the destination library will be the CompanyLibrary we made earlier. Because you can send documents to libraries outside this site (such as a different subsite, site collection, or even a different Web application), you need to specify the correct URL for the destination library's location.

4. In the Destination section, enter the URL for the destination library. My example specifies http://sp2/companylibrary, because that is the URL of the site where the library is located and the library name. You don't need to cut and paste the library's URL here. You can use the library's real name, even if it has spaces in it. Just keep in mind that Share-Point specifies sites by their URL, not their title. So it's best to get in the habit of using a URL.

FIGURE 6.53
Preparing to send a copy of a document to a different library

FIGURE 6.54
Sending a copy of the document to a different library

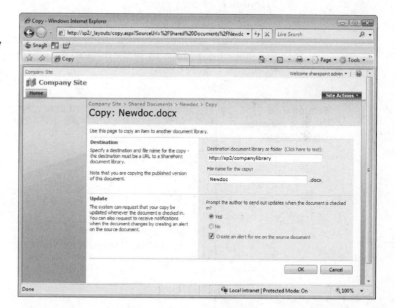

CONFIRMING THE URL

If you're not sure of the URL or library name, click the (Click here to test) link to open a window to the location. If an incorrect library comes up, correct the address and try again.

The Update section is where you decide whether or not the copy should keep a link with its original. To make this copy a linked copy to send updates from the original, choose "Prompt the author to send out updates when the document is checked in." That option implies that a prompt will pop up when you are updating an original, but it won't. It is really just meant to link the copy.

IF YOU DON'T NEED A LINK

If you don't want a copy to be linked, choose No for "Prompt the author to send out updates when the document is checked in." Also keep in mind you can unlink a copy from its original at any time.

The Update section also has the option to create an alert for the original document's library, so you can get an email to remind you that the document has been changed. This will let you make sure that, if you need to keep the copy updated, you know when to force the update.

5. Choose Yes to prompt the author to send out updates. You can always unlink the copy later. You can also enable an alert on the original so you will be aware when changes are made.

6. Once you've entered the correct location for the document copy and other settings, click OK to continue the copy process.

7. A Copy Progress dialog box will appear. Check the path and make sure it is the correct document. If you are sure, click OK to complete the copy. The dialog box will process for a few moments, add a copy of the original document to the other library, and then announce its success (Figure 6.55).

FIGURE 6.55
The copy operation was successful

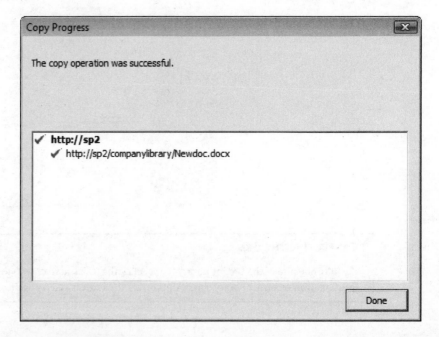

8. To confirm that the Send To worked, open the library where the copy was sent (Company Library in my example). The copied document should be there. You may notice that, looking at the document, it doesn't indicate it is a copy. One easy way to tell if a document is a copy is if the Go to Source Item option appears in the item selection menu (Figure 6.56).

FIGURE 6.56
The copied document is in the new library

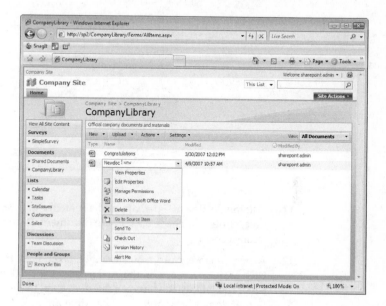

9. Click Go to Source Item. It will take you to the View Properties page for the original document. In the View Properties page of the original document, the Action bar has the option Manage Copies. You may have noticed this option previously, but it had no real use until now. This is one place you can check to see what copies of a document you have made, and you can manually update copies from here. When you update a copy of a document, you are literally saving over or *overwriting* the copy with the changes from the original. If versioning is enabled in the copy's library, the changes will be saved as the most current version.

DON'T CHECK OUT COPIES

Never enable Require Check Out on a destination library for copies. If you do, the updates will not work.

Now that we're are on the original document in the originating library, let's check it out, make changes, and then check the document back in.

10. You can open a document for editing from within a document's View Properties page by clicking on the document's filename (figure 6.57). It works the way it would if you clicked the filename in the library's content page. The link is exactly the same. However, it may not prompt you to check out the document to edit it. It may open the file as a read-only copy until you click the Check Out button in the information panel or link in the task pane. This is why I tend to check out the document there manually so it can be edited. Make certain the document is checked out first.

FIGURE 6.57
The original document's
View Properties page

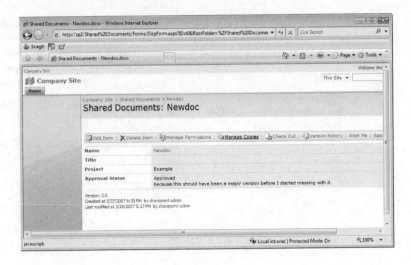

11. Edit the document—perhaps add a sentence to the end of the text, as I do in my example—save, close, and check back in the document. It does not matter if the change is a major or minor version.

12. After you close Word, you should be taken back the original View Properties page. If you click Manage Copies on the Action bar, it will take you to a Manage Copies page (Figure 6.58). You will see the copies of this document that either prompt for updates (that are linked) or that do not prompt for updates (that are unlinked). You should have a document listed in the linked documents section.

FIGURE 6.58
The Manage Copies page

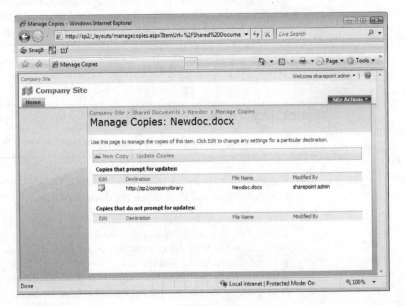

UNLINKING AND RELINKING DOCUMENTS

If you need to unlink a document copy, or relink it by prompting for updates, you can edit its properties using its Edit button. Although it says that you can request to receive an alert to be notified when the original document changes, there is no setting there for enabling an alert.

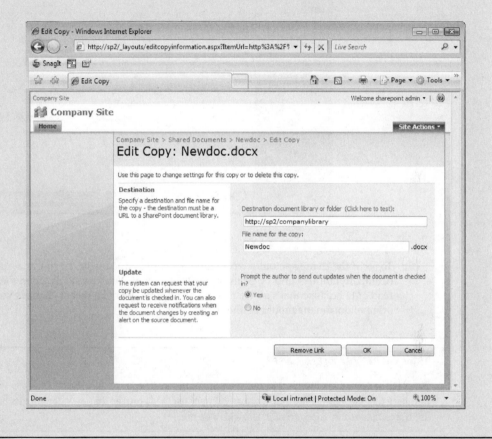

13. You can force an update of the changes made to the original document to the copy by clicking Update Copies on the Action bar. This will take you to the Update Copies page, where you can select to update particular linked copies or update all at once (Figure 6.59). Simply select the copy you want to update, and then click OK. The Copy Progress dialog box will appear again, proving that it simply will overwrite a newer copy of the original over the first copy. It's that simple. Click OK in the Copy Progress dialog box to continue the process.

14. Click Done when the copy is successful to close the dialog box. This will take you back to the original document's View Properties page.

FIGURE 6.59
Update Copy page

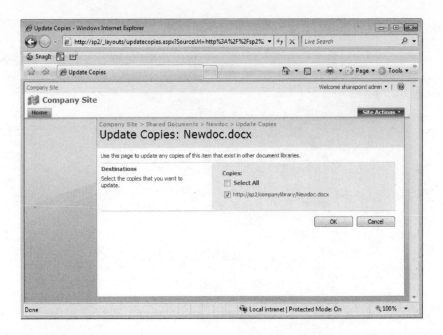

15. To see if the change actually worked on the copied document, go to the destination library (CompanyLibrary) and open the copied document. You can safely open the document as read only because that's all we need to do with it. The most recent changes you made to the original document should be there.

TEMPLATE? WHAT TEMPLATE?

Because the copied document was not created using the New button, it doesn't use the nifty custom template that documents for that CompanyLibrary use. This proves that new documents in the library use the template, and those created elsewhere do not.

There is an additional, and easier, way to update copies from an original in the content page of a library. This is probably what you are going to use most often. Just follow these steps:

1. Go back to the original library (Shared Documents).

2. Move your cursor over the document you copied (my example is Newdoc), click on the selection box, and in the dropdown menu, select Send to.

3. In the Send To menu popup, you'll see the Existing Copies option (Figure 6.60). If you click on that it will take you to the same Update Copies page that you used earlier from the Manage Copies page. Feel free to update any copies you'd like. In our case, it's not really necessary but it's nice to know the option is here.

FIGURE 6.60
Existing Copies option on original document

A FEW MORE SEND TO DETAILS

If you simply want to make a copy of a document in another library without being able to update that copy, simply send that copy to the other location but choose No to the prompt for updates.

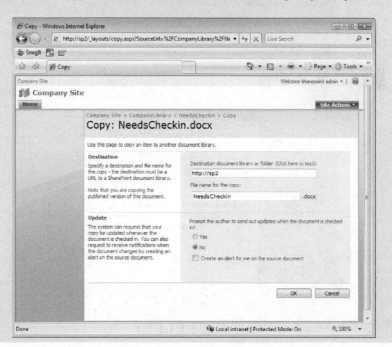

Then, if you check the item selection menu, there will be no Send to, Existing Copies option because you chose No for the prompt for updates action.

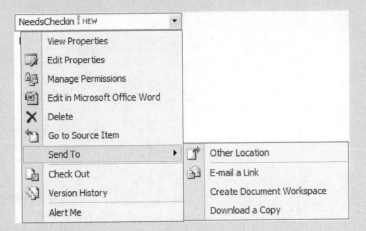

If you go to the Manage Copies page for that document, you will see that the document is listed under Copies that do not prompt for updates.

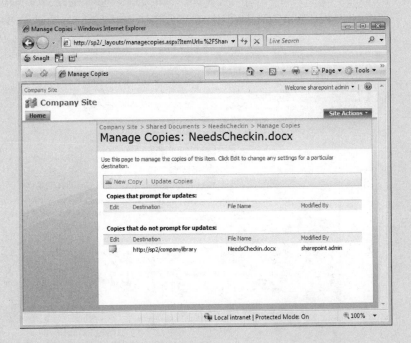

This means that that copy cannot be updated.

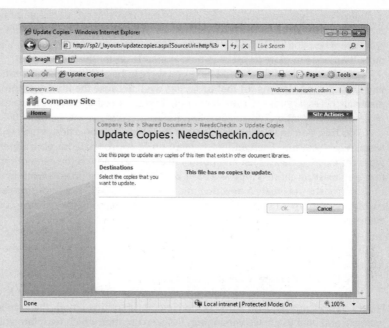

However if you want to, you can set that copy to prompt for updates—and therefore be able to be updated from the original—by just editing its properties.

Another quirk of Send To is that if you are going to change the update options of a copy, you must change them at the original document's properties, not the copy's properties. If the original library requires check out (as my example does), you must check out the document before you make any changes to a copy's settings, despite the fact that that copy exists in a different library.

Content Types

You know how to use an existing document library, how to create a new document library, how to add a custom template to a library so all new documents created there can take advantage of it, and you know how to send copies of documents from one library to another for archiving purposes. Now it's time to work with another useful feature in the list and library repertoire—content types. Content types are basically templates of standard list or library items. Item properties include the fields of that item, the template that might be associated with it, even what kind of workflow works with that item.

Content types are actually stored in a gallery for the entire site collection. So if you create a content type to be used for a particular library, realize that, once built, it's actually available to be used in a different list or library elsewhere in the collection if you'd like.

Because content types are general item templates available to the whole site collection, the fields they use must be available site collection wide as well. This is why content type fields are made up of site columns. Site columns are available from their own gallery, and can be used anywhere in the site collection as well. Therefore, if you want to add a field to a content type, it will have to be available as a site column (or you can make a site column specifically to use in your content type).

Before we began sending copies, I mentioned that you can define a library by its template. This means that that library will always create new documents that use that library's associated template when you click the New button. However, content types allow a library (or list) to have more than one template or list item type available under the New button.

A good example of this would be if you were to have a library that contained documents for a project and presentations for that project as well. Because the library would be focused on the materials necessary for the project overall, it would need to contain templates for both the written project documentation (Word 2007) and the project slides (PowerPoint 2007).

To do this, you enable content types in the library's properties, which will disable the single template association. Then add the content types appropriate for your library. Many of the content types for existing default list and library items are already in the content types gallery. So it is easy to use an existing content type as a base, and customize it a little to work in your new list or library.

First, we should create a new document library that will hold your project work. Next, we will enable content types on that library, and then choose among the existing content types to make available two different kinds of templates for the library.

To create a new document library, go to Site Actions at the top left of the page and select Create from the dropdown menu.

Click Document Library on the Create page.

On the New page, fill in the fields necessary to create the new library. My example uses the library name **Projects**. Add a description, enable incoming email (the alias in my case will be *projects*), and enable simple versioning. It doesn't matter which template you select during the library setup because it will be disabled when you enable content types. (See Figure 6.61.) Click Create when configuration is done.

FIGURE 6.61
Creating a new document library

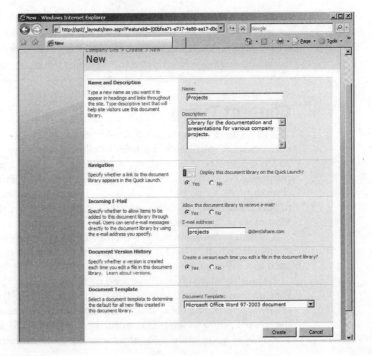

Enable Content Types

On the new library, let's enable content types. Normally a library has only one type of library item, and that item will be associated with the library's default template. To have more than one library item for a library, and therefore have the opportunity to associate more than one template with the library, you must enable content types. To do so, follow these steps:

1. Go to Settings on the Action bar, and select Document Library Settings from the dropdown menu.

2. On the Customize page, click Advanced Settings. On the Advanced Settings page, select Yes in the Content Types section. Click OK to finish. It's that simple. That will change the Customize page, adding a Content Types section that did not exist before they were enabled.

On the Customize page, you can see that the Content Types section already has one item; Document. This is the default library item, which in this case is a library item with a Word 97/2003 template associated with it. It is the default library item assigned when the library was created. We will be, conveniently, keeping this library item.

Also notice in Figure 6.62 that there is a brief description of content types under the section title. Basically, the library can now contain different list item types complete with their own associated file templates, fields, workflows, and more. This example is a simple way to use them, but hopefully this will introduce you to the concept in case it is something you might need. All lists and libraries have items (or more precisely, records), but with content types, they can have more than one kind of item if necessary.

FIGURE 6.62
The Content Types section

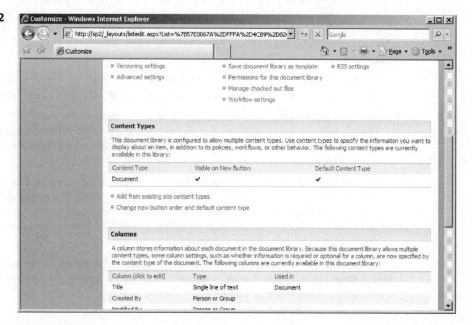

FOLDERS AS CONTENT TYPES

To make things more complicated, folders are considered items in a list or library, which means their properties can be modified and they can be used as content types. This is how they work in discussion lists. There are online articles and books dedicated to working with lists and libraries, and integrating them with Office 2007. They go into more detail about content types and folders than we can here.

Although we already have a nice, default, blank template for our documentation files, we need to add a library item with a template for project-specific slides. We should use a customized template for the project's PowerPoint presentations so users can simply get started with the correct slide layout when they are working with this project library.

Create a New Content Type

When you create a new content type, it has to have a parent content type to be based on. That's why there are so many default types to choose from. So when we create a new content type, say for a document library, we can use the default document item content type as the base. Then we can configure it, such as specifying particular fields or the template that will be associated with it to make it unique. Once a content type is created, it can become a base for other new content types if necessary.

Parent content types available by default in SharePoint fall under certain headings:

Custom Content Types   This is the content type group where content types that you create are listed, unless you specify otherwise.

Document Content Types   These content types are what are likely to be stored in a document library, such as a Document (the default content type for a library, contains default fields and is associated to the template assigned to the library), Web Page, Picture, even Master Pages. There is also the link content type, that is used to a link to a file in a different location, a la Send To linking.

Folder Content Types   This list of content types is short. There is the folder content type associated with discussions, and the default for simply creating a new folder.

List Content Types   The content types in this group are the standard items applied to most default lists, such as Contacts, Announcement, Issues, and Tasks. Included is the option *Item*, which is used in custom lists as the default for list items and enforces the Title field requirement (now you know).

Special Content Types   There is only one content type listed in this group by default, the Unknown Content Type. This content type, associated with libraries by default, allows libraries to accept any file that is uploaded to the library regardless of file type (unless it is blocked administratively). If you can't upload files to the library, but you used to, make certain that this content type was not removed from the library's settings.

In our case we are going to need to create a content type, based on the standard document library item, but associate it with a custom PowerPoint template. To do this we'll need to go to the site collection's content type gallery.

To create a new content type, follow these steps:

1. Go to the top of the Customize page, click Site Actions, and then select Site Settings.

2. On the Site Settings page (Figure 6.63), select Site content types from the Galleries category. As with the Site Columns page, you can see that the site content types are organized in groups.

FIGURE 6.63
The Site Content
Type Gallery

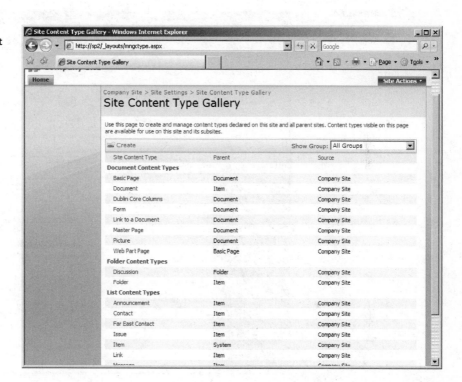

3. You can look through this list and see that there doesn't seem to be a content type for creating PowerPoint presentations listed. Therefore, we are going to have to create one ourselves. To create the new content type, click Create on the Action bar (it's the only thing listed there).

   When you create a content type, you generally base it on a parent or an existing content type to save time. In this case, you just need a standard document library item, but with a different template.

4. To that end, on the New Site Content Type page (which opened when you clicked Create), in the Name and Description section, name the new content type—ProjectSlides for my example—and describe it as *Document content type to be associated with a PowerPoint template.*

5. Under Parent Content Type, you can see that, in the Select Parent content type from field, there are several groups of base content types listed. Because you are working with a document library, you should choose Document Content Types. Because you chose that group, in the Parent Content Type field below (see Figure 6.64), you can choose *Document*. That means that it will be prepared to be associated with the preferred template, and it will have the same fields as the content type that is the default for the library.

FIGURE 6.64
The new Site
Content Type page

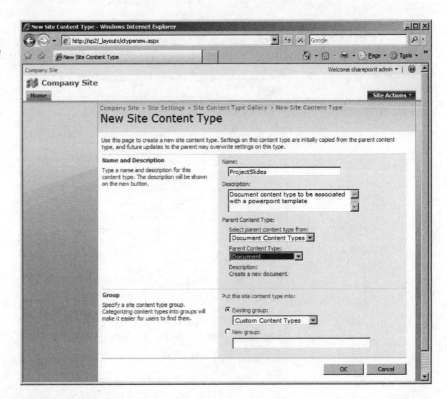

ORGANIZING FOR LISTS AS FIELDS VIEWS

List views can be organized by fields. If the library or list items have no fields in common, trying to organize those items in a view will be challenging.

6. You can decide if you want to list your new content type under the general Group heading Custom Content Types or you can create one yourself. My example uses the default. If all the settings are good, click OK to create your new content type.

7. This will take you to the new content type's settings page (Figure 6.65). There you can change the name and description, set up the workflow you want to be used with this content type, delete the content type, or configure its advanced settings, which is what we are going to modify.

FIGURE 6.65
The Content Type Settings page

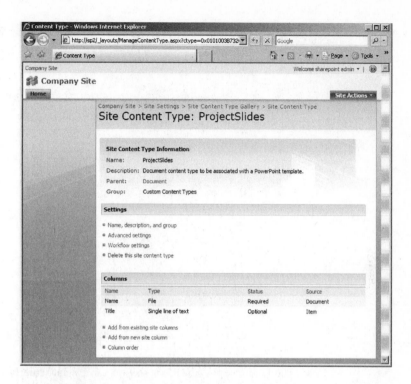

8. Click Advanced settings. The Content Type Advanced Settings page has three sections: Document Template, Read Only, and Update Sites and Lists.

   ◆ The Document Template section is where you specify the template that will be associated with this content type. This is a convenient place for you to upload the template to Share-Point that will be used for this content type. My example has the Dem0tek PowerPoint template located in a folder on my local drive, but you can browse to wherever you have your template located (see Figure 6.66 for my example).

   ◆ The Read Only section restricts the editing of the content type's settings. If you do want the content type to be read only and unmodifiable, keep in mind that this setting can be changed by someone with the right to edit content types. My example does not make the content type read only.

SOME TIPS ABOUT THAT READ ONLY SETTING

If a content type is set to read only, on the content type's settings page, all configuration settings you might have wanted to use disappear except for the Advanced settings page (the page you need to be able to access to disable read only). In addition, if you do set a content type to read only, and change your mind, disabling read only might disconnect any workflows that might be associated with that content type. Be sure to specify the workflow association again after disabling read only.

FIGURE 6.66

The Site Content Type Advanced
Settings

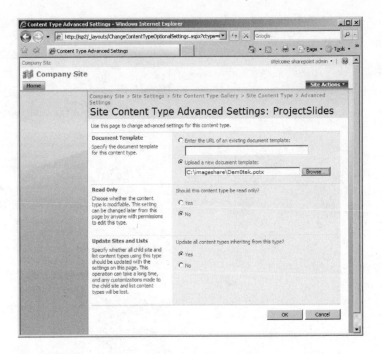

- ◆ The Update Sites and Lists section can be particularly useful setting. As you know, you create new content types by basing them on existing content types. What you might not have considered is the fact that SharePoint remembers that connection. And if you change a parent content type, those changes can trickle down to all content types based on that parent. It is in this section that you can choose to allow changes made to this content type to be inherited by all content types based on it, or not. The default is Yes, and that's fine for now.

9. For the Document Template section we need to upload a template for this content type. So enter the path to your template in the field or browse to it. For my example I am going to use a PowerPoint template called `Dem0tek.potx`. Otherwise keep the defaults for the Read Only and Update Sites and Lists sections and click OK to finish the Advanced Settings for this content type.

The advanced settings are the only thing changing at this time for this content type; however, keep in mind that you can make changes at any time, including adding more fields if you'd like from either existing site columns or site columns that you create yourself.

Now that we have created a new content type, let's apply it to our library:

1. Go to the new library you created (my example is *Projects*). The easiest way to do that from a site gallery is to click the Home tab on the top-link bar. On the home page, click on the library name in the Quick Launch bar.

2. In the library, click Settings on the Action bar, and then click Document Library Settings in the dropdown menu.

3. On the Customize page, in the Content Types section, click Add from existing content types.

4. In the Add Content Types page, in the Select content types from field, choose the Custom Content Types group—because that's where we put the new content type, if yours is in a different group choose that one.

5. In the Available Site Content Types, select the new content type (my example is *ProjectSlides*, as you can see in Figure 6.67), and add it to the Content types to add box. Then click OK.

FIGURE 6.67
Add Content Types to the library

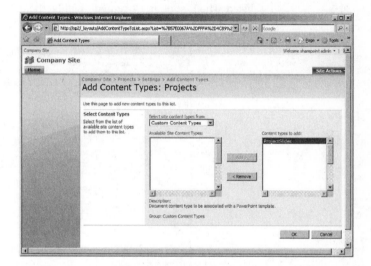

You should be back on the Customize page for the library. In Figure 6.68, you can see two content types for the library. The default is the document type, and they are both visible under the New button. We could change the order of the content types under the button, making the new one the default. However, I am fine with the document being the default, as that will probably be the template the users will use the most.

FIGURE 6.68
Two content types for the new library

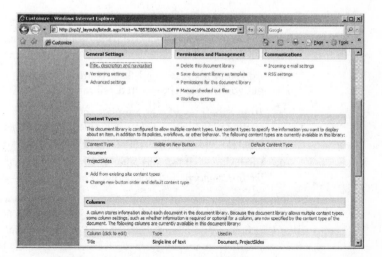

Now that the library has its two different templates associated with it, let's use our content types for the library:

1. Go out to the library's content page by clicking its name in the breadcrumb above the title of the settings page.

2. Back on the content page of the library, click the little down arrow next to the New button in the Action bar. In Figure 6.69, you can see that two items (other than Folder) are now listed. The first item, Document, will be the default if you click New without going to the down arrow.

FIGURE 6.69

Two templates options under the New button

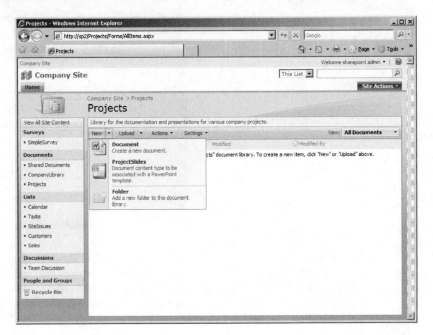

3. To prove this, click away from the dropdown menu, and then click New. SharePoint will use the default blank document template for Word.

4. Add some text, save, and close. Name the document, my example is *Firstproject*. That should put your new document in the library.

5. To use the PowerPoint template, click the down arrow next to New and select the new content type's template (my example is called *ProjectSlides*). This will open a presentation in PowerPoint using the template you uploaded (see Figure 6.70 for my example).

6. Create some slides, and enter whatever text you'd like. Then save the file (my example is *Firstpresentation*) and close PowerPoint.

On the content page of the library, you can see that two documents are stored there (Figure 6.71). In the Document Type column, notice that the two file types are different. *Firstproject* is a Word document, and *Firstpresentation* is a PowerPoint file.

FIGURE 6.70
The custom
PowerPoint template
from the new content
type

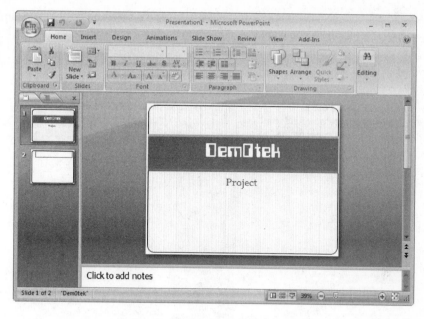

FIGURE 6.71
Two different content
type items in library

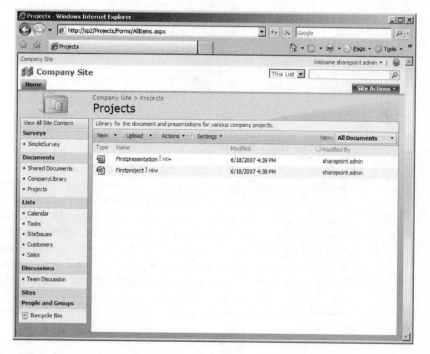

Because these content types are based on the same parent (Document), they have the same fields. If you want to add fields to the library, they can be added to both content types as if they were one kind of library item. While you are creating the field simply select *Add to all content types* at the bottom of the Create Column page, as you can see in my example of a new field for Projects in Figure 6.72.

FIGURE 6.72

Adding a new field to all content types on the Create Column page

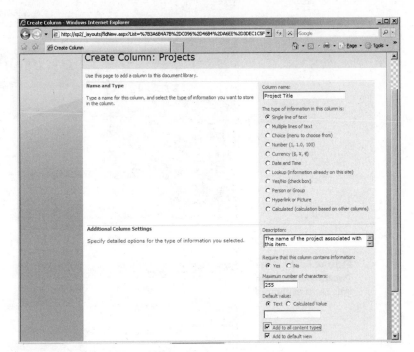

WHEN IN DOUBT, RELINK

If you change the template used by a content type in a library, you may have to relink documents that were using the template to reflect the change. Otherwise, they may not open properly when users try to read or edit the document. If you have changed a template and are now having problems opening files in a library, go to Explorer View in the View menu. In the Explorer view, open the Forms folder, and double-click the `repair.aspx` icon. This will open the Repair page for that library in which you can select the file that needs to be relinked to its template. The library will check the file for its content type, and then check that content type's template. If the URL pointer for that file's template doesn't match the updated one for the content type, the file's pointer will be changed to match. That should fix the problem. Remember, `repair.aspx` is your friend.

And that's about all I am going to cover for document libraries. However, there are a few other kinds of libraries available in SharePoint. They are very similar to a document library; they simply were meant to store and manage different particular file types.

Picture Library

Picture libraries were meant to store all the pictures a site or site collection might require (with thumbnail views, download options, and slideshow). All image files stored in a picture library will have a URL so you can use them elsewhere. This comes in handy if you have a contact list of employees and pictures for each employee in a picture library. You can then use the Hyperlink/Picture field (conveniently part of the contact list by default) to point to the picture's URL for each employee.

To see how a picture library works, let's create one.

Just click Site Actions, and then click Create from the dropdown menu. On the Create page, click Picture Library in the Libraries category.

As you can see in Figure 6.73, the settings for a new picture library are very similar to those of any other library. You can enable incoming email and versioning, and you can determine whether or not the link for the library will be on the Quick Launch bar. Name the library (mine will be *CompanyPictures* for this example), give it a description, and enable incoming email (my example's alias is *pictures*). Otherwise, keep the defaults for navigation and versioning. When the settings are complete, click OK.

FIGURE 6.73
New Picture Library Settings

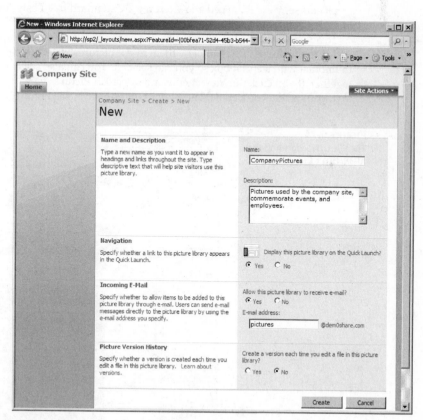

This will take you to the new picture library. The library will look no different than any other. However, the New button has only a folder under it. You can't create pictures from a template there. To get pictures to the picture library, you have to upload them. Some new, picture-library–specific actions are under the Actions button:

Edit   This will open your operating system's default application to edit image files. It prefers the Microsoft Office Picture Manager.

Delete   This will delete a selected picture.

Download   This is the opposite of upload, of course. It will copy the selected picture to your local computer.

Send To   This is not the Send To you were expecting. It inserts a selected picture in an email or document.

View Slideshow   This uses the Slideshow view to cycle through the pictures in the library.

Open with Windows Explorer   Just like any library, this will open an Explorer window so you can drag and drop image files into the library conveniently.

Of course, View RSS Feed and Alert me are standard in all lists and libraries and are on the menu as well.

To add an image to the library, you can either upload it or use Explorer view. Once images are added to the library, you can view them in All Pictures view, which shows each picture as a thumbnail with a check box so you can select it. You can also select particular images to view together. If you click the View menu, and select All Pictures view, an alternate menu will appear; in it, you can choose Details, Thumbnails, or Filmstrip (see Figure 6.74 for an example).

FIGURE 6.74
The Filmstrip view and the
All Pictures View menu

Remember that to upload multiple pictures at one time the machine you are using to access the picture library must have an Office 2003 or 2007 product installed.

Wiki Page Library

The Wiki Page Library is just a library of Web pages. To create a wiki library go to Create on the Site Action menu, and then select Wiki Library from the Libraries category. On the New page you can simply specify the name and description of the library, and whether or not to display the library on the Quick Launch bar. Wiki libraries don't support incoming email, and like the picture library, can't be assigned a template. For wiki libraries, versioning is enabled by default, so the option just isn't available during creation. And all wiki pages are going to be HTML pages, which is why the option to choose a different template isn't available. Wiki libraries are very simple libraries meant to do one thing, contain web pages that link to one another.

As you can see in Figure 6.75, the wiki library in my example is called CompanyWiki. One of the more unusual things about a wiki library is its default view. A wiki library opens with a view that displays a default file in the library named Home as its first view. The wiki library has versioning enabled by default. On what is essentially the home page of the library are links to edit the Home document and view its Version History. Because wiki pages are specifically supposed to be linked to other pages in the library, you can check what links the Home file contains. On the bottom left, below the Quick Launch bar, are some additional navigation features: a link for recent changes, a list of the documents in the wiki library, and a link to go to the Library content page.

FIGURE 6.75
The new wiki library

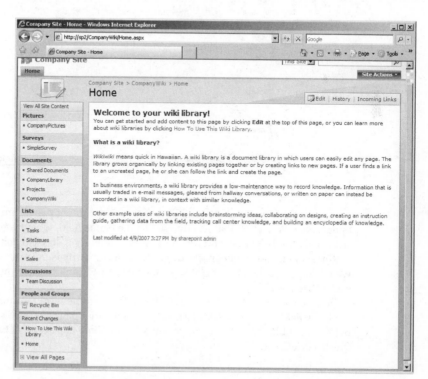

To see the library's content page, you can to look to the breadcrumb and click on the library's name (my example is CompanyWiki) or go to View All Pages at the bottom of the Quick Launch, Recent Changes bar. That will take you to the library proper (Figure 6.76). In the item selection menu for an item, you can see that the wiki library is like any other, except that the product used to edit the files is not Word, Excel, or PowerPoint; it's SharePoint Designer. This indicates that the documents in the library are considered a sort of Web page.

FIGURE 6.76
The wiki library's content

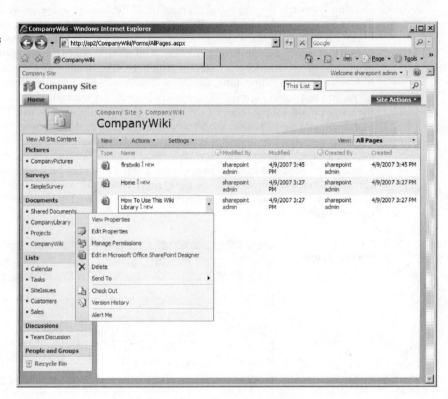

To add a document to the wiki library from the content page, simply click New. It will open a New Wiki Page that has two fields: the Name field, which is required because it's essentially the Title field, and the Body field. The Body field is an enhanced rich-text field, so pictures and tables can be inserted; however, it primarily is meant to have HTML elements as well. It supports the convenient wiki-specific tags for linking documents in the library with each other.

To create a wiki document, simply name the document (my example is **firstwiki**). Then in the Body field, add some text. To create links to other pages in the library, simply use their name between double brackets. To create a link to the home page type **[[home]]** (see Figure 6.77). To finish, click Create.

FIGURE 6.77
Creating a wiki document

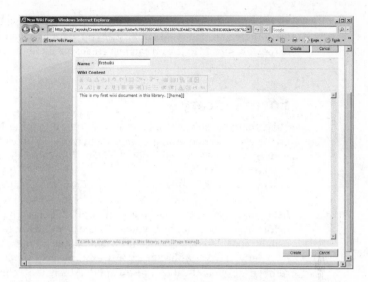

Then if you view the page, you'll see that there is a link to home from there (Figure 6.78). If you create a wiki link to a page that doesn't exist, the library will indicate the link is empty by putting a dotted line under it. When you click it, it will try to get you to create content for that page.

FIGURE 6.78
The new wiki document

For more about wiki libraries, check out Chapter 7, which covers wiki sites, that, coincidentally, are centered around a wiki library. If you want to have wiki documents, you don't have to dedicate a subsite to it. You can just create a wiki library.

Form Library

This library doesn't get a lot of press because it requires Microsoft InfoPath to be installed locally on the user's computer in order for them to use it (unless you have a InfoPath Forms Server on your network). However, if you are using InfoPath extensively at your company, you might want to take a look at it.

This library is created like any other. From the Create page, select the Form Library link.

The New page has your standard fields for library creation. It even has a Document Template field, but the only option is to use an InfoPath Form template. That is because the template is just a holder and, using InfoPath, you will need to publish a form template up to the library. Forms are usually considered *templates,* and when people fill out a form, it is considered a *form instance.*

After you create your library (my example is CompanyForm), it will look like any other. All the settings are generally the same except that there is a Relink documents to this library setting on the library's Settings page because it is not uncommon for forms to become unlinked from their parent template.

To use the library, you must first publish a form template to the library. Meaning you have to open InfoPath, create a form, save it, and then publish it.

In my example, I opened InfoPath and used a sample template (See the Status Report in Figure 6.79). It was saved as `status.xsn` locally.

FIGURE 6.79
The Status Report template in InfoPath

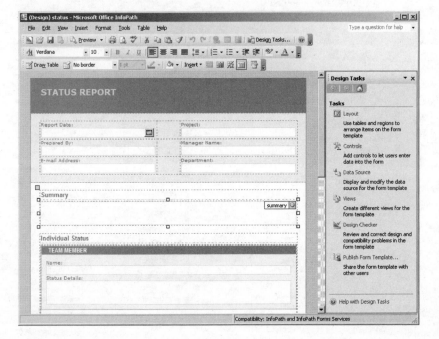

Once the form template is designed the way you like it and you've saved it locally, the form is ready to be published to the library:

1. In InfoPath, click Publish Form Template in the Design Tasks pane, or click Publish under the File menu.

2. This opens a Publishing Wizard dialog box for you to choose where you want the template to be published. Choose To a SharePoint Server with or without InfoPath Forms Services (Figure 6.80). Click Next to continue.

FIGURE 6.80
The Publishing Wizard

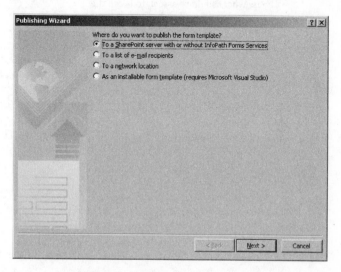

3. The next screen (Figure 6.81) for the wizard asks for the site URL for the form library. My example uses http://sp2. Enter the URL and click Next.

FIGURE 6.81
Enter the path for the site

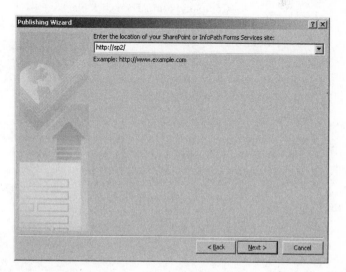

The next screen (Figure 6.82) wants to know if the form will be associated with a library or a content type. SharePoint considers a form library to be a document library because it is essentially a document library for forms. Although InfoPath forms can be browser-enabled, the site does not support it. The user must use InfoPath to fill out forms in a form library (since this server does not have InfoPath services on it, and we are assuming there is no convenient InfoPath server on the network).

FIGURE 6.82
Choose what should be associated with the template

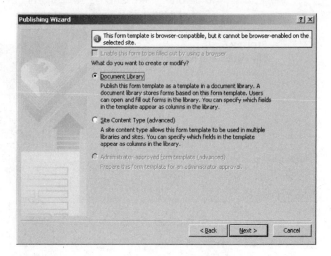

4. Choose Document Library and click Next.

5. In the next screen of the Publishing Wizard, you can see that InfoPath has found all of the possible libraries that might need a form template (Figure 6.83). Choose Update the Form Template in an existing document library, and select your Form Library (my example is CompanyForm). Then click Next.

FIGURE 6.83
Choose the form library to which to publish the form template

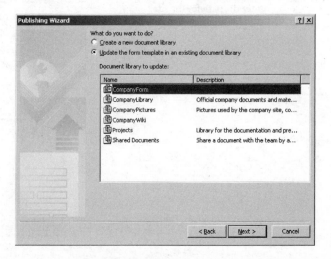

6. The next screen shows the fields that will be available for the library list item itself (the form's metadata if you will). You can add or remove fields here. Doing so does not affect the form template's fields. For this example, let's leave them as is and click Next.

7. The last screen is to verify if the settings are correct. If they are correct (Figure 6.84), click Publish to publish the form to the form library.

FIGURE 6.84
Verify the publishing settings

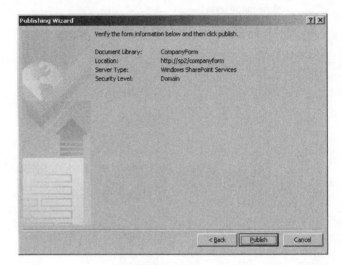

8. After the Form template publishes to the library, you will get a "Your form template was successfully published" screen. You can open the form library from there if you'd like (InfoPath still insists it's a document library), or you can click Close to finish. Click Close and return to the form library.

Back on the form library, you'll see that there is now a form template (Figure 6.85). In my example it is called *status*.

FIGURE 6.85
The Form template published to the form library

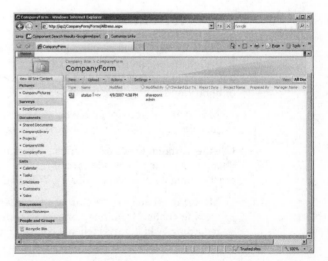

If you click on it, it doesn't open the template, it opens a form instance. Also, if you click the New button, it too simply uses the newly published Form template to create a form instance that a user can fill in (Figure 6.86).

FIGURE 6.86
The Travel Request form made from the Form template

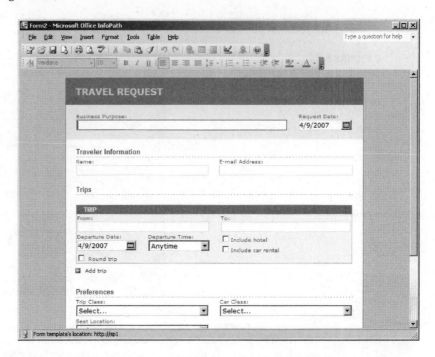

So that's about it for libraries in general. I hope this chapter has given you a basic understanding about how to use libraries, what they are, what they are meant to do, and what they actually do.

The Bottom Line

Create a library   A library is a kind of list that focuses primarily on the files that are attached to the list items. There are several different types of libraries, depending on the type of file they are intended to store. Creating a library is as easy as opening the Create page, selecting the type of library, and configuring it. There are several different types of libraries.

Master It   If you do not have any Microsoft Office 2003 or 2007 products installed on your machine, what two main features of document libraries are not available?

Use the different kinds of libraries   Document libraries can be created for any type of file, but SharePoint has four main kinds of libraries with different features and views. These four libraries are: Document library, Form library, Wiki Page library, and Picture library.

Master It   You're restructuring the content of some of your libraries, and are planning on moving content from one library to another. What key facts do you need to keep in mind regarding Wiki libraries when it comes to moving or uploading files?

Set check out, content approval and versioning.   Require Check Out forces users of a document library to check out a document if they intend to edit it. This helps enforce version management by allowing only one person to edit a document at a time. When a document is checked out, it can be only be read by other users, but they cannot edit the document until the person with it checked out, checks it back in.

Content approval can allows items to remain invisible to most list or library viewers until someone with approval rights approves the item. In a library with content approval and major and minor versions enabled, only major versions of a document can be approved.

Versioning means that whenever a list or library item (or its attached document) is changed, that change is saved as a different version. That means that if an edit was a mistake, you can restore a previous version.

> **Master It**   Brian has left the company, but some of the documents in your Shared Documents library are still checked out by him. Several of the documents have multiple versions stored, but one was a brand new document that Brian uploaded to the server recently. What three methods are available to check these documents back in?

Manage content types   By default each library (or most lists for that matter) has one content type. The content type of a library item is one that can have a single template associated with it such as Word documents, PowerPoint presentations, or Excel spreadsheets. However, it is possible to have a document library with multiple content types, allowing the library to create a mix of documents and multiple templates.

> **Master It**   You have a general document library for the Public relations department. They wish to use the library to manage a large number of different document types – from Word to pictures to movie clips to more obscure things. More importantly, the type of files they're going to use is likely to change over time. How should you configure the content types for this library?

Chapter 7

Sites, Subsites, and Workspaces

You've seen what you can do with a SharePoint site and all the amazing things you can configure with lists and libraries. Now it's time to look at what you can do to the site overall and how to leverage SharePoint to provide multiple sites for multiple purposes and users. Adding new sites to a site collection is easy, and you can customize these sites to do almost anything. From adding additional Team sites to providing blogging and wiki services, SharePoint offers numerous site types and configuration offerings.

In this chapter, you'll learn how to:

◆ Create and customize a new site

◆ Adjust Site Settings for administrative purposes

◆ Understand the different types of SharePoint sites available by default

◆ Add additional site templates and definitions

Definitions and Concepts

In order to better understand the different types of SharePoint sites, it's best to first review some core definitions and concepts.

Site Definition   Each SharePoint site is based on a site definition. The site definition determines what all sites based on that definition can do, what custom list fields exist, what web parts are available, whether any custom features are loaded, and how libraries and lists are configured. The site definition is the underlying framework for SharePoint sites. Site templates are based on site definitions. They essentially refine the potential of a site definition into discrete sites for different purposes.

Site Template   A site template is similar to the site definition, in that it determines how a site is displayed and what premade lists, libraries, and web parts are made, and what settings and configuration is available. However, a template is very different from a definition. For one thing, templates are based on definitions. A site template is used to generate the site and is applied when a site is created; once the site is created, the template is done and the site can be customized beyond the template. All templates have, as their base, a site definition. And because of that, regardless of what template you use for a site, they all actually have the same capabilities set by the site definition, they only differ in what capabilities have been applied; what is prebuilt, how it is laid out, and how it looks.

SITES CAN BE BASED ON TEMPLATES OR SITE DEFINITIONS

The sites we will be looking at are those created by the default templates available with WSS 3.0. However, it is possible, if you are a developer, to create a great site definition and simply use it to create a site, avoiding the need for a template. Site definitions can even contain information for separate basic sites based on its settings and features (which is what meeting workspaces use). The details are beyond the scope of this book, but I wanted to let you know that you can download and use really fancy site definitions to be applied to new sites. Most often though, for the convenience, people create templates based on an existing site definition and use those instead.

Site Collection   The site collection is a collection of sites. The first site in the collection is called the top-level site and all subsequent sites below that are called *subsites*. All sites in a site collection can share users and permissions, galleries, and reside in the same basic path. Each site is created based on a template, including a blank one if you simply want to customize it from the ground up in SharePoint Designer. Site collections are contained in web applications. There can be more than one site collection per web application.

Top-Level Site   The first and "top" site in a site collection. All site collections require at least one site: the top-level site. The top-level site is the site that holds the settings for administering the entire site collection. Although the top level site is created based on a template just like all others, its security settings and galleries can effect all other sites in the collection.

Site   A site is simply a shorter way of saying a SharePoint website. A site in SharePoint is either a top-level site or a subsite in a site collection.

Subsite   A site that resides under another site. Often the upper site is called the *parent site* and the subsite is called a *child site*. All sites and their subsites reside in a site collection.

Self-Service Site   A site collection (not a site) that is user-created and user-controlled.

When creating SharePoint sites (whether top-level sites, or subsites), you will use site templates based on site definitions to easily configure the new site to do exactly what you need it to do. By default, SharePoint has several existing site templates.

- Team Site
- Document Workspace
- Wiki
- Blog
- Meeting Workspace
- Custom

Before we dig deeper into what these sites can do, and how they differ from each other, let's first take a closer look at how to create a new subsite and apply different settings from custom themes to site administration. Once you've seen how you can modify all the sites, we'll examine each of the different default template types and even add some new ones.

Creating a New Subsite

Before creating a new subsite, you need to keep the overall structure of your site collection in mind. At first, creating a new subsite below your main site is straightforward—but as your SharePoint deployment grows, you'll need to keep track of where a subsite is located relative to other sites. In a similar fashion to designing the organizational units (OUs) in Active Directory, it pays to plan ahead before creating a new subsite. Consider the purpose of the new site, user access desired, and how long you intend the site to exist. Subsites can be created with the intention of being temporary, such as a workspace for a project, or permanent, such as team site for a particular department or organization.

For my example, we'll build a new Team site for the Human Resources department to give them a place to work and share documents without cluttering the main site. It will need to be just like the main Company site, but designed specifically for Human Resources.

To create a new site, follow these steps:

1. Go to the Create Page by clicking on the Site Action button and choosing Create as shown in Figure 7.1. For this example the site will be created off the top-level site.

FIGURE 7.1
The Site Action menu

THE CREATE BASIC PAGE LINK

Despite what its name implies, the Create Basic Page link does not let you create a new web page within your SharePoint site. The Create Basic Page link merely creates a new web page for storage in an existing document library, just like adding a new Word document to an existing library.

---

2. On the Create Page, go to the Web Pages category and choose Sites And Workspaces. See Figure 7.2.

3. The New SharePoint Site page will appear, as shown in Figure 7.3. This is where you enter the initial settings for the new site.

4. The Title And Description section is pretty clear. Enter a name for the site (my example is **HR team site**). For the description, enter something useful to describe the purpose of the site, my example is **Site will contain forms, data, and documents pertaining to Human Resources. This site is intended to be a resource for all employees and staff.**

5. For Web Site Address, you can set the URL for the site. SharePoint has a limit of 255 characters in a single URL, so keep this short—you could end up placing more sites, libraries, and workspaces below the new site. Typically, this is a one-word URL without spaces. Enter an appropriate web page name, my example uses **HRteam**.

FIGURE 7.2
Sites and Workspaces

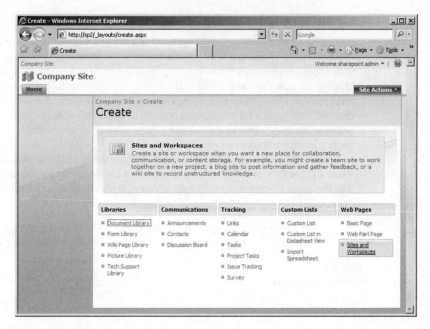

FIGURE 7.3
The new SharePoint
site

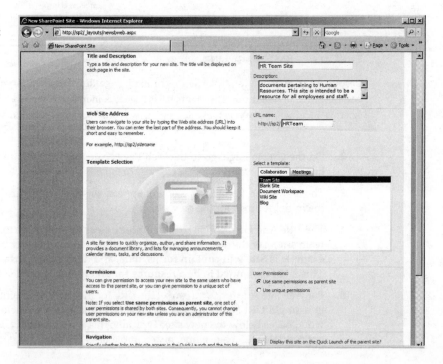

6. Under Template Selection, there are a number of templates you can use to speed up the design and layout of your new site. Each Template pulls data from a site definition. Under Collaboration, you'll see templates for Team Site, Document Workspace, Wiki, Blogs, and Blank Site. The Blank Site option creates a completely blank site so that you can customize it using SharePoint Designer. Under Meetings are the choices for each Meeting Workspace definition. For this example choose Team Site to create a main site for the HR Team. This template has, as you know, a lot of useful lists and web parts already pre-made and is a perfect for HR's uses.

7. For Permissions, you have two basic choices: Inherit or Custom. You can choose Inherit to have this site use permissions from the parent site. Choosing Custom will force you to manually create the permissions. If you choose to inherit permissions, you can later edit the site, break inheritance, and move to a custom permission set if you need to. For more details on Permissions, see Chapter 11, "Users and Permissions." For now, leave the default in place and use the same permissions as the parent.

WHAT IF YOU CHANGE YOUR MIND?

Don't worry. All of these settings, even the web page name can be changed after the new page is created. You can change it later if necessary.

The only option you can't change is the template used. After a site is created, you can't reapply a different template. That being said, anything on the Create page is available anywhere in the site collection. This means that you want a list for yor subsite, but it doesn't seem to be available by default, you can easily create it from resources available for all sites in the collection.

---

8. For Navigation, you have the option to have this new site appear as a link on the parent site's Quick Launch bar and Top Link bar. Adding the links lets people who go to the main site easily move to the HRteam site. Selecting No for both will not place the link on the Quick Launch bar or Top Link bar, but people can still get to the new site by using View All Site Content on the main page, or by entering the URL directly in their web browser (`http://sp2/HRteam/`). Leave both these options set to Yes so users can easily visit the HRteam site from the top-level site.

9. The Navigation Inheritance option sets the new site's Top Link bar to be the same as the parent site's Top Link bar. This is not always a good idea; it really depends on the new site's intended use. Consider your new site's role and if the top-level site's Top Link bar is appropriate. Choosing No will give the new site a brand new Top Link bar, with a default Home link that goes to the top page of the new subsite (and not the parent site). Choosing Yes will mean this site won't have its own bar; it will use the bar from the parent site (in which case the Home link goes to the parent site). Leave this option set to the default Yes. When you have finished with your settings click Create.

That's it! You now have a new site for Human Resources, as shown in Figure 7.4. It looks just like the main site. Remember to keep your current path in mind (using the breadcrumbs) so you keep track of these sites and the page you're using. Another thing to consider is changing the theme of the subsite to make it easy to distinguish whether or not you are on the top-level Team site or the Human Resources Team subsite.

FIGURE 7.4
The HR Team site

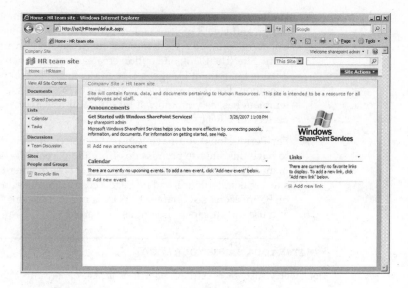

Site Settings

Your new site is obviously a lot like the old site because it's based on the same template.
Fortunately, SharePoint is very customizable, and you can do a lot to the sites to make them
unique without having to do any web development, from both a user and an administrator
perspective. Let's take a closer look at the different settings. To edit the Site's Settings, go to the Site
Actions menu (on the upper-right side of the screen) and choose Site Settings. You'll see the page
shown in Figure 7.5.

FIGURE 7.5
Site Settings

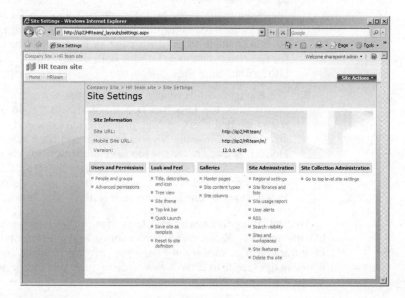

CUSTOMIZING THE CORRECT SITE

Keep in mind that when you make changes under Site Settings, they apply to the current site only. Before you make any changes, check your Site URL or breadcrumb path to ensure that you edit the HRteam site and not the main Company site. The following examples go through all of the categories discussed here, so that you can get an idea of what you can change and the ramifications of those changes.

Users and Permissions

Users and permissions are covered in more detail in Chapter 11, so for now let's just see how they relate to the new HRteam site versus the main Company site.

PEOPLE AND GROUPS

This page indicates who has what permissions to the site and what groups they belong to. Remember that if you chose to inherit permissions from the parent, any changes made here will actually be made in the Site Settings for the Company site (the top-level and parent site in this example), not to this HRteam subsite. (This is mentioned below the title in Figure 7.6 with the single line "Use this group to give people contribute permissions to the SharePoint site: Company Site".) Anything you do on this page—adding groups, users, etc.—is actually done to the Permissions for the Company site. This is because the HRTeam subsite doesn't have its own permissions so if you want to see what permissions are affecting it, of course its going to reflect the permissions of the parent site.

FIGURE 7.6
People and Groups

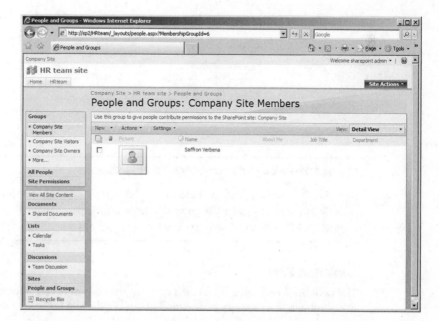

If you want to break inheritance (and have this site use its own, custom permissions), you need to click Site Permissions on the Quick Launch bar, which will take you to the same page as the Advanced Permissions link on the Site Settings page.

ADVANCED PERMISSIONS

Advanced Permissions is the page that displays what permission levels are being applied to the groups of the parent site, and therefore the subsite as well. This is where you can drill down to see what permissions and permission levels are being applied to the subsite, to the parent site, to manage those settings on the parent, or break that inheritance between the two. To break inheritance click Actions and choose Edit Permissions, as shown in Figure 7.7. (We're just looking at this point, so don't break inheritance and leave everything alone for now.)

FIGURE 7.7
Edit the advanced permissions

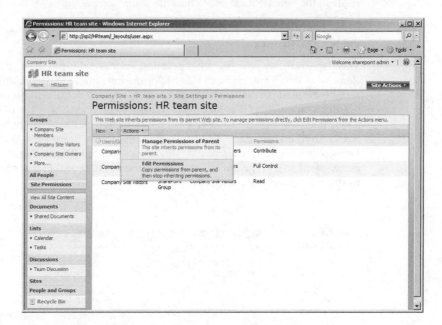

MOVING FROM CUSTOM TO INHERITED PERMISSIONS

If you break inheritance and use custom permissions (or start out with custom permissions from initial creation) and then later decide you want to inherit permissions from the parent site, enabling inheritance will wipe any custom permissions you might have.

Look and Feel

The Look And Feel category focuses on what the end users care about: the actual user interface. Everything in this category is designed to modify the site for ease of use and layout.

TITLE, DESCRIPTION, AND ICON

This section allows you to edit the site's Title and Description. The fields are identical to the fields on the Create page.

The page also lets you change the website address (the site's URL). Changing the URL will cause searches to fail until the next time the index service runs (because all of the paths will change). For details on setting the index frequency, see Chapter 2, "Installation."

Finally, this section has a new feature for WSS 3.0: Logo URL and Description. This feature wasn't present during creation, and it is a great way to customize a new site. The new icon replaces the SharePoint "play-toy people" icon in the top-left corner of the page. You can enter a URL to a new image hosted elsewhere, but you probably have a company logo or team photograph you'd like to place on the web server directly. In which case, the full path to the suggested location is `C:\Program Files\Common Files\Microsoft Shared\Web Server Extensions\12\templates\images\`. You can also navigate to this location in the IIS Manager (see Figure 7.8).

FIGURE 7.8
The IIS images location

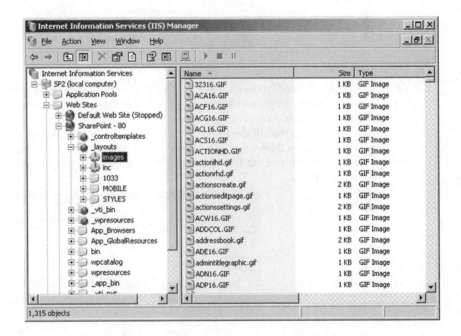

For this example, place your new logo in this directory. It can be any image file you like, but consider its size. Because it's going to be placed at the top-left of every page in the site, you'll probably want to use something small. Once the logo is in place, you can use a relative path in the Logo URL field.

Go ahead and change the logo for the site. My example uses a small JPG, you can use whatever you like.

For the logo URL, enter **/layouts/images/<imagefile>** and click OK. See Figure 7.9. The site icon will change immediately and you'll have a custom icon for the site.

FIGURE 7.9
Editing the logo

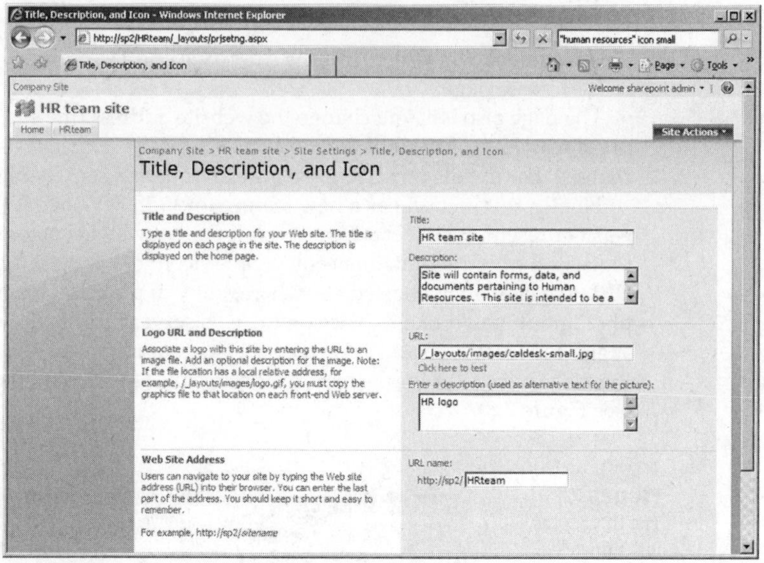

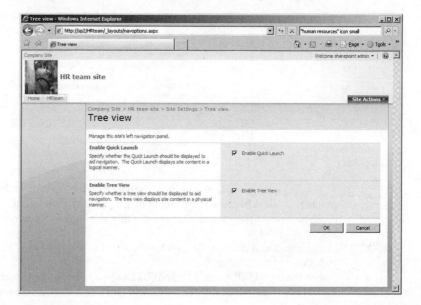

TREE VIEW

By default all SharePoint sites have the Quick Launch bar for navigation on the left side of most pages. However, there is an alternative; Tree View. Tree view can be used instead of or in addition to the Quick Launch bar. The Quick Launch bar contains site links grouped logically, whereas the Tree view shows the full site hierarchy in a physical sense. It behaves the same way as the tree pane in Windows Explorer or most MMC consoles. You can enable just the Quick Launch bar (this is default), enable just the Tree view, enable both, or enable neither. See Figure 7.10.

FIGURE 7.10
The Tree View page

When you enable both settings a new section will be added to the Quick Launch bar called "Site Hierarchy," which shows the Tree view. Enabling neither doesn't reclaim that space; it just leaves the View All Site Content link and the Recycle Bin in place, removing everything else. This flexibility in controlling what links are on the Quick Launch bar, what order they go in, whether there should be a display of site hierarchy, or even if there should be much of anything there at *all* allows you more control over what the users see conveniently, and therefore what they *use* conveniently. And keep in mind that that navigation design decision affects *all* pages on the site except administrative ones. So you might want to give it some serious thought when planning your subsites.

For this example let's go ahead and enable both.

TREE VIEW IS A POWERFUL THING

We've created a subsite beneath the top-level site. And because location has its privilege, and the child sites directly beneath top-level sites are added to the parent site's Quick Launch and Top Link bars.

However, if the child site spawned a child site, such as the HRTeam site having a HR blog subsite (called HR in Action! in this example), that subsite would not be on the Top Link bar of the HRTeam site. And ironically, if the blog subsite is inheriting the Top Link bar from its parent, it won't even be on its own Top Link bar.

This is because the HR blog is inheriting the top links from its parent site, which is inheriting its top links from the level above it. This means that the HR blog has the same Top Link bar as HRTeam, HRTeam has the same Top Link bar as the top-level site (Company Site in my case), and that site has no idea the HR blog exists.

The bottom line is that sub-subsite are not naturally listed in the Quick Launch bar or Top Link bar on the top-level site or any level above the subsite's parent. The only site that will have a link to it (if you don't disable it) is the sub-subsite's parent. So to get to the HR blog, you would first have to know that you need to go to the HRTeam site, then click in the Quick Launch bar to get to the HR blog.

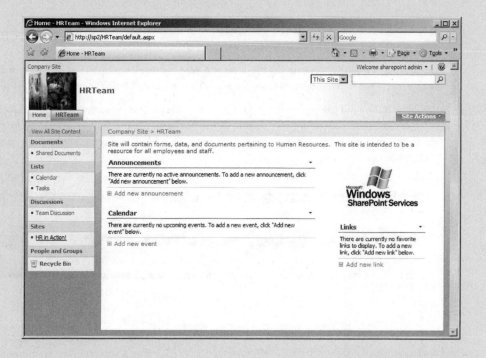

If you wanted users to be able to find and access all subsites in the site collection more conveniently, then consider enabling Tree View for the top-level site. If you enable Tree View, it will add the Site Hierarchy to the Quick Launch bar area. (It can take up a lot of space and clutter the Quick Launch bar, which is why so many people leave it off.) However, if you have the Site Hierarchy on (which is what the Tree View is called when enabled), you can use it to see what sites are where at any level throughout the site collection. And if you had your subsites inheriting the Quick Launch bar from the top-level site, they would automatically have the Site Hierarchy available as well.

In the Site Hierarchy, the lists, libraries, and subsites are displayed. Subsites are indicated first, with the rest of the local content displayed below. Subsites have plus signs next to them so you can expand them in the hierarchy to see what content they have available. If the subsite has sites beneath it, they will be displayed with plus signs so you can expand them as well.

So if you have a lot of subsites with subsites and you don't want to have to add them manually to the Top Link bar or to the Links List View web part of the top-level site, then consider Tree View.

SITE THEME

Site Themes are a convenient and dramatic way to change the appearance of a SharePoint site. Because SharePoint pages are rendered on the fly, changing the appearance using themes is easy. The theme changes colors, graphics, banners, and borders. It does not change the actual content in any way. There are 18 built-in themes, but web designers can create themes using SharePoint Designer or by directly modifying the CSS (Cascading Style Sheet) files.

CSS SAVVY—CREATING YOUR OWN THEME

Site Themes are a lot of fun. However, finding the perfect one with what's immediately available is difficult. Fortunately, a lot of free downloadable themes are available online from Microsoft and from many helpful people and third-party companies. If you absolutely must make your own theme, you'll need some way to edit the CSS sheets and you'll need to know what to edit where.

Editing or creating CSS files is beyond the scope of this book; however, if you know how to edit Cascading Style Sheets, you can use the locations and relevant files for SharePoint.

Themes are kept in the following location:

```
C:\Program Files\Common Files\Microsoft Shared\web server
    extensions\12\TEMPLATE\THEMES
```

It's usually easier to edit a copy of an existing theme than to make one completely from scratch. Make a copy of a theme folder, name it whatever you want your theme to be called, and play with that first.

Each theme folder contains an INF file. Rename it to match the folder name (and your new theme name). Open the newly renamed INF file and look in the [Info] section for `title=name`. Change *name* to your new theme name. Save and close the file.

Your theme will need to appear in the Site Theme section of Site Settings. This list is located in the `SPTHEMES.XML` file found in:

```
C:\Program Files\Common Files\Microsoft Shared\web server
    extensions\12\ TEMLATE\LAYOUTS\1033
```

Edit the `SPTHEMES.XML` file to include your new theme's info.

```
SPTHEMES.XML - Notepad
File Edit Format View Help
                <Preview>images/thvintage.gif</Preview>
        </Templates>
        <Templates>
                <TemplateID>wheat</TemplateID>
                <DisplayName>wheat</DisplayName>
                <Description>wheat has a golden background with brown control
areas.</Description>
                <Thumbnail>images/thwheat.gif</Thumbnail>
                <Preview>images/thwheat.gif</Preview>
        </Templates>
        <Templates>
                <TemplateID>DemOtek</TemplateID>
                <DisplayName>DemOtek</DisplayName>
                <Description>An example of a custom theme using a simple copy of
Jet.</Description>
                <Thumbnail>images/thjet.gif</Thumbnail>
                <Preview>images/thjet.gif</Preview>
        </Templates>
</SPThemes>
```

The new theme should appear on the list in Site Settings ➤ Site Theme. Of course, you still need to edit that theme's CSS file and images to make the theme unique (and not just a copy of an existing theme) by adding whatever new image files you'd like to use, then making changes to the folder's theme.css file, changing the background images and colors, font colors, hover images, and more. And just as a heads up, themes can be overwritten by service packs and upgrades, so always backup your favorite themes, just in case.

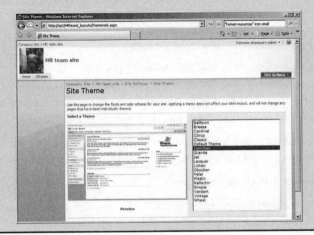

FIGURE 7.11
The newly themed
HRteam

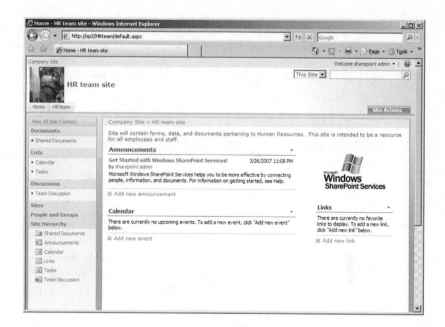

Browse through the themes, pick one you like, and change your site. My example uses Jet. After you apply your theme, go back to the HR Team site to check it out, as in Figure 7.11. The site now has custom logo, a new theme, and the Site Hierarchy section should appear on the Quick Launch bar.

TOP LINK BAR

If a site inherits the Top Link bar from its parent site, the only choice you have is to Stop Inheriting Links if you want to customize it (if you do stop inheriting links, you can change your mind and go back to the Top Link bar settings and use links from parent again). However, if this is the top site, or the subsite is not inheriting the Top Link bar, then you can add, edit, and delete links from the bar. The HR Team site is inheriting the bar, so to edit the Top link bar (without breaking inheritance) we have to go to the top-level site (Company site). To do this go into the top-level site's Site Settings, and Select Top link bar, as shown in Figure 7.12.

GOING YOUR OWN WAY WITH THE TOP LINK BAR

When a subsite doesn't inherit its Top Link bar from its parent, it cuts the bar off from all sites above it and reverts to considering itself to be a "top" site. Meaning that there will be only one link in its Top Link bar, and that will be the "home" tab that points to itself. All subsites that stem off of that site, if they inherit the Top Link bar, will consider that parent subsite to be the top, Home tab of their Top Link bar. This can be used to create a kind of mini site collection, where you can have a collection of subsites that don't use the Top Link bar to conveniently point back up the collection to the more top-level sites.

However, keep in mind that the global breadcrumb at the top of all SharePoint pages will always have a link to the top-level site, regardless of whatever you do with the Quick Launch and Top Link bars. As a matter of fact, this is a good example as to why there is that built in, navigational redundancy.

FIGURE 7.12
The Top Link Bar settings

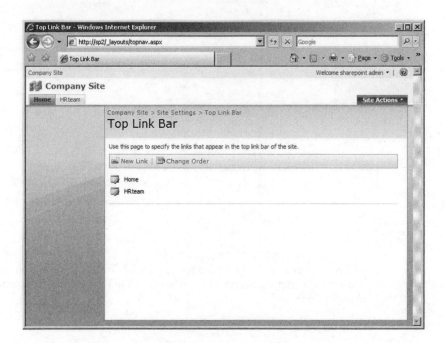

To add a link, use the New Link button. To edit or delete a link, click the Edit button next to that link. To change the order in which the links appear on the bar, click Change Order.

The Home and the HRteam links were auto-created links because you chose that option when creating the HRteam site. Auto-created links cannot be deleted or changed, only renamed; they are *managed*. If the page is deleted, the link is also deleted.

Links that you create yourself are manual links. A manual link can be any browser-readable link. It can be part of the SharePoint site, an external link, or anything else your browser can read. The Top Link bar doesn't *manage* these links. If you manually create a link to a page that later disappears, the link will stay. This includes manual links to pages within this site collection or site.

Let's create a new link to an external website (for example, your company's site, local news, weather, etc.). My example creates a link to Google, as shown in Figure 7.13. Put the URL for the link in the Web address field, and then type in a description. The description is what will be in the top link tab, so keep it short. When you are done, click OK to create the new link.

A Google link appears on the Top Link bar in Figure 7.14. Clicking this link will take you to www.google.com. Obviously, this will cause your browser to leave your SharePoint site. The only way to return to SharePoint is to use your browser's Back button.

FIGURE 7.13
The new link

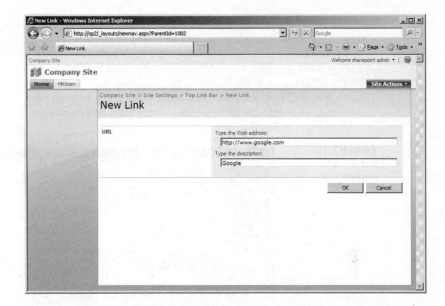

FIGURE 7.14
The modified Top Link
bar

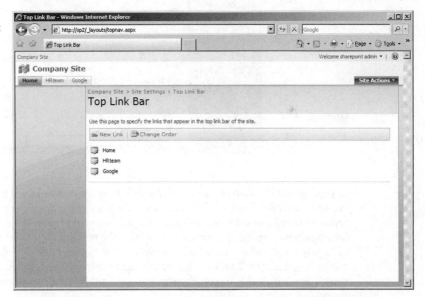

WATCH YOUR ACTIVE SITE

We've been moving back and forth between the Company site and the HRteam site. Remember to keep an eye on your breadcrumbs and ensure you're editing the correct site. It's a good thing you have a different logo and theme!

QUICK LAUNCH

The Quick Launch link lets you add, edit, and delete links from the Quick Launch bar. It is similar to the Top Link bar in this way, except it also includes convenient headings to organize the links. Let's go back to HRteam's Site Settings and look at the Quick Launch settings in Figure 7.15 (click on the HRTeam tab in the Top Link bar, click Site Actions, select Site Settings, then select Quick Launch in the Look and Feel category). On the Quick Launch page are links to add new links, new headings, or change the order of the existing links and headings.

FIGURE 7.15
The Quick Launch settings

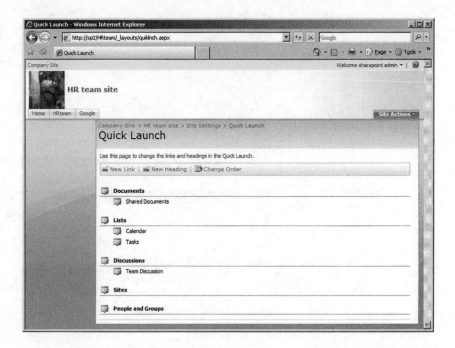

Just like the links on the Top Link bar, the auto-created links are managed. They'll disappear if the referenced list, library, or site are deleted. However, manually created links (even links to pages on the SharePoint site) are unmanaged, and will remain if the referenced page is deleted. Adding a new link will prompt you to choose the heading you want it under (along with the usual URL settings of web address and description, see Figure 7.16).

You'll notice there's no mention of the Site Hierarchy header, which was created under Tree View. Therefore, this is the one header you can't modify, delete, or change the order in which it's placed.

To demonstrate how easy it is to remove links or headings from the Quick Launch bar, let's delete the People And Groups heading. Maybe it's company policy to remove it from the Quick Launch to avoid distracting the users with a page they can't do much with. Getting that heading off the Quick Launch bar will help keep things neat. To delete the heading click the Edit button next to the People And Groups heading, and then choose Delete. See Figure 7.17.

Deleting a heading will also delete any links underneath it. If you ever want to delete a heading and retain the links, you'll need to edit each link and move it to a new heading.

FIGURE 7.16
A new Quick Launch link

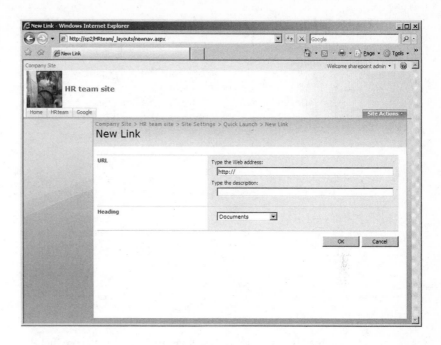

FIGURE 7.17
The Edit Heading page

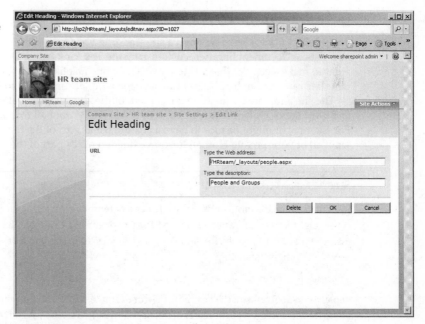

FIGURE 7.18
The Modified Quick
Launch bar with no
People and Groups

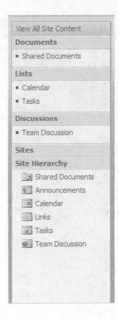

On the HR team site, shown in Figure 7.18, you can see that the People and Groups heading is no longer on the Quick Launch bar.

SAVE SITE AS TEMPLATE

After you've done a lot of work on a site—adding your custom logo, adjusting a theme, creating new lists or document libraries, customizing the Top Link bar or Quick Launch bar—you may want to make a copy of that site to make a new one just like it later. This is where saving it as a template can come in handy. You can save the template and use it to create new sites.

The site template can include the content of the site, including all the lists, document libraries, and workflows. Only include the content if you really want all this data to be part of the template. For example, it might be nice to have a custom list as part of the template, but you probably don't want all of your private Human Resource documents as part of the template.

SITE TEMPLATE LIMITATIONS

By default, there is a 10MB limit to the size of a site template. Anything larger will fail to be created. You can change this size limitation using the STSADM command-line tool. The limit can be adjusted up to a maximum of 500MB, but no further. To change the size limit, drop to a DOS prompt on your SharePoint server and run the following:

```
stsadm -o setproperty -pn max-template-document-size -pv size-in-bytes
```

Replace *size-in-bytes* with the desired size—for example, 100000000 would be approximately 100MB. STSADM will be discussed in greater detail in Chapter 13, "STSADM: A Look at the SharePoint Command-Line Tool."

To create a template out of the HRTeam site, and save what you've done so far as a template, on the Save Site as Template page enter a title and description for the template. In this example, you don't need to include the content. See Figure 7.19 for an example. Then click OK at the bottom of the page to complete the process.

FIGURE 7.19
Save the site as a template

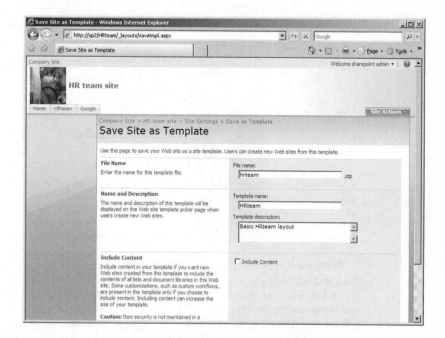

We'll come back to this template shortly, and see where it resides and how to use it. For now let's move on.

CONTENT FOR EVERYONE; WHY SECURE CONTENT SHOULDN'T BE SAVED IN TEMPLATES

Keep in mind that saving the contents of a site in a template means that data might be available to anyone allowed to create a site elsewhere in the collection because a site's security settings are not saved with the template for the site. Beware of the temptation of saving secure content with a site template unless you intend to download it from the gallery and remove it from the list later before anyone gets to use it for nefarious purposes.

RESET TO SITE DEFINITION

This is a link that, although it effects the Look And Feel of a site, may be better suited under Site Administration; but for whatever reason, here it is.

Resetting a site to the default definition completely removes any extensive customization of that site. As you can see in Figure 7.20, there is no "Undo" button.

FIGURE 7.20
Reset to site
definition

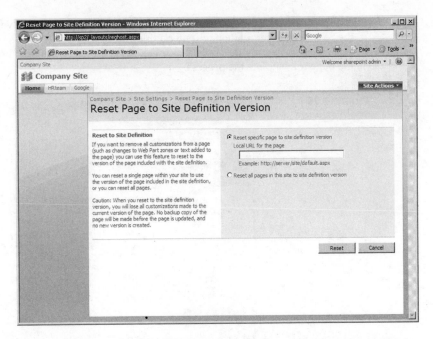

That's the bad news. The good news is that *customization* doesn't mean exactly what you might think it does. Nothing you've done so far—the custom logo, the theme, the Top Link bar, and the Quick Launch—has edited the site's definition. From a site definition perspective, you've done *nothing* to customize this site, you've only changed some settings and maybe augmented it. It's still a Team site. Resetting its definition won't change anything. However, if the site had been customized using SharePoint Designer, clicking the Reset button would reset it back to the default. This is sometimes handy if someone completely corrupts a site using SharePoint Designer (see Microsoft KB article: 832811).

SITE DEFINITIONS VERSUS SITE TEMPLATES

Site templates are used to speed up new site creation. You've looked at them briefly and even created a custom template from the HRteam site. So what's a *site definition*?

Templates are used when you're creating a site—and that's it. Once a site is created, the template no longer matters. You can customize the site well beyond the template.

Site definitions are more important. The site definition defines what can and cannot be available in a template based on it. The site definition controls what *type* of site the site is—a meeting, a blog, a wiki, a Team site, or even Central Administration. Site definitions are the underlying XML and ASPX files used to generate the page regardless of what kind of theme, logo, or change you apply to the site. Under the hood, every site still adheres to the site definition of its template. The core files are located in `C:\Program Files\Common Files\Microsoft Shared\web server extensions\12\TEMPLATES\SiteTemplates` in their own folders.

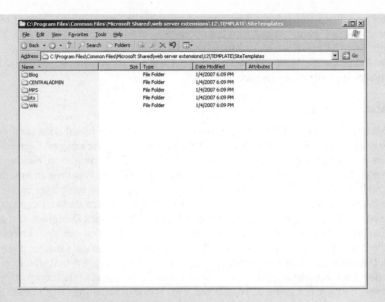

There are five existing site definitions:

◆ Blog (for blog sites)

◆ CENTRALADMIN (for the Central Administration site)

◆ MPS (for Meeting sites)

◆ sts (for SharePoint Team sites)

◆ Wiki (for Wiki sites)

Site definitions each have their own `default.master` file, which is a master page that determines the layout of the web page.

Site templates take all the potential of their site definition and narrow it down to their own application of the layout, theme, prebuilt lists, web parts, etc. of that definition. So, for example you can have a meeting workplace site definition, and from that make a template for a social, basic, or decision meeting workplace. Each one is based on the same definition but laid out differently based on the presumed use. All with the same potential, just applying it differently for your convenience. This explains why everything in SharePoint looks so similar and has the same interface. Many of the sites are using the same site definition under their particular theme and template. It also explains why meetings, wikis, and blogs look different from normal Team sites. Site definitions can be created or edited in SharePoint Designer or using the SharePoint Software Development Kit.

Galleries

Galleries are for storing customized lists, sites, web parts, and more (usually in the form of template files, but there are exceptions). There are even galleries for custom columns and content types. Galleries are generally document libraries, used to organize and make available those files for download, upload, etc. There are seven galleries, three are available at all site levels (as you can see back in Figure 7.4) and four are accessible only from the top-level site. The items available at this level trickle down to all subsites. Items from the site collection level are available, but items added to the site level galleries are for that site and its subsites specifically. The galleries that are available at all site levels are:

MASTER PAGES

Master pages are HTML files that reference the ASP.NET-based code (and possibly a little javascript as well) that controls general features for the site's pages. General features in this case are things that appear on every page of the site, such as navigation, header, footer, and content areas. The Master page has the code for the Top Link bar, Welcome menu, the Help icon, and the Quick Launch bar. Site definitions have a master page, and templates create an initial master page when a new site is first created. Every site has, by default, a `default.master` file. You can add custom master pages (or create and edit them in SharePoint Designer) and add them to the site using the Master Page Gallery, as shown in Figure 7.21. You can also download them and import them into other sites or even other servers. When you change a master page for a site, be it a top-level site or a subsite, it only changes that master page for that site. Even though there may be other sites in the site collection using the same template, and their own copy of the same master page, they are not going to be affected. This is one of the things that stands out from a site definition. If you change a site's master page, it only affects that site. If you change a site definition, the change will be reflected in all sites that are based on that site definition.

FIGURE 7.21
Master Page Gallery

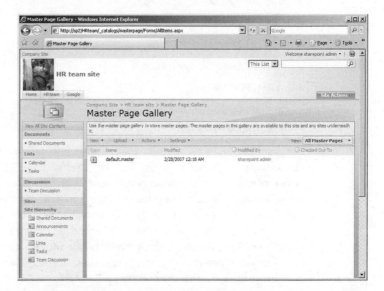

SO WHAT'S THE DIFFERENCE BETWEEN A THEME AND A MASTER PAGE?

Sites can be defined by their master page; standardizing the layout, the tools available on the pages, as well as the background, color, and images. Themes are essentially cascading style sheets (CSS) that modify the background or color scheme when applied to a master page.

Themes change the "look" of a site's pages, without modifying the underlying standardization of the master page. If you want to do more than change the color scheme, such as rearrange the components on the page, then editing the master page (SharePoint Designer is the tool for that) is right for you. For more about customizing a master page using SharePoint Designer, check out Microsoft's SharePoint Designer 2007 demos (http://office.microsoft.com/en-us/sharepointdesigner/HA102199841033.aspx).

SITE CONTENT TYPES

This gallery contains all the content types for this site. Content types are a kind of list item template. Or more precisely, they are the definition files for site list items, as well as the documents and pages that can be stored in document libraries, like basic web pages and master pages. The gallery is available to the site and all subsites, and shows the content types inherited from the parent site. Chapter 6, "Introduction to Libraries," explains content types in more detail.

SITE COLUMNS

This gallery collects all the premade columns available to the lists and libraries in the site (think convenient templates for list fields). Once again, this gallery shows inherited columns, and everything here is available to all subsites. More details about columns can be found in Chapter 5, "Introduction to Lists."

The galleries that are available only at the site collection's top-level site are listed below. To get to the top-level site's Site Settings (my example is called "Company Site" as shown in Figure 7.22), either click on the Go to top-level site settings link in the Site Settings of the subsite, or just navigate to the top-level site, click Site Actions and select Site Settings. There you'll see the additional galleries.

FIGURE 7.22
The top-level Site Settings

SITE TEMPLATES

Site templates are used to create new sites. You used one of the default templates when you made HRteam. You also created a custom template based on the HRteam site. If you go into site templates (see Figure 7.23), you can see this custom template residing safely in the gallery. The Site Template Gallery will only show the templates you add to the gallery, not the defaults. Those are not available here because this gallery was meant for you to manage the templates you add to your site collection.

FIGURE 7.23
The site templates

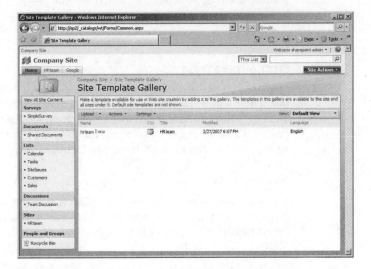

Site templates are simply files that reside in the gallery the way Word documents reside in a document library. This means they can be downloaded, uploaded, backed up, and restored. Chapter 12, "Maintenance and Monitoring," discusses restoring a site template in greater detail.

There is no way to edit site templates directly in this gallery. You can change the properties (Name, Title, and Description), but that's it. To use the template when you create a new site, simply choose it from the Custom tab on the Create New SharePoint Site page, as shown in Figure 7.24.

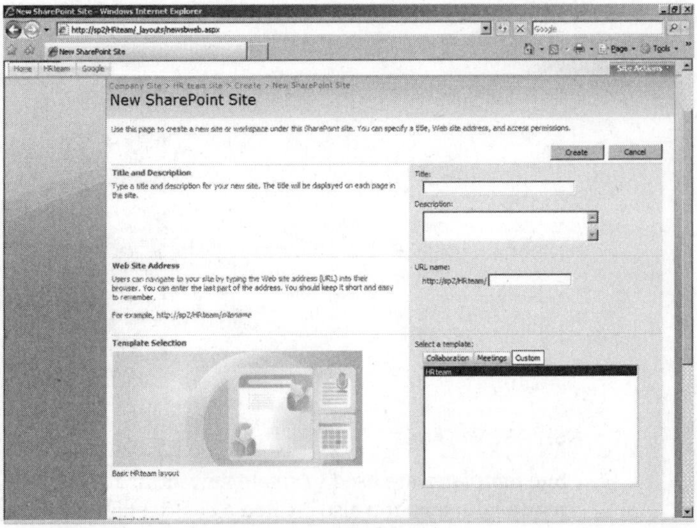

FIGURE 7.24
Choosing a custom
site template

LIST TEMPLATES

As with sites, you can save customized lists as templates. They are stored in this List Templates Gallery for use when creating a new list. The gallery will show you the name, date, title, language, and version of the list template. Any list that is saved as a template is saved to the list gallery. And like any library you can upload list templates to the gallery, as well as edit their title and description properties. But you cannot actually edit the list template from there. You can also download list templates from the gallery by clicking on their title. This is good for backing up the template in case of emergency. If you create a new list template, it will appear on the Create page just like the original template it was based on (and in the correct category as well). However, unlike the prebuilt lists, the list templates you create may need to be deleted or renamed, thus they have their own gallery. See Chapter 5 for more on how to create lists, and Chapter 12 for more on creating list templates.

WEB PARTS

The Web Parts Gallery holds all the web parts available to the site (except for the list view web parts of course, those are unique to the lists for the site and not available in the gallery). You can add, edit, and delete the web parts from it. Anything in this gallery is available for use in the entire site collection and all subsites. More information about web parts can be found in Chapter 4, "Introduction to Web Parts."

WORKFLOWS

Despite being in the Gallery category, this isn't actually a gallery. It's merely a rendered list of all the current workflows on the site collection. You cannot make any changes from here. Unlike a normal gallery (which is just a document library), there's no way to add, edit, or delete workflows from this gallery. WSS 3.0 comes with one workflow by default: the three-state workflow (MOSS 2007 has several more). It is used with Issue Tracking or any other list with a Choice menu of three or more choices. Other Workflows can be obtained from third party software developers or built using SharePoint Designer. For more information on Workflows, see Chapter 5.

Site Administration

This category is for back-end administration and maintenance of the site. These are settings that end users are not necessarily interested in, but they are invaluable for the server administrator. Site Administration does include settings that affect the end users from a features perspective; they are site-wide changes to the way the site behaves and what it allows.

Let's go back at HRteam Site Settings where we can customize them for even more control over the site (click the HRTeam tab in the Top Link bar, then click Site Actions, then select Site Settings from the dropdown menu).

REGIONAL SETTINGS

The Regional Settings page deals with location-specific settings, such as Time Zone, Date, Calendar, etc. By default, a new site is given the same settings as its parent site. So it's a good idea to examine these settings (shown in Figure 7.25), especially settings like Define Your Work Week which can really impact the way the Calendar works for all site participants unless they explicitly override it with their own regional settings. Letting the site know your company's daily start and end times will assist in tracking appointments (or overtime) and ensure that the calendars are created with the correct settings.

FIGURE 7.25
The Regional Settings page

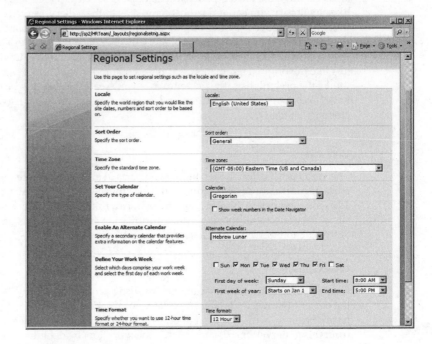

The settings you can adjust here include:

Locale   This setting determines the world region, such as English (US) or English (UK). This will determine such things as the way dates are displayed (3/28/2007 versus 28/3/2007), decimal points or decimal commas, and other regional-specific modifiers.

Sort Order   This setting changes the sort order for lists and libraries. The sort order determines the way alphabetically sorted lists are handled. Certain languages have different sort orders for characters. Although American English speakers are used to seeing X-Y-Z at the end of the alphabet, users in other regions may not be.

PERSONAL REGIONAL SETTINGS

By clicking the Welcome menu and choosing My Settings, an individual user can adjust their regional settings to differ from the site's regional settings. For example, a user can set their time zone to PST even though the site is in the EST zone. The only exception is Sort Order, which cannot be adjusted by individual users.

Time Zone   The setting ensures that all posted announcements, modification dates, and other time listings are adjusted for your local time zone.

Set Your Calendar   This setting determines the calendar you use in your daily life. Most people will use Gregorian, but you can adjust this for custom calendars (such as Buddhist, which is on year 2550 as of the time this book was written).

Enable An Alternate Calendar   If you need to track dates in two calendar forms, this setting allows you to have one calendar that easily shows both forms—for example, if you need Gregorian and also need the Hebrew Lunar calendar, enable the alternate calendar for Hebrew Lunar and easily see both in Figure 7.26.

FIGURE 7.26
The alternate
calendar

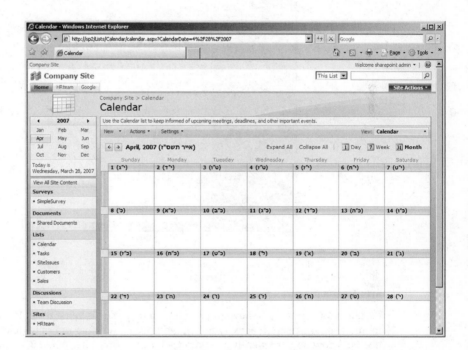

Define Your Work Week   With this setting, you can choose which days are considered "work" days (such as Monday through Friday) and when work starts and stops (such as 8:00 A.M. through 5:00 P.M.). You can start the week on Sunday or Monday—or even Thursday if you like.

Time Format   With this setting, you can choose whether you want 12-hour or 24-hour time displayed. This setting can change automatically if you change the Locale setting, so make sure you double-check it if you make any changes to this page.

SITE LIBRARIES AND LISTS

This setting's page seen in Figure 7.27, provides you with an easy list of all the site's lists and libraries, with easy links to the Customize page for each one as well. These links take you to the same places that the specific list or library's Settings will take you. For more details about customizing lists and libraries, see Chapters 5 and 6.

FIGURE 7.27
The Site Libraries
And Lists page

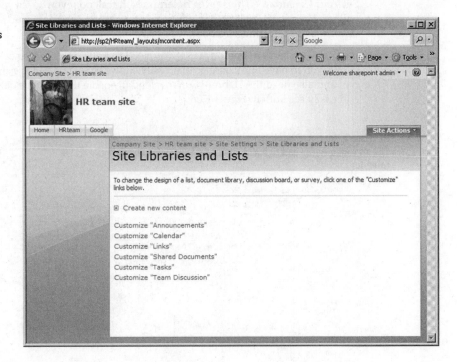

SITE USAGE REPORT

It's always a good idea to keep track of how much a site is being used. Perhaps you need to monitor some sites for inactivity to help you decide whether or not to delete them, or maybe you need to know how frequently a certain user accesses the site. When usage analysis is enabled in Central Administration, the Site Usage Report becomes available for all sites in the server farm.

HEY, WHAT HAPPENED TO MY SITE USAGE REPORT?

In order to use the Site Usage Report and the Site Collection Usage Summary, you need to enable Usage Analysis Processing. This is done in SharePoint 3.0 Central Administration. To do that, follow these steps:

1. Connect to Central Administration.

2. Once you've logged into Central Administration, navigate to Operations, Logging and Reporting category, Usage Analysis Processing. This will take you to the page in the graphic below.

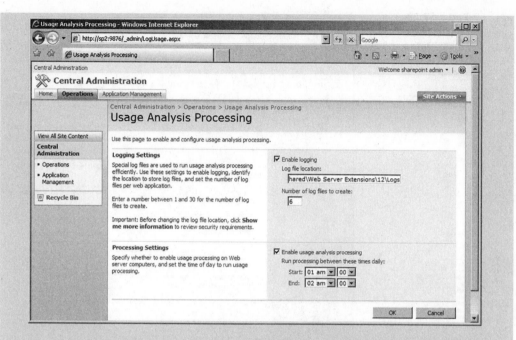

3. Check the Enable Logging box. You can change the Log File Location or leave the default in place:

   ```
   C:\Program Files\Common Files\Microsoft Shared\web server
        extensions\12\Logs.
   ```

   My example leaves the default in place.

4. Determine the number of log files you want created per day. Some people prefer one large log file for the day, and other people prefer to chop it up into smaller segments. My example uses six log files, one every 4 hours. The number of log files will not impact the reporting at all; however, if you need to manually look at the logs for something, it might be easier to have some smaller logs. Also keep in mind that you can always just have logs without the analysis if your server is low on resources.

5. Check the Enable Usage Analysis Processing box. For the Processing Settings section, you need to keep in mind that these processes are pretty demanding, so you want it to run the reports at off-peak hours. My example uses between 1:00 A.M. and 2:00 P.M. The usage report process runs only once per day. When you first turn it on, you still won't be able to run any reports until after the Usage Analysis Processes have run at least once (sometimes twice, depending on site usage).

6. Go ahead and click OK. You've enabled usage reports. Now all you need to do is wait a day or two before you can check them out.

At the main SharePoint site, let's look at the Company site's usage reports. See Figure 7.28. Five kinds of reports are available from the Select Report dropdown menu:

FIGURE 7.28
The Site Usage
Report page

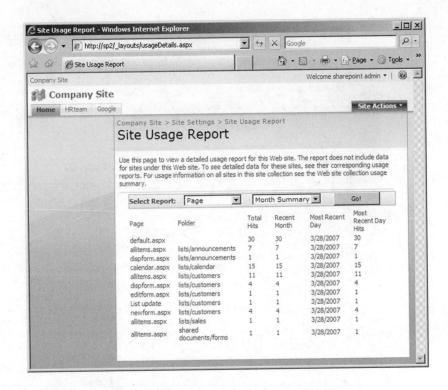

Page Shows the number of hits each page has received in the site.

User Displays the number of times each user has accessed the site. This is by user name, not machine IP.

OS Lists the number of times the site has been access by OS type.

Browser Displays what browser the users were using to access the site.

Referrer URL Shows a list of what URLs directed people to the site. This is probably the least-used report, because most SharePoint sites are accessed directly.

Each report can render this information in a monthly summary or on a table showing day-by-day information for the month.

USAGE REPORTS INDICATE WINDOWS NT 4 AND IE4!

You've set up a SharePoint server, enabled Usage Logging, and after you've let it run overnight, you see Windows NT listed under the OS report. You also see a corresponding number of hits under the Browser report for Internet Explorer 4.0.1. You're pretty darn sure there's no NT box on your network, so what gives?

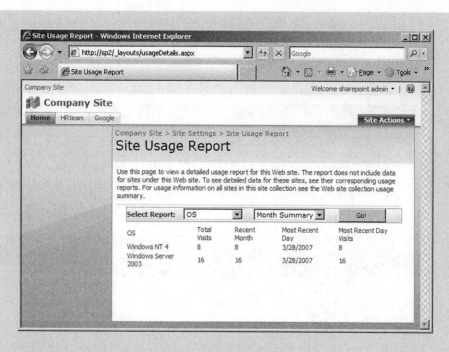

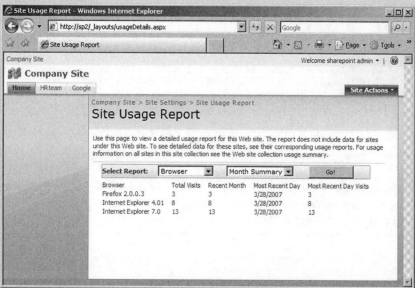

The answer is the indexing service. A look at the Users report will show you matching hits for the Content Access (Index) account (either the account assigned for a server farm, or the LocalService account for a standalone server).

To see why the indexing service shows up as NT 4, check the actual log files, stored in `C:\Program Files\Common Files\ Microsoft Shared \ web server extensions\12\Logs\ <guid>\ <date>\`. You can spot the actual site hit by searching for the content access account name, or by searching for **Robot**.

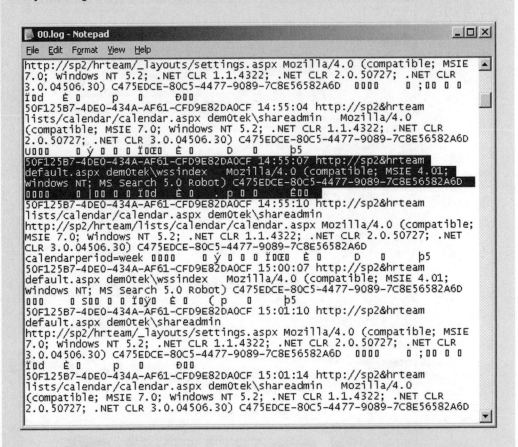

The identified "browser" for the process is MSIE 4.0.1; Windows NT; and MS Search 5.0 Robot. The reports simply collate the data in the log files, so that when the indexing service indexes the site, those hits register as having used Internet Explorer 4.0.1 and Windows NT 4.

USER ALERTS

This setting gives you an easy way to see user alerts on lists or libraries. You can't see a complete list of all alerts for the site, but you can display alerts for individual users (see Figure 7.29). The only thing you can do to an alert from here is delete it; no editing or creation is possible.

FIGURE 7.29
The User Alerts page

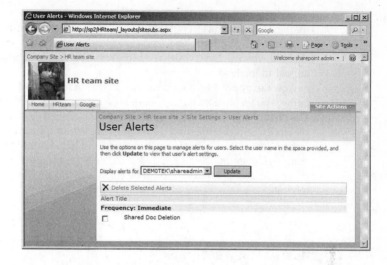

RSS

This setting is available under the category of Site Administration at every site, from top-level to the lowest subsite. However at the subsite level, it allows you to enable or disable RSS feeds for the site, and to specify channel elements for the RSS feeds on the site. On the top-level site however, the settings are the same but there is an extra option to allow or disallow RSS feeds for the *entire* site collection from there, not just the top-level site. So make certain that that option (see Figure 7.30) is not disallowed if you want RSS to work at all for any site in the site collection. If RSS is disabled at the Site Collection level, the RSS option will not appear under Site Settings for any of the subsites in the collection.

FIGURE 7.30
The top-level RSS settings

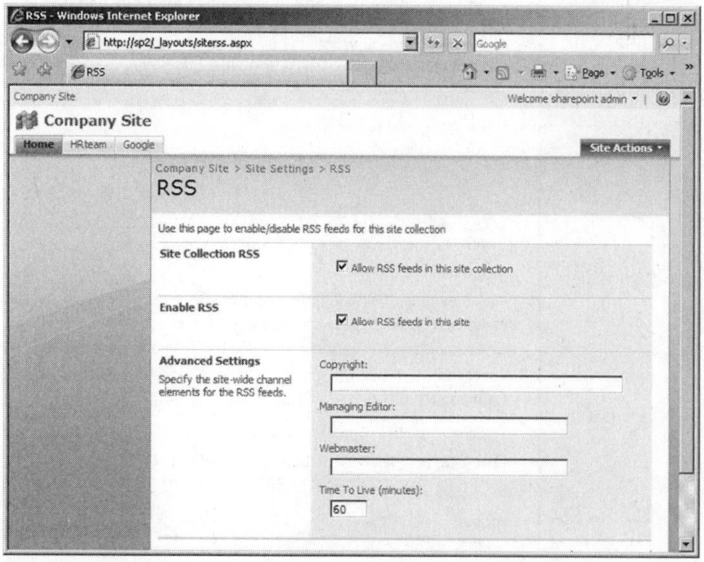

RSS (Really Simple Syndication) is the protocol for what are commonly called *web feeds*, which frequently update web content you can subscribe to so your computer will automatically download any updates. RSS feeds are frequently used for the Announcements list. With RSS enabled, you can have your web browser subscribe to this list so any new announcements will appear in the feed.

You can apply additional channel elements to the feed, tagging it with a copyright, editor name, and webmaster name. These tags are seen by some RSS readers and are a good idea to have. The elements entered in this location will be applied to all RSS feeds throughout the site.

The Time To Live setting determines the minimum *refresh time* permitted for the site. The refresh rate is the shortest amount of time an RSS reader has to wait between update checks. Although it sounds like a good idea to keep this rate low so updates are frequent, remember that every RSS reader out there could be constantly hitting the site for updates if you make this setting too low.

How Do I View RSS Feeds?

You can view an RSS feed in Internet Explorer by clicking on the RSS Feed button. This button is active only when you're looking at a page that has a corresponding feed. When you click on the button, the page changes to the RSS view.

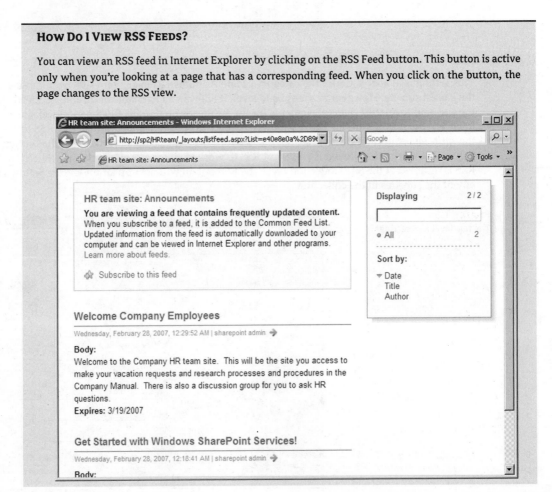

Click Subscribe To This Feed to add the feed to your browser list of feeds, and place the feed in a folder. Doing so works similarly to making a Favorite (or bookmark).

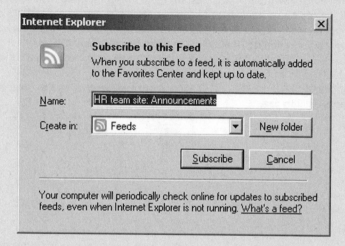

When you've subscribed, you can see the RSS feed in your Feed tab under Favorites.

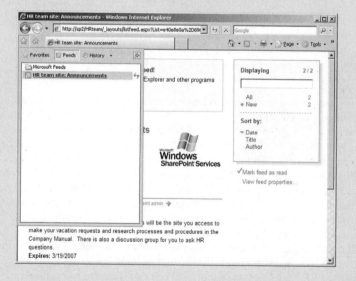

Note that Internet Explorer does not support authenticated feeds; it only supports NTLM/Kerberos credential pass-through. This means that the feed will be able to auto-update only if you are logged in to the local machine with the same account that you use for SharePoint.

A lot of third-party RSS viewers, including other web browsers and custom applications, are available as well, if you would rather use something other than IE.

SEARCH VISIBILITY

As shown in Figure 7.31, you can disable search indexing if you don't want this site or any of its contents to show up in search results. Note that Search is already permissions-aware, and users will not see results they do not have permission to see. In general, it's okay to leave indexing turned on (even on sites with private information) because unauthorized users can't search the site anyway. However, sites using fine-grained permissions or linked web parts with different permissions *can* allow unauthorized users to see restricted items in their search results.

FIGURE 7.31
The Search Visibility page

Fine-grained permissions are when you restrict parts of a site above and beyond the main site permissions. For example, if you have a document library (with certain inherited permissions) and you decide to change the permissions on one document item in the library to make it more restrictive then the rest of the library. In that case, users with permission to the document library will see this restricted document in their search results. They won't be able to open it (the link will fail), but even seeing the name of the document could be a security concern.

Another security concern occurs when web parts link to another web part containing different permissions. For example, a list of Contacts (with relatively open permissions) linked to a list of performance evaluations (with more restrictive permissions) could cause the more restricted information to be listed in the search results when they shouldn't.

It is unfortunate, but in the case that you need to use such fine-grained permissions or web part linkages, Microsoft recommends that you disable the indexing for the site. Fortunately, the Indexing ASPX Page Content section will tell you if you're using fine-grained permissions, and SharePoint has the default behavior of disabling indexing if such permissions exist. Mind you, this also explains why, suddenly search does not work for a site's new information when it did before you enabled unique permissions on a list item.

Most of the time you'll want to leave the default in place, and allow indexing for most sites, and disallow indexing on those sites with fine-grain permissions or linked web parts. However, if being able to search is more important than letting users see the search results for list items and files they can't open anyway, then you can enable search to always index ASPX pages regardless.

SITES AND WORKSPACES

The Sites And Workspaces page (shown in Figure 7.32) displays a list of subsites below the current site. Because the HRteam site has no subsites, let's look at this section under the main Company site.

FIGURE 7.32
The Sites And Workspaces page

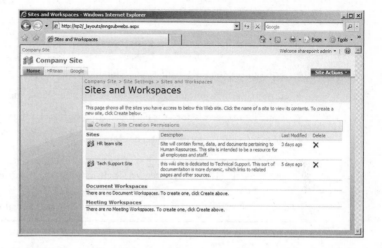

Two subsites, the HR Team site you created and a second one for tech support (this was added to the site as an example), are displayed. Clicking the site's name takes you to that site. Clicking the Create button takes you to the New SharePoint Site page.

On the top level site the Sites and Workspaces page also has a handy Site Creation Permissions button on the Action bar (subsites don't have this feature, even if they themselves have subsites beneath them, if they are all inheriting permissions from the top-level site). Clicking on the Site Creation Permissions button will display a partial list of Permission Levels for the site (see Figure 7.33).

FIGURE 7.33
Granting Create Site permission

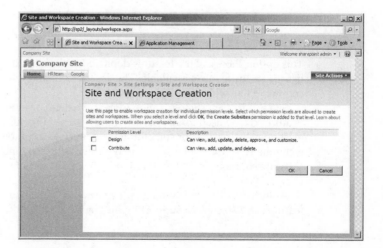

PERMISSION LEVELS

Permission levels are not user groups: they are bundles of permissions (formerly called *site groups* in WSS 2.0) that define what kind of control and access a user or group has to sites, lists, and libraries. Users are assigned to groups, groups are assigned permission levels, and those levels can be edited to provide a custom set of permissions.

SharePoint has five default Permission levels:

◆ Full Control (has all permissions available to the site)

◆ Design (permissions for customizing pages, sites, lists, and web parts)

◆ Contribute (permissions for personalizing pages, working with list and library content)

◆ Read (can only view items and content)

◆ Limited Access (Guest, which is often a user that does not have permission to access the whole site but is passing through to access a single list, library, or subsite)

By default, only Full Control has the permission to create subsites.

By checking the box beside a permission level and clicking OK you're assigning the Create Subsites permission for that Permission Level (and therefore giving the power to create new subsites to any groups or users with that permission level). The site owners group already has the right to create subsites, and by default the visitors group is not given the option here to have the right to create subsites because they only have read rights to the site as it is.

Under Advanced Permissions, you can also manually edit the permission levels to give each level the specific permissions you want. See Chapter 11 for more on permissions.

SITE FEATURES

This option shows all the features deployed to the site. All you can do on this page is activate or deactivate the features available. The deployment and retraction of site features is done from the command line with STSADM.

Site features are customization tools that extend or modify the existing SharePoint site. Features can be used for almost anything—something minor such as a change to one of the existing menu options or something major such as a complete overhaul of SharePoint to provide e-commerce solutions. Features are typically written by third-party companies to integrate their software solutions into SharePoint or by helpful developers, many of whom give them away free over the Web.

At the core of a site feature is a `feature.xml` file, which tells SharePoint what to do. Each feature can also contain supporting files (additional XMLs, ASPX, DLL, or other files) if needed, but they aren't required. Many features do everything they need to do in the single `feature.xml` file. Everything involved with a feature is tucked away in a named folder that is stored in:

```
C:\Program Files\Common Files\Microsoft Shared\web
    serverextensions\12\TEMPLATES\FEATURES\
```

Features are usually provided by installation packages called *solutions.* Solutions can appear as custom SharePoint installation files (`*.wsp`) or a simple cabinet files (`*.cab`). The only way to install a new feature—either as part of a solution or even just a lone feature—is via the `STSADM.EXE` command. Step-by-step instructions for installing additional features can be found in Chapter 13.

DELETE THIS SITE

The last Site Administration option is to simply delete the site, as shown in Figure 7.34.

FIGURE 7.34
The Delete This Site page

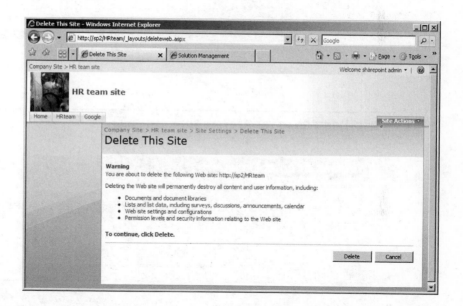

Deleting a site is not something you do lightly; doing so deletes the entire site—all web parts, lists, discussions, document libraries, documents in the libraries, customizations, unique permissions, you name it. Make sure you've salvaged anything you need from the site before you destroy it. For example, if you're about to delete a document workspace because the document is finished, make sure you copy the final version of the document to the parent site first.

Deleting a site collection, which is what happens if you delete a top-level site, (see Figure 7.35) is even larger—not only will you delete the site and everything in or below it, but you'll also completely delete the security information (users, groups, permission levels, etc.). You might want to make a backup before you delete a site at any level—just in case.

FIGURE 7.35
Delete a site
collection

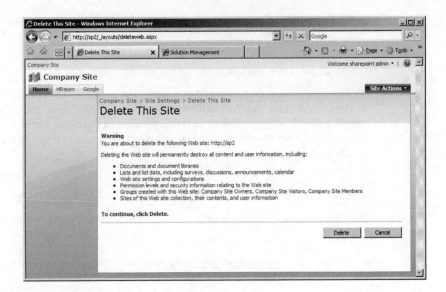

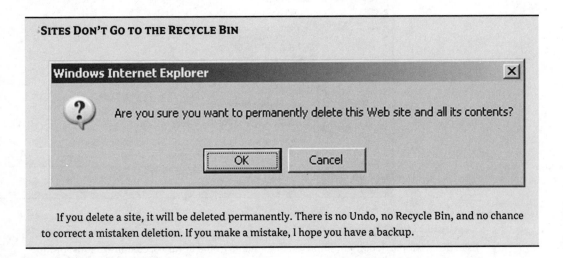

SITES DON'T GO TO THE RECYCLE BIN

If you delete a site, it will be deleted permanently. There is no Undo, no Recycle Bin, and no chance to correct a mistaken deletion. If you make a mistake, I hope you have a backup.

Site Collection Administration

Site collections can be administered only from the top-level site in the site collection. The HRteam subsite has a category called Site Collection Administration that provides one link, Go To Top Level Site Settings. Clicking this link takes you to the Site Settings page for the Company site in my example, because it's the top-level site. On this page (see Figure 7.36), you'll see the Site Collection Administration tools.

FIGURE 7.36
The top-level Site
Settings page

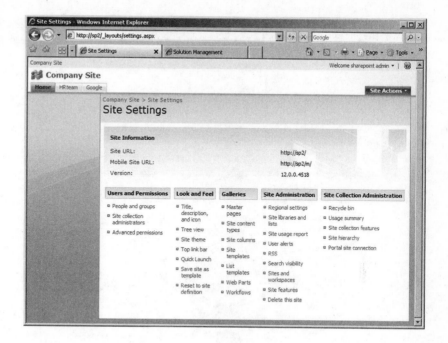

RECYCLE BIN

The Site Collection Recycle Bin shows everything deleted from the site collection—except sites. When your users delete a document or list item and then suddenly realize they made a mistake, you can easily recover the document or list item from the Recycle Bin rather than having to restore from a backup. This is one of the coolest things in WSS 3.0.

Each user has their own Recycle Bin per site, which is why it is often called the End user Recycle Bin. Their bin shows them only what they personally deleted (or more precisely they can only see the contents of the site Recycle bin that they deleted).

Site administrators have their own End user Recycle Bin if they delete something on the site, but they can also access the overall End user Recycle Bin at the site collection level, which shows everything deleted by all users in the site collection. See Figure 7.37. The site collection level user recycle bin is particularly useful if a user deleted something from somewhere in the site collection but they can't remember which site. They can ask the site collection administrator to check the End user Recycle Bin which lists all things deleted in the site collection, regardless of which site it was.

When an item is deleted, it goes to the End user Recycle Bin, where it will sit happily for 30 days before being permanently destroyed. If a user goes to their Recycle Bin and deletes items from it, the items that were in it are not completely gone, they are moved to the real second stage, site collection level Recycle Bin. This Recycle Bin contains only items deleted from the End user recycle bins at the site level. As you can see the elusive second stage, site collection level Recycle Bin (Figure 7.38) is under the Deleted From End User Recycle Bin view.

If an item is deleted from this second recycle bin, it's gone for good. Basically, you can restore anything (except sites) that were deleted less then 30 days ago (or whatever the recycle bin default is), even if the user also emptied their Recycle Bin by checking the Site Collection's Recycle Bin.

FIGURE 7.37
The Site Collection
Recycle Bin

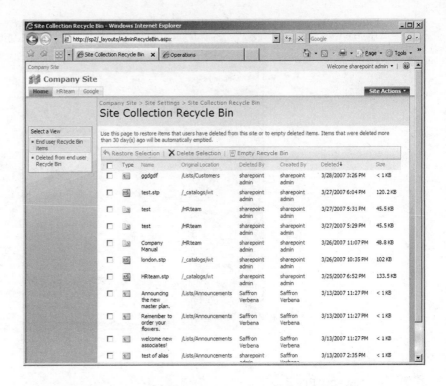

FIGURE 7.38
Items deleted from the
Recycle Bin

FIGURE 7.39

The Site Collection Usage Summary page

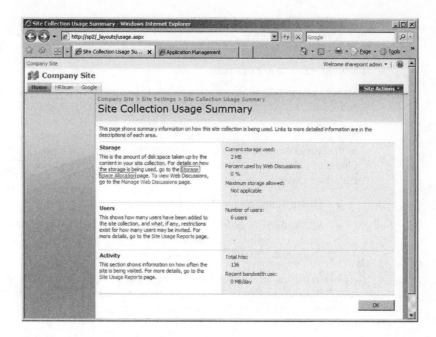

USAGE SUMMARY

The Site Collection Usage Summary (Figure 7.39) is a useful tool for checking site or page access and provides a nice overview—with statistics on storage, users, and activity—of how the site collection is being used.

MISSING USAGE SUMMARY OPTION

The Usage Summary option will not be available under Site Collection Administration if Usage Analysis Processing is not enabled in Central Administration. This setting is explored in Chapter 10, "Central Administration: Operations." Basically, if SharePoint is not processing usage, then no usage reports and summaries can be generated. This can be a good thing because usage analysis is very processor and RAM intensive. Although I find the reports to be useful enough to risk the resource hit, if you don't need the information then don't enable usage analysis.

Storage   Shows the amount of space consumed by the site collection and the maximum storage permitted under the site collection's storage quota. If the site collection has no storage quota assigned, then the maximum storage is listed as Not Applicable. Additional statistics can be displayed by following the Storage Space Allocation link in the description or by using the main Site Collection Administration category list. Following the Site Usage Report link just takes you to the reports found under Site Settings Site Administration Site Usage Report.

Users   Total number of users on the site collection.

Activity   Displays the number of hits that have been recorded for the entire collection and the recent bandwidth use.

STORAGE SPACE ALLOCATION

Storage Space Allocation appears on the list only if a storage quota has been enabled for the site collection. If no quota is assigned to the site collection, this link will not appear.

Storage quotas are ways to limit the growth of a site collection by setting a hard limit on how big they can get. To set a storage quota, there are two sections of Central Administration in the Application Management ➤ SharePoint Site Management category ➤ Quota Templates. Quota templates are used to create storage quotas that can be applied when creating new site collections later.

◆ **Quota Templates**: used to create a quota template.

◆ **Site collection quotas and locks**: used to assign the template to a site collection or set the quota on a site collection manually. More information on these settings can be found in Chapter 8, "Site Collections and Web Applications."

When quotas are enabled, the Storage Space Allocation page shows how the storage is being handled. Examine Figure 7.40; in it, you can see the size of each document library, list, document, and item in the Recycle Bin. The Show Only dropdown menu just filters the list by those view options.

FIGURE 7.40
The Storage
Space Allocation
page

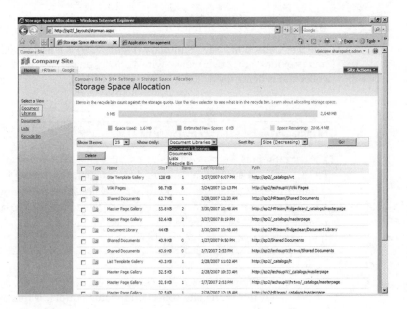

SITE COLLECTION FEATURES

Site collection features are just like site features, except they're designed to be available for or affect (once activated) the entire site collection (see Figure 7.41). The only site collection feature installed by default is the three-state workflow. This feature is simple; it provides access to that workflow to all the sites residing in the site collection.

FIGURE 7.41
The Site
Collection
Features page

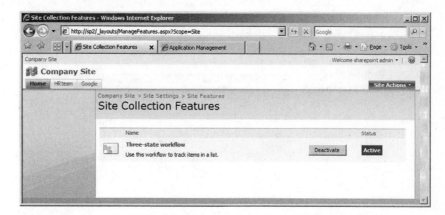

As with site features, site collection features can be installed and deployed via STSADM.EXE.

SITE HIERARCHY

This page (see Figure 7.42) provides a nice list of all the subsites that have been created in the site collection. From the Site Hierarchy page, you can go to a subsite's home page (by clicking the URL) or to the subsite's Site Settings page (by clicking on the Manage link). This page is an example of SharePoint reusing a term and has nothing really to do with the Tree View in the Quick Launch bar.

FIGURE 7.42
The Site Hierarchy
page

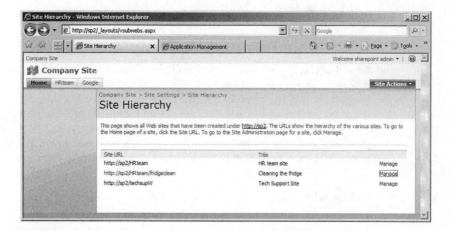

PORTAL SITE CONNECTION

Connecting to a portal site is applicable only if you have a Microsoft Office SharePoint server on your network. In that case, you can attach this WSS 3.0 site collection to the MOSS portal (see

Figure 7.43). Interestingly this setting can be used to add a link, any link, to the beginning of a site collection's global breadcrumb. It will precede the site collection's own top-level site's home page as first link there. Any link can be used, but usually it should be used for a central site that needs to be accessed from anywhere in the site collection (and that site should have a link back to the site collection that refers to it).

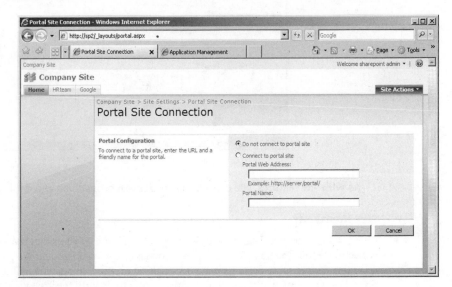

Additional Default Site Templates

Now that you've seen all the ways to customize and control sites, let's take a closer look at the different types of sites available in SharePoint and how they differ from each other. Choosing a template during site creation will pre-build the site with lists, libraries, and custom features designed for that type of site. This speeds up the customization process, since you're starting from a pre-built default that will (hopefully) contain what you need. There are several existing site templates, and each contains key differences in layout and intent. The following templates are available choices during site creation, starting with the most common, Team Site.

Team Site

The Team site is the SharePoint workhorse. So far everything you've done has been in a Team site. Team sites are the most general and the most common sites. They're typically what administrators choose for the main site from which all other sites branch. Containing lists, libraries, some web parts, and a nice custom theme, they're perfect for your all-purpose SharePoint site. If you just need a site, you're looking for a Team site.

Document Workspace

A document workspace is all about managing one document. There are two ways to create a document workspace: either through the usual New SharePoint Site page (under Site Actions ➤ Create ➤ Sites And Workspaces) or from the actual Document directly by selecting Create a Document Workspace from the document's dropdown menu as shown in Figure 7.44.

FIGURE 7.44
Creating a workspace

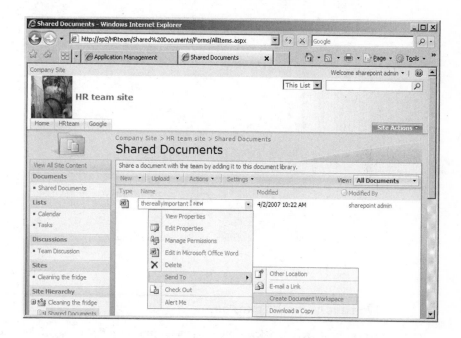

Why would you want to have a separate site for one document? Say you have a large number of people working on one file—a legal brief, screenplay, or other complex document. That sort of collaboration would require discussion, versioning additional documents, and other collaboration; all of which can be done in a library on the main Team site. But why have all of that work on that document clutter the main site? It's better to give the document its own space so you can add supporting documents, discussions boards, and assign tasks separately from the rest of the site.

When the document workspace (Figure 7.45) is first created, a copy of the document is placed in the workspace's Shared Documents library. The creating user is added to the workspace users list. All other users who need to work on the document need to be added to the Workspace Members list; it does not inherit the permissions of the parent site. Fortunately, there is a link on the main page of the document workspace to do this. Users without permission to access the workspace will not even see it in the site hierarchy.

A document workspace comes prebuilt with the document library containing the document, a Tasks list to assign tasks to members, a calendar to track deadlines and milestones, and a Links list to add relevant links to the document.

FIGURE 7.45
The document
workspace

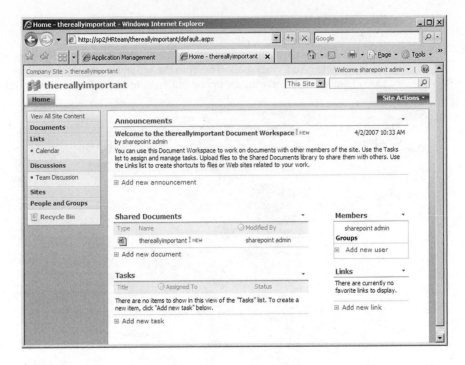

FIGURE 7.45
The document
workspace

WORKING ON THE WRONG COPY

When you're creating a document workspace, remember that a copy of the document is still sitting in the original document library. It's important to keep track of which copy is the primary one and keep that copy in the document workspace. Why else have it? The last thing you want is to have someone working on the original copy while a group is also working on a copy in the workspace. You may want to remove or check out the copy from the original Shared Document Library to prevent confusion.

Once the document is finished and the purpose of the workspace is completed, you may want to remove the workspace to keep the server clean. Before you do so, make sure you copy everything you want to keep (in particular, the actual final document) to the parent site. Once the workspace is deleted, it's gone. Sites don't go to the Recycle Bin.

Wiki

A Wiki site is a collaborative, usually user-managed site that can contain entries with direct links to one another. Wikis are used mostly for information sharing, such as a knowledge base or encyclopedia. You've probably encountered Wiki sites online, and now Microsoft has added a wiki site definition to SharePoint. A good use for a wiki is as a tech support site with documents detailing common issues and solutions. Such a site is shown in Figure 7.46.

FIGURE 7.46
A tech support
Wiki site

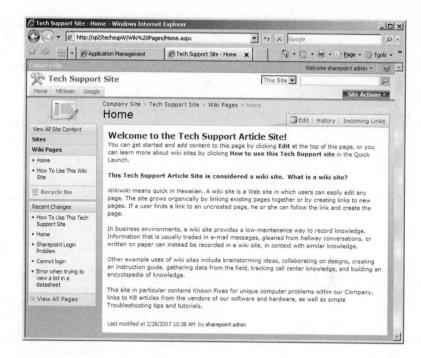

A Wiki site is simple in design. It contains a modified document library for wiki pages. Wiki pages are web pages, which support inline images and links to other pages. To create a new wiki page, click the Wiki Pages link on the Quick Launch bar. This will take you to the document library where you can choose New to create a new page (see Figure 7.47).

FIGURE 7.47
Create a new wiki page

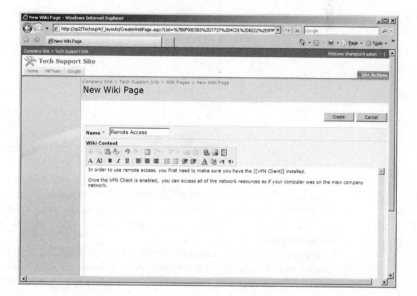

Name the new page (my example is Remote Access), and enter the content for that page. When entering content, you can create links by enclosing the word or phrase in double-brackets. For example, to create a link of the words *VPN Client,* I entered the following:

In order to use the remote access, you first need to make sure you have the [[VPN Client]] installed.

The double-brackets will turn the words *VPN client* into a link to a wiki page called VPN Client (well, the page doesn't exist yet, but you optimistically have a link to it).

When you're done, click Create and the new page will be posted.

In Figure 7.48, the VPN Client link has a dashed line below it. This means that although the link exists, the page it references does not exist. With a Wiki site, this is okay. When you're creating a new wiki page, it's not a bad idea to create links to any significant word or phase, even if the corresponding wiki page does not exist yet. When the missing wiki page is created, the link will automatically be active. Because wikis are intended to be user-created content, clicking on a forwarding link that does not go anywhere will not result in an error; rather the user will be taken to a New Wiki Page creation page for that link (see Figure 7.49), so the user can create the needed site if they so choose. As a matter of fact, most new pages in a Wiki come to be because of a link like that.

FIGURE 7.48
The newly created page

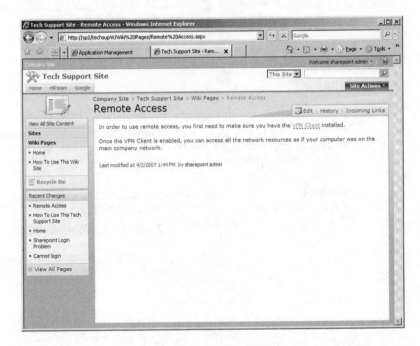

Wiki pages also come with a type of versioning called History, which lets you view previous versions of the page and, if needed, revert to an earlier version. By clicking History, you can see the different changes made to the page through all the versions. See Figure 7.50. Because wiki pages are intended to contain user-created content, some inaccuracies might slip in—this makes Versioning rather critical.

Otherwise, Wiki sites are very similar to Team sites, but with a focus on the Wiki Document Library so that you can turn on approval requirements, add themes, etc. It may take some time to build a full Wiki site, but once it's in place, it's easy to keep it updated, relevant, and useful for users.

FIGURE 7.49
Completing the link

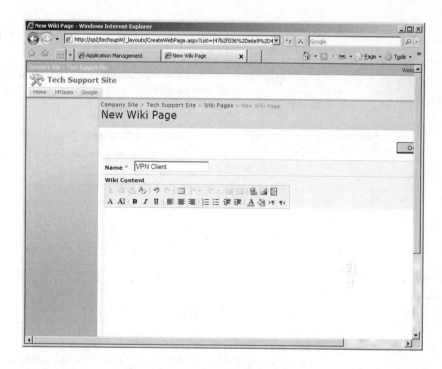

FIGURE 7.50
Wiki versioning

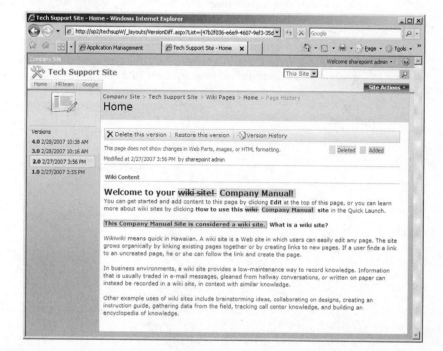

Blog

In addition to adding wiki pages to SharePoint, Microsoft has added blogging support. Blogs, probably the most notorious form of website, are basically public diaries and journals with frequent postings listed in reverse chronological order. SharePoint blogs support comments so users can comment on posts, with categories to organize the posts, and Permalinks, which are fixed-links to posts.

FIGURE 7.51
A SharePoint blog

On the left side of the page is a modified Quick Launch bar, unique to the Blog template's home page. On the right side of the page (Figure 7.51) are the administrative links to create, edit, or maintain the posts and comments on the site. They appear only when you are logged in as the blog's creator or another user with rights to create posts. Clicking Create a post will take you to the New Post page, as shown in Figure 7.52. To create a post you can enter a title and text in the body of the post. You can assign a category, and specify a publish date for the post. The post can be saved as a draft or you can publish it. When published, the post appears on the home page of the blog. Blogs are based on a Posts list with content approval enabled, as well as lists for Comments and Categories.

FIGURE 7.52
A new post

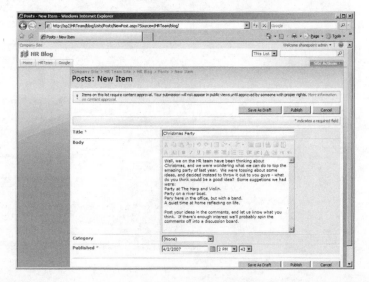

FIGURE 7.53
A blog with a post

In addition to creating the actual post content, you can assign a category and edit the post date from here, which will determine where in the chronological list the post appears. Once the post is created, it will appear on the main page. An example is shown in Figure 7.53. To edit the categories and add more, click on the Categories heading in the Quick Launch bar. That will take you to the Categories list.

Blog posts have support for comments, which are feedback posts that are linked to the main post and are typically created by other users. When looking at the main page, you can see the Comments link below each post, with a number showing the current comment count. Clicking this link will take you to the comments (see Figure 7.54) and let you add a new comment.

Comments are actually stored in the Comments list and referenced to the main post with a lookup field to the Posts list column called Post Title. The Posts list also contains a linked field called Number of Comments, which looks up the Comments list and does a count of comments that are related to the Post's title.

SharePoint blogs can be edited with any SharePoint-compatible blog-editing software, such as Word 2007 or Windows Live Writer.

FIGURE 7.54
Comments

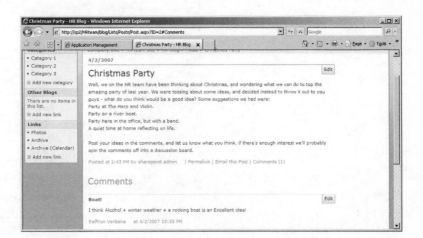

Meeting Workspace

No one likes to be told they have to attend a meeting without knowing what it's about or who else is going to be there. No one likes to leave a meeting unsure of what was accomplished and who's supposed to do what to move the project forward. Typically, meeting agendas are emailed, and people look at the email's CC field to see who is attending. SharePoint has meeting workspace templates that were designed with the needs of the meeting organizer in mind.

With a meeting workspace, you can organize the meeting attendees, agenda, objectives, post any required documents, resolve task assignments, and record any decisions made. There are several types of meeting workspaces and different templates that adjust the site for particular needs. All Meeting Workspaces are based on the same site definition. This is what gives meeting workspaces their unique layout and shortcomings, I mean, streamlined feature. Meeting workspaces usually appear to have only one page. There are several standard lists that are made available to users as List View web parts on the workspace's home page. Meeting Workspaces' home page is actually a content page that can contain multiple sets of web part pages displayed in the content area. Each page is indicated (and accessed) by its tab in the content area. To start, regardless of the type of Meeting Workspace template you choose, each will have at least one page considered the home page.

Creating a meeting workspace can be done several ways. The first is through the now familiar New SharePoint Site page (using a template from under the Meetings tab). The other ways are more common, and they are creating the meeting workspace based on an event, or based on a meeting. When creating a new meeting request from a SharePoint aware product, like Outlook 2007, you can also create a meeting workspace for it, which helps manage the attendees. You can also create a new workspace from an event in a calendar on the SharePoint site as shown in Figure 7.55. Because when creating a new event in a calendar, there is an option for creating a new meeting workspace as well.

FIGURE 7.55
The new calendar event

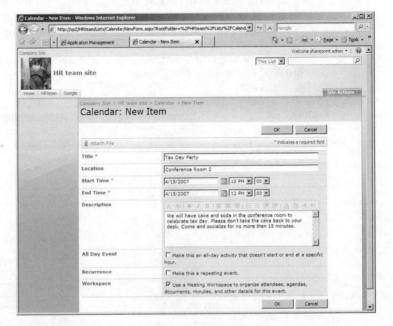

REPEATING MEETINGS

If you create a repeating calendar event and then select to create a meeting workspace for it, the workspace will be aware of the recurrence, although it has an interesting way of showing it. It creates separate instances of the workspace (so the pages look the same but they aren't) for each meeting.

On the left side of the workspace (regardless of the template you choose) will be a list of the dates of the recurring event. You select the correct date, and the workspace will bring up the instance for that date. It's kind of slick and allows someone who doesn't want to create a workspace for the meeting then add a page for each new date to avoid that extra effort.

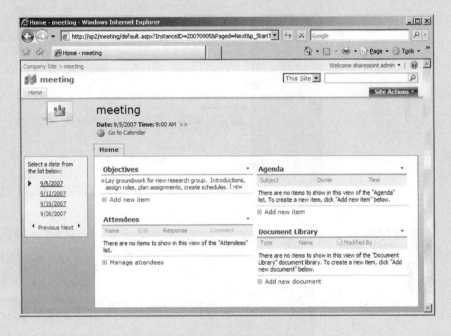

Checking the box in the Workspace section when creating a Calendar event for example, will take you to the New Or Existing Meeting Workspace page shown in Figure 7.56; there you can create the new meeting workspace.

Once you've entered the meeting information and click OK, you will be prompted to choose the desired template (see Figure 7.57); these templates are the same templates as those listed under the Meetings tab on the New SharePoint Site page. All Meeting Workspaces are based on the Meeting Workspace (MPS) site definition. This is why they have a different look and feel than your standard document workspace or Team site. Actually, technically, meeting workspaces refer directly to the site definition and don't even have templates, but Microsoft tends to take liberties concerning referring to the different workspaces as templates.

So let's take a look at how these templates differ from one another, and see what you can do with them.

FIGURE 7.56
The new meeting
workspace

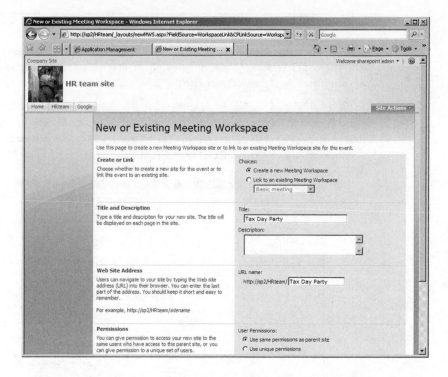

FIGURE 7.57
Selecting a template

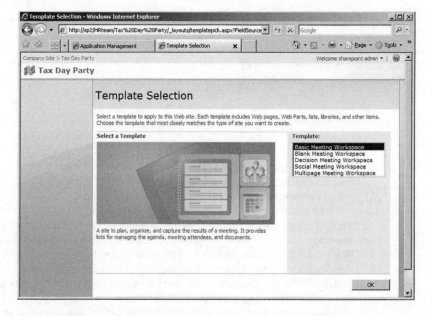

LINKING A CALENDAR EVENT TO AN EXISTING MEETING WORKSPACE

Often times there are meetings to plan other meetings or meetings that are follow ups from other meetings.

You may have noticed in Figure 7.56 that there was an option in the first section to link an event to an existing meeting workspace or to create a whole new workspace for it.

If you choose to link the event to an existing meeting, then you would have to choose the meeting from the dropdown menu. The catch is the meetings available as choices must be directly off of the site you are creating the calendar event on.

When you choose the meeting to link the event to, that meeting workspace's home page gets altered slightly to list the event and offer a link to it in the calendar.

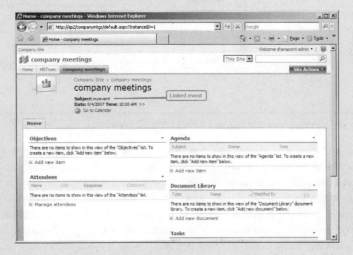

This offers an alternative if you want to link a followup event to a meeting workspace, but don't want to actually create a full blown workspace for it.

BASIC

The Basic meeting workspace (shown in Figure 7.58) is the general template based on the Meeting Workspace site definition. This is why the home page for the site is so fundamentally different from the Team site. It still has most of the features of a team site except for the Quick Launch bar. Most scheduled meetings will be fine with basic. The Basic workspace includes some prebuilt lists, such as Agenda, Objectives, and Attendees. It also includes a document library for storing related documents for the meeting.

The Objectives list is a simple list for notes used to list objectives for the meeting.

The Agenda list item has a required Subject field, an Owner field (for whoever posted the agenda item), a Time field (for how long should this Agenda item should take to discuss during the meeting), and a Notes field.

FIGURE 7.58
The Basic Meeting page

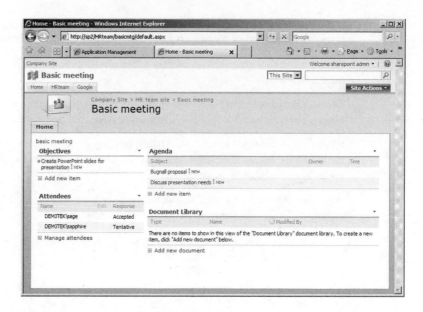

SOME ATTENDEES ARE MORE EQUAL THAN OTHERS

You may notice in Figure 7.60 that several of the names of the invited attendees were formatted in a domain\username fashion and one (Saffron's) was formatted in the standard first name, last name kind of way. This is because people can be invited to a meeting without actually having access to SharePoint. Saffron was already a user of the site collection, so SharePoint had already parsed her friendly name from Active Directory. However, the other two attendees have accounts in Active Directory, but are not existing members of this site collection. So if an attendee's name does not resolve to a friendly name in the attendee list, that means they do not already have permissions to use the SharePoint site. This doesn't necessarily mean they can't go to the meeting, it just means that they don't have access to the Workspace. This could be intentional, or it could mean that this workspace needs to break permission inheritance to add those attendees to the workspace as members to at least view its contents.

The Attendees list is a place to list the users who are going to attend the meeting. When you add a new user, two additional fields, Response and Attendance, are required. They appear in Figure 7.59.

The Response field, which the list creator will probably leave set to Tentative, is simply the user's response to the meeting request: Accepted, Tentative, or Declined.

These Meeting Workspaces are simple sites. There is no automated way for a user to email a response and have their Response field change by default. The meeting organizer (or the attendee themselves if they have the permission to) will have to change that field manually. Also note that the attendees have to have permission to access the site in order to see it. Make certain the attendees can actually log in as at least visitors of the site.

FIGURE 7.59
The New Attendee item

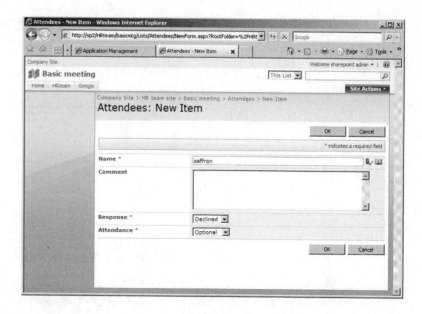

Attendance also has three options: Required, Optional, and Organizer, which is a polite way of saying "really required because you're calling the meeting."

A quick glance at the Attendees list will show you who's supposed to attend, if they can make it, and who's running the show (see Figure 7.60).

FIGURE 7.60
The Attendees list

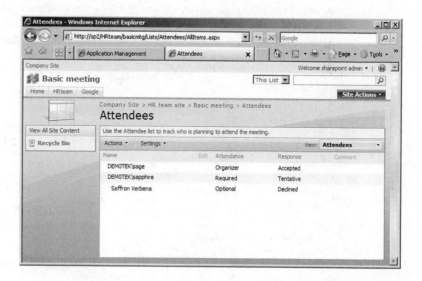

In addition, you can add other Lists and therefore List View web parts to a meeting to add Tasks, Issue Tracking, and pretty much whatever else you need. Just as with Team sites, you can adapt a meeting workspace to meet your needs. See Figure 7.61.

FIGURE 7.61
Adding to the meeting
workspace

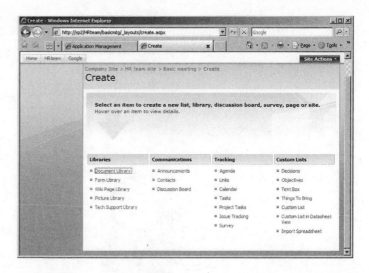

THE CONVENIENCE OF HAVING ALL MEETINGS IN THE SAME PLACE

As many of us know all too well, meetings can be either regularly recurring or there can be meetings that stem from other meetings that cause yet more meetings.

The team site template treats each list and library as if they were their own pages with links to them from the home page. The meeting workspace template treats each list available on that site as a web part, and considers pages to be separate content areas on the main workspace page, indicated by their own tabs. This is because you can add "pages" to the workspace. These pages can be used for separate meetings, each with their own lists, such as tasks, discussions, objectives, and attendees.

Most meeting workspaces start out with a home page (indicated with a tab in the content area named Home).

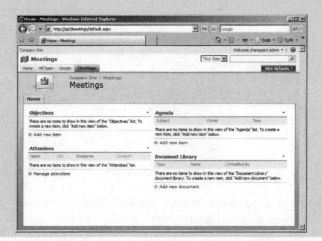

But you aren't limited to one page, you can add another page by going to Site Actions, Add Page. This lets you add a page for each meeting. Note that the Site Actions menu allows you to go to the Site Settings, and Edit the page you're on, as well as Add or Manage Pages.

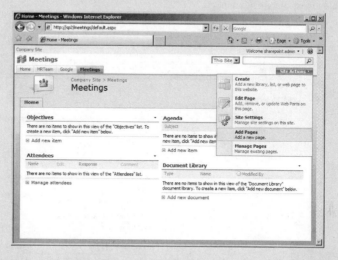

When you add a page to a meeting workplace it will use the familiar Tool Pane (which is usually used to do work with web parts), but in Page mode (yes, tool panes have modes) for you to name and manage pages. After you create a page, it starts in edit mode so you can then add web parts to the new page such as a document library, an attendees list, or links, then populate them with data pertinent to that meeting. Or, later you can click Site Actions, then Edit page (just like an other web part page), and add web parts to the web part zones. For each page the List View web parts for the meeting are incremented. So the home page has Objectives, Agenda, Attendees, etc., the page you add will have Objectives1, Agenda1, etc.

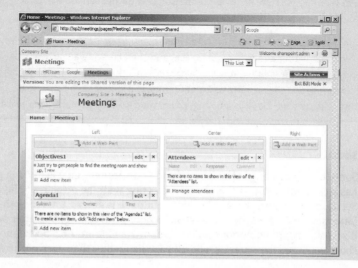

Back on the Home page, if there is more than one meeting listed, you can add the web parts from the other meeting pages (they're all just lists on the same site). This gives you the opportunity to combine, conveniently, the web parts from the other meetings—such as their discussions, document libraries, or objectives—on one home page.

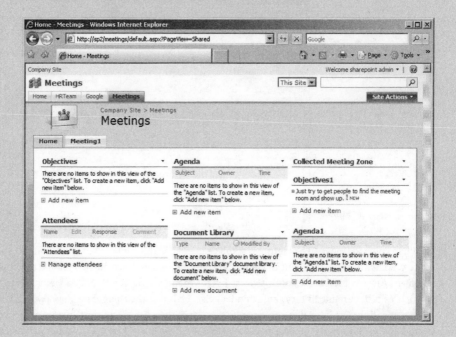

This can give you one central page to go for historical, or shared data between the different meetings, and then the separate pages are there to access for the collected details about the individual meetings themselves.

Just something to think about when creating workspaces for those endlessly spawning meetings. Instead of creating a meeting workspace, and then creating a sub-workspace for the next one, and the next . . . consider creating one workspace for meetings, and simply adding each meeting as a separate tabbed page in that workspace's content area. It might save time, space, and give the attendees one simple place to go for each meeting, rather than a different workspace every time.

SOCIAL

Sometimes a meeting is less serious and your primary goal is making sure everyone attends and has a good time. Rather than create a meeting with the objective "Have a party," why not create a Social meeting workspace? The Social template is geared toward both the before-party planning (attendees, who needs to bring what, location, and timing) and after-party reminiscence, with a discussion board and photo gallery as shown in Figure 7.62. Social meetings are considered one shots, so it uses the separate tabs for each list, rather than each occurrence of a meeting.

FIGURE 7.62
The social meeting

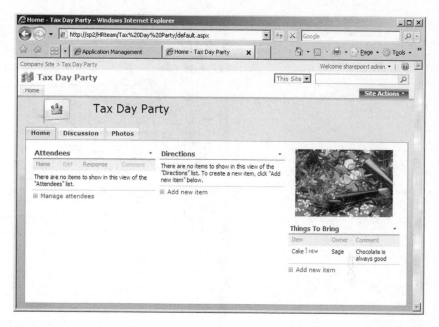

DECISION

The Decision template is focused on resolving questions or issues. See Figure 7.63. It contains the base web parts of the Basic template, but it adds additional Tasks and Decisions lists.

The Tasks list allows tasks to be assigned, progress to be tracked, and a deadline set for the task as shown in Figure 7.64.

The Decisions list is used when decisions are actually being made. Each decision has a Contact and a Status field that can contain Proposed, Pending Approval, or Final.

FIGURE 7.63
A decision meeting

FIGURE 7.64
A new task item

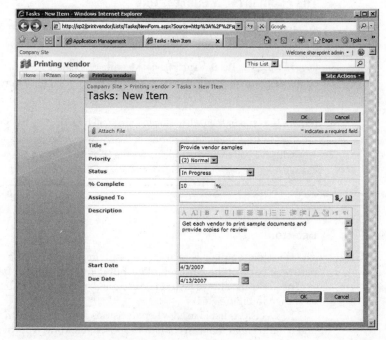

MULTIPAGE

A MultiPage template (see Figure 7.65) is simply a Basic template with two additional blank pages provided to do with as you see fit. The home page of the MultiPage site is a basic site, minus the document library.

The two blank pages are really, really blank (Figure 7.66). You'll want to customize these pages by adding web parts to them before opening the workspace to users.

FIGURE 7.65
A MultiPage meeting

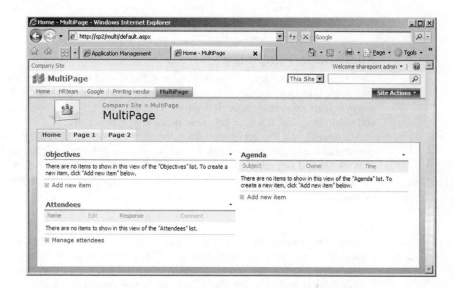

FIGURE 7.66
A seriously blank page

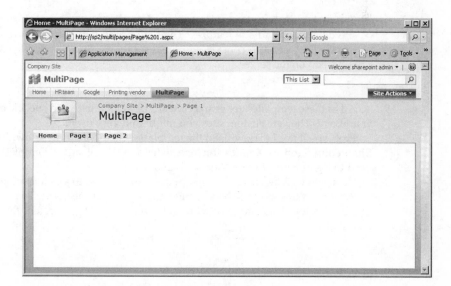

Even More Sites

SharePoint can make a custom site for almost every need. The default sites are only the beginning. Thanks to such tools as Site Definitions, Solutions, Features, and Templates almost any kind of site can exist in SharePoint. You can install prebuilt site templates or new site definitions; if an existing site definition or template doesn't do quite what you want, odds are that there's one out there somewhere that will. In fact, there are so many SharePoint possibilities that you might want to let your users make their own site collections. Here's a closer look at two ways to extend SharePoint into new waters.

Application Templates

We've discussed site definitions and site templates, and talked about how one is a fundamental way a site is built and designed, and ultimately what it can do, and how the other is a template using at least aspects of those definitions to apply to a new site. You've heard about site features and solutions. Now it's time get some real use of them.

Microsoft has a free set of *application templates* for WSS 3.0 available for download. These applications take the basics found in the default site definitions with an out of the box installation of WSS 3.0, and improves upon them. Adding functionality, features, and custom lists to increase the usefulness of the standard site definitions and templates. These application templates come in two types:

Site Admin Templates Standard site templates can be uploaded into the Site Template Gallery and made available to create new sites. These templates can be uploaded to the gallery by any site administrator. Because they reside in a Site Template Gallery, you can install them in a single site collection. These templates, are still based on the original site definitions that come with WSS 3.0.

Server Admin Templates These templates are more advanced, and they provide additional site definitions and site features. They are pretty hefty and require a server administrator to install. They are also considered global solutions, so when deployed they effect to every site collection on the server.

All of these templates are geared toward particular uses and specific deployment scenarios of SharePoint. They are custom sites you might find very useful.

First, you'll need to download the templates. Go to Microsoft's download section and search for **SharePoint Services Application Templates** and download All Templates. (To do this, you might need to log in with a Live account or Passport).

Once you've downloaded the templates, extract them to a folder somewhere. See Figure 7.67. At the time of this writing, there are 40 templates, 20 of each type. They are listed in Table 7.1. There are a lot of sites to play with, but before we can get started, they first need to be installed.

FIGURE 7.67
Microsoft Application Templates

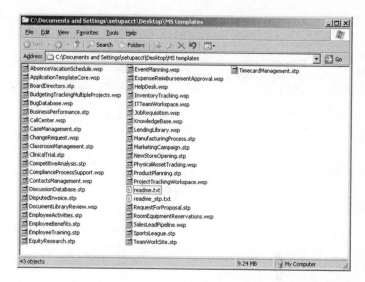

TABLE 7.1: Application Templates

SITE ADMIN TEMPLATES	SERVER ADMIN TEMPLATES
Board of Directors	Absence Request and Vacation Schedule Management
Employee Training Scheduling and Materials	Help Desk
Business Performance Rating	Budgeting and Tracking Multiple Projects
Equity Research	Inventory Tracking
Case Management for Government Agencies	Bug Database
Integrated Marketing Campaign Tracking	IT Team Workspace
Classroom Management	Call Center
Manufacturing Process Management	Job Requisition and Interview Management
Clinical Trial Initiation and Management	Change Request Management
New Store Opening	Knowledge Base
Competitive Analysis Site	Compliance Process Support Site
Product and Marketing Requirements Planning	Lending Library
Discussion Database	Contacts Management
Request for Proposal	Physical Asset Tracking and Management
Disputed Invoice Management	Document Library and Review
Sports League	Project Tracking Workspace
Employee Activities Site	Event Planning
Team Work Site	Room and Equipment Reservations
Employee Self-Service Benefits	Expense Reimbursement and Approval Site
Timecard Management	Sales Lead Pipeline

INSTALLING SITE ADMIN TEMPLATES

Site Admin templates are just site templates, like the team site template, or the HR Team site you created. Installing a Site Admin template is simple.

1. Navigate to the Site Template Gallery of your top-level site under Site Settings. This should look familiar, but just in case see Figure 7.68.

FIGURE 7.68

The Site Template Gallery

2. Click Upload. If you have Microsoft Office installed, go to Upload Multiple Files. If not, you'll need to upload them individually by choosing Upload Document.

3. Browse to where you extracted the application templates and select the template files (they end with `the file extenstion.stp`) and click OK. Once they've all been uploaded, you should see them in your Site Template Gallery.

4. At this point, in my example, all 20 site templates (Figure 7.69) are installed at the site collection level, and are ready to use. When you select Create ➤ Sites And Workspaces, you'll see them under Custom, ready for selection.

FIGURE 7.69

The new templates are added

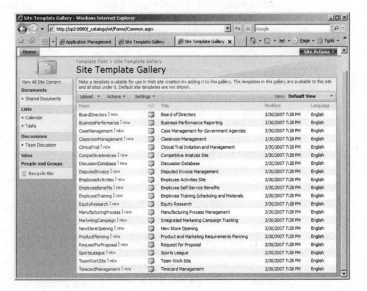

Installing Server Admin Templates

The Server Admin templates are the challenging set to install. They are packaged as `*.wsp` solutions. They contain new site definitions and site features. Remember, these solutions can only be deployed globally; they will be applied to every site collection on the server. Not all solutions are global, but all of the ones provided in this downloaded package are global.

The Application Template Core solution is the most important. It is required before any of the others can be installed, so it has to be installed first.

There are three steps to this: installation, deployment, and copying the contents of the `/app/bin/folder` to the web.config file.

1. At the command prompt (you can only install Solutions using STSADM at the command prompt), enter the following:

STSADM Is Not Recognized

Remember, these commands assume that `STSADM.EXE` is in either your current directory or in the `PATH` statement. If you've forgotten where that is, it's:

```
C:\Program Files\Common Files\Microsoft Shared\web
    server extensions\12\bin.
```

```
STSADM.exe -o addsolution -filename
<path to the applicationtemplatecore.wsp file>
```

This will add the application template to the server where it will be displayed in Central Administration, under Solution Management.

2. Enter the following:

```
Stsadm.exe -o deploysolution -name
ApplicationTemplateCore.wsp -allowgacdeployment
```

There are other settings for the deploysolution operation that might be useful in your environment (you may be prompted to use operations such as -immediate). This step is what actually deploys the applicationtemplatecore for the whole SharePoint farm. See Chapter 13 for more details. For now this simple command is effective as a good example.

3. Enter the following:

```
Stsadm.exe -o copyappbincontent
```

This operation modifies a web.config file for all web applications in the farm based on the changes added to the app\bin folder during the installation and deployment of the solution. This allows all of web applications to make use of the new solution.

The Application Template Core should now be installed and deployed. Note that you could have also deployed this solution (after adding it at the command line) via the Central Administration site (Operations ➢ Solution Management), but the command line is faster. If you want to go to Central Administration and check, you will see the Solution is deployed. Clicking on it will give you more information, as shown in Figure 7.70.

FIGURE 7.70
The Solution Properties
page

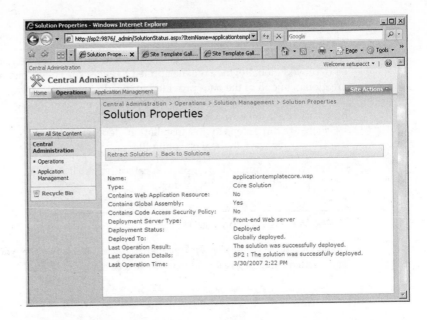

You can also tell it's deployed by checking your top-level Site Settings under Site Collection
Features; you should see at least one new feature. Check out Figure 7.71.

FIGURE 7.71
The new Site Collection
Features page

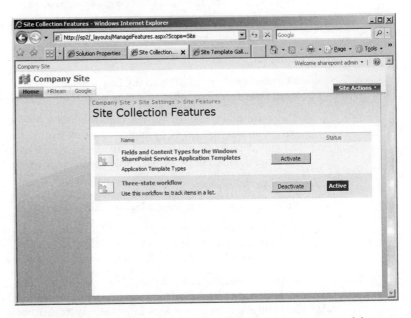

The new feature is not active; it doesn't have to be unless you are actually using one of the new
site definitions, which you haven't installed yet.

To install one of the Server Admin templates (now that you have ApplicationTemplateCore installed), you need to basically use the same commands, but using the template's filename and skipping the last step:

```
STSADM.exe -o addsolution -filename
    <path/to/filename.wsp>
STSADM.exe -o deploysolution -name
    filename.wsp -allowgacdeployment
```

If you plan to install all of them, you may want to batch-file this, or use the %f variable at the prompt (as I am in this example). The following examples assume the WSP files are in the current directory:

```
for %f in (*.wsp) do STSADM.exe -o
    addsolution -filename %f
for %f in (*.wsp) do STSADM.exe -o
    deploysolution -name %f -allowgacdeployment
```

Once you have installed and deployed the templates you're interested in, you need to wait a few minutes for everything to run, then reset IIS:

```
iisreset /noforce
```

At this point, all the solutions you installed should be deployed and ready to go. You can verify this in Central Administration again, or you can go to your site and check Site Settings ➢ Site Features (Figure 7.72). These features are all associated with at least one of the new templates you've installed.

FIGURE 7.72
The new site features

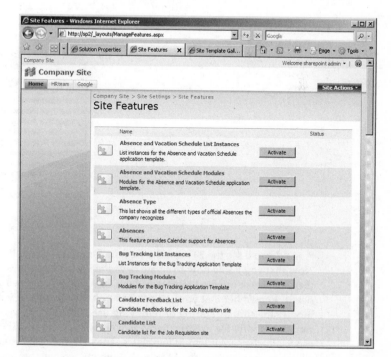

SITE FEATURE ACTIVATION

You don't need to activate any of these features by hand. When you create a new site based on a site definition that requires a certain feature, it will activate that feature automatically on the new site.

So how do you use these fancy Templates now that they are installed? Select Site Actions ➢ Create ➢ Sites and Workspaces. You'll see the 20 new Server Admin Templates (which are actually new site definitions) under their tab, Application Templates (see Figure 7.73):

FIGURE 7.73
The new Server Admin Templates

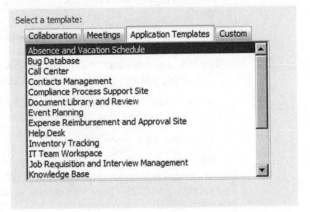

FIGURE 7.74
The new site templates

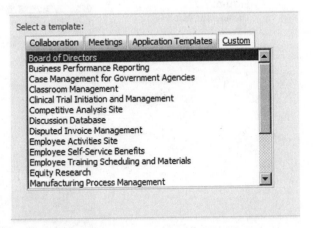

And you'll see the 20 new Site Admin Templates under the Custom tab (see Figure 7.74): Now that you know how to create new sites using templates, it will be easy to get started and take these new task oriented templates for a spin. See which ones are the most appropriate for your needs. Remember that you can permanently delete a site if you don't want to keep it, you can modify the sites by adding or removing lists, libraries, or web parts, and by the same token, you can also modify the existing items as well. Remember that these sites can have new nifty features, especially the server admin templates. They are not called solutions for nothing. You have all the skills you need at this point to check them out, so feel free and make them your own.

Self-Service Site Creation

Ironically Self-Service Site Creation, which seems to be a shoo-in for this chapter, is *not* about creating subsites. Self-Service Site Creation allows a user to create their own site *collections* (which is why it is covered so thoroughly in the next chapter). That being said, with all these different sites, and all the possible templates and site definitions, you could easily find yourself doing nothing all day but creating new subsites for people; new meetings, blogs, document workspaces, etc. You might be tempted to give more users the Create Subsites permissions, so they can create their own subsites. Of course, then you'll have the nightmare of all these subsites popping up with no organization, and you'll need to deal with them (keep in mind that each subsite eats into the site collection's storage quota, if there is one). As an alternative to letting your users create subsites on your main site collection, you can enable Self-Service Site Creation. Then you can more easily apply a storage quota to each of their site collections (they'll probably only ever use the top-level site) and there is an automated deletion feature that can be used to delete unused site collections.

ALLOWING USERS TO CREATE SITE COLLECTIONS GIVING YOU CHILLS?

Of course, giving users the right to create their own site collections (versus creating subsites) presents its own problems. Site collections are easier to manage from Central Administration, but they are fully functional site collections, with a top-level site, the capacity to have lots of subsites of all kinds, and their own users and permissions. So there is a trade off, ease of management versus giving users carte blanche over their own collection of sites.

ENABLING SELF-SERVICE SITE CREATION

Self-Service Site Creation is a web application wide setting configured in Central Administration under Application Management (to get to the Central Administration site, go to Start, Administratrative Tools, SharePoint 3.0 Central Administration on the SharePoint server). Once there click the Self-Service Site management link to go to the page as you can see in Figure 7.75. Here you can enable Self-Service Site Creation for a particular Web Application. When it is enabled, all Permission Levels with the Self-Service Site Creation permission set (by default, everyone but a visitor, or user account with only read rights) allow users to create their own site collections.

Creating a Self-Service Site Creation site collection is a little different than creating a site collection from Central Administration (you'll learn all about it in the next chapter). Namely, site collections are built administratively from Central Administration. But with Self-Service Site Creation enabled, users without access to Central Administration can create site collections. In addition during the creation process the users will not get to choose their path or their storage quota. The default managed path and storage quota set at the Central Administration level will be applied for them.

Whoever creates the site collection is by default the owner of the site collection, and they can add, edit, and remove other people, groups, permissions, permission levels, subsites, and all site content. However, they still do not have any administrative rights to the original, main parent site or access to Central Administration. They're only a big fish in their own pond. But they are still big enough to impact storage as they add to their site collections and the build up activity as the people they add join them there. It is important to regularly monitor usage to see where growth is happening. Keep in mind that Self-Service Site Creation gives users the opportunity to create a site collection of their very own, but it doesn't limit them to just one.

FIGURE 7.75
Self-Service Site
Creation

When enabling Self-Service Site Creation, you will want to consider setting some limits in order to manage the possible storage load that all of those user site collections could pose on whatever server is hosting the web application's data. The first thing is to place a default storage quota on your web application for all newly created site collections. Go to Central Administration➢ Application Management➢ Web Application General Settings (see Figure 7.76). More about storage quotas in chapter 8, "Site Collections and Web Applications."

The other key settings to consider are for automatic deletion and usage notifications under Site Use Confirmation and Deletion. These settings are shown in Figure 7.77. A lot of users will create new site collections, use them once, and leave them to linger forever. You can prevent this by enabling automatic deletion.

Automatic deletion is simple. It is based on notifications (you cannot set site collections to be automatically deleted without first enabling usage notification). You first set the number of days that SharePoint should wait before sending notifications (minimum 30, maximum 365), then you set how often after that date notices are sent. Then you set how many notifications must be sent without a confirmation response before the site creation is permanently deleted. As you know, when a site is deleted, it's gone. No Recycle Bin exists for sites.

Usage a Notifications are meant to prevent accidental deletion of site collections. After a site collection has existed for the number of days you set, the owner(s) will receive a notification email asking if the site is still in use. The email will contain a confirmation link: clicking this link resets the countdown timer for automatic deletion. If the site owner(s) do nothing, after a set amount of time and repeated email notifications, the site is deleted.

If you enable auto-deletion, you are strongly encouraged to require a secondary administrative contact for site collection creation. The last thing you want is to have a site collection deleted because the one person getting the email notifications is on vacation. For much more about Site Use Confirmation and Deletion, see Chapter 8, "Site Collections and Web Applications." You may also want to review Chapter 12 "Maintenance and Monitoring," as well.

FIGURE 7.76
Setting storage limits

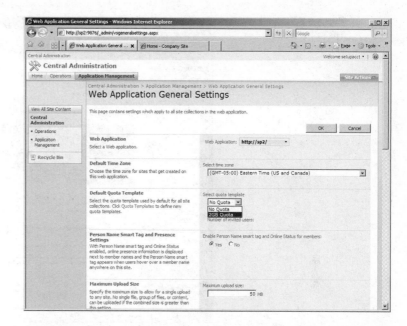

FIGURE 7.77
Enabling Site Use
Confirmation Deletion

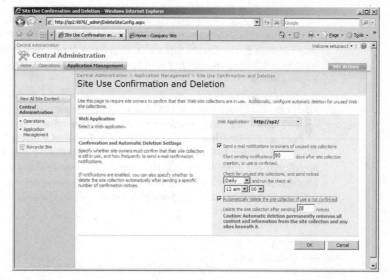

CREATING A SELF-SERVICE SITE COLLECTION

When Self-Service Site Creation is enabled, a new announcement will appear on the main page of your site collection (see Figure 7.78). This announcement contains a link to create a new site collection, starting with the top-level site. This is the only way users can use Self-Service Site Creation, so don't delete this link. If needed, you can add it to the Links web part, Top Link bar, or Quick Launch bar.

FIGURE 7.78
The self-service
announcement

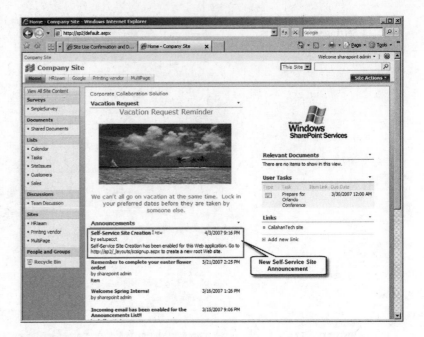

Clicking this link takes the user to a modified New SharePoint Site page. Ironically it does not take the user to the Create Site Collection page. If you notice, in the address bar, the page is `scsignup.aspx`, meaning it is in fact the site collection sign up page and not going to just create a new subsite.

However, the page is almost exactly like any other Create Site Collection page, except there is no option to choose a site quota or specify the owner (as the person creating it is the ipso facto owner). You'll see much more about creating site collections in the next chapter.

Because it's creating a new site collection (not just a SharePoint site as the page title suggests), there is no option to inherit permissions or navigation; instead, there is a new section to assign any additional site administrators. That setting is the only thing uniquely Self-Service. If you configured Self-Service Site Creation to require a secondary contact (as shown in Figure 7.79), this field must have at least one person listed in order to be able to create the site collection.

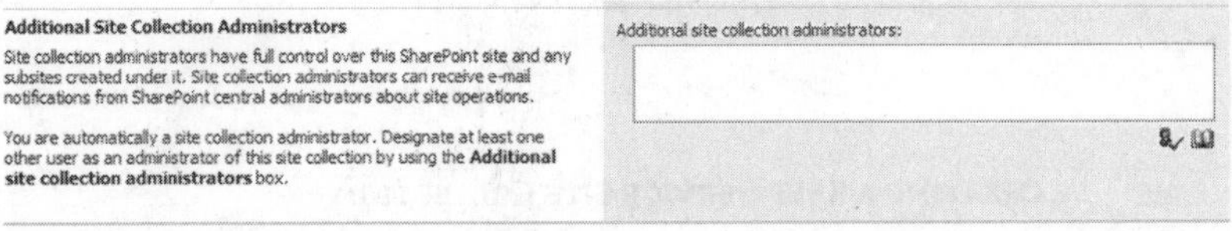

FIGURE 7.79
Second administrative
contact

Additional Site Collection Administrators

Site collection administrators have full control over this SharePoint site and any subsites created under it. Site collection administrators can receive e-mail notifications from SharePoint central administrators about site operations.

You are automatically a site collection administrator. Designate at least one other user as an administrator of this site collection by using the **Additional site collection administrators** box.

Additional site collection administrators:

Once the site is created, it will take the user to a Set Up Groups for this Site page (see Figure 7.80) where they can quickly add users to the default SharePoint groups for their site. Once that's done, the site is fully created and can be accessed from the main URL. No link to it is created on the first site collection site; if you want a link there, you'll need to add one manually.

FIGURE 7.80
People and groups

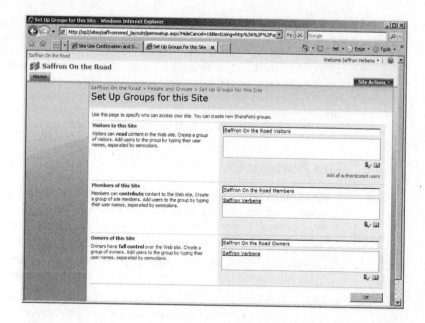

As a matter of fact, remember that site collections are an island, they don't have convenient links to other sites or site collections outside of themselves. You may want to consider configuring the Portal Connection setting in the top-level site of any new site collection to link to the company's primary site collection so the users can get back to the site collection they started from.

Once you've finished setting up the groups, click OK to actually access the top-level site of the new site collection (Figure 7.81).

FIGURE 7.81
New Self-Service Site
Collection

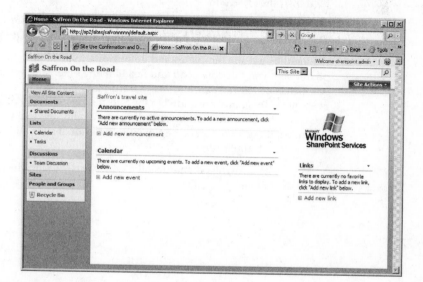

So you've learned what subsites are, and how to create them. You not only explored the different default templates, but you've discovered how to install additional application templates. And finally, you've learned what Self-Service Site Creation is, that it actually creates site collections, as well as how to use the feature once it's enabled. Remember, Self-Service Site Creation creates site collections, not single sites. However, it was intended to at least give users access to their own top-level site. They may be happy with their top-level site and never make any subsites, but the option is there. Now that you have mastered all that is site related, it's time to really delve into what site collections and web applications really are.

The Bottom Line

Create and customize a new site.   Using the New SharePoint Site page, you can create a new subsite from one of several templates or site definitions (in the case of Meeting Workspaces), or you can create a new Workspace from an existing document or calendar event. The site can be customized using themes, custom logos, lists and libraries.

Master It   Create a new blogging site, give it a unique logo and theme, and add a discussion list for users to have their own discussions beyond the comments.

Adjust Site Settings for administrative purposes.   You can configure sites to inherit or set unique permissions on a site. You can also configure subsites to add a storage quota, enable alerts, place the site on the Top Link bar, adjust regional settings, and enable features such as RSS and usage reports.

Master It   Enable RSS feeds for the new blog, confirm search visibility, and check Usage reports.

Understand the different types of SharePoint sites available by default.   By default, Share-Point can create Team sites, document workspaces, blogs, wikis, and meeting workspaces (Basic, Decision, Social, and MultiPage). These can all be created as subsites or new top-level sites in their own site collection.

Master It   Explain the core differences between a Team site and a document workspace, and the difference between a Basic meeting workspace and a Decision meeting workspace.

Add additional site templates and definitions.   In addition to the default sites included with SharePoint, you can download and install many other site templates and definitions. Microsoft has a pack of 40 available, and many third-party companies and helpful coders have provided even more. Templates are added to the Site Template Gallery of a site collection. Site definitions are usually added as solutions using the command-line tool and can be deployed via Central Administration. They can be deployed to individual site collections (if possible) or globally to the entire web application.

Master It   Download and install a new site definition. Test it by creating a new site using the definition.

Chapter 8

Site Collections and Web Applications

Until this point, you've done all of your work in the first site collection that you created when you installed SharePoint. You've explored web parts, lists, and libraries, and you've even built some subsites. You've done all of that in that single site collection within its web application. Now it's time to branch out and learn how and why to create additional site collections and additional web applications.

In this chapter, you'll learn how to:

◆ Create and customize a new site collection

◆ Use managed paths

◆ Create a new web application

◆ Configure Anonymous Access

◆ Set different zones for different access

Site Collections

We've mentioned site collections before; a separate top-level site and corresponding subsites form the SharePoint site collection used throughout this book. A separate site collection is obviously very different from a subsite. But from a user perspective, it looks the same. A site's a site, it's all just different URLs. Otherwise a top-level site looks like a subsite. It is possible to create all new site collections, with their own top-level site and subsites, but why would you want to do such a thing?

Unlike a new site or subsite, a new site collection does not inherit anything from the previous sites—although they all share global settings and web-application settings, which will be discussed later. This lack of inheritance can be very useful when you want to separate a batch of SharePoint sites from your main site collection.

Having multiple site collections allows you to set different settings on the collections from your main site collection. A separate site collection lets you:

◆ Allow an entirely different group of people to be administrators for the site collection.

◆ Use separate, unique users, groups, and permissions.

◆ Back up just that site collection.

◆ Have unique workflows, site templates, list templates, content types, and site columns.

◆ Specify different storage quotas.

For example, say you have a branch office; a different location with its own group of people, unique needs, and documents. At first, you might be tempted to just give that location its own subsite off your main top-level site. However, there will be times when this arrangement is less than optimal. For example, you'd have to give those subsite users permissions in the site collection and handle the increased administration required to restrict their account groups to just their subsite.

With a new site collection, you have a whole new top-level site, with new users and groups. You could then give the branch office's IT department administrative rights to that site collection. The branch office administrator could then manage that office's own sites, permissions, and subsites—without having access to your main SharePoint site. They could have their own templates, navigation, permissions, logo, and whatever they like, and you wouldn't have to worry about them. And, of course, don't forget that you can apply storage quotas, as well as Usage Notification and Deletion to site collections. Having their own storage quota means that that branch office has more control over their storage, as opposed to having to share with, and impact, all the other sites in the site collection if they had only a subsite. As far as usage notification and deletion, it would be inappropriate if the site collection were intended to be permanent and was active to constantly threaten to delete it, but it gives the server farm administrator another way to shift the responsibility of tracking site collection activity from their shoulders and require the branch office's administrator to respond to the notifications or risk their site collection being deleted.

Creating a Site Collection

Normally new site collections are created in Central Administration. To create one, follow these steps:

1. Open Central Administration and navigate to Application Management.

2. The Create Site Collection link is under the SharePoint Site Management category.

3. Click this link to go to the Create Site Collection page, as shown in Figure 8.1.

   Configure your new site collection and the required top-level site that will start this collection.

FIGURE 8.1
The Create Site Collection page

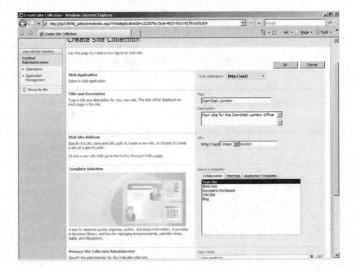

4. The first step is to choose the web application on which you want the site collection to be created. We'll discuss web applications later in the chapter, so for now leave the web application set to the default (and in my example, only) web application.

5. The Title and Description fields are treated the same as when you create a site. This is actually for the top-level site in the new site collection. Enter a title for your new top-level site (and a description if you require). My example creates a new site collection for the London office, so it uses **Dem0tek London,** with the description **Main site for the Dem0tek London Office.**

6. The Web Site Address field is where you enter the URL for the new top-level site. Unlike the URL for a subsite (which is placed in the path of the parent site), this URL starts at the top of the web application and uses a *managed path* as the location for the new site. The default managed path is /sites/; we'll discuss how and why to change this path later. For our purposes this path is fine, just enter your desired URL. My example uses **london**.

The templates in the Template Selection section are identical to those available when you create a new subsite; but this time we are choosing the template for the site collection's top-level site. Any custom site templates you installed into the first site collection will not be available here, because this is a new site collection and not part of the first one.

However, if you installed and deployed any application templates to the farm (like the server application templates installed in the last chapter) they would be available to any site collection in any web application under the Application Templates tab. But, in order to keep it simple, I am going to stick with the default templates available with SharePoint out of the box.

7. So in the Template Selection section, I am assuming that you at least have Collaboration or Meeting tabs from which to choose your site template. From those options you'd typically, for a top-level site, want to choose the Team Site template, which is what I am going to use in my example.

    The Primary Site Collection administrator is the owner of this new site collection. New site collections do not inherit any permissions from any other collections; therefore, unless you enter someone's username in this box, no one will be able to log on to the new top-level site or administer it. For my example, *shareadmin* is the primary administrator. The Secondary Site Collection administrator is a second administrative account, and it's a good idea to have a second account in case something happens to the primary account or administrator. My example adds Nigella, the London Office's network administrator.

    The Quota Template field lets you choose which Quota template to apply to the site collection. This quota will determine how large the site collection can get (in MegaBytes) and is needed for storage reports on the individual sites within the collection, as shown in Chapter 7, "Sites, Subsites, and Workspaces." My example uses No Quota because we haven't created on yet. However, I can always apply a quota later.

8. Once you're done, click OK. The new site will be created in the managed path (for my example, http://sp2/sites/).

    Going to the root of the server (http://sp2/) will take you to the main site collection, where there is no hint that the new site collection even exists. Even under View All Site Content, you won't see the new London site. It's completely separate, and the only way to get there is to use the new URL (http://sp2/sites/london). See Figure 8.2.

FIGURE 8.2
The new top-level
site

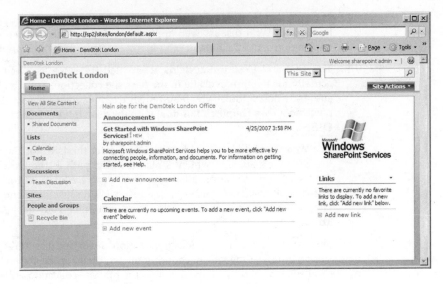

You should have a fresh, new top-level site ready to configure and build on.

WHAT IF THE SITE COLLECTION ADMINSTRATOR HAS BEGUN TO RUN AMOK?

If the fact that only site collection administrators can access a site collection (and you aren't allowed to make yourself one) makes you uneasy, take heart. There are things you can do, of course, to gain access to any site collection in case of emergency. Truly, the only user accounts that will be listed and available to log in to the site collection just after creation will be the site collection administrators, but there are always ways around that if necessary. The hope is, you'll never need them, but here are some alternate ways to access site collections even if you aren't the site collection administrator:

◆ Any Farm Administrator can take over ownership of a site collection by using the Site collection administrators setting on the Application Management page of Central Administration. On that page the Farm Administrator can select the site collection, then see (and change) who the primary and secondary administrators are.

◆ Use Policy for Web Application under Application Management to add an account to the web application with administrative control over all site collections therein. This page is used to apply user policies to web applications effecting everything they contain. On the Policy for Web Application page, you can select the web application that contains the site collection(s) that you want to be able to access (regardless of who the assigned administrators are), then add the account you are going to use, assigning it full control (which is the permission level that administrators have). That will give it administrative rights over all site collections in the selected web application. (For more about Policy for Web Application, see Chapter 10, "Central Administration: Application Management.")

- ◆ As a last resort (otherwise you should never, ever log in with these) you can use:

  - ◆ The web application's application pool account (accesses the web application's content database)

  - ◆ The Farm Account (the account that accesses the configuration database and runs the SharePoint timer jobs)

  - ◆ Search related accounts: Search service and the indexing for search (called the Content Access account).

All of these service accounts, by default, must have access to all sites, although the search related accounts only have read access. They are not listed in People and Groups anywhere, (as a matter of fact, the web application pool and Farm accounts are considered *system accounts*) but you can still use them to access a site collection. Do not use any of them to log into SharePoint except in an extreme emergency.

Site Collection Site Settings

Before we go to town on the new site collection—customizing the theme, adding subsites, and installing new templates— let's take a look at the settings that distinguish site collections. These are settings that will apply to the entire site collection, from the top-level site down. You'll recognize a lot of the options from previous chapters, so let's focus on those settings that apply to site collections rather than simply sites. To view the site settings, click the Site Actions menu and choose Site Settings. On the Site Settings page for the top-level site of the site collection, there are settings in each category that are actually significant because of the fact that they effect the entire site collection.

USER PERMISSIONS

First and foremost, you need to add the users to the new site. Right now only two people have access to the site: the two site collection administrators. Just as you configured your first site, you'll need to go through the initial setup of this new site collection, and that includes adding users and giving them the appropriate permission levels. You do this in the same relative location as on any site: Site Settings ➢ Users and Permissions (or you could go to People and Groups in the Quick Launch Bar). At a minimum, you should make sure anyone who needs to view or contribute to the site has access. At a maximum you might want to consider what users you want for the entire site collection. This is where inheriting permissions comes into its own. You can add users to the top-level site that will be able to access any other site in the collection if that site inherits permissions. In addition, you can create your own permission levels and modify the defaults that can affect all inheriting subsites but no other site collection. This is why a site collection can be considered a permissions boundary.

More details on permissions can be found in Chapter 11, "Users and Permissions."

GALLERIES

The previous chapter clarified the difference between site galleries and top-level site galleries. The galleries that appear only on the top-level site apply to all sites in a site collection.

While individual sites can have unique master pages, content types, and columns, the top-level galleries apply to every site in the collection and contain the same items regardless of the site they are accessed from.

To review, these galleries are:

- Site templates
- List templates
- Web parts
- Workflows

If you want certain sites to have certain content in those galleries, you'll need to put them in different site collections.

Looking at site templates, for example, will show any custom templates installed in the site collection.

Recall that the original site collection (Company Site) had a template for HRteam (Figure 8.3) as well as Site Admin Templates in the gallery in chapter 7.

FIGURE 8.3

The "Company Site" Site Gallery

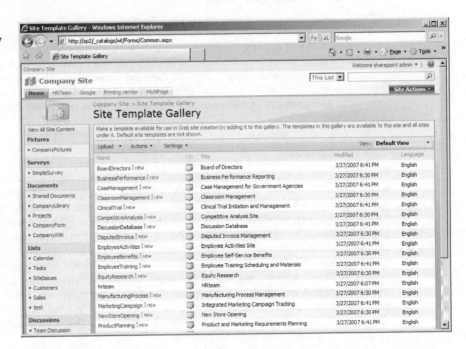

This template is available whenever you create a new site within the Company Site site collection; however, this template does not exist in the new Dem0tek London site collection (see Figure 8.4).

All the other top-level site galleries (list templates, web parts, and workflows) operate in the same way. They are for individual site collections only. These galleries are covered in more detail in Chapter 7, "Sites, Subsites, and Workspaces."

FIGURE 8.4
The Demotek London
Site Gallery

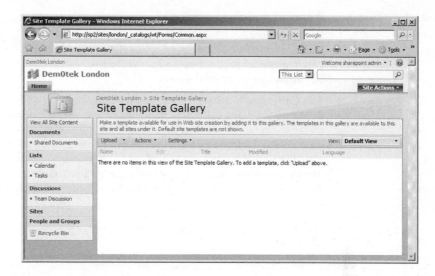

SITE COLLECTION ADMINISTRATION

Returning to Site Settings, on the right side of the page is the Site Collection Administration category. As you can tell by the title, all of the options under this category apply to the entire site collection explicitly. This means that each site collection has its own Recycle Bin, can run separate usage reports, and each site collection has its own list of site collection features, a separate hierarchy, and separate portal connections.

To review, the site collection administration settings are:

◆ **The Recycle Bin**. The Recycle Bin (SharePoint's, not the desktop recycle bin) has two stages; the site stage and the site collection stage. It is at the site level Recycle Bin where the items users delete are stored. The users, due to security filtering, can only see the items in that bin that they deleted. This leaves them to think of the site Recycle Bin as their own and because of this it is named the End user Recycle Bin. The Site Collection Recycle Bin allows the administrators of the site collection to see *all* of the deleted items in the site level Recycle Bin, including anything accidentally deleted from that Recycle Bin. The administrators can view the contents of that second stage, site collection Recycle Bin which will hold items deleted from the site level Recycle Bin for a set number of days, and restore items if necessary.

◆ **Usage Summary**. If Usage Analysis Processing is enabled for the SharePoint server (or server farm), then usage data is collected, collated, and made available for each site collection and site in all web applications. At the site level, each has a detailed Usage report, indicating site usage. At the site collection level, usage is tabulated and reported as part of a Usage Summary. This summarizes the overall activity for the site collection, with links to storage information (if a storage quota have been applied) for the site collection.

◆ **Storage Space Allocation**. If the site collection has a storage quota applied to it, then the Storage Space Allocation report will be able to display how much storage space the site collection is currently using versus the quota. The report details how much space each list, document library (which include the template galleries), individual documents, and the End user Recycle Bin use. The End user Recycle Bin takes up space in the site collection and does need to be monitored (especially if something unexpectedly large ends up there). It can have a time limit (usually 30 days) to hold deleted items before removing them forever. However you might want to check from time to time to be certain that there is nothing there that could be permanently removed sooner.

◆ **Site Collection Features**. If Features were installed (or a Solution containing features) and deployed to the site collection, then they would be listed on this setting's page. It is here that features can be activated or deactivated for the site collection. When activated the feature becomes available to all sites in the collection. Features are additional functionality added to a site collection, like a print option added to a menu on an Action bar, or an additional workflow (the default three-state workflow is activated by default for site collections in SharePoint). Anything that can add to the performance of a site can be considered a feature.

FEATURE CONFUSION

There is a little overlap with what is a Feature and what is a Solution. They are both installed, deployed, and activated. But a Solution is essentially a large and more complex Feature (or set of features). It improves and increases functionality but generally has more moving parts and can include entire custom site definitions. Solutions are usually deployed at the server level. Features are more flexible and can be deployed at either the server level or the site collection level, depending on whether you want to make them available to all site collections in the server farm, or if you want to just add the Feature to a particular site collection.

◆ **Site Hierarchy**. Ironically has nothing to do with the Tree View setting for the Quick Launch bar despite having the same name, Site Hierarchy opens a page displaying the URLs of every single subsite (no matter if they are several sub-sub-subsites below the top-level site). Each URL is a link giving the administrators access to those sites, all from one place. Useful if you are planning on deleting a subsite and need to be sure there are no subsites beneath it.

◆ **Portal Site Connection**. A setting primarily meant to point a site collection at a MOSS portal site; to create a navigational link between the two. However, what this setting really does is add whatever link you use for the Portal Site Connection to the front of the global breadcrumb that is always at the very top of every page in a site collection. It will precede the top-level site's link so that it appears that it is "home" for even the top of the site collection. This is useful if you want to link site collections together with a single top site collection.

These features were also covered in Chapter 7, but it's important to note they are unique to site collections.

Configuring Site Collections

You can make several changes to a site collection to customize how it behaves and what is permitted. These configuration changes are all done through Central Administration, on the Application Management page. Just as with the site collection settings, these changes affect the entire site collection and can vary between site collections.

Configuring a site collection (such as creating storage quotas or managing paths) is a server-level administrative task, and it is not something you'd expect the site collection administrator to handle. Site collection administrators do not necessarily have access to Central Administration. In my example, Nigella (the London Office network administrator) does not have access to these settings. These settings should be configured before, during, or immediately after the initial creation of a new site collection by a qualified farm administrator. The site collection administrator's responsibilities should occur in the site collection interface itself, and focus on managing users, permissions, settings, and content of the sites and subsites in her care. Central Administration can be accessed from the SharePoint server by going to Administrative Tools ➢ SharePoint 3.0 Central Administration. Then navigate to the Application Management page.

MANAGED PATHS

As discussed in Chapter 1, Windows SharePoint Services uses Internet Information Server (IIS) to host and publish all of its websites. This means that everything you see through the web browser is being hosted on or accessed by IIS and is, therefore, bound by the rules of IIS.

IIS usually stores all websites in the file system. If you have a normal webpage with the URL `http://www.mycompany.com/sales/default.html`, a sales folder containing the file `default.html` will reside somewhere on the IIS server (by default in the `WWWroot` folder). All your website content—images, pages, scripts, etc.—will reside somewhere in the file system, nested within the root path assigned in the IIS Web Site settings.

SharePoint, on the other hand, compiles its webpages on-the-fly based on the content in the content database. This means there is no need for separate files to be stored in the local file system for each and every page. If you create new content, such as a list named Order, or upload a document to a library, everything will be stored in the database, not in the file system. In other words, the Order list's `Allitems.aspx` page is compiled from the master page and other components that exist in the file system by default (depending on the site template or definition), but the unique data and settings for that list are all stored in the content database for the site. SharePoint web applications do have a virtual directory that do contain necessary components to display web content, but most of it is information for compiling pages on the fly.

The new London site is located at `http://sp2/sites/london` because the path for the URL defaulted to `/sites/` when the site collection was created.

No matter where you look in the local file system, you'll never find a London folder with HTML (or ASPX) files in it. Instead, all that data will be in the content database and otherwise all pages for the site will be compiled when requested.

IIS and SharePoint distinguish between paths that are normal IIS websites (and exist in the file system) and paths that are SharePoint sites (and exist in the database) by using managed paths. A *managed path* is a path for which SharePoint tells IIS, "I'll handle this request."

With Windows SharePoint Services 3.0, all unspecified paths are by default *excluded*—they are not managed. In order for a path to be used by SharePoint (and available as a path for site collections to specify), it needs to be set as a managed path. On installation, SharePoint creates two managed paths. They can be viewed in Central Administration, under Application Management. In the SharePoint Web Application Management category, click Define Managed Paths. See Figure 8.5.

FIGURE 8.5
The Define Managed Paths page

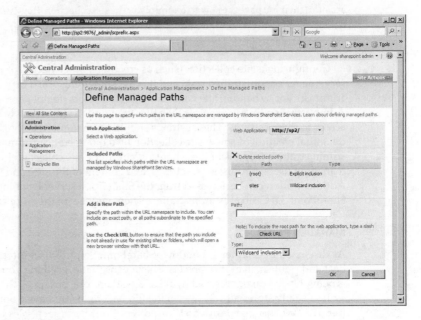

WINDOWS SHAREPOINT SERVICES 2.0 VERSUS 3.0

Under WSS 2.0, all paths were managed by default. This meant that all paths could be defined as *included* (paths you were allowed to be used for new site collections) or *excluded* (ignored by SharePoint). You had to explicitly set excluded paths to let IIS take control of them, rather than having SharePoint control them. WSS 2.0 had an option to define excluded paths.

With WSS 3.0, all paths are unmanaged by default. They're automatically *excluded* and don't need to be explicitly defined as such any more. WSS 3.0 can only define *included* paths, which are now simply called Managed Paths.

There are two types of managed paths, explicit and wildcard.

Explicit Managed Path An *explicit* managed path is a path that is itself a SharePoint site. Root is an explicit path because, if you enter the root of the server into a browser (for example, http://sp2/), you'd get to a SharePoint site.

Wildcard Managed Path A *wildcard* managed path is a URL that contains multiple sites. Sites is a wildcard managed path because any site URL that starts with http://sp2/sites/ is a SharePoint site, but the managed path its self is not a site. For example, http://sp2/sites/london is a SharePoint site, but http://sp2/sites is not.

When you create a new managed path, it needs to be *explicit* for that path to host a single SharePoint site (think of it as an explicit address, "Your site address is "`http://sp2/`"). If you want to host multiple sites inside the managed path, you need to make it a *wildcard* managed path. Making it a more general address, as in "Your site is somewhere under `/sites/`."

To create a new managed path, simply specify the web application's URL for the base, then you can type the path (such as sales) in the Add New Path section of the page. You can specify if the path is explicit or managed, and then click OK. When you create a managed path it stays on the page, assuming that you are going to do several. You can also test the URL to make certain it works and isn't already in use somehow by clicking the Check URL button.

TO SLASH OR NOT TO SLASH

The Define Managed Paths page says you have to precede paths that start at the root address of the web application with a forward slash. In my experience this isn't necessary. I just thought you should know.

To specify a managed path, you have to type in each path from the web application address forward. For example, it is possible that you might want to provision some longer managed paths for members of a presales presentation team to use Self-Service Site Creation to create their blogs. In that case, if you want the address to be
`http://sp2/mktg/presentteam/<theuser'sname>`, you will have to enter the entire path from the web application to the end of the path, for example "`mktg/presentteam`" (Figure 8.6). Then the users could use their names to specify their blog address, such as
`http://sp2/mktg/presentteam/BasilMullien` (Figure 8.7).

FIGURE 8.6
Creating a long new managed path

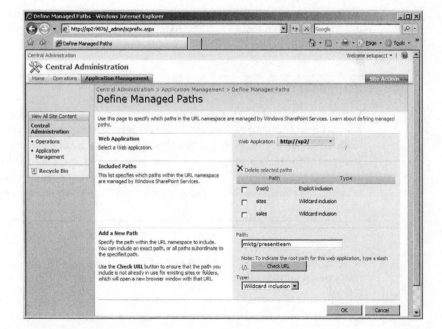

FIGURE 8.7
Site Collection
using new
managed path

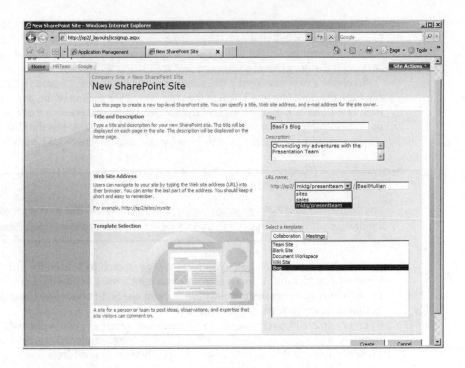

There is no short way to specify a long managed path, which should be useful discouragement in and of itself. Remember the 255 character limit for URLs when creating paths.

DON'T GO MANAGED PATH CRAZY

Keep in mind that these paths are for site collections and are available for anyone creating a site collection, at Central Administration or Self-Service. Subsite addresses within site collections are *appended* to site collection addresses. This means that if you had a site collection at `http://sp2/sales` and you wanted to create a subsite for presales projects, you don't need to create a managed path for `sales/presales` to put that subsite at that address. If you add a presales subsite to the site collection at `http://sp2/sales`, it's address will be `http://sp2/sales/presales` without additional effort.

A managed path is more than just the URL you use for site collections, it's a critical piece of the relationship between WSS and IIS. Letting IIS know what addresses to expect SharePoint to take care of.

USING EXCLUDED PATHS

If you'd like to place a traditional little website in an excluded path on the IIS server while keeping the default port 80, you need to do a couple of things to make IIS display the site outside of SharePoint.

For example (and I am intentionally keeping this simple), say you want the URL `http://sp2/sales/` to go to a standard website, rather than to a SharePoint site. First make certain that the site's path is not a managed path (in our case we'd have to delete it from the list of included paths). The next thing to do is place the website files in the correct location—the root of whatever IIS Web Site is hosting port 80. As you may remember from Chapter 2, "Installation," the default site was disabled and port 80 was (and still is) used by the Web Site SharePoint-80 instead.

Launch Internet Information Services (IIS) Manager and expand the Web Sites folder. You'll see the SharePoint-80 Web Site. Under the Home Directory tab, look at the properties of this site to see the directory for the site. Mine is:

```
C:\Inetpub\wwwroot\wss\VirtualDirectories\80\
```

Copy your website to this location. Keep it in its own folder (my example uses sales for the folder).

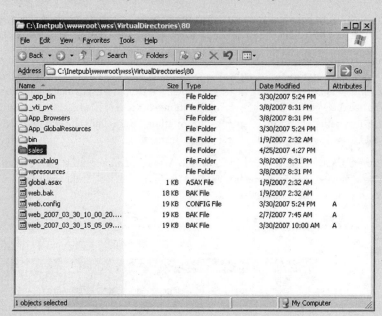

In this case you'll have a Sales folder containing your website files (HTML, images, etc.). This example has only one file in there, `default.htm`.

In order for IIS to know that the new path is there, you may need to restart it. From the command prompt, enter

```
iisreset /noforce
```

This will restart IIS, and `http://sp2/sales/` will lead to the static `default.htm` file. It will not go to SharePoint.

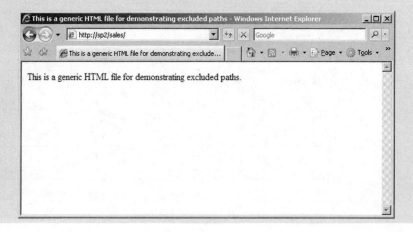

Keep in mind that everything that is hosted this way uses the same IIS Web Site, which is called SharePoint-80 in this case, and is used by SharePoint. Therefore, any IIS settings you have for the web application, such as Authentication (allowing or disallowing Anonymous Access) will also apply to this excluded path. If you want to change these settings just for the excluded path, you'll need to create a new IIS website for the path and not use one of SharePoint's.

QUOTA TEMPLATES

Because SharePoint is meant for users to store data and documents, it can take up more space than expected very quickly. The two main ways to prevent site collections from consuming too much storage space are quotas and locks. Both can be configured on a per-site collection basis, so you can have different disk quotas for different site collections, and you can lock specific site collections without locking others.

Q Site quotas can be manually set on a particular site collection, or you can create Quota templates to use for quick assignment (or to have a quota automatically assigned during Self-Service Site Creation). It's a good idea to create site quota templates rather than manually entering the quota on each site collection, so you have some consistency and don't need to keep entering quota settings for each collection.

Chapter 7 discussed site quotas and showed how to check the storage usage of a site collection. Now that you're creating new site collections, it's a good idea to create at least one quota template to have handy.

To create a new Quota template, go to Central Administration's Application Management page, and in the SharePoint Site Management category, click Quota Templates. This will take you to the page in Figure 8.8.

FIGURE 8.8
Create a Quota template

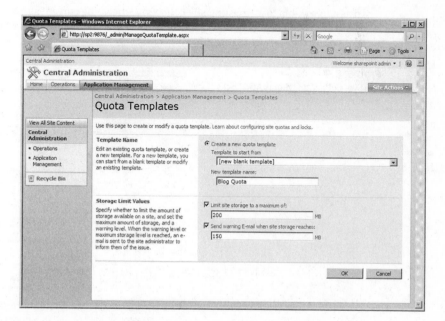

Using this page, you can create a new template or edit an existing one. Each template needs a name and a storage size limit. You can also set the server to email the site administrators when the site collection reaches a certain size, to warn them that they are approaching that limit.

LIMITED INVITATION

If you had Active Directory Account Creation mode enabled, it is also here that you would set the limit on the number of users that can be invited to a site collection. It is not applicable otherwise.

For my example I am going to create a quota for site collections meant to contain blogs. Later in the chapter, I will provide a web application for blogging site collections, and it would be nice to have a storage quota for them. Name the quota by entering it in the New template name field, mine uses **Blog Quota**. For the quota limits, set the limit to 200MB, with a warning at 150MB.

You can edit existing quota templates on this page, delete a template, as well as create a new template based on an existing one. Quota templates, despite being meant to be applied to site collections, are a farm wide setting.

EDIT AND DELETE ARE MISSING.

Don't be alarmed if you notice (as you can see in Figure 8.6) that there doesn't seem to be any settings for editing or deleting a quota template. If there are any existing templates in the farm, the options to edit a template, as well as the delete button, will become available.

SITE QUOTAS AND LOCKS

To assign a quota to an existing site collection, check the current storage used, or to lock the site collection, click Site Collection Quotas and Locks on the Application Management page. This will take you to the page in Figure 8.9.

FIGURE 8.9
The Site Collection Quotas And Locks page

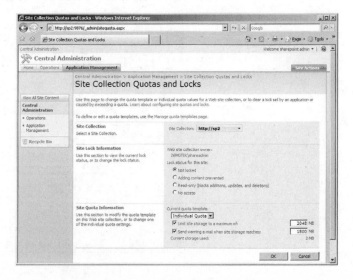

Check the Site Collection section to make sure you're editing the correct site collection before you apply a quota or lock (and change it if necessary).

To apply a quota or quota template to the selected site collection, go to the Site Quota Information section at the bottom of the page. You have the option to either select a quota template that you've previously created on the Quota Template page, or you can choose the Individual Quota option. The individual quota option lets you set the storage quota limits on this individual site collection (as I have for http://sp2). This is useful if the site collection requires quota settings that don't fit with current quota templates.

On this page, you can also set a *site lock* on the site collection (or check its lock status).

"HE CAN SEE *HIS* SITE COLLECTION, WHY CAN'T I SEE MINE?"

When troubleshooting why a site collection can not be accessed when others can, always check here to eliminate the chance that the site collection has gone over quota or has been manually locked.

Site locks are quick ways to prevent access to a site collection without having to go into the Site Settings for that site collection and edit everyone's permission level. By default, site collections are unlocked. Access to the site collection, in that case, is determined by the permission level the user has in the Site Settings for that site. Other Site Lock settings are:

Adding Content Prevented   The site collection can still be viewed, and existing content can be updated or deleted. No new content (even a new field for a list item) can be added to the site collection. This is the Lock setting that is automatically triggered when a Site Quota limit is reached.

Read-Only   The site collection can be viewed, but no additions, edits, or deletions are permitted.

No Access   The site is completely locked and cannot even be viewed.

When you change a site lock to any of these three options (anything but Unlocked), the Additional Lock Information text box will appear on the page, shown in Figure 8.10. This box is required for any lock to be placed on a site collection. The text in this box is shown to your users when they try and access the locked site (or perform a locked action). Always enter some information explaining to your users why you've locked the site.

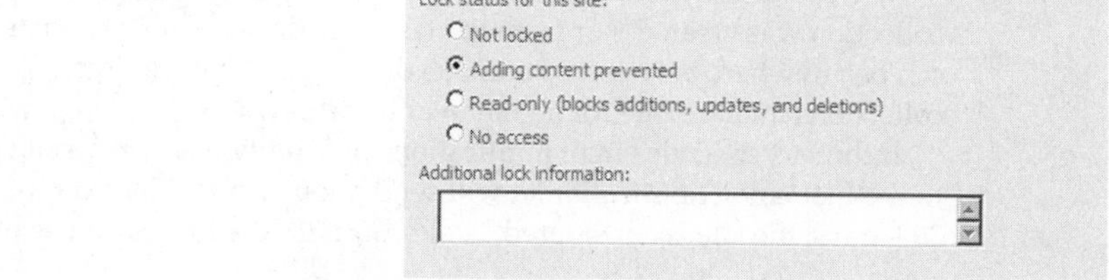

FIGURE 8.10
The Additional Lock Information box

Site Lock Information

Use this section to view the current lock status, or to change the lock status.

Web site collection owner:
DEMOTEK\shareadmin
Lock status for this site:

- ○ Not locked
- ⦿ Adding content prevented
- ○ Read-only (blocks additions, updates, and deletions)
- ○ No access

Additional lock information:

SITE QUOTA TIPS

◆ Let's say you create a quota template for a particular type of site collection (for example, personal blogging sites for users) and set it to 300MB. Then you create a bunch of site collections using that quota. Later you decide to upgrade everyone's disk space to 500MB, so you edit the template to reflect the change. Any new site collections created with this template will be set to 500MB. This will not, however, change the settings for any existing site collection that has already had the template applied. Those collections will stay at a 300MB limit until you manually reapply the quota to the site collections. It is possible (but not easy) to update quotas on a large number of existing site collections by using the SharePoint SDK (Software Development Kit).

◆ A site collection's quota is for everything in that site collection, including the End User Recycle Bin. Therefore, having people delete stuff won't free up any space unless they the deleted items are also emptied from of the Recycle Bin. The second-stage Recycle Bin, which only Administrators can see, does not count toward the quota; instead it's limited to a configurable percentage of the quota (above and beyond the collection's quota). The exact percentage is configured at the web-application level, as discussed later in the chapter.

◆ If you add a quota limit to a site collection that is already bigger than the quota limit allows, the site collection will immediately be locked. Therefore, if you're not sure, check the size of an existing site collection before applying a quota.

SITE USE CONFIRMATION AND DELETION

For each web application on the server, you can enable Site Use Confirmation notification and Automatic Deletion. These settings are found in Central Administration, under Application Management. In the SharePoint Site Management category, click the Site Use Confirmation and Deletion link. This will take you to the page shown in Figure 8.11.

Site Confirmation and Deletion is focused on enabling usage confirmation first, sending a notification email to the site collection administrators for confirmation about the site. However, you can also, once confirmation is enabled, enable automatic deletion of site collections that don't get confirmation of activity over a certain number of notifications. Turning on email notifications will send the emails on a set schedule, prompting them to either confirm the site collection is in use or to delete the site collection. This email is seen in Figure 8.12.

This page is a bit misleading because it implies that it will send notifications to only those site collections that it senses, somehow, are not active. This is not the case. When sending email notifications is enabled, every single site, regardless of popularity, will be subjected to notification emails.

The emails are sent after the number of days you specify have passed from when the site collection was created—or from the last time the administrator confirmed use. This specified time can be anywhere between 30 and 365 days. The server can scan for, and send email to, site collections that are due for an email notification on a daily, weekly, or monthly basis.

If the server sends email notifications on a daily basis and a site administrator does not respond to the first email notification, it will send another one the next day. The server won't wait another 30+ days, the site is considered "stale" until it's confirmed in use or deleted.

FIGURE 8.11

The Site Use
Confirmation and
Deletion page

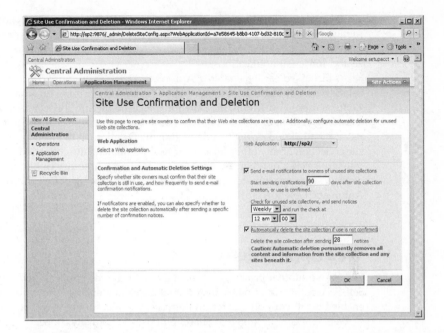

FIGURE 8.12

The notification
email

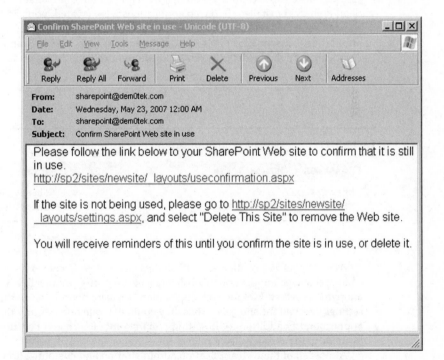

You can also turn on Automatic Deletion (deletion isn't required, but to delete, notification is required first). After a set number of email notifications have been sent with no response, the server will automatically delete the site collection. This set number of notifications can be between 28 and 168 email notifications.

As discussed earlier, enabling Automatic Deletion is a wise decision if you're going to enable Self-Service Site Creation. However, there is a risk to turning on Automatic Deletion: Site Use Confirmations and Automatic Deletion affects all the site collections in a web application, including your main site (Company Site in my example). Because of this, it is strongly recommended you do *not* enable Automatic Deletion on the web application that hosts your main site collection or any other mission critical permanent site collections. Instead, if you need it for self-service sites or other reasons, such as hosting temporary public site collections, you should create a separate web application and put those temporary site collections there, then enable Automatic Deletion for them.

Web Applications

Let's move another layer up the chain and look at web applications. Say you do want to enable Self-Service Site Creation, with Automatic Deletion enabled, but you don't want auto-deletion enabled on all your other sites. In this case, you'll need a new web application.

Web applications are what SharePoint uses to hold site collections. Every site collection has to reside in a web application, although a web application can contain many site collections. When SharePoint was installed, two web applications were created: your first site (in my example that's `http://sp2/`) and Central Administration (in this case, `http://sp2:9876/`). A web application is essentially comprised of two items that reside in IIS: an IIS Web Site and an Application Pool. The default web applications and their corresponding names in IIS are shown in Table 8.1.

TABLE 8.1:   Default Web Applications

SHAREPOINT WEB APPLICATION	IIS WEBSITE AND APPLICATION POOL
`http://sp2/`	SharePoint-80
`http://sp2:`*uniqueport*	SharePoint Central Administration v3

Any settings you configure in IIS on these web sites affect every site collection in the comparable web application. IIS Web Sites host security settings like SSL, authentication, and anonymous access. Making web applications security boundaries in the sense that their security settings effect all the site collections they contain, while not affecting the security of other web applications. In addition to IIS settings, SharePoint offers a lot of additional configuration that can be made at the web-application level.

Almost all of the web application administration and customization is done in Central Administration under Application Management, as shown in Figure 8.13.

FIGURE 8.13

The Application Management page

Creating a New Web Application

The first link on the Application Management page under, conveniently enough, the SharePoint Web Application Management category, is to create or extend a web application. Extending a web application to a new server will be covered later in the chapter in the "Alternate Access Mapping" section, but let's see what you need to do to create a new one.

Let's create a new web application for user blogs—one with a main site collection for the Administration blogs and other information (like an announcement to allow site members to make their own site collections), with Self-Service Site Creation turned on so that the users can create blogs of their own from there (yes, they'll likely only use the top-level site of the collection and not be aware that they can do more, but still, it's easy to do and easy to clean up after).

When you enable Self-Service Site Creation, there needs to be an existing site collection. It's that first site collection's users that are given the Self-Service permission, and have access to the link to the Self-Service Site Creation page on the top-level site's Announcements list. So you add the users you want to give the right to create their own site collections to that first site collection. Then they can use that site collection as the staging area for their own collections.

HOME SITE HOME

To make that first site collection a place to come back to for those users, consider configuring the Portal Connection setting on their site collections to point back to that staging site collection's URL. It will give all pages on their sites a link back to that original site collection's home page. This way they always have a convenient link back to that location. However, if you do that, be sure to create a link back to their site collection(s) so you don't, navigationally speaking, strand them there.

1. To create a new web application, make sure you are on the Application Management page and click the Create or Extend Web Application link. It will take you to a new page with two options: Create a new Web application and Extend an Existing Web application.

2. Click on the Create a new Web application link, which will take you to the Create New Web Application page shown in Figure 8.14.

FIGURE 8.14

The Create New Web Application page

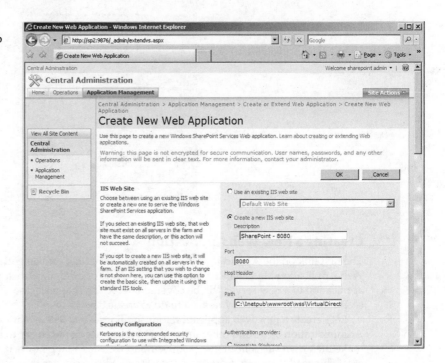

We need to work with a lot of settings to create a new web application, so let's go through them all with the new blogging web application in mind.

IIS Web Site   We need to specify which IIS Web Site the new web application will use. On the off chance you already created a Web Site in IIS for this web application, you could choose it from the list. In this case we have not, so we need to create a new one.

To create a new web application, you need to enter the following information:

Description   A descriptive name for the IIS Web Site, usually something such as `SharePoint-portnumber`.

3. This field will change to reflect your port or host header selections later in the settings. You can choose to manually enter a description as well. My example uses `SharePoint-8080` for this web application (I didn't type that in, if you change the port or host header it changes for you).

Port   The port on which the new web application will listen. IIS Web Sites must be unique in some way in order to receive traffic. Web Sites can be unique either by port number or by host header (you can't mess with unique IPs in this interface). Using a port number to make a Web Site is adequate for demonstration purposes, but does require that users type in a port number next to the server name in their browser to access the top-level site.

4. The port suggested by default is certain not to be already in use by the server. However, you can specify a port if you know it is available. Because port 80 is taken by the first web application, SharePoint-80, my example is specifying port 8080.

Host Header   A host header is a way to change the expected URL of the web application. Normally, because port 80 is already taken by the SharePoint- 80 Web Site (which is our first web application for this SharePoint server), you would not be able to have any more Web Sites on that port. But Host Headers allow you to specify a unique URL for the Web Site that listens on port 80. As long as the host header is unique in IIS, IIS can capture user requests on port 80 for it and redirect the correct traffic to that Site. This will be covered later in the chapter.

5. For this web application, my example leaves this blank because we are using a unique port instead.

Path   Where the SharePoint configuration files are to be kept. My example uses the default settings. By default, IIS places the files in a folder which is named, by default, whatever the port or host header is for the web application. For example: `C:\Inetpub\wwwroot\wss\Virtual Directories\8080`.

6. Although you can specify a different path for your web application's data, for this example, keep the default.

Security Configuration   There are several ways you can configure security on the new web application, as shown in Figure 8.15.

FIGURE 8.15
The Security
Configuration
settings

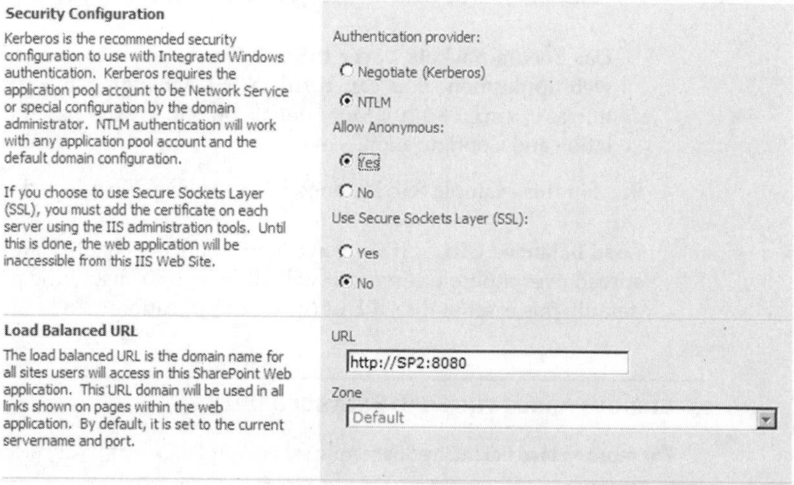

Security Configuration

Kerberos is the recommended security configuration to use with Integrated Windows authentication. Kerberos requires the application pool account to be Network Service or special configuration by the domain administrator. NTLM authentication will work with any application pool account and the default domain configuration.

If you choose to use Secure Sockets Layer (SSL), you must add the certificate on each server using the IIS administration tools. Until this is done, the web application will be inaccessible from this IIS Web Site.

Authentication provider:

○ Negotiate (Kerberos)

◉ NTLM

Allow Anonymous:

◉ Yes

○ No

Use Secure Sockets Layer (SSL):

○ Yes

◉ No

Load Balanced URL

The load balanced URL is the domain name for all sites users will access in this SharePoint Web application. This URL domain will be used in all links shown on pages within the web application. By default, it is set to the current servername and port.

URL

`http://SP2:8080`

Zone

`Default`

Authentication Provider   It is here that you can select what kind of authentication the web application should use when authenticating users. This was covered in Chapter 2 during the installation of SharePoint (you had to choose it for that first, SharePoint-80, web application). You have two options: Kerberos and NTLM. In most cases, the default choice of NTLM. Microsoft suggests this option as a best practice because using Kerberos for authentication requires you to configure server principal names for the server. Kerberos is also very time sensitive and all servers and clients must have the same time in order for the tickets that Kerberos uses to be time-stamped correctly. This means that external users will likely have a problem with this authentication model.

7.   Because we don't require Kerberos for authentication, let's keep NTLM selected.

SHAREPOINT DOESN'T AUTHENTICATE

Remember that SharePoint does not do authentication; only authorization. SharePoint uses outside processes, like Active Directory, to store user accounts and authenticate those accounts. Then SharePoint authorizes those authenticated users to access its resources.

Allow Anonymous   This setting turns Anonymous Access on or off in the IIS Web Site for the web application. Enabling Anonymous Access adjusts IIS settings to allow the web application to offer anonymous access as an option to the site collections, or just the subsites, or even individual lists and libraries. If there is a site collection or subsite (if it doesn't inherit permissions) in the web application that wants to take advantage of this, the administrator has to choose to enable anonymous access at that level. Lists and Libraries can be explicitly given anonymous access, but that option (to give particular lists or libraries unique anonymous access) must be enabled at the site collection or subsite where the list or library is located as well as at the web application level.

8.   In this example, allow anonymous by selecting Yes (the default is No) so the user blogs have the option to be read by everyone on the network without logging in.

Use Secure Sockets Layer (SSL)   If you want to use SSL to encrypt all the sites in the web application, you can turn on SSL (changing the path from `http://sp2:8080` to `https://sp2:8080`). More details on SSL are discussed in Chapter 15, "Advanced Installation and Configuration."

9.   For this example SSL is unnecessary, so keep No selected for this setting.

Load Balanced URL   If you have load balancing enabled, and the web application needs to be spread over multiple servers, it will allow you to ensure the paths displayed are consistent. By default, this is set to the URL of the web application.

CURIOUS ABOUT THE LOAD BALANCED URL?

For more on load balancing SharePoint, check out Chapter 15, "Advanced Installation and Configuration."

10. Using the default URL is fine for this example, so leave this setting at its default.

Application Pool You need to establish which Application Pool in IIS is going to be used by the IIS Web Site. Application Pools in IIS access resources on behalf of the Web Site using an account identity that you specify. This Application Pool will be used by the web application to access its content database. Generally, you'll want to create a new one to keep it separate from the existing Application Pools. If you do create a new Application Pool, you will also have to provide the security account it will use to access its content database. On a single-server install, this can be the Network Service account. However, on a server farm, you'll probably want to create a new domain user just for this web application, or you could use the account you created for the original web application after installing SharePoint.

11. For this demonstration I am going to keep the suggested Application pool name (it usually matches the description of the web application) and use the domain account dem0tek\blogcontent. See Figure 8.16.

FIGURE 8.16
The Application Pool section

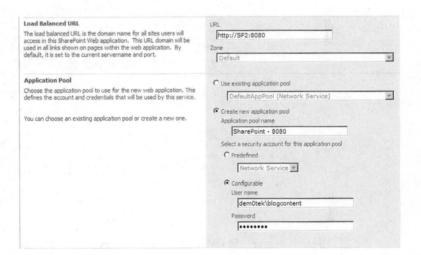

Reset Internet Information Services This section is active only if you have a server farm. In order for a new web application to be created, IIS needs to be restarted on every web server in the farm. The local server (the one you're currently on) needs to be restarted manually, but it's possible to have the server restart IIS on the rest of the farm automatically.

12. The current setting for this section is to restart manually, which is fine in this case because you should always reset the local server anyway, so keep the default.

Database Name and Authentication The web application needs a content database to store everything in—just as the SharePoint-80 web application did during the initial installation of SharePoint (as discussed in Chapter 2). You need to choose which SQL server you want the database to be stored on; of course, with a Basic or Stand-alone server install, you'll need to use the default provided as it points to the Windows Internal Database on the server. You can leave the database name as the default or rename it to something more intuitive if you wish (the default creates a unique GUID for the database, which is hard to remember). You'll also need to decide how the web application will authenticate to the database. Again, you'll most likely want to use the default Windows Authentication, but if your SQL server does not use Windows Authentication, you'll need to supply a username and password.

13. Make certain the correct database server is specified, that the database name is acceptable, and that your web application can authenticate to access the database. My example uses WSSBlog_Content for the database name, otherwise the default database server and authentication method are fine, as shown in Figure 8.17.

FIGURE 8.17
The Database Name And
Authentication section

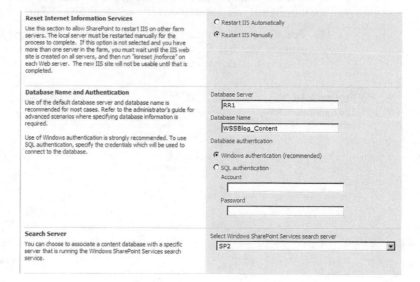

Search Server In order for the search service to index the content database for this new web application a search server must be assigned. The dropdown list shows only those servers running the Windows SharePoint Services search service.

14. Select a search server for the content database. For this example, there is only one choice (SP2), but it is possible to move search to another server (or have search on more than one server for that matter), as discussed in Chapter 15, "Advanced Installation and Configuration."

Once you've set everything to your satisfaction, click OK and wait while the new web application is built. Once the operation completes, you'll need to take some more steps to finish the creation.

15. To complete the web application creation process you need to manually restart IIS on the server so it finishes building the new IIS Web Site. Open a command prompt and enter `iisreset /noforce`.

Because we chose to restart IIS manually, if there are other SharePoint servers in the farm, you will need to run the IISRESET command for each of them as well. If you don't their IIS won't realize that they should also have a copy of the new web application.

When IIS restarts, go ahead and open Internet Information Services (IIS) Manager, which is found in Administrative Tools on the Start Menu. You'll see your new IIS website and application pool, as shown in Figure 8.18.

FIGURE 8.18
IIS shows the new website

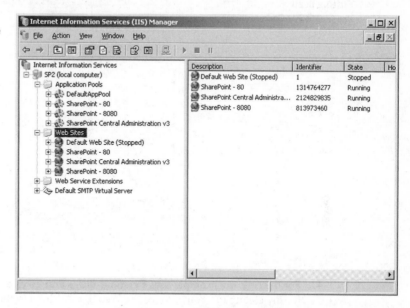

Your new web application is up and running in IIS and available to SharePoint. Of course, it's completely empty. Going to the URL won't show anything—after all, you have no actual site there. The next step is to create a new site collection for the web application and fill it with the top-level site.

1. To create the first site collection for the new web application, go back to Central Administration, Application Management, and under the SharePoint Site Management category, click Create Site Collection.

2. On the Create Site Collection page, you need to change the web application to your new one (SharePoint-8080), so the new site collection will go in this new web application. So in the first section of the page, click on the web application's name and choose Change Web Application. This will take you to the Select Web Application page shown in Figure 8.19.

FIGURE 8.19
The Select Web
Application page

Name	URL
SharePoint - 80	http://sp2/
SharePoint - 8080	**http://sp2:8080/**

Select Web Application -- Webpage Dialog

Select Web Application

Cancel

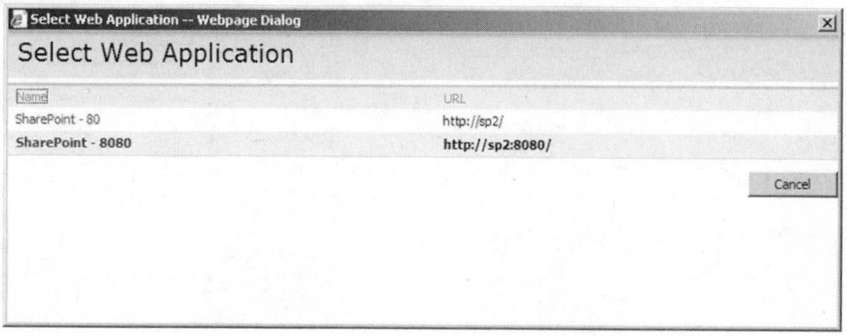

3. Choose your new web application and click OK. You will be taken back to the familiar Create Site Collection page, but now the page shows the new web application. See Figure 8.20.

FIGURE 8.20
The Create Site Collection page

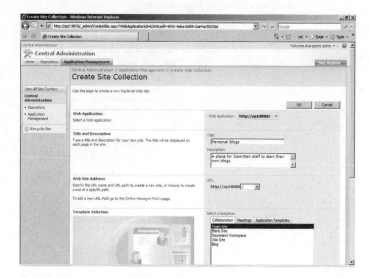

4. For the title, my example uses **Personal Blogs** and gives a brief description (see Figure 8.20 for my example) . You'll notice the Web Site Address is showing the new URL for the web application. We're going to make this site collection the root of the web application, so the complete URL is `http://sp2:8080/`.

5. Go ahead and create a new top-level site using the Team Site template (it makes a good portal for the user blog site collections that will be created from there), use your account (mine is *shareadmin*) as the Primary administrator, and apply a Quota template. (My example uses the Blog Quota we created earlier.), then click OK. When you're done, browse to your new site collection, as shown in Figure 8.21.

FIGURE 8.21
The new site on `http://sp2:8080`

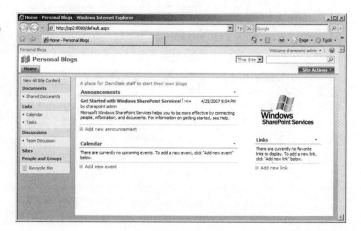

Now, to fill out the site collection (after all, is it really a collection if there is only a top-level site?) let's create a subsite of the top-level site. This subsite will actually be a blog for the administrators of the site collection for this example. It is intended to teach users what a blog is and how to use one before they create their own.

Use the Site Actions menu to get to the Create page. Once there select Sites and Workspaces, and on the New SharePoint Site page, name the site (I'am using Admin Blog), and use the Blog template. For the URL, add **adminblog** to the path. In my example that would look like `http://sp2:8080/adminblog`. Be sure to place it on the Quick Launch and Top Link bar of the parent site. When you are finished, click OK. When it's done, you should have a nice blog site to display to users in addition to the main Personal Blogs top-level site, as shown in Figure 8.22. For more details on how to create a subsite, see Chapter 7, "Sites, Subsites, and Workspaces".

FIGURE 8.22
The Admin Blog site

Web Application Settings

Now you have a new web application, holding a new site collection with a basic top-level site and one subsite. As we did with site collections, let's take a look at the unique things you can do with a web application. All of these settings are found in Central Administration on the Application Management page (to access Central Administration open Internet Explorer and type in the server address and unique port for the site, such as http:// sp2:9876).

SELF-SERVICE SITE CREATION

The web application in this case was created so users could have their own blogs. There are basically two ways of going about allowing users to create their own blog site: Allow them to create subsites in one site collection; or enable Self-Service Site Creation. They both have their pros and cons.

If you allow users to create subsites in a site collection then they can create as many as they want there. Because when you enable the permission there is no inherent limit to how many they can create. But they at least can only overload one site collection.

On the plus side, that one site collection with all the subsites is pretty easy to back up and restore. Also, the users don't need to know how to manage their own securities if they simply inherit them from the parent site. They also can use any custom templates you may have added to the site collection. On the other hand, if you have users abusing the permission to create subsites, you will have to track down the subsites they create and delete them manually. Also the site collection quota will effect all of the subsites in the collection, meaning that one person's overloaded subsite can lock the site collection for everyone.

If you enable Self-Service Site Creation, yes, the users can create their own site collections (with their own users and security). As a matter of fact they can create as many as they want (once enabled, there is no way to limit how many site collections the users can create), and that's pretty powerful. But you can also set up Usage Notification and Automatic Deletion, which will automate the deletion process, freeing you from having to hunt down and delete unused site collections yourself. Not to mention that each site collection will have its own storage quota, so no one will be locking anyone else's sites with their data overload (they will be limited by the quota as well). Also keep in mind that they will have to set up their own users and security for this site collections as well (which gets tiresome after a while).

Because the users are permitted to have considerable independence concerning what they add to their blogs in this scenario, we are going to enable Self-Service Site Creation for this web application. But in addition, we will make the users responsible for regularly indicating their site is being used. If they don't respond quickly enough, the site collection triggering the confirmation notice will be deleted.

Site collections need to reside in a web application, therefore, the Self-Service Site Creation setting needs to be applied at the web application level. It is enabled in Central Administration, under the Application Security category, by clicking the Self-Service Site Management link.

In this example we'll turn it on for the selected web application by selecting On and clicking OK, so individual users can create their own blog site collections. See Figure 8.23.

FIGURE 8.23
The Enable Self-Service
Site Creation section

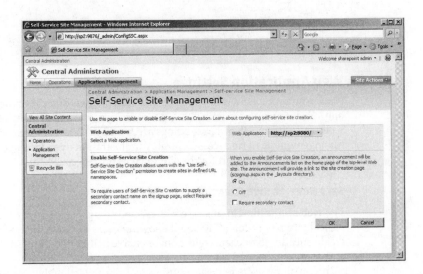

When Self-Service Site Creation is on, an entry will be added to the announcements list on the top-level site of the first site collection with a link to the site creation page (scsignup.aspx, as you can see in Figure 8.24).

FIGURE 8.24
Self-Service Sign up link

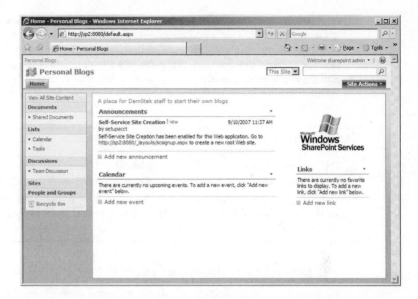

When the user accesses that page to create their site collection, it will look like they are creating a subsite, but it will say at the top of the page that they are creating a top-level site (as a matter of fact, if you look closely in Figure 8.25, you'll notice that is says the user can specify an owner, which is not true, the creator is the owner by default). They will be able to specify their site collection's path (based on managed paths), top-level site's template, but not the storage quota because the default quota is already applied at the web application level.

FIGURE 8.25
Self-Service site collection creation

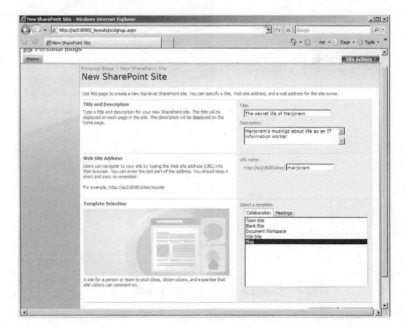

After the user creates the site collection, they will be prompted to add users to the three default groups, Visitors, Owners, and Members. The accounts are pulled from Active Directory by default and there is, unfortunately, no way no limit the number of users they can add. When they are done and click OK on that Set Up Groups for this Site page, their site collection will open in the browser and they will be able to begin. Keep in mind that the user will be the owner of the site collection, where there is a lot of configuration settings available. Some training might be in order.

MISSING SECONDARY ADMINISTRATOR FIELD

Self-Service site collections are based on the defaults set in Central Administration for their web application. If the web application setting is not enabled to require a secondary administrator (and this one didn't), then there will be no option for it during creation from the user's perspective. This is one of those subtle signs of how SharePoint changes interfaces several layers away from the settings that caused it at the server level.

WEB APPLICATION OUTGOING E-MAIL SETTINGS

By default, a web application uses the same email settings you created at the Operations level during the installation, but it is possible to give a web application unique email settings. Do this under SharePoint Web Application Management. Click on the Web application outgoing email settings, which will take you to the page in Figure 8.26. You'll probably want to keep the same mail server, but you might find it useful to change the sender address to be unique for this web application. My example uses `blogserver@dem0tek.com`. (Make certain, of course, that that email address exists on your email server.)

FIGURE 8.26
The Web Application
E-mail settings

WEB APPLICATION GENERAL SETTINGS

The Web Application General Settings link takes you to the page in Figure 8.27.

FIGURE 8.27
The Web Application
General Settings page

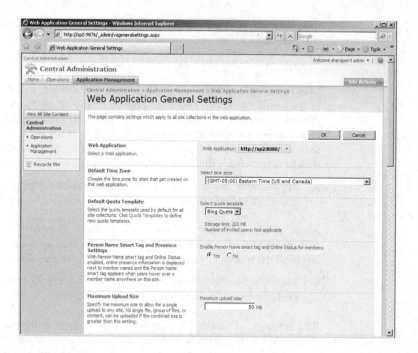

This page contains a large number of sections for configuration. Everything you see here will apply to all the site collections and sites within the web application. Some of these settings are defaults for the sites, which means they apply to site creation but can be changed on individual site collections post creation. Most of these settings, however, are applied to the web application and cannot be changed later for individual site collections.

Web Application   Choose the web application you want to modify.

1. In my example, the `http://sp2:8080` web application is edited. Select the correct web application to which to apply these settings.

Default Time Zone   Set the default time zone for newly created sites. This is only a default setting; individual sites can be edited to change the time zone from the default to reflect local time.

2. Select the default time zone for all sites in the web application. My example uses the main office's time zone: EST.

Default Quota Template   Set the default Quota template for newly created site collections. This setting is also a default. You can still change the Quota template assigned to a site collection manually, as discussed in the "Site Collections" section of this chapter.

3. My example uses the Blog Quota template, so self-service sites that are created on this web application automatically get this quota.

Person Name Smart Tag and Presence Settings   This option requires MSN Messenger or Windows Messenger. Person Name Smart Tags are small popups that appear when a user hovers their cursor over a name on the SharePoint server. The tags indicate whether the person is online currently, and if they're available for chat.

4. This option is on by default, which is fine in this case.

Maximum Upload Size This is the maximum amount that can be uploaded in a single process to the web application. This limit applies to any single file upload, or any group of files being uploaded together. For example, if you're using the Explorer view to copy and paste 50 documents to a document library in one go, you'll need to make sure the combined size of the files is less than this limit. If you're planning to transfer a large amount of data to a SharePoint site, you should first increase this limit and then decrease it when you're done.

5. My example leaves the default of 50MB in place. Apply the maximum upload size that is appropriate for your environment.

Alerts User alerts are discussed in Chapter 5. They can be very useful, but you really don't want to let a user set thousands of alerts (your email server might complain). Here is where you can limit the number of alerts a user can set, or you can disable User Alerts altogether.

6. My example, changes the default of 500 to a mere 50, so the users can't go crazy with alerts. Feel free to set the limit to fit your environment.

RSS Settings Disabling RSS feeds means that there will be no RSS for any of the site collections on that web application. In fact, when RSS is disabled at the web-application level, the RSS link on the Site Settings page for enclosed site collections won't even appear.

7. For this example, leave RSS turned on.

Blog API Settings With the rise of blogging, a large amount of third-party blog-writing software has been developed. In an effort to allow blog-writing software to connect seamlessly with actual blog servers, an RFC has been written for two application programming interfaces (APIs): Blogger API and MetaWeblog API. Blogger API, an older standard, dealt only with accessing the text on a blog. The newer standard, MetaWeblog API, also handles extra data such as common RSS-built metadata such as Author, Title, Comment, etc.

SharePoint supports MetaWeblog API; when it's enabled on the web application, users can update, edit, or create blog posts via third-party software. If you accept usernames and passwords via the MetaWeblog API, these programs can also log in to perform the updates. Otherwise, the default authentication for the site is used.

If you do enable the API and allow the username and password to be accepted, note that these credentials are sent in cleartext. Enabling SSL on the web application can reduce this security risk, as will be discussed later in the chapter.

8. Leave the Blog API enabled, and turn on username and password acceptance.

USING WINDOWS LIVE WRITER WITH SHAREPOINT BLOGS

Windows Live Writer from Microsoft is an excellent example of a MetaWeblog API—compatible program (and is still in beta at the writing of this book). You can download it from Microsoft's `get.live.com` website.

In order to set up Live Writer for use with a SharePoint blog, you'll need to configure a new blogging profile as follows:

1. When you open Live Writer for the first time it will prompt you to create a Windows Live Spaces blog. And if you click Next (because you already have a blog, thank you) it will ask you for the blog type you are writing to. If the account you use to log into the local machine is the one you use to access your SharePoint blog, then choose **SharePoint Blog**. At that point Live Writer will ask for you blog address, then access your blog, and will be ready to begin.

   However, if you want to be able to specify an account, select **Another weblog service** (which is what I prefer), and click Next.

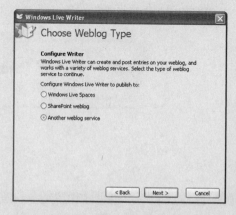

2. If you choose Another weblog service, it will take you to a screen to enter the URL for your blog (for example, `http://server/myblog`) and provide your username and password (assuming authentication via the API is enabled on the SharePoint server), and click Next.

3. It will check to see if there is a web page at that address and when you are prompted for a service provider, choose **MetaWeblog API**.

4. For the remote posting URL, you'll need to tack `/_layouts/metaweblog.aspx` to the end of your blog's URL (for example, `http://server/myblog/_layouts/metaweblog.aspx`).

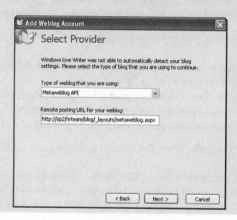

5. Confirm the settings, name the profile, and click Finish.

From that point on it is easy to create blog entries using this (or many other) MetaWeblog API compatible program, the configuration should be the hardest part.

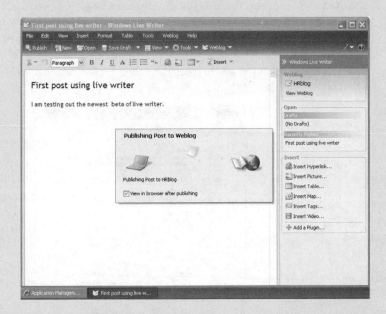

Remember that MetaWeblog API is a web-application setting; therefore, enabling it will provide this kind of integration for all blogs on all sites in all site collections residing in that web application.

Web Page Security Validation This is a legacy setting left over from WSS 2.0, where the security validation timeout determined how long a user could remain idle before having to login again. At the time of this writing, this setting no longer applies under WSS 3.0 (see KB article 888828). This may change in a future update or service pack for SharePoint.

9. As the setting seems to have no effect on SharePoint, leave the default setting.

Send User Name and Password in E-mail This setting is relevant only if Active Directory Account Creation mode (ADAC) is enabled.

When this setting is enabled, and when an account is created for a user, they will receive a notification email detailing their username and password. Without this setting enabled, the user will require an administrator to reset the password in Active Directory.

10. For my example, leave the default in place.

Backward-Compatible Event Handlers *Event handlers* are custom code written and triggered by events in document libraries. Under Windows SharePoint Services 2.0, these handlers could be applied only to document libraries. With Windows SharePoint Services 3.0, they can be applied to other components, such as lists, files, and even sites. There are other significant changes in how the code works and needs to be written. To assist in the transition to version 3.0, this setting lets you retain your older 2.0 event handlers until you can redo them for 3.0.

11. My example leaves the default in place; as we've got no custom event handlers at this point.

Change Log The *change log* is a new feature in Windows SharePoint Services 3.0 and is a part of the new Search features. The server keeps a log of any recent changes to the site in the change log. This allows Search services to quickly provide up-to-date search results without having to re-index the entire site.

12. You can specify how long entries should be kept in the log, or you can disable the log completely. My example leaves the default of 15 days in place.

Recycle Bin You can customize the Recycle Bin for the entire web application. These changes apply to every site collection and site in the web application. You can adjust how long items sit in the End User Recycle Bin and the second-stage Recycle Bin before deletion, set the Recycle Bins to never delete anything automatically, or disable the Recycle Bins completely.

13. My example leaves the defaults in place. Items are left in the Recycle Bin for 30 days before they are deleted, and the second-stage Recycle Bin is set at 50 percent of the site quota. This means the second stage recycle bin adds 50% of the site collection's quota to the space taken in the content database.

When you're done configuring the general settings, click OK. You will be taken back to the Application Management page of Central Administration.

DELETE WEB APPLICATION

If you need to delete a web application, go to Central Administration's Application Management page. Under the SharePoint Web Application Management section, click Delete Web application. This will take you to the page shown in Figure 8.28.

FIGURE 8.28
The Delete Web application page

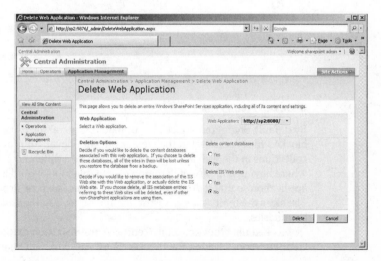

Make sure you're set to delete the right web application. If not, change it before you change any settings on the page. If you do accidentally delete the wrong application, check Chapter 12, "Maintenance and Monitoring," for how to restore from backup (that is assuming you *made* a backup).

When deleting the web application, you can choose to delete the associated Web Site in IIS and/or delete the content database. Deleting the IIS Web Site will remove both the Web Site and the corresponding Application Pool from IIS—even if they are being used by another website. Deleting the content database will destroy everything in that database, including all your sites and documents. If you choose to not delete the database, you can create a new web application and reattach it later. Content databases will be covered in more detail later in this chapter.

MANAGE WEB APPLICATION FEATURES

Just as with sites and site collections, web applications have Features that apply to the entire web application (and the site collections therein). These can be provided by third-party companies to integrate their products into SharePoint, or as part of an overall solution to customize SharePoint functionality. These features are displayed by clicking Manage Web application features, which will take you to the page shown in Figure 8.29. If there are features installed that were scoped to apply to a web application, they would be manageable here.

FIGURE 8.29
The Manage Web Application
Features page

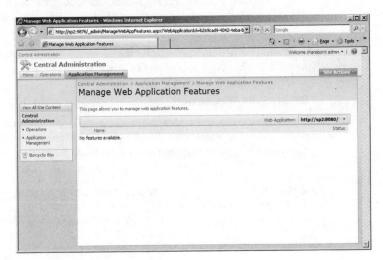

BLOCKED FILE TYPES

By default, SharePoint blocks the upload of several file types based on the file extension. The list of blocked file types is set at the web-application level. You can block all *.exe files for all site collections in the web application. Then create a different, private "IT tech team" web application, where having a library of common executable tools would be handy. You can also restrict a web application so that it doesn't permit media files (such as .mpg, .mov, or .wmv files) to be uploaded. The sky's the limit as far as restricting file types. Another reason web applications are security boundaries.

Blocked file types are set in Central Administration on the Operations page under Security Configuration. Clicking the Blocked File Types link will take you to the page shown in Figure 8.30.

FIGURE 8.30
The Blocked File Types
page

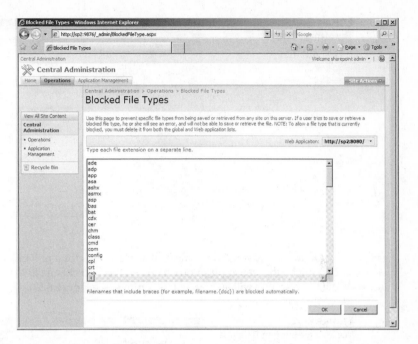

On the Blocked File Types page, you can edit the list of file extensions to block. First make sure you're editing the correct web application. If you need to make changes to all the web applications, you'll need to edit the list for each one. You can permit previously blocked file extensions by simply removing them from the list, and you can block new file extensions by adding them to the list (note that you only add the characters for the extension, not the period).

SharePoint doesn't check a file beyond the extension; therefore, if a user changes a blocked extension to a permitted extension, they'll be able to upload the file. For example, someone could take **evilhack.exe**, rename it evilhack.doc, and successfully upload it to a document library.

Content Databases

During the install process in Chapter 2, you worked with content databases, and you even created a new one while creating a new web application. Now let's take a closer look at what you can do with content databases in regard to web applications. Web applications need at least one content database to put everything in, but they can support additional content databases. As mentioned in Chapter 2, content databases on a simple install reside in

```
%windir%\SYSMSI\SSEE\MSSQL.2005\MSSQL\Data\
```

With a server farm install, they are located on the SQL server you specified during installation.

EDITING CONTENT DATABASE SETTINGS

To manage content databases, go to Central Administration's Application Management page and click Content databases. This will take you to the Manage Content Databases page, shown in Figure 8.31.

FIGURE 8.31

The Manage Content
Databases page

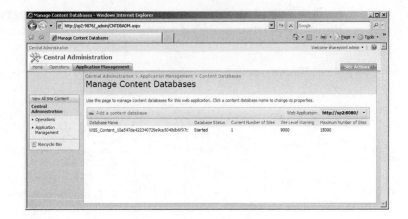

On this page, you can see the content databases for a particular web application. As always, clicking on the web application's name will let you change to a different one. Clicking on a content database's name will let you edit its settings (see Figure 8.32).

FIGURE 8.32

The Manage Content Database
Settings

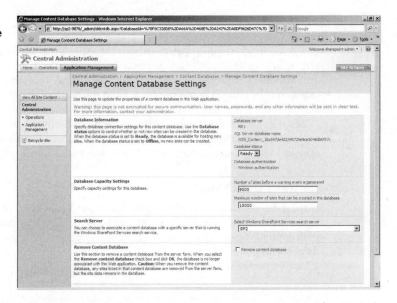

Database Information   A content database can be in two states: Ready and Offline.

The default setting is Ready, which allows new sites to be created in the content database. Obviously, you'll want this if you plan to add site collections to the web application and this is the only content database for that web application.

The other setting is Offline. This setting prevents any new site collections from being created in the content database. Existing site collections can still be used, including creating new subsites within that collection, but the limit has been reached and no more new ones can be added.

When a database is placed Offline and someone attempts to create a new site collection (either via Central Administration or through Self-Service Site Creation), the error message in Figure 8.33 will appear.

FIGURE 8.33
Database offline error

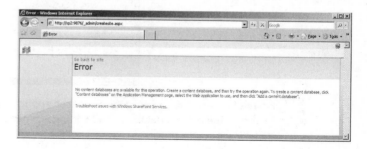

Database Capacity Settings To prevent a database from growing too much and getting out of hand, you can limit the number of site collections that are created in a single content database. The default number is 15,000, but it can be set to whatever you like. There is also an option to send out a notification if a certain number of site collections are reached. You obviously want this to be lower then the actual limit, and the default is 9,000.

Note that on this page, the word "site" is used when describing the limit and warning level. This is a misnomer; the settings apply to site collections, not to individual sites.

When a database reaches the warning level, an event is generated in the log file, as shown in Figure 8.34.

FIGURE 8.34
Site capacity warning event

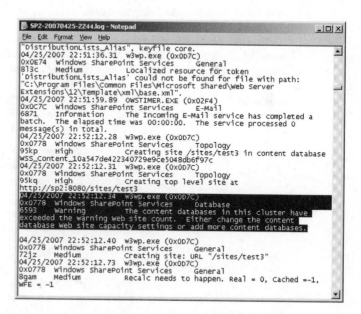

When the database hits its capacity, it will behave in the same manner as an Offline database—no new site collections are permitted. The error message generated is different and clearly shows the issue is capacity (see Figure 8.35).

FIGURE 8.35

A site capacity error generated during creation

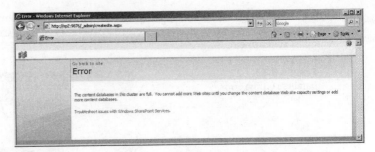

Search Server When you created the web application, you were prompted to choose a Search server for the content database. This setting is where you can change that choice if you want to transfer the search process to another Search server.

Remove Content Database Removing a content database from a web application does not delete that database; it just disassociates it from the web application. The database still exists, just as when you delete a web application and elect to not delete the content database.

A removed content database can be added to a web application later or used when you create a new web application.

ADDING A NEW CONTENT DATABASE

When the content database gets too large, or hits its capacity limit, you may want to add a second content database to the web application. In this case, additional site collections can be added to the new database while still being part of the web application. A web application can have numerous databases to accommodate increases in data storage.

To add a new content database, go to Central Administration's Application Management page and click Content databases. Click the Add a Content Database button on the Action bar. This will take you to the Add Content Database page, as shown in Figure 8.36.

FIGURE 8.36

The Add Content Database page

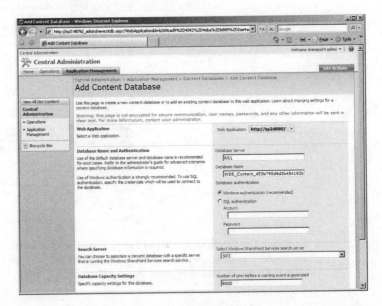

This page asks you to fill out the same information the content database required during the creation of a new web application; in addition, it lets you specify the capacity site limit and warning event level. Once you provide the needed information, click OK. You'll see the new content database listed on the Manage Content Databases pages. See Figure 8.37.

FIGURE 8.37
Content databases

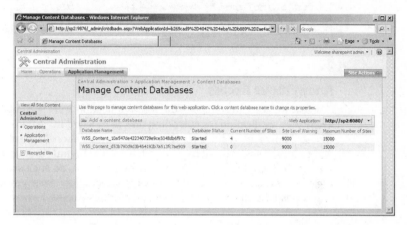

At this point, any new site collection created inside the web application will go to whichever database has the most available space for site collections. The available space isn't calculated by storage capacity, but by subtracting the existing number of sites in the database from the database's site limit.

USING AN EXISTING CONTENT DATABASE

It's possible to use an existing content database. It could be one that was previously removed from a web application, or it could simply have not been deleted when its web application was deleted.

In some cases, when the web application becomes horribly corrupt and unusable, you could be forced to remove it—but, of course, that would never happen.

If you want to bring a preexisting content database back online, and resurrect the sites contained in the database, you can do so by creating a new web application and entering the content database in the "Database Name and Authentication" section.

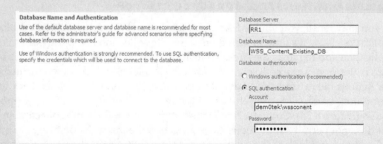

Of course, you'll need to know the name of the existing database and the SQL server on which it's located.

When the web application is created, you do *not* want to create a new site collection to complete the install; after all, the content database already has the site collections and enclosed sites. Instead, just reset IIS by running:

```
iisreset /noforce
```

Then go to your new web application URL, where you'll see the old sites from the content database.

Anonymous Access

One feature you can control at the web-application level is Anonymous Access. When creating a new web application (or extending one, as detailed in "Alternate Access Mapping"), you can choose Allow Anonymous for the new web application. This selection does not turn Anonymous Access for the site collections on or off; it merely permits that option for each site collection. If a web application does not allow Anonymous Access, no enclosed site collection can have Anonymous Access. If the web application does allow Anonymous Access, then the enclosed site collections have the *option* to Allow Anonymous Access; however, it's still turned off by default.

ADDING ANONYMOUS ACCESS TO AN EXISTING WEB APPLICATION

If you don't enable Allow Anonymous Access during the creation of a web application, you can enable it later. Go to Central Administration's Application Management page and click Authentication providers.

Make sure you choose the web application you want to edit, and then click the zone on which you want to Allow Anonymous Access. (Zones are discussed in the "Alternate Access Mapping" section. For now, you have only the default zone). When you click the zone, you will be taken to the Edit Authentication page.

Check the Enable Anonymous Access box and click Save to permit Anonymous Access for this web application.

The Authentication Providers page is covered in more detail in Chapter 10, "Central Administration: Application Management."

ENABLING ANONYMOUS ACCESS ON A SITE COLLECTION

As you may recall, you allowed Anonymous Access when you created the blogging web application. Now it's time to turn it on at the site collection level. Browse to your new web application and log in as the site administrator (my example uses http://sp2:8080 and the login is dem0tek\shareadmin) to reach the top-level site. If you go to Site Settings (under the Site Actions menu) and click Advanced permissions, you will be taken back to the familiar Permissions page. Click the Settings button in the Action bar to see a new option, Anonymous Access (Figure 8.38). Compare this to the Settings menu for a site collection in a web application that does not permit Anonymous Access, such as the main site on http://sp2 (see Figure 8.39).

Go ahead and look at the Anonymous Access settings for the site collection (mine is http://sp2:8080). Click the link in the Settings menu to go to the Change Anonymous Access Settings page (shown in Figure 8.40).

FIGURE 8.38
Site Permissions on a web application that allows Anonymous Access

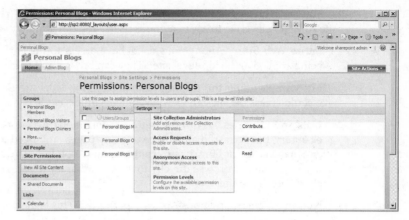

FIGURE 8.39
Site Permissions on a web application that does not allow Anonymous Access

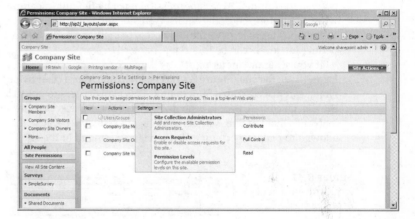

FIGURE 8.40
The Change Anonymous Access Settings page

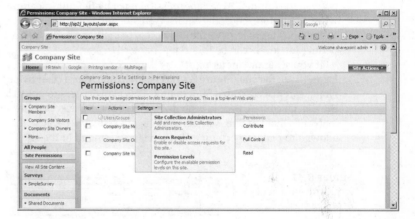

You have three options for how you want this site collection (remember, this is at the site-collection level) to treat anonymous users. You can grant anonymous users access to:

Entire Web Site   Anonymous users have access to the entire site collection (because this is being applied at the top-level site). They can browse and read all pages, lists, and libraries.

My example grants this for the Personal Blogs top-level site. So in this demonstration anyone who could access the site can view all contents unless explicitly set to allow otherwise.

Lists and Libraries   With this setting, anonymous Access is available to be enabled per list or library, but not set to allow access to any pages. You need to manually edit the permissions on whatever list or library you want to grant Anonymous Access. And even then anonymous users will have to browse directly to the list or library to see it because they will not be allowed elsewhere in the site.

Nothing   No Anonymous Access is permitted. This is the default.

When Anonymous Access is granted by using the Entire Web Site setting, the anonymous user is given the Limited Access permission level by default (meaning they can only read and not write). Therefore, choosing Entire Web Site will not give them full control, but will merely allow anonymous users to have limited access to view the entire site collection. More information about permission levels can be found in Chapter 11.

If you set anonymous access to allow access to the entire site, a visiting user does not need to log in to see the site (Figure 8.41). The Welcome Menu (that usually indicates the logged in user's name) is replaced with a Sign in link. This allows users to opt to log in if they wish to contribute to the site. Of course, people who do not have a valid user account to the site will not be able to log in. Notice that the Site Actions menu is not available because the unauthenticated user is not allowed to make any changes to the view or content of the site.

FIGURE 8.41
A site with Anonymous
Access enabled

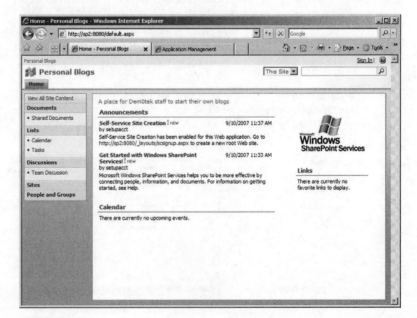

EDITING ANONYMOUS USER PERMISSIONS ON A LIST OR LIBRARY

If Entire Web Site or Lists and Libraries is selected, you can still edit the anonymous user rights to individual lists or libraries (it isn't an either or situation, you can change the anonymous access to individual lists and library. You can give anonymous users access (if you selected Lists and Libraries) or you can change the permissions from the default Limited Access (if you selected Entire Web Site).

At this point, all visitors can view all content on the site, but they cannot contribute. Which is basically good, we don't want visitors adding posts, but we do want them to be able to comment. So let's give the anonymous users the right to only add comments to the Admin Blog. All comments will be stored in the Comments list.

1. Browse to your Admin Blog (at `http://sp2:8080/adminblog/` in my example), and navigate to the Comments List, which can be found under View All Site Content on the Quick Launch bar. (If you are not using a blog template for your site, any list will do.)

2. Once on the list, click the Settings button on the Action bar and choose List Settings. On the Customize Comments page, click Permissions for this list. (List settings are fully covered in Chapter 5, "Introduction to Lists," and permissions are covered in more detail in Chapter 11.)

3. Because the list will inherit permissions from the parent site (meaning everyone can read but anonymous can't contribute), you need to break that inheritance so you can set custom permissions for the list. Go to the Actions button and choose Edit permissions.

4. A dialog box will remind you that this breaks inheritance. Click OK.

    The Permissions: Comments page will show the unique permissions for this list. If you click the Settings button on the Action bar, you'll see the new Anonymous Access option (see Figure 8.42).

FIGURE 8.42
List permissions

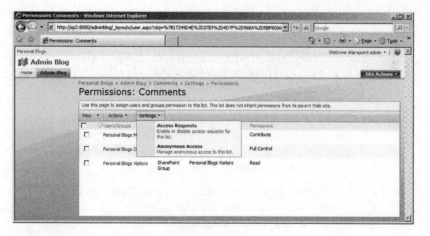

5. Click Anonymous Access on the Settings dropdown menu.

    On this page (shown in Figure 8.43), you can adjust the rights of an anonymous user on this particular list. The available permissions are:

Add Items   The ability to add a new item to the list or to add a new document to a library (in this example, the ability to add a new comment)

Edit Items   The ability to edit an existing item, such as an existing comment, in the list or library

Delete Items   The ability to delete an existing item

View Items   The ability to view items in the list

FIGURE 8.43
The Change Anonymous
Access Settings page

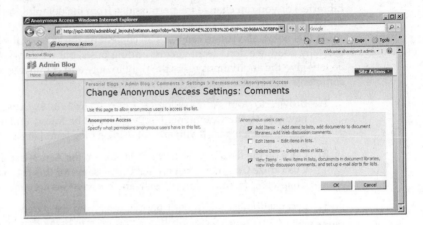

When you selected Entire Web Site for the Anonymous Access settings at the site-collection level, the server gave anonymous users the View Item permission, so it will be already checked here. If you set the anonymous access for the site collection to Lists and Libraries, none of these will be checked.

6. For the comments, you'll want to give anonymous users rights to Add Items and View Items (which they currently already have), but not Edit or Delete, because you don't want people to edit or delete other people's comments. Since they are all anonymous SharePoint can't keep track of what anonymous user wrote what, so it's best they don't edit anything. Check the Add Items box and click OK.

BIG BROTHER SAYS NO

You can force all site collections in a given web application to comply with a policy that just doesn't allow anonymous contribution, no matter what the site collections want, by using Policy for Web Application at the Central Administration level.

Anonymous access is simply turned on at the Web Application level. The more granular anonymous access settings are set at the site level (or the site-collection level) and can grant anonymous users the ability to add new content to the sites.

But if you have a lot of site collection administrators (for example, if you have a web application running Self-Service Site Creation), you may want to force Anonymous Access to be read only for all site collections in the web application. In other words, you'll want to give the sites Anonymous Access, but you won't want the site administrators to grant anonymous users the ability to modify content (Add, Edit, or Delete Items).

This is where Policy for Web Application can be helpful, as discussed in Chapter 10. You can restrict Anonymous Access to be write-only at the web-application level, meaning that no matter what settings the site collection administrators set on their sites, anonymous users will never be able to create new content.

Permissions can be tricky. You might change the permissions on a list to grant anonymous users the ability to Add Items, only to find it doesn't work because a web application Authentication Policy is in place. So if it happens to you, check that overriding policy and see if you've been blocked, invisibly, at a higher level. See Chapter 10 for more details.

You should now have a Personal Blogs site, with an Admin Blogs subsite, that allows Anonymous Access. Open a new browser window and go to `http://sp2:8080`. You should be able to see the site without having to log in. As you can see in Figure 8.44, the button at the top right no longer shows your name, but it provides you the option to Sign In.

FIGURE 8.44
Viewing a site anonymously

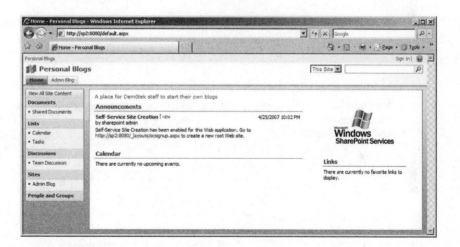

For this example, let's see if we can comment on that Add Item enabled list. Browse to the Admin Blog (or whatever you named your subsite) and see if you can add a list item. In my case I am going to add a comment to the default post "Welcome to your Blog." To do that click the Admin Blog link, and click the Comments link at the bottom of the post. You'll be taken to the Comments list for that post. See Figure 8.45.

You can immediately tell if anonymous users are permitted to create comments. The Add comment fields will be available at the bottom of the page: that link does not appear if you don't have permission to add a comment. Go ahead and add a comment, and click Submit Comment. The new comment will be posted with no username listed (as you can see with my sample mystery comment in Figure 8.46).

As always, think carefully before enabling Anonymous Access. Even though this web application isn't currently accessible from outside your network, someone could still add inappropriate comments.

FIGURE 8.45
The Comments list

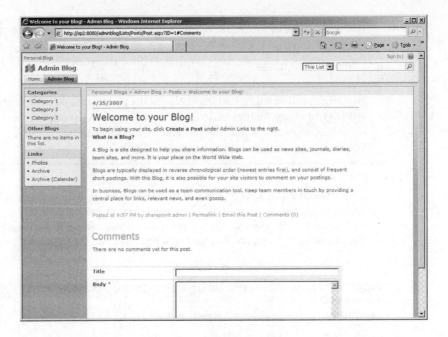

FIGURE 8.46
An anonymous
comment is posted

Host Headers

Once you've started building multiple web applications on your server, you'll quickly realize that having the same URL but different port numbers for all those web applications can be confusing. You also might be thinking about how great it would be if you could host websites with completely different URLs, especially if you would like your server to be referred to by something other than its internal network server name. Host headers, an IIS feature that SharePoint is more than happy to take advantage of, can help organize the confusion.

Host headers allow you to map a web application to a custom URL. For example, rather than creating a web application with the URL `http://sp2:27445/`, you could set it to the URL `http://tech/` or the live, external DNS name `http://tech.dem0share.com/`. The really nice thing is that both of these URLs can run on port 80 rather than a custom port, which simplifies browser use. Because 80 is the default port for HTTP, the user won't need to specify a port in their browser's address bar, just the URL.

UNIQUE IS BETTER THAN GOOD, IT'S NECESSARY

Keep in mind that each IIS Web Site (and therefore each web application) must be completely unique in the way it identifies itself so IIS can pass it the correct user requests. Thus the Web Site must have a unique URL, unique port, or if the server has multiple network cards, it can have its own IP address. Above all else the Web Site must be uniquely identifiable by IIS in order to work.

And, if you are working with host headers, the IIS server will never get the request for that URL if DNS does not have a record for it that resolves to that server's address. If the URL is used on the internet, that domain should be registered to your company and listed on a DNS or *Name* server on the internet. In addition to having a record in the internal DNS.

Host headers should be set when a web application is created or extended.

1. So create a new web application (Central Administration ➤ Application Management ➤ Create or Extend a Web Application ➤ Create New Web Application).

2. On the New SharePoint Site, SharePoint will suggest a random port, so change the suggested port back to 80 and enter the URL to which you want the web application to respond in the Host Header field. See Figure 8.47.

FIGURE 8.47

Setting a host header in the Create New Web Application page

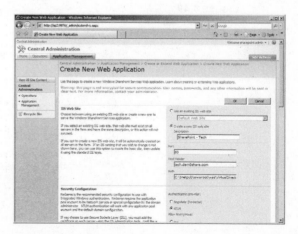

3. Configure the other sections as you would any new web application; Security, Application pool, Database, Search, etc. Then click OK.

After the web application is generated, you'll need to create the initial site collection (my example is *techsite* to keep with the tech theme) and run `iisreset /noforce`, just as we did earlier in this chapter. Keep in mind that in order for users to successfully browse to this URL, they'll need to be able to resolve it in DNS to the IP address of your SharePoint server (so make certain that there is a record in DNS that resolves to the server's IP). Once everything is created and IIS has been reset, you'll be able to see the host header information in IIS.

Open Internet Information Services (IIS) Manager and browse to Web Sites in the tree pane, right-click the new website, go to Properties, and look under the Web Site tab. The default port of 80 will be listed for the site. Click Advanced to see the host header URL, as shown in Figure 8.48.

Of course, browsing to the new URL (in my case http://tech.dem0share.com) will take you to the new site. See Figure 8.49.

FIGURE 8.48
The host header of the new Web Site in IIS

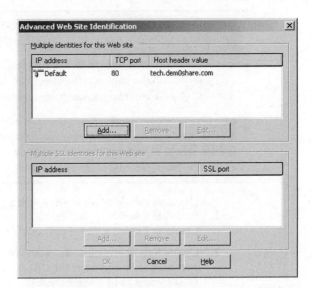

FIGURE 8.49
The new URL site

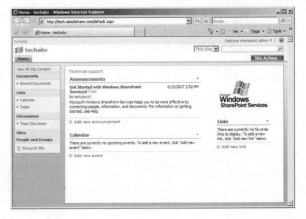

SITE COLLECTIONS AND HOST HEADERS

Officially, you need to create a new web application to use a host header; however, the STSADM command has an undocumented feature (or should we say, *underdocumented*) that lets you create a new site collection using a host header. In the previous version of WSS it was called Scaleable hosting mode, required that SharePoint be installed from the command line with a switch indicating the mode, and it could only apply to one web application. With WSS 3.0 all web applications are allowed to have both site collections that follow the standard path conventions for addressing, and for hosted site collections.

Remember, site collections reside in web applications, and adding a new site collection to the web application usually means you have to place the new site collection in one of the managed paths for that web application (by default, the /sites/ path). However, you can add a site collection to a web application and have that site collection use its own host header, instead of using the managed path.

Using STSADM, the command to create a new site collection normally is as follows:

```
STSADM -o createsite -url http://server/sites/newsite -owneremail
    name@domain.com -ownerlogin DOMAIN\username
```

Other switches, such as -sitetemplate to pre-specify the top-level site's template, are covered in Chapter 13.

Therefore, if you want to create a new site called http://sp2/sites/camper without using a host header and using the http://sp2 web application with *shareadmin* as the owner, use the following command:

```
STSADM -o createsite -url http://sp2/sites/camper -owneremail sh.aread-
    min@dem0share.com -ownerlogin dem0tek\shareadmin
```

If you go to that site in your browser, you'll be asked to choose the template you want to use and enter some users and groups (just as you did with Self-Service Site Creation). After you enter the users and groups, you'll be taken to the new site, where you'll see the normal, expected, URL in the Address bar.

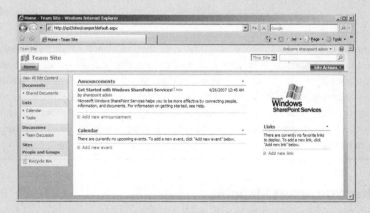

You can create the same site using a host header for the site collection itself (instead of for the web application). It's still in the `http://sp2` web application and must abide by that web application's settings; however, the URL would be `http://camper.dem0tek.lcl` rather than `http://sp2/sites/camper`. Think of it essentially *masking* the real normal web application based address of the site collection with the host header.

The command for this would be

```
STSADM -o createsite -url http://camper.dem0tek.lcl -owneremail
    shareadmin@dem0share.com -ownerlogin dem0tek\shareadmin -hhurl
    http://sp2
```

You'll notice two changes. The `-url` switch displays the desired host header URL (rather than the web application's managed path) and the `-hhurl` switch, which needs to point to the web application in which you want to create the site collection.

Once again, if you browse to `http://camper.demotek.lcl`, you'll be prompted to choose a Site template and add users and groups. Then you'll be taken to the new site, displayed with the nice host header URL in the address bar.

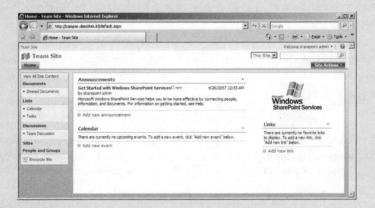

Keep in mind this new site collection is in an existing web application, so you only want to do this if you want the site collection to be constrained by the web application settings (like anonymous access, user permissions, etc.). As a last caveat, also note that SSL will not work for a host header site collection unless it is using a wildcard certificate and the host header is in the same domain. Because site collection host headers are not listed in Alternate Access Mapping, search may also return unexpected links in query results. Despite these shortcomings, the option to use site collections with their own host headers is here if you need it.

Alternate Access Mapping

With the creation of multiple web applications, multiple sites, host headers, and a complex SharePoint deployment, there will come a time when you want to start providing access to

SharePoint sites from multiple places and for multiple people. At the very least, you might want to open your server to outside access; opening a port in your firewall, and forward it to the SharePoint server. Of course, no one in the outside world is going to browse to your server using the URL `http://sp2/` or `http://sp2.dem0tek.lcl`. They're going to use a real address, such as `http://blogs.dem0share.com`. You know how to make a new web application with this URL, but what about adding the URL to an existing web application? This is done through alternate access mapping.

Alternate access mapping lets you:

◆ Map a new URL to an existing web application.

◆ Send a URL other than the one received back to the client browser.

◆ Allow different security policies, based on the URL, for a single web application's content (with zones and extended web applications).

◆ Provide access to a web application's content on a second port.

To understand how alternate access mapping works, you first need to establish how SharePoint treats URLs. Fundamentally, a URL is how a user gets to a SharePoint site. The URL is also used by SharePoint to generate links on the page. A good example of this is with search results. The links in SharePoint aren't hard-coded in an HTML file somewhere; they're generated on the fly, just as SharePoint pages are. When you perform a search request on a SharePoint site, and you get back some possible results, each result shows you a clickable link to that result's location. The links have to have the correct path to work. See Figure 8.50.

FIGURE 8.50
Search results with links

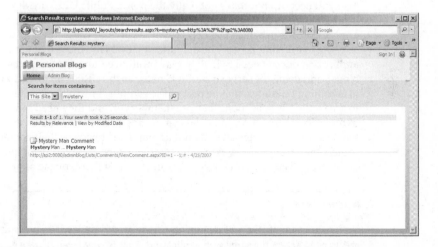

Notice that the result link has the site's path (`http://sp2:8080/<pathtoresult>`) in it. This link works great if the user can resolve the URL `http://sp2:8080/`, but it would be pretty useless if the user were connecting to the server from outside your firewall and couldn't resolve `http://sp2:8080/`. In that case, all those search result links would be dead.

SharePoint resolves this issue by using alternate access mapping, allowing each web application to have up to five different public URLs. That means that the same web application, with all the enclosed site collections, can be accessed from multiple URLs, and SharePoint is smart enough to use the corresponding public URL in all its internal links and paths, making them useful again. For example, the web application `http://sp2:8080` could also respond to the URL `http://blogs.dem0share.com`. As such, you would have two different URLs, both pointing at the same web application content.

In order to work with alternate access mapping, you need to be familiar with some terms:

Public URL   The public URL is the URL that SharePoint displays in the Address bar of the browser and in all the paths and links generated on the page.

Internal URL   The internal URL is the URL that is presented to SharePoint during the request for a page. This is often, but not always, the same as the public URL that SharePoint sends back.

Zone   Each public URL for a web application is associated with a *zone*. Zones are just an easy way to keep track of which public URLs go to which internal URL. When you first create a web application, the URL used becomes the public URL for the Default zone. The other four zones are named Intranet, Internet, Custom, and Extranet. The different zones don't have any intrinsic differences. The names are just for clarity and the zones can be used for whatever you like. Zones are also used to address extended web applications. In otherwords, you can take an existing web application's content databases and make a new web application (essentially a new IIS Web Site) that points to those databases. Allowing two different URLs to access the same data.

CREATING A NEW PUBLIC URL (BY EXTENDING A WEB APPLICATION)

You can create a new public URL by going to the Alternate Access Mappings page and typing one in order to associate it with an existing web application (and we will do that later, in case you need it). But that's not really the point. Public URLs are associated with zones because it is possible that you might want to offer a web application's contents to users that require different kinds of security, such as SSL or anonymous access. These kinds of users can be thought of as being in different zones. The default zone users are those that are in the local office. They're web application doesn't need SSL, they may be allowed anonymous access (to read their coworkers' blogs), and using the server's NetBIOS name as the URL is fine. The intranet users could be the ones in adjoining buildings, maybe part of the campus, but not in the office; they should authenticate to access the site collections they are members of, and they need to use a URL that resolves outside of the office. Extranet could be the commuting users, accessing content over the internet; they too need to use an external URL and authenticate to access their content, but they also need SSL to protect their transactions. While the Internet users could be customers or partners also accessing the web application's content over the internet, while requiring anonymous access and SSL.

ANONYMOUS?

Notice that anonymous access is being offered to certain kinds of users depending on the zone they are using to access the same web application. That is why, even though anonymous can be enabled at the web application level, it is additionally allowed or disallowed at the site collection level. Those site collections meant to contain private company data would never enable anonymous on any site, list or library therein, despite the option being available depending on what URL accesses the site collections.

In order to create a new, public URL for accessing a web application using different security settings than the original, that web application needs to be extended to a different IIS Web Site. As you know from creating a new web application, the IIS Web Site determines the URL for the web application, either by setting a custom port for the main URL (such as `http://sp2:8080`) or by using a host header to give the web application a custom URL (such as `http://tech.dem0share.com`). The IIS Web Site also determines which kind of authentication is to be used (NTLM, Kerberos, allowing Anonymous Access) and if SSL is going to be used.

Extending a web application creates a new IIS Web Site based on an existing web application's content. This new IIS Web Site uses the same Application Pool and, therefore, the same content database as the existing web application. But extending a web application lets you add another URL and other IIS Web Site-based settings to access the existing web application's content. This allows you to create a new public URL for the web application and adjust the security settings for that public URL without changing the existing security settings for your web application's default public URL.

For the example, we can take the blogging site collection, running in the web application `http://sp2:8080`, and extend it to the public URL of `blogs.dem0share.com`, which, in this example, is accessible from the outside world through the firewall. While we're at it, we can set the new URL so that it doesn't permit Anonymous Access. This way only people with log in accounts (the company's employees) will be able to access the blogs from outside the firewall. The default, internal URL settings (for `http://sp2:8080`) will stay the same, and Anonymous Access will be permitted there.

To extend a web application, follow these steps:

DNS Is Still Critical

We're going to be doing a lot of work with new URLs, both public and internal. All of these URLs are still dependent on DNS to function. Make sure your DNS server can resolve any URL you create and it points the client to the SharePoint server. Remember that all URLs need to map to an IP address eventually.

---

1. To extend a web application in Central Administration, click the Create or Extend a Web Application link on the Application Management page in the SharePoint Web Application Management category.

2. Instead of choosing to Create a New Web Application (as you did earlier), click Extend an Existing Web Application. This will take you to the Extend Web Application to another IIS Web Site page. See Figure 8.51.

3. Select the web application you want to extend (my example is `http://sp2:8080`).

4. Under IIS Web Site, create a new IIS website, mine is called **Blogs Outside** in the description. Assign it to port 80, and enter the URL you'd like it to have, my example is **blogs.dem0share.com**, in the Host Header field.

5. Under Security Configuration, leave NTLM selected, leave Allow Anonymous Access disabled, and leave SSL disabled.

6. Under Load Balanced URL, leave the new default (mine is `http://blogs.dem0share.com:80`) and set the Zone to Internet. You can set the zone to any of the five zones that have not already been used. The *default* zone is being used by the main URL (`http://sp2:8080` in my example), so it's not an available choice. After you're done creating this extended web application, the *Internet* zone will no longer be available should you ever choose to extend the existing web application again.

FIGURE 8.51
The Extend Web Application page

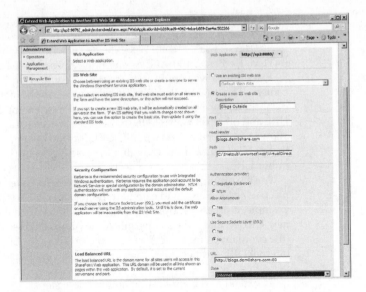

7. Once you've configured the extended web application the way you like, click OK. SharePoint will extend the web application to the new IIS Web Site (not need to add any site collections). If you have DNS set up to point the URL to the server, browsing to it will show the same site, but with a new URL in the Address bar and the corrected links and paths will display on the page. See Figure 8.52.

FIGURE 8.52
The same site as http://sp2:8080 with a new URL

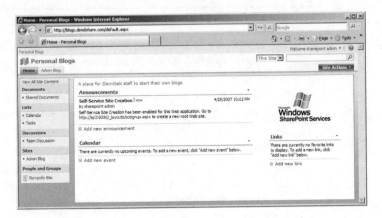

Unlike browsing to `http://sp2:8080`, using this new URL will prompt for authentication because Anonymous Access was disabled for the new IIS Web Site.

CHANGES TO IIS

You can see what changes occurred in to IIS from extending a web site, by going into Internet Information Services (IIS) Manager and checking out the new website, as shown in Figure 8.53.

FIGURE 8.53
The new IIS Web Site

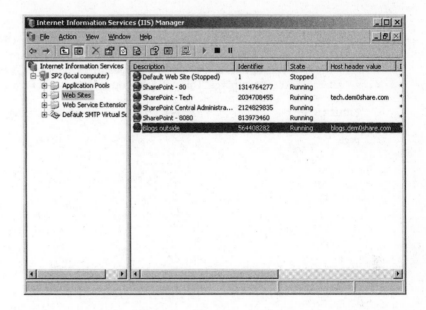

Go to the Properties of this new IIS Web Site to verify that it is listening on port 80. The Advanced button will show the expected host header. Click the Home Directory tab to see that it is using the same application pool as the original IIS Web Site (SharePoint-8080). This means all traffic bound for this new IIS Web Site will be directed to the same content database as traffic bound for the original SharePoint-8080 Web Site. The SharePoint-8080 Application Pool will list the new Web Site's Root and layout paths, as shown in Figure 8.54.

FIGURE 8.54
Application Pool changes

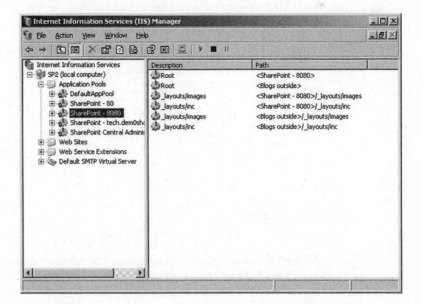

CHANGES TO ALTERNATE ACCESS MAPPINGS

Let's take a look at what SharePoint shows with this new public URL. Go to Central Administration's Operations page because Alternate Access Mappings, although specifically for addressing web applications, effect the whole farm. Under the Global Configuration section, click Alternate access mappings. This will take you to the page in Figure 8.55.

FIGURE 8.55
The Alternate Access Mappings page

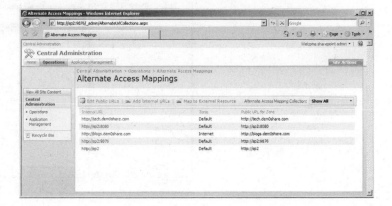

This page lists all the current internal URLs and public URLs on the SharePoint server. Any incoming request is examined to see if it matches one of the internal URLs. If it does, the server responds with the path shown in the corresponding public URL. If the request doesn't match an internal URL, the server responds with the public URL of the default zone on whatever port the request was received on.

If you click the View menu (default view of this list is Show All), you can filter the view to display the mappings for a particular web application. Let's look at the original web application we extended (mine is `http://sp2:8080`), as shown in Figure 8.56.

FIGURE 8.56
The `http://sp2:8080` URLs

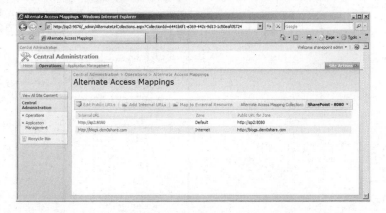

The original web application now has two alternate access mappings, one for the default zone and one for the Internet zone. Both mappings have an internal URL and a public URL. Therefore, any request sent to the server as `http://blogs.dem0share.com` in my example will come back to the requester's browser showing `http://blogs.dem0share.com` in the Address bar and for all the paths and links on the page—which means they'll work fine through the firewall.

POLICIES FOR ZONES

You'll also spot a change to SharePoint in Central Administration, on the Application Management page, in the Policy for Web Application link. Policy for Web Application is well named (although a bit vague). It was meant to allow farm administrators to create user policies, manage anonymous access, and manage permissions that are above and beyond the permissions to be applied for normal users of the site collections. When you add a new user to the policy for the web application, the new zone will appear in the dropdown menu, as shown in the graphic below, so you can apply policies to it separately. For much more about adding users to the policy, see Chapter 10, "Central Administration: Application Management."

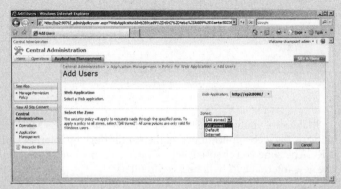

You can also see the effects of zones on the Authentication Providers page (also accessed from the Application Management page). It's here that Zones come into their own, as you can change authentication settings for a particular zone (always representing an extended web application in this case).

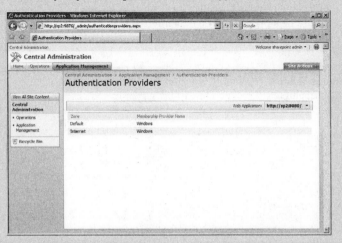

CREATING A NEW INTERNAL URL

Although you can have only five public URLs for a web application (one for each zone), it's possible to have several internal URLs for each public URL. Remember that internal URLs are the addresses that SharePoint responds to for a particular web application, and public URLs are what are returned to populate the address bar of the client's browser. To create a new internal URL for a public URL, go to Central Administration's Operations page, click Alternate Access Mappings to get back to the Alternate Access Mappings page. Click the Add Internal URLs link on the Action bar. This will take you to the page shown in Figure 8.57.

FIGURE 8.57
Create a new
Internal URL

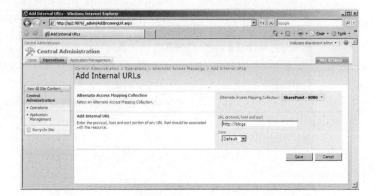

Make sure you've chosen the correct Alternate Access Mapping Collection, which is the same thing as the web application, and then enter the new internal URL and chose the zone for this URL. The zone you choose needs to have a corresponding public URL (if you don't specify one, the new internal URL will be used to fill it).

My example uses a new internal URL called `http://blogs` for the default zone. As such, internal users who previously had to enter `http://sp2:8080` will only need to enter **blogs** (which is easier for them to remember) into their web browser to go to the Personal Blogs Site Collection. When they get there, it'll kick back the default zone's public URL of `http://sp2:8080`, which is fine because they can resolve that URL (if they were outside the firewall, this would be a problem). The new internal URL is displayed on the Alternate Access Mappings page (see Figure 8.58).

FIGURE 8.58
The new internal
URL mappings

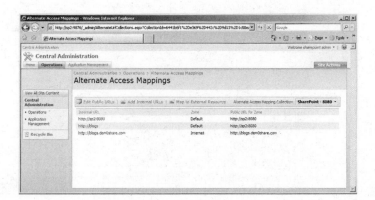

Just as you do with all URLs, you need to make sure new internal URLs exist in DNS and point to the server.

MANUALLY ADDING A PUBLIC URL

You can also edit public URLs from the Alternate Access Mapping page. For example, you can quickly add a new public URL for an unused zone (or change the URL for an existing zone) and save the changes. The public URL will be added to the web application and automatically generate a new internal URL to match. For example, you could use the URL `http://blogserver/` as the Extranet zone for the web application `http://sp2:8080`. See Figure 8.59.

FIGURE 8.59
Editing a public URL

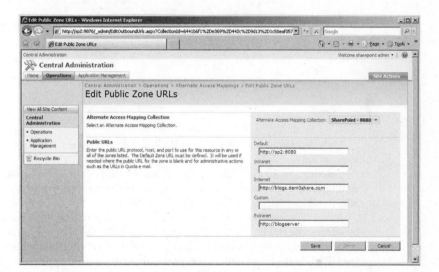

While this method will work for browsing the web application, it has one key difference from the full Extend a Web Application process: it doesn't create a new IIS Web Site for the new public URL. This means that there is no new security policy available for the URL, and no host header exists in IIS to direct traffic to the correct web application (SharePoint does the redirect on the backend). Although editing *existing* public URLs is fine if they are extended web applications, you really shouldn't create new public URLs this way. It simply doesn't allow you the flexibility of being able to enable unique authentication or policy settings for the URL because it doesn't have a corresponding Web Site in IIS.

REMOVING A PUBLIC URL (BY REMOVING AN EXTENDED WEB APPLICATION)

You could, conceiveably just delete the entry for a public URL, regardless of whether or not it is associated with an extended web application. But if you want to correctly remove an extended web application's public URL from a web application's mapping, you should use the Remove SharePoint from IIS Web Site link in Central Administration (under Application Management).

It either just removes the association of the web application with the IIS Web Site in SharePoint, or removes the Web Site altogether. This will also allow you to remove the public URL from the list in Alternate Access Mapping. See Figure 8.60.

FIGURE 8.60
Remove SharePoint
from the IIS Web Site

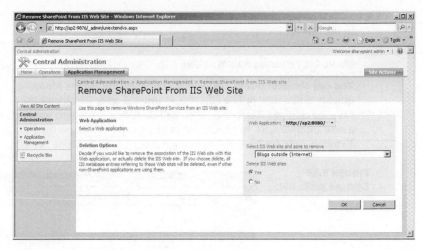

Make sure you select the correct IIS Web Site and zone to remove from the extended web application.

Deleting the IIS Web Site deletes, unsurprisingly, the Web Site, which removes any custom settings you might have—but it also keeps IIS nice and clean. If you chose not to delete the IIS Web Site, the IIS server places the Web Site into the stopped state; so it's still there, it's just not running.

Again it is possible to delete the public URL from within the Alternate Access Mapping page, by editing the Public URLs and simply clearing the field. However, doing so is not recommended because it makes no change to IIS. This leaves the website running, so it accepts connections for the URL (via the host header) and points them at the web application. In this case, because the public URL has been deleted, SharePoint serves the web pages with the default URL (for example, `http://sp2:8080`), but it doesn't stop service, it just doesn't return the former public URL.

So you've learned what a site collection is, how to create one and how to manage it, as well as what web applications are and their configuration. At this point you have covered how to use SharePoint from web parts to web applications. It's now time to move on to how to administer SharePoint, from Central Administration to Maintenance and Monitoring.

The Bottom Line

Create and customize a new site collection.   A new site collection has separate permissions, its own Recycle Bin, its own storage quota, and its own site collection galleries. You can change the regional settings and grant someone site administrator rights on a new site collection without compromising your existing sites.

Master It   Create a new site collection, apply a Site Quota template, and restrict the new site collection to 1GB.

Use managed paths.   SharePoint uses managed paths to tell IIS which paths in a URL are handled by SharePoint and are, therefore, *managed*. All other paths are considered *excluded*, and

IIS is free to use them with traditional websites. You can add your own managed paths, adjusting the URL of site collections.

By default, SharePoint site collections have two managed paths: the path (root), which is explicit, and the path /sites/, which is a wildcard path.

Master It Define the difference between an *explicit* managed path and a *wildcard* managed path.

Create a new web application. A new web application is fundamentally a new IIS Web Site. Using a new IIS Web Site allows you to change the port for accessing the web application, use a host header, and adjust the IIS-level authentication such as Anonymous Access. Web applications in addition to being a security boundary, are also a boundary for settings such as RSS, sending alerts, upload size limits, and blocked file types that effect all contained site collections. All SharePoint site collections must reside in a web application. At this level, serious changes can effect the way the site collections are accessed and controlled.

Master It Create a new web application using a host header, and set up two content databases, both limited to 10,000 sites.

Configure Anonymous Access. One of the main features of web applications is the ability to allow Anonymous Access to the site collections they contain. Anonymous Access can allow the site to be viewed without requiring a login while retaining all the needed permissions for authenticated users to add, edit, modify, or delete site content. Anonymous Access is enabled in two core steps: first by permitting anonymous access at the web-application level, and then by enabling anonymous access at the site-collection level.

Master It Someone else has allowed Anonymous Access on a web application, and you're configuring your site collection. You want anonymous users to view only the Status list and nothing else. How do you configure the site?

Set different zones for different access. Each web application can support up to five public URLs that it displays in the Address bar and on the page in links and paths. Four of the public URLs can be used for manually entered alternate web addresses or created by extending the web application to a new IIS Web Site, providing a new URL (including a new port if desired), and applying different authentication policies to the same site. For example, one site collection within the local network can permit Anonymous Access, but authentication can be required for anyone accessing the site through the Internet public URL. The five public URLs are identified by their *zone*, and additional internal URLs can be mapped to each zone.

Master It Extend a web application to a new IIS website with a port of 18080, and set it to the Extranet zone.

Part III

Administering Windows SharePoint Services 3.0

Chapter 9

Central Administration: Operations

This chapter is intended to give you a reference point for all of those settings links on the Central Administration site. Chances are good that you will never use a few of them, but it's nice to know what they are, just in case. Many of these settings were covered extensively in previous chapters (they will be pointed out to you), but some haven't, so this chapter will pull them all together in one spot.

In this chapter, you'll learn how to:

- Understand Central Administration's organization
- Use the settings on the Operations page
- Manage Solutions and Features
- Set the Server Farm's default database
- Determine where to stop and start farm services
- Change a web application's service account

Central Administration Organization

As you know, SharePoint creates an Administrative web application during installation. All SharePoint administration that applies to the farm as a whole, or web applications and site collections in particular, are configured in this application.

This administrative web application is called Central Administration. When this web application is created, it is assigned a unique port number for security reasons; this helps obscure the site from casual browsers. Central Administration also contains one top-level site in its only site collection.

To access Central Administration, simply open a browser (preferably Internet Explorer 6 or higher), enter the SharePoint server address that is hosting the Central Administration site (it is often the first SharePoint server on a farm if you are not using a standalone server), and then add the port number. My example uses `http://sp2:9876`. (As you may remember, when we installed this SharePoint server in Chapter 2, that port number was chosen because it was easy to remember.) This means that you can access the Central Administration site from any machine with a browser on your network, rather than being limited to accessing it only from the SharePoint server. However, if you want to access the Central Administration site from the server where you installed SharePoint, you can use the shortcut that SharePoint adds to the Administrative Tools menu (Start ➤ Administrative Tools ➤ SharePoint 3.0 Central Administration). That shortcut just opens the browser to the site's address, such as `http://sp2: 9876` (the same address my example just used). Regardless, the shortcut is useful if you have forgotten the port number for the site.

When you install SharePoint, the Central Administration site is created with your setup account as the only owner. However, unlike any other site collection, Central Administration also allows, by default, the built-in Administrators group to also log in (in case of emergency, such as when the farm administrator's password is forgotten). This means that if you are a domain administrator, the local server's administrator, or using the setup account, you can log in to Central Administration. My example, uses the setup account, `dem0tek\setupacct`, to log in, as you'll see on the welcome menu on the home page of the site.

WHY SETUP ACCOUNT?

Keep in mind that I am using the setup account to log in for simplicity's sake, this is the one account I know you can use to log in, otherwise SharePoint wouldn't be installed. Otherwise, under normal circumstances, you should never use the SharePoint setup account for anything at all but installing and configuring SharePoint. I've mentioned it elsewhere, but it bears repeating.

It is dead easy to add Farm Administrators, just go to the Update farm administrator's group setting on the Operations page (it's mentioned a little later in the chapter). The setting will take you to the People and Groups: Farm Administrators page, where you can click New and add as many users from Active Directory to the group as you'd like. This will ensure that you will be logging in with a different account next time. Whatever account (or accounts) you choose, be sure that they are also either local administrators on the SharePoint servers or domain admins. Otherwise, as farm administrators, they will not be able to configure settings that affect the underlying OS or modify IIS. Those settings will simply be missing from the pages for them in Central Administration.

In Figure 9.1, you can see that the site has all of the standard interface features. At the top left of the page are the global breadcrumb indicating that you are at the top site for this site collection. Beneath that are the site title and the Top Link bar indicating that Central Administration has essentially three main pages: Home, Operations, and Application Management. Although you might think they are sites because of their links on the Top Link bar, they are not. At the top right are the Welcome menu and the Help button.

NO SEARCH FOR CENTRAL ADMINISTRATION

There is absolutely no Search. That's right. No searching is available for this site despite the fact that it has its own content database, as you've seen in previous chapters. This is probably due to the fact that Central Administration is primarily composed of Settings pages, which are generally never searchable. Beneath the area where the Search field should be is the ubiquitous Site Actions menu.

FIGURE 9.1
The Central
Administration home
page

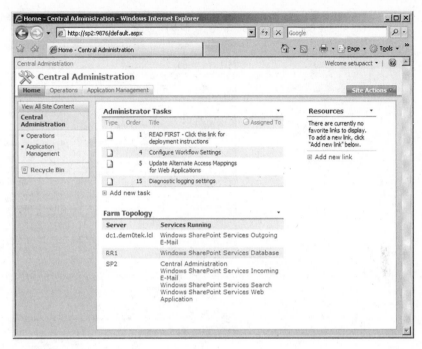

FIGURE 9.1

The Central Administration home page

In the content area of the page are the Web Part zones with three web parts specific for Central Administration. Alone in the right Web Part zone is the Links List View web part, which has been renamed *Resources*. As you know, hyperlink fields can be used to open anything, including file shares, Word documents, and links to websites. This web part gives the administrators to add a few additional resources that might be appropriate for working on SharePoint (such as a link to the Microsoft SharePoint sites, or the TechNet Windows SharePoint Services 3.0 technical library online).

The Administrator Tasks and Farm Topology web parts are in the left Web Part zone of the home page. The Administrator Tasks web part is actually the Administrator Tasks List View web part. That list is pre-populated with likely configuration task list items when Central Administration is created. The Farm Topology web part is a List View web part of the Servers in farm list (accessed, usually, from the Operations page). Farm Topology lets you know at a glance what servers SharePoint is aware of on the network and what it thinks is handling required services. This web part comes in handy when you are trying to figure out what server is hosting the Central Administration pages, managing Search, or handling incoming email.

The Quick Launch bar is on the left side of the Web Part zones of the Central Administration home page. It echoes the Top Link bar with links to the Central Administration home page, Operations, and Application Management pages. At the top of the Quick Launch is the View All Site Content page. This is where you can really see what the site can do. If you click on the View All Site Content link, you'll see what lists, libraries, and sites Central Administration holds.

FIGURE 9.2
The All Site Content page
for Central
Administration

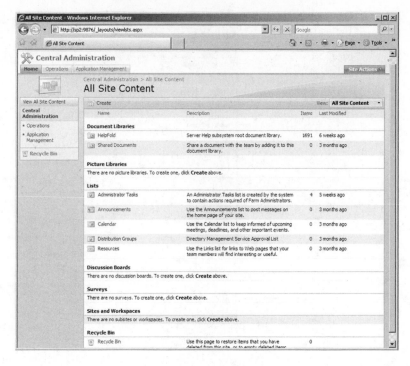

In Figure 9.2, you can see that Central Administration has the Help files in a document library (see Chapter 2, "Installation" for more about those help collections), and it has a shared document library as well. It also has the Administrator Tasks list (which you can tell by the description is just a default Tasks list), a Calendar list, Announcements, the Links list called Resources, and a Distribution Groups list if you choose to enable Directory Management Services (see Chapter 15, "Advanced Installation and Configuration"). Note that Central Administration has no subsites, despite the fact that the Top Link bar has links.

You may be tempted to use Central Administration as a SharePoint site for administrators, but remember—and never forget—that you can't recover this site, as you can any other SharePoint site. Because it is so closely tied to the configuration database, Microsoft treats it differently. Although it can be backed up using SharePoint Backup and Restore, you can't restore it from backup. You have to reinstall it from scratch so you'll have a completely fresh configuration database on which to rebuild. This is why you should create a unique web application for the SharePoint administrators; so you can have calendars, discussions, document libraries, wikis, and the like to foster communication between administrators and leave Central Administration for configuration settings only.

DOCUMENT THE SETTINGS

Always, always, always document the settings you make in Central Administration, as well as at the site collection, site, and even list level of SharePoint. Documentation never hurts when it comes to restoring SharePoint.

Obviously, SharePoint's Central Administration site contains three main pages. Home is a Web Part page, containing the Administrator Tasks, Farm Topology, and Resources web parts. You could add web parts for announcements, a calendar, or more. You could create more lists and you could use the Shared Documents Library, but keep in mind that this site is so closely tied to the configuration database for the server/server farm that it won't be easily recoverable in case of disaster.

IF YOU ABSOLUTELY, POSITIVELY HAVE TO

Your best bet to safeguard your data, if you succumb to the temptation of adding useful data to the site's lists and libraries, is to either backup the lists or libraries you use as templates with content, or make a subsite from Central Administration, put that information there, then backup that subsite independently (and regularly) at the command line. Then if the Central Administration site is lost, they can be restored after the site is rebuilt. It takes more effort, but the option is there.

The Operations page and Application Management pages are essentially Settings pages (like a Site Settings or List Settings page). This is why they are formatted to contain links to other pages laid out in categories. The other pages used by the site are specifically for configuring settings. The Operations settings are concerned mainly with things associated with SharePoint as a whole (either the SharePoint settings for the server if it is a standalone install, or the settings that affect the entire server farm). Therefore, a setting on the Operations page will likely affect every web application (and all site collections the web applications contain) for all of SharePoint.

The Application Management page contains settings that apply to creating, deleting, and managing web applications, as well as managing their site collections. Settings on the Application Management page generally affect only the web applications you specify, or possibly those of their site collections. Therefore, there is a certain logic to where configuration settings are as they pertain to SharePoint overall or a site collection or web application in particular. As a matter of fact, the fact that the settings are split logically between the two pages is quite an improvement over the previous version of SharePoint.

Keep in mind that certain settings available in Central Administration are only there as "hooks" to connect Windows SharePoint Services 3.0 with SharePoint Server 2007 (MOSS 2007). You need to be aware of them so they don't surprise you when they appear, even though you aren't doing anything with them. There are also settings that require third-party products that may not be available at this point or that vary so greatly that you'll need to check with your vendor to see how to integrate them with SharePoint.

Operations

To get to the Operations page, you can either click the Operations link in the Top Link bar or in the Quick Launch bar. Once on the page, take a second to familiarize yourself (see Figure 9.3).

The settings are divided into general categories, as described in detail in the following sections.

Topology and Services   This category covers the general services that are fundamental to SharePoint, such as incoming and outgoing email, and basic services, such as Search. It also has a link to let you see what servers are doing what for SharePoint.

FIGURE 9.3
The Operations page

Security Configuration   This category actually contains the Service Accounts settings. It also contains what Microsoft feels should be under the security heading, such as Information Rights Management (if you have an Information Rights Management (IRM) server handy on your domain), blocked file types (it can actually be set per web application), and antivirus protection (which is one of those settings dependent on third party software).

Logging and Reporting   This short category contains the settings for diagnostic logging and usage analysis processing. As you can see, SharePoint in its current form doesn't really have much in terms of logging, reporting, and general monitoring.

Global Configuration   By definition, all settings here are global; such as usage analysis, backup and restore jobs, alternate access mappings, as well as farm features and solutions. These settings affect all web applications and their site collections.

Backup and Restore   This category is pretty straightforward; it contains the settings for backing up and restoring SharePoint. You can back up and restore a single web application if you'd like; however, this category is considered a SharePoint server/server farm operation because you can back up and restore all of the web applications (their content databases) and the Search instances in a farm.

Data Configuration   This is another short category that contains the settings for specifying a default SQL database server, and Data Retrieval Service for SharePoint services, SOAP, XML, and OLEDB.

And now that you have a feel for what the general categories were intended to contain, let's go through them and briefly cover each setting. Many will be also covered elsewhere in the book, but it's still good, while we're here, to get an idea of what each setting is meant to do.

Topology and Services

The Topology and Services category is especially useful if someone has several web front-end SharePoint servers in a server farm. In that case, one server could host the Central Administration page, one could host Search, and the others could just be there as an extra web front end server for load balancing (which is the whole reason for having a farm). Given that scenario, if you had to take one of the servers offline, those services would need to be assigned to a different SharePoint server in the farm. Suddenly, it would become useful to know where your services are, what server is hosting them, and how to stop and or move a service, as well as how to remove a server from service in the SharePoint farm.

SERVERS IN FARM

This settings page lets you see what servers SharePoint believes are running which SharePoint required services. In Figure 9.4, you can see that my domain controller (DC1) is the outgoing email server, that RR1 is the SQL server (which is correct), and that SP2 is the only SharePoint server and is carrying all the SharePoint roles at this point. Notice also that it lists the name of the configuration database for this server farm (of which there is currently only one server), the version number for this version of SharePoint (nowhere in there is the number three), and the database server for the configuration database (which is useful if you have more than one SQL server on your network).

FIGURE 9.4
The Servers In Farm page

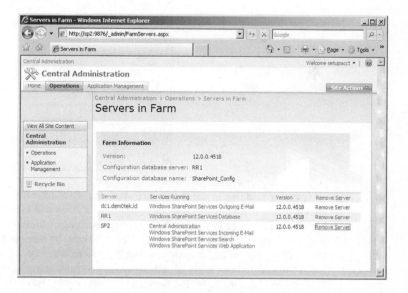

This page will help you figure out where the services are for the server farm. If a server has been decommissioned or has become irreparably damaged, you can remove it from the server farm here by clicking the Remove Server link. When you remove a server from the server farm, all it actually does is remove the server's entry in the configuration database for the farm, making whatever services it was responsible for available for reassignment to other servers (such as Central Administration or Search). What it does not do is uninstall SharePoint from the removed server, so if that server comes back online, it will not be recognized by the SharePoint server farm because it is no longer listed in the configuration database. You really should uninstall SharePoint on a server (if there is a chance that that server may ever be used on the network again) before you remove it from the server farm.

SERVICES ON SERVER

The Services On Server page is used to manage the services running on a particular SharePoint server directly. As you can see in Figure 9.5, the server services displayed by default belong to the first SharePoint server (which in my example is called SP2). We set up both these services (the Search service, as well as Incoming and Outgoing email) in Chapter 2. The Central Administration service was configured during install automatically, so the server can host the Central Administration site; as well as the Web Application service, so it can host SharePoint Web Applications.

FIGURE 9.5
The Services On Server page

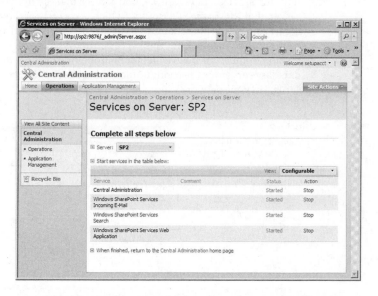

If you would like to see the services running on a different server in the farm topology, you can click the Server menu, and select Change Server. This will take you to a page where you can select the server you'd prefer (Figure 9.6). This type of page is used to change the selection of Settings pages throughout Central Administration. Options, be they servers, web applications, or alternate access mapping collections, are laid out as links to select on a background of alternating stripes (with the selected one highlighted in orange). Simply select your option and it will filter the Settings page accordingly. The Services on Server page is where you start and stop services on a particular server. For an example of this, check out Chapter 15, "Advanced Installation and Configuration," where you'll learn how to move or add the search service to a second server on the farm.

FIGURE 9.6
The Select Server page

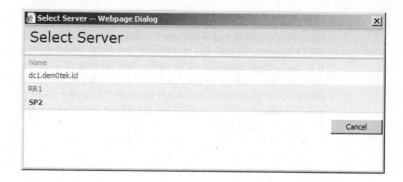

OUTGOING E-MAIL SETTINGS

SharePoint uses outgoing email to send notifications and alerts to users, site owners, and administrators. As you can see in Figure 9.7, you only need to let the server know the address of the outbound email server, the From address (which can be fictional), the Reply-to address (which has to be a real address, and one someone checks regularly), and the character set for the email (UTF-8 is a good default in many cases; use what is correct for the language of your network).

OUTGOING E-MAIL SETTINGS

The outgoing email settings for SharePoint can be set per web application. Therefore, if a web application needs a different character set for its region, it can override the global setting here.

FIGURE 9.7
The Outgoing E-Mail Settings page

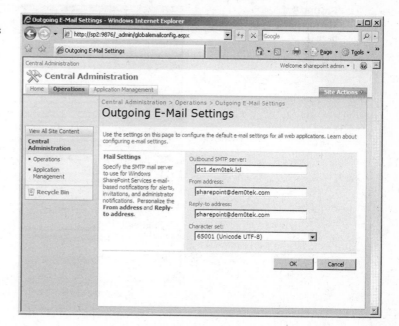

INCOMING E-MAIL SETTINGS

Incoming email is a new feature for this version of SharePoint. Using the defaults built into IIS's SMTP service, SharePoint can gather incoming email from a drop box on the local server and add it to the appropriate lists or libraries. Not all lists and libraries can handle incoming email, because the email fields must be mapped to the list's fields in order to be useful. You can create your own email event handlers if you want to make incoming email possible for your custom lists; however, you can simply reuse existing list templates that already support incoming email and modify them to suit your needs.

In addition to setting up incoming email, you also can enable something called Directory Management Service. This feature ties SharePoint in with Active Directory to allow SharePoint to create contact items and distribution list objects in a specific Organizational Unit (OU). It requires Exchange 2003 and Active Directory, of course. Contrary to popular belief, Directory Management Service does not have to be enabled for incoming email to work.

As you can see in Figure 9.8, to enable incoming email for the server farm, you simply choose Yes in the Enable Incoming E-Mail section. If you leave the Settings mode at Automatic, the SMTP default location for the email drop folder is used for incoming email. Use Advanced mode only if you are not using the SMTP default drop folder for incoming email on the server. Then in the E-Mail Server Display Address, enter the address of the server itself (which is the server's default) or the alias you would like to use for the server to receive email (see Chapter 2, "Installation"). In the last section, Safe E-Mail Servers, you can choose "Accept mail from all e-mail servers" or specify the address of those servers allowed to forward email to SharePoint. Email works perfectly fine without Directory Management Service. However, the incoming email service cannot run on a SharePoint server that is also hosting Exchange, because Exchange listens on the same port as the SMTP service that SharePoint uses, rendering the SMTP service useless.

FIGURE 9.8
The Incoming E-Mail Settings page

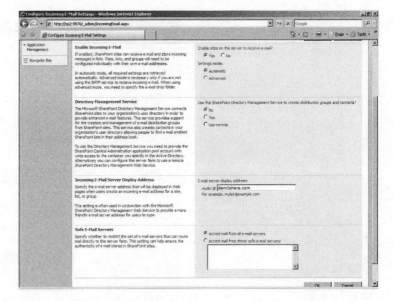

To see more about setting up incoming email, see Chapter 2, in the "Post Configuration Tasks" section.

APPROVE/REJECT DISTRIBUTION GROUPS

This settings page is useful if you have enabled Directory Management Services as part of the incoming email settings. (This service is not required to enable incoming email, and it requires Exchange 2003 somewhere on your network in order to function properly.) If you enable DMS, it will create an email contact item in an OU you specify for your incoming email-enabled lists and libraries, as well as make it possible to have distribution lists for groups. In order to keep groups from getting out of control, those distribution lists can be set for approval, requiring a Farm administrator (meaning any domain administrator, local administrator, or any account explicitly added as a farm administrator in Central Administration) to approve the new distribution list before the object is added to Active Directory.

Security Configuration Settings

The Security Configuration settings category contains settings that range from managing service accounts for web applications' application pools to managing members of the Farm Administrator's group. Most of these settings have global consequences, but keep in mind that the Blocked File types can be set per web application.

SERVICE ACCOUNTS

This is a very useful Operations setting link. It is the place to go when someone accidentally changes the password of the service account you are using for the content database access account (otherwise known here as the web application account).

If you click the Service Accounts link, it opens a page that gives you the opportunity to select the web application for which you'd like to change the service account. You can change the account if you need to, or keep the same account and change the password.

Unfortunately, you can change only the standard SharePoint web-application *service account* (the application pool account that accesses that web application's content databases) and no other service account on this page. Additional services are scarce for WSS unless you upgrade to MOSS. If you were to do so, the Service Accounts page is one of those that would significantly change. In other words, this is one of those settings that is meant to be used more extensively with MOSS.

As you can see in Figure 9.9, the Windows service and Web application pool dropdowns appear in the "Select the component to update" setting. Unfortunately the Windows service field has no available options with WSS; it apparently is there for MOSS only. To change the service account for one of your web application pools, you'll need to choose Web service first. In this example, there is only one option: Windows SharePoint Services Web Application Service, which all SharePoint web front end servers run. This service manages the SharePoint web applications, particularly their application pools. When the web application service is selected, the option to select a particular web application's application pool becomes available.

FIGURE 9.9
The Service Accounts page

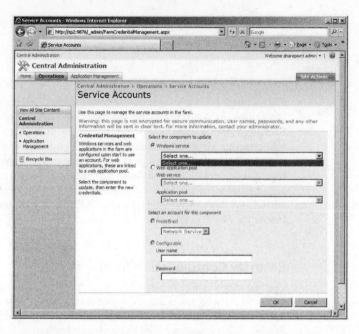

Once you choose the correct web application you'd like to update, you will be given the chance to either update the password of the existing account (see Figure 9.10) or type over the existing account with a new account (and of course enter the account's password). The Service Accounts page is also useful to see what SharePoint thinks the application pool service account is for a particular web application.

FIGURE 9.10
Changing the application pool
service account

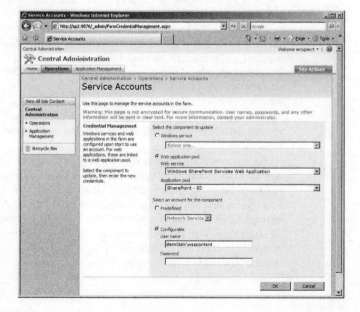

WHAT SHAREPOINT ACTUALLY MEANS . . .

When you perform a standalone server installation of SharePoint, it assigns the local network service account to most SharePoint services. SharePoint doesn't like the fact that the Central Administration pool and any other web application might have the same account. Therefore, in the Administrator Tasks web part on the home page of Central Administration, it propagates a list item with the cryptic title of Central Administration must have a unique application pool. Then it directs you to the Service Accounts page—but the joke is on you, because you can't actually change the service account for the Central Administration pool and make it unique there. When it dumps you on the Service Accounts page, SharePoint really means that you need to change the service accounts for your web applications so that they are not using the same account as Central Administration.

INFORMATION RIGHTS MANAGEMENT

SharePoint can be Information Rights Management (IRM) savvy using this setting. However, as you can see in Figure 9.11, you must have the Windows Rights Management (WRM) client (service pack 2 or higher) installed on the server, and you should have a Rights Management server on your network for SharePoint to confer with concerning information rights. In addition, each file type that is going to be protected with Information Rights Management must have a *protector* (a file that encrypts and decrypts a particular file format in a list or library that is IRM-enabled) installed on the server that will be IRM-enabled. Rights management is applied at a list or library level, not for each individual file. Files are encrypted and restricted based on the SharePoint user's rights to access and use the file in the list or library where it is stored. When a user downloads a file from an IRM-enabled list or library, it is restricted by their SharePoint user access rights for that library or list. Common restrictions include making the file read only and preventing the text from being copied, printed, or saved as a local copy. IRM is not really a SharePoint thing; it's a different server function altogether. See the online document about Information Rights Management for more information.

FIGURE 9.11

The Information Rights Management page

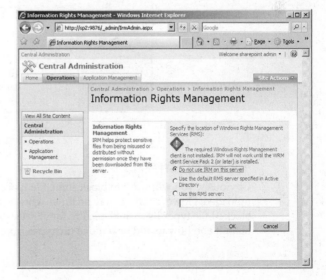

ANTIVIRUS

This setting requires that you have a SharePoint-aware antivirus program installed on *all* front-end web servers on the farm. Once that software is installed, you must use this setting in Central Administration to allow SharePoint to scan uploaded or downloaded documents, attempt to clean infected documents, or even allow infected documents to be downloaded (I am not sure why anyone would want to do that, but it's there). Using the antivirus software takes up resources on the SharePoint servers and can cause lagging and delays, so you can set the default timeout period (300 seconds, which is 5 minutes) to wait before the antivirus scan times out (Figure 9.12). You can also decide how many processor threads a virus scanner can use on the server to curtail the amount of processor resources a single scan can consume. The default is 5, but you can experiment with that to see what's right for you.

FIGURE 9.12
The Antivirus page

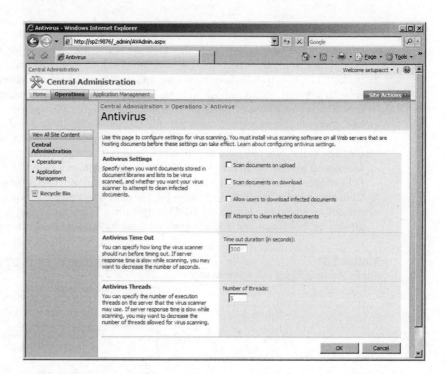

BLOCKED FILE TYPES

Obviously, you will want to block some file types, such as malicious executable files, from being uploaded. However, there may be times when your users will need to upload files that are on the blocked file types list. You'll need to familiarize yourself with what file types are blocked by default and how to add or remove file types from the list.

As you can see in Figure 9.13, this page is really simple. On the right, above the blocked file type list, you can see that blocked file types are applied by web application. This means that this setting can be applied to one web application and not effect the other web applications. The list of file types being blocked is just a multiple-line text box. To add a file extension to the list, simply scroll down to the last entry in the text box, put the cursor at the end of the entry, and press Enter. That will create a new line where you can type the extension you want to block—or you can go to whatever point in the list you'd like and add the extension there (alphanumerics only, no periods). To remove an extension, select the correct web application to apply the change to, then select the file extension in the list, and delete it.

FIGURE 9.13
The Blocked File Types page

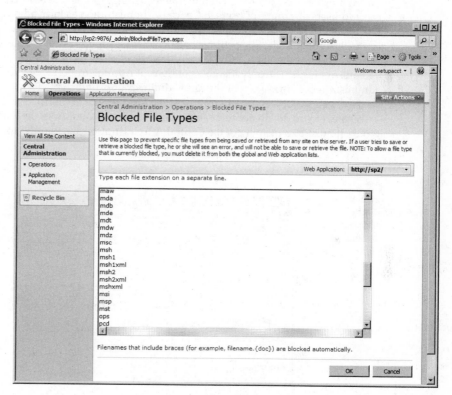

On the page there is some text saying that you need to delete an extension from the global list then the web application list to be able to upload an originally blocked file type. In this version of SharePoint there is no longer a global list of blocked file extensions, so removing them from the web application's listing in this interface does the trick.

For more information, see Chapter 8, "Site Collections and Web Applications."

EVADING BLOCKED FILES

As you can see, this is a pretty rudimentary way to block file uploads. It obviously only checks the file extension and not the file contents. This means that a clever user only needs to change a file's extension before they upload it to avoid the file being blocked.

UPDATE FARM ADMINISTRATOR'S GROUP

This settings link is very useful and definitely belongs on the Operations page. This is where you can add users or groups of users to Central Administration as farm administrators. The setting link takes you to the site's People And Groups page (see Figure 9.14) to add users or groups (instead of going to the Site Settings page). No other groups are available to use Central Administration other than Farm Administrators; in other words, there are no contributors, visitors, or guests. The only members of Central Administration are by default the built-in administrators of the server or the farm administrators (which by default contains the setup account, `setupacct` in my example, and the farm service account).

Whatever you do, do not remove the farm service account from the Farm Administrators group. It must be a member of the Central Administration site in order for Central Administration to work.

FIGURE 9.14
The Farm
Administrator's
People and
Groups page

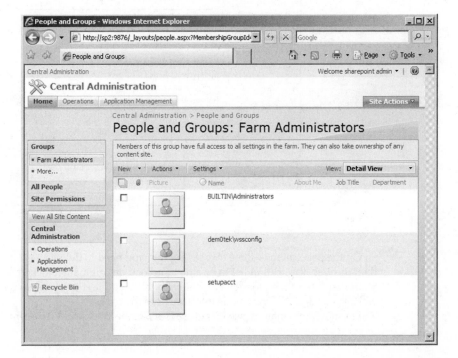

HELPGROUP

Interestingly, there is a group in Central Administration for accessing the Help Files Document Library called HelpGroup. Members of that group are the service account for the farm and the Content database account. I strongly suggest you don't mess with that group.

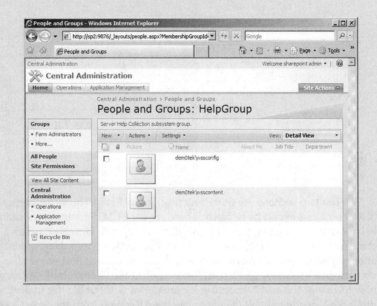

It goes without saying that you should not add all authenticated users to Central Administration as farm administrators, although the option is still there when you are on the Add Users page. See Chapter 11, "Users and Permissions," for more about adding users and user permissions. Also, keep in mind that Central Administration is at the top of its own site collection (in its own web application as well for added security), which means there can be users assigned as site collection administrators if necessary, but the likelihood that you would have someone do that who is not also a Farm Administrator is slim.

Logging and Reporting

This category is brief and covers the few tools that SharePoint offers in terms of logs and reports.

DIAGNOSTIC LOGGING

The Diagnostic Logging page (Figure 9.15) is an interesting one. The first two sections, Customer Experience Improvement Program and Error Reports, are designed to send Microsoft as much information from your use of SharePoint as possible.

FIGURE 9.15
The Diagnostic Logging page

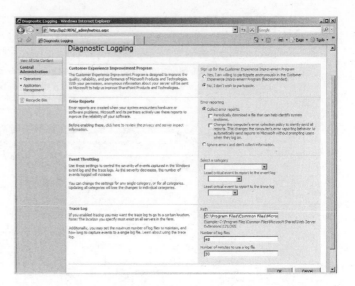

The last two sections are more practical. In the Event Throttling section, you can control how SharePoint logs events by severity. There are about 24 different event categories (see Figure 9.16) to choose from, or you can set an overall severity level. However, here's a trick: if you do want to change the severity of the events that an individual category uses, you have to click the OK button after you set it, and you have to do that after each change or it won't take. That's inconvenient, but you can check Chapter 13, "STSADM: A Look at the SharePoint Command-Line Tool," to learn how to change the event throttling for categories without having to deal with the GUI's limitations. Further, if you decide to use the All option from the Select a category setting, it will overwrite any of the individual settings you made.

FIGURE 9.16
The Event Throttling categories

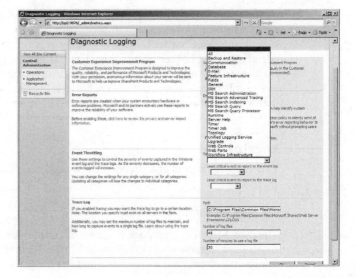

If you are sick of having the application log of the Event Viewer overrun with idle SharePoint event chatter, you can throttle the kinds of entries that show up there by eliminating the least critical events in order to lighten the log's load. Event types are listed from most critical to least critical, so you can chose the bottom-most type of event you would like reported to the event log. If you don't need to receive all of those informational events or audit successes that clog your application log, select the event above the level you want to throttle, which is Audit Failure in my example, to eliminate the Information And Audit Success events from the event log (Figure 9.17).

FIGURE 9.17
The Audit levels to throttle

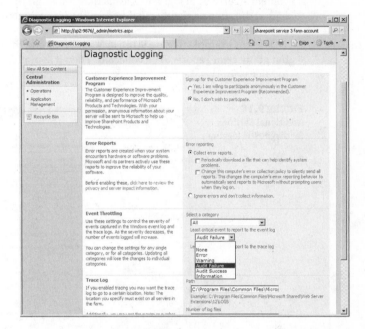

The severity levels by which you can throttle your events are the basic event types for the logs; such as Error, Warning, Audit Failure, etc. They are displayed in most-critical to least-critical order.

Trace logs report what the application is doing, and are most often used by developers. You can throttle the trace logs by Unexpected, Monitorable, High, Medium, and Verbose; they also appear in most- to least-critical order.

TRACE LOGS AND DIAGNOSTIC LOGS

Keep in mind that the trace logs (located in %Program Files%\Common files\Microsoft Shared\web server extension\12\LOGS) can take up 40 MB very quickly on a single, nearly inactive server. For this reason, the trace logs can be moved to a different location, which must be the same on all web front-end servers. Also note that if you move the trace logs, the PSCDiagnostics logs that are created whenever Central Administration is opened will also go along. This is part of what adds to the weight of the trace logs' folder. Make certain that the location for the logs has the same permissions as the previous location so the necessary SharePoint services can still access it. (WSS_ADMIN_WPG is the local group needed to generate those reports.)

Trace logs are created in real time, and by default, a new log is started evey 30 minutes. Also by default, 96 logs are in the folder at any given time. (Together that is about two days' worth of data.) This is one of the reasons they take up so much space. The trace logs are created, written for the expected duration, saved, and then a new one is created and filled with the next duration's worth of data, saved, and so on. When the limit of logs is reached, the oldest one is deleted and the newest is created to keep the maximum number. These logs can be storage hogs, which is why you can limit the number of trace logs that can be created and the duration (and therefore approximate content size) of each log. This means that, although the default is 96, you can create fewer logs of a higher duration or simply cut down on the logs altogether—if you are not worried about missing something.

For this example (Figure 9.18), let's avoid joining the customer experience improvement club but allow error reports to be collected. Then if something crashes we'll be asked to send the report to Microsoft.

FIGURE 9.18
Additional Settings
for diagnostic logging

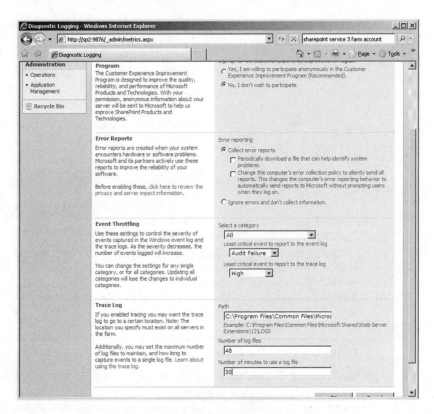

For Event Throttling, let's set All categories to log only the events that are bad news by setting the least critical event to Audit Failure. (Avoiding Audit Success and Information.) For the trace logs, set the least-critical event to High and avoid Verbose and Medium. That should help a little bit to keep the trace logs smaller in size.

In the Trace Log section, I am going to keep the trace logs in their default location. This will be fine for me right now; at least I know where it is. For number of logs, it's a toss-up. Some people prefer fewer larger files, some prefer a lot of smaller files, some people like having two days' worth of trace logs at any given time, and others prefer one day's worth because chances are good that they'll know something is wrong well within that 24-hour time limit. How you handle your trace logs is up to you, but my example uses 48 logs, each filled with 30 minutes' worth of data, so the logs will always span the most-recent 24 hours).

USAGE ANALYSIS PROCESSING

This is one of those settings that has system-wide significance. On the Usage Analysis Processing page, you make it possible to track the usage reports for sites and site collections throughout the SharePoint server farm. Usage Analysis Processing is definitely a global setting.

Some of the things you need to realize about Usage Analysis Processing:

◆ Usage analysis processing is a two-step process. It stores logs and then it analyzes them, taking up considerable resources in the process.

◆ It takes about 200 bytes to record a hit on a web page. That means that if your site gets a million hits a day, your log could be 200MB for 24 hours.

◆ To process a log, SharePoint reads it all into RAM until it is done with it. At that time, the first line of the log is amended with an ampersand (&) to indicate that it has been processed. This means if a log is 200MB, then 200MB of RAM is used for the task during usage analysis processing. This is why it might behoove you to use more than one log per day for usage analysis processing. One log per day is the default: however, depending on your environment, it may make sense to have more. Also, because of the stress on the server's resources, it's a good idea to schedule the process during a low usage time for your servers. It's also not a bad idea to make the window of time in which processing should occur large enough for SharePoint to finish analyzing the logs.

◆ Usage Analysis does not seem to delete logs in a cycle any less than 31 days for daily logs. It takes much longer for monthly logs, about 31 months. If you don't need usage data that is that historical, feel free to delete the older logs.

◆ Usage Analysis generally needs to wait to collect its first 24 hours of data, then it will process what it finds for the first day's analysis. If a site or site collection hasn't had activity in that time, they will not be able to display any data in the site's usage report. A site will also report that it has no usage data if it has not had any activity within the last 31 days.

◆ If you move the usage analysis logs (which makes sense if your sites get a lot of traffic and therefore generate large usage logs), you must make certain that you give the local server group WSS_ADMIN_WPG read, write, and modify access to the location you are moving them to. Their default location is in the same Logs folder as the diagnostic logs (%Program Files%\Common files\Microsoft Shared\web server extension\ 12\LOGS).

As you can see in Figure 9.19, both logging and processing are enabled. Yes, you can just create the logs without processing them if you are so inclined. I opted for 4 logs to be created a day (the default is 6). They are broken up into 6-hour chunks in my example. The usage analysis processing schedule is set to start at 1:00 A.M. and end at 3:00 A.M. daily in my example (the default is from 1:00 A.M to 2:00 A.M), giving it plenty of time to process those logs.

FIGURE 9.19
The Usage Analysis
Processing page

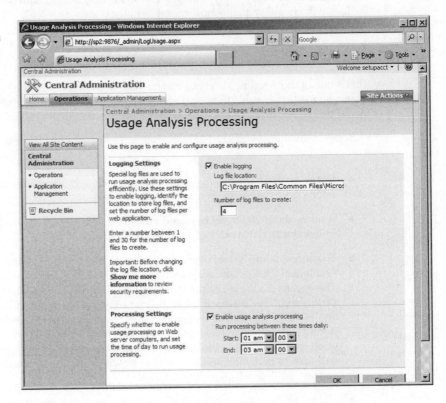

As you know if you read Chapter 7, "Sites, Subsites, and Workspaces," your sites and site collections can generate usage reports if you enable Usage Analysis Processing at the server farm level. Usage reports are a convenient way to see which sites are being used frequently and which are not being used, so you can determine which sites are obsolete and subject to deletion and which need to be watched in case utilization increases, bumping the edges of that site collection's storage quota. To get to the Site Usage Report for a site, simply go to that site's settings under the Site Action menu. The Site Settings page has a link for the Site Usage Report under the Site Administration category. The Site Usage Report can display usage data in a daily or monthly; summary, filtered by OS, Browser, User, Page, and even Referrer URL. The Referrer URL is the URL that referred the visitor to the site. In Figure 9.20, you can see the monthly summary page usage report for the Company site. The top-level site also has an added Usage Summary that summarizes the activity for a site collection based on the data gathered by Usage Analysis.

FIGURE 9.20
The Site Usage
Report page

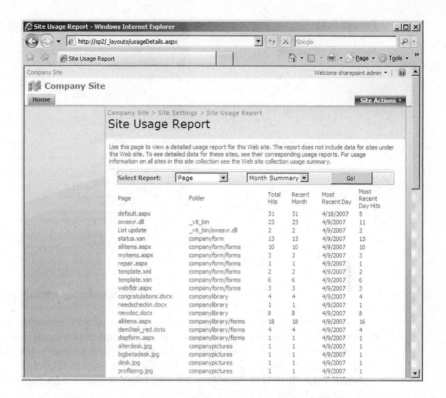

Global Configuration

It's in this section that you manage global settings, such as troubleshooting Timer job tasks that SharePoint is supposed to be doing and managing the web address (or addresses if it suits your fancy) of your web applications. It's also the only place to manage the SharePoint features and solutions that you might install for use by your entire SharePoint farm.

TIMER JOB STATUS

SharePoint uses the Timer service to run tasks that may be scheduled, such as site deletion notification, incoming email checking, and even "one-time" jobs, such as backup or restore. When SharePoint starts a job, that job is added to the list of job titles as the server prepares to begin. This list is where you can see if a job has initialized, what progress it has had, and whether (when done) it has succeeded or failed.

Figure 9.21 illustrates the Timer Job Status page with a backup job initializing. As you can see, several timed tasks are listed there, including the CEIP (Customer Experience Improvement Program) data collection. That job is not supposed to send data if you do not allow it; however, it has succeeded in collecting the data anyway. Do not be surprised if you see some timer jobs that you have not enabled, such as disk quotas or usage analysis. They are built into SharePoint and are ready to complete their tasks as soon as you enable them.

FIGURE 9.21
The Timer Job Status page with a
backup job initializing

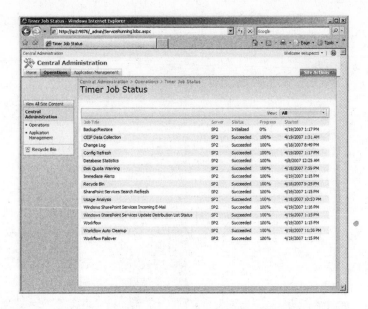

This page has multiple views; the default view, as with any other list, is the All view. However, you can limit it by web application or even the kind of service. If you click on the View menu and choose one of the other options (besides All), you will probably get a blank list until you choose the web application or service type by which you want to filter. In Figure 9.22, the Timer Job Status list is filtered to show only the jobs being performed by the SharePoint Timer Service. This is just an example, but it illustrates how you can filter the list by web application or service, which should help you learn what job is associated with what. This can give you an idea of what jobs might fail in a given scenario. Understand that timer jobs can be created as part of a solution or feature that you might have added to the farm, increasing the number of jobs in the status list. This also would give you good reason to considering filtering your view of the jobs to save time.

FIGURE 9.22
The filtered Timer Job Status page

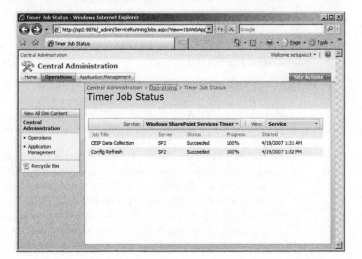

If you do have a job that doesn't seem to behave properly, you can see if that job has succeeded or failed here. Then you can check the trace logs to find any errors related to the job, and/or you can go to the Timer Job Definitions page.

TIMER JOB DEFINITIONS

The Timer Job Definitions page is a less passive report of which timer jobs are available for SharePoint. This page lists only the title of each job, the web application for each timer job, and each job's schedule type (Figure 9.23). If no specific web application is associated with the job, the web application will be N/A, especially if the job is global. This page also has filtered views for the timer jobs under the View menu. Like the Timer Job Status page, you can filter the view by web application or service.

FIGURE 9.23

The Timer Job Definitions page

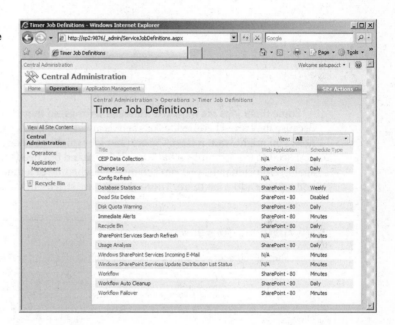

The Timer Job Definitions page is not quite as passive as the status page because each timer job title is a link to an Edit Timer Job page where you can change that job's title, and either delete or disable the job (Figure 9.24).

EXECADMSVCJOBS

You can make some changes to the properties of several of the timer jobs using STSADM, as well as force all administrative service jobs to execute (should one be lagging). For more information about doing that, you might also want to check out the STSADM operation `execadmsvcjobs`.

FIGURE 9.24
The Edit Timer Job page

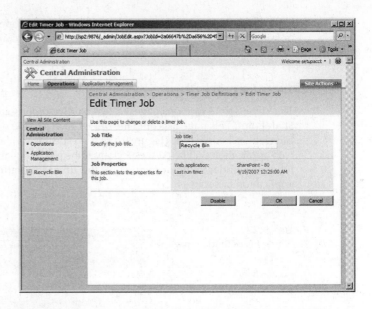

Some timer jobs are required for some settings, so they can only be disabled and not deleted. Because they are scheduled tasks, there is always the chance that although you don't want it now, you might want it later. Other timer jobs might be one-time jobs that you can delete if you need to (for example, a backup job that failed but needs to be deleted before you can try again). Unfortunately, you can't change the schedule of a timer job in the Edit Timer Job interface, nor can you add a job there. Those changes are strictly in the domain of the developer.

IF A TIMER JOB GOES BAD

What should you do if you start a timer job, such as a backup, and it fails?

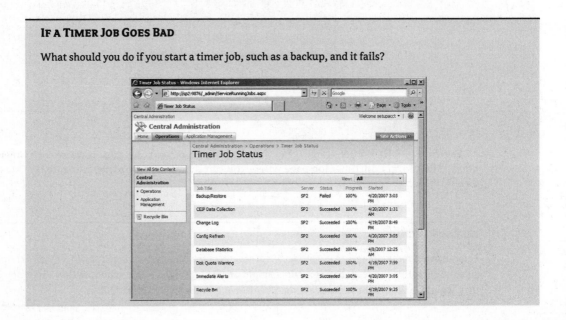

If you simply try to do the task again, you will get an error because the job failed and you won't be able to do it again until it has been removed. When a timer job fails, it remains in the queue, so you will know what has happened. However, this procedure can be inconvenient.

If a timer job fails, go to the Timer Job Definitions page and select the title of the job that failed. This will give you the chance to delete the offending job and clear the failure from the definitions list so you can try again.

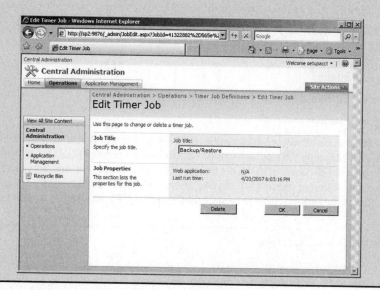

ALTERNATE ACCESS MAPPINGS

This settings link opens to a page that can be a little confusing (Figure 9.25). Alternate access mappings are also extensively used in Chapter 8.

FIGURE 9.25
The Alternate Access Mappings page

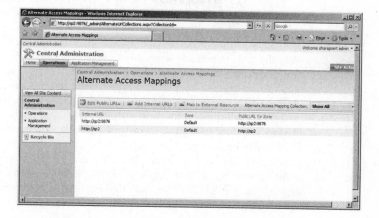

Alternate access mappings are generally associated with web applications. Here's a basic idea of how it works:

Internal URL   A URL that the SharePoint server can accept to give users access to a particular web application.

Public URL   A URL that the SharePoint server returns to the user when she accesses the server using a particular Internal URL.

Public URLs are associated with web applications and come in five flavors (called zones):

◆ Default (Don't change this because it is the real address of the web application.)

◆ Intranet

◆ Internet

◆ Custom

◆ Extranet

This means that each web application—or as SharePoint calls them in this instance, Alternate Access Mapping Collection—can have four unique public URLs.

Internal URLs are what users use to access the SharePoint site. You can map an internal URL to return a different public URL, or you can have them both match. Most people create a new public URL for the server with a corresponding internal URL for users to access the server.

PUBLIC URLS IN ACTION

You've probably seen public URLs in action when you type in a site address, such as **www.microsoft.com**, and get to the page you want, but the address in the address bar is actually `js1.windows.microsoft.com`. The address you typed was essentially an internal URL, but that URL had a public URL of `js1.windows.microsoft.com`.

Those are the fundamentals of internal and public URLs. Of course, SharePoint takes that simple concept and makes it more complicated, but that's the general gist.

Figure 9.25 shows a simple example with just the Central Administration site's address and the main SharePoint-80 site. On the top right of the list is the View menu (now called the Alternate Access Mapping Collection). By default, this menu is set to display all possible internal URLs of all web applications and external mapped resources. These addresses in my example are simply the defaults and are nothing fancy. My Central Administration address is `http://sp2:9876`, and my SharePoint-80 web application's address is `http://sp2`. Because only the defaults are shown, you can see that the internal and public URLs are the same. That's kind of the point of the default public URL; it at least returns the original internal URL's address to the user.

Like the View menu for most settings pages, you can filter the list by clicking the Alternate Access Mapping Collection menu and selecting Change Alternate Access Mapping Collection. That will open a separate window in which you can select the web application for which you want to see the URLs (Figure 9.26). If you choose a particular web application to work with (my example uses SharePoint-80), it will limit the view of the alternate access mappings only to that web application's URLs. You may find it easier to work with the internal and public URLs of each web application individually.

FIGURE 9.26
Select an Alternate Access Mapping
Collection page

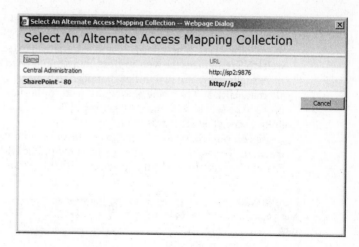

To see what public URLs that web application is using, click Edit Public URLs in the Action bar. It will open the Edit Public Zone URLs page (see Figure 9.27). As you can see, there is only an entry for the default URL for the web application itself, and the other four zones are empty. Feel free to cancel out of the page.

FIGURE 9.27
The default public URL for the
SharePoint-80 web application

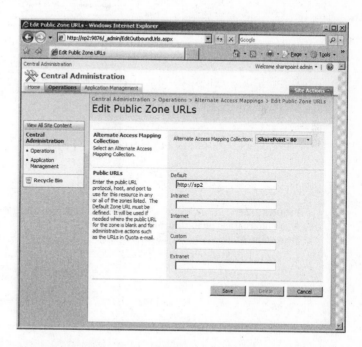

Back on the Alternate Access Mappings page itself, it now makes sense that the internal URL has a default-zone public URL that is the same thing. Throughout this book, this is why the same address was returned when the URL `http://sp2` was used to access the primary site collection for the SharePoint-80 web application.

What if you want that web application to respond to a different URL, such as an external URL instead of `http://sp2`? You will, of course, need DNS records for the new URL to resolve to the SharePoint server, both internally and externally if external access is needed. But regardless of how well DNS recognizes the web address, more things need to be done in SharePoint to get this to work.

Actually, there are two things that need to happen. First, the user needs to be able to enter that alternate URL and have the SharePoint web application accept it as valid. Next, that alternate URL needs to be sent back to the user as the public URL, so the search results use that public URL in the links it sends back to the user.

As you can tell, you will need to create a new, internal URL address and a new, public URL to match it. To make it easy, if you create a new public URL for the web application (Figure 9.28), SharePoint will also make it a new internal URL (Figure 9.29).

FIGURE 9.28
Add a new public URL to the Internet zone

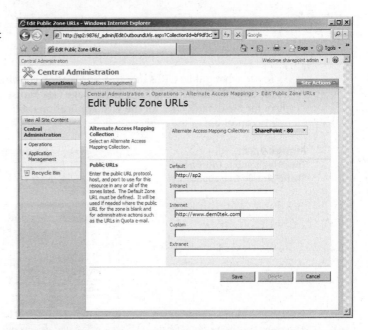

FIGURE 9.29
A new internal and public URL for SharePoint-80

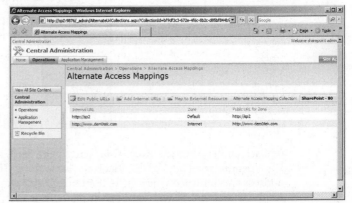

Because SharePoint sees that URL as a valid URL for the web application, it works when you use it in a browser—assuming that DNS is set up properly (Figure 9.30).

FIGURE 9.30
The SharePoint site accessed using a new internal URL

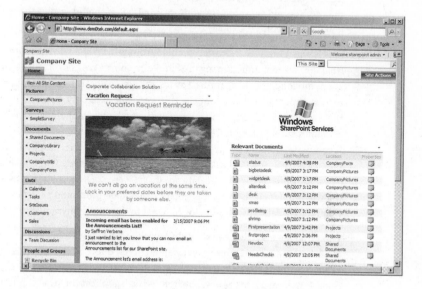

YOU CAN'T JUST MASK A PORT NUMBER WITH A PRETTY URL

Now that you have an understanding of Alternate Access Mapping you might be tempted to get creative with it, and when you do it may seem to work strangely.

The text example shows the easy way to give external users access to the SharePoint server from outside the office. Users coming in from the Internet cannot use `http://sp2` to access the server, but they can use `http://www.dem0tek.com`. That means the web application responds to the URL request because both the default `http://sp2` and the public URL `http://www.dem0tek.com` are meant to be captured using port 80.

To be clear, IIS captures HTTP requests that are sent to a server by listening on the correct ports for its Web Sites. If you have a SharePoint web application on port 80, as in my example, that web application's security settings affect what IIS does with the request sent to that port. All HTTP requests, unless they specify the port in the URL, always go to port 80 by default. Therefore, if the web application on port 80 requires Windows authentication, the user's request will prompt for a login. In my example, we just wanted to get to that web application with an alternate URL. So the alternate address works perfectly, as expected.

But a problem can come up if you take that concept a bit further and have a web application that uses a unique port to identify itself, but try to use Alternate Access Mapping to associate a public URL (which will get a matching internal URL) with it that doesn't use the port number in its address.

Say you wanted users to be able to access **http://sp2:8080** by using an alternate address, such as **www.dem0tek.com**. You could be tempted to create a public URL of **www.dem0tek.com** to map to http://sp2:8080. That public URL would create a corresponding internal URL so users could type in the address; and as long as the address is in DNS, it should resolve to the mapped web application—and it will, eventually.

This is when the authentication problem comes in. When you first enter the URL www.dem0tek.com (that, as you remember, maps in SharePoint to http://sp2:8080 in this example, which is set for anonymous access), it is captured by IIS. IIS, which doesn't really care about SharePoint's fancy alternate access mappings, will see that the URL does not explicitly specify a port. Therefore, IIS will send it to the web application listening on *port 80* (in our example that would be http://sp2), which requires Windows authentication. The user will see a login prompt and have to log in to port 80. When the login is complete, the web application will then see that the URL the client was using is not mapped its own public URL list, it will check the Alternate access mappings list, and will pass the client request to the correct address (accessing the data on http://sp2:8080). At that time, the user will be able to access the site anonymously (which is good or they'd be prompted to log in again). Regardless, they will be frustrated because they had to log in to get to the site anonymously.

What that means is that you shouldn't mask a web application's URL that specifies a port with a URL that doesn't (there is some trickery you can do in IIS, but that's not the point). It means you should use host headers from the start if you don't want the users to remember port numbers. This is especially, critically, important if you want the new or extended web application to have different security requirements than the one listening on port 80.

As you know if you've been through Chapter 8, there is something else you can do with the public URLs. When you extend a web application, you are really creating a new IIS Web Site that uses the same application pool account and content database of an existing web application. That web application's URL is considered a public URL (or *zone*) of the existing web application. (That's why public URLs are also referred to as zones.) Because two IIS Web Sites point to the same content, the second or extended web application is not considered a full-fledged web application in its own right, and it is instead subordinate to the first web application. In SharePoint, it is indicated as one of the public URLs of the main web application, as if it were just an alternate address for a real web application– which it is. That means that you can fill in the fields of a web application's public URLs manually, or if you extend that web application, you can choose which Public URL zone that that extended web application's address would fill.

WHEN IS A ZONE NOT REALLY A ZONE?

Primarily, public URLs were meant to be used by extended web applications. SharePoint expects you to create extended web applications so you can associate a public URL and its zone to particular IIS security settings—like a particular kind of authentication (forms-based, or Kerberos for example), anonymous access, or SSL.

This is why, when you add a public URL manually to a zone field, it doesn't show up as a zone to be managed in the Authentication Provider page or Policy For Web Application page. Because only websites in IIS can have independent security, an alternate access mapped URL is essentially one of the URLs for a web application and will have the security of its existing web application applied to it.

Therefore, if you have a public URL in a zone field, and it doesn't have a corresponding Web Site in IIS, chances are it is not an extended web application and therefore cannot have its own security settings.

Finally, there is one more setting for alternate access mapping, Map to External Resource. This setting is really meant to be used by Microsoft Office SharePoint Server 2007 or third-party products because it is intended to give a SharePoint administrator a means to mask URLs to alternative network resources.

DELETE THE COLLECTION

If you use the Map To External Resource setting and create a new Alternate Access Mapping Collection (which is what it does) by accident and want to delete it, you need to view that new collection's public URLs. The Delete button on that settings page does not delete a selected public URL, but instead deletes the collection.

MANAGE FARM FEATURES

Features can be scoped to be applied at the farm level, web application level, site collection, or even at the site level. This capability is specified in the feature's contents and can not be forced during install. This setting displays the Features that are scoped to be available at the farm level.

A Feature can be a single addition to the functionality of SharePoint (such as adding an item to the Site Actions menu) or more. It usually consists of one `feature.xml` file and occasional supporting files that are installed in SharePoint's Features folder (where all default features are located). They are then activated per their scope (that's why you can manage features at the farm, web application, site collection, or site level).

The only place you can install or uninstall Features is at the command line using STSADM. However, if you have added features to your SharePoint server, they'll be listed here if they are scoped to. For more about adding features to a server, see Chapter 13.

If a feature is applied, you can activate it either at the command line or in the Features page at the level for which it was scoped.

For example, if a feature was scoped for a site you can activate it at the site's settings by going to that site's Site Settings page under the Site Actions menu, and going to Site Features in the Site Administration category.

On the Site Features page (Figure 9.31), you can see if there are any Features available at that level. In my example you can see that a new feature (Central Admin Link by SharePoint Solutions) is available for this site, but has not been activated. Remember, features can be added to SharePoint as features on their own or as part of a larger solution. Features simply change or add to the functions that a SharePoint can do.

FIGURE 9.31
The Site Features
page

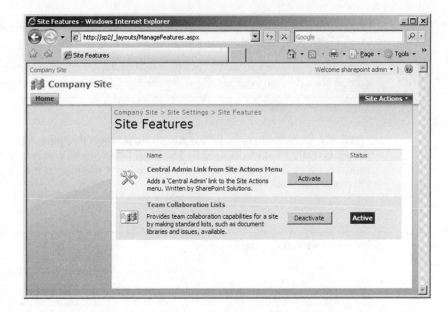

To activate a feature, simply click the Activate button. That will make the function available for use at the level it was scoped, which is the site in this case (Figure 9.32). To deactivate a feature, simply go back to the Site Features page and click the Deactivate button, which replaces the Activate button when the feature is active. It will warn you that you are about to deactivate a feature. Click the link on the warning page to continue, and the feature will be deactivated.

FIGURE 9.32
A new feature in action on
the Site Actions menu

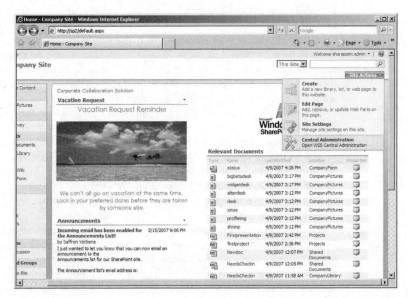

INSTALLED, ADDED, WHAT'S THE DIFFERENCE?

Keep in mind that Features are installed and then activated; Solutions are added, then deployed, *then* activated. Despite the apparent extra step, Solutions are easy to create and deploy so expect to add many more Solutions for your farm than Features.

SOLUTION MANAGEMENT

This settings page is very much like the Manage Farm Features in that you need to use STSADM to add the solution (and delete it for that matter). However, you can choose to deploy or retract a solution once it's added to SharePoint using the Solution Management page.

In my example, two solutions are deployed (see Figure 9.33). *Solutions* are really files packaged together in a CAB file with the `.wsp` extension. A solution can be as big as a site definition, site templates, and their features and web parts, or as small as a single feature and its supporting files. The newer solution in my example is the Central Administration link feature that was activated at the site level in the previous section. Solutions are often made of features that can be scoped to be activated at different levels of SharePoint. So they can add workflows to site collection level Feature lists, new menu options to sites, and more. When a Solution is deployed to a web application, that only means that all of the site collections or sites in that particular web application can have access to the new Features, depending on how they're written.

FIGURE 9.33
The Solution
Management page

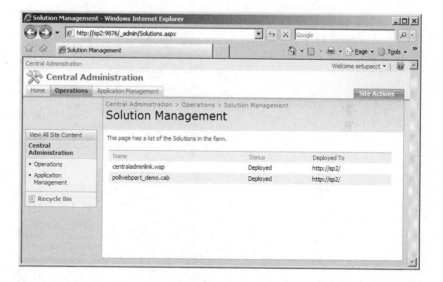

In my example the solution was added using STSADM (I deployed it there too). Once added to SharePoint, the solution is available to be viewed and managed on the Solution Management page.

To manage a particular solution, click it on the page. You will be taken to that solution's Properties page.

As you can see in Figure 9.34, you can check the solution properties, such as whether or not it was deployed, and what web application it was deployed to (in my example, that web application is `http://sp2`).

FIGURE 9.34
The Solution Properties page

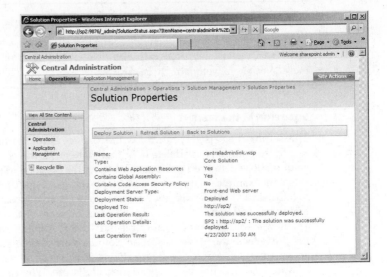

From there, you can deploy the solution to a new web application by clicking the Deploy Solution link in the Action bar. This will give you the option to deploy the solution to a specific web application.

FIGURE 9.35
The Deploy Solution page

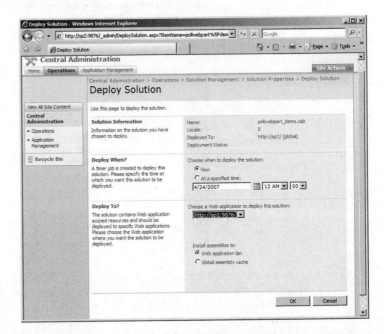

As you can see in Figure 9.35, you can deploy the solution now or at a time that might put less strain on the server. You can deploy it to the global assembly cache (this is particularly useful if your solution needs to use secure controls) or to a particular web application's bin folder. If you previously deployed a solution to the global assembly cache for use by a web application, SharePoint will assume you want to use that deployment option with all other web applications. Therefore, you will not be given the option to deploy the solution to a web application's bin. In addition, when you choose Global assembly cache as the location for the solution, you will be warned that everything in there is trusted. The global assembly cache is useful because it's globally accessible and it's a high-level security location so all solutions there run in a highly trusted context. That also means you shouldn't just download any old solution from the Internet and install it to the global assembly cache.

Of course, if you can add, you can take away by retracting a solution from a web application or all of them on the farm. To check this, select Retract Solution on the Solution Management page (Figure 9.36).

FIGURE 9.36
The Retract
Solution page

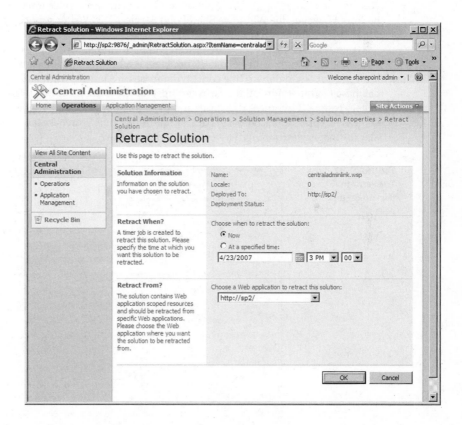

This will take you to a page that lets you choose when to retract the solution (now or at a scheduled time) and the web applications from which to retract. If your solution contains features that are running on sites, you should deactivate the feature there before you retract its solution from the web application in which the site is stored.

Backup and Restore

This category is where you go to do farm or web application backup and restore in Central Administration. Remember, you can also backup and restore using the STSADM command-line tool. See Chapter 13 for more information. Chapter 12, "Maintenance and Monitoring" has additional information that specifically addresses SharePoint backup and restore.

PERFORM A BACKUP

The Perform A Backup settings link will take you to a page where you can begin the two-step process of backing up the SharePoint farm or certain web applications and databases of the SharePoint farm. SharePoint Backup uses the Windows SharePoint Services Administration Service to access local server resources, and it uses the Volume Shadow Copy service of both the local server and possibly the SQL server that is hosting SharePoint's databases (depending on how you installed SharePoint). This is why the Administration service must be running when you do a backup. However, the Windows SharePoint Services VSS Writer service can be on Manual and will run if SharePoint needs it.

As you can see Figure 9.37, the first step in performing a backup is choosing what part (or whole) of the farm you'd like to back up. Here is a tip though; you cannot restore the Admin_content database (the content database for Central Administration) or the configuration database (and therefore all the farm settings) for the farm. Basically, that information is backed up to help restore the content databases and their web applications properly. Notice that, in addition to the web applications, you can back up the SharePoint Search instance, which includes the index files for the server running the service, and its database.

FIGURE 9.37
The Perform A Backup-Step 1 Of 2 page

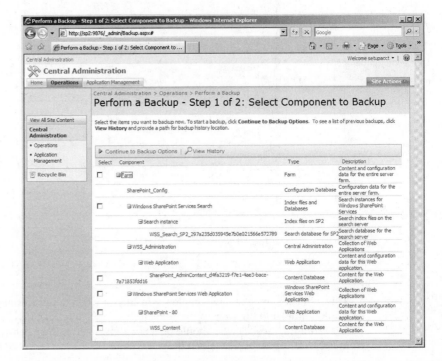

Generally, it's a good idea to create a full farm backup as soon as the farm is up and healthy. After that, you can perform differential backups. You can even create backups of particular parts of the farm (such as a specific web application) if you feel it's necessary.

To do a whole farm backup, just select the checkbox next to the Farm component and click Continue to Backup Options. This will automatically select all farm components and then take you to the second step of the backup process, which is selecting the backup options.

As you can see in Figure 9.38, you can confirm what you are backing up and change your mind in the Backup Content section—my example says Farm because that's what I selected in Step 1. There are only two ways to perform a backup in SharePoint; Full and Differential.

FIGURE 9.38
The Start Backup-Step 2 Of 2 page

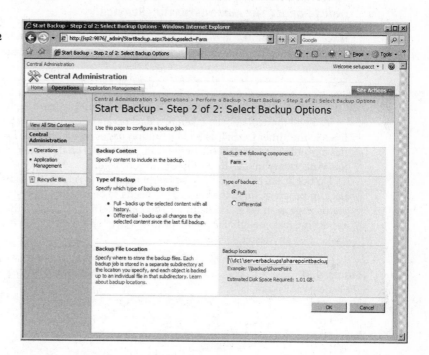

Full   Backs up everything selected as it is at the time of backup.

Differential   Backs up all changes since the last full backup.

WHEN DIFFERENTIAL WON'T DO

If you make a big change, like adding a new content database or a new web application, then you can't do a differential backup until you do another full one.

Let's leave this set at Full. The last section, Backup Location, is where you specify the directory where you will be storing the backup files. As you know, you need to store the backup somewhere other than the backed-up server, in case of emergency. Therefore, never back up to the same server that is hosting SharePoint.

However, if you are backing up to a different server or location on the network, the appropriate user accounts must have the correct permissions to that directory in order for the backup to succeed. In my example, those accounts are the farm account (dem0tek\wssconfig), and the SQL Server service account. If you are going to use STSADM to perform backups, the account you are going to use to run the command needs to have read and write access to the file share as well.

DON'T FORGET THE ADMINISTRATION SERVICE

Make certain that the Windows SharePoint Services Administration service is started. This is particularly important for restoring SharePoint because the search instance will not restore properly without it.

Once the correct backup location is listed, click OK to start the backup.

You will immediately be taken to a Backup and Restore Status page (Figure 9.39). This page has links to the Timer Job Status and Definition pages so you can see how the backup job is going. If it has a problem, you can confirm the status of the job on the Timer Job Status page and delete the job, if necessary on the Timer Job Definition page.

Do not be surprised if it takes several minutes to refresh the Status page and show you the backup progress. First, the backup job needs to be created, then started, and then displayed in the status page, so it takes a little time. There is a Refresh button on the page's Action bar if it isn't refreshing fast enough. However, hitting it over and over like an elevator button will really not make it go any faster.

FIGURE 9.39
The Backup and Restore Status page

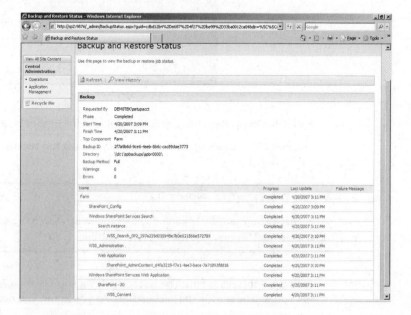

Now that you know how to do a full backup, feel free to do differentials as well. Remember, backups require a pretty big resource load, so don't perform them in the middle of the day. Also remember that backups record only the changes that occurred before the backup begins, and any changes after the backup will not be captured. In order to restore a differential backup, you must first restore a recent full backup and then restore the differential to catch up.

EVERYTHING BUT THE KITCHEN SINK

Also keep in mind that it is a good idea to backup other SharePoint components like the virtual directories and configuration files used by SharePoint in IIS, SSL certificates (if you have any), as well as the SharePoint hive 12 folders to backup any customizations you might have made (like adding Features and Solutions).

BACKUP AND RESTORE HISTORY

When SharePoint creates a full backup, it adds an spbrtoc.xml file to the backup location listing all the backups stored there, their components, and whether they are full or differential. All of these taken together comprise the backup history of all the backups located there. This is handy if you want to see what backups you have where. You can simply go to the Backup and Restore History page and see what backups are available (the page simply reads the spbrtoc.xml page for the information).

By default, the Backup and Restore History page will display the history of backups in the location you most recently backed up to (Figure 9.40). However, if you are looking for a specific backup somewhere else, you can change the directory (from the link in the Action bar), which will let you choose a new location to see the backup history stored there.

FIGURE 9.40
The Backup And Restore History page

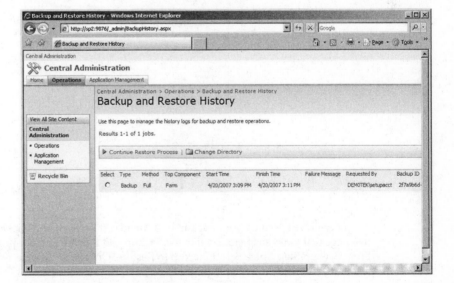

SUCCESSFUL RESTORES

Each backup you do is contained in its own folder, with its own XML file to record what files are in the folder. The Restore process uses that XML file (usually called `spbackup.xml`) to identify all of those backup files in the correct order and their exact location in relation to itself. Therefore, the restore won't work if any of the files have been moved to a location that that XML file does not expect. This means that if you need to move the backups, instead of moving the individual backup files, move the folder they are contained in. Or better yet, make a copy of the entire directory where the backups are, so you preserve the backup history of the location with the spbrtoc.xml, and retain each backup folder in its pristine state.

Also, because you might decide to restore a backup from the History page, you can select a backup on that page and start the restore process from there if you'd like. For more about backing up SharePoint and its required components, see Chapter 12, "Maintenance and Monitoring," which is primarily dedicated to monitoring SharePoint and preparing to recover from disaster.

RESTORE FROM BACKUP

This link takes you to the beginning of the four-step Restore process. The first page (Figure 9.41) simply contains the field for specifying the location of the SharePoint backup files you'd like to restore.

FIGURE 9.41
The Restore From Backup: Step 1 of 4 page

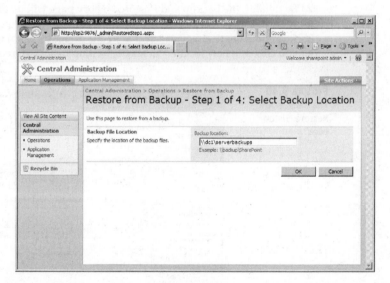

Once you've specified your backup location to restore from and clicked OK, you will be taken to a page that looks suspiciously like the Backup and Restore History page, but it is called Restore From Backup-Step 2 of 4: Select Backup to Restore. On it, you can select the backup from the location you specified in Step 1 (Figure 9.42).

FIGURE 9.42
The Restore From
Backup: Step 2 of 4
page

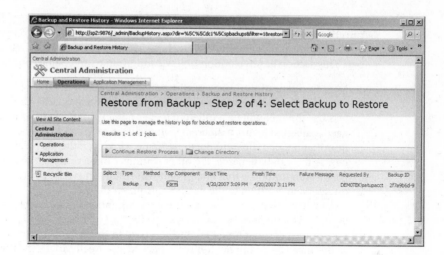

Once you've selected the backup you want to restore, click Continue Restore Process in the Action bar. The next page is Step 3 of 4: Select Component to Restore, as you can see in Figure 9.43. On this page, you can choose the component or components from the backup to restore. It basically reports the backup history for the backup you chose, complete with failure information if a component failed to be fully backed up (and can't be restored). Once you've chosen what to restore from backup, click Continue Restore Process.

FIGURE 9.43
The Restore From
Backup: Step 3 of 4
page

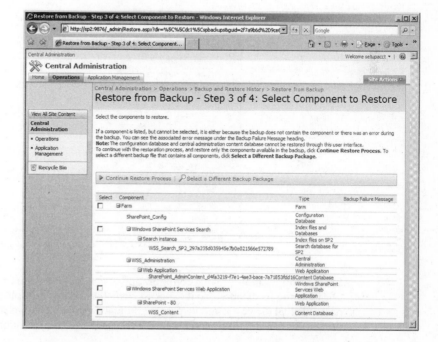

The Restore From Backup - Step 4 of 4: Select Restore Options page has the specific options you can choose when restoring SharePoint components. The Restore Component section is where you can confirm the component you chose in Step 3. The Restore Options section is an important one. This section has two options: New configuration and Same configuration.

New Configuration　New configuration is generally used if you are restoring components to a new server and need to specify a new description and URL for the web applications, possibly because the root will be a different server name; or if you are using a different SQL server (and need a different login), a different virtual directory location for the web application's IIS Web Site information, or a different database name. However, the only thing that is really required to be new is the database name, the other settings can be reused. The nice thing about restoring to a New configuration is that SharePoint will restore the web application data in IIS and the virtual directory, in addition to the database, from scratch.

As you can see in Figure 9.44, New configuration is the default, making it possible to use the existing data in the New Names section for the components you are restoring but mostly giving you an idea of what type of data should go in those fields based on the existing, working data at the time the component(s) were backed up. Really that's mostly informational, SharePoint expects you to type new data in those fields.

FIGURE 9.44
The Restore From Backup:
Step 4 Of 4 page

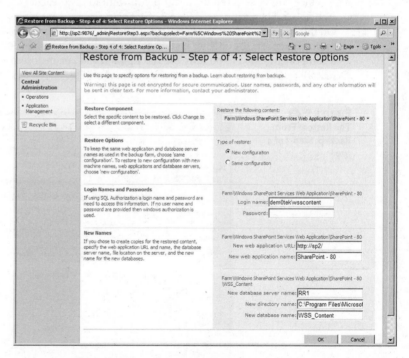

Same Configuration　Same configuration is generally used to overwrite an existing web application and its database, so it expects *exactly* the same web application data (URL, application name, virtual directory, and its path) and database to which to restore. It will not re-create anything if it is missing. As a matter of fact, if you use Same configuration for your restore, all options in the New Names section, except for the content database access account login and password will be grayed out, and you will be warned that all components being restored are simply going to be written over as is. That means that it will not use its backup information to create anything anew, even if it needs that information.

Once you click OK at the bottom of the page, you will be taken to the Backup and Restore Status page, where you may need to wait several minutes until it starts reporting the progress of the restore process. If any of the components fail to restore, the failure will be reported in the failure message column, just as for the backup process.

BACKUP AND RESTORE JOB STATUS

This settings link takes you to the page that is used by both the Backup and Restore processes to report the status of jobs. If you were to leave or close the job status page during a backup or restore, you could get back to that page by going to this link to see what has been happening (or has happened) with the most recent Backup or Restore task. If you are not backing up or restoring a SharePoint component, this link will still take you to a page populated by the most recent status information of the last backup or restore job.

Data Configuration

This category is small but does contain a useful means to save time while creating new web applications by assigning a global default database server for the server farm. In addition, Data Retrieval Service allows you to see at a glance what data source controls and retrieval services are running on your server farm or specific web application.

DEFAULT DATABASE SERVER

SharePoint obviously needs to use SQL databases for both configuration and content data. When you create new web applications, a new content database can also be created—if you aren't reusing an existing one, and either way, SharePoint needs to know where that database should be. And since that is a requirement for every database, it is convenient to have the database server field already filled in by default. That is what the Default Database Server setting is for, so you can specify a default database server for the server farm. It can be overridden without a problem during web application creation, but at least the option is available to accept the default. As an added bonus, this setting lets you see, at a glance, what the name of at least one database server is for a new network with which you might be unfamiliar.

DATA RETRIEVAL SERVICE

Data retrieval services are technologies that use Simple Object Access Protocol (SOAP) or XML to pass data from a source to the data consumer. This settings page is actually prepopulated by default and doesn't give you much leeway to modify it, although you can register a third-party service by using the `bindservice` operation in STSADM. On the Data Retrieval Service page (Figure 9.45), you can see that the data retrieval services supported by default are Windows SharePoint Services, OLEDB, SOAP Passthrough, and XML-URL. You can enable or disable these services entirely as a group. There is no option to pick and choose among them. Under normal circumstances you should not disable those services. Other settings on this page are basically about the size (in kilobytes) that the data source returns to the data retrieval service that requested it. The default service is OLEDB. You can enable OLEDB update queries here; it is off by default.

You can also set the data source time-out period in seconds (the default is 30). This refers to how long it takes the data source to respond to a retrieval service request. You can also enable or disable the data source controls for the retrieval services to process query requests. If you disable either the data source controls or the data retrieval services, no query requests will occur. Therefore, no data will be passed from the data sources to the data retrieval services and then on to you, ultimately. You don't want that to happen.

FIGURE 9.45
The Data Retrieval Service page

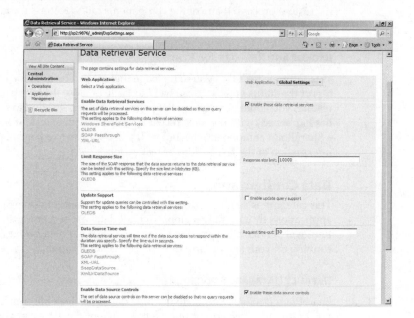

The Bottom Line

Understand Central Administration's Organization   SharePoint's Central Administration is organized in two pages, Operations and Application Management, with a home page that has several useful web parts.

Master It   Is it a good idea to use Central Administration to hold shared library content, lists, and calendars? Why?

Use the Settings on the Operations Page   The Operations page is intended to contain settings specific to the administration of SharePoint as whole. It contains settings pertaining to defaults that govern all servers, web applications, etc, for the entire server (or server farm). The use and application of those settings vary, but the interface used to access them is much more consistent that it was with the previous version.

Master It   Can you configure blocked file types at a global level or only at the web application level?

Manage Solutions and Features   The settings for managing solutions and features are available on the Operations page under Global Configuration. Managing Farm Features page allows you to see what Features are active (or inactive but available) at the Farm level. Solutions Management allows you to see what solutions have been added to SharePoint, as well as deploy or retract them.

Master It Can you install a feature or add a solution to SharePoint from the Manage Features or Solution Management pages?

How to Set the Server Farm's Default Database Server In SharePoint an administrator is often going to be doing work that involves databases. For this reason, having a default database server specified for the server farm is a great convenience.

Master It If you are creating a new web application, can you specify a different database server other than the default set for the server farm?

Determine Where to Stop and Start Farm Services The Server Farm Services are not ones that can be managed from the server's Services management console. The Server Farm Services can be started and stopped from the Services on Server Settings page under Topology and Services on the Operations page.

Master It Name a server farm service that can be stopped or started from the Services on Server Settings page.

How to Change a Web Application Service Account If a web application's service account's password has been changed or you need to change the account altogether, go to the Service Accounts Settings page, select the web application that requires the change, and make the account updates there.

Master It What is a good indication that the service account password has changed on a web application's application pool?

Chapter 10

Central Administration: Application Management

This chapter gives you a reference point for all of those settings links on the Central Administration's Application Management site. The odds are good that you'll never use a few of them, but it's nice to know what they are, just in case. Many of these settings were covered extensively in previous chapters (and if that is the case, I'll let you know), but a few haven't. This chapter pulls them all together in one place.

In this chapter, you'll learn how to:

◆ Navigate Application Management

◆ Manage site collections

◆ Configure Person Name Smart Tags and Presence Settings

◆ Manage web application content databases

◆ Change a web application's authentication method

Overview

The Application Management page was meant to contain all SharePoint server farm settings that pertain to web applications and their site collections; however, a few of them ended up on the Operations page as well. Application Management is really a key part of administering SharePoint overall. The Operations page was all about managing SharePoint servers as a whole; managing their services, default settings, timer jobs, backup and restore, and more. But the Application Management page is where you actually create, delete, and manage the web applications that make it possible to have SharePoint sites. It is also here that you can create and manage the site collections within the web applications (also critical to the use of SharePoint), apply security, and integrate with MOSS servers and external services. This page is essentially the foundation of SharePoint web application and site collection administration.

The Application Management page is organized by categories:

SharePoint Web Application Management   This category contains the settings for managing, creating, extending, and deleting the SharePoint web applications.

Application Security   As the name implies, all things relating to web application security—from authentication, anonymous access, to securing web parts—are located in this category.

Workflow Management   This is a short category containing only one settings link. Here you can set, per web application, whether or not a user can create workflows from the templates available on the site, and whether or not those workflows are allowed to send files to people external to SharePoint if they are assigned a task due to a workflow (the answer to that, for many reasons, is usually no).

SharePoint Site Management   This category is all about the site collections. It allows you to conveniently see the list of site collections for a particular web application and also create, delete, and manage site collections.

External Service Connections   As the word *external* implies, this category has more to do with the MOSS version of SharePoint than Windows SharePoint Services. When MOSS is added to WSS, it offers settings to access external records center or document conversion service application servers. However, HTML Viewer is still a service available for use on a single WSS server (to a certain degree).

In this chapter, as in the preceding chapter, we'll work through all of the settings for each category. Generally, the descriptions will be brief because much of what's here was covered in detail in Chapter 8, "Site Collections and Web Applications."

To get to the Application Management page of Central Administration, open a browser (specifically, a Level 1 browser that supports ActiveX controls such as Internet Explorer 6.0 or higher). Enter the URL and port number of the Central Administration site, or if you are on the SharePoint server hosting Central Administration, use the SharePoint 3.0 Central Administration shortcut on the Start menu.

In my example, the default farm administrator (dem0tek\setupacct) is the account that installed SharePoint and the one with which I am logged in. After you've opened Central Administration and logged in, click the Application Management link either on the Quick Launch bar or the Top Link bar. Either way, you'll end up on the Application Management page (Figure 10.1).

FIGURE 10.1
The Application Management page

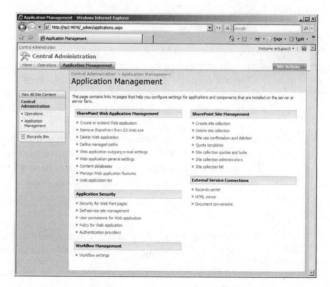

LOGIN EXPLANATION

Mind you I am using the setup account to log in as a convenience (it is one I *know* you have otherwise SharePoint wouldn't be installed). It is obviously a better practice not to use that account for anything but installing SharePoint. So if you have a qualified Farm Administrator account to log in with, please do. In order to be able to create or extend web applications, the Farm Administrators account that you use must also be at least a local administrator on the SharePoint servers. Otherwise the links pertaining to creating and modifying web applications will not be available on the page—something to keep in mind if you would like to have a Farm Adminstrator who is allowed to manage the farm but shouldn't be allowed to create web applications.

Sharepoint Web Application Management

The SharePoint Web Application Management category is the meat and potatoes of web application management. Focused on creating, deleting, and extending web applications, this category also covers web application features, what web applications are available on the server farm, managing content databases, and the settings to override the default settings applied at the Operations level for individual web applications.

Create Or Extend Web Application

This link is where the action is, making it possible to create new web applications in the SharePoint GUI as well as extend an existing web application's content over to another IIS website. This setting (along with most of the settings on this page) was covered in detail in Chapter 8, but just to be thorough, let's take a look at it as a quick reference.

Clicking the Create Or Extend Web Application link will take you to a sort of interim page with two options: See Figure 10.2.

◆ Create a new Web application actually creates a new IIS website and application pool, as well as a new content database for that application pool to access.

◆ Extend an existing Web application simply creates a new IIS website to use the same application pool to access the same content database. Extending a web application allows you to give more people access to the content of the original IIS website, which is useful if you are getting too much traffic. Because the extended IIS website has its own security settings (SSL, Anonymous Access, etc.), it allows you to apply different security to users accessing the same content but using a different URL. Therefore, those using the original web application's URL can have less restrictive authentication applied to them, and those who want to access the content from outside of the network can use the extended web application's URL and have that web application be set with stricter authentication.

FIGURE 10.2
Create or Extend Web
Application

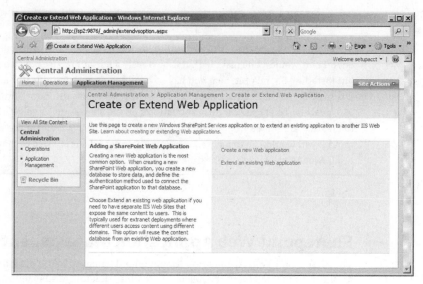

CREATE A NEW WEB APPLICATION

If you click Create a new Web application on the Create Or Extend Web Application page, you'll go to the Create New Web Application page. This page has seven sections that allow you to specify the IIS Web Site for the web application:

♦ Its port, host header, and virtual directory

♦ The security configuration settings such as authentication providers (NTLM is usually a safe bet because it requires less configuration than Kerberos), enabling anonymous access, or SSL

♦ The load-balanced URL (useful only if you are doing network load balancing between Share-Point servers)

♦ The Application pool name and account

♦ The database name and authentication for the content database

♦ The search server

♦ Whether or not to reset IIS on the rest of the servers on the farm manually or automatically when the web application is created

The Load Balanced URL section has a setting that refers to a zone. It is grayed out because it is actually for extended web applications, which you will see in a moment.

MORE DETAILS

For more on extending or creating web applications, see Chapter 8, "Site Collections and Web Applications."

EXTEND A WEB APPLICATION

If you click Extend an existing Web application, it will take you to a slightly different page that offers you slightly different choices (Figure 10.3).

FIGURE 10.3
The Extend Web Application page

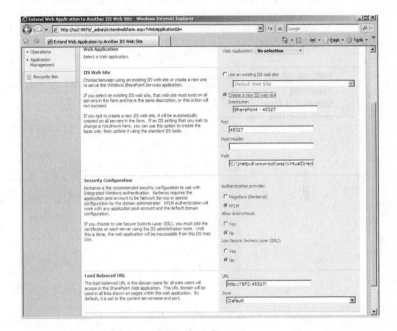

On the Extend Web Application to Another IIS Web Site page, you first have to choose the existing web application with which you are going to have this web application share an application pool and content database. Next, you need to specify the details of the IIS Web Site for this extended web application (port or host header, virtual directory path), as well as the security configuration and load-balanced URL. For an extended web application, you are now able to choose a zone; this specifically relates to alternate access mapping, which is covered in Chapters 8 and 9. The zone you choose with be essentially that extended web application's identity in SharePoint.

Once those settings are complete, you can create your extended web application. It will not have its own listing in the web application list, and it cannot be managed like a standard web application because it does not have its own content database and, therefore, cannot store its own site collections and content. Everything done at its URL is shunted to the content database it is sharing with the main web application. Extended web applications are referred to in SharePoint by their URL and zone in Alternate access mappings.

Remove SharePoint from an IIS Web Site

This page is used to remove the SharePoint files from an IIS Web Site that is currently hosting a SharePoint web application's information. Although you *can* simply remove the SharePoint files and association with that IIS Web Site/web application, this is really where you go to get rid of an *extended* web application (the Deleting a Web Application is for *real* web applications only). Why this setting is not called "Remove Extended Web Application" I just don't know.

To use it you specify the SharePoint web application and then choose which of the zones associated with it that should be removed. The default selection for the zone is, well, Default, in which case you will remove SharePoint from the real web application's Web Site—so make sure you select the correct zone. This setting let's you delete only the SharePoint bits from the IIS website (and SharePoint's association with it), or you can delete the whole IIS Web Site as well (Figure 10.4).

FIGURE 10.4
Removing
SharePoint from
an IIS Web Site

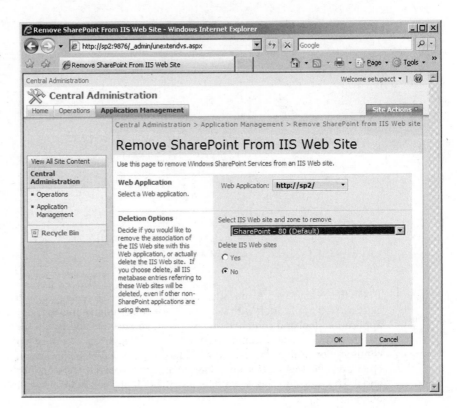

Delete Web Application

This link seems very similar to the Remove SharePoint from an IIS Web Site link. However, instead of just removing the web application's bits from an IIS Web Site, you can use this link to delete all traces of it in the configuration database of SharePoint, from IIS, and from SQL. This setting was obviously meant for real, non-extended web applications only. Nowhere on this page is there an option to apply it to a particular zone

On the Delete Web Application page (Figure 10.5), you just select the web application you want to delete, and then decide if you want to delete the Web Site of the web application from IIS or just disassociate from it in SharePoint; delete the content database for the web application or just detach it, or both.

FIGURE 10.5
The Delete Web
Application page

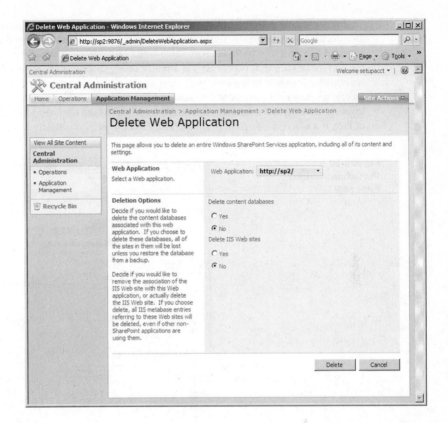

Define Managed Paths

This page specifies what data SharePoint explicitly manages and what data it doesn't. More importantly, it specifies what managed paths are available, per web application, to make site collections. By default, in SharePoint, the first site collection made in a web application gets the coveted `root` path. That means that its URL is at the root of the web application, just as the Company site is at the root of SharePoint-80, at `http://sp2`.

SharePoint has a default managed path (`http://server/sites`) set up as a default for any other site collections you might make in a particular web application. This means that if you create another site collection in the SharePoint-80 web application, it will default to being in the `http://sp2/sites/` path.

JUST A TIP

SharePoint prefers that there is always a site collection at the root of a web application. If you decide to use the /sites/ path for all of your site collections for some reason, search may not work. Weird but true.

If that default path is a little too boring or doesn't match your plans for the design and architecture of your SharePoint sites, you can specify unique managed paths. To do that, enter the name of the alternate path, such as **sales** (see Figure 10.6). If you do create a new path, test the URL to make sure that no content is already being displayed there by clicking Check URL. This will open a browser to the new path and, hopefully, fail to display any data, see Figure 10.7. Don't worry, the test is not supposed to succeed because you haven't put a site collection there yet. The important thing is the address in the Address bar. Make sure that there are no typos. As a matter of fact, if a site comes up on that address, then the path is already in use, so try something else.

FIGURE 10.6
The Define Managed
Paths page

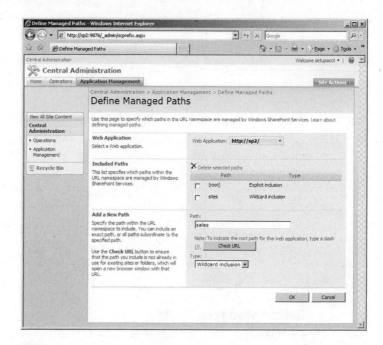

FIGURE 10.7
Checking the URL of a new path

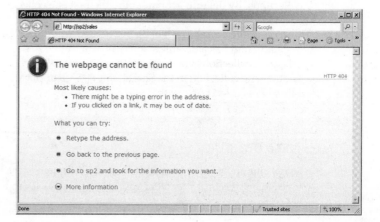

Another setting on the Managed Paths page lets you decide whether the path is a wildcard path or explicit. A wildcard path is one that is intended to host multiple site collections within that path. For example, `http://sp2/sites` is a wildcard path and can be used for `http://sp2/sites/blogs`, `http://sp2/sites/marketing`, etc. It can be used for whatever other site collections you would like to put there. You can use an explicit managed path to specify an absolute path that points to one and only one specific site collection. For example, creating an explicit path of `http://sp2/humanresources` will let you create one site collection in that web application with that explicit path—period. You cannot put any other site collections under that, so to speak (like `http://sp2/humanresources/manuals`). Keep in mind though that this sort of path can be used for a subsite within the human resources site collection as well. So when creating explicit managed paths, realize that there could be overlap. That's part of the reason why the Check URL button is there.

If you use `sales` as a wildcard path by entering it in the Path field and clicking OK, you could use it the next time you created a site collection for that web application (Figure 10.8). Keep in mind that you can make as many managed paths as you'd like, but there is a character limit of 255 characters for a web address (which will include the name of the page the user is on while there), so keep your paths as brief as you can.

FIGURE 10.8
A new path is available during site collection creation

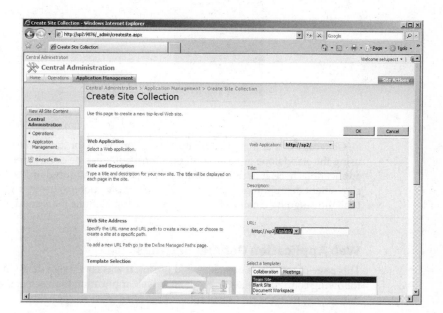

When you specify a wildcard path for a site collection, it's referred to as a site prefix.

Web Application Outgoing E-Mail Settings

This page, shown in Figure 10.9, is for web applications that might need a different email account, character type, or even email server to send out their email notifications.

FIGURE 10.9

The Web Application Outgoing E-Mail Settings page

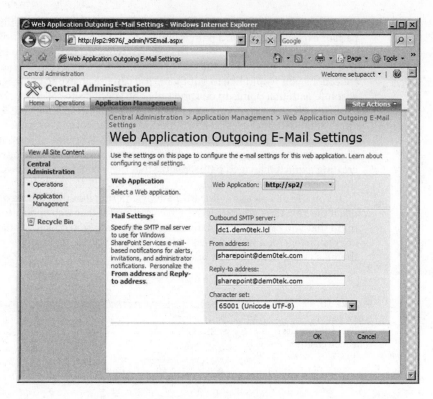

Generally this option is set on the Operations page for the whole farm (or server if you were using the standalone or basic configuration), but it can be overridden by individual web applications here, if necessary. Think of the setting configured on the Operations page as a convenient default in case you want all web applications to use it, and this setting is here to fine tune the outgoing email settings for the web applications that require it.

Web Application General Settings

This page of settings is extensive and useful. It was covered in detail in Chapter 8, and contains the following configurable settings for each web application (you select the web application to apply the settings to in the first section):

Default Time Zone   Set the default Time Zone for all enclosed site collections.

Default Quota   Have a specific storage quota template be applied to new site collections by default.

Person Name Smart Tag and Presence Settings   Enable or disable online status icons. Requires one of the Messenger programs and/or Outlook.

ONLINE PRESENCE AND PERSON NAME SMART TAG

The Person Name Smart Tags and Presence setting is more complex then the single enable box would indicate. This setting has been enabled throughout the exercises in this book, but you haven't seen it do anything in any of the screenshots.

Online Presence is all about Messenger (MSN Messenger, Windows Messenger, Live Messenger, whatever it's called this month). If the user is running Messenger using the same email account as the one in their user information in SharePoint, and their friends in SharePoint are doing the same, and the friends are part of the first user's buddies list, they will appear as online for that first user and vice versa—if the first user is listed as a contact in Messenger for their buddies, of course. Online Presence is evident in lists that have a column that displays usernames. The usernames will display a colored ball (or sometimes a chess piece if you are using the most up-to-date OS and Office system) if the users are signed into Messenger and are on your Messenger Contact list.

If a person is online, the icon will be green. Red is for Busy or On The Phone; half red or half green means the user has been idle for a while; light orange is for Be Right Back, Out To Lunch, or Away; and gray is for Appear Offline and for when they are actually offline.

SharePoint accounts that do not have email addresses (such as the setup account, or the search, farm, and content database accounts) will not have icons next to their names.

The Person Name Smart tag works only if the user accesses SharePoint from a computer that has Outlook installed. (Outlook Express will not cut it.) Under those circumstances, a username link displayed anywhere (in the Created By field, in a People and Groups field, etc.) becomes active. That means that when you move your mouse over the name of a user who has an email address in SharePoint, a dropdown list will appear (on the left of the name, or over the Online Presence icon if present). Click the down arrow to see a list of the collaboration options that Outlook and Messenger offer.

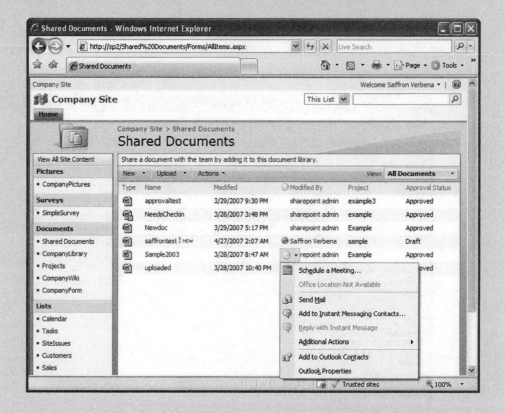

The bottom line is that if the users are not using Outlook or Messenger, enabling Person Smart Tags and Online Presence will make no change for them. Further, if a Messenger user doesn't have anyone from SharePoint in their Buddies list, the presence icons will not mean anything either.

Maximum Upload Size   Restrict uploads to a certain size. The default is 50MB.

Alerts   Enable (or disable) alerts for all enclosed site collections, and limit the number of alerts permitted per user for the entire web application. By default, alerts are enabled and limited to

500 per user. Notice that setting alerts limits is done at the web application level, not at any lower level, unfortunately.

RSS Settings   Permit RSS settings for all site collections in the selected web application.

Blog API Settings   The API that SharePoint uses is the common MetaWebLog API, which makes it possible for the users (when this setting is enabled) to use third-party editors like Windows Live Writer to write their blog entries and post them to their SharePoint blogs. It can also pass through whatever authentication SharePoint is using if necessary. Be aware that some blog editors do send login information in cleartext, which can cause a problem with authentication.

Web Page Security Validation   This setting was a painful one in the earlier version of Share-Point. Now it works differently. Web Page Security Validation is supposed to set the length of time a user can sit on a web page idly before it times out and the user needs to re-authenticate. This was a pain if the page was full of fields to fill out or required considerable thought, like a survey, and the user ran out of time filling it out and had to start over. With the current version of SharePoint however, it seems that the setting simply promises to never go stale and require validation below that set period (in minutes), but could in fact wait a very long time on a page without timing out (if it goes stale at all, often it simply never times out regardless of the limit you enter). This may change with a later service patch or update.

Send User Name and Password in E-Mail   This setting is specifically for SharePoint installations that are using Active Directory Account Creation Mode (ADAC) and will be discussed in Chapter 15, "Advanced Installation and Configuration." If a user is added to a site collection in that scenario, an email should be sent to the user letting them know what their username and password is to access the site collection. The password is generated randomly, and without that email, the user would never know how to log in until an administrator manually changes their password.

Backward Compatible Event Handlers   This setting allows event handlers created for previous versions of SharePoint to work with this version.

Change Log   Configures how long to store entries in the change log used by the SharePoint search service. The default is 15 days.

Recycle Bin   Configures the Recycle Bins for all enclosed site collections. You can set how long items remain in the end-user Recycle Bin before they are deleted. Then you can apply a storage limit to the second-stage Recycle Bin based on a percentage of each site collection's storage quota. Alternatively, you can disable the second-stage recycle bin completely, so anything deleted from the end-user recycle bin is completely deleted.

Content Databases

The Manage Content Databases page is where you can add, remove, and manage the content databases of your web applications without using STSADM. This page actually focuses on two different things: adding new databases and managing existing ones.

If you go to the Manage Content Databases page by clicking the link, you'll be taken to a page that lists all the content databases for a given web application (Figure 10.10).

FIGURE 10.10
The Manage Content
Databases page

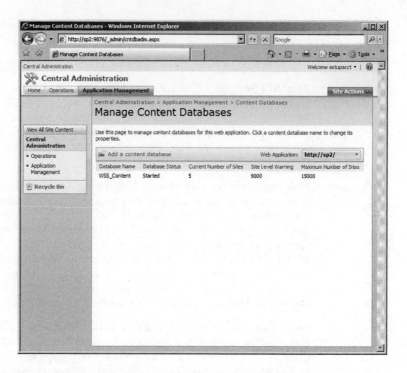

As discussed in detail in Chapter 8, you can have more than one database per web application, so it stands to reason that there would need to be a list of them somewhere.

To view the settings for an existing content database, just click the database name in the list of content databases. This will open a page containing the settings for that content database (Figure 10.11):

◆ Its status (whether it is Offline or Ready).

◆ The number of sites the database can contain before reaching a warning level (that generates an alert) or a maximum level that causes the database to go offline and be inaccessible.

◆ The setting that specifies which search server (if there is more than one in your network) will service this content database.

◆ A setting to remove this database (and all enclosed sites and content for this web application) from SharePoint.

If you are smart, you'll add a second database to a web application when you reach the warning level of the first database's capacity. To add that database, go back to the Manage Content Databases page, and click Add a content database in the Action bar. After making certain you are adding the database to the correct web application in the Web Application section (see Figure 10.12), you can specify the database server, the database name (you can change the default into something more recognizable if you'd like), and the database authentication (if your SQL server uses Windows Authentication or has its own). In order for the database's contents to be searchable, you'll need to specify the search server. To help manage the size of the new database you are adding, there are settings for the warning level and maximum number of site collections.

FIGURE 10.11
The Manage Content Database Settings page

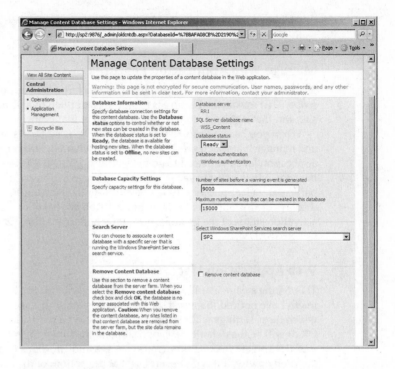

FIGURE 10.12
The Add Content Database page

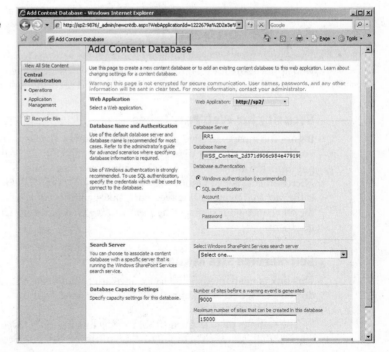

Chapter 8 has more details about what happens when you add a content database to a web application.

Manage Web Application Features

SharePoint Features can be created to run in a farm, web application, site collection, or single site scope. That means the Feature is meant to be applied to a farm, web application, site collection, or site, and that it can be activated or managed at that point.

When you have a Feature that is meant to be used for a site collection or site, you simply see it and manage it at that level. However, to see what Features are applied at the farm- or web-application level, you need to go to Central Administration—of course. Just as obviously, this is the page where you can see what Features are available in SharePoint that are scoped to affect a particular web application (you select it from the Web application menu). The page itself simply displays the installed Features scoped for web applications with a column to indicate the activation status of the Features. Installing and unistalling Features is done at the command line using STSADM.

Web Application List

This setting's page literally lists what web applications are available in SharePoint. By now, you might have noticed that most settings pages start with a section specifying the web application to which those settings will be applied. If you select a particular web application in this list and click OK, it will be the default web application at the top of the settings pages. This is particularly useful if you are making numerous changes and additions to one web application. And begs the question of why, if it is that useful, is it at the bottom of the category?

Application Security

The Application Security category contains the settings for the user permissions to be allowed per web application, for assigning authentication providers, creating overriding user and anonymous access policies, self-service site collections, and securing web parts.

Security for Web Part Pages

It's not the most extensive settings page; however, the Security for Web Parts Pages page is where you can either allow or disallow Web Part connections. It is also where you determine whether or not users are allowed to access the online Web Part Gallery. At the time of this writing, there is no Microsoft supported Online Web Part Gallery for WSS 3.0. However, the real point of that setting is the fact that using online web parts takes a fair bit of resources, and can be slow to load. So on the off chance your users get access to online web parts, you still may want to disable the option to use them.

Self-Service Site Management

This link is misnamed; Self-service sites are actually site collections, and the web application set to do Self-Service Site Creation allows users to create their own site collections, with all the autonomy that implies.

The settings page (Figure 10.13) for this link has only three settings in the Enable Self-Service Site Creation section: On or Off (the default), and Require Secondary Contact (which is always a good idea). See both Chapters 7 and 8 for more on Self-Service Site Creation.

FIGURE 10.13
The Self-Service Site
Management page

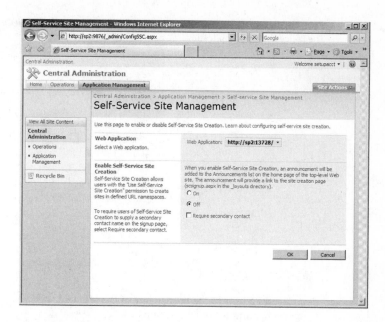

User Permissions for Web Application

This settings page contains all the user permissions that SharePoint offers. Organized by List permissions, Site permissions, and Personal permissions; any item selected will be available to be applied at the site-collection level or lower within the web application. For more about user permissions, see Chapter 11, "Users and Permissions."

Policy for Web Application

Policy for Web Application is another of those interesting settings in SharePoint. It essentially does triple duty:

◆ It lets you create user, permission, and anonymous access levels that override or overlap whatever settings might occur at the site-collection level of a web application.

◆ It lets you specify those overriding or overlapping anonymous-, user-, and permission-level policies for the parent web application or specific extended web applications, which are referred to as *zones* of a parent web application.

◆ You can set policies that apply to *all* zones of a web application, which means the parent web application and any of its extended web applications are affected.

The interesting thing about policies for web applications is that you can set a policy so there are users and permission levels for site collections that, at the site-collection level, you *cannot* see.

For example, on the Policy for Web Application page (Figure 10.14), there is an Action bar with Add Users, Delete selected Users, and Edit Permissions of Selected Users. The users listed for the web application are NT Authority/Local Service and the Search Crawling (Index) Service (dem0tek\ wssindex in my example), both with Full Read permissions. This means that all site collections in the web application will give read-only permissions to these accounts, even if they do not actually show up on the All People list on the sites themselves.

FIGURE 10.14
The Policy For Web Application page

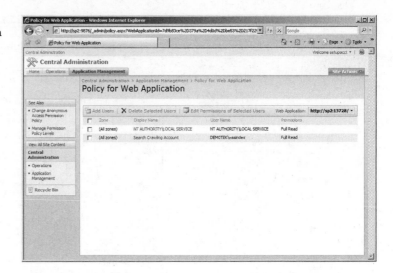

To add a user to the user policy of the selected web application, simply click Add Users in the Action bar and follow these steps:

1. On the Add Users page (Figure 10.15), you can see that it will be a two-step process. First, you need to confirm that you are working in the correct web application, and then you need verify the zone of that web application to which you want this user policy to apply. If you choose (All Zones), no matter how many extended web applications you make from this web application, all of them will all be affected by this added user policy. My example explicitly applies this change to only the parent web application by specifying Default. Once you're sure about your web application and zone, click Next to continue.

FIGURE 10.15
The Add Users page

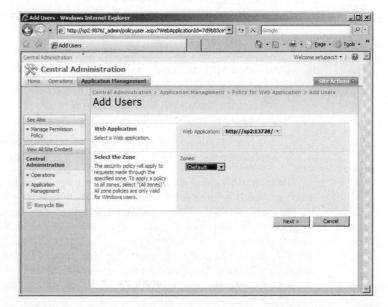

2. On the next page of Add Users (Figure 10.16), you can see the web application and zone to which this user policy will be added. In Choose Users, you can enter the username (from Active Directory of course, unless you are running in AD Account Creation mode) in the People Picker.

If you'd like, you can check the name to make sure it is spelled right by clicking the Check Names icon under the People Picker, or you can click the Address Book icon (called Browse), so you can enter the name and choose from near matches in AD. Either way, once you have the users or AD group you want, you need to select the permission level that will affect them throughout the web application zone. By default, the only permission levels available are somewhat limited:

◆ **Full Control.** This is exactly like giving ownership or administrator permission.

◆ **Full Read.** When this setting says Full Read, it means it. This permission level allows users to read *everything*, every setting, list, library, and document, but they cannot change a darn thing anywhere. It's basically an auditor setting.

◆ **Deny Write.** This is not what you probably think it is. You might think that the Deny Write permission-level policy gives someone the equivalent of a visitor's status on a site collection, but it doesn't. This setting is an "explicit deny," and it does not grant access to anything. Instead, it waits for a site or site collection to add the user (users, or group, whatever is added to the People Picker) as a contributor, full control, or some other permission level that allows viewing, editing, deleting, or adding of items, and then it forcibly and invisibly blocks those permissions and allows that user(s) to read only. It is an absolute deny from the web-application level, regardless of the settings on the enclosed site collections.

◆ **Deny All.** This permission level, if chosen, trumps anything done at the site collection. In other words, it blacklists whomever it is applied to; even if a site collection owner adds them explicitly to their site, they will not be able to log in.

3. After you've chosen your user, you need to apply permissions to them. My example gives the user account the Full Control permission level. This ensures that, no matter what the site collection owner does, the user will always be able to log in and control the site with this account.

FIGURE 10.16
The second Add Users page

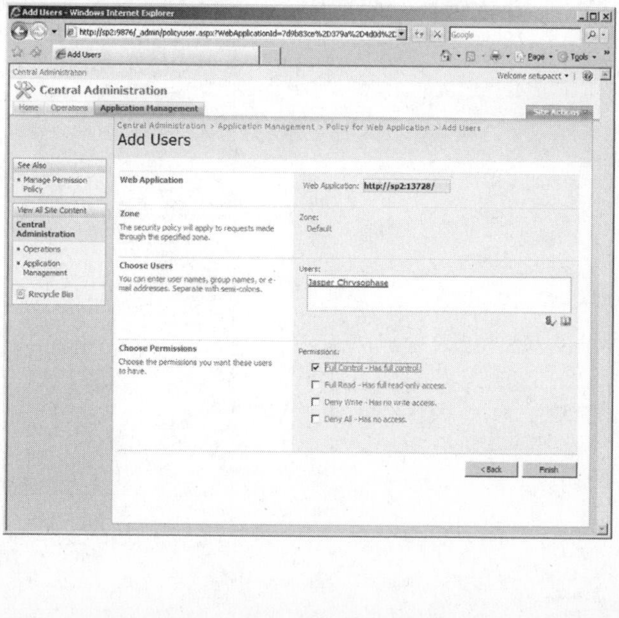

Now that the user is added, they can log in to a site with the Full Control permission level—despite the fact that the site does not explicitly have them added as a member or a site collection administrator (Figure 10.17).

FIGURE 10.17
All People does not show the user with web application policy applied.

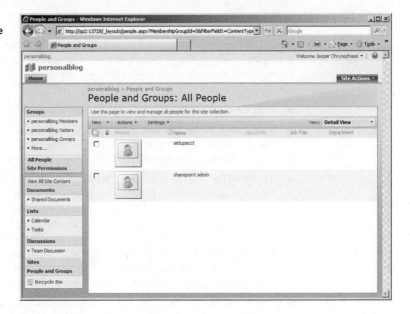

If you want to have a custom permission policy level to apply to users (in other words, if the default permissions aren't enough for you), you can do so. Simply click Manage Permission Policy Levels in the See Also bar on the left side of the Policy for Web Application page (Figure 10.18).

FIGURE 10.18
The Manage Permission Policy Levels page

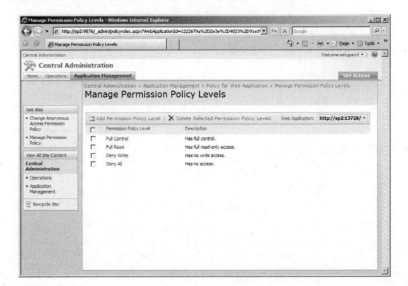

On this page, you can see what permission policy levels already exist. On the Action bar are Add Permission Policy Level and Delete Selected Permission Policy Levels (levels is plural because you can check more than one at a time). If you click on a particular existing level in the list, it will open a page indicating what permissions it is explicitly allowing or denying.

On the Manage Permission Policy Levels, to continue creating a new policy level, simply click Add Permission Policy Level in the Action bar.

The page that opens looks a lot like the User Permission page used to specify the permissions to be admissible for a web application, except for two things:

◆ Each permission has two columns to check: an explicit Grant (or allow) and an explicit Deny.

◆ There is a section called Site Collection Permissions, which conveniently lets you just choose an existing Administrator (Full Control) or Auditor (Full Read) permission with which to begin.

My example creates a List Manager permission policy level so you can force site collections to allow the users to whom you assign this permission policy level to manage lists even if they are not explicitly added as site members. As you can guess from Figure 10.19, you can simply grant all of the List Permissions to the level and then click OK.

FIGURE 10.19
The Edit Permission Policy Level page

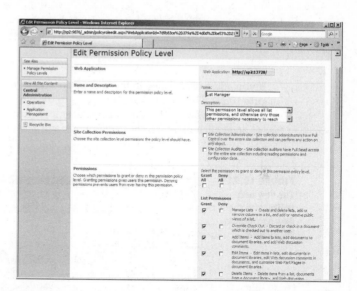

PERMISSIONS CAN OVERLAP

You can have a permission policy level that gives a user rights to a site collection. However, if that person is also added to the site as a user with a different permission level, those two levels can merge, giving them more permissions than you might have expected.

Use Deny if you need to ensure that certain permissions are never attainable by the users to whom the permission policy level are assigned. For more on the effects of user permissions, see Chapter 11.

Back on the Manage Permission Policy Levels page, there is a new permission policy level (see Figure 10.20).

FIGURE 10.20
The new List
Manager
Permission
Policy level

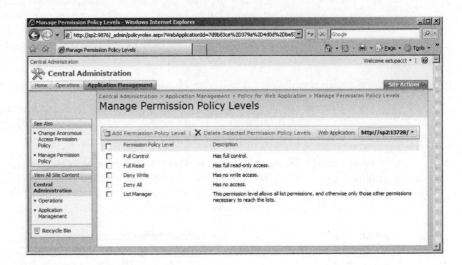

If you add a user policy to the web application, you can apply the new permission policy level (Figure 10.21). This grants the user access to the web application (and the site collections it contains) in the selected zone, so if the user logs in to a contained site collection that does not have her as an explicit member, she can still manage lists using her account (Figure 10.22).

FIGURE 10.21
The new user
policy with the
new permission
policy level

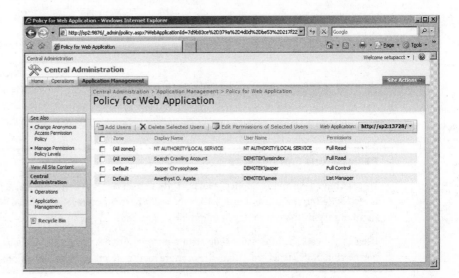

FIGURE 10.22
Logged in as a
web-application policy user
with List Manager
permissions

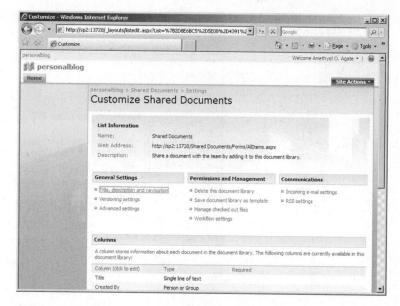

The Policy for Web Application page also manages (and overrides) the default anonymous access behavior for site collections in a selected web application or its individual zones. For this setting to be applied, the web application must have anonymous access enabled.

Normally, when a web application enables anonymous access in addition to Windows authentication, site collections still need to explicitly allow anonymous access in order for it to work. This is a fail safe in case there are secure items in any site collection. However, if anonymous access is allowed, then site-collection owners, subsite owners, and even list or library managers with the right to change permissions could enable anonymous access at their level. To more strictly lock down how anonymous can be handled at those levels from the web-application level, you can click Change Anonymous Access Permission Policy in the See Also bar on the Policy for Web Application page.

This will bring up the Anonymous User Policy page (Figure 10.23), where you can choose the web application and zone this policy will affect. You can apply one of three settings for the anonymous user policy:

None—No policy   This policy will not override anything happening at the site-collection level.

Deny Write—Has No Write Access   If this policy is selected, the only option that site administrators can enable for anonymous users is View Items. All other permissions for anonymous users cannot be applied. This policy does not explicitly allow anonymous access in its own right; it simply denies the permissions that might let someone contribute to a site anonymously.

Deny All—Has No Access   This option, if selected, means that even if anonymous is enabled at the web application at any point, anonymous access will still be unavailable at the site collection level.

In this example (Figure 10.23), Deny Write is selected for a default (parent web application) zone. This means while accessing the site with that URL, that even if you enable anonymous on a site collection contained there, you can't enable more than view item on any list or library, no matter what you try to do at the site-collection level (Figure 10.24).

FIGURE 10.23
The Anonymous User
Policy page

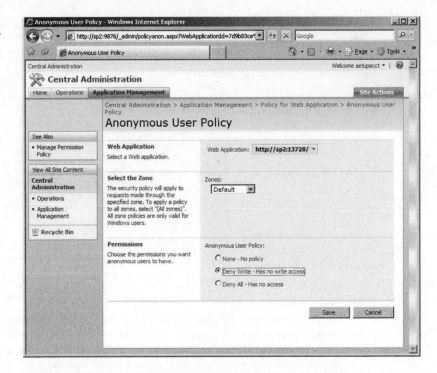

FIGURE 10.24
The Anonymous
settings allow only
View Items

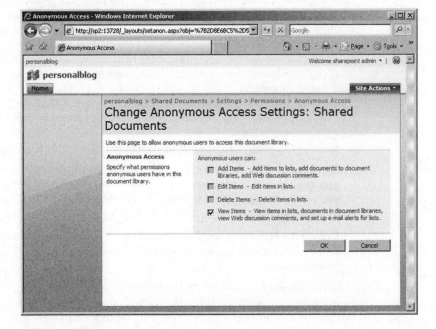

Authentication Providers

The Authentication Providers settings page is where you can change the authentication settings of a web application or zone (extended web application). When you click Authentication Providers, you will be taken to a page where you can confirm the web application you want to work in and the zones available for that web application (Figure 10.25).

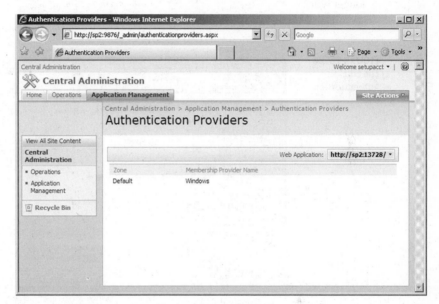

FIGURE 10.25
The Authentication Providers page

In my example the `http://sp2:13728` web application has no extended web applications yet, so it has only one zone. To see the authentication settings of a zone, simply select it.

MEMBERSHIP PROVIDERS AND ZONES

The membership provider name is listed next to the zone on the Authentication Providers page. In my example it indicates that the zone uses Windows authentication. If it were using forms-based authentication, that would be indicated instead.

Here is where using extended web applications really comes into its own. If you want to use different methods of authentication for users to access the same content, you can create multiple, extended web applications, assign them to different zones (one to a zone), and then return here to select different authentication methods for each zone. This means that when users use the Public URL for the zone, they are authenticated by the method selected for the zone.

Once you've selected a zone, the Edit Authentication page (Figure 10.26) will open. On it, you can enable or disable anonymous access and choose the kind of Windows authentication method you'd like to use (NTLM, Kerberos, or even Basic). You can enable or disable Client Integration as well, meaning you can allow or disallow users to automatically trigger the appropriate application to edit a document or file in a library. Client Integration doesn't always work well with forms-based authentication; however, if the option is disabled, users will have to download files to work on them and then upload them to save any changes because integration with Office will no longer work.

FIGURE 10.26
The Edit
Authentication
page

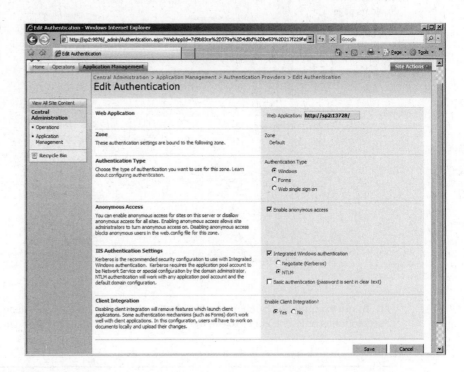

The most important setting here is the Authentication Type. Generally, Windows authentication is used because you are on a Windows network and SharePoint is a Windows product.

However, if you have external users with no corresponding Active Directory account (or you don't want them to have one), you could use forms-based authentication. Although SharePoint supports forms-based authentication because it uses ASP.NET 2.0, you will have to build or customize your own. SharePoint does not come with any in stock out of the box. You can build your own form using an ASP.NET 2.0 Membership Provider. ASP.NET 2.0 comes with a SQL Server Provider, but the details of how to do it are outside the scope of this book.

Although the Web single sign on option appears on the page, it is meant for MOSS (Microsoft Office SharePoint Server) and does not work for Windows SharePoint Services.

Workflow Management

The Workflow Management category is teeny tiny for a reason. In Windows SharePoint Services 3.0, not much is done with workflows at the web-application level.

Workflow Settings

This setting page is the only one in this category. In Figure 10.27, you can see that only a few settings are available for managing workflows.

◆ Allow the users to build custom workflows from existing workflow pieces deployed to the site (but not necessarily add their own).

◆ Alert internal users who do not have site access when they are assigned a workflow task.

◆ Allow external users to participate in a document workflow by emailing them the document.

FIGURE 10.27
The Workflow
Settings page

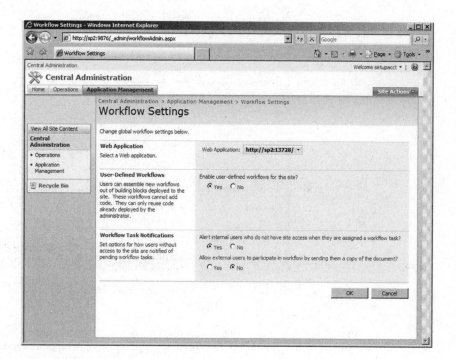

SharePoint Site Management

The SharePoint Site Management category is all about creating, deleting, and managing site collections. In this category, you can create, delete, and manage quotas and locks; enable site collection confirmation and deletion; and add or remove site administrators, which can be very useful if there happens to be a problem with the site collection and its management.

Create Site Collection

The Create site collection link is pretty self-explanatory. If you click the link, it will open a page that looks suspiciously as though you are simply creating a site—and you are. As you know if you looked through Chapter 8, when you create a new site collection, you are creating a new top-level address space and a site to put there. As you can see in Figure 10.28, you can enter a title, a description, and the URL path for the site. All other subsites below it will start with the path chosen for the top-level site. My example creates a new site collection (with the URL http://sp2/sites/newsite) for the HR team.

FIGURE 10.28
The Create Site
Collection page

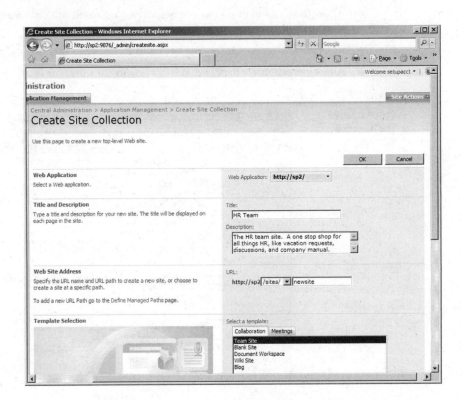

In addition, site collections can be used as user account and group boundaries (otherwise known as permission boundaries) because permissions can be inherited from the top-level site of a site collection throughout the libraries, lists, and subsites. This makes them convenient for branch offices or regions, because you can add users at the top-level site of a collection unique to that site collection, and have them easily propagate through all the subsites below it.

Delete Site Collection

The Delete site collection page contains options that are pretty straightforward (Figure 10.29). To start, you must specify the site collection to delete by clicking in the Site Collection selection box, and then selecting Change Site Collection.

FIGURE 10.29

The Delete Site Collection page

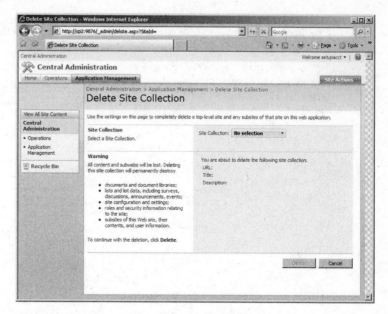

In the left pane on the Select Site Collection page, select the site collection you plan to delete (make certain you are in the correct web application). More detailed information about it will appear in the right pane (Figure 10.30). If you're sure that's the site collection you want to delete, click OK.

FIGURE 10.30

The Select Site Collection page

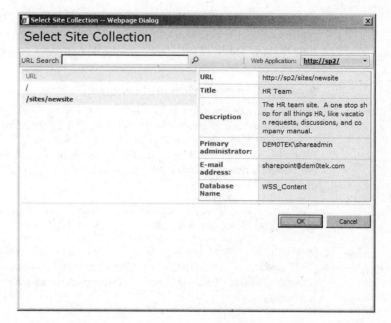

That'll take you back to the Delete Site Collection page, which will be propagated with the site collection's information. To continue with the site collection deletion, click Delete at the bottom of the page (Figure 10.31).

FIGURE 10.31
Delete the selected site collection.

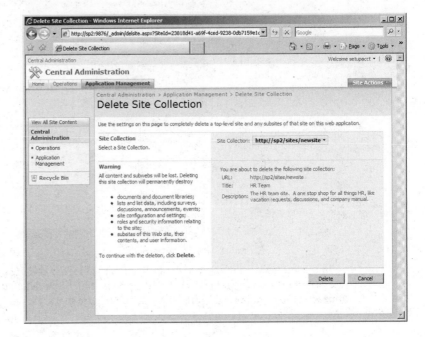

That will permanently delete the site collection and everything it contained. Before doing something so drastic, it is always a good idea to make a backup, just in case.

Site Use Confirmation and Deletion

The Site Use Confirmation and Deletion page setting is useful when users create their own site collections. Although this method is not the most useful or fanciest, Site Use Confirmation and Deletion lets you determine if and when site collection owners should be contacted to confirm that their site collection is still being used. You can even set it so that the site collection can be permanently deleted if the contact does not respond to the confirmation email in a certain number of requests.

SITE VERSUS SITE COLLECTION

Sometimes SharePoint says *site* when it really means *site collection*, as is the case with the Site Use Confirmation and Deletion page. This is because in prior versions of SharePoint, and in IIS, a *site* is a site collection and a *subsite* is called a *web* or *subweb*. These old naming conventions also exist in the STSADM commands.

As you can see in Figure 10.32, the settings on this page are pretty rudimentary. There is the option to enable site use confirmation emails, and there is a setting to delete the site collections.

FIGURE 10.32
The Site Use Confirmation and Deletion page

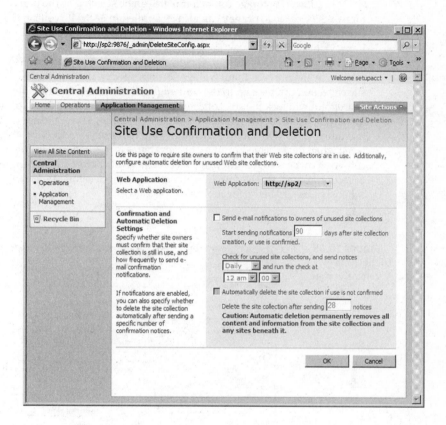

If you enable the site confirmation emails, you'll need to specify how long a site collection needs to have been running before the confirmation requests are sent to the site contacts (that can be both the primary and secondary administrators). Then you'll need to specify how often and when they are sent. Confirmation emails can get really annoying if the people you are contacting are busy, so daily may not be a good thing.

If you enable the email notifications, you can also set how many of those notifications can go unconfirmed before the site collection is deleted. If the delete option is not enabled, confirmation emails can continue indefinitely without anything happening to the site collection—defeating the purpose of the notification. However, always keep in mind that when a site collection is deleted, it is permanently deleted. You won't find it in the Recycle Bin. If you enable the delete option, make sure you have a backup of the site collections to be deleted in case the site-collection contact calls you in a panic, wondering where it went.

For detailed step-by-steps instructions and descriptions about site use and confirmation, see Chapter 8.

Quota Templates

This is another page that focuses on controlling the growth of site collections. Here is where you can create storage-limit templates for site collections. (Although SharePoint says sites, it means site collections.) A storage quota template can be selected as the default for site collections (useful for Self-Service sites) or they can also be applied to each site collection specifically. If you click the Quota Templates link, it will take you to a page with two sections: Template Name and Storage Limit Values.

As you can see in Figure 10.33, you should enter a template name in the Template Name section. In the Storage Limit Values section, specify the maximum size in megabytes that the site collection can take up in the content database. When the site collection hits that maximum, SharePoint will lock the site collection, prevent the addition of new content, and refuse all changes to that site—although it will allow you to delete things until the site collection falls beneath the maximum limit. (Do not forget to empty the End user Recycle Bin). You can also set a warning level; when the specified number of megabytes is reached, a warning email will be sent to the site collection owners so that they can act preemptively before the maximum is reached. When a site collection contact receives notification that they are reaching their limit, make sure they take it seriously (see Chapter 8 for more about quotas).

FIGURE 10.33
The Quota
Templates page

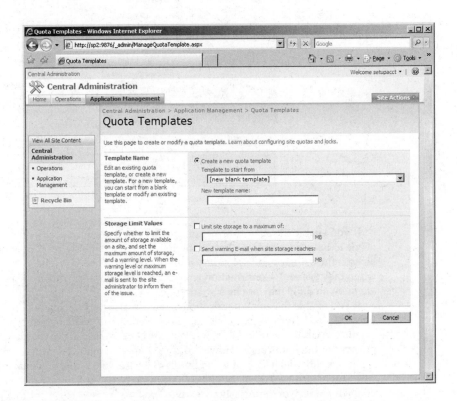

You can make as many templates as you'd like to apply to different site collection situations.

Site Collection Quotas and Locks

The Site Collection Quotas and Locks page does two things:

◆ It lets you apply a Quota template to a site collection or apply a custom quota to the site collection, instead of applying an existing Quota template.

◆ It shows you the lock status of a given site collection and allows you to change it.

In Figure 10.34, you can see that the page contains settings for Site Lock Information and Site Quota Information—and of course, the site collection selection itself.

FIGURE 10.34
The Site Collection Quotas and Locks page

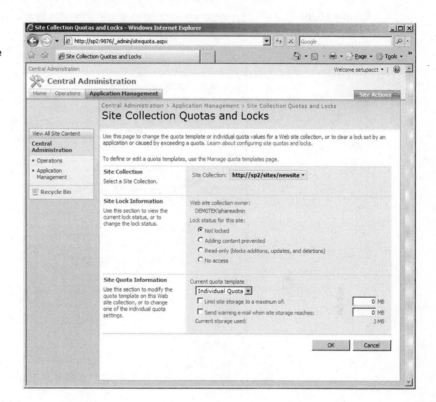

In the Site Lock Information section, there are four lock states:

◆ Not Locked

◆ Adding Content Prevented

◆ Read-Only (Blocks Additions, Updates, And Deletions)

◆ No Access

Here is where you can check the status of a site collection *and* change its lock state. This ability is very useful if, for instance, you have a rogue user doing bad things and you need to block all access to the site collection until the situation is contained.

In the Site Quota Information section, you can set the selected site collection's storage quota individually or assign an existing template to it if you'd like. This setting is useful if you want to change the quota assigned to a site collection during its creation.

Site Collection Administrators

As you can see in Figure 10.35, this link simply opens a page where you can see the primary and secondary administrators for the selected site collection.

FIGURE 10.35
The Site Collection Administrators page

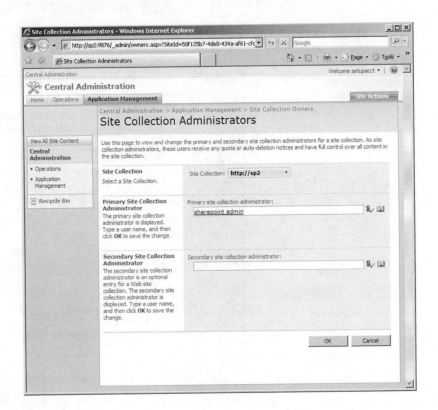

AN ADMINISTRATOR BY ANY OTHER NAME

SharePoint has a habit of using several different names to refer to *site administrators*, including *site owners* and *site contacts*.

This setting is here is so a farm administrator can see who is supposed to own a particular site collection and reassign ownership if necessary—or take one over if they must.

To change the site collection you want to manage, click the Site Collection menu, select Change Site Collection, pick the site collection you plan to check, and click OK.

Site Collection List

The Site collection list link simply lists all the site collections for a particular web application (Figure 10.36). This information is very handy when you're troubleshooting why users can no longer access a site collection. If you come here and find that a site collection is gone, you'll know what the problem is. Ironically, considering it's the last setting on the page, if you come to this setting first and select a site collection from the list, that site collection will be the default site collection selected in the Site Collection menu of most of the pages in this category. Coincidentally, this page is identical to the Select Site Collection page used to select a site collection to delete.

FIGURE 10.36

The Site Collection List page

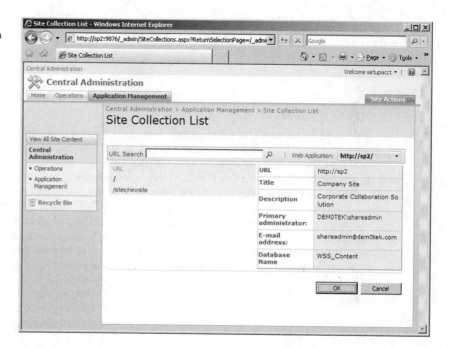

External Service Connections

Primarily focused on external applications, the External Service Connections category contains links mainly useful for those using Windows SharePoint Services with Microsoft Office SharePoint Server 2007.

Records Center

This settings page is useful only if you are using Microsoft Office SharePoint Server 2007 (MOSS). The Records Center is a MOSS site template meant to be used as a central repository for the long term storage of a company's records. If you were running MOSS, you'd use this page to let Central Administration know what the path of the Records Center was (Figure 10.37).

FIGURE 10.37
The Configure Connection To Records
Center page

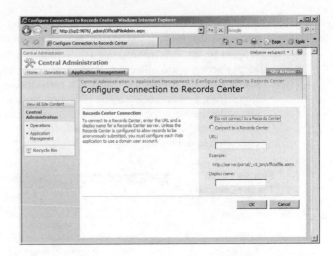

HTML Viewer

This could be a pretty cool set of settings but currently it requires an HTML Viewer file that is difficult to find, it currently only supports Office 2003, and needs to be updated to support Office 2007 (but Microsoft does not seem to be offering to do so). Essentially this setting is only intended to be used by already existing HTML Viewer configurations.

HTML viewing is intended to give users who do not have Office installed on their computers the ability to view documents in their browser. An HTML Viewer service converts those documents on-the-fly from their original file type to HTML. Most of the original formatting is kept, and the document is at least readable. The HTML Viewer service must be acquired, and installed on a computer that will bear the brunt of having to make those file conversions; therefore, it should be installed on a network computer other than the SharePoint server. As you can see in Figure 10.38, you are expected to enter the path in the Path to HTML Viewer Server field; SharePoint knows you aren't going to run the HTML Viewer service locally.

FIGURE 10.38
The HTML Viewer page

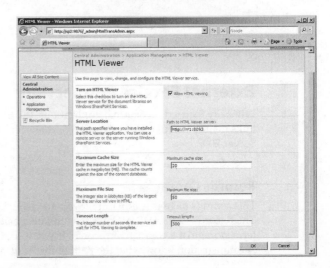

Once the HTML Viewer service software is installed on a network computer (and configured with a custom installation of Office), you can use the HTML Viewer page to point to the path of that computer and turn on the service for all document libraries in the server farm. There are maximum size settings (in megabytes) for how large the HTML cache file should be and for the maximum size file that can be converted to HTML. There is also a timeout limit for how long, in seconds, the conversion should take. The default is 5 minutes (displayed as 300 seconds).

Document Conversions

Document conversions are set on individual web applications and make it possible to do document-type conversions within SharePoint. A Document converter allows you to take a document of one type (such as a Word document) and convert it into another type (such as a PowerPoint document or PDF) Primarily for MOSS, this capability requires converter files and two services to be running and configured for this process to be successful. The files and two services already exist for MOSS, but you have to make them for WSS. See the Microsoft Developers Network website (MSDN), for more information. The Document Conversion Load Balancer Service is in charge of accepting and balancing conversion requests for the server farm. The Document Conversion Launcher Service is actually in charge of converting the document. The document conversion process requires the Document Conversion Launcher service have access to the appropriate converter files so that it knows what it is converting from and what it's converting to.

If you examine Figure 10.39, you'll understand why a load-balancer server is required. This is not network load balancing, but instead SharePoint wants to know what SharePoint server on the farm is running the document conversion load-balancing service. Otherwise, you simply enable document conversion and set the schedule for when conversions should be processed.

FIGURE 10.39
The Configure Document Conversions page

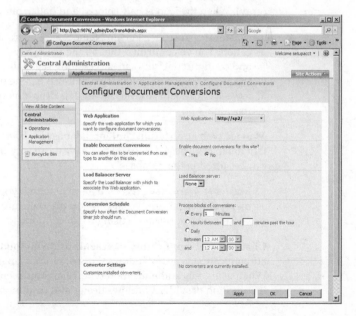

The Bottom Line

Navigate Application Management   The Application Management page in Central Administration is divided into five categories, and each category has several links focused on Web Applications, their site collections, and additional customization tools.

Master It   You want to ensure members of the Active Directory security group "Corporate Auditors" have full read access to every site collection in a Web Application, but cannot make any changes to anything within the site collections, regardless of what the site administrators do. Which setting would you use to do that, and how would that be done?

Manage site collections   The SharePoint Site Management category is focused on site collections. Here you can add, delete, and customize site collections. Site collections can have their administrators changed, storage quotas assigned (either from a template or directly) and can be locked. You can enable site usage notifications and automated deletion there as well.

Master It   Two popular configuration options are Site quotas and Site Use Confirmation. One of these options can apply different settings for individual site collections while the other is set at the web application level and applies the same settings to all enclosed site collections. Which is which?

Configure Person Name Smart Tags and Presence Settings   Person Name Smart Tags require Outlook be installed and configured for the SharePoint users. It creates a drop-down menu on every username in the SharePoint site collections allowing direct emailing and other communication options.

Online Presence requires Messenger be installed and configured for the SharePoint users. It creates a small icon beside every username in the SharePoint site collections, showing the user's current online presence. This can be Online (green), Busy (red), Away (light orange), or Offline (gray). When the icon is half-colored and half-white, the user is also Idle.

Master It   You have Person Name Smart Tags and Presence Settings enabled on a web application. You've confirmed that all the users have Outlook and Windows Messenger installed and configured. Users can successfully see Online Presence icons for each other, and can use the Smart Tag drop-down menu. However, one user, Jasper, cannot see any Online Presence icons but can still use the Smart Tag drop-down menu. What might be wrong on Jasper's machine?

Manage web application content databases   Each web application can have one or more content database. These databases can have a capacity limit that restricts how many site collections can be stored in the database.

Master It   You have received a warning that your web application's database is reaching its maximum size limit. What can you do to ensure that the database does not become locked and the web application using it can continue to function?

Change a web application's authentication method   Web Applications can have one of three authentication types: Windows, Forms, or Web single sign on. The most common is Windows. When using this authentication type, SharePoint sends authentication requests to whatever authentication provider Windows designates (commonly Active Directory). These requests can be sent using one of three authentication methods—NTLM, Kerberos, or Basic. This is configured in Authentication Providers.

Master It   You have a web application configured to use the Windows authentication type and the Kerberos authentication method. You are planning on providing access to the web application for some remote users and you want to use NTLM as the authentication method for these remote users while keeping Kerberos for your local users. How do you configure SharePoint to allow for both methods?

Chapter 11

Users and Permissions

Controlling user access is a fundamental concern to SharePoint Administrators and it is where they earn a lot of our bread and butter. I mean, really, what good is SharePoint if no one can use it? But nothing is worse than having users unable to get to the information they need or allowing someone to get to information that they are not supposed to see. Access management is a prime area of focus in the administrator's life, if you plan and implement user access correctly, life goes much more smoothly. WSS 3.0 user security is improved over the previous version with a finer level of granularity and more authentication options.

In this chapter, you'll learn how to:

◆ Define users and groups in SharePoint

◆ Add users and groups in SharePoint

◆ Define permissions and permission levels in SharePoint

◆ Set Permissions on a Site/List/List item for a user or a group

◆ Plan user access in SharePoint

What Are Users, Groups, and Permissions?

When you start looking at security, chances are good that you start with the basics: who is allowed to access SharePoint resources, what resources are they allowed to see, what resources are they allowed to use, and how are they allowed to use them.

The people who are allowed access to SharePoint are commonly referred to as users. To add user accounts, SharePoint utilizes the services of an authentication provider, such as Windows integrated Authentication (which on a domain uses Active Directory, on a stand-alone server it is that server's security account manager database). Active Directory (AD) stores its own user accounts, and people use it to log into their workstations to access network resources all the time. SharePoint uses that authentication source for user accounts when setting up users in its own environment, which allows administrators to use accounts already available in AD to populate its users and group. And, when a user logs into SharePoint, SharePoint passes the authentication information to the authentication provider. If that account is okay with the provider and they authenticate it, then SharePoint either lets the user get to the site they are trying to access, or if the account is not a member of the site, they are rejected. Once there, SharePoint uses groups, permission levels, permissions, and other security to authorize the user to access the resources they were meant to, and blocks access to those they weren't.

This is why the term "user account" is used in two ways:

◆ **Domain user accounts** refer directly to the accounts in AD.

◆ **SharePoint user accounts** refer to the user accounts added to SharePoint from AD (or other authentication source).

SharePoint manages what a user account can do with *permissions*. There is a large list of set permissions that are available at the web application level. These permissions, when applied to a user account, govern what it can do. Permissions are generally grouped together in what are called *permission levels*, to be applied to users based on the type of role they will play, or tasks they will perform in SharePoint. There are a few default permission levels, such as full control (which usually is applied to administrators who require all permissions to be enabled), or contribute (which is usually applied to users who will be viewing content, adding content, editing content, etc.). Individual permissions can't be applied to users directly, but permission levels can.

For the convenience of administrators, in addition to permission levels putting together useful permissions into role based combinations, SharePoint uses another convention; the SharePoint group (sometimes known as a site group). SharePoint groups are useful because they are associated with particular permission levels (or even combinations of permission levels if necessary), so when the users are added to the group they are all given the same permissions. Changing a group's permissions changes them for all users contained therein. Groups are an excellent organizational device (which is why Microsoft keeps using them), allowing users to be grouped together by applied permissions so they can all be added to a resource's access list in one go (and removed that way as well). In addition, SharePoint has a People and Groups page that displays the users in a particular group. Members of the group can go to that page and see the other members and access their user information (if they have permission to). If Directory Management Service is enabled, the group can have a distribution list associated with it in AD, allowing someone to email all members of the group at once.

You can add users individually to SharePoint groups, or you can take advantage of Active Directory by adding entire security groups (such as adding the Sales_Dept security group as members of the Sales site collection). This is a good thing from a SharePoint administrative point of view, because SharePoint can only handle so many security objects (otherwise known as *security principals*). As far as SharePoint is concerned, both a single user account and a security group are security objects, even though the security group can contain many user accounts. Using security groups to add users to SharePoint groups does add an extra layer of administration, because any change to that security group in AD (such as removing a user) could have an obvious affect on whether or not that user can access SharePoint. However, if you focus on managing users in groups at the AD level, then it's a snap to simply add their security groups to SharePoint and not really worry about the individual users and whether or not they've been demoted, promoted, or fired at that level. The changes occur in AD and then are reflected in SharePoint. All this talk of groups leaves you with two different kinds of groups to consider:

◆ **Domain security groups**, created and controlled by the AD administrators. A domain security group contains users and is a method for applying security uniformly to all users it contains.

◆ **SharePoint groups**, controlled, and that can be created by site collection administrators in SharePoint. Intended to more easily apply permissions to groups of users at once. Secondarily, can be used to indentify contained users by the role they play in SharePoint.

AUTHENTICATION VARIES

Keep in mind that, although I am using Windows Authentication with Active Directory as my example, SharePoint is easily meant to support other forms of authentication. As a matter of fact, SharePoint was built to be authentication independent so it can take advantage of multiple different kinds of authentication providers. One of the most useful is called Forms based authentication, which takes advantage of a SQL database for its authentication source. It's a convenient, alternate form of authentication if Windows Authentication is not a viable option for you. It takes a little work to configure, but once done, it works like any other authentication provider.

All SharePoint groups are created at the site collection level and are available to any subsite in the site collection. However, you can choose to create a SharePoint group that has permissions only on a particular subsite, if you don't want it to inherit permissions from the parent site. Although sites that are built on Windows SharePoint Services can, of course, have additional SharePoint groups, Windows SharePoint Services 3.0 provides three default SharePoint groups:

◆ Site name Owners (such as Company Site Owners, default permission level: Full Control)

◆ Site name Members (default permission level: Contribute)

◆ Site name Visitors (default permission level: Read)

Each of these SharePoint groups is associated with a default permission level, but you can change the permission level for any SharePoint group as needed. Anyone who is assigned a permission level that includes the Create Groups permission can create custom SharePoint groups.

Before you start working with permissions or creating, editing, and changing groups, you need to clearly understand authentication and authorization. They are critical to a good fundamental understanding of security. *Authentication* is the process of establishing identity; in a security context, this is assessing the credentials of a user seeking access to resources under the control of the authentication provider. You can compare this to matching up someone's face to the picture on their passport to make sure that they are the same. Authentication verifies that they are who they claim to be and you can proceed to the next stage, which is authorization. People frequently talk about authentication and authorization as if they were the same thing, but they most definitely are not. *Authorization* allows a user to do something with or to the resources their authentication gave them access to. It is the permission to do a particular task in a system, such as opening a page, reading a document, or managing permissions. All permissions make up the level of authorization for a user. That level of authorization can be considered a permission level inside of SharePoint.

Permissions are the authorization to perform specific actions, such as viewing pages, opening items, and creating subsites. WSS 3.0 provides 33 predefined permissions that you can use to allow users to perform specific actions. For example, users assigned the View Items permission can view items in a list. Each permission belongs to one of the following categories: List, Site, or Personal. Permissions are not assigned directly to users or SharePoint groups. Instead, permissions are enabled in one or more permission levels, which are in turn assigned to users and SharePoint groups. Permissions can be included in multiple permission levels, and it is possible to apply multiple permission levels to a single SharePoint group, user, or domain group. Permission levels will be covered later in the Permission Levels section.

Individual Permissions

Permissions are rights to do something; to view, create, delete, or edit something. Permissions are allowed or disallowed at the web application level using the User permissions for Web applications setting on the Application Management page, in Central Administration. SharePoint breaks these permissions down into categories for assignment to users and groups. 33 separate permissions are divided across three categories (Site, List, and Personal). The following sections will describe them all. Table 11.1 is divided into four columns. The Permission Name is what appears on the pages where you select the permissions. The Description explains what the permission allows you to do. The Required permissions are additional permissions that the permission needs to have also enabled to function. The Permission Levels by Default lists the default permission levels containing this permission. This is also a useful guide to selecting or creating permission levels.

The permissions are shown Figure 11.1 and described in Table 11.1.

FIGURE 11.1
Permission Level List permissions

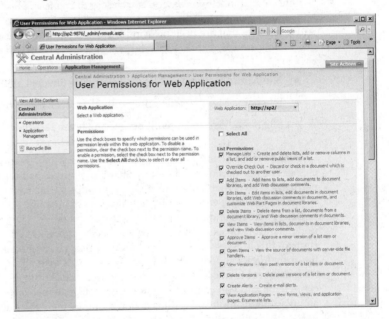

The List permissions govern the actions available to users in lists and on list items. You can combine them to reach your particular goals, but be careful about being overly gracious with what they are allowed to do, such as assuming that someone who needs to manage versioning and approve items should also Manage lists. Also, keep in mind that when you look at List permissions, they will be dependent on the choices made for the lists. For instance, View Versions will work only if you have Versioning turned on for the list; you could have permission to view versions but no ability to view them if versioning is turned off. Another interesting thing about the list permissions is that what you can do to a list item is broken out explicitly, but there are no explicit create list, delete list or change list permissions; they are all lumped under the Manage List permission. Therefore if you want someone to just be able to edit an existing list's settings or add columns, they also have to be allowed to create more lists. Currently permissions are not quite as granular as they could be, and that alone is useful to know.

TABLE 11.1:   List Permissions

PERMISSION NAME	DESCRIPTION	REQUIRED PERMISSIONS	PERMISSION LEVELS BY DEFAULT
Manage Lists	Create and delete lists, add or remove columns in a list, and add or remove public views of a list. This is the main control permission to allow control of the lists on the site.	View Items, View Pages, Open, Manage Personal Views	Design, Full Control
Override Check Out	Discard or check in a document that is checked out to another user without saving the current changes. This is actually a key administration feature, because it allows those who have the permission to effectively discard a check out and return the document to available status.	View Items, View Pages, Open	Design, Full Control
Add Items	Add items to lists, add documents to document libraries, and add web discussion comments. A Basic Member Level right, allowing the user to interact with the contents of the site.	View Items, View Pages, Open	Contribute, Design, Full Control
Edit Items	Edit items in lists, edit documents in document libraries, edit web discussion comments in documents, and customize Web Part pages in document libraries. A Basic Member Level right, allowing the user to interact with the contents of the site.	View Items, View Pages, Open	Contribute, Design, Full Control
Delete Items	Delete items from a list, documents from a document library, and web discussion comments in documents. A Basic Member Level right, allowing the user to interact with the contents of the site.	View Items, View Pages, Open	Contribute, Design, Full Control
View Items	View items in lists, documents in document libraries, and view web discussion comments. To use any of the items on the site you must be able to view them first.	View Pages, Open	Read, Contribute, Design, Full Control
Approve Items	Approve minor versions of list items or documents. Versioning would need to be enabled for this to be in effect.	Edit Items, View Items, View Pages, Open	Design, Full Control
Open Items	View the source of documents with server-side file handlers. This allows the user to open the document in the source application, such as Word or Excel.	View Items, View Pages, Open	Read, Contribute, Design, Full Control

(Continued)

TABLE 11.1: List Permissions (*Continued*)

PERMISSION NAME	DESCRIPTION	REQUIRED PERMISSIONS	PERMISSION LEVELS BY DEFAULT
View Versions	View past versions of list items or documents. Versioning would need to be enabled for this to be in effect.	View Items, Open Items, View Pages, Open	Read, Contribute, Design, Full Control
Delete Versions	Delete past versions of list items or documents. Versioning would need to be enabled for this to be in effect.	View Items, View Versions, View Pages, Open	Contribute, Design, Full Control
Create Alerts	Create email alerts, so that the user can be notified via Outlook that something has changed in the item.	View Items, View Pages, Open	Read, Contribute, Design, Full Control
View Application Pages	View forms, views, and application pages. Enumerate lists. This allows you to open and use any pages, which is basic to all other functions.	Open	All

The second category of permissions is Site permissions. These permissions govern the user's access at the site and subsite level and what they can do concerning sites there. The permissions for the SharePoint site are shown in Figure 11.2 and described in Table 11.2.

FIGURE 11.2
The SharePoint Site permissions

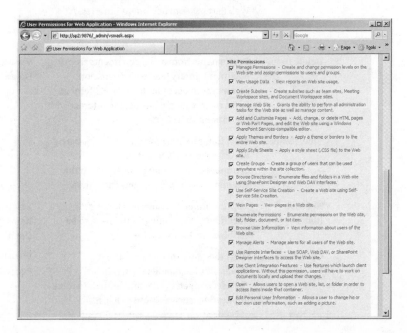

TABLE 11.2:   SharePoint Site Permissions

Permission Name	Description	Required Permissions	Permission Levels by Default
Manage Permissions	Create and change permission levels on the website and assign permissions to users and groups. This permission enables control of other permissions. It is typically reserved for administration-level people.	View Items, Open Items, View Versions, Browse Directories, View Pages, Enumerate Permissions, Browse User Information, Open	Full Control
View Usage Data	View reports on website usage. A key method of gathering metric data on the site. This permission is typically reserved for administration-level people.	View Pages, Open	Full Control
Create Subsites	Create subsites such as Team sites, Meeting Workspace sites, and Document Workspace sites. This permission deals with the structure of the site and should be reserved for administration-level people to allow for the tightest control of the environment.	View Pages, Browse User Information, Open	Full Control
Manage Web Site	Perform all administration tasks for the website and manage content. This permission is the high-level control permission that gives full administration control to the holder.	View Items, Add and Customize Pages, Browse Directories, View Pages, Enumerate Permissions, Browse User Information, Open	Full Control
Add and Customize Pages	Add, change, or delete HTML pages or Web Part pages, and edit the website by using a Windows SharePoint Services–compatible editor, such as SharePoint Designer. This permission enables more site changes.	View Items, Browse Directories, View Pages, Open	Design, Full Control

(Continued)

TABLE 11.2:   SharePoint Site Permissions (*Continued*)

PERMISSION NAME	DESCRIPTION	REQUIRED PERMISSIONS	PERMISSION LEVELS BY DEFAULT
Apply Themes And Borders	Apply a theme or borders to the entire website. As this permission deals with presentation and design, it is not restricted to administration-level people but should also include the designers and developers.	View Pages, Open	Design, Full Control
Apply Style Sheets	Apply a style sheet (css file) to the website. As this permission deals with presentation and design, it is not restricted to administration-level people but should also include the designers and developers.	View Pages, Open	Design, Full Control
Create Groups	Create a group of users that can be used anywhere within the site collection. This is a security-based permission that will allow control of access to the site. This is administration level.	View Pages, Browse User Information, Open	Full Control
Browse Directories	Enumerate files and folders in a website by using Microsoft Office SharePoint Designer and Web DAV interfaces.	View Pages, Open	Contribute, Design, Full Control
Use Self-Service Site Creation	Create a website by using Self-Service Site Creation. This permission allows users to create a site. This permission is only active if Self-Service Site Creation is enabled on the web application, otherwise it is ignored.	View Pages, Browse User Information, Open	Read, Contribute, Design, Full Control
View Pages	View pages in a website. This permission is for everyone.	Open	Read, Contribute, Design, Full Control
Enumerate Permissions	Enumerate permissions on the website, list, folder, document, or list item. This is a security-based permission that will allow control of access to the site. This is an administration-level permission.	Browse Directories, View Pages, Browse User Information, Open	Full Control

(Continued)

TABLE 11.2:   SharePoint Site Permissions (*Continued*)

PERMISSION NAME	DESCRIPTION	REQUIRED PERMISSIONS	PERMISSION LEVELS BY DEFAULT
Browse User Information	View information about users of the website. This permission allows users to discover public information about other users and engage in social networking.	Open	All
Manage Alerts	Manage alerts for all users of the website. This is an overriding permission to the List Permission Create Alerts permission. It allows the administrator to change what other alerts are doing.	View Items, View Pages, Open	Full Control
Use Remote Interfaces	Use SOAP, Web DAV, or Office SharePoint Designer interfaces to access the website. This permission just allows external access to the site from other SharePoint component pieces.	Open	All
Use Client Integration Features	Use features that launch client applications. Without this permission, users must work on documents locally and then upload their changes. This permission enables the web-enabled collaboration that is the heart of WSS 3.0.	Use Remote Interfaces, Open	All
Open	Open a website, list, or folder to access items inside that container. This one is needed for almost all other permissions to function.	None	All
Edit Personal User Information	Users can change their own user information, such as adding a picture. This permission is the one that allows users to make public the information others might browse if they have the Browse Information permission.	Browse User Information, Open	Contribute, Design, Full Control

Site permissions are the basis of control at the site level. Combinations of these permissions are what define user's effective control of their environment. This category of permissions contains powerful, administrative capabilities, such as managing permissions and seeing site usage information, versus the ability to open documents using the correct client or see document libraries using webDAV (Explorer View) for users.

As a matter of fact, if a user cannot use Explorer View, make certain they have the Use Remote Interfaces permission. Despite the fact that that permission also makes it possible for them to open the page in SharePoint Designer, it's needed for all browsing of libraries with Explorer.

SELF-SERVICE SITE CREATION BLOCKING

If you would like to block the possibility of Self-Service Site Creation ever being used in a particular web application, deny its permission here. Then, even if it is enabled in Central Administration, no user will be able to use it. It will piss people off when they try, but it is a fail safe way of avoiding an "accidental" onslaught of new site collections. Another thing you can do is disable the permission in particular permission levels, allowing Self-Service Site Creation only to the permission levels you choose, as opposed to all of them.

The third category of permissions is Personal permissions. The Personal permissions from the SharePoint site are shown in Figure 11.3 and described in Table 11.3.

FIGURE 11.3
The SharePoint Personal permissions

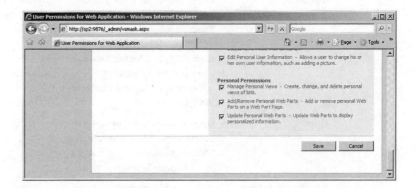

Personal permissions deal with an individual user's view of the website, including being about to manage their own personal view of lists, libraries, and web part pages (particularly the home page). Unfortunately, if you allow users the permission to change web parts, intending to let them personalize the home page, they can also modify web parts on the list and library pages as well. So consider carefully the ramifications of what personalizations you allow them to do.

Permissions, individually, are never applied to users or groups. Instead Permission levels are created by making combinations of these permissions, and those permission levels are applied to users and groups. Therefore, it is only fitting that we take a look at permission levels next.

TABLE 11.3:   SharePoint Personal Permissions

PERMISSION NAME	DESCRIPTION	REQUIRED PERMISSIONS	PERMISSION LEVELS BY DEFAULT
Manage Personal Views	Create, change, and delete personal views of lists.	View Items, View Pages, Open	Contribute, Design, Full Control
Add/Remove Personal Web Parts	Add or remove personal web parts on a Web Part page.	View Items, View Pages, Open, Update Personal Web Parts	Contribute, Design, Full Control
Update Personal Web Parts	Update web parts to display personalized information.	View Items, View Pages, Open	Contribute, Design, Full Control

Permission Levels

Permission levels enable you to assign a set of permissions to users and SharePoint groups so that they can perform specific actions or *tasks* on your site. Most permission levels (and SharePoint groups for that matter) are role related, aligning the set of permissions with a task that must be performed. With permission levels, you can control which permissions are granted to users and SharePoint groups on your site. For example, by default, the Read permission level includes the View Items, Open Items, View Pages, and View Versions permissions (among others), all of which are needed to read documents, items, and pages on a SharePoint site.

The following permission levels are provided by default: Full Control, Design, Contribute, Read, and Limited Access. Anyone assigned a permission level that includes the Manage Permissions permission can customize permission levels (except for the Full Control and Limited Access) or create new ones. Site owners are assigned the Manage Permissions permission, by default.

The defaults each have their own uses and purposes, which are described in Table 11.4.

As you look at the levels and try to decide what to do with them, remember you always want to give the minimum amount of permission to do a task that the user will need. You can see in the table that each succeeding level has all the permissions of the level before it and then adds more. You cannot directly edit either the Full Control or Limited Access permission levels, the two far ends of the spectrum, but they can be changed at the Web Application level in the Central Administration tool.

REMOVING A PERMISSION REMOVES IT COMPLETELY

Now that you know about permissions at the web application level you can see another reason why a web application is considered a security boundary. Not only can each web application specify its own authentication, anonymous access, or whether or not it uses SSL, but it can also control exactly what permission are or are not available for all site collections contained therein.

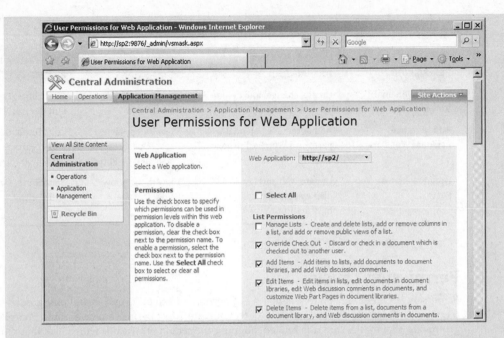

If you disable a permission at the web application level, at the site collection level absolutely no permission level will have that permission available (not even Full Control).

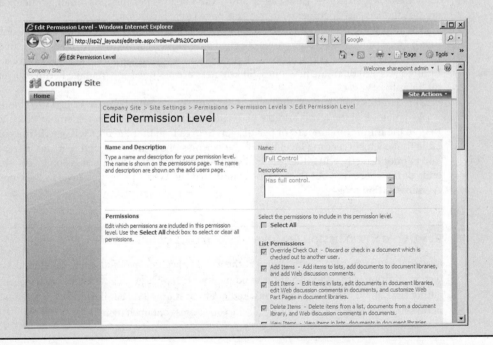

TABLE 11.4: WSS 3.0 Default Permission Levels

PERMISSION LEVEL	DESCRIPTION	INCLUDED PERMISSIONS
Limited Access	This level is designed to be combined with fine-grained permissions to give users access to a specific list, document library, item, or document, without giving users access to the entire site. This level allows very focused control of access. *Cannot be customized or deleted.*	View Application Pages Browse User Information Use Remote Interfaces Use Client Integration Features Open
Read	Read-only access to the website. This is a default for <<*Site name*>> Visitors group. Not intended to add, edit, or delete items, or be able to personalize their views.	Limited Access permissions plus: View Items Open Items View Versions Create Alerts Use Self-Service Site Creation (when enabled at web application) Browse User Information View Application Pages User Remote Interfaces Use Client Integration Features View Pages
Contribute	Can add and edit items in existing lists and libraries, and personalize page views. This is a default for <<*Site name*>> Members group. Not intended to manage lists, create subsites, or manage permissions.	Read permissions plus: Add Items Edit Items Delete Items Delete Versions Browse Directories Edit Personal User Information Manage Personal Views Add/Remove Personal Web Parts Update Personal Web Parts
Design	Can create (and if necessary, manage) lists and document libraries, and edit pages in the website. This would generally be used for modifying the look and feel of your pages in the site. Cannot create or manage groups, alerts, sites, or permissions.	Contribute permissions plus: Manage Lists Override Check Out Approve Items Add and Customize pages Apply Themes and Borders Apply Style Sheets User Remote Interfaces Use Client Integration Features Manage Lists
Full Control	Has all permissions enabled. Specifically, can manage and create sites, permission levels, alerts, groups, and view usage data. This is the default for <<*Site name*>> Owners group. *Cannot be customized or deleted either.* Required for full site management.	All permissions without restriction

Manage Permission Levels

Now that you've seen the out-of-the-box permission levels, you might need to do some customization. The Read, Design, and Contribute permission levels can be copied or modified, and otherwise new permission levels can be created for a site. In other words; you can use the pre-made permission levels as they are; you can use those levels but modify them; you can copy those levels, then modify the copy; or you can apply your own and ignore the default levels (with the exception of Limited Access). For example, if you have a SharePoint server with a large number of users and groups assigned the Read permission level and you decide you want to restrict these users further (or give them more control), you can edit the Read permission level to provide the precise combination of permissions desired, without having to give all these users a new permission level. On the other hand, if you create a new site, or want to add a lot of new users with unique permission needs to an existing site, you can create a new permission level with the correct permissions; either by using an existing level as a template or by creating one from scratch. Permission levels were meant to be easy to manage; as long as you know what the individual permissions actually do (particularly in combination) you can have a lot of control over your SharePoint resources, and therefore over your users.

Permission levels are most often modified at the site collection's top-level site and then inherited by the subsites below it. So most of the exercises will be done at the top-level site of the site collection (which in my case is Company Site). Be aware that you can break inheritance at any subsite, where they then can do as they wish with their SharePoint groups and permission levels at that point.

VIEWING SITE PERMISSIONS

To work with permission levels, you must get to the Permissions page for the site. Both the Advanced Permissions link in Site Settings for the site, and the last option on the Quick Launch bar, Site Permissions, will take you to the Permissions page. This page (Figure 11.4) will allow you to see all the groups and security principals on your site to which permission levels have been assigned directly, what those permissions are, and the type of object they are (user, SharePoint group, etc).

FIGURE 11.4
The Permissions page

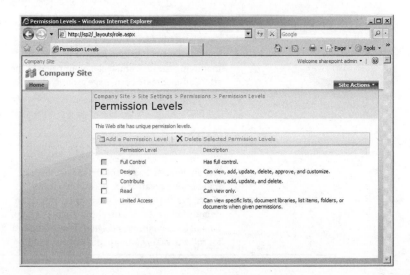

Typically this list will simply be a list of your SharePoint groups only, but it can also contain individual user accounts or security groups as well. During the adding of a new user, if you had elected to assign permissions to the new user or domain security group directly (instead of adding them to a SharePoint group), they would then appear in this list. This is because, usually, user permissions are managed for the users in their respective groups, but if you apply a permission level directly to the account, they need to be listed somewhere so they can also be managed. Site Permissions is the last bastion of hope for them in that case.

On a Permissions page for the site (my example is the top-level, Company Site), the standard Quick Launch bar is moved down and the Groups Quick Launch bar replaces it on the top left of the page. This bar lists the SharePoint groups available on this site; a More . . . link, which takes you to a page listing all groups (including, oddly enough, any security groups you might have added to any SharePoint groups); an All People link which lists all users for the site, regardless of their group affiliation; and a Site Permissions link, which takes you to, conveniently, to the Permission page you are on now.

The Action bar has the standard three buttons; New, Actions, and Settings.

- ◆ **New** allows you to add either a new user or a new group.

- ◆ **Actions** allows you to either edit or remove the permissions of a selected group.

- ◆ **Settings** allows you to manage site collection administrators, enable or disable access requests, and configure permission levels.

ACCESS REQUESTS

Access Request is generally enabled by default, is a site level feature, and allows users to, when faced with a denial of access, if it's a missing menu item or a blocked list item, click Request Access in the Welcome menu, but if they are completely denied access to a list, library, or subsite; an Access Denied page will come up with a link to request access available for them.

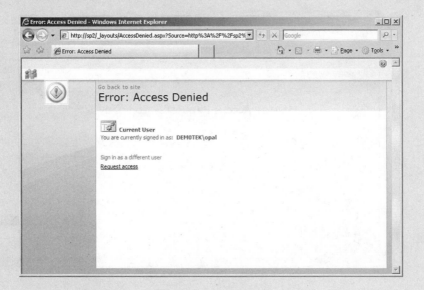

If they click it they can request access and send the request. It is obviously up to the user to explain what they need access to and why they need that access.

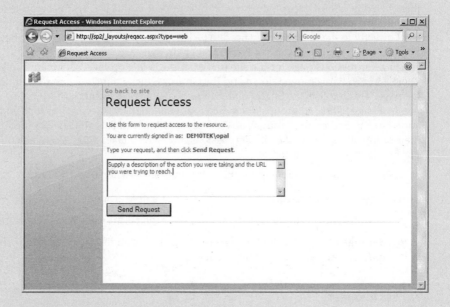

According to the menu option, the request will be sent to the site administrator, but actually it will be send to the address in the Access Request Settings section. This address is by default is the original site collection administrator, but it can be changed.

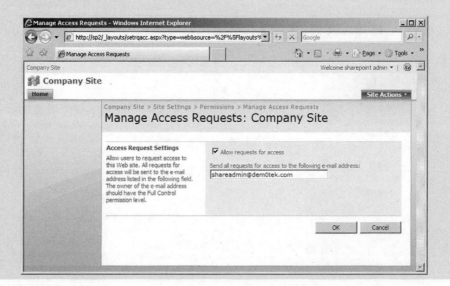

This feature is a double-edged sword. It lets you know what lists, libraries, or subsites users would like to use, but it is also frustrating if they are denied access for a good reason that will not change. Obviously those requests for access can be disabled on the site level by going to the Permissions page, Settings menu, Access Requests.

EDIT AN EXISTING PERMISSION LEVEL

To customize an existing permission level you take a permission level that is almost what you need and you edit it. You can include or exclude specific permissions as necessary. Editing an existing permission level will replace the existing level with your new permission level. Although I prefer to create a copy of the original and work with that, there may be times when your company requires that there be as few permission levels as possible, requiring that you modify the existing levels to better suit your needs.

Doing this will require a few steps:

1. Navigate to the Permissions page for the site (such as going to the Site Settings page for the site, then clicking on the Advanced Permissions link in the Users and Permissions category).

2. On the Action bar, select Settings ➢ Permission Levels (see Figure 11.5).

FIGURE 11.5
Select
Permission
Levels

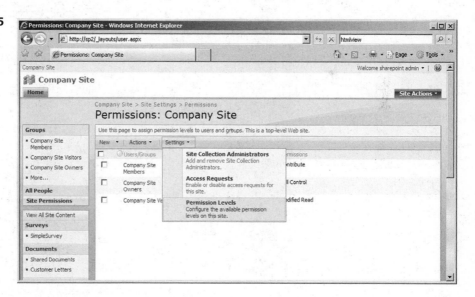

3. In the list of permission levels, click the name of the permission level you want to customize. This example uses the Read level (see Figure 11.6).

FIGURE 11.6
Choose the Read level

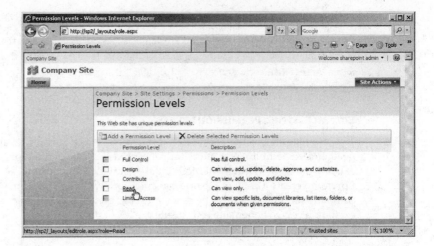

When you click on the permission level, the Edit Permission Level page opens (see Figure 11.7).

FIGURE 11.7
Edit the current
permission level

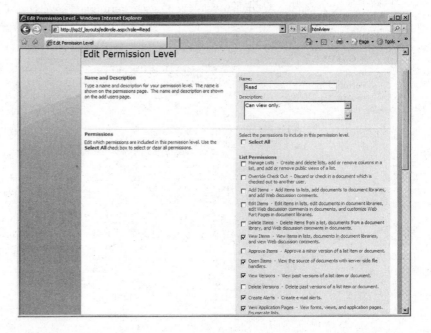

4. On the Edit Permission Level page, enter a name for the modified permission level in the Name box (see Figure 11.8). While changing the name of the level is not required, it is recommended so you can easily see the permission level has been modified from the default. My example uses, imaginatively enough, **Modified Read**.

5. Adjust the permissions that are applied to this permission level, adding or removing select permissions until Modified Read provides the exact permissions you desire. This will change the permission level, and any user or group with this permission level assigned will receive the new permissions (my example adds the Edit Items permission).

FIGURE 11.8
The modified name

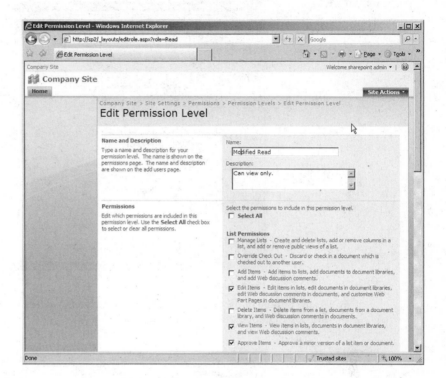

6. Click Submit at the bottom of the page, and the modified permission level will be saved. This will overwrite the Read permission level with the new Modified Read permission level.

COPY AN EXISTING PERMISSION LEVEL

As I mentioned, the preferred method of modifying a permission level is to copy and modify an existing one. If the custom permission level that you want is similar to an existing default permission level, and you need to use both the default permission level and your custom permission level, you can copy the default permission level, modify the copy, and save it as a new permission level.

To do this, follow these steps:

1. Get to the Permissions page whatever way you choose; by using the Quick Launch bar ➤ People and Groups ➤ Site Permissions; or on the Site Settings page, under Users And Permissions, click Advanced Permissions.

2. On the Action bar in the Permissions page, select Settings ➤ Permission Levels.

3. In the list of permission levels, click the name of the permission level you want to copy (see Figure 11.9). My example will copy Modified Read, since we are already familiar with it.

FIGURE 11.9
Choose the
Permission level to
copy

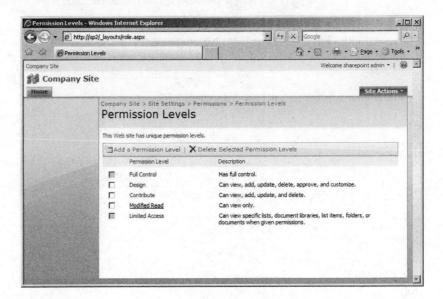

4. At the bottom of the page, click Copy Permission Level (see Figure 11.10). This will display the Copy Permission Level page (see Figure 11.11).

FIGURE 11.10
Select the Copy
Permission level

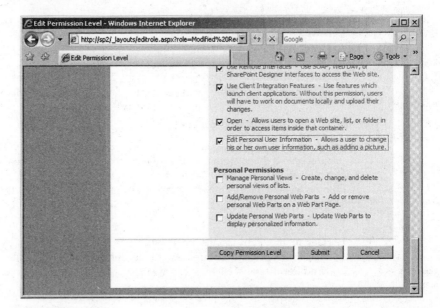

FIGURE 11.11
The Copy Permission
Level page

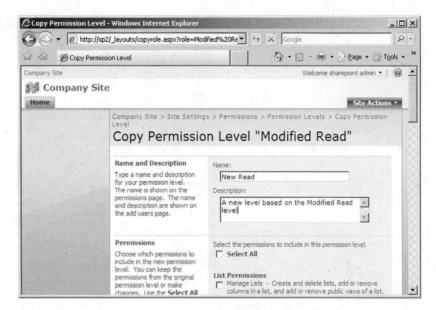

5. On the Copy Permission Level page, enter a name in the Name box for the new permission level. My example uses **New Read**.

6. In the Description box, enter a description for the new permission level.

7. From the list of permissions, select or clear the checkboxes to add permissions to or remove permissions from the permission level. As you may remember, some permissions have prerequisites, so pay attention to what you enable.

8. To create your new custom, copied permission level, click Create at the bottom of the page.

By using this method, you have created a new permission level while keeping the existing one in place, allowing you to use both permission levels in the site collection.

CREATE A NEW PERMISSION LEVEL

Creating a permission level from scratch is a good idea when none of the existing permission levels are close to what you need. You can create a permission level that will include exactly what you require. To create a brand new level, follow these steps:

1. Navigate to the Permissions page. For example, on the Site Settings page, under Users And Permissions, click Advanced Permissions.

2. On the Action bar in the Permissions page, select Settings ➢ Permission Levels.

3. On the Action bar, click Add A Permission Level (see Figure 11.12).

FIGURE 11.12
The Permission Levels page

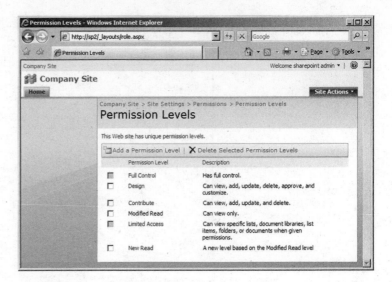

4. In the Name box on the Add A Permission Level page, enter a name for the new permission level (see Figure 11.13). My example will be a new permission level for **List managers**.

FIGURE 11.13
The Add A Permission Level page

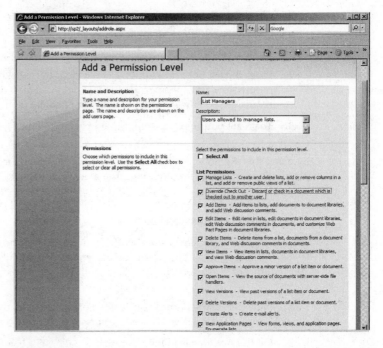

5. In the Description box, type a description for the new permission level.

6. In the list of permissions, select the checkboxes to add permissions to the permission level. If you want to create a level with almost Full Control, click Select All and then uncheck the permissions you want to remove. You can create as flexible a structure as you would like, but you should plan for consolidation because permission levels that are custom created are often duplicates of others already in the system. In my case I am enabling all of the list permissions to allow the list managers to freely work on lists in whatever capacity they require.

7. Click the Create button at the bottom to create your custom level.

At this point you know how to check the current permission levels of your sites to see what permissions they actually have; how to modify existing permission levels (and which you can't); how to create copies of existing permission levels for customization; and finally, you know how to create your own permission levels to combine exactly the permissions you want into a permission level.

Users and Groups

Now that you understand the foundation of permissions in SharePoint, it's time to start looking at them inside the SharePoint site collection.

When adding users to SharePoint, Microsoft recommends you add Active Directory security groups (domain groups) to SharePoint groups rather then individual users as much as possible. SharePoint has a limit of 2,000 security principals (users and groups) for a website. According to Microsoft, going beyond this limit has not been tested and could cause performance issues. However, adding Active Directory security groups allows the number of supported users (assuming they are all in no more then 2,000 AD security groups) to scale to 2 million.

Adding domain groups rather then individual users provides another distinct advantage: ease of administration. Rather than having to manage users in two places, you only need to manage Active Directory group membership.

For example, you can add all the managers in your organization to a Managers security group in Active Directory, then add that domain group to a Managers SharePoint group that you created. You want these managers to have read and write access on the Sales Events subsite, read-only access on the Accounting subsite, and full control access on the Management subsite. You can accomplish this by adding the Managers AD security group to a Managers group on the top-level site, then assigning the permissions you want for the Managers SharePoint group separately on each subsite. As managers join the team, you add them to the Managers Active Directory security group, the way you normally would without SharePoint on the network. This automatically makes them part of the Managers SharePoint group, without having to manually add them to SharePoint as an individual user. There is also no need to specify the permissions they have on different sites, because you have already assigned the permissions you want to the Managers SharePoint group for all three sites. If the manager leaves or gets transferred, you just remove the user account from the Managers Active Directory security group. And they will no longer be a member of the Managers SharePoint group. On the other hand, if you choose to add each manager directly to a site instead of using a domain group and a SharePoint group, you must assign each manager the appropriate permissions on each of the three sites. If they then change job roles in the company, you need to manually change their permissions for each site.

CROSS-SITE GROUPS

In earlier versions of Windows SharePoint Services, there were no site collection-wide groups, so there were no groups that just were inherited from the top-level down. Each site's groups had to be managed at that site level. There were two types of groups; site groups, and cross site groups. A Site group was used to add users to a site and apply permissions, very like a SharePoint group now only at the site level exclusively. A cross site group was just a list of users that could be added to any of the site groups. This was to compensate for the fact that many of the same users were going to need to access more than one site. The cross site groups would still need to be applied for each site they required access to.

In this version of SharePoint, site groups and cross site groups have been done away with, and there are only SharePoint groups. SharePoint groups are created at the site collection level and can be inherited to be applied to each subsite as well (although those subsites can choose to have different groups if they wish). So if you plan your SharePoint groups well, the subsites should have the right people, in the right places, able to do the right things with little to no additional effort.

Editing Site Administrators

Before we get started with viewing, modifying, and creating groups, site administrators should be mentioned. When a site collection is created, you are given the option to enter primary and secondary user accounts for site collection administration. However, once the site collection is up and running, you can add more site collection administrators. And this is where it's done.

Site collection administrators not only have full control permissions to the site collection, but they are considered responsible for the site collection in Central Administration and are the primary contacts for notification about the site collection. Ironically however, site collection administrators are not members of the Owners SharePoint group (except for the account assigned at the creation of the site collection), despite their having full control of the site. They stand apart from the real members of the site collection.

To get a look at the existing site collection administrators and make changes to the list if necessary, follow these steps:

1. From the home page of your site, go to Site Actions and choose Site Settings. The Site Settings page will appear (see Figure 11.14).

2. By now this page is probably pretty familiar to you. You are going to be looking at the first column of course; Users And Permissions. It has three links underneath it: People And Groups, Site Collection Administrators, and Advanced Permissions. We've seen where the Advanced Permissions goes, now it's time to explore the other two links.

FIGURE 11.14
The Site Settings page

3. Go ahead and click the Site Collection Administrators link to open that page (see Figure 11.15).

FIGURE 11.15
The Site Collection
Administrators page

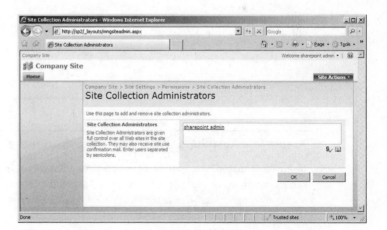

This page shows you the account (or accounts if you have a secondary) that are the current administrators. My example shows my default user, sharepoint admin (*share admin*).

4. If you wanted to add another administrator or two, you could type in their AD user account names (separated by semicolons) in the people picker field, or you could click the Browse button, which looks like an address book, and use the Select People page to find the correct account. The Select People page (as well as the people picker) pulls accounts from the authentication source configured for the web application. In my case, if I were to type in a user name (see Figure 11.16), and click Find, the page will query Active Directory for the account name, and return accounts that match. From the list of found people (I have only one match), you can select the one that you want and click Add at the bottom of the page, then click OK to add the user to the site collection administrators people picker field. Remember, once the account is added to the people picker field on the Site Collection Administrator's page, to click OK there as well to keep the change.

FIGURE 11.16
Select People page

ASSIGN SITE ADMINISTRATORS IN CENTRAL ADMINISTRATION

If, for some reason, you need to have access to a SharePoint site collection as an administrator you can always access this information from the SharePoint Central Administration site. The Applications Management page has a link to the Site collection administrators page where you can change or remove the existing administrators.

Viewing People and Groups

Now that you have seen where you can go to add site administrators, let's visit the People and Groups page and see where you go to manage user accounts. Either make certain you are on the

Site Settings page and click on the People and Groups link or, if you are on a page that has a Quick Launch bar, click on the People and Groups link there. Either way, find you way to the People and Groups page (see Figure 11.17).

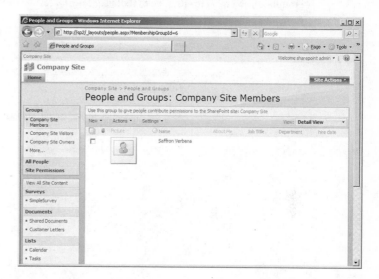

This page is essentially a list of the people and groups for the current site and generally defaults to displaying the users in the Members group (Saffron is there in my example because we added her in chapter 2). It allows you to manage the users in the groups as well as manage the groups themselves. On the Group Quick Launch bar, you can see the three default groups that SharePoint added to the site: Company Site Members, Company Site Visitors, and Company Site Owners. The Company Site Owners SharePoint group has the Full Control permission level assigned, the Company Site Members SharePoint group has been assigned the Contribute permission level, and the Company Site Visitors SharePoint group has the Read permission level assigned.

The action bar for the People and Groups page generally relates to the group it is displaying, except for the New button.

The New button for any group offers the choice of creating a new user or a new group. Both of these open to the respective New object page, regardless of what page you chose them from.

The Actions button for the People and Groups page offers:

◆ **Email Users**: opens the local email client and using the email address in the user's information, prepares an email message to the selected user(s). All of these options are plural because you can select more than one user at a time.

◆ **Call/Message Selected Users**: requires a SIP (session initiation protocol) address in the user information of the selected users, but will try to place an online call to the intended users. Requires additional configuration.

◆ **Remove Users from Group**: This option will delete the selected user (or security group) from the group. However, that user will stay in the all people list for the site, they just won't have any permissions applied to them. They will have to be added to back to the site so they can have permissions applied to them again.

Bye Bye. No seriously, buh *bye* . . .

In order to remove a user entirely from the site collection (instead of having them hanging around groupless), you need to either go to that user's user information in People and Groups and select Delete from Site Collection.

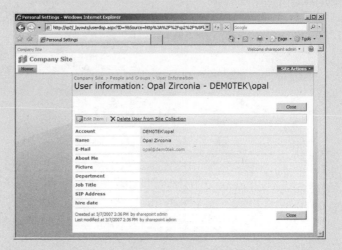

Or on the All People page, select the user or users you want to remove from the site collection, and under Actions, select Delete Users from Site Collection.

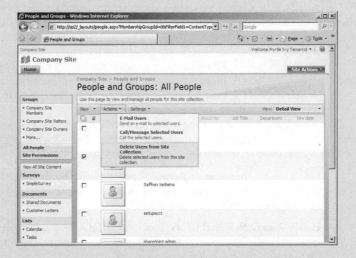

Once you have done this the user account will be gone from the SharePoint site collection completely (unless there is a subsite that is not inheriting permissions and is using that account).

The Settings button for the People and Groups page offers:

◆ **Group Settings**: This page lets you edit the Group's settings with a page almost exactly like the one we will use to create groups. It allows the name, description, group owner, who can view the group, whether users can request membership, and permissions to be edited.

◆ **View Group Permissions**: This will trigger a popup window that will conveniently show the URLs of the site collection that this group has access to, as well as what permissions are applied to the group there. In addition, if there are any subsites that are not inheriting permissions, but are using the group, they will appear in the list as well. I broke inheritance with the tech support wiki site in this example, and as you can see in Figure 11.18 it is listed separately.

FIGURE 11.18
View Group
Permissions

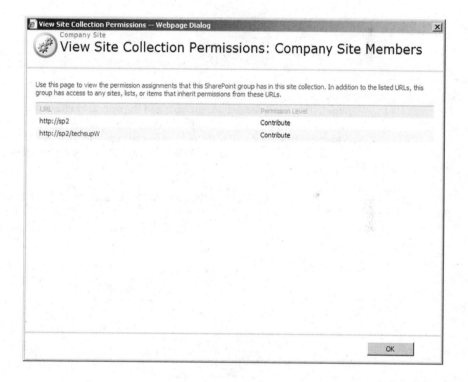

◆ **Edit Group Quick Launch**: From any of the Group pages in People and Groups, this settings is available. This makes it possible to remove (or add) a group to the launch bar, as well as rearrange them. The Edit Group Quick Launch page is not fancy; the groups are displayed in a text field, in order, separated by semicolons (See Figure 11.19).

FIGURE 11.19
Edit Group Quick Launch
page

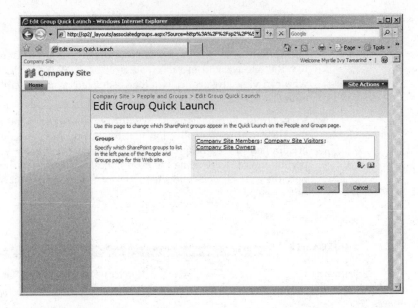

◆ **Set Up Groups**: This page is actually pretty interesting, I'm not sure why it is here. It opens a page listing the three default groups, and the option to either use the existing default groups or create new ones (Figure 11.20). It is the page used for Self-Service Site creation to quickly add users to a new site collection. It is convenient at the subsite level if you want to add an existing default group to the level without having to re-establish inheritance with the parent site.

FIGURE 11.20
Set Up Groups page

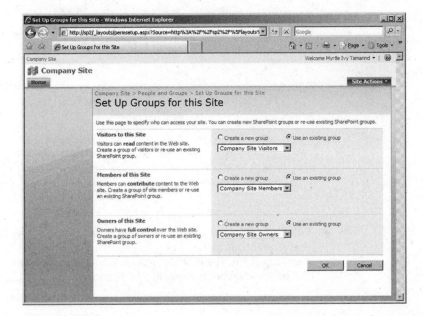

◆ **List Settings**: Because the Group page for people and groups is just a list (a very custom list, but a list nonetheless), you can manage it like a list; adding columns, changing views, etc. This option is available at the top-level site only.

LOCATION, LOCATION, LOCATION

Note that members of the Company Site Owners group for a top-level website can control more options than site owners of a subsite. For example, they can perform actions such as specifying settings for web document discussions or alerts and viewing usage and quota data for the top-level site and all subsites.

Creating a New SharePoint Group

In Chapter 2, as one of the post configuration tasks, we added a user to the Company Site Members group, as an example. It's easy to add users to existing SharePoint groups. But if you'd like to use a group that has different permission levels than the defaults, you'll need to create it.

1. While you are on the People and Groups page click the New dropdown button on the menu (see Figure 11.21).

FIGURE 11.21
The People and Groups,
New menu

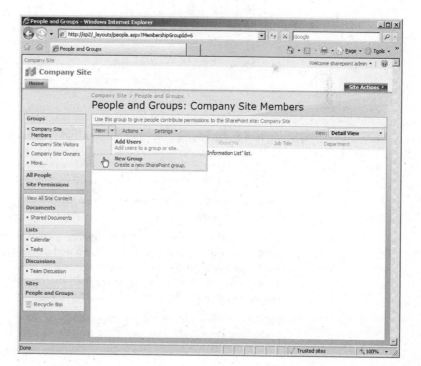

2. Click New Group. This will allow you to add a new Group to the site. When you click it, the New Group Page will open (see Figure 11.22).

FIGURE 11.22
The New Group
page

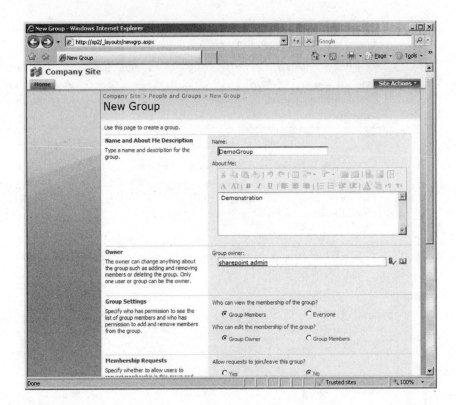

The top half of the page has several options that you can fill out:

◆ The first option is the Group Name. Always use a unique name for the group. My example uses **DemoGroup**.

◆ Directly under the Group Name is About Me, which is the description. My example uses **Demonstration**.

◆ The next section for the group is Owner. The owner can be any user, SharePoint group, or domain security group. But keep in mind that owner is not plural, there can only be one item in that field, even if it is actually a group of users. The owner will have full control of the group by default. My example uses sharepoint Admin (`shareadmin`). The field will default to the user name of the person creating the group.

◆ The next section is about the group members' settings, specifically who can view the group members (only that group or everyone) and who can edit the group members (only the owners or all members). The defaults are as shown, with the group members being able to view group membership and the group owner being able to edit the group members. Those defaults are fine for this example.

The bottom half of the page deals with the final options for the group, as shown in Figure 11.23.

FIGURE 11.23
The bottom of the
New Group page

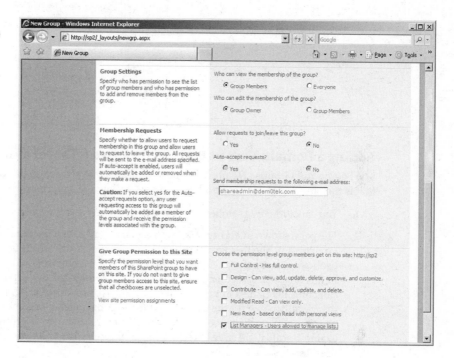

♦ The Membership Requests section is where you indicate whether or not you will allow requests to join or leave the group and whether or not you will automatically accept requests if they are allowed. The email address box is typically filled with the group owner or site administrator's email address, although the request can be sent to anyone who has authorization to edit the group. The defaults are fine for our example also.

♦ The Give Group Permission to this Site section is where you specify the permission levels for the group for the site to which the group is being added. My example assigns the new List Managers permission level for this group.

3. Once you have made all your entries, click Create and the group will be created and displayed (see Figure 11.24). By default, because a group cannot be empty of users, the owner/creator of the group is always the first member.

FIGURE 11.24
The DemoGroup members

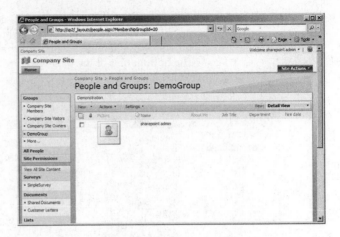

Adding a Domain User or Domain Group to a SharePoint Group

The People and Groups : DemoGroup page indicates that the group has one member, in my case that is the SharePoint admin. To add new users, follow the steps below:

1. You can add new members by going back to the New button and clicking Add User.

2. The page shown in Figure 11.25 allows you to add a new user or domain group to the Share-Point group. The first entry box is the People Picker into which you can add usernames. The username can be any existing SharePoint user, Domain user or Domain group in the system. In this box, you can enter multiple users and domain groups separated by semi colons. You can enter the names in the format of *Domain\UserName* or *Domain\GroupName*, just use the friendly name for the user and have the people picker resolve it to the user name in AD, or you could even use the email address listed for the user or group in Active Directory. My example adds the Active Directory security group **dem0tek\managers** and the individual user **dem0tek\citrine**.

FIGURE 11.25
Adding a new user

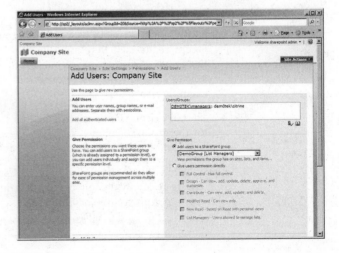

There is a link in the Add Users section to add all authenticated users for the authentication provider if you don't feel like adding individuals. Generally all domain users are not added to SharePoint in this way, but it is a way to add a lot of users at once, all without adding as many security principal objects. One NT AUTHORITY\Authenticated Users security group containing a hundred users is easier than adding them all by hand, and easier on SharePoint than a hundred individual user accounts. Of course, we are not using this feature in this example.

CHECKING NAMES

After each entry, it's a good idea to check the name immediately so that you can confirm the name is valid before trying to add them to the group. You can use the Check Names button just below the entry box to verify that you typed the name correctly. In my example, `dem0tek\managers` has been checked; Citrine has not yet been checked. When checked, the entered user account will change to show a user's full name. Checked names are also underlined.

---

3. Then choose the sharepoint group or permission level that the new user and domain group will use on the site. Typically, you will choose to add them to a SharePoint group. Because you were on the DemoGroup page when you clicked New User, it defaults to adding the user and domain group to that SharePoint group. If you don't want to add them to a SharePoint group, you can directly apply a permission level to them. This is generally not recommended because you should use SharePoint groups to control permission levels. In this case, they were meant to be added to the DemoGroup, so keep the default.

4. The last dialog box can be used to send a welcome message to users to let them know they have been added to a group (Figure 11.26). My example leaves this option in place.

FIGURE 11.26
Welcome message setting

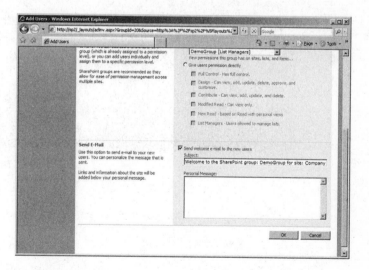

5. Once you click OK, you will be taken back to the Group page (see Figure 11.27). It will have three members in the group: sharepoint admin, Citrine, and the `dem0tek\managers` domain group.

FIGURE 11.27
The group has three members

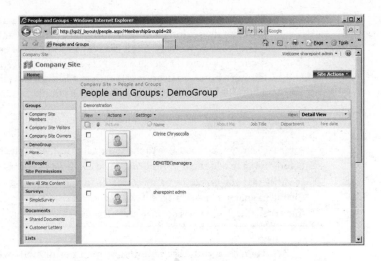

Removing a Domain User or Domain Group from a SharePoint Group

You can also remove a user or domain group from the SharePoint group in case they have been added incorrectly, have changed job functions, or no longer need to have the SharePoint permissions granted to the SharePoint group.

1. To do this, select the user or domain group in the list, go to the Actions menu, and choose Remove Users From Group (see Figure 11.28). My example will remove Citrine, one of the newly added members.

FIGURE 11.28
Remove a user from the group

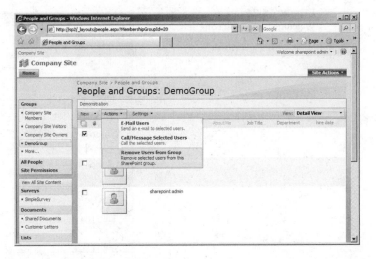

2. You will get a dialog box warning you that you are about to remove members from the SharePoint group permanently (see Figure 11.29). Once you click OK, the user and domain group will be removed from the SharePoint group. The user will not be deleted from the site, just from the current SharePoint group membership.

FIGURE 11.29
The Remove User Warning
dialog box

Viewing All People

This page was meant to allow you to see all users who have ever had the permission to access the site, regardless of their group affiliation. This is a quick way to find a user, then see what group they belong to (or not if their group has been deleted; those users are considered *orphaned*).

On the People and Groups page, select All People from the Quick Launch bar on the left to list all of the users in the site (see Figure 11.30). This page will allow you to edit individual user information (such as their job title), but you will not be able to directly edit the user's authorization. For example, on this page there is no way to add an existing user to a SharePoint group, or apply permissions directly to the user. However, from here you can delete users from the entire site collection rather than simply remove them from a SharePoint group. You will notice that Citrine, previously removed from DemoGroup, still exists in the site as a user object. But since she has no permission level assigned and is not a member of any SharePoint group she cannot log in. If you want to add her to another SharePoint group or to assign a permission level directly to her account you will need to go through the New User process again. There is no other mechanism to simply give her permissions, unfortunately.

FIGURE 11.30
The All People page

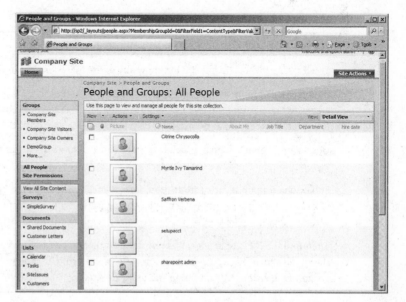

Domain security groups added to the SharePoint site do not show up in All People; only individual user accounts do. In order to see the added domain security groups, you need to view the All Groups page for the site. The All Groups page, shown in Figure 11.31, is reached by clicking the More... link in the Groups Quick Launch bar. Here you will notice that dem0tek\managers still exists.

FIGURE 11.31
The All Groups page

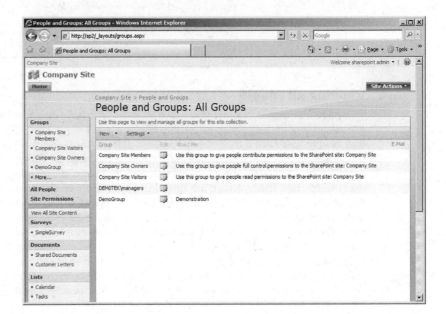

DOMAIN GROUP MEMBERS AND ALL PEOPLE

You'll notice that All People did not show any of the members of demotek\managers.

Because this domain security group was added to SharePoint, all the members of this group now have access to SharePoint (with whatever permission levels are eventually granted to demotek\managers). However, SharePoint has no reason to care about these users until they actually log in.

Once a member of a domain group logs into SharePoint and begins using the site, they will appear in All People.

Should the domain security group (demotek\managers) be removed from the site completely, members of this security group that have previously logged in will remain in All People but will no longer be assigned to a SharePoint Group or have any permissions (just like Citrine).

Therefore the All People page does not show all the people who necessarily have permissions to access the site; it shows only those people who were added explicitly and those members of an added security group who have actually logged in and used the site.

Applying Permissions

Now that we have covered a good bit of ground, it is time to set permissions on the stuff inside SharePoint. Several different objects that can be secured are in the SharePoint system. A securable object is an object upon which permissions can be configured (for example, a site, list, library, folder within a list or library, list item, or document). Permissions for users and SharePoint groups can be assigned to any securable object. The SharePoint system defaults to assigning permissions at the Site level, and those permissions filter down through permission inheritance to the contained objects such as lists, list items, and the like. A user with the Manage Permissions permission can edit the permissions for any of the contained objects, breaking the hierarchy of inheritance chain. This permission is assigned to the Site Owners group by default.

Inheritance

Inheritance means that a site and its contents inherit their permissions from their parent object; so subsites get their permission from their parent site; the subsite's lists and libraries get their permissions from the subsite, and list and library items get their permissions from the list or library in which they reside. This chain of inheritance makes it possible to administer permissions for entire site collection from one place and have those changes trickle down to all other objects contained therein.

Figure 11.32 shows a top-level site with a set of permissions called Permission Set A. The two subsites underneath it also have Permission Set A, as do the lists and list items underneath the sites. All of the objects in my example are shown inheriting permissions from the top-level site.

FIGURE 11.32
Inherited Permissions

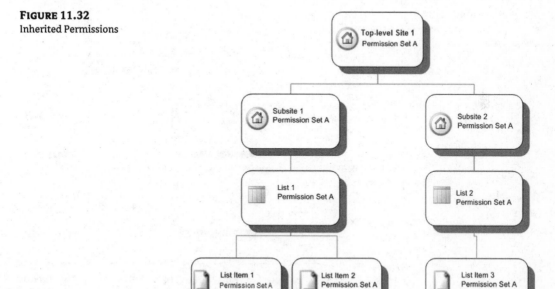

If you change the permissions set on Subsite 2, the permissions for the list contained there will also change so that they both will have Permission Set B. See Figure 11.33.

FIGURE 11.33
Subsite 2 permissions change

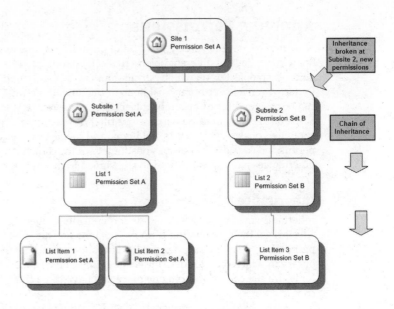

You could also change the permissions on List Item 2 to a different set of permissions, Permission Set C (see Figure 11.34).

FIGURE 11.34
List Item 2 permissions change

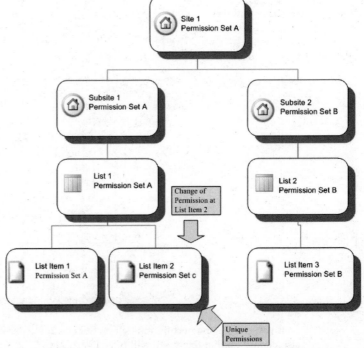

And on a larger scale, instead of drilling down on the permissions of a site versus a single list item, the permissions of sites and subsites also have a bit of flexibility.

Figure 11.35 shows a top-level site with a set of permissions we'll call Permission Set A. Subsites 2 and all subsites beneath it are configured to inherit permissions, and therefore also use Permission Set A throughout their pages, lists, and libraries.

However, there are times when you need a set of subsites that break inheritance in order to have their own, unique permissions. In this diagram, one of the subsites two levels below the top-level site, subsite 1-A, has broken inheritance to use its own permissions. For the sake of discussion, we'll call its permissions, Permission Set B. That means that all lists and libraries on that site will be effected Permission Set B (unless set to do otherwise). If any subsites are created beneath subsite 1-A, and are set to inherit permissions, they will inherit Permission Set B. This gives subsite 1-A permission capabilities akin to a top level site. Changes to the permissions at that level trickle to the other two subsites.

FIGURE 11.35
Subsites with different inherited permissions

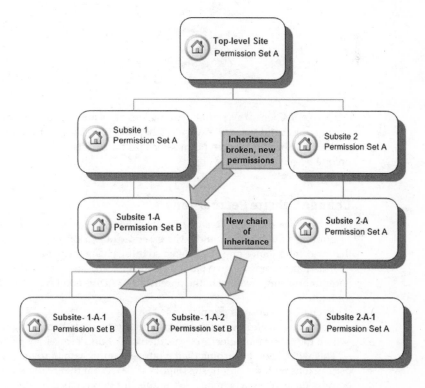

One of the nice things about WSS 3.0 is that it will actually allow you to reestablish the inheritance relationship. Anywhere inheritance can be applied, from the site level to the item level, inheritance can always be restored. This means that these decisions are not unchangeable. On the Permissions page where you make the change, you can choose to inherit permissions, as shown in Figure 11.36.

FIGURE 11.36
The Edit Permissions
option

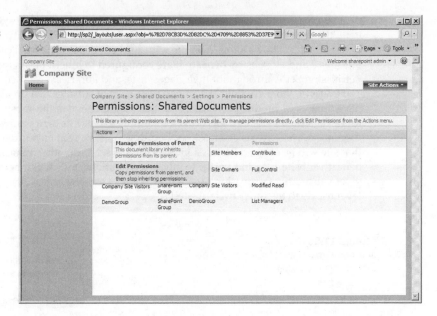

Once you choose this option, you will lose any and all customizations you have made to the current object and you will revert to inheriting permissions from the parent object. Should you decide to go back to custom permissions from inherited permissions, you would need to redo the unique permissions for the object.

Change Subsite Permissions

Occasionally a subsite is created in a site collection that requires unique permissions, such as an accounting subsite that should be accessed by only a subset of the users in the Members group. In that case, inheritance must be broken so those changes can be made.

Inheritance comes in two parts. The subsite can choose to have its own groups and users without breaking away from the parent site's permission levels, or you can break inheritance for both.

To change a subsite's permissions:

Go to the subsite's permissions page (in my example I am using my Tech Support Wiki site), and on the action bar, select Actions, then click Edit Permissions (Figure 11.37).

This will trigger a warning dialog box reminding you that you will be breaking inherited permissions with the parent site (Figure 11.38). What that really means is a copy of all groups and permission levels will be made on the site, but the connection with the parent will be severed at that point, so if changes are made to permissions at the parent level, they will not affect this site. Click OK.

At that point, all the groups will be there to be changed as you would at a top-level site. So you can add groups, change the groups copied there, even remove groups. As you can see in Figure 11.39, inheritance has been broken with the parent on this site for Groups.

However, if you try to change a permission level, you will find that you haven't *quite* broken inheritance.

FIGURE 11.37
Edit Permission on
subsite

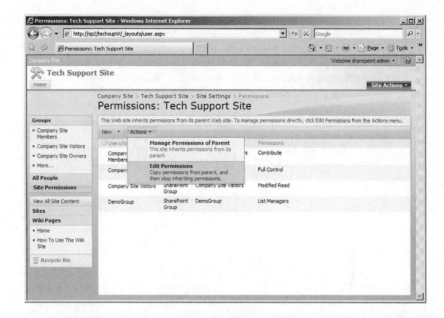

FIGURE 11.38
Breaking Inheritance
warning

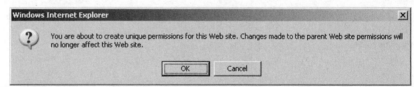

FIGURE 11.39
Web Site does not
inherit permissions

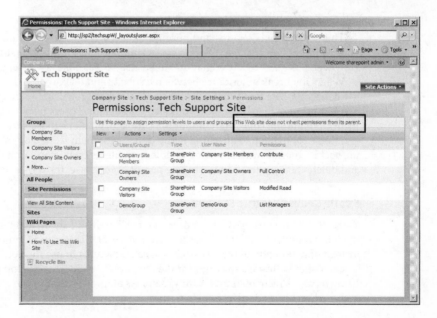

Click on Permission Levels on the Settings menu of the action bar. When you reach the Permission Levels page, you will see in Figure 11.40, that permission levels are still being inherited. To edit permission levels at this site, you will need to click the Edit Permission Levels link in the action bar. This will trigger another dialog box warning you that you are about to break inheritance. After clicking OK you will be able to create your own permission levels, and customize or delete the ones copied from the parent.

FIGURE 11.40
Permission levels still need to be disinherited

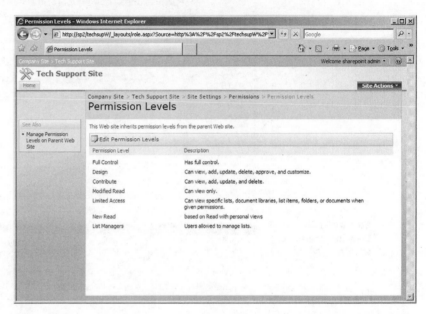

This separation of groups and permission levels allows a site administrator to break from the parent site enough to have different users and different groups, but still keep permission levels. However, it is good to know that making a clean break takes two steps.

When you break inheritance between a subsite and its parent, it does not really take it out of the site collection. The users that exist for the site collection will show up in the All People page, even if you don't give them access on your site (and deleting users from the All People page deletes them from the site collection). If that is a problem, just take those extra users out of your groups and don't apply them to anything if you don't want them using your site. Breaking inheritance just unshackles the subsite from being unable to create its own SharePoint groups or permission levels, and delete the ones forced on it by the parent (in my case, the top-level site).

SET UP GROUPS FOR THE SUBSITE

If you check the subsite's Groups quick launch bar, it still shows the parent site's groups (you see them in Figure 11.39). If you want to create Member, Visitor, and Owner groups for the site itself, instead of making them from scratch, the easiest way is to use the Set Up Groups option.

Go to any of the Group pages (or the All Groups page from the top of the Groups Quick Launch bar—which, not surprisingly, displays all groups for the site collection), click on Settings in the action bar, and select Set Up Group.

On the Set Up Groups page (Figure 11.41), there are sections for applying the standard permission levels for Visitors, Members, and Owners groups. Instead of using the existing SharePoint groups, select Create a new group for each of the sections you desire.

The sections will drop and allow you to name the group and add users (as you can see in Figure 11.42, I added a number of users and confirmed their names). Notice that, in the Visitors section, you can add all authenticated users if you wish (which I don't).

After entering your data for the groups, click OK. Back on the Groups page, you'll see that there are now three new groups (Figure 11.43). Now you have groups of your own devising, containing users you want for the site. Feel free to keep the groups copied from the parent but not use them (unless you want to), or you can delete them. Keep in mind that you are removing them from the site, not the site collection.

FIGURE 11.43
Three New Groups on People and Groups page

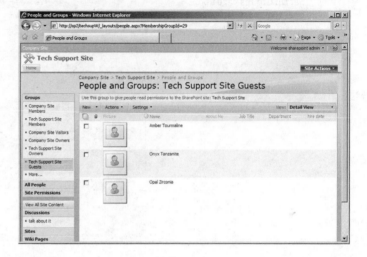

REMOVE INHERITED GROUPS

To conveniently remove the groups that were copied from the parent site, simply go to the Permissions page, select the groups, click on Actions, and select Remove User Permissions. As you can see in Figure 11.44, it will pop up a dialog box warning you that you are removing the groups from the site (which can reassure you that you are not deleting them from the site collection).

FIGURE 11.44
Remove Groups from subsite

Now, the groups from the parent site, despite their being removed from the site itself, will still show up in the Groups Quick Launch bar (and the All Groups page). To get rid of them, from the Quick Launch bar simply edit the Groups Quick Launch off of the Settings menu on any Group page. However, even if those groups do show up on the Groups Quick Launch bar, they are truly gone. For example, if you were to view the permissions of a list on the site, the parent groups that were removed would not be listed (Figure 11.45).

FIGURE 11.45
Permissions on the site after removing groups

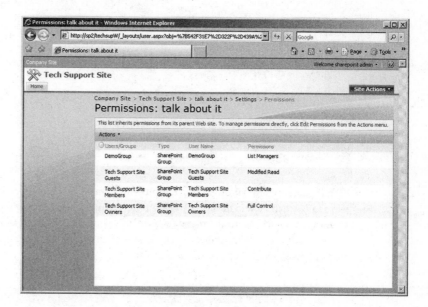

Hopefully this gives you an idea of how to break inheritance at the subsite level. Changing permission levels (once you break inheritance there) is more straightforward than messing with groups. And always remember, you can always re-establish inheritance by going to the permissions page, Actions menu, and choosing Inherit Permissions. The same goes for the permission levels.

THROUGH THE USERS' EYES

Generally, as administrators, we will rarely log into a SharePoint site with less than administrative privileges. But, because security filter works in this version, for a user with deprecated privileges, such as Visitors (with the Read permission level) or Members (with the Contribute permission level), logs in, features that we take for granted are missing.

When a user logs on with only the permissions available with the Read permission level, they cannot personalize any pages or change any site settings, so the Site Actions menu is missing altogether. The Welcome menu does not offer the user the chance to personalize the page. On lists and libraries, the New and Settings menus are gone, and the only button on the action bar is Actions, allowing the visitor to be able to set an alert, open the list in Explorer, export to a spreadsheet, or set an RSS feed.

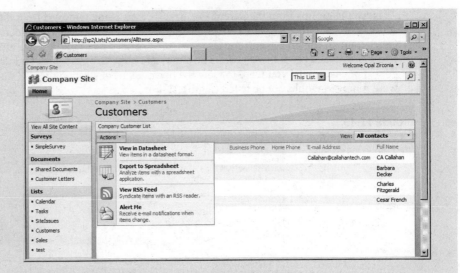

When a user logs in with the Contribute permission level (Members have this by default), they can personalize their view of the home page, but not change the site settings or create new pages, so there is a new option on the Welcome menu for them to personalize the page, but Edit is the only option. On a list or library, they are not allowed to change the settings, so that menu is completely missing for them, but both the New and Actions menus are available.

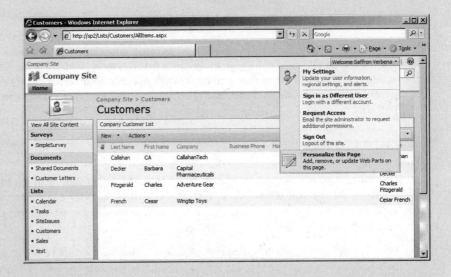

Just keep in mind, when using and applying permission levels, that the user experience will vary considerably, depending on the permissions they have.

Change List or Library Permissions

Sometimes the need to customize occurs, not at the subsite level, but at the list or library level. Often is the case that a document library needs to be created that will hold secure documents that the users that otherwise populate the site should not see. Because of this, it needs to have custom permissions.

To change permissions on a List or Library, you need to break the inheritance chain from the parent site before you can set custom permissions.

1. Open the list or library on which you want to change permissions. My example uses the Shared Documents library. Select Settings ➤ Document Library Settings.

2. When the Document Library Settings page opens, click Permissions for this Document Library under the Permissions and Management category (see Figure 11.46).

FIGURE 11.46
The Document Library Settings page

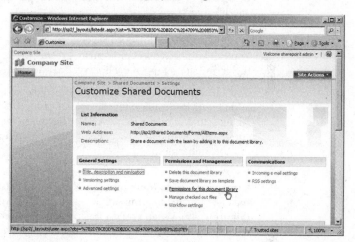

3. The Permissions: Shared Documents page will open. This page contains the permissions currently inherited from the parent site. Choose the Actions menu and select Edit Permissions (see Figure 11.47).

FIGURE 11.47
The Permissions page and Actions menu

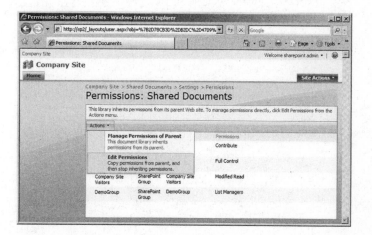

4. After you select Edit Permissions, a dialog box will warn you that you are about to create unique permissions for this library (see Figure 11.48).

FIGURE 11.48
The Permission Changes
warning

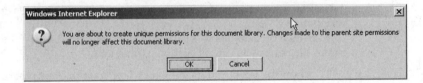

5. After you click OK on the warning box, the Permissions page will open again. You can select any of the entries and modify their permissions. Use the Action menu to make your modification.

Once you have broken inheritance:

◆ You can add new users or security groups to the library. To do this simply click on New on the permissions page of the library, and add the user or security group via the new user page.

◆ You can remove a SharePoint group allowed to access the library (or user if they were added with permission levels instead of a group), by selecting the group or user, going to Actions, and selecting Remove User Permissions. The person or the people in the group will summarily be unable to access that library from that point (but still easily access the rest of the site, unharmed).

◆ You can edit the permission levels applied to the SharePoint groups for the list. In my example I am going to add (only for the sake of demonstration, I don't suggest you do this at home) the List Managers permission level to all of the contributors to the Shared Documents library (Figure 11.49). When you do this on a list or library that has broken inheritance, it does not change the true permission levels applied anywhere else on the site.

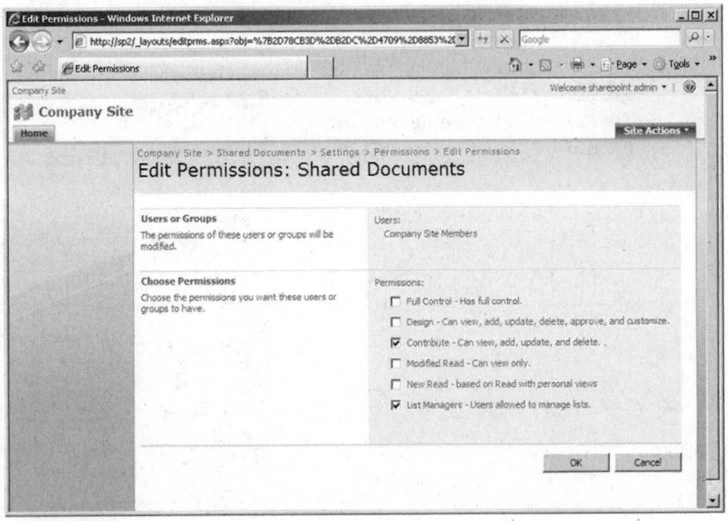

FIGURE 11.49
Editing the permission levels
for a Group at the library level

- You *cannot* simply create a new SharePoint group for the library.

- You *cannot* create anew or modify the permission levels applicable for the library.

Keep in mind that you can always change your mind and restore inheritance by choosing Inherit Permissions at any time from the Actions menu on the list or library's Permissions page. All changes you made during the non-inheriting time will be undone.

Change List Item or Library Item Permissions

New to WSS 3.0 is the ability to set custom permissions at the Item level. In the previous version, you were limited to the Library or List level. This is a definite step forward in security measures, but it does entail more overhead because you have another level of permissions and controls to worry about. Changing the permissions on an item is fairly easy.

PERMISSION LEVELS AND HIERARCHICAL LEVELS

When discussing levels of permissions, keep in mind there are two definitions for the word *level*. Permission Levels are groupings of permissions (Full Control, Contribute, etc.) while hierarchical levels, such as the ones discussed here, refer to the depth of control. Items reside in Lists or Libraries, which reside in Sites, which are contained by Site collections, then web applications. Each of these objects can be referred to as levels (such as the Item level or Site level). So setting permissions at the List or Library level is referencing a hierarchy, while customizing permissions for the Read level is referencing a permission level.

In my example, the Tasks list contains a Security Test item which has been selected. See Figure 11.50.

FIGURE 11.50
The Security Test Item menu

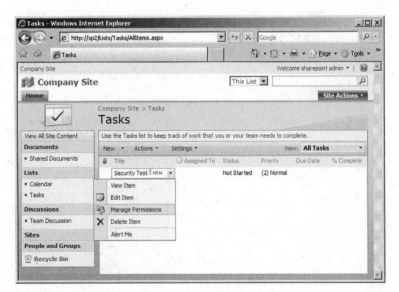

On the dropdown menu, you can see the Manage Permissions option, which is the means to manage permissions on a single item. When you click it, you'll get the Permissions: Security Test (where Security Test is the name of your Item) page, as shown in Figure 11.51.

FIGURE 11.51
The Permissions Item page

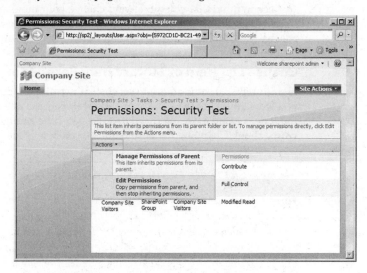

From this page, you can select the Actions menu, which has two items on it. Manage Permissions of Parent will allow you to manage the Lists permissions. To break inheritance choose Edit Permissions; you will again get the Warning dialog box that says you are creating Unique Permissions for the item.

After you click OK on the Warning dialog box, the Permissions page will redisplay. On it, you will be able to select a user (if you added one to the site collection without adding them to a group) or SharePoint group and modify their permission level for the items (including remove users or groups that are currently allowed to access this item). See Figure 11.52.

FIGURE 11.52
The Permissions page with
selectable options

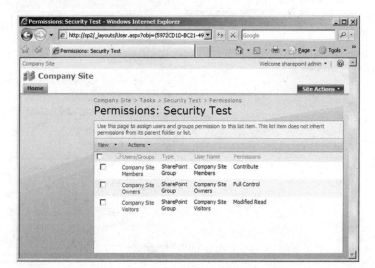

To modify a user or group's assigned permission level, select that user or group and go to the Action menu and select Edit Permissions (you can also remove the selected users from this menu).

The next page that will appear is Edit Permissions: Item Security Test (where Security Test is the name of the item), shown in Figure 11.53. It will list the user or group you selected and their currently assigned permission levels. You can choose any available permission level for them, and that will assign them that level on this item. It will not affect any other items in the list. This is the *item-level granularity* that is available in WSS 3.0.

FIGURE 11.53
Edit Permissions:
Item Security Test

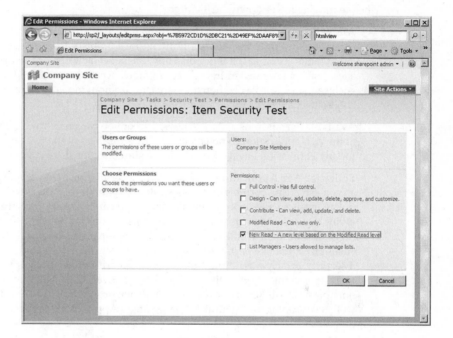

Planning User Access

SharePoint user access takes a considerable amount of planning. Security starts at the web application level, affecting user access with permissions and policies. Then the effect trickles down to the site collections, sites, lists, and even list items. The top levels can affect the permissions and security of the lower levels, so it's a good idea to know what settings are where when you are responsible for SharePoint authorization.

AUTHORIZATION, NOT AUTHENTICATION

Remember that permissions are all about authorization, and control what a user is permitted to do on the site. Authentication has nothing to do with permissions as they pertain to SharePoint.

User Access at the Web Application Level

The first place to plan user access and authorization is at the Web Application level. If you already have a web application that provides the exact configuration you need (from allowing or disallowing the correct permissions to enabling SSL), you may want to place your new site collections there. Otherwise you will need to create a new web application to provide the exact settings you require. The configuration of a web application is covered in Chapter 8, "Site Collections and Web Applications."

When planning user access, first examine these considerations at the web application level before moving lower down the hierarchy.

Allow Access to Anonymous Users   You may want to enable anonymous access. If anonymous access is allowed for the web application, site administrators can decide whether or not to grant anonymous access at the Site Collection, Site level, at a List or Library level, or to block it from sites, lists or libraries entirely. If anonymous access is prohibited at the web application, no enclosed sites can have anonymous users. If anonymous is enabled, each site collection can choose to enable it or not at their level.

Available Permissions   As discussed earlier you can enable and disable available permissions at the web application. When a permission is disabled at the web application, it is not available for any Permission Level on the enclosed site collections.

Policy for Web Application   You can create permission policy levels at the web application, just as you can create permission levels at site collection level. You can then apply those permission policy levels to a security principal (user or security group) directly for that web application, giving that security principal that level of permissions to all site collections in the web application, regardless of the site collections' settings. These permission policy levels can be modified and customized just like permission levels for site collections. Creating a web application policy for a security principal will grant that user or security group the applied permission policy level to every site collection in the web application, even if they are never added to the site and do not appear in All People or All Groups. Policies can modify the effects of anonymous access as well. See Chapter 10, "Central Administration: Application Management," for more information on Policies.

Additional Configuration   There are several other settings at the web application level that affect and define user access that can require a separate web application. For example, Alternate-Access Mapping, Kerberos, and SSL. These are related to how the user connects to the site and to authentication, but not necessarily to authorization and permissions. See Chapters 8 and 15 for more details.

User Access at the Site Collection Level

When a site collection is created, user access needs to be carefully planned. Finding the balance between ease of administration, performance, and the need to control specific permissions for individual items is important. If fine-grained permissions are used everywhere in your sites and subsites, you will spend significantly more time managing the permissions, and users may experience slower performance when they try to access site content (not to mention the potential problems with search displaying secured list items in the results—even if the user does not have the permissions to open it). When planning user access on a site collection, it is also important to follow the principle of "least privilege" when it comes to authorizing access to the site: Only give users the permission levels they need to use to accomplish their assigned tasks. It is generally a good idea to begin by using the standard groups (such as Site Members, Site Visitors, and Site Owners) and controlling permissions at the site collection level for the easiest administration experience. Most users will be best served by being members of the Visitors or Members groups. Always limit the number of people in the Owners group to those users who need to change the structure of the site or change site settings and appearance. You should design your site collections, and the collection's sites, lists, and libraries with set groups for user permissions in mind.

If particular subsites, lists, libraries, folders, items, or documents contain more sensitive data and must be even more secure, you can then choose to break inheritance and create custom permissions. There is a big caveat though: there is no single page that shows a user's personal permissions specific to lists, libraries, folders, items, or documents within a site. This means that it is difficult to quickly determine who has exactly which permissions on which objects, and it is also difficult to reset any fine-grained permissions in bulk.

PLAN FOR PERMISSION INHERITANCE

It is easiest to manage permissions when there is a clear hierarchy of permissions and inherited permissions. Managing permissions gets more difficult when some lists within a site have fine-grained permissions applied, and when some sites have subsites with unique permissions and some with inherited permissions. As much as possible, arrange site collections so their enclosed sites, subsites, lists, and libraries can inherit permission levels. Separate sensitive data into their own lists, libraries, subsites, or even a new site collection. Keep in mind that search can accidentally display secured list items in the results if security is too granular. Unless you intend to disable search for aspx pages, keep the fine-grained permissions as rare as possible. This will just make permission management easier on you.

ACTIVE DIRECTORY SECURITY GROUPS

For easier user management, you should always assign permission levels to SharePoint groups rather than to individual users (although we have broken that rule for demonstration purposes a time or two in this chapter, this rule is still a good one to remember).

When adding members to the SharePoint group, look for an existing Active Directory security group rather than adding individual domain users to the SharePoint group.

If you can include the domain group itself and not the individual members of the group, Active Directory manages the users for you. This does mean you need to work with your Network Administrators to verify members of the Active Directory security groups.

Each organization sets up its Windows security groups differently, but often the existing Active Directory group structure will closely match your desired SharePoint groups. For those cases where you need unique groupings for SharePoint, create a new SharePoint group and add the users individually.

Another example of exploiting the AD user structure, if you decide that you want all users within your domain to be able to view the content on the site collection, you should consider adding all authenticated users, or the *Domain Users* security group, to the *Company Site Visitors* SharePoint group. This would give everyone in the domain the Read permission level for the site collection with very little effort.

DECIDE WHICH GROUPS TO USE

Deciding how to organize your users and what permission levels to assign them is important in SharePoint. You have already learned that SharePoint has several default groups to help you organize your users based on their roles; however, you might have unique requirements that will cause them to fall outside the scope of the default SharePoint groups. Your first step should be to review the available default groups and then add additional groups if needed. SharePoint groups can be composed of many individual users, can hold security groups, or can be some combination of the two. SharePoint groups confer no specific rights to the site (their permission levels do that); they are merely a means to contain a set of users. Depending on the size and complexity of your organization, you can organize your users into a few, several, or many groups; the choice is yours.

The decision to create custom SharePoint groups is an organizational one. You should create custom SharePoint groups instead of using the default groups if any of the following situations apply:

◆ You have more (or fewer) user roles within your organization than are apparent in the default groups.

◆ If there are well-known names for unique roles within your organization that perform very different tasks. For the sake of familiarity, it may be a good idea to use those role names for the SharePoint groups.

◆ If you want to preserve a one-to-one relationship between Windows security groups and the SharePoint groups.

Otherwise you can consider keeping the defaults and expanding on them. Or you could simply modify the existing defaults, such as changing the group name. Maybe Visitors doesn't work for you; feel free to change it.

DECIDE WHICH PERMISSION LEVELS TO USE

Each SharePoint group needs to have a permission level assigned. Permission levels are designed to provide a general collection of permissions, covering a wide range of permitted actions. While SharePoint groups are role-based, permission levels are more task-based. However, they might not map exactly to your particular authorization needs. If the default permission levels do not exactly match the desired permissions for a SharePoint group, you can modify the permissions included in specific permission levels, or create custom permission levels.

The decision to customize permission levels is less straightforward than the decision to customize SharePoint groups. If you customize the permissions within a particular permission level, you must keep track of that change, verify that it works for all groups and sites affected by that change, and ensure that the change does not negatively affect your security or your server capacity and performance.

For example, if you customize the Contribute permission level to include the Create Subsites permission, contributors can create and own subsites, potentially creating large numbers of unused subsites. If you allow the Read permission level to keep the Create Alerts permission, all members of the Visitors group can create alerts, which might overload your servers.

You should copy and modify the default permission levels if either of the following applies:

◆ A default permission level includes all permissions except a few that your users need to do their jobs, and you want to add those permissions (and they don't allow more than you want the users to do).

◆ A default permission level includes a few permissions that your users do not need. It is easy to deselect the permissions you don't want the users to have.

Otherwise, if there is no existing permission level that is appropriate as a template, add a completely new permission level. Hopefully this chapter has given you an idea of how to better manage your users and their access to SharePoint's resources.

The Bottom Line

Define users and groups in SharePoint   SharePoint users are individuals with user accounts that can be authenticated by SharePoint server. Users can be stored in one or more groups. SharePoint understands two types of groups: SharePoint groups and Domain groups.

> **Master It**   Differentiate between the SharePoint group and the Domain group. Determine the preferred method for adding users to SharePoint.

Add users and groups in SharePoint   New SharePoint groups can be created to organize user access to websites. User accounts and domain groups from Active Directory can be added to the SharePoint server directly or by being placed into a SharePoint group.

> **Master It**   If you add a domain group to a SharePoint group, and then later delete that SharePoint group, how do you apply a permission level to the domain group directly?

Define permissions and permission levels in SharePoint   Authorization in SharePoint is handled by 33 distinct permissions. These permissions provide user access to lists, sites, and personal settings. They also determine if the user's access is restricted to simply reading or browsing, can allow editing of objects, or even permit creation of new objects.

Permission levels are simply groups of permissions. A permission level can contain any or all of the 33 permissions, and can depend on prerequisite permissions. The permission level is then applied to SharePoint groups to provide authorization to members of that group. They can also be applied directly to users and security groups.

> **Master It**   Describe what the Manage Permission permission does and what dependant permissions it requires. What permission level contains manage permissions by default?

Set Permissions on a Site/List/List item for a user or a group   Permission Levels are assigned to SharePoint groups, domain groups, or individual users starting at the Top-level site of the site collection. By default, these users and groups (along with their assigned permission levels) propagate throughout the site collection using permission inheritance. You can go to any object (site, list, library, or item) in the site collection and break inheritance, adding users and groups to the object manually, and then give them different permission levels.

> **Master It**   If you break inheritance on a subsite of the main Company Site and start using custom permissions for that subsite, do the lists on the subsite retain their original permission settings from Company Site, or do they also gain the custom permissions set on the subsite?

Plan user access in SharePoint   Planning user access for SharePoint needs to be done from the top down. Start with the web application and move down the hierarchy, changing the user access settings, authorized users and groups or permission levels only where needed. Before placing a new site collection into an existing web application, confirm the new site collection requires the same security settings as the existing site collections in that web application. Before adding a new site to a site collection, determine if the inherited groups, users, and permission levels are desired, or if a new site collection would be more appropriate. Try to balance the ease of administration that inheritance provides with the granular control of custom permissions.

Master It   Which is the better option?

1. Permitting anonymous access at the Web Application level, and then enabling anonymous access to a select few site collections within the web application.

2. Denying anonymous access at the Web Application level, and then enabling anonymous access to a select few site collections within the web application.

Chapter 12

Maintenance and Monitoring

As a SharePoint administrator, your job is never done, particularly once the server is set up and functioning. You have servers to nurture and protect, databases to manage, and websites to control. Lists are being built, data is being processed, and web pages are being accessed. SharePoint was meant to grow, and grow it will. Now is the time to create a baseline of how your SharePoint services work optimally and prepare for possible emergencies. It's beneficial to recognize what your server looks like on a good day, when all is working well, so you can anticipate when things are going to start lagging before the users start to complain.

Tools to monitor your SharePoint server's health are built into both Server 2003 and SharePoint itself. There are, of course, many third-party products you could use for monitoring as well, but let's start with what we all should have.

SharePoint itself can be resource intensive, putting a strain on the server's hardware from the beginning. Because it is very processor and RAM sensitive, SharePoint will begin to show signs of stress if your server's hardware struggles to support it. In addition, SharePoint is very dependent on network access. If you can't reach the server because its network card (NIC) is overwhelmed or the network itself is too busy, SharePoint is broken as far as users are concerned. The hard drive can be pelted by paging requests if the system's RAM is not up to SharePoint's activity requirements (not to mention the extra RAM requirements each web application adds). SharePoint's databases can fill quickly with mission-critical data that requires practically 24/7 user access. It's a closed circle, Processor-RAM-Hard Disk-Network card, so you must watch for these things.

To monitor your server, you first need to create a baseline. To do so, you need to be familiar with the Performance Monitor. This server tool has been around for a long time, and you should already be using it to monitor your existing systems.

In this chapter, you will learn how to:

◆ Monitor server performance

◆ Use SharePoint Backup and Restore

◆ Backup separate SharePoint components

◆ Recover from disaster

Performance Monitor

To open the Performance Monitor, go to Start ➤ Run, enter **perfmon**, and press Enter, or you can go to Start ➤ Administrative Tools ➤ Performance. The Performance Monitor appears in Figure 12.1.

FIGURE 12.1
The Performance
Monitor

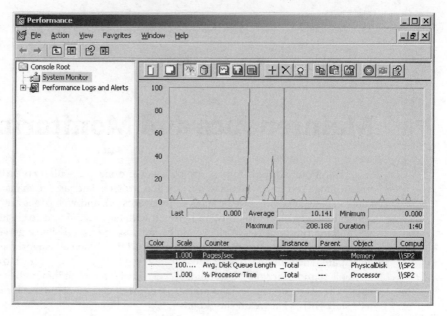

Once Performance Monitor comes up, the System Monitor portion of the console runs several default counters in a graph so you can tell how your server is doing. This graph shows you in real time what is happening on your server to the performance counters listed beneath the graph. The counters each have a color that corresponds to their line in the graph; the long, vertical red line running the height of the graph always indicates the current activity. These counters allow you to see at a glance if your server is choking, because they check the processor's total usage, measure the size of the queue for things the disk must do, and how much paging the RAM is doing to the hard drive per second.

This means from the start, that you are essentially covering the processor, RAM, and hard drive (three of the four critical parts of the server), so all you really need to add is a counter to check the health of the network card. Although the graph itself indicates each counter with a different color, you can select the counter from the list below the chart and click the Highlight button (the one with the light bulb) to highlight the selected counter with a thick white or black line to make it stand out from the rest. One of the counters is highlighted in Figure 12.4, if you would like an example.

Adding a Counter to System Monitor

To add a counter to the System Monitor, just click the button with the plus sign over the graph. The Add Counters dialog box (see Figure 12.2) contains many counters based on all of the objects available on your server.

The Add Counters dialog box allows you to pull the performance objects and their counters from the local computer, or you can specify a different computer (if you have the permissions). By default, it specifies the local computer for the counters.

FIGURE 12.2
Add a counter

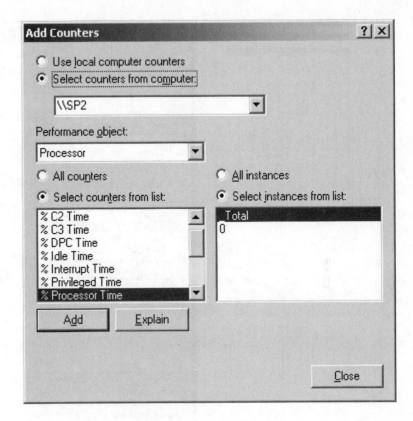

The Performance Objects dropdown list is huge. By default, it shows you the processor counters, but it actually contains a list of all objects that can be monitored with Windows Server 2003. You choose an object in the list, and the corresponding counters will appear in the counters list below beneath it. As you can see in Figure 12.2, the Percent Processor Time Total counter is already being monitored in the System Monitor.

To add the network interface counter to monitor its performance, just click on the Performance Object dropdown list and scroll up to Network Interface. Note just how many things you can monitor. The number will vary from server to server depending on their roles. Many Microsoft products add their own counters to the monitor, and SharePoint is no exception.

The network interface counters populate the counter list once that object is chosen. There are so many counters that you may not be sure what to choose. If that is the case, simply pick a counter such as Bytes Total/Sec (as shown in Figure 12.3), and click the Explain button. A small window will display a brief explanation of the counter. This window is not attached to the dialog box, but it's handy to keep it at the bottom of the dialog box for easy reference. While the Explain Text dialog box is open, the Explain button will be inactive.

In the counters list, choose Bytes Total/Sec to track the network activity. In the instances list, if you have more than one NIC, choose the one you want to monitor. Once you have made your selection, click the Add button to add it to the System Monitor.

FIGURE 12.3
Network interface counters
with explanation dialog box

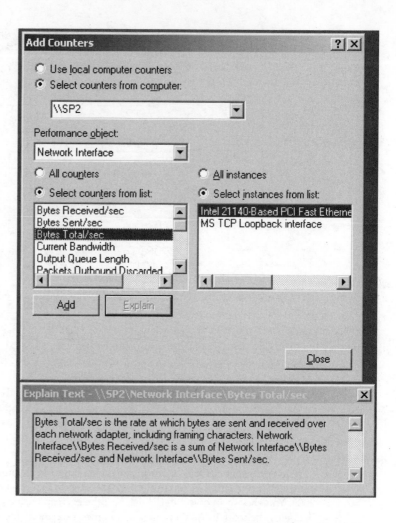

As you can see, the System Monitor in Figure 12.4 shows a lot of activity, and the NIC counter has been highlighted in white. The Bytes/sec counter is showing an average of 14819.254 (or approx. 15KB/sec) and a maximum of 177112.138 (or approx. 177KB/sec) calculated over the last one minute and 40 seconds (1:40).

The sample server is running in a virtual machine with as little RAM as possible to keep it going. This gives you a chance to see what a stressed-out SharePoint server looks like when people access it. The network card, highlighted with a thick white line at the bottom of the graph, is obviously not being overtaxed at this time.

Being able to see what's going on with the System Monitor is great. After you've surfed through all the performance objects and read all the explanations of the counters, you may be tempted to try to monitor all of them with the System Monitor. Don't. The monitor will become too crowded and hard to read. Keep it simple, maybe no more than six or so counters as a maximum.

FIGURE 12.4
A network Interface counter
added to the System Monitor

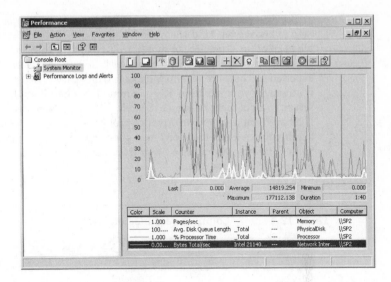

Creating a Counter Log

What if you want to keep track of more than six significant counters, or you want a longer sample time? In that case, you'll need a baseline report that collects data over time to give you the big picture of what your server is doing. It will give you the chance to spot trends using multiple counters and anticipate the need for upgrades and repairs before the users complain. To build a baseline report you'll first need to create a performance log (or *counter log* as it is called in the Performance Monitor).

To create counter logs, or logs used to track the activity of a group of counters, follow these steps:

1. Double click Performance Logs and Alerts in the Performance console.

2. Right-click the Counter Logs, and select New Log Settings.

3. You'll be prompted to name the log. My example, is going to use it to track the baseline performance of the SharePoint server. Name the log **WSS3_Baseline**.

4. Click OK in the New Counter Log dialog box.

The Counter Log dialog box opens with the name of your new counter log in the title bar. You can see the log filename and default location in the current log filename field. The Counters field is in the center, and the Add Object and Add Counters buttons are below it.

ADD OBJECTS

You don't actually need to add objects in the New Counter Log dialog box. Each individual counter will add the object it requires when you add them. Although if you are curious about a particular Object (as opposed to a counter), click the Add Objects button; it will give you an Explain button for each performance object on your system.

Because you are going to use this log to create a performance baseline for your server, it would help to know what kind of counters you should choose. There is no list of official counters to use when creating a baseline for monitoring a Windows server, and the optimum collection of counters will vary from server to server based on hardware, environment, and previous experience. There are several Microsoft white papers that can assist you in picking the right counters for your situation. Keep in mind that SharePoint has added custom counters to the server, most of them relating to Search, which can be added as well.

SharePoint counter performance problems are often corroborated by events in the application log. If you see levels that don't look good in your logs, remember that you should see what events SharePoint has generated to better troubleshoot the problem. Table 12.1 lists some counters you can use for your baseline.

TABLE 12.1: Common Baseline Counters

PERFORMANCE OBJECT	COUNTER	LOOK FOR THESE MAXIMUMS
Memory	%Committed Bytes in Use	Greater than 80% can mean you don't have enough RAM.
Memory	Available MB	Less than 50MB is bad because the default file maximum for uploads is 50MB, at least 128 to 256MB is better.
Memory	Pages/Sec	If your server is paging memory at 220 pages per second or more, you need to increase the RAM.
Logical Disk	%Idle Time	Less than 20% means that the disk is being overworked. Each partition can be measured as an instance.
Network Interface	Bytes Total/Sec	If you are using more than 50% of your NIC's total bandwidth, you could have real problems during peak times. If you are monitoring a 100MB NIC, that would be 50MB, or 536,870,912 bytes, give or take.
Physical Disk	%Disk Time	Indicates the percentage of time a disk is busy. If it is busy 80% of the time, you've got a bottleneck (you can also do this for logical disks). Can count all disks total or individual disks as instances.
Physical Disk	Avg Disk Queue Length	A standard counter for the physical disk. If it's above 2 or 3 per hard disk (depending on your environment), you either need more RAM or faster disks. Also can measure each disk individually as an instance.
Processor	%processor time_total	Total of all processors on the server. Greater than 80% means it's overutilized. You can also measure the performance of individual processors if you think one is failing.
System	Processor Queue Length	Greater than 10 threads may mean that your processor is too slow or overworked.

Performance Object	Counter	Look for these Maximums
Web Service	Connection Attempts/Sec	500 or more a second could mean that you need to think about adding another server to your farm. There is an instance for each web application.
SharePoint Search Archival Plug-in*	Error Documents	Indicates how many documents had errors being indexed by Search. This could indicate that the document was too large or that Search is malfunctioning. Retried documents can be measured in conjunction to see if the documents eventually get indexed.
SharePoint Search Indexer Catalog*	Queries Succeeded	Used to see how many successful search queries were made during your sample interval.
SharePoint Search Indexer Catalog*	Queries Failed	Used to see how many search queries failed during the sample interval. Used in comparison to the successful queries value. This value needs to be far outnumbered by successes. If this value grows to be significantly higher than it was at the original baseline, check the event logs.
SharePoint Search Gatherer*	Heartbeats/Heartbeats Rate	Gatherer heartbeats occur every 10 seconds. If the number of ticks does not increment for this counter, the Gatherer's heart isn't beating and therefore it is not running. Check the event logs for errors, and make sure the search service is running somewhere on your farm. This counter is good for alerts.

*SharePoint counters require the log to run as an administrator on the domain. The other counters can run as the local system (the default) without a problem.

To add these counters to the log, follow these steps:

1. Click the Add Counters button. The Add Counters dialog box will open.

2. Select each of the performance objects from Table 12.1, then select the correct counter in the Counters list (and instance where applicable), and click Add. The dialog box will stay open until you close it manually.

   For example, select Memory from the Performance Object list. Then select %Committed Bytes In Use from the Counters list.

3. There are no additional instances for this counter, so click Add to add it to the log.

4. Repeat steps 1 through 3 for each counter.

5. When you are done, click Close to leave the Add Counters dialog box. This will return you to the Property settings for the WSS3_Baseline log (see Figure 12.5). A lot of counters now appear in the list.

FIGURE 12.5
WSS3_Baseline log
counters

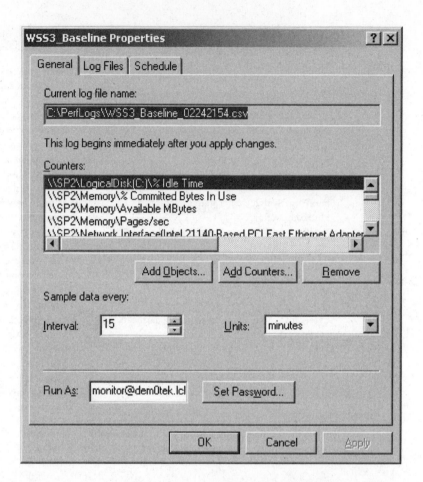

SPEAKING OF COUNTERS

You may think some of the counters from Table 12.1 are redundant, and that's fine. Running a lean log does make the log easier to read and uses fewer machine resources. However, you do need to know the various counter options that can assist you in assessing your server's performance. Once you get the hang of using counters feel free to experiment with your own baseline monitoring until you use only the counters that are right for you. Remember, monitoring takes resources, so keep your sampling intervals as long as you can (I prefer not to go under 15 seconds unless absolutely necessary) and try to save the logs to a drive other than the one that is being sampled. Remember that the real-time System Monitor does take resources, so just using logs and not running the monitor helps conserve resources.

Also note that all the maximum values listed in Table 12.1 can be used as Alert triggers to warn you when an unacceptable performance threshold has been met. Those values are not only so you can interpret the baseline logs you will create, but so you can be alerted. Alerts will be covered in the section "Setting a Performance Counter Alert."

The General tab has more options of which you need to be aware. Interval actually indicates the interval of time for which the log will *sample* counter data (that is, collect counter data). In this case, you should consider sampling at least every 5 minutes or so. You don't want to add extra processing strain on a server you might already be worried about, which is why you should consider avoiding a sampling interval that is too short, especially in the long run. For this example, since we are going to be making a baseline of performance over a longer period of time, let's set it for 15 minute sample intervals. To do that, set the Interval for 15, and set the Units to Minutes.

Using the Run As field you can monitor counters from other computers on the network or monitor counters that are managed by services with domain accounts that access network resources. To do that successfully, you may need to run the log under a domain account with the permission to access the services and resources necessary to measure performance. To use the SharePoint counters in my example, you need this log to run in a context that is allowed to access the SQL server, the SharePoint databases, and local services. My example uses the monitor@dem0tek.lcl account for the SharePoint server. This account was created as a member of domain admins.

To commit your counters to the log, click Apply. A dialog box will open and warn you that the default path for the log does not exist. It will ask if would you like to create it (see Figure 12.6). Click Yes.

FIGURE 12.6
The Create Folder warning

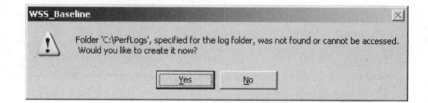

APPLY SETTINGS BEFORE MOVING ON

Why should you apply your settings now before you've examined the other two tabs? Because if you accidentally press Esc at this point, the dialog box will close and you will have to start all over again. If you escape after clicking Apply, even though you may not have changed the default settings for the log, you'll at least have a valid log and won't have to start over. This explains why my example will end up with a log file in the default file type and another one in a custom type.

The Log Files tab is where you can choose your log file format (see Figure 12.7). If you are going to use the System Monitor to graph the log data, you can keep it in binary. If you are going to import it into Excel to work on, save the file as a comma-delimited or tab-delimited file. You can also decide how the baseline logs will be named, either by consecutive number or date.

My example saves the file as a comma-delimited text file and ends the filename with the date. You can change the filename and file location by clicking the Configure button, which opens the Configure Log Files dialog box where you can also set the maximum log file size. It's never a bad thing to limit a log file so it doesn't grow too large, so my example will set the Log File Size to 8MB (see Figure 12.8). When you set a limit, the counter log will start a new log file after the first one becomes full, if necessary.

FIGURE 12.7
The Log Files tab

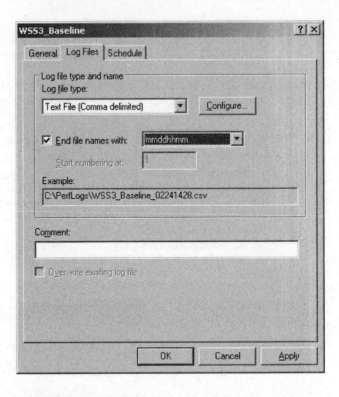

FIGURE 12.8
The Configure Log Files dialog box

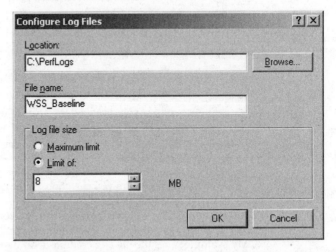

Finally, you need to schedule when your log is going to run, so go to the Schedule tab. As you can see in Figure 12.9, you can set the log to start manually, end manually, and you can even run a command when a log file closes. For my example, set the log to start immediately. (The default is to start immediately, and the time is generally when you started creating the log, so it will start immediately after you finish configuring the log.)

FIGURE 12.9
Scheduling the log

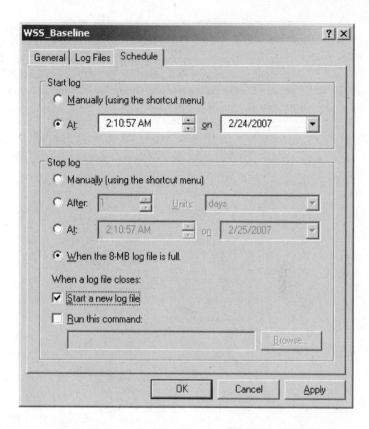

You want the log to stop when each log reaches its 8MB limit and then start again with a new log file. To do that, choose to stop logging when the 8MB log is full. In the When a Log File Closes section, put a check mark next to Start A New Log File. When you're done scheduling your log, click OK to finish the process.

To make certain that your logs have been created, open Windows Explorer and navigate to your log file location (in my example, it's `c:\perflogs` as you can see in Figure 12.10).

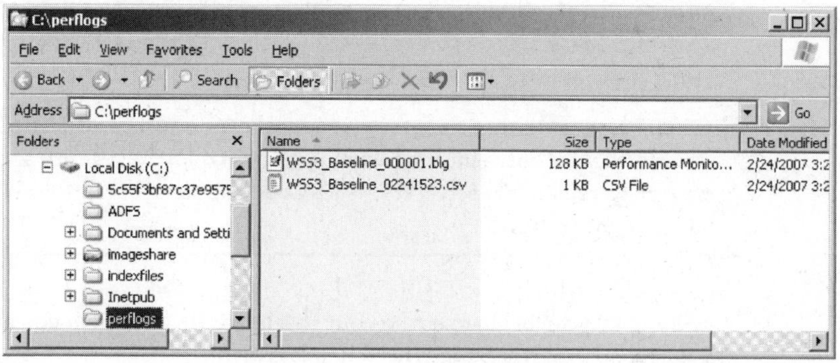

FIGURE 12.10
Log files that have
been created

ANALYZING YOUR LOG FILES

You've got some quiet time on a Friday night, so why not spend some time analyzing your log files? For example, you could open the comma-delimited log file in Excel and conditionally format the results so you can tell at a glance if any totals are outside your acceptable range. It's easy and only takes a second in Excel 2007.

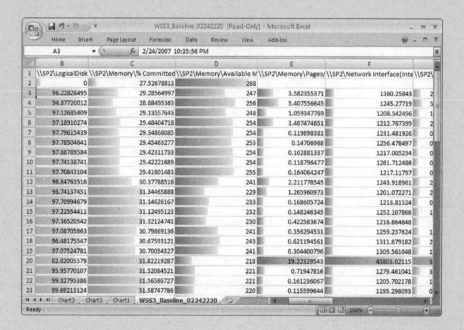

Just keep in mind that you don't have to open your comma-delimited log file and read it as a text file. The point is to have it parsed elsewhere. You can open it in Access to make a database out of it, or you can choose an SQL database file type for your logs so you can query them with SQL. Logs aren't just simple text files anymore. Logs are only as useful as you make them. If you don't analyze them, they are just taking up space.

All sorts of free tools and utilities are available to help you interpret log files. Log Parser 2.2 or higher is a free Microsoft utility that is available online. It will apply an SQL query to practically any log file type, giving you another tool to dig through your logs.

Another good tool is the Server 2003 (SP1) Server Performance Advisor 2.0 (another free download from Microsoft). This utility generates some great reports based on Performance Monitor counters, and it has reporting templates for server roles such as domain controller, DNS, Terminal Services, and Internet Information Services (IIS).

Now you can begin to create your baselines. This will give you an idea of what is going on with your server and what might need improvement.

To be sure the log is running, click on the Counter Logs node in the Performance console. In the content pane, notice that the new log is listed and the icon for it is green (although in grayscale it does look dark gray, but in color it's green). This indicates that it is running (see Figure 12.11). If you want to turn it off, you can simply right-click it and select Stop from the contextual menu.

FIGURE 12.11
Running the counter
log in a console

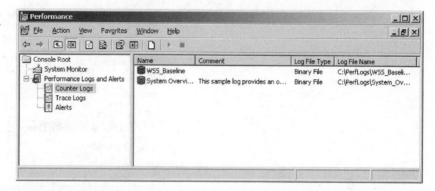

Setting a Performance Counter Alert

Now that you've created your baseline, you must wait for it to build up some data. After a while, when data has been collected, you'll have to look at it. That's good, but what if one of those counters passed a threshold you think is dangerous and you didn't have time to check the log at that particular moment? Wouldn't you like to know if something catastrophic may be brewing? That's why you can set alerts for performance counters. To do so, follow these steps:

1. To set an alert, right-click Alerts in the Performance console, and select New Alert Settings.

2. A dialog box will come up so you can name the alert. My example calls the alert **free disk space**. Click OK.

3. In the dialog box for the alert, you can add a comment and counters. My example adds the comment **This alert triggers when the logical disk is running out of space**.

4. To add the counter for this alert, click Add to bring up the Add Counters dialog box.

5. Because you are adding a counter for the logical disk, you can use that value to select in the Performance Object list, and select % Free Space in the Counters list.

6. In the Instance field, choose a drive as the logical partition that you want to monitor (see Figure 12.12); my example selects the C: drive.

7. Click Add to add this counter to the alert. You could add more, but all of their values would have to be triggered for the alert to go off. Therefore, it's a good idea to create alerts based on as few counters as possible.

8. The *alert value*, or the value that the counter needs to reach in order to trigger the alert, is set in the Alert dialog box. The alert can be triggered when a value is either over or under the specified value. For this example, set the alert value to Under 30. The alert will trigger when the % of free space on the C: partition is less than 30%. Set the sample Interval to 5 minutes (see Figure 12.13). Notice the interval is 5 minutes, you can experiment and see if a longer interval will work for you.

FIGURE 12.12
Configure the % Free Space counter

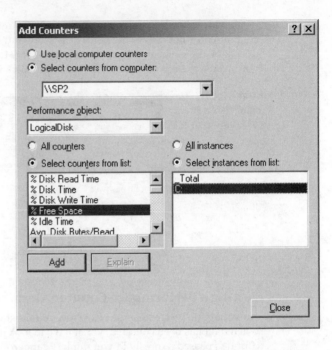

FIGURE 12.13
Setting an alert value and sample interval

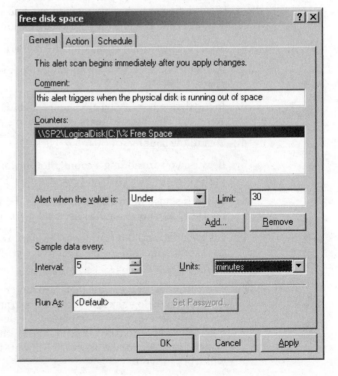

9. Click Apply, and then go to the Action tab. This is where you specify what happens when the trigger value is reached. The alert can log an entry in the application event log, send a network message, start a performance data log, or run a program (Figure 12.14). Set the alert to add an entry in the application event log.

FIGURE 12.14
An alert action

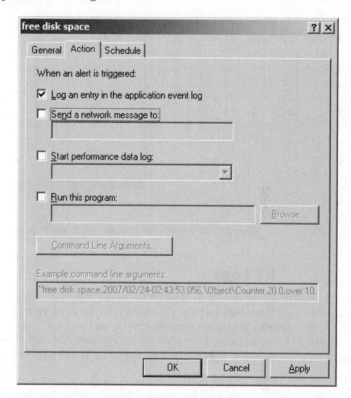

SENDING AN ALERT MESSAGE

If you choose to have an alert send you a network message, the server *must* be running the messenger service. Network messages are sent to a user account, and appear as dialog boxes.

10. To set the schedule for this alert, go to the Schedule tab. Alerts start monitoring immediately by default, but you can change that on the Schedule tab. You can also manage how to stop the alert and start it again after the scheduled stop as if it were a log file. For my example, the schedule start and stop are both set to Manual.

11. Click OK to finish setting up the alert.

12. To start the alert (if it you didn't have it start immediately), click Alerts in the console. Verify that the new alert is in the content pane. It should be red because it requires a manual start. To start the alert, right-click it and select Start (Figure 12.15), or you can select the alert and click the Start button in the toolbar (it has a right arrow icon on it).

FIGURE 12.15
Start an alert manually

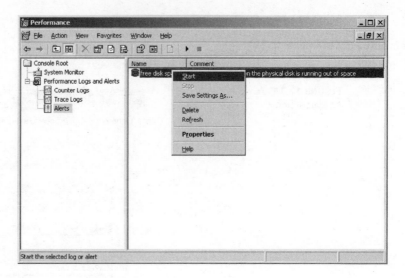

After the alert starts, its icon will turn green to indicate that it is active.

IIS Logs

By default, IIS keeps logs for all IIS Web Sites, which means it keeps logs for each web application. These logs keep approximately the same information as the SharePoint Usage Analysis does (another means to monitor your sites and site collections, by the way). However, you can have more control over what the IIS log does and does not track and more control over how you look at it. To see what the IIS logs are for each web application, just follow these steps:

1. Open the IIS console on the SharePoint server by choosing Start ➤ Administrative Tools ➤ Internet Information Services (IIS) Manager.

2. Inside the console, expand the tree pane so you can see your website icons.

3. Right-click on one of the SharePoint web applications (my example uses SharePoint-80), and select Properties in the popup menu.

4. In the Enable Logging section of the Web Site tab of the Properties dialog box for the IIS Web Site (Figure 12.16), you'll see that logging is Enabled by default. The format for the log is W3C Extended Log File Format. This is the default format for IIS log files, and its use is highly recommended (see the IIS Help files for lots of information about logging and log file formats).

5. To do anything with the log file, you first need to find out where the log file is and what it is called. To do that (because that information isn't conveniently located on the Web Site tab), click the Properties button next to the Active Log Format field.

6. On the General tab of Logging Properties (Figure 12.17), you can see its location (and change it if you'd like) and the filename itself, which is often composed of difficult to remember alphanumerics. Also on the General tab you can change the schedule of the log. The default is Daily, which is fine for this example.

FIGURE 12.16
The Enable Logging option on the
Web Site tab

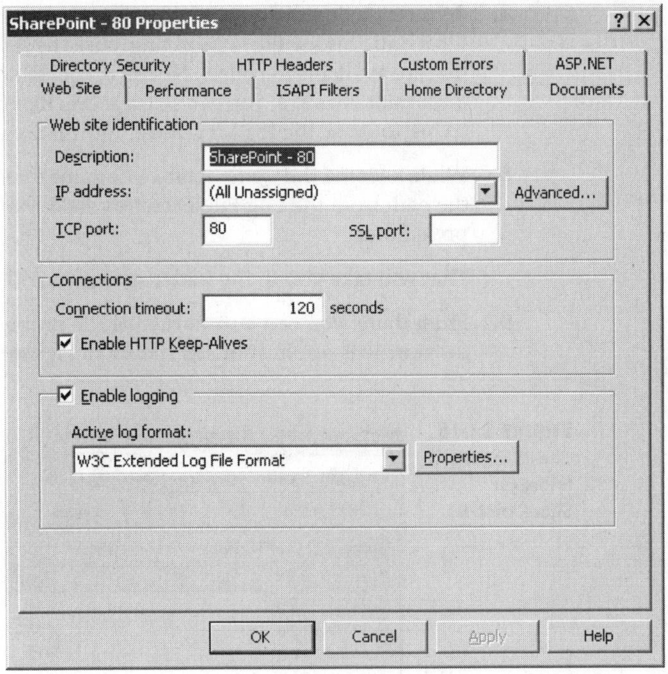

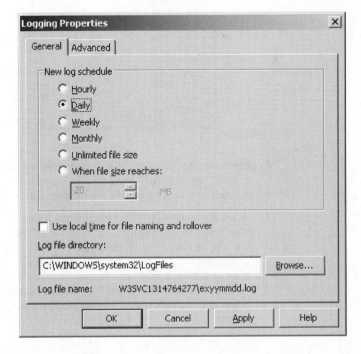

FIGURE 12.17
Log file properties

7. Because the log file type is W3C extended, the log can contain extended information. To see what data this log file is collecting, click the Advanced tab. You will see the extended options that are available to collect. Not all of the fields are selected by default, but many of the most important ones are. You can select more. Remember this. It can be useful later when you are trying to parse the log for critical information.

8. While keeping the General tab of Logging Properties open, open an Explorer window. Copy the path from the Log File Directory field into the address bar of the Explorer window and press Enter.

   That will take you to the folder where your IIS log files are located.

9. From there, you can look at the log file properties again and see the name of the log folder for your web application (as shown in Figure 12.18).

FIGURE 12.18
The IIS log file folder for SharePoint-80

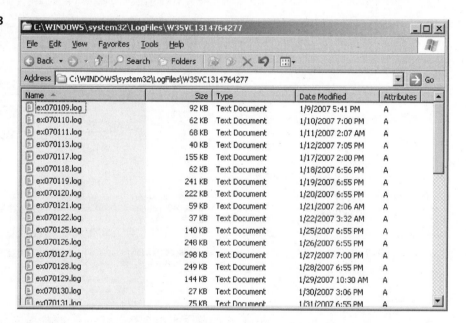

10. Open the log file folder that matches the log filename for your web application. You'll see a list of log files (how long the list is depends on how long the web application has been running and what schedule the log files use).

11. A log file is actually a text document. To see its contents, you can just open the file. Open your most recent log file. The very top of the text file lists the headings for data that the log will be collecting, in the order it will be reported for each entry. The activities that IIS recorded for that particular web application are listed below that. As you scroll, you'll see a lot of GET and POST commands. You'll see the browsers that people used to access the web application, what pages they went to, and what account they used. You can even see the pages that the Index service accessed (yet another good reason to give each service its own account).

These log files can be long, tedious, and full of stuff. This is why using a log parsing tool can be useful. It's also why SharePoint collects the same sort of data to display in its usage analysis; the IIS logs are kind of ponderous. Nonetheless, they are priceless during times of trouble.

OTHER HELPFUL TOOLS

If you are familiar with SQL queries, you can use the Log Parser 2.2 utility from Microsoft to actually run queries against the logs to make them more useful.

Using GUI interfaces can save time and make reviewing the logs easier for others. IIS Log Parser is a little GUI tool that works on top of Log Parser 2.2. You can find it at `http://devtools.10try.com`. Its log queries work well, and they have some nice defaults. It might be right for you.

You might also want to try the Server Performance Advisor. It has a performance template and a specific set of reports designed specifically for monitoring servers running IIS. The Server Performance Advisor is available for download from Microsoft's website.

Event Viewer

The Event Viewer is another important tool in your arsenal. This console can be used in conjunction with the Performance Monitor to see what events SharePoint is reporting in the system's event logs. If you get any extreme readings in the log files, or alerts for unacceptable thresholds, the next place you should go is Event Viewer to see if there are any error events that may shed light on how these log anomalies are affecting SharePoint.

This means you'll need to take a quick trip to the Event Viewer. To open Event Viewer, go to Start ➤ Administrative Tools ➤ Event Viewer. The Event Viewer console contains at least three event logs (there may be more depending on what your server is running). The Application event log (see Figure 12.19) is particularly important in this example. It's where SharePoint will record its significant application events. Any SharePoint source and category can report an error, but the figure shows some things you should look for; you should check the Event Viewer regularly as part of your monitoring rituals.

FIGURE 12.19
The Event Viewer

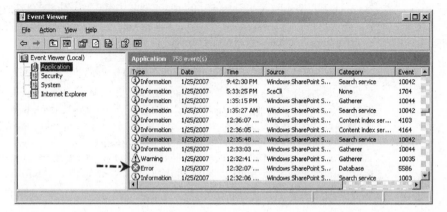

SharePoint tends to be a bit verbose, so expect to see a fair number of informational event entries in the application log. They will at least let you know when things are going well. Of course, SharePoint is not shy about announcing when something is not going well, even if the problem is temporary. (Figure 12.19 shows an example of a momentary blip in the connection with SQL.)

Common Application Event Errors

In the application log, you should look for events referring to the SharePoint Services, DCOM, and ASP. NET, such as:

DCOM, System Log Event, No Category   The standard DCOM event, usually number 10016, means that SharePoint did not give the farm account, or a content database account, the local activation right to the IIS WAMREG Admin Service DCOM. For some reason it most often does this when creating web applications. Often it forgets to give the web application's application pool account local activation rights to that DCOM component. So if, when creating a new web application, and you happen to use a unique user account for the application pool, check the Application logs for DCOM errors.

A PRACTICAL ROMP THROUGH COMPONENT SERVICES

For those of you suffering from the DCOM error 10016 (if the CLSID starts with 61738644), it's easy to fix.

Follow these steps:

1. Open the Component Services console (Start ≻ Administrative Tools ≻ Component Services), and click Component Services.

2. Under the Computers folder, double-click the Computer icon.

3. Open the DCOM Config folder, and scroll to the IIS WAMREG Admin Service icon (application ID just so happens to start with 61738644, which is what's listed in the error).

4. Right-click it, and select Properties from the popup menu.

5. Go to the Security tab, and click Edit in the Launch and Activation Permissions section.

6. In the Launch Permission dialog box, add the service accounts listed in the DCOM errors, giving them explicit Allow Local Activation rights.

This will stop the DCOM error and may also help you troubleshoot search errors.

If you get a DCOM error with a CLSID that does not start with 61738644, chances are good that you'll have to search the registry to resolve the CLSID to the correct DCOM application ID (which is what the DCOM applications are listed by in the Component Services console). Open the registry editor (type regedit at the command prompt or in the Run window). In the registry editor, do a search for the CLSID that the DCOM error displays. You may have to click Next a few times, but it will eventually display the friendly name and AppID mapped to the CLSID. Then use that AppID to find the correct DCOM application to modify in the console.

ASP.NET 2.0.50727.0, Web Event and File Monitoring Errors   This type of error can occur in association with the corruption (or even deletion) of a particular virtual directory that is supposed to be used by one of SharePoint's web applications. To fix this, you can restore the troubled virtual directories from backup. You may have to restart the ASP.NET service and IIS in order to clear this issue. Try to restore the virtual directory first, restart the web application (because it may have stopped due to problems with the virtual directory), then reset IIS, and finally restart ASP.NET. If this does not work, you may want to consider restoring the web application from SharePoint backup.

Windows SharePoint, Gatherer Category Errors   These errors usually mean that the Index service cannot figure out the web address of the web application or site it is supposed to be indexing, or that Search cannot index data from the content databases it has been assigned to, or that Search can't access its own search database where it catalogs the data it has found. There can be several causes for this database issue, so check to see if any other SharePoint services are having a problem accessing the SQL server. If so, the SQL server may have been rebooted, may currently be down, network access to that server may have failed, or the service accounts those services are running under may not be able to log in to their respective databases (check to see if there have been any unauthorized password changes).

The Index service can also be paused when Backup is used to back up files on the server. Indexing is resource sensitive and will stop on its own if the computer does not have the resources available to index data properly. (This is another good reason to monitor your server's resources.) The Index service prefers to authenticate using NTLM, so it can also have a hard time accessing data on sites that use Kerberos exclusively.

Gatherer errors also occur due to web-addressing problems. When you create a web address host header for a web application, make certain that there is an appropriate alternate access mapping for it. The Gatherer uses Alternate Access Mappings (AAM) to be sure that the links it returns to a user are appropriate for the zone they are in (such as Extranet versus Intranet). When you restore web applications, the alternate access mappings may not be restored as well, so be sure to check them after recovering the server (or migrating the web applications to a different server or network), and add the correct alternate access mappings where necessary.

SUSPICIOUS COMPANY

I have had problems getting Gatherer and Search errors in conjunction with VSS (Volume Shadow Copy Service) errors. If that occurs, and an IISreset didn't help, then you may want to consider rebooting your SharePoint server. I don't exactly know why that occurs—and maybe in the future a service pack or two will fix the problem—but for now, a reboot seems to fix it when nothing else does.

Windows SharePoint Service, Database Category Errors   A Database error entry inevitably means that SharePoint has lost contact or can't establish contact with SQL in general or its databases in particular. Make certain that network access to the SQL server is still available. Make certain that the SQL Server service has not stopped.

This error category can also be caused by a security issue if a service account that needs to access the database in question has been corrupted, deleted, or had its password changed. The offending database will be listed as not found, and the account it used to access the database has failed to login. This error event can happen after a web application is restored. Sometimes it seems that the restoration process doesn't quite add the accounts it should. This usually means the service account meant to access the database, or the farm account, has not been added to the restored database with ownership rights. Check the SQL server's Event Viewer logs. If there are corresponding failure audits (meaning that an account failed to log in to access the restored databases), you may have to add the accounts manually. That's generally all it takes to get everything up and running. Also, if a content database has reached its maximum capacity, a warning using the database category will be issued.

Windows SharePoint, Timer Category Errors   This error relates to the Timer job service and often is due to lack of access to the SQL databases required to do a task, or because a task it tried to perform failed. The Timer service will also record an error if you are trying to rerun a failed restore. Remember to delete a failed restore from the Timer Definitions list before you try again.

SharePoint error events are usually pretty self-explanatory (which is good because Microsoft doesn't have any online help for SharePoint events at the writing of this book) and often inform you whether an action failed because a service isn't running (just as restores will fail without the administrative service), or if the problem is database access. Often the event log entry will suggest ways to fix the problem right in the description of the problem.

Event IDs will vary, but the root cause of many SharePoint problems is with the databases or access to SQL. If you reboot the SQL server (say, because you innocently installed a security update), SharePoint will panic because its access to SQL was broken, even momentarily, and you will see error events. Search, Gatherer, and Timer will all throw errors if their access to their SQL is broken for any length of time. If you see these errors, make certain that SharePoint was able to re-establish its connection with SQL after the reboot, and that all is well. Another cause is if you change the password of the service accounts that access databases, such as the Search, Content Database, or the Configuration database (which also is used by the Timer service). The service whose password you changed will no longer be able to log in to SQL to access its databases, causing an issue in SharePoint until you update the password for those service accounts in the SharePoint GUI (or STSADM if you prefer the command line). Additionally, when you restore a web application and its database, make certain that the access accounts have the correct permissions to the correct databases.

Backing Up and Restoring SharePoint

What do you do if you keep getting critical event errors about SharePoint in the application and system logs? What if, despite your careful monitoring of the server, something goes awry? Can it be fixed? Can you recover from a crisis?

At this point, you have some tools to recognize a crisis and why it might be happening. Now is the time to marshal those tools to prepare for catastrophes before they happen, so you can recover your data and get SharePoint back up and running when it fails.

To start with, SharePoint has a couple of points of failure, IIS and SQL.

SharePoint depends on IIS to hold and maintain the web application data necessary to give users web access to SharePoint. Without IIS's configuration data about the SharePoint sites (and their virtual directories), there are no SharePoint websites. Therefore, backing up IIS, as well as the IIS virtual directory information for those web applications, is critical for continued web access to SharePoint. It's good to have that information, just in case.

In addition, SharePoint desperately depends on its databases; therefore, backing them up independently is also good in case they become corrupt or are otherwise damaged and lost.

Finally, Microsoft has wisely given SharePoint a means to defend itself from catastrophe with built-in Backup and Restore capabilities. Knowing that SharePoint needs the IIS configuration data virtual directories, and content databases, SharePoint backs up the IIS configuration for each of the farm's web applications, the virtual directories for those web applications, and the content databases used by those web applications. Restoring those web applications is just a matter of getting to the Central Administration site, selecting what to restore and where to restore it to (you can write over a web application, or simply create a new one if you wish), and then actually running the restore. IIS web application information will be modified with the recovery information (possibly creating a new IIS Web Site and virtual directory with the new location for the restored data). The content database will be recovered or copied with a new name to be associated with the new web application, so you'll have recovered the data you required. All in all, it's a good way to protect all of your hard work and the work of the users.

Although SharePoint does have its own means to back up its data, it is always a good idea to individually back up all the components that you can. In other words, don't put all your data in one basket. Back up SharePoint using SharePoint's tools, back up the databases individually, back up the IIS metabase and configuration data, as well as the virtual directories, and even back up the folder that SharePoint stores its templates and site definitions. Be ready for any eventuality. If a content database goes bad, you can try to replace it by doing a SharePoint restore. But if the SharePoint backup is corrupted for some reason (we all know it happens), you could be out of luck if you don't have an extra backup of that SQL database. Back up everything, and back up often. Keep a copy on site and a copy offsite.

There are several ways to perform backups with SharePoint, and each has its merits. However, the first and foremost method is to use SharePoint's own backup and restore features. SharePoint uses IIS configuration data and SQL databases, and that's what SharePoint's backup tools focus on. This means that you can do full backups of SharePoint's IIS configuration data for each web application, each web application's content database, and even the virtual directory information. The built-in backup also works equally well on a standalone installation as a server farm (well, it is faster and easier when it's all on one box). SharePoint can back up a whole farm, but it can't actually restore the configuration database or its administrative site.

Why? Microsoft decided that the configuration database was awfully complex, and it contains all of the settings and configuration information for the entire farm in absolute terms. To restore the configuration database, all servers on the farm, and their configurations, must be identical to the state of the backed-up configuration database so the configuration data will match. Microsoft felt it would be easier for you to reinstall SharePoint, create a new, almost blank configuration database, and set it up "real quick." Then you can simply restore all of the web applications on the farm and you'll be up and running.

Nonetheless, SharePoint's backup and restore capabilities are extensive when it comes to backing up and restoring the SharePoint web applications and their contents in place. So having, backups are good. As a matter of fact, consider backing up your backups.

Your first backup of anything should always be a *full backup*. SharePoint will allow you to choose, in the interface, whether or not to back up the whole farm (all of the web applications in one shot) or just the web applications of your choice. Whenever a backup is done in SharePoint, a folder is created containing a series of backup files and an XML file that catalogs all of the folder's contents. If you ever need to move those backups, move the entire folder structure.

Once you've made a full backup, you can do *differential backups*. Differentials only back up the changes since the last full backup. This means that you should be able to restore a server by applying the most recent full backup, and then the most recent differential. Because differential backups take less time, you can perform differential backups more frequently than full backups.

Backups and restores take considerable RAM and processor power to perform, so they are not something to undertake in the middle of a busy production day. Wait until down times (such as 3:00 A.M.) to do backups. Don't do backups at the same time you perform usage process analysis. SharePoint backups can be a little fragile, which is why making a backup of your SharePoint backups is a good thing.

Back Up SharePoint

Making backups with SharePoint does have a few gotchas. To help avoid some of them, remember these tips:

♦ Make sure the Windows SharePoint Services 3.0 Administrative Service is running. This service is often stopped on single-server installs. If you are doing a restore on a server farm, make certain that the Administrative service is running on all the frontend servers in the farm for the duration of the backup or restore.

♦ The VSS services of both SharePoint and SQL are used during the backup process. If there are problems, make sure they are running. (Theoretically, they are supposed to be triggered to start by the backup or restore process. If that doesn't happen, at least you know what they are and can start them in the Services console.) Make certain that there are no VSS errors in the event logs before you back up your SharePoint server.

♦ Make certain that the SQL Server service account is a domain account. If the service account is a local account on the server, you'll need to give the SQL server's machine account permissions to the file share where the backups are to be stored. There is no guarantee that that will always work. It's easier just to give the SQL Server service account a domain account and then give *it* permission to the file share.

♦ Make certain that the location where you are going to save the backup (and probably restore from there as well) has enough disk space, as well as read and right permissions assigned to:

♦ The Timer service account, which should also be the Central Administration pool account (my example is dem0tek\wssconfig). If you are running a SharePoint standalone or basic installation, the computer account must have access (for example, dem0tek\sp1$).

♦ The SQL Server service for the SQL server that contains the SharePoint databases. Again, if you are running on a standalone SharePoint server, then the SQL Server Embedded Edition (SSEE) database is running in the local computer's context and, therefore, must have access to the share as the computer account.

♦ Make certain all necessary accounts have at least Change and Read share permissions for the file share.

To get to SharePoint's backup and restore interface, open the Central Administration website. Select Start ➤ Administrative Tools ➤ SharePoint 3.0 Central Administration on the SharePoint server. Then follow these steps:

1. On the Central Administration home page, click the link or tab for Operations.

2. On the Operations page, click on the Perform a backup link in the Backup and Restore section.

FIGURE 12.20
The Perform A Backup Step
1 of 2 page

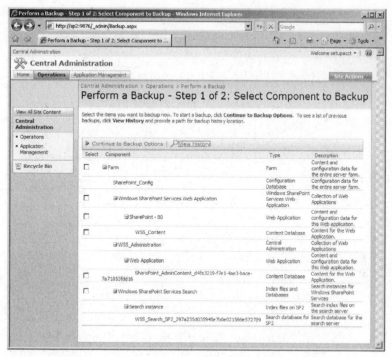

3. On the Perform a Backup Step 1 of 2 page (see Figure 12.20), the layout of the components to back up basically conform to the databases that are used by SharePoint, either as content databases for the web applications or the database used by Search. To back up everything SharePoint will let us, select Farm. Everything on the page will be selected. This is a good idea to do as a first backup in SharePoint.

4. If Farm is selected, then click Continue to Backup Options in the action bar.

5. On the Start Backup Step 2 of 2 page, the first section confirms that you selected to backup the entire Farm. You can change your mind by clicking Farm and selecting Change Backup Component from the drop-down menu if you'd like, which would be the equivalent of clicking the Back button. Leave it set to Farm.

6. We are going to do a full backup. However, you could do regular differential backups in the future, if it suits your environment. *Differential backups* just back up the changes since the last full backup. They are faster to do. However, when you restore, you'll need to restore a full backup first and then a differential. For this example leave the Type of Backup option set to Full.

7. In the last Backup File Location section, specify your backup location. My example is on a file share on the network (see Figure 12.21). Conveniently, SharePoint even lets you know how large the file is going to be (estimated disk space). Make certain that the Timer service account has read, write, and modify rights to that location.

8. Once you have specified the location for your backup, click OK to begin.

FIGURE 12.21
Specify the backup location

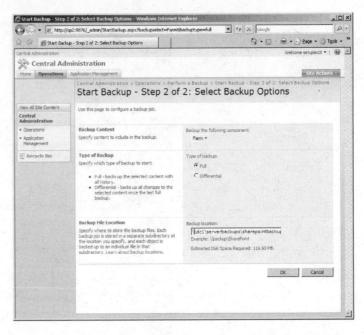

The Backup and Restore Status page will appear. It will take a moment, as the SharePoint Timer job gets the backup task and begins it. This page will refresh occasionally and let you know what is happening with the backup. This is where you will find out if your backup is working (Figure 12.22). For your first backup, try not to get distracted until it is complete, so you can fix issues immediately.

FIGURE 12.22
The Backup and Restore
Status page

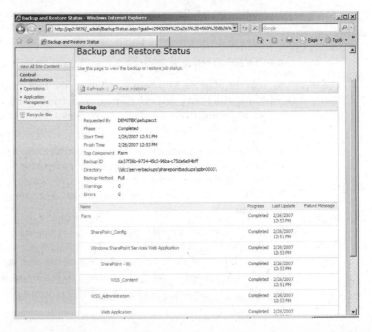

Now that you have performed a backup, it will be listed in the backup history. For most backup and restore pages, the link to the backup history is usually on the action bar. There is also a link to it on the Operations page. From here, just click the View History link in the action bar. The History page will have a listing for your backup. This data is pulled from the last location where you stored backups. To display SharePoint backups from a different location, you'll need to click the Change Directory link in the action bar (see Figure 12.23).

FIGURE 12.23
The Backup And
Restore History page

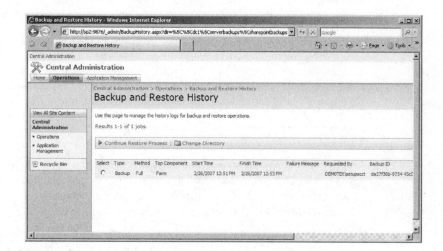

The folders and files that were created when you did a backup were named automatically; you had no choice in the matter. If you go to the location where the backups were made (see Figure 12.24), you will see that there is a folder containing the separate backup files for this particular backup. These backup folders' names are prefaced with spbr followed with a four-digit number. The four-digit number will increment by 1 for each additional backup. In addition, in the backup location, there is always a backup history document or spbr toc, which is the backup XML file. Always move all of the folders and the TOC file together. The TOC lists exactly where all backups are in the folders. If you move the backups away from their TOC file, SharePoint restore may not know how to restore them because they can't be listed in the location's history. In each backup folder is also a critical XML file indicating all the individual backup files and their order.

FIGURE 12.24
Backup files

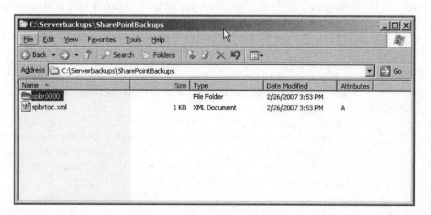

Once you've backed up your SharePoint server farm, you can recover it should something go wrong with your web applications. Although you did a full-farm backup, that backup is structured so you can perform restores of any individual web application or the Search service and database.

Now you are prepared for a catastrophe. Catastrophes come in many forms. Someone could ruin the contents of a web application, delete a few site collections and deface a few more. The application's IIS Web Site could become corrupted, or the database could throw errors and become inaccessible according to the Gatherer errors in the event logs.

The beauty of SharePoint backups is that they are complete. They cover the IIS configuration data for the web applications and their virtual directories, as well as that web application's database. They are *full fidelity*, meaning they keep all the content and settings they can (alternate access mapping will have to be reset) and all the user security settings that are possible. The backups can be used to restore all of the web applications for a server farm, or whichever one you need to recover. The web applications can be restored to the same server, to a different server, and even to a different server farm. They are your first stop in restoring SharePoint functionality.

TWO WAYS TO RESTORE

Keep in mind that there are two distinct ways to perform SharePoint restores: to the same configuration or to a new configuration. SharePoint remembers the exact configuration of the web applications, the exact web address (which for the first web application is often the server name itself), port, service account, virtual directory, database server, and database name.

If you are simply overwriting a web application, use the Same configuration. If you are restoring the backup to a different server, you must use the New configuration setting and specify the new server name in the web address (or addresses if you are restoring more than one web application at a time). When you perform a new configuration restore, you can use the same web address as before, but you usually must use a different database name.

Restore SharePoint

When there are errors in the event logs, when content databases seem to have gone sour, when IIS doesn't seem to remember your SharePoint website (it's there, but not quite working), or when the application pool seems to have forgotten its identity, often the best thing to do is restore from SharePoint backup. Sometimes it is faster and easier to restore from backup than it is to spend fruitless hours trying to fix a bizarre problem.

This example demonstrates the simplicity and power of restoring from an existing backup. In it, I've drastically changed the theme for the home page of the http://sp2 site (see Figure 12.25). This theme change is to visually emulate a possible corruption of the content database that is causing unexpected changes to the sites. Fortunately, this happened after the last full backup was made to the site (otherwise, you could restore the most recent full backup and then the most recent differential).

Recovering the same configuration of the site from backup will restore the content database of the web application and put it in its pre-backup, pre-corruption condition.

To begin the recovery process, first make certain that the Administrative service is running and that all the necessary accounts have access to the file share. Then restore the web application using the Farm backup made within SharePoint.

FIGURE 12.25

The Home page in Black, simulating a formatting catastrophe

To do that, go back to Central Administration (select Start ➢ Administrative Tools ➢ SharePoint 3.0 Central Administration on the SharePoint server or use the correct server address and port in Internet Explorer). Then follow these steps:

1. On the Central Administration home page, click the Operations link or tab.

2. On the Operations page that appears, go to the Restore from Backup link in the Backup and Restore section.

3. On the Restore From Backup—Step 1 Of 4 page (see Figure 12.26), you can use the default location of your last backup as your restore location, or you can specify a different one if you'd like (if you have one). My example keeps the default. Click OK to continue.

FIGURE 12.26

The Restore From Backup Step 1 Of 4 page

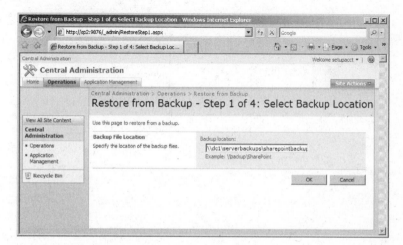

4. On the Step 2 of 4 page, choose the backup from which you'd like to restore. My example has only the restore that was just created, so it displays only that one (see Figure 12.27). Notice that it is a full-farm backup. Once you've selected your backup, click Continue Restore Process on the action bar.

FIGURE 12.27
Choose a backup

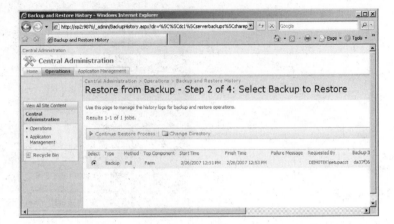

5. On the Restore Backup—Step 3 Of 4 page, you can see the list of web applications that can be restored using the full-farm backup. The backup contains everything to restore all web applications for the SharePoint farm, but you can pick and choose what you want. In my example, we only need to restore the SharePoint-80 web application. So let's select the web application we need to recover. You can just restore the content database if you'd like, or you can recover the web application information as well as the database (just in case). Both are selected in Figure 12.28. When you've selected what you want to restore, click Continue Restore Process.

FIGURE 12.28
Restore the selection

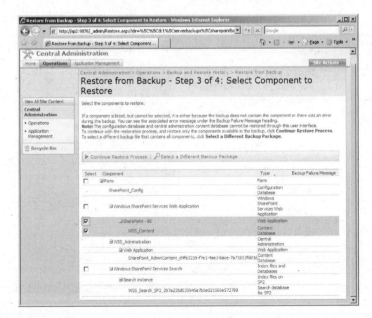

6. The Restore From Backup—Step 4 Of 4 page is where you indicate where you are going to restore the selected backup data. You can restore over the existing data (to repair or replace something), or you can create a new web application and content database. In this example, we are going to restore the good data over the top of the bad data in the existing web application. However, if you want to simply recover the web application without disturbing the existing one, you can recover to a New Configuration. This is also useful if you just want to restore to a clean slate, because SharePoint will treat the recovered information like a completely different web application that just happens to contain the same data. The page's sections can be seen in Figure 12.29.

FIGURE 12.29
The Restore
Settings page

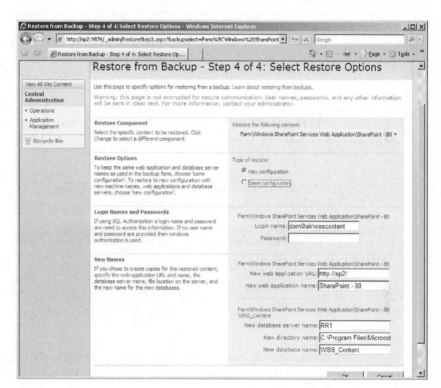

Those four sections are explained here:

- The first section of the page simply confirms what you are restoring.

- The second section contains the restore options. The default is New Configuration.

- In the third section, because New Configuration is still chosen above, you can specify the application pool account for the new web application. It will need to have content database permissions to the SQL server. My example will not need to do this, since the plan is to overwrite the existing location.

- The fourth section contains information pertaining to the web application's name and URL, as well as the name of the new database and the server where it will reside.

THE WEB APPLICATION NAME AND URL

If you choose to restore to a new web application and use the same default URL as the original SharePoint site (in my case `http://sp2`) then SharePoint has no choice but to give the new configuration of the web application a different port number. This page has a condensed version of the information used when you are creating a new web application. So it is here you either specify the host header for the web application or the URL based on a managed path. If you want to use a port number and use the default web address, then specify that port in the new web application field (although I've seen SharePoint assign its own despite that).

In order to change these settings to use the existing location, you need to select **Same Configuration** in the Restore Options section to specify that you are going to keep the same configuration and simply restore over the existing data. You may get an overwrite warning dialog box here, click OK to move on.

7. The last section of the page will gray out because you are not going to change that data. You will be left with the option to specify the username and password of the content database access account. This example uses the account that is already specified for this particular web application, so all I need to do is to enter the account password.

8. If all the data on the Restore From Backup—Step 4 Of 4 page is complete, click OK to begin the restore process. You'll get a warning that all selected components will be overwritten (see Figure 12.30). That's fine, so click OK.

FIGURE 12.30
Overwrite
warning

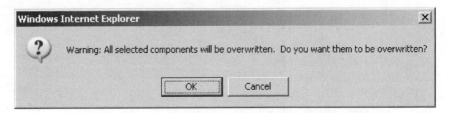

9. Check the Backup and Restore Status page and wait for the backup to complete. Then, wait several more minutes. Do not panic if sites in the web application do not come back up right away.

10. Using your browser, open a web page on the web application you just restored to make certain that everything is okay. In my example, a change was made to the top-level site theme (back on Figure 12.25) that needs to be undone. That means I just go to the URL that was restored, `HTTP://sp2`, and the old theme is back (Figure 12.31). All of the changes, potential corruptions, and other problems are replaced with the data from the backup.

There are some rules of thumb as to how SharePoint backup behaves. Same Configuration restores are primarily for the restoration of existing content. If your IIS Web Site or application pool for a web application are deleted or are corrupted, a Same Configuration restore will not fix them. Same Configuration just applies the existing settings and content database information to existing IIS Web Sites and content databases. The application pool identity is not reset. This is when restoring the IIS metabase (or IIS Web Site configuration data) comes in handy.

FIGURE 12.31
Site theme
returned,
catastrophe
averted

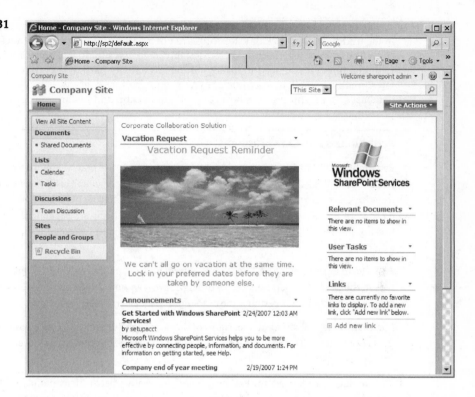

To rebuild the IIS Web Site, IIS Application Pool, and database of a SharePoint web application (or even more than one) using SharePoint, you must use the New Configuration option. New Configuration tells SharePoint to create a new IIS Web Site and application pool for the new web application in IIS, and to create a new content database in SQL based on the backup information. You can use the same IIS Web Site settings (port, host header, etc.) as the deleted web application you are trying to recover, but you cannot use the same content database. New Configuration restores require that the database be unique and, therefore, you must use a different database name (unless the database itself is also missing). New Configuration restores can be used to restore a web application side by side with the existing one, in case you want to recover something from the backup but not overwrite the existing web application. However, they can be used to completely rebuild the web applications of a server farm as well. When doing a SharePoint restore, the New Configuration setting (which is the default) makes it possible to restore SharePoint entirely should you have a disaster.

Remember, if web application content has been ruined, do an in-place content database restore using Same Configuration. If you need to rebuild the web application from scratch, use New Configuration to create a new web application with a new port or host header and, specifying the SQL server, a new database and even a new content database service account. Usually, when you are restoring SharePoint to a different server, you will need to do a New Configuration restore anyway, because the server name (and therefore the web address for the sites) will be different than the backup's configured server name.

Performing a restore in SharePoint pushes that server's resources, so be careful about restoring in the middle of the work day. Restores are not a game. If you just want to restore a single site collection, site, or list, there are better less invasive ways to do it. Think of this sort of restore as a sledgehammer. If you need to hit something large really hard, it is perfect; however, if you need to tap something small, it's too much. If you need to restore every web application and their content databases for an entire server farm, SharePoint backup and restore can do it.

SCHEDULING FOR CATASTROPHES

Remember, STSADM can do anything at the command line that SharePoint does in the GUI—and more. The GUI is simply executing STSADM commands for you. This means that if you would like to write a script to schedule your SharePoint site collection or web application backups, you can do so with STSADM. Because SharePoint doesn't have scheduling capabilities available for the GUI backup and restore, you have to use the STSADM command for doing backups and schedule it as a task.

To perform a catastrophic backup (that is, a farm or web application backup), just create a text file and type in the STSADM operation to do a backup, save it as a batch file, and then create a schedule task to trigger the batch file at a certain time or to repeat over a certain period.

I generally schedule differential backups of the farm nightly (because I can choose to restore individual items from a single farm backup, I don't need to do separate backups for each web application), and full backups weekly.

To schedule these SharePoint backups, I need to create a batch file containing the command I want to run, and then I need to schedule that command to run daily, at about 3:00 A.M. starting tonight. To do that:

1. Open a text file in Notepad. For the differential backup of the farm enter:

   ```
   "C:\Program Files\Common Files\Microsoft Shared\web server
      extensions\12\BIN\stsadm" -o backup -directory
      \\dc1\Holding\WSSbackups\sp4back -backupmethod differential
   ```

   Where -directory is the file share where the backup should be stored, and -backupmethod can either full or differential. In this case, I am performing a differential backup.

2. Save the text file as farmdiff.bat.

3. Once the file is saved, create a new scheduled task (Start ➢ Accessories ➢ System Tools ➢ Scheduled Tasks), and double-click the Add Scheduled Task to start the wizard.

4. In the Schedule Task Wizard that opens, click Next to choose the program you want to schedule. Of course, the batch file isn't be on the list, so browse and select your batch file (mine is farmdiff.bat).

5. The wizard will prompt you to name the task (I am keeping farmdiff for simplicity's sake) and set up the schedule as to how often the task is performed. In my case, I am going to choose Daily and click Next.

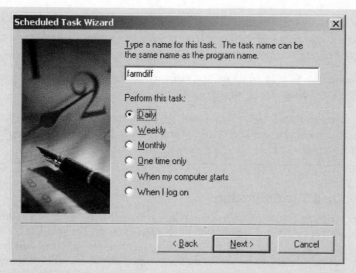

6. In the next wizard screen, choose a time of day to do the differential farm backups. Be careful to schedule this when as few activities as possible are happening on the network, the SharePoint server, and the SQL server. It is also a good idea to keep in mind when your usage analysis processing is scheduled, so you can avoid that time for the backups. With that in mind, 3:00 A.M. will be the time I schedule to start today. Click Next.

7. The next screen in the wizard requires the username and password of the account that will run these tasks. This account must be a Farm Administrator on the Central Administration site, a domain admin or local administrator to run commands locally on the SharePoint server, and must have read, modify, and write rights on the file share where the backup will go. Enter an account with these rights (and its password). For my example, this will be dem0tek\shareadmin.

8. Once you've entered an appropriate username and password, click Next.

9. After verifying the task name and schedule, click Next to create the scheduled task.

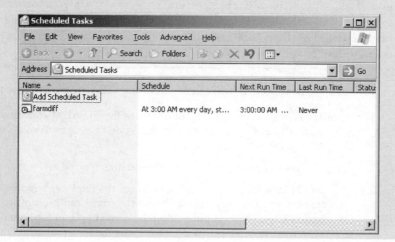

When the task's schedule time occurs, a command prompt will open, the STSADM backup command will execute, activity information will scroll down the command prompt window until the command completes, and then the window will close.

Remember that you can create the same sort of thing for your full backups, or you can create separate backups for each web application if you'd like.

You can restore from these backups in the GUI just as you would any you created there using the GUI. If you'd like, you can restore using STSADM just as easily. Check out Chapter 13, "STSADM: A Look at the SharePoint Command Line Tool," for more STSADM details.

Back Up a Site Collection

There are probably going to be times when you need to back up and restore smaller things than an entire web application. Luckily, you have a few choices. The smallest component of SharePoint that you can actually back up and restore is an entire *site collection*, which means a top-level site and all of its subsites. Otherwise, smaller components of SharePoint are export/imported or made into templates, but not officially backed up or restored.

Site collection backups are full fidelity, meaning they keep as many custom and security settings as possible. They can be restored to repair or recover the same web application by overwriting it; or to the same web application but under a different URL (if you want to recover some bits without altering the existing version); or even be restored to a completely different server in a different domain (in that case, security will have to be reconfigured, of course).

The SharePoint GUI does not have a place to back up and restore site collections. Just like scheduling backups, running a backup job of a single site collection is something that can only be done using the STSADM command.

WHO YOU ARE MATTERS

STSADM can only run locally, and it is a command-line executable, so it runs in the context of the person executing it. To use it, you need to be logged in as someone with administrative rights to the SharePoint server where you are running the command, and administrative or ownership rights to the site collection itself. You might be able to back up with STSADM using a local administrator account, but you can't restore without being the owner/admin of the site collection itself.

To back up a site collection (while easily accessing STSADM), just follow these steps.

1. Open Windows Explorer, navigate to where the STSADM command is located, which is `%Program Files%\Common Files\Microsoft Shared\web server extensions\12\BIN`.

2. Open a command prompt. On the command line, type **cd** and a space.

3. Click on the little folder in the address bar of the Explorer window that is displaying the contents of the path in Step 1. Drag it into the command prompt window and press Enter (see Figure 12.32). This will put you on the correct path in the command prompt window, so you can work with STSADM without typing the long path to get there (but that option is open to you if you prefer it).

4. Now that you are at the command prompt, enter **STSADM** and press Enter. A long list of information about STSADM will scroll by. For this example, you only need to know how to back up and restore site collections, which use the STSADM operations of backup and restore.

The syntax for these operations using STSADM are listed in Figure 12.33. Notice that there are two different types of backup and restore for SharePoint: site collection backup and catastrophic backup. The site collection backup is for site collections, and the catastrophic backup is the command-line version of the SharePoint backup and restore that you do in the GUI. That's all, not really catastrophic, hopefully. It backs up and restores web application IIS data, virtual directories, and content databases.

FIGURE 12.33
Syntax for STSADM's backup
and restore operations

```
C:\Program Files\Common Files\Microsoft Shared\web server extensions\12\BIN>stsa
dm -help backup

For site collection backup:
    stsadm.exe -o backup
        -url <url>
        -filename <filename>
        [-overwrite]

For catastrophic backup:
    stsadm.exe -o backup
        -directory <UNC path>
        -backupmethod <full | differential>
        [-item <created path from tree>]
        [-percentage <integer between 1 and 100>]
        [-backupthreads <integer between 1 and 10>]
        [-showtree]
        [-quiet]

C:\Program Files\Common Files\Microsoft Shared\web server extensions\12\BIN>stsa
dm -help restore

For site collection restore:
    stsadm.exe -o restore
        -url <url>
        -filename <filename>
        [-hostheaderwebapplicationurl <web application url>]
        [-overwrite]

For catastrophic restore:
    stsadm.exe -o restore
        -directory <UNC path>
        -restoremethod <overwrite | new>
        [-backupid <Id from backuphistory, see stsadm -help backuphistory>]
        [-item <created path from tree>]
        [-percentage <integer between 1 and 100>]
        [-showtree]
        [-suppressprompt]
        [-username <username>]
        [-password <password>]
        [-newdatabaseserver <new database server name>]
        [-quiet]
```

Fundamentally, for site collection backup STSADM needs the URL for the site collection's top-level site, and the filename that will be used for the backup. There is also the option to overwrite the previous backup by the same name if you'd like. For restore, STSADM needs the name of the backup file and the URL of where it is going. If the site collection is being restored to a web application that uses a host header, that needs to be specified as well. Finally, you need to specify whether or not you are overwriting an existing site collection. If you are, then you must specify that with the -overwrite parameter or the restore will, reasonably enough, fail (you can't have two site collections with the exact same URL in a server farm).

To start, let's back up a simple, site collection in the SharePoint server farm. For this example, the server's name is SP2. To access the home page of the top-level site of the site collection, we'll use HTTP://SP2, which is the URL for that site collection since it backs up from the top-level site downwards.

Therefore, to back up that site collection using STSADM, you should use the following syntax:

```
STSADM -o Backup -url HTTP://SP2 -filename
  \\dc1\serverbackups\sp2backups\sitecollections\sp2top.bak -overwrite
```

-o
Indicates that STSADM is going to act on an operation (-help means it is going to display the help information for the operation)

backup
The operation

-url
The parameter that specifies the URL of the top-level site of a site collection to back up

-filename
The path to where you will put the backup (my example is a file share on the DC1 server) and what you will name it

-overwrite
The parameter indicating that another backup in that location with the same name should be overwritten. This is great for scripting a backup so you can schedule it as a task. You can simply overwrite the backup from time to time to keep the site collection backup as recent as possible.

At the command prompt, you should type the previous command, all in one line (see Figure 12.34), using your site collection's URL and your backup location instead of the example.

FIGURE 12.34
Successful completion of site collection backup

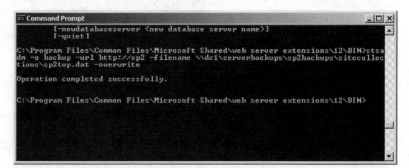

The backup for the site collection in this example has been saved to the network share, so if the running site collection is ruined, it can be restored from backup.

To really prove the backup works, do something to visibly alter (or if you are particularly daring, really ruin) the site collection. In my example I am going to delete the Shared Documents Library and change the theme of the site to something different than the default (see Figure 12.35).

HERE'S AN EXAMPLE OF HOW I ALTERED THE SITE FOR THIS EXAMPLE

If you'd like to see the changes I made to the site in color, follow along using these steps:

1. Go to the site collection you backed up, in this case first site collection of the first web application (my example is at `HTTP://SP2`). Click on the link in the Quick Launch bar for Shared Documents. On the Shared Documents list, click Settings in the action bar, and select Document Library Settings from the dropdown.

2. From the Document Library settings page, click Delete This Document Library. It will warn you that the document library will go to the Recycle Bin. Click OK.

3. Go back to the home page. The Shared Documents Library will no longer be listed on the Quick Launch bar.

4. Click Site Actions and go to Site Settings.

5. In the Look And Feel section, click on Site Theme and choose a theme very unlike the original. Click Apply.

Now we've made changes to this site collection (see Figure 12.34). If you are feeling courageous, you can do even more damage; just make sure you can access your site collection backup to restore.

FIGURE 12.35
The site uses a different theme and is missing Shared Documents

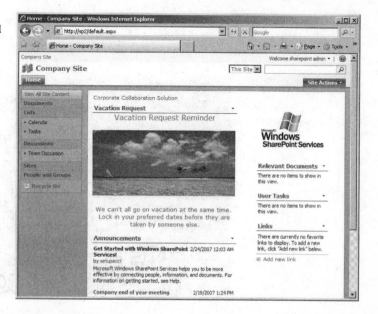

Restore a Site Collection

To restore a site collection after it has been damaged; simply use the STSADM command at the command prompt.

The STSADM operation syntax for restoring a site collection backup is

```
Stsadm -o restore -url -filename -overwrite
```

If the web application this site collection resides in uses a host header, you need to use the -hostheaderwebapplicationurl parameter as well, to specify the host header address.

My example will restore a site collection over that site collection that was ruined. The site is at the URL HTTP://SP2, and the filename of the backup is \\Dc1\serverbackups\ sp2backups\sitecollections\sp2top.dat. This means to restore the site collection from backup, you need to use (all on one line):

```
STSADM -o restore -url HTTP://SP2 -filename
    \\dc1\serverbackups\sp2backups\sitecollections\sp2top.bak -overwrite
```

The restore may take a moment and leave you sitting at the command prompt wondering what error might be waiting to appear. However, the chances are good you will end up with a operation completed successfully notice like the one in Figure 12.36.

FIGURE 12.36
The restore was completed successfully

When you browse to the restored site collection's home page, you will be greeted with a restored Shared Documents Library, and the site theme will return to the one it originally had (Figure 12.37).

FIGURE 12.37
The restored site collection in the browser

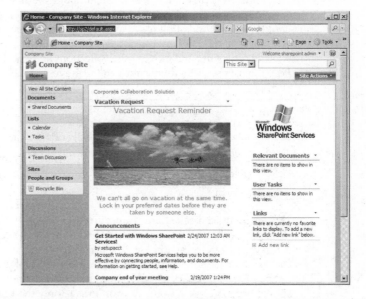

OUTDATED TERMINOLOGY

There's a funny thing about STSADM: it's old school. It calls web applications "sites" (as in IIS websites), and it calls subsites "subwebs." This becomes more relevant as you use operations that specifically request information about site collections and subsites. Don't be confused; it's just language from another time.

Export and Import Site Collections and Subsites

Export and import are STSADM operations that kind of cross the boundary between backing up and restoring site collections, and backing up and restoring subsites. They aren't officially considered backup and restore, but they do very similar things. Importing and exporting work on either site collections or subsites. *Export* saves a site or site collection so it can be exported from its current location and imported to a new web application or server. Export is full fidelity, saving as many settings and as much security as possible.

IMPORTING AND EXPORTING VERSUS SITE TEMPLATES

The nice thing about import and export is that it doesn't have the size limit of a template. When you make a site template with saved content, it can only be so big, so that can be a problem. On the other hand, to import a site, you must first create a site for it to import over, so that can be inconvenient as well. Site Templates are covered in Chapter 7, "Sites, Subsites, and Workspaces."

This set of operations is new to this version of SharePoint's STSADM. The set makes it possible to create a content migration package (or .cmp) file of your favorite site collection or subsite. Those .cmp files can be stored for future use and restored with all settings intact on the same server or on a completely different server farm (although alerts will be lost and the user permissions might be a little worse for wear if the accounts it thinks it should be using aren't in that domain's Active Directory). This operation may have been added to compensate for the fact that version 3.0 of Windows SharePoint Services no longer supports the SMIGRATE command of version 2.0, which allowed for saving and moving site collections and subsites. However, this version lets you keep the user security information in the move, so in a way, this can be considered a step up.

USING THE .CAB EXTENSION

Content migration package files are essentially cabinet files (.cab) files. If you don't want to use the default extension for your export file, .cab will work. As a matter of fact, if you give the export file the .cab extension, you will be able to open it and see what makes it tick—provided you have the user permission to do so.

Here's a quick peek at how Importing and Exporting works.

Export will save a site based on its URL, saving all content starting from the URL and heading down the hierarchy. In other words, if a site collection is located at the root address for the server, such as http://sp2, Export will save all sites and pages from that web address as well as http://sp2/hrteam, http://sp2/hrteam/timeclock, and so on. This means the whole site collection gets saved. If you want to save only the timeclock subsite, specify that Export begin from the http://sp2/hrteam/timeclock URL, which would capture only that site's files and settings from that address downward.

When you import a site or site collection from an exported .cmp file, you need to have some place to import it. Like its predecessor, SMIGRATE, the Import operation of STSADM requires that you create a target site for the import to fill. Then you specify the URL to import the .cmp file to, which propagates the exported site information into the new site, as completely as possible (but unfortunately losing alerts).

As a matter of fact, say you created a subsite under the main company site that you now wish you'd put in its own site collection. You can export that subsite (with *its* subsites if it has any), create a site collection, and import the subsite to be the top-level site of that new site collection. Then that subsite would have its own site collection and you could delete it safely from its original location. Be sure to check the user permissions to make certain they are correct, and remember that alerts will have to be reset.

EXPORTING AND IMPORTING WITH THE STSADM COMMAND

Keep in mind that, in order to successfully export and import, you must run the stsadm command from a command prompt using an account that is an owner of the site you want to export. It also helps if that account is allowed to run commands on the SharePoint server.

EXPORT A SITE

Let's export the HR Team site out from under the top-level Company site and export it to its own site collection (where it will be the top-level site). This will help the design, and it can be used to recover data without actually doing anything invasive to the original HR Team site. Follow these steps:

1. To run STSADM, you must open a command prompt (generally as the site owner of the site collection from which you'd like to export, and later as the site owner of the site to which you'd like to import). Be sure that you either use the path to the STSADM command or that it is part of the system's PATH environmental variable.

2. At the prompt, to see what the syntax and parameters are for import and export, enter **STSADM -help import** and press Enter. This will display the syntax and parameters for the import operation (see Figure 12.38). Do the same for export, to familiarize yourself with it as well.

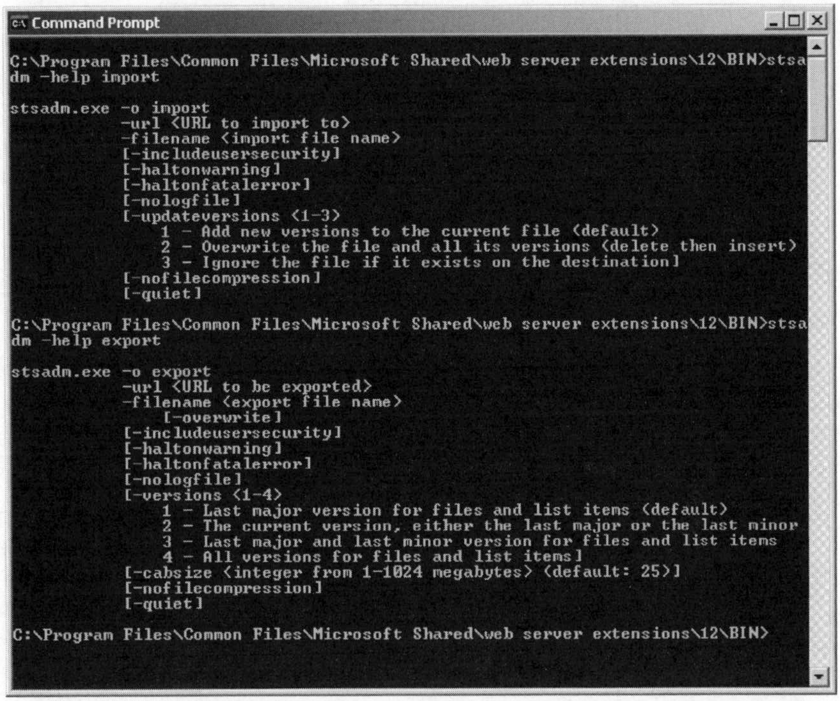

FIGURE 12.38
The STSADM import and export syntax

```
C:\Program Files\Common Files\Microsoft Shared\web server extensions\12\BIN>stsa
dm -help import

stsadm.exe -o import
          -url <URL to import to>
          -filename <import file name>
          [-includeusersecurity]
          [-haltonwarning]
          [-haltonfatalerror]
          [-nologfile]
          [-updateversions <1-3>
              1 - Add new versions to the current file (default)
              2 - Overwrite the file and all its versions (delete then insert)
              3 - Ignore the file if it exists on the destination]
          [-nofilecompression]
          [-quiet]

C:\Program Files\Common Files\Microsoft Shared\web server extensions\12\BIN>stsa
dm -help export

stsadm.exe -o export
          -url <URL to be exported>
          -filename <export file name>
              [-overwrite]
          [-includeusersecurity]
          [-haltonwarning]
          [-haltonfatalerror]
          [-nologfile]
          [-versions <1-4>
              1 - Last major version for files and list items (default)
              2 - The current version, either the last major or the last minor
              3 - Last major and last minor version for files and list items
              4 - All versions for files and list items]
          [-cabsize <integer from 1-1024 megabytes> (default: 25)]
          [-nofilecompression]
          [-quiet]

C:\Program Files\Common Files\Microsoft Shared\web server extensions\12\BIN>
```

For my example, we'll export the site first. The syntax (all in one line) for exporting a site or site collection is:

```
STSADM -o export -url http://sp2/HRteam -filename
\\sp2\exports\teamsite -overwrite -includeusersecurity -versions 4
-cabsize 600
```

This example does not use every single parameter available for the operation, but those demonstrated here are:

-url
The web address of the site or site collection you are going to export. The example is the Human Resources subsite of the Company site collection, http://sp2/HRteam.

-filename

The path and filename for the `.cmp` file. My example will save the `.cmp` file to the local file share `\\sp2\exports\teamsite`. Remember, if you want the file extension to be a CAB file, you must explicitly name your export file with a `.cab` extension. Otherwise it will default to a CMP file, as it will in my example.

-overwrite

The parameter to overwrite a file of the same name if that file already exists at the location to which you are saving the exported `.cab` file. This is useful if you are going to create a schedule for this task.

-includeusersecurity

A unique parameter meaning that when the site is imported to its new location, it will do so with its timestamps and security settings intact (or as best they can be given they could be imported to a different domain).

-versions

A parameter that lets you specify how many of the item or library file versions are retained in the lists and libraries that the site or site collection might hold. The options available for this parameter are:

1 - Last major versions for all items or files.

2 - Current version only.

3 - Last major and minor versions of all items and files.

4 - All versions of files and list item.

My example uses option 4, so you can keep everything, just in case.

-cabsize

The parameter that lets you specify the maximum size of the `.cmp` files for this export. Basically, the default is 25MB, but it can go to 1GB if you want. In the example, 600MB is more than large enough for the site. If the site is big enough, a couple of files may be needed to export it all (each being the limit you set). In that case, to import the site, refer to the first filename for the export and it will pull all of the extras when needed. Just be sure that all of the `.cmp` or `.cab` files from the export are all in the same location when importing.

CHECKING THE SIZE BEFORE EXPORTING

To see how large the site or site collection is before you export it, check the Site Usage Report for it in the Site Settings (if you have Usage Analysis Processing enabled in Central Administration).

At the command prompt, run your STSADM `-o export` command. Don't be surprised if it takes a moment, as export reports each part of the site that is being exported. If you don't have a long list of things being done during export, check to make certain that the account you are using to run the command has ownership rights to the site being exported. As you can see in Figure 12.39, the HRteam site exported successfully.

FIGURE 12.39
A successful export of the
HRteam site

FIGURE 12.39
A successful export of the
HRteam site

The export created a .cmp file and an associated log file in the backup location (Figure 12.40).

FIGURE 12.40
Files the export created

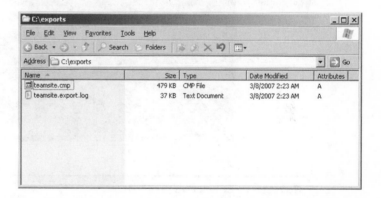

Now, you can use the site export to recover a site that has been corrupted by importing over the original URL. What if you want to import that subsite as the top-level site of a new site collection? It can be done. You can even import the site or site collection to a different web application or even a different server.

IMPORT A SITE

Importing an exported site or site collection can require two steps. The first step is to ensure that there is a site to import to. This can be an existing site (which will be written over), or a new site you created. In our case we are going to quickly create a new site collection, then import our HRteam site to it as the top level site. This will allow us, in the very least, to recover any data that might have been lost for the original site, without actually changing that site.

To do this, you first need to create a new site collection. At this point, you should know how to go to Central Administration and create a new site collection. However, because the command prompt is open, let's use STSADM to create a site collection quickly. (Remember, you can do with STADM practically anything that you can do with the GUI.)

To create a site collection with STSADM, the syntax is, for example:

```
STSADM -o createsite -url http://sp2/sites/newsite -owneremail
 SharePoint@dem0tek.com -ownerlogin dem0tek\shareadmin
```

Where:

- ◆ -url is the new site collection's URL.
- ◆ -ownermail is the email contact information for the site owner and is required.
- ◆ -ownerlogin is the domain\username of the site owner.

This operation has other parameters, but these are all we need for our purposes.

Running the STSADM command (see Figure 12.41) generates a brand new site collection, minus a site template (one wasn't specified because my example is just importing a site over it anyway).

FIGURE 12.41
The Create Site operation was successful

NO NEED TO CHECK THE SITE IN IE

If you tried to use Internet Explorer to open the new site right now, it would try to finish the site-creation process by requesting you choose a template. There is no reason to do that step, because a full site's contents will be applied to the site during the import. This is why I am not going to go to the site to see if it's there. The fact that it is there will be proven when the import works momentarily.

To import the exported site to the new site collection, use the following example (substitute your site collection address and account information) as an illustration of the syntax:

```
STSADM -o import -url http://sp2/sites/newsite -filename
  \\sp2\exports\teamsite.cmp -includeusersecurity -haltonwarning
  -updateversions 3
```

◆ `-url` is the target site to for the import data.

◆ `-filename` is the path and filename of the export file to be imported. In this case, you must specify the filename and extension.

◆ `-includeusersecurity` keeps the security settings and timestamps of the site, and the site's list, library, and list items.

◆ `-haltonwarning` will cause the import process to stop at the first warning it receives of a problem. Instead of waiting for the whole import process to attempt to finish, this allows you to fix the problem and try again. It just saves time. There is a `-haltonfatalerror` parameter as well.

◆ `-updateversions` indicates how to handle file or item versions on the import. Because imports are often done to recover the site or site collection it was exported from, there is a chance that there will be file version conflicts (especially when overwriting). This parameter gives you the opportunity to decide the default behavior when it comes to versions:

1. Add new versions. (The default. It leaves the old versions as is and simply adds the import versions as new rather than overwriting.)

2. Overwrite the file and all its versions. (Basically, it deletes the items or files it finds and inserts its version as the only one.)

3. Ignore the file if it exists already. (Otherwise, the import will only add files to libraries or items to lists that do not exist on the target version of the site.) This is the setting used for my example.

There are other parameters for this operation, but these are the ones my example uses to import the site. For more information on STSADM, see Chapter 13.

After you run the import command, open the new site collection to confirm that the import was successful. See Figure 12.42 for proof that the new site collection contains the old HR Team site content. Notice the address bar.

FIGURE 12.42
Newly imported HRteam subsite in new site collection

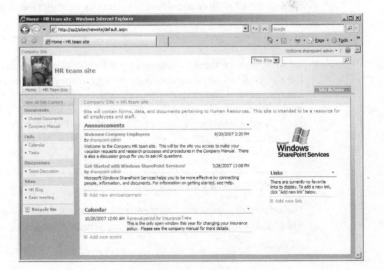

When you perform an import, make sure to check the security settings and file versions in the site libraries to be certain that the `updateversions` parameter worked. Remember that the alerts will need to be reset.

Back Up an Individual Subsite to a Template

There is a simpler way to quickly back up a subsite: make it a template. For example, let's say that that ever popular HR Team subsite has been improved greatly because the Human Resource department has been carefully working on it for weeks. When it is finished, it will have a custom document library containing all the data from the employee manual. They want to back it up just as it is, for safe keeping.

You can't back up the site using SharePoint backup and restore; the smallest component it does is site collections. STSADM can do it using an export/import; however, you would have to import over the existing site or create a new site into which you would import the export.

Site templates were meant to allow you to capture the design of a great site to reuse, but it can be used to capture the site's contents as well, to a limited degree. It does have its limitations. The backup doesn't keep its security settings and by default it can have a 10MB size limit (that can be overcome). But it is easy to make and easy to use. Just create a template of the site, complete with content, move it to the target site collection's Site Templates Gallery, then apply it by making a new subsite. Or you can simply create the template, with content, and download it in order to store it elsewhere for recovery later.

Templates are stored upon creation at the site-collection level and made available to all subsites. This means that template size impacts the overall size of a site collection. This is good reason to remove the template from the site collection's gallery and store it elsewhere until it is needed again.

WIKIS AND WORKSPACES CANNOT SAVE CONTENT

Almost all sites, except for wiki sites and meeting workspaces, can be made into templates with all the content included. Wikis and meeting workspaces can still be made into templates, but without the content included. Because wiki sites are merely sites that facilitate a wiki document library, you can just back up the site's library if you need to protect its contents.

Another nice thing about making a template out of a site is that it can easily be restored as a different subsite, into a site collection, web application, or even server farm. The template is independent of the configuration database. On the other hand, because of this, a template backup is not full fidelity because the user accounts and security settings are not preserved. You'll need to reset those when you restore the template. Just make sure you give the site a unique name when you restore it.

BREAK THE 10MB TEMPLATE LIMIT

The default maximum size limit of templates is a property of SharePoint. You can increase it up to 500MB (the absolute limit) by using the following STSADM operation:

```
STSADM -o setproperty -pn max-template-document-size -pv 500000000
```

-pn max-template-document-size is the property name you want to set, and -pv is the property value in bytes (500MB). This affects all templates, be they site or list. Remember this value, and reduce it if you need to tighten up the amount of hard-drive space your site collections utilize. Also, in the other direction, keep in mind that there are cases where a single document in a library exceeds that total, so be sure to check the usage report for the site before trying to make a template, including content, out of it.

MAKE A SITE TEMPLATE

To make a site template, simply go to the site in question, in this case, the HR Team site (see Figure 12.43):

FIGURE 12.43
HR Team subsite's Site Settings

1. Click Site Actions on the home page, and select Site Settings.

2. On the Site Settings page, click Save site as template under the Look And Feel category.

3. The Save Site as Template page has three sections: File Name, Name and Description, and Include Content. The filename should be reasonably short (notice the file type is .stp for SharePoint template), but the template name and description should be as descriptive as possible. This is what you see when you use the template in the SharePoint GUI. Figure 12.44 shows the filename, as well as the template name and description.

FIGURE 12.44
The Save Site As
Template page

4. Make certain there is a check mark next to Include Content if you want to back up the content of the site with the template.

5. Once you've named your site template file, given the template a name and description, and selected Include Content you click OK.

POSSIBLE SECURITY THREAT?

All information in the site's libraries and lists will be preserved in this backup. This could be a security issue, because a site template does not keep its security settings. When the template is used to create a new site, the new site can inherit the settings of its parent site. This means, potentially, that users who should not have access to the site and its contents, could have access. You will see in a moment how to export a site template from a SharePoint site. I strongly suggest you do that and delete the template from the readily available site collection's site gallery. Then import the template to the gallery only when you need it.

In a moment, the Operation Completed Successfully page will appear, letting you know that the site has been saved to the Site Template Gallery. This means you have successfully backed up your site. If you'd like, you can stop there, with the HR team site safely stored in the Site Template Gallery. Keep in mind that the Site Template Gallery is to store templates. You cannot use the templates to create new subsites from there, but instead should use the Create page.

However, you might be concerned that by having that site as a template, anyone with the right to create their own site can use that template. You might want to back up the site template somewhere other than the Site Template Gallery (or even somewhere other than that server) and then delete that template from the gallery.

EXPORT A SITE TEMPLATE

In order to back up the site template outside of SharePoint, you need to access the Site Template Gallery. Click the Site Template Gallery link on the Operation Completed Successfully page (or go to the top-level site and access it from the Site Settings page there).

You might notice that the Site Template Gallery is nothing more than a list (or a modified document library to be more exact). It has an action bar and views. The site template itself is listed in the default view, with the filename as the link to trigger a download for the item and an Edit icon for editing the item's metadata.

This means that if you click on the site template in the Template Gallery, you will be prompted as to where to save it. Exporting the template to a different drive location is that simple.

To export, or save, the template to a different location, click on the site template's filename (in my example, that would be HRteam, as you can see in Figure 12.45). A dialog box will ask you where you want to save the template file. Click the Save button and browse to the location where you would like to safely save the HRteam site template. My location is a network share that is backed up nightly (see Figure 12.46). Make certain that the account you are logged in with has the right to access that location, and make certain that when you are adding the template to the site later, you can still access it.

FIGURE 12.45
The Site Template Gallery

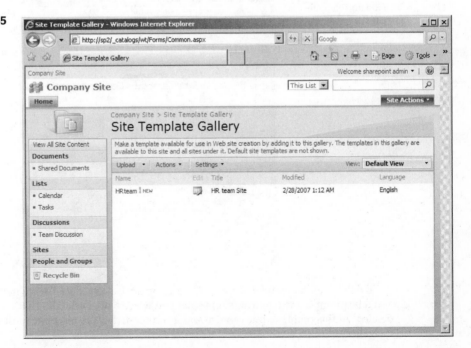

FIGURE 12.46
Back up the site template
to the file share location

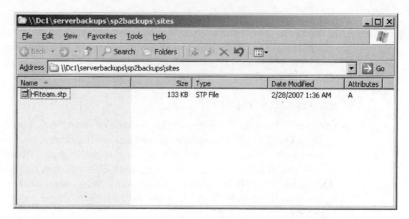

Now that you have saved the site template file to a location that is regularly backed up, you can safely free up space in the site collection by deleting the template there.

DELETE A TEMPLATE FROM THE SITE TEMPLATE GALLERY

To delete a site template from the site gallery, you have to edit the template's metadata. To do that, click the Edit icon for the site template in the gallery list. That will take you to the site template's Edit page. Notice in Figure 12.47, that the page has a Delete Item link and a Check Out link in the action bar. The Delete Item link is the only way in the gallery to delete a site template.

FIGURE 12.47
The HRteam Template
Edit page

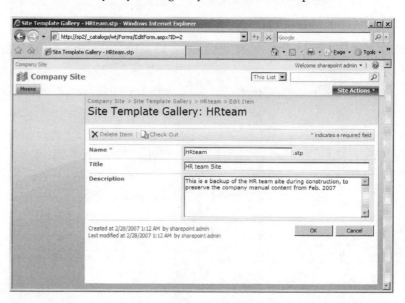

To delete the site template from the Site Template Gallery, click Delete Item in the action bar. You'll be prompted to confirm that is what you want to do; click OK. That's it; the site template is deleted. At this point, no one can use it as a content-laden site template until you upload it back to the gallery.

Restore an Individual Subsite from a Template

Now that you have a template backup of the subsite you can use it in any server farm, on any domain. You can also use it anywhere in any site collection, including the one it came from. It is completely independent of such considerations as content databases or URLs. This makes templates a really convenient thing to restore.

So if the site the template is based on is accidentally deleted, don't panic; you have a site template that can restore it (and the content from the point the template was made).

UPLOAD A TEMPLATE TO A SITE TEMPLATE GALLERY

For SharePoint to be able to use the site template, you first must upload it to the Site Template Gallery for the site collection where you want it to be located. Then just follow these steps:

1. Go to the Site Template Gallery for the top-level site (Site Actions ➤ Site Settings ➤ Galleries Category ➤ Site Templates).

2. Click the Upload button on the action bar. It will open an Upload Template page, which looks like any other upload page, complete with an Overwrite checkbox.

3. Simply browse to the location where you saved the site template (which is for me a really long path: \\dc1\serverbackups\sp2backups\sites\HRteam.stp, as you can see in Figure 12.48), select the template file, and click Open.

FIGURE 12.48
The Site Template path to upload

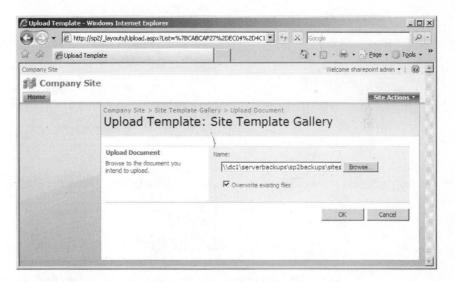

4. On the Upload Site Template page, click OK. The Edit page of the template will appear (in case you want to change the metadata, the name, title, or description). To keep the metadata as is, click OK.

Voilà! Your HRteam site template is back in the gallery. The first part of restoring the subsite is done.

The next part is to actually create a new site and use the template. It is a good idea to restore a site using a site template (as opposed to simply just using the template to simply create a new site) side by side with the old one, and then delete the old one. Keep in mind that, since you can't have two sites at the same URL with the same name, the new site name has to be at least slightly different (if not completely different). Having both lets you check to see if all of the information you need is in the second site, for example, you can make list or library templates and move them to the new site, or do a Send to for documents in libraries you might be missing. If having the variation in the name is a problem, then after you delete the first site, go to Site Settings, Title, Icon, and Description, and change the web address for the site to match the old one. This will help make certain that anyone with a static link to the site will still be able to access it without a hitch.

RESTORE A SUBSITE FROM TEMPLATE

This particular example restores the HRteam subsite to a slightly different name, just in case there is something on the original that the team actually needs to keep that they don't mention until it is gone. Follow these steps:

1. To restore the subsite, go to the home page of the site you want to be the parent site (my example is the top-level site).

2. Click Site Actions, and then click Create in the dropdown menu.

3. On the Create page, click on the Sites and Workspaces link in the Web Pages category (see Figure 12.49).

FIGURE 12.49
The Create Sites And
Workspaces link

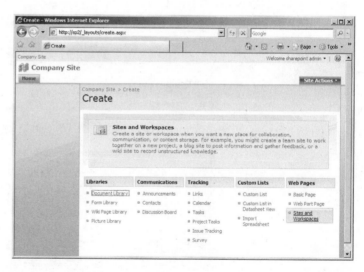

4. In the Title and Description, and Web Site Address sections, enter a title, description, and URL for the new subsite. The URL must be unique; it cannot be the same as an existing site. For my example, the new name is **HR Team** (notice the space) as the title, a brief description about the HR site, and the URL **HR_Team**.

5. On the New SharePoint Site page, there is a tab called Custom you'll see in the Select a Template list. That tab is where site templates that have been added to the Site Template Gallery are displayed. To use the newly uploaded template, click the Custom tab in the Select a template list and select your HR Team site template (see Figure 12.50).

FIGURE 12.50
Creating new site based
on backed-up HR team
site template

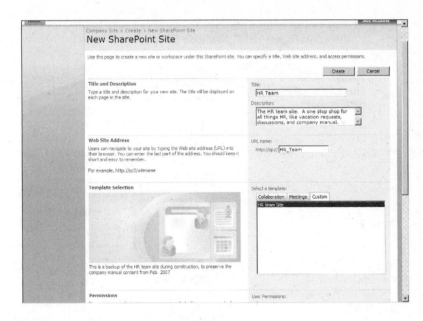

FIGURE 12.50
Creating new site based
on backed-up HR team
site template

6. Leave all of the defaults for permissions and navigation. Verify that the title, description, URL, and template are correct. Click Create to create the new subsite.

There you go; the HR team site has been reborn, in the same state as it was when you saved the site as a template (except the custom title icon, that is returned to the default). Pay particular attention to the URL in the address bar. In Figure 12.51, that the address is HR_Team, not HRteam, which is still the address of the original, supposedly damaged, HR team subsite.

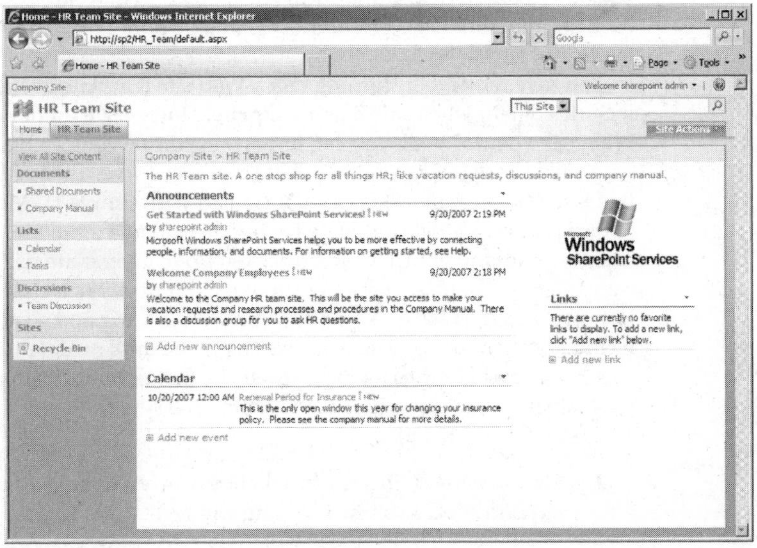

FIGURE 12.51
The new address for
recovered subsite

If you go to the Company Manual Document Library for the new subsite, the content is still there (see Figure 12.52), available for use.

FIGURE 12.52
The Company Manual content remains

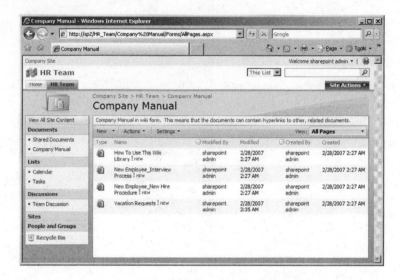

Now you have backed up and restored an individual subsite both by using Export/Import and making a site template. Keep in mind that there is a hard size limit to a template by default. If you want to increase that limit, go to your SharePoint server and use the STSADM command to change the setting.

Back Up a List or Library Template

So you've backed data at the Farm level, down to individual subsites. But what if you needed to back up individual lists or libraries? Can it be done? Yes (to a point). Lists and Libraries can be made into templates too.

You may remember learning that a Wiki site template is one of two site types that cannot include content when saved as a template. However, a lot of people will want to save their wikis. What can you do? Well, you can import/export or you can backup the wiki's library.

A wiki site is really a small subsite that focuses on a wiki library. A wiki library is usually not that large (in megabytes) because it is filled with simple HTML documents. Therefore, a wiki library is often a good candidate for backing up to a template.

Sites, lists, and libraries can be backed up to a template with content for safe keeping and convenience. Templates were meant to let you preserve a clever or complex list or library so, if lost, you wouldn't have to spend the time rebuilding and customizing it. But, list templates can include content too. Unless you change it, the template default maximum size is 10MB, and it affects lists and libraries too (not just sites). List templates can be uploaded to any site, but the template must have a unique name within the site.

To create a list template:

1. Go to the list or library of your choice. (My example uses a document library on my technical support wiki, as shown in Figure 12.53.)

FIGURE 12.53
The Tech Support Wiki Library

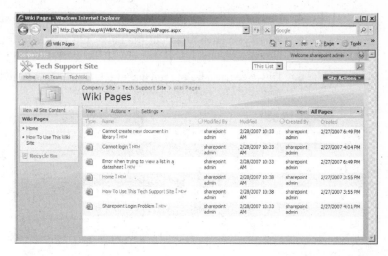

2. Click the Settings button on the action bar, and then click Document Library Settings in the dropdown menu.

3. On the Document Library Settings page, under Permissions and Management, click Save document library as template. The Save as Template page will appear.

This page should look familiar, as it is the same page used to save the site templates (notice in Figure 12.54 that even the file extension is the same). This is why it is a good idea to specify when a template is a list or library rather than a site. It is also why we are using `TechSupL` for the filename and Technical Support Library for the title.

FIGURE 12.54
Save the Tech Support Library as a template

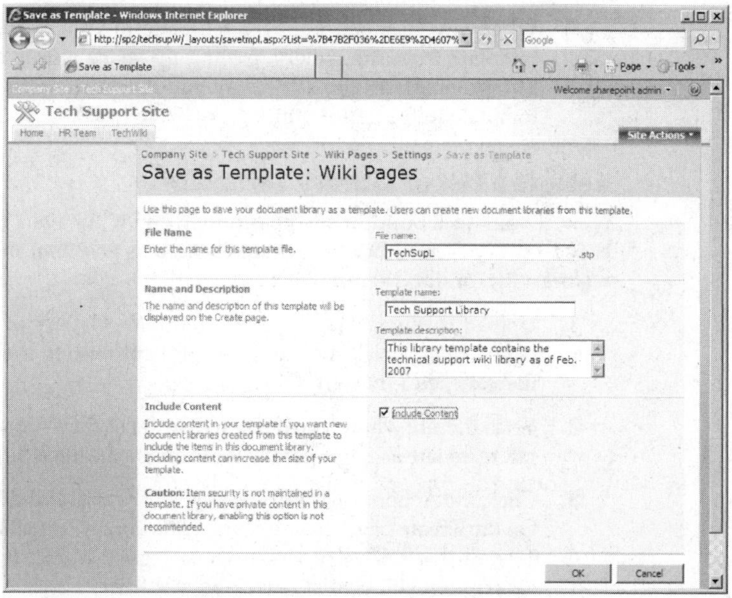

4. Feel free to enter a useful description, and make sure you enable Include Contents.

5. When you have filled out the fields and selected Include Content, click OK to create the library template. It will take you to the Operation Completed Successfully page.

6. The page has a link to the list template gallery (because libraries are lists), click that link to go to the List Template Gallery. See Figure 12.55.

FIGURE 12.55
The operation was successful for the library template

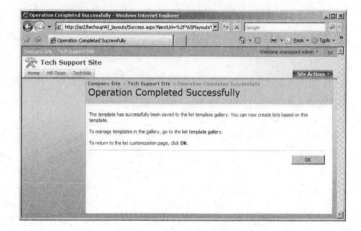

7. On the List Template Gallery, select the filename for the template you just created (my example is TechSupL).

8. When the File Download dialog box appears, click Save. Choose a location to store the list template.

9. When you've saved your list template to your storage location, you can safely delete the template from the gallery, freeing up space within the site collection. You delete list and library templates the same way you delete site templates (click the edit button for the list template in the gallery, and click Delete Item).

Restore a List or Library Template

Now, if your Tech Support site goes down, you will have a backup of the site's main library for easy recovery. Remember to back up as often as possible, and back up the backups regularly. To restore a list (or library) template:

1. Upload the template to the List Template Gallery of the site collection (go to the List Template Gallery, click the Upload button, browse to the saved template, click OK, confirm the filename, etc., then click OK).

2. Go to the site where you'd like to use the library's contents. My example uses my ubiquitous HR team site as a temporary location for the Tech Support Wiki Library.

3. Click Site Actions on the home page of the site, and then click Create in the dropdown menu. On the Create page that appears, your library template should be listed under Libraries (the Tech Support Library is shown in Figure 12.56). If you move your mouse over it, your description will be displayed above the list.

FIGURE 12.56
A unique library template, made
from backup, in the Create list

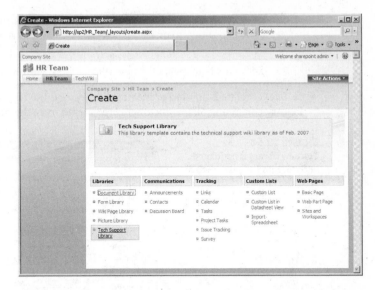

FIGURE 12.56
A unique library template, made
from backup, in the Create list

4. Select the list template you uploaded (mine is the Tech Support Library template) from the list.

5. On the New page, enter a name and description of the library. Remember to keep it short and try to keep it to one word (or combo word) because the name will be used for this list's URL. Enter a description as well. Here is where you can indicate that it is a backup and include the date (see Figure 12.57 for an idea of what I mean). This will help the staff realize why it's there.

FIGURE 12.57
A new library made
from a template

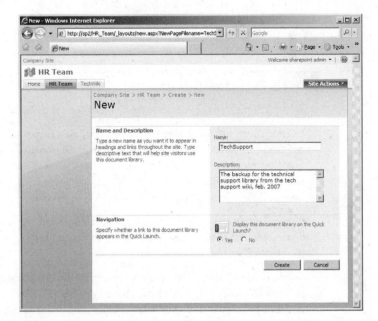

6. Once you have entered a name and description for the library, decide whether you want this library to show up on the Quick Launch bar. It is fine for my example, so leave it at the Yes default.

7. Click Create to create the new library from your template.

The template is applied to the new library, and the HR Team site now has a Tech Support Library containing all the documents recovered from the original wiki site (Figure 12.58).

FIGURE 12.58
The new library is populated with content from the original Wiki Site Library

Backup and Restore Using Other Tools

Although this chapter focused on how to back up and restore using SharePoint's tools, you can restore data in other ways. Let's look at IIS to start. All IIS Web Sites have configuration data, application pools, and file data. The configurations are stored in the IIS metabase (although you can separately backup individual Web Site and application pool configuration files). This is the data that you see in the IIS console or the Properties dialog box for an IIS Web Site. This means if someone accidentally deletes a website from the IIS console, you can recover it easily and SharePoint need never know it was missing.

BEST PRACTICES

SharePoint seems to resent it when you restore IIS or an SQL database without using its backup (Microsoft cryptically hints at the fact in its TechNet documents). This means, because SharePoint does not like to work with a mix of backups (databases, IIS metabase, etc.), when you are forced to do a backup of that type, it might be a good idea to do a new SharePoint backup to incorporate the changes into a new SharePoint backup folder.

Always test your restores. I cannot emphasize this enough. Use a test environment that echoes the real one, even if only on a small scale simply to periodically test your backup and restore scheme. Try restoring the IIS metabase or configuration files, and see if you can restore SharePoint properly. Then try to restore a SharePoint backup to ensure it will work. Test your database backup and restores, and watch your event logs and Performance Monitor to see if any issues were introduced after the restore. Check to make sure everything is running smoothly as part of your regular maintenance program, and you will always know if you are ready for an emergency.

Back Up the IIS Metabase

The IIS metabase is a complete backup of all of the configuration information for all website and application pools for the server. Although powerful, complete, and easy to use, this kind of backup does have the drawback of being server specific; if you backup the IIS metabase of one server, it can only be restored for that one server, and cannot be restored anywhere else. For a server farm, this means that metabase backups would have to be made for each individual server.

To back up an IIS metabase, open the IIS Management console:

1. Choose Start ➢ Administrative Tools ➢ Internet Information Services (IIS) Manager.

2. In the console, right-click the Local Server icon, go to All Tasks in the popup menu, and select Backup/Restore Configuration.

3. In the Configuration Backup/Restore dialog box that appears (see Figure 12.59), you can see that IIS does its own automatic backups. However, to back up the IIS metabase yourself, click Create Backup, and then assign a name to the backup. **ManualBackup224** is the configuration name in my example (see Figure 12.60). You can choose to encrypt the backup with a password. If you choose this option, the file cannot be restored without this password to unlock it.

4. The password may not be necessary in some environments. My example does not provide a password for the backup, so click OK to create the backup. It takes mere moments to return to the Backup/Restore dialog box with your new backup displayed in the list. That's it. The backup is done.

FIGURE 12.59
The Backup/Restore dialog box

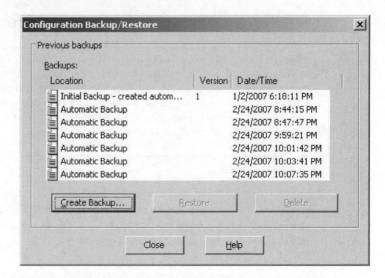

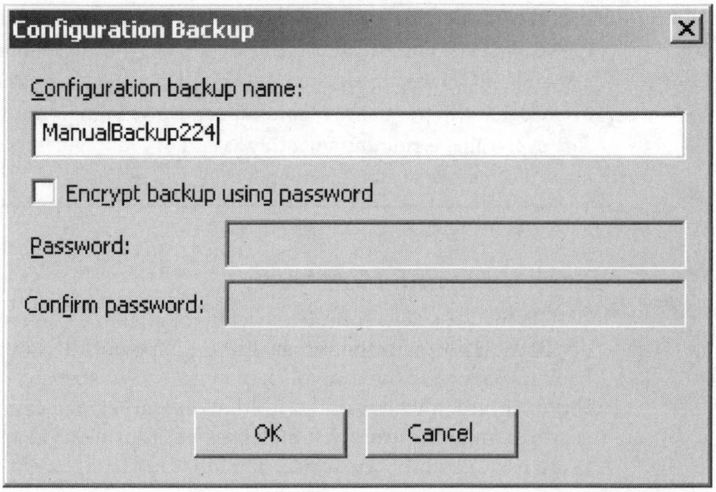

FIGURE 12.60
The Configuration Backup
dialog box

ENCRYPTING YOUR BACKUPS

Encrypting your backups is always a good idea, but that is just the tip of the iceberg. Remember to secure your backups as if they contained your personal information, because in a way they do. They generally always contain data you don't want strangers, clients, or competitors to access—so protect them. In my environment, it is unlikely that anyone else is going to access my machines or network. A business environment, however, is more dangerous. Pay attention to where you put your backups. Don't make them available to just anyone. From cleaning staff to disgruntled employees, you just never know who might be considering the value of your data.

What exactly was backed up? The configuration settings for all application pools, Web Sites (even FTP Sites), and references to virtual directories in IIS were backed up. The metabase data can be restored in case of an emergency. Where did the backup go? IIS saves backup files to `%windir%\System32\inetsrv\MetaBack` *only*. Each backup has two files. If you are going to copy those backups to another location for safe keeping, don't split up the pairs; they are both required to restore IIS. Remember that Metabases are unique per server, so keep one for each server in the farm if necessary, and label them accordingly.

Restore the IIS Metabase

When you restore the IIS metabase, it overwrites everything in the console. Be aware of that. To help avoid damaging the rest of what may be in IIS (and make it possible to restore to different servers), SharePoint's restore specifically only backs up configuration data for each individual web application. The metabase is nothing to mess with, but it is a good last defense when all else fails, because it can return everything in the console back to a functional state.

How do you restore an IIS metabase? Let's say that the application pool for the `http://sp2` web application was accidentally deleted by an overzealous junior administrator. Even worse, he doesn't really know *what else* he did, but it's obvious that nothing is working. Everyone needs to learn, but you don't have the time it will take to find out all of the IIS settings he changed or time to try to re-create the application pool.

That sort of situation really could use a metabase restore (mind you, currently my farm has one SharePoint server). That's right, if no changes have been made to web applications since the last metabase backup, restore the application pool (and undo all the administrative mistakes) by restoring an IIS metabase backup. To do so, follow these steps:

1. Go to the IIS console (Start ➢ Administrative Tools ➢ Internet Information Server (IIS) manager), and right-click the icon for the local computer.

2. In the popup menu that appears, select All Tasks, and then Backup/Restore Configuration.

3. In the Configuration Backup/Restore dialog box that opens, select the backup file we made earlier, and click Restore. If you moved the file, you will have to put it back into the correct directory, `%windir%\System32\inetsrv\MetaBack` in order for the metabase restore to list it.

4. A dialog box will warn you that restoring the metabase is a lengthy process and may cause all internet services to be stopped (Figure 12.61). To continue with the restore process, you must click Yes (remember that this process needs to be done for each SharePoint server as well).

FIGURE 12.61
The Metabase restore warning

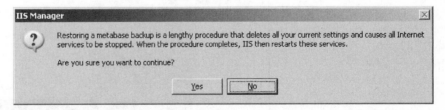

5. IIS can take several minutes and cause a significant slowdown on the server as it rebuilds all of the site and application pool data. Eventually, you should receive an Operation Completed Successfully dialog box. Click OK to get back to your now fully restored IIS console.

Back Up a Web Application by Saving its Configuration File

The IIS metabase is easy to back up because doing so is an automatic feature of IIS, but you can back up the IIS configuration file for each individual web application as well (the application pools too). Originally meant to be able to export an IIS Web Site's configuration and application pool information from one server and import it quickly to a different server, the configuration files can also be used to rebuild a deleted IIS Web Site, or write over one that has been misconfigured.

The IIS Web Site configuration files are what SharePoint's built-in Backup and Restore feature backs up for each web application (instead of the whole IIS metabase). When you back up a single IIS Web Site, it saves the site's configuration file. When you restore that configuration file, you get a choice to write over the existing IIS Web Site, or create a new site. In SharePoint's case, it really only uses the configuration file information to create a new site (a possible bug). You can try to mess up an IIS Web Site for a web application by changing the password of an application pool, the name of the site, and the security settings to see if SharePoint's built-in Backup and Restore will fix it with a Same Configuration restore, but it won't. The Same Configuration restore of a web application does not use the backed-up configuration file for the web application's IIS Web Site to fix what might be ailing that site. Instead, it apparently ignores it and only restores the content database.

This is why keeping a backup of each web application's IIS Web Site configuration file is a good idea. You can also backup the application pool's configuration but it so easy to create application pools that it might not be worth it. If you have a problem with a web application and a Same Configuration restore in SharePoint fails to fix the problem, then the issue probably lies in either IIS or the virtual directory folder. This means that restoring the configuration file for the offending web application's IIS Web Site would likely do the trick. (If it doesn't, consider restoring the web application's virtual directory from backup.)

To save an IIS Web Site's configuration file:

1. Simply right-click the website in the IIS console, go to All Tasks, and select Save Configuration to a File (see Figure 12.62).

FIGURE 12.62
Selecting a website to save configuration

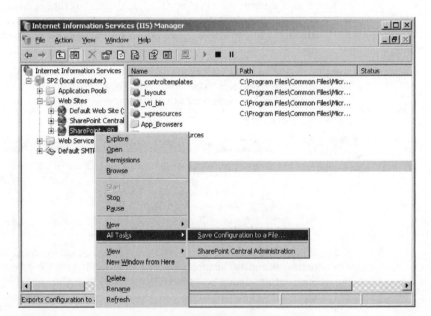

2. The Save Configuration to a File dialog box will allow you to name the file and choose where to store it. The default (which we will use for this demonstration) is the `%windir%\system32\inetsrv` folder. You can choose a different location by clicking Browse (as you can see in Figure 12.63), giving you the chance to specify the network location where this file should be stored.

FIGURE 12.63
The Save Configuration To A File dialog box

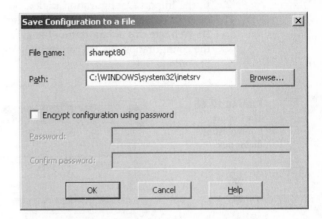

3. After naming the file (I used **sharept80**) and keeping the default location, click OK to save the configuration file (you can also encrypt it with a password if you'd like).

That will safely backup the configuration information about that website, ready to be restored should disaster strike.

Restore a Web Application Using a Configuration File

The configuration backup contains the data necessary to restore an IIS Web Site to full function from a number of indignities. For example, let's say that, not long after the configuration was saved in the previous section, someone else made horrible changes to the SharePoint -80 IIS Web Site. You can see the more superficial effects in Figure 12.64. The website name was changed, hinting at nefarious changes to the security settings, ports, and host header. In this case it is likely that the website requires restoration.

FIGURE 12.64
The vandalized SharePoint-80
IIS Web Site

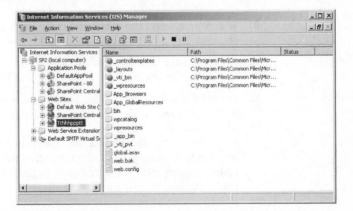

To fix all of those problems and restore the web application to functionality, just follow these steps:

1. Right-click on the damaged Web Site node in IIS, and in the popup menu, go to New, Web Sites from File.

2. In the Import Configuration dialog box that opens, browse to the configuration file and open it. To confirm that it is indeed the correct file, click Read File, which will display the IIS Web Site this configuration file is for (this is useful if the name under which you saved the configuration file isn't intuitive). You can see the site configuration in Figure 12.65 is SharePoint -80.

FIGURE 12.65
The Import Configuration dialog box

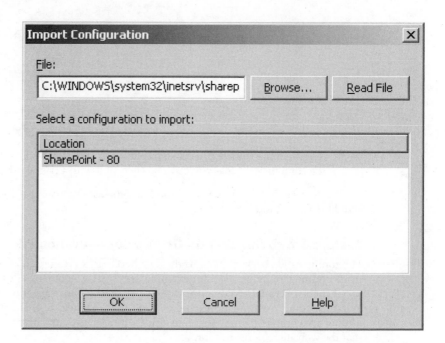

3. To continue, select the configuration to import (I only have SharePoint -80 to choose from) and click OK.

4. Another dialog box will open and ask if you would like to replace the existing site or create a new one. For my example, choose Replace The Existing Site and click OK.

5. In the IIS console, the IIS Web Site has been returned to its original name (as you can see in Figure 12.66). Under the hood, all changes that were made have been undone. When an IIS Web Site has been replaced, it may need to be started manually, but that in no way means the replacement failed. IIS is just giving you a chance to check it over before bringing it online. Simply select the site, and click the Start button in the Console toolbar (it looks like a right arrow button), or right-click the IIS Web Site and select Start from the popup menu.

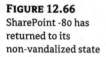
FIGURE 12.66
SharePoint -80 has
returned to its
non-vandalized state

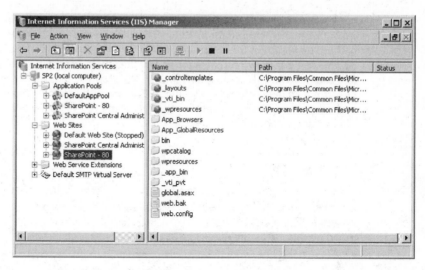

Now you know how to recover a particular web application's IIS Web Site should it become damaged or deleted. You can either replace a site or create a new site with the saved configuration. This can be done on a local server or migrated to a different server in case of calamity.

A LITTLE MORE ABOUT CONFIGURATION FILES IN IIS

You can create configuration files for all of the websites at one time in IIS by right clicking the websites node in the tree pane and selecting New, Configuration File. It will create a configuration file that has copies of configuration files for all websites under it. Then, when you restore it, you can choose to Read file and select the correct website if you wish, or restore them all.

Application pools can have their own Configuration Files as well if you'd like to backup and restore them. You might want to consider backing up the configuration files of the Application pools when you do them for the websites. They can be backed up individually or as a group, just like the Web Sites. I don't always have good luck with Application pools restored from configuration files (hey, everyone has something they're not good at). I have found it easier to create new application pools than restore from configuration file, but the option is there. There is a lot of flexibility when it comes to backing up IIS information, so use it.

Back Up Virtual Directories and SharePoint's folders

The other part of the backing up of SharePoint web applications is the virtual directories and the SharePoint specific folders in the file system. Backing up the IIS Metabase will store configuration information about virtual directories, but not the *contents* of those directories. Virtual directories contain the actual ASPX pages, images, layout information, and more. You can't have an IIS Web Site for SharePoint without virtual directories anymore than a SharePoint web application is of any use without a site collection.

The virtual directories are located in a folder called, intuitively enough, `virtualdirecto-ries` under a folder used for all things IIS called `Inetpub` (I'll show you that in a moment). When backing up your files for IIS (and therefore, by extension, SharePoint) it is always good to actually backup, not just the virtual directories, but the whole `Inetpub` folder. Why? The `Inetpub` folder also contains the files used by SMTP. So in one step you backup both your virtual directories and the drop mail folder (in case anything goes awry with incoming email). I will be demonstrating backing up using `Inetpub`, but if you don't want to, feel free to only back up the virtual directories instead. It's your call.

JUST ONE MORE FOLDER

There is one folder that SharePoint uses that is outside of the 12 hive, and that is the wpresources folder. This folder contains, at minimum, a web.config file that is used for web part resources and Global Assembly Cache (GAC). This folder is particulary useful if you have custom web parts. If you do, consider backing up this folder, it is located in the same directory as the 12 hive.

In addition to the virtual directory files, SharePoint uses other files to define its website. These files are located in the SharePoint folders, starting with a folder named 12, at the path: `%ProgramFiles%\Common Files\Microsoft Shared\web server extensions\12\`. This path contains so much critical SharePoint stuff that it is actually referred to as the *12 hive*, as if it were part of the registry. The folders most critical for SharePoint IIS Web Sites to function are under the `TEMPLATE` and `ISAPI` folders in the 12 hive.

To back up those essential folders and the files they contain, you could go directly to the folders that I suggest and directly copy them to a file share, or you can use backup software. In this example I am going to use a file system backup product that I know we all have—because we have to be using Windows Server 2003 (or higher)—NTBackup. Once you see how this works you can easily use this information with whatever backup solution you prefer. And for those of you who don't have any backup solution, well, these instructions are particularly for you. NTBackup, as simple as it is, works better than nothing.

1. There are several ways to access NTBackup; go to a command prompt, or Start ➢ Run, and enter **NTBackup**, or you can go to Start ➢ All Programs ➢ Accessories ➢ System Tools ➢ Backup. They all take you to the same place: The Backup or Restore Wizard.

2. Once the Backup or Restore Wizard opens, it will ask you if you want to continue with the wizard or go to Advanced mode. Administrators generally prefer advanced modes because they often give more options than a wizard. This situation is no exception, so click the Advanced Mode link (see Figure 12.67).

   Advanced mode takes you behind the wizard and opens the Backup Utility window where the Welcome tab has three buttons: Backup Wizard (Advanced), Restore Wizard (Advanced), and Automated System Recovery Wizard. These wizards basically hold your hand and walk you through using the three tabs in this window—Backup, Restore And Manage Media, and Schedule Jobs. The first button, Backup Wizard (Advanced) triggers a wizard that will help you back up files, the second button is what you would use to restore the files you've backed up with this utility, and the third button is for Automated System Recovery, which we will be discussing briefly later.

FIGURE 12.67
The Backup Or Restore Wizard

3. To save time, avoid using the Backup Wizard, and just click the Backup tab in the Backup Utility window (Figure 12.68).

FIGURE 12.68
The Backup Utility window

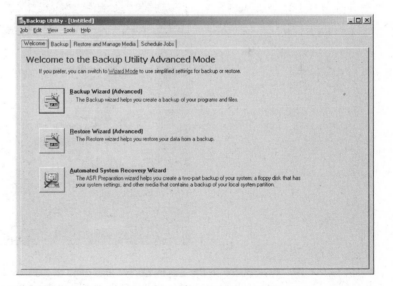

On the Backup tab, you'll see a standard file system tree with checkboxes next to each storage location for your server. We just need to back up the Inetpub and 12 hive files, so navigate to the two locations.

HEY! I DON'T RECOGNIZE THAT NUMBER

In Figure 12.68, the folder name for the SharePoint web application's folder is 80 (meaning the port number) but the Central Administration site's folder is 17372. You may have noticed that, throughout the book, the port for Central Administration is 9876, so why 17372? There is actually a funny story behind that. When I was installing SharePoint, I was given the choice to either take the default random port that SharePoint wanted to assign for the Central Administration site or create my own. I chose to specify 9876, but SharePoint remembered its suggestion and named the virtual directory after the port number it suggested I give the site.

6. To start, backup `Inetpub` and all of its subfolders (now that you know what's in there). To do this, simply put a check mark next to `Inetpub` in the file system tree on the left of the Backup window (Figure 12.69).

SPACE A CONCERN?

Keep in mind that if space is a premium, you can always just back up the `virtualdirectories` folder if you want to simply preserve the virtual directories.

FIGURE 12.69
Backing up Inetpub

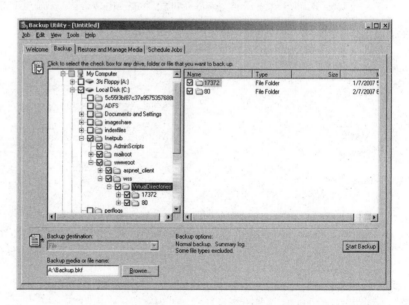

7. In addition to the `Inetpub`, we also need to back up the SharePoint 12 hive templates and site definitions (this is particularly useful if you have customized anything). Those files are usually buried deep under `%ProgramFiles%\Common Files\Microsoft Shared\web server extensions\12\`. All of the files and subfolders in that location should be backed up in case of catastrophe, so make sure all subfolders are selected (Figure 12.70).

Pay attention to the web parts, features, solutions, and templates you may add to SharePoint over time. Usually they are put in one of the subfolders beneath the `Template` folder, but pay attention to where they might end up on your server and back them up as well.

Once you've chosen what to back up, you need to choose both the location for the backup file (everything is backed up and stored in one file) and what to name it. To do that, you need to go to the bottom-left of the window, to the Backup Media or Filename field (the Backup Destination field is grayed out in my example because my system doesn't have a backup device attached to it).

8. In the Backup Media or Filename field, specify a location that is not on the local drive to store your backup file. My example uses a network share called `serverbackups`. The floppy drive is the default backup media, which obviously is not a good idea.

9. In addition to where to put the file, you need to name it something reasonably intuitive. It's pretty important to have a naming scheme for your backups. For my simple example I am going to name the file **WSS3filebackup**.

IT JUST CAN'T FORGET THE FLOPPY DRIVE

If you don't type in the path to the backup location and choose to click Browse instead, you'll be prompted to insert a disk in the floppy drive (because it was the default value in that field). Just click Cancel, and it should take you to an Open dialog box, where you can browse to your backup location.

---

10. Once you've chosen your location and named your backup file, you'll be ready to perform the backup. My example of the full path is `\\DC1\Serverbackups\sp2backups\WSS3filebackup.bkf`, as you can almost see in Figure 12.70. To start the process, just click the Start Backup button on the bottom-right side of the window.

FIGURE 12.70
The Backup location

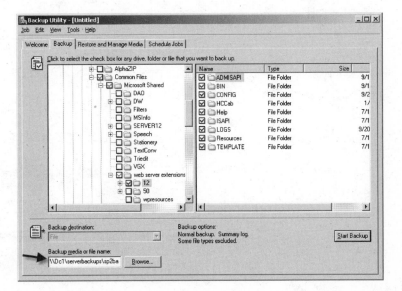

BACKUP OPTIONS

Near the bottom of Figure 12.69, you can see that the backup type will be Normal, with a summary log and some file types excluded. If you want to change those settings, go to Tools ➤ Options. In the Options dialog box, you can set the default behavior for backups, such as verifying the data when backup is complete and specifying the backup type (Normal, Copy, Differential, Incremental, and even Daily). For this example, Normal is fine. To see what files are excluded from backup (and add or remove exclusions), go to the Exclude Files tab.

Just before the backup process begins, you'll be prompted to verify the type of backup you'd like to do and if you'd like the data verified. However, using the Options dialog box lets you set those preferences once and then you change them only when necessary.

---

11. A Backup Job Information dialog box will popup, offering you all kinds of options to modify the backup. For this example we don't need change the defaults of all of those options, we are just doing a simple, normal backup. Just click Start Backup.

The backup will prepare to back up using volume shadow copy, and it will copy the backup files to the backup location (see Figure 12.71). This may take several minutes depending on the size and number of files to back up. Make certain your backup location is large enough to accommodate the backup.

FIGURE 12.71
The Backup Progress dialog box

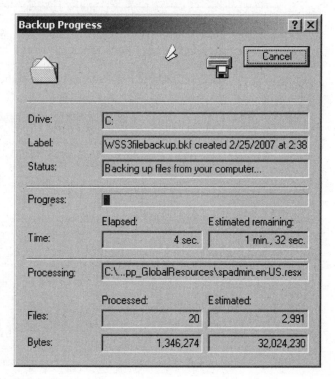

12. The Backup Progress dialog box indicates when the backup is done, with a quick report as to how long it took, how many files got backed up, and their sizes. It should say the backup is complete. If not, click the Report button to see what happened; otherwise, click Close.

Your backup of the `Inetpub` and `Template` folders is complete. You should consider scheduling regular backups of the virtual directories (or all of `Inetpub`), as well as the `Template` folder for all of your SharePoint servers in case of emergency.

Restore a Virtual Directory from Backup

What do you do if somehow a virtual directory on one of your SharePoint servers has gone missing? Replace it with the backup you made.

In this example, we'll restore the virtual directory for the beleaguered SharePoint- 80 virtual directory. As you can see in Figure 12.72, critical files normally contained in the virtual directory (like `web.config` or `global.aspx`) are missing. To recover them, we'll restore the website's virtual directory.

FIGURE 12.72
Files missing for SharePoint-80

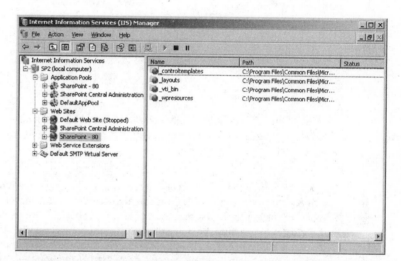

1. Open NTBackup again (Start ➤ Run, type **ntbackup**, and press Enter).

2. Click the Advanced Mode link in the wizard to open the Backup Utility interface (if necessary).

3. Click on the Restore and Manage Media tab. It should display the backup you recently did (my example is `WSS3filebackup.bkf`).

4. Click the plus sign next to the backup file in the media pane. This will expand the path of the backup job's contents, starting with a folder for the local drive.

5. Double-click each storage area until you navigate to and select the virtual directory you need to restore (my example is 80, as you can see in Figure 12.73).

FIGURE 12.73

The Restore And Media tab, where you select the directory to restore

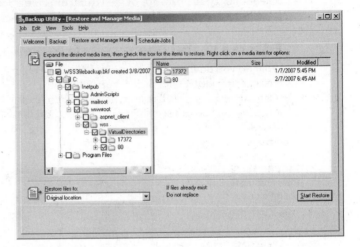

6. Once the directory that needs to be restored is selected, make sure that the Restore Files to setting is set to Original Location, and click Start Restore. A dialog box offering advanced settings might appear, but those settings aren't necessary for this example, so just click OK to continue.

The restore will begin and take a few moments. Check the Virtual Directories folder to verify that 80 is back (Figure 12.74). You can also browse to the SharePoint -80 site, which is actually the more important part. Remember, SharePoint web applications need IIS Web Sites and their virtual directories to function. Back up these components frequently, store them in an external location (network share, external drive, SAN, etc.), and be prepared to use them to restore. Label your backups intuitively. Baffling backup names don't really help.

FIGURE 12.74

Files recovered for SharePoint -80

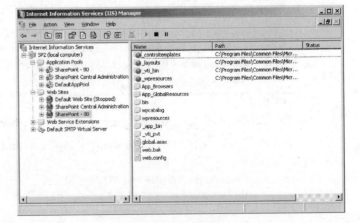

Backup Standalone Server Databases

At this point, the files that are associated with SharePoint's web front end are prepared for catastrophe, but what about the databases? How they are backed up depends on whether you are running the Windows Internal Database (SSEE) locally on your standalone SharePoint server, or if you are using a SQL server on the network to host your databases.

When running a standalone install of SharePoint, there are two ways to back up embedded databases:

◆ Turn off the services that might be using the databases (and consider taking the databases offline in SharePoint), and then copy those databases and their log files to a different location for safekeeping. Then turn the services back on (and bring the databases back to a Ready state).

◆ Use good old NTBackup because it uses Volume Shadow Copy to create a backup and, therefore, doesn't cause any locking issues by messing with an active database.

MANUAL BACKUP OF THE DATABASE

To be cautious with SharePoint, you can turn all the services off when you are copying a database on a standalone server. Remember, stopping SharePoint stops it for everyone, so certainly don't do this during business hours.

To turn off the services and copy the databases manually:

1. Open the Services console, and choose Start ➤ Administrative Tools ➤ Services.

2. Scroll to the SharePoint services and stop them, particularly the Administration, Search, and Timer services.

3. Then scroll to the SQL Server 2005 Embedded Edition (Microsoft##SSEE) service and stop it as well.

4. Now that the services are stopped, navigate to the folder that contains the databases: `%Windows%\SYSMSI\SSEE\MSSQL.2005\MSSQL\Data` (Figure 12.75).

FIGURE 12.75
The folder containing the embedded databases

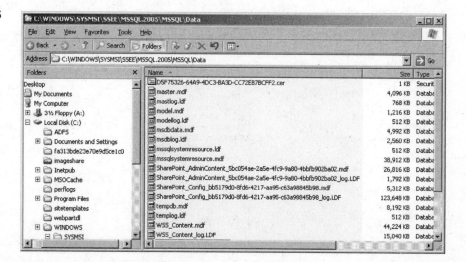

SUPERSTITION

Technically you only need to turn off the SQL SSEE service, but I always turn off the SharePoint services to avoid having it try to access a database in mid-timer job. Also, when backing up or restoring databases, if I can, I will try to take the database offline for the web application (so if it's trying to limp along, it knows it's going down) by going to Application Management in Central Administration, selecting Content Databases, and clicking on the content database that is having issues. This will bring up the database settings page for that database where I change the Database status to Offline (if it isn't already) and click OK at the bottom of the page.

Mind you, none of these things are necessarily *required* for most backup or restores, I just feel it's better to be safe than sorry. And once you're done, be sure to return the databases to a Ready state.

5. Because the databases are not being used, they are allowed to be copied. Keep in mind that the databases must have their corresponding log files with them. For the standalone or basic install for SharePoint the databases will be named something like:

- ◆ SharePoint_AdminContent (and a long GUID)
- ◆ SharePoint_Config (and a long GUID)
- ◆ WSS_Content
- ◆ WSS_Search_(servername)

6. Select the databases (with the .mfd extension) and their corresponding log files (.ldf extension) that you want to back up (remember, you may have created more web applications with SharePoint, and therefore you may need to back up more than what is listed here) and copy them to your backup location (you can see my example here in Figure 12.76). These are complete copies of the databases, they just need to be copied back with the same steps only in reverse to recover the databases to the state they were when you copied them.

FIGURE 12.76
Copied databases

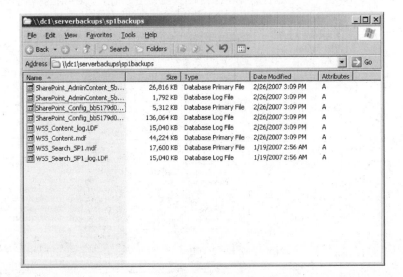

7. When you are done copying the databases, remember to start the services that you stopped, starting with SQL Server 2005 Embedded Edition (Microsoft##SSEE), and then the Share-Point services. If you took the databases offline in SharePoint, be sure to return them to the Ready state.

So that's it for the old school "stop all services and copy the databases" method for backing up the SSEE databases. Do not forget to turn your services back on; I won't mention how many times that's caused me problems. Always check the Event logs to make certain you haven't forgotten anything.

This process works in reverse when recovering a database with a copy (as opposed to restoring a missing database). When restoring the databases, be sure to turn off the services again, and if the database is a high traffic one, make sure that it is Offline in Central Administration ➢ Application Management ➢ Content Databases, so the web application is aware that it's not available. Remember that databases have a log file and the database file itself, they are a pair, so if you replace a bad database with a clean copy of it, use both the .mdf file and the .ldf files. Then restart the services (and bring the content database back to its Ready state). You may need to go to the Content Databases page and add the restored database back to its web application.

USING A BACKUP UTILITY TO BACKUP THE DATABASE

Of course, there is a much easier way to backup embedded databases now that Server 2003 has volume shadow copy. Simply use NTBackup (or some other 3rd party backup software, preferably VSS aware) and backup the databases instead. To back up your SQL Embedded Edition databases:

1. Open NTbackup by choosing Start ➢ All Programs ➢ Accessories ➢ System Tools Backup (or you can go to the command prompt or the Run dialog box and enter **NTBackup**).

2. Go to Advanced mode.

3. Go to the Backup tab.

4. Browse to %Windirows%\SYSMSI\SSEE\MSSQL.2005\MSSQL\Data (see Figure 12.77). The SharePoint default database names are:

   ◆ SharePoint_AdminContent (and a long GUID)

   ◆ SharePoint_Config (and a long GUID)

   ◆ WSS_Content

   ◆ WSS_Search_(servername)

5. Select the databases and their log files you want to back up. (Back up the .mdf files and their corresponding .ldf log files, which should be restored together.)

6. Make certain the options for your backup are the ones you want (verify data, full backup, etc.). Choose the location where you want the backup stored, name the backup file, and click Start Backup. The backup prepares a volume shadow copy (which is why it can do the backup while the database is running) and then begins backing up.

When the backup is complete, close the Backup Progress dialog box. That's it. You've backed up your SharePoint databases in case of emergency. Should one of them get damaged, you have a replacement. Make sure you back up the databases on a regular basis.

BACKING UP THE CONFIGURATION DATABASE

Restoring the configuration database is dangerous if your backup does not match the current server's configuration in terms of new web applications, etc. If you're planning to do anything that significantly changes the configuration, I strongly suggest you back up the configuration database first. Then if you do need to restore the configuration database, it will match the current setup. Otherwise, focus on backing up the data that is stored in the content databases.

RESTORING A DATABASE ON A STANDALONE SERVER

Restoring databases on a standalone SharePoint server is pretty easy, thankfully. Thanks to volume shadow copy, the easiest way to restore is NTbackup (or other 3rd party VSS aware backup utility). Consider taking the content databases that you are restoring Offline in SharePoint to let the web applications know what's going on—then remember to set their state back to Ready when the restore is complete.

1. Open NTbackup by using a command prompt or by entering **ntbackup** in the Run dialog box and pressing Enter.

2. You can use the Backup and Restore Wizard to navigate to the most recent database backups. You can also use Advanced mode instead, if you want to avoid the wizard. On the Restore and Manage Media tab, select the backup file you want to use (my example is in the file share `\\dc1\sp1backups\backupexec\sp1DBbackup2.bkf`, as you can see in Figure 12.77).

3. Navigate through the backup file if you'd like by double-clicking the file, and then double-clicking each location listed beneath it, to get to the database and log files you need. For my example, we are going to restore all files including the configuration database, because no configuration changes have been made to SharePoint since we made this backup. If changes had been made, we would exclude the configuration database, the admin-content database and their logs.

FIGURE 12.77
Restore databases in the
Backup Utility

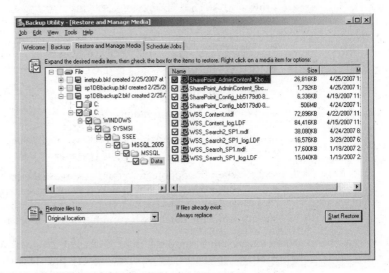

MORE WIZARDRY

Sometimes the Backup and Restore Wizard is actually more useful than the Advanced mode (for example, if your backup isn't listed on the Backup And Restore Media tab in the Backup Utility window). If you use the wizard to do a restore, on the third screen, after choosing to restore files and settings, you are given the option to browse to your backup file.

4. Make certain the restore location for your databases (and logs) is the original location and the restore option is Always Replace, and then click Start Restore. After your restore is complete, NTbackup might require you to reboot, so be prepared.

That's how easy it is to back up and restore the critical databases of a standalone installation of SharePoint. Despite the fact that having both SharePoint and its critical data on one machine offers one point of failure, restoring that single point isn't that difficult to do. Just be sure to back up the server very regularly, in SharePoint, at the IIS level, file level, and particularly the database level.

Backup Your SQL Databases in a Server Farm Install

In a server farm, by definition, SharePoint will use SQL Server 2000 or 2005. This well-documented Microsoft product can be used to back up and restore any databases you might have stored there. SQL has its own built-in options, the details of which have filled their own books. However, here are some suggestions about backing up SQL 2005 databases.

ADVANCED SQL BACKUP

The following operation is a database-by-database backup. I am going to demonstrate the simplest way to back up these databases and restore them, but SQL comes with much more extensive backup and recovery options than I am going to demonstrate here. In particular, I am fond of the Database Maintenance Plan Wizard (which creates a thorough maintenance schedule for backing up SQL databases).

Also look into recovery models, and transaction logs (how to roll forward is a good thing to know). Covering the details of SQL is far outside the scope of this book, but the details are still well worth knowing if you are going to be responsible for your SQL databases. Again, it is better to be safe than sorry.

To manually back up individual databases from an SQL 2005 server, do the following:

1. Open the SQL Management Studio.

2. In the Object Explorer pane, beneath the icon for the SQL server, expand the Databases node.

   On the SQL server 2005 for SharePoint, we are planning to back up the Admin_Content, WSS_Config, WSS_Content, and the WSS_Search_SP2 databases. Your SQL server may contain other databases, but for the time being let's stick to those that are required by SharePoint (you might have more content databases, but for this example I am sticking with the minimum defaults).

3. Right-click one of the databases you intend to back up (the example uses WSS_Content). From the dropdown menu, select Tasks and then Backup (Figure 12.78).

FIGURE 12.78
Selecting to back up a database
in SQL 2005

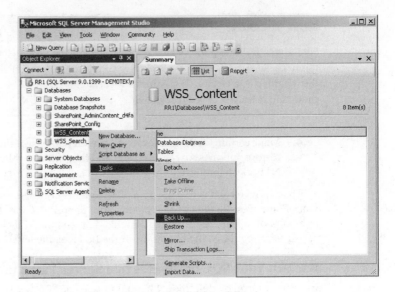

4. The Backup Database window will allow you to choose the source of the backup (the database you right-clicked), what you will name your backup (the backup set), and the destination of the backup file itself (see Figure 12.79).

FIGURE 12.79
The Back Up Database window

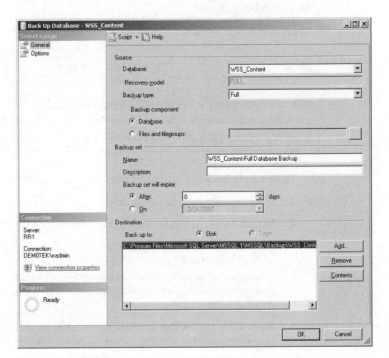

Default information is provided here for your convenience. The default type of backup is Full, which is good; we are going to do a full backup at this time. The backup component is Database, and there is a default Backup Set name, which is the name of the database plus the backup type. The Backup Set name is the name of the backup as it will appear in the Restore window in SQL, if you select the backup file to be restored, it should be informative. There is no expiration date by default for this backup, and the default backup location is the default for SQL, which is on the local drive. This is not a good thing, so we need to change that. Otherwise, the default settings are fine for this example.

5. To change the default location of the backup of the database, select Add in the Destination section of the Back Up Database window. It will bring up a dialog box where you can specify the path for the backup file.

6. Currently it's the local default; however, you should replace it with the path to the location where you want to store the database backup. You also have to name the backup, hopefully with an intuitive, useful name. My example is going to be a network share on DC1 (see Figure 12.80), and is going to call the backup **wsscontent**.

7. Click OK to commit to the location.

USE THE UNC PATH, NOT A MAPPED DRIVE

To back up and restore files in SQL, you must use a UNC path to specify the location. The SQL Server service account should have full control of the share where the backups will go (this means the service account must not be a local account).

FIGURE 12.80
The Select Backup
Destination dialog box

8. The new location should be listed in the Destinations list on the Back Up Database window. Delete the old destination by clicking the Remove button, because you have a better destination now.

9. Make certain that you are backing up the correct database, with the correct backup type, set name, and destination. Click OK at the bottom of the window to do the backup. It should start executing, and then you should get a dialog box telling you the backup is complete (Figure 12.81).

FIGURE 12.81
The backup was successful

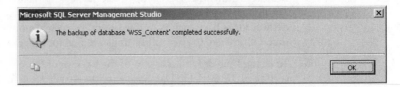

Now you know how to back up the separate components of SharePoint. If anything happens in IIS or SQL, you are ready to restore their respective components.

Restore a SQL Database

What if one of the content databases becomes corrupt and you don't have a recent SharePoint backup of it? What if you have a more recent full backup of the content database instead? You can restore it in SQL. You will probably need to reconnect the restored database to the web application in SharePoint, but that is yet another way to cover your bases during a catastrophe. To restore a database in SQL, follow these steps:

1. At SharePoint's Central Administration, be sure to let the SharePoint web application know that the database is going to be offline. To do so, go to Application Management, select Content Databases, and click on the content database that is having issues (my example is WSS_Content). This will bring up the database settings page for that database. Make certain the Database status is Offline and click OK at the bottom of the page (if it is damaged, it will likely be offline).

2. On the SQL server, open the SQL Management Studio.

3. In the Object Explorer pane, beneath the icon for the SQL server, expand the Databases node.

DIFFERENT STEPS FOR DIFFERENT VERSIONS

Obviously, I am using SQL 2005, but the backup process is approximately the same in SQL 2000 as well. Check your SQL documentation for more detailed instructions about the ins and outs of SQL backup and restore.

In my example, we are going to restore the content database for the SharePoint -80 web application. It has begun to generate errors that make it unusable. We don't have a Share-Point backup more current than the database backup, so we are going to use the database backup of WSS_Content that we created. If the database were simply missing (maybe accidentally deleted), you could just restore it, but in this case we need to replace an existing, malfunctioning database.

The WSS_Content database is still listed, but it's not working. Detach the database to drop any connections with SharePoint, and then restore it from backup.

4. To do this, right-click the database you are going to eventually restore (my example is WSS_Content), go to Tasks and select Detach. See Figure 12.82.

FIGURE 12.82

Select the database to restore

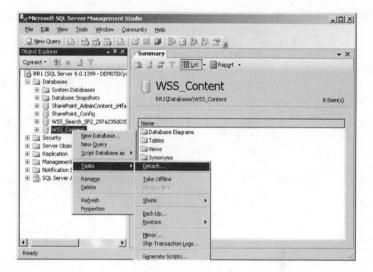

5. In the Detach Database window (Figure 12.83), you can see two connections active to the database. This would cause the restore of this database to fail, so put a check in the box for the Drop Connections column, and click OK.

FIGURE 12.83

The Detach database

6. The database will disappear from the window because it has been detached. To restore it, right-click the Databases node, and select Restore Database from the popup menu.

7. In the To Database field, type the name of the database you are restoring to (my example is WSS_Content).

8. In the From Database field, select the database you are trying to restore (WSS_Content is listed in my example). When you select the database that you want to restore, the most recent backup for that database will appear in the Select The Backup Sets To Restore box.

9. That is convenient for us, because that is the backup we want to restore from, so make sure there is a check mark in the Restore column next to the backup you'd like restore. If there are more than one there (if you have done several backups of that database), choose the most recent one (see Figure 12.84).

FIGURE 12.84
Restore a detached database

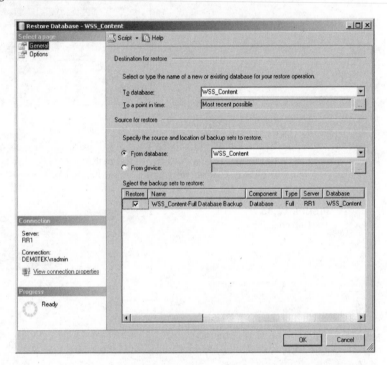

10. The database you detached and want to restore is technically still on the server; it's just not displayed in the console. In order for this restore to succeed, you need to give it permission to overwrite its predecessor (if the database were gone, you don't need to worry about overwriting anything). To do that, go to the top right of the Restore Database window and click Options.

11. On the Options page, put a check mark in the first checkbox, next to Overwrite the Existing Database.

12. Click OK to finish the restore.

13. In a few minutes (depending on the size of the database), a dialog box will appear, either giving you an error report if it fails or an announcement that the restore completed successfully. Click OK to finish the process. The database will be restored to the SQL Management Studio console.

14. Now that the database is restored (and reattached) in SQL, it's time to put it back online in SharePoint. To do that, go back to SharePoint's Central Administration site, Application Management page. Then select Content databases, confirm the correct web application is selected, select the content database you just restored, change its database status from Offline to Ready, and click OK. If it's missing, use the Add a content database to return it to the list.

That's all it should take to restore that SharePoint web application to functionality. This demonstrates that there are several ways to help keep SharePoint healthy and restore it should calamity strike. Utilize every way possible to back up SharePoint, and you will very likely be ready to restore SharePoint should anything go awry.

Suggested Recovery Scenarios

You know how to prepare for the loss or corruption of a site collection, subsite, list, and even a web application or two. You can even recover the server farm data by using the SharePoint backup and restore capability. But what if the entire server goes down? Here are some suggestions on how to handle that based on the knowledge you already have (or should have).

For a Full Recovery of a Single Server Installation

Restore from image or Automated System Recovery (ASR) backup. This means you simply restore the entire server's OS and all applications whole cloth. This scenario assumes that a regular Automated System Recovery backup (see the sidebar at the end of the chapter for step by step information) or other full image is made of the SharePoint server. It makes sense in this situation because all of the SharePoint services are running on one computer.

If you have an image or ASR backup of the server, that can restore the server fully to the point in time the backup was made. But if you have added web applications and databases since then:

Do a SharePoint Restore of the web applications, New Configuration. If you have more recent full backups, you can re-create the web applications that are missing from the backup by restoring them with the New Configuration settings. This will re-create the databases and all other information necessary to get the web applications back up and running. Doing a SharePoint restore is always a good starting point, if you have one.

Do an IIS metabase restore of the most recent backup you have for the server. If you don't have a full SharePoint restore available you can restore the missing bits from scratch, starting with restoring the IIS metabase. This means you will need to copy your IIS metabase backup files for that particular server (there are two, as you know) to the %windir%\system32\ inetsrv\metaback folder. Then open the IIS console, right-click the icon for the local server, and choose All Tasks ➤ Backup/Restore Configuration. Select your backup and click Restore. That should restore the settings in IIS to exactly the state of the last IIS backup. Complete with application pools and correct settings for all.

DON'T HAVE A METABASE HANDY?

Using the IIS metabase is very convenient for disaster recovery, but if you have configuration files for the Web Sites and Application pools, you can also use them to recover. It's just a little more tedious. You'll have to restore the Application pools and the Web Sites individually, then point the Web Sites to their correct Application pools when you're done.

To recover the Web Sites with a configuration file, right click the Web Sites node, select New ➤ Web Site (from file). In the dialog box, browse to the backup file, then click the Read File button, select the correct Web Site Configuration file, and click OK.

To recover the Application pool from Configuration file, follow the same steps as above, using the application pool's configuration instead of the Web Site's.

If you don't have a configuration file backup of your application pools, or they don't work quite as they should, you can create new application pools for the Web Sites.

◆ Right click Application Pools, select New ➤ Application Pool.

◆ In the dialog box, name it and select what it will be based on; either use default settings or copy an existing application pool, if you have one handy. Enter the correct application pool identity, and click OK.

In case you need to create the application pool with the default settings—the standard settings for a SharePoint application pool are: Recycle Worker processes at a particular time (click add and a unique time will be generated), make sure only Request Queue Limit at 1000 is selected for the Performance tab, and for Health, enable pinging (30 seconds), and rapid-fail protection (5 failures and 5 minute time period).

Once the application pools have been created or restored, go to the properties of each of the restored Web Sites, select the Home Directory tab, and select the correct application pool at the bottom of the dialog box, then click OK.

Keep in mind also, that if the Web Sites are missing any files in the virtual directories, be sure to restore them and the SharePoint 12 hive first, before starting the Web Sites.

Restore the virtual directories (and customizations) from a recent backup.   After you restore your IIS metabase, if there are new web applications that weren't there when you did the ASR backup, you will need to restore their virtual directories. In the IIS console, right-click each new IIS Web Site, go to Properties, and check the Home Directory tab for the path to the web application's virtual directory. Once you know which ones you need, restore them using your virtual directories backup. If there were any customizations, you should return them to the 12 hive folders as well.

Do a restore of the most recent backups of the embedded databases.   Simply restore the backups of the databases. It's that easy. You could also stop all SQL and SharePoint services, replace the existing databases, and then restart the services again, but in this case, NTbackup (or other third party utility) really works.

Make sure that each web application in SharePoint indicates that it is connected to the correct database and that those databases have the status of Ready.

DO A FULL REINSTALLATION

If you don't have a full image backup of the server, you are not entirely out of luck. You can do a complete recovery anyway. If you can reinstall the server and get it back up and running, simply reinstall SharePoint using the Basic Install. Then do a full farm recovery, New Configuration. This will restore SharePoint to the point when the backup was made.

If you don't have a full farm backup, you can, since SharePoint is running, create new web applications, remove their new databases (since they're empty and not that useful) and add the existing databases that you backed up instead.

To do that use STSADM and add the databases manually to each web application at the command line (remember that this is for the Basic, single server install):

```
STSADM -o addcontentdb -url <web address of web application>
  -databasename <name of the database you want to restore>
  -databaseserver <servername>\Microsoft##SSEE
```

You can also optionally specify the site warning and maximum levels, as well as the search server in the command as well.

If you had any customizations; new solutions, features, or web parts, you should restore the wpresources folder and 12 hive as well. You might have to reconfigure the features, solutions and other customizations manually (yes that's a pain but its better than losing them altogether).

For a Web Front End Server

In this scenario, using ASR or some other full-system image is a good idea. This server does not contain a lot of data per se because all of the data is on an SQL server elsewhere, but it does contain the web parts, customizations, images, solutions, and features saved locally. If the SQL databases are perfectly intact, all you'll need to do is bring the server back online and the services on the server itself, otherwise they'll use the databases as if nothing happened.

Restore IIS. You can either restore the IIS metabase for that server (metabases are server specific) or restore the configuration files for the web applications that may have been created since the ASR backup. Remember to make the corresponding application pools.

Restore virtual directories and customizations. Use your ntbackups (or other third party product) to restore whatever virtual directories or custom web parts, templates, etc., that might be required by the new web applications. However, the databases on SQL were never compromised and are likely not going to need restoration.

IF ALL ELSE FAILS

If you don't have a full image backup of the Web Front End server, there is another easy way to recover that server. After the operating system has been reinstalled, and the machine added to the domain, prepare for and install SharePoint on the server. Then select to do an Advanced, Web Front End installation. Add it to the existing farm. SharePoint will add the necessary files where they need to go, and configure IIS for you (you may need to do an IISRESET/noforce), bringing the server into alignment again. Be sure to reconfigure those items that are outside of the scope of a SharePoint installation; network load balancing, SSL certificates, and Kerberos, if necessary.

For a Full Recovery of a Server farm

If your SharePoint server and the SQL server—even if your entire network—suffers a disaster, you can still rebuild it if you have your backups.

First, make certain that you have a domain available with DNS. Then make sure you also have the necessary service accounts (with the setup account correctly configured in SQL), with a SQL server up, running on the domain, and accessible from the new SharePoint server.

Install SharePoint   Do a server farm installation of SharePoint on a qualified server (running 2003 SP1 on a domain, with IIS and SMTP installed, and .NET Framework 3.0), and choose to do an Advanced install, new server farm. This will create a new configuration database, as well as the Central Administration site and its content database. That gives you the foundation to re-create your whole SharePoint farm by just resetting your configurations, restoring the web applications, and maybe restoring the customizations, alternate access mappings, etc.

Use the most Recent SharePoint restores   When that server farm installation is complete, do a full restore from your most recent backup of all of the web applications. Make sure you do New Configuration restores, because there will be a new database server and possibly a new server name for the SharePoint server. If you've done a differential restore since the full backup, apply it if necessary. Check your configuration settings to ensure they are all there, and reset your alternate access mapping (don't forget your DNS settings to access any host header sites). Then copy over whatever files were used for your customizations.

TIPS AND TRICKS FOR RESTORING WEB APPLICATIONS TO A NEW FARM

Sometimes when SharePoint does a restore on a new server, it does not correctly add all of the security accounts to their respective databases. This may well occur if restored databases are attached to the SQL instance with the old security intact, and without the new accounts added. If this occurs, you will have a successful restore except for the databases. If you check the logs, as well as the event log for both the SharePoint server and the SQL server, they will all indicate that the farm account cannot access the restored content database, and that possibly the new content database access account cannot log in either.

To fix this, simply add the necessary accounts as database owners of the correct databases. Then, in Central Administration, be sure to add the now functional databases to the restored web applications to which they belong.

The problem is due to the fact that the web applications did not get to finish the process of connecting to their databases because the SharePoint service accounts could not take ownership properly. If this does not give the web applications access to the databases within about five minutes, you may need to take the databases offline, and then set them to Ready again to force the connection. Resetting IIS and even restarting the SharePoint or SQL services might be necessary to make certain all the services involved are clearly aware of the change.

There are more backup and recovery troubleshooting tips in the "Troubleshoot backup and recovery for Windows SharePoint Services 3.0" article in the Windows SharePoint Services 30. Technical Library online.

You should now have plenty of ideas on how to monitor and maintain your SharePoint servers and help you prepare for any disaster. Being unprepared is not an option. No one will think it's acceptable that you simply didn't think a catastrophe could happen.

Make sure you have plenty of storage space for your backups, make sure they are always readily accessible, and test them as often as you can. Monitor your servers to prepare for any problems that might arise. *Do* your backups; scheduled tasks are your friends.

If you can, back up your backups. Have a strategy in place that is appropriate for the value of your data, how long it would take to recover, and how much money and productivity would be lost during that time. If possible, have extra, regularly scheduled backups of the backups stored offsite (in case of fire, flood, or earthquake). Have a hot-swappable virtual twin of your network to go online in case of emergency. Mirror your SQL databases, and more. You cannot be too protected. From saving a list to saving a farm, it's all worth it when disaster strikes.

SPEAKING OF DISASTER: NEED TO BACKUP AN ENTIRE SERVER?

A lot of people have purchased third-party imaging software to create copies of their servers in case of emergency. However, Windows Server 2003 (and higher) comes with a backup and restore feature that will basically create a server image for free. Because it does a mini plug-and-play setup before the restore, you can have hardware that isn't necessarily identical (although it helps to be close if you can) to the original server's hardware.

I am talking about *Automated System Recovery* (ASR). To use it on your SharePoint server make certain that:

◆ You are logged in as an administrator on the server you are backing up.

◆ The account has read and write access to the backup location.

◆ The backup location is large enough to accommodate the ASR backup. ASR backs up everything on a server's system hard drive, every partition and file. That means that if the server took up 4GB originally, the ASR backup file will be 4GB as well. When it restores, it will wipe all partitions on the drive you are restoring to, and lay down all partitions and data from the backup just as it was for the original server.

◆ You have a floppy drive and disk for the backup configuration information. Yes, ASR requires a formatted floppy disk. Make certain you have a floppy on hand (and maybe an USB floppy drive if the server doesn't have one) to successfully do an ASR backup. Do not lose it either, or else the ASR restore will fail. Back up the floppy if you can.

◆ To restore a server from an ASR backup, you will first have to boot from a Windows Server 2003 CD and press F2 right at the beginning (watch for it, it comes right after the prompt for F6) to go into Automated System Restore mode. This means, to restore from ASR backup, in addition to the floppy disk containing the configuration data for the backup, you must also have a Windows Server 2003 CD handy as well.

Backing up to an external drive is the most convenient because you can simply attach it to the server to which you would like to restore it. However, you can save your ASR backup file to a network location if you have DHCP running on the target network when you restore. During the ASR recovery process the mini-setup will configure the network settings, but it won't give *you* a chance to configure the settings if you need a static IP. During the restore, you might get a warning that the backup file cannot be found. That generally means that ASR cannot log in to the network share on its own. Simply click Browse when prompted for the data source, enter the UNC path to the backup file, and click Open, which will prompt you for authentication. From that point, the restore will work fine.

The restoration process can be lengthy. It can take more than 30 minutes to prepare the operating system (OS) for restoration (ASR basically installs the Windows Server OS) and then more than 30 minutes to apply the complete ASR restoration of the server backup. Sure, it can take a while, but after an hour or so, the entire server will be back up in running order, just as you left it when you backed it up.

1. To start, you need to create the ASR backup by opening NTBackup (from the System Tools under Accessories off of the Start menu, by typing **ntbackup** at the command prompt, or by typing **ntbackup** in a Run dialog box—take your pick).

   You can use the Backup Wizard to do an ASR backup—just make certain you choose All Information on this Computer. However, I prefer the Advanced mode, which opens the Backup Utility. If you have the Backup Utility window open, click the Automated System Recovery Wizard button on the Welcome tab.

2. In the Automated System Recovery Wizard, click Next on the Welcome Screen to get to the backup destination screen. You will use it to specify the location of your backup. I am going to back up to an external drive and use the filename **sp2ASRbackup**. Once you've chosen your backup location and filename, click Next.

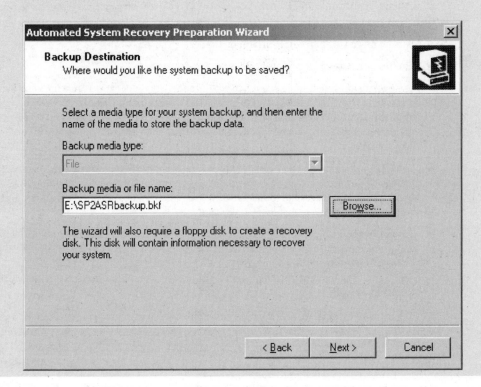

3. Have your floppy disk handy, and click Finish to start the backup. Once you click Finish, the backup will begin by checking the drive, preparing the volume shadow copy, and estimating the size of the drive. The backup process will take quite a while, depending on the size of your drive and how many partitions there are.

4. Toward the end of the backup, ASR will use the floppy disk to write the necessary restore system data. When the backup is done, be sure to label the floppy and store it carefully.

Now, that you have a complete system backup, if that server completely dies, you can re-create it on a different server entirely. Be absolutely certain that you have access to the careful and thorough backups you created of SharePoint, its IIS configuration data, its virtual directories, and its databases. Although, in this scenario, all you really need is the most recent SharePoint Full (and maybe differential) backups.

If you need to restore a SharePoint server from an ASR backup, make sure you have a server with a drive at least as large as the one on the original server so you can restore the server's backup to it. The server does not need to be identical to the original, just make it as close as you can. During installation, ASR does go through a plug-and-play process (see the ASR documentation about adding custom drivers to use during restore if that is necessary in your environment) to compensate for hardware variations.

1. To begin the restoration of your ASR backup, turn on the server to which you intend to apply the restore. Verify that the drive is big enough to accommodate the backup, and that you have a floppy drive and the ASR configuration floppy disk for the backup. Boot up the server with the Windows Server 2003 installation CD/DVD (or disk one of the 2003 R2 disk set). Be ready to press F2 as soon as you are prompted, basically moments after the blue screen environment of the Windows installation starts.

2. Moments after you press F2, you will be prompted to for your ASR floppy disk. Insert it and press any key to continue.

3. Soon after that, you will be prompted to format the new server's drive. This will wipe out all partitions on the target system drive in preparation to apply the ASR restore. There are no other options, either you wipe the drive or you quit the restore. To continue the restore, type C. The drive will be formatted, and then the system will reboot (remember to remove the floppy).

4. Prepare to do plug and play for components and do a mini-setup of the OS in preparation to apply the ASR restore. This could take 30 minutes or more, so be prepared.

5. After the mini-setup is complete, the ASR recovery process will automatically look for the restore files based on the information on the configuration disk. My backup drive was on an external disk, which I simply attached to the new server prior to booting it up. The restore process found the drive, and immediately starting restoring from it.

6. Then the restore will start the Automated System Recovery Wizard to confirm your backup location. Make certain that the correct backup file is listed. If you are restoring from a network location, you will have to browse to the path and specify the location of the file. The wizard cannot authenticate to the share, so it will fail to find the file until you browse to the path for the file and authenticate manually. Once the file is found, click Next, and then click Finish to start the restore.

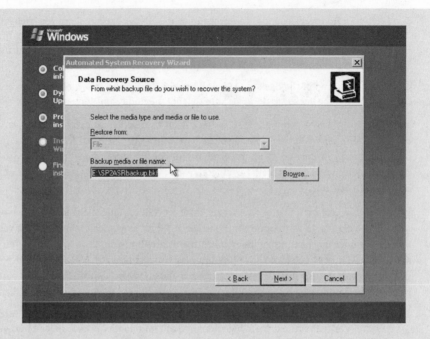

The restore can take 30 minutes or more (probably about as long as it took to do the backup). When it is finished, it will reboot automatically.

At that point, you will have a completely recovered server. All you normally would need to do is open SharePoint and run a full SharePoint restore from there. However, I have found that some ASR restorations enable Windows Firewall, so check to make certain that is disabled before trying to access SharePoint. Often accessing a SharePoint server after ASR restore can be problematic because the firewall is on, so be sure to disable it before you consider the installation to be complete. Consider yourself warned.

The Bottom Line

Monitor server performance   Use the Performance Monitor's System Monitor to view real-time server performance or create a counter log to measure performance over time. You can create custom alerts that read the logs and warn you if something passes a counter limit.

> **Master It**   You have an existing server which has been tasked as your new SharePoint server. The installation is done, and it's about to go live. Because it's an existing server, you're worried that the addition of SharePoint will require more RAM then the server has installed. Build a performance alert that will register an event in the Application Event log if the available RAM ever gets below 50MB.

Use SharePoint Backup and Restore   SharePoint has its own backup and restore features — both in the GUI and using the STSADM command. These tools allow you to back up individual site collections, web applications, or even the whole server farm. The GUI has some easy to use steps found in Central Administration, while the STSADM commands can be scripted, allowing for automation and scheduling.

Master It   You are getting ready to decommission a site collection and wish to make a final backup of it in case it needs to be referenced or resurrected in the future. This archive needs to be done in such a fashion that you are able to restore it to a different SharePoint server (in case this server is gone by the time the archive is needed). How do you go about creating this final backup?

Backup separate SharePoint components   In addition to SharePoint's built-in backup and recovery options, you can back up individual components of SharePoint using a variety of different tools. At a more granular level than a site collections alone, it is possible to use templates and import/export to backup individual lists, libraries, and subsites. You can also use the backup features of IIS and SQL to backup SharePoint's IIS Web Sites and SQL databases.

Master It   After a large amount of work was done to a list on the SharePoint server, one of the users has accidentally deleted it. It's been too soon for the list to be backed up using the nightly STSADM script, but there's a possibility the list was exported as a template. What's the first step you should take to recover this deleted list?

Recover from disaster   SharePoint can be recovered from catastrophe several ways. The Share-Point built-in back up has an option to perform a catastrophic backup (and back up the entire farm). IIS Web Sites can be moved to a new web front-end server, and SQL Databases can be transferred to a new database server. Finally, ASR is available to completely rebuild the Windows Server (and SharePoint), even to disparate hardware.

Master It   It's been raining, the ceiling has burst, and your server room has just been given an impromptu shower. Now the SharePoint server is a smoking, dripping ruin and SharePoint is "down for routine maintenance." You had a full ASR backup, but its corresponding floppy disk was in an envelope taped to the rack's door and is also destroyed. You do have a recent SharePoint catastrophic backup on an external hard drive (stored offsite at your house) and access to a freshly installed Windows server at your co-location site. What's the fastest way to get SharePoint back up and running?

Part IV

Special Topics in Windows SharePoint Services 3.0

STSADM: A Look at the SharePoint Command Line Tool

In earlier chapters you have probably noticed references to something called STSADM.EXE, and this thought may have entered your mind: "What is STSADM.EXE, and why should I care?"

The answer to the first part of the question—in case you haven't figured it out by now—STSADM.EXE is the command-line administration tool for WSS. The name is a bit of a throwback to when WSS was known as SharePoint Team Services (STS), but nonetheless it is the command-line tool for performing SharePoint administration.

Almost all of the tasks that you have learned to do using the various SharePoint administration tools can be done with STSADM. Quite a few things can be done only with STSADM.

As for the second part of the question, it's really quite simple. There are four main reasons that you need to be aware of STSADM.EXE.

1. There are some management tasks that are only able to be done with these tools. The good folks at Microsoft—for various reasons—did not see fit to include some of these tasks in the administration website.

2. Some tasks are repetitive in nature and may need to be scheduled for off-peak times. Thus, the ability to create some kind of script file is of great use.

3. You are managing a large number of web farms or front-end servers in a web farm, and the ability to quickly reproduce a given activity may be of great value. Again, the ability to script these activities is of great use.

4. Impress your friends at parties!

In this chapter, you'll learn how to:

◆ Make sure everything is in place to run this tool

◆ Use the basic STSADM syntax

◆ Complete common management tasks with STSADM

STSADM Setup Information

On an x86-based server, the default location of `STSADM.EXE` is the `c:\program files\ common files\microsoft shared\web server extensions\12\bin` directory. If WSS was installed on the x64 platform, there is a slight variation, and the default location is the `c:\Program Files (x86)\Common Files\ Microsoft Shared\web server extensions\12\bin` directory.

SHORTENING THE PATH

In order to make life easier and to free up screen real estate when you're using STSADM, you may want to adjust the default path statement and work from the root of C: while at the command prompt.

The following illustration demonstrates how to adjust the path.

The `PATH` entry at the end of the third line tells the computer to add all the already defined paths to your new one. Without it, all of the other paths would be removed.

You can also add the path statement to the `PATH` environment variable. This can be adjusted in the System Control Panel.

If you don't use the tool very often, you can create a shortcut to `cmd.exe`, and make the appropriate directory the working directory for that CMD session.

To create a command prompt shortcut with the STSADM working directory:

1. Right-click on the Desktop (or wherever you want to place the shortcut). A popup menu will appear.

2. Choose New ➢ Shortcut from the popup menu. The Create Shortcut Wizard will launch.

3. On the first screen of the Create Shortcut Wizard, enter **cmd.exe**. Then click the Next button.

4. On the Select A Title For The Program page of the wizard, type in whatever name you would like this shortcut to have. It will default to `cmd`. Then click the Finish button.

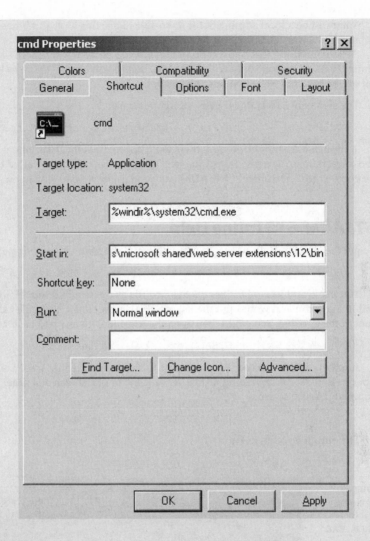

5. Find the shortcut in the location in which you saved it, and then right-click the shortcut and choose Properties. This will bring up the properties of the shortcut and focus on the Shortcut page.

6. In the Start In field, enter `c:\program files\common files\microsoft shared\web server extensions\12\bin`.

7. Click the OK button.

There are other ways within Windows to create easier access to long directory paths. As long as you are comfortable with the way you are choosing to employ, it shouldn't really make much difference.

You must be a local administrator to be able to use this tool, and it needs to be run locally. In other words, you can't use it for remote administration.

Almost anything that one can do in the GUI can be done via STSADM, and there are a few things that can be done only with STSADM. Before you head into the task-specific topics, a little bit on the basics of STSADM might be useful.

The syntax of STSADM is pretty straightforward:

```
STSADM.exe -o <operation> [parameters required for the operation]
```

Although it is straightforward, there are a approximately 110 different operations, and most of those operations have several parameters. Once you've committed all of those to memory, you'll be good to go... fortunately, STSADM has good inline help to assist you.

STSADM.EXE Inline Help

To get the list of operations that are available, use the following command:

```
STSADM.exe -help or STSADM.exe -?
```

You may want to pipe the results to a text file as the results zoom by too quickly on screen. The following command would put the list of STSADM operations in a file called `stsadm.txt` on the root of the C: drive. You could then open the text file with any text editor.

```
STSADM.exe -help >c:\stsadm.txt
```

Another option is to use the |more pipe to show only the first screen of the results and give you options to view the remaining text either one line or one screen at a time. Use the following command to use more:

```
STSADM.EXE -help |more
```

The output appears in Figure 13.1.

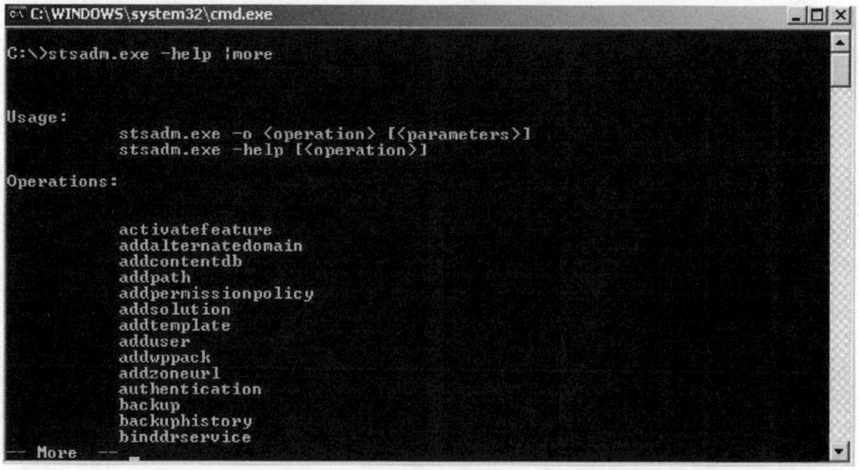

FIGURE 13.1
Using the more pipe with STSADM.EXE

At the—More—prompt, you can press the Enter key to advance one more line or press the spacebar to advance one screen. Select Ctrl+C to exit out of the pipe entirely.

Once you have found the operation you are looking for, you may need to get the proper syntax for that particular operation. To get the full syntax for a single operation use the following command:

```
STSADM.exe -help <operation>
```

The output of this command appears in Figure 13.2.

FIGURE 13.2
Using the inline help with the *CREATESITE* operation

```
C:\>stsadm.exe -help createsite

stsadm.exe -o createsite
            -url <url>
            -owneremail <someone@example.com>
            [-ownerlogin <DOMAIN\name>]
            [-ownername <display name>]
            [-secondaryemail <someone@example.com>]
            [-secondarylogin <DOMAIN\name>]
            [-secondaryname <display name>]
            [-lcid <language>]
            [-sitetemplate <site template>]
            [-title <site title>]
            [-description <site description>]
            [-hostheaderwebapplicationurl <web application url>]
            [-quota <quota template>]

C:\>_
```

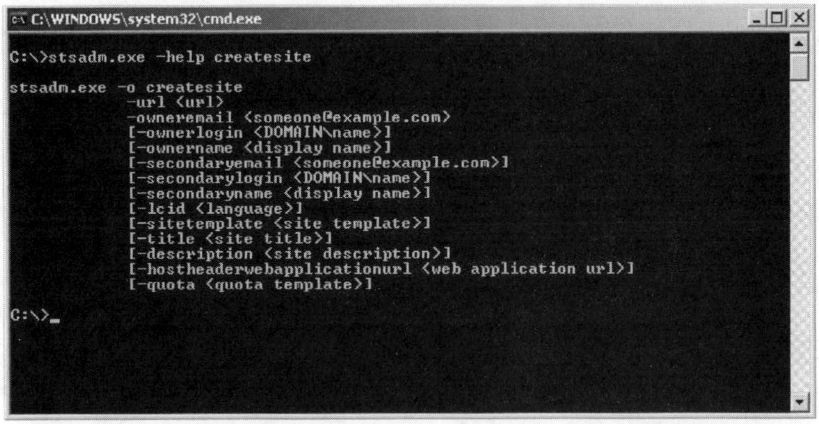

The screen shows all of the parameters for the createsite operation. Parameters without brackets (in this case -url and -owneremail) are mandatory parameters for the operation to be completed. Conversely, parameters with brackets are optional.

SIMPLIFYING *STSADM.EXE* WITH SCRIPTING

Most administrators know only a small fraction of the STSADM operations, usually the ones that they need to use frequently. Many operations have multiple parameters. The result can be commands that are quite long, to the tune of two to three lines at the command prompt. Being a command-line tool, STSADM is unforgiving of even the smallest typing mistakes.

For example, the command to create a new personal site for Sage Tarragon on the SP1 web server could look something like this:

```
stsadm.exe -o createsite -url http://SP1/sites/SageT -ownerlogin
    dem0tek\SageT -owneremail SageT@dem0tek.lcl -sitetemplate
    "Dem0tek Personal Site" -title "SageT Personal Site" -description
    "Personal site for SageT" -quota "200 MB"
```

That's a lot to type correctly, even once. Imagine you need to do this every time a new staff member is added. Smart administrators make things easier on themselves by using batch files or scripts to simplify frequently used stsadm commands.

The following batch file would have the same effect as the command above:

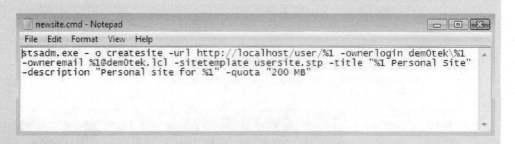

However, to use this batch file, you need to enter the following command. One thing to note is that for this particular batch file to run you will either have to run it from the same location as stsadm.exe or have adjusted the path.

Newsite.cmd <*username*>

The ***username*** that is provided is passed as the variable (%1) that is referenced within the batch file itself. In other words, if the administrator enters **Newsite.cmd SageT**, then SageT is substituted for every instance of %1 in the file when it runs.

If you prefer to work with VBScript, you can use this very simple VBScript that does basically the same thing:

```
'Create variables used in script
Dim oShell
Dim sUser, sCommand

'Instantiate the shell library required to run commands
Set oShell = CreateObject("WScript.Shell")

'The next line creates a prompt for the administrator to type in the
  logon name of the user that the personal site is for.
sUser = InputBox ("Enter the logon name of the user:","Personal Site
  Creation")

'Build the text string that is the entire STSADM command required to
  create a new site
'Chr(34) is the character code for double quotes, which are needed for
  this string to execute properly.
scommand = "stsadm.exe -o createsite -url http://localhost/users/" &
  sUser & " -ownerlogin dem0tek\" & sUser & " -owneremail " & sUser
  & "@dem0tek.lcl -sitetemplate usersite.stp -title "& Chr(34) &
  sUser & " Personal Site" & Chr(34) & " -description " & Chr(34) &
  "Personal site for " & sUser & Chr(34) &" -quota " & Chr(34) & "200
  MB" & Chr(34)
```

```
'Run the stsadm command
oShell.run scommand
```

This script does not require the person running it to provide any arguments at the command line, but it will prompt for the logon name of the user for whom the site is being created.

STSADM-Only Tasks

As we've discussed earlier in this chapter, there are several activities that can only be done via STSADM. In some cases, these tasks make up part of a bigger picture (i.e., they are one step in a process). In other cases, the tasks are the sum total. In the end, it doesn't really matter which of these is the case. Either way, you need to have your typing fingers ready.

MORE STSADM TASKS

In this section, you're going to learn some tasks that have to be done using STSADM. In many—but not all—of these cases there will be no indicator in the WSS Central Administration or Site Administration tools that this task must be done via STSADM. If you'd like a complete list of the tasks that can be done only with STSADM, you can go online to the Windows SharePoint Services Technical Library ➢ Technical Reference for Windows SharePoint Services 3.0 Technology ➢ Stsadm Command Line Tool (Windows SharePoint Services) article.

Two operations are of particular note: the GETPROPERTY and SETPROPERTY operations. Although most STSADM operations have multiple potential parameters that can be specified, each operation affects only a single activity; i.e., it creates a site or renames a web). However, these two operations can be used to retrieve or set the values for more than 75 properties of the server farm and virtual servers (otherwise known as web applications). These properties cover a wide range of topics—from workflow CPU throttling to Recycle Bin retention time to the number of days that the !New icon displays. It may well be worth your time to use the inline help to review the list of properties that are available to you through these operations. You might find something that pleasantly surprises you.

The Getproperty and Setproperty operations illustrate another common occurrence with STSADM: the operation is something that can be done with the appropriate GUI tool, but there are some options that are available only by using STSADM. For a different example, you can create a web application by using Central Administration (Chapter 8, "Site Collections and Web Applications"), and it has quite a few options. However, it doesn't have the ability to define the template that should be used to create the site collection or the owner of the site. In STSADM, the Extendvs operation (which is used to create a new web application) has parameters that allow you do both of these tasks when extending the IIS Web Site.

There's a very real chance that the extra tasks/options will not be mentioned at all in the GUI tools.

Site Template Management with *STSADM.EXE*

In Chapter 8, "Site Collections and Web Applications," you learned how to import and export site templates for use within a site or site collection. However, what should you do if you need to make a template available to all site collections within the server farm? If you wanted to, you could add it for each site collection via the GUI tools. However, using STSADM.EXE might be a little more efficient in this instance, because there is no means to do this as a single operation within the WSS Site Settings pages.

Within STSADM.EXE, there are three primary operations that deal with templates:

◆ Enumtemplates

◆ Addtemplate

◆ Deletetemplate

All of these operations have a fairly simple syntax, as shown in Table 13.1.

TABLE 13.1: Template Management Operations Reference

OPERATION	PARAMETERS
Addtemplate	-title <template title>
	[-description <template description>]
Deletetemplate	-title <template title>
	[-lcid <language code>]
Enumtemplates	[-lcid <language code>]

You might notice that each operation has relatively few parameters and each parameter is reasonably self-descriptive. The only parameter that isn't fairly obvious is the -lcid parameter used in the Deletetemplate and Enumtemplate operations. Because WSS allows for multiple languages, it is also possible for a template to use a particular language. In both of those operations, if you need to filter out the templates by a particular language, you will need to use the optional -lcid parameter and feed it the language code. You'll see in "Listing the Site Templates for the Farm" how you can find out the language code for a given template.

Adding a Template to the Server Farm

Again, you should already have the template you want to add to your farm. You can acquire it using any of the methods discussed in Chapter 8. Once you've acquired it and are ready to add it to the farm, you can use the AddTemplate operation. If you want to add a new meeting site template customized for Dem0tek (dem0mtg.stp for example), use the following command:

```
STSADM.EXE -o Addtemplate -filename c:\dem0mtg.stp -title Dem0tek
    Meeting" -description "All meetings organized by Dem0tek staff
    should use this template"
```

The results of running that command are shown in Figure 13.3.

The results include a message stating that you will need to restart IIS for the change to take effect, and you are given instructions on how to do that using IISreset (you could also do an IIStreet/noforce). This has already been done in Figure 13.3, but it is something you might need to be aware of when adding site templates to the server. You may need to schedule this type of activity during off-peak hours to lessen the impact of the IIS restart.

FIGURE 13.3
Add a site template to
WSS and then run IISreset

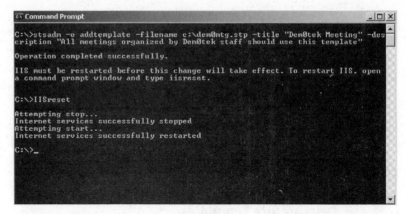

You can see the effect of adding this template in the Site Administration pages when you create a new site. Again, this process is outlined in detail in Chapter 8. Notice the Custom tab toward the bottom of the page where you choose which template to use; that is where you find the title of your newly added template. You may also notice that the added optional description appears on the left, underneath the graphic (see Figure 13.4).

FIGURE 13.4
The new template as it
appears in the SharePoint
Administration pages

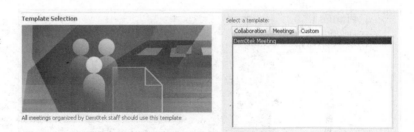

Listing the Site Templates for the Farm

As you might guess, to get a list of templates that have been loaded for the server farm, you use the following command:

```
STSADM.EXE -o Enumtemplates [-lcid:language]
```

The one optional parameter allows you to filter the results for templates based on a particular language set. If you are unsure what the correct language code is for the templates you want listed, you may want to run this command without that parameter. The output of this command looks something like what appears in Figure 13.5:

FIGURE 13.5
The results of the
Enumtemplates
operation

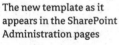

The output of this command is pretty basic, but there is some useful information in there. It shows the title of the template as it appears in the GUI, as well as the description, but it also gives us the language code (used in the `-lcid` parameter).

ENUMTEMPLATES LIMITATIONS

One important thing to remember about the `Enumtemplates` operation is that it will only return any custom templates that have been loaded to the farm. The result set does not include the default templates.

Deleting Site Templates

Now that you know the title (and if required, the language ID) of all the custom templates loaded into the farm, deleting one of them is just a matter of using the last operation of this section, `Deletetemplate` (see Figure 13.6).

```
STSADM.exe -o Deletetemplate -title "Dem0tek Meeting"
```

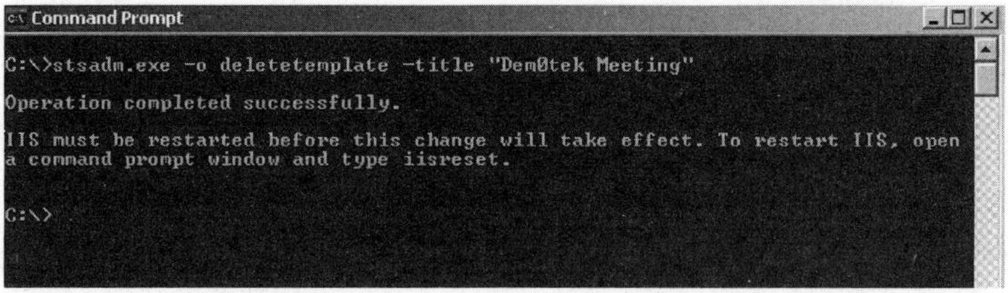

FIGURE 13.6
Deleting a site template using **STSADM.EXE**

Just as with the `Addtemplate` operation, you will need to run IISreset for the change to take effect. Once that has been done, the template will no longer appear in the list of Custom templates on the Site Creation pages.

IISRESET

IISReset is not technically a WSS command-line tool; it is an IIS command-line tool that has been around for a few years. As you can probably guess, it is used to restart (or reset) IIS. It doesn't fully unload the `HTTP.SYS` driver, but it has a similar effect as going into the Services tool and restarting the World Wide Web service.

At its most basic, it is very simple to use: simply open a command prompt and enter **IISReset**. However, there is quite a bit more to this utility than first meets the eye.

For example, IISReset can be used remotely by supplying the computer name of a particular computer. IISReset can also be used to either start or stop the web services (although the default is to restart) or to force a reboot of the computer.

To see a complete list of options available with this tool, simply enter **IISReset/?** from within a command window.

Managing Web Parts with STSADM

Web parts are one of the core components of any SharePoint deployment. In many ways, they are the building blocks of quite a bit of the content. In Chapter 4, "Introduction to Web Parts", you learned how to manipulate web parts within your pages and sites. However, as you probably noticed, there are some limitations to what you are able to do and some limits to where the parts you added to a site can be used later. Typically, a new web part introduced in that manner is limited to use in that site collection and its subsites.

How do you make a particular web part available to all the site collections and web applications? This is where STSADM comes in very handy. STSADM has several operations available to let you manage prepackaged web parts; they are known as *web part packs* in your WSS infrastructure.

Chapter 4 covers the various ways you can acquire a web part package, so there's little need to go into it here. However, keep in mind that the web part packs you are going to install using STSADM are CAB files, not the .dwp files that you imported directly into WSS in the GUIs.

Table 13.2 shows a list of web part management operations:

TABLE 13.2:   Web Part Management Operations Reference

OPERATION	PARAMETER
Addwppack	-filename <Web Part Package filename> [-lcid <language code>] [-url <url>] [-globalinstall] [-force] [-nodeploy]
Addwppack	-name <name of Web Part Package> [-lcid <language code>] [-url <url>] [-globalinstall] [-force]
Deletewppack	-name <name of Web Part Package> [-lcid <language code>] [-url <url>]

(Continued)

TABLE 13.2: Web Part Management Operations Reference *(Continued)*

OPERATION	PARAMETER
Deploywppack	-name <name of Web Part Package> [-url <web application url. [-time <time to retract at>] [-immediate] [-local] [-lcid <language code>] [-globalinstall] [-force]
Enumwppacks	[-name <name of Web Part Package>] [-url <virtual server url>] [-farm]
Retractwppack	-name <name of Web Part Package> [-url < web application url. [-time <time to retract at>] [-immediate] [-local] [-lcid <language code>]

Adding a Web Part Package

The Addwppack operation is the main operation you'll use to add a web part package (or wppack) to your WSS infrastructure. However, it can be used in one of two ways.

The first method of using ADDWPPACK allows you to import a web part pack into the infrastructure. The parameters are much as you would expect. To import the Poll web part pack (such as the poll web part by ACAR for example, that you already saved as c:\pollwebpart\pollwebpart_demo.cab), you might use this command:

```
STSADM -o Addwppack -filename
    c:\pollwebpart\pollwebpart_demo.cab -globalinstall
```

This command will install the resulting web part or parts into the global assembly cache (the -globalinstall parameter), making them available to all site collections in the web application. If you only want it to be available to a certain web application, you can use the -url parameter instead.

Once this had been added, when you add web parts to a site or page in WSS, you should find the web part listed as it appears in Figure 13.7.

You can confirm that the Poll web part is the one you added by clicking on the Advanced Web Part Gallery And Options link in the lower-right corner of the dialog box. That will load the traditional Add Web Parts box on the right side of the page. You can see the new web part listed in the Server Gallery section, as shown in Figure 13.8 (remember that you used the -globalinstall parameter).

FIGURE 13.7
Using the newly added Poll web part

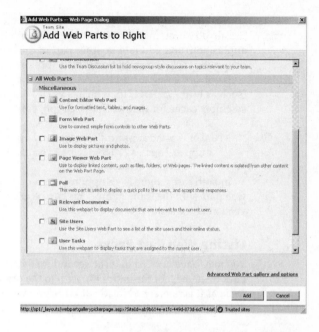

FIGURE 13.8
The Poll web part viewed in the gallery in which it is installed

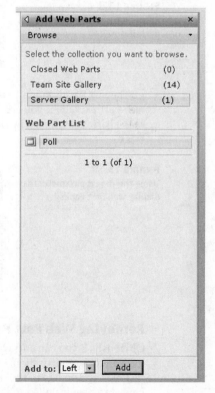

The second method of using the `Addwppack` operation allows you to take a web part pack that has already been introduced into the infrastructure (usually installed into the default web application) and add it to another part of the infrastructure, either into the global assembly cache or specific URL of an additional web application.

If you are going to add the Poll web part pack to an additional web application in the farm (such as http://sp1:44215, which is what I am using for this example), again in the global assembly cache for that web application, you would use the command like this:

```
STSADM -o Addwppack -name pollwebpart_demo.cab -url
    http://sp1:42215-globalinstall
```

In both cases, there is an optional `-force` parameter that can be used to overwrite an existing web part with the same name. This can be useful if you are replacing a web part with a new version of the same part.

Listing Web Part Packs

You may have noticed that the second method to add a web part pack referenced the web part pack by name, not the entire file path to the original CAB file. To get the name of the web part pack, as it is referenced inside of WSS, you will need to use the `Enumwppacks` operation. Figure 13.9 shows the syntax for the `Enumwppacks` operation.

FIGURE 13.9
Enumerating web part
packages

The `-url` and `-name` parameters allow you to filter the results for a single web application or web part package if you choose. The `-farm` parameter, shown in Figure 13.10, has the same scope as the basic syntax seen in Figure 13.9, but it also displays the web part ID, as referenced within WSS.

FIGURE 13.10
Using the `-farm` parameter to
display web part packages

Removing Web Part Packages

Obviously, if you can add web part packages, you must be able to remove them. For each use of the `Addwppack` operation, there is a corresponding removal operation.

If you would like to remove a web part package from a particular web application, but still have it remain installed in the WSS infrastructure, then use the `Retractwppack` operation. The following command in my example will remove the Poll web part package that you added to the second web application. The `-immediate` parameter tells the SharePoint Timer Service to execute as quickly as possible. A `-time` parameter can be used to specify a particular time that the SharePoint Timer Service should execute the command.

```
STSADM -o retractwppack -name pollwebpart_demo.cab -url
    http://sp1:42214 -immediate
```

To completely remove a web part package, you would need to use the `Deletewppack` operation. Its syntax and parameters are considerably simpler that the `RETRACTWPPACK` operation, merely offering the option to specify a particular URL to delete it from, as well as a particular language code.

EXECADMSVCJOBS AND THE WINDOWS SHAREPOINT TIMER SERVICE

After the `RETRACTWPPACK` operation is run, you may get a message stating the timed event (even if you use the `-immediate` switch) will fail because the Windows SharePoint Administration service is not running. Don't panic. This is normal. By default, the Windows SharePoint Administration Service (which schedules things for the Windows SharePoint Timer service, among other things) is configured for manual startup. You can change that setting and avoid that error in the future, or you can run the following command:

```
STSADM -o execadmsvcjobs
```

This will automatically trigger any waiting jobs. Remember that these jobs may have been sent from other commands and administrators, so be careful when forcing your hand like this—it could have unintended consequences.

To completely remove the Poll web part package you installed earlier, the following command will work:

```
STSADM -o Deletewppack -name pollwebpart_demo.cab
```

Managing Features and Solutions with STSADM

One of the new features in WSS 3.0 is the ability to deploy Features and Solutions. In the past, developers could create site definitions that consisted of a directory on the web servers that held some XML files and all the other files related to the site definition. These had to be manually installed into all of the web servers (if there were multiple servers) and were limited in scope as to what they could be used to define. In WSS 3.0, this has been addressed through what is now called *Solutions* and *Features*.

One of the main benefits of Features is that they are smaller in scale than entire Site Definitions. In other words, as the name implies, they can deal with a part, or component of a site (or a feature of the site, if you will), rather than an entire site itself. These modular components can then be activated for any sites in the farm. You have the means to activate Features through the GUI tools, but not the means to install Features on their own.

Of course, Features can be part of another new deployment mechanism known as *Solutions*. Solutions are similar in concept to a web part package, in that they are CAB or WSP files that contains all of the files necessary to implement the Solution. Solutions are unlike a web part package though, in that they can include site definitions and features and anything else required for the Solution to function properly. Solution installation and removal must be done via STSADM (see Table 13.3), while deployment and retraction can be handled in the GUI or via STSADM (see Table 13.4).

TABLE 13.3: Solution Management

OPERATIONS	PARAMETERS
Addsolution	-filename <solution filename> [-lcid <language code>]
Canceldeployment	
Copyappbincontent	
Deletesolution	-name <solution name> [-override] [-lcid <language code>]
Deploysolution	-name <solution name> [-url <virtual server url>] [-allcontenturls} [-time <time to deploy at>] [-immediate] [-local] [-allowgacdeployment] [-allowcaspolicies] [-lcid <language code>] [-force]
Displaysolution	-name <solution name>
Enumdeployments	
Enumsolutions	
Removesolutiondeploymentlock	
Retractsolution	-name <solution name> [-url <virtual server url>] [-allcontenturls} [-time <time to retract at>] [-immediate] [-local] [-lcid <language code>]
Syncsolution	
Upgradesolution	-name <solution name> -filename <upgrade filename> [-time <time to deploy at>] [-immediate] [-local] [-allowgacdeployment] [-allowcaspolicies] [-lcid <language code>]

TABLE 13.4:   Feature Management

OPERATION	PARAMETERS
Activatefeature	-filename <relative path to Feature.xml> OR -name <feature folder> OR -id <feature Id> [-url <url>] [-force}
Deactivatefeature	-filename <relative path to Feature.xml> OR -name <feature folder> OR -id <feature Id> [-url <url>] [-force]
Installfeature	-filename <relative path to feature.xml from system feature directory> OR -name <feature folder> [-force]
Scanforfeatures	[-solutionid <id of Solution>] [-displayonly]
Uninstallfeature	-filename <relative path to feature.xml from system feature directory> OR -name <feature folder> [-force]

Adding Solutions

Adding or deleting a Solution is actually relatively straightforward. The syntax of both of these commands, while not identical, is very similar.

For example, to add the SharePoint Learning Kit solution (a sample solution you would have downloaded and saved as `c:\install\release\sharepointlearningkit.wsp`) to the SharePoint site, run the following command:

```
STSADM -o addsolution -filename
    "c:\install\release\sharepointlearningkit.wsp"
```

One thing to note is that the Solution will have a name for itself as part of its definitions. You will need to discover this name before you can delete a Solution from the farm. You can use the `Enumsolutions` operation for that. There are no parameters for this command, so

```
STSADM -o enumsolutions
```

will generate a list of Solutions that are currently being employed. The results set would be something like what appears in Figure 13.11.

A perusal of the results reveals a few interesting tidbits. In addition to the name and ID (which you would kind of expect), there are a few attributes toward the bottom of the each entry that may prove of value to you later—the `ContainsGlobalAssembly` and `Contains CodeAccessSecurityPolicies` properties to be specific. When we are ready to deploy the Solution, you'll want to keep those properties in mind.

Deleting Solutions

Now that you have the names of the Solutions that have been installed, you can use that information in other operations, namely `Deletesolution`. This operation has a simple syntax, much like the `Addsolution` operation.

```
STSADM -o Deletesolution -name <solution name> -override
```

However, using this syntax to delete a Solution only works if the Solution is no longer deployed to any virtual servers. The optional `override` parameter can be used in cases where you need to delete a Solution without first retracting it from all the deployed URLs. Be careful though, because if you use the `override` parameter, you will be unable to retract those Solutions later.

Deployment of Solutions

Now that the Solution has been installed into the SharePoint infrastructure, you're ready for the next bit—deploying the solution to sites and servers within the SharePoint infrastructure.

Unlike the `Addsolution` and `Deletesolution` operations, the `Deploysolution` and `Retractsolution` operations are a little more complex.

If you look at the parameters available for these two operations, it can be a bit daunting. You have to remember that the vast majority of them are optional and are simply there to give you some flexibility.

One of the key decisions you will have to make about deploying a Solution has to do with the scope in which you want to make it available. If you need the Solution available to all the web applications (*virtual servers* in STSADM), then you will want to use the `-allcontenturls` parameter, rather than specifying a specific web application, which requires the use of the `-url` parameter. An additional component that provides a great deal of flexibility for the administrator is the `-time` parameter. As you might guess, it allows you to run the STSADM command at your leisure, but the actual deployment will be scheduled to occur at the time you specify, using the built-in scheduling capabilities of WSS.

Anyway, a common use of the `Deploysolution` operation for the Solution you added earlier might look like this:

```
STSADM -o Deploysolution -name sharepointlearningkit.wsp -url
    http://sp1 -immediate -allowgacdeployment
```

In this example, you don't use every parameter that you could, but you have done enough to specify which Solution (`-name sharepointlearningkit.wsp`), which virtual server (`-url http://sp1`) and when (`-immediate`), and that it should be added to the global assembly cache (`-allowgacdeployment`).

The results of this command should look something like what appears in Figure 13.12.

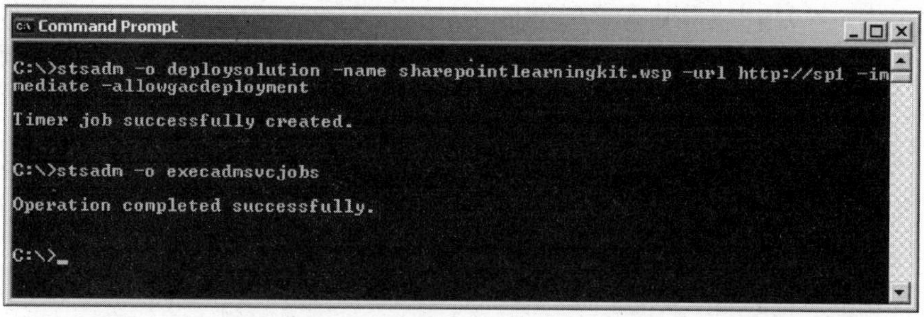

FIGURE 13.12
Deploying a
Solution

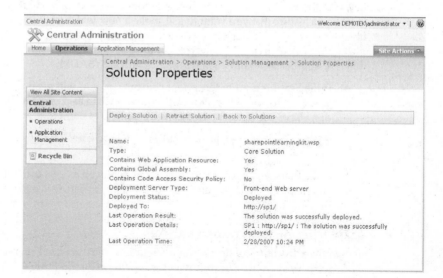

You can see the results of the deployment in the Central Administration tool in Figure 13.13.

At some point in time, however, you may want to leave the Solution available in the infrastructure, but stop it from being used in a particular web application. This is where the `Retractsolution` operation comes into use.

FIGURE 13.13
The same Solution
displayed in the
Central
Administration site

You have probably noticed that the parameters for this Solution are very similar to the ones available for the `Deploysolution` parameter. As a result, the use of this operation would look like this:

```
STSADM -o Retractsolution -name "Sharepoint Learning Kit" -url
    http://sp1 -immediate
```

DEACTIVATE FEATURES

An important thing to remember about using this operation is that any activated Features that were part of the Solution need to be deactivated before you can retract the deployment.

Upgrading Solutions

If the Solution provider notifies you that they have made a few changes that need to be deployed, don't worry. If they've done their job properly, they should be able to provide you with a Solution upgrade file. If you have this, the only command you will need is this:

```
STSADM -o Upgradesolution -name <solution name> -filename <path to the
    upgrade file>
```

You will want to note that this operation has mostly the same parameters as `Deploysolution`, specifically regarding the time aspects and whether or not to allow global assembly cache access and code access security (CAS) profiles.

Adding Features

As we discussed earlier, Features are a new aspect of WSS that allows developers to be a little more granular when managing and creating additional functionality for SharePoint sites. In other words, they don't have to create an entire new site definition just to add a single type of functionality. Now developers can create a Feature. However, it's important to remember that Features can be packaged as part of Solutions as well as being free-standing components. If you have a feature that you want to use, make a new folder for it in the FEATURES folder of the 12 hive (where the BIN folder is for STSADM) and copy it there.

Because Features can either be freestanding or packaged as part of a Solution, there are a few different approaches to how you manage them via STSADM.

- If the Feature is an independent component, you will need to use the following command to get it into your SharePoint structure (you can also use -filename instead of -name, if you don't have a folder containing the feature file to point to):

```
STSADM -o Installfeature -name <folder where the feature files are
    located>
```

- If the Feature you want to manage was deployed as part of a Solution, you may not need to run that command. Regardless, now that your Feature is installed into the infrastructure, it needs to be activated.

Activating/Deactivating Features

In both the activation and deactivation operations (`Activatefeature` and `Deactivativefeature`, respectively), you will need to indicate where/which Feature you are running the operation against. One way to find out some of the information you might need to activate these features is by running the following command:

```
STSADM -o Scanforfeatures [-solutionid <solutionid>]
```

If used without the optional parameter, it will return all of the Features that are available for management. If you want to specify the Features from a specific Solution, use the -solutionid parameter. You won't find the solution ID in the Central Administration tool. You will need to use the Enumsolutions operation to get that information.

Once you know how to identify the Feature you're interested in, you can activate that Feature for all URLs or for a given URL within your SharePoint site by using the following command:

```
STSADM -o Activatefeature -filename <relative path to Feature.xml> OR
    -name <feature folder> OR -id <feature Id> [-url <url>]
```

THE SAME PARAMETERS

The parameters to deactivate a Feature are identical to those used to activate a Feature. In practical terms, this means that you can activate a Feature for an entire site collection (by not specifying a specific URL) but still deactivate it for those sites within the web application that do not require that Feature. (Remember that you can also activate Features for particular sites via the Site Administration tools, as mentioned in Chapter 8.)

RETRACT, DELETE, DEPLOY, OH MY!

By now your head is probably spinning just a bit from all this talk about Features, Solutions, and everything else. That's perfectly normal. A bit of a summary of the relation between these two items and the order in which you need to deal with them is probably in order.

There are three key points to remember here:

◆ *Solutions* are a collection of many related components (with the goal of adding some kind of capability to your SharePoint installation) and can include Features, along with site definitions and many other things. When you install a Solution those components are also installed.

◆ *Features* can be part of Solutions or can be entities that are installed and managed unto themselves.

◆ For both Solutions and Features, there is a specific order of activities for their installation and removal. Those orders (and the basic command-line operation that accompanies each step) are listed here.

INSTALL A SOLUTION THAT INCLUDES A FEATURE

1. Install the Solution:

   ```
   Stsadm -o Addsolution
   ```

2. Deploy the Solution to a particular web application:

   ```
   Stsadm -o Deploysolution
   ```

3. Activate a Feature that is part of the Solution:

   `Stsadm -o Activatefeature`

INSTALL AN INDIVIDUAL FEATURE

1. Install the Feature:

   `Stsadm -o Installfeature`

2. Activate the Feature:

   `Stsadm -o Activatefeature`

REMOVE AN INDIVIDUAL FEATURE

1. Deactivate the Feature:

   `Stsadm -o Deactivatefeature`

2. Remove the Feature:

   `Stsadm -o Uninstallfeature`

REMOVE A SOLUTION THAT CONTAINS A FEATURE

1. Deactivate the Feature:

   `Stsadm -o Deactivatefeature`

2. Retract the Solution:

   `Stsadm -o Retractsolution`

3. Delete the Solution:

   `Stsadm -o Deletesolution`

What happens if you don't get the order quite right or forget to retract before deleting? It depends.

If you happened to use the `-override` parameter on your deletion operation, the Solution or Feature will uninstall, and you will be unable to deploy it to any other web applications. In fact, you will be unable to manage it in any way because you will not have a reference to it in the WSS infrastructure.

Web Application Management

If you are managing a small WSS implementation, you may find that you have little need to manage your web applications using STSADM. There aren't any significant differences between what can be achieved with each respective tool either the GUI or command line.

However, if you are lucky enough to be able to manage WSS configured as part of a web farm, the STSADM method may allow you to more quickly and consistently reproduce tasks, specifically in the area of creating/extending your virtual servers (web applications). Also keep in mind that you can provision Alternate Access Mappings or Zones using STSADM as well. Table 13.5 shows a list of operations you can use.

TABLE 13.5: Web Application Operations Reference

OPERATIONS	PARAMETERS

Addalternatedomain	`-url <protocol://existing.WebApplication.URLdomain>`
	`-incomingurl <protocol://incoming.url.domain>`
	`-urlzone<default, extranet, internet, intranet, custom>`
	`-resourcename <non-web application resource name>`

Addzoneurl	`-url <protocol://existing.WebApplication.URLdomain>`
	`-urlzone <default, extranet, internet, intranet, custom>`
	`-zonemappedurl <protocol://outgoing.url.domain>`
	`-resourcename <non-web application resource name>`

Createadminvs	`[-admapidname <app pool name>]`
	`[-admapidtype <configurableid|NetworkService>]`
	`[-admapidlogin <Domain\name>]`
	`[-admapidpwd <app pool password>]`

Deletealternate domain	`-url <ignored>` `-incomingurl <protocol://incoming.url.domain>`
Deleteadminvs	

Deletezoneurl	`-url <protocol://existing.WebApplication.URLdomain>`
	`-urlzone <default, extranet, internet, intranet, custom>`
	`-resourcename <non-web application resource name>`

Enumalternate domains	`-url <protocol://existing.WebApplication.URLdomain>` `-resourcename <non-web application resource name>`
Enumsubwebs	`-url <Starting URL>`
Enumzoneurls	`[-url <web.application url>]` `-resourcename <non-web application resource name>]`

Extendvs	`-url <url>`
	`-ownerlogin <domain\name>`
	`-owneremail <owner@email.name>`
	`[-exclusivelyusentlm]`
	`[-ownername <display name>]`
	`[-databaseuser <database user>]`
	`[-databaseserver <database server>]`
	`[-databasename <database name>]`
	`[-lcid <language id>]`
	`[-sitetemplate <site template>]`
	`[-donotcreatesite}`
	`[-description <iis web site name>]`
	`[-sethostheader]`
	`[-apidname <app pool name>]`
	`[-apidtype <configurableid|NetworkService>]`
	`[-apidlogin <Domain\name>]`
	`[-apidpwd <app pool password>]`
	`[-allowanonymous}`

(Continued)

TABLE 13.5: Web Application Operations Reference (*Continued*)

OPERATIONS	PARAMETERS

Extendvsinwebfarm	`-url <url>`
	`-vsname <web application name>`
	`[-exclusivelyusentlm]`
	`[-apidname <app pool name>]`
	`[-apidtype <configurableid|NetworkService>]`
	`[-apidlogin <Domain\name>]`
	`[-apidpwd <app pool password>]`
	`[-allowanonymous`

Getproperty	`-propertyname <name of property>` `[-url <url of virtual server>]`
Geturlzone	`-url <protocol://incoming.url.domain>`

Setproperty	`-propertyname <name of property>`
	`-propertyvalue <value>`
	`[-url <url of virtual server>]`

Unextendvs	`-url <url>`
	`[-deletecontent]`
	`[-deleteiissites]`

Upgradetargetwebapplication	`-url <URL to upgrade>`
	`-relocationurl <new URL for non-upgraded content>`
	`-apidname <new app pool name>`
	`[-apidtype <configurableid/NetworkService>]`
	`[-apidlogin <DOMAIN\name>]`
	`[-apidpwd <app pool password>]`
	`[-exclusivelyusentlm]`

Creating a Web Application

When you create a web application in the Central Administration site, you are given a few options, mainly revolving around security and databases. All of these options can be handled using STSADM, but STSADM also gives you the ability to create your initial site collection, choose which template you'd like, and set the owner information. These things can be done via the GUI, but it does take extra steps.

Although it is not obvious from the syntax, you can create all the important components (such as the IIS Web Site or the content database) for your new web application in advance or have them created on the fly for you. In either case, you have to use the correct parameters for the Extendvs operation. If you specify a particular component in the right parameter, WSS will look for it. If it's not there—and you have the appropriate permissions—WSS will create the component if possible.

The one thing that STSADM does not give you the option to do is to restart IIS. You will need to use `IISReset/noforce` for this.

If you want to create a new IIS Web Site that listens on port 49000, add SharePoint files to it, have the site collection be created based on the Dem0tek Meeting template, and create a new database called WSS_WebApp4, you can use the following command:

```
STSADM -o Extendvs -url http://sp1:49000 -ownerlogin
   dem0tek\Administrator -owneremail administrator@dem0tek.lcl
   -exclusivelyusentlm -databaseserver sp1\Microsoft##SSEE
   -databasename WSS_WebApp4 -sitetemplate dem0mtg.stp
```

Given all that this command is doing—creating an IIS Web Site, creating a new content database, extending the IIS Web Site (adding SharePoint components to the Web Site), and creating the initial site collection—you should expect it to take a little while (a few minutes) to return any results in your command window. Go out, take a walk, and get some fresh air.

If you had created the IIS Web Site and database in advance, the command would be exactly the same, but you would expect the command to execute a bit more quickly.

Eventually, you would expect to get results similar to what appears in Figure 13.14.

FIGURE 13.14 The results of the **`Extendvs`** operation

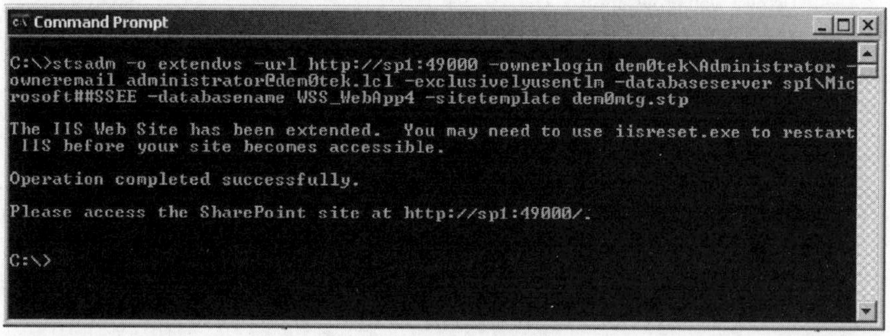

GIVE ALL THE INFO

There is no secret way to get the information you need to fill in the parameters (things such as the database server name or Application Pool details). It's up to you to make sure you provide STSADM with all the information it needs to run properly.

You can verify that the new site was created simply by looking in IIS (see Figure 13.15) or browsing to the new site itself (see Figure 13.16).

FIGURE 13.15
Using IIS to verify that the new site was created

FIGURE 13.16
Using a web browser to verify that the new site was created

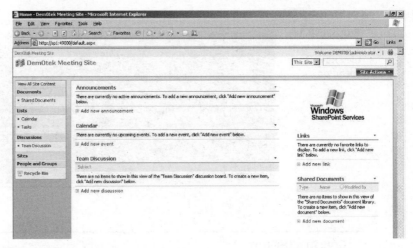

EXTENDING IN THE WEB FARM CONFIGURATION

This is the equivalent to the Central Administration, Extend a web application option in the GUI. If you need to extend a current web application to either a new IIS site in a web frontend server or to a different IIS Web Site on the same server, use the Extendvsinwebfarm operation. It has a slightly simpler syntax, mainly because most of the details of the web application have already been established. In this scenario, you might be able to get by as simply as this:

```
STSADM -o Extendvsinwebfarm -url <url of Web Front End> -vsname
    <web application name>
```

The trick to watch out for here is to make sure you get the URL of the IIS Web Site correct of the web application for the vsname, and if the name (not the URL) of the web application contains spaces, you will need to put the web application name in quotes. Don't forget to do an IISreset to complete the process.

Creating New Administration Websites

If you need multiple administration websites—perhaps to better deal with firewall issues, load balancing, or network utilization—STSADM gives you the tools to extend the Central Administration website to additional IIS sites. The syntax is very simple. If you are happy with the default Application Pool settings, then all you will need to run is

```
STSADM -o Createadminvs
```

It's important to note that this is not something you can do via the Central Administration tool itself.

Removing Web Applications

As you might expect, removing web applications is a bit simpler than adding them. However, you need to remember—and this is very important—that you, as the administrator, need to ensure that the web application is clean before you remove it. Once you remove the web application, its content is no longer available.

If you want to remove a test web application, all of its content, and its IIS site (my example is using http://sp1:39000), then use the following command:

```
STSADM -o unextendvs -url http://sp1:39000 -deletecontent
    -deleteiissites
```

Depending on the amount of content within your site, this may take a few minutes. If all goes well, you will get a single line reading "Operation completed successfully."

Listing Your Web Applications

You may have noticed that there is no simple way in STSADM to get a list of the web applications that are present. You might think that the ENUMSITES operation that was discussed earlier would do the trick–but you would be wrong. That would be too obvious.

However, Enumzoneurls will do the trick. Although this isn't necessarily intended to be the way to list your web applications (it's designed to say what zone—default, Intranet, etc.—each URL you are using is categorized as), it works very well for a simple listing of the web applications that are present. Its usage and results for this example are shown in Figure 13.17.

You'll notice that the output of this is properly formed XML. This can be very handy if you want to pipe the results into a text file for later manipulation or review.

In Figure 13.17, you may have noticed that the last web application has several URLs listed. This is the result of setting alternative access URLs for the web application. If you want the listings for a single web application, then use the -url parameter with the default URL of the web application.

If you want a complete list of all the subwebs that are in a web application, you can use the Enumsubwebs operation, using the URL you got from Enumzoneurls. These results are also properly formed XML. The syntax for Enumsubwebs is very simple.

```
STSADM -o Enumsubwebs -url <starting URL>
```

FIGURE 13.17
Displaying the list of web applications

Unfortunately, there is no obvious way to take your list of sites and pipe it through to the Enumsubwebs operation. It is possible to do this using VBScript and the WSS object model, but it would not be a simple operation.

Ongoing Management and Maintenance

Web applications have a great many settings, spread across many different pages in the Central Administration tool. Much like the GUI, the operations involved in adjusting the properties of a web application are spread out quite a bit in STSADM, too. This chapter doesn't cover in detail every single operation that can be done with STSADM. We are primarily concerned with two operations that cover a lot of ground, Setproperty and Getproperty.

Running STSADM -help Setproperty or STSADM -help Getproperty reveals quite a list. If you review that list created with help, you'll find that quite a few of the parameters are reasonably self-explanatory (such as max-file-upload-size), others you might find less so. This chapter is not going to go over every single property, but it will hit the settings that are unique to the SETPROPERTY operation.

A closer look at the list reveals that the properties have been split into two sections: the SharePoint Cluster Properties section and the SharePoint Virtual Server Properties section. The first section deals with global, or farm properties, and those are discussed in the "Farm Management" section. The second section, however, is of more interest to this chapter.

SERVER VERSUS FARM

A closer look at the list of properties that can be adjusted using Setproperty reveals that there are quite a few properties that be adjusted at either the farm ("cluster") or the web application level. You will need to be clear what scope you want to change when you run STSADM -o Setproperty. If you need the property to only affect a single web application, then you must specify the appropriate website by using the -url parameter. If you choose to not use the -url property, the change may affect all servers in the web farm.

If you aren't sure exactly which property needs to be adjusted, use the Getproperty operation. This operation is used to output what the setting is for a specified property. The properties that can be viewed are exactly the same as those that can be modified with Setproperty.

Forty-one virtual server properties can be accessed by this operation. Many of them reflect options in the Application Management pages of the Central Administration site, and quite a few in the Operations Management section. You won't find a few of them in the Central Administration site at all. We're going to start with the properties you can't set anywhere else.

TIMED JOBS

The `Setproperty` operation has nine virtual server properties that can be used to schedule the time that certain WSS internal jobs are to be executed. Many of these jobs have a default schedule of "Between 10 P.M. and 6 A.M. every day." If that works for you, that's great. You won't need to touch these properties. However, if that does not work for you, you will need to adjust these settings here, as the Central Administration site allows you to see and delete the timed jobs that are scheduled, but it doesn't give you a centralized tool to adjust the times themselves.

The syntax for using these timed job properties is as follows:

```
Stsadm -o Setproperty -url <web app url> -propertyname job-<jobname>
    -propertyvalue
```

An important thing to remember is that all of the timed job properties have names that are hyphenated, which sometimes makes it a bit confusing with all those hyphens flying around.

One way to shorten and simplify the `Setproperty` and `Getproperty` operations is to substitute `-pn` and `-pv` for `-propertyname` and `-propertyvalue`.

If you want to set the time to run your deleted sites cleanup to 11:00 P.M. for the root web application on server SP1, the syntax would look like this:

```
STSADM -o Setproperty -url http://sp1 -pn job-dead-site-delete
    -pv "daily at 23:00:00"
```

It's important to note that the actual time that is set is expressed as a text string, the reference to the time is listed using the 24-hour clock, and it can be set down to the second.

It is also possible to schedule some of these tasks to occur during a block of time. The overall syntax of the command doesn't change, but you will need to express the property value a little bit differently. If you are going to configure SP1 to do its disk-quota warning notifications between the hours of 8 P.M. and midnight every day, use this syntax:

```
STSADM -o Setproperty -url http://sp1 -propertyname job-diskquota-
    warning -propertyvalue "Daily between 20:00:00 and 00:00:00"
```

In either case, the resulting screen output is the benign Operation Completed Successfully message.

SETTING THE TIME

The Timer Job properties are very useful and allow you a great deal of control, but you need to make sure that you properly express the times (otherwise known as a schedule or recurrence) you desire in a textual way. Here are some samples to help you get the time right.

◆ **Every day at the same time** "Daily at 20:00:00"

◆ **Every day within a block of time** "Daily between 20:00:00 and 00:00:00"

◆ **Every Monday at the same time** "Weekly at Mon 23:00:00"

◆   **Every Tuesday night, overnight** "Weekly between Tue 22:00:00 and Wed 6:00:00"

◆   **Every 15 minutes** "Every 15 minutes between 0 and 59"

If you're not exactly sure if you've got the schedule you want expressed properly, don't worry. If the Timer Service doesn't like what you've written, it will reject the command with the error "The specified schedule recurrence string is invalid: `<string>`". You'll then have the chance to figure out what the error was and try again.

Here's the list of all the virtual server–based timer jobs that can be managed with the `Setproperty` operation:

```
job-change-log-expiration    job-dead-site-delete
job-immediate-alerts         job-recycle-bin-cleanup
job-diskquota-warning        job-usage-analysis
job-workflow                 job-workflow-autoclean
job-workflow-failover
```

Most of these are pretty self-explanatory, but you may not be as familiar with the workflow properties. The job-workflow properties are referring to any scheduled activities relating to workflows that are being run in your SharePoint sites. By default, workflow activities (such as email the department head when a new form is submitted) are scheduled to run every 5 minutes, but this is configurable with the "job-workflow" property listed.

ADJUSTING THE PEOPLE PICKER

You know, when I think about the people picker properties, all I can think about is "Peter Piper picked a peck of pickled people, A peck of pickled people is what Peter Piper picked . . . " and "One-eyed, one-horned flying purple People Pickers . . . "

There, now you've got that running through your head too. My work here is done.

As interesting as it would be if the People Picker were one-eyed, one-horned, flying, and purple, the reality is a little more boring, although probably a lot more useful.

The People Picker is the tool you use to select users when setting permissions in SharePoint's various GUI management tools. If you have a fairly simple Active Directory (AD) infrastructure (such as a single-domain forest) or a fully trusted AD enterprise, you may not need to worry about adjusting the People Picker. However, if either of those scenarios does *not* describe your WSS implementation, you may want to continue reading.

As stated earlier, if you have a fully trusted AD infrastructure, the People Picker will allow you to choose users and groups from any domain in your infrastructure. However, if you do not, you will need to use the People Picker properties to configure your WSS web application to connect properly.

For example, if your business wants to allow their strategic partner, Findog Enterprises (`Findog.lcl`), access to various parts of their WSS sites that are running on SP1, the following command would give administrators the ability to select users from the Findog forest (this is, of course, assuming that all other technical issues such as network connectivity etc. have already been dealt with).

```
STSADM -o Setproperty -url http://sp1 -propertyname peoplepicker-
    searchadforests -propertyvalue "forest:Findog.lcl;
    domain: Findog.lcl", PartnerLogin, Pa$$w0rd
```

It's important to note that in the `propertyvalue`, the forest and the domain had to be listed separately. You may also want to note that you need to get the username and password (`Partner-Login` and `Pa$$w0rd`, respectively) for connection from the Findog Enterprises administrators.

As you have probably surmised, given the separate listings for the target domain and forest, you can have different connection settings for different domains within the same forest.

Another set of properties (`peoplepicker-activedirectorysearchtimeout` and `peoplepicker-searchadcustomquery`) may come in handy for many administrators. The `peoplepicker-activedirectorysearchtimeout` property is pretty self-explanatory and sets the time in seconds before it is considered a timeout. You may need to adjust this if there are slow links involved in querying your AD infrastructure. The default value is 30 seconds.

However, the `peoplepicker-searchadcustomquery` property allows you to customize the query sent to the AD servers. Whatever AD attributes you set in the `peoplepicker-searchadcustomquery` will be appended to the query that is generated by the GUI. This would allow you to query for users in a specific OU or with a particular property. You will need to be very careful with this one, as a mistyped or misspelled attribute may result in the People Picker not being able to see any accounts. You will need to find out the correct attribute name(s) to successfully use this command.

To have the People Picker for SP1:49000 only choose users from New Zealand, the syntax would look like this:

```
STSADM -o Setproperty -url http://sp1:49000 -propertyname
    peoplepicker-searchadcustomquery -propertyvalue "(c={New Zealand})"
```

You will need to find out the correct name of the value you want to query on (in this case, the country attribute is called c within AD).

MORE INFORMATION ON PEOPLE PICKER

If you'd like more detailed information regarding the People Picker properties, a good place to start would be:

```
http://blogs.msdn.com/joelo/archive/2007/01/18/multi-forest-cross-
    forest-people-picker-peoplepicker-searchadcustomquery.aspx.
```

!New Content Icon

One somewhat unexpected property that can be set is the length of time that the !New graphic appears next to new content. The default time is two days, but this is the property to adjust if you need to change that. The only real value needed is the number of days that things should be listed as "!New." To shorten the notice to one day for SP1, (you can also disable it entirely by specifying zero days) use the following syntax:

```
STSADM -o setproperty -url http://sp1 -propertyname days-to-show-
    new-icon -propertyvalue 1.
```

Database Management

The database management activities that are available within WSS beyond the initial creation of a database, whether at install or web application creation time, are focused primarily around backup/restore issues of sites. For anything above and beyond that, you are looking at management using SQL tools.

The backup and restore processes are covered extensively in Chapter 12, "Maintenance and Monitoring," so they won't be covered here. Our focus will be purely on understanding the options within STSADM, not necessarily when to use it.

Table 13.6 shows a list of database management operations.

TABLE 13.6:　　　Database Management Operations Reference

OPERATION	PARAMETERS
Addcontentdb	-url \<web application url> -databasename \<database name> [-databaseserver \<database server name>] [-databaseuser \<Domain\User>] [-databasepassword \<databaseuser password>] [-sitewarning \<site warning count>] [-sitemax \<max number of site collections>]
Backup **(site collection)**	-url \<url> -filename \<filename> [-overwrite]
Backup **(catastrophic)**	-directory \<UNC path> -backupmethod \<full|differential> [-item \<created path from tree>] [-percentage \<integer between 1 and 100>] [-backupthreads \<integer between 1 and 10>] [-showtree] [-quiet]
Backuphistory	-directory \<UNC path> [-backup] [-restore]
Databaserepair	-url \<url> -databasename \<database name> [-deletecorruption]
Deleteconfigdb	
Deletecontentdb	-url \<url> -databasename \<database name> [-databaseserver \<database server name>]
Enumcontentdbs	-url \<url>
Export	-url \<url to be exported> -filename \<export file name> [-includeusersecurity]

OPERATION	PARAMETERS

	`[-haltonwarning]`
	`[-haltonfatalerror]`
	`[-nologfile]`
	`[-versions <1-4>]`
	`[-cabsize <1-1024> (default is 25)]`
	`[-nofilecompression]`
	`[-quiet]`

Import	`-url <URL to import to>`
	`-filename <import file name>`
	`[-includeusersecurity]`
	`[-haltonwarning]`
	`[-haltonfatalerror]`
	`[-nologfile]`
	`[-update versions <1-3>]`
	`[-nofilecompression]`
	`[-quiet]`

Restore
(Site collection)
	`-url <url>`
	`-filename <filename>`
	`[-hostheaderwebapplicationurl <url>]`
	`[-overwrite]`

Restore
(catastrophic)
	`-directory <UNC path>`
	`-restoremethod <overwrite|new>`
	`[-backupid <id from backuphistory>]`
	`[-item <created path from tree>]`
	`[-percentage <1 to 100>]`
	`[-showtree]`
	`[-suppressprompt]`
	`[-username <username>]`
	`[-password <password>]`
	`[-newdatabaseserver <new database server name>]`
	`[-quiet]`

Setconfigdb	`[-connect]`
	`-databaseserver <database server>`
	`[-databaseuser <database user>]`
	`[-databasepassword <database user password>]`
	`[-databasename <database name>]`
	`[-exclusivelyusentlm]`
	`[-farmuser]`
	`[-farmpassword]`
	`[-adcreation]`
	`[-addomain <Active Directory domain>]`
	`[-adou <Active Directory OU>]`

Connecting and Disconnecting Databases

WSS differentiates between the content databases and the configuration database. As a result, there are two sets of commands for dealing with the connection and disconnection of databases, one for each type.

To connect a content database to a web application, Addcontentdb is the operation for you.

```
STSADM -o addcontentdb -url <web application url> -databasename
    <database name>
```

This is the bare minimum for this command. It is working under the following assumptions:

◆ The command is being run on the database server

◆ The default credentials (running as local system) are sufficient

If either of those assumptions is not true, you may need to use some of the optional parameters listed to specify different credentials and/or the name of the database server.

Additionally, you can limit the number of site collections that can be stored within a database, as well as when WSS should generate a warning about the number of site collections. That warning will be in the application event log. The warning count should probably be slightly smaller than the maximum.

To create a configuration database from the command line, use the Setconfigdb operation. It has a similar syntax to Addcontendb, but with additional parameters that relate to the type of authentication mechanism for the WSS farm, farm security parameters, and parameters relating to Account Creation mode.

The two deletion operations, Deleteconfigdb and Deletecontentdb, are used to disconnect a web application or the configuration site from its respective databases. There are no parameters required to disconnect the configuration database from the server (considered *unprovisioning*) and deleting it, but you do need to provide the relevant web application URL and content database name, and usually the database server name to delete a content database. Also keep in mind that configuration database deletion is best done using the psconfig command.

BACKUP/RESTORE

Both the Backup and Restore operations have a bit of a split personality. They can be focused on a single site collection, or what WSS refers to as a "catastrophic"—where you can deal with the anything from the entire farm on down to a single web application. In the GUI backup mechanisms, this is handled by using *check boxes*. In STSADM, this is handled by your choice of parameters.

Site Collection Backup and Restore

To backup and restore a site collection (http://sp1/sites/dem0tekmtg), the syntax is very straightforward.

To backup, use:

```
STSADM -o Backup -url http://sp1/sites/dem0tekmtg -filename
    c:\dem0tekmtg -overwrite
```

To restore, use:

```
STSADM -o Restore -url http://sp1/sites/dem0tekmtg -filename
    c:\dem0tekmtg -overwrite
```

The only difference between the syntax is that `Restore` has an additional optional parameter, `-hostheaderwebapplicationurl`, which can be specified if the web application IIS Web Site references a host header URL.

Catastrophic Backup

The syntax for catastrophic backup and restore is more complex, as you might expect, given the greater scale of the operation.

To perform a catastrophic backup, use:

```
STSADM -o backup -directory \\sp1\backup -backupmethod full
```

If you need to backup only a particular web application, you can add specify which web application by using the `-item` parameter. However, to use this, you will need to know how to reference the web application. You can get the proper reference by using the `-showtree` parameter first.

Figure 13.18 shows that the `-showtree` parameter was used in the first command to get the proper path, which was then used in the second command to do a full backup of only the default web application. You'll want to note that because of the spaces and hyphen (-) in the path name, the entire path had to be enclosed in quotation marks.

FIGURE 13.18

Backing up a single web application

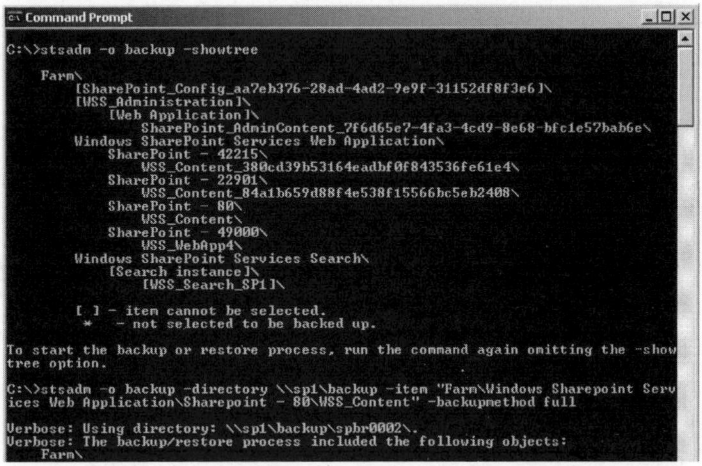

The output from the `backup` command goes on for several screens. At the end of the output, you'll find a listing of the entire farm, with all components except the web applications marked with an asterisk, which signifies that they were not backed up.

If you run a second backup of the same item, you can choose to use the `-backupmethod differential` parameter instead.

The other parameters for backup `-backupthreads` allow you to control the amount of system resources the backup process will consume. The default number of backup threads is 1, and increasing this should speed up the backup process, but it will increase the workload on the server. The `-percentage` parameter dictates how often the backup process will generate a progress report. The default is 5; making it less frequent (i.e., setting the number higher) will improve the performance of the backup nominally.

Catastrophic Restore

A review of the parameters for the catastrophic RESTORE operation will show that the parameters are very similar, although not identical to the parameters for the Backup operation.

The base syntax is what you would expect:

```
STSADM -o Restore -directory \\sp1\backup -restoremethod overwrite
```

This command takes the most recent backup found in the directory and restores it over the top of the current content of whatever content database is in the backup. There is a confirmation prompt, which can be suppressed with the -suppressprompt parameter. If you are unable to restore over the top, you may want to use "new" as the restore method, instead of "overwrite."

If you need to restore it to a different SQL server, you may need to use the optional parameters that specify the new database server, as well as providing appropriate credentials.

```
STSADM -o Restore -directory \\sp1\backup -restoremethod new
    -newdatabaseserver <server name> -user <domain\user> -password
    <password>
```

You may also need to use the -user and -password parameters any time you need to provide credentials other than what you are logged on with to do the restore.

If you need to restore a different backup in the same location, you will need to add the -backupid parameter and give it the ID of the backup you need to use. You will need to use the BACKUPHISTORY operation to get this list of backup ID (see Figure 13.19).

```
STSADM -o Backuphistory -directory \\sp1\backup
```

The output doesn't fit in a command prompt particularly well, so you may want to pipe this to a text file (append command with >textfilename.txt) for easier viewing, as well as the ability to copy and paste the ID.

FIGURE 13.19
Retrieving and displaying the backup history

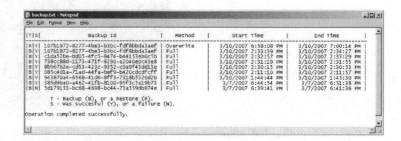

Once you have the backup ID you need, you can then run a restore command to use that particular backup.

```
STSADM -o Restore -directory \\sp1\backup -restoremethod overwrite
    -backupid "385d9ba0-a462-41fb-8100-95f3c5a19b73" -suppressprompt
```

IMPORT/EXPORT

The Backup and Restore operations only allow you to move data around with limited granularity and only down to the site collection level. If you want to move data around down to the individual subweb or library level, you will want to look at your choices using `Import` and `Export`. With these operations, you specify the part of your site you want to use with a URL and the file from where or to where you want to move the data. These operations have almost identical parameters, so if you are comfortable with one, you should be comfortable with the other.

The following command will export a blog site to a CAB file on the root of the E: drive.

```
STSADM -o Export -url http://sp1/sites/newsite3/blog -filename e:\blog
```

That code created a file called `e:\blog.cmp` and a log file called `e:\blog.export.log` on the root of E:.

The optional parameters for `Import` and `Export` control the basic behavior of the operation, such as whether to produce a log file, what to do if errors are encountered, and whether or not security settings should be exported.

The one parameter that may not be quite as obvious is the `-versions` parameter (when Importing it is -updateversions instead, with 3 options: Add, Overwrite, and Ignore). This parameter controls how version-controlled data (such as files in document libraries) should be handled. The options are as follows:

1. Last major version

2. The current version

3. Last major and last minor version

4. All versions

With export, the selected versions are applicable, and with import the version specified will be updated (should there be any conflicts). In smaller sites, you may not need to adjust these parameters at all, but be aware of their presence, especially if you are dealing with large amounts of data.

Search Management

The ability to search for content within your SharePoint installation is one of the most important tools for the end users who will be accessing the sites and libraries on a daily basis.

Microsoft has made some pretty drastic changes to the search service in WSS 3.0. However, most of the changes are kind of "under the hood," so they are not obvious. One of the big changes is that WSS no longer uses the SQL Search Engine. Microsoft is making a big push to consolidate the search engines, and one of the results of that is that the Windows Desktop Search, Live Search, and SharePoint Search engines are now driven by the same technologies. This means content providers only have to develop a single protocol handler (the code that lets the search service attach to a particular type of storage, such as Exchange Public Folders) and iFilter (the code that tells the search service how to "crack open" the files themselves (for example, the iFilter for Adobe Acrobat files).

In WSS, Microsoft hides most of this stuff away, and administrators are given very little ability to adjust or control the search component of WSS. The Central Administration site allows you to manage the following things:

◆ The Service Account, which defaults to "Local Service" for a Basic install, otherwise should be a domain account.

◆ The Content Access Account (i.e., the index account, with credentials used to connect to data sources), also defaults to "Local Service" for Basic, and otherwise should be a domain account.

◆ The Search Database, which you can't move but can change the authentication method (defaults to Windows Authentication).

◆ The Indexing Schedule, which defaults to every 5 minutes.

Now that you're thouroughly underwhelmed by the amount of control you've been granted in Central Administration it's nice to know that you have a little more control when you use STSADM.

In STSADM, you have the ability to manually trigger full crawls, add content databases (rather than clicking through the GUI), and change the location of the index files and search database, among other things.

Table 13.7 lists the search management operations.

TABLE 13.7:   Search Management Operations Reference

OPERATION	PARAMETERS

Spsearch	`[-action <action to perform>]`
	`[-f <suppress prompts>]`
	`[-farmperformancelevel`
	`  <Reduced|PartlyReduced|Maximum>]`
	`[-farmserviceaccount <DOMAIN\name>`
	`  <service credentials>]`
	`[-farmservicepassword <password>]`
	`[-farmcontentaccessaccount <DOMAIN\name>]`
	`[-farmcontentaccesspassword <password>]`
	`[-indexlocation <new index location>]`
	`[-databaseserver <server\instance>]`
	`[-databasename <database name>]`
	`[-sqlauthlogin <SQL authenticated database`
	`  user>]`
	`[-sqlauthpassword <password>]`

Spsearchdiacriticsensitive	`[-setstatus <True|False>]`
	`[-noreset]`
	`[-force]`

Searching Content in More Than One Language

If documents in your SharePoint sites contain multiple languages, you may need to configure the SharePoint Search Service to pay attention to the letters with *diacritics*, the extra marks on top. Fluent speakers of languages who use diacritics in their alphabets will tell you that the difference between these letters is important. If you want your searches to reflect this, then you will need to tell your search server to do so.

```
STSADM -o Spsearchdiacriticsensitive -setstatus True
```

The results of that command may ask if you if you want to reset the index. Be very careful, because resetting the index involves wiping all data from the index and rebuilding it. If you say "Yes," your users will be unable to search for content until the index finishes its rebuild. If this is not something you want to have happen at this time, make sure you say "No," or add the optional

-noreset parameter. On the other hand, if you want to force the reset without being asked, use the -force parameter.

If you run STSADM -o Spsearchdiacriticsensitive without any of the optional parameters, it will return what your status is on the search server, which will be either "On" or "Off."

Managing the Search Service

All of the management settings you can control with the Central Administration site can also be controlled using STSADM. A quick perusal of the parameters for the SPSEARCH operation will reveal that most of those have a parameter (such as, -farmserviceaccount and -farmcontentaccessacount) of their own.

However, there is one specific property (-farmperformancelevel) that does not map to a GUI setting. The farm performance level can be set to one of three options: Reduced, Partly Reduced, or Maximum. Adjusting this property adjusts the amount of stress that indexing will put on the WSS content database while it indexes. If you find that the end-user experience suffers while the content is being indexed, then one option would be to adjust this property downward, which will increase the time it takes to index but not impact the database server's resources so harshly. Of course another option includes changing the indexing schedule in the GUI to avoid indexing at peak use times.

However, if you choose to adjust the Search Service to "Partly Reduced," the syntax is very straightforward.

```
STSADM -o Spsearch -farmperformancelevel PartlyReduced
```

If you aren't having any issues with this particular scenario, don't adjust the property needlessly, because reducing the load on the database also increases the time it takes to index, and increases the chance that the index will become inaccurate.

Moving the Index

One of the "under the hood" changes that Microsoft made to the search service relates to how it stores the indexing results. The results are split in two. The actual content index is stored as a file on the machine running the search service. It's commonly located in c:\Program files\ common files\ Microsoft shared\web server extensions\data\ applications\ <GUID>. The properties of the files that have been indexed are stored in the SQL database, which is commonly called the "property database." If you need to move the index files, you will have to use STSADM. There is no provision in the GUI to do this. You can view the location of the search database in the GUI, but you can't view the index location in the GUI.

To view the index location, as well as the properties confirm the name and location of the search database, you can use the -action list parameter of Spsearch, as discussed in the next section.

If you want to move the index files themselves, say to a folder on a second hard disk (E:\index), you can use the following command:

```
STSADM -o -Spsearch -indexlocation e:\index
```

This will temporarily stop the search service, copy the index folder from its original location to the new location, and then restart the service. In Figure 13.20, the -action list parameter is used to verify the move.

FIGURE 13.20

Retrieving the search catalog configuration and then moving the index files

You can also verify the move by checking to see if the index files are in the new location. If you look in the location you specified in the command, you should find a folder with a 32-byte GUID for its name, and inside that the files and folders used for the index itself.

Action!

The two remaining parameters (-action and -f) are generally used together. The -action parameter needs to be followed by one of these actions listed in Table 13.8.

TABLE 13.8: The Action Parameters

ACTION	EXPLANATION
Fullcrawlstart	Triggers a full indexing run
Start	Enables searching
Attachcontentdatabase	Adds a WSS content database to the search corpus
Fullcrawlstop	Ends a full indexing run
Stop	Disables searching
Detachcontentdatabase	Removes a WSS content database from the search corpus
List	List the configuration of WSS search

You don't need a lot of imagination to figure out what the actions in the first column do. Fullcrawlstart triggers a full indexing run, outside of the scheduled time. Fullcrawlstop ends one. These two parameters could be very useful if you have a conservative indexing schedule and need to add new content outside of the schedule. These actions may prompt the administrator for confirmation. If you want to skip that step (say you're putting this in a batch file that will run on a schedule), then simply add the -f. The -f parameter is meant to suppress prompts and warnings.

Here is the syntax to trigger a new full content crawl:

```
STSADM -o Spsearch -action fullcrawlstart
```

The "stop" and "start" actions aren't quite what they seem on the surface—especially the stop action. Using the stop action will completely disable the Search Service and delete the indexes and database. Fortunately, you are prompted with a warning and it gives you the chance to cancel. Unfortunately, if you used the -f parameter, you aren't.

The attachcontentdatabase and detachcontentdatabase actions throw up a bit more of a challenge.

In WSS, all content databases for your web applications can be set for indexing during creation or through the GUI. There is no way to add content from outside your SharePoint installation. You aren't given any choice. However, in certain recovery scenarios, you may desire the capability to manually add the content sources for the index, at the command line, rather than having to click through the GUI.

STSADM allows you to do this.

```
STSADM -o Spsearch -action attachcontentdatabase -databaseserver
    <server\instance> -databasename <content database name>
```

If you are running this command against a machine that is using the built-in SSEE database, you will not need to use the -databaseserver parameter, as it will default to its own database location.

If you are unsure about what the database server or content database names are, remember that you can discover this information by looking it up in the GUI or simply by entering:

```
STSADM -o Enumcontentdbs -url <url of the web application in question>
```

This will return the name of the server and the name of the database, which can then be used in the attachcontentdatabase or detachcontentdatabase actions.

Perhaps the most useful option of all is the one that allows you to see how your search service is configured, as well as the list of all the content databases that are being indexed.

```
STSADM -o Spsearch -action list
```

This command returns data that looks like what is shown in Figure 13.21:

FIGURE 13.21
Retrieving the search service configuration

You will note that everything you can manage is listed here, including the farm performance level and the diacritic character handling. The only noticeable absence is the indexing schedule. That can be found and adjusted via the Central Administration site.

Site and Subweb Management

One of the most common administrative categories within SharePoint is the management of site collections and their subwebs. As you'd expect, there are quite a few operations in STSADM that deal with this, as shown in Table 13.9. Keep in mind that you can't administer a site collection unless you are a site collection administrator as well.

TABLE 13.9:   Site and Subweb Operations Reference

OPERATIONS	PARAMETERS
Createsite	-url <url> -owneremail <someone@example.com> [-ownerlogin <DOMAIN\name>] [-ownername <display name>] [-secondaryemail <someone@example.com>] [-secondarylogin <DOMAIN\name>] [-secondaryname <display name>] [-lcid <language>] [-sitetemplate <site template>] [-title <site title>] [-description <site description>] [-hostheaderwebapplicationurl <web application url>] [-quota <quota template>]
Createsiteinnewdb	-url <url> -owneremail <someone@example.com> [-ownerlogin <DOMAIN\name>] [-ownername <display name>] [-secondaryemail <someone@example.com>] [-secondarylogin <DOMAIN\name>] [-secondaryname <display name>] [-lcid <language>] [-sitetemplate <site template>] [-title <site title>] [-description <site description>] [-hostheaderwebapplicationurl <web application url>] [-quota <quota template>] [-databaseuser <database username>] [-databasepassword <database password>] [-databaseserver <database server name>] [-databasename <database name>]

OPERATIONS	PARAMETERS

Createweb	`-url <url>`
	`[-lcid <language>]`
	`[-sitetemplate <site template>]`
	`[-title <site title>]`
	`[-description <site description>]`
	`[-convert]`
	`[-unique]`

Deletesite	`-url <url>` `-deleteadaccounts <true/false>`
Deleteweb	`-url <url>`

Enumsites	`-url <virtual server url>`
	`-showlocks`
	`-redirectedsites`

Enumsubwebs	`-url <url>`
Renameweb	`-url <url>` `-newname <new subsite name>`

One of the issues you have to deal with is that there is a bit of inconsistency within the various administrative tools regarding naming. In the Central Administration site, you create site collections. Within STSADM, site collections are usually referred to as sites. Of course, what is referred to as a "site" within Central Administration and Site Settings is referred to as a "subweb" within STSADM. It's not a huge deal, but important to remember to avoid confusion.

Listing Site Collections and Sites

Many of the operations rely on identifying a particular site collection or site, so one of the first things you need to know is how to get that information. Additionally, STSADM provides more information about these than you will find in Central Administration or Site Settings, which makes these very handy for your server documentation.

If you need to list the site collections for your web application at `http://sp1`, use the following command:

```
STSADM -o Enumsites -url http://sp1
```

The result is an XML string that looks similar to Figure 13.22.

You probably have noticed that quite a bit of information is included in the results, most notably the size and size quotas. Compare that with the list of site collections as viewed in Central Administration and shown in Figure 13.23.

Once you know the site collections that exist within a web application, you can use the Enumsubwebs to get a list of all the sites and workspaces that are in that site collection.

FIGURE 13.22
Retrieving and listing the site collections for the **http://sp1** web application

FIGURE 13.23
The Site Collection list in Central Administration

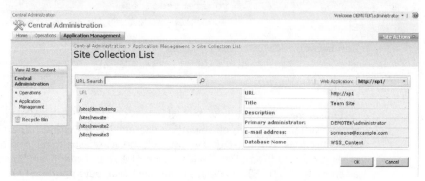

To see what sites are in the NewSite3 site collection, use the following command:

```
STSADM -o Enumsubwebs -url http://sp1/sites/newsite3
```

One shortcoming of this command is that it only lists the next level down, and there isn't an option to traverse through the site tree. If you want to know what subsites exist in a given site, you will need to run this command against each site.

If you want to get a complete list all the way down, you'll need to write a fairly complex script that analyzes the result set of the site collection, and then list the subwebs of each node, analyze that result set, and then list the subwebs, etc. It might be easier to write a pure VBScript and use the SharePoint object model. Either way, it's way outside the scope of what we're covering here.

USING YOUR LIST OF SITE COLLECTIONS

You may have noticed that the output from these two operations (actually the output of most operations) is well-formed XML. If you were to pipe your command out to an XML file, you could use it to create a quick and easy site directory in your WSS site, using an XSL style sheet.

To do this:

1. Create a directory to hold the XML and XSL files. Make sure that folder is an IIS directory, but is not a path that is managed by SharePoint. Create or save your XSL style sheet into this directory.

2. Schedule a task that runs `STSADM -o enumsites -url http://<url of your web application>` and creates a well-formed XML file that refers to your XSL style sheet.

3. Add a link in your SharePoint site to the XML file.

Now you have a quick and dirty list of all the site collections for your web application at SP1, and this list will be updated every time the scheduled task runs. You could do the same thing for each set of sites within a given site collection as well.

The basic process is pretty easy, but it will require that you do a little bit of coding, both to build a well-formed XML file and develop the style sheet.

Here is a basic VBScript that gets the site collections from the web application `http://SP1` and creates the XML file. It refers to an XSL style sheet that has already been created.

```
'Create variables used in script
Dim oShell,oFSO, oXML, oExec
Dim sCommand,sResults

'Instantiate the libraries required to run commands
Set oShell = CreateObject("WScript.Shell")
Set oFSO = CreateObject("Scripting.FileSystemObject")

'Build the text string that is the entire STSADM command that lists
   the site collections
'Then run the command (Using the .exec method lets you capture the
   output)
'and capture the output.
sCommand = "stsadm.exe -o enumsites -url http://sp1"
Set oExec = oshell.Exec (sCommand)
sResults = oExec.StdOut.ReadAll

'Create a new well-formed xml file in our IIS virtual directory
'The first two writeline instructions add standard xml header
   information
'and specifies the name of the xsl style sheet that should be applied.
'The next line opens the xml tag, and the last writeline instruction
   closes it.
'The only write instruction inserts the xml that was captured from
   stsadm
'Chr(34) is the character code that puts quotes in a text String
Set oXML = oFSO.CreateTextFile
("c:\inetpub\wwwroot\mysites\sp1.xml",true)
```

```
oXML.writeline "<?xml version=" & Chr(34) & "1.0" & Chr(34) & "?>"
oXML.Writeline "<?xml-stylesheet type=" & Chr(34) & "text/xsl" &
    Chr(34) & " href=" & Chr(34) & "sp1.xsl" & Chr(34) & "?>"
oXML.writeline "<xml>"
oXML.write sResults
oXML.Writeline "</xml>"

'Close the files
oXML.close
```

SharePoint Designer is one of many tools you can use to create the XSL style sheet. Use whatever tool makes you feel the most comfortable. The real point of the XSL style sheet is to take the raw data and make it look nice. XSL files are basically filled with HTML. The XSL files can be as simple or complex as you like.

Creating Site Collections and Sites

Site creation is one of the more common management activities that you will do in SharePoint. No one would argue that it is particularly difficult to do using Central Administration, but if you use some of the scripting methods discussed earlier it can be easily done using STSADM as well. This may be of particular interest to you if your company wants its staff to be part of the blogging masses, as you may want or need to create a blog site for all new employees and want to add it to your user provisioning process without using Self-Service Site Creation.

The syntax for creating a new site in an existing site collection using the `Createweb` operation is pretty simple. At its simplest (`STSADM -o Createweb -url http://<full url of new site>`), it will create the site at the URL you specify. The first time you open that site in a web browser, SharePoint will take you to a configuration page where you can set the template for the site.

However, wouldn't it be easier to get some of that detail out of the way right from the start? STSADM allows you to create your new site with almost all the options you have in the GUI, including implementing a site template and setting the site to use unique permissions (as opposed to inherited from its parent site).

To create a new blog site for Sage Tarragon in a blogging area that was created for the Dem0tek staff, you could use the following command.

```
STSADM -o Createweb -url http://sp1/sites/newsite3/blogs/SageT
    -sitetemplate blog#0 -description "Sage Tarragon's Blog" -unique
```

The syntax for creating a new site collection in an existing web application looks a little more daunting; however, if you take the time to look at the optional parameters for the `Createsite` operation, you'll find that they are reasonably self-explanatory.

To create a new site collection based on the Team Site template for the marketing department on the `http://sp1` web application, you can use this command.

```
STSADM -o Createsite -url http://sp1/sites/Marketing -owneremail
    administrator@dem0tek.lcl -ownerlogin dem0tek\administrator
    -sitetemplate STS#0 -title "Marketing Home" -description "Marketing
    Team Site" -quota "200 MB"
```

The optional -quota parameter refers to quota templates that have been created by you. SharePoint doesn't have any quota templates by default. If you want to limit the amount of data that a site collection can contain, you will need to create a quota template and then use it when creating the site collection.

DEFAULT SITE TEMPLATE NAMES

In the GUI tools, you get to pick the site template you want from a list. But that's the easy way, and you don't want to do things the easy way, do you?

You may have noticed by now that the site template name that you need to use in STSADM is not the same as the name that's displayed in the GUI. So how do you find out the names of the default site templates so you can use them in STSADM?

There are two main ways. The first way is to find the XML file in WSS that lists all the available templates. This is where the GUI gets its info. That file is found in c:\program files\ common files\Microsoft shared\web server extensions\ 12\template\1033\ xml\webtemp.xml. (You might need to use a different language ID if you have site templates for languages other than English.) You will need to combine the template name (STS or MPS, for example) with the configuration ID (0 or 1), with a pound sign (#) between the two. For example, the Document Workspace site template is part of the STS template, and it has a configuration ID of 2, so in STSADM it is referred to as STS#2.

The second way is to refer to this list.

GUI Name	STSADM Name
◆ Team Site	STS#0
◆ Blank Site	STS#1
◆ Document Workspace	STS#2
◆ Basic Meeting Workspace	MPS#0
◆ Blank Meeting Workspace	MPS#1
◆ Decision Meeting Workspace	MPS#2
◆ Social Meeting Workspace	MPS#3
◆ Multipage Meeting Workspace	MPS#4
◆ Blog Site	BLOG#0
◆ Wiki Site	WIKI#0

If you've added other site templates, you can retrieve the same information for those templates by using the Enumtemplates operation. The custom templates will always have a template name with _Global_, so their reference for STSADM will look something like _Global_#1. The actual number will depend on how many custom templates you have added and the order in which you added them.

The other operation to create a site collection has all the same options as `Createsite`, but it adds options that let you create a new content database for the web application to hold the content for the site collection (as opposed to putting it in the content database for the web application like any other site collection). Amazingly enough, this operation is `Createsiteinnewdb`. The only difference is the four extra parameters that are used to identify the name of the database server, the database name itself, and the user credentials to use when connecting. Keep in mind that it doesn't allow you to specify the search server for the new database.

Renaming a Site

You can rename a site (but not a site collection) using the `Renameweb` operation.

```
STSADM -o Renameweb -url <current url of site> -newname <new name>
```

About the only thing you need to be aware of for this operation is that you need the full URL for the `-url` parameter, but you only need the new relative path name of the site (not the full URL) for the `-newname` parameter.

For example, this command renames the poorly named site "mps" to "Sales."

```
STSADM -o Renameweb -url http://sp1/sites/newsite3/mps -newname Sales
```

Deleting Site Collections and Sites

Deletions are the simplest operations to perform. At their most basic, the deletion command line consists of:

```
STSADM -o Deletesite -url <url of site collection>
```

to delete a site collection, and

```
STSADM -o Deleteweb -url <url of site>
```

to delete a site. The only optional parameter to consider is whether or not you need to delete any Active Directory user accounts that are connected to the site collection you are deleting. The default is to *not* delete them. Unless you are absolutely certain that you want to do that, you should probably leave that alone.

Security Management

For an in-depth discussion of the user permissions and security, you should refer back to Chapter 11, "Users and Permissions." However, if you're confident that you understand the "why's" of security and permissions management and the structure (i.e., users and groups are assigned roles on a given site, and those roles are made up of particular activities, how inheritance works, etc.), and you just want to know how to do those things with STSADM, then you've come to the right place.

Table 13.10 shows the security operations at your disposal.

TABLE 13.10:   Security Operations Reference

OPERATIONS	PARAMETERS

Addpermissionpolicy	`-url <url>`
	`-userlogin <login name>`
	`-permissionlevel <permission policy level>`
	`[-zone <URL zone>]`
	`[-username <display name>]`

Adduser	`-url <url>`
	`-userlogin <DOMAIN\user>`
	`-useremail <someone@example.com>`
	`-role <role name> / -group <group name>`
	`-username <display name>`
	`[-siteadmin]`

Authentication	`-url <url>`
	`-type <windows/forms/websso>`
	`[-usebasic (valid only in windows authentication`
	`  mode)]`
	`[-usewindowsintegrated (valid only in windows`
	`  authentication mode)]`
	`[-exclusivelyusentlm (valid only in windows`
	`  authentication mode)]`
	`[-membershipprovider <membership provider name>]`
	`[-rolemanager <role manager name>]`
	`[-enableclientintegration]`
	`[-allowanonymous]`

Changepermissionpolicy	`-url <url>` `-userlogin <DOMAIN\name>` `[-zone <URL zone>]` `[-username <display name>]` `[{ -add	-delete }` `-permissionlevel <permission policy level>]`

CreateGroup	`-url <url>`
	`-name <group name>`
	`-description <description>`
	`-ownerlogin <DOMAIN\name or group name>`
	`[-type member|visitor|owner]`

DeleteGroup	`-url <url>` `-name <group name>`

DeleteUser	`-url <url>`
	`-userlogin <DOMAIN\name>`
	`[-group <group>]`

Deletepermissionpolicy	`-url <url>`
	`-userlogin <login name>`
	`[-zone <URL zone>]`

(Continued)

TABLE 13.10:   Security Operations Reference *(Continued)*

OPERATIONS	PARAMETERS
Enumgroups	-url \<url\>
Enumroles	-url \<url\>
Enumusers	-url \<url\>
Getsitelock	-url \<url\>
Managepermissionpolicylevel	-url \<url\>
	-name \<permission policy level name\>
	[{ -add | -delete }]
	[-description \<description\>]
	[-siteadmin \<true | false\>]
	[-siteauditor \<true | false\>]
	[-grantpermissions \<comma-separated list of permissions\>]
	[-denypermissions \<comma-separated list of permissions\>]
Migrateuser	-oldlogin \<DOMAIN\name\>
	-newlogin \<DOMAIN\name\>
	[-ignoresidhistory]
Setsitelock	-url \<url\>
	-lock \<none | noadditions | readonly | noaccess\>
Siteowner	-url \<url\>
	[-ownerlogin \<DOMAIN\name\>]
	[-secondarylogin \<DOMAIN\name\>]
Userrole	-url \<url\>
	-userlogin \<DOMAIN\name\>
	-role \<role name\>
	[-add]
	[-delete]

User Management

User and Group Management is one of the most common aspects of managing security for WSS installations. STSADM gives you the ability to handle this easily. This can come in handy when trying to reproduce settings from your test environment to your production environments or in user provisioning processes.

Use the Adduser operation to add a user or domain group to a WSS site and assign them a particular role (permission level) or assign them to a SharePoint group (which probably already has a role associated with it). To give Sage Tarragon designer permissions on the blog site on SP1, use the command like this:

```
STSADDM -o Adduser -url http://sp1/sites/newsite3/blog -userlogin
    Dem0tek\SageT -useremail SageT@dem0tek.lcl -role Design -username
    "Sage Tarragon"
```

If you wanted to put Sage into an existing site group, do not use the `-role` parameter, but use the `-group` parameter instead.

In both cases, it is assumed that the conditions required to run the command exist—in other words, the SharePoint group or permission level exists. You will also need to know how to reference the various components. The correct enumeration operations (`Enumgroups`, `Enumroles`) will provide you with this information.

If you need to adjust the permission level for a user that has already had one explicitly assigned to them, you can use the `Userrole` operation.

```
STSADM -o Userrole -url http://sp1/sites/newsite3 -userlogin
    dem0tek\SageT -role "Full Control" -add
```

This command will add the Full Control role to Sage. To delete a role, use the same command, except use `-delete` instead of add.

Deleting users or SharePoint groups via STSADM doesn't really offer any challenge, and you'll find the syntax very simple.

```
STSADM -o Deleteuser|deletegroup -url <url of site> -name <name of
    user or group>
```

SharePoint Group Management

This is one area where the GUI tools give you considerably more flexibility than the command line. The only real operations you have for SharePoint groups are `Creategroup`, `Deletegroup`, and `Enumgroups`. A quick review of the parameters for `Creategroup` reveals only the most basic of options (although it does give you the option to add the group to one of the three basic types; member, owner, visitor, which the New Group page does not). Compare Figure 13.24 to the options available when creating a SharePoint group using the Site Administration tools.

FIGURE 13.24
SharePoint Group creation in Central Administration

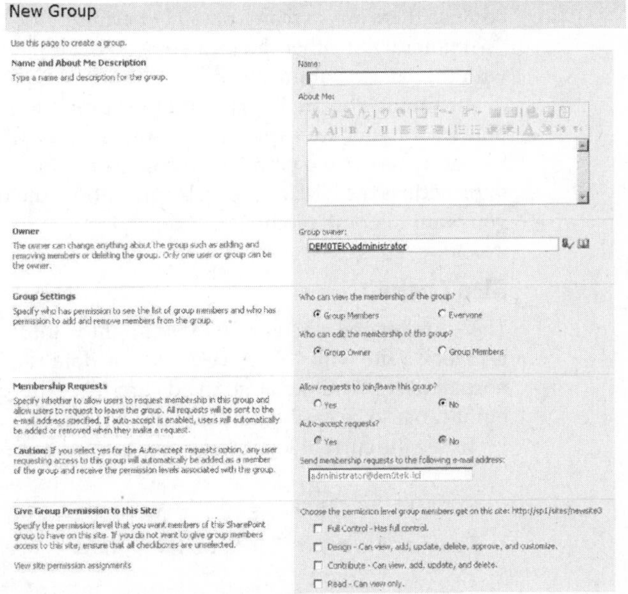

You have considerably more control over the group settings, including the permission level, when using the GUI. Add to that the fact that there is no operation for editing existing groups for STSADM, and it really points to using the GUI.

Permission Policy Management

Permission policies are set at the web application level, and you have four operations that allow you to manage them:

- Addpermissionpolicy
- Changepermissionpolicy
- Deletepermissionpolicy
- Managepermissionpolicylevel

Much like group management, you may find that the GUI is actually a better interface for doing this work, especially given the relative infrequency with which you are likely to be configuring these settings.

Having said that, the first thing you may want to do is add new permission policy levels or modify the existing levels (assuming that you are unhappy with the default options). In either case, use the Managepermissionpolicylevel operation.

```
STSADM -o Managepermissionpolicylevel -url http://sp1 -name "SP1
    Admin" -description "Full Control of SP1 Web App" -add -siteadmin
    true
```

There is an optional parameter that allows you to deny and grant permissions (using a comma-separated string), but you might actually find it easier to adjust these settings in the GUI, because there are so many possible permissions.

If you do not either the -add or -delete parameters, you will edit the policy you identify with the -name parameter.

Assuming you are happy with the permission policy levels, you can then create the permission policies for your web application, such as using Addpermissionpolicy to add a user policy.

The syntax of the permission policy operations is very basic and self-explanatory. All you need to provide is the URL of the web application, the user's login, and the name of the permission level you want to grant, modify, or delete.

Site Locks

There are several reasons why you might want to lock a site. One of the tasks in restore scenarios is to lock a site with "No Access," so the data can be restored properly. This setting can override normal user permissions, so tread carefully. This can be done via the Central Administration tool, but it can also be easily handled with STSADM.

To see the current lock status on a site via STSADM, use:

```
STSADM -o Getsitelock -url http://sp1/sites/newsite3
```

To set a "No Access" lock on the same site, use:

```
STSADM -o Setsitelock -url http://sp1/sites/newsite3 -lock noaccess
```

To remove the lock after the restore is finished, use:

```
STSADM -o Setsitelock -url http://sp1/sites/newsite3 -lock none
```

There are two other locks: `readonly` and `noadditions`. They do pretty much what you would expect. The former only allows you to read anything in the site. The latter allows you to edit existing things, but not add anything new to the site, including subsites and pages.

Farm Management

The majority of the operations that STSADM provides deal with managing the various aspects of specific web applications, site collections, or sites. However, you shouldn't forget that there are some settings that cross all of these boundaries and apply to all the servers in your farm. (Remember that even a standalone server is still considered a farm, albeit a very small one—more like a vegetable garden or flowerbox.)

DIAGNOSTIC AND TRACE LOGGING LEVELS

In Central Administration, you have the ability to set the Event Log and Trace Logging levels, but you must do it one category at a time. You cannot configure them in a single action. Therefore, this is a very time-consuming process (hours) if you follow best practice and set every level. Also, setting `Category=ALL` overwrites all of your previous settings. Did I mention that there are some hidden categories as well?

First, you can run:

```
stsadm.exe -o Listlogginglevels -showhidden
```

This will list all of your current levels. You might want to pipe this out to a text file for reference and future use.

When you are ready to change logging levels en masse, you use:

```
stsadm.exe -o Setlogginglevel -category <category name> -tracelevel
    <level> -windowslogginglevel <level>
```

Create a batch file that has a line for every category you want to set. If the service has spaces, surround the category with quotes. Although writing this batch file is time consuming, it only needs to be done once. The file can then be reused in multiple farms, or in the same farm when performing Disaster Recovery.

If you feel a burning urge to do it all with a single command, you can add multiple categories on one line, separated by a semicolon. For example:

```
stsadm.exe -o Setlogginglevel -category query; "Query Processor"
    -tracelevel unexpected -windowslogginglevel error
```

This example changed `query` and `Query Processor` simultaneously. Note that all categories given in a single command must use the same trace/log levels.

Table 13.11 lists all the levels as they need to be referenced within STSADM.

TABLE 13.11:   Log and Trace Levels

WINDOWS LOGGING LEVELS	TRACE LEVELS
None	None
ErrorServiceUnavailable	Unexpected
ErrorSecurityBreach	Monitorable
ErrorCritical	High
Error	Medium
Warning	Verbose
FailureAudit	
SuccessAudit	
Information	
Success	

Table 13.12 lists all of the farm-level operations. Most of them have a single purpose, but remember that the Getproperty and Setproperty operations have a pretty large set of options, which are listed in Table 13.13. A detailed explanation of the syntax of those two commands appears earlier in this chapter.

TABLE 13.12:   Farm Operations Reference

OPERATION	DESCRIPTION	PARAMETERS

Addpath	Create a managed path rule	`-url <path to be added>`
		`-type <explicitinclusion|`
		`  wildcardinclusion>`

Binddrservice	Set the data retrieval service	`-servicename <data retrieval`
		`  service name>`
		`-setting <data retrieval setting>`

Blockedfilelist	Manage the blocked file types	`-extension <file extension>`
		`-add|-delete`
		`[-url <url>]`

Disablessc	Disable self-service site creation	`-url <url of web app>`

Email	Configure the email server that SharePoint will use	`-outmtpserver <smtp server>`
		`-fromaddress <email@email.address>`
		`-replytoaddress <email@email.`
		`  address>`
		`-codepage <65001 is Unicode UTF>`
		`[-url <url>]`

Enablessc	Enable self-service site creation	`-url <url of web app>` `[-requiresecondarycontact]`
Enumservices	List the services being provided by the server	

OPERATION	DESCRIPTION	PARAMETERS
Getadminport	Retrieve the port number of the administration website	
Getproperty	Retrieve properties of the web farm or site collection	`-propertyname <property>` `[-url <url>]`
Listlogginglevel	Show the current event and trace logging levels	`[-showhidden]`
Localupgradestatus	Retrieve upgrade status of a server	

Provisionservice	Manage a service to a server	`-action <start|stop>`
		`-servicetype <namespace or`
		`  assembly qualified name>`
		`[-servicename <service name>]`

Refreshdms	Refresh the Directory Management Service	`-url <url>`
Refreshsitedms	Refresh the site-level Directory Management Service	`-url <url of site>`
Registerwsswriter	Register and start the SharePoint VSS Writer service on a server	

Removedrservice	Remove the data retrieval service	`-servicename <data retrieval`
		`  service name>`
		`-setting <data retrieval`
		`  services setting>`

Renameserver	Rename a server (useful in recovery scenarios)	`-oldservername <old server name>` `-newservername <new server name>`

Setadminport	Set the Central Administration port number	`-port <port>`
		`[-ssl]`
		`[-admapcreatenew]`
		`[-admapidname <app pool name>]`

Setapppassword	Set application password	`-password <password>`

Setlogginglevel	Adjust the current event and/or tracelogging levels	`[-category <category name from`
		`  logging list>]`
		`-default|-tracelevel <level>`
		`[-windowslogginglevel <level>]`

Setworkflowconfig	General workflow configurations for a web application	`-url <url>`
		`-emailtonopermissionparticipants`
		`  <enable|disable>`
		`-externalparticipants`
		`  <enable|disable>`
		`-userdefinedworkflows`
		`  <enable|disable>`

(Continued)

TABLE 13.12:   Farm Operations Reference *(Continued)*

OPERATION	DESCRIPTION	PARAMETERS
Unregisterwsswriter	Unregister and stop the SharePoint VSS Writer service on a server	
Updateaccountpassword	Update the service account password	`-userlogin <domain\name>` `-password <password>` `[-noadmin]`
Updatealerttemplates	Load modified alert template files	`-url <url>` `[-filename <filename>]` `[-lcid <language id>]`
Updatefarmcredentials	Update service credentials	`[-identitytype <configurableid\` `  Networkservice>]` `[-userlogin <domain\name>]` `[-password <password>]` `[-local [-keyonly]]`

TABLE 13.13:   Farm Properties in **Getproperty** and **Setproperty**

Avallowdownload	Delete-web-send-email
Avcleaningenabled	Irmaddinsenabled
Avdownloadscanenabled	Irmrmscertserver
Avnumberofthreads	Irmrmsusead
Avtimeout	Job-ceip-datacollection
Avuploadscanenabled	Job-config-refresh
Command-line-upgrade-running	Job-database-statistics
Database-command-timeout	Job-dead-site-delete
Data-retrieval-services-enabled	Job-usage-analysis
Data-retrieval-services-oledb-providers	Job-watson-trigger
Data-retrieval-services-response-size	Large-file-chunk-size
Data-retrieval-services-timeout	Token-timeout
Data-retrieval-services-update	Worklow-cpu-throttle
Data-source-controls-enabled	Workflow-eventdelivery-batchsize
Dead-site-auto-delete	Workflow-eventdelivery-throttle
Dead-site-notify-after	Workflow-eventdelivery timeout
Dead-site-num-notifications	Workflow-timerjob-cpu-throttle
Defaultcontentdb-password	Workitem-eventdelivery-batchsize
Defaultcontentdb-server	Workitem-eventdelivery-throttle
Defaultcontentdb-user	

The Bottom Line

Make sure everything is in place to run this tool   STSADM provides the SharePoint administrator with the means to schedule, automate, and replicate many administrative and configuration tasks. This may be especially important in farm configurations, disaster recovery, and when moving configurations from test to production.

Master It   Verify the location for STSADM.EXE on your server and create an easy way to access it.

Basic STSADM syntax   One of the features of STSADM is that the syntax is consistent from one operation to the next, although there are a large number of operations.

Master It   Retrieve the list of all operations from STSADM.EXE and then create hard documentation for that list. Find the operation that you would use to create a new site collection, and create the hard documentation for that operation.

Complete common management tasks with STSADM   Just about everything that can be done in the SharePoint GUI management tools can be done via STSADM.EXE (but that doesn't necessarily mean it should).

Master It   Your company has decided that all employees will have a blog site on the company intranet, but in order to keep things under control each blog will be limited to 50MB using a quota template named "50MB Limit". These blogs will be created inside an existing Site Collection, http://sp1.dem0tek.lcl/blogs. Each employee's blog will use their username from Active Directory as the name of the blog site. You need to create these sites for all existing employees and add the creation of the blogs to the existing user provisioning process for new users.

Chapter 14

Migrating from WSS 2.0 to WSS 3.0

Migrating from WSS version 2.0 to 3.0 is a complicated but inevitable chore you must undertake. Migration (winged or not) can turn into a mess that makes a used kitty litter box smell fresh. Also, like some cats, "gotchas" will be waiting in the process of your migration to snag you out of the air like lunch time is here. The good news is that, like the birds, if you know where you are going and take some time to get ready in advance, you have a great chance to avoid or (if necessary) escape when they pounce.

In this chapter, you'll learn how to:

◆ Decide which migration method is right for you

◆ Ready yourself and your current environment for migration

◆ Avoid pitfalls that may impede the migration

◆ Perform the migration process

◆ Perform follow-up steps after the migration

TEAM SERVICES 1.0 TO SHAREPOINT 3.0

If your current setup is operating on SharePoint Team Services 1.0 and you want to upgrade it to 3.0, you will need to bring it up to the 2.0 version first. If you want a more direct migration, the alternative would be to hire a developer with a thorough knowledge of both versions to code an upgrade utility and lay out the migration path for you. Such a project is beyond the scope of this book and, in almost all cases, is a waste of resources that could be put to better use making sure the steps from versions 1.0 to 2.0 and then from 2.0 to 3.0 go smoothly. If you migrate directly from version 1.0, you will have to pay much greater attention to the details to avoid the issues you may run into when incompatible items are upgraded.

PLANNING STAGE COMPLETE?

If all of your migration planning is complete and all of your decision points have been passed, you can skip directly to the "Performing the Migration" section later in this chapter. However, this chapter does contain good information you may want to review for future migrations and to review your current one.

Migration Basics

Let's begin with the basics. A SharePoint migration has far too many potential potholes to fall into for a large-scale software change to be done in a haphazard way. For now, let's look at a good approach for making the migration plunge. After that, feel free to walk away with what works for you and leave the rest behind.

MIGRATE VERSUS UPGRADE: THE GREAT LINGUISTIC DEBATE

Let's get a quick bit of terminology clarified. This chapter uses the terms "upgrade" and "migrate" interchangeably, and it uses the proper term based on which section I am discussing. In the modern world, the two words have picked up the same connotation in many instances. The truth is that most upgrades are not migrations, and many migrations are not upgrades. This chapter uses "upgrade" because an *upgrade* implies that you are gaining more features or added performance in some fashion. *Migration*, on the other hand, implies at least a conceptual change of location or the base on which something rests. This chapter discusses moving from SharePoint 2.0 to SharePoint 3.0. One can hope that no one would plan on the transition from one to the other without an expectation of gain. On the flipside, in order to do this there is no choice but to follow the upgrade path.

The Joy of Justification: Why Migrate?

You are going to have to figure out a few things before you migrate between versions. Why do you want to migrate? Knowing this will ease your decision process. Organizations migrate for many different reasons, but the bottom line is that the migration must benefit the company. (If there were no potential benefit in migrating, the odds are high that only people who were gluttons for punishment would bother to get involved in the process.) These are some of the more common reasons and the drivers behind them.

New SharePoint features have brought with them potential new benefits. Perhaps your organization sees a lot of overhead and/or risk in the centralized administration model of your current version. This could be a drive to push some of the administrative responsibility closer to the users or physical sites associated with a particular set of your SharePoint infrastructure. One great benefit of this is that the administrator may actually be more productive. Perhaps your organization gets a lot of use from SharePoint Services, but wishes the layout of the administration and site screens was more intuitive. The user interface for the 3.0 version of SharePoint is orders of magnitude easier to navigate. Besides being better organized, you are often never more than two clicks from the setting you need. Or maybe added features like RSS feeds or wikis may be too good to avoid.

Perhaps you've decided that it's just upgrade time. Many large organizations keep themselves on a periodic upgrade cycle. These cycles can be for hardware, software, or processes. Cycling helps keep them technologically current with a predictable schedule so that their organizations can put tools in place to assist with the transition. This also keeps them from trying to manage unsupported resources. For example, finding replacement parts or software for an IBM 386 would be difficult today.

Or maybe a political shift has triggered a non-periodic upgrade. This frequently happens when a new CEO or CIO has taken over company operations and decided it is time to upgrade. This maybe because of personal preference or for budgeting reasons. Some company leaders want their businesses (in all or part) to be on the cutting edge of technology.

Possibly, upgrading is something that your organization is doing to assist or solve a legal tracking or auditing issue. Most industries have systems in place to act in a regulatory fashion. More regulations mean compliance documentation becomes of greater importance. Today's headlines are filled with reports of breakdowns of such systems. With the advent of the Enron and WorldCom scandals, perhaps you work for a publicly traded company and have to meet the requirements set down in Sarbanes-Oxley (SOX). Perhaps your organization has access to medical information (difficult to avoid if you have a Human Resources department or offer medical insurance) and has to comply with HIPPA regulations. Maybe you work for an accredited educational institution or you are ISO 9000-certified and would like a better way to manage those pieces of information. New features in SharePoint 3.0 were designed with that in mind.

Of course there are always the "softer" and less practical reasons to migrate, which seem to occur just as often. Maybe it just seemed like a cool idea. You looked at the content and abilities of SharePoint 3.0 and said "I have to have that." The other "soft" reason is the downward flow from upper management. A decision was implemented at corporate level to standardize across the organization. (There is, of course, nothing inherently "wrong" with any of these reasons.)

At this point, you need to make two important decisions:

◆ Firstly, if you have valid reasons for migrating, that the effort wil be worth it.

◆ Secondly, that you are going to migrate– the only question is how.

For example, if you know that your organization is going to move some departments to new locations and you have multiple servers, you should plan for the hardware migration and the new software installation. Maybe some technologies aren't being used in the system and won't be in the future. This could be a time to disable or remove those items during the transition, and while you're at it, consider improvements- like upgrading SharePoint. And it is these considerations that will drive the choices you make during the migration.

Which Way to the New World? Types of Upgrades

The next decision point concerns what type of migration you are going to perform. Migration is usually broken down into three different types, each with its own benefits and drawbacks.

◆ *In-place migration*, which in a lot of ways boils down to keeping everything the same and overwriting but not wiping out the original. With an in-place migration, you essentially install SharePoint 3.0 over the existing 2.0 installation.

◆ *Gradual migration*, in which version 3.0 is installed on the same hardware as version 2.0, and the older version is transitioned over to the newer version in pieces (usually by site collection) until the original disappears. In this type of migration, you have two versions running until the migration is complete.

◆ *Database migration method* where SharePoint 3.0 is installed on a different system and the content databases are manually moved over to the new system (either literally for a stand-alone server, or figuratively, attaching the databases to the new version). This last method is more complicated; however, the structure of your current environment may make it a necessity. Thanks to some good design work on this aspect of SharePoint 3.0, even the database migration method is much easier than a lot of upgrades, unless you have a lot of outside customizations.

In the pages ahead I am going to describe the pros, cons, and important details of each type of migration, as well as what preparations are necessary before walking through the implementation of them. This will give you a chance to look over each option before diving into the step-by-step instructions.

KNOW WHY FIRST: READ THE DIRECTIONS BEFORE THE PRESCAN

The "Performing the Migration" section will discuss the Prescan utility. You should use the report from the utility to help decide which migration method to use but you should know what the migration types are before using the tool so you know what the report information means and how you can use it.

IN-PLACE MIGRATION

You may be planning to migrate in place and lay one version of SharePoint on top of the other for any number of reasons. One good reason is if you have only one server off of which you can run SharePoint. Or perhaps you are in a transition cycle and your organization's SharePoint 2.0 setup was just a place to prototype features and layouts until SharePoint 3.0 hit its final release. If the latter is the case, you should look into wiping the earlier version out completely and starting from a new base install. But, as is often the case, if the prototype has become part of production, upgrading in place is a good, option. Keep in mind that, with an in-place migration, your development team has their hands in the system, so always thoroughly review what they have done. The results may have to be altered by those developers to work with the new version.

Whatever the reason, your plan is to do the migration in place and overlay one version on the other. This is a practice that people have used for decades with operating systems and software. As a result, the concept should be an easy one to grasp.

What advantages does this method give you? Migrating in this manner means all of the work is done as one continuous unit. You won't have to upgrade part of the system and keep the older portion synchronized or communicating in a friendly manner with the new version. If you need to apply patches to the system over time, you won't have to constantly monitor which version is operating on which part of the system and what compatibility issues might arise. You won't have to support two environments. You won't have to communicate regularly with the users about which portions of the system they can reach when some parts have to be brought down during upgrades. In most situations, you should be able to bring it down and back up outside of business hours. From a hardware and software perspective, this is the least expensive option. SharePoint (well, WSS 3.0) is a free download if you don't have it on media. In addition, because you intend to use the same hardware, there is no cost other than the time to plan, perform, and validate the upgrade.

You may wonder why you should choose any other option if in-place migration is so good. Think this through for a moment. Could the upgrade break something? In this form of migration, there is no opportunity to simply flip a switch and roll things back. (Always be mindful of the value of a good backup.) What if your SharePoint setup is integrated into your public website or is mission-critical for 24/7 operation and, therefore, cannot be brought down for any significant amount of time without harming business? (This situation is becoming increasingly common due to the mass globalization of companies and communication.) Perhaps your current deployment is simply so widespread that pulling the upgrade trigger across the board would essentially bring down your infrastructure. In addition, if your SharePoint 2.0 installation is running in Active Directory Account Creation mode, then an in-place migration is not supported. Scaleable hosting mode is also not supposed to be supported.

BEING VIRTUALLY THERE: A WAY TO SAVE TIME AND SANITY

Upgrades and migrations are two instances where virtualization rules the day. This is true whether you are using hosted systems live as your servers or merely have access to the software to produce a virtual environment. Most virtualization options have systems in place for two technologies that are significant in these scenarios. One is the ability to take an existing hard drive and turn it into a virtual drive. The other uses *differencing drives* (sometimes called *delta drives*, after the Greek letter symbolizing change).

These two technologies offer a golden opportunity to protect yourself and test your upgrade and migration implementations. First, use the software to create a snapshot of your current running SharePoint environment to use as the base image for your virtual environment. Secondly, set the virtualization product to create a differencing drive with that base image as its core (differencing is when you use a virtual drive image as a base or *parent* image and create other *differential* images based on that parent, that can be changed without affecting the parent image). Finally, experiment with your installs, upgrades, and migrations on the virtual differential images. It doesn't hurt the original server, or even the base virtual image of the server, if you mess up. Depending on whom you are doing this transition for you may be able to temporarily turn off the main server and use the virtual server as a live production box for a time, just to make certain everything is working properly.

Once this is done, be sure to do rigorous testing of the differential image you just created. If everything works and everyone signs off on it, life is good. Depending on the virtualization product you are using you can then take that well-functioning virtual machine and use it to create an image to apply to the physical server. In the very least you can make copies of that virtual machine as a backup or archive it as a proof of concept before you repeat your success on the actual physical server.

On the flip side, if the system you built for testing collapses (that's why you're testing it), or it is not performing up to par for some reason, all you have to do is delete the differential image of the drive environment and start over with a new differential image from the clean base image you built from your real environment.

GRADUAL MIGRATION: INCH BY INCH THE TASK IS A CINCH

Now we come to the most common method, the gradual migration transition. This falls somewhere between the drastic switch of the migration in place and the complexity of the database moving method. This particular method does have a lot of advantages. Because both databases and versions are running in parallel, an easy rollback is possible if a transition should fail. When a transition is being performed, the only sites that are down are those being migrated. Another frequently overlooked advantage of this method, as well as the next one, is the hardware itself. If your current system hardware meets the new requirements, you can transition it later and have another server boost your output. As an alternative, it can be used as a failover server or as a server for another system that requires less power.

Of course, every method has its disadvantages. Although you can perform this type of migration on a single box, it has the potential to cause some performance and storage issues, many of which will be dependent on your hardware. The issue is tied to the need for multiple databases and serving instances. During the migration, you will be running the two setups in parallel and the migration itself will be using a third, temporary database for transitioning the contents from one version to the other. If you are doing this at a rapid clip—perhaps using this method as an alternative to the upgrade-in-place method—you will be in a situation where two SharePoint versions are rendering content while three independent databases are communicating on the same box. This is not usually the ideal environment for high performance. If you are not going to do the gradual migration on a single box, you will either have to invest in managing the gradual upgrade of multiple servers. The last major disadvantage has to do with URLs. When performing a gradual upgrade, it is necessary to assign an alternate URL to the sites in the old verion and point the standard URL to the new version. This makes sense because the URLs for the sites cannot have the same name, so usually a DNS entry is made for an alternate URL for the older version of the sites. This means that there can be two URLs accessing approximately the same data, one for the old version and one for the new, untill the migration is final. Another thing to keep in mind is you cannot do a gradual upgrade if your SharePoint 2.0 server is operating in Scaleable Hosting or Active Directory Account Creation mode.

SINGLE SERVER GOTCHA

If you only have one SharePoint 2.0 server installed with the Typical install, then the option to do a gradual upgrade is unavailable. For that sort of installation the only option is to either do an in-place upgrade or to do a true side-by-side install of SharePoint 3.0 while not touching the original 2.0 installation.

If you do the side-by-side installation, the SharePoint 3.0 installation will stop the default first site in IIS and create its own SharePoint-80 site on that port. You will need to change the port of the default site (or give it a host header) in IIS and restart it in order to have access to that SharePoint 2.0 IIS site again.

DATABASE MOVE MIGRATION: MAKE THE MOVE TO A NEW HOUSE

This method has some advantages that can be very valuable if you are either doing major redesigns and restructures of your environment or if you have a lot of customizations in place. This procedure is much like a disaster recovery drill for the SharePoint 2.0 content databases that you are migrating. The basic process involves switching the databases to read-only status, creating a backup of the database, and then restoring it to the new system. This all occurs outside of the SharePoint GUI, meaning the original installation of SharePoint isn't touched- its content database will simply be coppied. This allows you to transition, restructure, upgrade, and migrate entire server farms in pieces. You won't have to worry about migrating the configuration database, because one will already exists the new environment by virtue of having SharePoint 3.0 installed there. If there is a problem, the old environment will still be up and running so you can always switch back with ease. If you opted to create your SharePoint 2.0 setup in scalable hosting mode (the -hh install option) or you have SharePoint automatically creating Active directory accounts for you, this is supposed to be your only option. In other words, you can't simply use the SharePoint installer's migration options to upgrade your Active Directory Account Creation or Scaleable Hosting mode SharePoint 2.0 installations. The option in those cases is to go from 2.0 to 3.0 and to move just the content databases from the old server to the new one. If you are going to use the same SQL server for both the SharePoint server running 2.0 and the one running 3.0, then make copies of the databases (rename them) and use those copies for the newer server, so the two different versions of SharePoint are using two different sets of databases.

I must mention that it has been my experience that detaching and attaching databases when using scaleable hosting mode causes problems. If you do have scaleable hosting mode running on your SharePoint 2.0 server, please see KB article 928305 for more info. If you get the database from a scaleable hosting mode virtual server to attach to a SharePoint 3.0 web application, *do not* detach it if you plan on using it again.

THERE ALWAYS HAS TO BE SOMETHING . . .

The only time that migrating by moving the databases won't work is if you are running Microsoft Office Web Components on your 2.0 server. The only way to get them to work in SharePoint 3.0 is to do an in-place or gradual upgrade. Why? The web components cannot be *installed* in version 3.0. They must be installed on version 2.0, then upgraded in order to work in version 3.0.

The only major disadvantages to this method are procedural. The procedure for performing the transition is complex to keep track of and almost entirely manual. You must have the command-line utilities and know how to use them for SQL Server 2000 or SQL Server 2005, and SharePoint 3.0. This method almost presents a paradox. In principle, it is very simple. If you can back it up, you can bring it up. In practice, it gets quite complicated because you have a great deal of manual activity and a great amount of information to track.

CAN I DO THAT, PLEASE? OR, KNOW YOUR PERMISSIONS

When performing a migration at any level, the person performing the migration must have the appropriate permissions to complete the task. This can affect many areas. For example, if they do not have permission to the local file system, they will not be able to move and/or reattach a database. If they aren't a member of the Farm Administrators group at the Central Administration level, they will not be able to migrate the entire farm . Always be mindful of permissions. Without the proper ones, it could bring new meaning to "Losing the farm."

Preparing for the Migration: What do I Need in Place?

The first thing to do is to check that you meet the minimum requirements for hardware and software. The requirements for the previous version of SharePoint were not as high as the requirements for SharePoint 3.0. Your basic requirements are as follows:

◆ **CPU:** 2.5 GHZ

◆ **Memory:** 1GB

◆ **Drive Space:** 3GB

◆ **Monitor:** 1024 × 768

◆ **Network Speed:** 56K

◆ A DVD drive

These, of course, are the minimum requirements and aren't really adequate as an actual production box. If you intend to deploy a standalone server, the recommended specs are as follows:

◆ **CPU:** 2 processors at 3 GHZ

◆ **Memory:** 2GB

◆ **Drive space:** 3GB plus enough space to hold the sites you intend to host

◆ **Network Speed:** 56K (preferably higher)

◆ A DVD drive or a network share holding the install material

All of these specifications are right out of the documentation. Your final specifications should be determined as if you were doing a new install and should be based on your environment. The items above are merely a guideline to keep you on the proper runway. Never underestimate the value of a good network infrastructure and good hardware setup. If the server can send 100 pages per second but your connection will allow only one page per second throughput (obviously an example of extreme disparity), there was a failure somewhere in the planning process. You could also gain an advantage in the new 64-bit processing systems. This will be especially true of whichever box is hosting your database because it now has the ability to take advantage of such items as the new memory addressing model. Alternatively, you may want to explore the possibilities opened up by the new dual- and quad-core processors.

Check the Software

Now let's move on to checking the software. Because you already have SharePoint 2.0 in place, we can assume a couple of things:

◆ You already have a version of Windows Server 2003 and IIS 6.0 running.

◆ You are running either SQL Server 2000 or Microsoft SQL Server 2000 Desktop Engine (Windows) (WMSDE) as a base for this system.

Here's what you may have to change depending on your setup. Your version of Windows Server 2003 must be SP1 or higher (see Figure 14.1).

FIGURE 14.1
An error message appears if you try to install SharePoint without Windows Server 2003 SP1

If your SQL Server 2000 is not up to Service Pack 3a or you have SQL Server 2005 but it is below SP1, you will need to bring your database software up to these levels. If you are using WMSDE and intend to upgrade to the SQL Server 2005 Embedded Edition (SSEE) or Windows Internal Database (WID), you can read about that later in this chapter. Make certain that you have service pack 2 for SharePoint installed. Obviously, you already have ASP.NET active with at least version 1.1 of the .NET framework in place. If you do not already have the 3.0 version of the .NET framework in place, you will have to install it and make sure that ASP.NET 2.0 is enabled. If you don't have these installed, you will receive another error (see Figure 14.2).

So make certain that you have IIS 6.0 installed (which of course you do), ASP .NET 2.0 installed and enabled in IIS, and .NET Framework 3.0 is on board before migrating.

FIGURE 14.2
You'll receive this error message if you try to install SharePoint without .NET framework 3.0

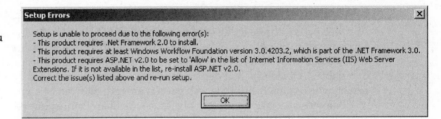

Setup Errors

Setup is unable to proceed due to the following error(s):
- This product requires .Net Framework 2.0 to install.
- This product requires at least Windows Workflow Foundation version 3.0.4203.2, which is part of the .NET Framework 3.0.
- This product requires ASP.NET v2.0 to be set to 'Allow' in the list of Internet Information Services (IIS) Web Server Extensions. If it is not available in the list, re-install ASP.NET v2.0.
Correct the issue(s) listed above and re-run setup.

OK

Define Your Key Sharepoint Users

Your key SharePoint users should include a large enough and diverse enough base of people that, as a whole, they can test most (hopefully all) of the critical processes and usage tied to the system. This base of users should include someone from the IT staff who is either familiar or will become familiar with SharePoint to help find, prioritize, and solve issues. These users will be the ones tasked with really testing the new migration to find any discrepancies before production staff.

Define Your Regression Testing

You should meet with the key users and map out (or have them map out) how the current version is used and how it works. With this map in place, you will know what needs to be done to make sure that the migration goes smoothly. Once your regression tests are defined, you can use any of several software packages that allow you to script and automate these procedures. This is of great benefit as it allows you to easily run the tests as many times as necessary against the migration to confirm it, at least, matches the previous version's performance and eliminate much human error. This process can also generate a user acceptance plan that can be used at the end of the process to ensure a successful migration.

Document Everything

You should also document all of this information and get all of the parties involved, especially management, to sign off on approval of this information. The information you have gathered from your users is an essential tool for you and your team to have so that you know when to begin the migration process. Proper documentation also helps you define your goals. When people are looking for someone to blame, good documentation will allow you to prove what was required of you. If something in the outcome definition was missed, you'll be in a better position to get the time and resources you need without being blamed. If someone signed off on the process and you have met the stated goals, you should be covered. Good documentation is also a way to prevent *scope creep*. You can document what is eating up all of your time when someone wants you to take on a new project. In addition, good documentation is useful for generating a testing plan of the migration when it is done. Then everything will be documented, and all points will be covered.

Communication Is Key

Always communicate with your users. Let them know when machines and sites will be up and down. Let them know when they can test. Let them know when things are complete. If you communicate and do well by them, your users can become your biggest advocates and assets.

Evaluate Custom Web Parts

Any web parts intrinsic to the earlier version should be automatically upgraded or replaced. Custom web parts can always be a potential issue. If you have a custom web part that has proven to be a strain on system resources, this would probably be an appropriate time to replace, rebuild, or remove it. Obviously, that decision will be based on the need for it and your environment. If the person who originally built the web parts is around, they can be a great asset.

Code access security is another big issue with SharePoint applications. To prevent errors when accessing sites that use them, anything you added to previous `web.config` files for custom web parts should be added to the corresponding configuration files and sections. As a benefit of this transition, with the advent of the 2.0 version of the .NET framework, a command-line utility (`aspnet_regiis.exe`) will allow you to encrypt sections of the `web.config` files. The bigger problem comes with web parts that have been obfuscated to a level that makes them incompatible with the new version. These files may have to be rebuilt and redeployed. This will also give the developer a chance to upgrade or convert any custom web parts before attempting to redeploy them.

OBFUSCATION: A DELIBERATE AND LEGITIMATE FORM OF CODE CONFUSION

Currently, .NET executables are deployed after they have been coded in a format that is much easier to reverse engineer than natively compiled code. This is greatly beneficial if somehow the source code is lost or if you need to view the metadata stored with the application. In order to make stealing the code more difficult, programs called *obfuscation utilities* (or just *obfuscators*) are used. These utilities take the programs that they are obfuscating and do such tasks as replacing variable names with ones that are random or generic, then scrambling the file so that the information is scattered and unreadable. The trick is that this is not encryption. The program is still fully capable of running as is, but is altered to the point that it cannot be translated back to human or human-readable computer languages in any reasonable amount of time. The point is to make the program so garbled that it would be easier for a person to build a new version from the ground up than to decode the existing one.

Keep Rollbacks in Place

It is essential to always have a rollback position in place. This can be anything from keeping the old setup running until the new one has passed acceptance testing, to having a complete set of backups that will allow you to rebuild the system at any time. The biggest determining factors for this will be what kind of business continuity you must maintain during the transition, how much work loss is acceptable in the case of disaster, and what kind of resources you have access to for maintaining your rollback position.

TEST, TEST, TEST: A TRUE STORY

Many companies must perform monthly closing processes. During the closing process, all of the company's financial information is calculated and placed into the ledgers for that time frame. During the slowest months, the closing process for one particular company usually ran between 2 and 4 hours (a testament to the people running it due to the volume it handled.) After the process started one month, it kept running and running. After 28 days, the penalties paid for filing late, interest paid on late payments (which is huge on such a large volume), and paying multiple high-priced specialty consultants for two weeks, they finally found the problem. It all came down to one overconfident developer. He had inserted a small line of code into the processing routines for the close (a query hint). He firmly believed that the piece of code he inserted would improve performance. He never tested it and deployed it directly to the production system, with the previously mentioned disastrous result. The mantra should be "Test, Test, Test." Establish a fallback point, test the fallback, and then deploy.

In that same light, take nothing for granted. Try things out first or at least know a trusted source. All the migration paths in this chapter have been tested. That does not mean that your environment may not have a variable that makes it act differently, and there is no way to test the infinite number of possible custom setups.

Consider Improving the System

When you are performing a migration, especially on a large scale, opportunities to improve the system invariably present themselves. These improvements tend to revolve around either poor use of resources or removing bottlenecks. One big question should be, "What resides in this system or on this box and should it be moved somewhere else or eliminated completely?"

If you have large files that are accessed frequently, and every time they are accessed either the network bandwidth is choked or the SharePoint server grinds to a complete halt, you may need a change. Depending on where the actual bottleneck exists, it may be time to look into moving those files to another machine with better hardware, setting up a Storage Area Network (SAN), or upgrading your network equipment.

Take a detailed look at your environment. When you are gathering requirements, treat the upgrade as a new install. Never assume that just because something worked before, it is a good idea to keep going with it. Make sure that your server is up to your needs for such things as page throughput and storage capacity. Make sure that you have monitors, logging, audits, and alerts put into place so that the server can be at peak performance with minimal effort (for more about monitoring your SharePoint server, check out Chapter 12, "Maintenance and Monitoring"). After all, every IT professional in the world has probably heard the adage "Do more with less" and been required, at least at some point, to determine how to accomplish that goal.

For example, you support a legal department whose responsibility is solely reviewing contracts with no graphical data. This environment has a lot of documents that can be thoroughly indexed and version-controlled inside the SharePoint environment. The documents don't take up nearly as much space as graphic file types and, unless you have a policy requirement to keep the documents external of the database, then they can be stored in the content database, and have little effect on search services. In that case, there is no excessive additional storage space or the processor resources search indexing would require. However, if after the migration, graphics will be introduced to those documents, and being able to search by extensive metadata will become critical, then this would be a good time to adjust the hardware accordingly.

Then there is the opposite scenario. You work for a cartography/mapping or geological survey company. You will have large files, many probably multiple GB in size. These files will be difficult to index and the odds are high that you don't want to place them as documents in the database. There are multiple ways that you can handle a situation like this. The most likely way is simply to leave things as they are (stored somewhere on the network but not in SharePoint) and change your environment later if it actually becomes an issue. In other words, leave the files on the server they are on now (assuming it has enough storage space to handle them) and don't plan to add them to the SharePoint server's storage load. If the figures are on the SharePoint server, now might not be a bad time to consider storing them elsewhere.

When planning for a migration or simply installing SharePoint, you need to be realistic as to the nature of your data. It is important to realistically plan for the added resources necessary for the added tasks a SharePoint server might be required to do after a migration. But instead of trying to see how you can wedge everything into SharePoint, you should consider whether or not it belongs on the SharePoint server at all. There are always ways to offer links to the files from SharePoint, using hyperlink fields, web parts, wiki documents, and more. It just may not be reasonable to stuff them into SharePoint's databases at all.

PLUS SIZE FILES

In terms of large files, if you want to improve your usage and take advantage of SharePoint's capabilities, you have a couple of options:

◆ Store the oversized files (such as large images) on a share and link it into a document (Microsoft Word would do nicely) that contains the information on which you want the binary file indexed. This way SharePoint searches based on the document, and then you use it as a jump to the image. Or you could create a list with custom fields for metadata, and use a hyperlink field to link to the files. Then searches could be based on the metadata. This has the added bonus or being able to group or filter data in the list by that metadata.

◆ Change your file format to something that allows better indexing. Versions of the CGM (Common Graphics Metafile) format, for example, are based largely on internal text-based tag information that can be read, rendered, and indexed as plaintext (this will require a custom filter).

Performing the Migration: Can I Get My Hands Dirty Now?

STSADM.EXE, OSQL.EXE, AND SQLCMD.EXE: ARE YOU FRIENDS

If you haven't become familiar with these three command-line executables, you should. They have a lot of options and capabilities that involve managing SharePoint, and there are situations where they are the only means of performing necessary tasks (for example, when migrating databases that need to be upgraded into new SharePoint instances).

`Stsadm.exe` is your SharePoint administration command-line utility. It will be used to merge databases and perform certain administrative tasks that cannot be handled from the GUI. This utility is covered in Chapter 13, "STSADM: A Look at the SharePoint Command-Line Tool."

`Osql.exe` is the command-line version of the SQL query analyzer. It will let you execute scripts or commands from a command prompt, including detaching databases from the SQL Server or WMSDE to be reattached where necessary.

`Sqlcmd.exe` replaces both `isql.exe` and `osql.exe` in the SQL server 2005 environment. `isql.exe` and `osql.exe` will still work, but they have been deprecated and may be removed altogether in future versions. For more on these utilities, look for books on the versions of SQL Server or research it in the SQL server books online.

Now we get to the mechanics of the upgrade process. We have ended up with five basic scenarios:

◆ The three different migrations:

  ◆ In-place

  ◆ Gradual

  ◆ Content database move

◆ Each of those migrations has

  ◆ A single server deployment

  ◆ A multiple server deployment

TWO WITH THE WIZARD AND ONE WITHOUT

Basically keep in mind that the in-place migration and gradual migration both require that you install SharePoint 3.0 over the existing 2.0 installation. The installation wizard will realize that the earlier version is there and give you three options; either to do a gradual update, an in-place upgrade, or simply install version 3.0 but leave version 2.0 untouched.

However, when doing a database move from one version to the other, then it is not necessary to run the installer (unless you just want to in order to get the Prescan utility). All you need to do is move the 2.0 databases either to the new SharePoint 3.0 server if they were local or make copies (or create a new instance) and add them to SQL. When the databases are attached to web applications in SharePoint 3.0, SharePoint will sense that they are the wrong version and update them then.

If there are any significant differences between the upgrade of the single and server farm setups, I will attempt to clarify them in the following steps.

The first three migration steps will be essentially the same for any upgrade you are performing. Step 3 *can* actually be run before Steps 1 and 2. Personally, I always perform backups before beginning any part of an upgrade procedure. Read through all of the steps before you actually begin the procedure.

1. Use the `Stsadm.exe` utility to back up your SharePoint sites. Specify the `overwrite` option if you want to replace a previous backup file (remember that with WSS 2.0 there is no catastrophic backup).

   ```
   stsadm.exe -o backup <site_url_to_backup> -filename
     <name_of_file_to_create> -overwrite
   ```

2. Back up the rest of your system. The extent of the backup and the methodology used for it will depend on your environment. Most people prefer to back up both the machine and the database so that they have plenty of fallback room where necessary. If you are backing up a WMSDE database for your server, your best bet is to detach it at the command line. (See the "Database Move Migration:WMSDE to WID" section later in this chapter for details.) Because such a database can't be marked as read only, as a full SQL Server database can be, detaching will prevent changes from occurring in the SharePoint sites while you are performing the backup. For a SQL Server database, this should be a *full* backup to retain all needed information.

3. Run the Prescan utility. The Prescan utility is part of the SharePoint installation package. So you could get the utility by running the SharePoint installation but not running the configuration wizard. However, I prefer to download the prescan utility from the Microsoft downloads and run the prescan before running the installation software. Why? Two reasons; one is that it's easier to find because you can indicate where the file goes when you download it, and the second reason is because as soon as you run the sharepoint installer it will immediately be aware of the older SharePoint version there and give you the option to upgrade. Now the upgrade process really starts when you begin the configuration wizard, but I prefer to run the installer only after I have done the prescan (very much the chicken-or-the-egg-scenario). The file that does the prescan is named, conveniently enough, `prescan.exe`. To find where the installation put it (if you used the installation to get it), the easiest thing to do is a filesystem search. To run the Prescan utility, open a command window and change to the directory on the machine containing the file "`prescan.exe`." When you run it, a report will be generated (you will need to pay attention to where the prescan puts it) that indicates items in your SharePoint environment that could present issues during the upgrade. These issues could include such things as custom components or objects that are orphaned in the system. You should try to address them if possible and run the utility again before the migration. If the tool identifies an item, such as a custom web part, that you cannot address, you can leave it and proceed with the upgrade. You will just have to be aware that it may pose a problem later. If it shows you no problems then you are ready to proceed. This is a required step. This means if there is a problem, consult the report. Fix the problem and run the prescan again. For an idea as to what is in the prescan report, see Figure 14.3. Notice that there are entries for broken sites, broken webs, custom templates, and unghosted (which means customized) pages. These are the sort of things that need to be taken into account when migrating SharePoint. If you rerun the scan you will see that the customizations will not continue to generate errors because sharepoint assumes that you got the point with the last scan and won't keep reminding you.

FIGURE 14.3
A clean Prescan report

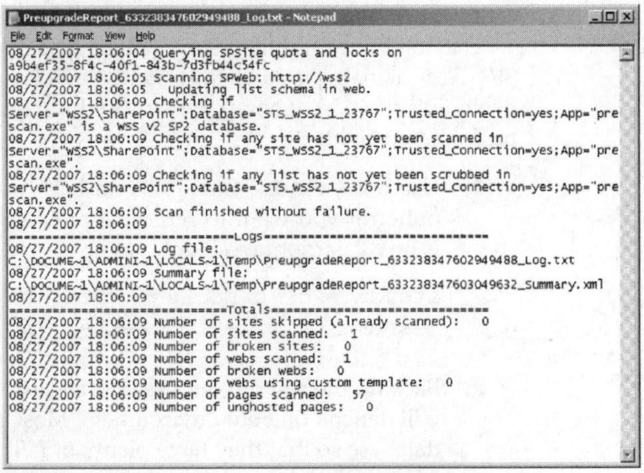
PreupgradeReport_633238347602949488_Log.txt - Notepad
File Edit Format View Help

```
08/27/2007 18:06:04 Querying SPSite quota and locks on
a9b4ef35-8f4c-40f1-843b-7d3fb44c54fc
08/27/2007 18:06:05 Scanning SPWeb: http://wss2
08/27/2007 18:06:05   Updating list schema in web.
08/27/2007 18:06:09 Checking if
Server="WSS2\SharePoint";Database="STS_WSS2_1_23767";Trusted_Connection=yes;App="pre
scan.exe" is a WSS V2 SP2 database.
08/27/2007 18:06:09 Checking if any site has not yet been scanned in
Server="WSS2\SharePoint";Database="STS_WSS2_1_23767";Trusted_Connection=yes;App="pre
scan.exe".
08/27/2007 18:06:09 Checking if any list has not yet been scrubbed in
Server="WSS2\SharePoint";Database="STS_WSS2_1_23767";Trusted_Connection=yes;App="pre
scan.exe".
08/27/2007 18:06:09 Scan finished without failure.
08/27/2007 18:06:09
===============================Logs================================
08/27/2007 18:06:09 Log file:
C:\DOCUME~1\ADMINI~1\LOCALS~1\Temp\PreupgradeReport_633238347602949488_Log.txt
08/27/2007 18:06:09 Summary file:
C:\DOCUME~1\ADMINI~1\LOCALS~1\Temp\PreupgradeReport_633238347603049632_Summary.xml
08/27/2007 18:06:09
==============================Totals===============================
08/27/2007 18:06:09 Number of sites skipped (already scanned):   0
08/27/2007 18:06:09 Number of sites scanned:   1
08/27/2007 18:06:09 Number of broken sites:   0
08/27/2007 18:06:09 Number of webs scanned:   1
08/27/2007 18:06:09 Number of broken webs:   0
08/27/2007 18:06:09 Number of webs using custom template:   0
08/27/2007 18:06:09 Number of pages scanned:   57
08/27/2007 18:06:09 Number of unghosted pages:   0
```

As the Prescan utility processes the SharePoint database, it will make alterations to let the upgrade utilities know that it has been scanned. One result of this (and a good reason not to run it until you are ready for the upgrade) is that much of the content will be marked as having been updated. For example, if you have a retirement plan set up in SharePoint that is set up to eliminate old content, the dates will now be skewed. If you attempt to scan the wrong database or scan on a system without SharePoint 2.0, you will receive an error message (see Figure 14.4).

NOTE: After step 3 above, the instructions for continuing the migration differ depending on the type of migration you are performing, and will be covered in separate sub-sections below.

FIGURE 14.4

A prescan in the wrong environment

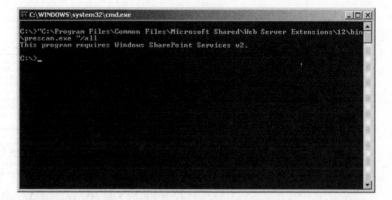

A LITTLE ADDED CONVENIENCE

I usually like to create a directory on one of my root-level drives for all of the command-line utilities that I may have to run during an upgrade or any large scale system procedure. This way I won't have to type any huge lengths of path information when I need to run items from the command line repeatedly. The one thing you need to remember is that you must make sure any files the command-line utilities need to run are either copied into the same directory or are in a directory that is part of the system's path variable. Once I have completed the process, I can remove all of my install files just by deleting the executables.

Migration In Place

Before you do this migration, remember to run the Prescan utility (see the initial three steps of the section above for instructions). Assuming that your hardware and software are up to spec and that you are in an environment with few or no customizations, this will be the easiest part of your migration. You will essentially connect the dots by clicking Next and filling in a few options. If you have a large amount of customization, there are issues that can occur. Many of them are covered in the next section.

1. Install SharePoint 3.0 on the server or servers that make up your current installation by executing the `SharepointServices.exe` file, which is downloadable from the Microsoft website. (The next several steps will be the same for most of the migration paths. Procedural changes will be noted.) At this point, the installation files will extract.

    The main installer window will appear, and the program will begin processing the extracted files for the installation.

2. Check the box to accept the End User License Agreement (EULA). See Figure 14.5.

FIGURE 14.5
Accept the EULA

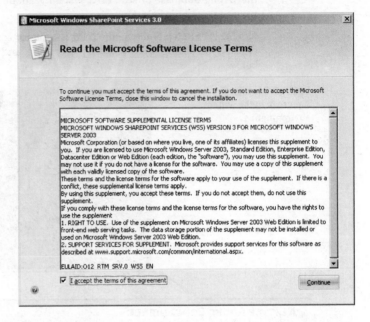

3. For this installation, select the second option to perform an automated, in-place upgrade (see Figure 14.6). This will be the first point in the install where the procedure will deviate based on the type of migration you are performing.

FIGURE 14.6
Select the option to upgrade the installation in place

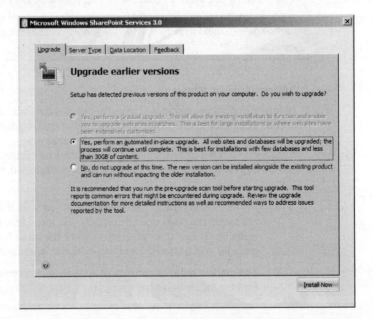

4. At this time, you may also want to use the Data Location tab to indicate where you want the server to store Search indices (see Figure 14.7).

FIGURE 14.7
The Data Location tab

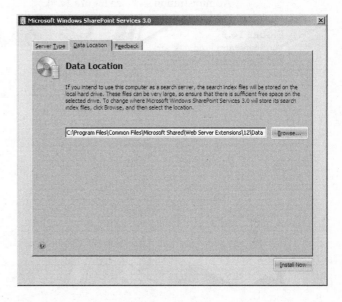

5. Once you have selected the parameters for the install, click the Install Now button at the bottom right. The installation will continue automatically until it is complete.

6. Once the installation is complete, a notification will appear with a checkbox indicating that you want to launch the SharePoint Products and Technologies Configuration Wizard (see Figure 14.8). To proceed with the configuration, leave it checked and click the Close button; otherwise, uncheck the box and you can launch the wizard later from the Administrative Tools menu.

FIGURE 14.8
The installation is complete

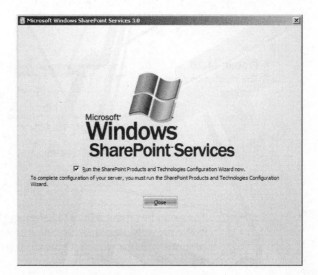

7. When you are ready, run the SharePoint Products and Technologies Configuration Wizard on all frontend web and search servers beginning with the web server containing your Central Administration site (see Figure 14.9).

FIGURE 14.9
The SharePoint Products and Technologies Wizard

8. The SharePoint Products and Technologies Wizard will give you two warnings. The first one tells you which services may have to be stopped and restarted during the install (see Figure 14.10). This is a good time to warn people about the migration, if you haven't already done so.

FIGURE 14.10
The affected services warining

The second warning relates to Language Template Packs (see Figure 14.11). If you used them in the previous version, this is the time to download and install the new ones before you continue with the wizard. Otherwise, click OK.

FIGURE 14.11
The Language Pack
warning

9. At this point the wizard will essentially take over and go through several steps upgrading and configuring your system for the new platform while migrating your old content and configurations.

10. When Step 9 is complete, you will receive a message indicating that the wizard has finished and that once you close it, you will be sent to your Central Administration page for the server. It may require you to log in. You must use the name/password combination that you used to log onto this machine with administrative rights.

11. When login is complete, you will be taken to Central Administration under the Operations tab. A timer-based job will be running to perform the final upgrade. The screen will be cycling on a 1-minute interval and showing you the status of the upgrade (see Figure 14.12).

FIGURE 14.12
The Upgrade Job
Monitor page

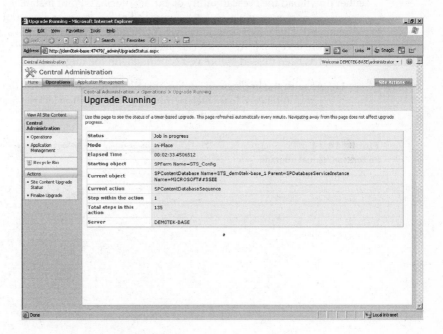

12. Assuming all of these steps completed without trouble, the in-place migration is now complete. The Job Monitoring screen will indicate that the upgrade is no longer running (see Figure 14.13). All that is left is to test everything, review the process, and decide where to go from here.

FIGURE 14.13
The upgrade is completed

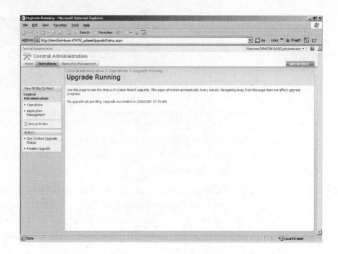

Gradual Migration

Keep in mind that a Prescan should be run for this migration as well. Remember that you need to either download the Prescan utility or extract the SharePoint installation files in order to access the prescan.exe executable. Run the command at the command prompt, and assess the report that is generated. This will let you know what you need to change to make it right. Make the changes you feel are necessary. Always rerun the prescan when you've made suggested changes to ensure nothing has been missed before you continue with the migration.

1. As with the in-place migration, install SharePoint 3.0 on all the 2.0 servers to be migrated. The difference is that when performing this install, select the first option indicating that you want to perform a Gradual upgrade (see Figure 14.14).

FIGURE 14.14
Perform a Gradual upgrade

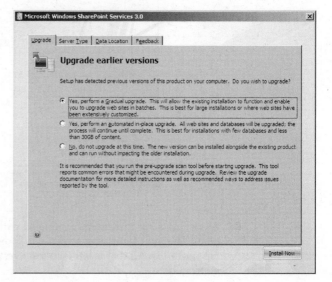

2. If you are performing a gradual migration on a server farm, start the installation with the server that contains Central Administration. The wizard will generate the message shown in Figure 14.15. This message also appears if you are performing an in-place migration on a server farm.

FIGURE 14.15
A message telling you to upgrade the components on servers in the farm will appear

3. On the first server you update (which should be the one running the Central Administration service), select Complete in the Server Type tab. Select Web Front End on the Server Type tab for the installation on all other servers in the farm (see Figure 14.16). This will hold true for all server farm migrations of any type.

FIGURE 14.16
Select the server type

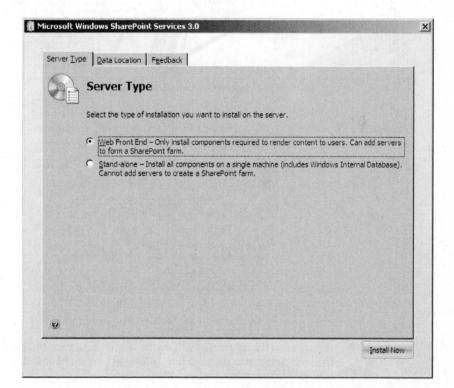

4. Proceed through the wizard to the last screen, as described in the previous section on the in-place migration. Complete these pre-configuration install steps on all of the servers in the farm.

5. Beginning with the server that will contain Central Administration for the setup (whether it is an individual server or a farm), launch the SharePoint Products and Technologies Configuration Wizard.

6. When prompted, if installing on the server supporting Central Administration, select the "No-I want to create a new server farm" option. For all other servers, select the "Yes-I want to connect to an existing server farm" option and connect to the first server's configuration database.

7. You will now need to specify the Configuration Database Settings. You will need to identify the server where the Configuration Database sits and the name of that database. You will also need to specify the database access account (see Figure 14.17).

FIGURE 14.17
You will need to
specify the
Configuration
Database settings

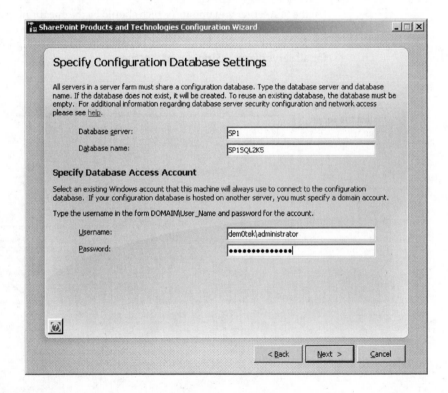

8. If you are on the server that will contain Central Administration, you will need to configure the Web Application, giving it an alternate port number if desired, and choose NTLM or Kerberos Security (see Figure 14.18).

FIGURE 14.18
Configure Central Administration Web
Application

9. The next screen allows you to view the settings you have selected. Clicking Next confirms and applies them (see Figure 14.19). If you need to adjust the HOSTS entry for the site, you can click the Advanced Settings button to do so.

FIGURE 14.19
Confirm the settings

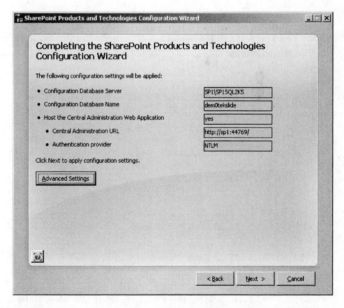

10. If all goes well, you will be presented with a screen indicating that your configuration was successful (see Figure 14.20). Clicking the Finish button will take you to the Central Administration home page.

FIGURE 14.20
Configuration completed
successfully

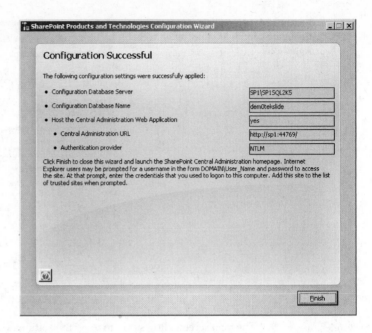

On the Central Administration home page, you will be presented with an Administrator
Tasks list with links detailing what your next steps should be (see Figure 14.21).

FIGURE 14.21
The Central Administration home
page Tasks list

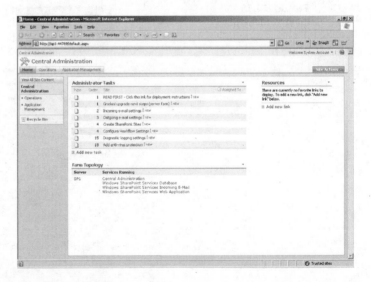

11. Clicking the Gradual upgrade next steps task link in the Administrator Tasks list will
take you to the task specifically customized for the particular type of migration you are
performing. In Figure 14.22, you can see the first Task item in the list for a gradual server
farm migration.

FIGURE 14.22
Tasks list detail

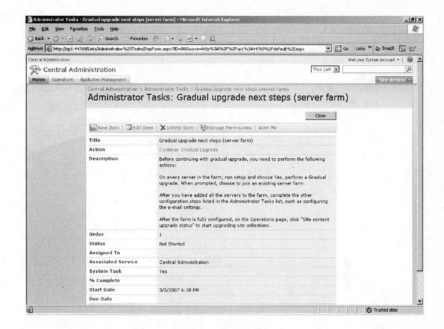

12. As you can see, the first Task will of course be to finish connecting all of the servers to the farm, so make certain their installation and configuration as members of the farm are complete (see Figure 14.23). Make note of the description of the task and click Close.

FIGURE 14.23
All servers are connected to farm

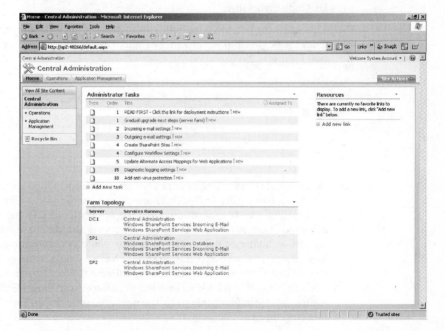

13. Once the servers are all connected (or if you are not implementing a farm), you will need to go to the Operations page to continue the migration (see Figure 14.24). First you upgrade the web applications, then the site collections within.

FIGURE 14.24

The Operations page

14. The Upgrade and Migration menu is at the bottom left of the screen. Click the Site Content Upgrade Status link.

15. This will bring you to a page with a list of the existing web applications that you can upgrade. Click the Begin Upgrade link to the right of the web application you want to start upgrading (see Figure 14.25)

FIGURE 14.25

List of sites to upgrade

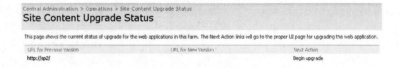

16. You will be taken to a page where you can enter information for the selected web application to migrate (see Figure 14.26). This page contains settings very similar to the standard settings for creating a web application, with the option to specify the application pool and pool account. There is also a section for specifying the database names. This means you can allow the databases to be auto-named or you can specify names. You may think that, at least to start, the web application should have a single database, but in a gradual upgrade, there will be a transitional database, and the final, actual, upgraded database, both of which you can name if you'd like. Choosing to name the databases (instead of accepting defaults) means, after you leave this page, the next one will ask you to, well, name the databases for this target web application.

FIGURE 14.26
Set the target web application

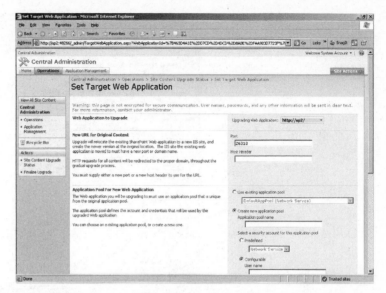

There is also a section that is very specific to the gradual upgrade on this page, and that is New URL from Original Content. It is here that you enter the URL for the *old* web application, not the new one. The upgraded web application will be taking on the old URL for continuity for the users, and therefore you must specify a new URL for the old content. Once you are done with your settings, click OK.

YOU DON'T HAVE TO STOP AT JUST ONE

You can repeat this process for each virtual server you would like to migrate. When Central Administration means Site content, they mean IIS Web Site content, expecting you to migrate virtual servers, then their contents.

If you haven't entered anything in error, a dialog page will appear asking you to wait while your settings are processed.

17. The next page (if you allowed the databases to be auto-named) will show a list of sites available for upgrade with checkboxes beside them (see Figure 14.27) from the old version of SharePoint. Check the ones you want to upgrade and clear the boxes on any you may be eliminating (in case there are any old sites you just don't want to upgrade or simply don't want to upgrade at this time). Click the Upgrade Sites button.

ALWAYS START AT THE ROOT

Keep in mind that you must always upgrade the root site collection of a web application before you can upgrade any others.

FIGURE 14.27
Select the sites to upgrade

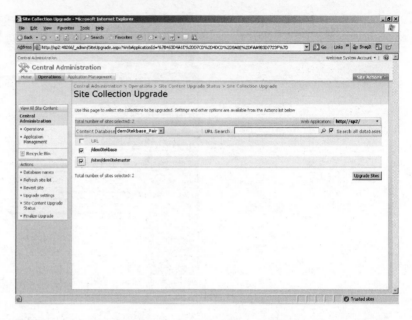

18. The next page is your last chance to back out of the upgrade procedure. If you are ready to start it (which I'm sure by now you would be), click the Upgrade Sites button. If you aren't ready, click Cancel (see Figure 14.28).

FIGURE 14.28
Begin upgrading sites in a
web application

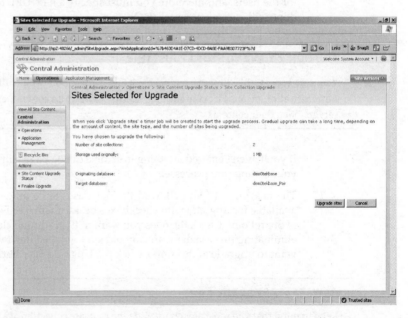

Just as in the in-place migration, you will be taken to a page monitoring the upgrade's timer job. It will track the status of the upgrade (see Figure 14.29).

FIGURE 14.29
The upgrade status

FIGURE 14.29
The upgrade status

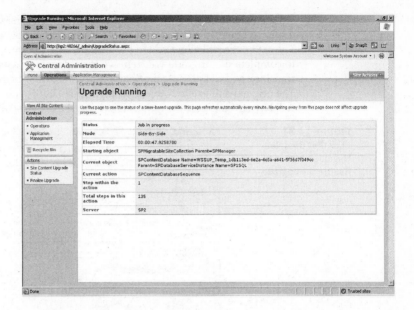

Depending on the size of your web application (and the selected site collections), this part of the process could take quite a while. Once it is done, the monitoring screen will display a message indicating that there are no more upgrade jobs running.

19. Once this is done, you will have access to your original content upgraded into the new version (see Figure 14.30).

FIGURE 14.30
The original Team site

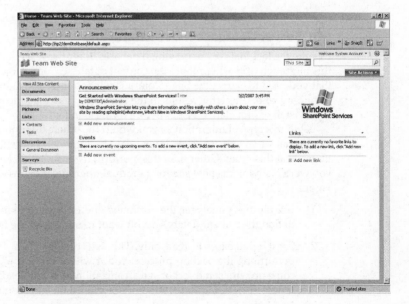

20. After you have migrated all of your sites to the new version, return to the Upgrade and Migration menu on the Operations screen. Click the Complete Upgrade link (see Figure 14.31). The next page will allow you to perform the finalization. Clicking the button on this screen to complete the upgrade will remove the temporary database that has been used for the transition and all links into the SharePoint 2.0 setup, so be sure you are truly done migrating. The original still exists at the alternative URL, but if you want to repeat the upgrade, you will have to eliminate the new version and start from scratch.

FIGURE 14.31
Click the "Complete Upgrade" button to finalize the upgrade

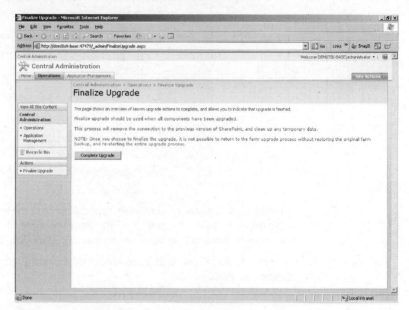

SQL Server Database Move Migration

Despite the fact that we are moving databases, it is always a good idea to do a Prescan before even this migration (this will prepare the content databases for upgrade). To do the prescan, remember that you need to extract the SharePoint installation files, and at the command prompt run prescan.exe. Check the results in the report generated by the prescan and make certain that your install has no glaring issues before trying *any* migration.

Begin this type of migration as you would the others by running the SharePoint installation, except that when you are asked if you want to upgrade, choose the third option "No, do not upgrade at this time." Other than this, perform the installation and configuration procedure as if you were readying the new site for a gradual upgrade, in terms of selecting server type, etc. (see Figure 14.32).

1. Use the query analyzer, the command line, or whatever kind of SQL GUI interface you prefer to find the content databases you want to migrate to the new system.

2. Set the databases to read only. This will prevent them from being altered while you are performing the backup process, and it will allow you to migrate them without having to come up with some sort of synchronization method. Reads inside SharePoint can still occur if necessary, but updates will not occur until the new content site is up and running.

FIGURE 14.32
Select the "No, do
not upgrade" option

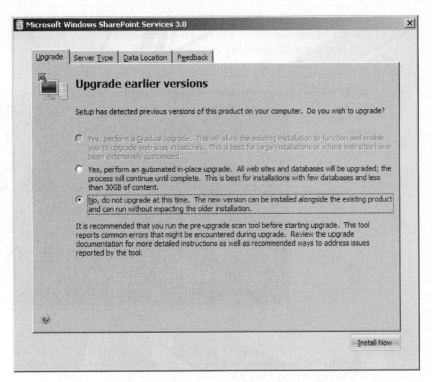

Remember only to work with the content databases. If a screen appears like that (in
Figure 14.33) when you try to attach the migrated database, you most likely made the mistake of
backing up the configuration database and trying to add it to SharePoint as content.

FIGURE 14.33
Adding a
configuration
database causes an
error

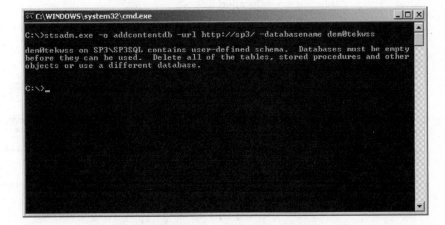

Also remember that, although this method has its conveniences, it does not allow you to skip steps. Make sure that you have run the Prescan utility, or you will get an error when you attempt to restore the database (see Figure 14.34).

FIGURE 14.34
You must run the Prescan Utility

THIS FEELS FAMILIAR . . .

As previously stated, this procedure is much like disaster recovery for a SQL Server database. The primary differences being that this situation shouldn't be an emergency (regardless of what other departments may think, and that you are only interacting with the content databases).

---

3. Create a backup of the content database using your preferred method, and copy the backup file to the new location.

4. From within the SQL Server for the target SharePoint 3.0 system, restore the file, selecting the option of restoring it to the most recent point in time.

DATABASE BACKUP AND RESTORE HELP

For detailed steps on how to perform the database backup and restore, see *Mastering Microsoft SQL Server 2005* (Sybex, 2005).

---

5. Create a web application inside SharePoint to act as a receiver for the sites being transferred in the content databases (see Figure 14.35). Then remove the empty database you gave it during creation in preparation for adding a migrating one.

FIGURE 14.35
Create a new web
application

FIGURE 14.35
Create a new web
application

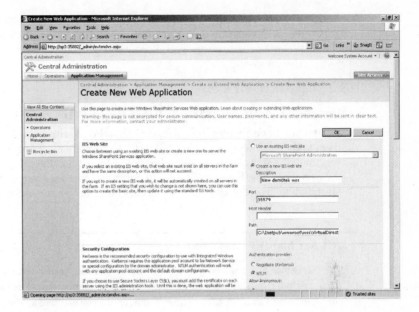

6. Once the web application has been created, you will have to add the content database you are migrating the web application. This will have to be done from the command line as follows. Make sure that the root site is the first one restored and added, or the sites will not fall into place properly.

```
stsadm.exe -o addcontentdb -url <URL> -databasename
    <Name_Of_The_Restored_Content_Database>
```

You can also specify the database servername and password, as well as site limits and search server. This procedure could take a while, as the command line is performing a similar routine as the gradual migration tools shown in the GUI; however, it will let you know when it has finished successfully (see Figure 14.36).

FIGURE 14.36
The database attachment
is completed

7. If you first attempt to access the migrated content is too soon after attaching the database, you will be greeted by the processing screen. This is simply SharePoint finalizing the upgrade. When it's done, so are you. Repeat this process for each web application until all contents are restored.

Database Move Migration: WMSDE to WID

What if you have a typical installation of SharePoint with databases in WMSDE and want to move them to the WID setup for SharePoint 3.0? This is actually a fairly simple procedure that is a variant of the standard database migration. Most of the difference is in the greater need and use of the command line. First, you'll have to perform a standard, one-server install (see Chapter 2, "Installation.") on the server to host SharePoint 3.0, and run a prescan. Then follow these steps:

IT's ALL ABOUT PERSPECTIVE

The mechanics of a migration from WMSDE to WID are not complicated if you are experienced with these or similar procedures. To do this properly, you must know or be willing to learn in detail the command-line administration of SharePoint, which you can find in Chapter 13, "STSADM: A Look at the SharePoint Command-Line Tool." You'll also need to be familiar with whichever version of SQL Server you are using, which is beyond the scope of this book.

---

8. Because a WMSDE database cannot be marked as read only (as the databases in a full SQL 2000 or 2005 Server database can), you will have to detach it from the instance of SQL. This requires a simple command-line entry. Type the following at a command prompt and press enter (note that the options are case sensitive):

```
Osql -S <Servername>\<sharepoint> -E
```

The -S is followed by the server and instance to connect to, and the -E option designates the use of a trusted connection. The user doing this must be a member of the local administrators group where this is being done. Once done, enter the following for each of your content databases:

```
EXEC sp_detach_db "<content database name>"
  go
```

The "<content database name>" tag specifies the content database you want to migrate. The tag does need to be surrounded by quotes. Obviously, you can leave behind any you don't want to retain. Don't bother detaching the configuration stores; you have already created new ones in the SharePoint 3.0 setup you installed.

9. Now it is time to attach the old database to the new version. If you do not have it already, you will need to obtain the SQL Server native client and the SQLCMD utility, which can be downloaded from the Microsoft website. Install them on the machine

running SharePoint 3.0 server first, then SQLCMD. Copy your database into the `WINDOWS\` `SYSMSI\SSEE\MSSQL.2005\MSSQL\Data` directory on the drive where you have installed SharePoint 3.0. Make sure that you are logged into the system as a member of the administrators group. Open a command window and enter the following:

```
sqlcmd -S
  \\.\pipe\mssql$microsoft##ssee\sql\query -E
```

10. This will open a tunnel onto the local WID so that you can attach the content databases. For each one that you want to attach, enter the following (using the correct content database name):

```
EXEC sp_attach_db @dbname = N'Content_Database_name',
  @filename1=N'%WINDIR%\SYSMSI\SSEE\MSSQL.2005\MSSQL\Data\<DBname>.mdf',
  @filename2=N'%WINDIR%\SYSMSI\SSEE\MSSQL.2005\MSSQL\Data
  \<DBname>_log.ldf'
```

The EXEC command should be entered as one continuous line. Press Enter. Then type **GO** and press Enter.

Type `"exit"` and press Enter to disconnect from the utility. After that, add the content databases to the web applications as you did for the SQL database upgrade.

Post-Update Steps: Testing for success

Just because you made it through the mechanical stages of a migration doesn't mean you are finished or safe. Give yourself a pat on the back for handling it as well as you have, but now it's the time to see just how well you really did.

In the carpentry world, the adage is "Measure twice, cut once." In the IT world, it should be "Test, test, test, and test again." All of your servers are up, running, and kicking out pages. At the beginning of all of this process, you probably got together with users and managers and planned exactly what it would look like if this migration was successful. Now it is time to go back through your documentation and make sure that all of the sites you expect to come up do so. Make sure that anything you have migrated works, do your regression testing (if you didn't already do that virtually). Test all of your custom web parts to make sure they still function. Check the access settings for users. After you have done all of that, get your key users to go through and do the same. Inevitably, there will be someone in the company who uses some portion of the system once per year that is critical to business when it is used. He will probably be the one person who was not consulted when laying out the migration plan, so make sure he can do his job and get as many eyes on it as possible. Now is the time to implement the test plan you documented before the migration, as well as the user acceptance plan. Those plans were created with (hopefully) everyone's input, so they will go far in silencing those who forgot to mention what they critically need now that the new system is in place.

What if your tests fail? What if something goes wrong? What you need to do depends on the migration method you used and what the actual issue is. If it turns out that it was something that you didn't know about because your end users did not inform you, then you still have to fix it. However, the onus is on them to let you know—thanks to your good planning and documentation. If it is a minor glitch that can be quickly fixed, do so. If a custom web part no longer works, you can kill it, clean it, or copy it. In other words, remove it and find an alternative, find and fix the offending code, or create a new version of it which replicates the functionality. If none of this can be done, then you will realize why you established those fallback points and why backups are good.

The Bottom Line

Decide which migration method is right for you   Choosing the method by which you are going to migrate can be one of the most critical decisions you make. It will influence the environment you lay down as well as where it can go in the future. Once this decision point is passed, many of your other decisions can be made and supported easily.

Master It   When planning for migration, what method would be better suited for single server implementation than it would be for a server farm?

Ready yourself and your current environment for migration   It has been said that most failures are caused by poor planning. By getting all of your planning out of the way—including such things as disaster recovery, rollback positions, and what pieces to migrate how and when—you have set yourself up with the best chance for success. Stick to the plans. When the expected occurs, you will be ready. When the unexpected occurs, there will be no wasted energy or resources, so you'll be able to deal with the issue at hand.

Master It   Once you have decided how you want to upgrade, what will you need to prepare your organization and environment for the transition?

Avoid pitfalls that may impede the migration   With good planning, preparation, and research, you'll be ready for the hills and valleys of the transitional process. Knowing some of the more common issues will help you get there more smoothly.

Master It   Look again at your environment and what decisions you have made up to now. What are the some common points of failure that could occur during the transition.

Perform the migration process   There are three different types of migrations to choose from when moving from WSS 2.0 to 3.0: in-place, gradual, and database migration. Which you choose must depend on what will be appropriate for your resources and environment.

Master It   Now that you have planned it all out, give it a try. Put together a test environment that presents scenarios as close as possible to the real thing and perform a trial migration.

Perform follow-up steps after the migration   You are finished, it's over, and it's done. Now look back and see whether you accomplished your goals and how well you did. These steps will vary depending on your environment but usually involve gathering user data, getting user acceptance, reviewing process successes and pitfalls, and completing documentation. Finally get final sign off approval to complete the migration.

Master It   What is a key thing to do after migration has taken place? Who should you involve in the post installation process?

Chapter 15

Advanced Installation and Configuration

Generally you install SharePoint on your network for a reason. Maybe you intend to use it for document storage, collaboration, data gathering, or calendar and contact management. But behind the scenes you might need more than the default settings allow. You may need your users to *not* have preexisting accounts in Active Directory. Your data might need the security of SSL, or you might need Kerberos authentication. You might be planning on having tens of thousands of users and require multiple front end servers managed centrally from one Central Administration site. These requirements involve a more complicated SharePoint installation and configuration. They also may (who am I kidding? They will) have limitations that must be considered before implementation.

This chapter was intended to cover the more advanced features, configurations, and settings that were not appropriate earlier in the book. It will show you what happens when you enable Active Directory Account Creation mode during an advanced installation of SharePoint. With a brief foray into installing additional web front end servers on a server farm. Then demonstrate some of the more advanced configurations such as Network Load Balancing (which is the whole point of having a server farm), Directory Management Service, using SSL with SharePoint, and enabling Kerberos as an authentication method.

In this chapter, you'll learn how to:

◆ Understand Active Directory Account Creation mode.

◆ Set a service principal name.

◆ Configure Network Load Balancing.

◆ Configure Directory Management Service and understand its requirements.

Advanced Installation

As if having three different types of SharePoint installation; Basic, Advanced Stand-alone and Server Farm, were not enough, there are a couple other kinds of installation that need to be mentioned.

Depending on your needs, how you install SharePoint is integral to its function. A single mouse click, a single missed button will change a web front end server's function, even the whole farm's function, if you are not careful.

Take, for instance, Active Directory Account Creation Mode. This user mode can only be enabled and written to the configuration database of the server farm during installation. It cannot be changed, it cannot be set later.

Another example is installing SharePoint with the intent to use it in a SharePoint server farm configuration. In that case you might expect to install at least a second SharePoint front end server. That installation of the second web front end server is a bit different than the installation for the first server in the farm, as is its configuration. Up to this point, we've used a server farm installation to give us access to an SQL server to store the SharePoint databases. That is a fine reason to use the Advanced web front end installation, but to really benefit from features of a SharePoint server farm, like doing network load balancing or having more than one server host services, you need to install additional servers.

Active Directory Account Creation Mode SharePoint Installation

When you install SharePoint using any of the standard Basic or Advanced installation configurations, you will, by default, be using the Active Directory Domain account mode. When SharePoint finishes the installation and opens, you can start adding users from Active Directory, because SharePoint uses the user accounts from Active Directory automatically.

AUTHORIZATION VERSUS AUTHENTICATION

SharePoint authorizes its users to access its resources after they authenticate using some other authentication provider. During install, SharePoint focuses on Windows Authentication (Central Administration *always* uses Domain account mode), but you can create web applications that use Forms-based authentication, or some other third-party authentication provider. Active Directory Domain account mode is a misnomer to a certain degree—if you have a SharePoint server that is not in a domain, SharePoint will use the server's security account manager (SAM) database for accounts instead of Active Directory.

Of course, that's due to the fact that SharePoint opts to use Active Directory Domain Account Mode (usually just called Domain Account Mode) by default. That account mode simply accesses Active Directory for user accounts and authentication. But what if you don't want to do that? What if you want to have outside users access SharePoint? What if you want to create accounts in SharePoint first, and have them added to AD second?

In that case, you can enable Active Directory Account Creation (ADAC) mode.

When you choose to use ADAC, the user mode will be written to SharePoint's configuration database at the point the database is being built. It is a one-shot setting, no give-backs. Once a server farm is installed using ADAC, you can't change back to using Domain account mode unless you uninstall and reinstall SharePoint with a new configuration database. When you use ADAC, SharePoint considers it a non-Windows authentication mode, as if you were using a third-party forms-based authentication for the farm.

Normally, ADAC is enabled for those SharePoint installations that have primarily, if not exclusively, external users; users that do not have, or should not have, user accounts in the company Active Directory. That allows the SharePoint administrator to add a user to SharePoint without requiring them to already have an account in Active Directory. When a user is added to SharePoint, a corresponding user object gets created in an Active Directory Organizational Unit (OU) specifically for SharePoint.

ADAC is site collection-centric, meaning that ADAC user accounts are applied per site collection, which can actually be limited to a certain number of invited users. It is an often overlooked point that in ADAC user accounts will be confined to logging into a particular site collection. In order for the same user to access a different site collection, they will need to create a different account in the OU to access the additional site collection. The same account cannot be used to log into two or more site collections.

SITE COLLECTION-CENTRIC

You might think that once an account is created in the ADAC OU, it would be available to all site collections in SharePoint, just as an account would be if you were using Domain account mode; however, that's not so. Because SharePoint considers ADAC to be a non-Windows authentication mode, SharePoint does not let the People Picker field see or accept preexisting accounts in AD when adding users, *even* if they are in the special ADAC OU.

This is why I think that SharePoint developers designed the ADAC mode to be used to let external users access separate site collections without accessing any sites other than the one they originally were invited to use.

To make matters worse, by default, usernames are based on the aliases of their email addresses. That means the user who wants access to two different site collections should use two different email addresses. They can use the same email account for both, but the second alias will have a number appended to the end, possibly confusing the user as they try to remember which site collection requires the username with a number at the end of it.

Also consider if the only email address you have for someone who needs access to a site collection is `sexydog1109`, then the user account is going to be `sexydog1109`. However, you can change the display name in SharePoint if you want, but their unfortunate email address will still be the same and really the primary way they are identified.

You might consider, instead of ADAC, allowing anonymous access. But by authenticating (rather than accessing the site anonymously), the users will be able to contribute to lists, libraries, blogs, and wikis while using individual user accounts, so their activities can be attributed to them and you can apply particular permissions to them. Anonymous users don't have user accounts per se, and therefore no individual accountability.

When in ADAC mode, SharePoint creates a domain account for a user when you create an account in SharePoint. To do this, SharePoint takes the email address you supply when creating the SharePoint account, checks to see if that alias already exists as a username, appends a number if the username already exists, and creates a new user in Active Directory (AD) in the OU you put aside just for ADAC. When the new user wants to log into the SharePoint site collection they've been given access to, they'll have to use the `domain\username` format just as any other user would. In my example, the login is `dem0tek\`*username*. You can create a user quota for each site collection to help avoid bloating the OU.

As discussed in Chapter 8, "Site Collections and Web Applications," and Chapter 10, "Central Administration: Application Management," there is a *Send username and password in an email* setting in each web application's general settings that enables an email to be sent to new users, giving them their username and password to access SharePoint. This setting is usually ignored, but with ADAC it is the only way to get the SharePoint users names and passwords to the users. This is no small thing, and it is on by default.

When SharePoint creates a user account for a new SharePoint user, it sends an email to the user's email address. The email gives them their username and the randomly generated password that SharePoint gave the account when it was made in Active Directory. If no email is generated, the user will not know their username and password and will be unable to log into SharePoint. If that happens, you will have to find out what account SharePoint generated for the user, reset the password (because there's no way for you to know the random one either), and send the information to the user yourself.

When the user receives the email invitation to SharePoint, they can click the link in the invitation to go to the site collection of which they are a member. When they get there after logging in, they can go to their User Information and change their password. They will not receive explicit instructions on where to go or how to change their password. However, if they know to go to User Information, they can use the Change password link in the Action bar to change their passwords with impunity. They just have to know where to look.

Before you can get SharePoint to work efficiently, you'll need to tend to a few technical details:

◆ ADAC is not an option if you choose to install SharePoint in a Basic or Standalone configuration. Neither of them (at this point) will allow you to stop the configuration process and select Active Directory Account Creation mode. Only the Advanced, Web Front End installation option will do that. This means that you can use ADAC only if you are installing SharePoint with the intention of using SQL Server to host its databases and possibly will have more than one web front-end server.

◆ ADAC is not supported by MOSS. Just in case you decide to use MOSS in your company instead of or in addition to WSS, MOSS cannot use Active Directory Account Creation mode for its users.

◆ If you are running ADAC, certain SharePoint features and certain parts of the Central Administration interface are disabled. If you are running ADAC, you absolutely cannot do Self-Service Site Creation; for that function to work the person creating the site collection must already have an account in AD, but ADAC creates a brand new account for the owner of the new site collection when that site collection is made. ADAC can't use existing accounts, even in its own, special, ADAC-specific OU. In addition, you cannot use the link to create a new site collection in the graphic interface of Central Administration. To create a site collection, you must use STSADM at the command line. This is not a real hardship, but it is something to keep in mind.

◆ For SharePoint to be able to create Active Directory user accounts, it must have access to Active Directory. For this to work, you create an Organizational Unit (OU) in Active Directory specifically for SharePoint. Do not put *anything* else in there—no contacts, no distribution groups, nothing. The OU should be dedicated to SharePoint's users. This is not a hard and steadfast requirement. You could get sloppy and put other stuff in the OU; however, if you stick to the rule, it will make it easier to troubleshoot.

Once you've created the OU, you'll need to give SharePoint access to it. To start, the Farm account must have at least Delegate Control rights to create, change, and delete user accounts, and the right to read all information in the OU (the Farm account, Database Access account, Configuration database account, and Central Administration Application Pool account are all the same thing).

When you create new web applications, their Content Database Access accounts must be given the same Delegate Control rights to the OU as the Farm account. Otherwise, the site collection owner cannot add new users to the site collection themselves. That's obviously inefficient, so make sure each web application's Content Database Access account (the account that accesses the web application's content database, also known as the web application's application pool account) has access to the OU as well. The need to delegate control to the Farm account and Content Database Access accounts is why some preplanning is in order. First, make sure you have an OU in Active Directory specifically for SharePoint. Then verify that you have created domain user accounts for the Farm account and for your Web Application Database Access account (for each web application you create). Then delegate control of the OU to those accounts. At that point you are ready to do a standard Advanced, Web Front end installation of SharePoint, well, almost.

Installing SharePoint with ADAC enabled *is* essentially doing an Advanced, Web Front End installation except for one thing; you must click the Advanced settings button at the correct point in the initial configuration process. If you miss that button, you cannot enable ADAC, you'll have to uninstall and start over. Remember, you can only choose to use Active Directory Account Creation mode once, during the install. At that point, it is burned into the configuration database, changing how it handles site collections and user accounts permanently.

PREPARE FOR ACTIVE DIRECTORY ACCOUNT CREATION MODE

This section won't walk you through the installation process again (we did that twice in Chapter 2), but it will show you when you must enable ADAC during the process. Before you begin the installation, you must create the unique OU in Active Directory that ADAC will use.

IF YOU AREN'T THE AD ADMINISTRATOR

If you are not an AD administrator (someone with the right to access and change Active Directory), you won't be able to create the Organizational Unit. The AD administrator will have to do this part for you. However, knowing the following information will help you tell them what you need and why.

CREATE THE ADAC ORGANIZATIONAL UNIT

To start, you'll need to access the Active Directory Users and Computers console. Once you are there, right-click the Domain icon, go to New in the popup menu, and then select Organizational Unit. In the New Object-Organizational Unit dialog box, name your OU (my example uses **ADACsp4**). Then click OK to create the OU. Your new OU should be in the console, as you can see in Figure 15.1.

FIGURE 15.1
New OU for ADAC

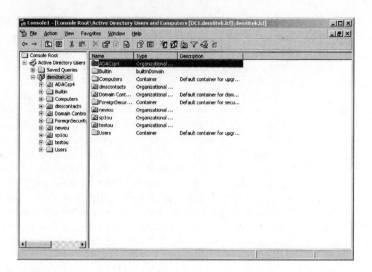

WHAT'S WITH ALL OF THE SP-SOMETHING SERVERS?

For those of you keeping track, this is the fourth installation of SharePoint for this book. SP1 was a Standalone, Basic install. SP2 was the Server Farm installation using RR1 as my SQL 2005 server. SP2 is used for most of the book's screenshots. SP3 is going to be used as the second web front end in the server farm with SP2, and it is going to be used to demonstrate how to set up network load balancing. SP4 will be used to demonstrate how to install SharePoint in Active Directory Account Creation mode. So now you know why there are so many SP-something servers in this book.

CREATE THE SERVICE ACCOUNTS

Once you've created your OU, you'll need to create your accounts to give access to the OU and then delegate control of the OU to them.

Just as a quick reminder, click the New User icon in the toolbar (it looks like a guy in a blue shirt with a star on the back of his head). In the New User dialog box, enter the user information (user first name, last name, and especially the user login name) for the Farm account for your new SharePoint server farm. In my example, it is called **wsssp4cfg**. When you are done entering the account information, click Next.

In the second dialog box, enter the password you want for the account. Make absolutely certain that you disable User must change password at next logon, because SharePoint doesn't have the means to do that. While you are there, set the password to never expire, so the user cannot change the password unless your environment requires it. Once you have completed those changes, click Next. It will take you to a Summary dialog box displaying your settings. If they look in order, click Finish.

Repeat the process for the Content Database account and give it a different account name, of course. My example uses **wsssp4con.**

Don't forget to create the accounts for the Search and Index services for this server. They just don't need to have access to the OU.

DELEGATE CONTROL OF THE OU TO THE SERVICE ACCOUNTS

After your accounts have been created, you'll need to delegate control of the OU to them so that ADAC will work. To do that, right-click the OU you created earlier, and select Delegate Control (Figure 15.2).

FIGURE 15.2
Select Delegate Control to manage the ADAC OU

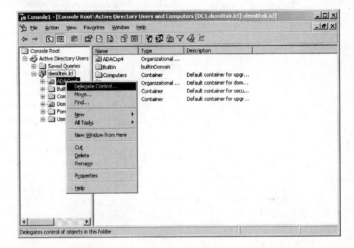

In the Delegation of Control Wizard, click Next to move beyond the Welcome screen. On the Users and Groups screen, you'll need to add the service accounts you created, so click the Add button. In the Select Users, Computers, and Groups dialog box, enter the user accounts (separated by a semicolon) and click Check Names to confirm that they are correct. If they are, click OK.

Back on the Delegation of Control Wizard, the accounts should be displayed in the Users or Groups box (Figure 15.3).

FIGURE 15.3
Users to whom control of the OU will be delgated

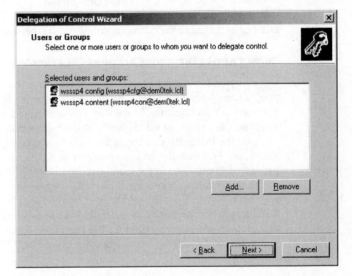

If they are correct, click Next to continue to delegate control. On the Tasks To Delegate screen (Figure 15.4), select the create, delete, and manage user accounts and Read all user information options, and then click Next.

FIGURE 15.4
Tasks to delegate to
the OU users

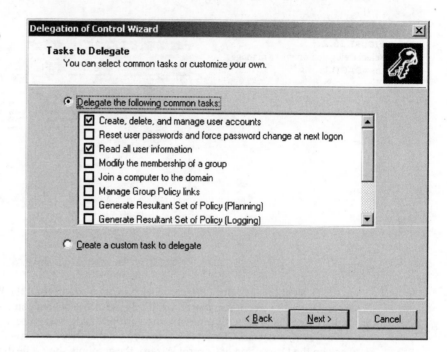

On the Completing The Delegation of Control Wizard screen, check the summary, make sure your settings are correct, and then click Finish.

When you're done, you'll have an OU to which to assign ADAC in SharePoint and control of it will be delegated to the correct accounts. You'll be ready to install SharePoint.

ENABLE ACTIVE DIRECTORY ACCOUNT CREATION MODE DURING INSTALLATION

Use Chapter 2 as a guideline to confirm you have the preinstallation requirements in place. When you've completed those steps, download the correct SharePoint installer (SharePoint.exe) for your server's architecture. Make sure you are logged in and running the installation using the setup account you created explicitly for installing SharePoint.

After the installation of the SharePoint files is complete and you've chosen to do an Advanced, Web Front End installation (you cannot use ADAC mode with a Basic install), you will be prompted to move on to the Configuration Wizard. In the wizard, make sure that you are creating a new server farm, choose the correct SQL server, name your database (or keep the default, whichever works for you), and then enter the Farm account that you created earlier as the Database Access account (my example is **wsssp4cfg**). From there, choose your port and the default authentication method for the farm (and specifically for Central Administration). At that point, you will reach the Completing the SharePoint Products and Technologies Configuration

Wizard. This summary page gives you the chance to verify your choices because this is the last time you will get to go back and change anything. Stop, do **not** click Next!

On the Completing the SharePoint Products and Technologies Configuration Wizard screen, don't do anything yet. Do not click Next. Do not finish unless you want to lose your chance to enable Account Creation mode. This is the only place you will be able to make that change. You can't see it in Figure 15.5, but the opportunity for ADAC is there.

FIGURE 15.5
Completing
Configuration screen,
Advanced Settings
button

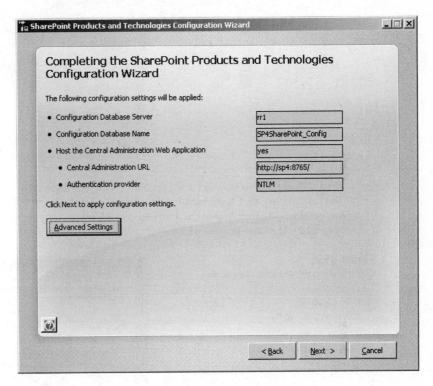

The ADAC setting is hidden beneath the Advanced Settings button. To enable it, click the Advanced Settings button.

On the Advanced Settings screen, you'll see the settings for Active Directory Account Creation mode. Click the check box to enable Active Directory Account Creation Mode. Once that is enabled, you'll need to enter the domain and the Organizational Unit that ADAC is going to use.

For the domain, use the single-word NetBIOS name for the domain. Do not try to use anything vaguely like an FQDN. Use a single word only. In my example, the domain name is dem0tek.

For the Active Directory Organizational Unit, my example uses ADACsp4, which is the one created earlier in the chapter. Use the OU that is correct for you, the one you delegated to your Farm and Content Database accounts so they could control it (see Figure 15.6 for an example).

FIGURE 15.6
Enable ADAC on the Advanced Settings Screen

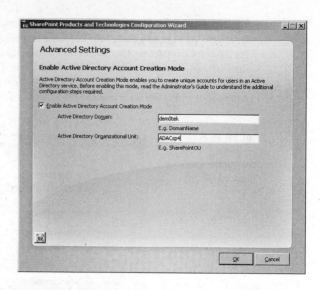

After you enter your domain and OU, click OK to continue.

The Completing the SharePoint Products and Technologies Configuration Wizard summary screen will indicate that Active Directory Account Creation mode has been enabled and list the domain and OU names (Figure 15.7).

FIGURE 15.7
Configuration Wizard Summary Screen

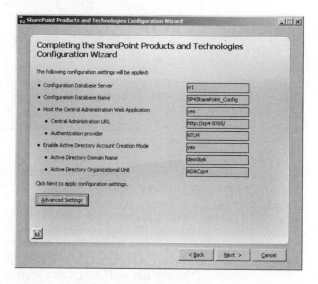

If all of the settings are correct (they are in my example), click Next. Keep in mind, this is the last time you can go back and make any changes.

After you click Next, you will be taken to a final summary screen. When you click Finish on it, Central Administration will open. Log in with your setup account because no other accounts have been created yet.

Using SharePoint in Active Directory

ACCOUNT CREATION MODE

Once you've logged in and added the server to your browser's trusted sites, you can do your post installation configuration tasks as you wish. However, ADAC absolutely requires that you set up outgoing email before you try to create any site collections because it expects to send out invitations to the new site collection owners, members, and the like.

You have already seen how to do the configuration tasks necessary for a SharePoint site in previous chapters, so this section will cover the differences between using Domain account mode and ADAC in SharePoint. To start, after you've configured your incoming and outgoing email, create your first web application as you normally would. My example uses the default SharePoint-80 settings at the root path. Be sure to specify the Application Pool account for the web application as the account you created for that purpose, and is the one that you delegated control to the ADAC OU.

ADAC IS FOR USERS, DUDE

Even though SharePoint is running in ADAC mode, Central Administration does not use that mode. It still runs in Domain account mode. Therefore, if the ADAC OU is accidentally deleted, Central Administration will still work. It has to do that in order to be able to create a web application and the Central Administration site collection without human interaction.

Most of Central Administration works normally in ADAC mode except for Self-Site Creation and manual Site Collection creation and deletion. Creating and deleting site collections must be done at the command line using STSADM.

CREATE A SITE COLLECTION IN ADAC MODE

Once you've created a web application, it can contain site collections. If you try to add a site collection to a web application by clicking Create Site, it will take you to an error page (Figure 15.8).

FIGURE 15.8
Create Site error page for ADAC

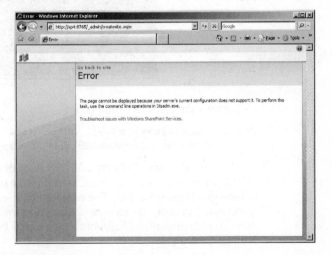

This means you have to go to a server on the server farm that has SharePoint installed locally and create site collections there. Remember, STSADM cannot work remotely. Keep in mind that you must be logged in with an account that is a farm administrator and at least a local administrator of the SharePoint server to run STSADM and add site collections.

From a SharePoint server, open a command prompt and navigate to the path where STSADM resides—or add it to your system's path, whatever works for you. Then use STSADM to create a site.

Now remember, SharePoint is doing Active Directory Account Creation, and that means that it only wants user email addresses so it can generate accounts from them. That includes the site collection owner. I'm not kidding. Remember that the user must already have an active email account with an *alias* (the first part of the email address) that can be used as their account name.

Here is the syntax to create a site collection:

```
STSADM -o createsite -url
      http:// pathtothesitecollection -owneremail
      theirexistingemail@somewhere.com
```

You can also optionally specify a template if you'd like. My example uses one of my own email addresses for this because I need to receive the invitation email myself. In my example, the *owneremail* will be `callahan@callahantech.com` (see Figure 15.9). Because this is going to be the first site collection in the web application, the path will be `http://sp4`, which is basically the root of the web application.

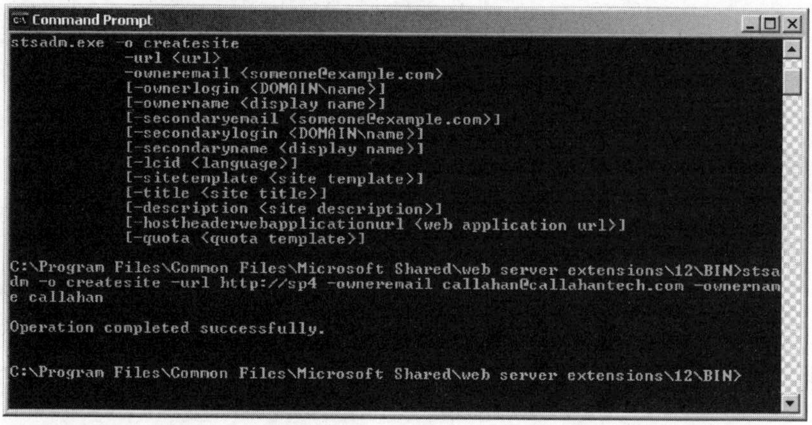

FIGURE 15.9

Creating a site
collection using
STSADM

For my example, you would enter:

**Stsadm -o createsite -url http://sp4 -owneremail
      callahan@callahantech.com -ownername callahan**

The site collection will be created with the path `http://sp4`. The *owneremail* will be `callahan@callahantech.com`, meaning that the user account created for the owner of this site collection will be `callahan`. The parameter *ownername* is also specified. Doing so was unnecessary because the account name will be `callahan`, but my example demonstrates that this is one way to display, in SharePoint, a username that is more appropriate or easier to remember than an email alias.

TEMPLATE-LESS SITE COLLECTION

When I do create a site collection at the command line, SharePoint will give me the opportunity to choose my template after I log in. This is useful if you are giving someone a site collection to do with as they please. Otherwise, you can assign them a template by using the `sitetemplate` parameter. (See Chapter 13 "STSADM: A Look at the SharePoint Command-Line Tool," for more on STSADM.) Keep in mind that there are other options when you create site collections at the command line. I am keeping it simple.

Once the site collection is created successfully, the new owner will be sent an invitation email and an account with a randomly generated password will be created.

In the AD Users and Computers console, you can see the new user account object in the ADAC OU (Figure 15.10).

FIGURE 15.10
New User in ADAC OU

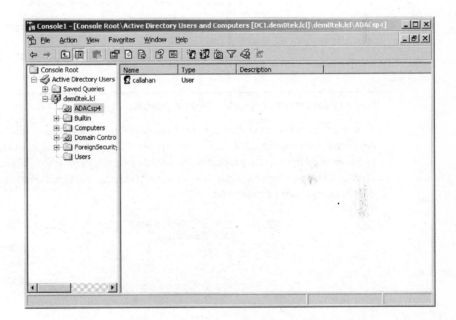

And as you can see in Figure 15.11, user `callahan` received an email invitation to the new site collection with their username and password. Notice that there is a link to change the password as soon as possible. There are no explicit instructions on how to change the password while on the site. However, it's really easy to do.

When you get your username, password, and URL to the site, feel free to take it for a spin. When you browse to the site, you'll be prompted to log in using your username and random password, which you can cut and pasted from the email. Remember that the format for logging in to SharePoint is still `domain\username` because it is still using Windows authentication.

FIGURE 15.11
Email Invitation to New User

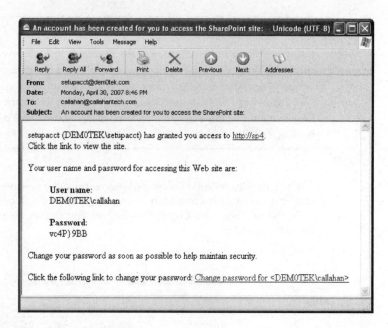

YOU ARE INVITED TO CHANGE YOUR PASSWORD

If the users want to change their password before doing anything else on the site, they can follow the link in the email invitation. When they do so, they will, of course, have to use the randomly generated password to get in. Once they log in they'll be taken directly to a `password.aspx` page to change their password. This password page can also be accessed from the user's User Information page, if they should want to change their password later.

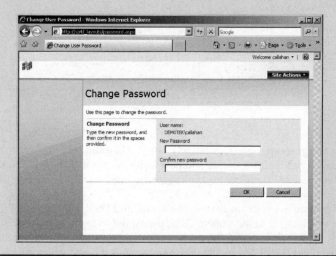

Once you log in, you will be prompted to choose a template. For convenience sake, this example is going to use the good old Team Site template. It will take a few minutes to process, but eventually you will be taken to an interesting "add users" page, Set Up Groups. As you can see in Figure 15.12, the page has three sections, one for each default group: Visitors, Members, and Owners. Notice that the site owner is a member of both the Members and Owners groups. Also notice that a Create button appears in the bottom-right of the People Picker field of each section. The button says Create, not Add, because SharePoint knows you will be creating AD accounts from here.

FIGURE 15.12
Adding Users to the Site, ADAC style

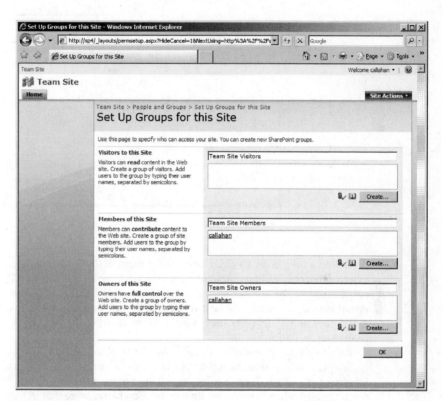

CREATE A NEW USER ACCOUNT IN SHAREPOINT TO ADD TO AD

To add a new user to the Members group, for example, click the Create button for that section. It will take you to a Create Active Directory Account dialog box. Notice the older version look and feel of it in Figure 15.13. Remember that the email address needs to be unique. If it already exists in Active Directory, SharePoint will append a number to the end of the name and add it to the OU, giving that person two accounts in the domain. Having two accounts is unavoidable if you want a member of the domain to have access to a SharePoint site using ADAC (they'll have a user account, and an account based on their email address in the OU), because you should be using this for external users only.

FIGURE 15.13
The Create Active
Directory Account
dialog box

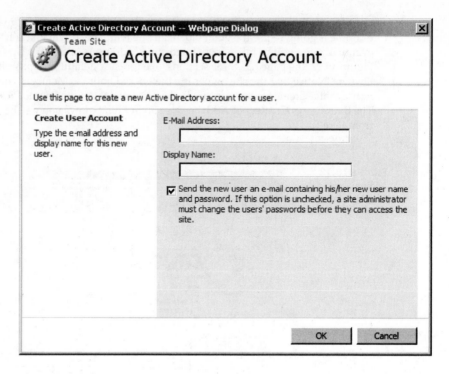

To add a user, enter an email address for them in the E-mail address field. My example uses an external, telecommuting employee who doesn't have an account in AD but has a dem0tek.com email account, juniper@dem0tek.com. When this email is added as a user in the Members group his display name will be **Juniper** (although you can specify a different display name if you'd like), and a Juniper user object will be added to the ADAC OU in AD. The user will then receive an invitation email.

If that's all that needs to be added now, click OK to continue.

That will take you to the top-level site for the new site collection, using the Team Site template. Of course, the title is Team Site by default, and there is no description because you didn't use the option to add one when you set up the site. You can change that in the site settings though, so no harm done. If you really wanted a description, you could have used parameters in STSADM to do so when you created the site.

As you can see in Figure 15.14 the Welcome menu indicates that my user, *callahan* is logged in and everything else seems in order. The site will function as any site should; you can build lists, libraries, web parts, etc. You can configure it to accept anonymous access, give lists and libraries unique permissions—the whole shebang. The only difference is how users are added to the site. Of course, you can also change your password (Figure 15.15) by going to User Information for your account and clicking Change Password on the Action bar.

To add a user to the site collection now that you're here, go to People And Groups by clicking the link on the Quick Launch bar.

FIGURE 15.14
New user logged into new site

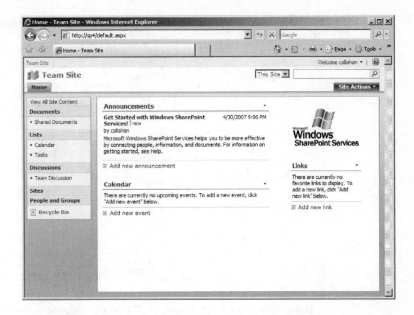

FIGURE 15.15
User Information Page

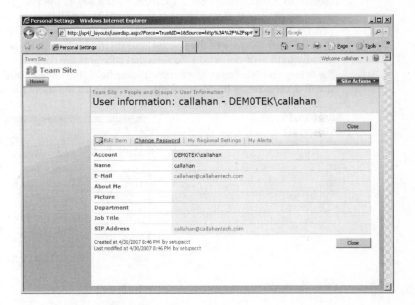

In People And Groups, the Team Site Members group will probably end up displaying by default. As you can see in Figure 15.16, there are two members: the `callahan` account and the one created in the example, `Juniper`. To add another account, simply click the New button.

FIGURE 15.16
Two SharePoint site members

On the Add Users page (Figure 15.17), you can see that everything looks as it should; nothing specific to ADAC, except for the Create button below the People Picker field. If you were to try to use an account that you know is in the ADAC OU but was created for a different site collection, you would not find it when you checked the name because it doesn't exist for the *site collection*. The People Picker, because of the special account mode SharePoint is using, will see only those accounts already in the site collection. To see what accounts are considered part of the site collection, click the Browse button below the People Picker field (the Browse button looks like an address book). It will open a dialog box displaying, by default, all the users for the site collection (Figure 15.18).

FIGURE 15.17
Add Users page

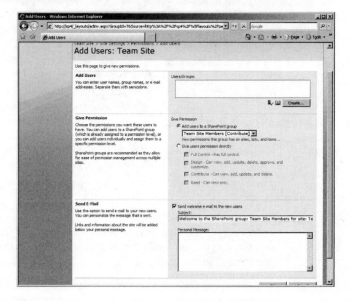

FIGURE 15.18
Browsing Site Collection Users

SERVICE ACCOUNTS ARE WELCOME TOO

Notice that the Setup account and the Search Index account—(I set up the Search service for the farm)—are considered users of the site collection. This is because the Setup account created the site collection at the command line on the server because that was the account logged into the server locally at that time. Also, at the Policy for Web Application level, the "Search Crawling account" (sometimes known as the *content access account* or *index account*) is given read access to all content in the web application's content database.

ADAC was meant to be used to make it possible for users outside of Active Directory to be added as users to access site collections. And, as it happens, it is possible that a site collection administrator could get a little out of hand as to how many people they invite to access their sites.

To avoid having a user account overload in the ADAC OU in Active Directory, you can curtail the number of invited users a site collection can have. Just like limiting the amount of storage a site collection can take, you can specify a user invitation quota.

To do this, go to Central Administration ➤ Application Management, and select Quota Templates under SharePoint Site Management.

On the Quota Templates page, you can see the standard settings for creating or editing quota templates. If you create a quota template (which, of course, I encourage), you'll see a new section at the bottom of the page that only exists for ADAC installation; Invite User Limits (see Figure 15.19). This section allows you to enable a user quota, and specify a limit to the number of users a site collection can contain. If you reach that limit and try to add another user, you will be unable to until you remove a user account or two to get back under the limit.

FIGURE 15.19
Invite User Limits

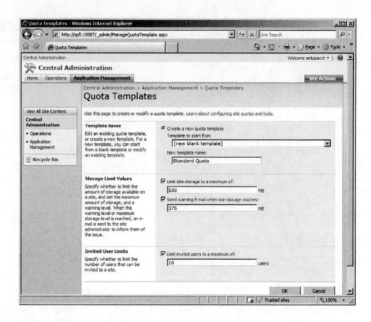

So that's Active Directory Account Creation mode in a nutshell. It does change the way accounts are handled in the interface, as well as how SharePoint handles site creation. However, when you need to have the option of adding users to SharePoint without them first having an account in AD, ADAC is there for you.

WINDOWS MOBILE USERS

By now you've probably noticed every SharePoint site shows two URLs on the Site Settings page—a Site URL and a mobile Site URL. These two URLs can be found for every site, listed at the top of the Site Settings page.

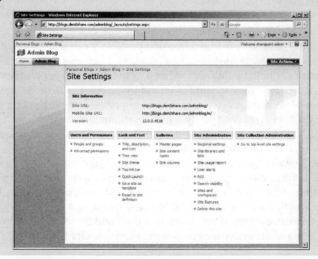

The mobile site URL is the same as the Site URL but with an addition - `/m/`. So the site `http://blogs.demoshare.com/adminblog/` has a mobile site with the URL `http://blogs.demoshare.com/adminblog/m/`.

The Mobile URL is designed for mobile devices—commonly Smartphones or PDAs using Windows Mobile. The Mobile URL provides a slimmed down version of the website with text-only links and data for rapid review on the smaller screen of the mobile device.

Windows Mobile supports TCP/IP access, and most SmartPhones and PDAs can connect to the web wirelessly through WiFi or a phone network, and some support wired Ethernet connections. SharePoint automatically formats all websites for optimal mobile use, and so by default your SharePoint server is mobile-ready.

If you take the example AdminBlog page shown below, you can see the full site on a regular web browser by going to `http://blogs.demoshare.com/adminblog/`

The site has two blog entries—the default one created with the site and a second one talking about a server migration. You can also see this site on a Windows Mobile device by launching Internet Explorer (Windows Mobile has its own version of IE) and going to `http://blogs.demoshare.com/adminblog/m/`.

You can see the site has been dramatically simplified, and only shows the titles for the two blog entries. Clicking on the link for Server Migration on Saturday in this example takes you to that blog entry.

Now, it is possible to go to the site's main URL in the Windows Mobile version of IE, but because the screen is so small, the site is nearly unusable. It's not something you're going to browse easily.

So it's best to stick to the mobile URLs for any phone or PDA based browsing.

Windows Mobile users are just like other users—they browse the site using a URL (which needs to exist in DNS and have an internal and Public URL in a Web Application's zone), authenticate, and are restricted by whatever permissions you set on the site. Since they are by definition mobile, you will probably want the sites they visit to be accessible via the Internet, so review Alternate Access Mapping in Chapter 8.

Installing an Additional SharePoint Server on a Server Farm

Because SharePoint was meant to be able to support tens of thousands of users, it can be deployed in a server farm fashion. Up to this point, we have been using a server farm/web front end installation of SharePoint for our single SharePoint server to make use of SQL 2005 for the SharePoint databases (instead of using the Windows Internal Database locally). But the real point of having a SharePoint server farm is to have multiple, identical, front end web servers offering the same content for uninterrupted user access, and to spread out the services that might consume extra processor time, like search, among those servers.

To make this possible, you must install more web front end servers, or at least, a second web front end server. This server will simply access the same configuration and content databases of the first SharePoint server, with the intention of being used to continue to offer SharePoint to clients without a hitch or break in service, should the first server become busy or unresponsive (exactly how that works depends on your load balancing product). The additional server will literally be a mirror of the first SharePoint server and is not really intended to independently host web applications and sites on its own.

SOMETIMES YOU FEEL LIKE MIRRORING, SOMETIMES YOU DON'T

If you want to manage your resources by splitting web applications between the first server and additional servers, then you may not want to add the extra servers to the existing server farm. Instead, if you want them to be accessible individually, install them each as independent server farms (or if it works for you, as stand-alone servers).

The problem then becomes trying to remember what site is on what server, and teaching users which server to access for what resource.

When offering load balancing by having all the servers mirror the first, all of the web applications are identical among the servers. This allows, with load balancing, the users to learn one server address to access their SharePoint resources. Then, if the first server becomes overloaded or non-responsive, the users are transparently sent to one of the other servers who can host the same data.

Each option has its strengths and weaknesses, so choose carefully before you install SharePoint on any additional servers.

Installing SharePoint on a server intended to be part of a farm is easy. It's just like installing SharePoint on a server intended to be the first in a server farm, except that, during the configuration wizard, you choose to connect to an existing configuration database, rather than creating a new one.

When you install SharePoint on the first server of the farm, you need to enable all of the services on that server if you want to use them. However, when other SharePoint servers are added to the farm, some of those services can be assigned to those servers instead, easing the strain on the resources of the first server.

When installing SharePoint on a server intended to be an addition to the SharePoint server farm, you need to be sure that the server meets the minimum hardware requirements or better, and is running Windows 2003 SP1 (or higher). IIS 6.0 (with SMTP to share the email load) and .NET Framework 3.0 also need to be installed, and ASP .NET 2.0 (installs with the .NET Framework 3.0) must be enabled in IIS.

ADD A SHAREPOINT SERVER TO AN EXISTING SERVER FARM

When installing the SharePoint software itself; make certain you are logged in as the setup account. When you double-click the SharePoint.exe installer, you will go through the wizard screens just as you would any other server farm install; accept the EULA, choose Advanced, select Web Front End as the Server Type, and click Install Now. It is only when you get to the Configuration Wizard that you get to specify that this will be an additional server and not a new server farm installation.

INSTALLATION LOCATION MATTERS

Something to keep in mind about installing SharePoint on additional servers in a server farm is the need to install it on the same drive for each server. SharePoint has some file location information written to the configuration database that requires that the same SharePoint files be in the same location on each web front end server.

So after you choose to run the SharePoint Products and Technologies Configuration Wizard (you can see why I just call it the Configuration Wizard), you'll need to click Next past the welcome screen, and click OK on the warning dialog box, to reach the screen where you make the choice that decides whether or not the server will be part of an existing farm or beginning a new farm.

On that Connect to a server farm screen (Figure 15.20) you have two choices; to make this installation part of an existing server farm or create a new farm. To make this installation part of an existing server farm, make certain "Yes, I want to connect to an existing server farm" is chosen. It is the default, conveniently enough. To continue the installation, click Next.

FIGURE 15.20
Connect to a
Server Farm

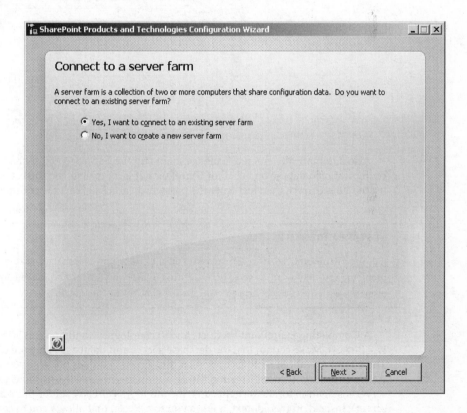

On the Specify Configuration Database Settings screen, enter the SQL server name (my example is RR1). To confirm that the server can be found from here, click Retrieve Database Names. This will also, once the database server is found, populate the Database name field with the most likely configuration databases that are available on that server. In my case it was correct, choosing SharePoint_Config from the databases on my SQL 2005 server (Figure 15.21).

FIGURE 15.21
Specify Configuration
Database Settings

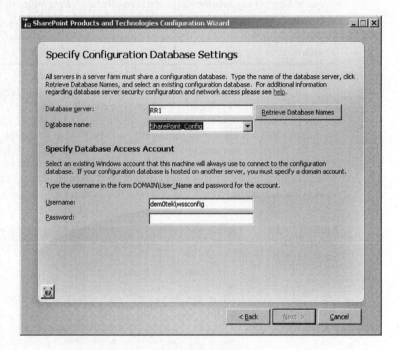

Also automatically entered is the username for the Farm account that accesses the configuration database on behalf of SharePoint. It is, of course, the correct one in my case. If the username is correct, then just enter the password and click Next to continue the installation.

MISTAKEN IDENTITY

If the username is not correct, you can fix it and click Next, however that mistake could indicate a greater problem. You may want to go to your existing SharePoint server and make certain it is functioning properly, with the correct Farm account, before continuing the install.

A Completing SharePoint Products and Technologies Configuration Wizard Summary screen will be next. Make certain that the database server and database name are correct (Figure 15.22). There is an Advanced Settings button on this screen that does not give you the option to use Active Directory Account Creation Mode, as you might have learned to expect from the first server installation for the farm (it can't, the mode was already set for this server farm with the first server). Instead, in this context, it takes you to a screen that allows you to configure whether or not this server will be used to also host the Central Administration website. Although this server is being installed on a second server to mirror the content of the SharePoint sites on the original server, we are not going to load balance the Central Administration site (we'll do that later).

FIGURE 15.22
Completing Configuration Wizard
Summary screen

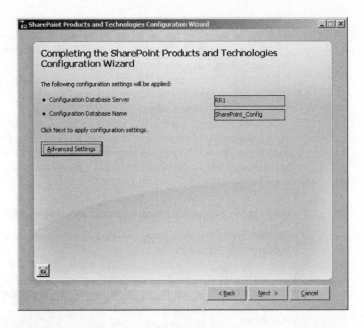

So if we were to click on the Advanced Settings button, we'd see that the option to not use this machine to host the Central Administration website is selected by default (Figure 15.23). This means that the Central Administration web application will not be created in IIS on this Server. If load balancing Central Administration was required for the server farm, then using the server to host the website on this machine would be necessary. Often the site is isolated to one server for security's sake.

FIGURE 15.23
Advanced Settings, host Central
Administration screen

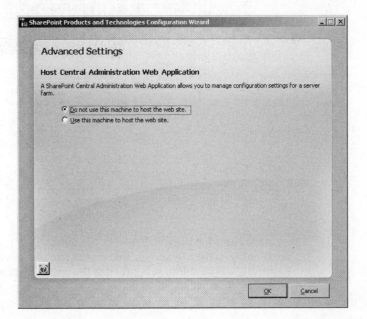

After you make your choice, you can either click OK to save the change, or Cancel to just go back to the summary screen. Once on the summary screen, click Next to continue the installation.

At that point the Configuration Wizard will connect to the configuration database, and do the necessary things to get SharePoint up and running.

Once the Configuration Wizard is done, you should get a Configuration Successful screen. Click Finish to open the default browser on the server (hopefully Internet Explorer) to go to the Central Administration site.

You may be prompted to log into the Central Administration site. Central Administration, with our configuration, is only located on the original SharePoint server. Use the setup account if you'd like, or whatever account you might have added as a farm administrator. Remember to make the site a trusted site in the browser, if you haven't already.

CONFIRM THE NEW SERVER IN CENTRAL ADMINISTRATION

On the Central Administration home page, the new server is displayed as part of the Topology of the farm (see Figure 15.24).

FIGURE 15.24
New Server in
Farm Topology

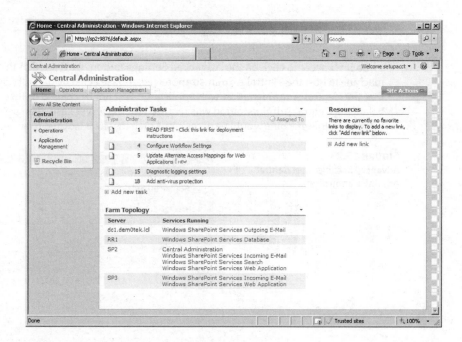

In the Farm Topology web part, notice that Incoming E-Mail and the Web Application services are running on the new server. That means that this server, when used with network load balancing, will be able to support all of the web application services that the first server does, as well as accept email if necessary.

SOME SERVICES WERE MEANT FOR FAILOVER

Incoming email wasn't necessarily intended to be load balanced, but if the first server's incoming email goes down, the service can be stopped there and shifted to the second server. It's more of a fail over feature than a load balancing one. In this case, Central Administration is really just reporting that SMTP is running on the second server.

Also added to the home page are two Administrator Tasks: the READ FIRST and "Update Alternate Access Mappings for Web Applications." Both of these items were returned to the list in response to the addition of the new server to the topology. They are new server tasks triggered by the installation of the new server.

The additional server was literally meant to either host services that may need to be shared with or removed from the first server; or to work with that first server in a load balanced environment; or possibly do a bit of both. It does have the same web applications in IIS locally that the first server has, but they were meant to be used to keep service to the SharePoint clients seamlessly effective, offering its web application pages when the first server's load might slow it down.

To see what services are available to be configured on a server, you need to go that server's Services on Server page. From Central Administration's home page, the easiest way to do that is to click on the server's name in the Farm Topology web part.

That will open the Services on Server page for that server (Figure 15.25).

FIGURE 15.25
Services on Server
page

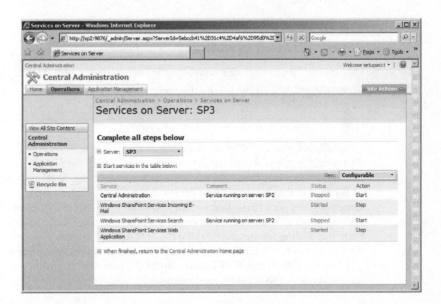

On the Services on Server page is a Server field in which you can choose the server you want to manage (if the one displayed isn't the one you want). There is also a View menu so you can see only the Configurable services for a server (the default view), or All services (even the ones you can do nothing about). Beneath that are the services displayed in the chosen view for that particular server, with columns for the current status of the service on the server, and an action column, containing the actions available concerning the service. Services that are not configured or running on the server are considered Stopped, those that are configured or running locally are considered Started, and those that are stopped locally but are running on a different server on the farm are indicated.

In my example, the configurable services for the new server (SP3) are:

Central Administration   This service both adds the Central Administration web application to the server, but manages it as well.

Windows SharePoint Services Incoming E-Mail   This service is available on this server because the SMTP service is enabled in IIS for this server. However, in the Incoming E-Mail settings, this server is not indicated as the incoming email server for the farm. It can be though, should something occur to the first server.

Windows SharePoint Services Search   This service is not enabled on this server. When enabled it runs the search and index services in order for data to be indexed from the content databases and accessed via search query. Currently this services is being hosted by the first server in the farm.

Windows SharePoint Services Web Application   This service will be running by default on any web front end server. This service is what adds the SharePoint web applications to this server in IIS, and keeps this server's IIS synchronized with changes that might occur on the server farm.

A FRONTLESS FRONT END SERVER

Theoretically, if you want this server to only host services such as search or incoming email, you can disable the web application service to conserve server resources. The server will then be on the farm to run those services and nothing else.

Additional services that are available on the server that you cannot configure are Windows SharePoint Services Administration (which is basically the SPAdmin service) and the Windows SharePoint Services Timer (which is the SPTimer service). These cannot be disabled in this GUI.

Right now this server is not supporting the Central Administration service. But, what if, in case something happens to the first server, you want to add that service to this server as well? There are some settings in SharePoint that, once you miss your chance at configuring it, you can never get it back. But adding (or *provisioning*) the Central Administration service to a server is not one of them. As a matter of fact, you can start or stop this server whenever you need to.

First, to confirm that the Central Administration web application is, in fact, not supported on this server, let's check the IIS management console.

CONFIRM SHAREPOINT WEB SITES IN IIS

To check what SharePoint did or did not add to IIS for the additional server, open the IIS management console (Start ➢ Administrative Tools ➢ Internet Information Services (IIS) Manager). In the console, open the Web Sites node to view the IIS Web Sites available (Figure 15.26). You'll see that the default Web Site is stopped, and that there is only SharePoint-80.

FIGURE 15.26
IIS Web Sites on additional
SharePoint server

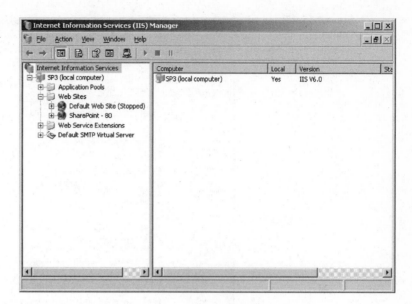

This confirms that Central Administration is not being supported on this server.

KEEPING IT SIMPLE

For this section, to keep things simple, I have removed any of the extra web applications that were created in previous chapters, so the install of SharePoint looks exactly as it would be after you did a fresh install. So if you are looking for SharePoint-8080 or SharePoint-Tech (from Chapter 8), they are not there for this example.

ENABLE THE CENTRAL ADMINISTRATION SERVICE ON THE NEW SERVER

In this example, Central Administration is not listed on the server because we chose not to support it during the installation (it is running on the other server however). Central Administration is not a service that required to run on only one server on the farm. Because of this, it is up to you as to how many servers on your farm end up running Central Administration. It is suggested that it be enabled on at least two servers on the farm or more, for redundancy's sake. However, this point can be hotly contested by those who feel Central Administration should be secured on one server only. But it's always good to know how to do it, even if you don't end up implementing it.

To enable the Central Administration service on the additional server, simply return to the Services on Server page in your browser, find Central Administration in the services table for the additional server, and click the **Start** link next to it in the Action column.

Initially the status of the service will change to Starting while the web application is added to IIS, then the status will change to started (Figure 15.27). Also notice that, once the service is started on this server, the indicator that the service is available on a different server disappears. This does not mean that that service was disabled, it just isn't necessary, apparently, to mention it, now that the service is running locally.

FIGURE 15.27
Central
Administration started
on new server in server
farm

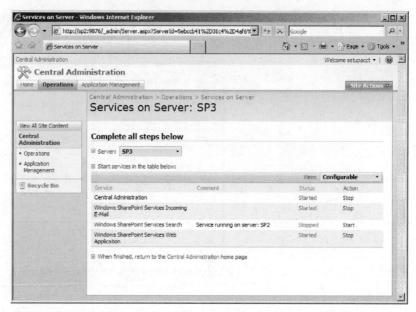

And if you go to the IIS management console on the new server (Figure 15.28), it will now contain the Central Administration Web Site (no need for an iisreset).

FIGURE 15.28
Central
Administration
Web Site on new
server in server farm

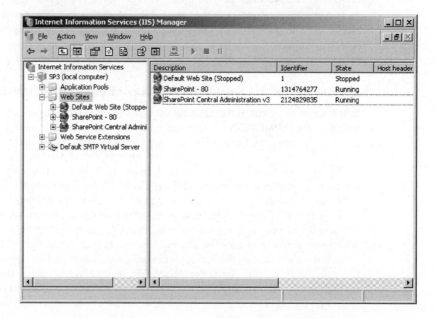

So now the new server is also hosting Central Administration. If necessary the Central Administration site can be assigned a load balanced URL and accessed even when the first server is unresponsive. This is an example of enabling a service on an additional server.

There are many reasons why a SharePoint server might be slow in its response to clients, not the least of which is during the time that SharePoint is indexing the content databases for the search service. If the server that is running search is underpowered, it might be a good idea to move that service to a different, more powerful server on the SharePoint farm.

MOVE A SERVICE FROM ONE SHAREPOINT SERVER TO ANOTHER SERVER ON THE FARM

To move a service from one server to another is easy, but does take some planning. In most cases, the service would need to be stopped on the original server, which means that service would be unavailable to SharePoint users until the move is complete. Once the service is stopped on the original server, it then needs to be configured and started on the target server. In the circumstance of the Search service, the service doesn't necessarily need to be stopped on the first server (search will happily work on both servers) but affected web applications in the farm would need to be assigned the new server for their search needs after the change is complete. Then the new server would need time to index those content databases before search will actually begin to work again for the users. Obviously this is not something to undertake during times of high activity on the servers. So plan to move or add services during times of low to no SharePoint access (such as the middle of the night, or over a holiday weekend).

To demonstrate moving SharePoint services, I am going to move the search service from one server to another. In my example, search has been hosted on the first server, SP2. However, now that the additional server is up and running, I'd like to move search over to it to free up resources on SP2. The newer server can run search more easily, and I would rather simply remove the service from the first server.

First, I am going to stop the service on the original server. To do this, open the Central Administration site and log in as a Farm administrator. On the home page you can click on the server's name in the Farm Topology web part, or you can go to the Operations page and click Services on Server then select the original server from the server menu. Either way you need to open the Services on Server page and display the services of the original server (Figure 15.29).

CAN'T STOP ROCKIN'

It is not absolutely mandatory to stop search on the first server when moving it to another server. However, I have found it helps to disable search on the first server, and then start it on the other server. It clearly indicates which server will do indexing, and avoids any conflicts if the service account names or passwords are changed.

However, if there is a web application that absolutely must remain searchable during this process, you can keep the search service running on the first server while enabling it on the second (and keep that web application's content database associated with that server until the move is complete). However, that means you must use exactly the same search and content access service accounts for the additional server that are running on the first.

FIGURE 15.29
Services on original server

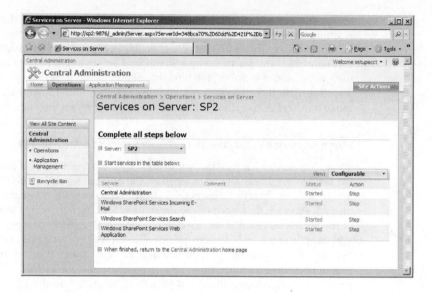

On the page, notice that the Search service is started. To stop it, simply click Stop in the Action column for that service.

A warning dialog box will come up (Figure 15.30), informing you that if the service is stopped the index files will be deleted and the service itself will be uninstalled.

WARNING ADDENDUM

What it doesn't tell you is if you want to re-enable the service it will be unable to use the database it has now. Search cannot reuse search databases. Once you disable search, and then re-enable it, you must delete the old database or specify a different database name for search so it can create a new one.

FIGURE 15.30
Warning dialog box when stopping the search service

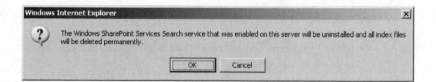

Click OK. It may take a few minutes to completely remove search from the server. But when it is done, you will see that Search on the original server has been stopped. Also displayed, as shown in Figure 15.31, is a notice that the service is required on the farm. That is not exactly true. If you do not want your users to every be able to search, then you can leave this service disabled. That isn't really practical in most circumstances however, so once the service is disabled on the first server, it should be enabled on the target server.

FIGURE 15.31
Search removed from original server on farm

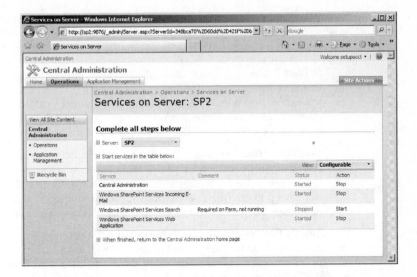

To do that, change the server displayed in the Server menu by clicking on it and selecting Change Server from the dropdown menu.

On the Select Server page, will be displayed all servers associated with the SharePoint farm in some way (such as the database and email server) not just web front end servers. Make certain that you select the server you will be moving the search service to (in my case that would be SP3). Once you select the server, you will be returned to the Services on Server page, only the services displayed will be those for the selected server.

Currently, there is no search running on the server farm, as is indicated in Figure 15.32. To remedy this, and start the search service on this target server, click Start in the Action column next to the listing for the Search service.

FIGURE 15.32
Additional Server displays no search service on SharePoint farm

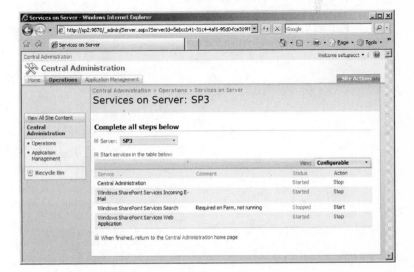

When you click Start, it will take you to the configuration page for the Search service on the server. You may already be familiar with this page because you originally configured search for the original server. But as a brief overview, here are the settings for this page:

Service Account   This section let's you enter the user account that the search service will use to access the search database and index files when a user generates a search query. On a domain, it needs to be a domain user, and on a stand-alone workgroup server, that must be an account on the local server. The account does not need special permissions, any permissions they need to SharePoint resources will be given to them by SharePoint during configuration.

Content Access Account   This section is for entering the user account to be used to index the data that will be searched. It crawls the content databases (that are assigned to it) and creates the index files on the local computer, to be merged to the search database at regular intervals. You don't need to give this user account special permissions. It does need read access to all content databases, but that will be set by SharePoint during configuration.

Search Database   This section contains the settings for specifying the database server and database name for the Search database, as well a the authentication information for the database (in case the SQL server is not using Windows Integrated Authentication, this section gives you the opportunity to specify the username and password to access SQL).

Indexing Schedule   This section allows you to set the interval in which the search service indexes SharePoint data. Although a high frequency rate is the most convenient, indexing is resource intensive, so it might be best to opt for a longer indexing schedule to conserve resources.

In order to configure search on the server, you need to enter a username and password for the Search account and Content Access account. The username must be in domain\username format.

Enter the server name and a search database name (or keep the default) in the Search Database section. The default is to access SQL using Windows Integrated Authentication. If you have SQL set up to use SQL authentication, be sure to enter the that information in the Search Database section as well. The database server in my example is RR1, and I am going to keep the default database name (Figure 15.33).

FIGURE 15.33
Search service configuration settings

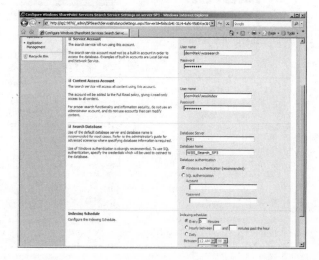

In the Indexing Schedule section, set the schedule you want the content access (index) service to use to index new data. In my case, I am leaving it at the default of five minutes. In my environment, the convenience of only having to wait five minutes for a list item or document to be searchable is worth it. However, I don't suggest you make your SharePoint server index your SharePoint content every five minutes unless you are certain the server can handle it without a drop in performance.

Once all of the settings are configured, click Start to, well, start the service. That will take you back to the Services on Server page, where the status of the service will be Starting (Figure 15.34). It will take a few minutes to create the index files, add the accounts to SQL (if you need to) with the correct permissions, and create the Search database. Eventually Starting will change to Started, which means that you can now assign this server to host search for your web applications.

FIGURE 15.34
Starting the search service on the new server

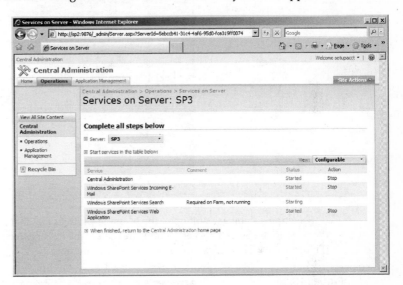

SEARCH REPAIR

If you find that you need to change the password of either account used by search, to make the change without stopping search and having to start over with a new database, click on the name of the service, Windows SharePoint Services Search, instead of the Action for it. This will open the configuration page for the service, allowing you to change only the account information and index schedule.

As a matter of fact, right now search will not work on your existing web applications (and any site collections contained therein). They lost their search settings because the server they were assigned to stopped its search service. (And if you hadn't stopped the service on the first server, you would still need to transfer the content database associations to the new search server.)

This is why the third step in moving the search service is to assign it to the existing web application databases.

To do that, while on the Central Administration site, go to the Application Management page, and click the Content databases link in the SharePoint Web Application Management category.

On the Manage Content Database are the databases for each of your web applications. There is a web application menu to choose the web application you would like to search enable, with the database or databases associated with that web application listed below it.

To enable search on a web application's database, select the database in the list (my example in Figure 15.35 is WSS_Content for the `http://sp2` web application).

FIGURE 15.35
Manage Content Database page

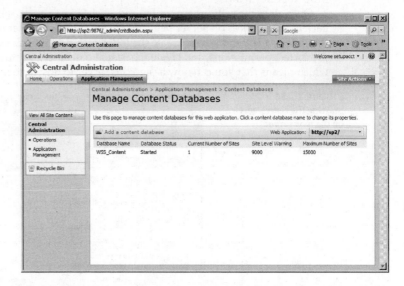

Selecting a database will open the Manage Content Database Settings page for it. Scroll down the page to the Search Server section, and select the new search server from the drop down list (Figure 15.36). Then click OK to finish the assignment.

FIGURE 15.36
Configuring new search server for content database

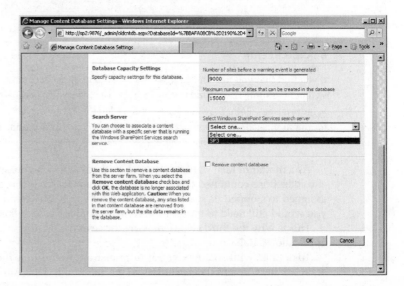

Remember to assign a search server for each web application and database that you need to be able to search.

THE SECRET LIFE OF WINDOWS SHAREPOINT SERVICES HELP SEARCH

Have you noticed that, sometimes, when you start the search service on a SharePoint server it calls itself Windows SharePoint Services Help Search for a while? Ever wonder why?

If you were to check online you would find that Windows SharePoint Services Help Search is considered by MOSS to be the equivalent of the Windows SharePoint Services 3.0 Search service. It is supposed to only search the help files. It doesn't use the normal index files. So when you first enable search on a WSS server, it may call itself Windows SharePoint Services Help Search until it has been assigned to a web application's content database or two, and then finished indexing them.

So after you start the search service, wait for the web applications to be indexed and then check the Services on Server list for that server, and you will likely see that it has changed from Windows SharePoint Services Help Search to plain, old Windows SharePoint Service Search.

Something to keep in mind is, unlike web content, services like search cannot be load balanced. Because of their programmatic nature, they are confined to running on a particular server or servers individually, and are assigned specifically to content databases. If you select a particular server to be the search server for a web application and that server goes down, then search for that web application's content will not work.

SO, YOU WANT MORE THAN ONE SEARCH SERVER ON YOUR NETWORK?

I know that the SharePoint documentation says both that you cannot have more than one index server on the network, and that you can have more than one search server.

But how can that be? In WSS 3.0 there is only one search service and it combines both functions. They are not two separate services that can be assigned independently—so how can you have one server that does indexing, and more than one search server on a server farm if the only search service available contains both?

The fact is, it's pretty simple. You *can* have more than one server on the farm run search. That makes sense, otherwise why bother being able to specify what search server you would like to associate with a given content database?

The trick is, when the second search server is enabled it takes over indexing. The first server keeps copies of the index files, but the second server actually does the indexing tasks. You can see it in the Application event logs; the first server stops generating master merge events, and the second server starts doing them instead.

The second and most important trick is there can be only one Search Service account and only one Content Access (or *Index*) account for the farm. Do not try to start search on the additional SharePoint server using different accounts (which you might be tempted to do for security and troubleshooting convenience). If you do, it will cause the first server's search service to fail.

At the command line, if you use STSADM to manage search, the parameter to specify the service accounts to configure and start search are called `farmserviceaccount` and `farmcontentaccessaccount`. That's it. One of each for the farm, and no more. Nowhere in the GUI does it mention that fact.

Therefore, if you want to enable search on more than one SharePoint server in the server farm, you must use the same accounts as those specified for the first server.

Otherwise it will fail.

This also means that indexing can never, actually, be redundant. But search can. Now you know.

A second server has been added to the farm. The Search service for the server farm has been moved from the original server to the new server. You've seen that the new server mirrors the web applications of the original server, and you've learned how easy it is to make a SharePoint server host the Central Administration site.

But what you may not realize is, short of its supporting the search service or a spare copy of the Central Administration site, this server is not really useful until Network Load Balancing is enabled on the web front end servers of the farm. The reason for this is the web applications hosted on the new server are not actually accessible on that server without explicitly configuring the server's address in Alternate Access Mapping (AAM). Of course, you would think that if the SharePoint-80 Web Site is hosted on this server, that we should be able to open a browser and access it on this server's address. But that is not the case. The new server's Web Sites are not meant to be accessed directly, but only as load balanced content.

In SharePoint, Alternate Access Mapping controls what URLs are accepted by web applications. Up to this point, our internal URL for the main SharePoint-80 web application has been the first server's address. In this example that is `http://sp2`. This address is the correct address for that site, if it were on only one server. But now it is echoed identically on a second server as well. The same web application, in two places. This is essentially step one of load balancing, to have two web servers with identical content. Step two is to have a shared URL so that both servers recognize and accept that URL to access that identical data. When you create a new web application, you can specify its load balanced URL. By default, SharePoint fills in that field for you with the URL you configured for that web application (including port, host header, whatever). But you can, and should, change it to the real shared address that you specify when implement network load balancing. However, in our case, with SharePoint-80, the server's URL was left as the default (the original server's address) for the load balanced URL because load balancing hasn't been enabled and it was the only server on the network.

This is why, in AAM, the internal URL for the SharePoint-80 web application is `http://sp2`. It is assumed by SharePoint to be the load balanced URL, even though it's not, and pointing to one server. You can see this by going to the Central Administration, Operations page, and clicking Alternate access mapping under Global Configuration. On that page you can see the internal URLs for the SharePoint-80 web application and Central Administration (Figure 15.37). These addresses are the default zone for those web applications, and under normal circumstances the default zone for a web application is also its load balanced URL. And since there is already a load balanced URL for these web applications, SharePoint didn't need to enter the new server's address into AAM. That server should be responding to the load balanced URL anyway.

FIGURE 15.37
URLs listed in
Alternate Access
Mappings page

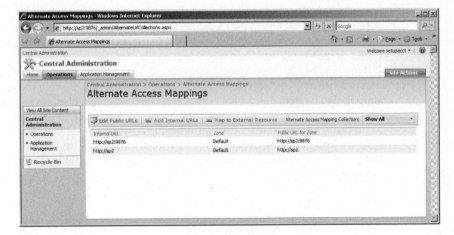

If you try to access the SharePoint web applications on the new server directly by using its address in the address bar of the browser, my example is `http://sp3`, SharePoint will assume it should send you to the load balanced URL (which in my case is `http://sp2`), where you will be authenticated by that server (Figure 15.38). The site will then load in the browser, with the load balanced URL displayed in the address bar.

FIGURE 15.38
Access to site on
additional server
redirects to load
balanced URL

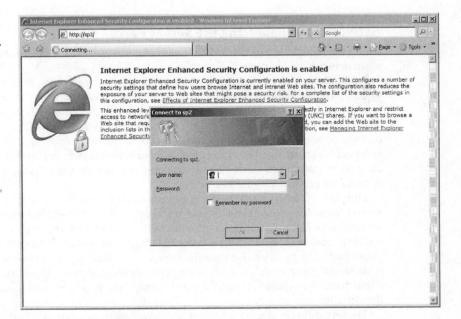

To identify why you cannot access the additional server on its own, you will need to check out Alternate Access Mapping.

Go back to the Alternate Access Mappings page. If you closed out, log into Central Administration, and go to the Operations page.

On the Operations page, click the Alternate access mappings link in the Global Configuration category.

Nowhere in Alternate Access Mapping is a listing for the new server (Figure 15.36). Which makes sense now that you know the default address for the server farms Internal URLs are supposed to be shared, load balanced URLs. And when load balancing's enabled, and the correct load balancing URL is used, that default zone URL will work for both servers.

To really demonstrate this, we need to enable network load balancing. There are numerous network load balancing products, both hardware and software, on the market today. However, for our purposes, the network load balancing functionality built into Windows Server 2003 will do just fine.

Advanced Configuration

Now that you are familiar with some advanced installations, it's time to become conversant in some of the advanced configurations available with SharePoint. Not the least of which are the practical concepts behind network load balancing SharePoint. Securing SharePoint with SSL and enabling Kerberos as an authentication method are also concepts any administrator should master. Finally, Directory Management Service, a new capability harnessing the power of Exchange and Active Directory, should round out your advanced configuration arsenal. This section will be exploring each of these concepts for your administrative enjoyment.

Network Load Balancing the Server Farm

Now that we have two servers in our SharePoint server farm, its time to see what SharePoint does when network load balanced.

First, network load balancing must be enabled. In order to install SharePoint, the operating system must be Windows Server 2003 Service Pack 1 or higher. That server has the capability to network load balance built in. As it is something we all should have in common, I am going to demonstrate how to enable load balancing using Windows Network Load Balancing (NLB), in order to demonstrate how it applies to SharePoint. However, once you have the concept down, it is applicable to any load balancing product your business may use instead. NLB is not the most complex or feature rich load balancer out there, so you may want to shop around to find the most appropriate product for your needs.

The point of network load balancing is to balance the network load between web front end servers (considered, together, a cluster) by distributing network traffic among the servers to increase availability, scalability, and performance. The servers are set up to all respond to a shared virtual IP address and full internet name. Among the servers, each has a unique identifier called a priority number, but they also keep their dedicated addresses to respond to any packets directly addressed to them as well as address any outbound connections. In addition, the full internet name that will be shared among the load balanced server must be configured in DNS to resolve to the virtual IP.

The servers in the cluster, when network load balancing, share a Virtual IP (VIP) and a virtual MAC (Media Access Control) address. Essentially it looks like they all have the same network card and IP address to the clients outside the cluster. Because of this, the NLB settings among the servers in the cluster must be identical. NLB will work for servers with a single network card (the servers in this example are single card machines). However, each server should be multi-homed (have multiple network cards), with one dedicated to, and configured for, NLB.

If the servers are multi-homed, with a dedicated NLB network card, then they should run in Unicast Mode. The shortcoming of Unicast mode is a network card configured to use it cannot communicate directly with other hosts in the cluster, because Unicast basically means that card will be Borg'd to the NLB collective, or to be less nerdy, it will be dedicated to solely support incoming NLB traffic and not be able to speak to the other members of the cluster (because, as far as unicast is concerned, they are all the same computer). This is not a problem if the servers have other network cards installed, the other network cards can be used to communicate within the cluster. However, if the servers only have one network card each (or at least one server in the cluster has only one card, because all of their clustering parameters must match) they should use Multicast mode, because that mode allows the servers within the cluster to communicate with one another directly. The shortcoming of multicast mode is it can cause some switch flooding issues under certain circumstances (see the Windows Server's Network Load Balancing help for more information).

TESTING, TESTING . . . IS THIS THING ON?

Single network card hosts for NLB cluster hosts are fine for testing and demonstration. To prove it works and get practice before installing a second network card to be used in production, it is often a good idea to use multicast mode on the single network card the servers have. Then, if it works, invest in the time, effort, and money to add additional network cards to the load balanced servers to dedicate to NLB.

Generally NLB is a Network Connection property (i.e., a feature added to the function of a network card). The network card's TCP/IP properties do need to be configured in that connection's properties. However, when actually configuring NLB itself, you should use the Network Load Balancing Manager console. Although the settings for enabling NLB are available in both places; the properties of the network card in Network Connections, and in the Network Load Manager; it is strongly recommended that you use only the console to create and manage NLB clusters.

If a server has two network cards, only enable NLB on one of them. Once NLB is configured, it should be managed using the Network Load Manager console. The servers that will be in the cluster must be on the same subnet. Also keep in mind that Windows NLB can only support up to 32 different hosts. If you need to load balance more, then it is time to look elsewhere for a more sophisticated load balancing product.

When configuring NLB, keep in mind that there will be Cluster parameters, Host parameter, and Port Rules.

- ◆ Cluster parameters are the shared virtual IP, its subnet mask, cluster mode (unicast or multicast), and whether or not remote access (to manage the cluster from a machine outside of the cluster—not a good idea security-wise) will be enabled.

- ◆ Host parameters are the dedicated IP address and subnet mask of the host, as well as the initial state the server will be in when it re-enters the cluster.

◆ Port Rules, which can be configured per host or per cluster, are similar to the rules or policies used to filter packets on a router, internet authentication service, or firewall. The port rules are used to set the Cluster IP addresses (if there is more than one), the port range and protocols that the cluster will listen for and respond to, as well as the filter mode. Filter mode indicates if the cluster contains a single server or multiple servers, Affinity and Load Weight. Affinity can be set to none, single, and class C. Affinity means allowing a connection to be "sticky" or continue to try to keep a connection with the server who answered their request throughout a session. Setting Affinity to none means the client can be shifted from one server to another during a session to load balance, setting it to single (the default when UDP protocol is being supported) means that affinity will stick a connection to the single server who responded for the entire session, and setting it to Class C means affinity will try to keep client session, from within a specific class C subnet, stuck to the correct server (useful if the client accesses the server through proxy servers). Load weight can also be set as a port rule, which specifies the relative load weight this host would hold in a cluster. A Load Weight of zero means the server will handle no client traffic.

CONFIGURE NETWORK LOAD BALANCING

Network Load Balancing should be configured almost exactly the same way on every server intended to be in the NLB cluster. Each server needs to enable and configure Network Load Balancing. Initially the network card that will be used for Network Load Balancing needs to be configured in its TCP/IP settings to not register its IP address in DNS, because now it will have two IP addresses, one of which it shares with a different server. Sharing is bad in DNS. The other reason to configure TCP/IP for NLB is that shared, virtual IP needs to be added to the network card's IP addresses.

To enable NLB and configure it, open Network Connections (Start ➢ Control Panel ➢ Network Connections), right click the icon for the network card you intend to use for Network Load Balancing, and select Properties from the menu.

In the Properties for the network card you first need to be certain the TCP/IP information is configured correctly before configuring NLB.

1. To make certain that those settings are correct, select Internet Protocol (TCP/IP) from the This connection uses the following items list. Then click the Properties button.

2. On the Internet Protocol (TCP/IP) Properties General tab, make certain the IP address for the server is a static one (assigned manually, not by obtaining an address from DHCP). Confirm that the IP address, subnet mask, default gateway, and addresses to the DNS servers are correct.

If they are all correct, then it's time to bind a second IP to the network connection—the NLB virtual IP (VIP). In this case we are just going to prepare the network card for enabling NLB. There are a number of additional steps before NLB configuration is complete.

3. To add the VIP to the network card's TCP/IP settings, click the Advanced button on the General tab of the Internet Protocol (TCP/IP) Properties dialog box. It will open another dialog box to configure the Advanced TCP/IP settings for the server's network connection. In the dialog box, click the Add button beneath the IP Addresses box (Figure 15.39).

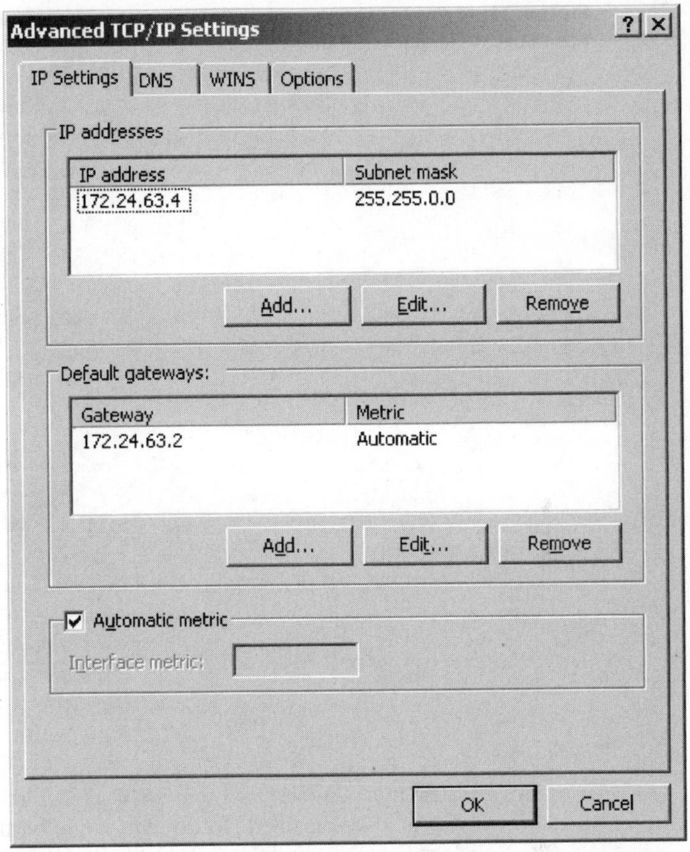

FIGURE 15.39
Advanced TCP/IP settings

4. A little dialog box will popup with a field to fill for the IP address and subnet mask. Enter the address you intend to be the shared address for the network load balanced server (mine is `172.24.63.10`), and its subnet mask. Then Click Add.

The IP Addresses box will now contain both addresses (Figure 15.40). Make certain that the server's IP address is at the top of the list, essentially the first IP. That should be the server's dedicated IP address that will be sending outgoing data and must be the server's address for outbound connections.

NOTE FOR THE MULTI-HOMED

If you are setting up NLB on a server with multiple network cards, and have a card dedicated to NLB, then you should clear the DNS and WINS entries on that dedicated card, as well as disable the setting for the server to register its address in DNS.

FIGURE 15.40
Additional IP address for server

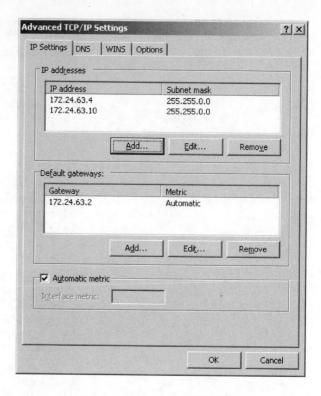

5. Because this network card will be NLB enabled, the option to automatically register with DNS has to be disabled. To do that, while on the Advanced TCP/IP settings dialog box, click on the DNS tab, and uncheck the Register this connection's addresses in DNS checkbox (realize that you will need to add the shared NLB A record to DNS manually).

6. Then click OK to finish preparing TCP/IP for Network Load Balancing. Then click OK on the Internet Protocol (TCP/IP) properties dialog box.

You should be back on the network card's Properties dialog box, and may be tempted to configure network load balancing here (the option is listed in the This connection uses the following items box). Don't do it. Most Microsoft documentation implies that it is always better to actually configure NLB using the Network Load Balancing Manager console. And believe me its true.

To open Network Load Balancing Manager, go to Start ➤ Run, type **nlbmgr**, and hit enter.

It will open the NLB Manager console. In the tree pane on the left there is an icon for the Network Load Balancing Clusters. On the right is the details pane, and across the bottom is a pane containing log information concerning NLB activities.

1. To continue to configure NLB and create the NLB cluster, right click the Network Load Balancing Clusters icon. In the popout menu, select New Cluster (Figure 15.41). This will walk you through the three steps of preparing new cluster: Cluster Parameters, Host Parameters, and Port Rules.

FIGURE 15.41
Create new cluster in NLB
Manager console

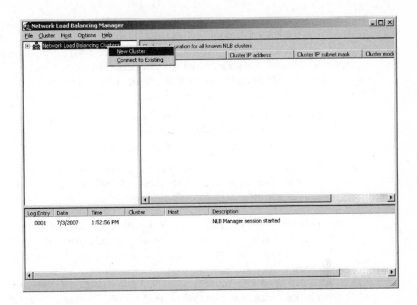

The first step of creating a new cluster will begin with a Cluster Parameters dialog box (Figure 15.42). When you configure network load balancing, keep in mind that the Cluster parameters—the virtual IP, the full internet name, and the cluster operation mode must be identical for all servers in the cluster.

FIGURE 15.42
Network Load Balancing, Clustering Parameters

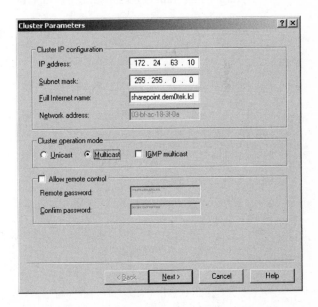

2. In the Cluster Parameters, enter the Network Load Balancing Virtual IP that you bound as the second IP address on the network card properties, its subnet mask, and the full internet name

for the Virtual IP. This name is what will be used as the basis for the load balanced URL for web applications in SharePoint and must be compatible with, and configured in, your business's DNS structure. So be sure to add an A record for the load balanced URL to the correct zone in DNS for your network. In my case I have an A record in DNS for SharePoint.dem0tek.lcl on 172.24.63.10. So the full internet name for my example is SharePoint.dem0tek.lcl. Notice that below this section is the automatically generated virtual MAC address.

3. In the Cluster Operating mode section, select Multicast. *Do not* keep the default of Unicast, unless you want the SharePoint servers with only one network card to be unable to directly communicate with each other for this cluster.

4. Click Next to continue configuring NLB. Because there can be additional virtual IP addresses assigned for the cluster, this screen allows you the option of defining them. There is no need for additional IPs for this demonstration, so click Next.

This will bring you to the Port Rules screen. Notice that at the top is the list of Port Rules for this cluster (each host must have almost identical port rules settings). The settings for Port Rules are similar to the rules or policies used to filter packets on a router, internet authentication service, or firewall.

To add or edit a port rule, click the Add or Edit buttons below the Port Rules list. The Add/Edit Port Rules dialog box contains settings for the Cluster IP address (or all if there are more than one Virtual IP for the network card), port range, protocols, and filtering mode. The default Port Rule settings, shown in Figure 15.43, will load balance all virtual IPs for the server (which in our case is only one), all ports from 0 to 65535 as well as both UDP and TCP protocols. The default of multiple host filtering mode means there will be more than one server in this cluster, supporting UDP means that Affinity is set to Single by default.

FIGURE 15.43
Default NLB Port Rules settings

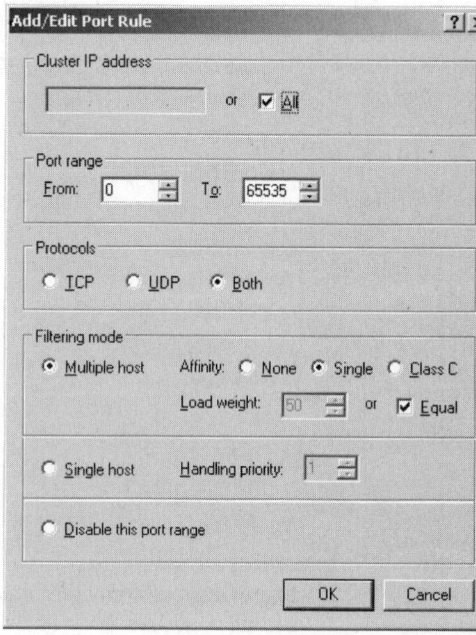

5. There are no settings that require editing in the Port Rule at this time, so click Next to continue.

HEAVY IS GOOD (WHEN TALKING ABOUT LOAD WEIGHT).

Load Weight is useful if you want to control which server answers a particular port, such as 443. Say only one server on the farm has an SSL certificate installed for a web application, then HTTPS traffic (port 443) should be directed to that server only. To do that, make its Load Weight 100 on a port rule that specifically targets port 443, and create a port rule on each other server that gives them a Load Weight of 0 for that port. That means the other servers will never answer 443 traffic, leaving the one server with the certificate (and the Load Weight of 100 for that port) as the only server responding to HTTPS requests.

---

6. On the Connect screen of this process, enter the IP address of one of the servers that will be added to this cluster and click the Connect button. This will display the server's network connections and their IP addresses. If the server had more than one network card installed, you could choose the one you wanted to apply Network Load Balancing to. However, as you can see in Figure 15.44), this server is a single network card machine. Select the dedicated IP of the network card that will be using NLB, and click Next.

FIGURE 15.44
Connect host to cluster

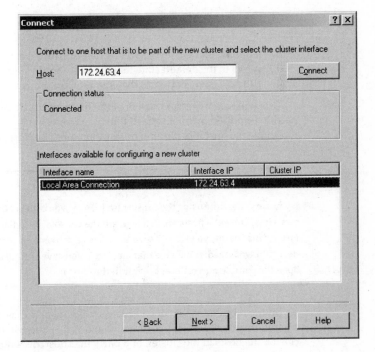

7. The next screen contains the Host Parameters for the host chosen in the previous screen. Each host must have a unique identifier. Keep the default of 1 (Figure 15.45).

FIGURE 15.45
Host Parameters settings

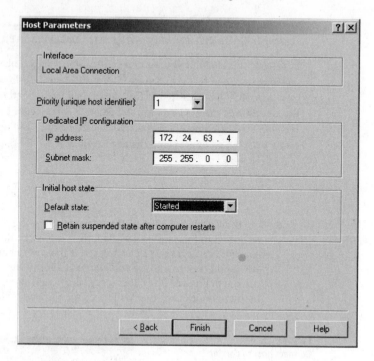

8. Confirm that the server's dedicated IP address and subnet mask are correct. Initial host state refers to the default state that the host should start in when being added to the cluster in the future. Leave Started as the default. Click Finish.

This will create the parameters of the first cluster, and add the first host. The other hosts will need to be added manually. Each time you open the console to manage the cluster, it will recognize the host it is running on, and the other host will need to be added.

HOST LIST CONVENIENCE

If you are going to be using the console frequently, you can create a host list to populate the console easily next time. Once the hosts are displayed in the console, click File in the menu bar, then select Save Host List. At that point, you simply save the file to a convenient location to be opened using the File menu next time you need to manage that cluster. If you save the host list to a file share, it can be used if you open the console on a different server in the cluster.

On the NLB Manager console, there will now be a cluster identified by the full internet name entered during the creation process. The details pane will contain general information about the cluster, the hosts in the cluster, or a particular host, depending on what is selected in the tree pane.

The tree pane should now also display the host you added, but it is obvious that the next host needs to be included to make load balancing work.

To add the second server (and any others) to the cluster, right-click the cluster icon and select Add Host to Cluster from the menu (Figure 15.46).

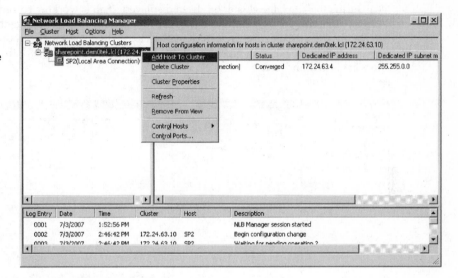

This will open a Connect dialog box. Enter the host IP address, click the Connect button, select the network connection that will be using NLB, and click Next. On the next screen, which contains the Host Parameters for the new host, the priority number (unique identifier) should be 2 or at least any number but 1. Confirm the dedicated host IP address and subnet mask, and leave the initial state for this host at the default Started state. Click Finish to add the host to the cluster.

In the console, there will now be two hosts listed, although the second host may take a few moments to update. In the log area at the bottom of the console, the status of the host being added to the console will be reported. You can also right-click a host and select Host Status for more information.

Check the Event logs for both servers to ensure that there are no WLBS errors. Make certain there are no typing errors, skipped steps, or possible DNS registration issues before continuing.

NETWORK LOAD BALANCING MANAGEMENT

Once Network Load Balancing is enabled on both servers, it is time to manage the cluster. The Network Load Balancing Manager console is where clusters are stopped, started, and administered. And in this particular example, we are going to use the Network Load Balancing Manager to make sure that NLB is running on the server cluster and what servers are reporting that they are in the cluster.

It is also here that we can test if clustering is working per host. In order to see if load balancing failover is functioning, you can simply turn off one of the servers and see if the cluster IP still services clients by using the other server. However, that is a little extreme (and can be time consuming to wait for the server to shut down gracefully, then boot back up). Instead, we will check to see if NLB is working by using the NLB manager and see if there is an interruption of service. If service (in this case we will ping the full internet name for the cluster) is interrupted, then we know that NLB is not working.

During this time, the cluster has been displayed (if all is working correctly) with the server icons outlined in green. This means they are functioning properly as members of the NLB cluster (trust me, even though Figure 15.47 is in black and white, the square around the server icons is green). If they are not both green, check the log entries at the bottom of the console for an idea as to what is malfunctioning.

FIGURE 15.47
Servers connected to cluster, displayed in NLB Manager console

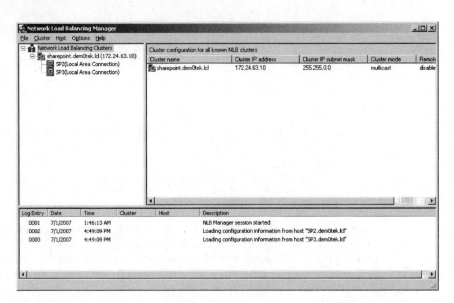

If the cluster icon is selected, you can see the host information in the details pane, which shows the status of the two servers. They both indicate that they have been converged, meaning they have been added to the cluster. Convergence occurs when a member is added or returned to a cluster. All members must realize there is a new member so they can figure out the relative weight of each other in the port rules and compare priority numbers.

Knowing that network load balancing is working by viewing it in the NLB manager console is one thing. But let's test it. In order for SharePoint to make use of network load balancing from a web server point of view, the full internet name for the cluster must work, and resolve correctly to the Virtual IP. To test this, ping the full internet name for the cluster.

Open a command prompt (Start ➢ Run, type cmd, hit enter).

At the command prompt type **ping**, space, and the cluster's name, such as, ping sharepoint (the domain part of the name is not necessary for this), then hit enter.

This will cause the server to resolve that DNS name to the virtual IP address, and send four sets of packets, then report the results. As you can see in Figure 15.48, my cluster internet name SharePoint resolved to the cluster's virtual IP of 172.24.63.10.

FIGURE 15.48
Test SharePoint NLB cluster virtual IP address

If the ping test did not work, the problem is likely (since NLB looks happy in the Manager console) that DNS does not have a Host (A record) for the full internet name of the cluster that resolves to the cluster's Virtual IP address (Figure 15.49). Check the event logs on the server to make certain there are no issues concerning communicating with the DNS server, then check DNS for the cluster's host record. Repeat the ping test when the issue is resolved.

FIGURE 15.49
A record in DNS to resolve cluster internet name

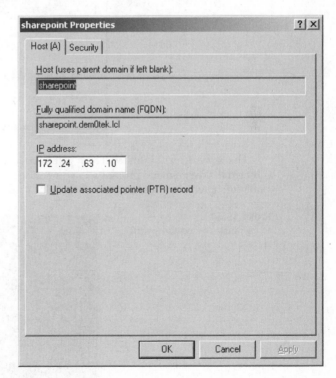

Now that we know that the cluster is working. Let's see what happens if we break it...or at least, *simulate* breaking it. This is a standard load balancing test of the cluster intended to demonstrate the failover capabilities of NLB. First we will do a ping test that continuously pings the cluster address. Then we will do something called Drainstop to one of the servers in the cluster. This cuts it off, temporarily, from the cluster, simulating a server failure. If NLB is working correctly, the ping test will not falter during the drainstop, because NLB will transparently, in milliseconds, transfer activity to the second server.

To do this, first start the ping test at the command prompt. Enter the ping command you used earlier but at the -t switch. For example:

```
ping sharepoint -t
```

Where SharePoint is the name of the cluster that resolves to the load balancing Virtual IP.

When the test is returning results, return to the NLB Manager console. Right click the first server (the one with the lowest number, and therefore highest priority), and from the popout menu, click Control Host, Drainstop (Figure 15.50).

FIGURE 15.50
Drainstop a host in the NLB Manager console to test cluster functionality

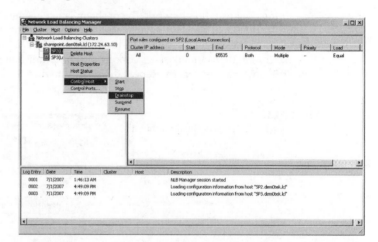

The server icon's outline will turn yellow as it stops, then red when it has stopped entirely. Return to the command prompt and you will see that the ping test is still going (see Figure 15.51), uninterrupted, at no loss in speed. This helps prove that NLB is working correctly.

FIGURE 15.51
Testing Cluster connectivity with Ping test

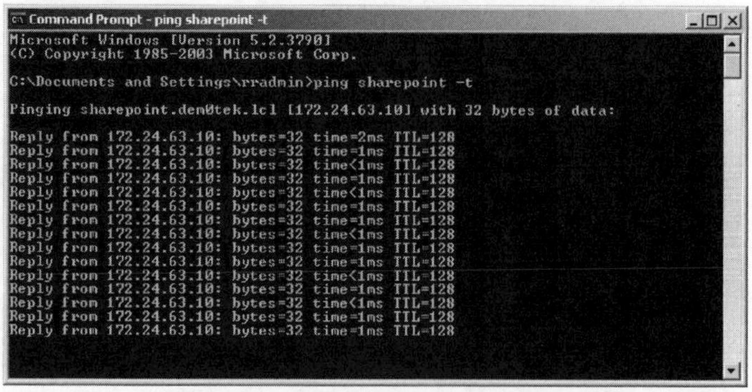

Of course, to do that we drainstopped one of the cluster's servers, meaning it is not responding to client requests on that IP. This is not a state we want to leave that server in. To return that server to the cluster, go back to the NLB Manager console, right click on the drainstopped server (see Figure 15.52) and select Start.

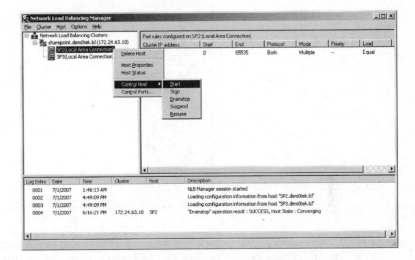

The server's icon outline will turn yellow while its status is converging, then after its status returns to converged, the outline will return to green (if you are impatient, you can hit refresh to speed up the color change). All the while, the cluster is still (because we haven't stopped pinging) responding to ping requests as if nothing had ever happened. To stop the ping test, you can close the command prompt window or select the window and type ctrl+c to cancel the command.

So now we know that NLB works between the servers for uninterrupted service. But in order for requests for SharePoint resources to be captured and filtered by the NLB, the load balanced URL must be used as the default zone for any web application you'd like to balance. Any web application that you do not want to be load balanced (such as Central Administration), do not use the load balanced URL for its default zone address.

CONFIGURE SHAREPOINT FOR NETWORK LOAD BALANCING

Currently this example of SharePoint has a Central Administration web application and a single SharePoint-80 web application. The SharePoint-80 web application has the default internal URL of `http://sp2`. This is the server's address, and works fine to access the sites in that web application. Now that we are using NLB, that default address needs to be changed to the internet name for the cluster. This will allow clients to always be able to access the web application, even if one of the servers is off.

To set up a load balanced URL for a web application after it has been created, you need to access Alternate Access Mappings. So go to Central Administration, Operations page, and click the Alternate Access Mappings link under Global Configuration.

On the Alternate Access Mapping page, click on the internal URL of the web application you'd like to change (my example is `http://sp2`). This will open a page that displays the current internal URL and its zone. Make certain the zone is set to Default (Figure 15.53).

FIGURE 15.53
Internal, default URL for web application

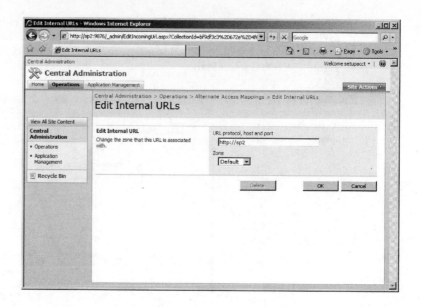

Change the URL to the internet name for the cluster (my example will be http://SharePoint because that will resolve to the full internet name and the virtual IP for the cluster), and click OK. That will take you to the Alternate Access Mappings page for the web application, displaying the new default URL (Figure 15.54). If you wanted the web application to also be accessible by the server address (in case NLB has a problem), enter that address in one of the other public zones for the site.

FIGURE 15.54
New load balancing URL for web application

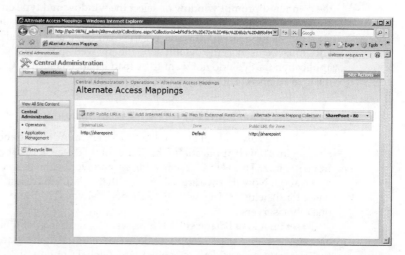

To test if the new URL works, go to a different server or workstation on the network than the SharePoint server (just to prove that the network load balancing service is working) and open Internet Explorer, and browse to http://sharepoint. You may be prompted for your username and password from SharePoint (not to the server itself, which is good), then the home page of the top level site will load without a problem (Figure 15.55).

FIGURE 15.55
SharePoint site now resolves to NLB cluster name rather than a single server

REAL ADMINS UNPLUG THE SERVER

To prove that load balancing works, you can open the NLB Manager console and do a drainstop on the server that hosts the original internal URL of that web application. But to better simulate a catastrophe (such as the network card failing on the server, or the server shutting down) in which the other server in the cluster must respond to client requests for that site, disable the server's network connection. You will still be able to access load balanced web applications by their load balanced, default zone URL if NLB and the other host on the cluster is working correctly.

To disable the network connection on the server, open the Network Connections window (Start ➢ Control Panel ➢ Network Connections). Right click the Local Area Connection icon (or whatever you named the network connection for that server's network card). In the drop down menu, select Disable. This will disable the network card, making it unable to be accessed from the network.

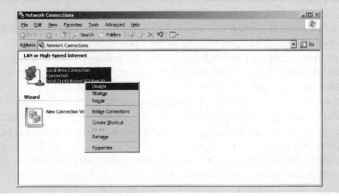

Go to a different server or workstation on the network. Log in and open Internet Explorer. In the address bar, type in the new, load balanced URL for the web application. It should let you log in (if necessary) and access the site without a hitch (although some web parts that display fileshares or images that are stored on the disconnected server may not display properly). This is because the NLB service sent the client request to the other server in the cluster. Re-enable the network connection after this exercise is complete.

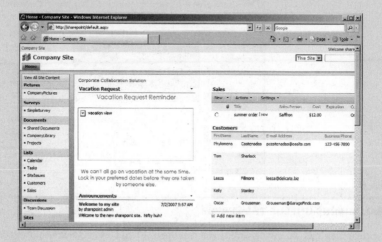

Keep in mind that load balancing for SharePoint works because the web applications are replicated between all SharePoint servers on the farm, but the file system is not. In other words, if there is a file, folder or service running on a server specifically, and that server becomes unavailable, then those unique items will become unavailable also. Load balancing depends on the servers hosting identical resources. If you use a distributed file system to store network resources or practice file level redundancy, if all necessary files and their fileshares are exactly the same on all SharePoint servers in the farm, then when catastrophe strikes and a server goes down, all file resources will be available regardless. However, services like search cannot be replicated that easily because the service is configured specifically to point at a particular server during set up.

From this point on, when you create new web applications for the SharePoint server farm, always use the cluster's internet name as the Load Balanced URL.

For example, create a new web application by going to the the Application Management page of Central Administration. Click the Create or extend Web application link in the SharePoint Web Application Management category.

On the Create or Extend Web Application page, select Create a new Web application link.

On the Create New Web Application page, configure the web application's address and other settings. In my example I am going to use the server name and unique port to address the web application, as you can see in Figure 15.56. In the Load Balanced URL section, notice that the default URL is the server name and the port number. That is not will not be load balanced because it is pointing specifically to the server's address. To configure it properly (now that we have load balancing in place), enter the cluster internet name rather than the server name.

FIGURE 15.56
Configuring new, load balanced
web application

FIGURE 15.56
Configuring new, load balanced
web application

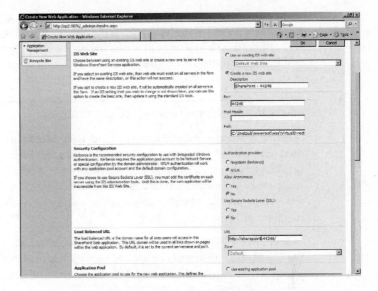

When you have completed the rest of the web application's configuration (including defining a content database access account, database name, and specifying a search server), click Create to finish. Create the site collection, then run iisreset /noforce at the command prompt of the SharePoint server.

ADDITIONAL INFO

For more about creating web applications, site collections, and alternate access mappings, check out Chapter 8, "Site Collections and Web Applications."

In the Alternate Access Mappings page, you'll see that the default internal URL for that web application is, in fact, the load balanced URL (Figure 15.57).

FIGURE 15.57
Internal URL reflects load balanced
URL for new web application

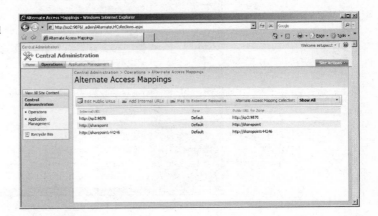

To access the site from any machine on the network, simply use the load balanced URL (Figure 15.58). As a matter of fact, that URL is the only web address that SharePoint will accept for the web application. If you want to access the new web application by any other addresses, be sure to add them as alternate access mappings.

CENTRAL ADMINISTRATION AND LOAD BALANCING

Speaking of access web applications by something other than the load balanced URL, you may realize that, since Central Administration is running on both servers, you can load balance it too. That is a possibility if high availability is a priority. However, it is considered a more secure practice to, instead, add the URLs of the additional servers that will be hosting Central Administration. The reasoning behind this is it obscures the Central Administration website's address that much more if it does not have the common, load balanced address.

To load balance Central Administration, make certain that all servers in the NLB cluster are hosting the site. Then change the default internal URL for the site to resolve to the cluster internet name (or whatever alias will resolve to the cluster virtual IP). In my case that would be changing `http://sp2:9876` to `http://SharePoint:9876`.

If you wanted to go the other way and simply make it possible for the Central Administration website on the additional server to be accessible by its own address if the original server were to go offline, simply add that server's address for the site as an internal URL. In my case that would mean adding `http://sp3:9876` to AAM.

FIGURE 15.58
New web application resolves to load balanced URL

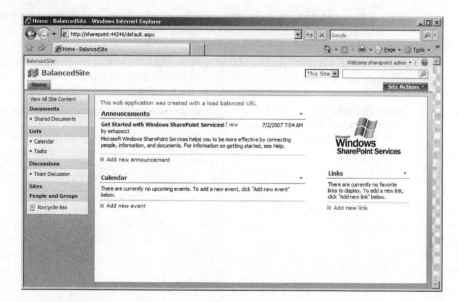

Although we have tested NLB by completely stopping access to one of the servers, remember that, in addition to failover capabilities, NLB also continuously monitors the activity of the cluster servers, and distributes client requests to the server with the least load at any given time. Keep in mind that Windows NLB is not application aware. If the web applications become unavailable in IIS on one of the servers, NLB will be unaware of it and continue to send that server client requests if it is next in line or the least busy of the cluster.

KERBEROS AND NLB

If you have web applications using Kerberos as the authentication method and want to enable NLB on your server farm, return the authentication method to NTLM until NLB is configured. Then register the cluster full internet name as a service principal name (SPN) in addition to each server in the cluster. This should allow the web applications to use Kerberos again; however, test it first because the combination has proven to be tricky. For more about how to set service principal names and enable Kerberos, see the Kerberos section later in this chapter.

Using SSL with SharePoint

Often external access to company data through SharePoint requires the additional protection of SSL. Secure Socket Layer (SSL) encrypts data sent over HTTP (making it HTTPS, the "S" meaning *secure*) to help avoid any tampering while in transit. SSL utilizes certificates, as well as public and private keys to encrypt and decrypt data. When a client requests access to a site that uses SSL, the server sends back the certificate and its public key. The client checks the certificate information to make certain it can be trusted (that the site is authentic and can be trusted to be who they say they are), then it creates a pre-master key of its own and encrypts that with the server's public key. The server gets the pre-master key, decrypts it with its private key, then uses that to create a master key (with the agreement of the client) to create a session key to encrypt all data to that client during that session. Both the client and the server know what the session key is that encrypts and decrypts the data that is traveling between them, but no one else does. This secures the traffic from snooping or any other exploitation while it is between destinations.

In order to use SSL to encrypt traffic to and from your SharePoint websites, the server (servers if you are using a load balanced server farm) must have a certificate. The URL that the certificate applies to must match the URL that the user is using to access a website. There are two kinds of SSL certificates that are really relevant under these circumstances: the wildcard certificate and the standard website certificate. A wild card certificate is more expensive and covers any site that uses the same domain name in the URL. A wildcard certificate for `*.dem0tek.com` would cover `SharePoint.dem0tek.com`, `sales.dem0tek.com`, `marketing.dem0tek.com`, and so on. A standard SSL certificate must match the full address exactly. So if there were a certificate for `marketing.dem0tek.com`, then that URL is the only one that could use it.

In this example, just to demonstrate how to enable SSL with SharePoint, we are going to use a standard certificate and secure a public facing web application. As a matter of fact, we are going to create a new web application, and use a host header to address it. This site will be accessed from outside of the office, and must have the data encrypted between the server and the client.

GETTING FANCY WITH HOST HEADERS AND NLB

This exercise will also demonstrate a more advanced use of load balancing. Instead of using the internet name for the web application, we are going to use a host header that resolves to the IP address using DNS. Create a new forward lookup zone for the external domain in DNS. Then create an alias for the new host header and map it to SharePoint.demotek.lcl (or whatever your cluster's internet name is).

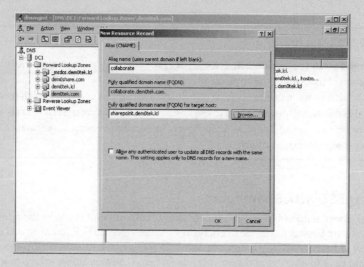

When you access the site using the host header, it will resolve (as this example will demonstrate) to the cluster's VIP and therefore be load balanced. Which is why its default address can also be the load balancing address.

Setting up for SSL requires three parts: Part one, which is decide on the URL. Part two, which is enable a web application to do SSL in SharePoint. Part three, configure SSL in ISS, generate the certificate request, and then add the certificate to the IIS Web Site. There is even an optional part four, which is export the certificate to import it to the web application on the other servers in the farm for load balancing purposes.

In part one of the process, it is important to decide what URL will be secured. In this example I am going to use *collaborate.dem0tek.com*. The domain dem0tek.com has been registered by the company with the correct DNS record to allow traffic to reach your internal SharePoint server. Internally, in this example, the router is configured to pass HTTP and HTTPS traffic to the SharePoint servers and DNS has a record for collaborate.dem0tek.com that resolves to the internal server's VIP address.

CREATE A WEB APPLICATION TO USE SSL

Part two of the process involves creating a web application and preparing it to use SSL.

1. To do that, go to the Central Administration website, Application Management page. Click on Create or extend Web application in the SharePoint Web Application Management category.

2. On the Create or Extend Web Application page, select Create a new Web application.

3. On the Create New Web Application page,

4. Once that selection is made, configure the new web application to use a host header that matches the URL to be used on the SSL certificate. As you can see in Figure 15.59, my example is `collaborate.dem0tek.com`. Make certain that the Port for this web application is 80.

FIGURE 15.59
Configuring new web application to use SSL

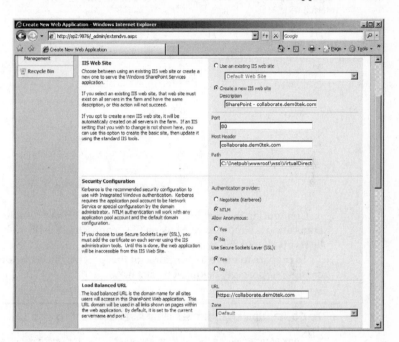

5. In the Security Configuration section, leave NTLM as the authentication method, do not enable anonymous (at this point), and select Yes to enable SSL for this web application.

In the Load Balanced URL field, the protocol at the beginning of the address changes from HTTP to HTTPS, and otherwise matches the host header address. That default is actually good for this example, because this is the address that will be used for the SSL certificate. In order for SSL to work, the users must type in an address for the web application that exactly matches the one used by the certificate. The host header is what we will be using and is an exact match (although you should remove the port number from the end, it's not necessary) of the Load Balanced URL. The Load Balanced URL will be the default zone for the web application in AAM, and therefore the only address (at least initially) that SharePoint will accept for that web application. The default (minus the port number) is good.

6. Configure the Content Database Access account, the database name, and select a search server. When configuration is complete, click OK.

7. Once the web application has been created, you will be prompted to create a site collection. Create a new site collection, then (do this on each SharePoint server in the farm) open a command prompt and run iisreset / noforce.

The new web application will be created with the new host header address as the default zone (in my example that's the `SharePoint-collaborate.dem0tek.com` web application), as you can see in Figure 15.60.

FIGURE 15.60
New web application's default, internal URL

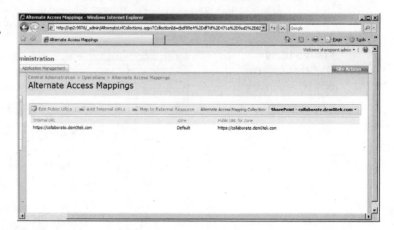

Configuring the new web application is not entirely complete. SharePoint, because the web application is supposed to be using SSL, configures the IIS Web Site for the new web application to be stopped until SSL is configured.

To prepare to move to part three of this process, the web application's IIS Web Site must be configured properly before you start it.

TO CONFIGURE AN EXISTING WEB APPLICATION TO USE SSL

You may wonder where the setting is to enable SSL for *existing* web applications. There really isn't one. You just change the URL in Alternate Access Mappings from HTTP to HTTPS. That's essentially all that enable SSL setting does when you create/extend a web application.

Keep in mind that enabling SSL on a SharePoint site requires that you enable SharePoint to accept requests for the web application using an HTTPS address, *then* you configure it in IIS.

CONFIGURE SSL FOR A SHAREPOINT WEB APPLICATION IN IIS

In part three of the process, with the web application created, you must get an SSL certificate and configure the IIS Web Site of the web application. You can use the Windows Certificate Authority console to create a certificate on your network. It may not be from one of the publicly trusted Certificate Authorities, but it can be trusted by your clients since you made it for them. Or you can use a trusted authority online, such as VeriSign or GeoTrust. These vendors do nothing but vouch for the authenticity of other people's websites and generate certificates for them. These authorities can put you through a rigorous application process from making certain you do own the domain, that your contact and company information is correct, to questions more appropriate when applying for security clearance.

Purchasing an SSL certificate from a third-party vendor is convenient, but potentially expensive (depending on the kind of certificate you choose). It is convenient because many of them are already trusted publishers of certificates, so Internet Explorer will accept their certificates readily, and because they offer additional support if the certificate expires (they generally are designed to expire), is lost, or becomes corrupt. Because companies often use third party certificates, that's the process this example will use.

CERTIFICATES GENERATED IN-HOUSE WORK

A certificate that is generated by the Certificate Authority on your network may cause users outside of the network to get a warning that it may have expired or is not known. Keep in mind that SSL does two things, sends a certificate to verify the site's authenticity, then negotiates the master key to encrypt the session traffic. It's a two step thing; authentication, then encryption. So if a user gets a warning in their browser about the certificate from your company's Certificate Authority not being trusted (because the browser knows nothing about your company) and they click to accept the certificate manually, then the key passing process will happen and all data between the two computers, server and client, will occur. If the user rejects the certificate, then they don't access the site.

Just because the browser doesn't like the look of a certificate does not mean it is automatically a problem if you know where it came from. The encryption will still work if it is accepted.

To get an SSL certificate, you first have to apply for one. IIS has a convenient wizard that helps you set up a certificate request that you can use to acquire a certificate from a trusted Certificate Authority. It is often a good idea to try out the certificate before you buy it, so most vendors offer trial certificates that expire in a few weeks.

1. To request a new certificate for a particular IIS Web Site, open the IIS Manager console (Start ➤ Administrative Tools ➤ Internet Information Server (IIS) Manager).

2. In the IIS Manager console tree pane, open the Web Sites node and right click the Web Site for the web application (in my example that is collaborate.dem0tek.com), and select Properties from the popup menu.

IT'S SUPPOSED TO BE STOPPED

You may notice that new web application is stopped. That is to be expected, SharePoint does that to keep anyone from accessing an SSL enabled web application until SSL is in place. After you finish configuring it to require SSL, you can start it.

---

3. On the general tab of the Properties dialog box, enter a port number for SSL. The default port for SSL traffic is 443, but some companies either intentionally use a custom port or, if you are applying SSL to multiple websites on the same IP address, they must each have a unique port for SSL. Apparently to be helpful SharePoint leaves the wrong value (port 80) in the field to force you to enter a value of your own choosing (Figure 15.61). I don't suggest using a different port number for SSL at this time, so for this example let's enter 443 in the SSL port number field. Keep in mind that if you don't enter a different value in that port than the one SharePoint put in there, you will be unable to continue configuring SSL.

FIGURE 15.61
Web Site Properties

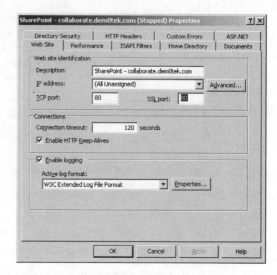

Also notice on this tab that the IP address is referred to as All Unassigned. A server can have more than one TCP/IP address (we have two for this example; the server's dedicated IP and the cluster's virtual IP), and you can have this website listen on all IP addresses on this server, or specify a particular one. All Unassigned works fine in this case.

ONE PORT PER CUSTOMER

In order for SSL to work, the URL the user types in their browser must exactly match the common name listed in the certificate for the site. SharePoint will let you get creative with URLs, accepting alternate addresses for a web application, allowing you to mask a port number or unsightly NetBIOS name. However, SSL does not.

There can be only one acceptable URL if you require secure channel communications per certificate. So when you are creating the certificate, the address you enter for the web application's URL (called a Common Name) is important. If the address changes, then you need to get a new certificate that matches the new address.

This is particularly important if you want to have multiple sites using host headers that require SSL on a single IP address, because each SSL IIS Web Site will need to use a SSL port that is unique. SSL, by definition, encrypts its traffic. IIS simply takes the data destined for the SSL port and passes the data to the site, without unencrypting the packets until they get there. If packets go to a site with a SSL certificate that doesn't match the request's host header, the connection will fail. This means that IIS can't have two sites with the same port number unless the sites are using the same SSL certificate (which is what wildcard certificates do).

So if you are planning to have a bunch of web applications with very different URLs or you do not want to pay for a wildcard certificate, you will need to make their SSL traffic clearly unique so IIS knows which Web Site to send it to.

You could simply specify a custom port for SSL on each Web Site. This works, but the users accessing the site will need to type the host header address and the port. Keep in mind that if you are using a custom SSL port, it must be added to the common name for the Web Site on the SSL certificate, the address must match exactly. It also means that the user must always remember, not only the host header for the site, but the port number.

Or you could get more creative. Another way to make the Web Site unique is to give it a different IP address. If the server is on a cluster, add more virtual IP addresses to the cluster to be used for Web Sites (if it is not, just add more IP addresses to the server directly). Then in the Web Site's properties, specify one of the IP addresses for the Web Site. That isolates traffic to the Web Site through that address and allows you to use port 443 for SSL traffic. It will help users avoid having to remember a custom port number, and make it possible for you not to have to specify the port in the Web Site's certificate. Traffic on that IP for that port will go to that Web Site specifically. Make certain that there is a record in DNS for the host header that resolves to the unique IP.

To keep it simple, I am creating one SSL secured web application on the farm, and therefore am able to use the default SSL port. However, in more complicated deployments, it may not be that easy.

4. Once you've entered a value for the SSL port, select the Directory Security Tab.

5. On the Directory Security tab, click the Server Certificate button to start the Web Server Certificate Wizard and request a SSL certificate for the IIS Web Site.

This wizard will step you through the process of collecting information to use for the certificate itself (which is intended to prove the authenticity of your web application's sites).

1. The wizard begins, as expected, with a Welcome screen, click Next.

2. On the Server Certificate screen, there are several options concerning web server certificates (Figure 15.62). Select the first option; Create a new certificate. Then click Next.

FIGURE 15.62
Web Server Certificate Wizard, Server Certificate screen

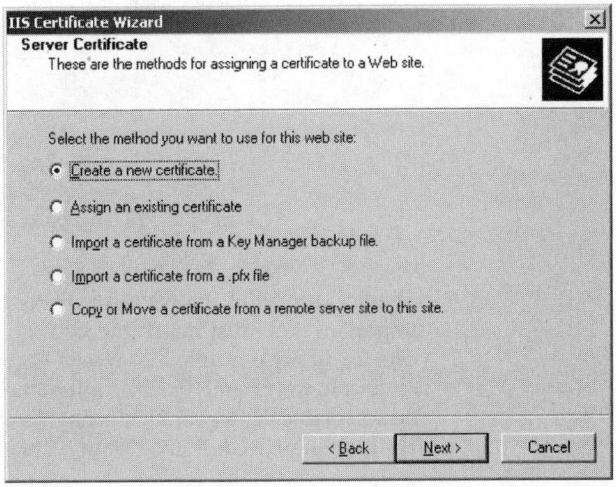

The next screen, Delayed or Immediate Request, only really has one option, and that is prepare the request now but send it later. This screen has several options grayed out because they are not relevant for the choice you made on the previous screen. The option to prepare the request now will generate a text document with the request in plain text within it. It is a complex string of characters with a header and footer for the information. The header and footer information are surrounded by two groups (apiece) of five dashes. Never cut off the dashes when you are cutting and pasting the text, or the certificate will not work.

3. In the Delayed or Immediate Request screen, your only option is to prepare the certificate now, but send it later. Click Next to continue.

4. In the Name and Security screen, enter the friendly name for the certificate (something you can remember). You can also choose the bit length of the certificate. For this example, keep the 1024 default. Click Next to continue.

5. For the Organization Information, enter the company name for the certificate. You also need to enter an Organizational Unit. Even if you don't really have one, make something up (but remember that all data in a certificate can be viewed by the user, so keep it professional—my example uses SharePoint in Figure 15.63). Click Next.

FIGURE 15.63
Organization
information for
certificate request

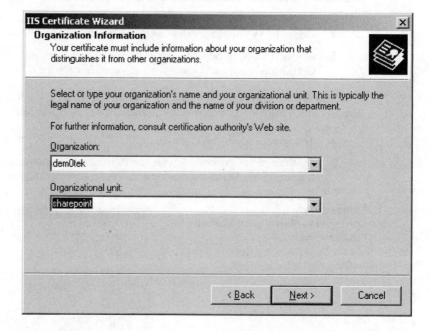

6. The next screen of the wizard asks for the Common Name for your site. This is critically important and must match the URL of the web application you are requesting the certificate for. In my example that would be `collaborate.dem0tek.com` (Figure 15.64). If the certificate were being used by internal clients only, then the server's NetBIOS name would be acceptable. However, that is not the case in this instance. Once you've entered your web application's URL into the Common Name field, click Next.

FIGURE 15.64
Common Name for SSL Certificate

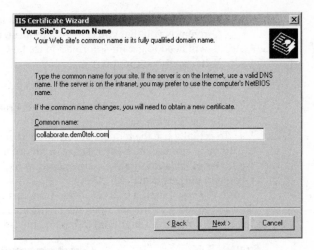

7. Enter your geographical information (country, state/province, city/locality) in this screen, and click Next.

8. On the Certificate Request File Name screen, name the file and enter the path to the location where you would like to save the file. The certification request information is just text that is intended to be copied and pasted into a field when using it to make your certificate request to the Certificate Authority. Therefore the file type is simply txt. The default is to save the file on the C: drive with the name certreq.txt (keep in mind that hackers know that default as well, so avoid using it if possible). Remember both where you put the file and what you named it because it will be important later.

9. Once you have entered the path and file name (or to accept the default), click Next.

10. The next screen of the wizard displays a summary of the information to be used in the certificate (see my example in Figure 15.65). Check it over carefully, and go back and fix whatever information might have been typed in incorrectly. If all of the information is correct, click Next.

FIGURE 15.65
Web Server Certificate Wizard summary screen

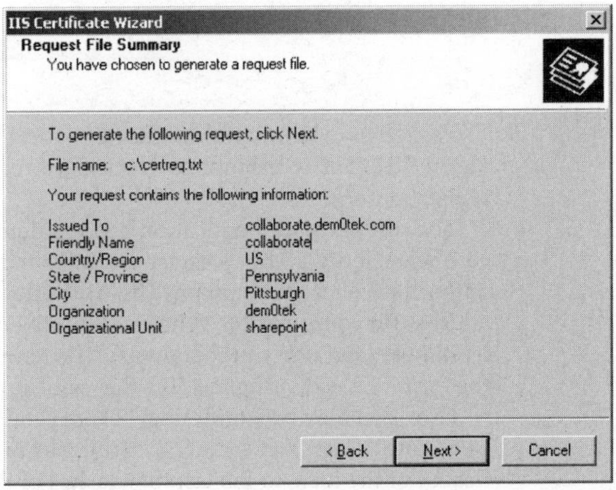

The final screen of the wizard indicates that the process to request a certificate is finished. It reminds you that you created a request, the location and file name of that file, and that you will need to get the information to the Certificate Authority in order for a real certificate to be generated for you.

11. Click Finish to complete the certificate request process.

The certificate request will have been generated, and you will find yourself back on the dialog box for the IIS Web Site.

To actually use the request information to get a certificate varies depending on what Certificate Authority you use. In many cases, you fill out a form with the name, phone number, and email address of the authoritative contact used to register the domain you are using for the common name in the certificate.

In my case I used a trial certificate from an online Certificate Authority.

To request a certificate, open the certificate request file that you just generated. Select the data (be sure not to miss anything) in the text file (see Figure 15.66).

FIGURE 15.66
Select text in certificate request text file

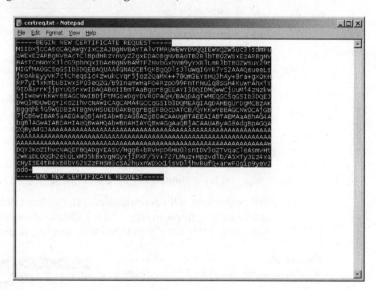

Paste that data into the certificate request field of the Certificate Authority you've chosen. See Figure 15.67 for an example of a standard request form might look like, and where to paste the request data.

The rest of the authentication process depends on the Authority. In my case, for the trial certificate, it did a whois query on my domain. It then returned the email address of the person authoritative for that domain. The Authority then sends an email to that authoritative email address for confirmation. When you get the email, click the link to confirm the certificate is legitimate (and one you requested). The new certificate will then be generated and sent to you in the form of a text string just like the request.

Now you may be wondering, "What can I do with this text? Where is the attached file that is the certificate?" That text *is* the SSL certificate. Simply copy (from five dashes of the Begin Certificate header of the data, to the last five dashes of the End Certificate footer) and paste it into a text file.

FIGURE 15.67
Sample request form at online Certificate Authority

Applicant Details
First Name:
CA
Last Name:
Callahan
Email Address:
callahan@callahantech.com
Phone Number:
1234567890
Server / Certificate Details
Your Certificate Signing Request:
(this is generated by the server you want to install the certificate on. For more information click here)
cNyISE4tR4XBRbY62sZzFHSm3
cSA2huxnWDXX1jsVDljhvRufQ
+arwF0g1p9yeV2
odo=
-----END NEW CERTIFICATE REQUEST-----
Common name or Fully Qualified domain name for certficate:
(as featured in CSR)
collaborate.dem0tek.com
(ie yourdomain.com or www.yourdomain.com)
Optional: Please tell us your server type - this can help us offer you faster support if needed.
Microsoft IIS 5.0 / Microsoft IIS 6.0
continue >
All fields are required. Click 'continue' to complete your order. Complete your order now and receive your certificate in just 10 minutes.

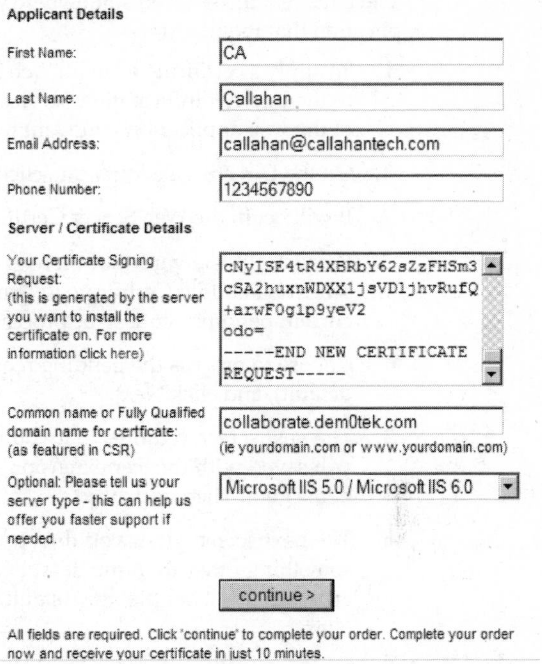

Name the text file something you can remember, with the file extension of .cer (see Figure 15.68 for my example). That indicates to Windows that the file contains certificate information, and the public and private key combination associated with that certificate (remember, SSL does two things, proves authenticity and encrypts data).

FIGURE 15.68
SSL Certificate from Certificate Authority

C:\
File Edit View Favorites Tools Help
Back Search Folders
Address C:\
Go
Name Size Type Date Modified Attributes
5c55f3bf87c37e9575357688f5 File Folder 1/3/2007 2:31 AM
ADFS File Folder 1/2/2007 7:20 PM
CentralAdminLinkFeature File Folder 4/22/2007 8:59 PM
Documents and Settings File Folder 1/8/2007 8:01 PM
imageshare File Folder 7/4/2007 9:15 PM
indexfiles File Folder 1/8/2007 8:02 PM
Inetpub File Folder 1/2/2007 7:20 PM
PortQryUI File Folder 1/6/2007 9:00 PM
PortQryV2 File Folder 1/6/2007 8:16 PM
Program Files File Folder 4/30/2007 11:45 PM R
WINDOWS File Folder 7/3/2007 4:52 PM
wmpub File Folder 12/1/2006 9:58 PM
certreq.txt 2 KB Text Document 7/5/2007 1:32 AM A
collaborate.cer 2 KB Security Certificate 7/5/2007 2:07 AM A

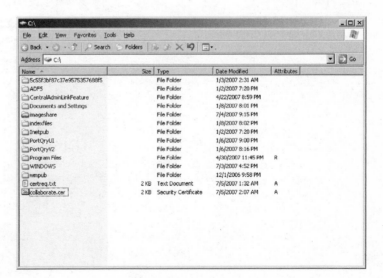

Once the text file is saved somewhere you can access it easily, it's time to add it to the web application that requested it.

1. To apply a certificate to an IIS Web Site (and therefore a SharePoint web application) go back to the Internet Information Services (IIS) Manager console. Open the Properties dialog box of the web application you want to require SSL, and go to the Directory Security tab.

2. On the Directory Security tab, click the Server Certificate button again.

3. It will begin the Web Server Certificate Wizard again, click Next on the Welcome screen.

   Because IIS is aware that there is a certificate request pending for this Web Site the next screen is Pending Certificate Request. On this screen you have the option to either delete the current pending request, or process the pending request and install the certificate.

4. Choose to process the pending request and install the certificate in this case (it is chosen by default), and click Next.

5. The next screen requires that you retrieve the Certificate Authority's response (the text file you saved with the .cer extension). Enter the file's path or browse to it in the Path and file name field. Then click Next.

6. The next screen gives you the opportunity to specify the SSL port, in case you would like something other than the default you specified on the General tab of the Web Site's properties. In this example, the default SSL port of 443 is preferable. Keep the default and click Next.

7. On the Certificate Summary screen is, of course, the summary of the certificate information based on your request. Click Next if the summary data is correct. And on the Completing the Web Server Wizard screen, just click Finish to complete the certificate process.

This will put you back on the Properties dialog box for the Web Site. To see what your certificate will look like to the users, click the View Certificate button. It will display the certificate's contents (Figure 15.69) as if it weren't based on a string of characters in a text file.

FIGURE 15.69
View new SSL Certificate

Congratulations, your web application now has its own SSL certificate.

There are a few steps left to complete this process. First the Web Site has to be started, and then it needs to be tested by accessing it with Internet Explorer (if it doesn't work, chances are good there is something wrong with the certificate).

If it works, then the certificate has to be exported. Why? Because the certificate has to be imported to the other SharePoint servers in the farm for the same web application. Remember, they all have to match, and that includes having the exact same certificate on all servers in the cluster. Then, after the certificate is imported to the other servers, the Web Site has to be started as well.

To start the IIS Web Site that we just configured to use SSL, click OK to close the Properties dialog box. Then, on the IIS Manager console, right click the Web Site and click Start in the popup menu.

Open Internet Explorer and type the web application's URL in the address bar, and hit enter. Be sure to use HTTPS instead of HTTP in the address.

It may prompt you to log in. Use the username you chose for the site collection administrator when you were configuring it. It may also prompt you to add the site to the Trusted Site zone on that computer. That is a very good sign and indicates that the browser found the site.

Once you have added the site to the Trusted sites zone, the home page for the SSL secured web application's first site collection should load (see Figure 15.70 for my example).

FIGURE 15.70
Website secured with
SSL Certificate

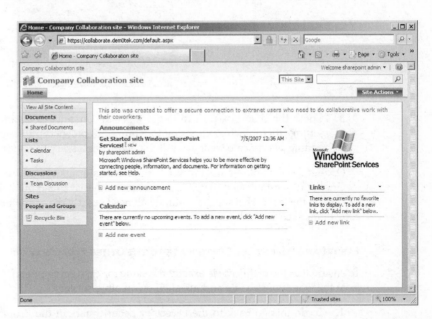

This indicates that SSL is working for the web application. To require SSL security to be used exclusively to access the site, go back to the IIS Manager console, and open the Properties dialog box (right click the Web Site and select Properties) for the SSL enabled Web Site we were just working on.

1. Select the Directory Security tab, then, in the Secure communications section, below the View Certificate button, click the Edit button.

2. It will open the Secure Communications dialog box (Figure 15.71).

FIGURE 15.71
Require SSL

3. Check the checkbox next to Require Secure Channel (SSL) and click OK. There are other settings there, such as choosing to require 128-bit encryption, ignoring client certificates, or adding a certificate trust list, but they aren't necessary to set for this example.

Open Internet Explorer and browse to the secure site again. Confirm that you can access the site. Once you've established that SSL is working with that site, it must be configured on all other servers on the farm. That means that they all need exactly the same certificate running on their copy of the Web Site to be secured.

EXPORT AND IMPORT SSL CERTIFICATE TO THE OTHER FARM SERVERS

To ensure that the certificate is exactly the same for each server, the certificate needs to be exported from the working Web Site and installed on all other servers.

1. To do this go back to the Directory Security tab, in the Properties dialog box of the SSL enabled Web Site.

2. Click on the Server Certificate button to start the Web Server Certificate Wizard, and then click Next at the Welcome screen.

Because the wizard is aware that a certificate is already installed for the Web Site, this screen now contains options pertaining to working with an existing certificate (as opposed to requesting or installing one).

3. As you can see in Figure 15.72, one of the option is to Export the current certificate to a .pfx file. Select that option and click Next.

FIGURE 15.72

Export current certificate

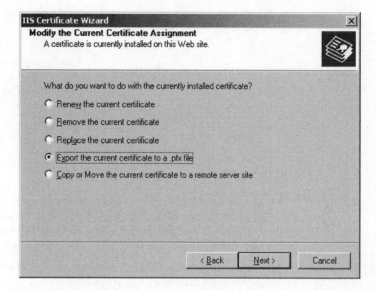

4. The next screen requires a file name and path for the exported file (or you can keep the default). Enter the path and file name you would like (it might be easier to save it to a fileshare so you can access it easily from the other servers on the farm). Click Next.

5. The .pfx file requires a password to extract. On this Certificate Password screen, enter the password you would like to use to extract the certificate. Click Next.

6. The Export Summary screen is next. It will display the data concerning the certificate and the path and file name for the exported file. Click Next if the information is correct.

Now that the certificate has been exported, it is time to add it to the second server on the farm. Use the same, surprisingly versatile Web Server Certificate Wizard, this time simply walking through the steps to import the certificate exported by the other server on the farm. Don't forget to set the SSL port on the General tab of the Web Site's properties. It must match the port of the other servers in the cluster hosting the Web Site.

1. Log into the second server on the SharePoint server farm. Open the IIS Manager console, and right click the stopped Web Site that requires SSL, select Properties in the popup menu.

2. Enter a port number for SSL, then click the Directory Security tab.

3. Click the Server Certificate button.

4. The Web Server Certificate Wizard will open, click Next to move past the Welcome Screen.

5. On the Server Certificate screen (Figure 15.73), instead of creating a new certificate, select Import a certificate from a .pfx file, and click Next.

FIGURE 15.73
Import Certificate

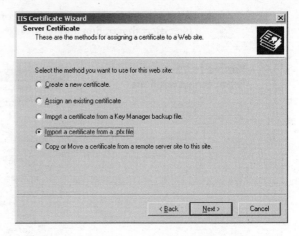

6. On the Import Certificate screen, browse to the .pfx file you exported earlier. You could mark the certificate as exportable if you'd like because usually the server that requested the certificate is the only one who can export. It is not necessary for this demonstration, so let's not enable it. Click Next.

7. On the Import Certificate Password screen, enter the password required to extract the certificate. Click Next.

8. Enter the SSL port for the Web Site. Click Next.

9. On the Import Certificate Summary screen, check to make certain that all of the certificate data is correct, then click Next.

10. Click Finish on the Completing the Web Server Certificate Wizard.

The certificate should now be enabled on this IIS Web Site. On the Directory Security tab in the Web Site's properties, click the Edit button and require secure channel (SSL). Click OK to close out of the Properties dialog box and save all changes.

Back on the console, right click the newly SSL enabled Web Site, and in the popup menu, select Start.

Repeat this process with each server in the farm.

Keep in mind that search may not work on the web application until the server that was selected for that web application has a working, SSL enabled IIS Web Site. Consider configuring that server's Web Site first.

Some things to keep in mind when using SSL:

◆ The IIS Web Site for each server on the farm will be stopped and require manual configuration before they are all functional.

◆ If there is a web applications already using the default SSL port, you will need to assign a different one. Each Web Site can have a different host header on port 80, but each Web Site must have a unique SSL port (or they need to either use a unique IP address or wildcard certificate). This is because traffic is *encrypted* when it gets to IIS, and therefore the host header information cannot be read to give IIS any change to figure out what Web Site to send the data to. Thus having a unique port for each site is critical. If you have any Port Rules governing the unique port, they will, obviously, have to change.

◆ If the IIS Web Site has to have a custom SSL port, then the SSL certificate must have the port as part of the common name (such as `collaborate.dem0tek.com:444`).

◆ Search may be delayed and errors may occur as each server is configured to start the new web application.

◆ The IIS certificate for each server's copy of the web application must be an exact duplicate of the others. Do not request a new certificate for each server. Even if they contain the same data, their keys will not be the same.

◆ Keep in mind that SSL session IDs linger in Internet Explorer. If you move away from an SSL site on a load balanced server farm, then try to go back, you may be redirected to a different server. However, IE will have a session ID for the other server it accessed earlier. Features of the page, like search or changing views, may not work properly. Try closing out of Internet Explorer altogether and then trying again. That will give IE a chance to clear the old session ID from its cache.

Using Kerberos for Authentication

When you are using Windows authentication, there are two primary authentication methods: NTLM and Kerberos (Negotiate). NTLM is the default Windows authentication method, and it requires no additional configuration to work in an Active Directory—or even a workgroup environment. Kerberos requires that both the client and server support that authentication method. Kerberos uses port 88 by default, so make certain, if you are using Kerberos authentication with external clients, that both the network firewall and the client's firewall allow Kerberos traffic on port 88. Also keep in mind that keeping exactly the same time is critical for Kerberos to work with external clients, so make certain they are pulling time from the same source and are updating their time adequately. Often issues of time are the biggest reason not to use Kerberos for authentication.

Kerberos is a ticket-based system, allowing an authenticated user to access resources based on their session ticket given by the key distribution center—usually the domain controller. However, sometimes a front-end product needs to be allowed to delegate authentication in order to give a user access to a back-end resource like the SQL server. This means that if someone logs into SharePoint, SharePoint needs to grant that user the right to access SharePoint resources in the SQL databases through a delegated service. For each web application that will be using Kerberos, the content database access account (otherwise known as the Application Pool account for that web application) must be given the right to access this data on behalf of the user. Only service principal accounts are allowed to delegate authentication with Kerberos. Which means that if you want to use Kerberos authentication, the content database access account must be registered as a service principal name (SPN) for the server (or servers) hosting its web application. Kerberos authentication has several bonuses. It is more secure, and in distributed environments, it works faster because of the session tickets.

Because there can be only one service principal name, per service class, per server registered; if you are going to enable Kerberos on more than one web application it is recommended that you register one account that will be used as a Content Database Access account for all of those web applications. This will make it more convenient to manage Kerberos and avoid duplicate principal name errors. Keep in mind that the same account can be registered as a service principal name on several different servers.

In addition to registering a service principal name, in more complex environments, you might need to also give the account *trusted for delegation rights* in Active Directory. Also keep in mind that the Search service (particularly the index service) often has problems authenticating using Kerberos. This is why it is considered common practice to have a main web application using NTLM authentication for the sake of search, and have everyone else access the content by using an extended web application, which will be using Kerberos for authentication.

Setting up for Kerberos is pretty easy to do. The main worry is that it does give a user account (or user accounts) that otherwise ran in a least-privilege context access to the network as a service principal.

In a single server installation of SharePoint, local services like Network Service already work with Kerberos. However, if they need to access network resources, you will need to register the computer object to be trusted for delegation and set as a service principal name on behalf of the local service. It is strongly suggested to use a domain account for web application application pools (Content Database Access accounts).

Using Setspn to Register Service Principal Names

Before you enable Kerberos authentication, you need to register the Content Database Access account as a service principal name in Active Directory. To do this, download and install setspn.exe from the Server 2003 Resource Kit on the SharePoint server. You can search for it online, or go to Microsoft's website.

Once you've downloaded and installed setspn.exe, you'll need to open a command prompt, go to the Resource Kit folder under Program files, and run the Setspn command with the following syntax:

```
Setspn -a http/servernamefqdn domain\contentdbaccessaccount
```

Where the *servernamefqdn* is the FQDN of the SharePoint server, *domain* is your domain name, and *contentdbaccessaccount* is the domain account that will be used as the application pool for accessing the content database of the web applications requiring Kerberos authentication.

This means you are going to register an arbitrary service principal, using the HTTP service class (because IIS needs to use it), for the server and the Content Database Access account.

In my example, that would be:

```
Setspn -a http/sp2.dem0tek.lcl dem0tek\wsscontent
```

This will allow SharePoint to access resources on behalf of a SharePoint user.

If you have one server, you can register the SPN for that server and be done. In Figure 15.74, you can see the example of setting the service principal name for my SP2 server for the Content Database Access account of dem0tek\wsscontent.

FIGURE 15.74
Registering an SPN for a server

However, if you are doing network load balancing, there is a little more labor involved. You will need to register the Content Database Access account as a service principal name for each NLB server in the cluster, and the cluster server internet name.

For example:

```
Setspn -a http/sp2.dem0tek.lcl dem0tek\wsscontent
Setspn -a http/sp3.dem0tek.lcl dem0tek\wsscontent
Setspn -a http/SharePoint.dem0tek.lcl dem0tek\wsscontent
```

QUIRKY KERBEROS

Kerberos can be a bit moody. I have worked with NLB networks that don't require the cluster internet name to be registered, and in others all clients but the SharePoint servers themselves can access the web application without the cluster name registered. The vast majority of SharePoint deployments don't need the Content Database Access account to be trusted to delegate, but a few (usually those with custom or complex web parts) do.

Kerberos does not report errors very well. Generally, if there are Kerberos (or key distribution center, KDC, errors) they will be on the domain controller. Otherwise the best way to know if there is a problem is to see if the web application can be accessed by all users and servers in the browser, and if search works.

If a web application is having any problems with authentication, Search is often the first to know. Check all Application logs on the servers hosting search for the Kerberos authenticated web applications. If search is having no problems, chances are good there are no problems.

To confirm the service principal names registrations for an account, use the list parameter for setspn:

```
Setspn -l accountname
```

Such as setspn -l wsscontent. That will, in my example, display all registrations for the dem0tek\wsscontent account (Figure 15.75).

FIGURE 15.75
Listing SPN registrations for a domain account

Once the registrations are complete, it is time to enable Kerberos on something.

ENABLING KERBEROS ON A WEB APPLICATION

You can enable Kerberos on a new web application (as long as it uses the Content Database Access Account that was registered as an SPN). But often it is the extended web application that gets set to use Kerberos. Also during the creation of a new web application, setting up Kerberos in the SharePoint interface means, in the Create Web Application page, scrolling to the IIS Authentication Settings section and selecting Negotiate (Kerberos). However, it is not as intuitive to change the authentication method of an existing web application, so this is what this section will demonstrate.

You can enable Kerberos on an existing web application (if its Content Database Access Account is the one registered as an SPN) by going to Authentication providers, on the Application Management page of Central Administration. On the Authentication Providers page, select the Web Application you would like to modify. When the web application has been selected, its zones will be displayed on the page. Remember that, in this context, the zones for the web application are the default zone, which is the true web application's address, and all other zones listed are extended web applications.

IT GOES WITHOUT SAYING

At this point I am assuming you have an extended web application to modify, and that you can log into the web application's top level site to make certain authentication is working.

In my example, I have a web application named, conveniently enough, `http://SharePoint`. This web application has an extended web application in the intranet zone (Figure 15.76).

FIGURE 15.76
web application zones in Authentication Providers page

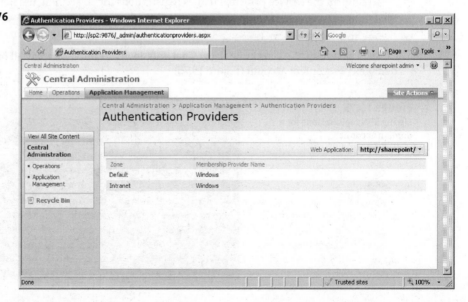

1. To configure an extended application to use Kerberos as its authentication method, select the zone for it.

2. In the Edit Authentication page for the zone, scroll down to the IIS Authentication Settings section (Figure 15.77). Make certain that Integrated Authentication is checked, then select Negotiate (Kerberos). When you are finished with that selection, click Save to finish.

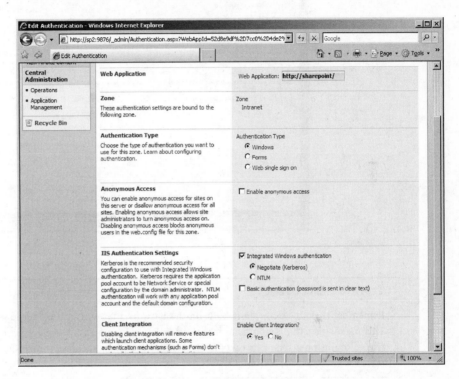

3. The extended web application will now be using Kerberos as its authentication method exclusively. To ensure this change was set in IIS, go to all servers in the cluster, and run iisreset/noforce at the command prompt.

Once IIS has been reset at all servers, log into a client on the network, and access the extended web application you just modified (in my example that would be `http://SharePoint:29834`). Log into the site as a user with at least contribute permissions, and bring up the top level site's home page. Once there, do some common tasks, such as add a list item and do a search (Figure 15.78). Make certain that authentication is truly working. Also, check the Event Viewer logs for errors on all servers in the cluster, as well as the domain controller. There should be no errors, but it never hurts to check. Sometimes it does take SharePoint a few minutes to realize that Kerberos is being used to access the content databases of the web application. So if search is not working, wait at least one indexing cycle and try again before beginning troubleshooting procedures.

FIGURE 15.78
Kerberos
authenticated
site, search
successful

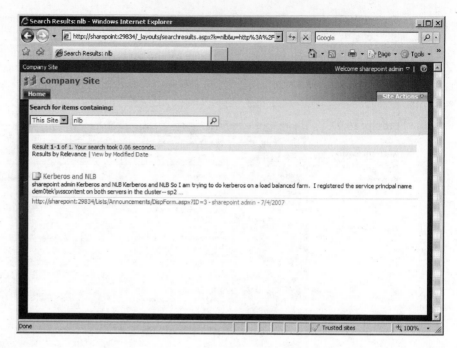

TESTING THE CLUSTER

Remember that this example is built on the network that was load balanced earlier in the chapter. This means that this Kerberos authentication is working across the cluster. In order to test it, feel free to drainstop a server or two (or disable its network connection) to confirm that load balancing is working.

If your SharePoint environment is more complex, with web parts that access external resources for example, you may need to set the Content Database Access account to be trusted for delegation in Active Directory. If this is the case, open the Active Directory Users and Computers console for the domain. Click on the Users node in the Tree pane of the console, then double-click the Content Database Access user account.

This will open its Properties dialog box. Select the Account tab (Figure 15.79). In the Account options list, check the checkbox for the Account is trusted for delegation item. Then click OK to commit the change. You may have to do an iisreset/noforce on the SharePoint servers for them to realize the change.

You should now be able to access the extended web application with no problems using Kerberos authentication. I have noticed that some of my servers do seem to perform ever so slightly better when Kerberos is enabled. Give it a try.

FIGURE 15.79

Configuring domain account for Trusted delegation

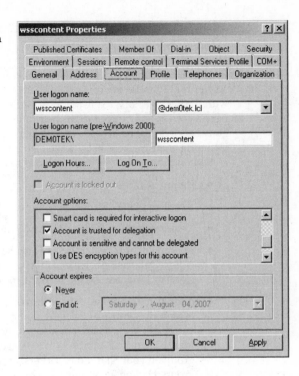

KERBEROS DOESN'T HAVE TO BE JUST FOR EXTENDED WEB APPLICATIONS

Enabling Kerberos on a new web application, as long as you use the Content Database Access account you've registered as a service principal name is easy. Although there are documents online stating that search cannot index a site that uses Kerberos exclusively, I have had no problems doing so. You can enable Kerberos in web applications that use host headers, they don't even have to match the internal domain, as well as web applications that use port numbers. However, if you run into a problem using search on a web application, you can just reset it to NTLM, create an extended web application of the original's contents, and enable Kerberos for that URL instead.

Authenticating is an important part of accessing shared resources on a network. Being able to conveniently access sites, lists, and libaries is what SharePoint is all about. Another convenience is being able to add items to lists and libraries using incoming email. With Directory Management Service, not only are lists and libraries able to have a contact listed in Active Directory and the Exchange Global Address List for easy use, but each SharePoint group can also have its own distribution list so users can send an email to the entire SharePoint group by finding its distribution group listing in the Exchange 2003 Global Address List as well.

Directory Management Service

Directory Management Service (DMS) is a feature that works in addition to Incoming E-mail. It integrates with Active Directory and Exchange 2003 to allow SharePoint to create an email contact for any list or library that has an incoming email alias. DMS will also create a distribution group in AD for any SharePoint group that has an email alias. Because Exchange is integrated so closely with Active Directory, if a list, library, or SharePoint group has an email alias then that alias will have a corresponding contact or distribution group in AD, and therefore, be listed in the Exchange global address list (GAL). This will make it easier for the SharePoint users to send email to incoming email enabled lists, as well as send email to everyone in a particular SharePoint group.

DMS has some caveats that you need to realize before you chose to enable it:

◆ Requires Exchange 2003.

◆ Requires that Exchange be configured to forward email correctly to the SharePoint server.

◆ Requires a unique Organizational Unit in Active Directory.

◆ Requires that the SharePoint Farm account (also known as the Configuration Database account, Database Access account, or Central Administration application pool account) and Content Database Access accounts be domain user accounts.

◆ The Farm Account must have the correct permissions for the OU. These permissions are pretty extensive, because of the work that must go on between SharePoint, AD, and Exchange at the enterprise level. There are also so many things that the Content Database Access accounts must have permission to do, it is most effective to either add them to the Local Administrator's group on your SharePoint servers, or if that is too onerous, add them to the Domain Admins group. Having an account that also accesses the content databases of your SharePoint web applications function with such elevated privileges may not comply with your company's security policies. Check before implementing DMS.

◆ Requires, of course, that SMTP be configured and working with incoming email on the SharePoint server. Keep in mind that email is not intended to be load balanced. This means that DMS is not load balanced either, and is intended to be run from one server in the farm (to the point where a remote server can be used to run DMS if necessary). This is why I refer to SP2 as the DMS server and not the NLB URL.

◆ When configuring incoming email to work with DMS, keep in mind that DMS will create the list or library contact based on the SMTP mail server address for the SharePoint server, not the display address. If you have the display address set up with a different domain alias, then the list, library, or distribution group could have two email addresses (SharePoint will accept either one); one with the list alias tacked onto the address you used in the SMTP mail server field, such as list@sp2.dem0tek.lcl, used by AD and Exchange; and one with the list alias tacked on to the display address, such as list@dem0share.com, which will be displayed in SharePoint as the list's incoming email address.

To prepare for DMS you need to create an OU and set up the correct account permissions.

CREATE THE DMS ORGANIZATIONAL UNIT

SharePoint has to have somewhere in Active Directory to put the contacts and distribution groups DMS will create. Thus, the need for a Directory Management Service OU. If you already have your OU created, you can skip the next three steps.

1. To create the OU, open the Active Directory Users and Computers (ADUC) management console.

2. Right click the icon for the domain that contains the accounts for SharePoint, and in the dropdown menu, select New, then Organizational Unit.

3. In the New Object dialog box, enter the name of the organizational unit that you are creating, then click OK. I entered *WSS_DMS* for my example.

In the management console, your new OU should be displayed (Figure 15.80).

FIGURE 15.80

New OU in console

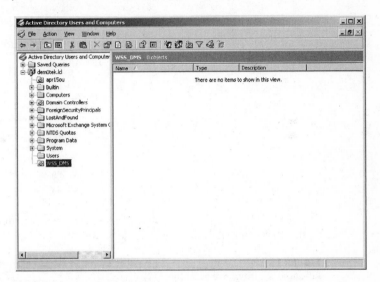

CONFIGURE ORGANIZATIONAL UNIT PERMISSIONS FOR DMS

Now that the OU has been created, it's time to give the necessary SharePoint accounts permission to allow Directory Management Service to work. The permissions are complex, so to keep things simple I work in two steps. Before we begin, make certain that the ADUC console is displaying advanced security by going to the View menu, and enabling Advanced Features.

Farm account

To start, the Farm Account (which in my case is dem0tek\wssconfig) must have access to the OU to create, delete, and manage objects. This has to include, not just the OU, but all child objects as well.

1. To configure the Farm Account's permissions on the new DMS OU, right click the OU (in my case that is WSS_DMS), and select Properties in the popup menu.

In the Properties dialog box, select the Security tab. You might be tempted to simply add the Farm account here and assign it permissions here. These are just general permissions that apply only to this object and not explicitly the child objects below it. We need more granular permission control than that.

2. On the Security tab (see Figure 15.81) click on the Advanced button on the bottom right, because we are going to need to drill down and apply some advanced permissions.

FIGURE 15.81
Security tab for the DMS OU

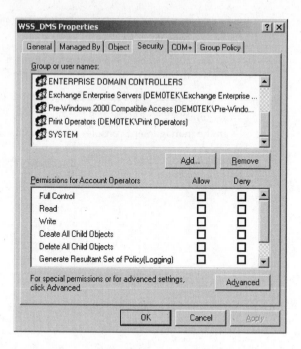

This will bring you to the Advanced Security Settings dialog box. You can see, in Figure 15.82, that the permissions displayed in the Security tab are listed here, but in more detail.

FIGURE 15.82
Advanced Security Settings for the DMS OU

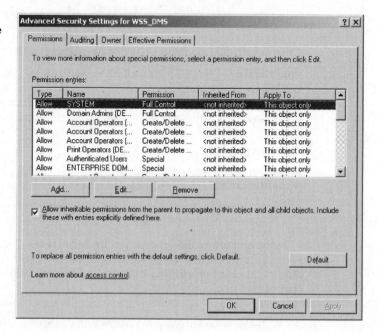

3. To add an advanced security entry for the Farm account, click the Add…button below the Permission entries list. In the Select User, Computer, or Group dialog box enter the username for the Farm Account (mine is `wssconfig`). If you are not sure of the spelling of your Farm account, click Check Name in the Select User, Computer, Group dialog box. If the username is correct, click OK.

This will open a Permission Entry dialog box for the entry. As you can see in Figure 15.83, This object and all child objects is selected in the Apply onto field.

FIGURE 15.83
Permissions for the Farm Account

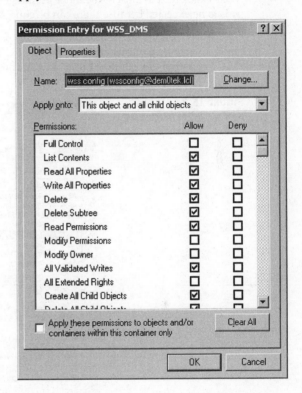

For permissions, the Farm account does not need full control but it does need the ability to Read, Write, and Create all child objects. In order for SharePoint to be able to delete objects, the Farm account also requires permission to Delete, Delete Subtree, and Delete All Child Objects.

4. To this end, allow the following:

- ◆ List Contents
- ◆ Read All Properties
- ◆ Write All Properties
- ◆ Delete
- ◆ Delete Subtree

◆ Read Permissions

◆ All Validated Writes

◆ Create All Child Objects

◆ Delete All Child Objects.

When you set the Create and Delete all child objects permissions, that will check the Allow checkbox next to most of the other permissions in the Permissions list relating to child objects. This is to be expected because there can be child objects in the OU.

5. When you have finished allowing permissions, click OK. That will return you to the Advanced Security Settings dialog box, where the Farm account should be listed with Special permissions for the object and all child objects (Figure 15.84).

FIGURE 15.84
New special permission for Farm account on OU

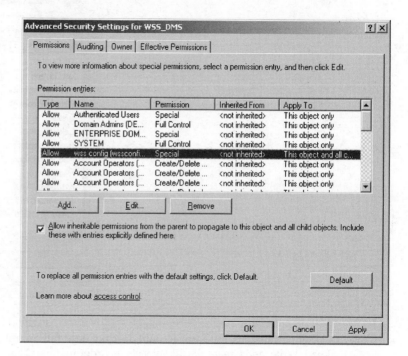

6. If the entry is listed correctly, click OK to close out of the Advanced Security Settings dialog box. Then click OK to close the Properties dialog box for the OU as well. This should return you to the management console.

Content Database Access Account

Additionally, the Content Database Access Accounts for any web application you would like to have work with DMS must also have elevated permissions. That account is the one that SharePoint actually uses to manage list, SharePoint group, and library settings. It is the account that really creates the contacts and distribution groups. Creating these email enabled objects means that the account has to interact with the network resources, and the SharePoint server, on an administrative level. Because the account needs to be so powerful, it has been my experience that you must add the Content Database Accounts to the SharePoint server's Local Administrator's group for each server in order to ensure that all necessary permissions have been applied. This obviously has some security drawbacks, and is a good reason to choose not to do DMS. Keep in mind that this must be done for each web application's content database access account.

1. To add the Content Access Database account to the Local Administrators group, go to the SharePoint server and open the Computer Management Console (Start ➤ Administrative Tools ➤ Computer Management).

2. Click on Local Users and Groups, then open the Groups folder in the content pane.

3. Double-click the Administrators group icon.

4. On the General tab, click the Add... button.

5. In the Select Users, Contacts, or Computers dialog box, enter the username (my example is wsscontent) for the Content Database Access account and click OK.

6. That will return you to the Administrators group Properties dialog box, with the Content Database Access account listed (Figure 15.85). Click OK to close the dialog box and return to the management console. Remember to do this for each Content Database Access account.

FIGURE 15.85
Content Database Access account added to the SharePoint Server's Local Administrator's group

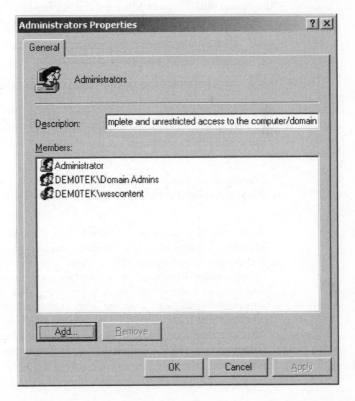

CONFIGURE DIRECTORY MANAGEMENT SERVICE

The Active Directory preparations for DMS are complete, now it's time to setup DMS in SharePoint and see what happens. Keep in mind that Directory Management Service is a feature of incoming email. You should enable incoming email and make certain it works, then enable DMS. Because they are two different features, it makes it easier to troubleshoot if you enable them one at a time. In this case, because incoming email was enabled in the Post Configuration Tasks section of Chapter 2, "Installation," I am going to assume that you already have incoming email up and running.

Open Central Administration (on the SharePoint server, go to Start ➢ Administrative Tools ➢ SharePoint 3.0 Central Administration) and log in with an account that has the right to administer the SharePoint farm.

Because enabling incoming email is a server farm level setting, and DMS is part of the incoming email feature, the setting is accessed from the Operations page.

So go to the Operations page, then click the Incoming e-mail settings link in the Topology and Services category.

It will open the Configuring Incoming E-Mail Settings page. You have configured most of the settings here long ago in order to enable incoming email for the lists and libraries that have email handlers (like Calendar, most libraries, and Announcements). However, you did not enable DMS then, and now it's time to do so.

Scroll down to the Directory Management Service section. Although there is a long description on the right of the section, it actually starts with only three options to the question "Use SharePoint Directory Management Service to create distribution groups and contacts?"

No This option, which is the default, means that there are no other settings for DMS displayed in the section and the feature is not enabled.

Yes This option propagates the section with the settings necessary to enable DMS on that server farm, to be managed by that server.

Use Remote This option allows you to point the server to another SharePoint server that is supporting DMS (primarily used with MOSS unfortunately).

If you select Yes, which is what we'll use for this demonstration, it will fill the section with settings related to configuring DMS on this SharePoint server. The settings will now be:

Active Directory container where the new distribution groups and contacts will be created: This field requires an Active Directory query syntax, so follow the example using the OU name and domain name separated by commas. For my example (in Figure 15.86) my OU is WSS_DMS in the dem0tek.lcl domain, so my syntax would be OU=WSS_DMS,DC=dem0tek,DC=lcl. Notice that I did not use spaces, so it is one long, run on series of characters. It indicates the OU you want to use, in a particular domain. Because there can be child domains, each part of the domain name that is separated by periods needs to be indicated, thus OU=WSS_DMS, and the domain name is indicated by DC=dem0tek and DC=lcl. If the domain name had more words separated by periods, each one of them would be preceded by DC = until the entire domain name were there.

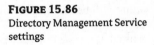

FIGURE 15.86
Directory Management Service settings

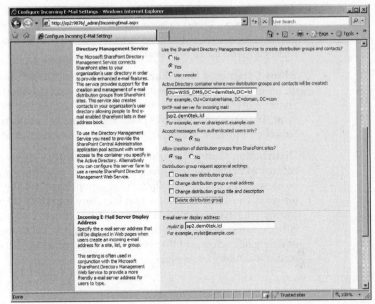

SMTP mail server for incoming email   This is usually the SharePoint server's fully qualified domain name, or FQDN (my example is SP2.dem0tek.lcl). This does not have to be the same as the Display Address. For simplicity's sake my example is going to have the server's address and the display address match.

ADVANCED CONCEPTS FOR INCOMING EMAIL ADDRESSING

Because DMS uses the mail server's address exclusively for the email address for incoming email enabled list, libraries, and for SharePoint groups, you can handle the SMTP mail server entry in several ways:

◆ Use a real server address so it shows up properly in AD, and have the display address match. If the internal domain is not internet accessible (it doesn't match the domain address registered and set up for email outside of the office), then that address will not work from outside the office.

◆ Use a domain alias (with correct DNS entries) instead of the real server name and have it show up, and work, with SharePoint and Exchange, but AD will leave the email field blank in the general properties of the contact or distribution list because it cannot resolve the address with its domain name. Then have the display address match the email server's address.

◆ Use the real server address, but use a different display name. The contact address will be different than the display address because DMS only uses the SMTP server name when creating the email address and contact. This will effectively give the contact or distribution group two email addresses, one that resolves to the server's address on the local domain, and one that resolves to the display address.

Accept Messages from Authenticated Users only   This setting will be enforced throughout the server farm. I tend to leave this setting at No, and then enforce this option at the individual list level. However, it is a good catchall security setting to ensure that no one but authenticated users can send email to SharePoint lists, libraries, or distribution groups.

Allow Creation of Distribution Groups from SharePoint Sites   This setting, with the choice of Yes or No, will add the option of creating a distribution group in the Group Settings of every SharePoint group in every site, in every site collection, in every web application on the server farm. If you want to enable DMS for incoming email capable lists and libraries, but not for SharePoint groups, set this option to No. I however, am of course going to enable it.

Distribution Group Request Approval Settings   If you enable distribution groups, you can control what distribution groups get created, changed, or deleted with these approval settings. So, despite the fact that all SharePoint groups can have the option of getting a distribution group for email in Active Directory (and therefore Exchange 2003), you (or a Farm administrator) can control what happens with the distribution group by requiring approval on it. The options are to either create a new distribution group, change its email address, change its title and description, or delete it. Each one of these options, if you select it, will cause the change to require approval before it actually takes place.

WITH THE POWER OF APPROVAL COMES GREAT RESPONSIBILITY

Remember, SharePoint site collection administrators (which can be practically anyone if you have Self-service site creation enabled) will be able to create whatever SharePoint group they want, and create, as well as name the distribution group anything they'd like. When they do that, those distribution groups get added to the Active Directory OU. If you want to control that and stop the spread of possibly inappropriate distribution group names, consider these approval settings.

But be warned. That means, when requiring approval, a Farm administrator will have to take the time to do approvals, such as approving the creation of a new distribution group, before that change can occur. If the danger of falling behind on approvals is greater than the danger of having a lot of uncontrolled distribution groups in the OU, then consider avoiding requiring approval.

So now that you know what the settings are for, it is time to configure DMS.

1. Make certain you have chosen Yes in response to the option to Use SharePoint Directory Management Service to create distribution groups and contacts.

2. In the Active Directory container field, enter the OU you will be using for DMS in the correct syntax, such as OU=WSS_DMS,DC=dem0tek,DC=lcl.

3. In the SMTP mail server for incoming email field, enter the FQDN for the SharePoint server hosting incoming email (unless you plan on doing something more fancy). My example is sp2.dem0tek.lcl.

4. For the Accept messages from authenticated users only, let's keep the default of No. In this case I am going to let unauthenticated users email the addresses at this level, and then lock down the incoming email at the list and library level.

5. For Allow creation of distribution groups from SharePoint sites, select Yes.

6. For Distribution group request approval setting, make certain that all of the option checkboxes are clear. For demonstration purposes, I would like to prove it works, then go back and show you what the settings do and where to manage distribution group approval.

7. If all settings are correct, click OK to enable DMS.

If you mistyped anything, or if the Farm account doesn't have access to the OU, then you will not be able to leave the page. Fix the problem and click OK until you can go back to the Operations page.

YOU JUST THINK YOU DID IT RIGHT . . .

Something to note, SharePoint is not actually that picky about letting you enable DMS. Your OU permissions can be wrong, but as long as the Farm account has access to the OU, SharePoint will let you save your settings. I guess it just needs to be sure you are willing to try to make it work, not necessarily if you got it right on the first go. When you make changes to the incoming email settings (this can include changing permissions in AD), if they don't seem to "take" go to the SharePoint server hosting the Incoming E-mail service, drop to the command prompt and do an iisreset/noforce.

Now that we have our OU with the correct permissions and DMS configured in SharePoint, it is time to use it.

ENABLE INCOMING EMAIL ON A LIST TO CREATE A CONTACT IN ACTIVE DIRECTORY

Keep in mind that, because Exchange is so closely integrated with Active Directory, any contact, user, or group object can have an email address assign to it that will have a corresponding address in Exchange, and therefore be added to Exchange's global address list. And now that DMS is enabled, all lists that become incoming email enabled will get a contact in the OU based on that list's email alias. SharePoint groups can get a distribution group with its email alias as well (the option not to create a distribution group for a SharePoint group is an option in the group's settings).

You may already know how to enable Incoming e-mail on a list or library because we covered that earlier in the book, but in this case we are enabling incoming email not just to allow users to add items to the list or library by email, but to create a contact in AD.

The process is the same; go to the SharePoint site of your choice in Internet Explorer (I am going to use http://sp2 for my example). Be sure to log in as someone who has the right to configure settings for the site.

On my Company site I am going to enable incoming email for the CompanyPictures library. To enable incoming email on a list or library, go to the content page and click List Settings in the action bar (for a library it will use the type of library Settings for the option instead).

On the Customize page for that list or library, select the Incoming e-mail settings link under Communications.

In the Incoming E-Mail Settings page, enable incoming email by clicking Yes in the Incoming E-Mail section.

Also in that section, give the list or library an email alias. In my case I am using the CompanyPictures library, so I am going to name it companypics (Figure 15.87).

FIGURE 15.87
Enabling Incoming
E-mail on a List to
create a contact in
Active Directory

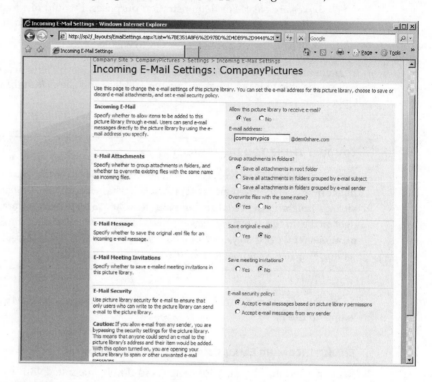

For the other incoming email settings, feel free to do as you wish. For this example, I am going to leave most of the defaults as they are. Notice the option to save email invitations to the list or library, within the list or library. This becomes a bigger deal when DMS is enabled because the list or library will be in the global address list in Exchange and therefore can be more easily, accidentally, invited to events by well meaning users.

Also note the setting where you can tighten the email security on the list by accepting email based on the list or library's permissions or accepting emails from any sender. Leave the default that accepts email based on the library's permissions.

If all the incoming email setting are correct, click OK to apply them.

Back on the Customize page, confirm that the correct email address is listed (that you didn't mistype the alias).

To confirm that the incoming email alias for the list or library actually did add a contact to the DMS OU, go back to the Active Directory Users and Computers management console, and select the DMS OU (my example is WSS_DMS). You should see the new contact displayed in the content pane (Figure 15.88). If you cannot see the contact, hit f5 to refresh the display.

FIGURE 15.88
New Contact in DMS OU

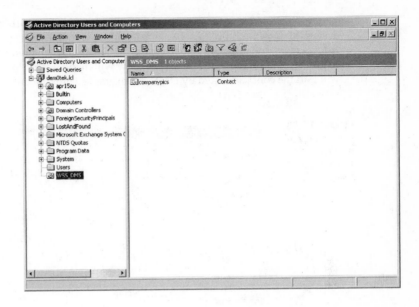

FIGURE 15.88
New Contact in DMS OU

If you double-click the contact, you will see that it has the expected email address (Figure 15.89).

FIGURE 15.89
New Contact properties

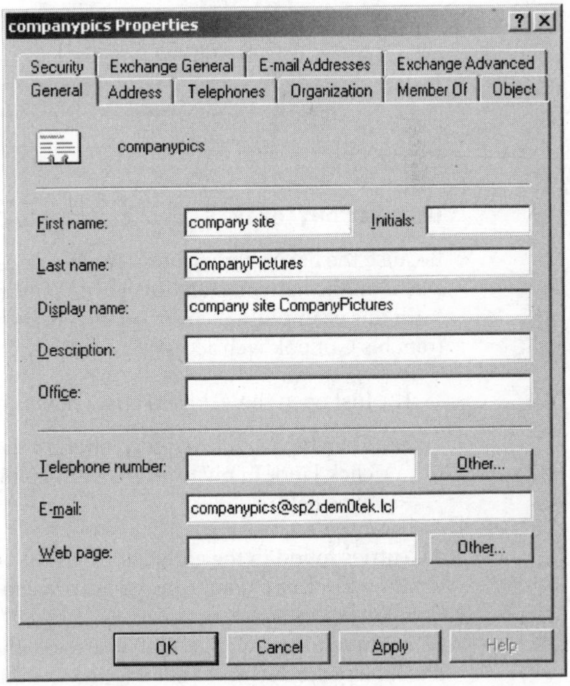

And, to see if the contact has made it to the global address list, you can open the Exchange System Manager and preview the global address list there by right clicking the Default Global Address List under Recipients, selecting Properties from the popup menu, then clicking Preview in the dialog box. The Address List preview will display the addresses, and if you scroll down you will find the contact created by DMS (my example, companypics, is displayed in Figure 15.90).

FIGURE 15.90
New Contact in the Global Address List Preview

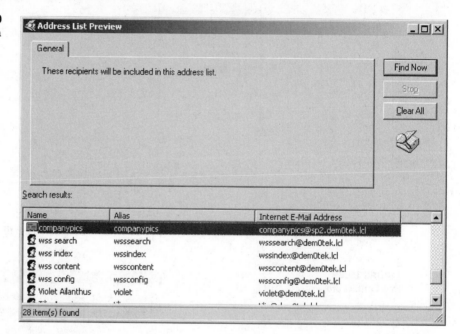

USE THE CONTACT DMS CREATED TO SEND CONTENT TO A LIST OR LIBRARY

Because the list or library has a contact in AD, and an entry in the global address list in Exchange, a user on the network can now easily send email to it.

In this example, a SharePoint user is going to send a picture to the CompanyPictures library from his Outlook web access.

1. Just open the Address book, make sure that the user is looking in the Global Address List.

2. Then type in the first few letters of the list or library's name in the display or alias fields, then click Find. In my example I am going to type the first two letters of the library name in the alias field.

All entries found in the global address list with that criteria will display at the bottom of the window. For this example, as you can see in Figure 15.91, there is only one entry, and that's my CompanyPictures contact.

If you send an email to that address with a picture attached (see Figure 15.92 for my example), it will be processed and added to the CompanyPictures library.

FIGURE 15.91
Contact listed in the GAL

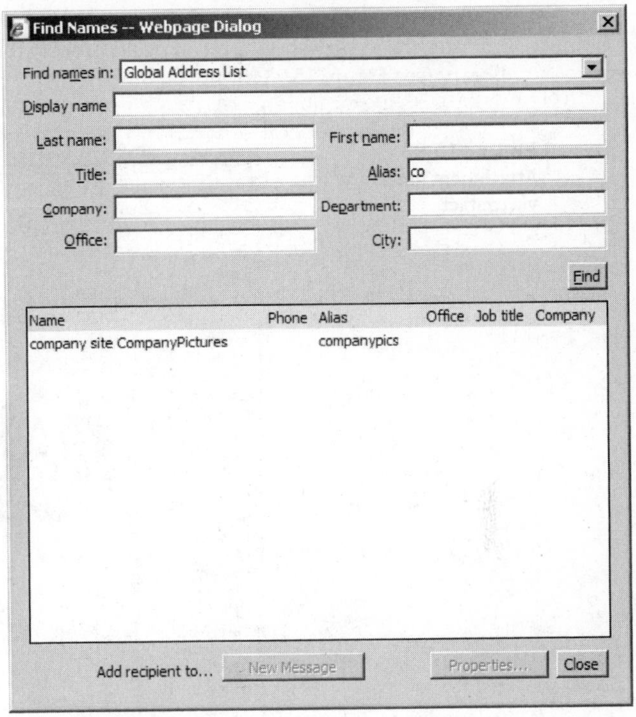

FIGURE 15.92
Email using contact to
Library

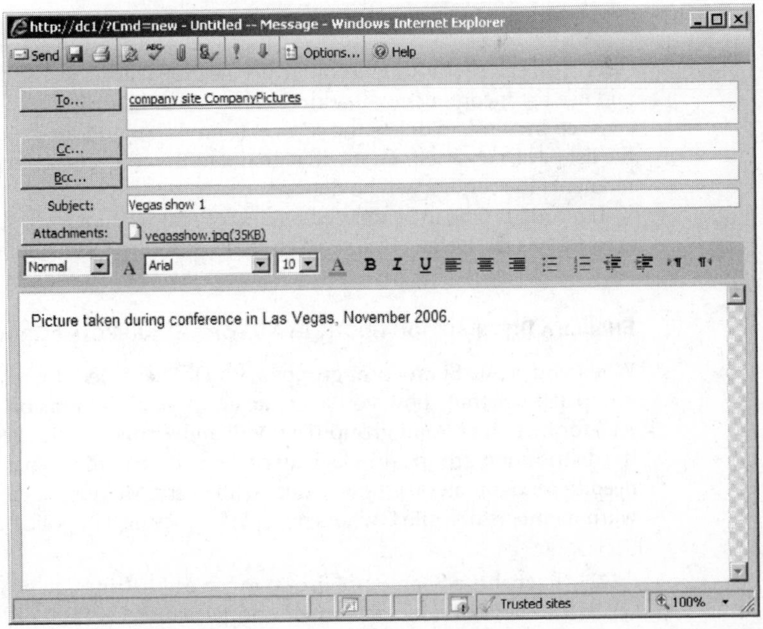

To see if the library received the email, you can go to the library in SharePoint. Within a few minutes the library should receive and process the email, and add the email's attachment to the library (see Figure 15.93 for my example).

FIGURE 15.93
Attachment in Library, sent via contact

As you can see, adding a contact to the global address list does make it easier for a user to find and use the incoming email address for a list or library.

Keep in mind, to delete the contact from AD, therefore the GAL, just disable incoming email for the list or library itself. That will signal that the contact must be removed from the OU, and in moments the contact will be deleted.

If a contact fails to be deleted by SharePoint when it is disabled, make certain that your Farm account has the Delete, Delete all child objects, and Delete Subtree permissions for the DMS OU.

ENABLE A DISTRIBUTION GROUP IN AD FOR A SHAREPOINT GROUP

When you create SharePoint groups with DMS enabled, there are a few options added to the group settings that allow you to create an email alias (and corresponding distribution group in AD) for that SharePoint group. That will allow anyone with access to the GAL to send an email to the distribution group and reach all of the people in the SharePoint group. This is useful if you need to send out an outage warning to all of the Members of a site collection, or if you need to warn members of a site Owners group of an upcoming policy change.

1. To enable a SharePoint group to have a distribution group in AD, go to People and Groups on the SharePoint site (my example is http://sp2).

2. Select the SharePoint group (my example is a group I created called ListManagers) that requires a distribution group, and click Settings on the action bar, then select Group Settings from the dropdown menu.

3. In the Group Settings page, scroll down to the bottom. There will be two new sections added because of DMS; E-mail Distribution List and Archive E-mail.

E-Mail Distribution List   This section simply has a Yes/No option for making the SharePoint Group Distribution list enabled (distribution list is essentially what an AD distribution group is), and the field in which you enter the distribution list's email alias.

Archive E-mail   SharePoint also gives you the option to conveniently store the emails sent to the SharePoint group (via its distribution group) in a list. You can choose an existing list, or have SharePoint create one with a name you enter, especially for this occasion. Note that the archive list will, by default, be set not to be displayed on the Quick Launch bar, so you will have to go to All Site Content to get to it. When you choose to create a new archive list for the SharePoint group's emails, SharePoint makes it a discussion list.

4. In the E-Mail Distribution List section, choose Yes. When that option is selected, then you can type an alias in the email address field—if the option is No, despite the fact that the field is not grayed out, you can't type in it.

5. In the Distribution list e-mail address field, enter the email alias you would like to use for the SharePoint group. In my example, I am going to use listmanagers as the alias (Figure 15.94).

FIGURE 15.94
Group Settings page, Distribution list settings

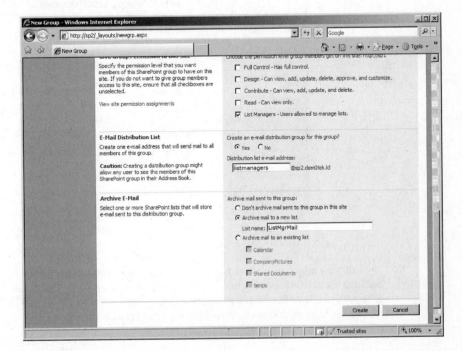

6. In the Archive E-Mail section, you can choose a list to archive the email, not archive the email, or create a list. In this example, let's choose to archive mail to a new list (which I am going to call ListMgrMail). This will create a discussion list on the site.

ARCHIVE IS FOREVER

Keep in mind that if you disable or delete distribution group or even delete the SharePoint group itself, it will not delete the archive list.

---

7. When you've finished your settings, click OK.

This should put you back on the content page for the SharePoint group you were configuring. Now at the top of the content area, the Group e-mail address and archive list will be displayed (Figure 15.95).

FIGURE 15.95
New Group
E-Mail Address
and E-Mail
Archive
Displayed on
SharePoint
Group page

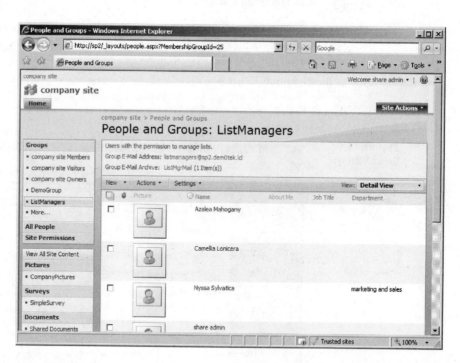

Now you might think that you created only a distribution group for the SharePoint group, but because the archive list also needs to be sent a copy of any email addressed to the distribution group, the archive list for the group was also given a contact object in AD. This makes it possible for the list to be added to the distribution group as a member.

You can confirm this by returning to the Active Directory Users and Computers management console (Figure 15.96). You'll see that DMS conveniently added a contact for the list as well.

FIGURE 15.96
New distribution group and contact in AD

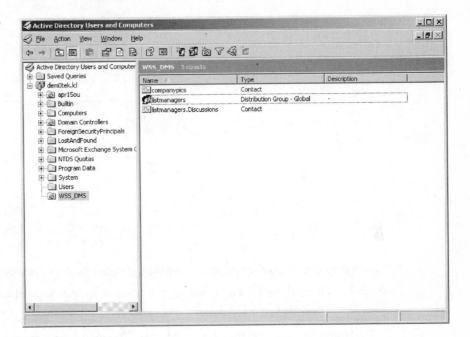

Now that the distribution group was created for the SharePoint group, anyone who is added to the group will be added to the distribution group members in AD and will receive a copy of any email addressed to the SharePoint group. If the user leaves the group, they will no longer be on the list of people who receive emails that are addressed to the SharePoint group's distribution list.

USE THE DISTRIBUTION GROUP TO SEND EMAIL TO MEMBERS OF A SHAREPOINT GROUP

Now that you know that the SharePoint group has a distribution group object in both AD and the Exchange GAL, let's see what happens when it's used.

To use the distribution group to send email to all of the members of the SharePoint group, simply open an email client that can access the Exchange global address list (my example is using Outlook Web Access).

Create a new email address, and for the To: address, use the Address book to find the distribution group in the GAL. In my example, I searched for "list" in the alias field.

You should see both the distribution group and its archive list contact displayed (Figure 15.97). Use only the distribution group at this time. Create the message and send it.

After the email is sent, open an email client that can receive email for one of the members of the SharePoint group you sent the email to above. You will receive the email sent to the distribution group.

FIGURE 15.97

Entries for SharePoint group in the GAL

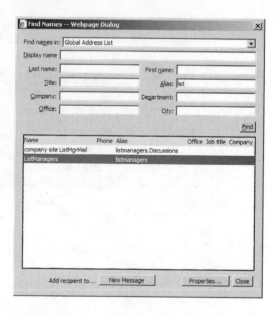

CONFIRM THAT THE SHAREPOINT GROUP'S EMAIL IS BEING SAVED IN THE ARCHIVE LIST

The point of the archive list is to store a copy of all email sent to the distribution group. This is done by creating an email contact in AD for the list and adding it to the membership of the distribution group.

To confirm that a copy of the email sent to the SharePoint group was archived in the list, open the list—it will not be on the Quick Launch bar, but you can click on the Discussions heading there. It will be listed on the All Site Content page under Discussion Boards.

In the list (ListMgrMail in my example, Figure 15.98), the email should be displayed.

FIGURE 15.98

Archive list containing copy of email to distribution group

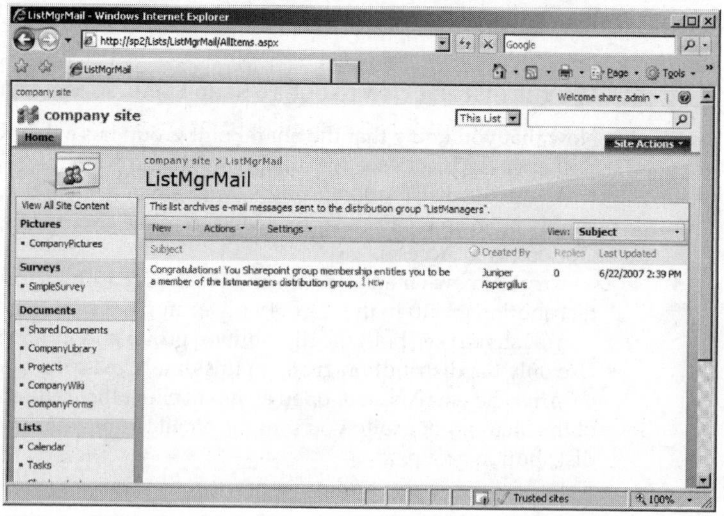

This proves that the permissions and settings for DMS works; the distribution groups and contacts in AD as well as the Exchange entries work; and the archive list for a SharePoint group's emails works.

There is really only one more thing that needs to be explored concerning DMS– distribution group approval settings.

TWO NAMES, THE SAME THING

Have you noticed that part of SharePoint Operations refers to distribution groups, but in the Share-Point group settings, the same thing is referred to as a distribution list? They are the same thing, but the reason why the name does not remain the same between the two settings page of SharePoint is a mystery.

MANAGE DISTRIBUTION GROUPS WITH DISTRIBUTION GROUP APPROVAL

Now that you can see how easy it is to enable distribution groups, and create discussion lists to archive email for those groups, let's take a look at how to enable and manage distribution group approval.

Just like content approval in a list is the interim step between an item being saved to a list and it being visible to the public. Group approval is an interim step between the enabling of a distribution group for a SharePoint Group and its creation in AD. You can also delay the approval of the deletion of a distribution group.

1. To enable distribution group approval, go back to the Incoming E-Mail settings page. To open it, first log into Central Administration, then go to the Operations page, and click the Incoming e-mail settings link in the Topology and Services category.

2. On the Configure Incoming E-Mail Settings page, scroll down to the Directory Management Service section. Near the bottom are the checkboxes for Distribution group request approval settings. The options are:

Create New Distribution Group   If this option is selected then the distribution group that should be created when the option is enabled on a SharePoint group, will instead wait for approval from a Farm Administrator before being added to AD.

Change Distribution Group E-mail Address   If this option is selected, if someone tries to change the distribution group's email address, the change should be delayed until approved.

Change Distribution Group Title and Description   This option delays the change of a distribution group's title and description (which means the SharePoint group's title and description) until approved.

Delete Distribution Group   This option will actually delay the deletion of a distribution group. If it is rejected, no deletion occurs. However, the approval entry remains in the list until the deleting request is approved. Then, at that point, the distribution group is deleted. In other words, you can block an accidental delete request by not approving it, but that request will remain in the list until it is approved. I would prefer that if a delete request was rejected, that the request would then leave the list.

3. For this example, select the Create a distribution group and Delete distribution group settings to require approval (Figure 15.99).

4. After making that selection, click OK.

FIGURE 15.99
Configuring Request Approval settings

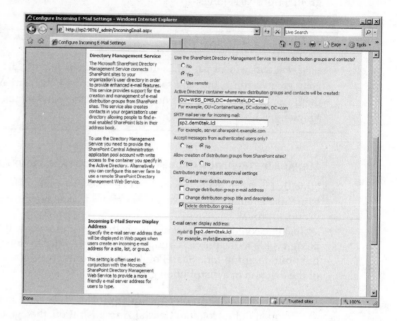

DISAPPROVING APPROVAL

Although the option is available, I have found the distribution group request approval feature to be a bit flaky. If you start seeing access denied status information on the settings page of the distribution lists after enabling request approval, disable the create new distribution group request approval setting and do an iisreset to see if that fixes the problem—before you start checking your permissions. Like a few other aspects of DMS, approval seems to be a work in progress.

Content approval in this context has three states: Pending, Rejected, and Approved. When a SharePoint is configured to create a distribution group, that request gets rerouted to the Distribution group list on the Central Administration site to await approval or rejection. The request starts in a pending state, and like a document in a draft state, the request simply stalls there, doing nothing until it is either approved or rejected by a Farm Administrator. Also, depending on what you configure, any change or deletion request also gets put in the Distribution group list pending approval or rejection. If a request is approved, then it gets processed and the change, deletion, or creation occurs. If a request is rejected, it is not removed from the list. It remains there, basically pending, until such time as it is approved.

The two requests that are the most extreme of the distribution group process are, of course, creation and deletion. As a matter of fact, I find the deletion request process to be the most interesting. Because of that I will cover both requests. I figure that if you can master those, the change requests will be old hat.

1. To see how approval works with distribution groups go back to the SharePoint site (my example is `http://sp2`).

2. Click People and Groups on the Quick Launch bar.

3. In the People and Groups page, choose a SharePoint group to assign a distribution group to. For my example, I am going to use the default Members group.

4. On the content page for the SharePoint group you've chosen, click the Settings button on the action bar, and select Group Settings.

5. On the Group Settings page, scroll to the E-mail Distribution List section and select Yes to create a distribution list for this SharePoint group. Also in this section, enter an alias for this group. I am going to use `members` for this example.

6. In the Archive email section, don't create an archive list at this time.

7. If your settings are complete, click OK. This will put you back on the content page for the SharePoint group. The new email alias will be displayed above the content area, but it won't work until the distribution group is approved.

So the request has been made to create a distribution group. To see what SharePoint does with it, go to the Central Administration site, log in. On the Operations page, click the Approve/reject distribution groups link, conveniently located just below the Incoming e-mail settings link.

NO CREATION BEFORE APPROVAL

You can prove that the distribution group has not been created before it is approved by going to Active Directory Users and Computers management console, and selecting the DMS OU. You will see that the distribution group will not be there yet.

This will take you to the Distribution Groups page (Figure 15.100).

FIGURE 15.100
Distribution Groups page

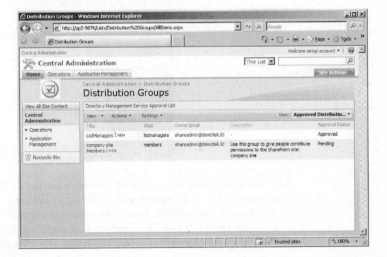

In the Distribution Group pages are all of the distribution groups that were made by SharePoint in AD. Right now my example displays the ListManagers group, which is approved because it was made before approval was required. The second group displayed is the one we just created. Its Approval status is Pending.

The Distribution Group page is a list like any other, and because of that the action bar has standard list buttons; New, Actions, Settings. This list was meant to display distribution groups so you can manage them. But you can create new distribution lists from here (maybe not the intended use for the list, but it can be done), organize the distribution groups by folder, and set an Alert or RSS feed on the list to keep informed as to changes might occur here.

The list also has several views. The default is called Approved Distribution Groups, but in fact is shows all distribution groups, with a column to indicate their approval status. There are several other views, all focused on the type of request the distribution group is waiting for; Create Requests, Delete Requests, and Modification Requests. These request-focused lists are important, because there is no field to add to the lists that indicate *why* the groups are in the list, or what will be done to it if it is approved.

To see what distribution groups are waiting to be created, click on the View menu and select Create Requests.

You will see our distribution group in the Create Requests view. This indicates what process will be done on this group when you approve it. Always make certain of what request view you are on when you approve something.

To see what you can do with a distribution group in this list setting, simply move your cursor over it, click on the selection box, and, on the dropdown menu, select Approve/reject, just as you would any list or library item (Figure 15.101). Of course, this list only has two things you can do with its items, View Item and Approve/reject (the default view allows you to either delete or view an item from the dropdown).

FIGURE 15.101
Create Request view with item selection menu

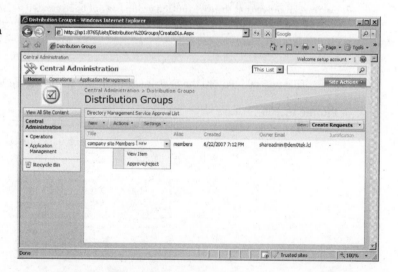

The View Item option let's you view the fields for the distribution group item. The interesting thing is there are two fields you can add data to; a justifications field, in case you want to add some sort of justification for the group to encourage approval, and a New Alias field. This field is a little unexpected and lets you change the distribution group's alias without having to go back into SharePoint, open the SharePoint group's settings, and change it there.

The Approve/reject option, the one we are going to use in this example, will open a page in which you can choose to approve or reject the request, with a comment field to explain your choice. To approve the group so it can be created in AD, on the dropdown menu, select Approve/reject. On the Manage Distribution Groups page, make certain that the Approve radio button is selected, and type a comment in the comment field (see Figure 15.102 for my example), and click OK.

FIGURE 15.102

Approve request in the Manage Distribution Groups

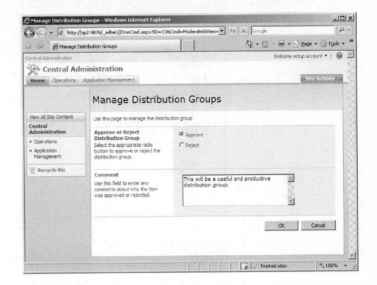

This will bring you back out to the Create Requests view of the Distribution Groups page. It should be empty because there are now no requests pending there.

Click on the View menu and select Approved Distribution Groups. This will open the default view for the list, and display the newly approved distribution group as Approved (Figure 15.103).

FIGURE 15.103

New distribution group is approved

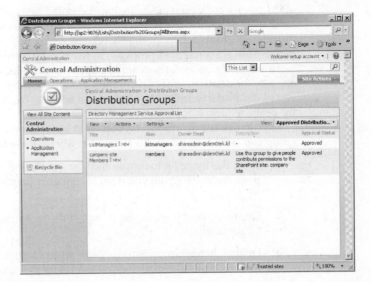

And, because the create request was approved, the new distribution group will now appear in the DMS OU in AD (Figure 15.104).

FIGURE 15.104
Newly created members distribution group in AD

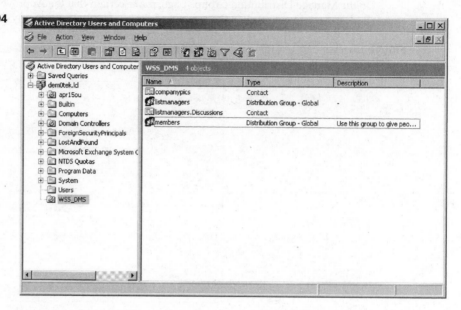

DELETE A DISTRIBUTION GROUP

Enabling DMS makes it possible to create distribution groups for each SharePoint group. If you decide to disable a SharePoint group's email capability, its corresponding distribution group object in AD must be deleted.

To delete a contact on incoming email enabled lists or libraries, you just disable incoming email for that list or library. To delete a distribution group, you simply disable the Create an e-mail distribution group option for the SharePoint group. Both will trigger SharePoint (if your permissions are configured properly) to remove the corresponding object in AD.

However, if you configured request approval on deleting distribution groups, then you have to approve the deletion before distribution groups are deleted. In the meantime, even if you think you've disabled a SharePoint group's email address, the distribution group will still be in AD until the delete request is approved.

First, to delete a distribution group (or at least start the request process), go to the SharePoint group you would like effect this change on. My example will be the Members group.

1. To do this by going to People and Groups on the SharePoint site. On the People and Groups page, select the group you want to configure (in my example, the Members group comes up by default).

2. On the content page of the group, click the Settings button on the Action bar, and select Group Settings.

3. On the Change Group Settings page, scroll down to the E-Mail Distribution List section, and for the Create an e-mail distribution list for this group? setting, select No.

STATUS REPORTS

In the E-Mail Distribution List section, there may be notice for the distribution group status. It displays the last status reported for the distribution group by SharePoint. Sometimes that report is obsolete.

4. Click OK to confirm this change.

If you don't have distribution group request approval set for deleting distribution groups in Central Administration, the distribution group would be deleted.

However, with that request approval set, you need to approve the deletion before it will actually occur.

1. To do that go to the Central Administration site, log in. Go to the Operations page and select Approve/reject distribution groups in the Topology and Services category.

On the Distribution Groups page, the distribution groups will be listed. The item you want to delete, which should now be Pending may still display as Approved. This is a quirk of content approval. Although changes to AD might be pending, only creating a new distribution group shows as pending.

However, this does not change the fact that the distribution group has still not been removed from AD.

A SECOND OPTION FOR ADDED SAFETY

If, for some reason, the distribution group that should be waiting to be approved for deletion does not show up in the Delete Requests view, you can still delete the distribution group.

You can delete a distribution group in two ways. One is to approve it on the Delete Requests page. The other is to simply move your cursor over it on the Distribution Groups page, click on its selection box, and then select, from the dropdown menu, Delete Item. That will take you to a Manage Distribution Groups page that will warn you that it will delete the item from the list and from AD. Click OK and the distribution group will be deleted.

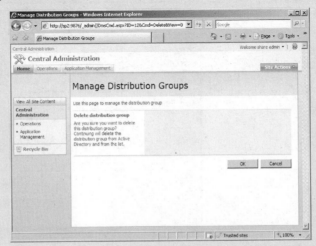

2. To approve the deletion request and delete the distribution group from AD, click on the View menu and select Delete Requests.

3. The distribution group you need to delete will be listed (Figure 15.105). Move your cursor over it, click in the selection box, and then select Approve/reject.

FIGURE 15.105

Distribution Group in Delete Requests View

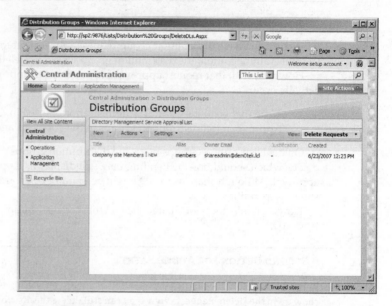

In the Manage Distribution Groups page (Figure 15.106), select Approve. You don't need to enter a comment because the item is going to be deleted. Then click OK to finish approving the delete request.

FIGURE 15.106

Approve the deletion of Distribution Group

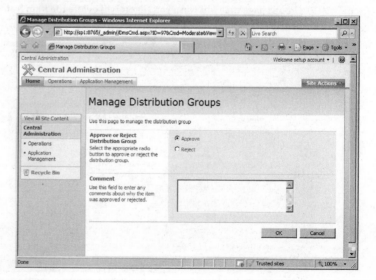

This will bring you back to the Delete Requests view of the Distribution Groups page. The distribution group you just approved will be gone.

If you check the Active Directory Users and Computers management console, the distribution group will be gone from there too (Figure 15.107).

FIGURE 15.107
Distribution group no longer in OU

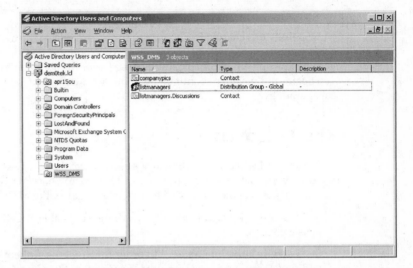

FIRST GENERATION GLITCHES

This is the first time that Directory Management Service has been released for SharePoint. And as is often the case with first releases, there are a few quirks to the way DMS works with content approval to keep in mind:

◆ Request Approval largely affects the way things function in AD. Often, when you remove the distribution group from the SharePoint group at the site, that change will appear to have worked there, despite there needing to be approved in Central Administration to remove the distribution group from AD.

◆ If a SharePoint Group's email alias is changed, it may show up in the Distribution group as a newly created distribution group, not as a modification request for an existing distribution group. If you approve the creation of the new email address based distribution group, be sure to delete the old one if you do not want it to be available.

◆ You can delete an approved distribution group from the Distribution Group page without changing it on the SharePoint site. And if you do, the SharePoint group on the site will not reflect this change.

◆ There is a glitch in the way that approval can be handled by SharePoint in which, after you approve a distribution group for creation, the SharePoint group's settings page still lists it as pending. This doesn't effect its function unless you try to change the email alias. This is not as bad as it sounds, because if you change a distribution group's alias it doesn't automatically delete the old one, so it's best to set the Create Distribution Group setting to No, delete the old Distribution group, then create a new one anyway.

◆ You can delete a distribution group object from the DMS OU in Active Directory. However, neither the Distribution Groups page nor the SharePoint Group settings on the SharePoint site will be aware that change occurred. The integration between SharePoint and Active Directory is pretty rudimentary at this point. Be prepared.

Hopefully this chapter has given you some insight into the more advanced installations and configurations of SharePoint. Always test your configurations in a lab before applying them to your production environment, always prepare for the shortcomings, tricks, and gotchas before you begin, and never be so intimidated you avoid trying it. Good luck with SharePoint and happy collaborating.

The Bottom Line

Understand what Active Directory Account Creation mode is   Active Directory Account Creation mode allows administrators to add users to SharePoint that are not in Active Directory. Those users will then be added to a specific Organizational Unit in Active Directory.

    Master It   What functionality is no longer available in Central Administration when ADAC is enabled?

Set a service principle name   In order for Kerberos authentication to work with SharePoint, additional configuration is required. The Content Database Access account for the web application using Kerberos must be registered as a service principal name for the SharePoint server (or servers).

    Master It   What program is used to register service principal names? How do you access it?

Configure Network Load Balancing   Network Load Balancing is a network connection feature, built into Windows Server 2003 (although there are other hardware and software solutions). It balances client requests and activity between servers in a cluster, effectively making them appear to be one computer from the client's perspective.

    Master It   What is a drainstop and what is it for?

Configure Directory Management Service and understand its requirements   Directory Management Service requires considerable planning and implementation in order to give users easy access to entries in an Exchange 2003 GAL for lists, libraries, and SharePoint groups.

    Master It   Are there any special security considerations if DMS is enabled?

Appendix

The Bottom Line

Each of The Bottom Line sections in the chapters challenge your understanding of the chapters' concepts and improve your skills. Generally there is only one possible Master It Solution, but you are encouraged to explore additional solutions and scenarios to improve your mastery of Windows SharePoint Services 3.0.

Chapter 1: Windows SharePoint Services 3.0 Under the Hood

Determine the software and hardware requirements you need for installing SharePoint Services 3.0   SharePoint has some stringent software and hardware requirements. Be sure you know what you need before you become the proud owner of your own SharePoint server or servers.

> **Master It**   What software must be on the server before you install SharePoint?

> **Master It Solution**   IIS 6.0 with ASP .NET 2.0 enabled, .NET Framework 3.0, and if incoming email will be enabled, SMTP service for IIS.

Choose the best of the three ways of installing SharePoint Services 3.0 for you   With SharePoint, how you choose to install it defines how it works. Making the wrong choice can come back to haunt you. Know what you're in for and choose the correct installation type for your business.

> **Master It**   If you were going to install SharePoint on one server (no existing SQL) for a small business of about 50 people, what installation type would you choose?

> **Master It Solution**   Basic or Advanced, Stand-alone because there will be only one server and so few users, and it will use SSEE to manage the databases.

Set up the necessary accounts that SharePoint needs to run   When SharePoint is installed on a domain, it needs user accounts to assign to its services. Knowing what permissions and roles those accounts require will help you avoid problems when installing and running SharePoint.

> **Master It**   What is a Database Access Account? Is it known by any other names?

> **Master It Solution**   It is the most powerful account in SharePoint. It is the application pool account for Central Administration and is used to access the configuration database for SharePoint (from a single server or an entire farm), and it is the account used by the SharePoint Timer Service to do tasks like backup/restore, Alerts, Incoming Email, and more. It is also known as the Server Farm Account (or Farm Account), and the Configuration Account.

Recognize the new features and requirements of SharePoint SharePoint has features that require additional planning and setup to function properly. Make sure you know what they are and what they require.

Master It What new feature of WSS 3.0 requires SMTP to be running locally on the Share-Point server?

Master It Solution Incoming Email. This feature allows lists and libraries that are incoming email enabled to have an email alias and accept item entries via email.

Plan for hardware requirements Don't let SharePoint outgrow its hardware before it really gets started. Prepare for growth. Establish your sharepoint server's baseline operations per second and storage needs before installing SharePoint.

Master It What is the formula to calculate the operations per second that a SharePoint server would be doing in a given environment?

Master It Solution User × Usage × Operations × Peak factor / 360,000 × Work hours. If, in a business, there were 200 employees, but only 60 percent would really use SharePoint, with about 50 operations a day, during a work day of 8 hours, and a peak factor of 4, the total operations per second would be 1 (or more precisely .972).

Chapter 2: Installation

Prepare for the installation of SharePoint SharePoint does have certain software and hardware requirements before it can be installed. In addition, some of those requirements vary depending on the type of installation you choose. It is good to know what to install, how to install them, and in what order to be prepared for installing SharePoint.

Master It Does SharePoint require SMTP?

Master It Solution No. If you do not want to enable incoming email, then you do not need SMTP. However, if you want the option to do incoming email, SMTP service must be available on the SharePoint server. There only needs to be one incoming email server per server farm.

Install SharePoint using the Basic and Advanced, Stand-Alone, and Advanced Server Farm Installation options There are several types of SharePoint installations available; Basic, which is a single server installation in which installs without intervention with all default settings and uses a Windows Internal Database; Advanced, Stand-alone, which is essentially the Basic Installation but you have a few basic configuration options before configuration begins; and Advanced, Web Front End (Server Farm) installation, which allows you to manage all configuration options and specify the SQL server that will manage the databases. Each installation type has its strengths and weaknesses, and it's good to know about them before you begin.

Master It Can you install and use SharePoint if you don't have SQL installed on your network?

Master It Solution Yes. You can use the Basic or Stand-alone installation types. They will install a scaled-down version of SQL 2005 locally, called the Windows Internal Database or SQL Server 2005 Embedded Edition (SSEE).

Determine what gets created when SharePoint installs   From Basic to Server Farm, it is good to know every step of the way, the repercussions of each installation, configuration, and service that SharePoint adds and/or enables.

> **Master It**   What is one way to confirm that the SharePoint services are running properly on the server?

> **Master It Solution**   Go to the Services console (Start ➤ Administrative Tools ➤ Services) and check for the SharePoint services; Administration, Timer, Search, Tracing, and VSS Writer.

Perform the initial configuration tasks after a SharePoint install (and understand why you perform them)   After installation, SharePoint can require additional configuration before you can call it your own. It is good to know what the necessary settings are to quickly get SharePoint up and running to the point where an administrator can start working on it.

> **Master It**   Does incoming email require Directory Management Service to function?

> **Master It Solution**   No. Incoming email can be configured, and works smoothly, without Directory Management Service.

Chapter 3: Introduction to the SharePoint Interface

Identify the SharePoint navigation tools and figure out how to use them   SharePoint makes a point of ensuring that a user always has a way to get where they need to go without using the Back button in the browser. Recognizing these features makes navigation easier and increases productivity.

> **Master It**   List three different ways to get back to the Home page should you be in a list or library on the top-level site.

> **Master It Solution**   Use the Home tab in the Top Link Bar. Use the breadcrumb above the page title. Use the global breadcrumb to get back to the home page of the top-level site.

Find a list or library   SharePoint uses the Quick Launch bar as a quick, convenient, and consistent way for users to find the SharePoint lists and libraries they need to access.

> **Master It**   How do you find a list or library if it is not on the Quick Launch bar?

> **Master It Solution**   Use the View All Contents link in the Quick Launch bar to open a page containing all the contents of the site.

Use the Quick Launch bar   The Quick Launch bar is more than a list of lists. It also contains an easy way to navigate through all contents of a site, access people and groups, check the Recycle Bin, and create new site contents.

> **Master It**   By default, when SharePoint is initially installed, the Quick Launch bar does not have Surveys as a heading. Why?

> **Master It Solution**   On install, SharePoint does not have a default Survey available. If a type of SharePoint content does not exist on a SharePoint site, the heading for that content will not be created in the Quick Launch bar.

Use a breadcrumb   Windows SharePoint Services 3.0 has instituted a navigation device that keeps track of where a user has been. This dynamic horizontal list lets a user jump back to where they started very conveniently without using the web browser's Back button.

Master It   Is there such a thing as a global breadcrumb? What is it?

Master It Solution   Yes, there is. A global breadcrumb resides at the very top left of every page in a SharePoint site. This unassuming list tracks what sites and subsites you have navigated to from the top-level site. It gives you a means to go back to a previous level site without have to click the Back button in the browser.

Understand a content page   Every list and library has a content page. This kind of page has a consistent layout to make working with it easy for users.

Master It   What is an Action bar? What's on it, and why would it be different in a library than it would be in a list?

Master It Solution   An Action bar is the bar of activities a user can engage in while in the content page of a list or library. This bar will contain different buttons and menu options depending on the intent and use of the list itself. A library will also have an Upload button (in addition to the standard New, Actions, and Settings buttons). Also, the New and Actions buttons will have different options beneath them for a library, because different activities are done there than are done in a list.

Chapter 4: Introduction to Web Parts

Identify Web Parts   Web parts are small, independent applications intended to quickly and conveniently display the contents of lists, libraries, folders, or pages.

Master It   What are List View web parts?

Master It Solution   List View web parts are web parts that get generated by default whenever a list or library is created in SharePoint. This sort of web part is intended to display a summary view of the contents of a list or library for convenient viewing on the home page or other web part page.

Use Edit Mode   In order to work on web parts in SharePoint, the page containing the web parts should be in Edit mode. Edit mode is a page state in which web parts can be moved, removed, added, imported, and edited. No data entry occurs in Edit mode.

Master It   How do you enter Edit mode to edit a Shared version of a page? How do you know for certain that you are editing the Shared version?

Master It Solution   To enter Edit mode for a shared version of a page, click Site Actions and then Edit Page. The information bar will tell you whether or not you are editing the Shared or Personal version of a page.

Distinguish Between Personal and Shared Versions   SharePoint offers the luxury of allowing users to have their own Personal version of any web part page; in which they can rearrange, remove, or add web parts to their version of the pages for their convenience.

Master It   How can a user tell if they are viewing the Personal or Shared version of a page?

Master It Solution   A user must personalize the page to have a Personal version of it. If they have, they can tell what version they are in by going to the Welcome menu. If there is an option for Show Personal View, then they are viewing the Shared version. If there isn't, they aren't.

Work with Web Parts   Adding, moving, removing, and customizing web parts while in the browser are all possible with SharePoint. There are built-in List View web parts to quickly populate the home page with web parts relevant to users. There are also built-in web part templates to easily customize web parts right in the browser, with nocoding necessary.

Master It   How do you change the title of a web part?

Master It Solution   Go into Edit mode on the page, and click Edit in the web part's title bar. Open the Appearance section of the tool pane, and change the Title. Click OK or Apply, and then exit Edit mode.

Export and Import Web Parts   Web parts aren't just static little applications. You can customize them, export them to a web part definition file, and import them to a different page or site collection.

Master It   How do you export a web part?

Master It Solution   Click the down arrow in the title bar of a web part, or Edit (in Edit mode), and select Export. Name the file, choose a location, and save it.

Chapter 5: Introduction to Lists

Use and modify a list   Lists are the collaboration core of SharePoint. With the content stored in a database, lists can be used to track data, hold discussions, manage issues, and more.

Master It   How do you get to a list if it isn't displayed on the home page? And, once you find it, how do you get to the list's settings to modify it?

Master It Solution   To access a list that is on neither the Quick Launch bar or displayed as a List View web part, go to All Site Content at the top of the Quick Launch bar and then select it on the All Site Content page. Once you are in the list, to change its settings, click the Settings button on the action bar, and select List Settings from the dropdown menu.

Modify a view and create a view   SharePoint uses views to display the content of lists. Much like reports, views can be modified to display any field in a list, in any order. Custom views can be created, with four different View formats to choose from.

Master It   What are the View formats, and which would you choose to display data grouped by a particular field?

Master It Solution   The View formats are Standard, Datasheet, Gantt, and Calendar. The type of view that most lends itself to displaying data grouped by a particular field is the Standard view.

Create a list from a template   SharePoint, in addition to a few convenient, pre-built lists, has ready to go templates of common lists. This makes it very easy to simply create a new list based on an existing template, then customize it; rather than having to create one like it from scratch.

Master It What list template creates a list that is meant to work with the Three-State Work-flow? How would you go about creating that list?

Master It Solution The list is Issue Tracking, and to create an Issue Tracking list from a template, go to the Create page by clicking Site Actions and selecting Create. On the Create page, click on the link for Issue Tracking. This will give you the opportunity to configure and create a new Issue Tracking list.

Create a custom list In addition to the pre-built lists and the templates, SharePoint has the option to create custom lists from scratch. Lists can be custom made in two ways: by importing from an Excel Spreadsheet, or by manually building one. All lists require at least one field (by default the *Title* field) and include system generated columns for *ID*, *Created By* and *Modified By*.

Master It You're creating a custom list for the Human Resources department to help manage employees. You've created the list, added a field for them to lookup employees from Active Directory, and another field for their department. As part of the process, you've decided to photograph all employees. These pictures are stored in a Picture Library and can be viewed by HR personnel. You'd like to provide HR a way to display these pictures on the list. You also want to indicate if the employee is full time or part time. How would you go about adding this information to the list?

Master It Solution You need to create two new columns for the list. Go to the List Settings for this list and click Create Column to add the two new columns (or you can just click Settings, Create Column on the list itself).

The first column needs to be a picture column for the employee photographs. Set the list column type as Hyperlink or Picture. Set it to format the URL as a Picture. Save the column.

The second column needs to be a Choice column for the employee status. Create this column as a Choice type and enter the two choices: Full Time and Part Time. Set the field to Radio Buttons or Drop-Down Menu so only one can be chosen. Save the column.

Now when HR adds someone to the list, they can choose the person from People and Groups using a people picker, add their department, type in the URL to their picture stored in the Library, and chose their status.

Chapter 6: Introduction to Libraries

Create a library A library is a kind of list that focuses primarily on the files that are attached to the list items. There are several different types of libraries, depending on the type of file they are intended to store. Creating a library is as easy as opening the Create page, selecting the type of library, and configuring it. There are several different types of libraries.

Master It If you do not have any Microsoft Office 2003 or 2007 products installed on your machine, what two main features of document libraries are not available?

Master It Solution Without Office installed, you cannot create a new document by using the New button and you have to upload/download documents to edit them. Also, without at least one Office product installed, you cannot upload multiple files to the library.

Use the different kinds of libraries Document libraries can contain any type of file, but Share-Point has four main kinds of libraries with different features and views. These four libraries are: Document library, Form library, Wiki Page library, and Picture library.

Master It   You're restructuring the content of some of your libraries, and are planning on moving content from one library to another. What key facts do you need to keep in mind regarding Wiki libraries when it comes to moving or uploading files?

Master It Solution   Wiki libraries do not support any form of uploading, so there is no way to place existing wiki pages into a library. If you need to move the content of a wiki library to a different site, consider moving the entire library as a whole.

Set check out, content approval and versioning   Require Check Out forces users of a document library to check out a document if they intend to edit it. This helps enforce version management by allowing only one person to edit a document at a time. When a document is checked out, it can only be be read by other users, but they cannot edit the document until the person with it checked out, checks it back in.

Content approval can allow items to remain invisible to most list or library viewers until someone with approval rights approves the item. In a library with content approval and major and minor versions enabled, only major versions of a document can be approved.

Versioning means that whenever a list or library item (or its attached file) is changed, that change is saved as a different version. That means that if an edit was a mistake, you can restore a previous version.

Master It   Brian has left the company, but some of the documents in your Shared Documents library are still checked out by him. Several of the documents have multiple versions stored, but one was a brand new document that Brian uploaded to the server recently. What three methods are available to check these documents back in?

Master It Solution   It is possible to check in all the documents by simply logging into the SharePoint server using Brian's account. Once logged in as Brian, you can check in all of them.

Without using his account, a site administrator can revert most of the documents to a previous (pre-check out) version, making this available to other users. Anything Brian has done to the document since the check-out would be lost.

For the new document which has no previous versions, the site administrator must first *take ownership* of the file, and then they can fill in the required fields and check it in.

Manage content types   By default each library (or most lists for that matter) has one content type. That content type of a library item is one that can have a template associated with it—such as Word documents, PowerPoint presentations, or Excel spreadsheets. However, it is possible to have a document library (or any list or library for that matter) with multiple content types, allowing the library to create a mix of documents from multiple templates.

Master It   You have a general document library for the Public relations department. They wish to use the library to manage a large number of different document types—from Word to pictures to movie clips to more obscure things. More importantly, the type of files they're going to use is likely to change over time. How should you configure the content types for this library?

Master It Solution   In this case, creating a content type for each kind of file the library will contain is not the necessary. Any library can have any file type uploaded to it (that has not been blocked), it does not depend on the content type. You can still set a default content type, or add some new content types to the library if you wish, but the majority of their unique files will need to be uploaded rather than created using a template.

Chapter 7: Sites, Subsites, and Workspaces

Create and customize a new site   Using the New SharePoint Site page, you can create a new subsite from one of several templates or site definitions (in the case of Meeting Workspaces), or you can create a new Workspace from an existing document or calendar event. The site can be customized using themes, custom logos, lists and libraries.

Master It   Create a new blogging site, give it a unique logo and theme, and add a discussion list for users to have their own discussions beyond the comments.

Master It Solution   Select Site Actions ➤ Create ➤ Sites and Workspaces, and create a new blog site. Edit the theme and logo under Site Settings ➤ Look & Feel. Add a new discussion list by clicking the Discussions heading in the Quick Launch bar and then clicking to Create and selecting the link to create it from there.

Adjust Site Settings for administrative purposes   You can configure sites to inherit or set unique permissions on a site. You can also configure subsites to add a storage quota, enable alerts, place the site on the Top Link bar, adjust regional settings, and enable features such as RSS and usage reports.

Master It   Enable RSS feeds for the new blog, confirm search visibility, and check Usage reports.

Master It Solution   Enable RSS under Site Settings ➤ RSS. Confirm search visibility and Check the usage reports under Site Settings ➤ Search visibility, and Site Settings ➤ Site Usage Reports.

Understand the different types of SharePoint sites available by default   By default, SharePoint can create Team sites, document workspaces, blogs, wikis, and meeting workspaces (Basic, Decision, Social, and MultiPage). These can all be created as subsites or new top-level sites in their own site collection.

Master It   Explain the core differences between a Team site and a document workspace, and the difference between a Basic meeting workspace and a Decision meeting workspace.

Master It Solution   A Team site is a generic all-purpose site, and useful as a top-level site. Document workspaces are geared around one document (copied to its Library), do not inherit site permissions, and include a Tasks list. They tend to be considered temporary, and are usually removed once the document is complete and published back to the main site.

A Decision meeting workspace is identical to a Basic meeting workspace except it includes a Tasks list and a Decisions list.

Add additional site templates and definitions   In addition to the default sites included with SharePoint, you can download and install many other site templates and definitions. Microsoft has a pack of 40 available, and many third-party companies and helpful coders have provided even more. Templates are added to the Site Template Gallery for the site collection. Site definitions are usually added as solutions using the command-line tool and then deployed via Central Administration. They can be deployed to individual site collections (if possible) or globally to the entire web application.

Master It   Download and install a new site definition. Test it by creating a new site using the definition.

Master It Solution   Extract the downloaded package and install it into the server using STSADM. Deploy the new solution to the site collection (or globally if required) either using STSADM or under Central Administration ➢ Operations ➢ Solution Management.

Test by creating a new site based on the definition, using the Create page ➢ Sites and Workspaces, and select the site template from the Select a template list.

Chapter 8: Site Collections and Web Applications

Create and customize a new site collection   A new site collection has separate permissions, its own Recycle Bin, its own storage quota, and its own site collection galleries. You can change the regional settings and grant someone site administrator rights on a new site collection without compromising your existing sites.

Master It   Create a new site collection, apply a Site Quota template, and restrict the new site collection to 1GB.

Master It Solution   Under Central Administration's Application Management page:

1. Go to Quota Templates, and create the new template with the 1GB restriction.
2. Click Create Site Collection, choose a web application, and enter the appropriate settings, making sure you apply the new Quota template.

Use managed paths   SharePoint uses managed paths to tell IIS which paths in a URL are handled by SharePoint and are, therefore, *managed*. All other paths are considered *excluded*, and IIS is free to use them with traditional websites. You can add your own managed paths, adjusting the URL of site collections.

By default, SharePoint site collections have two managed paths: the path (root), which is explicit, and the path /sites/, which is a wildcard path.

Master It   Define the difference between an *explicit* managed path and a *wildcard* managed path.

Master It Solution   *Explicit* managed paths are for a single site collection, and navigating to that path accesses the site collection. For example, if http://sp2/paris is an explicit path, entering this URL in a web browser will take you to the paris site collection.

Wildcard managed paths are for multiple site collections, and navigating to that path will not display a site collection. Instead, multiple URLs can start with that path.

For example, if http://sp2/paris is a wildcard path, then http://sp2/paris/tech and http://sp2/paris/sales will both take you to a site collection (two different collections actually). However, http://sp2/paris will fail to load anything.

Create a new web application   A new web application is fundamentally a new IIS Web Site with a database for content on the back end. Using a new IIS Web Site allows you to change the port for accessing the web application, use a host header, and adjust the IIS-level authentication such as Anonymous Access. Web applications are also a boundary for settings such as RSS, sending alerts, upload size limits, and blocked file types that effect all contained site collections. All SharePoint site collections must reside in a web application. At this level, serious changes can effect the way the site collections are accessed and controlled.

Master It   Create a new web application using a host header, and set up two content databases, both limited to 10,000 sites.

Master It Solution Create the new web application in Central Administration on the Application Management page. When creating the web application, change the suggested port back to 80 and enter a working host header (make sure it resolves in DNS). Once the web application is created, immediately create the first site collection and top-level site for the web application. Remember to reset IIS with the command:

```
iisreset /noforce
```

When the site is up and running, go back to Central Administration's Application Management page and click Manage Content Databases. Edit the existing database for that web application to set the capacity limit to 10,000 sites. Then add a new content database with the same limit, on to the existing SQL server (or local instance of SQL SSEE).

Configure Anonymous Access One of the features of web applications is the ability to allow Anonymous Access to the site collections they contain. Anonymous Access can allow the site to be viewed without requiring a login while retaining all the needed permissions for authenticated users to add, edit, modify, or delete site content. Anonymous Access is enabled in two core steps: first by permitting anonymous access at the web-application level, and then by enabling anonymous access at the site-collection level.

Master It Someone else has allowed Anonymous Access on a web application, and you're configuring your site collection. You want anonymous users to view only the Status list and nothing else. How do you configure the site?

Master It Solution In Site Settings for the top-level site, click Advanced Permissions. Then click the Settings button on the Action bar and choose Anonymous Access. Grant access to Lists and Libraries, and click OK.

Go to the Status list, click the Settings button on the Action bar, and choose List Settings. On the Customize Status page, click Permissions for this list. Break the inheritance by choosing Edit Permissions under the Actions menu.

Go to the Settings button on the Action bar, and choose Anonymous Access. Check the box to Grant View Items Permission and click OK.

Now anonymous users can go directly to the Status list, but they cannot browse anything else, including the root site of the collection.

Set different Zones for different access Each web application can support up to five public URLs that it displays in the Address bar and on the page in links and paths. Four of the public URLs can be used for manually entered alternate web addresses or created by extending the web application to a new IIS Web Site, providing a new URL (including a new port if desired), and applying different authentication policies to the same site. For example, one site collection accessed from within the local network can permit Anonymous Access, but authentication can be required for anyone accessing the site through the Internet public URL. The five public URLs are identified by their *zone*, and additional internal URLs can be mapped to each zone.

Master It Extend a web application to a new IIS website with a port of 18080, and set it to the Extranet zone.

Master It Solution On the Application Management page in Central Administration, click Create or Extend Web Application. Choose to extend an existing web application. Select a web application. Create a new IIS Web Site with a description and set it to the port 18080. Change the zone to Extranet, and click OK.

Chapter 9: Central Administrations: Operations

Understand Central Administration's Organization   SharePoint's Central Administration is organized in two pages, Operations and Application Management, with a home page that has several useful web parts.

Master It   Is it a good idea to use Central Administration to hold shared library content, lists, and calendars? Why?

Master It Solution   Although Central Administration has the capability to have these items available for the administrators who visit the site, it is strongly discouraged because this site cannot be restored by conventional means within SharePoint. If you must add content, consider creating a subsite off of Central Administration's top-level site, and back *it* up regularly. Then, if SharePoint has to be reinstalled, the subsite can be restored without data loss.

Use the Settings on the Operations Page   The Operations page is intended to contain settings specific to the administration of SharePoint as whole. It contains settings pertaining to defaults that govern all servers, web applications, etc., for the entire server farm (or server). The use and application of those settings vary, but the interface used to access them is much more consistent that it was with the previous version.

Master It   Can you configure blocked file types at a global level or only at the web application level?

Master It Solution   Blocked file types can only be configured at the web application level. In the previous version of SharePoint there was a text file of blocked file types that was applied at the global level, in addition to the ones used by the web applications. This is no longer the case.

Manage Solutions and Features   The settings for managing solutions and features are available on the Operations page under Global Configuration. The Managing Farm Features page allows you to see what Features are active (or inactive but available) at the Farm level. Solutions Management allows you to see what solutions have been added to SharePoint, as well as deploy or retract them.

Master It   Can you install a feature or add a solution to SharePoint from the Manage Features or Solution Management pages?

Master It Solution   No. Features and Solutions must still be added at the command line using STSADM.

How to Set the Server Farm's Default Database Server   In SharePoint an administrator is often going to be doing work that involves databases. For this reason, having a default database server specified for the server farm is a great convenience.

Master It   If you are creating a new web application, can you specify a different database server other than the default set for the server farm?

Master It Solution   Yes. The global setting for the server farm's default database is just a convenience.

Determine Where to Stop and Start Farm Services   The Server Farm Services are not ones that can be managed from the operating system's Services management console. The Server Farm Services can be started and stopped from the Services on Server Settings page under Topology and Services on the Operations page.

Master It Name a server farm service that can be stopped or started from the Services on Server Settings page.

Master It Solution

Central Administration

Windows SharePoint Services Incoming e-mail

Windows SharePoint Services Search

Windows SharePoint Services Web Application

How to Change a Web Application Service Account It can be useful to know how to manage web application service accounts. If a web application's service account's password has been changed or you need to change the account altogether, go to the Service Accounts Settings page, select the web application that requires the change, and make the account updates there.

Master It What is a good indication that the service account password has changed on a web application's application pool?

Master It Solution The web application will no longer be able to access its database.

Chapter 10: Central Administration: Application Management

Navigate Application Management The Application Management page in Central Administration is divided into five categories, and each category has several links focused on Web Applications, their site collections, and additional customization tools.

Master It You want to ensure members of the Active Directory security group "Corporate Auditors" have full read access to every site collection in a Web Application, but cannot make any changes to anything within the site collections, regardless of what the site administrators do. Which setting would you use to do that, and how would it be done?

Master It Solution Use Policy for Web Applications.

1. Go to the Policy for Web Application page and click Add Users.
2. Select the desired Web Application and (All Zones).
3. Click Next.
4. Add the *domain*\Corporate Auditors domain group and check both Full Read and Deny Write under Permissions.
5. Click Finish.

Alternately, you can create a new Permission Policy Level using the pre-existing Auditor site collection permissions (pre-made combination of permissions necessary for auditing), then apply it when adding the user. To do that:

1. In the Policy for Web Application page, select Manage Permission Policy Levels on the left side of the page.

2. Click Add Permission Policy Level.
3. In the Add Permission Policy Level page, enter a name and description for the Level, then select **Auditor** in the Site Collection Permissions section. Select a permission, such as Deny Overwrite Check Out (there has to be one selected, even if it is irrelevant, to save), click Save.
4. When you add the user, apply the Auditor permission level instead of Deny Write, Full Read.

Manage site collections   The SharePoint Site Management category is focused on site collections. Here you can add, delete, and customize site collections. Site collections can have their administrators changed, storage quotas assigned (either from a template or directly) and can be locked. You can enable site usage notifications and automated deletion there as well.

Master It   Two popular configuration options are Site Quotas and Site Use Confirmation. One of these options can apply different settings for individual site collections while the other is set at the web application level and applies the same settings to all enclosed site collections. Which is which?

Master It Solution   Site Quotas are set on individual site collections and limit the size of the collection in megabytes. Site Use Confirmation, like Automated Deletion, applies to every site collection in the web application and generates requests for confirmation of usage to site collection owners.

Configure Person Name Smart Tags and Presence Settings   Person Name Smart Tags require Outlook be installed and configured for the SharePoint users. It creates a drop-down menu on every username in the SharePoint site collections allowing direct emailing and other communication options.

Online Presence requires Messenger be installed, running, and configured for the SharePoint users. It creates a small icon beside every username in the SharePoint site collections, showing the user's current online presence. This can be Online (green), Busy (red), Away (light orange), or Offline (grey). When the icon is half-colored and half-white, the user is also Idle.

Master It   You have Person Name Smart Tags and Presence Settings enabled on a web application. You've confirmed that all the users have Outlook and Windows Messenger installed and configured. Users can successfully see Online Presence icons for each other, and can use the Smart Tag drop-down menu. However, one user, Jasper, cannot see any Online Presence icons but can still use the Smart Tag drop-down menu. What might be wrong on Jasper's machine?

Master It Solution   Jasper may simply not have Windows Messenger running. If Messenger is turned off, none of the Online Presence icons will be visible. If Messenger is running, check to make sure Jasper hasn't inadvertently deleted his contacts list. Smart Tags are based on Outlook and will continue to function regardless of Windows Messenger's status.

Manage web application content databases   Each web application can have one or more content database. These databases can have a capacity limit that restricts how many site collections can be stored in the database.

Master It   You have received a warning that your web application's database is reaching its maximum size limit. What can you do to ensure that the database does not become locked and the web application using it can continue to function?

Master It Solution   To ensure that the web application continues to function normally, including being able to add more site collections, add another content database to the web application.

Change a web application's authentication method   Web Applications can have one of three authentication types: Windows, Forms, or Web single sign on. The most common is Windows. When using this authentication type, SharePoint sends authentication requests to whatever authentication provider Windows designates (commonly Active Directory). These requests can be sent using one of three authentication methods—NTLM, Kerberos, or Basic. This is configured in Authentication Providers.

Master It   You have a web application configured to use the Windows authentication type and the Kerberos authentication method. You are planning on providing access to the web application for some remote users and you want to use NTLM as the authentication method for these remote users while keeping Kerberos for your local users. How do you configure SharePoint to allow for both methods?

Master It Solution   You need to extend the web application into a new IIS Web Site, creating a second zone intended for remote users. You can then go to the Authentication Providers page, choose this web application and change the authentication method to NTLM for the new zone without changing the authentication method for the default zone. Have the remote users use the second zone's web address to access the web application's data.

Chapter 11: Users and Permissions

Define users and groups in SharePoint   SharePoint users are individuals with user accounts that can be authenticated by SharePoint server. Users can be stored in one or more groups. SharePoint understands two types of groups: SharePoint groups and Domain groups.

Master It   Differentiate between the SharePoint group and the Domain group. Determine the preferred location for users.

Master It Solution   A SharePoint group is a one created inside SharePoint for organizing security principals (such as Windows users and domain security groups). A Domain security group is controlled by the authentication provider, such as Active Directory, and can be added to a SharePoint group to allow domain authenticated users to access SharePoint resources.

Users should be added to Active Directory Security Groups, and the Security Groups are added to SharePoint Groups. Permission levels would then be assigned to the SharePoint Groups.

Add users and groups in SharePoint   New SharePoint groups can be created to organize user access to websites. User accounts and domain groups from Active Directory can be added to the SharePoint server directly or by being placed into a SharePoint group.

Master It   If you add a domain group to a SharePoint group, and then later delete that SharePoint group, how do you apply a new permission level to the domain group directly?

Master It Solution   When a SharePoint group is deleted, or a member is removed from the group, the member does not get removed from the site completely. Users can still be found under All People, while domain groups can be found on the All Groups page (reached by clicking the More. . . link under the Groups category of the Quick Launch Bar).

However, to apply a permission level to the domain group you need to go through the New User Action menu option again, and essentially re-add the group to SharePoint.

Define permissions and permission levels in SharePoint   Authorization in SharePoint is handled by 33 distinct permissions. These permissions provide user access to lists, sites, and personal settings. They also determine if the user's access is restricted to simply reading or browsing, can allow editing of objects, or even permit creation of new objects.

Permission levels are simply groups of permissions. A permission level can contain any or all of the 33 permissions, depending on prerequisite permissions. The permission level is then applied to SharePoint groups to provide authorization to members of that group. They can also be applied directly to users and security groups.

Master It   Describe what the Manage Permission permission does and what dependant permissions it requires. What permission level contains manage permissions by default?

Master It Solution   Manage Permissions allows you to create and change permission levels on the website and assign permissions to users and groups. This permission enables user to control others' permissions. The required permissions are View Items, Open Items, View Versions, Browse Directories, View Pages, Enumerate Permissions, Browse User Information, and Open. By default it is enabled in the Full Control Permission Level.

Set Permissions on a Site/List/List item for a user or a group   Permission Levels are assigned to SharePoint groups, domain groups, or individual users starting at the Top-level site of the site collection. By default, these users and groups (along with their assigned permission levels) propagate throughout the site collection using permission inheritance. You can go to any object (subsite, list, library, or item) in the site collection and break inheritance, adding or removing users and groups to the object manually, and then give them different permission levels.

Master It   If you break inheritance on a subsite of the main Company Site and start using custom permissions for that subsite, do the lists on the subsite retain their original permission settings from Company Site, or do they also gain the custom permissions set on the subsite?

Master It Solution   The lists on the subsite gain the custom permissions set for the subsite. Because the lists are contained within the subsite, they are lower down the hierarchy and are impacted by any changes made at a higher level.

Plan user access in SharePoint   Planning user access for SharePoint should be done from the top down. Start with the web application and move down the hierarchy, changing the user access settings, authorized users and groups, or permission levels only where needed. Before placing a new site collection into an existing web application, confirm the new site collection requires the same security settings as the existing site collections in that web application. Before adding a new site to a site collection, determine if the inherited groups, users, and permission levels are desired, or if creating a new site collection would be more appropriate. Try to balance the ease of administration that inheritance provides with the granular control of custom permissions.

Master It   Which is the better option?

1. Permitting anonymous access at the Web Application level, and then enabling anonymous access to a select few site collections within the web application.
2. Denying anonymous access at the Web Application level, and then enabling anonymous access to a select few site collections within the web application.

Master It Solution   Option 1 is the only valid Solution. In order for **any** site collection in a web application to enable anonymous users, anonymous access must be permitted on the web application. Option 2 is simply not possible. You cannot enable anonymous access on a site collection that resides in a web application that does not permit anonymous access. You will need to either reconfigure the web application or move the site collection to a different web application.

Chapter 12: Maintenance and Monitoring

Monitor server performance   You can use the Performance Monitor's System Monitor to view real-time server performance or create a counter log to measure performance over time. You can create custom alerts that read the logs and warn you if something passes a counter limit.

Master It   You have an existing server which has been tasked as your new SharePoint server. The installation is done, and it's about to go live. Because it's an existing server, you're worried the addition of SharePoint will require more RAM then the server has installed. Build a performance alert that will register an event in the Application Event log if the available RAM ever gets below 50MB.

Master It Solution   First launch Performance Monitor (`perfmon`). Right-click on Alerts and click New Alert Settings.

Create an alert called "low memory" and add a counter.

Select the *memory* performance object and the *Available Mbytes* counter. Add this counter to the alert.

Set the alert value to **Under** the limit **50 MB.**

Double check the Run As field to make sure the user is a user with local admin permissions.

Under the Action tab, check the Log an event in the Application event log checkbox.

Under the Schedule tab, set the alert to start immediately, and to stop manually.

Use SharePoint Backup and Restore   SharePoint has its own backup and restore features—both in the GUI and using the STSADM command. These tools allow you to backup individual site collections, web applications, or even the whole server farm. The GUI has some easy to use steps found in Central Administration, while the STSADM command can be scripted, allowing for automation and scheduling.

Master It   You are getting ready to decommission a site collection and wish to make a final backup of it in case it needs to be referenced or resurrected in the future. This archive needs to be done in such a fashion that you are able to restore it to a different SharePoint server (in case this server is gone by the time the archive is needed). How do you go about creating this final backup?

Master It Solution   Site collections cannot be backed up in the GUI, so you will need to use STSADM. From a command prompt, type the following (with your relevant details):

```
STSADM -o Backup -url HTTP://path-to-site-collection -filename
    \\anotherserver\path-to-backup-location\backup.bak -overwrite
```

Then, for added protection, take the .bak file and burn it to a CD/DVD or store it in another safe place.

Backup separate SharePoint components In addition to SharePoint's built-in backup and recovery options, you can backup individual components of SharePoint using a variety of different tools. At a more granular level than site collections alone, it is possible to use templates and import/export to backup individual subsites, and list templates to backup lists and libraries too. You can also use the backup features of IIS and SQL to backup SharePoint's IIS Web Sites and SQL databases.

Master It After a large amount of work was done to a list on the SharePoint server, one of the users has accidentally deleted it. It's been too soon for the list to be backed up using the nightly STSADM script, but there's a possibility the list was exported as a template. What's the first step you should take to recover this deleted list?

Master It Solution Use the Recycle Bin. The list or library could also be restored from the recent template backup, but check the Recycle Bin first.

Recover from disaster SharePoint can be recovered from catastrophe several ways. The SharePoint built-in Backup has an option to perform a catastrophic backup (and back up the entire farm). IIS Web Sites can be moved to a new web front-end server, and SQL Databases can be transferred to a new database server. Finally, even ASR is available to completely rebuild the Windows Server (and SharePoint), even to disparate hardware.

Master It It's been raining, the ceiling has burst, and your server room has just been given an impromptu shower. Now the SharePoint server is a smoking, dripping ruin and SharePoint is "down for routine maintenance". You had a full ASR backup, but its corresponding floppy disk was in an envelope taped to the rack's door and is also destroyed. You do have a recent SharePoint catastrophic backup on an external hard drive (stored offsite at your house) and access to a freshly installed Windows server at your co-location site. What's the fastest way to get SharePoint back up and running?

Master It Solution Configure the new server with the same name as the old server (if necessary).

Install SharePoint using the advanced, New Server Farm option, on the fresh Windows 2003 Server (service pack 1 or, preferably, higher).

Then apply the most recent SharePoint restore, New Configuration. Verify that the databases have the correct login accounts and dbowners (and add them if necessary).

Then use Central Administration to make sure each web application is correctly connected to its content databases and that those databases are online.

Finally, redirect your DNS records and firewall rules to point all links to the new SharePoint server (if it doesn't have the same server name and IP).

Chapter 13: STSADM: A Look at the SharePoint Command Line Tool

Make sure everything is in place to run this tool STSADM provides the SharePoint administrator with the means to schedule, automate, and replicate many administrative and configuration tasks. This may be especially important in farm configurations, disaster recovery, and when moving configurations from test to production.

Master It Verify the location for STSADM.EXE on your server and create an easy way to access it.

Master It Solution Search, use Windows Explorer, or the command prompt to verify that either "c:\program files\common files\microsoft shared\web server extensions\12\bin" or "c:\Program Files (x86)\Common Files\ Microsoft Shared\web server extensions\12\bin" are present. Then adjust the %Path% environment variable or create a custom shortcut for CMD.EXE to reference the directory. You can also use the option of dragging and dropping the path from an Explorer window to a command prompt.

Basic STSADM syntax One of the features of STSADM is that the syntax is consistent from one operation to the next, although there are a large number of operations.

Master It Retrieve the list of all operations from STSADM.EXE and then create hard documentation for that list. Find the operation that you would use to create a new site collection, and create the hard documentation for that operation.

Master It Solution In the command window enter STSADM.EXE -help to retrieve the list of all operations. Create the text version of the same information by entering in STSADM.EXE -help > c:\stsadmhelp.txt

In that documentation you will find the Createsite operation. You can create the hard documentation for its syntax by entering STSADM.EXE -help Createsite > c:\Createsite.txt.

Complete common management tasks with STSADM Everything that can be done in the SharePoint GUI management tools can be done via STSADM.EXE (but that doesn't necessarily mean it should).

Master It Your company has decided that all employees will have a blog site on the company intranet, but in order to keep things under control the site collection will be limited to 50MB using a quota template named "50MB Limit". These blogs will be created inside an existing Site Collection, http://sp1.dem0tek.lcl/blogs. Each employee's blog will use their username from Active Directory as the name of the blog site. You need to create these sites for all existing employees and add the creation of the blogs to the existing user provisioning process for new users.

Master It Solution The quota template will need to be applied to the Site Collection if it hasn't been done already. To check this, enter

```
STSADM.EXE -o getproperty -propertyname defaultquotatemplate -url
http://sp1.dem0tek.lcl/blogs.
```

If the quota template has not been assigned to the blog site collection, enter

```
STSADM.EXE -o Setproperty -propertyname defaultquotateplate
    -propertyvalue "50MB Limit" -url http://sp1.dem0tek.lcl/blogs.
```

To create the sites for existing users, you will need to somehow extract the list of user accounts from Active Directory. There are several tools for this purpose. Once you have that list you will want to create either a batch file or vbscript that contains the following command:

```
STSADM.EXE -o Createweb -url http://sp1/blogs/<username>
    -sitetemplate blog#0 -description "<username>'s Blog" -title
    "<username>'s Blog"
```

You will need to replace every instance of `<username>` with the actual user name from Active Directory. Exactly how you would do this will vary depending on how much automation you wish to put into your batch file or script.

You will need to add this same line to your user provisioning script as well. Again, replacing `<username>` with the actual username in the most appropriate manner.

Chapter 14: Migrating from WSS 2.0 to WSS 3.0

Decide which migration method is right for you   Choosing the method by which you are going to migrate can be one of the most critical decisions you make. It will influence the environment you lay down as well as where it can go in the future. Once this decision point is passed, many of your other decisions can be made and supported more easily.

Master It   When planning for migration, what method would be better suited for a single server implementation that it would be for a server farm?

Master It Solution   In-place migration is often better suited to a single server implementation of SharePoint than it is for upgrading an entire server farm. The simpler the configuration, the more suited it is to the convenience of an in-place migration.

Ready yourself and your current environment for migration   It has been said that most failures are caused by poor planning. By getting all of your planning out of the way—including such things as disaster recovery, rollback positions, and what pieces to migrate, how and when—you have set yourself up with the best chance for success. Stick to the plans. When the expected occurs, you will be ready. When the unexpected occurs, there will be no wasted energy or resources, so you'll be able to deal with the issue at hand.

Master It   Once you have decided how you want to upgrade, what will you need to prepare your organization and environment for the transition?

Master It Solution   Prepare for the possible increased hardware requirements of the upgraded server. Create a plan for communications and documentation. Identify key users, and use them to test the migration and generate a user acceptance plan. Do regression testing to prepare for possible unexpected changes in customization performance. Plan for rolling back to the previous version if the upgrade fails for some reason, as well as backup and recovery before the upgrade even begins.

Avoid pitfalls that may impede the migration   With good planning, preparation, and research, you can be ready for the hills and valleys of the transitional process. Knowing some of the more common issues will help you get there more smoothly.

Master It   Look again at your environment and what decisions you have made up to now. What are some common points of failure that could occur during the transition?

Master It Solution   Some of the more common problems are customization issues, maintaining continuity, and being able to quickly recover from a failed step in the transition. Documentation and communication can also be an issue, make sure it is thorough and, especially, accurate.

Perform the migration process   There are three different types of migrations to choose from when moving from WSS 2.0 to 3.0: in-place, gradual, and database migration. Which you choose must depend on what will be appropriate for your resources and environment.

Master It Under what circumstances would it be best to use the database migration?

Master It Solution If your WSS 2.0 configuration includes scaleable hosting mode or Active Directory Account Creation mode. No other upgrade path from 2.0 to 3.0 supports those installation modes.

Perform follow-up steps after the migration You are finished, it's over, and it's done. Now look back and see whether you accomplished your goals and how well you did. These steps will vary depending on your environment but usually involve gathering user data, getting user acceptance, reviewing process successes and pitfalls, completing documentation. Finally get final sign off approval to complete the migration.

Master It What is a key thing to do after the migration has taken place? Who should you involve in the post installation process?

Master It Solution After a WSS migration, you should thoroughly test the system before pronouncing it complete. Test for user security and account access, customizations, design correctness, and usability. Be prepared for last minute requests. Always involve key users and management in the post migration process to cover user (and management) acceptance.

Chapter 15: Advanced Installation and Configuration

Understand what Active Directory Account Creation mode is Active Directory Account Creation mode allows administrators to add users to SharePoint that are not in Active Directory. Those users will then be added to a specific Organizational Unit in Active Directory.

Master It What functionality is no longer available in Central Administration when ADAC is enabled?

Master It Solution With ADAC enabled, all features relating to the creation of site collections must be done at the command line using STSADM. They are disabled in the GUI interface.

Set a service principal name In order for Kerberos authentication to work with SharePoint, additional configuration is required. The Content Database Access account for the web application using Kerberos must be registered as a service principal name for the SharePoint server (or servers).

Master It What program is used to register service principal names? How do you access it?

Master It Solution Setspn.exe is the command line tool used to register and manage service principal names. You must download it and install it to have access to it, it's not built into Windows Server 2003. It is also available as part of the Server 2003 Resource Kit.

Configure Network Load Balancing Network Load Balancing is a network connection feature, built into Windows Server 2003 (although there are other hardware and software solutions). It balances client requests and activity between servers in a cluster, effectively making them appear to be one computer from the client's perspective.

Master It What is a drainstop and what is it for?

Master It Solution Drainstopping is when a computer in the NLB cluster is intentionally cut off from the cluster and stops taking client requests on the cluster's virtual IP. This setting is managed from the NLB Manager console and is used when testing NLB functionality and failover capabilities.

Configure Directory Management Service and understand its requirements Directory Management Service requires considerable planning and implementation in order to give users easy access to entries in an Exchange (2003) GAL for lists, libraries, and SharePoint groups.

Master It Are there any special security considerations if DMS is enabled?

Master It Solution Yes, the SharePoint Farm account must have considerable permissions to the unique OU used by DMS. In addition, the Content Database Access accounts are added to the Local Administrators group of the SharePoint Server in order for DMS to function properly.

Index

Note to Reader: Throughout this index **boldfaced** page numbers indicate primary discussions of a topic. *Italicized* page numbers indicate illustrations.

A

AAM. *See* Alternate Access Mapping (AAM)
Accept Messages from Authenticated Users only setting, 992–993
access, **705**
  alternate mappings. *See* Alternate Access Mapping (AAM)
  at collection level, **706–709**
  database, **76**
  in versioning, **373–374**
  web applications, **540–546**, *541–546*, **706**
Access Denied page, 373, 667, *667*
access requests, **667–669**, *667–668*
Account tab, 982, *983*
accounts
  service
    ADAC, **906–908**, *907–908*, 919
    installation, **11–13**, **42–45**, *43*
    Organizational Unit for, **907–908**, *907–908*
    search service, 936
    security, **575–576**, *576–577*
  setup
    installation, **11–12**, **37–42**, *37–42*
    SQL, **64**
  user. *See* users and user accounts
Action bar
  libraries, **152–156**
  lists, **151**, **204–205**
Action tab, 725, *725*
Actions button
  groups, 679
  libraries, **154–155**
  lists, 152, **205**
  permissions, 667
Actions menu, **234–235**, *234–235*
Activatefeature operation, 823, **826–827**
activating/deactivating features, **826–827**

Active Directory, **707**
  contacts, **993–996**, *994–996*
  distribution groups in, **998–1001**, *999–1001*
  Organizational Unit in, 904–905
Active Directory Account Creation (ADAC) mode, **14**, **902–905**
  collections, **911–915**, *911–915*
  enabling, **908–910**, *909–910*
  mobile users, **920–923**, *920–923*
  OUs, **905**, *906*
  overview, **69–70**
  service accounts, **906–908**, *907–908*
  user accounts, 913, **915–920**, *916–920*
Active Directory container where the new distribution groups and contacts will be created setting, 990
Active Directory Users and Computers (ADUC) management console
  distribution groups, 1001, *1001*
    approval, 1005
    deleted, 1011, *1011*
    new, 1008, *1008*
    incoming email, 994, *994*
    Kerberos authentication, 982
    OUs, 985, *985*
active links for list view items, 210
Active Tasks view, 270
Activity statistics for collections, 462
ADAC. *See* Active Directory Account Creation (ADAC) mode
Add A Permission Level page, 673–675, *674–675*
Add a Web Part window, 185
Add A Workflow page, 284, *285*
Add and Customize Pages permission, **659**
Add Content Database page, 538, *538*, 626, *627*
Add Content Types page, 401, *401*
Add Counters dialog box, 712–713, *713*, *717*, *723*, *724*

Add/Edit Port Rules dialog box, 948, *948*
Add from Existing Columns option, **225**
Add Host to Cluster option, 951, *951*
Add Internal URLs page, 558, *558*
Add Items permission, 543, **657**
Add/Remove Personal Web Parts permission, **663**
Add Users page
  Active Directory, 918, *918*
  collections, 127–129, *128*
  groups, 686, *686*
  policies, 630–631, *630–631*
Add Web Parts window, 191–192
Add Web Parts To Main window, 185, *186*, 192–193, *193*, 195, *196*
Addalternatedomain operation, 829
Addcontentdb operation, 838, **840**
Adding Content Prevented setting, 513, 645
Adding Web Parts window, 195
Additional Column Settings section, 221, *222*
Additional Lock Information setting, 513, *513*
Addpath operation, 860
Addpermissionpolicy operation, 855, 858
Address List Preview screen, 996, *996*
Addsolution operation, 822
Addtemplate operation, 814
Adduser operation, 855–857
addwppack operation, 197, **817–820**, *819*
Addzoneurl operation, 829
AdminBlog page, 921, *921*
administration
  central. *See* Central Administration
  collections, **503–504**
  service
    in Basic installation, 56
    in Server Farm installation, 81
  websites, **833**
Administrator Tasks page
  email, 113–114, *113*
  migration, 888, *889*
  Read First task, 93, *93*
  sites, 99
administrators
  collections, **646**, *646*
  editing, **676–678**, *677–678*

Advanced backup mode, 778–779, *779*
advanced installation, **7–8**, *8*, **901–902**
  ADAC. *See* Active Directory Account Creation (ADAC) mode
  DMS. *See* Directory Management Service (DMS)
  Kerberos authentication, **977–978**
    limitations, **979**
    NLB, **961**
    Setspn for, **978–979**, *978–979*
    web applications, **980–983**, *980–983*
  NLB. *See* network load balancing (NLB)
  SSL, 102, 520, **961–962**
    certificates. *See* certificates
    configuring, *966–974*
    web applications, **962–964**, *963–964*
Advanced Security Settings dialog box, 986, *986*, 988, *988*
Advanced settings
  lists, **246**
  web parts, **174**
Advanced Settings screen
  ADAC, 909–910, *910*
  Central Administration, 927–928, *927*
Advanced TCP/IP Settings dialog box, 945–946, *945–946*
Affinity setting, 944, 948
aggregating content, 170
Alert Me option
  libraries, **331**
  lists, 208
alerts, 25
  collections, 624–625
  libraries, **331**
  limiting, 208
  lists, **258–264**, *259*, *261–263*
  messages, 725
  settings, **530**, **723–726**, *724–726*
  sites, 450, *451*
Alerts setting
  collections, 624–625
  web applications, **530**
aliases
  ADAC mode, 903
  incoming email, **119–121**, *120–121*, 991
All Events view, 265–266, *265*, *267*
All Groups page, 690, *690*
All People page, 689, *689*

All Site Content page, 146–147, *147–148*
  archive lists, 1002
  Central Administration, 567–568, *568*
  filtering, 148, *148*
  lists, 210–211, *211*
Allow Anonymous option, 102, **520**
Allow Anonymous Access option, 540
Allow Creation of Distribution Groups
      from SharePoint Sites setting,
      992–993
Alternate Access Mapping (AAM)
  moving services, **940–942**, *941*
  NLB, 955–956, 959, *959*
  overview, **21**
  settings, **591–597**, *591, 593–595*
  web applications, **550–552**, *551*
    changes, **556**, *556*
    IIS, **554–555**, *555*
    new URLs, **558–559**, *558*
    public URLs, **552–554**, *554*, **559–560**,
      559–560
    SSL, **964**, *964*
    zone policies, **557**, *557*
alternate calendar setting, 445, *445*
Announcements list
  contents, 204, *204*
  Team sites, 169
  template for, 278
anonymous access
  ADAC mode, 903
  overview, 15
  web applications, **540**
    collections, **540–542**, *551–552*
    lists and libraries, **543–545**, *543–546*
Anonymous User Policy page, 635, *636*
anonymous users, 706
Antivirus page, **578**, *578*
Appearance section for web parts, **172**
Application Created page, 109
Application Event log, 729, 730
Application Management, 516–517, *517*, **613**
  categories, **613–614**, *614*
  external service connections, **647–650**,
      648–649
  moving services, 937
  NLB, 958
  outgoing email, 114, *114*
  security, **628**

authentication providers, **637–638**, *637–638*
  Kerberos authentication, 980
  permissions, **629**
  policies, **629–635**, *630–636*
  self-service site management, **628**, *629*
  SSL, 962–963
  web part pages, **628**
site. *See* SharePoint Site Management section
web applications, **615**
  content databases, **625–628**, *626–628*
  creating and extending, **615–617**, *616–617*
  deleting, **618**, *619*
  features, **628**
  general settings, **622–625**, *623–624*
  lists, **628**
  managed paths, **619–621**, *620–621*
  outgoing email settings, **621–622**, *622*
  removal from IIS sites, **617–618**, *618*
workflow, **639**, *639*
application pools
  Basic installation, **51–55**, *52–53*
  Central Administration, **575**
  Kerberos, 977
  process account, **12**
  web applications, **103**, **521**, *521, 555, 555*
Application Security section, **628**
  Policy For Web Application page, **629–635**,
      629, 634
  Security for Web Part Pages page, **628**
  Self-Service Site Management page, **628**, *629*
  User Permissions for Web Application page,
      629
Application Server dialog box, 34–35, *35*
Application Server Options screen, 32, *33*
application templates, **484**
  Server Admin, **487–490**, *488–490*
  Site Admin, **484–486**, *485–486*
Apply Style Sheets permission, **660**
Apply Themes And Borders permission, **660**
applying
  collection quotas, **499**, **512–513**, *512*, **645–646**,
      646
  settings, 719
Approve Items permission, **657**
Approve/Reject Distribution Groups page, **575**
Approve/Reject Item view, 254–255, *255*
Approve/reject option, 1007
Approve/Reject page, 374, *374*

Approved Distribution Groups view, 1006
Approved state, 1004
architecture in installation, 46
Archive E-mail section, 999–1000
archive lists for email, **1002–1003**, *1002*
ASP.NET 2.0, 4
    error monitoring, 731
    in installation, **35–36**
ASR (Automated System Recovery) backups,
    798–802, *800*
Assigned To field for tasks, **269**
Attachcontentdatabase action, 846–847
Attachments section, 309
Attendees list, 477, *477*
Audience section, **238**
authentication
    and alternate access mappings, **595–596**
    vs. authorization, 705, 902
    groups, 655
    Kerberos, **16**, **977–978**
        limitations, **979**
        NLB, **961**
        Setspn for, **978–979**, *978–979*
        web applications, **980–983**, *980–983*
    methods, **15–16**
    options, 855
    providers, **520**, **637–638**, *637–638*
    support, 655
    web applications, **101–102**, **637–638**, *637–638*
Authentication Providers page
    settings, **637–638**, *637–638*
    web applications, 980, *980*
    zone effects, 557, *557*
authorization
    vs. authentication, 705, 902
    permissions, 655
auto-deletion of sites, 492, *493*
Automated System Recovery (ASR) backups,
    798–802, *800*
Automated System Recovery Wizard, *800*,
    801–802
Available MB counter, 716
Avg Disk Queue Length counter, 716

B
Backup And Restore Wizard, 788–789
Backup Database window, 790, *790*
Backup Job Information dialog box, 782

Backup Or Restore Wizard, 778–779, *779*
Backup Progress dialog box, 782, *784*
Backup/Restore dialog box, 771, *772*
Backup Utility window, 778–779, *779*
Backuphistory operation, 838, 842
backups, **732–734**
    Backup and Restore category, **602**
        Backup and Restore History page, **605–606**,
            605
        Backup and Restore Status page, 604–605,
            604, **609**
        Perform a Backup settings, **602–605**,
            602–603
    best practices, **771**
    collections, **746–749**, *747–749*, 840–841
    configuration, **774–775**, *774–775*, 788
    database
        catastrophic, **841**, *841*
        SQL, **789–792**, *790–792*
        standalone server, **785–788**, *785–786*
    encrypting, **772**
    guidelines, **734**
    IIS metabase, **771–773**, *772*
    lists and library, **766–768**, *767–768*
    Operations page
        Backup and Restore History page, 737, *737*
        Backup and Restore Status page, 736, *736*,
            742
    options, 838
    restore process. *See* restores
    scheduling, **744–746**, *745*
    servers, **798–802**, *800*, *802*
    settings, **602–605**, *602–604*
    steps, **734–738**, *735–739*
    subsites, **758–762**, *759–762*
    virtual directories, **777–783**, *779–782*
    web applications, **774–775**, *774–775*
    web parts, 183
backward-compatible event handlers, **532–533**,
    625
basic authentication, 15
Basic installation, **6**
    Central Administration site in, **56–57**
    IIS Web Site creation, **51–55**, *52–53*
    services in, **55–56**
    starting, **45–48**, *46–50*
Basic meeting workspace, **475–477**, *476–478*
Binddrservice operation, 860

blank date values, **251–252**
blocked file types
  Central Administration, **578–580**, *579*
  web applications, **534–535**, *535*
Blocked File Types page, **534–535**, *535*
Blockedfilelist operation, 860
Blog API setting, 625
Blogger API, 530
blogs
  mobile users, 922–923, *922–923*
  support, **470–471**, *470–471*
  web applications, **530**, 545, *546*
  Windows Live Writer for, **530–532**,
    531–532
Body field
  Team Discussion lists, 275–276
  Tracking lists, 287, *287*
bootstrap installers, 32
branching logic, **294–295**, *294*
Browse Directories permission, **660**
Browse User Information permission, **661**
browser-enabled documents, 380
Browser report, 448
built-in web parts
  adding, **176**, *177*
  configuring, **176–181**, *179–181*
bulk data entry for lists, **236**
bulk loading library files, 341
By Assigned To view, 270
By My Groups view, 270–271
Bytes Total/Sec counter, 716

C
.cab files, 752–754
-cabsize option in STSADM, 754
calculated fields
  Contacts list, **299–302**, *300–302*
  lists, **220–221**
Calendar and Calendar view
  importing to, 184–185, *185–186*
  lists, 169, 237
    Contacts, **307–308**, *307–308*
    modifying, **264–266**, *265–267*
    template for, 279
  regional settings, 445
Calendar page, 184–185, *185–186*
Call/Message Selected Groups option, 679
Canceldeployment operation, 822

capacity settings for content databases, **537**,
  537–538
Cascading Style Sheet (CSS) files, **429–430**, *430*
catastrophic backups, **841**, *841*
catastrophic restores, **842**, *842*
categories for list views
  filtering, **243–244**, *243–244*
  grouping, **236–243**, *237*, *241–242*
Central Administration, **565**
  with ADAC, 911
  Advanced Settings page, 927–928, *927*
  application pool and port, **53–55**, *54–55*
  applications. *See* Application Management
  in Basic installation, **56–57**
  database settings, **74–77**
  launching, **71–72**, *71–72*
  new servers, **928–930**, *928–929*
  NLB, **960**
  Operations. *See* Operations page
  organization, **565–569**, *567–568*, *570*
  outgoing email configuration, 113–114
  Server Farms
    installation, 64, *64*, **66–70**, *67–68*, *70*
    server additions, **931–933**, *932*
  web application, **9**
Central Administration page, 888, *888*
.cer files, 971–972
Certificate Authorities, 964–965, 969–971, *971*
Certificate Password screen, 975
Certificate Request File Name screen, 969
Certificate Summary screen, 972
certificates
  completed, **973–974**, *973*
  creating and purchasing, **964–967**, *966*
  exporting and importing, **974–977**, *975–976*
  requests, **970–972**, *970–971*
  trust problems, **965**
  types, 961
  viewing, 972, *972*
  web applications, 963
  Web Server Certificate Wizard, **967–970**,
    967–969, 972
Change Anonymous Access Settings page,
  540–543, *541*, *544*, 635, *636*
Change Distribution Group E-mail Address
  option, 1003
Change Distribution Group Title and
  Description option, 1003

Change Field Order page, 226, *227*
Change Group Settings page, 1008
Change Log setting, 625
change logs, **533**, 625
Change Password screen, 914, *914*
Change Type triggers, 260
Changepermissionpolicy operation, 858
Check In Comments dialog box, 350, *350*
Check In page, 354, *354*, 364, *364*
Check Out option, **331**
Checked Out Files page, 352, *353*
checking out documents
    checking in, **350–351**, *350*
    checking out, **344–350**, *345–349*
    discard check outs, **351–352**, *351*
    managing, **352–354**, *353–354*
    requiring, **343–344**, *344*
    with Send To feature, 387
child sites, 108, 418
choice fields
    lists, 218
    Tracking list, 285, *286*
Choose the installation you want screen, 46, *46*
circles in list views, 217
Close option for web parts, 173
closed web parts, 168
closing processes, **874–875**
Cluster Parameters dialog box, 947, *947*
clusters, NLB, 943, 946–947, *947*
.cmp files, 752, 754–755
code confusion, **874**
collections, 4, 418, **497–498**
    ADAC Mode, **911–915**, *911–915*
    Administration section, **503–504**
    administrators, **646**, *646*, **676–678**, *677–678*
    anonymous access, **540**
    backups, **746–749**, *747–749*, 840–841
    creating
        confirming, **107–109**, *107–109*, **642–643**, *643*
        Create Site Collection page, **640**, *640*
        process, **498–500**, *498, 500*
        STSADM, **852–854**
    deleting
        AAM, 597
        Delete Site Collection page, **640–642**, *641*
        Delete This Site page, 457, *458*
        STSADM, **854**
    excluded paths, 506, **509–511**, *509–510*
    exporting, **751–755**, *753, 755–757*
    features, **462–463**, *463*
    galleries, **501–502**, *502–503*
    host headers, **549–550**, *549*
    importing, **751–752**, **755–758**, *756–757*
    importing web parts to, **189–192**, *190–192*
    listing, **647**, *647*, **850–852**, *850*
    locks, **511–514**, *511–512*, **645–646**, *645*
    managed paths, **505–508**, *505–508*
    quotas
        applying, **499**, **512–513**, *512*, **645–646**, *646*
        creating, **511–512**, *511*, **644–646**, *644*
        settings, **111–115**, *112*
    Recycle Bin, **459**, *460*, **503**, 625
    restoring, **750–751**, *750–751*, 840–841
    Server Farm installation, **111–115**, *112*
    vs. sites, 642
    storage data, **462**, *463*
    usage summary, **461–462**, *461*
    user access, **501**, **706–709**
Column Headers, Action bar
    libraries, **156**
    lists, **152**
Column Ordering option, 225
columns, site, **441**
    Contacts list, **302–307**, *303–307*
    custom lists, **315–318**, *316–318*
Columns section, **238**
command line tool. *See* STSADM tool
comments
    blogs, 470–471, *471*, 545, *546*
    document check-in, 350, *350*
    permissions, 543, *543*
%Committed Bytes in Use counter, 716
common data in lists, **202–203**
Common Names for sites, 966, 968, *969*
communication in migration, 873
compatibility in libraries, 329
%Complete field, 269
Completing SharePoint Products and
        Technologies Configuration Wizard
        Summary screen, 926, *927*
Completing The Delegation of Control Wizard
        screen, 908
Completing The New Zone Wizard screen, 122
Completing the SharePoint Products and
        Technologies Configuration Wizard
        screen, 909–910, *909–910*

Completing the Web Server Certificate Wizard, 976

Completing the Web Server Wizard screen, 972

concatenating data, 300

configuration accounts, **12**

Configuration Backup dialog box, 771, *772*

Configuration Backup/Restore dialog box, 771–772, *772*

configuration files
  backups, 788
  restoring, **775–777**, *775–777*
  saving, **774–775**, *774–775*

Configuration Successful screen, 70, *70*, 928

Configure Central Administration Web Application page, 886, *887*

Configure Connection to Records Center page, 647, *648*

Configure Document Conversions page, 649, *649*

Configure Incoming E-Mail Settings page, 1003

Configure Log Files dialog box, 719, *720*

Configure Your Server wizard, 32–34, *33–34*

Configuring Incoming E-Mail Settings page, 116–127, 990

confirming
  collections, **642–643**, *643*
  names, 687
  server additions, **928–930**, *928–929*

Connect dialog box, 949, *949*, 951

Connect to a Server Farm page, 8, *8*, 62, *62*, 925, *925*

Connect to Server dialog box, 39, *39*

Connection Attempts/Sec counter, 717

connections
  databases, **840**
  external service, **647–650**, *648–649*
  NLB, 949, *949*, 951
  web parts and lists, **318–321**, *319–321*

contacts and Contacts list, **297–298**
  Active Directory, **993–996**, *994–996*
  advanced settings, **309–310**, *310*
  Calendar view, **307–308**, *307–308*
  fields
    calculated, **299–302**, *300–302*
    deleting, **298–299**, *299*
  sending content to lists and libraries, **996–998**, *997–998*

site columns, **302–307**, *303–307*
  template for, 278

content access accounts, **12**, 44
  ADAC mode, 905, 919
  Kerberos authentication, 977–979, 983
  permissions, **988–989**, *989*
  search service settings, 936
  web applications, 963

content approval
  distribution groups, 1004
  library files
    access with, **374**
    elevating minor versions to major versions, **370–375**, *371–372*, *374–375*
    enabling, **365–370**, *367–370*
    overview, **365**
  lists, **253–256**, *253*, *255–256*

content databases, **10–11**, 201
  accounts, 12, **44–45**
  adding, **538–539**, *538–539*
  deleting, **538**
  existing, **539–540**, *539*
  settings, **535–538**, *536–538*
  web applications, **535–540**, *536–539*, **625–628**, *627–628*

Content Editor web part, 170, 176–181, *177*

content for lists and libraries, **996–998**, *997–998*

content pages, 138, **150–151**
  edited, 184–185
  for lists, 201–202

content types, **393–394**, *394*
  Contacts list, 309
  galleries, **441**
  libraries, **393–395**
    creating, **396–404**, *397–404*
    enabling, **395–396**
    relinking, **402**
  for recycling, **273–274**
  templates, **379–380**

Contribute permission, 456, **665**

convergence in NLB, 952

conversions, document, **649**, *649*

Copy page, 384, *385*

Copy Permission Level page, 672–673, *672–673*

Copy Progress dialog box, 386, *386*

Copyappbincontent operation, 822

copying permissions, **671–673**, *672–673*

Counter Log dialog box, 715

counters
adding, **712–714**, *713–715*
alerts, **723–726**, *724–726*
deciding on, **716**
logs, **715–723**, *718–723*
CPU requirements for migration, 871
crawler accounts, 12
Create a new IIS Web Site option, **101**
Create Active Directory Account dialog box,
915–916, *916*
Create Alerts permission, **658**
Create Basic Page link, 419
Create Column option, 225
Create Document Workspace option, **383**
Create Groups permission, **660**
Create new application pool option, 103
Create New Distribution Group option, 1003
Create New Web Application page, 99, *100*, 518,
518, 615, 958, 963
Create Or Extend Web Application page,
615–617, *616*, 958, 963
Create page
Issue Tracking list, 279–280, *280*
libraries, 768–769, *769*
sites, **144–145**, *144*, 764, *764*
Create Requests view, 1006–1007
Create Shortcut Wizard, 808
Create Site Collection page, 109, *109*, 498, *498*,
523–524, *524*, **640**, *640*
Create Site option, 911
Create Subsites permission, **659**
Create View page, 236, *237*
Create Web Application page, 980
Createadminvs operation, 829, 833
CreateGroup operation, 855, 857
Createsite operation, 848, 852–854
Createsiteinnewdb operation, 848–849, 854
Createweb operation, 849, 852
cross-site groups, **676**
CSS (Cascading Style Sheet) files, **429–430**, *430*
currency fields for lists, 219
Custom Content Types section, 396
Custom Filter dialog box, 231, *231*
custom lists
creating, **244–248**, *245*, **310–312**, *311–312*
fields
editing, **312–313**
lookup, **315**

Person or Groups, **313–314**, *313*
single-line text, **314–315**
site columns, **315–318**, *316–318*
custom permissions, 424
Custom Send To Destination option, 380
custom zones, 592
Customize page for lists, 994
Customize Announcements page, 245, *245*

D
daily summaries for alerts, 260, *261*
Data Configuration category, **609–610**, *610*
Data Location tab, 59–60, *60*, 881, *881*
Data Retrieval Service page, **609–610**, *610*
Data section in web parts, **174–175**
Database Authentication setting, 104
Database category in error monitoring,
731–732
database engines, **7**
Database Maintenance Plan Wizard, 789
Database Name setting, 104
Database Name and Authentication settings,
104, *105*, **521–522**, *522*
Databaserepair operation, 838
databases, **10–11**
accounts, **12**, 43
backups
catastrophic, **841**, *841*
SQL, **789–792**, *790–792*
standalone server, **785–788**, *785–786*
connecting and disconnecting, **840**
content. *See* content databases
importing and exporting, **842–843**
migration
overview, **870–871**
process, **894–899**, *895–897*
restores
catastrophic, **842**, *842*
sites, 840–841
SQL, **792–795**, *793–794*
standalone servers, **788–789**, *788*
Server Farm installation, **74–80**, *75–80*
servers
default, **609**
web applications, 104
SQL Server Embedded Edition, 50, *51*
STSADM tool, **837–843**, *842*
datasheet view for lists, **229–237**, *229–235*

dates, lists
  blank, **251–252**
  setting, 219
DBOs (database owners), 12
DCOM events
  Event Viewer, **730**
  Server Farm installation, **83–86**, *83–85*
Deactivatefeature operation, 823
deactivating features, **826–827**
Deactivativefeature operation, 826–827
Decision meeting workspace, **481**, *482*
defaults
  database servers, **609**
  library templates, **378**
  list views, 239
  path statement, 808
  permissions, **456**, **663–665**
  quotas, 529, 622
  site template names, **853**
  time zones, 529, 622
  URL zones, 553, 592
  web parts, **169–171**
Define Managed Paths page, 505, *506*, **619–621**,
    620–621
Define Your Work Week setting, 445
Delayed or Immediate Request screen, 968
Delegation of Control Wizard, 907–908, *907–908*
Delete Distribution Group option, 1003
Delete from Site Collection option, 680
Delete Item option, 208
Delete Items permission, 544, **657**
Delete option for libraries, **331**, 406
Delete Requests page, 1009
Delete Requests view, 1010–1011
Delete Site Collection page, **640–642**, *641–642*
Delete This List link, 246
Delete This Site page, 457, *457–458*
Delete Users from Site Collection option, 680
Delete Versions permission, **658**
Delete Web Application page, **533–534**, *533*,
    618, *619*
Deleteadminvs operation, 829
Deletealternatedomain operation, 829
Deleteconfigdb operation, 838, 840
Deletecontentdb operation, 838, 840
deleted items, recovering, **770**
DeleteGroup operation, 855, 857
Deletepermissionpolicy operation, 855

Deletesite operation, 849, 854
Deletesolution operation, 822, **824**
Deletetemplate operation, 814, **816**
DeleteUser operation, 855, 857
Deleteweb operation, 849, 854
Deletewppack operation, 817, 821
Deletezoneurl operation, 829
deleting
  collections
    AAM, 597
    Delete Site Collection page, **640–642**, *641*
    Delete This Site page, 457, *458*
    STSADM, **854**
  contacts from AD, 998
  Contacts list fields, **298–299**, *299*
  content databases, **538**
  distribution groups, **1008–1012**, *1009–1011*
  features, **828**
  fields from views, **216**, *216*
  group users, **679–680**, *679*
  library documents, 332
  links, 246
  permissions, **663–664**, *664*
  picture library pictures, 406
  public URLs, **559–560**, *560*
  SharePoint from IIS web sites, **617–618**, *618*
  sites, **457**, *457–458*, 492, *493*, **854**
  solutions, **824**, **828**
  templates, **762**, *762*, **816**, *816*
  web applications, **533–534**, *533*, **618**, *619*, **833**
  web parts
    packages, **820–821**
    process, **195–196**, *196*
    from zones, **164**, *165*
delta drives, 869
Deny All–Has No Access policy, 635
Deny All permission, 631
Deny Write–Has No Write Access policy, 635
Deny Write permission, **631**
Deploy Solution page, 600–601, *600*
deployment of solutions, 600–601, *600*, **824–826**,
    825
Deploysolution operation, 822, **824–826**, *825*
Deploywppack operation, 818
descriptions
  collections, 499
  groups, 684
  IIS web sites, 518

descriptions (*Continued*)
  lists, 246
  permissions, 656, 673, 675
  sites, **425**, *425*
  tasks, 270
Design permission, 456, **665**
Destination section in Send To feature, 384, *385*
Detach Database window, 793, *793*
Detachcontentdatabase action, 846–847
diagnostic levels, **859–860**
Diagnostic Logging page, **581–585**, *582–584*
differencing drives, 869
differential backups, **603**, 735
digest authentication, 15
Directory Management Service (DMS), **118**, 984
  archive lists for email, **1002–1003**, *1002*
  configuring, **990–993**, *991*
  distribution groups, 992
    approval, **1003–1008**, *1004–1008*
    deleting, **1008–1012**, *1009–1011*
    for email, **1001**, *1002*
    enabling, **998–1001**, *999–1001*
  glitches, **1011–1012**
  incoming email, **993–996**, *994–996*
  OUs
    creating, **984–985**, *985*
    permissions, **985–989**, *986–989*
  sending content to lists and libraries, **996–998**, *997–998*
  warnings, **984**
Directory Security tab, 967, 972–976
Disablessc operation, 860
Discard Check Out option, **351–352**, *351*
disconnecting databases, **840**
Discussion lists, 169
  modifying, **273–278**, *275–277*
  template, 279
discussion topics, 152
Discussions link, 148
disk requirements, **23**, 871–872
%Disk Time counter, 716
display requirements, 23
Displaysolution operation, 822
Distribution Group Request Approval Settings, 992–993
distribution groups, 992
  approval, **1003–1008**, *1004–1008*
  deleting, **1008–1012**, *1009–1011*

  for email, **1001**, *1002*
  enabling, **998–1001**, *999–1001*
Distribution Groups page, 1005–1007, *1005–1007*, 1009–1011, *1010*
distribution lists, 999, *999*
DMS. *See* Directory Management Service (DMS)
DNS
  NLB, 953, *953*
  for URLs, 553
Document Content Types section, 396
Document Library Settings page, 701, *701*
Document Template section, **377**, **380–381**
Document Version History section, 377
documentation for migration, **873**
documents
  checking out. *See* checking out documents
  conversions, **649**, *649*
  libraries. *See* libraries
  size, **876**
  versions. *See* versions and versioning
  workspace, **465–466**, *465–466*
Documents link, 148
domain account modes, **14**
domain aliases for incoming email, **119–121**, *120–121*, 991
Domain groups
  adding to SharePoint groups, **686–687**, *686–688*
  removing from SharePoint groups, **688**, *688–689*
  security, 129, 654
domain users, 654
  adding to SharePoint groups, **686–687**, *686–688*
  removing from SharePoint groups, **688**, *688–689*
Download option, 406
Download a Copy option, **383–384**
downloading
  documents, **383–384**
  picture library pictures, 406
Draft Item Security setting, 373
drainstopping, **954–955**, *954–955*, 957
drive requirements, **23**, 871–872
drop folders, 118
dual identities, **140**

Due Date field
  Gantt view, 271
  Tasks lists, 270
Due Today view, 271
DVD drive requirements, 23

E
E-Mail Distribution List section, 999, *999*
E-mail Server Display Address setting, 118–119
Edit Authentication page, 638, *638*, 981, *981*
Edit Group Quick Launch option, 681, *682*
Edit in Datasheet option, 154
Edit in Microsoft Word option, 330
Edit Internal URLs screen, 955, *956*
Edit Item option, 208
Edit Items permission, 544, **657**
Edit mode for Web parts, **161–162**, *162*
Edit option for picture libraries, 406
Edit Page, **145**
Edit Permission Level page, 664, *664*, 670–671, *670–671*
Edit Permissions page, 705, *705*
Edit Personal User Information permission, **661**
Edit Properties option, 330
Edit Public Zones URLs page, 593–594, *593–594*
Edit Timer Job page, 589–591, *590–591*
Edit View page, *213*, 214–216
editing
  anonymous user rights, **543–545**, *543–546*
  documents with required fields, **334–338**, *334–337*
  lists
    Calendar, **264–266**, *265–267*
    fields, **218–221**, **224–229**, *227–229*, **312–313**
    items, **212–213**
    links, **267–268**, *268*
    prebuilt, **264**
    tasks, **269–273**, *270*, *272*
    views, **213–217**, *213–217*
  permission levels, **669–671**, *669–671*
  pictures, 406
  site administrators, **676–678**, *677–678*
  site settings, **422–423**, *422*
  Team Discussion lists, **273–278**, *275–277*
email, **20**
  advanced addressing concepts, **991**
  aliases, **119–121**, *120–121*
  archive lists for, **1002–1003**, *1002*

Central Administration
  incoming, **574–575**, *574*
  outgoing, **573**, *573*
collections
  confirmations, **642–643**, *643*
  notifications, 514–516, *515*
distribution groups for, **1001–1002**, *1002*
enabling on lists, **993–996**, *994–996*
libraries, 377, 382
lists, **248–253**, *249–252*
options, 860
safe servers, **119–127**, *120–126*
Server Farm installation
  incoming, **116–119**, *116–117*
  outgoing, **113–116**, *113–115*
web applications, **528**, *528*, **621–622**, *622*
Email a Link option, 383
Email Users option, 679
Enable Active Directory Account Creation Mode screen, 909, *910*
Enable An Alternate Calendar setting, 445
Enable Anonymous Access option, 540
Enable Incoming E-mail section, **117–118**
Enable Logging section, 726
Enablessc operation, 860
enabling
  ADAC Mode, **908–910**, *909–910*
  anonymous access, **540–542**, *541–542*
  content approval
    library files, **365–370**, *367–370*
    lists, **253–256**, *253*, *255–256*
  content types, **395–396**
  distribution groups, **998–1001**, *999–1001*
  IIS SMTP service, **34–35**
  incoming email, **248–253**, *249–252*, **993–996**, *994–996*
  Kerberos, **980–983**, *980–983*
  list versioning, **254**
  Self-Service Site Creation, **491–492**, *492–493*
encryption
  backups, **772**
  SSL, 102, 520, **961–962**
    certificates. *See* certificates
    configuring, **964–974**, *966–974*
    web applications, **962–964**, *963–964*
End User License Agreement (EULA), 880, *880*
Enumalternatedomains operation, 829
Enumcontentdbs operation, 838

Enumdeployments operation, 822
Enumerate Permissions permission, **660**
Enumgroups operation, 856–857
Enumroles operation, 856–857
Enumservices operation, 860
Enumsites operation, 849
Enumsolutions operation, 822
Enumsubwebs operation, 829, 833, 849
Enumtemplates operation, **814–816**, *815*
Enumusers operation, 856
Enumwppacks operation, 818, **820**
Enumzoneurls operation, 829, **833–834**, *834*
Error Documents counter, 717
errors
   ADAC, 911, *911*
   Kerberos, **979**
EULA (End User License Agreement), 880, *880*
Event Throttling section, **582–585**, *582*
Event Viewer, **729–730**, *729*
   events in, 730–732
   Kerberos authentication, 981
events
   calendar. *See* Calendar and Calendar view
   handlers, **532–533**
   Server Farm installation, **83–86**, *83–85*
exclamation points (!) for list items, 207
excluded paths for collections, 506, **509–511**,
   509–510
execadmsvcjobs operation, 589, 821
explicit managed paths, 506
Explorer, 154–155, *155*, **338–343**, *339–341*
Export dialog box, 182, *183*
Export option, 173
Export Summary screen, 975
exporting
   collections and subsites, **751–755**, *753,*
     755–757
   databases, **842–843**
   options, **838–839**
   site templates, **761–762**, *762*
   SSL certificates, **974–977**, *975–976*
   web parts, 173, **181–183**, *183*
Extend Web Application page, 553, *554*, 617,
   617
extending web applications, 553, *554*, **617**, *617*,
   832–833
Extendvs operation, 829, 831, *831*
Extendvsinwebfarm operation, 830, **832–833**

external drives for backups, 799
External Service Connections section, **647–650**,
   648–649
Extranet zones, 592

F
failover, 929
Farm Account permissions, **985–988**, *986–988*
Farm Administrators
   adding, **130**
   collections, 500
Farm Administrators group, **580–581**, *580*
farms. *See* Server Farms
features
   activating/deactivating, **826–827**
   adding, **826**
   collections, **462–463**, *463*
   installing, **828**
   removing, **828**
   sites, **456–457**, 489
   STSADM for, **826–828**
fields
   Contacts
     calculated, **299–302**, *300–302*
     deleting, **298–299**, *299*
   libraries, **332–338**, *333–337*
   list views, **215**, *215*
   lists
     adding, **221–224**, *221–224*
     editing, **218–221**, **224–229**, *227–229,*
       312–313
     lookup, **315**
     ordering, **224–229**, *229*
     Person or Groups, **313–314**, *313*
     single-line text, **314–315**
     site columns, **315–318**, *316–318*
   Server Property, 335
File In Use dialog box, 349, *349*
-filename option in STSADM, 754, 757
files. *See* documents
Filmstrip view, 406, *406*
Filter section, 238
filters, lists, 231, *231*, **238**, **243–244**, *243–244*
Flat view, 277
Folder Content Types section, 396
folders
   backups, **777–783**, *779–782*
   Contacts list, 309

as content types, 396
drop, 118
libraries, **381**
Folders section for lists, 240
Form Library, **410–414**, *411–414*
Form web part, 170
Forms folder, 155
forms libraries, **324**
FQDNs, 119
%Free Space counter, 723
front end servers in recovery, **797**
Full backups, 603
Full Control permission, 456, 631, **665**
full fidelity backups, 738
Full Read permission, 631
full recoveries, **798–799**
Full Screen reading mode, 347
Fullcrawlstart action, 846
Fullcrawlstop action, 846

G
galleries
    collections, **501–502**, *502–503*
    importing web parts to, **189–192**, *190–192*
    sites, **439–443**, *440–442*
    for web parts, 168
GALs (global address lists), 984, 1000, *1001*
Gantt view, 237, **271–273**, *272*
gatherer accounts, 12
Gatherer category in error monitoring, **731**
General settings
    lists, **246**
    System Monitor, 719
    web applications, **528–533**, *529*, **622–625**, *623–624*
Get Sort/Filter From option, 319
Getadminport operation, 861
Getproperty operation, 813, 830, 834, **861–862**
Getsitelock operation, 856, 858
Geturlzone operation, 830
Give Group Permission To This Site section, 685
global address lists (GALs), 984, 1000, *1001*
Global Configuration category, **587**
    Alternate Access Mappings page, **591–597**, *591, 593–595*
    farm management features, **597–598**, *598*
    Solution Management page, **599–601**, *599–600*

Timer Job Definitions page, **589–591**, *589*
Timer Job Status page, **587–589**, *588*
Go To Source Item option, 387
gradual migration, 867
    overview, **869–870**
    process, **884–894**, *884–894*
Group By section, **239–243**, *241*
group fields for lists, **219**
Group Settings page, 681, 999, *999*, 1005
groups, **653**
    adding to, **686–687**, *686–688*
    creating, **683–685**, *683–686*
    defined, **653–655**
    distribution, 992
        approval, **1003–1008**, *1004–1008*
        deleting, **1008–1012**, *1009–1011*
        for email, **1001**, *1002*
        enabling, **998–1001**, *999–1001*
    email for, **1001–1002**, *1002*
    lists, 219, **236–243**, *237, 241–242*
    overview, **675–676**
    permission levels, **663–665**
    removing from, **679–680**, *679*
    security, **707–708**
    STSADM for, **857–858**, *857*
    for subsites, **696–699**, *697–699*
    viewing, **678–683**, *679–682*, **689–690**, *689–690*
Groups Quick Launch bar
    for groups, 679
    for permissions, 667
guidelines of acceptable performance, 27

H
-haltonfatalerror option, 757
-haltonwarning option, 757
hardware requirements
    migration, **871–872**
    overview, **22–23**
Heartbeats/Heartbeats Rate counter, 717
help
    libraries, 91, *91*, 581, *581*
    limitations, 142
    searching, 939
    Server Farm installation, **90–93**, *91–92*
    STSADM tool, **810–811**, *810–811*
-help option in STSADM, 810–811
Help page, 142, *142*
Help Search service, **939**

HelpFold library, 91
HelpGroup group, 581, *581*
hierarchical levels vs. permission levels, 703
hierarchy, site, 463, *463*
histories
    Backup and Restore History page, **605–606**,
        605
    versions, 377
home page
    anatomy, **136–139**
    purpose, **135–136**, *136*
Home Directory page, 55, *55*, 509, *509*
host headers
    IIS sites, **101**, 519
    NLB, **962**, *962*
    SSL, 966
    web applications, **547–550**, *547–550*
host lists, 950
Host Parameters dialog box, 950–951, *950*
Host parameters in NLB, 943, 950–951,
        950
HTML Viewer, **648–649**, *648*
HTTPS protocol, 961, 973
huge lists, **226**
hyperlinks. *See* links

I
icons, site, **425**, *425*
identity swapping, **309**
Identity tab, 53, *53*
%Idle Time counter, 716
IFilters, 16, 20
IIS. *See* Internet Information Services (IIS)
IIS Authentication Settings section, 980
IIS Log Parser utility, 729
IISReset tool, **815–816**
Image web part, 170
Immediately alert option, 260
Import Certificate screen, 976
Import Certificate Password screen, 976
Import Certificate Summary screen, 976
Import Configuration dialog box, 776, *776*
importing
    collections and subsites, **751–752**, **755–758**,
        756–757
    configuration files, 776, *776*
    databases, **842–843**
    options, **839**

SSL certificates, **974–977**, *975–976*
web parts
    to collection galleries, **189–192**, *190–192*
    to single page, **184–188**, *184–189*
improvements with migration, **875–876**
in-place migration
    overview, **868**
    process, **879–883**, *880–884*
included paths for collections, 506
-includeusersecurity option in STSADM, 754,
        757
Incoming E-Mail Settings page
    contacts, 994, *994*
    distribution groups, 1003
    lists, 247–248, *249*
    Server Farm installation, 117, *117*
    settings, **574–575**, *574*
incoming email
    advanced addressing concepts, **991**
    aliases, **119–121**, *120–121*
    Central Administration, **574–575**, *574*
    enabling on lists, **993–996**, *994–996*
    libraries, 377, 382
    lists, **248–253**, *249–252*
    Server Farm installation, **116–119**, *116–117*
index accounts, 12, 919
Index Filters, 16, 20
index service, 18, 20
Indexed Columns option, **225**
indexes, 25
    list fields, **225**, **316**, *317*
    search, **845–846**, *846*, **936–937**
    in Server Farm installation, **86**, *86*
Indexfiles folder, 60, *60*
Indexing Schedule settings, **936–937**
Information Rights Management (IRM), **577**,
        577
inheritance of permissions, 424, **691–694**,
        691–694, **707**
inline help, **810–811**, *810–811*
Insert Image dialog box, 179, *179*
installation, **6**, **31**
    advanced. *See* advanced installation
    ASP.NET 2.0 in, **35–36**
    Basic. *See* Basic installation
    IIS and SMTP, **32–35**, *33–35*
    .NET Framework 3.0 in, **35–36**
    preparing for, **31–45**

Server Farm. *See* Server Farms
service accounts, **42–45**, *43*
setup accounts, **37–42**, *37–42*
Installfeature operation, 823, **826**
instances, form, 410
interface, **135**
    content pages, **150–151**
    Documents library, **152–156**, *153, 155*
    Help page, 142, *142*
    home page
        anatomy, **136–139**
        purpose, **135–136**, *136*
    lists, **151–152**, *151*
    page types, **138–139**
    Quick Launch bar, **146–149**, *146–149*
    Search field, **142–143**
    Site Actions menu, **143–145**, *144–145*
    Welcome menu, **139–141**, *139–141*
internal URLs
    alternate access mappings, 592–594
    web applications, 552, **558–559**, *558*
Internet access requirements, 32
Internet Explorer with imported sites, 756
Internet Information Services (IIS)
    configuration files
        restoring, **775–777**, *775–777*
        saving, **774–775**, *774–775*
    logs, **726–729**, *727–728*
    metabase
        backups, **771–773**, *772*
        restores, **773**, *773*, 795, 797
    requirements, **4**
    Restart Internet Information Services section, **104–107**, *105–106*
    Server Farms
        installation, **77–80**, *78–80*
        server additions, **930–931**, *931*
    SMTP for, **32–35**, *33–35*
    SSL configuration for, **964–974**, *966–974*
    web applications, **101**, **518–523**, *519, 521–523*, **554–555**, *555*
    web sites, removing SharePoint from, **617–618**, *618*
Internet Information Services dialog box, 34
Internet Protocol (TCP/IP) Properties dialog box, 944, *946*
Internet zones, 553, 592
Intranet zones, 592

Invite User Limits section, 919, *920*
IP addresses
    NLB, 944–950, *945–950*
    SSL traffic, 966–967
IRM (Information Rights Management), **577**, *577*
isql utility, 876
Issue Tracking lists, 273
    overview, **279–284**, *280–283*
    template for, 278–279
    three-state workflow, **284–291**, *285–291*
item-level granularity, 705
Item-Level Permissions section, 309, *310*
Item Limit section, 240

K
Kerberos authentication, **16**, **977–978**
    limitations, **979**
    NLB, **961**
    Setspn for, **978–979**, *978–979*
    web applications, **980–983**, *980–983*
key system users in migration, **873**
keys
    Kerberos, 977
    SSL, 961

L
language pack warning, 882, *883*
languages in searches, **844–845**
Launch Permission dialog box, 85, *85*
Layout section for web parts, **173**
libraries, **323**
    content types, **393–395**
        creating, **396–404**, *397–404*
        enabling, **395–396**
        relinking, **402**
    creating, **376–383**, *376, 378–379, 382*
    files
        checking out. *See* checking out documents
        content approval. *See* content approval
        creating, **328–332**, *329–330*
        opening and viewing, **338–343**, *339–341*
        uploading, **326–328**, *327–328*, 341
        versioning. *See* versions and versioning
    Form, **410–414**, *411–414*
    help, 91, *91*, 581, *581*
    opening, 154–155, *155*, **338–343**, *339–341*, 406, *406*

libraries (*Continued*)
    permissions, **543–545**, **701–705**, *701–705*
    picture
        headings, **148–149**
        overview, **405–407**, *405–406*
        purpose, **324**
    for recycling, **273–274**
    required fields, **332–338**, *333–337*
    requirements, 324–325
    Send To feature. *See* Send To feature for
        libraries
    sending content to, **996–998**, *997–998*
    Shared Documents, **152–156**, *153*, *155*
    templates, 279, **378–383**, *379*, *382*
        backups to, **766–768**, *767–768*
        restores from, **768–770**, *769–770*
    types, **324**
    web parts, **169**
    Wiki, **324**
        backing up to templates, **766–768**, *767–768*
        content, **408**, *408*
        creating, **407**, *407*
        documents, **408–410**, *409*
        restoring from templates, **768–770**, *769–770*
    for workflows, 325
Limited Access permission, 456, **665**
links, **219–220**
    deleting, 246
    lists, 169
        list view items, 210
        modifying, **267–268**, *268*
        template for, 279
    permissions, **247**
    Send To feature, 383, 386, 388
    Top Link bar, **137**, **431–433**, *432–433*
List action, 846
List Content Types section, 396
List Settings option, 682
List Settings page, 227, *227*
List Templates Gallery, **443**
List Versioning Settings page, 253–254, *253*
listing
    collections, **647**, *647*, **850–852**, *850*
    server farm templates, **815–816**, *815*
    sites, **850–851**
    solutions, **823–824**, *824*
    web applications, 628, **833–834**, *833*
    web part packages, **820**, *820*

Listlogginglevel operation, 861
Listlogginglevels operation, 859
lists, **151–152**, *151*, **201**
    Action bar, **204–205**
    Actions menu, **234–235**, *234–235*
    alerts, **258–264**, *259*, *261–263*
    backups, **766–768**, *767–768*
    bulk data entry, **236**
    Calendar, **264–266**, *265–267*
    common data, **202–203**
    Contacts. *See* contacts and Contacts list
    content approval, **253–256**, *253*, *255–256*
    creating from templates, **278–279**
    custom. *See* custom lists
    datasheet view, **229–237**, *229–235*
    fields. *See* fields
    huge, **226**
    incoming email, **248–253**, *249–253*, **993–996**,
        994–996
    indexing, **225**
    Issue Tracking, 273
        overview, **279–284**, *280–283*
        template for, 278–279
        three-state workflow, **284–291**, *285–291*
    items
        creating, **205–208**, *206–208*
        editing, **212–213**
        viewing, **208–212**, *209–212*
    links, 169
        list view items, 210
        modifying, **267–268**, *268*
        template for, 279
    overview, **201–202**
    permissions
        anonymous access, **543–545**, *543–546*
        changing, **701–705**, *701–705*
        Contacts, 309, *310*
        managing, 208
        overview, **656–658**, *656*
    for recycling, **273–274**
    RSS feeds, **256–258**, *257–258*
    sending content to, **996–998**, *997–998*
    surveys, **291–297**, *292*, *294–297*
    tasks, **269–273**, *270*, *272*
    Team Discussion, **273–278**, *275–277*
    templates
        backups to, **766–768**, *767–768*
        creating from, **278–279**

restores from, **768–770**, *769–770*
saving as, **246–247**, **443**
versioning, 246, **254**
views, 201–202
  fields, **215**, *215*
  filtering by category, **243–244**, *243–244*
  grouping by category, **236–243**, *237*,
    241–242
  modifying, **213–217**, *213–217*
  web parts, **169**
    adding, **166–167**, *166–167*
    connections, **318–321**, *319–321*
  workflow settings, **247**
Lists and Libraries View web parts, **169**
Lists link, 148
load balancing
  network. *See* network load balancing (NLB)
  Server Farms, 924
  URLs, **102–103**, *103*, **520–521**
Load Weight setting, 944, **949**
local document copies, 345
local security groups, **80–82**
Locale setting, 444
Localupgradestatus operation, 861
locks
  collections, **511–514**, *511–512*, **645–646**, *645*
  STSADM for, **858–859**
Log Files tab, 719, *720*
Log Parser 2.2 utility, 729
Logging and Reporting category, **581–586**,
    582–584, *586–587*
Logging Properties dialog box, 726–727, *727*
Logical Disk performance object, 716
login permissions, **699–700**, *700*
login screen, 48, *49*, 71, *71*
logs
  analyzing, **722**, *722*
  counter, **715–723**, *718–723*
  diagnostic, **581–585**, *582–584*
  IIS, **726–729**, *727–728*
  levels, **859–860**
  usage, 25
Look And Feel category, 424
lookup fields, 202–203, **219**, **315**

M
MAC (Media Access Control) addresses, 942
major versions
  documents, **359–362**, *360–362*
  elevating minor versions to, **370–375**,
    371–372, *374–375*
Manage Access Requests page, 668, *668*
Manage Alerts permission, **661**
Manage Content Database Settings page,
    626–627, *627*
  editing databases, 536, *536*
  searching databases, 938, *938*
Manage Content Databases page, **625–626**, *626*
  adding databases, 539, *539*
  editing databases, 535, *536*
  searching databases, 938, *938*
Manage Copies page, 388, *389*, 392, *392*
Manage Distribution Groups page, 1007, *1007*,
    1009–1010, *1009–1010*
Manage Lists permission, **657**
Manage Permission option, 330
Manage Permission Policy Levels page, 632,
    632, 634, *634*
Manage Permissions option, 208
Manage Permissions permission, **659**
Manage Personal Views permission, **663**
Manage Web Applications Features page, 534,
    534
Manage Web Site permission, **659**
managed links, 432
managed paths, **21–22**, 499
  collections, **505–508**, *505–508*
  defining, **619–621**, *620–621*
Managepermissionpolicylevel operation, 856,
    858
Map to External resource setting, 597
mapping. *See* Alternate Access Mapping
    (AAM)
Master Page Gallery, 440, *440*
Master pages, **440–441**
Maximum Upload Size setting, **530**, 624
Media Access Control (MAC) addresses, 942
meeting workspaces, **472–475**, *472–475*
  Basic, **475–477**, *476–478*
  benefits, **478–480**, *478–480*
  Decision, **481**, *482*
  MultiPage, **483**, *483*
  Social, **480**, *481*
  URLs, **481**
membership providers, 637
Membership Requests section, 685

Memory performance object, 716
memory requirements, 23, 871
messages, alert, 725
metadata, 59
MetaWeblog API, 530
Migrateuser operation, 856
migration from WSS 2.0 to WSS 3.0, **865**
 benefits, **866–867**
 database move
  overview, **870–871**
  process, **894–899**, *895–897*
 gradual
  overview, **869–870**
  process, **884–894**, *884–894*
 in-place
  overview, **868**
  process, **879–883**, *880–884*
 overview, **866**
 permissions, 871
 planning, **871–876**, *872*
 post-update steps, **899–900**
 process, **876–879**, *879*
 tests, **899–900**
 types, **867–868**
 vs. upgrading, **866**
 virtualization, **869**
Minimize option for web parts, 173
minor versions
 documents, **358–359**, *358–359*
 elevating to major versions, **370–375**,
  371–372, 374–375
mirroring with Server Farms, 924
missing library files, 369, *369*
Mobile section, 240
mobile users, **920–923**, *920–923*
Modify List RSS Settings page, 257, *257*
Modify Shared Web Part option, 173
Modify the Current Certificate Assignment
  screen, 975, *975*
Modify Web Part menu, 173, *173*
modifying. *See* editing
monitor requirements, 871
monitoring, **711**
 Event Viewer, **729–732**, *729*
 IIS logs, **726–729**, *727–728*
 performance, 25
 Performance Monitor. *See* Performance
  Monitor

more command, 810
MOSS
 with ADAC, 904
 searches, **143**
moving
 services on server farm servers, **933–942**,
  934–938, 941
 web parts, **163**, *163*
MS_WSS folder, 92–93
MS_WSS_ASMIN folder, 92
MSDE database engines, **7**
multi-homed servers, 942, 945
Multicast mode with NLB, 943, 948
MultiPage meeting workspace, **483**, *483*
multiple library file uploading, 327, 341
multiple lines of text
 datasheet view, **232–233**, *232–233*
 list fields, **218**
My Alerts On This Site page, 262, *263*
My Settings page, **140**, *140*, 444
My Tasks view, 271

N
Name and Security screen, 968
names
 certificates, 968
 confirming, 687
 groups, 684
 library, 376–377
 list views, **237–238**
 template, **853**
 users
  collections, 111
  web applications, 532
Navigation settings
 libraries, **377**
 lists, 246
 sites, **421**
.NET Framework 3.0, 5, **35–36**, *36*
Network Connection properties, 943
Network Connections window, 957, *957*
Network Interface counter, 716
network load balancing (NLB), 9, **942–944**
 Central Administration, **960**
 configuring, **944–951**, *945–951*
 host headers, **962**, *962*
 Kerberos with, **961**
 managing, **951–955**, *952–955*

SharePoint configuration for, **955–961**, *956–960*
testing, **957–958**, *957–958*
Network Load Balancing Manager console, 943, 946, **950–955**, *951–955*
network requirements, 23, 871–872
New Alert page, 259, *259*, 263, *263*
New button
 libraries, **154**
 lists, **151**, 205
 for permissions, 667
New Cluster option, 946
New configuration restore option, **608**
New Counter Log dialog box, 715
!New graphic, **837**
New Group page, 684–685, *684–685*
New Host dialog box, 123, *123*
New Item page
 announcements, 205, *206*, 228, *228*
 attendees, 477, *477*
 blogs, 470, *470*
 Calendar events, 266, *266*
 Issue Tracking list, 281, *282*
 links, 268, *268*
 tasks, 269, *270*
New Login window, 40
New menu for groups, 683, *683*
New Object dialog box, 985
New Object-Organizational Unit dialog box, 905
New Object-User dialog box, 38
New Or Existing Meeting Workspace page, 473, *474*
New page for content types, 394, *394*
New Question page, 292–293
New Resource Record dialog box, 124, *124*
New Row list option, 234
New SharePoint Site page, 419, *420*, 442, *442*, 764, *765*
New Site Content Type page, 397, *398*
New SMTP Domain Wizard, 120, *120*
New User dialog box, 906
New Wiki Page page, 468, *469*
New Zone Wizard, 121–122, *121–122*
No Access collection setting, 513
No Access lock state, 645
None–No policy policy, 635
Not Locked lock state, 645

Nothing permission, 542
NTBackup utility, **787–789**
NTLM authentication, 16, 977
number fields for lists, 219

O
obfuscation utilities, 874
Office program for libraries, 380
Online Presence, 217, **623–624**
Open Items permission, **657**
Open permission, **661**
opening libraries with Explorer, 154–155, *155*, **338–343**, *339–341*, 406, *406*
Operation In Progress page, 288
Operations page, **569–571**, *570*
 Alternate Access Mapping, 940, 942, 955
 Backup and Restore category, **602**
  Backup and Restore History page, **605–606**, *605*
  Backup and Restore Status page, 604–605, *604*, **609**
  Perform a Backup settings, **602–605**, *602–603*
 Backup and Restore History page, 737, *737*
 Backup and Restore Status page, 736, *736*, 742
 Data Configuration category, **609–610**, *610*
 distribution groups, 1005, 1009
 DMS, 990
 Global Configuration category. *See* Global Configuration category
 Logging and Reporting category, **581–586**, *582–584*, *586–587*
 in migration, 890, *890*
 moving services, 933
 Restore from Backup page, 739–742, *739–741*
 Security Configuration settings category, **575–581**, *576–581*
 Topology and Services category, **571–575**, *571–574*
Operations settings for outgoing email, 114, 116, *116*
Options dialog box for backups, 782
ordering
 list fields, **224–229**, *227–229*
 view fields, **216–217**, *217*
Organization information screen, 968

Organizational Units (OUs)
  in Active Directory, 904–905
  ADAC, **905**, *906*
  DMS
    creating, **984–985**, *985*
    permissions, **985–989**, *986–989*
  for service accounts, **907–908**, *907–908*
OS report, 448
osql utility, 876, 898
Other Location option, 383, *385*
Outgoing E-Mail Settings page
  Server Farm installation, **114–115**, *114*
  settings, **573**, *573*
outgoing email
  Central Administration, **573**, *573*
  Server Farm installation, **113–116**, *113–115*
  web applications, **528**, *528*, **621–622**, *622*
overlapping permissions, **633**
Override Check Out permission, **657**
-overwrite option, 754
overwriting with Send To feature, 387
-ownerlogin option, 756
-ownermail option, 756
owners, groups, 684

P
packages
  solution, 457
  web parts, 196–197
    adding, **817–820**, *819*
    listing, **820**, *820*
    removing, **820–821**
Page report, 448
page types, **138–139**
Page Viewer web part, 170
Pages/Sec counter, 716
panels, Word, 335
parent sites, 108, 396, 418
passwords
  ADAC mode, 904
  ADAC user accounts, **913–914**, *914*
  certificates, 975–976
  search services, 937
  service accounts, 906
  web applications, 532
PATH variable, **750**

paths
  excluded, 506, **509–511**, *509–510*
  exported certificates, 975
  Form Library, 410–411, *411*
  hyperlinks, 269
  IIS sites, 101, 519
  managed, **21–22**, 499
    collections, **505–508**, *505–508*
    defining, **619–621**, *620–621*
    STSADM, **750**, **808–809**
  UNC, 791
  virtual directories, 780
  WSS 2.0 vs. WSS 3.0, **506**
PDAs, 921
Pending approval state
  distribution groups, 1004
  documents, 370–374, *371–372*
Pending Certificate Request screen, 972
People and Groups page
  ADAC users, 917, *918*
  adding users, 127, *128*
  creating groups, 683, *683*
  distribution group approval, 1005
  distribution groups, 1008
  Farm Administrator's page, **580–581**, *580–581*
  groups, 697, *697*
  ListManagers, 1000, *1000*
  permissions, **423–424**, *423*
  removing from SharePoint groups, **688**, *688*
  viewing people and groups, **149**, *149*, **678–683**, *679–680*, **689–690**, *689–690*
People Picker tool, 314
  ADAC users, 918
  adjusting, **836–837**
Percent Complete field, 271
Perform a Backup page, 602, *602*, 735, *735*
performance
  considerations, **25**
  planning, **23–25**
Performance Monitor, **711–712**, *712*
  alerts, **723–726**, *724–726*
  counters
    adding, **712–714**, *713–715*
    logs, **715–723**, *718–723*
Permission Comments page, 543, *543*
Permission Entry dialog box, 987, *987*
Permission Levels page, 673, *674*

permissions and permission levels, **22**, 127, 129, **663**
  access requests, **667–669**, *667–668*
  applying, **691**
  collections, **501**
  copying, **671–673**, *672–673*
  creating, **673–675**
  deciding on, **708–709**
  default, **456**, **663–665**
  defined, **654–655**
  editing, **669–671**, *669–671*
  Explorer, **339–340**
  groups, 685
  vs. hierarchical levels, 703
  inheritance, **691–694**, *691–694*, **707**
  libraries, **543–545**, **701–705**, *701–705*
  links, **247**
  lists
    anonymous access, **543–545**, *543–546*
    changing, **701–705**, *701–705*
    Contacts, 309, *310*
    managing, 208
    overview, **656–658**, *656*
  login, **699–700**, *700*
  managing, **666**
  migration, 871
  OUs, **985–989**, *986–989*
  overlapping, **633**
  People and Groups page, **423–424**, *423*
  personal, **662–663**, *662*
  policies, **629–635**, *632–636*, **858**
  site, *455*, **456**, **658–662**, *658*
  STSADM for, **858**
  subsites, **694–699**, *695–699*
  viewing, **666–667**, *666*
  web applications, **540–543**, *541*, *543–546*, 706
  workspaces, *455*, **456**
Permissions for this List link, **247**
Permissions page, 424, *424*, 666–667, *666*
Person Name Smart Tag and Presence Settings
    option, 529–530, **622–624**, *623–624*
Person or Group field, **219**
Personal permissions, **662–663**, *662*
Personal version
  editing in, 185
  web parts in, 162
Personalize This Page link, **141**, *141*
.pfx files, 975

Physical Disk performance object, 716
picture fields for lists, **219**
picture libraries
  headings, **148–149**
  overview, **405–407**, *405–406*
  purpose, **324**
ping command, 952–955, *953–954*
policies
  anonymous access, **544–545**
  permissions, **858**
  web applications, **629–635**, *630–636*, **706**
  zones, **557**, *557*
Policy For Web Application page, 500, **629–635**, *629*, *634*
popups, Word, 335
Port Rules, **944**, 948
Portal Site Connection page, 463–464, *464*, **504**
PortQuery tool, 65–66, *65–66*
PortQueryUI tool, 66
ports
  Central Administration, **53–55**, *54–55*
  Kerberos, 977
  Server Farm installation, **65–66**, *65–66*
  sites, 101, 463–464, *464*, 519
  SSL traffic, **965–967**, *966*
  web applications, 742
post installation server farm configuration
    tasks, **113**
  incoming email, **116–119**, *116–117*
  outgoing email, **113–116**, *113–115*
  safe email servers, **119–127**, *120–126*
  users, **127–130**, *128–129*
post-update migration steps, **899–900**
posts, blogs, 470–471, *470–471*
pre-master SSL keys, 961
prebuilt lists
  Calendar, **264–266**, *265–267*
  links, **267–273**, *268*, *270*
  modifying, **264**
  Team Discussion, **273–278**, *275–277*
Prescan utility, **878**, *879*, 896, *896*
Preview Pane style, 239
Primary Site Collection Administrator, **110–111**, **499**
Priority field for tasks, 269
private SSL keys, 961
Processor performance object, 716
Processor Queue Length counter, 716

processor requirements, 23
%processor time_total counter, 716
Project Task template, 279
Protected mode in Explorer, 338
protectors, IRM, 577
Provide Row option, 319
providers, authentication, **637–638**, *637–638*
provisioning, 930
Provisionservice operation, 861
PSCONFIG command, **87–89**
public SSL keys, 961
public URLs
    adding, **559**, *559*
    creating, **552–554**, *554*
    deleting, **559–560**, *560*
    working with, **592–597**, *593–595*
Publishing Wizard dialog box, 411, *411–413*

Q
Queries Failed counter, 717
Queries Succeeded counter, 717
Question page, 292–293, *292*
questions for survey lists, **291–297**, *292*, *294–297*
Quick Launch bar, **138**, **146**, *146*
    Documents, Lists, Discussions, and Sites
        links, **148**
    People and Groups link, **149**, *149*
    View All Site Content link, **146–147**, *147–148*
Quick Launch link, **434–436**, *434–436*
Quick Start Guide, 93
Quota Template field, **499**
Quota Templates page, 511–512, *511*, **644–645**,
    644, 919, *920*
quotas and quota templates
    collections
        applying, **499**, **512–513**, *512*, **645–646**, *646*
        creating, **511–512**, *511*, **644–646**, *644*
        settings, **111–115**, *112*, 919, *920*
    web applications, 529

R
RAM requirements, 23
Read First task, **93–94**, *93*
Read Only lock state, 645
Read-Only setting
    collections, 513
    content type, 399
Read permission, 456, **665**

Really Simple Syndication (RSS)
    feeds, **248**, **256–258**, *257–258*
    permitting, 625
    settings, **451–453**, *451–453*
    web applications, 530
Records Center, **647**, *648*
recovery scenarios, **795**, **798–802**
Recycle Bin
    collections, **459**, *460*, **503**, 625
    recovering items from, **298–299**, *299*, **770**
    security for, **149–150**
    web applications, **533–534**
Recycle Bin setting, 625
recycling content, **273–274**
Referrer URL report, 448
Refresh Data option, **234**
Refreshdms operation, 861
Refreshsitedms operation, 861
Regional Settings page, **443–445**, *444–445*
Registerwsswriter operation, 861
regression tests, **873**
Rejected approval state, 1004
Related Issues field, 283, *283*
Relay Restrictions dialog box, 124–125, *125*
Relevant Documents tool pane, **173–174**, *173*, *175*
Relevant Documents web part, **170**
relinking
    content type, 402
    with Send To feature, 389
Remove SharePoint From IIS Web Site page,
    559, *560*, **617–618**, *618*
Remove Users from Group option, 679
Removedrservice operation, 861
Removesolutiondeploymentlock operation, 822
removing. *See* deleting
Renameserver operation, 862
Renameweb operation, 849, **854**
renaming sites, **854**
replacing library templates, **379–383**, *379*, *382*
replying in Team Discussion lists, **276–277**,
    276–277
Request Access page, 668, *668*
Request File Summary screen, 969, *969*
requests, certificate, **970–972**, *970–971*
Require Check Out setting, **343–344**, *344*
Require Secure Channel (SSL) option, 974, *974*,
    976
required library fields, **332–338**, *333–337*

required permissions, 656
requirements
  hardware, **22–23**
  libraries, 324–325
  migration, **871–872**
Reset Internet Information Services setting, **521**
Reset Page Content option, **167**, *168*
Reset Services Warning dialog box, 62, *62*
resetting site definitions, **437–439**, *438–439*
Restart Internet Information Services section,
  104–107, *105–106*
Restore And Media tab, 784, *784*, 789
Restore from Backup page, **606–609**, *606–609*,
  739–742, *739–741*
Restore Settings page, 741, *741*
restores
  ASR backups, **801–802**
  best practices, **771**
  collections, **750–751**, *750–751*, 840–841
  configuration files, **775–777**, *775–777*, 788
  database
    catastrophic, **842**, *842*
    sites, 840–841
    SQL, **792–795**, *793–794*
    standalone servers, **788–789**, *788*
  to farms, **798**
  IIS metabase, **773**, *773*, 795, 797
  lists and library from templates, **768–770**,
    769–770
  operations, **840–843**
  process, **606–609**, *606–609*, **738–746**, *739–741*
  recovery scenarios, **795**, **798–802**
  subsites to templates, **763–766**, *763–766*
  in versioning, **362–365**, *364*
  virtual directories, **783–784**, *783–784*, 796–797
  web applications, **775–777**, *775–777*, **798**
Retract Solution page, 601, *601*
Retractsolution operation, 822, 824
Retractwppack operation, 818, **820–821**
Retrieve Database Names option, 925
reuse of content, **273–274**
Rich Text Editor window, 178, *179*
rollbacks in migration, **874**
RSS (Really Simple Syndication)
  feeds, **248**, **256–258**, *257–258*
  permitting, 625
  settings, **451–453**, *451–453*
  web applications, 530

S
safe email servers, **119–127**, *120–126*
Same configuration restore option, **608–609**
sampling counter data, 717
Save As Template page, 767, *767*
Save Configuration to a File dialog box,
  774–775, *775*
Save Host List option, 950
Save List as Template link, **246–247**
Save Site as Template page, 437, *437*, 759,
  760
saving
  configuration files, **774–775**, *774–775*
  sites as templates, **436–437**, *437*, 759, *760*
Scanforfeatures operation, 823, 827
Schedule tab, 720, *721*, 725
Scheduled Task Wizard, 744–746, *745*
Scheduled Tasks dialog box, *745*
schedules
  alerts, 725
  backups, **744–746**, *745*
  logs, 720, *721*
  timed jobs, **587–589**, *588*, **835–836**
scope creep, 873
scripting, **811–813**
search accounts, **12**, 43
search and search servers, **16–20**, *17*
  in Basic installation, 56
  Central Administration, 566
  Contacts list, 310
  content databases, 538
  in help, **137**, **142–143**
  and Help Search service, **939**
  libraries, **380–381**
  moving, **933–942**, *934–938*, *941*
  multiple, **939–940**
  overview, **16–20**, *17*
  passwords, 937
  Server Farm installation, 81, **94–99**, *95–98*
  STSADM for, **843–848**, *846–847*
  visibility, **454**, *454*
  web applications, **104**, *105*, **522–525**, *523–525*
Search Database settings, 936
Search field, **137**, **142–143**
Search Visibility page, **454**, *454*
Secondary Site Collection Administrator
  section, 111
Secure Communications dialog box, 974, *974*

Secure Sockets Layer (SSL), 102, 520, **961–962**
  certificates. *See* certificates
  configuring, **964–974**, *966–974*
  web applications, **962–964**, *963–964*
security
  Active Directory, **707**
  antivirus, **578**, *578*
  Application Security section. *See* Application
    Security section
  blocked file types, **578–580**, *579*
  content approval, 373
  Farm Administrators group, **580–581**, *580*
  IRM, **577**, *577*
  permissions. *See* permissions and permission
    levels
  Recycle Bin, **149–150**
  safe email servers, **119–127**, *120–126*
  service accounts, **575–576**, *576–577*
  STSADM for, **854–859**, *857*
  templates, 760
  trimming, 20
  web applications
    anonymous access, **540–546**, *541–546*
    Kerberos for, **980–983**, *980–983*
    settings, **101–102**, **519–520**, *519*
    validation, **532**
  zones, **596–597**
Security Configuration section, 963, *963*
Security Configuration settings category,
  575–581, *576–581*
Security for Web Part Pages page, **628**
Security groups, 654
Security tab, 985, *986*
Select Backup Destination dialog box,
  791, *791*
Select Backup Location page, 606, *606*
Select Backup to Restore page, 606, *607*
Select Component to Restore page, 607, *607*
Select Group dialog box, 38, *38*
Select People and Groups dialog box, 918, *919*
Select People page, 678, *678*
Select Restore Options page, 608, *608*
Select Server page, 572, *573*, 935–936, *935*
Select Site Collection page, 641, *641*
Select User, Computer, or Group dialog box,
  987
Select Users, Computers, and Groups dialog
  box, 907, *907*

Select Users, Contacts, or Computers dialog
  box, 989
Select Web Application page, 523, *523*
Self-Service Site Creation feature
  blocking, **662**
  creating collections, **493–496**, *494–495*
  enabling, **491–492**, *492–493*
  web applications, **525–528**, *526–527*
Self-Service Site Management page, 526, *526*,
  628, *629*
self-service sites, **419**
Send Alerts for These Changes trigger, 260
Send In A Daily Summary alert option, 260
Send In A Weekly Summary alert option,
  260
Send To feature for libraries, **331**, **383**
  capabilities, **383**
  Create Document Workspace option, **383**
  Download a Copy option, **383–384**
  Email a Link option, 383
  guidelines, **391–393**, *391–393*
  Other Location option, **383**, *385*
  picture, 406
  steps, **384–391**, *385–391*
Send User Name and Password in E-mail
  setting, **532**, 625
sending content to lists and libraries, **996–998**,
  997–998
Server Admin templates, 484–485, **487–490**,
  488–490
Server Certificate screen, 967, 975
server databases
  backups, **785–788**, *785–786*
  default, **609**
  restores, **788–789**, *788*
  web applications, 104
Server Farms, 7–9, *8*
  accounts, **12**, **37–42**, *37–42*
  advanced installation, **57–64**, *58*, *60–63*
  backups, **798–802**, *800*, *802*
  Central Administration, **66–70**, *67–68*, *70*
  collections, **111–115**, *112*
  database creation, **74–80**, *75–80*
  DCOM problems, **83–86**, *83–85*
  finalizing installation, **88–89**, *89*
  help, **90–93**, *91–92*
  IIS in, **77–80**, *78–80*
  index files, **86**, *86*

management features, **597–598**, *598*

NLB. *See* network load balancing (NLB)

post installation configuration tasks, **113**
  incoming email, **116–119**, *116–117*
  outgoing email, **113–116**, *113–115*
  safe email servers, **119–127**, *120–126*
  users, **127–130**, *128–129*

PSCONFIG command, **87–89**

restores to, **798**

search, **94–99**, *95–98*

server additions, **923–924**
  Central Administration, **931–933**, *932*
  confirming, **928–930**, *928–929*
  IIS effects, **930–931**, *931*
  process, **924–928**, *925–927*
  services on, **933–942**, *934–938, 941*

services, **80–82**

SQL databases
  backups, **789–792**, *790–792*
  restores, **792–795**, *793–794*

STSADM tool, **859–862**

templates
  adding, **814–815**, *815*
  listing, **815–816**, *815*

web applications, **99–104**, *100, 105–109*, **107–109**

Server Performance Advisor, 722, 729

Server Property fields, 335

Server Type screen, 58, *58*, 885, *885*

Servers in Farm page, **571–572**, *571*

Service Accounts page, **575–576**, *576*

service principal names (SPNs), 961
  Kerberos, 977–978
  Setspn for, **978–979**, *978–979*

services
  accounts
    ADAC, **906–908**, *907–908*, 919
    installation, **11–13**, **42–45**, *43*
    OU for, **907–908**, *907–908*
    search, 936
    security, **575–576**, *576–577*
  in Basic installation, **55–56**
  data retrieval, **609–610**, *610*
  external connections, **647–650**, *648–649*
  IIS, **104–107**, *105–106*
  required, **13–14**
  server, **572**, *572*

Server Farms
  installation, **80–82**
  server additions, **933–942**, *934–938, 941*
  SharePoint as, 577

Services on Server page
  enabling services, 931, *932*
  managing services, **572**, *572*, 929–930, *929*
  moving services, 933–935, *934–935*, 937, *937*

session IDs, 977

session keys, 961

Set Target Web Application page, 890, *891*

Set Up Groups option, 682, *682*

Set Up Groups pages, 697, *697*

Set Up Groups For This Site page, 494–495, *495*

Set Your Calendar setting, 445

Setadminport operation, 862

Setapppassword operation, 862

Setconfigdb operation, 839

Setlogginglevel operation, 859, 862

Setproperty operation, 813, 830, **834–837**, **862**

Setsitelock operation, 856, 858–859

Setspn command, **978–979**, *978–979*

Settings button
  libraries, 155–156
  lists, 152, **205**
  for permissions, 667

setup accounts
  in installation, **11–12**, **37–42**, *37–42*
  SQL, **64**

Setup Errors window, 872, *872*

Setworkflowconfig operation, 862

severity levels for events, 583

shareadmin account, **44**

Shared Documents library, **152–156**, *153, 155, 325, 325*

Shared Documents list, 169, 278–279

Shared Documents page, 325–326, *326*, 353, *353*

Shared views, **168**

SharePoint_AdminContent_(GUID) database, 10

SharePoint_Config_(GUID) database, 10

SharePoint groups, **654–655**

SharePoint Products And Technologies Configuration Wizard, 47, *47*
  in-place migration, 881–882, *882*
  server farms
    installation, 60–63, *61–64*
    server additions, 924–928, *925–927*

SharePoint Search Archival Plugin performance object, 717
SharePoint Search Gatherer performance object, 717
SharePoint Search Indexer Catalog performance object, 717
SharePoint site, **9**
SharePoint Site Management section, **639**
  Create Site Collection page, **640**, *640*
  Delete Site Collection page, **640–642**, *641*
  Quota Templates page, **644–645**, *644*
  Site Collection Administrators page, **646**, *646*
  Site Collection List page, **647**, *647*
  Site Collection Quotas And Locks page, **645–646**, *645*
  Site Use Confirmation And Deletion page, **642–643**, *643*
sharing list fields, 220
Show in Standard View option, 234
Sign In As Different User option, 140
Sign Out page, 140, *141*
single lines of text
  custom lists, **314–315**
  list fields, **218**
single server installations, **7**
  advanced, **7–8**, *8*
  Basic install, **6**
  recovery scenario, **795–796**
Site Actions menu, **137–138**, **143–145**, *144–145*
Site Admin templates, **484–486**, *486*
site administrators
  collections, **499–501**
  editing, **676–678**, *677–678*
Site and Workspace Creation page, 455, *455*
Site Collection Administrators page, **646**, *646*, 677–678, *677*
site collection-centric accounts, 903
Site Collection Features page, 488, *489*
Site Collection Gallery, 169
Site Collection List page, **647**, *647*
Site Collection Quotas and Locks page, 512, *512*, **645–646**, *645*
Site Collection Recycle Bin, **459**, *460*
Site Collection Upgrade page, 891, *892*
Site Collection Usage Summary, **461–462**, *461*
site columns, **441**
  Contacts list, **302–307**, *303–307*
  custom lists, **315–318**, *316–318*

Site Columns Gallery page, 305, *305*
Site Content Type page, 398, *399*
Site Content Type Advanced Settings page, 399, *400*
Site Content Upgrade Status page, 890, *890*
Site Features page, *488*, 489, **597–598**, *598*
Site Hierarchy setting, 463, *463*, **504**
Site Libraries and Lists section, **445–446**, *446*
Site name Members group, 655
Site name Owners group, 655
Site name Readers group, 655
Site Settings page, 145, *145*
  collection administrators, 676–677, *677*
  collections, 458, *459*
  galleries, 189, *190*, 397, *397*
Site Template Gallery
  collections, 502, *502–503*
  deleting templates, **762**, *762*
  exporting templates, **761–762**, *761*
  Site Admin templates, 486, *486*
  template selection, 442, *442*
Site Themes, **429–431**, *430–431*
Site Usage Report page, 447–448, *448–449*, 586, *587*
Site Use Confirmation and Deletion page, **514–516**, *515*, **642–643**, *643*
Site User web part, **169–170**
Siteowner operation, 856
sites
  administration, **443**
    Regional Settings page, **443–445**, *444–445*
    Site Libraries and Lists section, **445–446**, *446*
    usage reports, **446–450**, *447–450*
  alerts, 450, *451*
  blogs, **470–471**, *470–471*
  vs. collections, 642
  collections. *See* collections
  creating, **419–421**, *419–420*, *422*, **852–854**
  definitions, 198, 417
    resetting, **437–439**, *438–439*
    vs. site templates, **438–439**
  deleting, **457**, *457–458*, 492, *493*, **854**
  document workspace, **465–466**, *465–466*
  features, **456–457**, 489
  galleries, **439–443**, *440–442*
  hierarchy, 463, *463*
  listing, **850–851**

locks, **858–859**
management
   central. *See* SharePoint Site Management
    section
   STSADM for, **848–852**, *850*
meeting workspaces, **472–475**, *472–475*
   Basic, **475–477**
   Decision, **481**, *482*
   MultiPage, **483**, *483*
   Social, **480**, *481*
   URLs, **481**
permissions, **658–662**, *658*
ports, 463–464, *464*
Quick Launch link, **434–436**, *434–436*
renaming, **854**
RSS, **451–453**, *451–453*
search visibility, **454**, *454*
Self-Service Site Creation, **491–496**, *492–496*
settings, **422–423**, *422*
Team, **464**
templates
   adding, **486**, *486*
   application, **484–491**, *485–486*, *488–490*
   creating, **760–761**, *761*
   default names, **853**
   exporting, **761–762**, *762*
   purpose, **441–442**, *442*, 502, *502–503*
   saving sites as, **436–437**, *437*
   vs. site definitions, **438–439**
   STSADM management, **814–817**, *815–816*
themes, **429–431**, *430–431*
Title, Description, and Icon section, **425**, *425*
Top Link bar, **431–433**, *432–433*
Tree view, **426–429**, *426–429*
Wiki, **466–469**, *467–470*
workspaces, **455–456**, *455*
Sites and Workspaces page, 419, *420*, **455–456**, *455*
Sites link, 148
Sites Selected For Upgrade page, 892, *892*
size
   exported files, 754
   files, **876**
   templates, **758–759**
   upload, **530**
Slideshow view, 406
smart tags, 529–530
SmartPhones, 921

SMTP, **32–35**, *33–35*, 249
SMTP mail server for incoming email setting, 991
Social meeting workspace, **480**, *481*
software
   limitations, **27–29**
   migration, **872**, *872*
   requirements, **4–6**
Solution Management page, **599–601**, *599–600*
solution packages, 457
Solution Properties page, 487, *488*, 600, *600*
solutions
   adding, **823–824**, *824*
   deleting, **824**, **828**
   deployment, 600–601, *600*, **824–826**, *825*
   installing, **827–828**
   listing, **823–824**, *824*
   overview, **827–828**
   with STSADM, **821–826**, *824–825*
   upgrading, **826**
Sort Order setting, 444
Sort section in list views, **238**
SPAdmin service, 13
   Basic installation, 56
   on new servers, 930
   Server Farm installation, 81
Special Content Types section, 396
Specify Configuration Database Settings page
   gradual migration, 886, *886*
   Server Farms
    installation, 63, *63*
    server additions, 925–926, *926*
SPNs (service principal names), 961
   Kerberos, 977–978
   Setspn for, **978–979**, *978–979*
Spsearch operation, **843–848**
SPSearch service, 13
   Basic installation, 56
   on new servers, 930
   Server Farm installation, 81
Spsearchdiacriticsensitive operation, 844
SPTimerV3 service, **13**
   Basic installation, 56
   on new servers, 930
   Server Farm installation, 81
SPTrace service, 13
   Basic installation, 56
   Server Farm installation, 81

SPWriter service, 14, 56
SQL 2005 Management Studio, 108
SQL databases, 13
    backups, **789–792**, *790–792*
    restores, **792–795**, *793–794*
    setup accounts for, **64**
SQL Server 2005 Surface Area Configuration
        window, 41–42, *41–42*
SQL Server Embedded Edition (SSEE), **5–7**, 50,
    51
SQL Server requirements, **5**
Sqlcmd utility, 876, 899
SSL (Secure Sockets Layer), 102, 520, **961–962**
    certificates. *See* certificates
    configuring, **964–974**, *966–974*
    web applications, **962–964**, *963–964*
stand-alone installation, **7–8**, *8*, **59**
standalone servers, **11–12**
    databases
        backups, **785–788**, *785–786*
        restores, **788–789**, *788*
Standard view for lists, 237
standard website certificates, 961
Start action, 846
Start Backup page, 603, *603*, **734–735**, *736*
Start Date field
    Gantt view, 271
    Tasks lists, 270
Status field for tasks, 269
Status Report template, 410, *411*
status reports for distribution groups, 1009
Stop action, 846
storage
    collection statistics, 461
    planning, **25–27**
Storage Limit Values section, **644**
Storage Space Allocation page, **462**, *462*
Storage Space Allocation reports, **503–504**
STSADM tool, **807**
    backups, **746–748**, *747–748*
    collections, **912**, *912*
    database management, **837–843**, *842*
    exporting and importing collections and
        subsites, **751–758**, *753*, *755–757*
    farm management, **859–862**
    for features, **826–828**
    inline help, **810–811**, *810–811*
    paths, **750**, *808–809*

restores, **750–751**, *750*
    scripting for, **811–813**
    search management, **843–848**, *846–847*
    search service, 940
    security management, **854–859**, *857*
    setup information, **808–810**, *808–809*
    site and subweb management, **848–852**, *850*
    site template management, **814–817**, *815–816*
    for solutions, **821–826**, *824–825*
    tasks, **813**
    web applications, **828–837**, *831–832*
    web parts, **817–821**, *819–820*
Style section for list views, 239
Subject field
    Team Discussion lists, 275
    Tracking lists, 287, *287*
subnet masks, NLB, 950
subsites, 418, 642
    backups, **758–762**, *759–762*
    exporting and importing, **751–758**, *753*,
        755–757
    groups for, **696–699**, *697–699*
    permissions, **694–699**, *695–699*
    restoring to templates, **763–766**, *763–766*
subweb management, **848–852**, *850*
summaries for alerts option, 260, *261*
Summary of Selections page, 33, *33*
surveys, **148–149**, **291–292**
    branching logic, **294–295**, *294*
    creating, **292–293**, *292*, *294*
    template for, 279
    using, **295–297**, *295–297*
Syncsolution operation, 822
System Monitor, 712, *712*
    counters
        adding, **712–714**, *713–715*
        logs, **715–723**, *718–723*
System performance object, 716

T
tags
    Person Name Smart Tag and Presence
        settings, 529–530, **622–624**, *623–624*
    web applications, 529–530
Task page, 99, *100*
Task pane, 234, *234*
tasks and Tasks lists
    Decision meeting workspace, 481, *482*

lists, 169
modifying, **269–273**, *270*, *272*
STSADM tool, **813**
template, 278
Tracking lists, 289–290, *289–290*
Tasks To Delegate screen, 908, *908*
TCP/IP information
mobile users, 921
NLB, 944
Team Discussion lists, 169
modifying, **273–278**, *275–277*
settings, **151–152**, *151*
template, 279
Team Discussion page, **151–152**, *151*
Team Services, **865**
Team site, **464**
Team Site Members group, 917, *918*
Template Name section, **644**
Template Selection section, **110**, **499**
templates
application, **484**
Server Admin, **487–490**, *488–490*
Site Admin, **484–486**, *485–486*
collection quotas, **111–115**, *112*
collections, 913
default names, **853**
deleting, **762**, *762*, **816**, *816*
forms as, 410
vs. importing and exporting, 751
libraries, **378–383**, *379*, *382*
backups to, **766–768**, *767–768*
restores from, **768–770**, *769–770*
limitations, **436**
for lists
backups to, **766–768**, *767–768*
creating, **278–279**
restores from, **768–770**, *769–770*
saving as, **246–247**, **443**
meetings, 473, *474*
Self-Service Site Creation, 526
server farms
adding, **814–815**, *815*
listing, **815–816**, *815*
site, 417
adding, 486, *486*
creating, **760–761**, *761*
default names, **853**
exporting, **761–762**, *762*

purpose, **441–442**, *442*, 502, *502–503*
saving sites as, **436–437**, *437*
vs. site definitions, **438–439**
STSADM management, **814–817**, *815–816*
size limits, **758–759**
subsite
backups for, **758–762**, *759–762*
restores to, **763–766**, *763–766*
Wikis and Workspaces, 758
tests
migration, **899–900**
NLB, **957–958**, *957–958*
regression, **873**
text fields
custom lists, **314–315**
Datasheet view, **232–233**, *232–233*
lists, **218**
themes, sites, **429–431**, *430–431*
third-party Certificate Authorities, 964–965
Threaded view, 277
Three-State workflow, **284–291**, *285–291*
throttling events, **582–585**, *582–583*
ticket-based system authentication, 16, 977
time
list fields, 219
setting, **835–836**
Time Format setting, 445
Time Zone setting, 445
time zones
setting, 445
web applications, 529
timed jobs, **835–836**
Timer category in error monitoring, **732**
Timer Job Definitions page, **589–591**, *589*, 604
Timer Job Status page, **587–589**, *588*, 604
timer service
Basic installation, 56
email, 117
and EXECADMSVCJOBS, 821
Server Farm installation, 81
Title, Description, and Icon section, **425**, *425*
Title and Description section, 110
Title field
Gantt view, 271
lists, 246, 269
titles
collections, 110, 499
sites, **425**, *425*

Top Level Site Successfully Created page, 111, *112*
top-level sites, 418
Top Link bar, **137**, **431–433**, *432–433*
topology, server farms, 928–929, *928*
Topology and Services category, **571–575**, *571–574*
Totals option for lists, 234
Totals section in list views, **239**, *241*
Trace Logging level, **859–860**
trace logs, **583–584**
tracing service
   Basic installation, 56
   Server Farm installation, 81
Tree view in sites, **426–429**, *426–429*
triggers for alerts, 260, **723–725**
trusted for delegation rights, 977

U
UNC paths, 791
undoing web part changes, **167**
Unextendvs operation, 830, **833**
Unicast Mode with NLB, 943, 948
Uninstallfeature operation, 823
Unknown Content Type, 396
unlinking with Send To, 384, 389
unprovisioning, 840
unpublishing major versions, **361–362**, *362*
Unregisterwsswriter operation, 863
Update Copies page, 389, *390*
Update Farm Administrator's Group link, **580–581**
Update Personal Web Parts permission, **663**
Update section in Send To, 386
Update Sites and Lists section, 400
Updateaccountpassword operation, 863
Updatealerttemplates operation, 863
Updatefarmcredentials operation, 863
-updateversions option in STSADM, 757
Upgrade Earlier Versions page, 884, *884*, 894, *895*
Upgrade Job Monitor page, 883, *883*
Upgrade Running page, 883, *884*, 892–893, *893*
Upgradesolution operation, 822
Upgradetargetwebapplication operation, 830
upgrading
   vs. migration, **866**

migration. *See* migration from WSS 2.0 to WSS 3.0
solutions, **826**
Upload button, 154
upload size setting, **530**
Upload Template page, 763, *763*
Upload Web Part page, 190, *191*
uploading
   library files, **326–328**, *327–328*, 341
   site templates, **763–764**, *763*
   size limitations, **530**
-url option in STSADM, 753, 756–757
URLs
   Alternate Access Mapping, **591–597**, *591*, *593–595*, 940–942, *941*
   certificates, 961–962
   host headers, 547–550, *548*
   meeting workspaces, **481**
   mobile users, 920–921
   NLB, 948, 955–956, *956*, 958–960, *959–960*
   public
      adding, **559**, *559*
      creating, **552–554**, *554*
      deleting, **559–560**, *560*
      working with, **592–597**, *593–595*
   Referrer URL report, 448
   Send To feature, 384–385
   for SSL, 966
   web applications, **551–552**, *551*
      changes with, **554–555**, *556*
      internal, **558–559**, *558*
      load balanced, **102–103**, *103*
      public, **552–554**, *554*, **559–560**, *559–560*
Usage Analysis Processing page
   collection settings, **503**
   site usage reports, 446–447, *447*, **585–586**, *586*
usage logs, 25
usage reports
   collections, **461–462**, *461*
   sites, **446–450**, *447–450*, **585–586**, *586*
Use an Existing Site option, **101**
Use Client Integration Features permission, **661**
Use Existing Application Pool option, 103
Use Remote Interfaces permission, **661**
Use Secure Sockets Layer (SSL) option, 102, 520
Use Self-Service Site Creation permission, **660**, **662**

Use SharePoint Directory Management Service to create distribution groups and contacts? option, 990
user alerts, 262, *262*, 450, *451*, **530**
User Alerts page, 450, *451*
user-aware web parts, **171–172**, *171–172*
User Information page, 262, *262*, 916, *917*
User Permissions for Web Application page, 629, 656, *656*, 664, *664*
User report, 448
User Tasks web part, **170**
Userrole operation, 856–857
Users and Groups screen, 907, *907*
users and user accounts, **653**
    access. *See* access
    account modes, **14**
    ADAC
        collections, **913–915**, *913–915*
        creating, **915–920**, *916–920*
        mobile, **920–923**, *920–923*
    adding
        to groups, **686–687**, *686–688*
        in installation, **127–130**, *128–129*
    collections, 461
    defined, **653–655**
    names
        ADAC mode, 903–904
        collections, 111
        server farm accounts, 926, 987
        web applications, 532
    overview, **675–676**
    permissions, **22**
        collections, **501**
        web applications, 629
    removing from groups, **679–680**, *679*
    STSADM for, **856–857**
    viewing, **678–683**, *679–682*, **689–690**, *689–690*

V
values, alert, 723
variables, script, 812
Versioning Settings page, 246
versions and versioning
    confirming in, 364
    history, 377
    library files, **355–357**, *356–357*
        limitations, **365**
        major versions, **359–362**, *360–362*

minor versions, **358–359**, *358–359*
        restoring, **362–365**, *364*
    lists, 246, **254**
    vs. views, 161
    Wiki sites, 468, *470*
-versions option in STSADM, 754
Versions Saved page, 359–360, *359–360*
View All Site Content link, **146–147**, *148–149*
View Application Pages permission, **658**
View Group Permissions option, 681, *681*
View Item option, 1006
View Item page, 208
View Items permission, 544, **657**
View menu
    libraries, **156**
    lists, 152, **271**
View Pages permission, **660**
View Properties option, 330
View Slideshow option, 406
View Usage Data permission, **659**
View Versions permission, **658**
viewing
    certificates, 972, *972*
    libraries, **338–343**, *339–341*
    list items, **208–212**, *209–212*
    permissions, **666–667**, *666*
    users and groups, **678–683**, *679–682*, **689–690**, *689–690*
views and view lists, 201–202
    distribution groups, 1006–1007
    fields, **215**, *215*
    filtering by category, **243–244**, *243–244*
    grouping by category, **236–243**, *237*, *241–242*
    modifying, **213–217**, *213–217*
    vs. versions, 161
virtual directories
    backups, **777–783**, *779–782*
    paths, 780
    restores, **783–784**, *783–784*, 796–797
Virtual IPs (VIPs), 942, 944, 947–948, 953
virtual servers, 4, 824
virtualization in migration, **869**
viruses, **578**, *578*
Volume Shadow Copy Service (VSS), 731
VSS Writer service
    Basic installation, 56
    Server Farm installation, 81

W

warnings
 language pack, 882, *883*
 services, 62, *62*
 version, **363**
Web Application General Settings page, 492, *493*
Web Application List page, 628
Web Application menu, 109
Web Application Outgoing E-Mail Settings page, **621–622**, *622*
web applications, 4, **516**, *517*
 access, **540**
  collections, **540–542**, *551–552*
  lists and libraries, **543–545**, *543–546*
 alternate access mapping. *See* Alternate Access Mapping (AAM)
 Application Pool section, **102–103**
 authentication, **637–638**, *637–638*
 backups, **774–775**, *774–775*
 blocked file types, **534–535**, *535*
 content databases, **535–540**, *536–539*, **625–628**, *627–628*
 creating
  for blogs, **517–525**, *518–519*, *521–525*
  settings, **616**, *616*
  STSADM, **830–833**, *831–832*
 deleting, **533–534**, *533*, **618**, *619*, **833**
 extending, 553, *554*, **617**, *617*, **832–833**
 features, **534**, *534*, **628**
 host headers, **547–550**, *547–550*
 IIS, **554–555**
 IIS sites for, **101**, **518–523**, *519*, *521–523*
 listing, 628, **833–834**, *833*
 managed paths, **619–621**, *620–621*
 management and maintenance, **834–835**
 people picker properties, **836–837**
 policies, **629–635**, *630–636*, **706**
 ports, 742
 removing, **617–618**, *618*, **833**
 restores, **775–777**, *775–777*, **798**
 search servers, **104**, *105*, **522–525**, *523–525*
 security
  anonymous access, **540–546**, *541–546*
  Kerberos for, **980–983**, *980–983*
  settings, **101–102**, **519–520**, *519*
  validation, **532**
 Server Farm installation, **99–104**, *100*

 settings, **525**
  General, **528–533**, *529*, **622–625**, *623–624*
  outgoing email, **528**, *528*, **621–622**, *622*
  Self-Service Site Creation, **525–528**, *526–527*
 SSL for, **962–964**, *963–964*
 STSADM for, **828–837**, *831–832*
 timed jobs, **835–836**
 URLs, **550–552**, *551*
  changes with, **554–555**, *556*
  internal, **558–559**, *558*
  load balanced, **102–103**, *103*
  public, **552–554**, *554*, **559–560**, *559–560*
 user access, **706–709**
Web Front End installs, *8*, **9**
web front end servers in recovery scenario, **797**
Web Page Security Validation setting, 625
Web Part Gallery page, 191, *191–192*
Web Part tool pane, **173–174**, *173*, *177*
web parts, 25, **138**, **159–160**, *160*
 adding, **196–198**
 backing up, 183
 built-in
  adding, **176**, *177*
  configuring, **176–181**, *179–181*
 for Calendar View, 264
 default, **169–171**
 deleting, **195–196**
 Edit mode, **161–162**, *162*
 exporting, **181–183**, *183*
 galleries for, 168
 importing
  to collection galleries, **189–192**, *190–192*
  to single page, **184–188**, *184–189*
 List View, **166–167**, *166–167*
 lists and libraries, 169
  adding, **166–167**, *166–167*
  connections, **318–321**, *319–321*
 migration, **874**
 moving, **163**, *163*
 packages
  adding, **817–820**, *819*
  listing, **820**, *820*
  removing, **820–821**
 removing from zones, **164**, *165*
 security, **628**
 STSADM for, **817–821**, *819–820*
 undoing changes, **167**, *168*
 user-aware, **171–172**, *171–172*

Web Parts Gallery, 443
Web Server Certificate Wizard, **967–970**, *967–969*, 972, 974–976, *975–976*
Web Service performance object, 717
Web Site Address section for collections, 110
Web Site tab, 726, *727*
weekly alert summaries, 260
Welcome menu, **139–141**, *139–141*
Wiki libraries, **324**
    backing up to templates, **766–768**, *767–768*
    content, **408**, *408*
    creating, **407**, *407*
    documents, **408–410**, *409*
    restoring from templates, **768–770**, *769–770*
Wiki sites, **466–469**, *467–470*
Wiki templates, 758
wildcard certificates, 961
Wildcard managed paths, **506–507**, *507–508*
Windows authentication, 15, 638
Windows Certificate Authority console, 964
Windows Component Wizard, 34–35
Windows Explorer, 154–155, 406, *406*
Windows Live Writer, **530–532**, *531–532*
Windows Mobile users, **920–923**, *920–923*
Windows SharePoint Services Incoming
        E-Mail, 930
Windows SharePoint Services Web
        Application, 930
Windows Workflow Foundation, **5**
WMSDE, **7**
WMSDE to WID migration, **898–899**
Word application
    document editing, **334–338**, *334–337*
    panels and popups, 335
    required fields, **337–338**
work week setting, 445
Workflow Management section, **639**, *639*
Workflow Settings page, **247**, 639, *639*
workflows
    galleries, **443**
    Issue Tracking list, **284–291**, *285–291*
    libraries for, 325
    settings, **247**, 639, *639*
Workflows option, 287, *287*

Workflows page, 288, *288*
workspaces
    document, **465–466**, *465–466*
    meeting, **472–475**, *472–475*
        Basic, **475–477**, *476–478*
        Decision, **481**, *482*
        MultiPage, **483**, *483*
        Social, **480**, *481*
        URLs, **481**
    Send To feature, **383**
    sites, **455–456**, *455*
    templates for, 758
workstations, 5
wpresources folder, 778
WSS_Admin_WPG security group, **82**
WSS_Content database, 10
WSS_Restricted_WPG security group, **82**
WSS_Search_Servername database, 10
WSS_WPG security group, **82**
Wssconfig account, 43
Wsscontent account, **44–45**
Wssindex account, 44
Wsssearch account, 43

X
XML web part, 170

Y
Yes/No fields, 219
Your Site's Common Name screen, 969, *969*

Z
Zone Name screen, 122, *122*
Zone Type screen, 121, *121*
zones
    Alternate Access Mapping, 955
    authentication, **637–638**, *637–638*
    incoming email, 121–122, *121–122*
    policies, **557**
    public URLs, 592
    removing web parts from, **164**, *165*
    security for, **596–597**
    URL, **552–553**